WITHDRAWN

MARKET SHARE REPORTER

ISSN 1052-9578

MARKET SHARE REPORTER

AN ANNUAL COMPILATION
OF REPORTED MARKET SHARE
DATA ON COMPANIES,
PRODUCTS, AND SERVICES

32nd Edition

Volume 2
ROBERT S. LAZICH, Editor

ELIHU BURRITT LIBRARY
CENTRAL CONNECTICUT STATE UNIVERSITY
NEW BRITAIN, CT 06050

Market Share Reporter, 32nd Edition

Robert S. Lazich, Editor

Project Editor: Virgil L. Burton III

Editorial: Joyce P. Simkin, Monique D. Magee

Manufacturing: Rita Wimberley

© 2022 Gale, a Cengage Company

ALL RIGHTS RESERVED. No part of this work covered by the copyright herein may be reproduced, transmitted, stored, or used in any form or by any means graphic, electronic, or mechanical, including but not limited to photocopying, recording, scanning, digitizing, taping, Web distribution, information networks, or information storage and retrieval systems, except as permitted under Section 107 or 108 of the 1976 United States Copyright Act, without the prior written permission of the publisher.

This publication is a creative work fully protected by all applicable copyright laws, as well as by misappropriation, trade secret, unfair competition, and other applicable laws. The authors and editors of this work have added value to the underlying factual material herein through one or more of the following: unique and original selection, coordination, expression, arrangement, and classification of the information.

For product information and technology assistance, contact us at
Gale Customer Support, 1-800-877-4253.
For permission to use material from this text or product,
submit all requests online at www.cengage.com/permissions.
Further permissions questions can be emailed to
permissionrequest@cengage.com

Cover images: Bar chart with a map of the world ©pedrosek/Shutterstock.com, 2012; Oil Diagram - 3D Rendering ©N-trash/Shutterstock.com, 2012; Stock Market Chart on Blue Background ©AshDesign/Shutterstock.com, 2012; Abstract Design inspired by Stock Market Exchange - EPS 10 ©xalex/Shutterstock.com, 2012; Financial Data on a Monitor ©isak55/Shutterstock.com

While every effort has been made to ensure the reliability of the information presented in this publication, Gale, a Cengage Company, does not guarantee the accuracy of the data contained herein. Gale accepts no payment for listing; and inclusion in the publication of any organization, agency, institution, publication, service, or individual does not imply endorsement of the editors or publisher. Errors brought to the attention of the publisher and verified to the satisfaction of the publisher will be corrected in future editions.

EDITORIAL DATA PRIVACY POLICY. Does this publication contain information about you as an individual? If so, for more information about our editorial data privacy policies, please see our Privacy Statement at www.gale.com.

Gale, a Cengage Company
27500 Drake Rd.
Farmington Hills, MI, 48331-3535

978-0-02-866957-1 (2 vol. set)
978-0-02-866958-8 (vol. 1)
978-0-02-866959-5 (vol. 2)

ISSN 1052-9578

Printed in Mexico
Print Number: 01   Print Year: 2022

TABLE OF CONTENTS

Table of Topics vii
Acronyms and Abbreviations xv
Introduction xxi

Volume I
Abrasives - Autos and Trucks 1
Baby Care - Butter and Spreads 101
Cabinets - Cut Stone and Stone Products 156
Dairy Industry - DVDs 275
E-Cigarettes - Eye Care 310
Fabric Mills - Fuses 338
Gallium - Gypsum 418
Hair and Nail Salons - Hydrogen and Fuel Cells 460
Ice - Isotropic Graphite 495
Janitorial Services - Luxury Industry 531

Volume II
Machine Tools - Musical Instruments and Supplies 569
Natural Products Retailers - Nylon String Trimmer Line 644
Oats - Over-the-Top Media 655
Packaging - Pumps 681
Racetracks - Rubber 753
Salt - Systems Integrators 784
T&D Equipment - Tutoring and Test Preparation 878
Unions - Voting Machines 919
Wallboard - Zoos and Botanical Gardens 931

Indexes
Source Index 965
Place Names Index 1023
Products, Services, Names, and Issues Index 1045
Company Index 1071
Brands Index 1123

Appendix I - Industrial Classifications
SIC Coverage 1141
NAICS Coverage 1153
ISIC Coverage 1167
Harmonized Code Coverage 1173

Appendix II - Annotated Source List 1175

TABLE OF TOPICS

The *Table of Topics* lists all topics used in *Market Share Reporter* in alphabetical order. One or more page references follow each topic; the page references identify the starting point where the topic is shown. The same topic name may be used under different SICs; therefore, in some cases, more than one page reference is provided. Roman numerals indicate volume number.

Abrasives, p. I-1
Accounting Services, p. I-2
Adhesives and Sealants, pp. I-3-5
Advertising, pp. I-5-13
Aerosols, pp. I-13-15
Agents and Managers, p. I-15
Aggregate, p. I-15
Agricultural Product Retailers, p. I-16
Air Care, pp. I-16-17
Aircraft, pp. I-17-21
Aircraft Engines, pp. I-21-23
Aircraft Leasing, p. I-23
Aircraft Parts, p. I-24
Airlines, pp. I-24-28
Airports, pp. I-28-29
Alcoholic Beverage Retailers, p. I-29
Alcoholic Beverages, p. I-29
All-Terrain Vehicles, p. I-29
Alternative Fueling Stations, pp. I-30-44
Alumina, p. I-45
Aluminum, pp. I-46-48
Aluminum Foil, p. I-48
Aluminum Foil Pans, p. I-48
Aluminum Ore, p. I-48
Ambulance Services, p. I-49
Ammunition, p. I-50
Amusement Parks, pp. I-50-51
Antimony, p. I-52
Apparel, pp. I-52-60
Apparel Retailers, pp. I-60-61
Appliance Repair and Maintenance Services, p. I-61
Appliance Retailers, pp. I-61-62
Appliances, pp. I-63-69
Apps, pp. I-70-72
Architectural Services, p. I-72
Arenas, p. I-72
Armored Vehicles and Tank Parts, p. I-73

Arsenic Trioxide, p. I-73
Art, pp. I-73-75
Art Supplies, p. I-75
Artificial Intelligence, p. I-76
Artificial Marble, p. I-76
Asbestos, p. I-77
Asphalt Paving Mixtures, pp. I-77-78
Asphalt Shingles and Coatings, pp. I-78-79
Audio, pp. I-79-81
Auto Auctions, pp. I-81-82
Auto Dealers, p. I-82
Auto Leasing, p. I-82
Auto Parts, pp. I-83-85
Auto Parts Retailers, p. I-85
Auto Rental, p. I-86
Auto Repair, p. I-86-87
Auto Services, p. I-87
Autoclaved Aerated Concrete, p. I-88
Automated Parking Systems, p. I-88
Automatic Soldering Machines, p. I-88
Automation Equipment, pp. I-88-89
Autos and Trucks, pp. I-89-100
Baby Care, pp. I-101-102
Baby Food, pp. I-102-103
Back Side Silver Paste, p. I-103
Bagels and Bialys, pp. I-103-104
Bakeries, p. I-104
Bakery Products, pp. I-104-108
Banking, pp. I-109-123
Barber Shops, p. I-123
Base Oils, p. I-124
Batteries, pp. I-124-125
Battery Binder Materials, p. I-125
Bearings, pp. I-126-127
Beauty Salons, p. I-127
Bed-and-Breakfasts, p. I-127
Beer, pp. I-127-130
Beverages, pp. I-130-131
Bicycles, pp. I-131-132

Biofuels, p. I-133
Biometrics Equipment, p. I-134
Bioplastics, p. I-134
Biotechnology, pp. I-134-135
Blood and Organ Banks, p. I-135
Boat Dealers, p. I-136
Boats, pp. I-136-137
Boilers, p. I-137
Bolts, Nuts, Screws, Rivets and Washers, p. I-137
Book Retailers, p. I-138
Books, pp. I-139-142
Boron, p. I-142
Bottled Water, pp. I-143-144
Bowling Centers, p. I-145
Boxes, pp. I-145-146
Bread and Rolls, pp. I-146-149
Bricks, p. I-149
Brooms, Brushes and Mops, pp. I-149-150
Building Product Distributors, p. I-150
Building Products, p. I-151
Buses, pp. I-151-153
Business and Secretarial Schools, p. I-153
Business Associations, p. I-153
Butter and Spreads, pp. I-153-155
Cabinets, p. I-156
Cable, pp. I-156-157
Cadmium, p. I-157
Calculators, p. I-158
Cameras, pp. I-158-159
Candles, p. I-159
Cannabidiol Retailers, p. I-160
Cannabis and Cannabidiol, pp. I-160-161
Canned Food, pp. I-161-162
Capacitors, p. I-162
Caps and Closures, p. I-163
Carbon Fiber, p. I-163

Carwashes, pp. I-163-164
Cash-in-Transit, p. I-164
Caskets, p. I-165
Castings, p. I-165
Cattle, pp. I-165-166
Cattle Feedlots, p. I-167
Ceiling Grids, p. I-167
Cellophane, p. I-167
Cellphone Retailers, p. I-168
Cellphones, pp. I-168-171
Cellular Connected Industrial Machines, p. I-171
Cement, pp. I-172-174
Ceramics, pp. I-175-176
Cereal, pp. I-176-177
Charcoal, p. I-177
Charities, pp. I-177-178
Cheese, pp. I-178-182
Chemicals and Allied Products, pp. I-182-190
Child Care, p. I-190
Chocolate, pp. I-190-194
Christmas Tree Retailers, p. I-194
Chromium, p. I-194
Cigar Wraps, p. I-194
Circuit Breakers, p. I-195
Clad Plate, p. I-195
Clays and Related Materials, p. I-195
Cleaning Products, pp. I-195-197
Clocks, p. I-197
Coal, pp. I-197-199
Cobalt, p. I-199
Cocoa Beans, p. I-200
Coffee, pp. I-200-202
Coffee Cups, p. I-202
Coffee Roasters, p. I-203
Coffee Shops, pp. I-203-205
Colocation Services, p. I-205
Comic Books, p. I-205
Commodity Contracts, p. I-206
Community Food Services, p. I-206
Compressors, p. I-207
Computer and Office Machine Repair and Maintenance, p. I-207
Computer Data Storage, p. I-208
Computer Facilities Management Services, p. I-208
Computer Peripherals, p. I-209
Computer Retailers, p. I-210
Computers, pp. I-210-212
Concert Tours, pp. I-212-213
Concrete, p. I-213
Concrete Blocks and Bricks, p. I-214

Confectionery and Nut Stores, p. I-214
Confectionery Product Wholesalers, p. I-214
Confectionery Products, pp. I-215-227
Construction Machinery, pp. I-227-229
Construction Sand and Gravel, p. I-229
Construction Work, pp. I-229-233
Consulting Services, p. I-234
Consumer Electronics, pp. I-235-239
Consumer Electronics Retailers, p. I-239
Contact Lenses, pp. I-239-240
Containers, p. I-240
Contracting Work, pp. I-240-246
Convenience Store Wholesalers, p. I-247
Convenience Stores, pp. I-247-248
Conventions and Trade Shows, pp. I-248-249
Conveyancing Services, p. I-250
Conveyors and Drive Belts, p. I-250
Cookware, Utensils, Cutlery, and Flatware, pp. I-250-251
Copper, pp. I-252-255
Cork, pp. I-255-256
Corn, pp. I-256-257
Cosmetics, pp. I-257-262
Cosmetics and Personal Care Retailers, p. I-263
Cotton, pp. I-263-264
Countertops, pp. I-264-265
Court Reporting and Stenotype, p. I-265
Crackers, pp. I-266-269
Cranes, pp. I-269-270
Credit Reporting Agencies, p. I-270
Credit Unions, p. I-271
Croutons, p. I-271
Crowdfunding, p. I-271
Cruise Lines, p. I-272
Crushed and Broken Granite, p. I-272
Crushed and Broken Limestone, p. I-273
Cryptocurrencies, p. I-273
Culinary Products, p. I-273
Cut Stone and Stone Products, p. I-274
Dairy Industry, p. I-275
Dance Companies, p. I-276

Data Processing and Hosting, p. I-276
Datacenters, p. I-276
Death Care Industry, p. I-277
Debt Collection, p. I-277
Decking, p. I-278
Defense, pp. I-278-280
Dental Laboratories, p. I-281
Department Stores, p. I-281
Design Industry, p. I-282
Detergents, pp. I-282-284
Devices, p. I-284
Diagnostic Imaging Centers, p. I-284
Diagnostics, pp. I-284-286
Diamonds, pp. I-286-287
Diet and Weight Loss Centers, p. I-287
Differential Thermal Analyzers, p. I-288
Dips, p. I-288
Direct Selling, pp. I-288-289
Directories and Mailing Lists, pp. I-289-290
Displays, pp. I-290-291
Document Management, p. I-291
Dollar Stores, p. I-292
Dough, pp. I-292-293
Drafting Services, p. I-293
Dried and Dehydrated Food, p. I-294
Driving Simulators, p. I-294
Drug Stores and Pharmacies, pp. I-294-297
Drugs, pp. I-297-303
Drugs, Over-the-Counter, pp. I-304-308
Dry Ice Pellet Machinery, p. I-308
Drycleaning and Laundry Services, p. I-308
DVD and Video Tape Rental and Leasing, p. I-308
DVDs, p. I-309
E-Cigarettes, p. I-310
E-Commerce, pp. I-311-316
E-Learning, p. I-317
E-Sports, p. I-317
Earthing Lightning Protection, p. I-317
Egg Rolls and Wonton Wrappers, p. I-317
Egg Substitutes, p. I-318
Eggs, pp. I-318-320
Electronic Shelf Labels, p. I-320
Electronics Distributors, p. I-320

Electroplating, Plating, Polishing, Anodizing, and Coloring, p. I-321
Elevators and Escalators, pp. I-321-322
Emergency Services, p. I-322
Energy, pp. I-323-329
Energy Drinks, pp. I-329-330
Energy Shots, p. I-330
Engineered Wood Products, p. I-330
Engines, pp. I-330-331
English Language Training, p. I-331
Entertainment, pp. I-332-333
Environmental Organizations, p. I-333
Environmental Services, pp. I-333-334
Escape Rooms, p. I-334
Events and Exhibitions, p. I-334
Exchanges, p. I-335
Executive Search Firms, p. I-335
Expert Witness Consulting Services, p. I-335
Explosion-Proof Control Stations, p. I-336
Explosives, p. I-336
Eye Care, p. I-337
Fabric Mills, pp. I-338-339
Fabricated Structural Metal, p. I-339
Facial Recognition, p. I-339
Fairs, p. I-340
Family Planning Centers, p. I-340
Fans and Blowers, p. I-340
Farm and Garden Machinery Wholesalers, p. I-341
Farm Machinery, pp. I-341-343
Farms, pp. I-343-344
Fats and Oils, pp. I-345-347
Feldspar, p. I-347
Fencing, p. I-348
Fertilizers, pp. I-349-351
Fibers and Filaments, pp. I-351-353
Financial Information, p. I-353
Firelogs, p. I-353
Fish and Seafood Wholesalers, p. I-353
Fish Farming, pp. I-354-355
Fishing, pp. I-355-356
Flavored Malt Beverages, p. I-357
Flavoring Syrups and Concentrates, p. I-357
Flight Simulators, pp. I-357-358
Flooring, pp. I-358-362
Flooring Distribution, pp. I-362-363
Flooring Retailers, p. I-363

Florist and Nursery Supply Wholesalers, p. I-364
Florists, p. I-364
Flour, pp. I-365-366
Flowers and Other Plants, pp. I-366-367
Fluid Power, p. I-367
Fluorspar, p. I-367
Food, pp. I-368-373
Food and Trash Bags, p. I-373
Food Delivery, pp. I-374-377
Foodservice, pp. I-377-380
Footwear, pp. I-380-381
Footwear Retailers, pp. I-381-382
Footwear Wholesalers, p. I-383
Forecourt Retailers, pp. I-383-385
Formal Wear and Costume Rental, p. I-385
Foundries, pp. I-385-386
Fragrances, pp. I-386-387
Franchising, pp. I-387-388
Frozen Food Wholesalers, p. I-388
Frozen Foods, pp. I-388-398
Fruit and Vegetable Markets, p. I-399
Fruit and Vegetable Wholesalers, p. I-399
Fruit Concentrates, p. I-399
Fruits and Vegetables, pp. I-399-410
Furniture, pp. I-410-414
Furniture Repair and Reupholstery, p. I-415
Furniture Retailers, pp. I-415-417
Fuses, p. I-417
Gallium, p. I-418
Gaming, pp. I-418-423
Garage Doors, p. I-423
Garage Storage Systems, p. I-423
Garbage Cans, p. I-423
Garnets, p. I-423
Gaskets, Packing and Sealing Devices, p. I-424
Gasoline Stations, p. I-424
Gearboxes, p. I-425
Gene Editing, p. I-425
General Merchandise, pp. I-425-429
Generators, p. I-429
Geosynthetics, p. I-429
Gift Cards, p. I-429
Glass, pp. I-430-433
Glassware, pp. I-433-434
Global Distribution Systems, p. I-434
Gold, pp. I-434-436

Golf Courses and Country Clubs, p. I-436
Government Contracting, pp. I-436-442
GPS, p. I-442
Grains, p. I-443
Granite, p. I-443
Graphite, pp. I-443-444
Greenhouses, p. I-444
Greeting Cards, pp. I-444-445
Grocery Retailers, pp. I-445-452
Grocery Wholesalers, p. I-452
Ground or Treated Mineral and Earth, p. I-453
Gum, pp. I-453-454
Guns and Ammunition, pp. I-454-455
Gutters and Downspouts, p. I-456
Gyms, pp. I-456-457
Gypsum, pp. I-457-458
Hair and Nail Care Salons, p. I-460
Hair Care, pp. I-460-461
Hair Restoration, p. I-461
Handbags and Purses, p. I-461
Hard Cider, p. I-462
Hardware, p. I-462
Hazardous Waste Removal, p. I-462
Headsets, p. I-462
Health Care, pp. I-463-467
Health Food Stores, p. I-467
Heating and Cooling, pp. I-468-469
Heavy Equipment Rental, pp. I-469-471
Historical Sites, pp. I-471-472
Hobbies and Crafts, p. I-472
Hobbies and Crafts Retailers, p. I-472
Hogs and Pigs, pp. I-473-474
Hoists, p. I-474
Holding Companies, p. I-475
Home Improvement Retailers, p. I-475
Home Organization Products, p. I-475
Home-Sharing Industry, p. I-476
Homefurnishings, pp. I-476-478
Homefurnishings Retailers, pp. I-478-483
Homefurnishings Wholesalers, p. I-483
Homeowners Associations, p. I-483
Honey, p. I-484
Hotels, pp. I-484-486
Housewares Retailers, p. I-487

Housing, pp. I-487-493
Hunting and Fishing, pp. I-493-494
Hydrogen and Fuel Cells, p. I-494
Ice, p. I-495
Ice Cream and Frozen Desserts, pp. I-495-498
Immunoglobulins, p. I-498
In-flight Entertainment, p. I-498
Indoor Air Quality Meters, p. I-498
Industrial Design Services, p. I-499
Industrial Fasteners, p. I-499
Industrial Feed, p. I-500
Industrial Gases, pp. I-501-502
Industrial Launderers, pp. I-502-503
Industrial Machinery Wholesalers, p. I-503
Industrial Molds, pp. I-503-504
Information Technology, pp. I-504-505
Infrastructure, p. I-505
Ink, pp. I-506-507
Insulation, pp. I-507-508
Insurance, pp. I-508-520
Integrated Circuits, pp. I-520-521
Interior Design, p. I-522
Internet of Things, p. I-522
Internet Sites, pp. I-522-525
Investigation Services, pp. I-525-526
Investment Banking, pp. I-526-528
Iodine, p. I-528
Iron and Steel Pipes and Tubes, p. I-528
Iron Ore, pp. I-528-530
Isotropic Graphite, p. I-530
Janitorial Services, p. I-531
Jewelry, pp. I-531-532
Jewelry and Watch Retailers, pp. I-532-533
Juices, pp. I-533-535
Kaolin and Ball Clays, p. I-536
Kegs, p. I-537
Kitchen Storage, p. I-537
Labels, pp. I-537-538
Laboratory Instruments, pp. I-538-539
Ladders, p. I-539
Laminates, p. I-539
Land, p. I-540
Laser Markers, p. I-540
Laser Processing Equipment, p. I-540
Lasers, p. I-540
Laundries and Drycleaners, p. I-541

Lawn and Garden Industry, pp. I-542-543
Lead, pp. I-543-544
Leasing, pp. I-544-545
Leather, pp. I-545-546
LED Video Walls, p. I-546
Legal Services, p. I-547
Lenses, p. I-547
Libraries and Archives, pp. I-547-548
Licensed Merchandise, p. I-549
Lift Trucks, p. I-550
Lighters, p. I-550
Lighting, pp. I-550-553
Lime, p. I-554
Limousine Services, p. I-555
Liquor, pp. I-555-558
Lithium, p. I-559
Livestreaming, p. I-559
Loans, pp. I-559-561
Lobbying Industry, pp. I-561-562
Locks, p. I-562
Locksmiths, p. I-562
Low-Voltage Power Distribution, p. I-562
Lubricants, pp. I-563-564
Luggage and Bags, p. I-565
Lumber, pp. I-565-567
Luxury Industry, pp. I-567-568
Machine Tools, p. II-569
Magazines, pp. II-569-570
Magnesium, p. II-570
Manga, p. II-570
Manganese, p. II-571
Manhole Covers, p. II-571
Mannequins, p. II-571
Marble, p. II-571
Marinated Vegetables and Fruits, p. II-572
Mass Transit, pp. II-572-576
Meal Kits, p. II-576
Meat, pp. II-576-592
Meat Alternatives, pp. II-592-593
Meat/Cheese/Cracker/Desserts, p. II-593
Meat Markets, p. II-593
Meat Wholesalers, p. II-593
Medical Equipment, pp. II-594-599
Medical Equipment Wholesalers, p. II-600
Medical Products, pp. II-600-603
Merchant Acquirers, p. II-604
Mercury, p. II-604
Mergers and Acquisitions, p. II-604

Metal Buildings, p. II-605
Metal Cans, pp. II-605-606
Metal Coating and Engraving, p. II-606
Metal Containers, p. II-607
Metal Crowns and Closures, pp. II-607-608
Metal Cutting Tools, p. II-608
Metal Framing, p. II-608
Metal Fuel Tanks, p. II-609
Metal Heat Treating, p. II-609
Metal Powders, pp. II-609-610
Metal Service Centers, p. II-610
Metal Stampings, pp. II-610-611
Metalcasting Industry, p. II-611
Meters, p. II-612
Mica, p. II-612
Microdisplays, p. II-612
Microgrids, p. II-612
Microswitches, p. II-613
Military Exchanges, p. II-613
Milk, pp. II-613-615
Milk Alternatives, pp. II-615-617
Mineral Wool, p. II-617
Mining Equipment, pp. II-617-618
Missiles and Space Vehicles, p. II-618
Mobile Food Services, pp. II-619-620
Mobile Gaming, pp. II-620-622
Mobile Payments, p. II-622
Modular Grippers, p. II-623
Molybdenum, p. II-623
Monetary Authorities, pp. II-623-624
Mortgages, pp. II-624-626
Motion Pictures, pp. II-626-629
Motor Vehicle Towing, p. II-629
Motorcycles, pp. II-629-631
Movie Theaters, pp. II-632-634
MRO Industry, p. II-634
Museums, p. II-635
Mushrooms, p. II-636
Music, pp. II-636-640
Music Streaming, p. II-641
Musical Instruments and Product Retailers, p. II-641
Musical Instruments and Supplies, pp. II-642-643
Natural Products Retailers, p. II-644
Navigational Equipment, p. II-644
Networking Equipment, pp. II-645-646
Newspapers, p. II-647
Nickel, pp. II-648-649

Nightclubs and Bars, p. II-649
Nonwovens, pp. II-649-650
Nuclear Waste Disposal, pp. II-650-651
Nuts, pp. II-651-653
Nylon String Trimmer Line, p. II-654
Oats, p. II-655
Office Equipment, pp. II-655-656
Oil and Gas, pp. II-656-660
Oil and Gas Drilling, p. II-661
Oil and Gas Liquids, pp. II-662-663
Oil and Gas Pipelines, p. II-663
Oil and Gas Services, p. II-663
Oil and Gas Storage, p. II-664
Oilseeds, pp. II-664-669
Online Education, p. II-669
Online Grocers, pp. II-670-671
Online Travel, p. II-671
Optical Goods, p. II-671
Optical Goods Retailers, p. II-672
Optical Transceivers, p. II-672
Oral Care, pp. II-672-673
Ornamental and Architectural Metal Work, pp. II-673-674
Outdoor Kitchens, p. II-674
Outdoor Living, p. II-675
Over-the-Top Media, pp. II-675-680
Packaging, pp. II-681-686
Packaging Machinery, p. II-687
Paint, Varnish and Supplies Wholesalers, p. II-687
Paint and Coatings, pp. II-688-690
Paint and Wallpaper Stores, p. II-690
Palladium, pp. II-690-691
Pallets, p. II-691
Pancake/French Toast/Waffle Mixes, p. II-692
Panels, p. II-692
Paper and Paperboard, pp. II-693-696
Paper Bags, and Coated and Treated Paper, p. II-696
Paper-Cutting Machines, p. II-696
Paper Wholesalers, p. II-697
Parcel Sorting Machines, p. II-697
Parking Lots and Garages, p. II-697
Parks, p. II-698
Pasta and Noodles, pp. II-698-699
Patents, p. II-699
Pay Television, pp. II-700-701
Payment Cards, pp. II-701-703
Pearls, p. II-703
Peat, p. II-704
Pelts, p. II-704

Pensions, pp. II-704-705
Peppers, Pimentos and Olives, p. II-705
Personal Care Products, pp. II-706-707
Personal Watercraft, p. II-708
Pest Control Industry, p. II-708
Pet Food, pp. II-709-714
Pet Products, p. II-714
Pet Services, p. II-714
Pet Stores, pp. II-715-716
Pets, pp. II-716-718
Pharmaceutical Refrigeration, p. II-718
Pharmacy Benefit Managers, p. II-719
Phosphate Rock, p. II-719
Photo Printing, p. II-719
Photocontrols, p. II-720
Photofinishing, p. II-720
Photographic and Photocopying Equipment, p. II-720
Photographic Equipment Wholesalers, p. II-721
Photographic Film and Supplies, p. II-721
Photography, p. II-722
Photonics, p. II-722
Photovoltaics, p. II-723
Pipe, pp. II-723-725
Plastics, pp. II-725-730
Plastics Machinery, pp. II-730-731
Plastics Wholesalers, p. II-731
Platinum, p. II-731
Playground Equipment, p. II-732
Plumbing Fixture Retailers, p. II-732
Plumbing Fixtures, pp. II-732-734
Pneumatic Cylinders, p. II-734
Pneumatic Tubes and Fittings, p. II-734
Podcasting, pp. II-734-736
Police, p. II-736
Ports, pp. II-736-737
POS Terminals, p. II-737
Postal Service, p. II-737
Potash, pp. II-737-738
Potatoes, pp. II-738-739
Pottery, pp. II-739-740
Power Distribution Blocks, p. II-740
Power Infrastructure, p. II-740
Powered Pressure Washers, p. II-740
Prepared Salads, Fruit and Coleslaw, p. II-741

Printed Circuit Boards, pp. II-741-742
Printing, pp. II-743-744
Prisons, p. II-745
Private Clubs, p. II-745
Private Label Industry, p. II-746
Private Mail Centers, pp. II-746-747
Promotional Products, p. II-747
Propane Retailers, p. II-747
Public Relations, p. II-748
Publishing, p. II-748
Pudding, Mousse, Gelatin and Parfait, p. II-749
Pulp, pp. II-749-750
Pumice, p. II-751
Pumps, pp. II-751-752
Racetracks, p. II-753
Radio Broadcasting, p. II-753
Radios, p. II-753
Railings, p. II-754
Railroad Equipment, pp. II-754-755
Railroads, p. II-756
Rare Earths, pp. II-756-757
Real Estate, pp. II-757-760
Receptacles, p. II-760
Recording Media, p. II-760
Recreation Management, p. II-761
Recreational Goods Rental, p. II-761
Recreational Vehicles, pp. II-761-762
Refrigeration Equipment Wholesalers, p. II-763
Relays and Industrial Controls, p. II-763
Religious Organizations, p. II-763
Remediation Services, p. II-764
Remittances, p. II-764
Rental Industry, p. II-764
Repossession Services, p. II-765
Research, pp. II-765-766
Residential Intellectual Disability Care, p. II-766
Restaurants, pp. II-766-772
Retailing, pp. II-772-775
Reverse Vending Machines, p. II-775
Rice, pp. II-776-777
Ride-Hailing, p. II-777
Robotics, pp. II-778-780
Roofing, pp. II-780-781
Rooming and Boarding Houses, p. II-781
Rope, Cordage, Twine, Tire Cord, and Tire Fabric, p. II-782
Rubber, p. II-782
Salt, p. II-784

Sand and Gravel, p. II-784
Sand Castings, p. II-785
Sanitary Paper Products, pp. II-785-789
Sanitaryware, p. II-789
Satellites, pp. II-790-791
Sauces, Dressings and Condiments, pp. II-791-793
Saw Blades and Handtools, p. II-793
Sawmill, Woodworking and Paper Machinery, p. II-794
Scales and Balances, p. II-794
School Buses, p. II-795
Schools, p. II-795
Seafood and Fish, pp. II-795-797
Search, Detection, and Navigation Apparatus, p. II-798
Seaweed, p. II-798
Secondhand Apparel, p. II-798
Security Equipment, p. II-799
Security Industry, pp. II-799-800
Seeds, p. II-801
Self-Checkout Terminals, p. II-801
Self-Storage Industry, p. II-801
Semiconductor Machinery, p. II-802
Semiconductors, pp. II-802-808
Sensors, p. II-809
Servers, p. II-810
Serviced Apartments, p. II-811
Sewage Treatment, p. II-811
Sheep and Goats, p. II-811
Sheet Metal, p. II-811
Shipping, pp. II-812-818
Ships, p. II-819
Siding, p. II-819
Sightseeing, p. II-819
Signs, pp. II-820-821
Silicon, p. II-821
Silk, p. II-821
Silver, pp. II-822-823
Silverware, p. II-823
Skiing Facilities, p. II-823
Skin Care, pp. II-823-825
Sleep Industry, p. II-826
Small Arms and Ordnance, p. II-826
Smart Technology, pp. II-826-828
Snacks, pp. II-828-836
Soap, pp. II-837-838
Soda Ash, p. II-839
Soft Drinks, pp. II-839-840
Software, pp. II-841-851
Sound Recording, p. II-851
Soup, pp. II-851-852
Sour Cream, p. II-852

Space Industry, p. II-852
Spas, p. II-853
Special Die and Tools, Die Set, Jigs and Fixtures, p. II-853
Specialized Storage and Warehousing, p. II-853
Spices and Extracts, pp. II-853-854
Sporting Goods, pp. II-854-856
Sporting Goods Retailers, p. II-857
Sports, pp. II-857-859
Sports Drinks, p. II-859
Spreads and Syrups, pp. II-859-860
Springs, p. II-860
Staffing Industry, pp. II-860-861
Stainless Steel, p. II-861
Stationery Products, p. II-862
Steam and Air-Conditioning Supply, p. II-862
Steel, pp. II-863-865
Stone, Sand and Gravel, p. II-865
Storage Industry, p. II-866
Streaming Media Devices, pp. II-866-867
Sugar, pp. II-867-869
Sugar Substitutes, p. II-869
Sulfur, p. II-869
Sunglasses, p. II-870
Superchargers, p. II-870
Supplements, pp. II-870-877
Surge Protectors, p. II-877
Swimming Pools, p. II-877
Switches, p. II-877
Systems Integrators, p. II-877
T&D Equipment, p. II-878
Tank Terminals, p. II-878
Tank Trucks, p. II-878
Tape, p. II-879
Tape Measures, p. II-879
Tattoos, pp. II-879-880
Tax Preparation, p. II-880
Tea, pp. II-880-882
Telecommunications Equipment, pp. II-882-883
Telecommunications Services, p. II-883
Teleproduction and Postproduction Services, p. II-883
Telescopes, p. II-884
Television Broadcasting, pp. II-884-887
Tents, Awnings and Canvas, p. II-887
Testing Instruments, p. II-887
Textile Machinery, p. II-887
Textile Rental Services, p. II-888

Textiles, pp. II-888-889
Theater Companies and Dinner Theaters, p. II-889
Theaters, p. II-889
3D Printing, p. II-889
Timber, pp. II-889-890
Tin, pp. II-890-891
Tire Retailers, pp. II-891-892
Tire Retreading, p. II-892
Tires, pp. II-893-894
Titanium, p. II-895
Tobacco and Tobacco Products, pp. II-895-899
Tobacco Stores, p. II-899
Toll Roads, pp. II-899-900
Tools, pp. II-900-903
Tortillas and Taco Kits, p. II-903
Tourism, p. II-903
Toy and Hobby Goods Wholesalers, p. II-904
Toys and Games, pp. II-904-906
Toys and Games Retailers, p. II-906
Trailers, pp. II-906-907
Training, pp. II-907-908
Transformer Monitoring Systems, p. II-908
Translation Services, p. II-908
Transponders, p. II-908
Travel, pp. II-909-910
Travel Retail, p. II-910
Trim, p. II-910
Trucking, pp. II-911-913
Trucks, pp. II-914-916
Tungsten, p. II-916
Turbines, pp. II-916-918
Tutoring and Test Preparation, p. II-918
Unions, p. II-919
Unmanned Aerial Vehicles, p. II-920
Uranium, pp. II-920-921
Utilities, p. II-921
Vaccines, pp. II-921-922
Valves, p. II-923
Vans, pp. II-923-924
Vegetarians, p. II-924
Vending Machines, pp. II-924-925
Veterinary Patient Monitoring Equipment, p. II-925
Veterinary Services, p. II-925
Video Game Industry, pp. II-926-928
Virtual Events, p. II-928
Vitamin and Supplement Retailers, p. II-928
Vitamins, p. II-929

Voting Machines, p. II-930
Wallboard, p. II-931
Wallpaper, p. II-931
Warehouse Clubs, p. II-931
Warehousing, pp. II-931-933
Waste Removal, p. II-934
Watches, p. II-934
Water Filtration, p. II-935
Water Industry, p. II-935
Water Parks, p. II-935
Water Transportation, pp. II-935-936
Water Treatment, p. II-936
Wearable Devices, pp. II-937-938
Weather Forecasting, p. II-939
Weatherproof Boxes, p. II-939
Weddings, p. II-939
Welding Industry, pp. II-939-940
Wet Corn, pp. II-941-942
Wheat, pp. II-942-943
Whipped Toppings, p. II-943
Windows and Doors, pp. II-943-945
Wine, pp. II-946-948
Wine Distribution, p. II-948
Wipes, pp. II-948-950
Wire and Cable, p. II-950
Wireless Services, pp. II-950-954
Wireless Towers, p. II-954
Wiring Ducts, p. II-954
Wood, pp. II-955-959
Wool, p. II-959
Writing Instruments, p. II-959
Yarn, p. II-960
Yogurt, p. II-961
Zinc, pp. II-961-963
Zoos and Botanical Gardens,
  p. II-963

ACRONYMS AND ABBREVIATIONS

3D	Three dimension	B/W	Black and white
AAFES	Army & Air Force Exchange Service	B2B	Business-to-business
ABC	Automatic boarder control	B2C	Business-to-consumer
ABS	Acylonitrile butadiene styrene (a plastic)	BEMS	Building energy management systems
AC	Alternating current	BHKP	Bleached hardwood kraft pulp
ACT	American College Test	BOPET	Biaxially-oriented polyethylene terephthalate
AD	Autonomous driving		
ADHD	Attention deficit hyperactivity disorder (medicine)	BSRD	Basic shaped refractory products from dolomite
aDSL	Asymmetric digital subscriber line (telecommunications)	BSRM	Basic shaped unfired refractory products from magnesite
ADW	Automated deposit wagering	BURD	Basic unshaped refractory products from dolomite
AES	Album equivalent sales	C2X	Consumer-to-small business
AFH	Away-from-home	C4ISR	Command, control, communications, computers, intelligence, surveillance and reconnaissance
AFIS	Automated fingerprint identification system		
AG	Arbeitsgruppe (German for Working Group)	CAD/CAM	Computer aided design/computer aided manufacturing
ALC	Automatic level control	CAFE	Corporate average fuel economy
AMI	Advanced metering infrastructure	CAGR	Compounded annual growth rate
AMR	Automatic meter reading	CBD	Cannabidiol
APU	Auxiliary power unit (power source in vehicles not involved in locomotion)	CD	Compact disk (electronic storage device) or certificate of deposit (banking)
AR	Augmented reality	CFL	Compact fluorescent lamp
ARRA	American Recovery and Reinvestment Act of 2009	CHF	Swiss Franc (currency)
		CIGS	Copper, Indium, Gallium, Selenide
ART	Assisted reproductive technologies	CIS	Commonwealth of Independent States
ASEAN	Association of Southeast Asian Nations	CIS	Copper, Indium, Sulphur
ASIC	Application-specific integrated circuit	CIS	Contact image sensor (semiconductors)
ASSP	Application-specific standard product	CMBS	Commercial mortgagebBacked securities
ATE	Automatic test equipment or advanced technology engine	CMP	Chemical mechanical planarization
		CMO	Contract manufacturing organization
ATV	All-terrain vehicle	CMOS	Complementary Metal Oxide Silicon
AUV	Autonomous underwater vehicle	CNY	Chinese Yuan (currency)
AVOD	Advertising video on demand		

COPD	Chronic obstructive pulmonary disease	EHR	Electronic health record
CPO	Crude palm oil	EMEA	Europe, Middle East, and Africa
CRM	Customer Resource Management	EMS	Electronics manufacturing services
CRO	Contract research organization	EPCI	Engineering Procurement Construction and Installation
Crore	Indian word signifying 10 million, used ahead or behind other numbers to modify these	EPDM	Ethylene propylene diene terepolymer
		EPROM	Erasable programmable read-only memory
CVD	Chemical vapor deposition		
CVT	Continuously variable transmission	EREV	Extended-range electric vehicle
CWT	Hundredweight (100 pounds)	ERP	Enterprise Resource Planning
CX	Customer experience	ERTMS	European Railway Traffic Management System
DAB	Digital audio broadcasting		
DCI	Digital Camera Initiatives (film and entertainment industry standard for cameras)	EST	Electronic sell-through
		ETCS	European Train Control System
		ETD	Explosives detection equipment
DCS	Distributed control system (control system with multiple nodes spatially separated)	ETF	Exchange-traded fund
		EU	European Union
		EVSE	Electric vehicle supply equipment
DDI	Device driver interface		
DDOS	Distributed denial of service	FAA	Federal Aviation Administration
DISMO	Distilled monoglyerides	FABLESS	Not fabricated or fabricationless
DKK	Danish Krone (currency)	FDA	Food & Drug Administration
DMFC	Direct methanol fuel cell	FGD	Flue-gas desulfurization
DRAM	Dynamic random access memory	FHA	Federal Housing Administration
D-SLR	Digital single-lens reflex (camera)	FHP	Fractional horsepower
DTT	Digital terrestrial television	FPGA	Field programmable gate array
DVD	Digital video disk	FTA	Free-to-air (communications and television)
DVR	Digital video recorder		
DWT	Deadweight (carrying capacity of ships, usually given in metric tons)	FTC	Federal Trade Commission
		FTTH	Fiber-to-the-home (fiber optic fiber replacing copper wire in communications)
E85	Fuel containing 85% ethanol, 15% gasoline		
		FTTP	Fiber-to-the-premises
ECNs	Electronic Communications Networks	FVOD	Free video-on-demand
ECP	Eyecare professional	GC	Gas chromatography
ECU	European Currency Units	GC - MS	Gas chromatography - mass spectrometry
EEA	European Economic Area, the EU plus a selection of other European countries	GGP	Global geodynamics project
		GLA	Gross leasable area
EEL	Edge Emitting Laser	GmbH	Gesellschaft mit beschraenkter Haftung (German limited liability corporation)
EFT	Electronic funds transfer		

GNMA	Government National Mortgage Association	IPTV	Internet protocol television (digitally delivered television)
GNSS	Global navigation satellite system	IQF	Individually quick frozen
GPU	Graphics processing unit	ITC	Investment tax credit
GSA	General Service Administration	IVD	In vitro diagnostics
GSE	Government sponsored enterprise	IVF	In vitro fertilization
GSLV	Geosynchronous satellite launch vehicle	JIT	Just in time (supply chain term)
GW	Gigawatts	JPEG	Joint Photographic Experts Group (file format and file extension)
HALE	High altitude long endurance (aviation)	JUA	Joint use agreement
HCFC	Hydrochlorofluorocarbon	KGaA	Kommanditgesellschaft auf Aktien (German corporate form based on shares)
HCM	Human capital management		
HDD	High-density disk	KT	Kiloton
HDI	High density interconnect	KVM	Keyboard-video-mouse
HDPE	High-density polyethylene	KW	Kilowatts
HECM	Home equity conversion mortgage	LCC	Low-cost carrier
HFCS	High-fructose corn syrup	LCD	Liquid crystal display
HID	High-intensity discharge	LDPE	Low-density polyethylene
HIV/AIDS	Human immunodeficiency virus/Acquired immunodeficiency syndrome	LED	Light-emitting diode
		LEED	Leadership in energy and environmental design
HOD	Home and office delivery		
HPC	High-performance composite	LFL	Linear fluorescent lamps
HPL	High-presure laminate	LLDPE	Linear low-density polyethylene
HSS	Hollow structure section	LMS	Learning management system
HVAC	Heating, ventilation, and air conditioning	LP	Liquefied petroleum
HVACR	Heating, ventilation, air conditioning and refrigeration	LPG	Liquefied petroleum gas
		LSR	Limited-service restaurant
IAAS	Infrastructure as a service	LT	Long ton (2,240 pounds)
IAD	Independent ATM deployer	LTL	Less than truckload (transportation)
IBD	Inflammatory bowel disease	LVT	Luxury vinyl tile
IBS	Irritable bowel syndrome	M&E	Mergers and acquisitions
IC	Integrated circuit (electronics) or independent contractor (labor markets)	MALE	Medium altitude long endurance (aviation)
IDM	Integrated device manufacture	MAT	Moving annual total
IED	Improvised explosive device	MCOT	Mobile cardiac outpatient telemetry
IoT	Internet of things	MEMS	Micro-electrical-mechanical systems
IOL	Intraocular lens or Implantable lenses (optics)	MENA	Middle East and North Africa
		MLB	Major League Baseball

MLCC	Multilayer ceramic capacitor	OCTG	Oil Country Tubular Goods (pipe and tube used in the petroleum industry)
MMDS	Multichannel, multipoint distribution services (television distribution system)	ODM	Original design manufacturer
MMOG	Massively multiplayer online game	OEM	Original equipment manufacturer
MNR/EPR	Nuclear Magnetic Resonance/Electronic Paramagnetic Resonance	OLED	Organic light-emitting diode or device
		OOH	Out-of-home (advertising)
MOBA	Multiplayer online battle arena (gaming term)	OSAT	Outsourced assembly and test
MOOC	Massive open online course	OSB	Oriented strandboard (wood board similar in function but differently made than plywood)
MOSFET	Metal-oxide semiconductor field-effect transistor		
		OTA	Over-the-air (advertising)
MP3	Moving Picture Experts Group Layer-3 Audio (audio file format/extension)	OTA	Online travel agent
		OTC	Over-the-counter
MRI	Magnetic resonance imaging (diagnostic instrument)	OTDR	Optical time-domain reflectometer
		OTT	Over-the-top content
MRO	Maintenance, repair and overhaul	PAAS	Platform as a Service
MT	Metric ton (1,000 kilograms or 2,205 pounds)	PACS	Picture archiving and communication system
MTBE	Methyl tertiary butyl ether	PAN	Polyacrylonitrile
MTO	Money transfer operator	PBX	Private branch exchange (telecommunications)
MUAV	Micro unmanned aerial vehicle		
MW	Megawatts	PCM	Phase-change material
NAFTA	North American Free Trade Area	PDF	Portable document format
NAICS	North American Industrial Classification System	PEMFC	Protein exchange membrane fuel cell
		PEO	Professional employer organization
NASA	National Aeronautical and Space Administration	PERS	Personal emergency response system
		PET	Polyethylene terephthalate
NBA	National Basketball Association	PHEV	Plug-in hybrid electric vehicle
NC	Numerically controlled	PLC	Programmable logic controller (computers)
NDT	Nondestructive testing		
NEC	Not elsewhere classified (Census abbreviation)	PLD	Programmable logic device
		PLF	Premium large format
NF	Nursing facility	PLM	Product lifecycle management
NFL	National Football League	PLU	Primary logical unit
NHL	National Hockey League	PND	Portable navigation device
NIMH	Nickel, metal hydride	POC	Point of care (medical practice)
NPCC	Nano-Precipitated Calcium Carbonate	POD	Print-on-demand
NSK	Not specified by kind (Census abbreviation)	POL	Physician office laboratories
OCD	Obsessive-compulsive disorder		

POP	Point of purchase	SAAR	Seasonally adjusted annualized rate
POS	Point of sale, point of service, or point and shoot	SaaS	Software as a service
		SAR	Saudi Arabian Riyal (currency)
PPV	Pay-per-view (television expression)	SAT	Scholastic Achievement Test
PSA	Pressure sensitive adhesive	SB	Styrene butadiene (latex)
PSLV	Polar satellite launch vehicle	SC	Supercalendered paper, uncoated and mechanically compressed
PTSD	Post-traumatic stress disorder		
Pty	Private (South African corporate status)	SCM	Supply chain management
PUR	Polyurethane	SCR	Selective Catalytic Reduction
PV	Photovoltaic	SIC	Standard Industrial Classification (replaced by NAICS)
PVA	Polyvinyl acetate		
PVC	Polyvinyl chloride	SKU	Stock keeping unit (accounting, warehousing)
PVD	Physical vapor deposition		
QAA	Quality assessment audit	SLR	Single-lense reflex (camera)
QIM	Quality index method	SME	Small and medium-sized enterprise
RAS	Recirculating aquaculture system	SMP	Silane-modified polymers
REIT	Real estate investment trust	SNAP	Supplemental Nutrition Assistance Program (food-stamp program)
Renminbi	Chinese currency, the basic unit of which is the Yuan		
		SNF	Skilled nursing facility
REO	Rare earth oxide	SONET/SDH	Synchronous Optical Network/Synchronous Digital Hierarchy
RES	Renewable energy standard		
RF	Radio frequency	SSD	Solid-state drive (data storage device)
RIB	Rigid-hulled inflatable boat	SSRI/SNRI	Selective serotonin inhibitors/serotonin-norepinephrine reuptake inhibitors (pharmaceuticals)
RMB	Chinese Renminbi (currency)		
ROV	Remotely operated vehicle		
RPK	Revenue passenger kilometers	ST	Short ton (2,000 pounds)
Rs	Indian Rupees (currency)	STEM	Science, technology, engineering and mathematics
RTA	Ready-to-assemble		
RTD	Ready-to-drink	STUAV	Small tactical unmanned aerial vehicle (military)
RTE	Ready-to-eat		
RTK	Revenue ton kilometer	SURF	Subsea Umbilicals Risers and Flowline
RUB	Russian Ruble (currency)	SUV	Sport utility vehicle
RVS	Rail vehicle system	SVOD	Subscription video-on-demand
RYO	Roll-your-own (tobacco)	T&D	Transmission and distribution
SA	Service Assurance or, in many parts of the world, a corporate designation translated as Autonomous Society	TEA	Track equivalent albums (music industry)
		TEU	Twenty-foot equivalent units
		TFL	Thermally fused laminate
		TFT	Thin-film-transistor (usually associated with LED displays)

THC	Tetrahydrocannabinol	WLAN	Wireless local area network
TIC	Testing, Inspection and Certification software	XaaS	Everything as a service
TNC	Trans-national corporation		
TUAV	Tactical unmanned aerial vehicle (military)		
TVOD	Transactional video-on-demand		
UAE	United Arab Emirates		
UAS	Unmanned aerial system (military)		
UAV	Unmanned aerial vehicle (military)		
UCAAS	Unified communications as a service		
UCAV	Unmanned combat aerial vehicle (military)		
UGV	Unmanned ground vehicle (military)		
UHT	Ultra-high temperature		
UK	United Kingdom		
UPS	Uninterruptible power supply (electrical device)		
USB	Universal serial bus		
USV	Unmanned surface vehicle (military)		
UTM	Unified Threat Management		
VA	Veterans Affairs		
VCM	Vinyl chloride monomer (a plastic)		
VCSEL	Vertical-cavity surface-emitting laser		
VLCC	Very large crude carrier (transportation)		
VOD	Video on demand (television expression)		
VOIP	Voice over Internet protocol		
VPN	Virtual private network		
VR	Virtual reality		
VRF	Variable refrigerant flow		
VSAT	Very small aperture terminal		
VSF	Viscose staple fiber		
VTOL-UAV	Vertical take-off and landing UAV (military)		
WAN	Wide area network		
WAP	Wireless application protocol		
WCDMS	Wide division code multiple access		
WFE	Wafer fabrication equipment		

M

★ 2136 ★
Machine Tools
SIC: 3541; NAICS: 333517

Leading Machine Tool Consumers Worldwide, 2020

Countries are ranked by sales in billions of dollars. Machine tool consumption reached $66.8 billion, a decline of $16.8 billion, or 20.1%, over 2019. This was the lowest consumption level since 2009. China's machine tool consumption exceeded its production by the smallest amount since 1999. A major reason for this is that its production was virtually unchanged from 2019.

	($ bil.)	Share
China	$ 21.31	31.90%
United States	8.33	12.47
Germany	5.19	7.77
Japan	4.17	6.24
Italy	3.12	4.67
South Korea	3.09	4.63
India	1.61	2.41
Taiwan	1.44	2.16
Russia	1.26	1.89
Mexico	1.21	1.81
Other	16.07	24.06

Source: *Modern Machine Shop*, May 2021, p. 74+, from Gardner Intelligence.

★ 2137 ★
Machine Tools
SIC: 3541; NAICS: 333517

Leading Press Machine Makers Worldwide, 2019

A press machine uses pressure to change the shape of a work piece. The industry is forecast to grow from $7.85 billion in 2020 to $9.8 billion in 2026.

Schuler Group	12.64%
Komatsu Ltd.	6.89
Aida	6.15
Other	74.32

Source: "Global Press Machine Sales Market Report 2020." [online] from http://www.qyresearch.com [Published November 2020], from QY Research.

★ 2138 ★
Magazines
SIC: 2721; NAICS: 51112

Leading Magazines by Circulation, 2020

Titles are ranked by total paid, verified and analyzed non-paid circulation for the six months ended June 30, 2020.

AARP Bulletin	22,669,110
Costco Connection	14,550,448
Better Homes and Gardens	7,649,079
Good Housekeeping	4,014,028
People	3,502,833
Reader's Digest	3,029,039
Southern Living	2,820,399
Shape	2,530,783
Cosmopolitan	2,461,192
Womans Day	2,452,766
Sports Illustrated	1,866,026

Source: "Magazine Media - Search Results." [online] from https://abcas3.auditedmedia.com/ecirc/magtitlesearch.asp [Accessed January 21, 2021], from Alliance for Audited Media.

★ 2139 ★
Magazines
SIC: 2721; NAICS: 51112

Magazine and Periodical Industry Revenue, 2015-2024

Figures are in millions of dollars.

2015	$ 30,963.0
2016	30,562.4
2017	30,019.6
2018	28,276.9
2019	27,058.8
2020	23,316.4
2021	22,930.7
2022	21,902.2
2023	20,770.2
2024	19,682.5

Source: "The Media Report Media & Entertainment Data in America." [online] from https://digitalcommons.pepperdine.edu/cgi/viewcontent.cgi?article=1026&context=graziadiowps [Published September 2020], from IBISWorld.

★ 2140 ★
Magazines
SIC: 2721; NAICS: 51112

New Print Magazine Titles, 2019

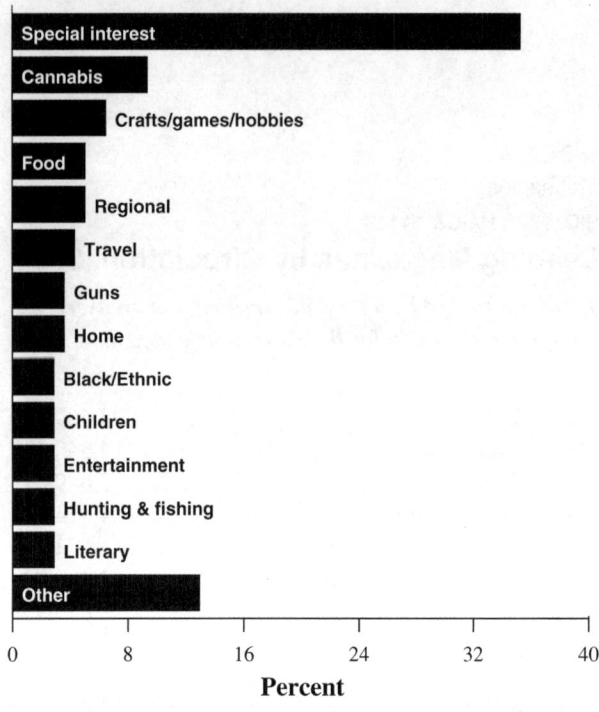

A total of 139 print magazines were launched in 2019. Approximately 228.9 million people reported reading a magazine in 2019 (both print and digital).

	Titles	Share
Special interest	49	35.25%
Cannabis	13	9.35
Crafts/games/hobbies	9	6.47
Food	7	5.04
Regional	7	5.04
Travel	6	4.32
Guns	5	3.60
Home	5	3.60
Black/Ethnic	4	2.88
Children	4	2.88
Entertainment	4	2.88
Hunting & fishing	4	2.88
Literary	4	2.88
Other	18	12.95

Source: "Magazine Media Factbook 2020." [online] from https://mpa.pressreader.com/magazine-media-fact-book-2020/20200629 [Accessed August 18, 2020], from Samir "Mr. Magazine" Husni Launch Monitor.

★ 2141 ★
Magnesium
SIC: 3341; NAICS: 331492

Leading End Markets for Magnesium Metal, 2020

In the United States, primary magnesium was produced by one company at an electrolytic process plant that recovered magnesium from brines from the Great Salt Lake. Secondary magnesium was recovered from scrap. About 67% of secondary magnesium was used in aluminum alloys and the other 33% was consumed for structural uses. Data show leading end markets for primary magnesium metal.

Castings	47.0%
Aluminum-base alloys for packaging, transportation and other applications	33.0
Desulfurization of iron and steel	16.0
Other	4.0

Source: "Mineral Commodity Summaries 2021." [online] from https://www.usgs.gov/centers/nmic/mineral-commodity-summaries [Published January 29, 2021], from U.S. Geological Survey.

★ 2142 ★
Manga
SIC: 2721; NAICS: 51112, 51913

Manga and Light Novel Sales in Japan, 2020

Data show manga and light novel sales by series for November 18, 2019 to November 21, 2020. Figures are in millions.

Kimetsu no Yaiba	82.34
Kingdom	8.25
One Piece	7.70
Haikyuu	7.21
Jujitsu Kaisen	6.70
Yakusoku no Neverland	6.36
5-Toubun no Hanayome	6.14
Boku no Hero Academia	6.00
Spy x Family	4.54
Shingeki no Kyojin	4.30

Source: "Japan's Yearly Manga and Light Novel Rankings for 2020." [online] from https://myanimelist.net/news/61260265 [Published November 29, 2020], from Anime News Network.

★ 2143 ★
Manganese
SIC: 3313; NAICS: 33111

Top Manganese Producing Countries, 2020

Countries are ranked by production in thousands of metric tons. Data for Kazakhstan and Ukraine refer to concentrate. "Other" does not include the United States. Manganese ore containing 20% or more manganese has not been produced in the United States since 1970. Production data are estimated.

	(000)	Share
South Africa	5,200	28.12%
Australia	3,300	17.85
Gabon	2,800	15.14
Ghana	1,400	7.57
China	1,300	7.03
Brazil	1,200	6.49
India	640	3.46
Ukraine	550	2.97
Côte d'Ivoire	460	2.49
Burma	400	2.16
Malaysia	350	1.89
Mexico	190	1.03
Georgia	150	0.81
Vietnam	150	0.81
Kazakhstan	130	0.70
Other	270	1.46

Source: "Mineral Commodity Summaries 2021." [online] from https://www.usgs.gov/centers/nmic/mineral-commodity-summaries [Published January 29, 2021], from U.S. Geological Survey.

★ 2144 ★
Manhole Covers
SIC: 3321; NAICS: 331511

Leading Manhole Cover Makers Worldwide, 2019

Market shares are shown based on revenue.

Baogai New Material	4.45%
Changsha Jinlong Casting	3.55
San Qun	3.41
Other	88.59

Source: "COVID-19 Impact on Global Manhole Covers Market Size Status and Forecast 2020-2026." [online] from http://reports.valuates.com [Published April 2020], from QY Research.

★ 2145 ★
Mannequins
SIC: 3999; NAICS: 339999

Leading Mannequin Makers Worldwide, 2019

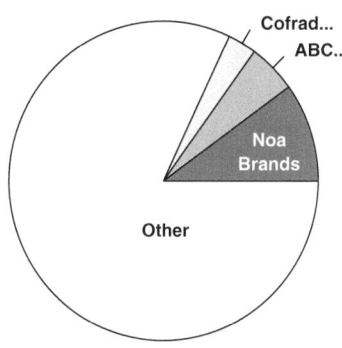

Mannequins, also known as dummies or dress forms, are used by window dressers, tailors, and others to display apparel. The industry is forecast to grow from $1.11 billion in 2019 to $1.42 billion in 2026. Market shares are shown based on revenue.

Noa Brands	10.37%
ABC Mannequins	5.07
Cofrad Mannequins	2.80
Other	81.76

Source: "Global Mannequin Market Size, Manufacturers, Supply Chain, Sales Channel and Clients, 2020-2026." [online] from http://www.qyresearch.com [Published July 2020], from QY Research.

★ 2146 ★
Marble
SIC: 1423; NAICS: 212313

U.S. Marble Imports, 2020

Data show imports for July 2020. Imports reached $47.66 million in July 2020, down from $55.32 million the same period in 2019.

	Sales	Share
China	$ 13,453,487	28.21%
Italy	10,497,986	22.02
Turkey	9,995,800	20.96
Mexico	2,854,506	5.99
Greece	1,340,625	2.81
Canada	1,295,852	2.72
Portugal	962,750	2.02
Other	7,282,168	15.27

Source: *Stone World*, November 2020, p. 20, from U.S. Department of Commerce.

★ 2147 ★
Marinated Vegetables and Fruits
SIC: 2099; NAICS: 311991

Leading Marinated Vegetable and Fruit Brands, 2020

Brands are ranked based on sales at supermarkets, drug stores, mass merchandisers, military commissaries, and select club and dollar chains for the 12 weeks ended September 6, 2020.

	Sales	Share
Nasoya	$ 2,731,433	27.84%
Seoul	2,063,073	21.03
DeLallo	546,826	5.57
Winter Gardens	394,516	4.02
Jo San	391,773	3.99
Wildbrine	349,755	3.57
Cedar's	342,542	3.49
Oh Snap! Pickling Co.	320,185	3.26
Mother in Law's Kimchi	318,900	3.25
Private label	727,409	7.42
Other	1,623,322	16.55

Source: *Frozen & Refrigerated Buyer*, November 2020, p. 10, from IRI.

★ 2148 ★
Mass Transit
SIC: 4141; NAICS: 48551

Charter Bus Industry Leaders, 2017

Data show the percent of industry sales held by the largest 4, 8, 20 and 50 firms in the sector. There are approximately 1,308 players operating in the industry generating employment for 35,210 people. According to Kentley Insights, the industry generated sales of $3.3 billion in 2019. The industry suffered in 2020 because of the reduced number of travelers due to the pandemic.

4 largest firms	14.2%
8 largest firms	20.0
20 largest firms	29.3
50 largest firms	43.7

Source: "Economic Census." [online] from https://www.census.gov/content/census/en/data/tables/2017/econ/economic-census/naics-sector-31-33.html [Accessed January 21, 2021], from U.S. Census Bureau.

★ 2149 ★
Mass Transit
SIC: 4111; NAICS: 485112

Largest Amtrak Stations, 2019

Stations are ranked by millions of passengers transported during the fiscal year.

New York Penn Station, NY	10.8
Washington D.C.	5.2
Philadelphia Gray 30th Street, PA	4.5
Chicago, IL	3.3
Boston South Station, MA	1.6
Los Angeles, CA	1.4
Sacramento, CA	1.1
Baltimore, MD	1.0
Albany-Rensselaer, NY	0.8
New Haven Union Station, CT	0.8

Source: "Pocket Guide to Transportation 2020." [online] from http://www.bts.gov [Published June 2020], from U.S. Department of Transportation and Amtrak Fact Sheet.

★ 2150 ★
Mass Transit
SIC: 4141; NAICS: 48551

Largest Bus Agencies, 2018

Companies are ranked by millions of unlinked passenger trips.

MTA New York City Transit	691.98
Los Angeles County Metropolitan Transportation Authority	273.62
Chicago Transit Authority	242.17
Southeastern Pennsylvania Transportation Authority	161.53
New Jersey Transit Corp.	151.64
MTA Bus Co.	137.61
Washington Metropolitan Area Transit Authority	119.68
San Francisco Municipal Railway	111.80
King County DOT - Mass Transit	104.26
Massachusetts Bay Transportation Authority	102.69

Source: "2020 Public Transportation Fact Book." [online] from https://www.apta.com/wp-content/uploads/APTA-2020-Fact-Book.pdf [Published March 2020], from American Public Transportation Association.

★ 2151 ★
Mass Transit
SIC: 4141; NAICS: 48551

Largest Bus Rapid Transit Agencies, 2018

Companies are ranked by millions of unlinked passenger trips.

MTA New York City Transit	30.27
Massachusetts Bay Transportation Authority	10.54
Los Angeles County Metropolitan Transportation Authority	7.16
Greater Cleveland Regional Transit Authority	3.76
Lane Transit District	3.49
Connecticut Department of Transportation	1.55
Transfort	1.46
Kansas City Area Transportation Authority	1.16
Central Florida Regional Transportation Authority	1.03
Roaring Fork Transportation Authority	0.92

Source: "2020 Public Transportation Fact Book." [online] from https://www.apta.com/wp-content/uploads/APTA-2020-Fact-Book.pdf [Published March 2020], from American Public Transportation Association.

★ 2152 ★
Mass Transit
SIC: 4119; NAICS: 485999

Largest Cable Car/Aerial Tramway/Inclined Plane Agencies, 2018

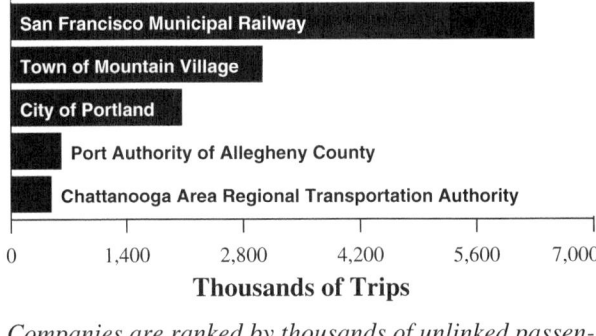

Thousands of Trips

Companies are ranked by thousands of unlinked passenger trips.

San Francisco Municipal Railway	6,292.3
Town of Mountain Village	3,026.1
City of Portland	2,068.0
Port Authority of Allegheny County	610.4
Chattanooga Area Regional Transportation Authority	489.5

Source: "2020 Public Transportation Fact Book." [online] from https://www.apta.com/wp-content/uploads/APTA-2020-Fact-Book.pdf [Published March 2020], from American Public Transportation Association.

★ 2153 ★
Mass Transit
SIC: 4119; NAICS: 485999

Largest Commuter Rail and Hybrid Rail Agencies, 2018

Companies are ranked by millions of unlinked passenger trips.

MTA Long Island Rail Road	105.53
MTA Metro-North Commuter Railroad	91.87
New Jersey Transit Corp.	87.05
Northeast Illinois Regional Commuter Railroad Corp.	68.44
Massachusetts Bay Transportation Authority	32.85
Southeastern Pennsylvania Transportation Authority	32.24
Peninsula Corridor Joint Powers Board	18.50
Southern California Regional Rail Authority	14.19
Maryland Transit Administration	9.32
Denver Regional Transportation District	7.61

Source: "2020 Public Transportation Fact Book." [online] from https://www.apta.com/wp-content/uploads/APTA-2020-Fact-Book.pdf [Published March 2020], from American Public Transportation Association.

★ 2154 ★
Mass Transit
SIC: 4141; NAICS: 48551

Largest Commuter Transit Bus Agencies, 2018

Companies are ranked by millions of unlinked passenger trips.

Central Puget Sound Regional Transit Authority	18.18
MTA New York City Transit	12.40
Metropolitan Transit Authority of Harris County, Texas	7.86
Hudson Transit Lines Inc.	4.31
Maryland Transit Administration	3.81
Academy Lines Inc.	3.28
Snohomish County PTBA Corp.	2.99
Alameda-Contra Costa Transit District	2.54
Suburban Transit Corp.	2.46
Rockland Coaches Inc.	1.99

Source: "2020 Public Transportation Fact Book." [online] from https://www.apta.com/wp-content/uploads/APTA-2020-Fact-Book.pdf [Published March 2020], from American Public Transportation Association.

★ 2155 ★
Mass Transit
SIC: 4119; NAICS: 485999

Largest Demand Response Agencies, 2018

Companies are ranked by millions of unlinked passenger trips.

MTA New York City Transit	5.08
Pace-Suburban Bus Division, ADA Para Services	3.84
Metro Mobility	2.29
Washington Metropolitan Area Transit Authority	2.26
Access Services	2.22
Maryland Transit Administration	2.14
Massachusetts Bay Transportation Authority	1.95
Metropolitan Transit Authority of Harris County, Texas	1.77
Miami-Dade Transit	1.74
New Jersey Transit Corp.	1.63

Source: "2020 Public Transportation Fact Book." [online] from https://www.apta.com/wp-content/uploads/APTA-2020-Fact-Book.pdf [Published March 2020], from American Public Transportation Association.

★ 2156 ★
Mass Transit
SIC: 4482; NAICS: 483114, 483212

Largest Ferryboat Agencies, 2018

Companies are ranked by millions of unlinked passenger trips. Port Imperial Ferry Corporation does business as NY Waterway.

Washington State Ferries	24.56
New York City Department of Transportation	24.49
Port Imperial Ferry Corporation	4.65
New York City Economic Development Corp.	4.10
Martha's Vineyard and Nantucket Steamship	3.05
San Francisco Bay Area Water Emergency Transportation authority	2.84
Golden Gate Bridge, Highway and Transportation District	2.57
BillyBey Ferry Co.	1.91
Massachusetts Bay Transportation Authority	1.49
Port Authority Trans-Hudson Corp.	1.37

Source: "2020 Public Transportation Fact Book." [online] from https://www.apta.com/wp-content/uploads/APTA-2020-Fact-Book.pdf [Published March 2020], from American Public Transportation Association.

★ 2157 ★
Mass Transit
SIC: 4119; NAICS: 485999

Largest Light Rail Agencies, 2018

Companies are ranked by millions of unlinked passenger trips.

Los Angeles County Metropolitan Transportation Authority	66.38
Massachusetts Bay Transportation Authority	56.76
San Francisco Municipal Railway	49.83
Tri-County Metropolitan Transportation District of Oregon	38.91
San Diego Metropolitan Transit System	36.99
Dallas Area Rapid Transit	28.87
Denver Regional Transportation District	25.32
Metro Transit (MN)	24.95
Central Puget Sound Regional Transit Authority	24.47
New Jersey Transit Corp.	20.95

Source: "2020 Public Transportation Fact Book." [online] from https://www.apta.com/wp-content/uploads/APTA-2020-Fact-Book.pdf [Published March 2020], from American Public Transportation Association.

★ 2158 ★
Mass Transit
SIC: 4119; NAICS: 485999

Largest Monorail and Automated Guideway Transit Agencies, 2018

Companies are ranked by thousands of unlinked passenger trips. The Detroit Transportation Corp. operates the Detroit People Mover.

Miami-Dade Transit	8,802.5
City of Seattle-Seattle Center Monorail Transit	2,021.8
West Virginia University	1,961.7
Detroit Transportation Corp.	1,952.5
San Francisco Bay Area Rapid Transit District	962.3

Source: "2020 Public Transportation Fact Book." [online] from https://www.apta.com/wp-content/uploads/APTA-2020-Fact-Book.pdf [Published March 2020], from American Public Transportation Association.

★ 2159 ★
Mass Transit
SIC: 4119; NAICS: 485999

Largest Streetcar Agencies, 2018

Companies are ranked by millions of unlinked passenger trips.

Southeastern Pennsylvania Transportation Authority	24.99
New Orleans Regional Transit Authority	7.74
San Francisco Municipal Railway	7.47
City of Portland	4.87
Kansas City, City of Missouri	2.01
King County Department of Transportation (King County Metro)	1.68
M-1 Rail	1.19
Progressive Transportation Services Administration	1.17
City of Tucson	0.89
Central Puget Sound Regional Transit Authority	0.85

Source: "2020 Public Transportation Fact Book." [online] from https://www.apta.com/wp-content/uploads/APTA-2020-Fact-Book.pdf [Published March 2020], from American Public Transportation Association.

★ 2160 ★
Mass Transit
SIC: 4119; NAICS: 485999

Largest Transit Vanpool Agencies, 2018

Companies are ranked by millions of unlinked passenger trips.

King County Department of Transportation	3.46
Los Angeles County Metropolitan Transportation Authority	3.42
California Vanpool Authority	3.17
Metropolitan Transit Authority of Harris County, Texas	1.87
San Diego Association of Governments	1.74
Pace-Suburban Bus Division	1.50
Potomac and Rappahannock Transportation Commission	1.35
Orange County Transportation Authority	1.28
Utah Transit Authority	1.17
Regional Public Transportation Authority	1.03

Source: "2020 Public Transportation Fact Book." [online] from https://www.apta.com/wp-content/uploads/APTA-2020-Fact-Book.pdf [Published March 2020], from American Public Transportation Association.

★ 2161 ★
Mass Transit
SIC: 4119; NAICS: 485999

Largest Trolleybus Agencies, 2018

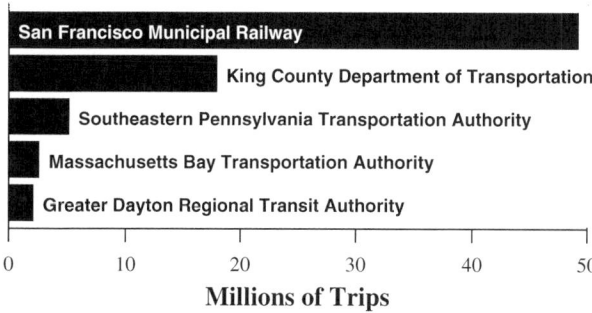

Companies are ranked by millions of unlinked passenger trips.

San Francisco Municipal Railway	49.19
King County Department of Transportation	17.95
Southeastern Pennsylvania Transportation Authority	5.08
Massachusetts Bay Transportation Authority	2.57
Greater Dayton Regional Transit Authority	2.08

Source: "2020 Public Transportation Fact Book." [online] from https://www.apta.com/wp-content/uploads/APTA-2020-Fact-Book.pdf [Published March 2020], from American Public Transportation Association.

★ 2162 ★
Mass Transit
SIC: 4119; NAICS: 48532, 48541

Leading Mass Transit Firms, 2018

Companies are ranked by millions of unlinked passenger trips.

MTA New York City Transit	3,368.10
Chicago Transit Authority	468.06
Los Angeles County Metropolitan Transportation Authority	394.36
Massachusetts Metropolitan Area Transit Authority	372.39
Washington Metropolitan Area Transit Authority	351.29
Southeastern Pennsylvania Transportation Authority	319.42
New Jersey Transit Corporation	264.67
San Francisco Municipal Railway	225.05
MTA Bus Co.	137.61
King County Department of Transportation	129.05

Source: "2020 Public Transportation Fact Book." [online] from https://www.apta.com/wp-content/uploads/APTA-2020-Fact-Book.pdf [Published March 2020], from American Public Transportation Association.

★ 2163 ★
Mass Transit
SIC: 4111; NAICS: 485112

Passenger Railway Undertakings in Europe, 2016-2018

Market shares are shown based on passenger-kilometers traveled. Total for 26 countries by year: 458 billion in 2016, 475 billion in 2017 to 480 billion in 2018. With the exception of five countries, the countries in the study all saw growth in 2018. Lithuania was the fastest-growing country because of the expansion of online sales.

	2016	2017	2018
Domestic incumbents	76.0%	77.0%	76.0%
Non-incumbents	16.0	14.0	15.0
Foreign incumbents	6.0	7.0	7.0
Principal RIJ	2.0	2.0	2.0

Source: *Railway Pro*, August 2020, p. 41, from IRG Rail, 8th RMM Report.

★ 2164 ★
Mass Transit
SIC: 4141; NAICS: 48551

Regional Bus Market in the United Kingdom, 2020

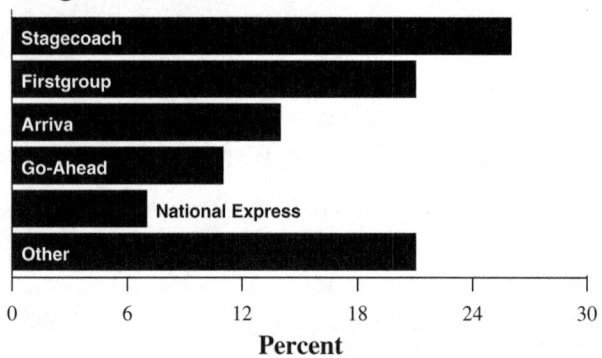

Market shares are shown in percent. Go-Ahead was the leader in the London market with a 24% share, followed by Arriva at 18%, Metroline with 17%, Stagecoach 13%, and other companies 28%.

Stagecoach	26.0%
Firstgroup	21.0
Arriva	14.0
Go-Ahead	11.0
National Express	7.0
Other	21.0

Source: "Go-Ahead Moving Communities Today Towards a Greener Tomorrow." [online] from https://gog-11615-s3.s3.eu-west-2.amazonaws.com/live/4016/0092/6016/The_Go_Ahead_Group_plc_Annual_Report_and_Accounts_2020.pdf [Published June 27, 2020].

★ 2165 ★
Meal Kits
SIC: 4215; NAICS: 49211, 49221

Leading Home Meal Solution Providers in Canada, 2020

Data show thousands of monthly visitors as of October 2020. According to Baum + Whiteman, an estimated 150 companies operate in the meal solution/kit market. Hexa Research expects this industry to be worth U.S. $8 billion in 2025.

Metro	2,400
IGA	1,900
Nofrills	1,900
Good Food	1,000
Instacart	960
Sobeys	940
Maxi	910
Loblaws	870
Hello Fresh	750
Safeway	410

Source: "Goodfood Investor Presentation." [online] from https://www.makegoodfood.ca/en/investisseurs/evenements [Published January 2021], from Similar Web.

★ 2166 ★
Meat
SIC: 2013; NAICS: 311612

Beef Production by Year, 2016-2021

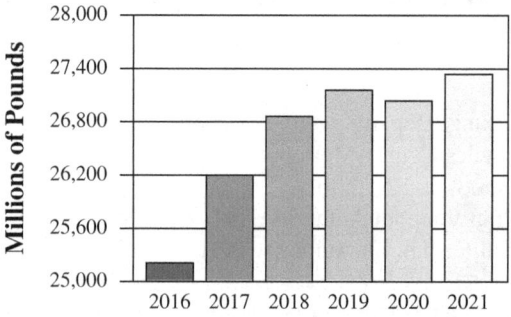

Production is shown in millions of pounds as of September 17, 2020. Figures for 2020-2021 are forecasts.

2016	25,221
2017	26,187
2018	26,872
2019	27,155
2020	27,048
2021	27,355

Source: *The National Provisioner*, October 2020, p. 19, from IRI and World Agricultural Supply and Demand estimates.

★ 2167 ★
Meat
SIC: 2013; NAICS: 311612

Beef Sales by Category, 2020

Figures are based on multi-outlet sales for the 52 weeks ended October 4, 2020. They are drawn from the IRI Syndicated Integrated Fresh database, which combines random- and fixed-weight brands/product types known to be sold in this department at the majority of retailers.

Ground beef	39.7%
Loin	14.6
Ribeye	12.0
Chuck	7.7
Round	7.2
Ingredient cuts	6.0
Sirloin	6.0
Brisket	2.4
Ribs	1.6
Offal	1.1
Flank	0.8

Source: *Winsight Grocery Business*, December 2020, p. H12, from IRI Syndicated Integrated Fresh database.

★ 2168 ★
Meat
SIC: 0251; NAICS: 11232

Broiler Production by Year, 2016-2021

Production is shown in millions of pounds as of September 17, 2020. Figures for 2020-2021 are forecasts.

2016	40,696
2017	41,662
2018	42,601
2019	43,905
2020	44,552
2021	45,020

Source: *The National Provisioner*, October 2020, p. 33, from IRI and World Agricultural Supply and Demand estimates.

★ 2169 ★
Meat
SIC: 2015; NAICS: 311615

Chicken Sales by Category, 2020

Figures are based on multi-outlet sales for the 52 weeks ended October 4, 2020. They are drawn from the IRI Syndicated Integrated Fresh database, which combines random- and fixed-weight brands/product types known to be sold in this department at the majority of retailers.

Breast	57.0%
Thighs	12.9
Wings	8.3%
Legs	8.0
Whole birds	5.7
Processed chicken	4.0
Ground chicken	1.5
Ingredient cuts	1.4
Cornish game hens	0.4
Giblets	0.4
Combo packs	0.3

Source: *Winsight Grocery Business*, December 2020, p. H12, from IRI Syndicated Integrated Fresh database.

★ 2170 ★
Meat
SIC: 2013; NAICS: 311612

Cultured Meat Sales, 2020

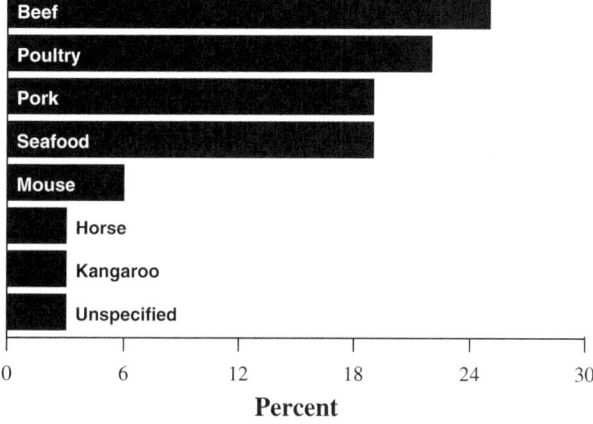

Cultured meats are produced by in vitro culture of animal cells. With the global population expected to reach 9.7 billion in 2050, cultured meat is one way to help meet the growing demand for food. As well, it helps make the food industry more sustainable, as meat production requires considerable land and water. The table refers to the cultured meat interests of 32 companies.

Beef	25.0%
Poultry	22.0
Pork	19.0
Seafood	19.0
Mouse	6.0
Horse	3.0
Kangaroo	3.0
Unspecified	3.0

Source: *Trends in Biotechnology*, June 2020, p. 573.

★ 2171 ★
Meat
SIC: 2013; NAICS: 311612

Fresh Meat Sales, 2020

Data show meat department sales for the 52 weeks ended October 4, 2020. Figures are based on multi-outlet sales and are drawn from the IRI Syndicated Integrated Fresh database, which combines random- and fixed-weight brands/product types known to be sold at this department at the majority of retailers.

Beef	54.2%
Chicken	25.4
Pork	13.1
Turkey	4.9
Alternative/substitutes	0.8
Other meat	1.6

Source: *Winsight Grocery Business*, December 2020, p. H12, from IRI Syndicated Integrated Fresh database.

★ 2172 ★
Meat
SIC: 2013; NAICS: 311612

Global Meat Sales, 2025-2040

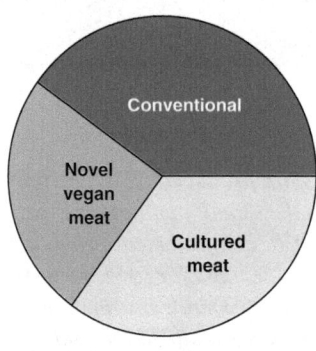

Spending is forecast to grow from $1.2 trillion in 2025 to $1.4 trillion in 2030 to $1.6 trillion to $1.8 billion trillion in 2040.

	2025	2030	2035	2040
Conventional	90.0%	72.0%	55.0%	40.0%
Novel vegan meat replacement	10.0	18.0	23.0	25.0
Cultured meat	0.0	10.0	22.0	35.0

Source: *South China Morning Post*, December 25, 2020, p. NA, from A.T. Kearney.

★ 2173 ★
Meat
SIC: 2013; NAICS: 311612

Leading Beef and Veal Consuming Regions, 2021

Figures are in thousands of metric tons (carcass weight equivalent). The meat of other types of bovines may be included for some countries.

	(000)	Share
United States	12,513	20.87%
China	9,730	16.23
Brazil	7,840	13.08
European Union	7,710	12.86
India	2,750	4.59
Argentina	2,344	3.91
Mexico	1,905	3.18
Pakistan	1,781	2.97
Russia	1,703	2.84
Canada	1,325	2.21
Other	10,349	17.26

Source: "Livestock and Poultry: World Markets and Trade." [online] from https://apps.fas.usda.gov/psdonline/circulars/livestock_poultry.pdf [Published October 9, 2020], from U.S. Department of Agriculture.

★ 2174 ★
Meat
SIC: 2013; NAICS: 311612

Leading Beef and Veal Producers Worldwide, 2021

Figures are in thousands of metric tons (carcass weight equivalent). The meat of other types of bovines may be included for some countries.

	(000)	Share
United States	12,479	20.31%
Brazil	10,470	17.04
European Union	7,730	12.58
China	6,900	11.23
India	3,950	6.43
Argentina	3,100	5.04
Mexico	2,130	3.47
Australia	2,050	3.34
Pakistan	1,840	2.99
Russia	1,385	2.25
Other	9,419	15.33

Source: "Livestock and Poultry: World Markets and Trade." [online] from https://apps.fas.usda.gov/psdonline/circulars/livestock_poultry.pdf [Published October 9, 2020], from U.S. Department of Agriculture.

★ 2175 ★
Meat
SIC: 2011; NAICS: 311611

Leading Braised Meat Brands in China, 2020

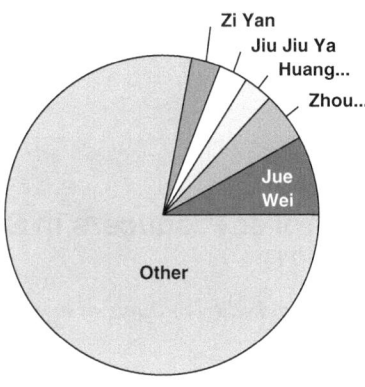

Meat snacks claimed 21.5% of overall snack sales in 2020, up from 13.5% in 2017. The source notes that the pandemic plays some role in this, as consumers were looking to consume heartier snacks and fewer meals. Popular types of braised meat include duck tongues, ducks and pork intestines.

Jue Wei	8.0%
Zhou Hei Ya	5.0
Huang Shang Huang	3.0
Jiu Jiu Ya	3.0
Zi Yan	3.0
Other	78.0

Source: "Meat Snacks in China: Meat Rose from 14% to 21% of Country's Snack Consumption in 2020." [online] from https://daxueconsulting.com/meat-snacks-in-china/ [Published March 2, 2021], from MobTech.

★ 2176 ★
Meat
SIC: 0251; NAICS: 11232

Leading Broiler Processors, 2020

Companies are ranked by average weekly slaughter in millions of pounds. Production reached 984.24 million pounds of ready-to-cook chicken.

	(mil.)	Share
Tyson Foods	230.30	23.40%
Pilgrim's Pride Corp.	179.82	18.27
Sanderson Farms Inc.	102.50	10.41
Perdue Foods	76.52	7.77
Koch Foods Inc.	72.31	7.35
Mountaire Farms Inc.	68.65	6.97%
Wayne Farms L.L.C.	54.60	5.55
Peco Foods	45.30	4.60
George's Inc.	35.23	3.58
House of Raeford Farms Inc.	34.90	3.55
Other	84.11	8.55

Source: WATTPoultry USA, March 2021, p. 21.

★ 2177 ★
Meat
SIC: 0251; NAICS: 11232

Leading Broiler Producers in Africa, 2019

Companies are ranked by millions of heads slaughtered annually.

Astral Foods	260.0
RCL Foods Ltd.	260.0
Cairo Poultry Co. (CPC)	75.0
Country Bird Holdings Ltd.	74.0
Sovereign Food Investments	70.0
Arab Poultry Breeders Co. (Ommat)	58.0
Daybreak Farms	52.0
Quantum Foods	40.8
Alf Sahel S.A.R.L.	30.0
Pyramid Poultry Co.	18.0

Source: Poultry International, October 2020, p. 12, from WATT Global Media.

★ 2178 ★
Meat
SIC: 0251; NAICS: 11232

Leading Broiler Producers in Asia, 2019

Companies are ranked by millions of heads slaughtered annually.

New Hope Liuhe	1,300.0
Wen's Food Group	748.0
CP Foods	685.0
Fujian Sunner Development Co. Ltd.	450.0
Dayoo Group	400.0
Suguna Foods	400.0
Harim Group	392.6
San Miguel Pure Foods	352.0
Japfa Ltd.	320.0
Jiangsu Lihua Animal Husbandry	261.0

Source: Poultry International, October 2020, p. 14, from WATT Global Media.

★ 2179 ★
Meat
SIC: 0251; NAICS: 11232

Leading Broiler Producers in Europe, 2019

Companies are ranked by millions of heads slaughtered annually.

LDC	578.5
MHP (Myronivsky Hliboproduct)	478.0
Plukon Food Group	426.4
Gruppo Veronesi	350.0
PHW Group	350.0
2 Sisters Food Group	323.0
Cherkizovo Group	318.8
Moy Park Ltd.	312.0
Resource Group of Companies	287.2
Amadori	250.0

Source: *Poultry International*, October 2020, p. 22, from WATT Global Media.

★ 2180 ★
Meat
SIC: 0251; NAICS: 11232

Leading Broiler Producers in North America, 2019

Companies are ranked by millions of heads slaughtered annually.

Tyson Foods	1,991.6
Pilgrim's Pride Corp.	1,575.6
Koch Foods Inc.	681.2
Perdue Farms	667.7
Sanderson Farms Inc.	622.4
Industrias Bachoco	622.0
Cargill Inc.	545.0
Wayne Farms L.L.C.	395.2
Mountaire Farms Inc.	394.7
George's Inc.	357.8

Source: *Poultry International*, October 2020, p. 34, from WATT Global Media.

★ 2181 ★
Meat
SIC: 0251; NAICS: 11232

Leading Broiler Producers in Oceania, 2019

Companies are ranked by millions of heads slaughtered annually.

Baiada Poultry	208.0
Inghams Enterprises PTY Ltd.	208.0
Turosi	75.0
Tegel Foods	58.0
The Golden Cockerel Group	44.0
Hazeldene's	35.3
P H Van Den Brink	15.0

Source: *Poultry International*, October 2020, p. 36, from WATT Global Media.

★ 2182 ★
Meat
SIC: 0251; NAICS: 11232

Leading Broiler Producers in South America, 2019

Companies are ranked by millions of heads slaughtered annually.

JBS S.A.	4,036.0
BRF S.A.	1,554.0
San Fernando	280.0
Aurora Alimentos	242.6
Granja Tres Arroyos	177.9
Copacol	172.3
Avidesa	150.0
Lar Cooperativa Agroindustrial	149.0
C Vale - Cooperativa Agroindustrial	144.7
Agrosuper	144.5

Source: *Poultry International*, October 2020, p. 38, from WATT Global Media.

★ 2183 ★
Meat
SIC: 0251; NAICS: 11232

Leading Broiler Producers in the Caribbean and Central America, 2019

Companies are ranked by millions of heads slaughtered annually.

Division Industial Pecuaria (DIP-CMI)	200.0
Cargill Proteína Latinoamérica	110.0
Jamaica Broilers Group Ltd.	54.4
Pollo Cibao	53.0
FRISA (Areca)	44.0
Productos Toledano	26.5
Grupo Melo	26.0
Coave	23.0
Grupo SuperAlba	20.0
Pollos Eccus	19.0

Source: *Poultry International*, October 2020, p. 18, from WATT Global Media.

★ 2184 ★
Meat
SIC: 0251; NAICS: 11232

Leading Broiler Producers in the Middle East, 2019

Companies are ranked by millions of heads slaughtered annually.

Arab Company for Livestock Development (ACOLID)	562
Al-Watania	300
Al-Fakieh Poultry Farms	200
Almarai Co.	189
Erpiliç	160
Keskinoglu	146
Beypiliç	121
Senpiliç Gida Sanayi	110
Banvit	90
Abalioglu Group	70

Source: *Poultry International*, October 2020, p. 30, from WATT Global Media.

★ 2185 ★
Meat
SIC: 0251; NAICS: 11232

Leading Broiler Producers Worldwide, 2019

Companies are ranked by millions of heads slaughtered annually.

JBS S.A.	4,036.0
Tyson Foods	1,991.6
BRF S.A.	1,554.0
New Hope Liuhe	1,300.0
Wen's Food Group	748.0
CP Group	685.0
Koch Foods Inc.	681.2
Perdue Farms	667.7
Sanderson Farms Inc.	622.4
Industrias Bachoco	622.0

Source: *Poultry International*, October 2020, p. 6, from WATT Global Media.

★ 2186 ★
Meat
SIC: 2013; NAICS: 311612

Leading Canned Ham Brands, 2020

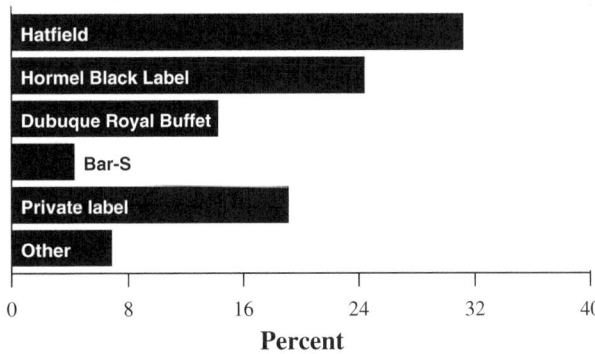

Brands are ranked based on sales at supermarkets, drug stores, mass merchandisers, military commissaries, and select club and dollar chains for the 12 weeks ended February 21, 2021.

	Sales	Share
Hatfield	$ 2,648,557	31.18%
Hormel Black Label	2,070,444	24.38
Dubuque Royal Buffet	1,210,323	14.25
Bar-S	360,113	4.24
Private label	1,624,438	19.12
Other	580,038	6.83

Source: *Frozen & Refrigerated Buyer*, April 2021, p. 10, from IRI.

★ 2187 ★
Meat
SIC: 2015; NAICS: 311615

Leading Chicken Meat Consumers Worldwide, 2021

Figures are in thousands of metric tons (ready-to-cook equivalent).

	(000)	Share
United States	17,189	17.07%
China	15,815	15.70

Continued on next page.

★ 2187 ★
[Continued]
Meat
SIC: 2015; NAICS: 311615

Leading Chicken Meat Consumers Worldwide, 2021

Figures are in thousands of metric tons (ready-to-cook equivalent).

	(000)	Share
European Union	11,850	11.77%
Brazil	10,238	10.17
Russia	4,715	4.68
Mexico	4,655	4.62
India	4,199	4.17
Japan	2,831	2.81
Thailand	2,420	2.40
Argentina	2,059	2.04
Malaysia	1,860	1.85
Other	22,881	22.72

Source: "Livestock and Poultry: World Markets and Trade." [online] from https://apps.fas.usda.gov/psdonline/circulars/livestock_poultry.pdf [Published October 9, 2020], from U.S. Department of Agriculture.

★ 2188 ★
Meat
SIC: 2015; NAICS: 311615

Leading Chicken Meat Consuming Regions, 2020-2021

Data are in thousands of metric tons. Figures are as of October 2020.

	(000)	Share
United States	17,189	17.07%
China	15,815	15.70
European Union	11,850	11.77
Brazil	10,238	10.17
Russia	4,715	4.68
Mexico	4,655	4.62
India	4,199	4.17
Japan	2,831	2.81
Thailand	2,420	2.40
Argentina	2,059	2.04
Malaysia	1,860	1.85
Other	22,881	22.72

Source: "Chicken Meat Production - Top Countries Summary." [online] from https://apps.fas.usda.gov/psdonline/app/index.html#/app/downloads [Published October 2020], from U.S. Department of Agriculture.

★ 2189 ★
Meat
SIC: 2015; NAICS: 311615

Leading Chicken Meat Exporting Regions, 2020-2021

Data are in thousands of metric tons of ready-to-cook equivalent. Figures are as of October 2020.

	(000)	Share
Brazil	3,940	32.33%
United States	3,331	27.34
European Union	1,470	12.06
Thailand	920	7.55
Turkey	470	3.86
Ukraine	430	3.53
China	410	3.36
Russia	220	1.81
Belarus	205	1.68
Argentina	165	1.35
Chile	150	1.23
Other	474	3.89

Source: "Chicken Meat Production - Top Countries Summary." [online] from https://apps.fas.usda.gov/psdonline/app/index.html#/app/downloads [Published October 2020], from U.S. Department of Agriculture.

★ 2190 ★
Meat
SIC: 2015; NAICS: 311615

Leading Chicken Meat Importing Regions, 2020-2021

Data are in thousands of metric tons of ready-to-cook equivalent. Figures are as of October 2020.

	(000)	Share
Japan	1,055	7.68%
China	925	6.73
Mexico	885	6.44
European Union	720	5.24
Saudi Arabia	625	4.55
Iraq	500	3.64
United Arab Emirates	400	2.91
Philippines	375	2.73
South Africa	325	2.37
Hong Kong	315	2.29
United States	61	0.44
Other	3,777	27.49

Source: "Chicken Meat Production - Top Countries Summary." [online] from https://apps.fas.usda.gov/psdonline/app/index.html#/app/downloads [Published October 2020], from U.S. Department of Agriculture.

★ 2191 ★
Meat
SIC: 2015; NAICS: 311615

Leading Chicken Meat Producers Worldwide, 2021

Figures are in thousands of metric tons (ready-to-cook equivalent).

	(000)	Share
China	15,300	14.96%
Brazil	14,175	13.86
European Union	12,600	12.32
United States	4,765	4.66
Russia	4,725	4.62
India	4,200	4.11
Mexico	3,775	3.69
Thailand	3,340	3.27
Turkey	2,250	2.20
Other	37,166	36.33

Source: "Livestock and Poultry: World Markets and Trade." [online] from https://apps.fas.usda.gov/psdonline/circulars/livestock_poultry.pdf [Published October 9, 2020], from U.S. Department of Agriculture.

★ 2192 ★
Meat
SIC: 2015; NAICS: 311615

Leading Chicken Meat Producing Regions, 2020-2021

Data are in thousands of metric tons. Figures are as of October 2020.

	(000)	Share
United States	20,465	19.89%
China	15,300	14.87
Brazil	14,175	13.77
European Union	12,600	12.24
Russia	4,725	4.59
India	4,200	4.08
Mexico	3,775	3.67
Thailand	3,340	3.25
Turkey	2,250	2.19
Argentina	2,220	2.16
Malaysia	1,800	1.75
Other	18,066	17.55

Source: "Chicken Meat Production - Top Countries Summary." [online] from https://apps.fas.usda.gov/psdonline/app/index.html#/app/downloads [Published October 2020], from U.S. Department of Agriculture.

★ 2193 ★
Meat
SIC: 2013; NAICS: 311612

Leading Dried Meat Snack Brands (No Jerky), 2020

Brands are ranked based on sales at supermarkets, drug stores, mass merchandisers, military commissaries, and select club and dollar chains for the 52 weeks ended September 6, 2020.

	($ mil.)	Share
Slim Jim	$ 660.54	35.49%
Jack Link's	466.36	25.06
Old Wisconsin	103.20	5.55
Jack Link's Wild	71.48	3.84
Duke's	54.83	2.95
Matador by Jack Link's	44.97	2.42
Tillamook Country Smoker	35.02	1.88
Penrose Big Mama	34.19	1.84
Old Trapper	27.24	1.46
Private label	53.38	2.87
Other	309.79	16.65

Source: *The National Provisioner*, October 2020, p. 21, from IRI.

★ 2194 ★
Meat
SIC: 2013; NAICS: 311612

Leading Dried Meat Snack Makers, 2020

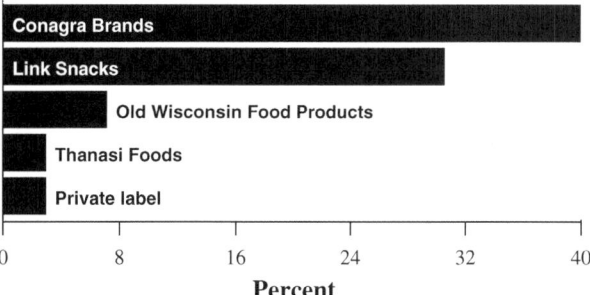

Companies are ranked based on sales at supermarkets, drug stores, mass merchandisers, military commissaries, and select club and dollar chains for the 52 weeks ended November 1, 2020.

	($ mil.)	Share
Conagra Brands	$ 755.3	39.9%
Link Snacks	577.0	30.5
Old Wisconsin Food Products	135.3	7.1
Thanasi Foods	54.7	2.9
Private label	55.0	2.9

Source: *The National Provisioner*, January 2021, p. 27, from IRI.

★ 2195 ★
Meat
SIC: 2013; NAICS: 311612

Leading Frozen Meat Brands (No Poultry), 2020

Brands are ranked based on sales at supermarkets, drug stores, mass merchandisers, military commissaries, and select club and dollar chains for the 52 weeks ended September 6, 2020.

	($ mil.)	Share
Bubba Burger	$ 181.18	8.87%
Cooked Perfect	102.53	5.02
Steak-umm	67.52	3.30
Philly Gourmet	50.43	2.47
Private label	920.90	45.07
Other	720.51	35.27

Source: *The National Provisioner*, October 2020, p. 13, from IRI.

★ 2196 ★
Meat
SIC: 2015; NAICS: 311615

Leading Frozen/Refrigerated Chicken/Chicken Substitute Brands, 2020

Brands are ranked based on sales at supermarkets, drug stores, mass merchandisers, military commissaries, and select club and dollar chains for the 52 weeks ended September 6, 2020.

	($ mil.)	Share
Tyson	$ 344.49	11.61%
Perdue	150.68	5.08
Kraft Heinz TGI Friday's	122.60	4.13
Just Bare	113.44	3.82
Barber Foods	103.36	3.48
Perdue Harvestland	90.06	3.04
Perdue Perfect Portions	89.21	3.01
Pilgrim's	56.55	1.91
Gold Leaf	54.13	1.82
Private label	1,134.09	38.22
Other	708.30	23.87

Source: *The National Provisioner*, October 2020, p. 33, from IRI.

★ 2197 ★
Meat
SIC: 2015; NAICS: 311615

Leading Frozen/Refrigerated Turkey/Turkey Substitute Brands, 2020

Brands are ranked based on sales at supermarkets, drug stores, mass merchandisers, military commissaries, and select club and dollar chains for the 52 weeks ended September 6, 2020.

	($ mil.)	Share
Jennie-O	$ 330.91	19.39%
Jennie-O All Natural	209.23	12.26
Butterball Everyday	202.11	11.85
Shady Brook Farms	160.35	9.40
Private label	338.68	19.85
Other	464.95	27.25

Source: *The National Provisioner*, October 2020, p. 39, from IRI.

★ 2198 ★
Meat
SIC: 2013; NAICS: 311612

Leading Jerky Brands, 2020

Brands are ranked based on sales at supermarkets, drug stores, mass merchandisers, military commissaries, and select club and dollar chains for the 52 weeks ended September 6, 2020.

	($ mil.)	Share
Jack Link's	$ 803.88	45.74%
Old Trapper	219.63	12.50
Bridgford Sweet Baby Ray's	107.40	6.11
Tillamook Country Smoker	50.39	2.87
Cattleman's Cut	41.53	2.36
No Man's Land	31.52	1.79
Oberto	28.59	1.63
Country Archer	19.57	1.11
Mingua Beef Jerky	17.60	1.00
Private label	174.77	9.95
Other	262.43	14.93

Source: *The National Provisioner*, October 2020, p. 20, from IRI.

★ 2199 ★
Meat
SIC: 2013; NAICS: 311612

Leading Jerky Makers, 2020

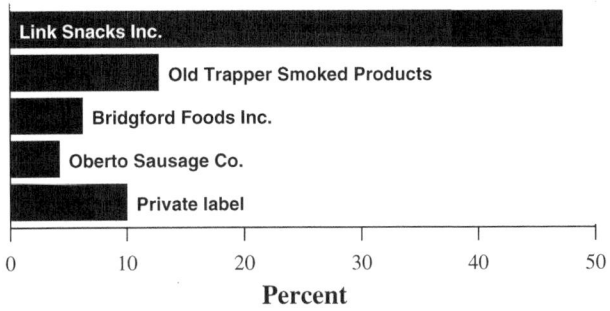

Companies are ranked based on sales at supermarkets, drug stores, mass merchandisers, military commissaries, and select club and dollar chains for the 52 weeks ended November 1, 2020.

	($ mil.)	Share
Link Snacks Inc.	$ 845.6	47.2%
Old Trapper Smoked Products	227.0	12.7
Bridgford Foods Inc.	111.1	6.2
Oberto Sausage Co.	76.0	4.2
Private label	178.7	10.0

Source: *The National Provisioner*, January 2021, p. 28, from IRI.

★ 2200 ★
Meat
SIC: 2015; NAICS: 311615

Leading Processed Frozen/Refrigerated Chicken/Chicken Substitute Brands, 2020

Brands are ranked based on sales at supermarkets, drug stores, mass merchandisers, military commissaries, and select club and dollar chains for the 52 weeks ended September 6, 2020.

	($ mil.)	Share
Tyson	$ 1,156.48	30.49%
Tyson Any'tizers	360.87	9.51
Perdue	233.82	6.16
Tyson Grilled & Ready	169.17	4.46
Foster Farms	154.50	4.07
John Soules Foods	136.31	3.59
Banquet	104.25	2.75
Perdue Short Cuts	99.20	2.62
Perdue Simply Smart Organics	89.27	2.35
Private label	619.38	16.33
Other	670.22	17.67

Source: *The National Provisioner*, October 2020, p. 34, from IRI.

★ 2201 ★
Meat
SIC: 2015; NAICS: 311615

Leading Processed Frozen/Refrigerated Turkey/Turkey Substitute Brands, 2020

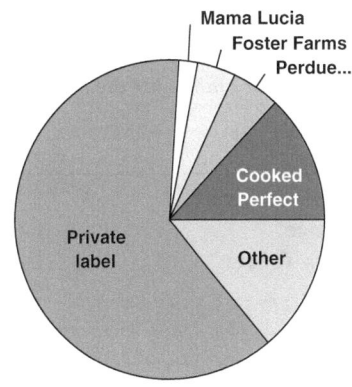

Brands are ranked based on sales at supermarkets, drug stores, mass merchandisers, military commissaries, and select club and dollar chains for the 52 weeks ended September 6, 2020.

	($ mil.)	Share
Cooked Perfect	$ 8.57	13.17%
Perdue Short Cuts	3.00	4.61
Foster Farms	2.33	3.58
Mama Lucia	1.48	2.28
Private label	40.62	62.44
Other	9.05	13.91

Source: *The National Provisioner*, October 2020, p. 40, from IRI.

★ 2202 ★
Meat
SIC: 2013; NAICS: 311612

Leading Refrigerated Sliced Lunchmeat Brands, 2020

Brands are ranked based on sales at supermarkets, drug stores, mass merchandisers, military commissaries, and select club and dollar chains for the 52 weeks ended September 6, 2020.

	($ mil.)	Share
Oscar Mayer Deli Fresh	$ 771.37	13.06%
Oscar Mayer	764.07	12.94
Hillshire Farm	598.98	10.14
Land O'Frost Premium	319.11	5.40
Private label	1,107.30	18.75
Other	2,346.16	39.72

Source: *The National Provisioner*, October 2020, p. 39, from IRI.

★ 2203 ★
Meat
SIC: 2011; NAICS: 311611

Leading Refrigerated Uncooked Meat Brands (No Poultry), 2020

Brands are ranked based on sales at supermarkets, drug stores, mass merchandisers, military commissaries, and select club and dollar chains for the 52 weeks ended September 6, 2020.

	($ mil.)	Share
No Brand Interstate Meat	$ 694.72	10.93%
Laura's Lean Beef	104.77	1.65
Hormel Always Tender	101.02	1.59
Smithfield	100.32	1.58
Private label	4,161.24	65.44
Other	1,196.42	18.82

Source: *The National Provisioner*, October 2020, p. 13, from IRI.

★ 2204 ★
Meat
SIC: 2013; NAICS: 311612

Processed Meat Sales, 2020

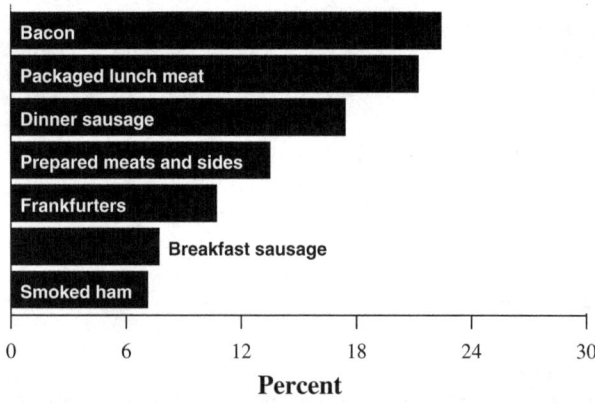

Figures are based on multi-outlet sales for the 52 weeks ended October 4, 2020. They are drawn from the IRI Syndicated Integrated Fresh database, which combines random- and fixed-weight brands/product types known to be sold in this department at the majority of retailers.

Bacon	22.4%
Packaged lunch meat	21.2
Dinner sausage	17.4
Prepared meats and sides	13.5
Frankfurters	10.7
Breakfast sausage	7.7
Smoked ham	7.1

Source: *Winsight Grocery Business*, December 2020, p. H12, from IRI Syndicated Integrated Fresh database.

★ 2205 ★
Meat
SIC: 2013; NAICS: 311612

Red Meat and Poultry Production by Year, 2016-2021

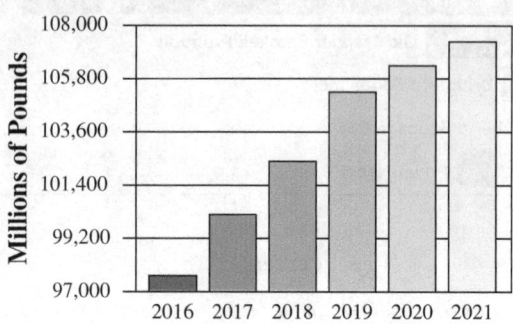

Production is shown in millions of pounds as of September 17, 2020. Figures for 2020-2021 are forecasts.

2016	97,614
2017	100,169
2018	102,435
2019	105,266
2020	106,296
2021	107,348

Source: *The National Provisioner*, October 2020, p. 14, from IRI and World Agricultural Supply and Demand estimates.

★ 2206 ★
Meat
SIC: 2013; NAICS: 311612

Top Bacon Brands (Refrigerated), 2020

Brands are ranked by sales at drug stores, supermarkets, mass merchandisers, military commissaries, and select club and dollar chains for the 52 weeks ended June 14, 2020.

	($ mil.)	Share
Oscar Mayer	$ 843.04	16.71%
Hormel	560.82	11.12
Wright	465.54	9.23
Smithfield	424.94	8.42
Farmland	177.13	3.51
Jimmy Dean	107.40	2.13
Bar-S	94.12	1.87
Farmer John	83.62	1.66
Sugardale	78.88	1.56
John Morrell	67.26	1.33
Private label	1,243.98	24.66
Other	898.01	17.80

Source: *The National Provisioner*, September 2020, p. 20, from IRI.

★ 2207 ★
Meat
SIC: 2013; NAICS: 311612

Top Bacon Brands (Shelf-Stable), 2020

Brands are ranked by sales at drug stores, supermarkets, mass merchandisers, military commissaries, and select club and dollar chains for the 52 weeks ended June 14, 2020.

	($ mil.)	Share
Hormel	$ 144.05	35.45%
Oscar Mayer	121.66	29.94
Boar's Head	19.27	4.74
Smithfield	11.83	2.91
Al Fresco	5.41	1.33
Jimmy Dean	4.44	1.09
Farmland	3.50	0.86
Sugardale	2.69	0.66
Butterball	2.44	0.60
Private label	89.39	22.00
Other	1.72	0.42

Source: *The National Provisioner*, September 2020, p. 24, from IRI.

★ 2208 ★
Meat
SIC: 0251; NAICS: 11232

Top Broiler Meat Firms in Russia, 2019

Industrialized commercial farms, also known as agricultural organizations, account for 93.4% of total poultry meat production; back yards and small peasant farms represent the balance of the market. Industrial production of poultry meat grew from 2.557 MMT (live weight) in 2015 to 6.197 MMT (live weight) in 2019. Figures exclude Crimea.

Cherkizovo	12.0%
GAP Resurs	10.0
Prioskolye	7.0
Agrokomplex named after N. Tkachyov	6.0
Belgrankorm	5.0
Poultry Growers Assets Trust	5.0
Severnaya	4.0
Prodo	3.0
Miratorg	2.0
Sfera	2.0
Other top 20	14.0
Other	30.0

Source: "Poultry and Products Annual." [online] from https://www.fas.usda.gov/data/russia-poultry-and-products-annual-3 [Published September 21, 2020], from FAS Moscow estimate based on data from Union of Poultry producers.

★ 2209 ★
Meat
SIC: 2013; NAICS: 311612

Top Frozen Sausage Brands, 2020

Brands are shown based on sales at supermarkets, drug stores, mass merchandisers, military commissaries, and select club and dollar chains for the 52 weeks ended May 17, 2020. Sausage sales grew 11.7% during this time period, outpacing total meat sales at 10.6%, as more people ate at home during the COVID-19 pandemic, preferring economical and convenient food choices.

	($ mil.)	Share
Banquet Brown 'N Serve	$ 166.4	31.97%
Applegate Naturals	42.6	8.18
Purnell Old Folks	40.2	7.72
Jimmy Dean	39.6	7.61
Jones Golden Brown	30.2	5.80
Smithfield	16.0	3.07
Williams	15.8	3.04
Ole South	9.3	1.79
Jones Dairy Farm	8.9	1.71
Private label	89.2	17.14
Other	62.3	11.97

Source: *The National Provisioner*, July 2020, p. 24, from IRI.

★ 2210 ★
Meat
SIC: 2013; NAICS: 311612

Top Frozen Sausage Makers, 2020

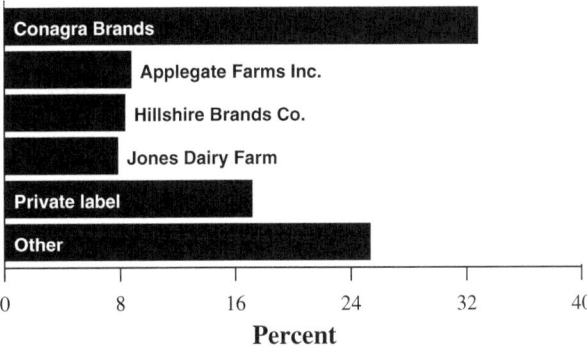

Brands are shown based on sales at supermarkets, drug stores, mass merchandisers, military commissaries, and select club and dollar chains for the 52 weeks ended May 17, 2020.

	($ mil.)	Share
Conagra Brands	$ 170.4	32.74%
Applegate Farms Inc.	45.4	8.72
Hillshire Brands Co.	43.2	8.30
Jones Dairy Farm	40.6	7.80
Private label	89.2	17.14
Other	131.7	25.30

Source: *The National Provisioner*, July 2020, p. 24, from IRI.

★ 2211 ★
Meat
SIC: 2013; NAICS: 311612
Top Organic Meat Firms, 2018

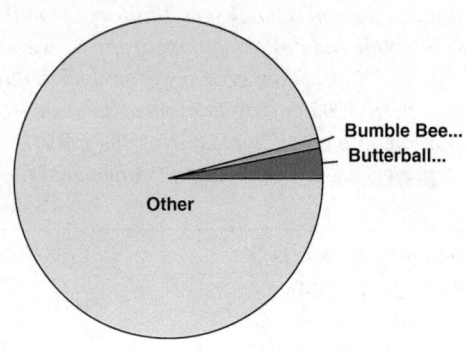

Market shares are shown in percent. Retail sales reached $2.58 billion.

Butterball L.L.C.	3.3%
Bumble Bee Seafoods	1.1
Other	94.2

Source: "Sector Trend Analysis — Organic Market Trend of Corn, Soya, Beans and Wheat Between Canada and the United States." [online] from https://www.agr.gc.ca/eng/international-trade/market-intelligence/reports/?id=1522931721523 [Published July 2020], from GlobalData Intelligence Center.

★ 2212 ★
Meat
SIC: 2013; NAICS: 311612
Top Pork Consumers Worldwide, 2021

Figures are in thousands of metric tons (carcass weight equivalent).

	(000)	Share
China	45,875	45.13%
European Union	20,420	20.09
United States	10,010	9.85
Russia	3,480	3.42
Brazil	3,030	2.98
Japan	2,725	2.68
Vietnam	2,490	2.45
Mexico	2,190	2.15
South Korea	1,955	1.92
Other	9,472	9.32

Source: "Livestock and Poultry: World Markets and Trade." [online] from https://apps.fas.usda.gov/psdonline/circulars/livestock_poultry.pdf [Published October 9, 2020], from U.S. Department of Agriculture.

★ 2213 ★
Meat
SIC: 2011; NAICS: 311611
Top Pork Exporting Regions, 2020-2021

Data are in thousands of metric tons of ready-to-cook equivalent. Figures are as of October 2020.

	(000)	Share
European Union	3,750	34.66%
United States	3,334	30.82
Canada	1,470	13.59
Brazil	1,250	11.55
Mexico	325	3.00
Chile	280	2.59
Russia	130	1.20
China	125	1.16
Argentina	48	0.44
Australia	35	0.32
South Africa	20	0.18
Other	52	0.48

Source: "Pork Production - Top Countries Summary." [online] from https://apps.fas.usda.gov/psdonline/app/index.html#/app/downloads [Published October 2020], from U.S. Department of Agriculture.

★ 2214 ★
Meat
SIC: 2011; NAICS: 311611
Top Pork Importing Regions, 2020-2021

Data are in thousands of metric tons of ready-to-cook equivalent. Figures are as of October 2020.

	(000)	Share
China	4,500	43.61%
Japan	1,445	14.00
Mexico	995	9.64
South Korea	615	5.96
United States	429	4.16
Hong Kong	360	3.49
Canada	270	2.62
Australia	230	2.23
Philippines	200	1.94
Vietnam	150	1.45
Chile	130	1.26
Other	995	9.64

Source: "Pork Production - Top Countries Summary." [online] from https://apps.fas.usda.gov/psdonline/app/index.html#/app/downloads [Published October 2020], from U.S. Department of Agriculture.

★ 2215 ★
Meat
SIC: 2011; NAICS: 311611

Top Pork Producers Worldwide, 2020

Companies are ranked by number of sows. Shares are shown based on the top 34 producers.

	Sows	Share
Wens Foodstuff Group	1,300,000	11.30%
Muyuan Foodstuffs Co. Ltd.	1,283,200	11.16
Smithfield Foods Inc.	1,241,000	10.79
CP Foods PCL	1,150,000	10.00
New Hope Group Co. Ltd.	500,000	4.35
Zhengbang Group Co. Ltd.	500,000	4.35
Triumph Foods L.L.C.	492,000	4.28
BRF S.A.	388,500	3.38
Pipestone Veterinary Services	385,000	3.35
Seaboard Foods L.P.	345,000	3.00
Other	3,915,300	34.05

Source: *National Hog Farmer*, June 2020, p. SS1-SS5.

★ 2216 ★
Meat
SIC: 2011; NAICS: 311611

Top Pork Producing Regions, 2020-2021

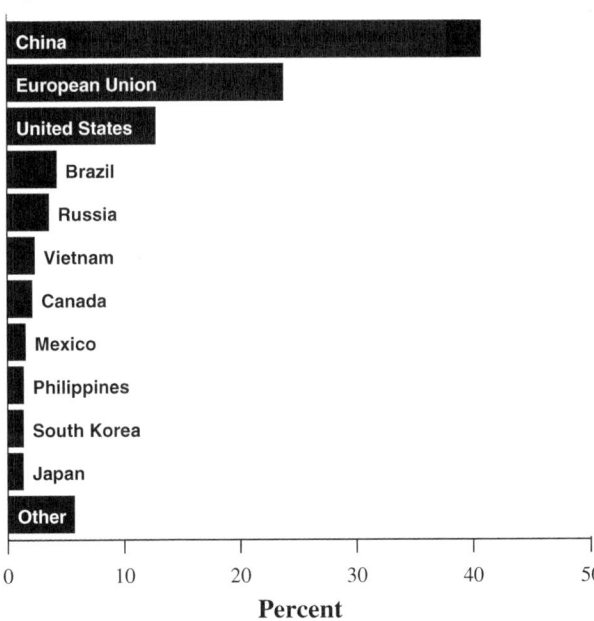

Data are in thousands of metric tons of ready-to-cook equivalent. Figures are as of October 2020.

	(000)	Share
China	41,500	40.62%
European Union	24,150	23.64
United States	12,938	12.66
Brazil	4,275	4.18%
Russia	3,600	3.52
Vietnam	2,350	2.30
Canada	2,110	2.07
Mexico	1,520	1.49
Philippines	1,350	1.32
South Korea	1,315	1.29
Japan	1,295	1.27
Other	5,757	5.64

Source: "Pork Production - Top Countries Summary." [online] from https://apps.fas.usda.gov/psdonline/app/index.html#/app/downloads [Published October 2020], from U.S. Department of Agriculture.

★ 2217 ★
Meat
SIC: 2013; NAICS: 311612

Top Pork Sales Categories, 2020

Figures are based on multi-outlet sales for the 52 weeks ended October 4, 2020. They are drawn from the IRI Syndicated Integrated Fresh database, which combines random- and fixed-weight brands/product types known to be sold in this department at the majority of retailers.

Loin	50.6%
Ribs	28.1
Shoulder	12.9
Ingredient cuts	4.1
Ground pork	2.4
Offal	1.4
Leg (fresh ham)	0.2
Other	0.1

Source: *Winsight Grocery Business*, December 2020, p. H12, from IRI Syndicated Integrated Fresh database.

★ 2218 ★
Meat
SIC: 2013; NAICS: 311612

Top Refrigerated Breakfast Sausage/Ham Brands, 2020

Brands are shown based on sales at supermarkets, drug stores, mass merchandisers, military commissaries, and select club and dollar chains for the 52 weeks ended May 17, 2020.

	($ mil.)	Share
Jimmy Dean	$ 608.7	30.91%
Johnsonville	221.0	11.22
Bob Evans Farm Fresh Goodness	125.6	6.38

Continued on next page.

★ 2218 ★
[Continued]
Meat
SIC: 2013; NAICS: 311612

Top Refrigerated Breakfast Sausage/Ham Brands, 2020

Brands are shown based on sales at supermarkets, drug stores, mass merchandisers, military commissaries, and select club and dollar chains for the 52 weeks ended May 17, 2020.

	($ mil.)	Share
Odom's Tennessee Pride	$ 119.9	6.09%
Swaggerty's Farm	80.1	4.07
Farmer John	36.6	1.86
Hatfield	33.7	1.71
Owens	32.4	1.65
Bob Evans	30.5	1.55
Private label	232.3	11.80
Other	448.5	22.77

Source: *The National Provisioner*, July 2020, p. 26, from IRI.

★ 2219 ★
Meat
SIC: 2013; NAICS: 311612

Top Refrigerated Breakfast Sausage/Ham Makers, 2020

Companies are shown based on sales at supermarkets, drug stores, mass merchandisers, military commissaries, and select club and dollar chains for the 52 weeks ended May 17, 2020.

	($ mil.)	Share
Hillshire Brands Co.	$ 612.6	31.11%
Johnsonville Sausage L.L.C.	223.6	11.35
Bob Evans Farms Inc.	195.8	9.94
Conagra Brands	123.0	6.25
Private label	232.3	11.80
Other	582.0	29.55

Source: *The National Provisioner*, July 2020, p. 26, from IRI.

★ 2220 ★
Meat
SIC: 2013; NAICS: 311612

Top Refrigerated Dinner Sausage Brands, 2020

Brands are shown based on sales at supermarkets, drug stores, mass merchandisers, military commissaries, and select club and dollar chains for the 52 weeks ended May 17, 2020.

	($ mil.)	Share
Johnsonville	$ 716.4	18.00%
Hillshire Farm	524.7	13.18
Eckrich	316.7	7.96
Hillshire Farm Lit'l Smokies	143.9	3.62
Johnsonville Beddar with Cheddar	121.9	3.06
Aidells	108.7	2.73
Premio	98.5	2.48
Bar-S	65.4	1.64
Conecuh	62.0	1.56
Private label	455.3	11.44
Other	1,366.2	34.33

Source: *The National Provisioner*, July 2020, p. 30, from IRI.

★ 2221 ★
Meat
SIC: 2013; NAICS: 311612

Top Refrigerated Dinner Sausage Makers, 2020

Companies are shown based on sales at supermarkets, drug stores, mass merchandisers, military commissaries, and select club and dollar chains for the 52 weeks ended May 17, 2020.

	($ mil.)	Share
Johnsonville Sausage L.L.C.	$ 872.2	21.92%
Hillshire Brands Co.	673.7	16.93
Armour Eckrich Meats L.L.C.	339.1	8.52
Aidells Sausage Co.	110.9	2.79
Private label	455.3	11.44
Other	1,528.5	38.41

Source: *The National Provisioner*, July 2020, p. 30, from IRI.

★ 2222 ★
Meat
SIC: 2013; NAICS: 311612

Top Refrigerated Hot Dog Brands, 2020

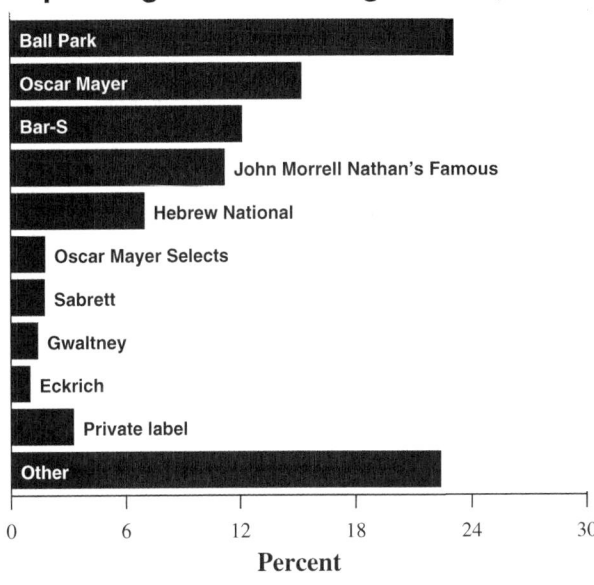

Brands are shown based on sales at supermarkets, drug stores, mass merchandisers, military commissaries, and select club and dollar chains for the 52 weeks ended May 17, 2020. Hot dog sales grew 10.6% over this time period.

	($ mil.)	Share
Ball Park	$ 597.9	23.05%
Oscar Mayer	394.3	15.20
Bar-S	313.8	12.10
John Morrell Nathan's Famous	290.2	11.19
Hebrew National	180.7	6.97
Oscar Mayer Selects	45.6	1.76
Sabrett	45.2	1.74
Gwaltney	35.7	1.38
Eckrich	25.3	0.98
Private label	84.2	3.25
Other	580.8	22.39

Source: *The National Provisioner*, July 2020, p. 27, from IRI.

★ 2223 ★
Meat
SIC: 2013; NAICS: 311612

Top Refrigerated Hot Dog Makers, 2020

Companies are shown based on sales at supermarkets, drug stores, mass merchandisers, military commissaries, and select club and dollar chains for the 52 weeks ended May 17, 2020. Hot dog sales grew 10.6% over this time period.

	($ mil.)	Share
Hillshire Brands Co.	$ 611.5	23.58%
Kraft Heinz Co.	440.0	16.96
Bar-S Foods Co.	317.2	12.23
Smithfield Packaged Meats	307.5	11.86
Conagra Brands	180.7	6.97
Other	736.8	28.41

Source: *The National Provisioner*, July 2020, p. 27, from IRI.

★ 2224 ★
Meat
SIC: 0253; NAICS: 11233

Turkey Processing by Company, 2020

Companies are ranked by production in millions of live pounds processed. Turkey production declined by 76 million pounds over 2019. The drop came from a decline in demand in the foodservice sector and the cancellation of winter holiday celebrations because of the pandemic.

Butterball L.L.C.	1,260
Jennie-O Turkey Store	1,220
Cargill Protein	900
Farbest Foods	630
Tyson Foods Inc.	376
Kraft Heinz Co.	308
Cooper Farms	301
Perdue Farms	300
Virginia Poultry Growers Cooperative Inc.	278
Michigan Turkey Producers	234

Source: *WATTPoultry USA*, March 2021, p. 54, from WATT Global Media.

★ 2225 ★
Meat
SIC: 0253; NAICS: 11233
Turkey Production by State, 2019-2020

States are ranked by millions of turkeys raised. Data include estimates from all known operations raising 1,000 or more turkeys annually. In 2020, a forecasted 222 million turkeys were raised, down 3% from 2019.

	2019	2020	Share
Minnesota	40.0	39.0	17.57%
Arkansas	30.0	31.0	13.96
North Carolina	31.0	30.0	13.51
Indiana	20.0	20.0	9.01
Virginia	16.0	16.3	7.34
Missouri	16.5	16.0	7.21
Iowa	11.7	11.7	5.27
California	8.5	8.0	3.60
Pennsylvania	6.2	6.6	2.97
Ohio	5.9	5.9	2.66
Michigan	5.3	5.4	2.43
South Dakota	4.5	4.5	2.03
West Virginia	3.1	3.3	1.49
Other	30.3	24.3	10.95

Source: "Turkeys Raised." [online] from https://usda.library.cornell.edu/concern/publications/0g354f23n?locale=en [Published September 24, 2020], from U.S. Department of Agriculture.

★ 2226 ★
Meat
SIC: 0253; NAICS: 11233
Turkey Production by Year, 2016-2021

Production is shown in millions of pounds as of September 17, 2020. Figures for 2020-2021 are forecasts.

2016	5,981
2017	5,981
2018	5,878
2019	5,818
2020	5,708
2021	5,770

Source: *The National Provisioner*, October 2020, p. 38, from IRI and World Agricultural Supply and Demand estimates.

★ 2227 ★
Meat
SIC: 2015; NAICS: 311615
Turkey Sales by Category, 2020

Figures are based on multi-outlet sales for the 52 weeks ended October 4, 2020. They are drawn from the IRI Syndicated Integrated Fresh database, which combines random- and fixed-weight brands/product types known to be sold in this department at the majority of retailers.

Ground turkey	56.2%
Whole bird	22.3
Breast	12.8
Wings	3.4
Legs	2.4
Backs and necks	1.4
Tails	0.6
Thighs	0.6
Ingredient cuts	0.3
Giblets	0.1

Source: *Winsight Grocery Business*, December 2020, p. H18, from IRI Syndicated Integrated Fresh database.

★ 2228 ★
Meat Alternatives
SIC: 2099; NAICS: 311991
Global Sales of Alternative Meat, 2018-2026

The market for meat alternatives has heated up in recent years. Reasons for this include the development of plant-based products that replicate the look and taste of beef, concerns about regular meat consumption on one's health, as well as concerns about the effect of meat production on the environment. Sales are shown in billions of dollars. Figures for 2019-2026 are forecast.

2018	$ 10.10
2019	11.59
2020	13.31
2021	15.28
2022	17.54
2023	20.14
2024	23.12
2025	26.54
2026	30.92

Source: "Growing Alternative Meat Market." [online] from http://news.kotra.or.kr [Published July 15, 2020], from Statista.

★ 2229 ★
Meat Alternatives
SIC: 2099; NAICS: 311991

Leading Refrigerated/Frozen Meat Substitute Brands, 2020

Brands are ranked based on sales at supermarkets, drug stores, mass merchandisers, military commissaries, and select club and dollar chains for the 52 weeks ended September 6, 2020.

	($ mil.)	Share
Morningstar Farms	$ 275.78	28.69%
Beyond Meat Beyond Burger	77.63	8.08
Gardein	75.98	7.90
Morningstar Farms Grillers	59.91	6.23
Beyond Meat Beyond Sausage	52.72	5.48
Other	419.16	43.61

Source: *The National Provisioner*, October 2020, p. 15, from IRI.

★ 2230 ★
Meat/Cheese/Cracker/Desserts
SIC: 2099; NAICS: 311999

Leading Meat/Cheese/Cracker/Dessert Brands, 2020

Brands are ranked based on sales at supermarkets, drug stores, mass merchandisers, military commissaries, and select club and dollar chains for the 52 weeks ended August 9, 2020.

	($ mil.)	Share
Lunchables	$ 254.23	46.06%
Sargento Balanced Breaks	37.99	6.88
Armour Lunch Makers Cracker Crunchers	33.39	6.05
Hillshire Snacking	32.72	5.93
Lunchables Uploaded	25.43	4.61
Hormel Gatherings	25.21	4.57
P3	24.81	4.49
Armour Lunch Makers	14.59	2.64
Hormel Party Tray	13.65	2.47
Private label	17.18	3.11
Other	72.78	13.19

Source: *Frozen & Refrigerated Buyer*, October 2020, p. 16, from IRI.

★ 2231 ★
Meat Markets
SIC: 5421; NAICS: 44521

Leading Meat Market Operators, 2019

Operators in this industry are butcher shops and delicatessens that primarily sell fresh, frozen and prepared meat and poultry to consumers and other establishments. It does not include seafood markets. Industry revenue reached $6.8 billion in 2019. This market faces challenges from other retail channels, as well as from consumers moving away from meat to other sources of protein. Supply chain shortages related to COVID-19 were an issue for this industry in 2020.

Omaha Steaks International Inc.	8.2%
Honey Baked Ham Company	2.4
Other	89.4

Source: "Meat Markets in the United States." [online] from http://www.ibisworld.com [Published December 2019], from IBISWorld.

★ 2232 ★
Meat Wholesalers
SIC: 5147; NAICS: 42447

Meat and Meat Product Merchant Wholesale Leaders, 2017

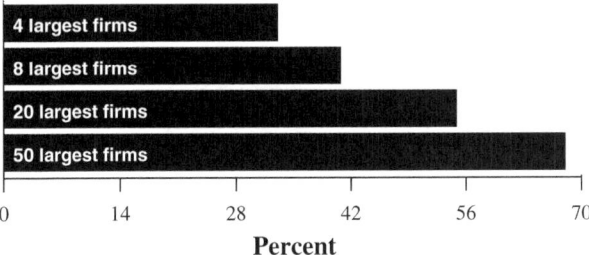

Data show the percent of industry sales held by the largest 4, 8, 20 and 50 firms in the sector. There are approximately 2,329 players operating in the industry generating employment for 47,325 people. The industry should see revenue of $91.4 billion in 2021, according to IBISWorld.

4 largest firms	33.0%
8 largest firms	40.7
20 largest firms	54.8
50 largest firms	68.0

Source: "Economic Census." [online] from https://www.census.gov/content/census/en/data/tables/2017/econ/economic-census/naics-sector-31-33.html [Accessed January 21, 2021], from U.S. Census Bureau.

★ 2233 ★
Medical Equipment
SIC: 3842; NAICS: 339113

Global Market for Electric Wheelchairs, 2020, 2023 and 2027

Figures are in millions of dollars.

	2020 ($ mil.)	2023 ($ mil.)	2027 ($ mil.)	Share
North America	$ 2,387.0	$ 3,202.0	$ 4,847.0	39.49%
Europe	1,663.4	2,205.3	3,284.5	26.76
Asia-Pacific	1,326.1	1,780.1	2,698.1	21.98
Latin America	396.5	521.5	768.1	6.26
Middle East	231.9	305.2	450.0	3.67
Africa	121.3	156.7	225.0	1.83

Source: "Electric Wheelchair Market." [online] from https://centaurrobotics.com/wp-content/uploads/2020/07/Report_Global-Electric-Wheelchair-Market_Coherent-Market-Insights.pdf [Accessed April 21, 2021], from Coherent Market Insights.

★ 2234 ★
Medical Equipment
SIC: 3841; NAICS: 339112

Global Market for Handheld Surgical Equipment, 2018

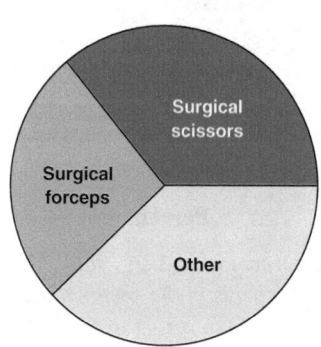

Market shares are shown by type. Obstetrics and gynecology claimed the largest share of the market by application, 25.72%, followed by orthotics with an 18.16% share. The market is forecast to grow from $4.1 billion in 2020 to $5.7 billion in 2026.

Surgical scissors	35.65%
Surgical forceps	25.96
Other	38.39

Source: "Handheld Surgical Instrument Market 2020-2026." [online] from http://www.qyresearch.com [Published February 2020], from QY Research.

★ 2235 ★
Medical Equipment
SIC: 3841; NAICS: 339112

Home Health Care Market, 2019-2020

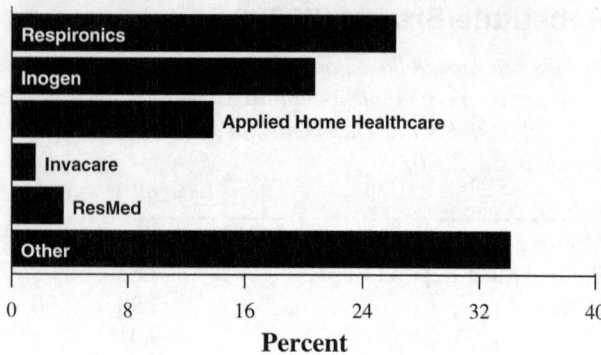

Data show current POC market share and the projected market share in 12 months. POC stands for point of care.

	Current	12 Months
Respironics	27.0%	26.2%
Inogen	16.8	20.7
Applied Home Healthcare	15.9	13.8
Invacare	6.2	1.6
ResMed	2.3	3.5
Other	31.9	34.1

Source: "4Q19 HME Oxygen, Sleep, And Complex Rehab Survey." [online] from https://cdn2.hubspot.net/hubfs/5670140/4Q19%20HME%20Sleep-Oxygen-Rehab%20Survey%2001-27-20.pdf [Published January 27, 2020], from Needham & Company 4Q19 HME Survey.

★ 2236 ★
Medical Equipment
SIC: 3842; NAICS: 339113

Leading Advanced Wound Management Firms Worldwide, 2019

The industry was valued at $9.4 billion.

The 3M Company	19.0%
Smith+Nephew Corp.	14.0
Molnlycke	9.0
Convatec	7.0
Other	51.0

Source: "Smith+Nephew Investor Presentation." [online] from https://www.smith-nephew.com/investor-centre/reporting/presentations-and-site-visits/ [Published October-December 2020], from public sources.

★ 2237 ★
Medical Equipment
SIC: 3845; NAICS: 334517

Leading Cardiac Rhythm Management Firms, 2018-2019

Market shares are shown based on U.S. hospitals.

	2018	2019
Medtronic Inc.	43.0%	42.9%
Abbott Laboratories	28.1	24.3
Boston Scientific Corp.	22.7	25.5
Biotronik	6.2	7.3
Other	< 0.1	< 0.1

Source: *Spotlight*, August 2020, p. 3, from Curvo Labs.

★ 2238 ★
Medical Equipment
SIC: 3845; NAICS: 334517

Leading Defibrillator Brands, 2018-2019

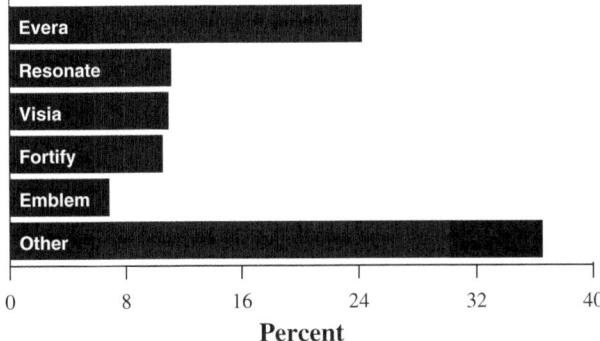

Market shares are shown based on U.S. hospitals.

	2018	2019
Evera	28.7%	24.2%
Resonate	8.4	11.1
Visia	12.0	10.9
Fortify	10.2	10.5
Emblem	6.4	6.8
Other	34.3	36.5

Source: *Spotlight*, August 2020, p. 3, from Curvo Labs.

★ 2239 ★
Medical Equipment
SIC: 3845; NAICS: 339113

Leading Dual Chamber Pacemaker Brands, 2018-2019

Market shares are shown based on U.S. hospitals.

	2018	2019
Azure	27.7%	33.8%
Assurity	26.0	30.0
Accolade	21.4%	23.5%
Edora	6.8	6.4
Advisa	10.4	3.2
Other	7.7	3.1

Source: *Spotlight*, August 2020, p. 3, from Curvo Labs.

★ 2240 ★
Medical Equipment
SIC: 3842; NAICS: 339113

Leading Hip and Knee Implant Makers Worldwide, 2019

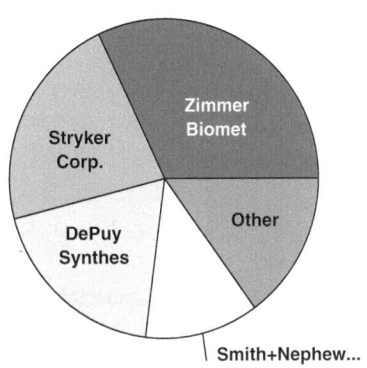

The industry was valued at $14.8 billion.

Zimmer Biomet	32.0%
Stryker Corp.	22.0
DePuy Synthes	19.0
Smith+Nephew Corp.	12.0
Other	15.0

Source: "Smith+Nephew Investor Presentation." [online] from https://www.smith-nephew.com/investor-centre/reporting/presentations-and-site-visits/ [Published October-December 2020], from public sources.

★ 2241 ★
Medical Equipment
SIC: 3845; NAICS: 334517

Leading Medical Imaging Equipment Makers Worldwide, 2019

The industry generated $38 billion in 2019. Data refer to equipment sales only, services and consumables are not included. X-rays claimed $17 billion (44.7%), endoscopy and ultrasound $6 billion each (15.7%), MRI $5 billion (13.1%), molecular imaging $3 billion (7.8%), and optical coherence tomagraphy $1 billion (2.6%).

GE Healthcare	20.0%
Siemens Healthineers	15.0

Continued on next page.

★ 2241 ★
[Continued]
Medical Equipment
SIC: 3845; NAICS: 334517

Leading Medical Imaging Equipment Makers Worldwide, 2019

The industry generated $38 billion in 2019. Data refer to equipment sales only, services and consumables are not included. X-rays claimed $17 billion (44.7%), endoscopy and ultrasound $6 billion each (15.7%), MRI $5 billion (13.1%), molecular imaging $3 billion (7.8%), and optical coherence tomography $1 billion (2.6%).

Philips N.V.	11.0%
Canon Inc.	8.0
Olympus Corp.	7.0
Karl Storz SE & Co.	4.0
Dentsply Sirona	3.0
Hologic Inc.	3.0
UnitedImaging	3.0
Hitachi Ltd.	2.0
Other	24.0

Source: "Medical Imaging: Semiconductor Technology is a Key Enabler for Truly Dedicated Solutions." [online] from http://www.yole.fr/MedicalImaging_Equipment_Detectors_Overview.aspx [Accessed May 1, 2021], from Yole Développement.

★ 2242 ★
Medical Equipment
SIC: 3842; NAICS: 339113

Leading Orthopedic Product Categories Worldwide, 2018-2019

Categories are ranked by sales in millions of dollars.

	2018 ($ mil.)	2019 ($ mil.)	Share
Spine	$9,324.7	$9,654.1	18.16%
Knees	9,058.2	9,324.2	17.54
Hips	7,582.3	7,788.8	14.65
Trauma	7,205.9	7,449.3	14.01
Sports medicine	5,614.4	5,920.7	11.14
Orthobiologics	5,088.0	5,291.1	9.95
Extremities	2,279.2	2,436.5	4.58
Other	5,075.0	5,288.2	9.95

Source: "Orthopedic Outlook: COVID-19's Impact on Industry Growth and Trends." [online] from https://www.bonezone-pub.com/2710-orthopedic-outlook-covid-19-s-impact-on-industry-growth-and-trends [Published June 19, 2020], from Orthoworld.

★ 2243 ★
Medical Equipment
SIC: 3842; NAICS: 339113

Leading Orthopedic Product Makers Worldwide, 2018-2019

Companies are ranked by sales in millions of dollars.

	2018 ($ mil.)	2019 ($ mil.)	Share
DePuy Synthes	$8,885.0	$8,839.00	16.63%
Stryker Corp.	7,331.6	7,741.50	14.56
Zimmer Biomet	7,081.7	7,112.30	13.38
Smith & Wesson Corp.	3,517.7	3,663.30	6.89
Medtronic PLC	3,101.2	3,167.00	5.96
Arthrex Corp.	2,514.3	2,699.30	5.08
NuVasive Corp.	1,101.7	1,168.10	2.20
Other	17,694.5	18,762.39	35.30

Source: "Orthopedic Outlook: COVID-19's Impact on Industry Growth and Trends." [online] from https://www.bonezone-pub.com/2710-orthopedic-outlook-covid-19-s-impact-on-industry-growth-and-trends [Published June 19, 2020], from Orthoworld.

★ 2244 ★
Medical Equipment
SIC: 3842; NAICS: 339113

Leading Orthopedic Sectors in China, 2018

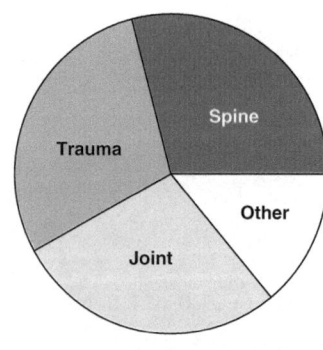

The market was estimated at 26.2 billion renminbi.

Spine	29.0%
Trauma	28.6
Joint	27.9
Other	14.5

Source: "Microsoft Scientific Corp." [online] from http://www.chinastock.com.hk/en/NC/CA/index.aspx [Published August 10, 2020], from *The Blue Book of Medical Device Industry in China, 2019*.

★ 2245 ★
Medical Equipment
SIC: 3842; NAICS: 339113

Leading Posture Corrector Makers Worldwide, 2019

A posture corrector is used to help people improve their postures and maintain an upright position. The industry is forecast to grow from $1.19 billion in 2019 to $1.74 billion in 2026. Market shares are shown based on revenue.

Babaka	3.58%
IntelliSkin	2.53
BackJoy Orthotics L.L.C.	1.40
Other	92.49

Source: "Global Posture Corrector Market Research Report 2020." [online] from http://www.qyresearch.com [Published July 2020], from QY Research.

★ 2246 ★
Medical Equipment
SIC: 3845; NAICS: 334517

Leading Single Chamber Pacemaker Brands, 2018-2019

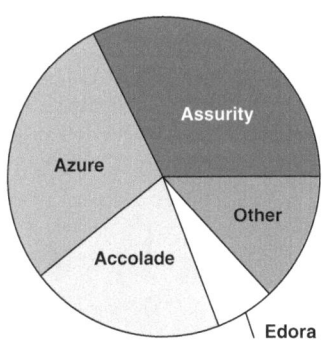

Market shares are shown based on U.S. hospitals.

	2018	2019
Assurity	33.0%	32.5%
Azure	19.0	28.5
Accolade	21.7	20.3
Edora	6.5	6.1
Other	19.8	12.6

Source: *Spotlight*, August 2020, p. 3, from Curvo Labs.

★ 2247 ★
Medical Equipment
SIC: 3842; NAICS: 339113

Leading Spinal Implant Makers Worldwide, 2019-2020

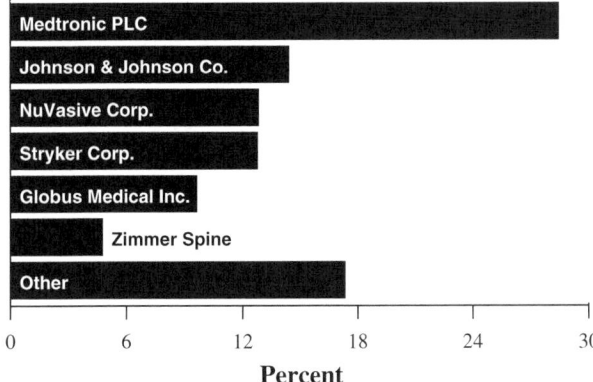

Companies are ranked by sales in millions of dollars.

	2019 ($ mil.)	2020 ($ mil.)	Share
Medtronic PLC	$ 2,715.0	$ 2,335.0	28.43%
Johnson & Johnson Co.	1,398.0	1,179.0	14.36
NuVasive Corp.	1,168.0	1,051.0	12.80
Stryker Corp.	1,157.0	1,047.0	12.75
Globus Medical Inc.	785.4	789.0	9.61
Zimmer Spine	433.3	389.3	4.74
Other	2,005.4	1,422.4	17.32

Source: "How Have the Market Shares in the Spine Market Changed After 2020 with COVID-19." [online] from http://thespinemarketgroup.com/how-have-the-market-shares-in-the-spine-market-changed-after-2020-with-covid-19/ [Accessed March 2, 2021], from Research and Markets.

★ 2248 ★
Medical Equipment
SIC: 3842; NAICS: 339113

Leading Sports Medicine Implant Makers Worldwide, 2019

The industry was valued at $5.3 billion.

Arthrex Corp.	33.0%
Smith+Nephew Corp.	26.0
DePuy Synthes	11.0
Stryker Corp.	11.0
Other	17.0

Source: "Smith+Nephew Investor Presentation." [online] from https://www.smith-nephew.com/investor-centre/reporting/presentations-and-site-visits/ [Published October-December 2020], from public sources.

★ 2249 ★
Medical Equipment
SIC: 3842; NAICS: 339113

Leading Sterilization Equipment Makers Worldwide, 2019

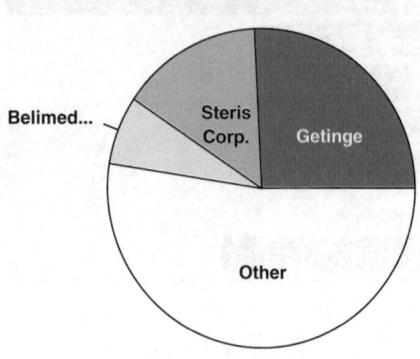

The industry was valued at $1.25 billion in 2019. Market shares are shown based on revenue.

Getinge	25.84%
Steris Corp.	14.62
Belimed AG	6.74
Other	52.80

Source: "Global Sterilization Equipment Market Research Report 2020." [online] from http://www.qyresearch.com [Published May 2020], from QY Research.

★ 2250 ★
Medical Equipment
SIC: 3841; NAICS: 339112

Leading Surgical Microscope Makers Worldwide, 2018

Surgical microscopes are used to perform microsurgeries in a number of fields, including neurosurgery, dentistry and oncology. The industry is forecast to grow from $1.34 billion in 2019. Market shares are shown based on revenue.

Carl Zeiss AG	49.12%
Leica Microsystems	23.39
Olympus Corp.	7.44
Other	20.05

Source: "Global Surgical Microscope Market Insights, Forecast to 2026." [online] from https://www.marketreportsworld.com/global-surgical-microscope-market-15561647 [Published October 2019].

★ 2251 ★
Medical Equipment
SIC: 3841; NAICS: 339112

Power Wheelchair Market, 2019-2020

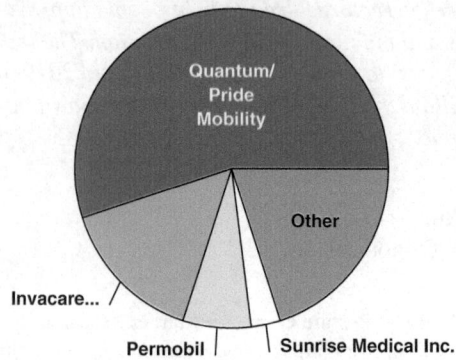

Data show current POC market share and the projected market share in 12 months. POC stands for point of care.

	Current	12 Months
Quantum/Pride Mobility	57.6%	54.6%
Invacare Corp.	14.1	15.4
Permobil	6.4	6.8
Sunrise Medical Inc.	1.8	3.2
Other	20.0	20.0

Source: "4Q19 HME Oxygen, Sleep, And Complex Rehab Survey." [online] from https://cdn2.hubspot.net/hubfs/5670140/4Q19%20HME%20Sleep-Oxygen-Rehab%20Survey%2001-27-20.pdf [Published January 27, 2020], from Needham & Company 4Q19 HME Survey.

★ 2252 ★
Medical Equipment
SIC: 3841; NAICS: 339112

Sleep Mask Market, 2019-2020

Data show current POC market share and the projected market share in 12 months. POC stands for point of care.

	Current	12 Months
Respironics	37.4%	38.3%
RedMed	37.3	34.5
Fisher & Paykel	23.2	24.1
Other	2.0	3.0

Source: "4Q19 HME Oxygen, Sleep, And Complex Rehab Survey." [online] from https://cdn2.hubspot.net/hubfs/5670140/4Q19%20HME%20Sleep-Oxygen-Rehab%20Survey%2001-27-20.pdf [Published January 27, 2020], from Needham & Company 4Q19 HME Survey.

★ 2253 ★
Medical Equipment
SIC: 3841; NAICS: 339112

Top Medical Device Makers, 2020

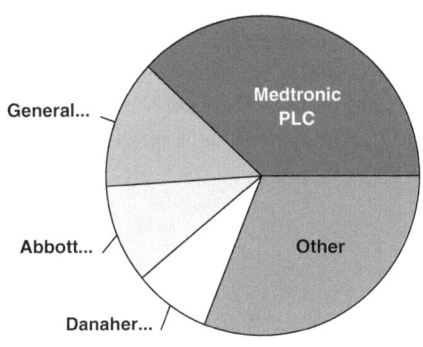

A total of 1,109 business establishments operate in this industry. Revenue reached $47 billion.

Medtronic PLC	38.4%
General Electric Healthcare	13.0
Abbott Laboratories	9.8
Danaher Corp.	7.9
Other	30.9

Source: "U.S. Medical Device Industry Trends." [online] from http://www.news.kotra.or.kr [Published December 2, 2020], from Hoover, KOTRA Dallas Trade Center and company websites.

★ 2254 ★
Medical Equipment
SIC: 3841; NAICS: 339112

Top Medical Device Makers Worldwide, 2020

The largest medtech companies are ranked by estimated revenue in billions of dollars. Figures for Johnson & Johnson and Abbott Co. are for the medical device sector. Cardinal's figure is for its medical sector. Danaher's figure is for the life sciences and diagnostics segments. Shares are shown based on revenue generated by the top 40 companies.

	($ mil.)	Share
Medtronic PLC	$ 28.91	8.07%
Johnson & Johnson Co.	25.96	7.25
Royal Philips	21.80	6.09
GE Healthcare	19.94	5.57
EssilorLuxottica S.A.	19.46	5.43
Siemens Healthineers	16.18	4.52
Cardinal Health Inc.	15.44	4.31
Stryker Corp.	14.88	4.15
Medline Industries Inc.	13.90	3.88
Danaher Corp.	$ 13.51	3.77%
Abbott HealthCare	12.23	3.41
Baxter International	11.36	3.17
Boston Scientific Corp.	10.74	3.00
Other	133.82	37.37

Source: *Medical Design & Outsourcing*, November 2020, p. 14.

★ 2255 ★
Medical Equipment
SIC: 3841; NAICS: 339113

Top Medical Device Markets in Europe, 2018

The industry was valued at €120 billion.

Germany	27.1%
France	14.6
United Kingdom	11.0
Italy	10.1
Spain	6.3
Netherlands	4.2
Switzerland	3.7
Belgium	2.7
Poland	2.6
Austria	2.5
Other	15.0

Source: "The European Medical Technology Industry in Figures 2020." [online] from https://www.medtecheurope.org/wp-content/uploads/2020/05/The-European-Medical-Technology-Industry-in-figures-2020.pdf [Accessed September 16, 2020], from Fitch Solutions.

★ 2256 ★
Medical Equipment
SIC: 3841; NAICS: 339112

Ventilator Market in China, 2019

Demand for ventilators has increased because of an aging population, the rise of bronchial diseases, and COVID-19 infections. Production increased from 4,100 units in 2012 to 9,900 units in 2019. But demand rose from 7,800 units to 18,200 over the same period. Market shares are shown by brand.

Dräger	17.53%
Mindray	14.03
Phillips	9.92
Maquet	7.82
Covidien	6.17
Hamilton	4.13
CareFusion	4.06

Continued on next page.

★ 2256 ★
[Continued]
Medical Equipment
SIC: 3841; NAICS: 339112

Ventilator Market in China, 2019

Demand for ventilators has increased because of an aging population, the rise of bronchial diseases, and COVID-19 infections. Production increased from 4,100 units in 2012 to 9,900 units in 2019. But demand rose from 7,800 units to 18,200 over the same period. Market shares are shown by brand.

Weinmann	3.61%
Comen	3.30
Aeonmed	3.19
Other	25.24

Source: "China Ventilator Market Trend." [online] from http://www.news.kotra.or.kr [Published December 15, 2020], from China Commerce Industry Research Institute.

★ 2257 ★
Medical Equipment Wholesalers
SIC: 5047; NAICS: 42345

Medical, Dental, and Hospital Equipment and Supplies Merchant Wholesale Leaders, 2017

Data show the percent of industry sales held by the largest 4, 8, 20 and 50 firms in the sector. There are approximately 10,305 players operating in the industry generating employment for 232,781 people.

4 largest firms	24.2%
8 largest firms	38.3
20 largest firms	61.3
50 largest firms	76.5

Source: "Economic Census." [online] from https://www.census.gov/content/census/en/data/tables/2017/econ/economic-census/naics-sector-31-33.html [Accessed January 21, 2021], from U.S. Census Bureau.

★ 2258 ★
Medical Products
SIC: 3842; NAICS: 339113

Breast Implant Market, 2018-2019

The industry was valued at $1.5 billion in 2019.

	2018	2019
Allergan (AbbVie)	57.9%	59.5%
Mentor (J&J)	39.1	29.9
Sientra Inc.	3.0	10.6

Source: *Spotlight*, May 2020, p. 3.

★ 2259 ★
Medical Products
SIC: 8099; NAICS: 621991

Corneal Transplants, 2010-2019

The source saw 57 eye banks reporting for its 2019 survey, the same as 2018. The number of whole globes and corneas donated grew from 133,576 in 2018 to 136,130 in 2019. The number of donors rose from 68,102 to 68,759 over the same period. Data show the number of corneal transplants provided by the United States.

2010	59,271
2011	67,590
2012	68,681
2013	72,736
2014	76,431
2015	79,304
2016	82,994
2017	84,297
2018	85,441
2019	85,601

Source: "2019 Eye Banking Statistical Report." [online] from https://restoresight.org/what-we-do/publications/statistical-report/ [Accessed March 10, 2021], from Eye Bank Association of America.

★ 2260 ★
Medical Products
SIC: 3842; NAICS: 339113

Face Mask Sales Worldwide by Demand, 2020

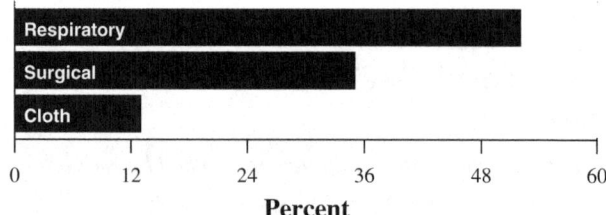

Market shares are estimated. Respiratory masks fit tightly and filter out small particles, viruses and bacteria. Demand is forecast to see a CAGR of 13% through 2025. Surgical masks are loose fitting and cover the nose, mouth and chin. The CAGR is approximately 9% through 2025. Face masks offer protection from dust and COVID-19. The market is forecast to see a CAGR of 6% through 2025.

Respiratory	52.0%
Surgical	35.0
Cloth	13.0

Source: "Boomer Essentials." [online] from http://www.lythampartners.com [Published October 2020].

★ 2261 ★
Medical Products
SIC: 3842; NAICS: 339113
Global Disposable Glove Market by Type, 2019

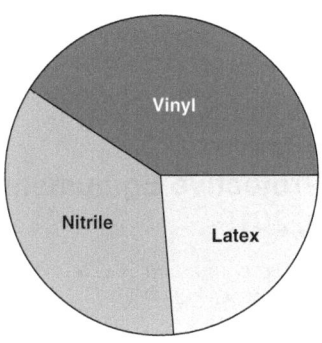

Distribution is shown based on shipments of 529 billion pieces. Europe claimed 30.1% of the total, the United States claimed 29.8%, the Asia-Pacific (excluding Japan) 14.2%, Latin America 7.1%, Japan 5.5% and other 13.3%.

Vinyl	37.5%
Nitrile	32.7
Latex	22.0

Source: "Industry Overview." [online] from https://www1.hkexnews.hk/app/sehk/2021/103148/a107477/sehk21012901518.pdf [Accessed April 19, 2021], from Frost & Sullivan.

★ 2262 ★
Medical Products
SIC: 3842; NAICS: 339113
Hearing Aid Shipments, 2020

Market shares are shown based on sales for the first three quarters of 2020. Hearing aid sales were down 6.2% in the third quarter of 2020 when compared to the same period in 2019. The source notes this is an improvement over the second quarter, when COVID-19 helped drive down sales 58.6% over second quarter 2019. A total of 96.4% of sales were classified as wireless hearing aids.

RIC/RITE	79.5%
BTE	8.2
Other	12.3

Source: *The Hearing Review*, October 12, 2020, p. 4, from Hearing Industries Association.

★ 2263 ★
Medical Products
SIC: 3842; NAICS: 339113
Leading Stent Makers in China, 2018

There were approximately 915,000 cases of coronary intervention surgery in China in 2018, up from 228,000 in 2009.

Lepu Medical Technology (Beijing) Co. Ltd.	20.0%
MicroPort	18.0
JW Medical Corp.	15.0
Abbott Laboratories	11.0
Medtronic PLC	10.0
Boston Scientific Corp.	6.0
Edwards Lifesciences	5.0
Other	15.0

Source: "Microsoft Scientific Corp." [online] from http://www.chinastock.com.hk/en/NC/CA/index.aspx [Published August 10, 2020], from *The Blue Book of Medical Device Industry in China, 2019.*

★ 2264 ★
Medical Products
SIC: 3842; NAICS: 339113
Leading Tattoo Aftercare Product Makers, 2019

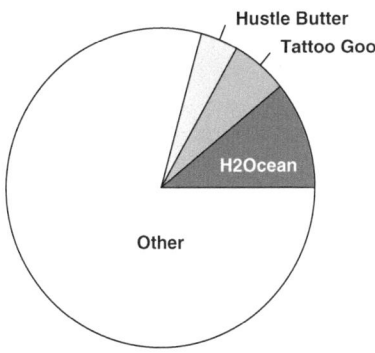

Tattoo aftercare products are used to protect the skin after tattooing. The industry is forecast to grow from $104.5 million in 2019 to $158.3 million in 2026.

H2Ocean	10.83%
Tattoo Goo	6.02
Hustle Butter	3.51
Other	79.64

Source: "Global Tattoo Aftercare Products Market Size, Manufacturer, Supply Chain, Sales Channel and Clients, 2020-2026." [online] from http://www.qyresearch.com [Published July 2020], from QY Research.

★ 2265 ★
Medical Products
SIC: 3841; NAICS: 339112

Market for Catheter-Directed Treatment for Blood Clots, 2019 and 2024

The market refers to the catheter-directed treatment for pulmonary embolism blood clots.

	2019	2024
Boston Scientific Corp.	55.0%	35.0%
Inari Medical	10.0	33.0
Penumbra Inc.	7.0	20.0
Other	28.0	12.0

Source: *IBD Weekly*, August 17, 2020, p. A6, from Canaccord Genuity.

★ 2266 ★
Medical Products
SIC: 3842; NAICS: 339113

Neurovascular Related Product Market Worldwide, 2018-2019

The market includes neurovascular coils and plug, thromectomy catheters, balloons, aneurysm clips, and intracranial vascular tents.

	2018	2019
Stryker Corp.	30.3%	35.0%
Medtronic PLC	34.6	30.7
Penumbra Inc.	13.0	10.4
Codman/Integra	7.3	8.4
Microvention/Terumo	3.7	4.8
Other	11.1	10.7

Source: *Spotlight*, February 2020, p. 3.

★ 2267 ★
Medical Products
SIC: 3842; NAICS: 339113

Personal Protective Equipment Consumption by Region, 2019

Regions are ranked by sales of personal protective equipment (PPE) consumed in the manufacturing, construction, mining and utilities sectors. The PPE market totaled $5.5 billion in 2019.

	($ mil.)	Share
South Atlantic	$1,027.75	18.56%
Northeast Central	918.49	16.58
Southwest Central	836.52	15.10
Pacific Coast	696.37	12.57
Mid-Atlantic	688.33	12.43
Mountain	401.14	7.24
Northwest Central	392.03	7.08
Southeast Central	343.93	6.21
Northeast Coastal	234.23	4.23

Source: *Industrial Supply*, November/December 2019, p. 43, from MDM Analytics.

★ 2268 ★
Medical Products
SIC: 3842; NAICS: 339113

Personal Protective Equipment Market Worldwide, 2019

Personal protective equipment is safety gear that protects the user from harm. Market shares are shown in percent.

Hand protection	34.0%
Respiratory	22.0
Clothing/apparel	14.0
Eye and face	8.0
Other	22.0

Source: "Global Personal Protective Equipment Market 2020-2025." [online] from https://mobilityforesights.com/product/personal-protective-equipment-market/ [Published May 2020], from Mobility Foresights.

★ 2269 ★
Medical Products
SIC: 3829; NAICS: 339112

Thermometer Sales by Type, 2020

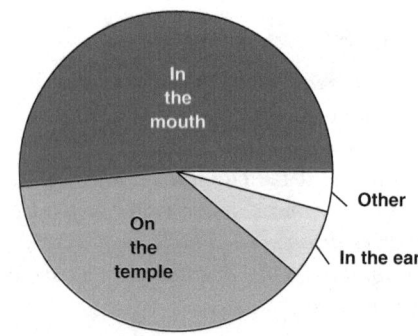

Market shares are shown for the three months ended December 2020.

In the mouth	51.3%
On the temple/forehead	36.9

Continued on next page.

★ 2269 ★
[Continued]
Medical Products
SIC: 3829; NAICS: 339112

Thermometer Sales by Type, 2020

Market shares are shown for the three months ended December 2020.

In the ear	7.3%
Other	4.5

Source: "Not All Products Are Created Equal: Thermometers." [online] from https://www.traqline.com/newsroom/blog/not-all-products-are-created-equal-thermometers/ [Published January 13, 2021], from TraQline Monthly Survey.

★ 2270 ★
Medical Products
SIC: 3842; NAICS: 339113

Top Disposable Glove Brands, 2020

Market shares are shown based on food store sales for the 52 weeks ended April 19, 2020. Sales of disposable gloves grew significantly from the previous year as demand for personal protective equipment and cleaning supplies soared at the beginning of the coronavirus pandemic in 2020. Playtex sales jumped more than 244% and Butler Mr. Clean Ultra Flex sales rose 130.9%. All other top-10 brands saw sales climb between 31.7% and 46.4% except for Butler Good Cook brand disposable gloves, used for food preparation. Its sales saw a 52.2% drop over this time period.

Butler Mr. Clean	11.49%
Playtex	5.35
Big Time Soft Scrub	4.74
Curad	3.68
Handi Works	2.10
Butler Mr. Clean Ultra Flex	1.56
Omni Safe	0.98
Butler Good Cook	0.83
Caring Hands Elegant Fare	0.80
Private label	60.89
Other	7.58

Source: *Non-Foods Management*, Annual 2020-2021, p. 224, from IRI.

★ 2271 ★
Medical Products
SIC: 3842; NAICS: 339113

Top First Aid Categories, 2020

Categories are ranked by sales in millions of dollars at supermarkets, drug stores, mass merchandisers, military commissaries, and select club and dollar chains for the 52 weeks ended October 4, 2020.

	($ mil.)	Share
Tape/bandage/gauze/cotton	$ 949.9	45.42%
Muscle/body support devices	803.8	38.44
Heat/ice packs	236.8	11.32
Aid kits	67.9	3.25
Electrotherapy devices	32.9	1.57

Source: *MMR*, November 16, 2020, p. 50, from IRI.

★ 2272 ★
Medical Products
SIC: 3842; NAICS: 339113

Top Medical/Body Support Brands, 2020

Market shares are shown based on drug store sales for the 52 weeks ended April 19, 2020.

Futuro	18.08%
Idea Village Copper Fit	5.62
Mueller Sport Care	4.87
Futuro Sport	4.75
Ace	4.47
Neo G	2.06
KT Tape Pro	1.53
KT Tape	1.42
Mueller	1.38
Private label	41.76
Other	14.06

Source: *DrugStore Management*, Annual 2020-2021, p. 95, from IRI.

★ 2273 ★
Medical Products
SIC: 3842; NAICS: 339113

Top Rubber Glove Makers Worldwide, 2020

Companies are ranked by estimated production capacity in billions of pieces. Rubber glove demand reached 360 billion pieces in 2020.

Top Glove Corp. Bhd.	85
Hartalega Holdings Bhd.	35
Sri Trang Gloves Thailand PLC	33

Continued on next page.

★ 2273 ★
[Continued]
Medical Products
SIC: 3842; NAICS: 339113

Top Rubber Glove Makers Worldwide, 2020

Companies are ranked by estimated production capacity in billions of pieces. Rubber glove demand reached 360 billion pieces in 2020.

Kossan Rubber Industries Bhd.	32
Supermax Healthcare Inc.	26

Source: "Sri Trang Gloves (Thailand) Public Company Limited Opportunity Day." [online] from https://www.sritranggloves.com/en/investor-relations/downloads/presentations-webcasts [Published September 16, 2020], from company reports.

★ 2274 ★
Merchant Acquirers
SIC: 6141; NAICS: 52221

Largest Merchant Acquirers Worldwide, 2019

Companies are ranked by billions of purchase transactions. Shares are shown based on 342.2 billion purchase transactions generated by the top 150 firms.

	(bil.)	Share
FIS (Worldpay)	36.72	10.73%
JPMorgan Chase & Co.	29.41	8.59
Sberbank	20.61	6.02
Fiserv (First Data)	20.36	5.95
Bank of America	18.56	5.42
Global Payments	16.19	4.73
Other	200.35	58.55

Source: *Nilson Report*, September 2020, p. 1.

★ 2275 ★
Merchant Acquirers
SIC: 6141; NAICS: 52221

Leading Merchant Acquirers in Latin America, 2018-2019

Companies are ranked by millions of transactions. Shares are shown for the group.

	2018	2019	Share
Cielo	5.30	5.50	29.43%
Rede	4.33	4.77	25.52
GetNet	1.84	2.05	10.97
BBVA Group	1.82	1.92	10.27
Transbank S.A.	1.48	1.82	9.74
Prisma Medios de Pago	1.31	1.37	7.33%
PagSeguro	0.99	1.26	6.74

Source: *Nilson Report*, August 2020, p. NA.

★ 2276 ★
Mercury
SIC: 1099; NAICS: 212299

Top Mercury Producing Countries, 2020

Countries are ranked by production in metric tons. Mexico's and Peru's figures refer to exports. In the United States, mercury has not been mined since 1992. Production data are estimated.

	MT	Share
China	3,400	91.77%
Tajikistan	100	2.70
Mexico	60	1.62
Argentina	50	1.35
Peru	40	1.08
Norway	20	0.54
Kyrgyzstan	15	0.40
Other	20	0.54

Source: "Mineral Commodity Summaries 2021." [online] from https://www.usgs.gov/centers/nmic/mineral-commodity-summaries [Published January 29, 2021], from U.S. Geological Survey.

★ 2277 ★
Mergers and Acquisitions
SIC: 4822; NAICS: 517311

Amazon's Major Acquisitions, 2021

Amazon agreed to acquire MGM Holdings in May 2021. The deal, valued at $6.5 billion, is one of Amazon's largest acquisitions, and analysts have noted that MGM's holdings, which includes the James Bond and Rocky films, would help Amazon boost its stagnant subscriber growth. Data show Amazon's largest acquisitions in billions of dollars. Figures exclude partial ownership stakes and debt.

Whole Foods Market	$ 13.60
MGM	6.50
Zappos.com	1.20
Ring	1.00
Twitch Interactive	0.97
Kiva Systems	0.78
PillPack	0.75
Souq.com	0.58
Quidsi	0.55

Continued on next page.

★ 2277 ★
[Continued]
Mergers and Acquisitions
SIC: 4822; NAICS: 517311

Amazon's Major Acquisitions, 2021

Amazon agreed to acquire MGM Holdings in May 2021. The deal, valued at $6.5 billion, is one of Amazon's largest acquisitions, and analysts have noted that MGM's holdings, which includes the James Bond and Rocky films, would help Amazon boost its stagnant subscriber growth. Data show Amazon's largest acquisitions in billions of dollars. Figures exclude partial ownership stakes and debt.

Elemental Technologies	$ 0.30
Audible	0.28

Source: *Wall Street Journal*, May 27, 2021, p. B1, from Dealogic and staff reports.

★ 2278 ★
Metal Buildings
SIC: 3448; NAICS: 332311

Leading Metal Building Makers, 2019

Companies are ranked by tonnage. Shares are shown based on the 205,109 tons built by the top 100 firms.

	Tonnage	Share
Span Construction & Engineering Inc.	26,708.80	13.02%
Keller Inc.	13,951.00	6.80
Steel Worx Solutions L.L.C.	12,980.00	6.33
Crossland Construction Co. Inc.	8,919.00	4.35
Precision Erection Co. Inc.	8,644.00	4.21
Baker Builders L.L.C.	6,534.80	3.19
Fast Track Erectors L.L.C.	5,225.00	2.55
Superior Metal Services	4,858.00	2.37
Big D Builders Inc.	4,543.00	2.21
S&S Structures Inc.	3,680.00	1.79
Other	109,065.41	53.17

Source: *Metal Construction News*, May 2020, p. 18.

★ 2279 ★
Metal Cans
SIC: 3411; NAICS: 332431

Metal Can Manufacturing, 2017

Total shipments were valued at $14.60 billion. The term "nec" stands for not elsewhere classified.

	($ 000)	Share
Manufacturing of aluminum cans (including lids, ends, and parts)	$ 9,169,097	63.51%
Manufacturing of steel cans and tinware end products (including ice cream cans, lids, ends, and parts)	5,265,700	36.47
Other manufacturing revenue, nec	2,785	0.02
Other metal processing and metalworking contract manufacturing services	275	<0.01
All other products and services, nec	31	<0.01

Source: "Economic Census." [online] from https://www.census.gov/programs-surveys/economic-census/data/tables.html [Accessed December 2, 2020], from U.S. Census Bureau.

★ 2280 ★
Metal Cans
SIC: 3411; NAICS: 332431

Metal Can Manufacturing Leaders, 2017

Data show the percent of industry sales held by the largest 4, 8, 20 and 50 firms in the sector. There are approximately 186 players operating in the industry generating employment for 17,529 people. According to Kentley Insights, the industry generated sales of $15.9 billion in 2019.

4 largest firms	71.1%
8 largest firms	89.5
20 largest firms	97.6
50 largest firms	100.0

Source: "Economic Census." [online] from https://www.census.gov/content/census/en/data/tables/2017/econ/economic-census/naics-sector-31-33.html [Accessed January 21, 2021], from U.S. Census Bureau.

★ 2281 ★
Metal Cans
SIC: 3411; NAICS: 332431

Metal Can Shipments, 2016-2018

Shipments are shown in millions of cans. "Other food" includes baby food, dairy, fruit/vegetable juices, seafood, and meat and poultry cans. In 2018, food claimed 50% of the market, vegetables 17.46%, pet food 15.05%, soup and misc. foods 8.85%, fruit (excl. juices) 1.38%, coffee 0.07%, and other categories 7.2%.

	2016	2017	2018
Food	26,960	26,602	26,328
Vegetables (excl. juices)	9,644	9,342	9,193
Pet food	7,464	7,676	7,923
Soup and misc. foods	4,744	4,672	4,660
Fruit (excl. juices)	868	876	726
Coffee	44	46	35
Other food	4,196	3,990	3,791

Source: "CMI Shipments Report 2018-2019." [online] from https://www.cancentral.com/media/publications/2019-cmi-annual-and-can-shipments-report [Published December 10, 2020], from Can Manufacturers Institute.

★ 2282 ★
Metal Coating and Engraving
SIC: 3479; NAICS: 332812

Metal Coating, Engraving (except Jewelry and Silverware), and Allied Services To Manufacturers, 2017

Total shipments were valued at $13.39 billion. "Manufacturing of weldments and fabricated steel plate for other purposes" excludes construction and mining. "Special-purpose coatings" includes all marine coatings, industrial, construction (excluding roofing and architectural coatings) and maintenance coatings, traffic marking paints, etc., but exclude roofing and architectural coatings, and maintenance. The term "nec" stands for not elsewhere classified.

	($ 000)	Share
Physical vapor deposition (PVD) thin film vacuum coating of metals	$ 961,593	7.24%
Electroplating, plating, polishing, anodizing, and coloring	370,919	2.79
Heat treating of metal for the trade (heat treating, pickling, annealing, brazing, shot peening, tempering, etc.)	285,686	2.15
Chemical vapor deposition (CVD) thin film vacuum coating of metals	$ 120,036	0.90%
Wholesale sales of recyclable ferrous metal scrap	23,773	0.18
Manufacturing of weldments and fabricated steel plate for other purposes	10,100	0.08
Machine shop job work and job order repairs	9,125	0.07
Retail sales of other goods, nec	4,343	0.03
Manufacturing of special-purpose coatings	2,718	0.02
Other metal processing and metalworking contract manufacturing services	518,799	3.91
Other manufacturing revenue, nec	67,155	0.51
Other service revenue, nec	14,247	0.11
All other metal coating, engraving and etching (excluding jewelry and silverware), and allied services to manufacturers	10,611,558	79.93
Other thin film vacuum coating (electronics, plastics, glass, etc.)	275,204	2.07

Source: "Economic Census." [online] from https://www.census.gov/programs-surveys/economic-census/data/tables.html [Accessed December 2, 2020], from U.S. Census Bureau.

★ 2283 ★
Metal Coating and Engraving
SIC: 3479; NAICS: 332812

Metal Coating, Engraving (except Jewelry and Silverware) Leaders, and Allied Services To Manufacturers, 2017

Data show the percent of industry sales held by the largest 4, 8, 20 and 50 firms in the sector. There are approximately 2,592 players operating in the industry generating employment for 51,221 people. According to Kentley Insights, the industry generated sales of $14.7 billion in 2019.

4 largest firms	21.4%
8 largest firms	33.4
20 largest firms	46.1
50 largest firms	59.0

Source: "Economic Census." [online] from https://www.census.gov/content/census/en/data/tables/2017/econ/economic-census/naics-sector-31-33.html [Accessed January 21, 2021], from U.S. Census Bureau.

★ 2284 ★
Metal Containers
SIC: 3412; NAICS: 332439

Top Metal Container Exporters Worldwide, 2019

Data show the major exporters of metal containers for storage or transport. Exports reached $20.2 billion in 2019, a 0.2% decrease from 2018.

China	13.6%
United States	9.5
Germany	8.8
Italy	5.2
Poland	3.9
Spain	3.8
United Kingdom	3.8
Czechia	3.4
Netherlands	3.3
South Korea	3.2
Other	41.5

Source: "2019 International Trade Statistics Yearbook." [online] from https://comtrade.un.org/pb/ [Published December 2020], from U.N. Comtrade.

★ 2285 ★
Metal Containers
SIC: 3412; NAICS: 332439

Top Metal Container Importers Worldwide, 2019

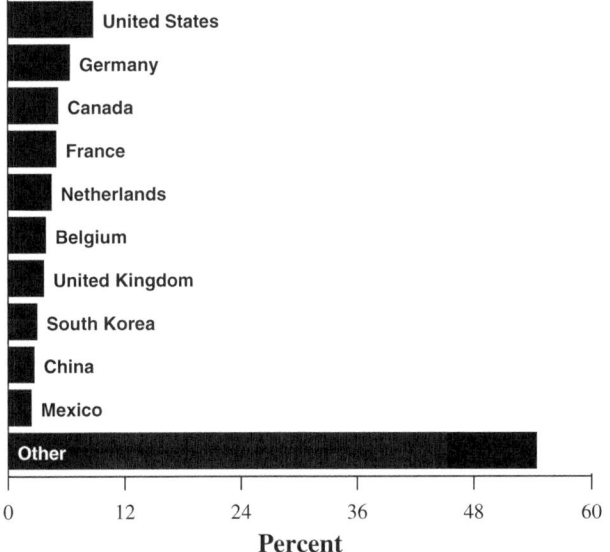

Data show the major importers of metal containers for storage or transport. Imports reached $18.9 billion in 2019, a 1.8% decrease from 2018.

United States	8.8%
Germany	6.4
Canada	5.2
France	5.0
Netherlands	4.5
Belgium	3.9
United Kingdom	3.7
South Korea	3.0
China	2.7
Mexico	2.4
Other	54.4

Source: "2019 International Trade Statistics Yearbook." [online] from https://comtrade.un.org/pb/ [Published December 2020], from U.N. Comtrade.

★ 2286 ★
Metal Crowns and Closures
SIC: 3466; NAICS: 332119

Metal Crown, Closure, and Other Metal Stamping (except Automotive), 2017

Total shipments were valued at $11.02 billion.

	($ 000)	Share
Metal electronic enclosures (stamped and pressed), excluding computer stampings	$ 420,298	5.71%
Metal and metal-composite closures, including home-canning closures	405,203	5.51
Other metal processing and metalworking contract manufacturing services	868,210	11.80
Other metal job stampings, excluding automotive	2,093,779	28.45
Other stamped and pressed metal end products for machinery, transportation, and other equipment, excluding spinning products	1,537,522	20.89
Other industrial equipment metal job stampings	1,082,355	14.71
All other metal closures, including metal crowns (including soft drinks and beer) and roll-ons	952,675	12.94

Source: "Economic Census." [online] from https://www.census.gov/programs-surveys/economic-census/data/tables.html [Accessed December 2, 2020], from U.S. Census Bureau.

★ 2287 ★
Metal Crowns and Closures
SIC: 3466; NAICS: 332119

Metal Crown, Closure, and Other Metal Stamping Leaders (except Automotive), 2017

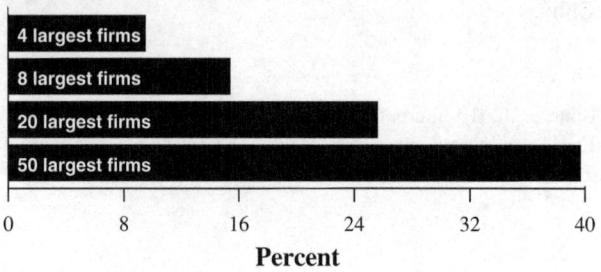

Data show the percent of industry sales held by the largest 4, 8, 20 and 50 firms in the sector. There are approximately 1,387 players operating in the industry generating employment for 48,817 people. According to Kentley Insights, the industry generated sales of $11.9 billion in 2019.

4 largest firms	9.5%
8 largest firms	15.4
20 largest firms	25.6
50 largest firms	39.7

Source: "Economic Census." [online] from https://www.census.gov/content/census/en/data/tables/2017/econ/economic-census/naics-sector-31-33.html [Accessed January 21, 2021], from U.S. Census Bureau.

★ 2288 ★
Metal Cutting Tools
SIC: 3545; NAICS: 333515

Consumption of Carbide Cutting Tools, 2019

Total consumption reached $3.66 billion. Figures are in millions of dollars.

	($ mil.)	Share
Northeast Central	$1,047.23	28.61%
South Atlantic	461.33	12.60
Pacific states	403.68	11.03
Southwest Central	395.61	10.81
Northwest Central	386.79	10.57
Mid-Atlantic states	382.76	10.46
Northeast Coastal	209.92	5.74
Southeast Central	207.12	5.66
Mountain states	165.57	4.52

Source: *Industrial Supply*, Jan-Feb 2020, p. 40, from MDM Analytics.

★ 2289 ★
Metal Cutting Tools
SIC: 3545; NAICS: 333515

Leading Metal Cutting Tool Makers Worldwide, 2017

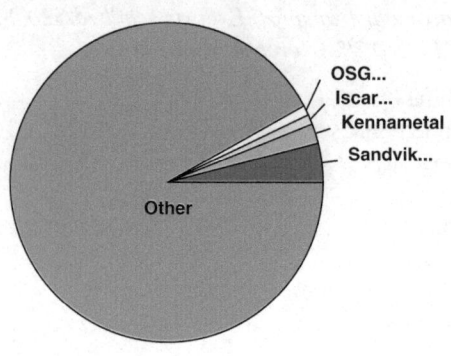

The market is forecast to grow from $35.81 billion in 2020 to $42.65 billion in 2026.

Sandvik AB	3.88%
Kennametal	1.62
Iscar Ltd.	1.24
OSG Corp.	1.06
Other	92.20

Source: "Global Cutting Tools Market Research Report 2020." [online] from https://www.360marketupdates.com/global-cutting-tools-market-14837730 [Published January 2020], from QY Research.

★ 2290 ★
Metal Framing
SIC: 3444; NAICS: 332439

Metal Framing by Finish, 2020

Market shares are shown based on dollar sales for the 12 months ended March 2020.

Pre-galvanized	62.6%
Stainless steel	11.4
Electroplated galvanized	8.1
Aluminum	5.7
Hot-dipped galvanized	3.6
Painted	3.4
Gold galvanized	2.5
Other	2.5

Source: *The Electrical Distributor*, April 2020, p. 58, from Epicor's Industry Data Analytics.

★ 2291 ★
Metal Fuel Tanks
SIC: 3443; NAICS: 33242

Metal Fuel Tank Market, 2019

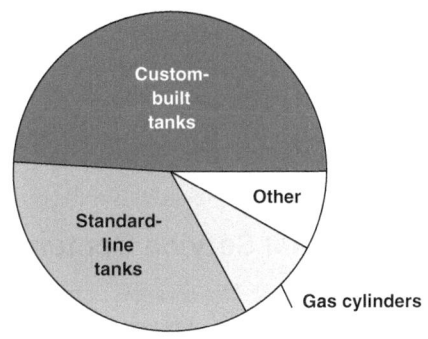

The industry was valued at $1.1 billion in 2019.

Custom-built tanks	49.2%
Standard-line tanks	33.8
Gas cylinders	8.7
Other	8.3

Source: "The Remarkable Expansion of the Custom Built Market." [online] from https://agbproducts.com/news/the-remarkable-expansion-of-the-custom-built-market/ [Published January 28, 2020], from IBISWorld.

★ 2292 ★
Metal Heat Treating
SIC: 3398; NAICS: 332811

Metal Heat Treating, 2017

Total shipments were valued at $4.95 billion. "Heat treating of metal for the trade" includes heat treating, pickling, annealing, brazing, shot peening, tempering, etc. The term "nec" stands for not elsewhere classified.

	($ 000)
Heat treating of metal for the trade	$ 4,458,104
Metal coating, engraving (excluding jewelry and silverware), and allied services to manufacturers	22,634
Wholesale sales of recyclable ferrous metal scrap	22,564
Machine shop job work and job order repairs	20,350
Electroplating, plating, polishing, anodizing, and coloring	19,014
Manufacturing of precision turned products (made on CNC equipment or screw machines), excluding automotive	7,909
Maintenance and repair services for industrial machinery and equipment	4,020
Other metal processing and metalworking contract manufacturing services	$ 229,462
Other manufacturing revenue, nec	2,899

Source: "Economic Census." [online] from https://www.census.gov/programs-surveys/economic-census/data/tables.html [Accessed December 2, 2020], from U.S. Census Bureau.

★ 2293 ★
Metal Heat Treating
SIC: 3398; NAICS: 332811

Metal Heat Treating Leaders, 2017

Data show the percent of industry sales held by the largest 4, 8, 20 and 50 firms in the sector. There are approximately 783 players operating in the industry generating employment for 20,407 people. According to Kentley Insights, the industry generated sales of $5.5 billion in 2019.

4 largest firms	27.8%
8 largest firms	39.9
20 largest firms	52.9
50 largest firms	66.2

Source: "Economic Census." [online] from https://www.census.gov/content/census/en/data/tables/2017/econ/economic-census/naics-sector-31-33.html [Accessed January 21, 2021], from U.S. Census Bureau.

★ 2294 ★
Metal Powders
SIC: 3499; NAICS: 332117

Copper Powder Shipments Worldwide, 2020

More than 1.4 million kilograms of copper powder, both pure copper and copper alloys, are to ship during the year for the copper additive manufacturing market.

General industry and tooling	28.3%
Aerospace	26.5
Service	23.0
Automotive	3.4
Energy	3.3
Oil and gas	3.3
Medical	2.8
Other	9.3

Source: "SmarTech Analysis: Over 1.4 Million Kg of AM Copper Powders to Ship by 2029." [online] from https://3dprint.com/267539/smartech-analysis-over-1-4-million-kg-of-am-copper-powders-to-ship-by-2029/ [Published May 19, 2020], from SmarTech Analysis.

★ 2295 ★
Metal Powders
SIC: 3499; NAICS: 332117

Metal Injection Molding Market in North America, 2019

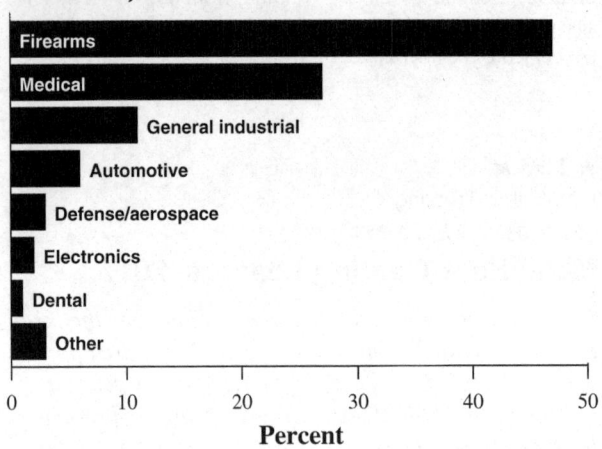

Distribution is shown based on weight of parts shipments.

Firearms	47.0%
Medical	27.0
General industrial	11.0
Automotive	6.0
Defense/aerospace	3.0
Electronics	2.0
Dental	1.0
Other	3.0

Source: *Powder Metallurgy Review*, Autumn/Fall 2020, p. 48.

★ 2296 ★
Metal Powders
SIC: 3499; NAICS: 332117

Metal Powder Shipments in North America, 2018-2019

Metal powder has a variety of applications, including transportation, electronics, construction and industrial. Data are in short tons. North America claimed approximately 40% of the global market for metal powders.

	2018 ST	2019 ST	Share
Iron and steel	433,203	388,351	85.29%
Aluminum	33,660	26,448	5.81
Copper and copper-base tin	18,500	16,900	3.71
Stainless steel	8,750	7,960	1.75
Tungsten carbide	8,590	7,919	1.74
Nickel	6,100	5,500	1.21
Tungsten	1,750	1,689	0.37%
Molybdenum	820	550	0.12

Source: "State of the PM Industry in North America - 2020." [online] from https://www.mpif.org/Resources/StateofthePM-Industry.aspx [Published July 2020], from Metal Powder Industries Federation.

★ 2297 ★
Metal Service Centers
SIC: 5051; NAICS: 42351

Leading Metal Service Centers, 2019

Companies are ranked by revenue in billions of dollars. Shares are shown based on revenue generated by the top 50 companies.

	($ bil.)	Share
Reliance Steel & Aluminum Co.	$ 11.00	19.06%
Ryerson Inc.	4.50	7.80
ThyssenKrupp Materials NA Inc.	3.20	5.55
Kloeckner Metals Corp.	2.95	5.11
Samuel, Son & Co Ltd.	2.80	4.85
Russel Metals Inc.	2.77	4.80
Toyota Tsusho America	2.47	4.28
O'Neal Industries Inc.	2.40	4.16
Steel Technologies L.L.C.	2.37	4.11
Worthington Industries	2.20	3.81
Alro Steel Corp.	1.98	3.43
Olympic Steel Inc.	1.58	2.74
Other	17.48	30.29

Source: *Metal Center News*, September 2020, p. 20.

★ 2298 ★
Metal Stampings
SIC: 3462; NAICS: 332111

Leading Metal Stamping and Forging Firms, 2018

According to an update by the source, the 2,075 companies in this industry generated revenue of $28 billion in 2020.

Precision Castparts Corp.	10.4%
Allegheny Technologies Inc.	5.1
Other	84.5

Source: "6 Things to Know About the Metal Stamping & Forging Industry." [online] from https://teamcoact.com/learning-center/metal-stamping-forging-industry/ [Accessed February 15, 2021], from IBISWorld.

★ 2299 ★
Metal Stampings
SIC: 3465; NAICS: 33637

Motor Vehicle Metal Stamping, 2017

Total shipments were valued at $36.65 billion. The term "nec" stands for not elsewhere classified.

	($ 000)	Share
Automotive job stampings (truck, bus, and passenger car)	$ 34,663,568	95.22%
Metalworking die and die sets	536,814	1.47
Manufacturing of other metal job stampings	385,375	1.06
Wholesale sales of recyclable ferrous metal scrap	188,783	0.52
Wholesale sales of metal castings, forgings, and stampings	167,163	0.46
Recreational vehicle and agricultural equipment metal job stampings	62,384	0.17
Wholesale sales of recyclable nonferrous metal scrap	58,258	0.16
Punches, die parts, and other special tooling	11,758	0.03
Furniture metal job stampings	5,147	0.01
Other manufacturing revenue, nec	149,916	0.41
Other transportation equipment contract manufacturing services	90,592	0.25
Other ammunition products, including industrial shells and cartridges, air gun ammunition, percussion caps	45,394	0.12
Other metal processing and metalworking contract manufacturing services	36,691	0.10

Source: "Economic Census." [online] from https://www.census.gov/programs-surveys/economic-census/data/tables.html [Accessed December 2, 2020], from U.S. Census Bureau.

★ 2300 ★
Metal Stampings
SIC: 3465; NAICS: 33637

Motor Vehicle Metal Stamping Leaders, 2017

Data show the percent of industry sales held by the largest 4, 8, 20 and 50 firms in the sector. There are approximately 756 players operating in the industry generating employment for 103,114 people. According to Kentley Insights, the industry generated sales of $39.6 billion in 2019.

4 largest firms	24.8%
8 largest firms	36.6
20 largest firms	54.3
50 largest firms	70.7

Source: "Economic Census." [online] from https://www.census.gov/content/census/en/data/tables/2017/econ/economic-census/naics-sector-31-33.html [Accessed January 21, 2021], from U.S. Census Bureau.

★ 2301 ★
Metalcasting Industry
SIC: 3369; NAICS: 331529

Metalcasting Industry Revenue, 2012-2021 and 2025

Industry revenue is shown in millions of dollars. Figures are forecast for 2021 through 2025. The number of facilities has been declining for some time, although the rate of this decline has slowed in recent years. There were 1,985 facilities in 2012, 1,800 in 2017, 1,745 in 2020, 1,730 in 2021, and 1,683 in 2025.

2012	$ 38,793
2013	38,715
2014	40,670
2015	38,889
2016	35,640
2017	37,835
2018	41,354
2019	44,290
2020	36,805
2021	44,056
2025	52,832

Source: *Casting Source*, January-February 2021, p. 28.

★ 2302 ★
Meters
SIC: 3825; NAICS: 334514

Top Smart Heat Meter Makers in China, 2019

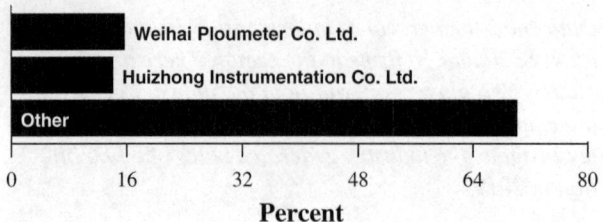

Smart heat meters generated sales of 3.65 million units. Market shares are estimated.

Weihai Ploumeter Co. Ltd.	15.7%
Huizhong Instrumentation Co. Ltd.	14.1
Other	70.2

Source: "Smart Heat Industry Report 2020-2026." [online] from http://www.researchinchina.com [Published May 2020], from Research in China.

★ 2303 ★
Mica
SIC: 1499; NAICS: 212399

Top Natural Mica Producing Countries, 2020

Countries are ranked by scrap and flake production in metric tons. In the United States, mica was mined in Georgia, North Carolina, and South Dakota. Eight companies produced about 57,000 tons of ground mica, most of which was used in joint compound, oil-well-drilling additives, paint, roofing and rubber products. Production data are estimated.

	MT	Share
China	95,000	27.10%
Finland	65,000	18.54
United States	35,000	9.99
Madagascar	30,000	8.56
South Korea	20,000	5.71
Canada	18,000	5.14
France	18,000	5.14
India	15,000	4.28
Turkey	5,500	1.57
Other	49,000	13.98

Source: "Mineral Commodity Summaries 2021." [online] from https://www.usgs.gov/centers/nmic/mineral-commodity-summaries [Published January 29, 2021], from U.S. Geological Survey.

★ 2304 ★
Microdisplays
SIC: 3679; NAICS: 33431

Demand for Microdisplays Worldwide, 2020 and 2025

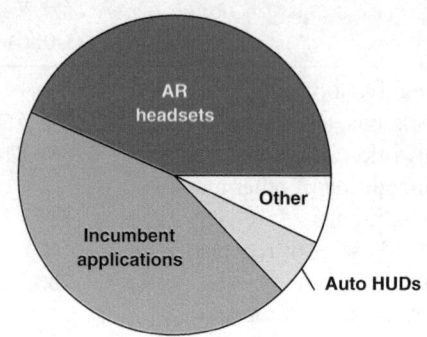

Spending is estimated in millions of dollars. The industry is forecast to grow from $1.9 billion in 2020 to $4.2 billion in 2025.

	2020 ($ mil.)	2025 ($ mil.)	Share
AR headsets	$ 45	$ 1,800	43.62%
Incumbent applications	1,800	1,800	43.62
Auto HUDs	34	242	5.86
Other	8	285	6.91

Source: "Microdisplay Industry: An Explosive Ecosystem Mining Technical Innovations, Strategy and Attractive Applications." [online] from http://www.yole.fr/iso_upload/News/2020/PR_MICRODISPLAYS_MarketUpdate_YOLE_Oct 2020.pdf [Press release October 1, 2020], from Yole Développement.

★ 2305 ★
Microgrids
SIC/NAICS: See frontmatter for explanation.

Leading Microgrid Makers Worldwide, 2018

A microgrid is a "localized power system comprised of distributed generation assets, energy storage devices, and smart distribution technologies that interoperates through controls and software-based intelligence systems." The industry generated revenue of $24.13 billion in 2019 and is expected to reach $51.47 billion in 2026.

ABB Inc.	8.59%
NEC Corp.	7.21
General Electric Co.	5.93
Other	78.27

Source: "Global Microgrid Market Size, Status and Forecast 2020-2026." [online] from http://www.qyresearch.com [Published February 2020], from QY Research.

★ 2306 ★
Microswitches
SIC: 3679; NAICS: 334419

Leading Microswitch Makers Worldwide, 2017

A microswitch, also known as a miniature snap-action switch, is a switch activated with little physical force. The industry was valued at $590 million in 2018.

Omron Corp.	7.50%
Alps Electric Co.	6.14
Johnson Electric (Burgess)	5.76
Panasonic Corp.	5.19
Other	75.41

Source: "Global Microswitch Market Insights, Forecast to 2025." [online] from https://www.qyresearch.com [Published March 2019], from QY Research.

★ 2307 ★
Military Exchanges
SIC: 5999; NAICS: 453998

Leading Military Exchanges, 2020

Exchanges are ranked by resale sales in thousands of dollars for the 52 or 53 weeks ended June 2020.

Army & Air Force Exchange	$ 667,000
Defense Commissary Exchange	341,670
Navy Exchange Service Command	206,212
Marine Corps. Exchange	97,263
Veterans Canteen Service	25,318
Coast Guard Exchange	19,582

Source: "Resale Snapshot." [online] from http://www.ebm-pubs.com/ECN/ecn_curis.asp [Accessed January 5, 2021].

★ 2308 ★
Milk
SIC: 2026; NAICS: 311511

Best-Selling Types of Milk, 2019

Distribution is shown based on volume of sales from December 1, 2018-December 1, 2019.

Whole milk	39.9%
2%	36.9
1%	15.7
Skim/fat-free	7.5

Source: *Northeast Dairy*, First Quarter 2020, p. 24, from Dairy Marketing Institute.

★ 2309 ★
Milk
SIC: 2026; NAICS: 311511

Leading Dairy Cream Brands, 2020

Brands are ranked based on sales at supermarkets, drug stores, mass merchandisers, military commissaries, and select club and dollar chains for the 12 weeks ended September 6, 2020.

	($ mil.)	Share
Hood	$ 6.19	15.18%
Cacique	5.21	12.78
Farmland	1.38	3.38
Silk Oat Yeah	1.09	2.67
Reddi-Whip	0.87	2.13
Private label	17.99	44.11
Other	8.05	19.74

Source: *Frozen & Refrigerated Buyer*, November 2020, p. 11, from IRI.

★ 2310 ★
Milk
SIC: 2026; NAICS: 311514

Leading Evaporated Milk Makers Worldwide, 2019

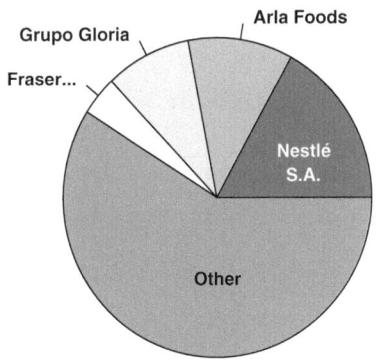

The industry is forecast to grow from $5.55 billion in 2020 to $7.23 billion in 2026. Market shares are shown based on revenue.

Nestlé S.A.	17.26%
Arla Foods	10.68
Grupo Gloria	8.94
Fraser and Neave	4.43
Other	58.69

Source: "Global Evaporated Milk Market Insights and Forecast to 2026." [online] from http://www.qyresearch.com [Published September 2020], from QY Research.

★ 2311 ★
Milk
SIC: 2026; NAICS: 311511

Leading Flavored Milk/Eggnog/Buttermilk Brands, 2020

Brands are ranked based on sales at supermarkets, drug stores, mass merchandisers, military commissaries, and select club and dollar chains for the 12 weeks ended August 9, 2020.

	($ mil.)	Share
All Dean Foods	$ 28.21	12.00%
All Fairlife	26.68	11.35
Prairie Farms	13.02	5.54
Hiland	10.99	4.67
Promised Land	8.75	3.72
Borden	8.62	3.67
Darigold	4.54	1.93
Private label	73.29	31.17
Other	61.05	25.96

Source: *Frozen & Refrigerated Buyer*, October 2020, p. 20, from IRI.

★ 2312 ★
Milk
SIC: 2026; NAICS: 311511

Top Cow's Milk Consuming Regions, 2020

Figures are in thousands of metric tons.

	(000)	Share
India	81,000	42.55%
European Union	33,260	17.47
United States	21,200	11.14
China	12,800	6.72
Belarus	11,250	5.91
Brazil	7,200	3.78
Ukraine	4,866	2.56
Mexico	4,145	2.18
Japan	3,999	2.10
Other	10,640	5.59

Source: "Dairy: World Markets and Trade." [online] from https://apps.fas.usda.gov/psdonline/circulars/dairy.pdf [Published July 2020], from U.S. Department of Agriculture.

★ 2313 ★
Milk
SIC: 2026; NAICS: 311511

Top Cow's Milk Producing Regions, 2020

Figures are in thousands of metric tons.

	(000)	Share
European Union	156,700	29.44%
United States	100,485	18.88
India	94,000	17.66
Russia	31,000	5.82
Brazil	24,950	4.69
New Zealand	21,900	4.11
Mexico	12,750	2.40
Argentina	11,100	2.09
Ukraine	9,690	1.82
Other	69,731	13.10

Source: "Dairy: World Markets and Trade." [online] from https://apps.fas.usda.gov/psdonline/circulars/dairy.pdf [Published July 2020], from U.S. Department of Agriculture.

★ 2314 ★
Milk
SIC: 2026; NAICS: 311511

Top Milk Makers in China, 2019

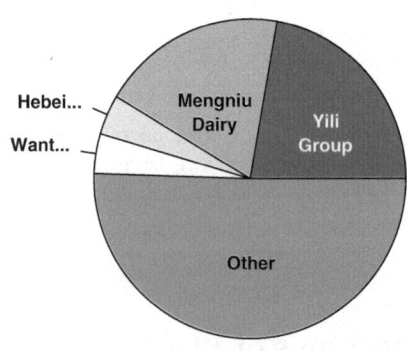

Milk sales reached 220 renminbi in 2019, up from 181.8 billion in 2017 and 203.4 billion in 2018. Milk sales by channel: supermarkets 44.3%, food wholesalers 23.8%, food retailers 16.8% and other channels 15.1%.

Yili Group	21.7%
Mengniu Dairy	19.4
Hebei Yangyuan Zhihui Beverage Co.	4.5

Continued on next page.

★ 2314 ★
[Continued]
Milk
SIC: 2026; NAICS: 311511

Top Milk Makers in China, 2019

Milk sales reached 220 renminbi in 2019, up from 181.8 billion in 2017 and 203.4 billion in 2018. Milk sales by channel: supermarkets 44.3%, food wholesalers 23.8%, food retailers 16.8% and other channels 15.1%.

Want Want Holdings Ltd.	4.3%
Other	50.1

Source: "The Milk Market in China: Consumers' Perception of Nutrition Has Sustained the Growth of This Sector." [online] from https://daxueconsulting.com/report-on-dairy-milk-market-in-china/ [Published July 24, 2020], from Euromonitor.

★ 2315 ★
Milk
SIC: 2026; NAICS: 311511

Top Refrigerated Skim/Low-Fat Milk Brands, 2020

Brands are ranked based on sales at supermarkets, drug stores, mass merchandisers, military commissaries, and select club and dollar chains for the 52 weeks ended September 6, 2020.

	($ mil.)	Share
All Dean Foods	$ 646.7	8.87%
Hood Lactaid	474.1	6.50
All Danone North America	312.5	4.29
Fairlife	235.9	3.23
Prairie Farms	170.0	2.33
Hiland	114.7	1.57
Organic Valley	82.9	1.14
Hood	82.2	1.13
Borden	66.3	0.91
Private label	4,172.1	57.21
Other	934.8	12.82

Source: *Dairy Foods*, November 2020, p. 33, from IRI.

★ 2316 ★
Milk
SIC: 2026; NAICS: 311511

Top Refrigerated Whole Milk Brands, 2020

Brands are ranked based on sales at supermarkets, drug stores, mass merchandisers, military commissaries, and select club and dollar chains for the 52 weeks ended September 6, 2020.

	($ mil.)	Share
All Dean Foods	$ 589.2	11.00%
All Danone North America	314.8	5.88
Hood Lactaid	204.0	3.81
Borden	120.7	2.25
Hiland	109.7	2.05
Prairie Farms	109.1	2.04
Fairlife	92.4	1.72
Organic Valley	75.4	1.41
Cream-O-Land	60.5	1.13
Private label	2,908.9	54.29
Other	773.3	14.43

Source: *Dairy Foods*, November 2020, p. 35, from IRI.

★ 2317 ★
Milk Alternatives
SIC: 2026; NAICS: 311511

Leading Dairy Half and Half Brands, 2020

Brands are ranked based on sales at supermarkets, drug stores, mass merchandisers, military commissaries, and select club and dollar chains for the 12 weeks ended August 9, 2020.

	($ mil.)	Share
All Danone U.S.	$ 45.99	19.67%
Organic Valley	11.31	4.84
All Dean Foods	6.15	2.63
Hood	5.88	2.51
Darigold	3.92	1.68
All Heartland Farms	2.96	1.27
Clover Sonoma	2.32	0.99
Prairie Farms	1.84	0.79
Shamrock Farms	1.38	0.59
Private label	134.15	57.36
Other	17.96	7.68

Source: *Frozen & Refrigerated Buyer*, October 2020, p. 20, from IRI.

★ 2318 ★
Milk Alternatives
SIC: 2026; NAICS: 311511

Leading Milk Alternative Drink Makers, 2020

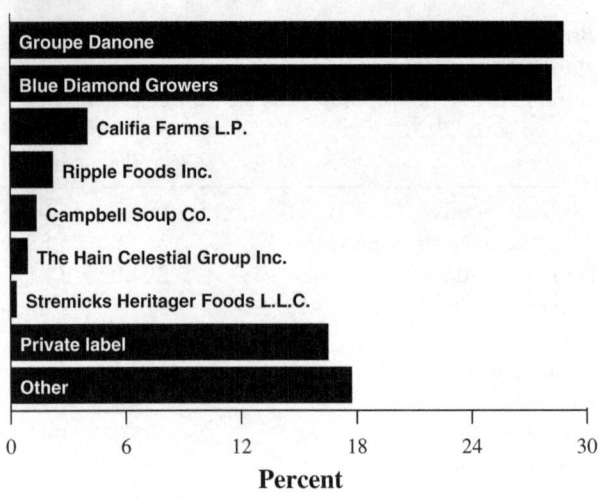

Companies are ranked by sales in millions of dollars.

	($ mil.)	Share
Groupe Danone	$ 825.0	28.80%
Blue Diamond Growers	807.6	28.19
Califia Farms L.P.	114.9	4.01
Ripple Foods Inc.	63.5	2.22
Campbell Soup Co.	38.9	1.36
The Hain Celestial Group Inc.	25.6	0.89
Stremicks Heritager Foods L.L.C.	9.0	0.31
Private label	472.7	16.50
Other	507.8	17.72

Source: "Milk Alternative Beverages in the United States and Canada." [online] from https://www.agr.gc.ca/eng/international-trade/market-intelligence/reports/?id=1522931721523 [Published May 2021], from Euromonitor.

★ 2319 ★
Milk Alternatives
SIC: 2026; NAICS: 311511

Milk Alternative Market in Western Europe, 2020

Market shares are shown in percent.

Alpro	25.1%
Oatly	9.2
Bjorg	5.0
Chufi	4.6
Provamel	3.8%
Other	52.3

Source: "Nestlé Introduces Plant-based Milk Brand to Rival Oatly, Alpro." [online] from https://www.bloomberg.com/news/articles/2021-05-04/nestle-introduces-plant-based-milk-brand-to-rival-oatly-alpro [Published May 4, 2021], from Euromonitor.

★ 2320 ★
Milk Alternatives
SIC: 2026; NAICS: 311511

Top Refrigerated Almond Milk Brands, 2020

Brands are ranked based on sales at supermarkets, drug stores, mass merchandisers, military commissaries, and select club and dollar chains for the 52 weeks ended May 17, 2020.

	($ mil.)	Share
Blue Diamond Almond Breeze	$ 554.25	39.6%
Danone	474.32	33.9
Califia Farms	88.48	6.3
Silk Almond Light	15.56	1.1
Private label	253.16	18.1
Other	15.07	1.0

Source: *Beverage Industry*, July 2020, p. SOI-32, from IRI.

★ 2321 ★
Milk Alternatives
SIC: 2026; NAICS: 311511

Top Refrigerated Milk Substitute Brands, 2020

Brands are ranked by multi-outlet sales in millions of dollars for the 52 weeks ended July 12, 2020. Shares are shown for the top 20 companies.

	($ mil.)	Share
All Oatly	$ 32.92	13.11%
All Danone U.S.	31.16	12.41
Ripple	27.84	11.09
Silk Oat Yeah	27.34	10.89
Meyenberg	24.35	9.70
Chobani	14.51	5.78
Good Karma	8.28	3.30
Califia Farms	7.97	3.17
William Bolthouse Farms	3.07	1.22

Continued on next page.

★ 2321 ★
[Continued]
Milk Alternatives
SIC: 2026; NAICS: 311511

Top Refrigerated Milk Substitute Brands, 2020

Brands are ranked by multi-outlet sales in millions of dollars for the 52 weeks ended July 12, 2020. Shares are shown for the top 20 companies.

	($ mil.)	Share
Hood	$ 1.74	0.69%
Mooala Brands L.L.C.	1.57	0.63
Redwood Hill Farm & Creamery	1.47	0.59
Mariani	0.83	0.33
Private label	4.28	1.70
Other HP Hood	51.27	20.42
Other	12.50	4.98

Source: *BevNet Magazine*, September-October 2020, p. 28, from IRI.

★ 2322 ★
Milk Alternatives
SIC: 2026; NAICS: 311511

Top Refrigerated Milk Substitute Brands (All Other), 2020

Brands are ranked based on sales at supermarkets, drug stores, mass merchandisers, military commissaries, and select club and dollar chains for the 52 weeks ended May 17, 2020. Danone was the only brand listed that saw sales decline from the previous year. Other HP Hood brands saw a 923.7% increase in dollar sales, followed by Silk Oat Yeah (668.6%), Oatly (370.2%) and Ripple (28.6%). This market may refer to non-almond milk; it is unclear from the source.

	($ mil.)	Share
Danone	$ 30.79	14.0%
Oatly	27.21	12.4
Ripple	26.68	12.1
Silk Oat Yeah	25.02	11.4
Other HP Hood	43.57	19.8
Other	66.84	30.3

Source: *Beverage Industry*, July 2020, p. SOI-33, from IRI.

★ 2323 ★
Mineral Wool
SIC: 3296; NAICS: 327993

Mineral Wool Manufacturing Leaders, 2017

Data show the percent of industry sales held by the largest 4, 8, 20 and 50 firms in the sector. There are approximately 258 players operating in the industry generating employment for 14,666 people. According to Kentley Insights, the industry generated sales of $6.4 billion in 2019.

4 largest firms	58.4%
8 largest firms	76.6
20 largest firms	90.8
50 largest firms	96.4

Source: "Economic Census." [online] from https://www.census.gov/content/census/en/data/tables/2017/econ/economic-census/naics-sector-31-33.html [Accessed January 21, 2021], from U.S. Census Bureau.

★ 2324 ★
Mining Equipment
SIC: 3532; NAICS: 333131

Leading Surface Mining Equipment Producers Worldwide, 2020

Data show share of underground fleet. Figures are as of May 2020.

Caterpillar Inc.	43.0%
Komatsu Ltd.	18.0
Volvo Construction AB	9.0
BEML Ltd.	5.0
Hitachi Machinery Construction Co. Ltd.	4.0
Atlas Copco AB	3.0
BelAZ	3.0
Liebherr-International AG	2.0
Scania AB	2.0
Sandvik AB	1.0
Other	10.0

Source: *Mine*, June 2020, p. NA, from GlobalData's Power Intelligence Centre.

★ 2325 ★
Mining Equipment
SIC: 3532; NAICS: 333131

Leading Underground Mining Equipment Producers Worldwide, 2020

Data show share of underground fleet. Figures are as of July 2020.

Sandvik AB	22.0%
Komatsu Ltd.	20.0
Caterpillar Inc.	17.0
Atlas Copco AB	13.0
Famur Group	9.0
Eimco Elecon (India) Ltd.	4.0
AARD Mining Equipment (Pty) Ltd.	1.0
J.H. Fletcher & Co.	1.0
Normet Group Oy	1.0
VLI Pty. Ltd.	1.0
Other	11.0

Source: *Mine*, August 2020, p. NA, from GlobalData's Power Intelligence Centre.

★ 2326 ★
Missiles and Space Vehicles
SIC: 3761; NAICS: 336414

Guided Missile and Space Vehicle Propulsion Unit and Parts Manufacturing, 2019

Total shipments were valued at $8.03 billion.

	($ 000)	Share
Manufacturing of complete missiles, space vehicle engines, and propulsion units for U.S. Government military customers	$ 4,055,431	50.50%
Developing and making prototypes of complete missiles, space vehicle engines, and propulsion units	2,220,296	27.65
Manufacturing of missile and space vehicle components, parts, and subassemblies for U.S. Government military customers	43,700	0.54
Manufacturing of all other miscellaneous electronic components	8,488	0.11
Manufacturing of missile and space vehicle components, parts, and subassemblies for other customers	$ 5,969	0.07%
Other	1,696,116	21.12

Source: "Annual Survey of Manufactures." [online] from https://www.census.gov/programs-surveys/asm/data/tables.html [Accessed March 18, 2021], from U.S. Department of Commerce.

★ 2327 ★
Missiles and Space Vehicles
SIC: 3761; NAICS: 336414

Leading Cruise Missile Makers Worldwide, 2018

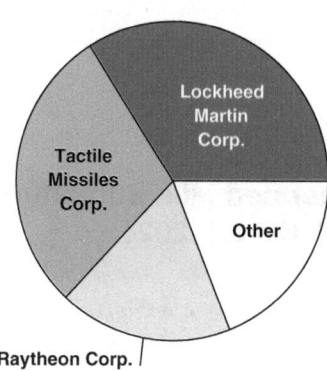

The industry is forecast to grow from $1.62 billion in 2018 to $2.46 billion in 2027. There are three types of cruise missiles: air-launched, land attack and other types. Air-launched claimed 61.77% of sales volume. Raytheon's share has declined recently because the U.S. government has reduced its purchases of the Tomahawk missile.

Lockheed Martin Corp.	33.90%
Tactile Missiles Corp.	29.06
Raytheon Corp.	18.01
Other	19.03

Source: "Cruise Missile Market Size Growth Opportunities, Driving Factors by Manufacturers, Regions, Type and Application." [online] from https://www.wicz.com/story/43544912/cruise-missile-market-size-growth-opportunities-driving-factors-by-manufacturer [Press release March 24, 2021].

★ 2328 ★
Mobile Food Services
SIC: 5963; NAICS: 72233

Mobile Food Service Leaders, 2017

Data show the percent of industry sales held by the largest 4, 8, 20 and 50 firms in the sector. There are approximately 5,211 players operating in the industry generating employment for 13,678 people. According to Kentley Insights, the industry generated sales of $1.4 billion in 2018.

4 largest firms	4.2%
8 largest firms	6.1
20 largest firms	9.9
50 largest firms	16.0

Source: "Economic Census." [online] from https://www.census.gov/content/census/en/data/tables/2017/econ/economic-census/naics-sector-31-33.html [Accessed January 21, 2021], from U.S. Census Bureau.

★ 2329 ★
Mobile Food Services
SIC: 5963; NAICS: 72233

Mobile Food Services, 2017

Total shipments were valued at $1.18 billion. The term "nec" stands for not elsewhere classified.

	($ 000)	Share
Meals, snacks, and other food items dispensed via mobile vending service	$ 918,360	77.91%
Nonalcoholic beverages dispensed via mobile vending service	77,371	6.56
Meals, snacks, and other food, without table service for consumption on the premises	53,469	4.54
Meals, snacks, other food items, and nonalcoholic beverages for catered events held on the customer's premises	50,129	4.25
Meals, snacks, and other food, for immediate consumption off the premises, except via drive-through service, including take-out, curbside pick-up, and delivery	19,237	1.63
Meals, snacks, and other food, prepared and served	13,647	1.16
Meals, snacks, other food, and nonalcoholic beverages prepared for catered events held on the caterer's premises	$ 9,599	0.81%
Meals, snacks, other food, and nonalcoholic beverages dropped off at the customer's event	8,101	0.69
Retail sales of soft drinks and nonalcoholic beverages	6,516	0.55
Nonalcoholic beverages, for immediate consumption off the premises, except via drive-through service, including take-out, curbside pick-up, and delivery	5,404	0.46
Nonalcoholic beverages, without table service for consumption on the premises	5,465	0.46
Retail sales of perishable prepared foods	4,293	0.36
Meals, snacks, and other food items, via drive-through service	1,996	0.17
Meals, snacks, other food items, and nonalcoholic beverages prepared for customer pick-up, including party platters	1,476	0.13
Meals, snacks, other food items, and beverages for immediate consumption, prepared under long-term contract	1,069	0.09
Nonalcoholic beverages, via drive-through service	996	0.08
Nonalcoholic beverages, prepared and served	953	0.08
Alcoholic beverages prepared for catered events	165	0.01
Retail sales of baked goods	118	0.01
Retail sales of food dry goods and other foods purchased for future consumption	163	0.01
Retail sales of other goods, nec	102	0.01
Local transportation and delivery of purchased or serviced items	49	< 0.01
Temporary staffing services	11	< 0.01

Source: "Economic Census." [online] from https://www.census.gov/programs-surveys/economic-census/data/tables.html [Accessed December 2, 2020], from U.S. Census Bureau.

★ 2330 ★
Mobile Food Services
SIC: 5812; NAICS: 722513

Popular Food Truck Cuisines, 2019

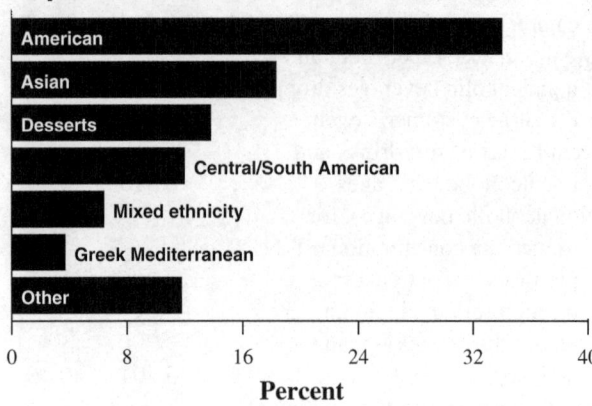

Industry revenue reached $1 billion in 2019. The source notes several important trends. With low barriers to entry, the industry is competitive. The number of businesses increased 12.8% from 2014-2019; revenue increased 6.8% over this same period. But revenue is expected to increase just 0.5% from 2019-2024. Cities are still modifying regulations to support food trucks in parking lots and similar areas. Food truck operators also need to have healthier options to address the needs of some consumers.

American	34.0%
Asian	18.3
Desserts	13.8
Central/South American	12.0
Mixed ethnicity	6.4
Greek Mediterranean	3.7
Other	11.8

Source: "Food Trucks in the U.S." [online] from http://www.ibisworld.com [Published March 2020], from IBISWorld.

★ 2331 ★
Mobile Gaming
SIC: 2741; NAICS: 51913

Leading Mobile Game Makers in China, 2020

Market shares are shown for the second quarter of 2020. Multiple battle arena games claimed 15.57% of sales by genre, 4X strategy 12.16%, turn-based role-playing games 10.7%, survival 1.23%, and other 60.34%.

Tencent Mobile Games	39.26%
NetEase Inc.	16.84
Lingxi Games Inc.	6.64
Shanghai Lilith Technology Co.	2.89
Perfect World	2.17%
FriendTimes Inc.	2.16
Supercell	1.83
Guangzhou Douyi Network Technology Co.	1.76
Shanghai Youzu Information Technology Corp.	1.65
Shanghai Hode Information Technology Co.	1.31
Other	23.49

Source: "Chinese Mobile Games Market 2020 vs. 2019." [online] from https://www.gamerefinery.com/chinese-mobile-games-market-2019-2020/ [Published October 13, 2020].

★ 2332 ★
Mobile Gaming
SIC: 2741; NAICS: 51913

Mobile Game Market, 2017-2025

Sales are shown in millions of dollars. Mobile gaming is expected to grow 12.1% from 2020 to 2021, benefiting from consumers looking for entertainment during the pandemic. The United States is the second largest mobile game market worldwide, behind China.

2017	$ 12,816
2018	13,849
2019	15,269
2020	18,250
2021	20,454
2022	22,828
2023	25,224
2024	27,510
2025	29,586

Source: "Corona 19 Accelerates U.S. Mobile Game Market Growth." [online] from http://www.news.kotra.or.kr [Published February 10, 2021], from Statista, December 2020.

★ 2333 ★
Mobile Gaming
SIC: 2741; NAICS: 51913

Mobile Game Market in China, 2020

There were 535.9 million mobile game players during the first six months of 2020. MOBA stands for multiplayer online battle arena game.

Role-playing	38.1%
MOBA	20.1
Simulation	8.7
Racing	8.5
First-person shooter	8.3
Puzzle	2.3
Card and board	2.1
Action-adventure	1.9

Continued on next page.

★ 2333 ★
[Continued]
Mobile Gaming
SIC: 2741; NAICS: 51913

Mobile Game Market in China, 2020

There were 535.9 million mobile game players during the first six months of 2020. MOBA stands for multiplayer online battle arena game.

Live simulation	1.9%
Other	8.1

Source: "Underestimated User Value, Initiate with Buy." [online] from http://www.pdf.dfcfw.com [Published October 7, 2020], from iResearch and Guotai Junan International.

★ 2334 ★
Mobile Gaming
SIC: 2741; NAICS: 51913

Mobile Gaming Industry Worldwide, 2017-2020

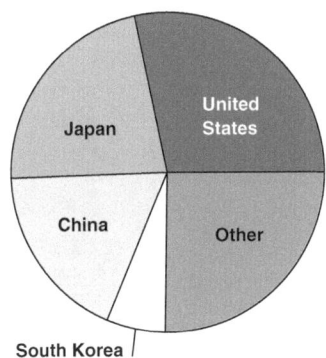

Market shares are shown based on revenue generated at the Google Play and Apple App Store. Data for 2020 are for the first three quarter of the year. Figures do not include revenue from third-party Android stores in China or other regions.

	2017	2018	2019	2020
United States	23.0%	24.0%	26.0%	28.0%
Japan	26.0	26.0	23.0	22.0
China	21.0	19.0	20.0	18.0
South Korea	7.0	6.0	6.0	6.0
Other	23.0	27.0	25.0	25.0

Source: "Mobile Games Market Spotlight: Japan Accounted for Nearly a Quarter of Global Revenue in First Nine Months of 2020." [online] from https://sensortower.com/blog/japan-mobile-games-market-spotlight [Published October 16, 2020], from Sensor Tower.

★ 2335 ★
Mobile Gaming
SIC: 2741; NAICS: 51913

Mobile Hyper-Casual Game Market, 2020

A hyper-casual game is easy to play and typically free. Market shares are shown based on revenue for the first three quarters of 2020.

Voodoo SAS	28.0%
AppLovin	16.0
SayGames	10.0
Good Job!	9.0
Crazy Labs	8.0
Playgendary	7.0
Rollic Games	7.0
Supersonic	7.0
Geisha Tokyo	4.0
Popcore	4.0

Source: "Merger Magic: How M&A is Shaking Up Category Leaders in Mobile Games." [online] from https://sensortower.com/blog/mobile-gaming-market-share-q4-2020 [Published October 30, 2020], from Sensor Tower.

★ 2336 ★
Mobile Gaming
SIC: 2741; NAICS: 51913

Mobile Puzzle Game Market, 2020

Market shares are shown based on revenue for the first three quarters of 2020.

King Ltd.	30.0%
Playrix Holding	27.0
Zynga Inc.	18.0
Jam City Inc.	5.0
Playtika Ltd.	4.0
Rovio Entertainment	4.0
Tactile Games	4.0
Firecraft Studios	3.0
PeopleFun	3.0
GSN Games	2.0

Source: "Merger Magic: How M&A is Shaking Up Category Leaders in Mobile Games." [online] from https://sensortower.com/blog/mobile-gaming-market-share-q4-2020 [Published October 30, 2020], from Sensor Tower.

★ 2337 ★
Mobile Gaming
SIC: 2741; NAICS: 51913

Pokémon GO Spending Worldwide, 2016-2020

Pokémon GO launched in 2016 and remains a popular title. Figures do not include revenue from third-thirty Android stores in China or other regions.

2016	$ 832
2017	589
2018	828
2019	902
2020	1,000

Source: "Pokémon GO Hits $1 Billion in 2020 as Lifetime Revenue Surpasses $4 Billion." [online] from https://sensortower.com/blog/pokemon-go-one-billion-revenue-2020 [Published November 3, 2020], from Sensor Tower Store Intelligence.

★ 2338 ★
Mobile Gaming
SIC: 2741; NAICS: 51913

Role-Playing Mobile Game Market, 2020

Market shares are shown based on revenue for the first three quarters of 2020.

Netmarble	18.0%
Bandai Namco	17.0
Scopely Inc.	17.0
Plarium	9.0
Electronic Arts Inc.	8.0
Zynga Inc.	8.0
Nexters	7.0
Gamevil	6.0
Lilith Games	5.0
Sony Corp.	5.0

Source: "Merger Magic: How M&A is Shaking Up Category Leaders in Mobile Games." [online] from https://sensortower.com/blog/mobile-gaming-market-share-q4-2020 [Published October 30, 2020], from Sensor Tower.

★ 2339 ★
Mobile Gaming
SIC: 2741; NAICS: 51913

Strategy Mobile Game Market, 2020

Market shares are shown based on revenue for the first three quarters of 2020.

Supercell Oy	22.0%
FunPlus	20.0
Lilith Games	10.0
Warner Bros.	9.0
Long Tech Network Ltd.	8.0%
Scopely Inc.	8.0
IGG Inc.	7.0
AppLovin	6.0
Camel Games	5.0
Yotta Games	4.0
Other	1.0

Source: "Merger Magic: How M&A is Shaking Up Category Leaders in Mobile Games." [online] from https://sensortower.com/blog/mobile-gaming-market-share-q4-2020 [Published October 30, 2020], from Sensor Tower.

★ 2340 ★
Mobile Gaming
SIC: 2741; NAICS: 51913

Top Downloaded Mobile Games, 2020

Titles are ranked by millions of downloads. PUBG was the leader in dollar spending at $2.7 billion, followed by Honor of Kings at $2.6 billion, and then Pokémon Go at $1.3 billion.

Among Us	282
Garena Free Fire	276
Subway Surfers	245
PUBG Mobile	240
Hunter Assassin	207
Gardenscapes	205
Brain Out	182
Ludo King	182
Tiles Hop	170
Homescapes	160
Roblox	160

Source: "5 Takeaways from Sensor Tower's New Mobile App Industry Trends Report." [online] from https://sensortower.com/blog/mobile-industry-trends-report-2021 [Published January 28, 2021], from Sensor Tower.

★ 2341 ★
Mobile Payments
SIC: 7372; NAICS: 334614, 51121

Leading Proximity Mobile Payment Providers, 2021

Data show millions of users. Figures refer to users 14 years of age and older; mobile phone users who have made at least one proximity mobile payments transaction in the last six months; includes point-of-sale transactions made by using mobile phones as a payment method; excludes transactions made by tablet.

Apple Pay	43.9
Starbucks Corp.	31.2

Continued on next page.

★ 2341 ★
[Continued]
Mobile Payments
SIC: 7372; NAICS: 334614, 51121

Leading Proximity Mobile Payment Providers, 2021

Data show millions of users. Figures refer to users 14 years of age and older; mobile phone users who have made at least one proximity mobile payments transaction in the last six months; includes point-of-sale transactions made by using mobile phones as a payment method; excludes transactions made by tablet.

Google Pay	25.0
Samsung Pay	16.3

Source: "U.S. Payment Users Will Surpass 100 Million This Year." [online] from https://www.emarketer.com/content/us-payment-users-will-surpass-100-million-this-year [Published March 30, 2021], from eMarketer.

★ 2342 ★
Modular Grippers
SIC: 3069; NAICS: 326299

Leading Modular Gripper Makers Worldwide, 2019

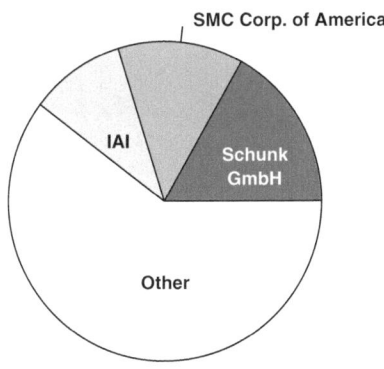

A gripper is a tool mounted on equipment to grip work pieces. A gripper might function through electric or pneumatic power. Market shares are shown based on revenue.

Schunk GmbH	16.53%
SMC Corp. of America	12.58
IAI	10.30
Other	60.59

Source: "Global Modular Gripper Market Research Report 2020." [online] from http://www.qyresearch.com [Published September 2020], from QY Research.

★ 2343 ★
Molybdenum
SIC: 1061; NAICS: 212299

Top Molybdenum Producing Countries, 2020

Countries are ranked by production in metric tons. Metallurgical applications claimed about 88% of total consumption. Production data are estimated.

	MT	Share
China	120,000	40.00%
Chile	58,000	19.33
United States	49,000	16.33
Peru	30,000	10.00
Mexico	17,000	5.67
Armenia	7,000	2.33
Iran	3,500	1.17
Russia	2,800	0.93
Canada	2,700	0.90
Mongolia	1,800	0.60
Turkey	400	0.13
Uzbekistan	200	0.07
Other	7,600	2.53

Source: "Mineral Commodity Summaries 2021." [online] from https://www.usgs.gov/centers/nmic/mineral-commodity-summaries [Published January 29, 2021], from U.S. Geological Survey.

★ 2344 ★
Monetary Authorities
SIC: 6011; NAICS: 52111

Monetary Authorities - Central Bank, 2017

Money Authorities perform central banking functions such as issuing currency, managing the nation's monetary supply, and acting as a fiscal agent for the central government. Total shipments were valued at $116.89 billion. The term "nec" stands for not elsewhere classified.

	($ 000)	Share
Trading debt instruments on own account	$ 93,261,074	79.78%
Trading equities on own account, including private equity	20,395,858	17.45
Trading foreign currency (wholesale) on own account	1,868,262	1.60
Cash handling and management services for business	588,238	0.50

Continued on next page.

★ 2344 ★
[Continued]
Monetary Authorities
SIC: 6011; NAICS: 52111

Monetary Authorities - Central Bank, 2017

Money Authorities perform central banking functions such as issuing currency, managing the nation's monetary supply, and acting as a fiscal agent for the central government. Total shipments were valued at $116.89 billion. The term "nec" stands for not elsewhere classified.

	($ 000)	Share
Automated clearing house (ACH) services	$ 368,042	0.31%
Loans to financial businesses	83,120	0.07
Support services for financial and commodity markets	28,854	0.02
Trading other securities and commodity contracts on own account	16,569	0.01
Regulation of credit markets	217	< 0.01
Other products supporting financial services	240,219	0.21
All other products and services, nec	48,056	0.04

Source: "Economic Census." [online] from https://www.census.gov/programs-surveys/economic-census/data/tables.html [Accessed December 2, 2020], from U.S. Census Bureau.

★ 2345 ★
Monetary Authorities
SIC: 6011; NAICS: 52111

Monetary Authorities Leaders - Central Bank, 2017

Money Authorities perform central banking functions such as issuing currency, managing the nation's monetary supply, and acting as a fiscal agent for the central government. Data show the percent of industry sales held by the largest 4, 8, 20 and 50 firms in the sector. There are approximately 57 players operating in the industry generating employment for 19,189 people.

4 largest firms	80.4%
8 largest firms	94.0
20 largest firms	100.0
50 largest firms	100.0

Source: "Economic Census." [online] from https://www.census.gov/content/census/en/data/tables/2017/econ/economic-census/naics-sector-31-33.html [Accessed January 21, 2021], from U.S. Census Bureau.

★ 2346 ★
Mortgages
SIC: 6162; NAICS: 522292

Leading Mortgage Firms, 2020

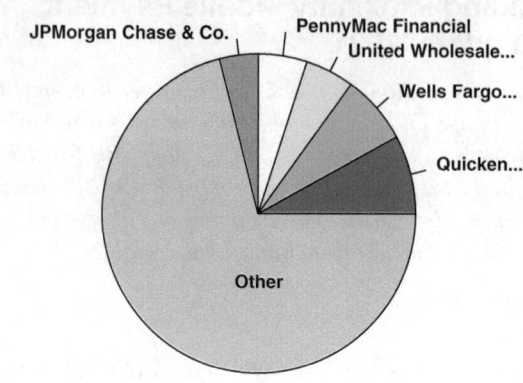

Market shares are shown based on originations from January 1-June 30, 2020.

Quicken Loans Inc.	8.1%
Wells Fargo Home Mortgage Inc.	6.9
United Wholesale Mortgage Corp.	5.4
PennyMac Financial	4.8
JPMorgan Chase & Co.	3.9
Other	70.9

Source: *Wall Street Journal*, August 6, 2020, p. A8, from Inside Mortgage Finance.

★ 2347 ★
Mortgages
SIC: 6162; NAICS: 522292

Leading Mortgage Firms in Baltimore, MD, 2020

Market shares are shown in percent.

Quicken Loans Inc.	5.52%
First Home Mortgage Corp.	4.36
Wells Fargo Home Mortgage Inc.	3.26
United Wholesale Mortgage Corp.	2.48
Primary Residential Mortgage Inc.	2.31
Other	82.07

Source: *Baltimore Business Journal*, April 6, 2021, p. NA, from http://www.mortgagedataweb.com.

★ 2348 ★
Mortgages
SIC: 6162; NAICS: 522292

Leading Mortgage Firms in Birmingham, AL, 2019

Market shares are shown based on value of loans as of June 24, 2020.

	($ bil.)	Share
Regions Bank	$ 384.55	6.14%
MortgageBanc/Fairway Independent Mortgage Corp.	354.17	5.66
Wells Fargo Bank	341.55	5.46
Renasant Bank	189.96	3.04
FirstBank Mortgage Partners	169.18	2.70

Source: *Birmingham Business Journal*, January 4, 2021, p. NA, from http://www.mortgagedataweb.com.

★ 2349 ★
Mortgages
SIC: 6162; NAICS: 522292

Leading Mortgage Firms in Central Florida, 2019

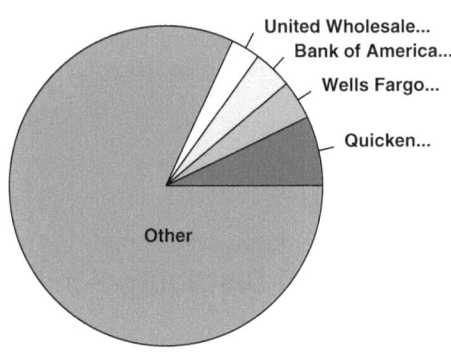

Market shares are shown based on mortgage volume. Figures are for conventional loans only, including purchase-money and refinance mortgages. Among government-insured loans, Quicken Loans claimed a 5.57% share, FBC Mortgage 4.68% and Universal American Mortgage 2.51%.

Quicken Loans Inc.	7.08%
Wells Fargo Home Mortgage Inc.	3.92
Bank of America Mortgage	3.75
United Wholesale Mortgage Corp.	3.48
Other	81.77

Source: *Orlando Business Journal*, March 6, 2020, p. NA, from http://www.mortgagedataweb.com.

★ 2350 ★
Mortgages
SIC: 6162; NAICS: 522292

Leading Mortgage Firms in Pittsburgh, PA, 2020

Market shares are shown based on mortgage volume for July 2019-June 2020.

PNC Bank NA	9.59%
Citizens Bank of Pennsylvania	6.17
Dollar Bank FSB	5.93
F.N.B. Corp.	4.34
Quicken Loans Inc.	4.30
Other	69.67

Source: *Pittsburgh Business Journal*, September 18, 2020, p. NA, from http://www.mortgagedataweb.com.

★ 2351 ★
Mortgages
SIC: 6162; NAICS: 522292

Leading Mortgage Firms in Sacramento, CA, 2019

Market shares are shown based on mortgage volume.

Quicken Loans Inc.	10.18%
United Wholesale Mortgage Corp.	10.00
Wells Fargo Home Mortgage Inc.	4.61
Finance of America	4.53
Guild Mortgage Co.	3.58
Other	67.10

Source: *Sacramento Business Journal*, March 6, 2020, p. NA, from http://www.mortgagedataweb.com.

★ 2352 ★
Mortgages
SIC: 6162; NAICS: 522292

Mortgage Industry in Canada, 2019

The big banks claimed 72% of the market in 2019, although this figure is down from 75% in 2018. The average loan was $220,650.

Big banks	72.0%
Mortgage finance companies	20.0
Credit unions	14.0
Private lenders/mortgage investment corps.	1.0

Source: "Big Banks Still Dominate Mortgage Market Share." [online] from https://www.canadianmortgagetrends.com/2020/09/big-banks-still-dominate-mortgage-market-share-says-cmhc/ [Published September 14, 2020], from Canada Mortgage and Housing Corp.

★ 2353 ★
Mortgages
SIC: 6162; NAICS: 522292

Mortgage Originations, 2014-2022

Figures are in trillions of dollars for one-to-four family properties. Figures are estimated for 2020-2022.

Year	
2014	$ 1.1
2015	1.6
2016	1.9
2017	1.7
2018	1.7
2019	2.2
2020	3.0
2021	2.6
2022	2.6

Source: "Rocket Mortgage." [online] from https://www.ml.com/content/dam/ML/ipo/equity_new_issues/Rocket-Companies.pdf [Published July 28, 2020], from Euromonitor, Mortgage Bankers Association and Zelman & Associates Research.

★ 2354 ★
Motion Pictures
SIC: 7812; NAICS: 51211

Documentary Industry in China, 2013-2020

Production is shown in billions of yuan. Figures are estimated for 2019 and 2020. The documentary industry saw noticeable growth from 2013-2015 as a result of favorable policy support and marketing efforts. A total of nine domestic and foreign documentaries were released on the big screen in 2017, up 50% from 2016. Total investment in documentary making reached an estimated $710 million in 2020.

Year	
2013	¥ 2.3
2014	3.0
2015	4.7
2016	5.2
2017	6.0
2018	6.4
2019	7.0
2020	7.9

Source: "Documentary Increases Stably in China." [online] from http://www.iresearchchina.com/content/details7_57986.html [Published October 15, 2019], from iResearch and Documentary Center.

★ 2355 ★
Motion Pictures
SIC: 7812; NAICS: 51211

Largest Motion Picture Markets Worldwide, 2020

Countries are ranked by box office receipts in billions of dollars. Global box office by year: $39.3 billion in 2016, $40.9 billion in 2017, $41.8 billion in 2018, $42.3 billion in 2019, and $12 billion in 2020.

	($ bil.)	Share
China	$ 3.0	25.00%
United States	2.2	18.33
Japan	1.3	10.83
Germany	0.4	3.33
India	0.4	3.33
South Korea	0.4	3.33
United Kingdom	0.4	3.33
Australia	0.3	2.50
Russia	0.3	2.50
Italy	0.2	1.67
Mexico	0.2	1.67
Netherlands	0.2	1.67
Spain	0.2	1.67
Other	2.5	20.83

Source: "2020 Theme Trends." [online] from https://www.motionpictures.org/wp-content/uploads/2021/03/MPA-2020-THEME-Report.pdf [Published March 2021], from comScore and Omdia.

★ 2356 ★
Motion Pictures
SIC: 7822; NAICS: 42399, 51212

Leading Film Distributors in North America, 2020

Market shares are shown based on box office for 2020. Figures include films released in previous years that made money in 2020 (for example, a film released at Thanksgiving or Christmas 2019 will make money in 2020). North America covers the United States, Canada, Puerto Rico and Guam.

	($ mil.)	Share
Sony Pictures	$ 429.83	20.96%
Universal	402.72	19.64
Warner Bros.	234.81	11.45
Walt Disney Co.	227.22	11.08
Paramount Pictures	180.56	8.81
20th Century Studios	89.19	4.35
Lionsgate	59.18	2.89
STX Entertainment	49.36	2.41
20th Century Fox	47.39	2.31

Continued on next page.

★ 2356 ★
[Continued]
Motion Pictures
SIC: 7822; NAICS: 42399, 51212

Leading Film Distributors in North America, 2020

Market shares are shown based on box office for 2020. Figures include films released in previous years that made money in 2020 (for example, a film released at Thanksgiving or Christmas 2019 will make money in 2020). North America covers the United States, Canada, Puerto Rico and Guam.

	($ mil.)	Share
Compass International	$ 47.24	2.30%
Neon	36.72	1.79
Focus Features	34.64	1.69
Solstice Studios	20.83	1.02
United Artists	19.46	0.95
101 Studios	19.00	0.93
Other	152.41	7.43

Source: "Market Share for Each Distributor in 2020." [online] from https://www.the-numbers.com/market/2020/summary [Accessed January 5, 2021].

★ 2357 ★
Motion Pictures
SIC: 7812; NAICS: 51211

Leading Film Genres in North America, 2020

Market shares are shown based on box office for 2020. Figures include films released in previous years that made money in 2020 (for example, a film released at Thanksgiving or Christmas 2019 will make money in 2020). North America covers the United States, Canada, Puerto Rico and Guam. Share of films by rating: R 39.48%, PG-13 32.51%, PG 26.64%, Not rated 0.81% and G 0.24%. Box office reached $2.05 billion; 223 million tickets were sold.

Adventure	34.63%
Action	21.27
Thriller/suspense	12.85
Horror	12.04
Drama	11.73
Comedy	3.97
Black comedy	2.14
Musical	0.53
Romantic comedy	0.35
Documentary	0.20
Other	0.29

Source: "Market Share for Each Distributor in 2020." [online] from https://www.the-numbers.com/market/2020/summary [Accessed January 5, 2021].

★ 2358 ★
Motion Pictures
SIC: 7812; NAICS: 51211

Motion Picture Industry in China, 2017-2020

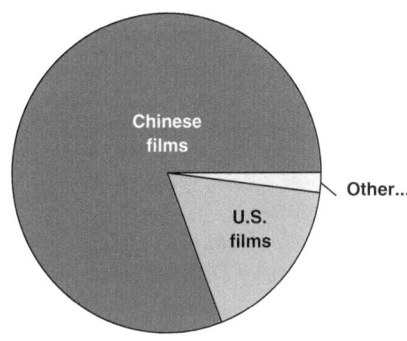

Figures show China's box office by the film's country of origin. Data show year-to-date for 2020. Hollywood films have steadily lost share, reflecting changing taste among moviegoers. China became largest film market in the world in 2021.

	2017	2018	2019	2020
Chinese films	53.8%	62.2%	64.1%	80.1%
U.S. films	36.0	32.4	30.2	16.8
Other imported	10.1	5.5	5.8	2.4

Source: *The Hollywood Reporter*, October 7, 2020, p. NA, from Artisan Gateway.

★ 2359 ★
Motion Pictures
SIC: 7812; NAICS: 51211

Top Films, 2020

Films are ranked by box office in millions of dollars.

Bad Boys for Life	$ 204.41
1917	157.90
Sonic the Hedgehog	146.06
Jumanji: The Next Level	124.73
Star Wars Episode IX: The Rise of Skywalker	124.49
Birds of Prey	84.15
Dolittle	77.04
Little Women	70.50
The Invisible Man	64.91
The Call of the Wild	62.34
Onward	61.55
Knives Out	49.65

Source: "Domestic Box Office for 2020." [online] from https://www.boxofficemojo.com/year/2020/?ref_=bo_lnav_hm_shrt [Accessed January 5, 2021], from Box Office Mojo.

★ 2360 ★
Motion Pictures
SIC: 7812; NAICS: 51211

Top Films in China, 2020

Films are ranked by box office receipts in millions of dollars in 2020. Moviegoers purchased 548 million tickets, bringing the box office to $3.13 billion. China surpassed North America in December to become the world's largest movie market, despite a 68% drop in box office over 2019 because of COVID-19 theater closures. Imported films represented about one-sixth of the industry.

The Eight Hundred	451.0
My People, My Homeland	410.0
Jiang Ziya: Legend of Deification	232.0
The Sacrifice	163.0
Leap	121.0
Shockwave	87.3
Caught in Time	77.9
Adoring	73.9
Love You Forever	73.2
Sheep Without A Shepherd	72.7

Source: *Screen Daily*, January 13, 2021, p. NA.

★ 2361 ★
Motion Pictures
SIC: 7812; NAICS: 51211

Top Films in France, 2020

Lockdowns closed theaters in Europe's largest movie market for 176 days. This drove admissions from 213 million in 2019 to 65.1 million, a decline of 70%. Box office reached $549 million. The top films are ranked by millions of admissions.

Tenet	2.3
1997	2.2
Sonic the Hedgehog	2.1
Bad Boys for Life	1.7
Star Wars Episode IX: The Rise of Skywalker	1.7
Docobu 3	1.4
Dolittle	1.2
The Call of the Wild	1.2
Ten Days Without Mom	1.1
30 Days Max	1.1

Source: *Variety*, January 5, 2021, p. NA.

★ 2362 ★
Motion Pictures
SIC: 7812; NAICS: 51211

Top Films in Spain, 2020

According to Comscore, COVID-19 lockdowns drove the box office down 72% over the year, from $738 million in 2019 to $207 million in 2020. Admissions fell from 105 million to 28.2 million, the lowest level since records began in 1965. The top films are ranked by box office in millions of dollars.

Father There is Only One 2	$ 15.7
1997	11.7
Tenet	9.2
Adú	8.1
Bad Boys for Life	8.1
Dolittle	7.4
Parasite	7.3
Sonic the Hedgehog	6.2
Star Wars Episode IX: The Rise of Skywalker	6.1
Jumanji: The Next Level	5.7

Source: *Variety*, January 5, 2021, p. NA.

★ 2363 ★
Motion Pictures
SIC: 7812; NAICS: 51211

Top Films in the United Kingdom and Ireland, 2020

Lockdowns from COVID-19 drove revenue down 76% in the region, from $1.83 billion in 2019 to $438.9 million in 2020. According to Comscore, this is the largest box office decline in Europe. The number of new releases fell from 938 to 441. One positive note: 31 new drive-in cinemas opened. The top films are ranked by box office in millions of dollars.

1917	$ 59.7
Sonic the Hedgehog	26.1
Tenet	23.6
Bad Boys for Life	22.0
Dolittle	21.5
The Gentlemen	16.5
Parasite	16.4
Little Women	15.3
Star Wars Episode IX: The Rise of Skywalker	15.3
Jumanji: The Next Level	14.9

Source: *Variety*, January 5, 2021, p. NA.

★ 2364 ★
Motion Pictures
SIC: 7812; NAICS: 51211

Top Films Worldwide, 2020

Films are ranked by global gross box office receipts in millions of dollars. Figures cover January 1, 2020-January 2, 2021.

The Eight Hundred	$ 451.0
Bad Boys for Life	430.5
My People, My Homeland	418.4
1917	385.3
Tenet	362.6
Demon Slayer: Mugen Train	334.6
Sonic the Hedgehog	319.5
Dolittle	246.1
Legend of Deification	232.5
Birds of Prey	202.1

Source: *The Hollywood Reporter*, January 6, 2021, p. 14, from comScore and Artisan Gateway Studios.

★ 2365 ★
Motion Pictures
SIC: 7812; NAICS: 51211

Top Streaming Films, 2020

Titles are ranked by estimated minutes streamed, in millions. Figures come from Netflix, Amazon Prime, Disney+ and Hulu. Viewers are U.S. viewers, aged 2+, and watching on televisions. Data cover December 30, 2019-December 27, 2020.

Frozen II	14,924
Moana	10,507
The Secret Life of Pets 2	9,123
Onward	8,367
Dr. Seuss' The Grinch	6,180
Hamilton	6,132
Spenser Confidential	5,374
Aladdin (2019)	5,172
Toy Story 4	4,416
Zootopia	4,400

Source: "2020 Theme Trends." [online] from https://www.motionpictures.org/wp-content/uploads/2021/03/MPA-2020-THEME-Report.pdf [Published March 2021], from Nielsen.

★ 2366 ★
Motor Vehicle Towing
SIC: 7549; NAICS: 48841

Motor Vehicle Towing Leaders, 2017

Data show the percent of industry sales held by the largest 4, 8, 20 and 50 firms in the sector. There are approximately 9,196 players operating in the industry generating employment for 64,472 people. According to Kentley Insights, the industry generated sales of $7.1 billion in 2018.

4 largest firms	2.2%
8 largest firms	3.4
20 largest firms	5.6
50 largest firms	9.6

Source: "Economic Census." [online] from https://www.census.gov/content/census/en/data/tables/2017/econ/economic-census/naics-sector-31-33.html [Accessed January 21, 2021], from U.S. Census Bureau.

★ 2367 ★
Motorcycles
SIC: 3751; NAICS: 336991

Demand for Motorcycles Worldwide, 2019

The market is forecast to grow 4.3% annually from 2019-2024. Major forces driving demand include rapid growth outside China in the e-bike sector, increasing availability of electric scooters and mopeds, and rising sales of medium and healthy models. Demand is shown by product.

Electric motorcycles	37.0%
ICE light motorcycles	35.0
ICE scooters, mopeds and motorbikes	25.0
ICE medium and heavy motorcycles	3.0

Source: "Motorcycles." [online] from http://www.freedoniagroup.com [Published May 2020], from The Freedonia Group Inc.

★ 2368 ★
Motorcycles
SIC: 3751; NAICS: 336991

Off-Road Motorcycle Sales by Generation, 2019-2020

Shares are shown based on unit purchases. Between August 1, 2019 and July 31, 2020, 109,000 new and pre-owned off-road motorcycles were sold.

	Aug. 2019	July 2020
Millennial	39.0%	46.0%
Generation X	38.0	33.0

Continued on next page.

★ 2368 ★
[Continued]
Motorcycles
SIC: 3751; NAICS: 336991

Off-Road Motorcycle Sales by Generation, 2019-2020

Shares are shown based on unit purchases. Between August 1, 2019 and July 31, 2020, 109,000 new and pre-owned off-road motorcycles were sold.

	Aug. 2019	July 2020
iGen/Generation Z	11.0%	12.0%
Baby boomer	12.0	10.0

Source: *PowerSports Business*, August 28, 2020, p. 27, from CDK Global Lightspeed.

★ 2369 ★
Motorcycles
SIC: 3751; NAICS: 336991

Top Motorcycle Brands in Argentina, 2020

Total sales reached 263,487. The country's economic situation helped drive the motorcycle into a decline from 2017 to September 2020, when the industry saw its first year-on-year increase.

	Sales	Share
Honda	60,246	22.86%
Motomel	36,456	13.84
Corven	34,028	12.91
Gilera	28,400	10.78
Keller	15,857	6.02
Yamaha	15,425	5.85
Zanella	13,138	4.99
Other	59,937	22.75

Source: "Argentina 2020. Honda Dominates Ahead of Local Manufacturers." [online] from https://www.motorcyclesdata.com/2021/01/18/argentine-motorcycles-market/ [Published January 18, 2021], from MotorCycles Data.

★ 2370 ★
Motorcycles
SIC: 3751; NAICS: 336991

Top Motorcycle Brands in France, 2020

Total sales were 295,100. France was the largest motorcycle market in Europe in 2020.

	Sales	Share
Yamaha	34,847	11.81%
Piaggio	28,533	9.67
Honda	27,083	9.18
Peugeot	18,554	6.29%
BMW	18,081	6.13
Kawasaki	14,024	4.75
SYM	11,723	3.97
Other	142,255	48.21

Source: "France 2020. Piaggio Gains the Second Place in a Market Down 4%." [online] from https://www.motorcyclesdata.com/2021/01/13/french-motorcycles/ [Published January 13, 2021].

★ 2371 ★
Motorcycles
SIC: 3751; NAICS: 336991

Top Motorcycle Brands in Germany, 2020

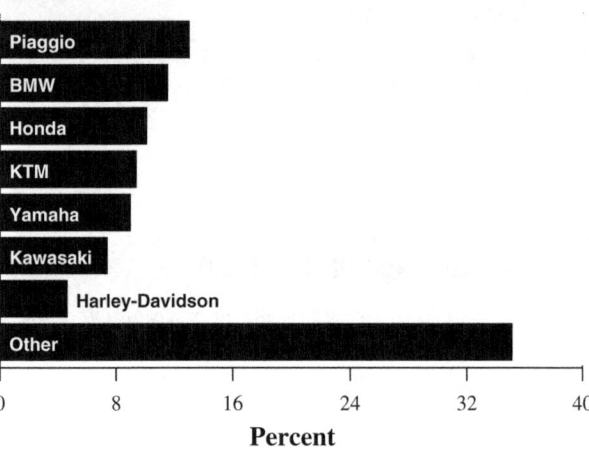

Total sales reached 241,134. Germany was the fourth largest motorcycle market in Europe in 2020.

	Sales	Share
Piaggio	31,362	13.01%
BMW	27,761	11.51
Honda	24,324	10.09
KTM	22,608	9.38
Yamaha	21,613	8.96
Kawasaki	17,774	7.37
Harley-Davidson	11,052	4.58
Other	84,640	35.10

Source: "Germany 2020. December Sales Boomed 309% Ending a Memorable Year." [online] from https://www.motorcyclesdata.com/2021/01/17/germany-motorcycles/ [Published January 17, 2021].

★ 2372 ★
Motorcycles
SIC: 3751; NAICS: 336991

Top Motorcycle Brands in Italy, 2020

Total sales of motorcycles and scooters reached 246,484. Motorcycle and scooter sales saw the first decline in sales in 2020 after five years of interrupted growth.

	Sales	Share
Honda	46,677	18.94%
Piaggio	38,064	15.44
Yamaha	27,220	11.04
Kymco	22,706	9.21
BMW	13,510	5.48
Other	98,307	39.88

Source: "Italy 2020. Honda Was Market Leader in a Market -5%. Ducati Lost 25%." [online] from https://www.motorcyclesdata.com/2021/01/14/italian-motorcycles/ [Published January 14, 2021], from MotorCycles Data.

★ 2373 ★
Motorcycles
SIC: 3751; NAICS: 336991

Top Motorcycle Brands in Pakistan, 2020

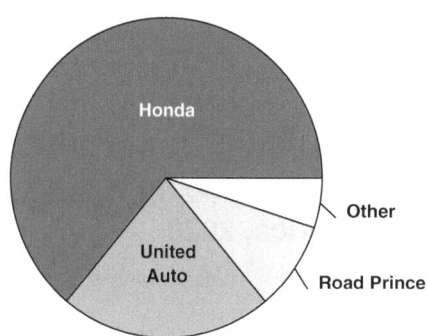

Pakistan is one of the fastest-growing motorcycle markets. Motorcycle sales reached 1.52 million, making it the fifth largest market worldwide.

	Sales	Share
Honda	976,000	64.21%
United Auto	334,000	21.97
Road Prince	135,000	8.88
Other	75,000	4.93

Source: "Pakistan 2020. Two & Three Wheeler Market Lost 8.9%" [online] from https://www.motorcyclesdata.com/2021/01/20/pakistan-motorcycles/ [Published January 20, 2021], from MotorCycles Data.

★ 2374 ★
Motorcycles
SIC: 3751; NAICS: 336991

Top Motorcycle Brands in Spain, 2020

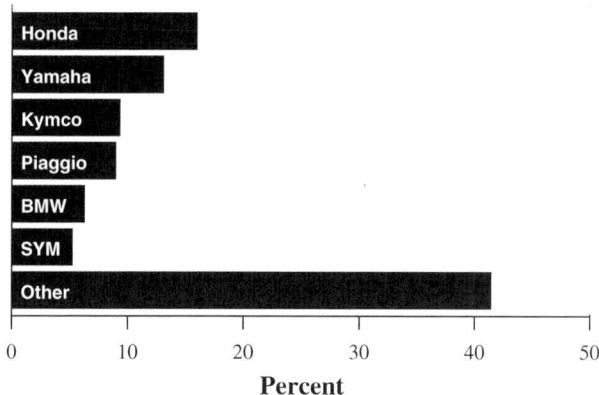

Spain was hit hard by COVID-19. This helped drive down sales in the market by 12.6% to 177,302.

	Sales	Share
Honda	28,264	15.94%
Yamaha	23,139	13.05
Kymco	16,461	9.28
Piaggio	15,815	8.92
BMW	11,019	6.21
SYM	9,172	5.17
Other	73,432	41.42

Source: "Spain 2020. Motorcycles Industry Hit More Than Other Top EU Markets (-12.6%)." [online] from https://www.motorcyclesdata.com/2021/01/15/spanish-motorcycles/ [Published January 15, 2021].

★ 2375 ★
Motorcycles
SIC: 3751; NAICS: 336991

Top Motorcycle Brands in Thailand, 2020

Thailand was the sixth largest motorcycle market worldwide in 2020. Total sales were 1.5 million.

	Sales	Share
Honda	1,180,000	78.67%
Yamaha	239,531	15.97
Piaggio	28,105	1.87
GPX	14,457	0.96
Kawasaki	12,155	0.81
Suzuki	11,996	0.80
Other	13,756	0.92

Source: "Thailand 2020. Two-Wheeler Market Lost 9.7%" [online] from https://www.motorcyclesdata.com/2021/01/19/thailand-motorcycles/ [Published January 19, 2021].

★ 2376 ★
Movie Theaters
SIC: 7832; NAICS: 512131

Digital 3D Screen Market, 2018-2020

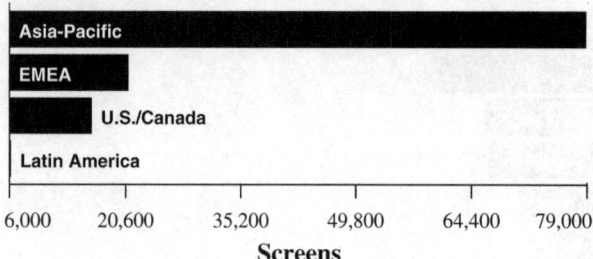

Screens

Data show the number of screens. In 2020, the Asia-Pacific region claimed 64.52% of the total, EMEA 17.12%, the United States and Canada 13.13%, and Latin America 5.04%.

	2018	2019	2020
Asia-Pacific	62,937	73,215	78,831
EMEA	20,711	20,884	20,913
U.S./Canada	16,972	16,586	16,284
Latin America	5,818	6,071	6,152

Source: "2020 Theme Trends." [online] from https://www.motionpictures.org/wp-content/uploads/2021/03/MPA-2020-THEME-Report.pdf [Published March 2021], from Omdia.

★ 2377 ★
Movie Theaters
SIC: 7833; NAICS: 512132

Drive-in Motion Picture Theater Leaders, 2017

Data show the percent of industry sales held by the largest 4, 8, 20 and 50 firms in the sector. There are approximately 191 players operating in the industry generating employment for 1,297 people. According to Kentley Insights, the industry generated sales of $500 million in 2019.

4 largest firms	40.9%
8 largest firms	48.1
20 largest firms	61.3
50 largest firms	79.9

Source: "Economic Census." [online] from https://www.census.gov/content/census/en/data/tables/2017/econ/economic-census/naics-sector-31-33.html [Accessed January 21, 2021], from U.S. Census Bureau.

★ 2378 ★
Movie Theaters
SIC: 7833; NAICS: 512132

Drive-in Motion Picture Theaters, 2017

Total sales were valued at $133.09 million. The term "nec" stands for not elsewhere classified. A total of 305 sites with 549 screens were in operation as of August 2019. This industry received a boost during the pandemic, as drive-in theater spaces allowed people to see movies, hear live music and attend church services while still social distancing.

	($ 000)	Share
Admissions to domestic films	$ 80,339	60.40%
Meals, snacks, other food items, and nonalcoholic beverages, prepared and served or dispensed, for immediate consumption	24,458	18.39
Retail sales of candy, prepackaged cookies, and snack foods	4,884	3.67
Rental and leasing of commercial space	2,299	1.73
Admissions to foreign films	115	0.09
Amusement park and arcade services	67	0.05
Other advertising space, time, and similar services	928	0.70
All other products and services, nec	19,920	14.98

Source: "Economic Census." [online] from https://www.census.gov/programs-surveys/economic-census/data/tables.html [Accessed December 2, 2020], from U.S. Census Bureau.

★ 2379 ★
Movie Theaters
SIC: 7832; NAICS: 512131

Largest Movie Theater Operators in North America, 2020

Companies are ranked by number of screens.

AMC Theatres	7,800
Regal Cinemas	6,989
Cinemark Holdings Inc.	4,517
Cineplex Entertainment	1,657
Marcus Theatres	1,097
Harkins Theatres	501
B&B Theatres	429
Malco Theatres Inc.	363
CMX Cinemas	341
Landmark Cinemas of Canada	334
National Amusements Inc.	321
Alamo Drafthouse Cinemas	317
Studio Movie Grill	294
Caribbean Cinemas	281
Cinépolis Luxury Cinemas	276

Source: *BoxOffice Pro*, Q1, 2021, p. 21+.

★ 2380 ★
Movie Theaters
SIC: 7832; NAICS: 512131

Leading Movie Theater Operators in Argentina, 2019

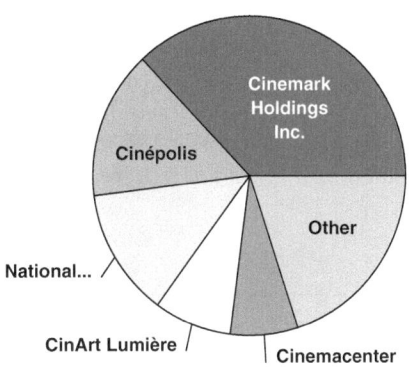

Market shares are shown based on fiscal year 2019 box office.

Cinemark Holdings Inc.	37.0%
Cinépolis	15.0
National Amusements Inc.	13.0
CinArt Lumière	8.0
Cinemacenter	7.0
Other	20.0

Source: "Cinemark Investor Presentation 2Q 2020." [online] from https://ir.cinemark.com/company-information/presentations [Published August 18, 2020].

★ 2381 ★
Movie Theaters
SIC: 7832; NAICS: 512131

Leading Movie Theater Operators in Brazil, 2019

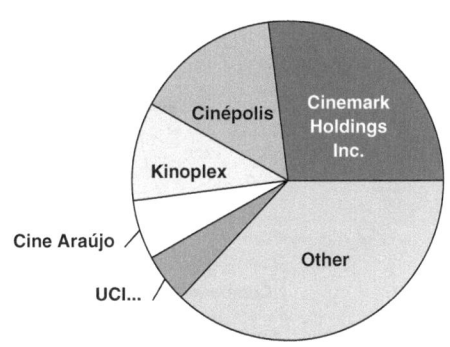

Market shares are shown based on fiscal year 2019 box office.

Cinemark Holdings Inc.	27.0%
Cinépolis	15.0
Kinoplex	10.0%
Cine Araújo	6.0
UCI Cinemas	5.0
Other	37.0

Source: "Cinemark Investor Presentation 2Q 2020." [online] from https://ir.cinemark.com/company-information/presentations [Published August 18, 2020].

★ 2382 ★
Movie Theaters
SIC: 7832; NAICS: 512131

Leading Movie Theater Operators in Chile, 2019

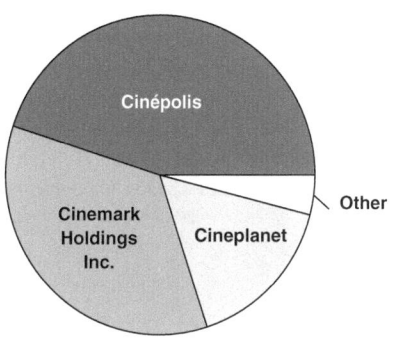

Market shares are shown based on fiscal year 2019 box office.

Cinépolis	45.0%
Cinemark Holdings Inc.	35.0
Cineplanet	16.0
Other	4.0

Source: "Cinemark Investor Presentation 2Q 2020." [online] from https://ir.cinemark.com/company-information/presentations [Published August 18, 2020].

★ 2383 ★
Movie Theaters
SIC: 7832; NAICS: 512131

Movie Theater Admissions in North America, 2011-2020

Data show billions of admissions. Box office is shown in billions of dollars.

	Admissions (bil.)	Box Office ($ bil.)
2011	1.28	$ 10.2
2012	1.36	10.8
2013	1.34	10.9

Continued on next page.

★ 2383 ★
[Continued]
Movie Theaters
SIC: 7832; NAICS: 512131

Movie Theater Admissions in North America, 2011-2020

Data show billions of admissions. Box office is shown in billions of dollars.

	Admissions (bil.)	Box Office ($ bil.)
2014	1.27	$ 10.4
2015	1.32	11.1
2016	1.32	11.4
2017	1.24	11.1
2018	1.30	11.9
2019	1.24	11.4
2020	0.24	2.2

Source: "2020 Theme Trends." [online] from https://www.motionpictures.org/wp-content/uploads/2021/03/MPA-2020-THEME-Report.pdf [Published March 2021], from comScore and National Association of Theatre Owners.

★ 2384 ★
Movie Theaters
SIC: 7832; NAICS: 512131

Movie Theater Attendance in Europe, 2019-2020

Countries are ranked by attendance.

	2019 (mil.)	2020 (mil.)	Share
France	213.1	65.1	22.09%
United Kingdom	176.1	44.0	14.93
Germany	118.6	38.1	12.93
Spain	104.9	21.6	7.33
Poland	60.6	17.1	5.80
Netherlands	36.6	16.8	5.70
Sweden	15.9	5.7	1.93
Belgium	19.9	5.5	1.87
Austria	13.7	3.9	1.32
Portugal	15.5	3.8	1.29
Other	232.1	73.1	24.80

Source: "E.U. & U.K. Cinema Attendance Down by 70.7% in 2020 Amid Global Pandemic." [online] from https://www.obs.coe.int/en/web/observatoire/home [Published February 25, 2021], from European Audiovisual Observatory.

★ 2385 ★
Movie Theaters
SIC: 7832; NAICS: 512131

Movie Theater Goers by Age Group, 2020

The source defines a moviegoer as someone who went to the movies at least once over the previous year. The table compares the age of moviegoers with the overall population of the United States. In terms of gender, 53% of moviegoers were men, while 47% were women. In terms of population, however, 51% were women and 49% were men.

	Movie-goers	Population
2-11	15.0%	13.0%
12-17	11.0	8.0
18-24	11.0	9.0
25-39	25.0	21.0
40-49	13.0	12.0
50-59	11.0	13.0
60+	14.0	24.0

Source: "2020 Theme Trends." [online] from https://www.motionpictures.org/wp-content/uploads/2021/03/MPA-2020-THEME-Report.pdf [Published March 2021], from Motion Picture Association and ENGINE.

★ 2386 ★
MRO Industry
SIC: 4512; NAICS: 481111, 481112

MRO Industry Worldwide, 2020 and 2030

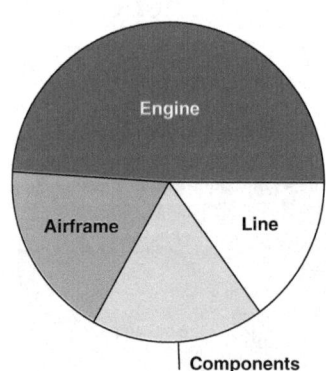

Data show value in billions of dollars.

	2020 ($ bil.)	2030 ($ bil.)	Share
Engine	$ 43.5	$ 64.2	49.23%
Airframe	17.4	24.0	18.40

Continued on next page.

★ 2386 ★
[Continued]
MRO Industry
SIC: 4512; NAICS: 481111, 481112

MRO Industry Worldwide, 2020 and 2030

Data show value in billions of dollars.

	2020 ($ bil.)	2030 ($ bil.)	Share
Components	$ 16.3	$ 23.1	17.71%
Line	13.5	19.1	14.65

Source: "Bigger Fleet. Bigger Challenges." [online] from http://www.oliverwyman.com [Published February 2020], from Oliver Wyman.

★ 2387 ★
Museums
SIC: 8412; NAICS: 71211

Museum Attendance, 2020

Attendance at the top 100 museums dropped from 230 million in 2019 to 54 million in 2020 because of the pandemic, a decline of 77%.

Musée de Louvre (Paris)	2,700,000
National Museum of China (Beijing)	1,600,000
Tate Modern (London)	1,432,991
Vatican Museums (Vatican City)	1,300,000
British Museum (London)	1,275,466
Museo Reina Sofia (Madrid)	1,248,486
State Russian Museum (St. Petersburg)	1,203,324
National Gallery (London)	1,197,143
Metropolitan Museum of Art (New York)	1,124,759
21st Century Museum of Contemporary Art (Kanazwana)	971,256

Source: *The Art Newspaper*, April 2021, p. NA.

★ 2388 ★
Museums
SIC: 8412; NAICS: 71211

Museum Revenues, 2017

Total revenues were valued at $13.19 billion. The term "nec" stands for not elsewhere classified.

	($ 000)	Share
Private contributions, gifts, and grants from individuals	$ 3,021,378	22.94%
Admissions to museums	2,017,909	15.32
Private contributions, gifts, and grants from foundations	1,313,852	9.98
Gains (losses) from non-financial assets sold	$ 1,110,707	8.43%
All other federal, state, county, and municipal contributions, gifts, and grants	946,434	7.19
Private contributions, gifts, and grants from business and industry	621,676	4.72
Trading securities and commodity contracts on own account	611,496	4.64
Membership services of performing arts societies and cultural institutions	543,939	4.13
Retail sales of other goods, nec	479,462	3.64
Program service revenue including government fees and contracts	432,516	3.28
Leisure, recreational, and athletic instructional programs	322,699	2.45
Rental and leasing of commercial space	249,118	1.89
School visits, children's parties and similar children's programs of cultural institutions	182,618	1.39
Meals, snacks, other food items, and nonalcoholic beverages, prepared and served or dispensed, for immediate consumption	168,143	1.28
Traveling exhibits	81,901	0.62
Parking services	59,957	0.46
Admissions to live performing arts performances	50,235	0.38
Tour guide services	30,078	0.23
Admissions to film exhibitions	26,895	0.20
Admissions to historic sites	26,220	0.20
Alcoholic beverages, prepared and served or dispensed for immediate consumption	25,570	0.19
Contributions, gifts, and grants from the National Endowment for the Arts	19,861	0.15
Conservation services for artistic, historical, and cultural works	4,002	0.03
Admissions to botanical gardens	15	< 0.01
Amusement park and arcade services	1,346	0.01
Other contributions, gifts, and grants, including from labor unions, etc.	512,068	3.89

Continued on next page.

★ 2388 ★
[Continued]
Museums
SIC: 8412; NAICS: 71211

Museum Revenues, 2017

Total revenues were valued at $13.19 billion. The term "nec" stands for not elsewhere classified.

	($ 000)	Share
Other nonoperating or tax-exempt revenue	$ 191,806	1.46%
Other products and services, nec	118,512	0.90

Source: "Economic Census." [online] from https://www.census.gov/programs-surveys/economic-census/data/tables.html [Accessed December 2, 2020], from U.S. Census Bureau.

★ 2389 ★
Mushrooms
SIC: 0182; NAICS: 111411

Best-Selling Types of Mushrooms, 2020

Market shares are shown based on multi-outlet dollar sales for the 52 weeks ended July 12, 2020. Sales reached $1.2 billion.

Regular	54.7%
Cremini/Brown	27.6
Portabella	10.5
Shiitake	2.8
Oyster	0.4
Chanterelle	0.1
Enoki	0.1
Morel	0.1
Other	3.9

Source: *Produce News*, August 3-17, 2020, p. 8, from IRI/FreshLook.

★ 2390 ★
Music
SIC: 3652; NAICS: 334614, 51225

Best-Selling Albums, 2020

Albums are ranked by millions of album sales. Sales include album sales, TEA (track equivalent album) and on-demand SEA (streaming equivalent album).

My Turn, Lil Baby	2.63
Folklore, Taylor Swift	2.20
Shoot for the Stars Aim for the Moon, Pop Smoke	2.19
After Hours, The Weeknd	2.03
Legends Never Die, Juice World	1.99
Hollywood's Bleeding, Post Malone	1.89
Eternal Take, Lil Uzi Vert	1.86
Please Excuse Me for Being Antisocial, Roddy Ricch	1.79
Fine Line, Harry Styles	1.52
What You See is What You Get, Luke Combs	1.47

Source: "MRC Data Year-End Report U.S. 2020." [online] from http://www.billboard.com [Accessed January 10, 2021], from MRC Data.

★ 2391 ★
Music
SIC: 3652; NAICS: 334614, 51225

Best-Selling Country Albums, 2020

Albums are ranked by album + TEA (track equivalent album) + on-demand SEA (streaming equivalent album) sales.

What You See is What You Get, Luke Combs	1,475,000
This One's for You, Luke Combs	993,000
If I Know Me, Morgan Wallen	944,000
SOUTHSIDE, Sam Hunt	607,000
Traveller, Chris Stapleton	595,000

Source: "MRC Data Year-End Report U.S. 2020." [online] from http://www.billboard.com [Accessed January 10, 2021], from MRC Data.

★ 2392 ★
Music
SIC: 3652; NAICS: 334614, 51225

Best-Selling Dance/Electronic Albums, 2020

Albums are ranked by album + TEA (track equivalent album) + on-demand SEA (streaming equivalent album) sales.

Chromatica, Lady Gaga	842,000
Golden Hour, Kygo	315,000
The Fame, Lady Gaga	290,000
Energy, Disclosure	270,000
Marshmello Fortnite Extended Set, Marshmello	238,000

Source: "MRC Data Year-End Report U.S. 2020." [online] from http://www.billboard.com [Accessed January 10, 2021], from MRC Data.

★ 2393 ★
Music
SIC: 3652; NAICS: 334614, 51225

Best-Selling Latin Albums, 2020

Albums are ranked by album + TEA (track equivalent album) + on-demand SEA (streaming equivalent album) sales.

YHLQMDLG, Bad Bunny	1,444,000
Emmanuel, Anuel AA	411,000
X 100PRE, Bad Bunny	410,000
El Último Tour Del Mundo, Bad Bunny	348,000
Las Que No Iban A Salir, Bad Bunny	315,000

Source: "MRC Data Year-End Report U.S. 2020." [online] from http://www.billboard.com [Accessed January 10, 2021], from MRC Data.

★ 2394 ★
Music
SIC: 3652; NAICS: 334614, 51225

Best-Selling R&B Albums, 2020

Albums are ranked by album + TEA (track equivalent album) + on-demand SEA (streaming equivalent album) sales.

After Hours, The Weeknd	2,032,000
Changes, Justin Bieber	1,088,000
Chilombo, Jhené Aiko	1,057,000
Over It, Summer Walker	930,000
Hot Pink, Doja Cat	845,000

Source: "MRC Data Year-End Report U.S. 2020." [online] from http://www.billboard.com [Accessed January 10, 2021], from MRC Data.

★ 2395 ★
Music
SIC: 3652; NAICS: 334614, 51225

Best-Selling Rap Albums, 2020

Albums are ranked by album + TEA (track equivalent album) + on-demand SEA (streaming equivalent album) sales. Figures are in millions.

My Turn, Lil Baby	2.63
Shoot for the Stars Aim for the Moon, Pop Smoke	2.19
Legends Never Die, Juice Wrld	1.99
Hollywood's Bleeding, Post Malone	1.89
Eternal Take, Lil Uzi Vert	1.86

Source: "MRC Data Year-End Report U.S. 2020." [online] from http://www.billboard.com [Accessed January 10, 2021], from MRC Data.

★ 2396 ★
Music
SIC: 3652; NAICS: 334614, 51225

Best-Selling Rock Albums, 2020

Albums are ranked by album + TEA (track equivalent album) + on-demand SEA (streaming equivalent album) sales.

Greatest Hits, Queen	929,000
Diamonds, Elton John	743,000
Rumours, Fleetwood Mac	721,000
Chronicle: The 20 Greatest Hits, Creedence Clearwater...	630,000
Journey's Greatest Hits, Journey	561,000

Source: "MRC Data Year-End Report U.S. 2020." [online] from http://www.billboard.com [Accessed January 10, 2021], from MRC Data.

★ 2397 ★
Music
SIC: 3652; NAICS: 334614, 51225

Best-Selling Vinyl Albums, 2020

Albums are ranked by millions of unit sales.

Fine Line, Harry Styles	232,000
When We Fall Asleep, Where Do We Go?, Billie Eilish	196,000
Greatest Hits, Queen	176,000
Abbey Road, The Beatles	161,000
Guardians of the Galaxy: Awesome Mix, Vol. 1, Soundtrack	152,000
Legend: the Best of..., Bob Marley & the Wailers	148,000
Rumours, Fleetwood Mac	138,000
Don't Smile at Me, Billie Eilish	126,000
Thriller, Michael Jackson	125,000
great kid, m.A.A.d city, Kendrick Lamar	117,000

Source: "MRC Data Year-End Report U.S. 2020." [online] from http://www.billboard.com [Accessed January 10, 2021], from MRC Data.

★ 2398 ★
Music
SIC: 3652; NAICS: 334614, 51225

Classical Music Market in China, 2015-2025

The classical music market consists of music licensing, online classical music subscription service, and live classical music performance. Figures are in millions of renminbi.

2015	1,040.4
2016	1,061.5

Continued on next page.

★ 2398 ★
[Continued]
Music
SIC: 3652; NAICS: 334614, 51225

Classical Music Market in China, 2015-2025

The classical music market consists of music licensing, online classical music subscription service, and live classical music performance. Figures are in millions of renminbi.

2017	1,196.5
2018	1,602.7
2019	1,736.4
2020	1,538.9
2021	1,696.0
2022	1,865.7
2023	2,042.7
2024	2,217.3
2025	2,396.6

Source: "Kuke Music Holding Ltd." [online] from https://www.sec.gov/Archives/edgar/data/1809158/000104746920 005717/a2242706zf-1.htm [Published December 18, 2020].

★ 2399 ★
Music
SIC: 3652; NAICS: 334614, 51225

Leading Music Distributors of AES (All Album) Sales, 2020

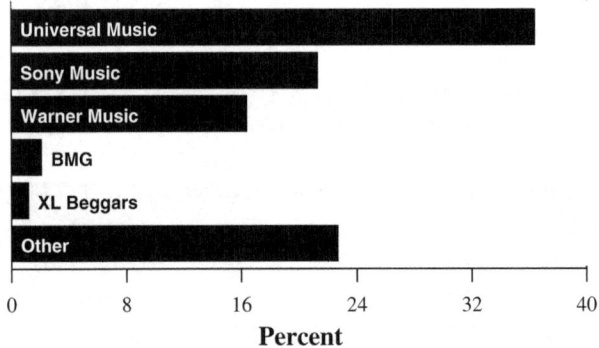

Corporate groups are ranked by market share for year-to-date. AES stands for Album Equivalent Sales.

Universal Music	36.4%
Sony Music	21.3
Warner Music	16.4
BMG	2.1
XL Beggars	1.2
Other	22.7

Source: *Music Week*, December 14, 2020, p. 51, from The Official Charts Company.

★ 2400 ★
Music
SIC: 3652; NAICS: 334614, 51225

Leading Music Distributors of AES (Artist Album) Sales, 2020

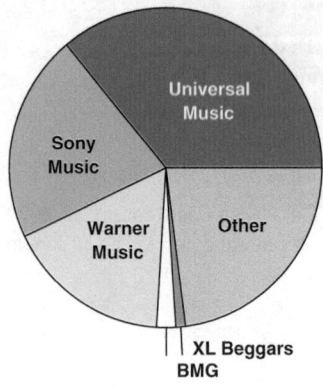

Corporate groups are ranked by market share for year-to-date. AES stands for Album Equivalent Sales.

Universal Music	36.3%
Sony Music	20.9
Warner Music	16.7
BMG	1.9
XL Beggars	1.2
Other	23.0

Source: *Music Week*, December 14, 2020, p. 51, from The Official Charts Company.

★ 2401 ★
Music
SIC: 3652; NAICS: 334614, 51225

Leading Music Distributors of Single Sales, 2020

Corporate groups are ranked by market share for year-to-date.

Universal Music	34.6%
Sony Music	21.5
Warner Music	17.3
BMG	2.2
XL Beggars	0.9
Other	23.5

Source: *Music Week*, December 14, 2020, p. 51, from The Official Charts Company.

★ 2402 ★
Music
SIC: 3652; NAICS: 334614, 51225

Leading Music Distributors of Single Streams, 2020

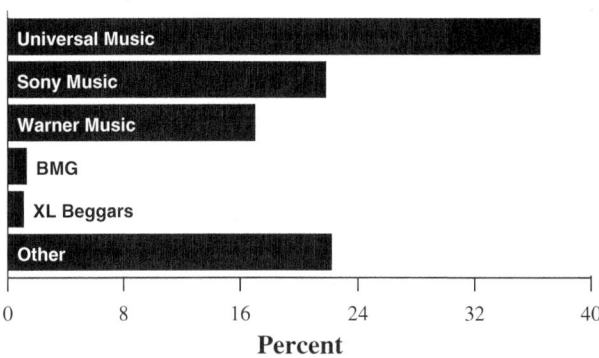

Market shares are shown by corporate group for year-to-date.

Universal Music	36.5%
Sony Music	21.8
Warner Music	17.0
BMG	1.3
XL Beggars	1.1
Other	22.2

Source: *Music Week*, December 14, 2020, p. 51, from The Official Charts Company.

★ 2403 ★
Music
SIC: 3652; NAICS: 334614, 51225

Leading Music Genres, 2020

Shares are shown based on sales volume (album + TEA and on-demand audio/video SEA).

R&B/hip-hop	28.2%
Rock	19.5
Pop	12.9
Country	7.9
Latin	4.7
Dance/electronic	3.2
Christian/Gospel	1.9
World music	1.8
Children	1.3
Jazz	1.1
Classical	1.0
Other	16.5

Source: "Year-End Report U.S. 2020." [online] from https://www.billboard.com/p/u-s-music-year-end-report-2020 [Accessed January 10, 2021], from MRC Data.

★ 2404 ★
Music
SIC: 3652; NAICS: 334614, 51225

Live Music Performance Market in China, 2020 and 2025

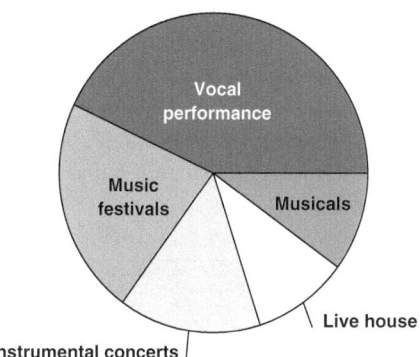

Figures are in billions of renminbi. The live music market relies on a number of factors, including rising income, growing urbanization, increased interest in classical music, and government policies that support the arts.

	2020 (bil.)	2025 (bil.)	Share
Vocal performance	2.3	3.1	43.06%
Music festivals	1.2	1.6	22.22
Instrumental concerts	0.8	1.1	15.28
Live house	0.3	0.7	9.72
Musicals	0.4	0.7	9.72

Source: "Kuke Music Holding Ltd." [online] from https://www.sec.gov/Archives/edgar/data/1809158/000104746920005717/a2242706zf-1.htm [Published December 18, 2020], from Frost & Sullivan.

★ 2405 ★
Music
SIC: 3652; NAICS: 334614, 51225

Music Sales by Category, 2019-2020

Data are in millions of units. Total audio consumption includes album + TEA+ on demand audio SEA. Total album sales include physical and digital sales. Physical albums include vinyl sales. Catalog music claimed 63.2% and 63.8% shares in 2019 and 2020, respectively. Current music sales claimed 36.8% and 36.2% of sales, respectively.

	2019	2020
On-demand audio song streams	745,900.0	872,600.0
Total audio consumption . .	678.1	756.8

Continued on next page.

★ 2405 ★
[Continued]
Music
SIC: 3652; NAICS: 334614, 51225
Music Sales by Category, 2019-2020

Data are in millions of units. Total audio consumption includes album + TEA+ on demand audio SEA. Total album sales include physical and digital sales. Physical albums include vinyl sales. Catalog music claimed 63.2% and 63.8% shares in 2019 and 2020, respectively. Current music sales claimed 36.8% and 36.2% of sales, respectively.

	2019	2020
Catalog audio consumption	428.3	483.2
Digital album sales	301.1	233.8
Current total audio consumption	249.8	273.6
Total album sales	112.7	102.4
Physical album sales	73.5	68.0
Digital album sales	39.3	34.4
Vinyl LP Sales	18.8	27.5

Source: "MRC Data Year-End Report U.S. 2020." [online] from http://www.billboard.com [Accessed January 10, 2021], from MRC Data.

★ 2406 ★
Music
SIC: 3652; NAICS: 334614, 51225
Music Sales by Category, 2020

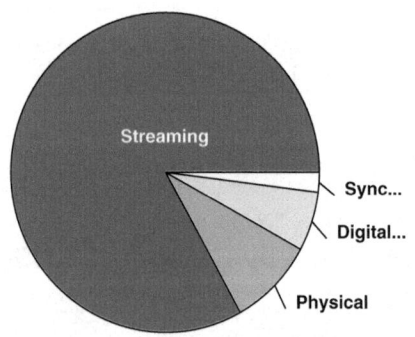

Shares are shown based on revenues of $12.2 billion.

Streaming	83.0%
Physical	9.0
Digital downloads	6.0
Synchronization royalties	2.0

Source: "Year-End 2020 RIAA Revenue Statistics." [online] from https://www.riaa.com/reports/2020-year-end-music-industry-revenue-report [Accessed March 26, 2021], from Recording Industry Association of America.

★ 2407 ★
Music
SIC: 3652; NAICS: 334614, 51225
Music Sales by Category Worldwide, 2017-2019

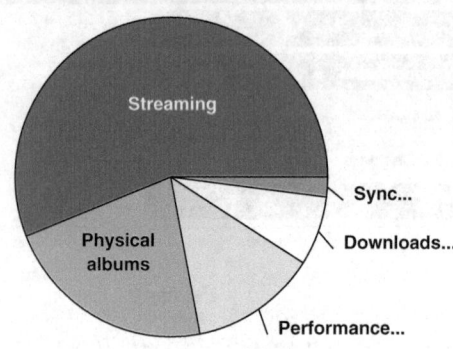

Global recorded music revenues totaled $20.2 billion in 2019, an increase of 8.2% from 2018. Revenues have grown each year since 2015. While physical album revenue declined 5.3%, streaming revenue grew 22.9%.

	2017	2018	2019	Share
Streaming	$6.5	$9.2	$11.4	55.88%
Physical albums	5.2	4.6	4.4	21.57
Performance rights	2.3	2.6	2.6	12.75
Downloads and other digital	2.6	1.7	1.5	7.35
Synchronization	0.4	0.5	0.5	2.45

Source: "IFPI Global Music Report 2020 - The Industry in 2019." [online] from https://www.ifpi.org/ifpi-issues-annual-global-music-report/ [Published May 4, 2020], from International Federation of the Phonographic Industry.

★ 2408 ★
Music
SIC: 3652; NAICS: 334614, 51225
Top Country Music Distributors, 2020

Market shares are shown based on chart presence for the week ended July 27, 2020.

Capitol Music Group	10.8%
Columbia	8.3
RCA	8.2
Bertelsmann Music Group	7.0
MCA Records	6.9
The Valory Music Co.	6.5
Big Loud	5.5
Warner/WAR	5.5
Broken Bow Records	5.4

Continued on next page.

★ 2408 ★
[Continued]
Music
SIC: 3652; NAICS: 334614, 51225

Top Country Music Distributors, 2020

Market shares are shown based on chart presence for the week ended July 27, 2020.

Warner/WEA	5.0%
Other	30.9

Source: *Country Aircheck*, July 27, 2020, p. 7.

★ 2409 ★
Music Streaming
SIC: 4832; NAICS: 515111, 515112

Leading Music Streaming Firms Worldwide, 2019

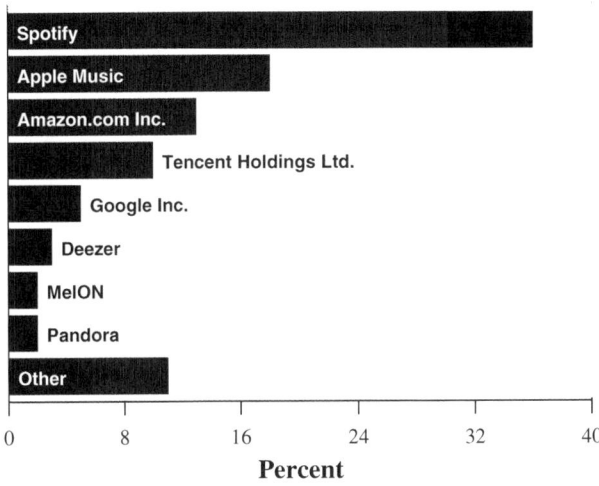

Market shares are shown in percent.

Spotify	36.0%
Apple Music	18.0
Amazon.com Inc.	13.0
Tencent Holdings Ltd.	10.0
Google Inc.	5.0
Deezer	3.0
MelON	2.0
Pandora	2.0
Other	11.0

Source: "Music Streaming Market Share." [online] from https://www.t4.ai/industry/music-streaming-market-share [Published August 16, 2020].

★ 2410 ★
Music Streaming
SIC: 4822; NAICS: 517311

Streaming Music Market Worldwide by Subscribers, 2019 and 2030

Market shares are estimated for 2030. Industry revenue is forecast to grow from $21.6 billion in 2019 to $75 billion in 2030.

	2019	2030
EM ex BRICs	11.0%	28.0%
China	12.0	20.0
United States	24.0	13.0
India	4.0	10.0
Brazil	4.0	4.0
United Kingdom	5.0	3.0
France	2.0	2.0
Germany	4.0	2.0
Japan	2.0	2.0
Mexico	3.0	2.0
Russia	3.0	2.0
Other DM	22.0	10.0

Source: "The Show Must Go On." [online] from http://www.goldmansachs.com [Published May 14, 2020], from *IFPI Global Music Report 2020* and Goldman Sachs Global Investment Research.

★ 2411 ★
Musical Instruments and Product Retailers
SIC: 5736; NAICS: 45114

Leading Musical Product Retailers, 2020

Companies are ranked by number of outlets. Shares are shown based on the top 60 chains. Guitar Center filed for bankruptcy in 2020. The company had been struggling even before the pandemic and had closed a number of stores in early 2020.

	Outlets	Share
Guitar Center Inc.	525	56.88%
Sam Ash Music Corp.	47	5.09
Music Go Round	37	4.01
Schmitt Music Co.	14	1.52
Steinway Hall	14	1.52
J.W. Pepper & Son Inc.	12	1.30
Brook Mays Music Co./H&H Music Co.	9	0.98
Eckroth Music Co.	9	0.98
Menchey Music Service	9	0.98
Piano Distributors	9	0.98

Continued on next page.

★ 2411 ★
[Continued]
Musical Instruments and Product Retailers
SIC: 5736; NAICS: 45114

Leading Musical Product Retailers, 2020

Companies are ranked by number of outlets. Shares are shown based on the top 60 chains. Guitar Center filed for bankruptcy in 2020. The company had been struggling even before the pandemic and had closed a number of stores in early 2020.

	Outlets	Share
Quinlan & Fabish Music Co.	9	0.98%
Other	229	24.81

Source: *Musical Merchandise Review*, December 2020, p. 20, from company data and *Musical Merchandise Review* estimates.

★ 2412 ★
Musical Instruments and Supplies
SIC: 3931; NAICS: 339992

Acoustic Guitar Sales, 2020

Data show share of unit sales for January 2020. Acoustic guitar sales grew 5.5% over 2018.

Under $200	41.8%
$200-$499.99	31.7
$500-$999.99	13.8
$1,000-$1,999.99	6.8
$2,000-$2,999.99	3.5
$3,000 and over	2.3

Source: *Music & Sound Retailer*, April 2020, p. 26, from Marketing Information Services Inc.

★ 2413 ★
Musical Instruments and Supplies
SIC: 3931; NAICS: 339992

Best-Selling Types of Guitar and Bass Straps, 2020

Market shares are shown based on unit sales. The most profitable brands for musical merchandise retailers were, in order, Levy's, D'Addario and Perri's.

Nylon	50.8%
Leather	23.8
Polyester	12.7
Cotton	11.1
Neoprene or memory foam	1.6

Source: *Musical Merchandise Review*, September 2020, p. 15.

★ 2414 ★
Musical Instruments and Supplies
SIC: 3931; NAICS: 339992

Electric Guitar Sales, 2020

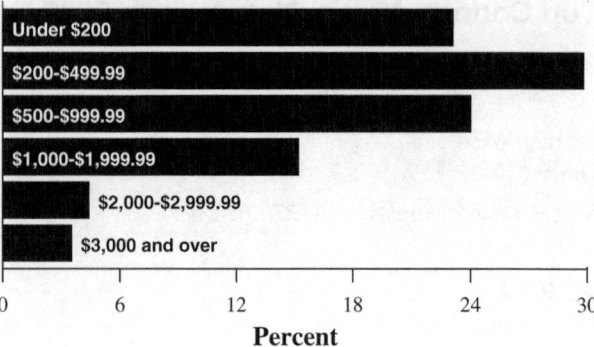

Data show share of unit sales for January 2020. Electric guitar sales grew 4.7% over 2018.

Under $200	23.1%
$200-$499.99	29.8
$500-$999.99	24.0
$1,000-$1,999.99	15.2
$2,000-$2,999.99	4.4
$3,000 and over	3.5

Source: *Music & Sound Retailer*, April 2020, p. 26, from Marketing Information Services Inc.

★ 2415 ★
Musical Instruments and Supplies
SIC: 3931; NAICS: 339992

Leading Musical Instrument and Product Makers Worldwide, 2020

Companies are ranked by sales in millions of dollars.

Yamaha Corp.	$ 3,866.39
Harman Professional Solutions (div. Samsung)	1,000.00
Sennheiser Electronic	876.00
Gold Peak Industries	872.00
Shure Inc.	740.00
Fender Musical Instruments	718.00
Kawai Musical Instruments Mfg. Co.	608.66
Steinway Musical Instruments	475.95
Roland Corp.	465.00
Music Tribe	425.00
Parsons Music	395.00
InMusic	350.00
JAM Industries	345.00
Gibson Guitars	310.00
Guangzhou Pearl River Piano Group	295.80

Source: *Music Trades*, Top 225 List, 2020, p. NA.

★ 2416 ★
Musical Instruments and Supplies
SIC: 3931; NAICS: 339992

Most Profitable Brands of Clarinet Ligatures, 2020

Data show the most profitable brands of clarinet ligatures based on a survey of dealers.

Rovner	83.3%
Vandoren	35.7
Bonade	28.6
American Plating (APM)	26.2
D'Addario Woodwinds/Rico	23.8
Luyben	23.8
Yamaha	23.8
BG	14.3
JodyJazz	11.9
Leblanc	11.6
Bois	9.5
Selmer Paris	9.5

Source: *Musical Merchandise Review*, January 2020, p. 36.

★ 2417 ★
Musical Instruments and Supplies
SIC: 3931; NAICS: 339992

Most Profitable Brands of Keyboard Stools and Benches, 2020

Data show the most profitable brands of keyboard stools and benches based on a survey of dealers.

On-Stage	56.8%
Roland	27.0
Yamaha	24.3
Casio	18.9
JamStands	13.8
Stagg	13.8
Quik-Lok	13.6
Jansen	13.5
K&M	13.5
Proline	2.7
Hidrau Model	2.1
GRK	1.2
Profile	1.0

Source: *Musical Merchandise Review*, April 2020, p. 36.

N

★ 2418 ★
Natural Products Retailers
SIC: 5999; NAICS: 446199

Leading Nutritional Product Retailers, 2019

Companies are ranked by nutrition sales in millions of dollars. "Other" includes specialty/gourmet, personal care (Body Shop, etc.), herb shops, mall stands, and other channels.

	($ mil.)	Share
Independents	$ 32,642	54.37%
Whole Foods Market	16,504	27.49
Sprouts Farmers Market	4,339	7.23
GNC Holdings Inc.	1,398	2.33
Natural Grocers by Vitamin Cottage	912	1.52
Vitamin Shoppe	891	1.48
Other	3,354	5.59

Source: *Natural Foods Merchandiser*, July 2020, p. 4, from *Natural Foods Merchandiser's Market Overview, 2020*.

★ 2419 ★
Natural Products Retailers
SIC: 5999; NAICS: 446199

Retail Sales of Natural Products, 2019

Sales of natural products grew from $128.8 billion in 2018 to $133.7 billion in 2019.

Conventional retailers	44.5%
Natural product retailers	36.2
Multilevel marketing	7.2
E-commerce	5.4
Practitioners	3.8
Mail order/direct response	2.9

Source: *Natural Foods Merchandiser*, July 2020, p. 4, from *Natural Foods Merchandiser's Market Overview, 2020* and *Nutrition Business Journal*.

★ 2420 ★
Navigational Equipment
SIC: 3812; NAICS: 334511

Leading Navigational Equipment Makers, 2019

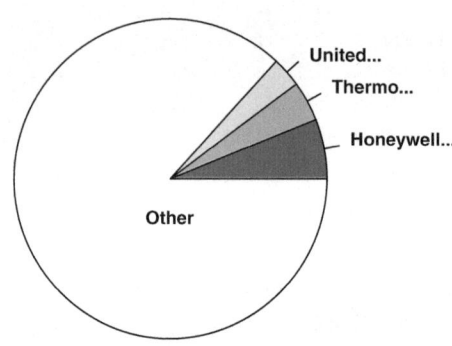

The production of navigational equipment includes search and navigational instruments, appliance regulators and controls, laboratory analytical instruments and physical properties testing equipment. A total of 4,213 businesses operated in this industry in 2019. Revenue is estimated to rise from $114.4 billion in 2019 to $120 billion in 2024. Exports represented 26.6% of industry revenue. California claimed 18.4% of businesses, Texas 7.1%, Massachusetts 6.1% and other states 68.4%

Honeywell International Inc.	6.5%
Thermo Fisher Scientific Inc.	4.1
United Technologies Corp.	3.0
Other	86.4

Source: "Trade Market Intelligence: Special Report Hotspots in the United States." [online] from http://www.novascotiabusiness.com [Published September 2019], from IBISWorld.

★ 2421 ★
Networking Equipment
SIC: 3669; NAICS: 33429

Best-of-Breed Equipment Market Worldwide, 2019

Technopedia refers to best-of-breed as "the best system in its referenced niche or category. Although it performs specialized functions better than an integrated system, this type of system is limited by its specialty area." Market shares are shown in percent.

Ceragon Networks Ltd.	15.0%
Huawei Technologies Corp.	15.0
NEC Corp.	14.0
Aviat Networks	9.0
SIAE Microelettronica	9.0
Ericsson Corp.	8.0
Intracom Holdings	7.0
Nokia Corp.	6.0
Other	17.0

Source: "The #1 Wireless Hauling Specialist Positioned to Lead in a Growing Market." [online] from http://www.ceragon.com [Published May 2020], from Ceragon analysis based on Sky Light Research, March 2020.

★ 2422 ★
Networking Equipment
SIC: 3669; NAICS: 33429

Cellular IoT Module Shipments Worldwide, 2020

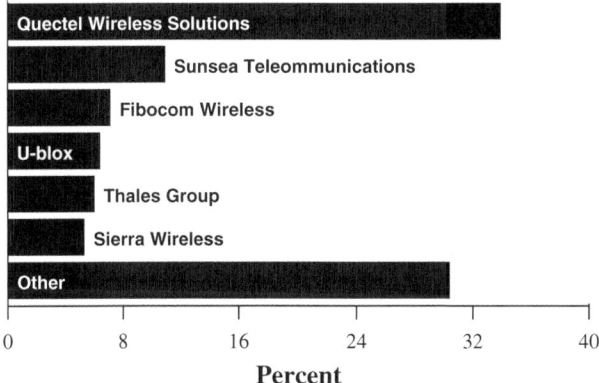

An IoT module is a small electronic device embedded in objects and modules that connect to wireless networks and send and receive data. Market shares are shown for the second quarter of 2020.

Quectel Wireless Solutions	33.9%
Sunsea Teleommunications	10.9
Fibocom Wireless	7.1
U-blox	6.4%
Thales Group	6.0
Sierra Wireless	5.3
Other	30.4

Source: "Quectel Widens Gap with Competition in Global Cellular IoT Module Market During Covid-Hit Q2 2020." [online] from https://www.counterpointresearch.com/quectel-widens-gap-with-competition-in-global-cellular-iot-module-market-during-q2-2020/ [Published October 28, 2020], from Counterpoint Research.

★ 2423 ★
Networking Equipment
SIC: 3669; NAICS: 33429

Global Market for Private LTE and 5G Networks, 2025

Market shares are shown in percent.

Manufacturing	25.0%
Energy & Utilites	24.0
Transportation and logistics	14.0
Public sector - government	10.0
Health care	8.0
Education	7.0
Retailing	7.0
Other	6.0

Source: "Omdia: The $5bn Ripple Effect of Private LTE and 5G Networks." [online] from https://omdia.tech.informa.com/pr/2021-feb/omdia---the-5bn-usd-ripple-effect-of-lte-and-5g [Published February 9, 2021], from Omdia.

★ 2424 ★
Networking Equipment
SIC: 3669; NAICS: 33429

Leading Ethernet Switch Makers in India, 2020

Market shares are shown based on revenue for the second quarter of 2020.

Cisco Systems Inc.	64.6%
Hewlett Packard Enterprise	4.1
Huawei Technologies Corp.	4.1
Dell Technologies	2.6
Nokia Corp.	2.5
Other	22.1

Source: "India Networking Market Showed a 9.6% YoY Decline in 2Q20." [online] from https://www.eetindia.co.in/india-networking-market-showed-a-9-6-yoy-decline-in-2q20/ [Published September 26, 2020], from IDC's Worldwide Quarterly Ethernet Switch Tracker.

★ 2425 ★
Networking Equipment
SIC: 3669; NAICS: 33429

Leading Router Makers in India, 2020

Market shares are shown based on revenue for the second quarter of 2020.

Cisco Systems Inc.	69.8%
Nokia Corp.	10.6
Juniper Networks	10.1
Huawei Technologies Corp.	9.3
Hewlett Packard Enterprise	0.6
Other	3.6

Source: "India Networking Market Showed a 9.6% YoY Decline in 2Q20." [online] from https://www.eetindia.co.in/india-networking-market-showed-a-9-6-yoy-decline-in-2q20/ [Published September 26, 2020], from IDC's Worldwide Quarterly Router Tracker.

★ 2426 ★
Networking Equipment
SIC: 3669; NAICS: 33429

Leading Router Makers in Japan, 2019

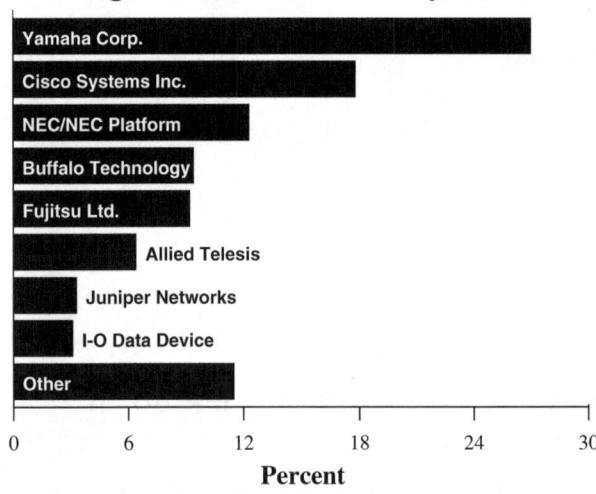

The source notes that the telecommunication equipment market is structured differently than in other countries, in that domestic companies tend to have large shares of the market.

Yamaha Corp.	27.0%
Cisco Systems Inc.	17.8
NEC/NEC Platform	12.3
Buffalo Technology	9.4
Fujitsu Ltd.	9.2
Allied Telesis	6.4
Juniper Networks	3.3
I-O Data Device	3.1%
Other	11.5

Source: "Trends in Japan's Telecommunications Equipment." [online] from https://workinjapan.today/hightech/trends-in-japans-telecommunications-equipment/ [Published January 21, 2020], from Nikkei XTech.

★ 2427 ★
Networking Equipment
SIC: 3669; NAICS: 33429

Leading Wireless LAN Makers in India, 2020

Market shares are shown based on revenue for the second quarter of 2020.

Cisco Systems Inc.	20.0%
TP-Link Technologies Co.	19.9
D-Link Corp.	19.1
Hewlett Packard Enterprise	10.7
Netgear Inc.	6.6
Other	23.7

Source: "India Networking Market Showed a 9.6% YoY Decline in 2Q20." [online] from https://www.eetindia.co.in/india-networking-market-showed-a-9-6-yoy-decline-in-2q20/ [Published September 26, 2020], from IDC's Worldwide Quarterly Wireless LAN Tracker.

★ 2428 ★
Networking Equipment
SIC: 3669; NAICS: 33429

Top KVM Switch Makers Worldwide, 2018

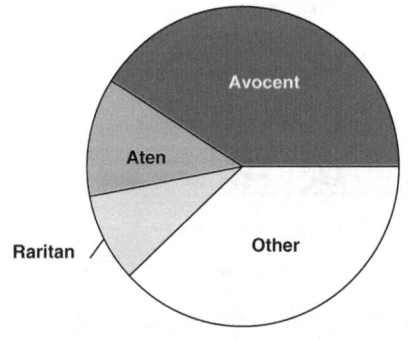

KVM switches allow IT personnel to use a single keyboard, video monitor and mouse (KVM) to control more than one computer at a time. Market shares are shown based on revenues of $943.3 million.

Avocent (Vertiv)	40.56%
Aten	12.40

Continued on next page.

★ 2428 ★
[Continued]
Networking Equipment
SIC: 3669; NAICS: 33429

Top KVM Switch Makers Worldwide, 2018

KVM switches allow IT personnel to use a single keyboard, video monitor and mouse (KVM) to control more than one computer at a time. Market shares are shown based on revenues of $943.3 million.

Raritan (Legrand)	8.93%
Other	38.11

Source: "Covid-19 Impact on Global KVM Switches Market Size, Status and Forecast 2020-2026." [online] from http://reports.valuates.com [Published April 2020], from QY Research.

★ 2429 ★
Newspapers
SIC: 2711; NAICS: 51111, 51913

Leading Newspaper Owners, 2019

Companies are ranked by number of total papers under ownership. Over the last 15 years, the number of news owners fell by more than one third, from 4,000 to 2,400. Twenty of the top 25 newspaper chains, as measured by number of newspapers owned, were private companies at the end of 2019. They owned nearly 1,000 newspapers.

Gannett/GateHouse Media	613
Digital First/Tribune	207
Lee Enterprises/BH Media	170
Adams Publishing Group	158
CNHI L.L.C.	112
Odgen Newspapers	84
Paxton Media Group	75
Boone Newspapers	65
Community Media Group	57
Landmark Media Enterprises	55

Source: "News Deserts and Ghost Newspapers: Will Local News Survive?" [online] from https://www.usnewsdeserts.com/reports/news-deserts-and-ghost-newspapers-will-local-news-survive/the-news-landscape-in-2020-transformed-and-diminished/the-new-media-giants/ [Published June 2020].

★ 2430 ★
Newspapers
SIC: 2711; NAICS: 51111, 51913

Leading Newspaper Publishers in Australia, 2020

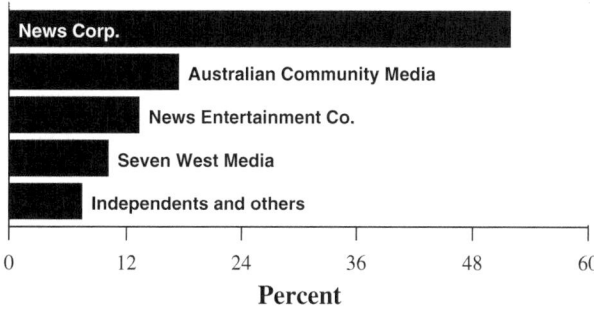

The newspaper market in Australia is one of the most concentrated in the world. Market shares are shown based on average issue readership. Industry growth was -9.5% for the five years leading up to 2020.

News Corp.	51.9%
Australian Community Media	17.4
News Entertainment Co.	13.3
Seven West Media	10.1
Independents and others	7.4

Source: *The Guardian*, November 13, 2020, p. NA, from IBISWorld.

★ 2431 ★
Newspapers
SIC: 2711; NAICS: 51111, 51913

Newspaper Industry Revenue, 2015-2024

Figures are in millions of dollars.

2015	$ 29,033.9
2016	27,326.2
2017	27,286.2
2018	25,568.1
2019	23,882.8
2020	19,950.1
2021	19,588.8
2022	18,674.6
2023	17,677.3
2024	16,735.9

Source: "The Media Report Media & Entertainment Data in America." [online] from https://digitalcommons.pepperdine.edu/cgi/viewcontent.cgi?article=1026&context=graziadiowps [Published September 2020], from IBISWorld.

★ 2432 ★
Nickel
SIC: 3341; NAICS: 331492

Leading High-Grade Nickel Producers Worldwide, 2019

Market shares are shown based on production.

Nornickel	24.0%
Jinchuan Group	17.0
Glencore PLC	15.0
Vale S.A.	14.0
BHP Billiton	8.0
Sherritt International	8.0
Sumitomo Metal Mining Co.	7.0
Other MMCs	7.0

Source: "Nornickel Expanding the Horizons of Sustainable Growth." [online] from http://ar2019.nornickel.com [Accessed December 10, 2020], from company reports.

★ 2433 ★
Nickel
SIC: 1061; NAICS: 21223

Leading Primary Nickel Producers Worldwide, 2019

Market shares are shown based on production.

Tsingshan Group	13.0%
Nornickel	9.0
Vale S.A.	8.0
Glencore PLC	7.0
Jiangsu Delong Nickel Industry Co.	7.0
Jinchuan Group	7.0
Shandong Xinhai Mining Technology	6.0
Sumitomo Metal Mining Co.	4.0
BHP	3.0
Sherritt International	3.0
Other MMCs	33.0

Source: "Nornickel Expanding the Horizons of Sustainable Growth." [online] from http://ar2019.nornickel.com [Accessed December 10, 2020], from company reports.

★ 2434 ★
Nickel
SIC: 3356; NAICS: 331491

Top Nickel Alloy Wire Makers Worldwide, 2019

The industry was worth $326.1 million in 2019. Nickel alloy wire is used for its corrosion and temperature resistance characteristics, as well as for its specific electrical resistance values.

Novametal Group	12.31%
Central Wire Industries	9.87
Sandvik Materials Technology	9.30%
Other	68.52

Source: "Global Nickel Alloy Wires Market Report, History and Forecast 2015-2026." [online] from http://www.qyresearch.com [Published July 2020], from QY Research.

★ 2435 ★
Nickel
SIC: 1061; NAICS: 21223

Top Nickel Exporters Worldwide, 2019

Data show the major exporters of nickel. Exports reached $16.5 billion in 2019, a 1.9% decrease from 2018.

United States	12.5%
Russian Federation	11.6
Canada	11.0
Germany	7.8
Norway	7.6
United Kingdom	6.0
China	5.3
Japan	4.4
Netherlands	4.4
Finland	3.9
Other	25.5

Source: "2019 International Trade Statistics Yearbook." [online] from https://comtrade.un.org/pb/ [Published December 2020], from U.N. Comtrade.

★ 2436 ★
Nickel
SIC: 1061; NAICS: 21223

Top Nickel Importers Worldwide, 2019

Data show the major importers of nickel. Imports reached $19.2 billion in 2019, a 1.8% increase from 2018.

China	19.4%
United States	11.6
Germany	8.1
France	5.9
South Korea	5.1
Japan	5.0
Italy	4.0
India	3.6
United Kingdom	3.4
Netherlands	2.9
Singapore	2.9
Other	28.1

Source: "2019 International Trade Statistics Yearbook." [online] from https://comtrade.un.org/pb/ [Published December 2020], from U.N. Comtrade.

★ 2437 ★
Nickel
SIC: 1061; NAICS: 21223

Top Nickel Producing Nations, 2020

Countries are ranked by production in metric tons. Production data are estimated.

	MT	Share
Indonesia	760,000	30.71%
Philippines	320,000	12.93
Russia	280,000	11.31
New Caledonia	200,000	8.08
Australia	170,000	6.87
Canada	150,000	6.06
China	120,000	4.85
Brazil	73,000	2.95
Cuba	49,000	1.98
Dominican Republic	47,000	1.90
United States	16,000	0.65
Other	290,000	11.72

Source: "Mineral Commodity Summaries 2021." [online] from https://www.usgs.gov/centers/nmic/mineral-commodity-summaries [Published January 29, 2021], from U.S. Geological Survey.

★ 2438 ★
Nightclubs and Bars
SIC: 5813; NAICS: 72241

Nightclub and Bar Market by Age Group, 2019

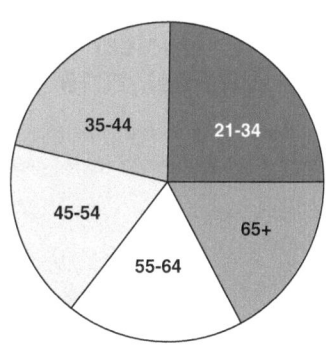

Nightclubs and bars offer limited foodservice and on-premise sales of alcoholic beverages. The industry generated revenue of approximately $26.6 billion in 2019. There are more than 36,000 single and multi-location establishments.

21-34	22.9%
35-44	19.8
45-54	17.4%
55-64	17.4
65+	16.0

Source: "Bars and Nightclubs." [online] from http://www.sdcnet.org/small-business-research-reports/bar-business-nightclub [Published June 2020], from IBISWorld.

★ 2439 ★
Nonwovens
SIC: 2297; NAICS: 31323

Demand for Carded Nonwovens, 2019

The industry was valued at $2.4 billion in 2019. The push for more sustainable products will help drive growth in this market. The pandemic has also helped drive growth in some markets, although it has hurt in others, such as autos and furniture.

Industrial	41.0%
Consumer	33.0
Filtration	9.0
Medical	9.0
Other	8.0

Source: "Carded Nonwovens." [online] from http://www.freedoniagroup.com [Published November 2020], from The Freedonia Group Inc.

★ 2440 ★
Nonwovens
SIC: 2297; NAICS: 31323

Demand for Filtration Nonwovens, 2019

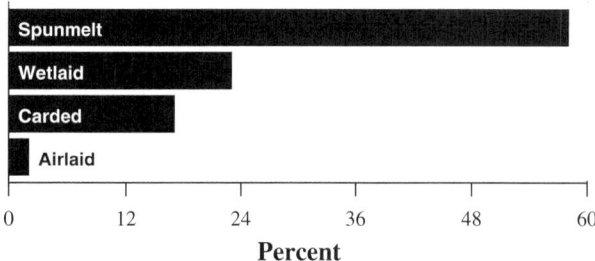

The market reached $1.3 billion in 2019. Major players include Ahlstrom-Munksjö, Berry Global, The Freudenberg Group, Johns Manville and Lydall Inc.

Spunmelt	58.0%
Wetlaid	23.0
Carded	17.0
Airlaid	2.0

Source: "Filtration Nonwovens." [online] from http://www.freedoniagroup.com [Published November 2020], from The Freedonia Group Inc.

★ 2441 ★
Nonwovens
SIC: 2297; NAICS: 31323

Demand for Medical Nonwovens, 2019

The market reached $1.3 billion in 2019. This figure covers surgical drapes, medical gowns, wipes, face masks, and other similar products. Major players include Ahlstrom-Munksjö, Berry Global, DuPont, Fibertex, Fitesa (Évora), Kimberly-Clark Corp. and Suominen.

Spunmelt	74.0%
Carded	16.0
Wetlaid	8.0
Airlaid	2.0

Source: "Medical Nonwovens." [online] from http://www.freedoniagroup.com [Published November 2020], from The Freedonia Group Inc.

★ 2442 ★
Nonwovens
SIC: 2297; NAICS: 31323

Leading Nonwoven Product Makers Worldwide, 2019

Companies are ranked by sales in millions of dollars. Shares are shown based on sales for the top 40 firms.

	($ mil.)	Share
Berry Global	$ 2,450	10.82%
Freudenberg Performance Materials	2,170	9.58
Ahlstrom-Munksjö	1,400	6.18
Kimberly-Clark Corp.	1,300	5.74
DuPont Inc.	1,000	4.42
Fitesa S.A.	980	4.33
Glatfelter	930	4.11
Lydall Inc.	837	3.70
Toray Inc.	801	3.54
Johns Manville	725	3.20
PFNonwovens	550	2.43
Suominen Nonwovens	491	2.17
TWEE Group	475	2.10
Low & Bonar	441	1.95
Avgol Industries	400	1.77
Other	7,691	33.97

Source: *Nonwovens Industry*, September 2020, p. 26.

★ 2443 ★
Nuclear Waste Disposal
SIC: 3272; NAICS: 32739

Global Market for Nuclear Waste Disposal of BWR Fuel, 2019

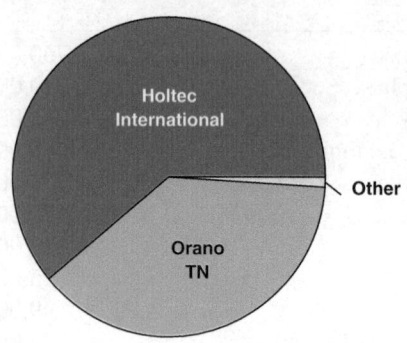

Market shares are shown for dual-purpose concrete systems. BWR stands for boiling water reactor.

Holtec International	61.0%
Orano TN	38.0
Other	1.0

Source: "Global Spent Fuel Overview." [online] from https://cdn.ymaws.com/inmm.org/resource/resmgr/docs/events/spentfuel2020/proceedings/greene_uxc_political_landsca.pdf [Published January 28, 2020], from StoreFUEL, January 2020.

★ 2444 ★
Nuclear Waste Disposal
SIC: 3272; NAICS: 32739

Global Market for Nuclear Waste Disposal of PWR Fuel, 2019

Market shares are shown for dual-purpose concrete systems. PWR stands for pressurized water reactor.

Orano TN	40.0%
Holtec International	36.0
NAC International	21.0
Other	3.0

Source: "Global Spent Fuel Overview." [online] from https://cdn.ymaws.com/inmm.org/resource/resmgr/docs/events/spentfuel2020/proceedings/greene_uxc_political_landsca.pdf [Published January 28, 2020], from StoreFUEL, January 2020.

★ 2445 ★
Nuclear Waste Disposal
SIC: 4953; NAICS: 562211

Leading Nuclear Waste Service Firms Worldwide, 2019

Companies are ranked by sector revenue in millions of dollars.

	($ mil.)	Share
AECOM	$1,044.7	28.52%
Bechtel	865.3	23.62
Jacobs	649.3	17.73
SNC-Lavalin Inc.	245.2	6.69
Leidos Holdings Inc.	136.9	3.74
Battelle	97.9	2.67
Navarro Research & Engineering Inc.	83.3	2.27
North Wind Group	76.1	2.08
Aptim Corp.	66.7	1.82
Mott Macdonald	60.5	1.65
Other	336.9	9.20

Source: *ENR*, July 20-27, 2020, p. 42.

★ 2446 ★
Nuclear Waste Disposal
SIC: 3272; NAICS: 32739

Nuclear Waste Disposal Market Worldwide for Shutdown Sites, 2019

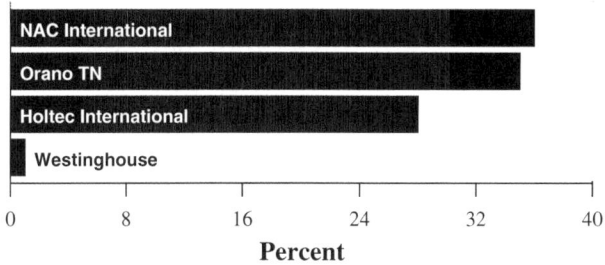

Market shares are shown in percent. As of August 2020, more than 180 commercial, experimental or prototype reactors, and several fuel cycle facilities have been retired from operation.

NAC International	36.0%
Orano TN	35.0
Holtec International	28.0
Westinghouse	1.0

Source: "Global Spent Fuel Overview." [online] from https://cdn.ymaws.com/inmm.org/resource/resmgr/docs/events/spentfuel2020/proceedings/greene_uxc_political_landsca.pdf [Published January 28, 2020], from StoreFUEL, January 2020.

★ 2447 ★
Nuts
SIC: 0173; NAICS: 111335

Leading Almond Producing Nations, 2020-2021

Countries are ranked by total production in metric tons, kernel basis.

	MT	Share
United States	1,562,626	81.40%
Spain	121,633	6.34
Australia	112,000	5.83
Turkey	20,000	1.04
Iran	16,000	0.83
Tunisia	16,000	0.83
Morocco	14,000	0.73
Chile	10,500	0.55
Italy	10,000	0.52
Greece	7,000	0.36
Other	30,000	1.56

Source: *Nutfruit Magazine*, July 2020, p. 70, from Almond Board of California, U.S. Department of Agriculture National Agricultural Statistics Service, Almond Board of Australia, AEOFRUSE and DESCALMENDRA, Aegean Exporters' Association, Greek Nuts and Fruits Trade Association and International Nut and Dried Fruit Council.

★ 2448 ★
Nuts
SIC: 0173; NAICS: 111335

Leading Brazil Nut Producing Nations, 2020-2021

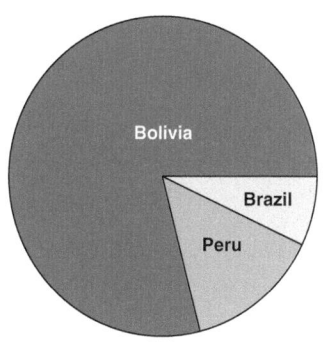

Countries are ranked by total production in metric tons, kernel basis.

	MT	Share
Bolivia	21,500	78.90%
Peru	3,800	13.94
Brazil	1,950	7.16

Source: *Nutfruit Magazine*, July 2020, p. 71, from International Nut and Dried Fruit Council.

★ 2449 ★
Nuts
SIC: 0173; NAICS: 111335

Leading Cashew Producing Nations, 2020-2021

Countries are ranked by raw cashew production in metric tons.

	MT	Share
Côte d'Ivoire	740,000	18.86%
India	731,000	18.63
Vietnam	495,000	12.61
Tanzania	367,000	9.35
Cambodia	250,000	6.37
Nigeria	225,000	5.73
Guinea-Bissau	200,000	5.10
Brazil	150,000	3.82
Benin	130,000	3.31
Burkina Faso	120,000	3.06
Other	516,000	13.15

Source: *Nutfruit Magazine*, July 2020, p. 72, from Global Cashew Council and International Nut and Dried Fruit Council.

★ 2450 ★
Nuts
SIC: 0173; NAICS: 111335

Leading Hazelnut Producing Nations, 2020-2021

Countries are ranked by total production in metric tons, kernel basis.

	MT	Share
Turkey	345,000	64.96%
Italy	65,800	12.39
United States	22,320	4.20
Azerbaijan	21,800	4.10
Georgia	18,330	3.45
Chile	17,640	3.32
Iran	9,092	1.71
Spain	6,830	1.29
China	6,565	1.24
France	4,250	0.80
Other	13,500	2.54

Source: *Nutfruit Magazine*, July 2020, p. 73, from Oregon Hazelnut Industry Office and International Nut and Dried Fruit Council.

★ 2451 ★
Nuts
SIC: 0173; NAICS: 111335

Leading Macadamia Producing Nations, 2020

Countries are ranked by total production in metric tons, kernel basis.

	MT	Share
South Africa	20,100	33.00%
Australia	11,000	18.06
Kenya	8,400	13.79
China	6,500	10.67
United States	4,000	6.57
Guatemala	3,150	5.17
Malawi	1,500	2.46
Brazil	1,380	2.27
Vietnam	450	0.74
Colombia	260	0.43
Other	4,160	6.83

Source: *Nutfruit Magazine*, July 2020, p. 74, from Macadamia Council, Macadamias South Africa, Australian Macadamia Society, Nut Processors Association of Kenya, China Chamber of Commerce for Import and Export of Foodstuffs, Brazilian Macadamia Association, Vietnam Macadamia Association and International Nut and Dried Fruit Council.

★ 2452 ★
Nuts
SIC: 0173; NAICS: 111335

Leading Peanut Producing Nations, 2020-2021

Countries are ranked by total production in thousands of metric tons, in-shell basis.

	MT (000)	Share
China	17,850	33.88%
India	6,063	11.51
Nigeria	4,300	8.16
United States	3,508	6.66
Indonesia	1,544	2.93
Argentina	1,200	2.28
Senegal	1,183	2.25
Ghana	656	1.25
Vietnam	644	1.22
Brazil	574	1.09
Mexico	396	0.75
Côte d'Ivoire	222	0.42
Nicaragua	182	0.35

Continued on next page.

★ 2452 ★
[Continued]
Nuts
SIC: 0173; NAICS: 111335

Leading Peanut Producing Nations, 2020-2021

Countries are ranked by total production in thousands of metric tons, in-shell basis.

	MT (000)	Share
South Africa	121	0.23%
Other	14,241	27.03

Source: *Nutfruit Magazine*, July 2020, p. 79, from China Chamber of Commerce for Import and Export Foodstuffs, U.S. Department of Agriculture, Argentine Chamber of Peanuts and International Nut and Dried Fruit Council.

★ 2453 ★
Nuts
SIC: 0173; NAICS: 111335

Leading Pecan Producing Nations, 2020-2021

Countries are ranked by total production in metric tons, kernel basis.

	MT	Share
United States	106,771	53.17%
Mexico	78,593	39.14
South Africa	11,028	5.49
Brazil	1,700	0.85
Australia	1,472	0.73
China	280	0.14
Other	952	0.47

Source: *Nutfruit Magazine*, July 2020, p. 75, from American Pecan Council, Brazilian Association of Nuts and Chestnuts, Brazilian Agricultural Research Corporation and International Nut and Dried Fruit Council.

★ 2454 ★
Nuts
SIC: 0173; NAICS: 111335

Leading Pine Nut Producing Nations, 2020-2021

Countries are ranked by total production in metric tons, kernel basis.

	MT	Share
Russia	12,150	30.96%
China	11,500	29.30
North Korea	8,750	22.29
Afghanistan	2,900	7.39%
Pakistan	2,800	7.13
Turkey	375	0.96
Portugal	300	0.76
Spain	250	0.64
Italy	125	0.32
Other	100	0.25

Source: *Nutfruit Magazine*, July 2020, p. 76, from China Chamber of Commerce for Import and Export Foodstuffs and International Nut and Dried Fruit Council.

★ 2455 ★
Nuts
SIC: 0173; NAICS: 111335

Leading Pistachio Producing Nations, 2020-2021

Countries are ranked by total production in metric tons, in-shell basis.

	MT	Share
United States	587,000	47.05%
Turkey	400,000	32.06
Iran	220,000	17.63
Syria	20,700	1.66
Greece	7,000	0.56
Afghanistan	4,500	0.36
Spain	2,500	0.20
Australia	2,200	0.18
Italy	2,200	0.18
China	1,500	0.12

Source: *Nutfruit Magazine*, July 2020, p. 77, from Iran Pistachio Association, Greek Nuts & Fruits Trade Association, Australia Pistachio Growers' Association and International Nut and Dried Fruit Council.

★ 2456 ★
Nuts
SIC: 0173; NAICS: 111335

Leading Walnut Producing Nations, 2020-2021

Countries are ranked by total production in metric tons, kernel basis.

	MT	Share
China	444,400	44.42%
United States	320,600	32.05
Chile	75,900	7.59
Ukraine	43,600	4.36
France	17,160	1.72

Continued on next page.

★ 2456 ★
[Continued]
Nuts
SIC: 0173; NAICS: 111335

Leading Walnut Producing Nations, 2020-2021

Countries are ranked by total production in metric tons, kernel basis.

	MT	Share
Romania	14,500	1.45%
India	14,114	1.41
Turkey	13,600	1.36
Iran	12,000	1.20
Italy	8,700	0.87
Argentina	8,600	0.86
Moldova	8,050	0.80
Australia	5,700	0.57
Hungary	4,700	0.47
Georgia	2,800	0.28
Other	6,000	0.60

Source: *Nutfruit Magazine*, July 2020, p. 78, from California Walnut Board and Commission, Ukrainian Walnut Association and International Nut and Dried Fruit Council.

★ 2457 ★
Nylon String Trimmer Line
SIC: 3087; NAICS: 325991

Leading Nylon String Trimmer Line Makers Worldwide, 2016

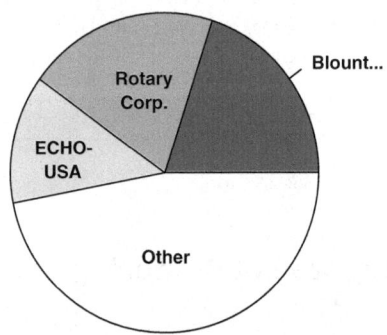

The cutting line in a string trimmer is used to cut through weeds and tall grass. The market is forecast to grow from $160 million in 2020 to $190 million in 2024.

Blount International (Oregon)	19.85%
Rotary Corp. (Desert & Maxpower)	19.75
ECHO-USA	13.16%
Other	47.24

Source: "Global Nylon String Trimmer Line Market 2020: Top Countries Data, Revenue Growth Development with COVID-19 Impact Analysis and Emerging Technologies with Forecasts to 2024." [online] from http://www.marketwatch.com [Press release August 11, 2020], from QY Research.

O

★ 2458 ★

Oats

SIC: 0119; NAICS: 111199

Leading Oat Consuming Regions, 2021

Data are in thousands of metric tons. Figures are for trade year as of October 2020.

	(000)	Share
European Union	7,930	33.58%
Russia	3,950	16.73
United States	2,492	10.55
Canada	2,400	10.16
Australia	1,050	4.45
China	980	4.15
Brazil	905	3.83
Argentina	630	2.67
Chile	575	2.44
Other	2,700	11.43

Source: "World Oats Production, Consumption and Stocks." [online] from https://apps.fas.usda.gov/psdonline/app/index.html#/app/downloads [Published October 2020], from U.S. Department of Agriculture.

★ 2459 ★

Oats

SIC: 0119; NAICS: 111199

Leading Oat Producing Regions, 2021

Data are in thousands of metric tons. Figures are for trade year as of October 2020.

	(000)	Share
European Union	8,150	33.74%
Canada	4,500	18.63
Russia	4,000	16.56
Australia	1,600	6.62
Brazil	970	4.02%
United States	949	3.93
Argentina	640	2.65
Chile	638	2.64
China	625	2.59
Other	2,082	8.62

Source: "World Oats Production, Consumption and Stocks." [online] from https://apps.fas.usda.gov/psdonline/app/index.html#/app/downloads [Published October 2020], from U.S. Department of Agriculture.

★ 2460 ★

Office Equipment

SIC: 3578; NAICS: 333318

Leading Office and Telecom Equipment Exporters Worldwide, 2019

Exports reached $1.75 trillion in 2019. China and Mexico figures include significant shipments through processing zones. Vietnam figure is a Secretariat estimate.

China	32.0%
European Union	18.3
United States	7.2
Chinese Taipei	7.1
South Korea	6.5
Singapore	5.9
Vietnam	4.8
Malaysia	3.8
Mexico	3.2
Other	11.2

Source: "World Trade Statistical Review 2020." [online] from https://www.wto.org/english/res_e/statis_e/wts2020_e/wts20_toc_e.htm [Accessed October 28, 2020], from World Trade Organization.

★ 2461 ★
Office Equipment
SIC: 3578; NAICS: 333318

Leading Office and Telecom Equipment Importers Worldwide, 2019

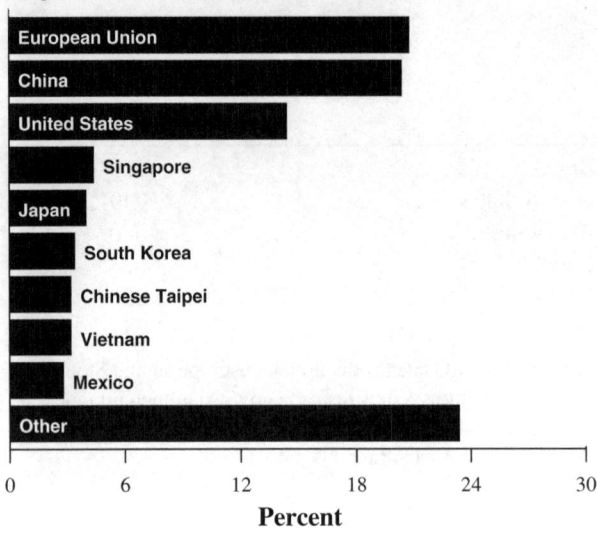

Imports reached $1.73 trillion in 2019. China's figure include significant shipments through processing zones.

European Union	20.8%
China	20.4
United States	14.4
Singapore	4.4
Japan	4.0
South Korea	3.4
Chinese Taipei	3.2
Vietnam	3.2
Mexico	2.8
Other	23.4

Source: "World Trade Statistical Review 2020." [online] from https://www.wto.org/english/res_e/statis_e/wts2020_e/wts20_toc_e.htm [Accessed October 28, 2020], from World Trade Organization.

★ 2462 ★
Oil and Gas
SIC: 1311; NAICS: 21113

Leading Natural Gas Firms (Reserves), 2019

Companies are ranked by reserves in billions of cubic feet.

ExxonMobil Corp.	19,026.0
EQT Corp.	16,677.2
Cabot Oil & Gas Corp.	12,903.0
Range Resources Corp.	12,115.0
Antero Resources Corp.	11,494.0
Southwestern Energy Co.	8,630.0
CNX Resources Corp.	7,938.4
Chesapeake Energy Corp.	6,566.0
Comstock Resources Inc.	5,341.5
Continental Resources Inc.	5,154.5

Source: *Oil & Gas Journal*, September 7, 2020, p. 22.

★ 2463 ★
Oil and Gas
SIC: 1311; NAICS: 21113

Leading Natural Gas Firms Worldwide (Reserves), 2019

Companies are ranked by reserves in billions of cubic feet.

ExxonMobil Corp.	32,924.0
Chevron Corp.	26,587.0
EQT Inc.	16,677.2
Cabot Oil & Gas Corp.	12,903.0
Range Resources Corp.	12,115.0
Antero Resources Corp.	11,494.0
Southwestern Energy Co.	8,630.0
Noble Energy Inc.	8,151.0
CNX Resources Corp.	7,938.4
ConocoPhillips	7,259.0

Source: *Oil & Gas Journal*, September 7, 2020, p. 22.

★ 2464 ★
Oil and Gas
SIC: 1311; NAICS: 21113

Leading Natural Gas Producers, 2019

Companies are ranked by production in billions of cubic feet.

EQT Inc.	1,435.1
ExxonMobil Corp.	1,103.0
Cabot Oil & Gas Corp.	865.0
Antero Resources Corp.	822.0
Chesapeake Energy Corp.	728.0
Southwestern Energy Co.	609.0
Range Resources Corp.	578.1
CNX Resources Corp.	505.4
EOG Resources Inc.	465.4
Gulfport Energy Corp.	458.2

Source: *Oil & Gas Journal*, September 7, 2020, p. 22.

★ 2465 ★
Oil and Gas
SIC: 1311; NAICS: 21113

Leading Natural Gas Producers Worldwide, 2019

Companies are ranked by production in billions of cubic feet.

ExxonMobil Corp.	2,434.0
Chevron Corp.	2,357.0
EQT Corp.	1,435.1
Cabot Oil & Gas Corp.	865.0
Antero Resources Corp.	822.0
ConocoPhillips	780.0
Chesapeake Energy Corp.	728.0
Southwestern Energy Co.	609.0
Range Resources Corp.	578.1
Occidental Petroleum Corp.	530.0

Source: *Oil & Gas Journal*, September 7, 2020, p. 22.

★ 2466 ★
Oil and Gas
SIC: 2911; NAICS: 32411

Leading Oil and Gas Refiners Worldwide, 2020

Companies are ranked by refinery capacity in millions of barrels per day.

China Petrochemical Corp.	5,909
China National Petroleum Corp.	4,832
ExxonMobil Corp.	4,798
Valero Energy Corp.	3,152
Marathon Petroleum Corp.	3,081
Royal Dutch Shell PLC	2,922
Saudi Arabian Oil Co.	2,908
Rosneft Oil Co.	2,900
Petróleos de Venezuela S.A. (PDVSA)	2,859
Petróleo Brasileiro S.A.	2,317

Source: *Offshore Technology Focus*, June 2020, p. NA, from GlobalData's Oil & Gas Intelligence Centre.

★ 2467 ★
Oil and Gas
SIC: 2911; NAICS: 32411

Leading Petroleum Refiners, 2020

Companies are ranked by capacity in barrels per calendar day as of January 1, 2020.

	bcd	Share
Marathon Petroleum Corp.	3,067,000	16.16%
Valero Energy Corp.	2,181,300	11.49
ExxonMobil Corp.	1,747,324	9.21
Phillips 66 Company	1,675,200	8.83%
Chevron Corp.	1,037,660	5.47
PBF Energy Co. L.L.C.	865,000	4.56
PDV America Inc.	764,765	4.03
BP PLC	683,500	3.60
Koch Industries Inc.	673,500	3.55
Saudi Aramco (Motiva)	607,000	3.20
HollyFrontier Corp.	514,630	2.71
Other	5,159,205	27.19

Source: "Table 5: Refiners' Total Operable Atmospheric Crude Oil Distillation Capacity as of January 1, 2020." [online] from https://www.eia.gov/petroleum/refinerycapacity/table5.pdf [Accessed August 25, 2020], from U.S. Department of Energy.

★ 2468 ★
Oil and Gas
SIC: 2911; NAICS: 32411

Leading Petroleum Refiners in China, 2018

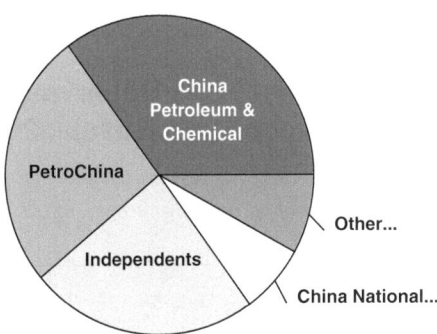

Diesel claimed 26% of demand by product, gasoline 22%, other light distillates 10%, jet fuel 7%, fuel oil 4%, and other products 31%.

China Petroleum & Chemical Corp.	35.0%
PetroChina	26.0
Independents	24.0
China National Offshore Oil Corp.	7.0
Other state-owned	8.0

Source: "Regional Energy: China Refining & Petrochemical Sector." [online] from https://www.dbs.id/id/corporate-id/aics/pdfController.page?pdfpath=/content/article/pdf/AIO/032020/200303_insights_reg_energy.pdf [Published March 3, 2020], from Sinopec and DBS Bank.

★ 2469 ★
Oil and Gas
SIC: 1321; NAICS: 21113

Proven Natural Gas Reserves in Africa, 2021

Countries are ranked by estimated proven reserves in billions of cubic feet as of January 1, 2021.

	bcf	Share
Nigeria	203,444	32.52%
Algeria	159,054	25.42
Mozambique	100,000	15.98
Egypt	63,000	10.07
Libya	53,144	8.49
Angola	12,113	1.94
Congo Brazzaville	10,029	1.60
Equatorial Guinea	4,909	0.78
Cameroon	4,770	0.76
Sudan and South Sudan	3,000	0.48
Other	12,154	1.94

Source: *Oil & Gas Journal*, December 7, 2020, p. 16.

★ 2470 ★
Oil and Gas
SIC: 1321; NAICS: 21113

Proven Natural Gas Reserves in Eastern Europe and Russia, 2021

Countries are ranked by estimated proven reserves in billions of cubic feet as of January 1, 2021.

	bcf	Share
Russia	1,688,228	71.88%
Turkmenistan	400,000	17.03
Kazakhstan	85,000	3.62
Uzbekistan	65,000	2.77
Azerbaijan	60,000	2.55
Ukraine	39,000	1.66
Romania	3,725	0.16
Poland	3,231	0.14
Serbia	1,700	0.07
Croatia	880	0.04
Other	1,973	0.08

Source: *Oil & Gas Journal*, December 7, 2020, p. 16.

★ 2471 ★
Oil and Gas
SIC: 1321; NAICS: 21113

Proven Natural Gas Reserves in the Asia-Pacific, 2021

Countries are ranked by estimated proven reserves in billions of cubic feet as of January 1, 2021.

	bcf	Share
China	234,993	39.82%
Australia	114,000	19.32
Indonesia	49,740	8.43
India	48,756	8.26
Malaysia	42,000	7.12
Vietnam	24,700	4.19
Myanmar	22,500	3.81
Pakistan	20,914	3.54
Brunei	9,200	1.56
Papua New Guinea	6,467	1.10
Other	16,880	2.86

Source: *Oil & Gas Journal*, December 7, 2020, p. 16.

★ 2472 ★
Oil and Gas
SIC: 1321; NAICS: 21113

Proven Natural Gas Reserves in the Middle East, 2021

Countries are ranked by estimated proven reserves in billions of cubic feet as of January 1, 2021.

	bcf	Share
Iran	1,200,252	42.22%
Qatar	842,627	29.64
Saudi Arabia	332,764	11.70
United Arab Emirates	215,098	7.57
Iraq	131,686	4.63
Kuwait	63,000	2.22
Oman	23,000	0.81
Yemen	16,900	0.59
Syria	8,500	0.30
Israel	6,216	0.22
Other	3,087	0.11

Source: *Oil & Gas Journal*, December 7, 2020, p. 16.

★ 2473 ★
Oil and Gas
SIC: 1321; NAICS: 21113

Proven Natural Gas Reserves in the Western Hemisphere, 2021

Countries are ranked by estimated proven reserves in billions of cubic feet as of January 1, 2021.

	bcf	Share
United States	457,897	56.83%
Venezuela	200,372	24.87
Canada	73,000	9.06
Argentina	14,000	1.74
Brazil	12,854	1.60
Bolivia	10,700	1.33
Peru	10,600	1.32
Trinidad and Tobago	10,526	1.31
Mexico	6,368	0.79
Chile	3,460	0.43
Other	5,990	0.74

Source: *Oil & Gas Journal*, December 7, 2020, p. 16.

★ 2474 ★
Oil and Gas
SIC: 1321; NAICS: 21113

Proven Natural Gas Reserves in Western Europe, 2021

Countries are ranked by estimated proven reserves in billions of cubic feet as of January 1, 2021.

	bcf	Share
Norway	54,542	77.75%
United Kingdom	6,380	9.09
Netherlands	4,683	6.68
Italy	1,616	2.30
Denmark	1,043	1.49
Germany	826	1.18
Ireland	350	0.50
France	275	0.39
Austria	178	0.25
Turkey	134	0.19
Other	126	0.18

Source: *Oil & Gas Journal*, December 7, 2020, p. 16.

★ 2475 ★
Oil and Gas
SIC: 1311; NAICS: 21112

Proven Oil Reserves in Africa, 2021

Countries are ranked by estimated proven reserves in millions of barrels as of January 1, 2021.

	(mil.)	Share
Libya	48,363.00	38.60%
Nigeria	36,890.00	29.45
Algeria	12,200.00	9.74
Angola	7,783.00	6.21
Sudan and South Sudan	5,000.00	3.99
Egypt	3,300.00	2.63
Congo Brazzaville	2,882.00	2.30
Uganda	2,500.00	2.00
Gabon	2,000.00	1.60
Chad	1,500.00	1.20
Other	2,859.11	2.28

Source: *Oil & Gas Journal*, December 7, 2020, p. 16.

★ 2476 ★
Oil and Gas
SIC: 1311; NAICS: 21112

Proven Oil Reserves in Eastern Europe and Russia, 2021

Countries are ranked by estimated proven reserves in thousands of barrels as of January 1, 2021.

	(000)	Share
Russia	80,000,000	66.70%
Kazakhstan	30,000,000	25.01
Azerbaijan	7,000,000	5.84
Romania	600,000	0.50
Uzbekistan	594,000	0.50
Ukraine	395,000	0.33
Belarus	198,000	0.17
Albania	150,000	0.13
Poland	113,000	0.09
Serbia	77,500	0.06
Turkmenistan	60,000	0.05
Other	761,096	0.63

Source: *Oil & Gas Journal*, December 7, 2020, p. 16.

★ 2477 ★
Oil and Gas
SIC: 1311; NAICS: 21112

Proven Oil Reserves in the Asia-Pacific, 2021

Countries are ranked by estimated proven reserves in thousands of barrels as of January 1, 2021.

	(000)	Share
China	26,022,600	56.57%
India	4,604,914	10.01
Vietnam	4,400,000	9.57
Malaysia	3,600,000	7.83
Indonesia	2,480,000	5.39
Australia	2,446,000	5.32
Pakistan	540,000	1.17
Thailand	252,750	0.55
Papua New Guinea	159,656	0.35
Japan	44,155	0.10
Other	1,448,832	3.15

Source: *Oil & Gas Journal*, December 7, 2020, p. 16.

★ 2478 ★
Oil and Gas
SIC: 1311; NAICS: 21112

Proven Oil Reserves in the Middle East, 2021

Countries are ranked by estimated proven reserves in millions of barrels as of January 1, 2021.

	(mil.)	Share
Saudi Arabia	258,600.00	30.50%
Iran	208,600.00	24.60
Iraq	145,019.00	17.10
Kuwait	101,500.00	11.97
United Arab Emirates	97,800.00	11.54
Qatar	25,244.00	2.98
Oman	5,373.00	0.63
Yemen	3,000.00	0.35
Other	2,700.25	0.32

Source: *Oil & Gas Journal*, December 7, 2020, p. 16.

★ 2479 ★
Oil and Gas
SIC: 1311; NAICS: 21112

Proven Oil Reserves in the Western Hemisphere, 2021

Countries are ranked by estimated proven reserves in thousands of barrels as of January 1, 2021.

	(000)	Share
Venezuela	303,806,000	52.69%
Canada	170,300,000	29.53
United States	69,442,720	12.04
Brazil	12,714,600	2.20
Ecuador	8,273,000	1.43
Mexico	5,786,100	1.00
Argentina	2,482,704	0.43
Colombia	2,036,000	0.35
Peru	858,890	0.15
Trinidad and Tobago	242,982	0.04
Other	698,560	0.12

Source: *Oil & Gas Journal*, December 7, 2020, p. 16.

★ 2480 ★
Oil and Gas
SIC: 1321; NAICS: 21113

Proven Oil Reserves in Western Europe, 2021

Countries are ranked by estimated proven reserves in thousands of barrels as of January 1, 2021.

	(000)	Share
Norway	8,122,151	65.31%
United Kingdom	2,500,000	20.10
Denmark	441,000	3.55
Turkey	366,000	2.94
Spain	150,000	1.21
Netherlands	137,747	1.11
France	61,719	0.50
Austria	35,200	0.28
Greece	10,000	0.08
Other	613,134	4.93

Source: *Oil & Gas Journal*, December 7, 2020, p. 16.

★ 2481 ★
Oil and Gas Drilling
SIC: 1381; NAICS: 213111

Floater Rigs by Current Activity, 2020

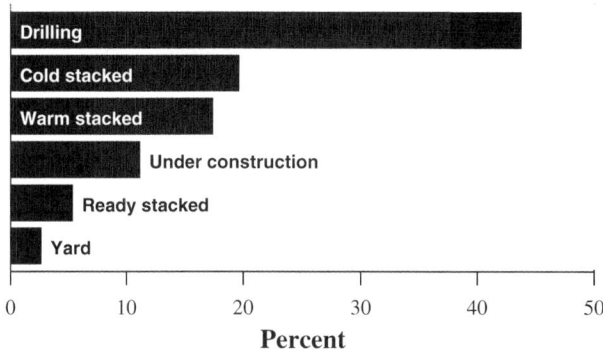

Floater rigs are not attached to or are resting on the ocean bottom. Data show the number of rigs by current activity.

	Rigs	Share
Drilling	98	43.75%
Cold stacked	44	19.64
Warm stacked	39	17.41
Under construction	25	11.16
Ready stacked	12	5.36
Yard	6	2.68

Source: *OGV Energy*, October 2020, p. 11, from Rystad Analytics.

★ 2482 ★
Oil and Gas Drilling
SIC: 1381; NAICS: 213111

Global Market for Horizontal Directional Drilling, 2018-2020

The oil and gas industry saw a drop in consumption, as well as a price war between Russia and Saudi Arabia. Data are estimated for 2020.

	2018	2019	2020
Telecommunications	24.3%	24.7%	25.9%
Water	19.0	19.8	19.9
Gas distribution	18.8	19.4	19.8
Electric transmission/ distribution	13.2	12.7	12.9
Sewers	9.0	8.9	9.0
Oil and gas transmission	8.0	9.9	7.6
Wind and solar	2.0	1.9	1.8
Other	5.7	2.7	3.1

Source: *Underground Construction*, June 2020, p. 18.

★ 2483 ★
Oil and Gas Drilling
SIC: 1381; NAICS: 213111

Jackup Rigs by Current Activity, 2020

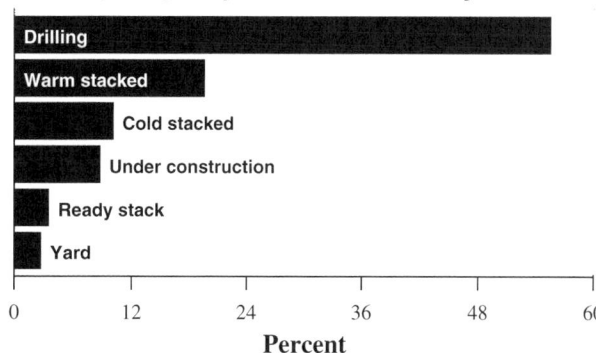

Jackup rigs, first built in 1954, are the most popular type of mobile offshore drilling unit, according to Rigzone. Data show the number of rigs by current activity.

	Rigs	Share
Drilling	287	55.51%
Warm stacked	101	19.54
Cold stacked	52	10.06
Under construction	45	8.70
Ready stack	18	3.48
Yard	14	2.71

Source: *OGV Energy*, October 2020, p. 11, from Rystad Analytics.

★ 2484 ★
Oil and Gas Drilling
SIC: 1381; NAICS: 213111

Leading Drilling Rig Contractors Worldwide (Offshore), 2019

Companies are ranked by total rigs managed as of December 31, 2019.

	Rigs	Share
Valaris PLC	70	7.66%
China Oilfield Services	55	6.02
Seadrill Ltd.	51	5.58
Transocean Ltd.	47	5.14
Shelf Drilling Ltd.	36	3.94
Borr Drilling	34	3.72
Noble Corp.	25	2.74
Petróleos de Venezuela S.A.	23	2.52
Maersk Drilling	22	2.41
ADNOC Drilling	20	2.19
Other	531	58.10

Source: *Offshore*, February 2020, p. 19, from IHS Markit.

★ 2485 ★
Oil and Gas Liquids
SIC: 1321; NAICS: 21113

Leading Natural Gas Liquid Firms (Reserves), 2019

Companies are ranked by reserves in billions of barrels.

ExxonMobil Corp.	3.08
EOG Resources Inc.	2.44
Chevron Corp.	2.43
ConocoPhillips	2.37
Occidental Petroleum Corp.	2.11
Antero Resources Corp.	1.23
Range Resources Corp.	1.01
DiamondEnergy Resources Inc.	0.94
Pioneer Natural Resources Co.	0.88
Marathon Oil Corp.	0.82

Source: *Oil & Gas Journal*, September 7, 2020, p. 22.

★ 2486 ★
Oil and Gas Liquids
SIC: 1321; NAICS: 21113

Leading Natural Gas Liquid Firms Worldwide (Reserves), 2019

Companies are ranked by reserves in billions of barrels.

ExxonMobil Corp.	13.10
Chevron Corp.	4.77
ConocoPhillips	2.92
Occidental Petroleum Corp.	2.72
EOG Resources Inc.	2.43
Antero Resources Group	1.23
Range Resources Corp.	1.01
Diamondback Energy Inc.	0.94
Haas Corp.	0.93
Pioneer Natural Resources Co.	0.88

Source: *Oil & Gas Journal*, September 7, 2020, p. 22.

★ 2487 ★
Oil and Gas Liquids
SIC: 1321; NAICS: 21113

Leading Natural Gas Liquid Producers, 2019

Companies are ranked by production in billions of barrels.

Chevron Corp.	264.0
EOG Resources Inc.	215.2
Occidental Resources Corp.	207.0
ConocoPhillips	202.0
ExxonMobil Corp.	168.0
Pioneer Natural Resources Co.	103.0
Marathon Oil Corp.	91.0
Diamondback Energy Inc.	87.0
Devon Energy Corp.	83.0
Conoco Resources Inc.	76.0

Source: *Oil & Gas Journal*, September 7, 2020, p. 22.

★ 2488 ★
Oil and Gas Liquids
SIC: 1321; NAICS: 21113

Leading Natural Gas Liquid Producers Worldwide, 2019

Companies are ranked by production in billions of barrels.

ExxonMobil Corp.	740.0
Chevron Corp.	550.0
ConocoPhillips	287.0
Occidental Petroleum Corp.	275.0
EOG Resources Inc.	215.5
Apache Corp.	113.3
Pioneer Natural Resources Co.	103.9
Marathon Oil Corp.	102.0
Diamondback Energy Corp.	87.0
Devon Energy Corp.	83.0

Source: *Oil & Gas Journal*, September 7, 2020, p. 22.

★ 2489 ★
Oil and Gas Liquids
SIC: 1321; NAICS: 21113

Top Liquefied Propane and Butane Exporters Worldwide, 2019

Data show the major exporters of liquefied propane and butane. Exports reached $60.7 billion in 2019, a 39.5% increase from 2018.

United Arab Emirates	39.8%
United States	25.0
Algeria	5.1
Kuwait	5.1
Canada	3.4
Iran	3.0
Norway	3.0
Russia	2.3
United Kingdom	1.9
Netherlands	1.3
Other	10.1

Source: "2019 International Trade Statistics Yearbook." [online] from https://comtrade.un.org/pb/ [Published December 2020], from U.N. Comtrade.

★ 2490 ★
Oil and Gas Liquids
SIC: 1321; NAICS: 21113

Top Liquefied Propane and Butane Importers Worldwide, 2019

Data show the major importers of liquefied propane and butane. Imports reached $50.5 billion in 2019, a 14.4% increase from 2018.

China	20.0%
India	14.3
Japan	9.7
South Korea	6.7
Indonesia	5.0
United States	3.5
Netherlands	3.2
Mexico	2.7
France	2.5
Morocco	2.4
Other	30.0

Source: "2019 International Trade Statistics Yearbook." [online] from https://comtrade.un.org/pb/ [Published December 2020], from U.N. Comtrade.

★ 2491 ★
Oil and Gas Pipelines
SIC: 4612; NAICS: 48611

Leading Crude Oil Liquid Pipelines, 2019

Companies are ranked by crude oil deliveries in thousands of barrels.

Plains Pipeline	1,731,436
Enterprise Crude Pipeline	1,443,310
Enbridge Energy	1,034,157
Marathon Pipe Line	678,666
Sunoco Pipeline	469,295
Seaway Crude Pipeline	416,985
LOCAP	382,255
ExxonMobil Pipeline	342,276
Mars Oil Pipeline	330,958
Zydeco Pipeline	326,983

Source: *Pipeline & Gas Journal*, November 2020, p. 32.

★ 2492 ★
Oil and Gas Pipelines
SIC: 4922; NAICS: 48621

Leading Transmission Pipelines by Gas Throughput, 2019

Companies are ranked by gas throughput in thousands of dekatherms annually.

Transcontinental Gas Pipe Line	5,617,379
Tennessee Gas Pipeline	4,527,426
Texas Eastern Transmission	4,424,196
Columbia Gas Transmission	3,144,459
ANR Pipeline	2,437,163
Natural Gas Pipeline of America	2,371,720
El Paso Natural Gas	2,065,674
Rover Pipeline	2,019,458
Gulf South Pipeline	2,000,784
Dominion Energy Transmission	1,962,770

Source: *Pipeline & Gas Journal*, November 2020, p. 33.

★ 2493 ★
Oil and Gas Services
SIC: 1389; NAICS: 213112

Leading Oil and Gas Service Firms Worldwide, 2016-2022

Market shares are shown based on revenue. Oil and gas services include drilling, maintenance and operation, seismic services, subsea services, and other services.

TechnipFMC	19.83%
Schlumberger Ltd.	17.87
Baker Hughes Co.	12.10
Saipem S.p.A.	10.19
Transocean Ltd.	8.03
Aker Solutions	7.33
Subsea 7	6.85
Halliburton Co.	6.16
Valaris	5.84
NOV Inc.	5.79

Source: *OGV Energy*, May 2021, p. 42, from Rystad Energy.

★ 2494 ★
Oil and Gas Storage
SIC: 1389; NAICS: 213112

Leading Oil and Gas Storage Firms at Fujairah, UAE, 2020

Fujairah is one of the world's largest refueling hubs because of its location just outside the Strait of Hormuz. Market shares are shown based on BPGIC's post Phase III construction plan, which will expand its capacity by 22 million barrels.

BPGIC	28.0%
Vopak Horizon Fujairah Ltd.	21.0
Fujairah Oil Terminal	18.0
VTTI BV	13.0
GPS Chemical Services	5.0
Gulf Petrochem Group	5.0
IPTF Terminals	5.0
Other	5.0

Source: "BPGIC Investor Presentation." [online] from https://sec.report/Document/0001213900-19-024529/ [Published November 2019], from IHS Markit.

★ 2495 ★
Oil and Gas Storage
SIC: 1389; NAICS: 213112

Leading Oil and Gas Storage Firms Worldwide, 2020

Companies are ranked by storage capacity in billions of barrels.

China Petroleum & Chemical Corp.	340
China National Petroleum Corp.	201
ENEOS Corp.	174
Korea National Oil Corp.	134
Saudi Arabian Oil Co.	131
Enbridge Inc.	118
Sinochem Group Co. Ltd.	99
Marathon Petroleum Corp.	91
ExxonMobil Corp.	89
PT Pertamina (Persero)	84

Source: *Offshore Technology Focus*, December 2020, p. NA, from GlobalData.

★ 2496 ★
Oilseeds
SIC: 2070; NAICS: 311224, 311225

Leading Oilseed Crushing Regions, 2020-2021

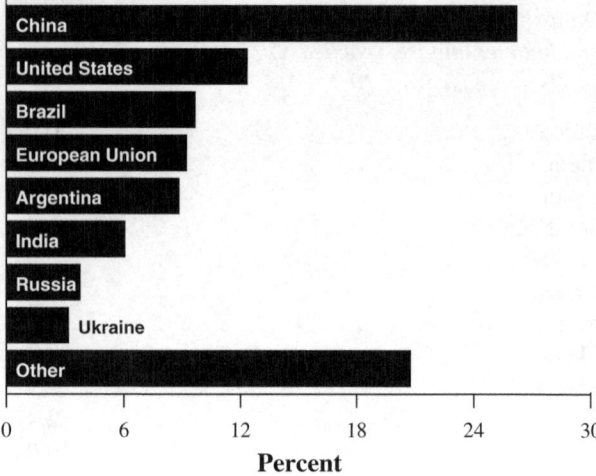

Percent

Crushings are estimated in millions of metric tons. Figures are as of October 2020.

	(mil.)	Share
China	134.85	26.19%
United States	63.57	12.35
Brazil	49.73	9.66
European Union	47.49	9.22
Argentina	45.44	8.83
India	31.18	6.06
Russia	19.30	3.75
Ukraine	16.28	3.16
Other	106.96	20.78

Source: "Major Oilseeds: World Supply and Distribution." [online] from https://apps.fas.usda.gov/psdonline/app/index.html#/app/downloads [Published October 2020], from U.S. Department of Agriculture.

★ 2497 ★
Oilseeds
SIC: 2070; NAICS: 311224, 311225

Leading Oilseed Exporting Regions, 2020-2021

Exports are estimated in millions of metric tons. Figures are as of October 2020.

	(mil.)	Share
Brazil	85.34	44.69%
United States	61.15	32.02
Canada	13.70	7.17

Continued on next page.

★ 2497 ★

[Continued]

Oilseeds

SIC: 2070; NAICS: 311224, 311225

Leading Oilseed Exporting Regions, 2020-2021

Exports are estimated in millions of metric tons. Figures are as of October 2020.

	(mil.)	Share
Argentina	8.13	4.26%
Paraguay	6.30	3.30
Ukraine	4.30	2.25
Australia	2.36	1.24
Other	9.69	5.07

Source: "Major Oilseeds: World Supply and Distribution." [online] from https://apps.fas.usda.gov/psdonline/app/index.html#/app/downloads [Published October 2020], from U.S. Department of Agriculture.

★ 2498 ★

Oilseeds

SIC: 2070; NAICS: 311224, 311225

Leading Oilseed Importing Regions, 2020-2021

Imports are estimated in millions of metric tons. Figures are as of October 2020.

	(mil.)	Share
China	103.80	55.40%
European Union	22.07	11.78
Mexico	7.85	4.19
Japan	5.93	3.17
Egypt	4.24	2.26
Argentina	4.00	2.14
Thailand	4.00	2.14
Turkey	3.80	2.03
Bangladesh	3.31	1.77
Indonesia	3.25	1.73
Other	25.10	13.40

Source: "Major Oilseeds: World Supply and Distribution." [online] from https://apps.fas.usda.gov/psdonline/app/index.html#/app/downloads [Published October 2020], from U.S. Department of Agriculture.

★ 2499 ★

Oilseeds

SIC: 2070; NAICS: 311224, 311225

Leading Oilseed Producers Worldwide, 2020-2021

Production is shown in millions of tons. Figures are as of February 2021.

	(mil.)	Share
Brazil	137.74	23.15%
United States	122.40	20.57
China	64.97	10.92
Argentina	52.59	8.84
India	37.92	6.37
Other	179.46	30.16

Source: "Oilseeds: World Markets and Trade." [online] from https://www.fas.usda.gov/data/oilseeds-world-markets-and-trade [Published February 2021], from U.S. Department of Agriculture.

★ 2500 ★

Oilseeds

SIC: 0116; NAICS: 11111

Leading Soybean Crushing Regions, 2020-2021

Crushings are estimated in thousands of metric tons. Figures are as of October 2020.

	(000)	Share
China	99,000	30.71%
United States	59,330	18.40
Brazil	45,500	14.11
Argentina	42,000	13.03
European Union	15,900	4.93
India	10,000	3.10
Mexico	6,400	1.99
Russia	4,750	1.47
Egypt	4,150	1.29
Paraguay	3,800	1.18
Other	31,585	9.80

Source: "Major Vegetable Oils: World Supply and Distribution." [online] from https://apps.fas.usda.gov/psdonline/app/index.html#/app/downloads [Published October 2020], from U.S. Department of Agriculture.

★ 2501 ★
Oilseeds
SIC: 0116; NAICS: 11111

Leading Soybean Exporters, 2020-2021

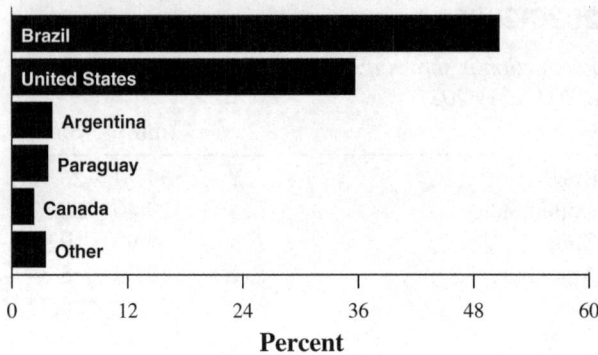

Exports are estimated in thousands of metric tons. Figures are as of October 2020.

	(000)	Share
Brazil	85,000	50.63%
United States	59,874	35.67
Argentina	7,000	4.17
Paraguay	6,300	3.75
Canada	3,850	2.29
Other	5,853	3.49

Source: "Major Vegetable Oils: World Supply and Distribution." [online] from https://apps.fas.usda.gov/psdonline/app/index.html#/app/downloads [Published October 2020], from U.S. Department of Agriculture.

★ 2502 ★
Oilseeds
SIC: 0116; NAICS: 311224

Leading Soybean Importers Worldwide, 2020-2021

Importers are shown in thousands of tons. Figures are as of February 2021.

	(000)	Share
China	100,000	59.90%
European Union	15,150	9.07
Mexico	6,200	3.71
Argentina	4,500	2.70
Egypt	4,150	2.49
Thailand	3,890	2.33
Japan	3,400	2.04
Turkey	3,000	1.80
Taiwan	2,900	1.74
Bangladesh	2,800	1.68
Other	20,955	12.55

Source: "Oilseeds: World Markets and Trade." [online] from https://www.fas.usda.gov/data/oilseeds-world-markets-and-trade [Published February 2021], from U.S. Department of Agriculture.

★ 2503 ★
Oilseeds
SIC: 2075; NAICS: 311224

Leading Soybean Oil Consumers Worldwide, 2020-2021

Consumption is shown in thousands of tons. Figures are as of February 2021.

	(000)	Share
China	18,691	31.37%
United States	10,569	17.74
Brazil	7,700	12.92
India	5,250	8.81
European Union	2,640	4.43
Argentina	2,004	3.36
Bangladesh	1,330	2.23
Mexico	1,300	2.18
Egypt	1,010	1.70
Other	9,091	15.26

Source: "Oilseeds: World Markets and Trade." [online] from https://www.fas.usda.gov/data/oilseeds-world-markets-and-trade [Published February 2021], from U.S. Department of Agriculture.

★ 2504 ★
Oilseeds
SIC: 2075; NAICS: 311224

Leading Soybean Oil Exporters Worldwide, 2020-2021

Exports are shown in thousands of tons. Figures are as of February 2021.

	(000)	Share
Argentina	5,750	47.44%
United States	1,247	10.29
Brazil	1,150	9.49
European Union	825	6.81

Continued on next page.

★ 2504 ★
[Continued]
Oilseeds
SIC: 2075; NAICS: 311224

Leading Soybean Oil Exporters Worldwide, 2020-2021

Exports are shown in thousands of tons. Figures are as of February 2021.

	(000)	Share
Paraguay	680	5.61%
Russia	600	4.95
Bolivia	375	3.09
Other	1,493	12.32

Source: "Oilseeds: World Markets and Trade." [online] from https://www.fas.usda.gov/data/oilseeds-world-markets-and-trade [Published February 2021], from U.S. Department of Agriculture.

★ 2505 ★
Oilseeds
SIC: 2075; NAICS: 311224

Leading Soybean Oil Importers Worldwide, 2020-2021

Imports are shown in thousands of tons. Figures are as of February 2021.

	(000)	Share
India	3,600	31.47%
China	1,100	9.62
Bangladesh	750	6.56
Algeria	650	5.68
Morocco	560	4.90
Peru	560	4.90
European Union	415	3.63
South Korea	400	3.50
Colombia	370	3.23
Egypt	300	2.62
Other	2,735	23.91

Source: "Oilseeds: World Markets and Trade." [online] from https://www.fas.usda.gov/data/oilseeds-world-markets-and-trade [Published February 2021], from U.S. Department of Agriculture.

★ 2506 ★
Oilseeds
SIC: 2075; NAICS: 311224

Leading Soybean Oil Producers Worldwide, 2020-2021

Production is shown in thousands of tons. Figures are as of February 2021.

	(000)	Share
China	17,741	29.42%
United States	11,596	19.23
Brazil	8,750	14.51
Argentina	7,720	12.80
European Union	3,202	5.31
India	1,710	2.84
Mexico	1,145	1.90
Other	8,438	13.99

Source: "Oilseeds: World Markets and Trade." [online] from https://www.fas.usda.gov/data/oilseeds-world-markets-and-trade [Published February 2021], from U.S. Department of Agriculture.

★ 2507 ★
Oilseeds
SIC: 0116; NAICS: 11111

Leading Soybean Producing Nations, 2020-2021

Production is estimated in thousands of metric tons. Figures are as of October 2020.

	(000)	Share
Brazil	133,000	36.10%
United States	116,153	31.52
Argentina	53,500	14.52
China	17,500	4.75
India	11,200	3.04
Paraguay	10,250	2.78
Canada	6,000	1.63
Other	20,866	5.66

Source: "Major Vegetable Oils: World Supply and Distribution." [online] from https://apps.fas.usda.gov/psdonline/app/index.html#/app/downloads [Published October 2020], from U.S. Department of Agriculture.

★ 2508 ★
Oilseeds
SIC: 2070; NAICS: 311224, 311225

Oilseed Crushings Worldwide, 2020-2021

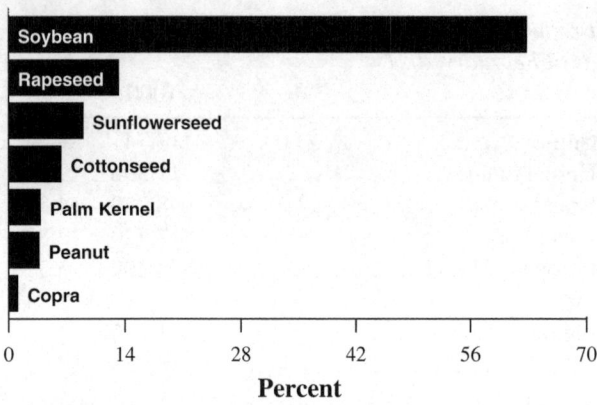

Crushings are shown in millions of tons. Figures are as of February 2021.

	(mil.)	Share
Soybean	321.98	62.77%
Rapeseed	67.99	13.25
Sunflowerseed	46.13	8.99
Cottonseed	32.49	6.33
Palm Kernel	19.75	3.85
Peanut	18.97	3.70
Copra	5.68	1.11

Source: "Oilseeds: World Markets and Trade." [online] from https://www.fas.usda.gov/data/oilseeds-world-markets-and-trade [Published February 2021], from U.S. Department of Agriculture.

★ 2510 ★
Oilseeds
SIC: 2070; NAICS: 311224, 311225

Oilseed Production Worldwide, 2020-2021

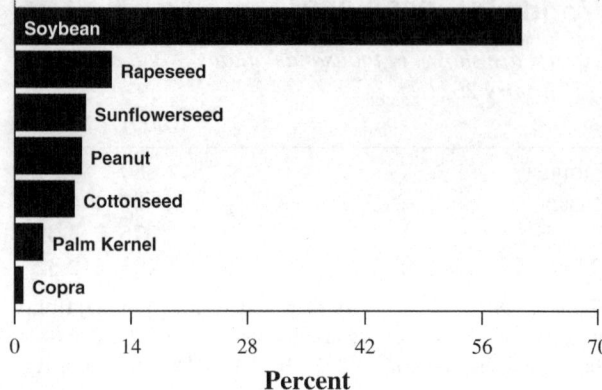

Production is shown in millions of tons. Figures are as of February 2021.

	(mil.)	Share
Soybean	361.08	60.68%
Rapeseed	68.93	11.58
Sunflowerseed	50.14	8.43
Peanut	47.32	7.95
Cottonseed	42.01	7.06
Palm Kernel	19.86	3.34
Copra	5.75	0.97

Source: "Oilseeds: World Markets and Trade." [online] from https://www.fas.usda.gov/data/oilseeds-world-markets-and-trade [Published February 2021], from U.S. Department of Agriculture.

★ 2509 ★
Oilseeds
SIC: 2070; NAICS: 311224, 311225

Oilseed Exports Worldwide, 2020-2021

Exports are shown in millions of tons. Figures are as of February 2021.

	(mil.)	Share
Soybeans	169.69	87.53%
Rapeseed	16.23	8.37
Peanut	4.16	2.15
Sunflowerseed	2.84	1.46
Cottonseed	0.63	0.32
Copra	0.24	0.12
Palm Kernel	0.08	0.04

Source: "Oilseeds: World Markets and Trade." [online] from https://www.fas.usda.gov/data/oilseeds-world-markets-and-trade [Published February 2021], from U.S. Department of Agriculture.

★ 2511 ★
Oilseeds
SIC: 2076; NAICS: 311224, 311225

Vegetable Oil Consumption Worldwide, 2020-2021

Consumption is shown in millions of tons. Figures are as of February 2021.

	(mil.)	Share
Palm	75.16	36.13%
Soybean	59.59	28.65
Rapeseed	27.60	13.27
Sunflowerseed	19.24	9.25
Palm Kernel	8.53	4.10
Peanut	6.21	2.99
Cottonseed	4.93	2.37

Continued on next page.

★ 2511 ★
[Continued]
Oilseeds
SIC: 2076; NAICS: 311224, 311225

Vegetable Oil Consumption Worldwide, 2020-2021

Consumption is shown in millions of tons. Figures are as of February 2021.

	(mil.)	Share
Coconut	3.65	1.75%
Olive	3.11	1.50

Source: "Oilseeds: World Markets and Trade." [online] from https://www.fas.usda.gov/data/oilseeds-world-markets-and-trade [Published February 2021], from U.S. Department of Agriculture.

★ 2512 ★
Oilseeds
SIC: 2076; NAICS: 311224, 311225

Vegetable Oil Exports Worldwide, 2020-2021

Exports are shown in millions of tons. Figures are as of February 2021.

	(mil.)	Share
Palm	51.34	59.20%
Soybean	12.12	13.97
Sunflowerseed	10.87	12.53
Rapeseed	5.60	6.46
Palm Kernel	3.25	3.75
Coconut	1.88	2.17
Olive	1.23	1.42
Peanut	0.35	0.40
Cottonseed	0.09	0.10

Source: "Oilseeds: World Markets and Trade." [online] from https://www.fas.usda.gov/data/oilseeds-world-markets-and-trade [Published February 2021], from U.S. Department of Agriculture.

★ 2513 ★
Oilseeds
SIC: 2076; NAICS: 311224, 311225

Vegetable Oil Imports Worldwide, 2020-2021

Imports are shown in millions of tons. Figures are as of February 2021.

	(mil.)	Share
Palm	49.93	60.13%
Soybean	11.44	13.78
Sunflowerseed	9.76	11.75%
Rapeseed	5.36	6.45
Palm Kernel	3.09	3.72
Coconut	1.87	2.25
Olive	1.15	1.38
Peanut	0.35	0.42
Cottonseed	0.09	0.11

Source: "Oilseeds: World Markets and Trade." [online] from https://www.fas.usda.gov/data/oilseeds-world-markets-and-trade [Published February 2021], from U.S. Department of Agriculture.

★ 2514 ★
Oilseeds
SIC: 2076; NAICS: 311224, 311225

Vegetable Oil Production Worldwide, 2020-2021

Production is shown in millions of tons. Figures are as of February 2021.

	(mil.)	Share
Palm	75.46	36.09%
Soybean	60.30	28.84
Rapeseed	27.83	13.31
Sunflowerseed	19.47	9.31
Palm Kernel	8.72	4.17
Peanut	6.14	2.94
Cottonseed	4.39	2.10
Coconut	3.57	1.71
Olive	3.20	1.53

Source: "Oilseeds: World Markets and Trade." [online] from https://www.fas.usda.gov/data/oilseeds-world-markets-and-trade [Published February 2021], from U.S. Department of Agriculture.

★ 2515 ★
Online Education
SIC: 8299; NAICS: 611519

Online Education Market in China, 2019

The industry grew from 70.5 billion yuan in 2012 to an estimated 313.4 billion in 2019 and 543.4 billion in 2024. Market shares are shown for the first half of 2019.

Higher education	49.6%
Vocational training	25.5
K-12 education	20.7
Online	4.2

Source: "Share of K12 in Online Education Market Rose to 20.7% in H1 2019." [online] from http://www.iresearchchina.com/content/details7_58124.html [Published October 22, 2019], from iResearch Global Group.

★ 2516 ★
Online Grocers
SIC: 5411; NAICS: 44511

Digital Grocery Shoppers by Year, 2018-2022

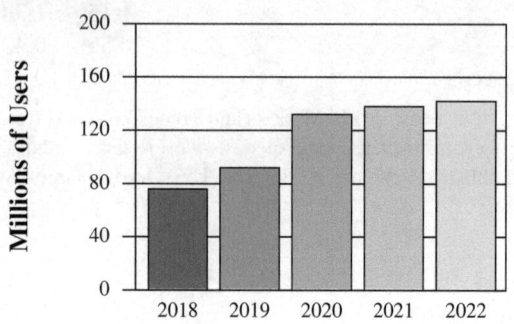

Data show millions of users. Figures include all shoppers age 14 and over. Digital buyers are defined as internet users who have made at least one grocery order via any digital channel during calendar year regardless of payment or fulfillment; includes grocery delivery and pickup.

2018	76.3
2019	92.3
2020	131.0
2021	137.4
2022	141.7

Source: "More Than Half of Internet Users Have Purchased Groceries Online." [online] from https://www.emarketer.com/content/nearly-half-of-internet-users-have-purchased-groceries-online [Published August 20, 2020], from eMarketer.

★ 2517 ★
Online Grocers
SIC: 5411; NAICS: 44511

Leading Online Grocers, 2020

Market shares are shown for June 2020.

Instacart	48.0%
Walmart Grocery	38.0
Shipt	7.0
FreshDirect	5.0
Peapod	2.0

Source: "Instacart Dominates Delivery, While Top Grocers See Little Shift in Market Share." [online] from https://secondmeasure.com/datapoints/grocery-spending-delivery-trends/ [Published August 13, 2020], from Second Measure.

★ 2518 ★
Online Grocers
SIC: 5411; NAICS: 44511

Leading Online Grocers in China, 2021

The first online grocery delivery firm in China was Yigou.com, which started operations in 2005. The industry had a variety of problems to solve, such as logistics and the development of an online payment system. Online grocery delivery has seen solid growth in recent years, especially in 2020 because of the pandemic. Operators are ranked by millions of unique users for January 2021. Market size in billions of yuan, by year: 130.83 in 2017, 204.53 in 2018, 279.62 in 2019 and 404.73 in 2020 (estimated).

Freshippo	10.47
Daojia.jd.com	9.55
MissFresh	8.41
Yonghui.com	4.10

Source: "What's Next for the Grocery Market in China After the Stay-at-Home Economy Slows?" [online] from https://daxueconsulting.com/online-grocery-market-in-china/ [Published April 23, 2021], from Daxue Consulting analysis.

★ 2519 ★
Online Grocers
SIC: 4215; NAICS: 517311

Leading Online Grocers in South Korea, 2019

South Korea boasts one of the largest and fastest-growing e-commerce markets, with roughly two-fifths of all purchases taking place online, by one estimate. Rice, pasta and noodles was the best-selling food category, followed by dairy, and then baby food. Online grocery sales grew from $7 billion in 2015 to $13 billion in 2020.

Coupang	21.9%
E-mart mall	14.8
Homeplus mall	9.9
Wemakeprice	9.4
Gmarket	8.0

Source: "South Korea: A Front Runner in E-Commerce." [online] from https://www.businessfinland.fi/49f3ab/globalassets/food/south-korea-mh-v1.pdf [Published June 12, 2020], from Statista.

★ 2520 ★
Online Grocers
SIC: 5411; NAICS: 44511

Online Grocery Sales (Pre- and Post-COVID-19), 2018-2025

Consumers turned to online shopping for groceries and other goods as a result of the pandemic. This helped push online grocery sales to claim a greater share of the overall grocery market. Grocery sales are in billions of dollars. Figures are projected for 2021-2025.

	Total Grocery	E-commerce Pre-COVID	E-commerce Post-COVID
2018	$ 993	$ 2.7	$ 0.0
2019	1,016	3.4	0.0
2020	1,039	4.3	10.2
2021	1,063	5.4	12.5
2022	1,087	6.8	14.6
2023	1,112	8.5	16.9
2024	1,138	10.7	19.1
2025	1,164	13.5	21.5

Source: "Online Grocery to More Than Double Market Share by 2025." [online] from https://www.supermarketnews.com/online-retail/online-grocery-more-double-market-share-2025 [Published September 18, 2020], from Mercatus and Incisiv.

★ 2521 ★
Online Travel
SIC: 4724; NAICS: 56151

Leading Online Travel Arrangers in China, 2019

The online travel industry started operating in 1997, helped along by the rapid growth of the internet. Outland travel also developed during this period. Market shares are shown in percent.

Trip.com	36.6%
Qunar	16.5
Fliggy	14.3
Meituan-Dianping	3.4
Tuniu Corp.	3.4
Other	25.8

Source: "Coronavirus to Increase Pressure on China's Already Vulnerable Travel Sector." [online] from https://equalocean.com/analysis/2020012813468 [Published January 28, 2020], from EqualOcean analysis.

★ 2522 ★
Online Travel
SIC: 4724; NAICS: 56151

Leading Online Travel Firms Worldwide, 2018-2019

Market shares are shown in percent.

	2018	2019
Booking Inc.	41.3%	40.7%
Expedia Group	31.9	32.6
Ctrip	12.9	13.8
Other	13.8	12.9

Source: "The State of Online Travel Agencies 2020." [online] from https://medium.com/traveltechmedia/the-state-of-online-travel-agencies-2020-f6acc899aca2 [Published July 24, 2020].

★ 2523 ★
Optical Goods
SIC: 3851; NAICS: 339115

Global Market for Eye Wear, 2019

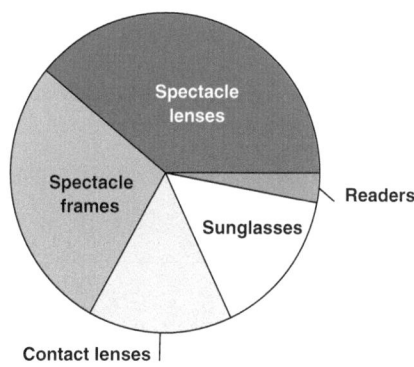

The market is estimated to be worth €100 billion.

Spectacle lenses	39.0%
Spectacle frames	28.0
Contact lenses	15.0
Sunglasses	15.0
Readers	3.0

Source: "EssilorLuxottica 2019 Universal Registration Document." [online] from http://www.essilorluxottica.com [Published April 2020], from Euromonitor and EssilorLuxottica estimates.

★ 2524 ★
Optical Goods Retailers
SIC: 5995; NAICS: 44613

Optical Goods Departments at Mass and Discount Merchandisers, 2019

Mass merchandisers and discount stores claimed about 10% of the overall vision care market. Companies are ranked by retail sales in millions of dollars. Figures include retailers' product sales, professional services, managed vision benefit revenue and e-commerce sales.

Walmart Inc.	$ 1,790.0
Costco Wholesale	1,256.7
Target/Super Target	410.0
Sam's Club	160.0
BJ's Wholesale	85.0
Shopko Optical	78.0
Fred Meyer	14.0

Source: *Vision Monday*, May 2020, p. 24, from Vision Monday's Top 50 Optical Retailers report.

★ 2525 ★
Optical Goods Retailers
SIC: 5995; NAICS: 44613

Retail Sales of Sports Eyewear, 2018-2020

Figures are based on a survey of 448 respondents at independent optical locations.

	2018	2019	2020
Sales representative	78.0%	75.0%	79.0%
Online	23.0	27.0	22.0
Optical trade shows	18.0	17.0	16.0
Other	10.0	10.0	6.0

Source: *20/20 Magazine*, April 2020, p. 21, from *2020 Sports Eyewear MarketPlus Survey*.

★ 2526 ★
Optical Transceivers
SIC: 3679; NAICS: 334419

Leading Optical Transceiver Makers Worldwide, 2019

The industry generated revenue of $17.7 billion.

II-VI (+ Finisar)	19.0%
Lumentum Holdings (+ Oclaire)	14.0
Accelink Technologies Co.	10.0
Foxconn International Technology	10.0
Innolight Technology Corp.	9.0
HG Genuine Optics Tech Co.	8.0
Sumitomo Corp.	7.0
Cisco Inc. (Acacia Communications)	6.0%
NeoPhotonics Corp.	4.0
Fujitu Optical Components	3.0
Other	10.0

Source: "The Optical Transceivers Market Will More Than Double by 2025 Driven by Heavy Investments in Data Centers." [online] from http://www.yole.fr [Accessed November 29, 2020], from Yole Développement.

★ 2527 ★
Oral Care
SIC: 2844; NAICS: 32562

Top Dental Care Categories, 2020

Categories are ranked by sales in millions of dollars at supermarkets, drug stores, mass merchandisers, military commissaries, and select club and dollar chains for the 52 weeks ended October 4, 2020.

	($ mil.)	Share
Tools	$ 917.4	33.01%
Manual toothbrushes	813.2	29.26
Power toothbrushes	591.3	21.28
Oral pain relief	222.6	8.01
Dental floss	186.6	6.71
Portable oral care	48.1	1.73

Source: *MMR*, November 16, 2020, p. 44, from IRI.

★ 2528 ★
Oral Care
SIC: 2844; NAICS: 32562

Top Dental Floss Makers in Japan, 2017

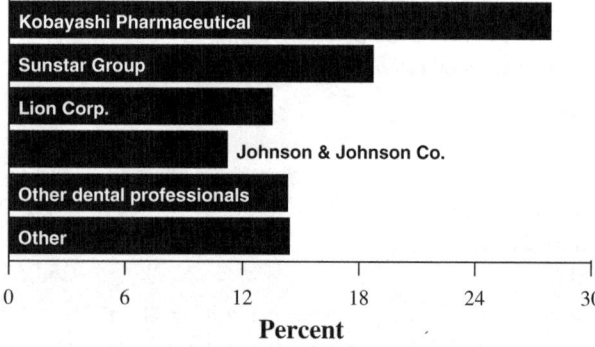

The market was valued at 12.5 billion yen in 2017 and forecast to reach 13.9 billion yen in 2019.

Kobayashi Pharmaceutical	27.9%
Sunstar Group	18.7
Lion Corp.	13.5
Johnson & Johnson Co.	11.2

Continued on next page.

★ 2528 ★
[Continued]
Oral Care
SIC: 2844; NAICS: 32562

Top Dental Floss Makers in Japan, 2017

The market was valued at 12.5 billion yen in 2017 and forecast to reach 13.9 billion yen in 2019.

Other dental professionals	14.3%
Other	14.4

Source: "Japanese Dental Floss Market Trend." [online] from http://www.news.kotra.or.kr [Published April 23, 2020], from Yano Economic Research Institute.

★ 2529 ★
Oral Care
SIC: 2844; NAICS: 32562

Top Mouthwash/Dental Rinse Brands, 2020

Market shares are shown based on drug store sales for the 52 weeks ended April 19, 2020.

Listerine	24.02%
Listerine Ultraclean	6.47
Listerine Total Care	5.22
Biotene	5.12
Therabreath	4.20
Smart Mouth	4.03
Crest Pro Health	3.11
Crest Pro Health Advanced	2.59
Crest Scope Outlast	2.55
Private label	10.20
Other	32.49

Source: *DrugStore Management*, Annual 2020-2021, p. 95, from IRI.

★ 2530 ★
Oral Care
SIC: 3991; NAICS: 339994

Top Toothbrush Makers in Japan, 2018

Companies are ranked by sales in millions of yen.

	(mil.)	Share
Lion Group	¥ 13,160	37.2%
Sunstar Group	6,370	18.0
Kao Corp.	4,250	12.0
Ebis Cosmetics	3,040	8.6
DentalPro	1,390	3.9
GlaxoSmithKline Consumer Healthcare	920	2.6
Procter & Gamble Japan	550	1.6
Omron Healthcare	530	1.5
Ginza Stefany	¥ 400	1.1%
Other	4,740	13.4

Source: "Japanese Toothbrush Market Trend." [online] from http://news.kotra.or.kr [Published October 2, 2020], from Fuji Economy.

★ 2531 ★
Oral Care
SIC: 2844; NAICS: 32562

Top Toothpaste Makers, 2020

Companies are ranked based on sales at supermarkets, drug stores, mass merchandisers, military commissaries, and select club and dollar chains for the 52 weeks ended October 4, 2020.

	($ mil.)	Share
Procter & Gamble Co.	$ 1,074.41	34.53%
Colgate-Palmolive Co.	966.42	31.06
GlaxoSmithKline PLC	677.54	21.78
Church & Dwight Co. Inc.	146.43	4.71
Tom's of Maine	74.68	2.40
Other	171.63	5.52

Source: *Household and Personal Products Industry*, November 2020, p. 52, from Market Advantage TSV and IRI Liquid Data.

★ 2532 ★
Ornamental and Architectural Metal Work
SIC: 3446; NAICS: 332323

Ornamental and Architectural Metal Work Leaders, 2017

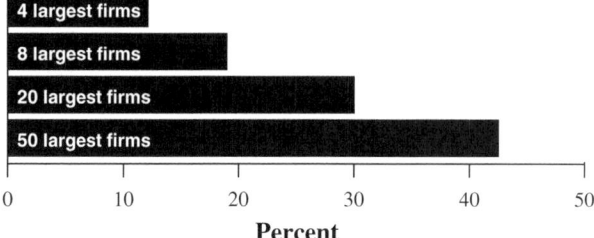

Data show the percent of industry sales held by the largest 4, 8, 20 and 50 firms in the sector. There are approximately 2,414 players operating in the industry generating employment for 35,146 people. According to Kentley Insights, the industry generated sales of $8.5 billion in 2019.

4 largest firms	12.1%
8 largest firms	19.0

Continued on next page.

★ 2532 ★
[Continued]
Ornamental and Architectural Metal Work
SIC: 3446; NAICS: 332323

Ornamental and Architectural Metal Work Leaders, 2017

Data show the percent of industry sales held by the largest 4, 8, 20 and 50 firms in the sector. There are approximately 2,414 players operating in the industry generating employment for 35,146 people. According to Kentley Insights, the industry generated sales of $8.5 billion in 2019.

20 largest firms	30.0%
50 largest firms	42.5

Source: "Economic Census." [online] from https://www.census.gov/content/census/en/data/tables/2017/econ/economic-census/naics-sector-31-33.html [Accessed January 21, 2021], from U.S. Census Bureau.

★ 2533 ★
Ornamental and Architectural Metal Work
SIC: 3446; NAICS: 332323

Ornamental and Architectural Metal Work Manufacturing, 2017

Total shipments were valued at $7.81 billion. "Wholesale sales of iron and steel bars and bar-size shapes" excludes reinforcement bars. "Metal coating, graving" excludes jewelry and silverware. "Swing and all other commercial, institutional, and industrial aluminum doors" exclude shower doors, tub enclosures, and storm doors. "Other" also includes grills, farm equipment, and other sectors. The term "nec" stands for not elsewhere classified.

	($ 000)	Share
Iron, steel, and aluminum stairs, staircases, and fire escapes and expanded metal plaster base accessories (including corner beads, screens, grounds, etc.)	$ 1,412,140	22.06%
Steel and aluminum fences, gates (other than wire), and railings and window guards	1,219,347	19.05
Open iron, steel, and aluminum flooring, grating, and studs for building construction	758,557	11.85
Metal scaffolding (suspended and access), shoring and forming for concrete work	375,358	5.86
Iron and steel warm air and air-conditioning grills, registers, and air diffusers	217,371	3.40
Metal stalls and corrals	$ 144,227	2.25%
Fabricated structural metal for bridges	21,061	0.33
Metal coating, engraving, and allied services to manufacturers	21,145	0.33
Aluminum and other sheet metal work	19,103	0.30
Steel and aluminum sheet metal awnings, canopies, carports, patios, cornices, domes, copings, soffits, fascia, and shutters	17,576	0.27
Wholesale sales of iron and steel bars and bar-size shapes	9,141	0.14
Wholesale sales of other goods, nec	8,721	0.14
Swing and all other commercial, institutional, and industrial aluminum doors	6,989	0.11
Wholesale sales of metal structural products	5,870	0.09
Other iron and steel architectural and ornamental work	2,163,477	33.80

Source: "Economic Census." [online] from https://www.census.gov/programs-surveys/economic-census/data/tables.html [Accessed December 2, 2020], from U.S. Census Bureau.

★ 2534 ★
Outdoor Kitchens
SIC/NAICS: See frontmatter for explanation.

Demand for Outdoor Kitchen Furniture and Appliances, 2019

The market is forecast to grow 6.3% annually from 2019-2024. Major factors driving growth include consumers' increasing interest in outdoor living, the rise of customizable products, and the growth of equipment with value-added features (smart lighting, etc.). Major players include Blaze Grills, Fisher & Paykel Appliances, Hestan Home and Middleby.

Cooking fixtures	50.0%
Islands, cabinets and storage	27.0
Refrigeration and cooling	14.0
Cocktail and bar centers	6.0
Sinks and faucets	2.0

Source: "Outdoor Kitchens." [online] from http://www.freedoniagroup.com [Published April 2020], from The Freedonia Group Inc.

★ 2535 ★
Outdoor Living
SIC/NAICS: See frontmatter for explanation.

Demand for Outdoor Living Products, 2020

The market grew 3.2% over 2019. Major factors driving growth: a move towards products that are easy to use and install, increased interest in low-maintenance landscapes, automation and products that emphasize water management.

Outdoor cooking and entertaining	33.0%
Lawn and yard maintenance	32.0
Gardening	24.0
Outdoor design and landscape	12.0

Source: "Outdoor Living." [online] from http://www.freedoniagroup.com [Published March 2020], from The Freedonia Group Inc.

★ 2536 ★
Over-the-Top Media
SIC: 4841; NAICS: 51521

How Consumers View OTT Streaming Video Worldwide, 2020

Data show share of time spent viewing OTT streaming video worldwide by device in the third quarter. Shares for the "connected device" sector: Roku 48%, Amazon Fire 28%, Apple TV 8.5%, Chromecast 6.8%, Android TV, and other 3.9%.

Connected TV devices	50.0%
Smart TVs	15.0
Gaming consoles	10.0
Laptops/desktops	10.0
Mobile phones	10.0
Tablets	5.0

Source: "The Majority of Time Spend Viewing OTT Streaming Video Occurs on CTV Device." [online] from https://www.emarketer.com/content/majority-of-time-spent-viewing-ott-streaming-video-occurs-on-ctv-devices [Published December 29, 2020], from Conviva, *State of Streaming Q3 2020*.

★ 2537 ★
Over-the-Top Media
SIC: 4841; NAICS: 51521

Leading Streaming Services by Advertising Spending, 2020

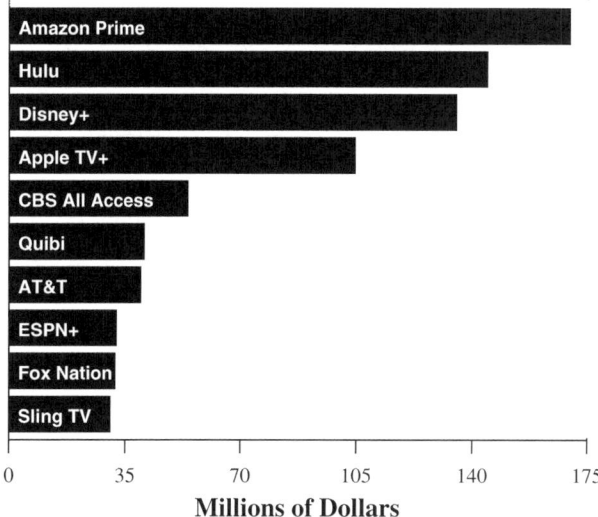

Millions of Dollars

Figures show estimated media value of ads placed by each streaming service in millions of dollars for the first six months of 2020.

Amazon Prime	$ 169.8
Hulu	144.6
Disney+	135.3
Apple TV+	104.7
CBS All Access	54.1
Quibi	40.8
AT&T	39.8
ESPN+	32.4
Fox Nation	32.0
Sling TV	30.5

Source: "Streaming Services Spend Heavily on Marketing amid Pandemic." [online] from https://www.emarketer.com/content/top-10-us-ecommerce-companies-2021-plus-6-key-takeaways-our-latest-forecast [Published October 21, 2020], from iSpot.tv.

★ 2538 ★
Over-the-Top Media
SIC: 4841; NAICS: 51521

Leading SVOD Firms, 2019 and 2025

Companies are ranked by thousands of SVOD subscriptions. SVOD stands for Subscription Video on Demand. HBO Now was discontinued on December 17, 2020 and replaced with HBO Max.

	2019	2025	Share
Netflix Inc.	61,043	71,022	22.41%
Amazon Prime Video	53,300	59,800	18.87
Disney+	22,800	49,800	15.72
Hulu	27,200	49,500	15.62
HBO Now	10,000	22,080	6.97
CBS All Access	6,200	18,400	5.81
Peacock	0	11,000	3.47
Other	22,147	35,266	11.13

Source: "U.S. to Reach 317 Million SVOD Subscriptions." [online] from http://www.digitaltvresearch.com/products [Press release September 2020], from Digital TV Research.

★ 2539 ★
Over-the-Top Media
SIC: 4841; NAICS: 51521

Leading SVOD Firms in Africa, 2020 and 2025

Operators are ranked by thousands of subscribers. Shares are estimated for 2025.

	2020 (000)	2025 (000)	Share
Netflix Inc.	1,991	5,698	43.96%
Disney+	0	2,707	20.89
Showmax	688	1,647	12.71
iRoko	331	586	4.52
Amazon Prime	100	456	3.52
Apple TV+	9	114	0.88
Other	739	1,753	13.53

Source: "African SVOD Subs to More than Quadruple." [online] from http://www.digitaltvresearch.com/products [Press release October 2020], from Digital TV Research.

★ 2540 ★
Over-the-Top Media
SIC: 4841; NAICS: 51521

Leading SVOD Firms in China, 2020-2026

Market shares are shown in percent.

	2020	2022	2024	2026
Tencent Video	38.0%	38.0%	38.0%	38.0%
IQIYI	31.0	27.0	25.0	25.0
Touku Premium	15.0	12.0	11.0	11.0
Mango TV	11.0	17.0	18.0	19.0
Other	5.0	6.0	8.0	7.0

Source: "Mango TV to Become China's Third Largest SVOD Service in 2021." [online] from https://www.ampereanalysis.com/insight/mango-tv-to-become-chinas-third-largest-svod-service-in-2021 [Published April 27, 2021], from Ampere Analysis.

★ 2541 ★
Over-the-Top Media
SIC: 4841; NAICS: 51521

Leading SVOD Firms in Denmark, 2020

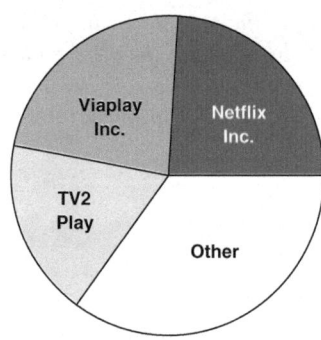

Market shares are shown based on subscribers. Total subscribers reached 3.82 million.

Netflix Inc.	24.0%
Viaplay Inc.	23.0
TV2 Play	18.0
Other	35.0

Source: "Trends in the VOD Market in EU-28." [online] from https://rm.coe.int/trends-in-the-vod-market-in-eu28-final-version/1680a1511a [Published January 2021], from Ampere Analysis.

★ 2542 ★
Over-the-Top Media
SIC: 4841; NAICS: 51521

Leading SVOD Firms in Eastern Europe, 2020 and 2025

Operators are ranked by thousands of subscribers. Shares are estimated for 2025.

	2020 (000)	2025 (000)	Share
Netflix Inc.	4,315	7,739	29.29%
Disney+	0	4,024	15.23
HBO	220	724	2.74
Amazon Prime	216	643	2.43
Apple TV+	39	403	1.53
Other	7,614	12,887	48.78

Source: "Eastern Europe to Add 16 Million SVOD Subs." [online] from http://www.digitaltvresearch.com/products [Press release September 2020], from Digital TV Research.

★ 2543 ★
Over-the-Top Media
SIC: 4841; NAICS: 51521

Leading SVOD Firms in France, 2020

Market shares are shown based on subscribers. Total subscribers reached 15.45 million.

Netflix Inc.	54.0%
Amazon Prime	26.0
Apple TV+	12.0
Other	8.0

Source: "Trends in the VOD Market in EU-28." [online] from https://rm.coe.int/trends-in-the-vod-market-in-eu28-final-version/1680a1511a [Published January 2021], from Ampere Analysis.

★ 2544 ★
Over-the-Top Media
SIC: 4841; NAICS: 51521

Leading SVOD Firms in India, 2019 and 2024

Companies are ranked by estimated millions of subscribers.

	2019 (mil.)	2024 (mil.)	Share
Hotstar Premium	15.00	25.95	28.11%
Eros Now	6.27	13.64	14.77
Amazon Prime Video	6.75	11.15	12.08
Zee5	4.64	8.05	8.72
ALT Balaji	3.70	6.50	7.04%
Other	9.79	27.03	29.28

Source: *Financial Express*, December 9, 2019, p. NA, from Ovum.

★ 2545 ★
Over-the-Top Media
SIC: 4841; NAICS: 51521

Leading SVOD Firms in Ireland, 2020

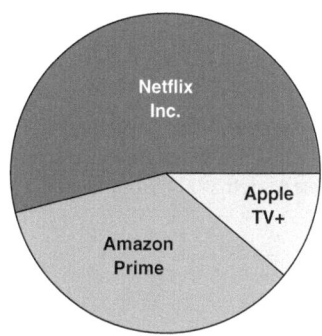

Market shares are shown based on subscribers. Total subscribers reached 978,000.

Netflix Inc.	54.0%
Amazon Prime	35.0
Apple TV+	11.0

Source: "Trends in the VOD Market in EU-28." [online] from https://rm.coe.int/trends-in-the-vod-market-in-eu28-final-version/1680a1511a [Published January 2021], from Ampere Analysis.

★ 2546 ★
Over-the-Top Media
SIC: 4841; NAICS: 51521

Leading SVOD Firms in Italy, 2020

Market shares are shown based on subscribers. Total subscribers reached 13.13 million.

Netflix Inc.	28.0%
Amazon Prime	18.0
TIM Vision	16.0
Other	38.0

Source: "Trends in the VOD Market in EU-28." [online] from https://rm.coe.int/trends-in-the-vod-market-in-eu28-final-version/1680a1511a [Published January 2021], from Ampere Analysis.

★ 2547 ★
Over-the-Top Media
SIC: 4841; NAICS: 51521

Leading SVOD Firms in Latin America, 2020-2021 and 2026

Companies are ranked by thousands of SVOD subscriptions. SVOD stands for Subscription Video on Demand.

	2020	2021	2026	Share
Netflix Inc.	37,530	41,022	49,070	42.42%
Disney+	2,197	12,216	33,277	28.77
Amazon Prime Video	5,371	7,230	14,442	12.49
HBO Max	843	1,389	5,051	4.37
Claro Video	2,678	2,974	3,431	2.97
Apple TV+	373	815	2,192	1.89
Other	3,787	4,956	8,211	7.10

Source: "Latin America to Add 63 Million SVOD Subscriptions." [online] from http://www.digitaltvresearch.com/products [Press release March 2021], from Digital TV Research.

★ 2548 ★
Over-the-Top Media
SIC: 4841; NAICS: 51521

Leading SVOD Firms in Spain, 2020

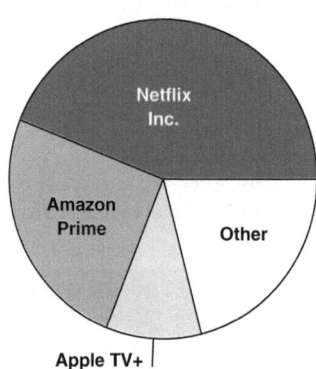

Market shares are shown based on subscribers. Total subscribers reached 10.82 million.

Netflix Inc.	44.0%
Amazon Prime	25.0
Apple TV+	10.0
Other	21.0

Source: "Trends in the VOD Market in EU-28." [online] from https://rm.coe.int/trends-in-the-vod-market-in-eu28-final-version/1680a1511a [Published January 2021], from Ampere Analysis.

★ 2549 ★
Over-the-Top Media
SIC: 4841; NAICS: 51521

Leading SVOD Firms in the EU-28, 2020

Companies are ranked by millions of subscribers.

	(mil.)	Share
Netflix Inc.	54.4	39.0%
Amazon Prime	40.3	29.0
Apple TV+	12.2	9.0
Disney+	10.0	7.0
DAZN	4.0	3.0
Viaplay Inc.	2.2	2.0
TIM Vision	2.1	1.0
Sky Now TV	1.9	1.0
HBO	1.6	1.0
IPLA	1.4	1.0
Other	10.6	7.0

Source: "Trends in the VOD Market in EU-28." [online] from https://rm.coe.int/trends-in-the-vod-market-in-eu28-final-version/1680a1511a [Published January 2021], from Ampere Analysis.

★ 2550 ★
Over-the-Top Media
SIC: 4841; NAICS: 51521

Leading SVOD Firms in the Middle East and North Africa, 2020 and 2025

Operators are ranked by thousands of subscribers. Shares are estimated for 2025.

	2020 (000)	2025 (000)	Share
Netflix Inc.	5,512	9,805	36.11%
Disney+	0	2,500	9.21
StarzPlay	1,293	2,393	8.81
OSN	348	2,283	8.41
Shahid VIP	574	1,049	3.86
Amazon Prime	299	983	3.62
Apple TV+	28	271	1.00
Other	5,366	7,871	28.99

Source: "MENA SVOD Subs to Grow by 148%." [online] from http://www.digitaltvresearch.com/products [Press release September 2020], from Digital TV Research.

★ 2551 ★
Over-the-Top Media
SIC: 4841; NAICS: 51521

Leading SVOD Firms in the United Kingdom, 2020

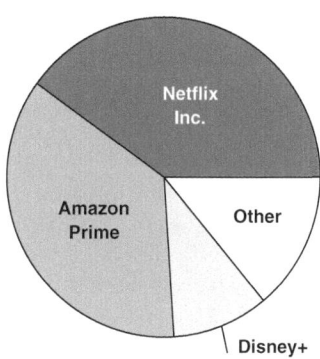

Market shares are shown based on subscribers. Total subscribers reached 31.79 million.

Netflix Inc.	40.0%
Amazon Prime	36.0
Disney+	10.0
Other	14.0

Source: "Trends in the VOD Market in EU-28." [online] from https://rm.coe.int/trends-in-the-vod-market-in-eu28-final-version/1680a1511a [Published January 2021], from Ampere Analysis.

★ 2552 ★
Over-the-Top Media
SIC: 4841; NAICS: 51521

Leading SVOD Firms in Western Europe, 2020 and 2025

Operators are ranked by thousands of subscribers. Shares are estimated for 2025.

	2020 (000)	2025 (000)	Share
Netflix Inc.	52,404	68,494	35.90%
Disney+	16,958	39,425	20.66
Amazon Prime	26,666	35,894	18.81
Apple TV+	524	3,970	2.08
HBO Max	1,971	2,772	1.45
Other	26,634	40,261	21.10

Source: "Western Europe to Add 101 Million SVOD Subs." [online] from http://www.digitaltvresearch.com/products [Press release September 2020], from Digital TV Research.

★ 2553 ★
Over-the-Top Media
SIC: 4841; NAICS: 51521

Leading SVOD Firms Worldwide, 2020 and 2025

Operators are ranked by thousands of subscribers. Shares are estimated for the group.

	2020 (000)	2025 (000)	Share
Netflix Inc.	201,183	274,144	40.46%
Disney+	82,336	194,382	28.69
Amazon Prime	116,861	167,071	24.66
HBO Max	16,188	28,519	4.21
Apple TV+	2,245	13,427	1.98

Source: "Disney+ to Add 112 Million Subscribers." [online] from http://www.digitaltvresearch.com/products [Press release November 2020], from Digital TV Research.

★ 2554 ★
Over-the-Top Media
SIC: 4841; NAICS: 51521

Leading SVOD Markets Worldwide, 2020 and 2025

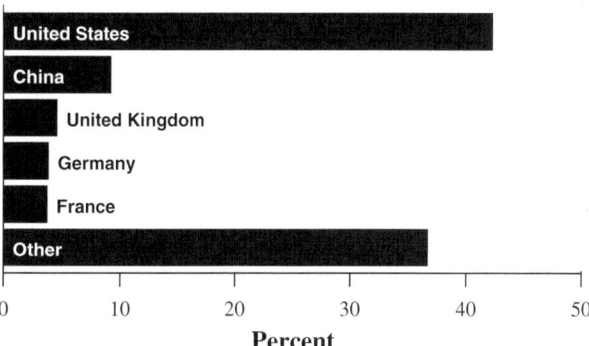

Markets are ranked by thousands of subscribers. Shares are estimated for 2025.

	2020 (000)	2025 (000)	Share
United States	29,580	42,061	42.25%
China	7,214	9,127	9.17
United Kingdom	2,919	4,476	4.50
Germany	2,186	3,755	3.77
France	1,938	3,645	3.66
Other	18,840	36,497	36.66

Source: "SVOD to Generate $100 Billion." [online] from http://www.digitaltvresearch.com/products [Press release September 2020], from Digital TV Research.

★ 2555 ★
Over-the-Top Media
SIC: 4841; NAICS: 51521

Over-the-Top Media Spending in North America, 2020-2021 and 2026

Data show OTT TV episode and movie revenues in millions of dollars. Revenues are expected to reach $94 billion in 2026, up from $49 billion in 2020. SVOD stands for Subscription Video on Demand. DTO stands for Direct-to-Own. AVOD stands for Advertising Video on Demand.

	2020	2021	2026	Share
SVOD	$32,522	$40,159	$54,391	58.05%
AVOD	10,695	13,636	32,613	34.81
DTO	3,077	3,247	3,916	4.18
Rental	2,486	2,562	2,771	2.96

Source: "North American OTT TV Revenues to Double." [online] from http://www.digitaltvresearch.com/products [Press release September 2020], from Digital TV Research.

★ 2556 ★
Over-the-Top Media
SIC: 4841; NAICS: 51521

Over-the-Top Media Subscribers by Year, 2017-2024

Data show millions of subscribers. Figures are estimated from 2020-2024.

Year	Subscribers
2017	127
2018	158
2019	207
2020	260
2021	302
2022	340
2023	372
2024	405

Source: "Entertainment Industry Market Update." [online] from https://hl.com/about-us/insights/insights-article/?id=17179871911 [Published Summer 2020], from Wall Street Research and Houlihan Lokey.

P-Q

★ 2557 ★
Packaging
SIC: 3089; NAICS: 326199

Demand for Bubble Packaging, 2019

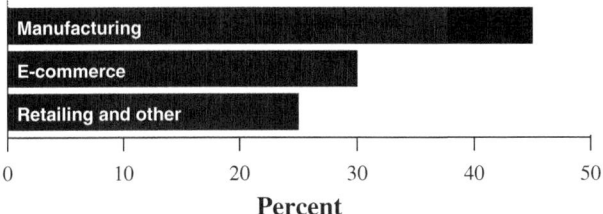

The market is forecast to see a CAGR of 4.0% from 2019-2024. Major factors driving growth include the continued rise of e-commerce and a push for sustainable products. COVID-19 is also shaping demand, as the pandemic has increased the number of packages being shipped. Major players include Polyair Inter Pack, Pregis, Sealed Air, Specialized Packaging Group and Storopack.

Manufacturing	45.0%
E-commerce	30.0
Retailing and other	25.0

Source: "Bubble Packaging." [online] from http://www.freedoniagroup.com [Published July 2020], from The Freedonia Group Inc.

★ 2558 ★
Packaging
SIC: 2673; NAICS: 326111

Demand for Candy and Snack Food Pouches, 2019

Pouches offer a number of attractive characteristics. They are resealable, and vacuum sealing helps ensure the product's freshness. Pouches also offer excellent graphics capabilities. Revenue is forecast to see a CAGR of 2.7% from 2019-2024. Major companies include Amcor, Printpack, ProAmpac, Sonoco Products and TC Transcontinental.

Savory snacks	37.0%
Candy and confectionery	27.0
Bakery snacks	16.0%
Other	20.0

Source: "Candy & Snack Food Pouches." [online] from http://www.freedoniagroup.com [Published November 2020], from The Freedonia Group Inc.

★ 2559 ★
Packaging
SIC: 2673; NAICS: 326111

Demand for Consumer Product Pouches, 2019

Pouches have been stealing market share from traditional rigid packaging. There a number of reasons for their popularity, such as they are lightweight and can be shipped flat. Revenue is forecast to see a CAGR of 6.7% from 2019-2024. Major companies include Berry Global, Mondi Group, Printpack, and TC Transcontinental.

Lawn and garden consumables	34.0%
Soaps and cleaning products	22.0
Wipes	20.0
Other	24.0

Source: "Consumer Product Pouches." [online] from http://www.freedoniagroup.com [Published November 2020], from The Freedonia Group Inc.

★ 2560 ★
Packaging
SIC/NAICS: See frontmatter for explanation.

Demand for E-Commerce Packaging Materials Worldwide, 2019

Market shares are estimated. Consumers turned to online shopping during the pandemic, a move that will help drive e-commerce sales to reach $5.4 trillion in 2022. Many analysts have called attention to the packaging materials used in shipping, and there has been a major push to use packaging that is friendlier to the environment.

Corrugated	80.0%
Secondary protective	15.0

Continued on next page.

★ 2560 ★
[Continued]
Packaging
SIC/NAICS: See frontmatter for explanation.

Demand for E-Commerce Packaging Materials Worldwide, 2019

Market shares are estimated. Consumers turned to online shopping during the pandemic, a move that will help drive e-commerce sales to reach $5.4 trillion in 2022. Many analysts have called attention to the packaging materials used in shipping, and there has been a major push to use packaging that is friendlier to the environment.

Flexibles	4.0%
Mailers	1.0

Source: "Stora Enso Investor Kit." [online] from https://www.storaenso.com/en/investors/reports-and-presentations [Published October 2020], from Sustainable Ecommerce Packaging.

★ 2561 ★
Packaging
SIC/NAICS: See frontmatter for explanation.

Demand for Egg Cartons, 2019

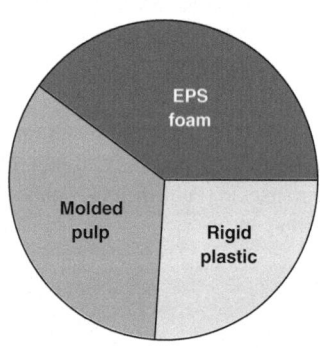

The market is forecast to see a CAGR of 3.6% from 2019-2024. Sales reached $544 million in 2019. The industry is seeing a major push for eco-friendly packaging, which has boosted demand for molded pulp cartons. Major players include CKF, Dolco Packaging (TekniPlex), Hartmann A/S, Highland Packaging Solutions (Sonoco Products), Huhtamäki and Pactiv (Reynolds Group).

EPS foam	40.0%
Molded pulp	34.0
Rigid plastic	26.0

Source: "Egg Cartons." [online] from http://www.freedoniagroup.com [Published July 2020], from The Freedonia Group Inc.

★ 2562 ★
Packaging
SIC/NAICS: See frontmatter for explanation.

Demand for Frozen Food Packaging, 2019

Revenue is forecast to see a CAGR of 3.5% from 2019-2024. As a result of the pandemic, consumers turned to frozen food as an easy meal. Some shoppers also stockpiled frozen items. Major companies include Amcor-Group, Berry Global, Georgia-Pacific L.L.C., Huhtamäki Oyj, International Paper, Pactiv Evergreen and WestRock.

Specialty foods	34.0%
Meat, poultry and seafood	30.0
Baked goods	12.0
Fruit, vegetables and juices	11.0
Ice cream and frozen desserts	11.0

Source: "Frozen Food Packaging." [online] from http://www.freedoniagroup.com [Published February 2021], from The Freedonia Group Inc.

★ 2563 ★
Packaging
SIC/NAICS: See frontmatter for explanation.

Demand for Frozen Food Tubs, Cups and Bowls Packaging, 2019

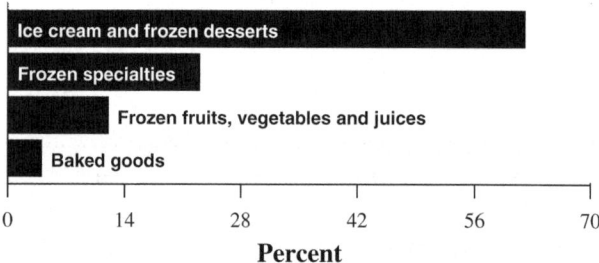

Revenue is forecast to see a CAGR of 3.8% from 2019-2024. Trends driving this growth include increasing demand for single-serve products, as well as dessert cups and bowls that help with portion control. Major companies include Berry Global, Huhtamäki Oyj, Pactiv Evergreen, Sabert and Sonoco Products.

Ice cream and frozen desserts	62.0%
Frozen specialties	23.0
Frozen fruits, vegetables and juices	12.0
Baked goods	4.0

Source: "Frozen Food Tubs, Cups & Bowls." [online] from http://www.freedoniagroup.com [Published February 2021], from The Freedonia Group Inc.

★ 2564 ★
Packaging
SIC/NAICS: See frontmatter for explanation.

Demand for Frozen Specialty Food Packaging, 2019

Revenue is forecast to see a CAGR of 4.0% from 2019-2024. Bowls are expected to see the fastest growth through this period due to the popularity of healthy meal bowls, but folding cartons and trays are to retain market leads. Major companies include Amcor, Berry Global, Georgia-Pacific L.L.C., Graphic Packaging, International Paper, Pactiv Evergreen, and WestRock.

Frozen dinners	32.0%
Frozen pizza	29.0
Frozen breakfast foods	14.0
Frozen entrées and side dishes	14.0
Other	11.0

Source: "Frozen Specialty Food Packaging." [online] from http://www.freedoniagroup.com [Published February 2021], from The Freedonia Group Inc.

★ 2565 ★
Packaging
SIC/NAICS: See frontmatter for explanation.

Demand for Ice Cream and Frozen Dessert Packaging, 2019

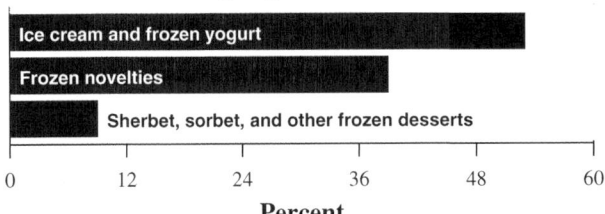

Revenue is forecast to see a CAGR of 3.1% from 2019-2024. Ice cream and frozen desserts are seen as an affordable luxury, and the industry has benefited from consumers in lockdown from COVID-19 looking for treats. Single serving portions have also helped drive sales. Major companies include Berry Global, Huhtamäki Oyj, Sonoco Products and WestRock.

Ice cream and frozen yogurt	53.0%
Frozen novelties	39.0
Sherbet, sorbet, and other frozen desserts	9.0

Source: "Ice Cream & Frozen Dessert Packaging." [online] from http://www.freedoniagroup.com [Published February 2021], from The Freedonia Group Inc.

★ 2566 ★
Packaging
SIC: 3089; NAICS: 326199

Demand for Insulated Containers and Shippers, 2019

The industry is forecast to see a CAGR of 3.5% from 2019-2024. Major factors driving this growth include demand from the drug and medical supplies sectors, as well as the increasing sales in the e-commerce market for meal kits and other perishables.

Manufacturing	80.0%
Retailing and other	11.0
E-commerce	9.0

Source: "Insulated Packaging Containers & Shippers." [online] from http://www.freedoniagroup.com [Published July 2020], from The Freedonia Group Inc.

★ 2567 ★
Packaging
SIC/NAICS: See frontmatter for explanation.

Demand for Packaging Worldwide, 2019

Distribution is shown based on an estimated market value of €850 billion.

Board-based industrial packaging	25.0%
Board-based consumer packaging	10.0
Other consumer packaging	40.0
Other industrial packaging	25.0

Source: "Meeting Consumer Demand for Eco-Friendly and Circular Solutions." [online] from https://www.storaenso.com/en/investors/reports-and-presentations [Published November 2020], from Stora Enso.

★ 2568 ★
Packaging
SIC/NAICS: See frontmatter for explanation.

Demand for Paper Packaging in North America, 2019

Demand is shown in millions of dollars.

	($ mil.)	Share
Containerboard	$ 30.6	64.83%
Boxboard	12.1	25.64
Wrapping	2.8	5.93
Industrial	1.7	3.60

Source: *Paper360°*, January/February 2021, p. 15, from Fastmarkets and Global Containerboard Outlook.

★ 2569 ★
Packaging
SIC: 2673; NAICS: 326111
Demand for Pouches, 2019

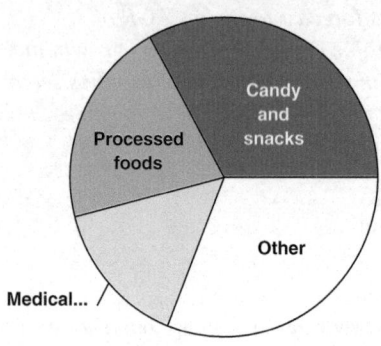

The industry is expected to see a CAGR of 3.7% from 2019-2024. Major forces driving this growth include new opportunities in the beverages, healthy snacks, and non-food markets, as well as the push to make the industry more sustainable.

Candy and snacks	33.0%
Processed foods	21.0
Medical and pharmaceutical	15.0
Other	31.0

Source: "Pouches." [online] from http://www.freedoniagroup.com [Published November 2020], from The Freedonia Group Inc.

★ 2570 ★
Packaging
SIC: 2673; NAICS: 326111
Demand for Processed Food Pouches, 2019

Revenue is forecast to see a CAGR of 4.0% from 2019-2024. Major companies include AmcorGroup, Berry Global, Printpack, ProAmpac, Sealed Air and TC Transcontinental.

Dry foods	60.0%
Frozen foods	19.0
Sauces and condiments	11.0
Other	10.0

Source: "Processed Food Pouches." [online] from http://www.freedoniagroup.com [Published November 2020], from The Freedonia Group Inc.

★ 2571 ★
Packaging
SIC: 2677; NAICS: 32223
Demand for Protective Mailers, 2019

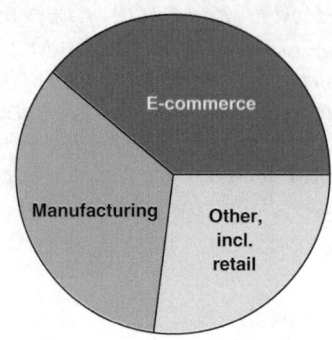

The market is forecast to see a CAGR of 5.0% from 2019-2024. The continued expansion of e-commerce will drive growth in this market. The push for sustainability will also be a concern. COVID-19 is also shaping demand, as the pandemic has increased the number of packages being shipped.

E-commerce	39.0%
Manufacturing	34.0
Other, incl. retail	27.0

Source: "Protective Mailers." [online] from http://www.freedoniagroup.com [Published July 2020], from The Freedonia Group Inc.

★ 2572 ★
Packaging
SIC/NAICS: See frontmatter for explanation.
Demand for Single-Use Foodservice Products, 2018

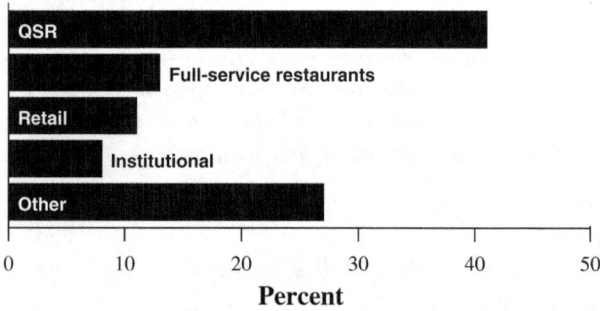

Single-use foodservice products include plastic to-go containers, alternative material clamshells, and paper carryout bags. The industry saw a CAGR of 3.4%.

QSR	41.0%
Full-service restaurants	13.0

Continued on next page.

★ 2572 ★
[Continued]
Packaging
SIC/NAICS: See frontmatter for explanation.
Demand for Single-Use Foodservice Products, 2018

Single-use foodservice products include plastic to-go containers, alternative material clamshells, and paper carryout bags. The industry saw a CAGR of 3.4%.

Retail	11.0%
Institutional	8.0
Other	27.0

Source: "Foodservice Single-Use Products." [online] from http://www.freedoniagroup.com [Published February 2020], from The Freedonia Group Inc.

★ 2573 ★
Packaging
SIC: 3089; NAICS: 326199
Demand for Vacuum Skin Packaging, 2019

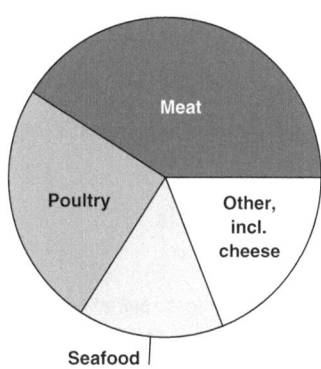

The market is forecast to see a CAGR of 7.9% from 2019-2024. Major players include Amcor, MULTIVAC, Plastopil, Sealed Air and Winpak.

Meat	41.0%
Poultry	25.0
Seafood	15.0
Other, incl. cheese	19.0

Source: "Vacuum Skin Packaging." [online] from http://www.freedoniagroup.com [Published July 2020], from The Freedonia Group Inc.

★ 2574 ★
Packaging
SIC/NAICS: See frontmatter for explanation.
Leading Aseptic Packaging Firms Worldwide, 2019

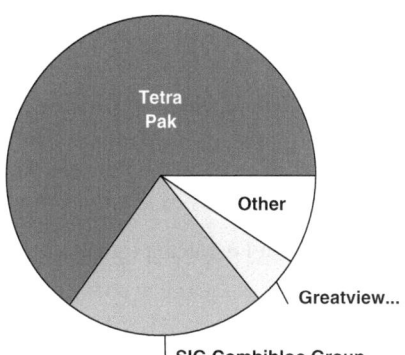

Aseptic packaging is a specialized manufacturing process in which food, pharmaceutical or other contents are sterilized separately from packaging. By one estimate, the market is forecast to grow from $38.16 billion in 2019 to $81.22 billion in 2027.

Tetra Pak	65.0%
SIG Combibloc Group	21.0
Greatview Aseptic Packaging Co.	5.0
Other	9.0

Source: "Greatview Aseptic: 10% Dividend for A Growing Company in an Industry With High Barriers to Entry." [online] from https://seekingalpha.com/article/4353191-greatview-aseptic-10-dividend-for-growing-company-in-industry-high-barriers-to-entry [Published June 10, 2020], from Euromonitor and SIG Combibloc Group.

★ 2575 ★
Packaging
SIC: 7389; NAICS: 56191
Packaging and Labeling Revenue, 2019

According to the source, operators primarily package "client-owned materials on a contract or outsource basis and provide labeling and imprinting package services. The industry excludes activity related to the manufacture of packaging or labeling products." The industry generated revenue of $10.3 billion. The source notes that there are no major players in this industry, but cites Sonoco Products as leading with a 2.9% share.

Food and beverages	38.0%
Cosmetics and personal care products	15.3

Continued on next page.

★ 2575 ★
[Continued]
Packaging
SIC: 7389; NAICS: 56191
Packaging and Labeling Revenue, 2019

According to the source, operators primarily package "client-owned materials on a contract or outsource basis and provide labeling and imprinting package services. The industry excludes activity related to the manufacture of packaging or labeling products." The industry generated revenue of $10.3 billion. The source notes that there are no major players in this industry, but cites Sonoco Products as leading with a 2.9% share.

Pharmaceuticals and medical products	8.6%
Hardware	2.9
Electronic goods	2.3
Apparel and textiles	1.3
Other	31.6

Source: "Packaging & Labeling in the U.S." [online] from http://www.ibisworld.com [Published May 2019], from IBISWorld.

★ 2576 ★
Packaging
SIC: 7389; NAICS: 56191
Packaging and Labeling Service Leaders, 2017

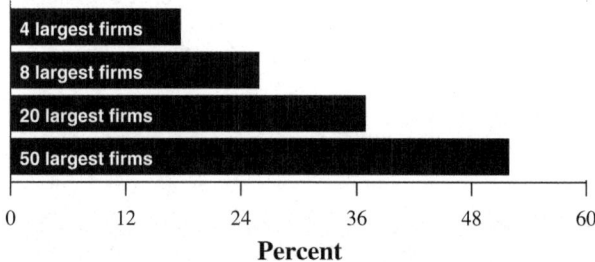

Data show the percent of industry sales held by the largest 4, 8, 20 and 50 firms in the sector. There are approximately 1,647 players operating in the industry generating employment for 43,714 people. According to Kentley Insights, the industry generated saless of $9.1 billion in 2019.

4 largest firms	17.7%
8 largest firms	25.9
20 largest firms	36.9
50 largest firms	51.9

Source: "Economic Census." [online] from https://www.census.gov/content/census/en/data/tables/2017/econ/economic-census/naics-sector-31-33.html [Accessed January 21, 2021], from U.S. Census Bureau.

★ 2577 ★
Packaging
SIC/NAICS: See frontmatter for explanation.
Pharmaceutical Packaging Market, 2019

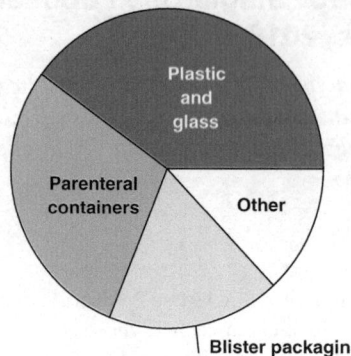

Demand is shown by primary container. The market is forecast to grow 3.9% annually from 2019 to reach $5.8 billion in 2024. Applications for solid oral and liquid medicines, nutritional preparations and dietary supplements will drive this growth. The introduction of new biologicals and biosimilars will cause parenteral containers to have the fastest growth.

Plastic and glass bottles	40.0%
Parenteral containers	29.0
Blister packaging	18.0
Other	13.0

Source: *Packaging Strategies*, September 2020, p. 8, from The Freedonia Group Inc.

★ 2578 ★
Packaging
SIC/NAICS: See frontmatter for explanation.
Reusable Transport Packaging Market Worldwide, 2017

The source defines the transport or transit packaging industry as the "movement of raw materials, commodities, or finished goods from point of production or processing to point of use in a manufacturing or commercial setting involving a business-to-business item transfer or a business-to-consumer item delivery." The industry was valued at $17.7 billion.

	($ bil.)	Share
Pallets	$ 62.3	62.24%
Rigid containers, crates, totes, trays and bins	17.7	17.68
Plastic-corrugated boxes, panels and sleeves	6.7	6.69
Reusable plastic containers	5.3	5.29

Continued on next page.

★ 2578 ★
[Continued]
Packaging
SIC/NAICS: See frontmatter for explanation.

Reusable Transport Packaging Market Worldwide, 2017

The source defines the transport or transit packaging industry as the "movement of raw materials, commodities, or finished goods from point of production or processing to point of use in a manufacturing or commercial setting involving a business-to-business item transfer or a business-to-consumer item delivery." The industry was valued at $17.7 billion.

	($ bil.)	Share
Tanks, drums and barrels	$ 3.8	3.80%
Intermediate bulk containers	3.4	3.40
Dunnage and cargo protection	0.5	0.50
Racks	0.3	0.30
Carts and dollies	0.1	0.10

Source: "Reusable Transport Packaging State of the Industry Report 2020." [online] from http://www.reusables.org [Accessed January 25, 2021], from Allied Market Research.

★ 2579 ★
Packaging Machinery
SIC: 3565; NAICS: 333993

Global Demand for Packaging Machinery, 2018

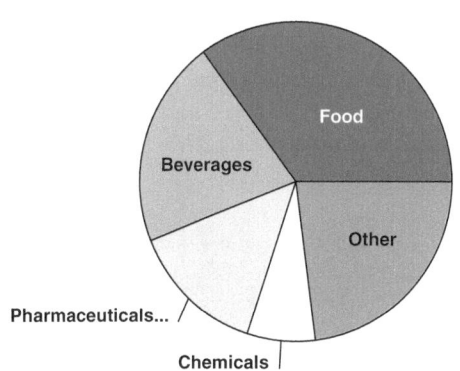

The market is forecast to see annual growth of 4.5% from 2019-2023. Rising manufacturing activity, increasing mechanization in developing countries and high-value sales of state-of-the-art equipment will drive this growth.

Food	35.0%
Beverages	21.0
Pharmaceuticals/personal care	14.0%
Chemicals	7.0
Other	23.0

Source: *Packaging Strategies*, September 2020, p. 8, from The Freedonia Group Inc.

★ 2580 ★
Packaging Machinery
SIC: 3565; NAICS: 333993

Packaging Machinery Manufacturing Leaders, 2017

Data show the percent of industry sales held by the largest 4, 8, 20 and 50 firms in the sector. There are approximately 519 players operating in the industry generating employment for 20,248 people. According to Kentley Insights, the industry generated sales of $7.3 billion in 2019.

4 largest firms	27.9%
8 largest firms	41.5
20 largest firms	59.4
50 largest firms	74.6

Source: "Economic Census." [online] from https://www.census.gov/content/census/en/data/tables/2017/econ/economic-census/naics-sector-31-33.html [Accessed January 21, 2021], from U.S. Census Bureau.

★ 2581 ★
Paint, Varnish and Supplies Wholesalers
SIC: 5198; NAICS: 42495

Paint, Varnish, and Supplies Merchant Wholesale Leaders, 2017

Data show the percent of industry sales held by the largest 4, 8, 20 and 50 firms in the sector. There are approximately 1,913 players operating in the industry generating employment for 21,226 people.

4 largest firms	48.7%
8 largest firms	64.9
20 largest firms	75.3
50 largest firms	83.7

Source: "Economic Census." [online] from https://www.census.gov/content/census/en/data/tables/2017/econ/economic-census/naics-sector-31-33.html [Accessed January 21, 2021], from U.S. Census Bureau.

★ 2582 ★
Paint and Coatings
SIC: 2851; NAICS: 32551

Architectural Paint Industry, 2019

Distribution is shown based on 831 million gallons.

DIY	37.0%
Residential repaint (pro)	30.0
Non-residential repaint (pro)	15.0
New residential	12.0
New non-residential	6.0

Source: "Sherwin-Williams Investor Presentation." [online] from https://s2.q4cdn.com/918177852/files/doc_presentations/2020/2020-Sherwin-Williams-Investor-Presentation.pdf [Accessed August 13, 2020], from American Coatings Association, U.S. Department of Commerce and Dodge Data & Analytics.

★ 2583 ★
Paint and Coatings
SIC: 2851; NAICS: 32551

Global Demand for Automotive Coatings, 2019

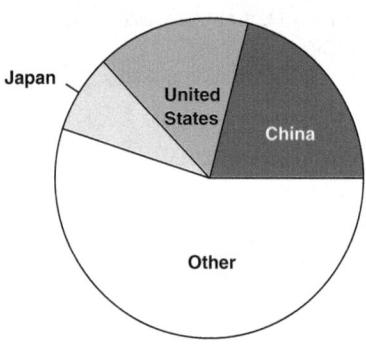

Demand reached 3.4 million metric tons.

China	21.0%
United States	16.0
Japan	8.0
Other	55.0

Source: "Automotive Coatings." [online] from https://www.freedoniagroup.com [Published May 2021], from The Freedonia Group Inc.

★ 2584 ★
Paint and Coatings
SIC: 2851; NAICS: 32551

Global Demand for Coatings, 2019

The industry was valued at $132 billion in 2019.

Architectural paints	40.0%
OEM coatings	40.0
Special purpose	20.0

Source: "Sherwin-Williams Investor Presentation 2020." [online] from https://investors.sherwin-williams.com/events-and-presentations/default.aspx [Accessed October 30, 2020], from KNG Research.

★ 2585 ★
Paint and Coatings
SIC: 2851; NAICS: 32551

Interior Liquid Paint Sales by Type, 2020

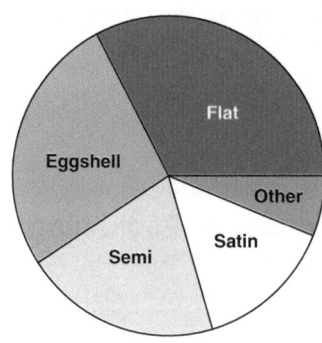

Sales are shown for the previous 12 months in the independent hardware channel. The top 5 items represented 12.6% of unit sales, the top 10 items 20%, the top 20 items 29%, and top 30 items 35.7%.

Flat	32.5%
Eggshell	26.3
Semi	20.5
Satin	14.4
Other	6.3

Source: *The Hardware Connection*, February 2020, p. 50, from Vista Information Services, division of Epicor Software Corp.

★ 2586 ★
Paint and Coatings
SIC: 2851; NAICS: 32551

Leading Paints and Coatings Makers in Europe, 2020

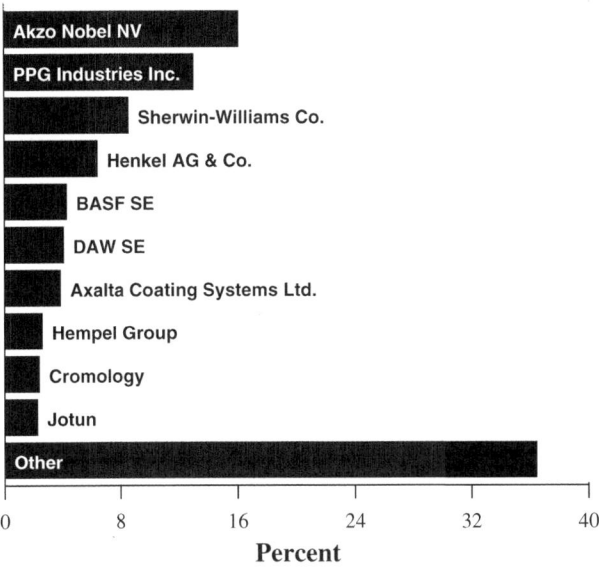

Market shares are estimated in percent.

Akzo Nobel NV	16.06%
PPG Industries Inc.	12.99
Sherwin-Williams Co.	8.57
Henkel AG & Co.	6.42
BASF SE	4.29
DAW SE	4.07
Axalta Coating Systems Ltd.	3.85
Hempel Group	2.60
Cromology	2.40
Jotun	2.27
Other	36.48

Source: "Global & European Paints & Coatings Market Highlights: 2020." [online] from https://www.akiresearch.com/post/global-european-paints-coatings-market-highlights-2020 [Published January 14, 2021], from AKI Research & Consulting.

★ 2587 ★
Paint and Coatings
SIC: 2851; NAICS: 32551

Paint and Coatings Market by Segment, 2019

Market shares are shown based on a $24.9 billion industry.

Architectural	50.0%
OEM	31.0
Special purpose	19.0

Source: *CoatingsTech*, August 2020, p. 23, from The ChemQuest Group.

★ 2588 ★
Paint and Coatings
SIC: 2851; NAICS: 32551

Paint Stripper and Removal Sales, 2020

Sales are shown for the previous 12 months in the independent hardware channel. The top 5 items represented 23.4% of unit sales, the top 10 items 36.1%, the top 20 items 51.2%, and top 30 items 62.2%.

Paint strippers	55.9%
Removers	36.8
Cleaners	5.8
Other	2.0

Source: *The Hardware Connection*, February 2021, p. 54, from Vista Information Services, division of Epicor Software Corp.

★ 2589 ★
Paint and Coatings
SIC: 2851; NAICS: 32551

Popular Automotive Colors Worldwide, 2020

Data show the leading colors, based on a survey by the source. White was the leading color in Asia with a 48% share, Africa with 46% and South America with 41%. Gray was the leader in Europe with a 25% share. Gray and black each had 19% shares in North America.

Solid white	27.0%
Gray	15.0
Effect black	14.0
Pearl white	11.0
Silver	9.0
Blue	7.0
Red	5.0
Solid black	5.0
Brown/beige	3.0
Yellow/gold	2.0
Green	1.0
Other	1.0

Source: "Global Automotive 2020 Color Popularity Report." [online] from https://www.axalta.com/content/dam/New%20Axalta%20Corporate%20Website/Documents/Brochures/axalta-2020-global-automotive-color-popularity-report.pdf [Published December 2020], from Axalta Coating Systems.

★ 2590 ★
Paint and Coatings
SIC: 2851; NAICS: 32551

Special Purpose Coatings Market, 2020

Market shares are estimated in percent. Special purpose coatings claimed about 19% of the overall paint and coatings industry.

Automotive refinish paints	41.9%
Industrial maintenance/protective coatings	30.6
Traffic marking paint	11.6
Marine paints	9.0
Aerosol paints	6.8

Source: *CoatingsTech*, August 2020, p. 27, from The ChemQuest Group.

★ 2591 ★
Paint and Coatings
SIC: 2851; NAICS: 32551

Top Coatings Firms in North America, 2019

Companies are ranked by estimated coatings sales in millions of dollars.

PPG Industries	$ 15,100
The Sherwin-Williams Co.	14,320
RPM International Inc.	5,600
Axalta Coating Systems	4,500
Behr Process Corp.	2,080
Benjamin Moore	828
Ennis-Flint Inc.	640
Shawcor Ltd.	510
Kelly-Moore Paint Co.	325
Innovative Chemical Products Group	300
Lanco Paints & Coatings (Blanco Group)	300

Source: *Paint & Coatings Industry*, July 2020, p. 25.

★ 2592 ★
Paint and Coatings
SIC: 2851; NAICS: 32551

Top Paint and Coatings Firms Worldwide, 2019

Companies are ranked by sales in billions of dollars.

	($ bil.)	Share
The Sherwin-Williams Co.	$ 17.9	10.88%
PPG Industries	15.1	9.18
AkzoNobel Ltd.	10.9	6.63
Nippon Paint Holdings Co.	5.6	3.40
Axalta Coating Systems	4.5	2.74
BASF Coatings	4.4	2.67
Kansai Paint Co. Ltd.	3.8	2.31
Masco Corp. (Behr)	$ 2.5	1.52%
Asian Paints Ltd.	2.3	1.40
The Jotun Group	2.2	1.34
Other	95.3	57.93

Source: *CoatingsTech*, August 2020, p. 24, from The ChemQuest Group.

★ 2593 ★
Paint and Wallpaper Stores
SIC: 5231; NAICS: 44412

Paint and Wallpaper Store Leaders, 2017

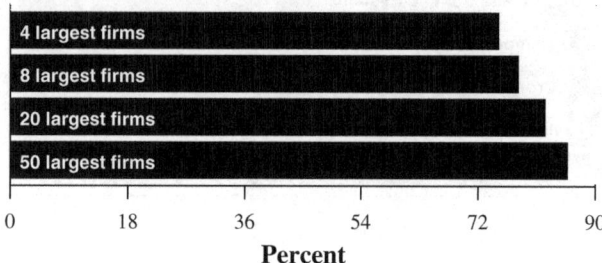

Data show the percent of industry sales held by the largest 4, 8, 20 and 50 firms in the sector. There are approximately 7,008 players operating in the industry generating employment for 37,180 people. In 2017, Sherwin-Williams was the largest paint store operator in North America with 41,141 stores, followed by PPG Paints with 960 stores, and Kelly-Moore Paints with 146 outlets.

4 largest firms	75.1%
8 largest firms	78.1
20 largest firms	82.3
50 largest firms	85.7

Source: "Economic Census." [online] from https://www.census.gov/content/census/en/data/tables/2017/econ/economic-census/naics-sector-31-33.html [Accessed January 21, 2021], from U.S. Census Bureau.

★ 2594 ★
Palladium
SIC: 1099; NAICS: 212299

Leading Palladium Markets Worldwide, 2019

Consumption is shown by industry. Total consumption was 357 tons.

Exhaust aftertreatment systems	82.0%
Electronics	6.0
Chemical catalysts	4.0

Continued on next page.

★ 2594 ★
[Continued]
Palladium
SIC: 1099; NAICS: 212299

Leading Palladium Markets Worldwide, 2019

Consumption is shown by industry. Total consumption was 357 tons.

Dental alloys	3.0%
Jewelry	2.0
Other	2.0

Source: "Nornickel Expanding the Horizons of Sustainable Growth." [online] from http://ar2019.nornickel.com [Accessed December 10, 2020], from company reports.

★ 2595 ★
Palladium
SIC: 1099; NAICS: 212299

Leading Palladium Producers Worldwide, 2019

Market shares are shown based on production. China claimed 28% of consumption, North America 26%, Europe 21%, Japan 12% and other regions 13%.

Nornickel	41.0%
Anglo Platinum	20.0
Sibanye-Stillwater	13.0
Implata Platinum	12.0
Glencore	3.0
Other MMCs	11.0

Source: "Nornickel Expanding the Horizons of Sustainable Growth." [online] from http://ar2019.nornickel.com [Accessed December 10, 2020], from company reports.

★ 2596 ★
Palladium
SIC: 1099; NAICS: 212299

Top Palladium Producing Nations, 2020

Countries are ranked by production in kilograms of platinum-group metal content. Palladium is used in catalytic converters because it has historically been lower in price than platinum; however, the price of palladium was higher than platinum in 2020. The price of palladium increased 38% from 2019 to 2020 while the price of platinum decreased for the fifth year in a row. Production data are estimated.

	kg	Share
Russia	91,000	43.42%
South Africa	70,000	33.40
Canada	20,000	9.54
United States	14,000	6.68%
Zimbabwe	12,000	5.73
Other	2,600	1.24

Source: "Mineral Commodity Summaries 2021." [online] from https://www.usgs.gov/centers/nmic/mineral-commodity-summaries [Published January 29, 2021], from U.S. Geological Survey.

★ 2597 ★
Pallets
SIC: 2448; NAICS: 32192

Demand for Pallets Worldwide, 2019

Demand is to see CAGR of 3.8% from 2019-2024 to reach 6.4 billion units. A major force driving growth is the expansion of pallet stocks worldwide, especially in the Asia-Pacific region. As well, the expansion of e-commerce sales is fueling demand for storage and distribution. Industry leaders are pushing to make the industry "greener" by emphasizing pallet recycling and rental.

Wood	92.0%
Plastics	5.0
Corrugated and molded pulp	3.0

Source: "Global Pallets." [online] from http://www.freedoniagroup.com [Published May 2020], from The Freedonia Group Inc.

★ 2598 ★
Pallets
SIC: 7359; NAICS: 53249

Top Pallet Pooling Rental Firms Worldwide, 2019

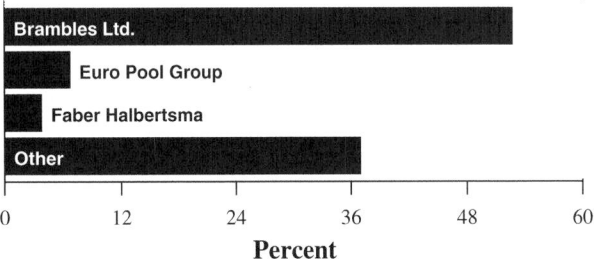

The industry refers to the renting or leasing of pallets from a managed pool. Market shares are estimated based on revenue of $7.4 billion in 2019.

Brambles Ltd.	52.67%
Euro Pool Group	6.65
Faber Halbertsma	3.72
Other	36.96

Source: "Global Pallet Pooling (Rental) Market Size, Status and Forecast." [online] from http://www.qyresearch.com [Published July 2020], from QY Research.

★ 2599 ★
Pancake/French Toast/Waffle Mixes
SIC: 2045; NAICS: 311824

Top Pancake/French Toast/Waffle Mix Makers, 2020

Companies are ranked by sales in millions of dollars at supermarkets, drug stores, mass merchandisers, gas and convenience stores, military commissaries, and select club and dollar chains for the 52 weeks ended April 19, 2020.

	($ mil.)	Share
Quaker Oats Co.	$ 151.78	25.22%
General Mills Inc.	127.55	21.19
Continental Mills Inc.	72.34	12.02
Baker Mills	69.62	11.57
Hometown Food Co.	45.52	7.56
Birch Bemnders	25.21	4.19
Pinnacle Foods Group	7.00	1.16
King Arthur Flour Co.	5.50	0.91
Bob's Red Mills Natural Foods	5.08	0.84
Private label	66.67	11.08
Other	25.58	4.25

Source: *Snack Food & Wholesale Bakery*, June 2020, p. 39, from IRI.

★ 2600 ★
Panels
SIC: 3679; NAICS: 334419

Computer LCD Monitor Panel Production Worldwide, 2020-2021

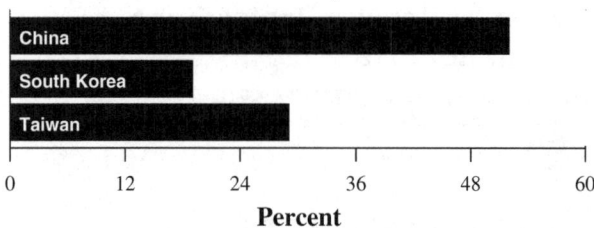

China display makers are expected to shift their LCD television lines to those of monitors. Shares are estimated for 2020 and forecast for 2021.

	2020	2021
China	39.0%	52.0%
South Korea	32.0	19.0
Taiwan	29.0	29.0

Source: "Chinese Panel Makers Expected to Occupy More Than 50% Share in Monitor Panel Market in 2021 Through Production Capacity Advantages, Says TrendForce." [online] from https://www.trendforce.com/presscenter/news/20201015-10511.html [Press release October 15, 2020], from TrendForce.

★ 2601 ★
Panels
SIC: 3679; NAICS: 334419

Computer LCD Notebook Panel Production Worldwide, 2020-2021

Shares are estimated for 2020 and forecast for 2021.

	2020	2021
Taiwan	44.0%	42.0%
China	36.0	39.0
South Korea	16.0	15.0
Japan	4.0	4.0

Source: "Chinese Panel Makers Expected to Occupy More Than 50% Share in Monitor Panel Market in 2021 Through Production Capacity Advantages, Says TrendForce." [online] from https://www.trendforce.com/presscenter/news/20201015-10511.html [Press release October 15, 2020], from TrendForce.

★ 2602 ★
Panels
SIC: 3679; NAICS: 334419

Leading TV Panel Makers Worldwide, 2020-2021

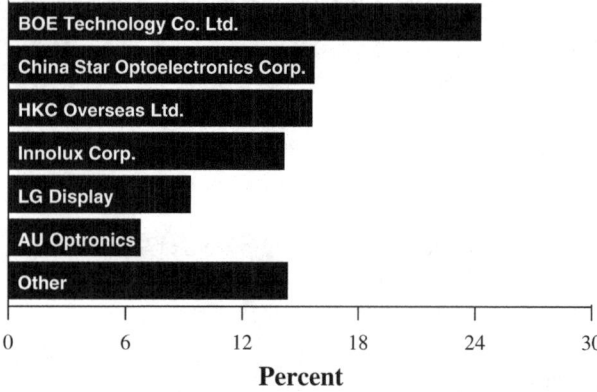

Companies are ranked by millions of units shipped. Shipments are expected to reach 269 million in 2020 and 268.9 million in 2021.

	2020 (mil.)	2021 (mil.)	Share
BOE Technology Co. Ltd.	47.2	65.2	24.25%
China Star Optoelectronics Corp.	39.7	42.2	15.69
HKC Overseas Ltd.	31.3	41.9	15.58
Innolux Corp.	42.0	38.0	14.13
LG Display	23.6	25.0	9.30

Continued on next page.

★ 2602 ★
[Continued]
Panels
SIC: 3679; NAICS: 334419

Leading TV Panel Makers Worldwide, 2020-2021

Companies are ranked by millions of units shipped. Shipments are expected to reach 269 million in 2020 and 268.9 million in 2021.

	2020 (mil.)	2021 (mil.)	Share
AU Optronics	20.1	18.1	6.73%
Other	65.1	38.5	14.32

Source: "Chinese Suppliers Take Top Three Spots in TV Panel Shipment Ranking, With Combined Shipment of More Than 50% of All Suppliers, Says TrendForce." [online] from https://www.trendforce.com/presscenter/news/20210409-10747.html [Press release April 9, 2021], from TrendForce, April 2021.

★ 2603 ★
Paper and Paperboard
SIC: 2621; NAICS: 322121

Global Tissue Consumption, 2019

Consumption reached an estimated 40.6 million tons. China recently passed Western Europe to become the largest tissue producer in 2015.

North America	23.9%
China	23.3
Western Europe	16.9
Latin America	11.1
Asia Far East	6.6
Eastern Europe	5.7
Japan	5.0
North Africa and Middle East	4.1
Africa	2.3
Oceania	1.1

Source: "Global Tissue Market Outlook." [online] from http://eventsrisiinfo.com [Published October 2020], from RISI.

★ 2604 ★
Paper and Paperboard
SIC: 2621; NAICS: 322121

Largest Paper and Paperboard Makers Worldwide, 2019

Companies are ranked by paper and board production in millions of metric tons.

International Paper Co.	20,951
Nine Dragons Paper Holdings Ltd.	15,900
WestRock	13,382
Oji Holdings Corp.	10,594
DS Smith PLC	9,307
UPM-Kymmene Oyj	8,326
Stora Enso Oyj	8,143
Smurfit Kappa Group	7,500
Lee & Man Paper Manufacturing Ltd.	6,291
Nippon Paper Industries Co. Ltd.	5,567

Source: *Paper360°*, September-October 2020, p. 13.

★ 2605 ★
Paper and Paperboard
SIC: 2631; NAICS: 32213

Leading Containerboard Makers in Indonesia, 2019

Market shares are shown based on 3.31 million metric tons.

Sinar Mas Group	31.5%
SCG Packaging (Fajar Paper)	25.0
Pakerin	8.9
Pelita	8.8
Mekabox	5.7
Buana Megah	3.0
Other	17.1

Source: "Independent Study on Packaging Products Market in Southeast Asia." [online] from http://ww2.frost.com [Published August 2020], from Frost & Sullivan.

★ 2606 ★
Paper and Paperboard
SIC: 2631; NAICS: 32213

Leading Containerboard Makers in Thailand, 2019

Market shares are shown based on 2.48 million metric tons.

SCG Packaging	50.2%
Panjapol Paper Industry	13.6
Elite Kraft & Mahachai	7.6
Asia Kraft Paper	6.2
United Paper	5.7
Other	16.7

Source: "Independent Study on Packaging Products Market in Southeast Asia." [online] from http://ww2.frost.com [Published August 2020], from Frost & Sullivan.

★ 2607 ★
Paper and Paperboard
SIC: 2631; NAICS: 32213

Leading CRB Paperboard Makers Worldwide, 2019

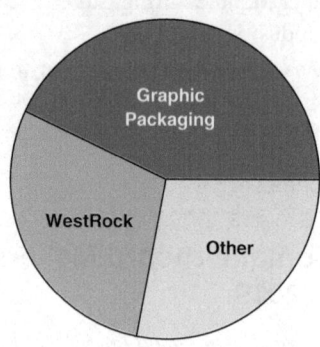

Market shares are shown in percent. CRB stands for coated recycled board.

Graphic Packaging	43.0%
WestRock	29.0
Other	28.0

Source: "Graphic Packaging Holding Co." [online] from https://www.theowlfund.com/s/Graphic-Packaging-Holding-Co-GPK_Initiating-Coverage-Report-13-Nov-2020-2.pdf [Published November 13, 2020], from Stephens Inc. and company data.

★ 2608 ★
Paper and Paperboard
SIC: 2631; NAICS: 32213

Leading CUK Paperboard Makers Worldwide, 2019

Market shares are shown in percent. CUK stands for coated bleached kraft.

Graphic Packaging	55.0%
WestRock	43.0
Other	2.0

Source: "Graphic Packaging Holding Co." [online] from https://www.theowlfund.com/s/Graphic-Packaging-Holding-Co-GPK_Initiating-Coverage-Report-13-Nov-2020-2.pdf [Published November 13, 2020], from Stephens Inc. and company data.

★ 2609 ★
Paper and Paperboard
SIC: 2631; NAICS: 32213

Leading SBS Paperboard Makers Worldwide, 2019

Market shares are shown in percent. SBS stands for solid bleached sulfate.

WestRock	33.0%
Graphic Packaging	20.0
Other	47.0

Source: "Graphic Packaging Holding Co." [online] from https://www.theowlfund.com/s/Graphic-Packaging-Holding-Co-GPK_Initiating-Coverage-Report-13-Nov-2020-2.pdf [Published November 13, 2020], from Stephens Inc. and company data.

★ 2610 ★
Paper and Paperboard
SIC: 2631; NAICS: 32213

Paperboard Mills, 2019

Total shipments were valued at $31.98 billion.

	($ 000)	Share
Unbleached kraft linerboard . .	$ 11,066,861	34.61%
Recycled linerboard and container chip and filler board	3,536,934	11.06
Recycled corrugating medium .	2,734,245	8.55
Bleached folding carton-type paperboard	2,162,380	6.76
Semichemical paperboard, including corrugating medium (75 percent or more virgin woodpulp)	1,219,383	3.81
Recycled clay-coated folding carton board	690,360	2.16
Bleached milk carton board . .	596,170	1.86
Special alpha and dissolving woodpulp (sulfite and sulfate for chemical conversion, papermaking, and other uses), sulfate woodpulp (including soda), sulfite woodpulp, and other woodpulp	281,962	0.88

Continued on next page.

★ 2610 ★
[Continued]
Paper and Paperboard
SIC: 2631; NAICS: 32213

Paperboard Mills, 2019

Total shipments were valued at $31.98 billion.

	($ 000)	Share
Bleached bristols and clay-coated, uncoated freesheet, cotton fiber, special industrial, packaging, and industrial converting papers	$ 139,906	0.44%
Turpentine, sulfate	18,200	0.06
Wholesale sales of recyclable paper and paperboard	13,917	0.04
Other solid bleached paperboard, including linerboard, heavyweight cup and round nested food container board, plate, dish, and tray stock, and paperboard for moist, liquid, and oily foods	4,342,494	13.58
Other unbleached kraft packaging and industrial converting paperboard, including tube, can, and drum paperboard, corrugating medium, folding carton-type board, etc.	3,501,649	10.95
Other recycled paperboard, including setup, tube, can, and drum stock, gypsum linerboard, panelboard and wallboard stock, and other special combination packaging and converting paperboard	1,375,384	4.30
Other pulp mill cooking liquor byproducts (skimmings, binders, fuel, etc.)	43,296	0.14
Other	256,860	0.80

Source: "Annual Survey of Manufactures." [online] from https://www.census.gov/programs-surveys/asm/data/tables.html [Accessed March 18, 2021], from U.S. Department of Commerce.

★ 2611 ★
Paper and Paperboard
SIC: 2621; NAICS: 322121

Tissue Consumption in Western Europe, 2017-2018

Consumption is shown in thousands of tons.

	2017 (000)	2018 (000)	Share
Germany	1,463	1,450	21.33%
United Kingdom	1,109	1,122	16.51
Italy	899	897	13.20
France	885	873	12.84
Spain	697	726	10.68
Netherlands	273	284	4.18
Belgium and Luxembourg	211	223	3.28
Sweden	199	195	2.87
Austria	168	170	2.50
Portugal	152	152	2.24
Switzerland	144	144	2.12
Denmark	100	101	1.49
Other	453	460	6.77

Source: *TissueMag*, May 2020, p. 8, from Fastmarkets RISI.

★ 2612 ★
Paper and Paperboard
SIC: 2675; NAICS: 322299

Top Corrugated Cardboard Makers in Japan, 2018

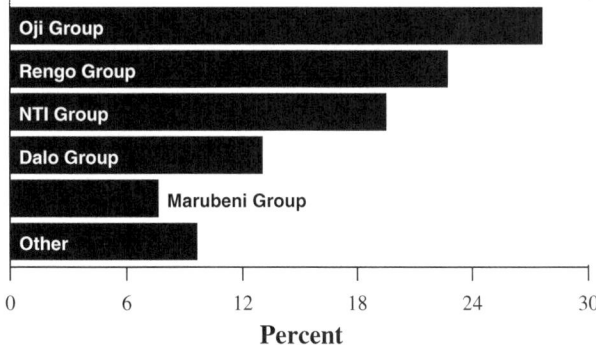

Production reached 14.4 billion cubic meters.

Oji Group	27.6%
Rengo Group	22.7
NTI Group	19.5
Dalo Group	13.0
Marubeni Group	7.6
Other	9.6

Source: "Japanese Corrugated Cardboard Market Trend." [online] from http://news.kotra.or.kr [Published October 2, 2020], from Yano Economic Research Institute.

★ 2613 ★
Paper and Paperboard
SIC: 2621; NAICS: 322121

Top Paper and Paperboard Producers in Europe, 2019

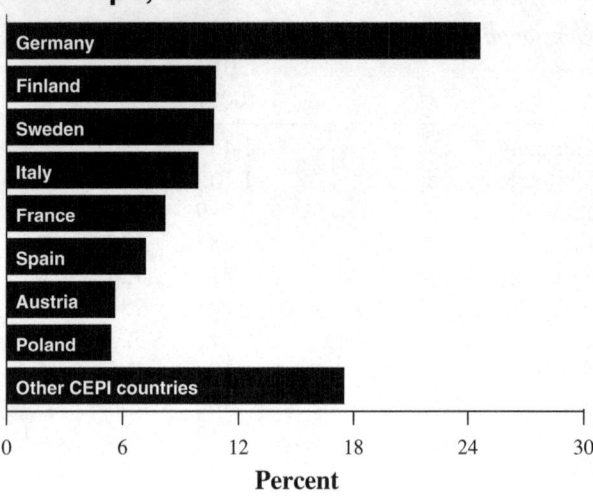

Percent

Production reached 89.6 million tons.

Germany	24.6%
Finland	10.8
Sweden	10.7
Italy	9.9
France	8.2
Spain	7.2
Austria	5.6
Poland	5.4
Other CEPI countries	17.5

Source: "European Pulp & Paper Industry Key Statistics 2019." [online] from https://www.cepi.org/key-statistics-2019/ [Accessed December 2, 2020], from Confederation of European Paper Industries and Alexander Watson Associates.

★ 2614 ★
Paper Bags, and Coated and Treated Paper
SIC: 2673; NAICS: 32222

Freezer Liner Market, 2019

Market shares are shown based on sales at drug stores, supermarkets, mass merchandisers, convenience stores, and select club and dollar chains for the 52 weeks ended September 28, 2019.

Reynolds Consumer Products	94.0%
Other	6.0

Source: "Reynolds Consumer Products." [online] from https://www.sec.gov/Archives/edgar/data/1786431/000119312520021414/d769843d424b4.htm [Published January 30, 2020], from Nielsen.

★ 2615 ★
Paper Bags, and Coated and Treated Paper
SIC: 2673; NAICS: 32222

Oven Bag Market, 2019

Market shares are shown based on sales at drug stores, supermarkets, mass merchandisers, convenience stores, and select club and dollar chains for the 52 weeks ended September 28, 2019.

Reynolds Consumer Products	93.0%
Other	7.0

Source: "Reynolds Consumer Products." [online] from https://www.sec.gov/Archives/edgar/data/1786431/000119312520021414/d769843d424b4.htm [Published January 30, 2020], from Nielsen.

★ 2616 ★
Paper Bags, and Coated and Treated Paper
SIC: 2671; NAICS: 32222

Paper Bag, and Coated and Treated Paper Manufacturing Leaders, 2017

Data show the percent of industry sales held by the largest 4, 8, 20 and 50 firms in the sector. There are approximately 751 players operating in the industry generating employment for 47,945 people. According to Kentley Insights, the industry generated sales of $20.8 billion in 2019.

4 largest firms	27.6%
8 largest firms	35.9
20 largest firms	51.1
50 largest firms	67.8

Source: "Economic Census." [online] from https://www.census.gov/content/census/en/data/tables/2017/econ/economic-census/naics-sector-31-33.html [Accessed January 21, 2021], from U.S. Census Bureau.

★ 2617 ★
Paper-Cutting Machines
SIC: 3554; NAICS: 333243

Leading Paper-Cutting Machine Makers in North America, 2019

The top three companies claimed more than 80% of production. Signs and cards marking and papercrafting use claimed 63.5% of the market.

Cricut/Brother/Silhouette	>80.0%
Other	20.0

Source: "Global Paper Cutting Machine Market Share 2026." [online] from http://www.qyresearch.com [Published September 2020], from QY Research.

★ 2618 ★
Paper Wholesalers
SIC: 5113; NAICS: 42413

Industrial and Personal Service Paper Merchant Wholesalers, 2017

Data show the percent of industry sales held by the largest 4, 8, 20 and 50 firms in the sector. There are approximately 4,545 players operating in the industry generating employment for 69,372 people. The industry generated revenue of $15 billion in 2020, according to IBISWorld. The move from paper to digital communications has had a negative effect on industry growth. The source estimates an annual revenue decline of 10.7% for the five years leading up to 2020.

4 largest firms	38.4%
8 largest firms	50.0
20 largest firms	65.4
50 largest firms	75.0

Source: "Economic Census." [online] from https://www.census.gov/content/census/en/data/tables/2017/econ/economic-census/naics-sector-31-33.html [Accessed January 21, 2021], from U.S. Census Bureau.

★ 2619 ★
Parcel Sorting Machines
SIC: 3559; NAICS: 333318

Leading Parcel Sorting Machine Markets Worldwide, 2018

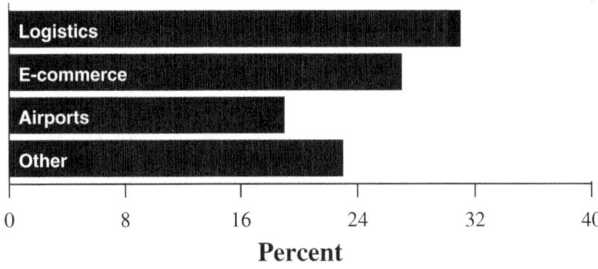

The industry is forecast to grow from $1.25 billion in 2020 to $2.67 billion in 2026. The Asia-Pacific region claimed a 42% market share, while Europe and North America followed with market shares of 26% and 23%, respectively.

Logistics	31.0%
E-commerce	27.0
Airports	19.0
Other	23.0

Source: "Global Parcel Sorting System Sales Market Report 2020." [online] from http://www.qyresearch.com [Published November 2020], from QY Research.

★ 2620 ★
Parking Lots and Garages
SIC: 7521; NAICS: 81293

Leading Parking Lot Operators, 2020

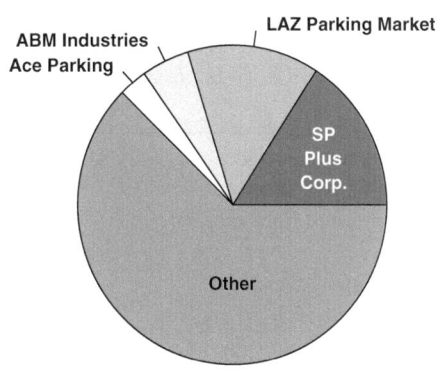

The industry was valued at $10.6 billion. Privately owned claimed 31.3%, shopping centers 11.6%, hotels and restaurants 10.3%, offices 8%, hospitals 7.1%, airports and rail 6.7%, and other sectors 25%.

SP Plus Corp.	15.9%
LAZ Parking Market	13.8
ABM Industries	4.6
Ace Parking	2.7
Other	63.0

Source: "Will COVID-19 Change the Parking Business?" [online] from https://thehustle.co/covid-19-business-of-parking-lots/ [Published April 26, 2020], from IBISWorld.

★ 2621 ★
Parking Lots and Garages
SIC: 7521; NAICS: 81293

Parking Lots and Garages, 2017

Total sales were valued at $9.64 billion. The term "nec" stands for not elsewhere classified.

	($ 000)	Share
Off-street parking services, hourly or daily	$ 4,569,860	48.12%
Valet parking services	1,644,182	17.31
Off-street parking services, weekly or monthly, in buildings	1,578,685	16.62
Off-street parking services, weekly or monthly, on lots	1,502,116	15.82
On-street parking services	89,717	0.94
Rental and leasing of nonresidential space in buildings or other facilities, except hosting of coin-operated self-service gambling machines	51,617	0.54

Continued on next page.

★ 2621 ★
[Continued]
Parking Lots and Garages
SIC: 7521; NAICS: 81293

Parking Lots and Garages, 2017

Total sales were valued at $9.64 billion. The term "nec" stands for not elsewhere classified.

	($ 000)	Share
Property management services	$ 22,045	0.23%
Washing and cleaning services for automobiles and light-duty trucks	3,381	0.04
Retail sales of other goods, nec	30	< 0.01
Other products and services, nec	29,763	0.31
Other road transportation support services	5,785	0.06

Source: "Economic Census." [online] from https://www.census.gov/programs-surveys/economic-census/data/tables.html [Accessed December 2, 2020], from U.S. Census Bureau.

★ 2622 ★
Parks
SIC: 8422; NAICS: 71219

Most-Visited National Parks, 2020

Data include parks administered by the National Park Service. Parks are ranked by millions of visitors.

Great Smoky Mountains National Park (NC-TN)	12.1
Yellowstone National Park (ID-MT-WY)	3.8
Zion National Park (UT)	3.6
Grand Teton National Park (WY)	3.3
Rocky Mountain National Park (CO)	3.3
Grand Canyon National Park (AZ)	2.9
Cuyahoga Valley National Park (OH)	2.8
Acadia National Park (ME)	2.7
Olympic National Park (WA)	2.5
Joshua Tree National Park (CA)	2.4

Source: "Visitation Numbers." [online] from https://www.nps.gov/aboutus/visitation-numbers.htm [Published February 25, 2021], from National Park Service.

★ 2623 ★
Parks
SIC: 8422; NAICS: 71219

Most-Visited Parks, 2020

Data include parks administered by the National Park Service. Parks are ranked by millions of visitors.

	(mil.)	Share
Blue Ridge Parkway (NC)	14.1	5.95%
Golden Gate National Recreation Area (CA)	12.4	5.23
Great Smoky Mountains National Park (NC-TN)	12.1	5.10
Gateway National Recreation Area (NJ-NY)	8.4	3.54
Lake Mead National Recreation Area (NV-AZ)	8.0	3.37
George Washington Memorial Parkway (VA)	6.2	2.61
Natchez Trace Parkway (TN-MS)	6.1	2.57
Chesapeake and Ohio Canal National Historic Park (DC-MD-WV)	4.9	2.07
Cape Cod National Seashore (MA)	4.1	1.73
Delaware Water Gap National Recreation Area (NJ-PA)	4.1	1.73
Other	156.7	66.09

Source: "Visitation Numbers." [online] from https://www.nps.gov/aboutus/visitation-numbers.htm [Published February 25, 2021], from National Park Service.

★ 2624 ★
Pasta and Noodles
SIC: 2098; NAICS: 311824

Italian Pasta Exports by Country, 2019

Countries are ranked based on exports from Italy valued at more than €10 million. The source notes that pasta demand has been strong worldwide. One reason is that people are cooking at home more because of the pandemic. Also, pasta is easy to prepare, low cost, and appeals to adults and children.

Germany	15.4%
France	14.2
United States	13.2
United Kingdom	12.5
Spain	4.4
Belgium	3.0
Japan	2.8
Sweden	2.7
Other	31.8

Source: Professional Pasta, July-September 2020, p. 31, from Nomisma.

★ 2625 ★
Pasta and Noodles
SIC: 2098; NAICS: 311824

Leading Pasta and Pasta Sauce Makers in Europe, 2019

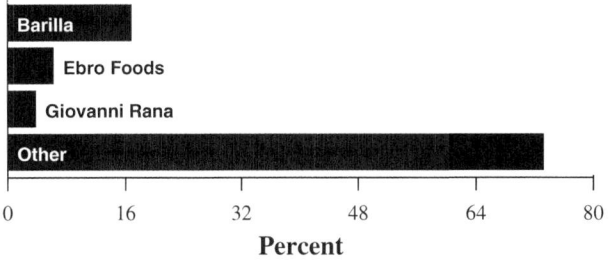

Market shares are shown in percent.

Barilla	16.8%
Ebro Foods	6.2
Giovanni Rana	3.8
Other	73.2

Source: "Pasta and Pasta Sauces Market in Europe: a 24 Country Analysis." [online] from https://www.globenewswire.com/news-release/2020/06/12/2047322/0/en/Pasta-and-Pasta-Sauces-Market-in-Europe-A-24-Country-Analysis.html [Published June 12, 2020], from Research and Markets.

★ 2626 ★
Pasta and Noodles
SIC: 2098; NAICS: 311824

Leading Refrigerated Pasta and Noodle Brands, 2020

Brands are ranked based on sales at supermarkets, drug stores, mass merchandisers, military commissaries, and select club and dollar chains for the 12 weeks ended September 6, 2020.

	($ mil.)	Share
Giovanni Rana	$ 50.84	45.93%
Buitoni	33.44	30.21
Three Bridges	2.76	2.49
La Pasta	1.31	1.18
Giovanni Rana Organic	1.18	1.07
O Sole Mio	1.03	0.93
Fortune Brands	0.70	0.63
Private label	14.41	13.02
Other	5.01	4.53

Source: *Frozen & Refrigerated Buyer*, November 2020, p. 11, from IRI.

★ 2627 ★
Pasta and Noodles
SIC: 2098; NAICS: 311824

Top Organic Pasta and Noodle Firms, 2018

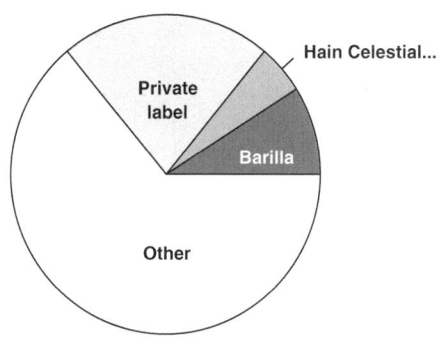

Market shares are shown in percent. Retail sales reached $324.2 million.

Barilla	9.2%
The Hain Celestial Group Inc.	5.4
Private label	21.9
Other	63.5

Source: "Sector Trend Analysis — Organic Market Trend of Corn, Soya, Beans and Wheat Between Canada and the United States." [online] from https://www.agr.gc.ca/eng/international-trade/market-intelligence/reports/?id=1522931721523 [Published July 2020], from GlobalData Intelligence Center.

★ 2628 ★
Patents
SIC: 6794; NAICS: 53311

Largest Patent Assignees, 2019-2020

Companies are ranked by number of patents.

	2019	2020
IBM	9,262	9,130
Samsung Electronics Co. Ltd.	6,469	6,415
Canon Inc.	3,548	3,225
Microsoft Technology Licensing	3,081	2,905
Intel Corp.	3,020	2,867
Taiwan Semiconductor Manufacturing Co.	2,331	2,833
LG Electronics	2,805	2,831
Apple Inc.	2,490	2,791
Huawei Technologies Co.	2,418	2,761
Qualcomm Inc.	2,348	2,276

Source: "Top 50 U.S. Patent Assignees." [online] from https://www.ificlaims.com/rankings-top-50-2020.htm [Accessed April 20, 2021], from IFI Claims Patent Office.

★ 2629 ★
Pay Television
SIC: 4841; NAICS: 51521

Largest Pay Television Services in Europe, 2020

Services are ranked by millions of subscribers as of March 2020.

Sky	23.93
Vodafone Germany	13.58
Tricolor	12.23
Orange France	7.31
Free	6.51
Rostelecom Telco	5.70
Cyfrowy Polsat	5.16
Rostelecom cable	4.79
Canal+France	4.55
Telefónica España	4.03

Source: *CSI Magazine*, September 2020, p. 11, from Informitv Multiscreen Index.

★ 2630 ★
Pay Television
SIC: 4841; NAICS: 51521

Leading Pay Television Markets Worldwide, 2020 and 2025

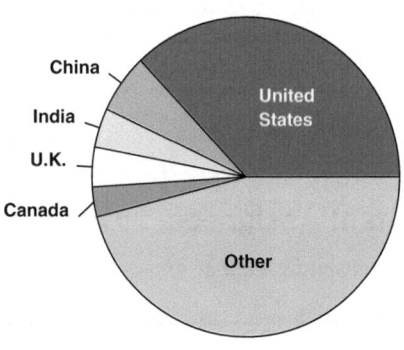

While some consumers are "cutting the cord," the pay television industry is still doing well in some markets. The industry is expected to add 34 million subscribers from 2019 to 2025. Markets are ranked by thousands of subscribers. Shares are estimated for 2025.

	2020 (000)	2025 (000)	Share
United States	79,241	56,019	36.90%
China	9,379	9,348	6.16
India	5,415	5,995	3.95
United Kingdom	6,349	5,780	3.81
Canada	5,698	5,130	3.38%
Other	70,835	69,559	45.81

Source: "Global Pay TV Revenues Down, Subscriptions Up." [online] from http://www.digitaltvresearch.com [Press release September 2020], from Digital TV Research.

★ 2631 ★
Pay Television
SIC: 4841; NAICS: 51521

Leading Pay Television Providers, 2020

Companies are ranked by subscribers at the end of fourth quarter 2020. Total subscribers through cable, satellite, phone and Internet-delivered services (vMVPD) reached 81,290,267, about 95% of the market. The number of subscribers declined by 5,118,633 over the previous year.

	Subscribers	Share
Comcast Corp.	19,846,000	24.41%
Charter Communications Inc.	16,200,000	19.93
DirecTV	13,000,000	15.99
DishTV	8,816,000	10.85
Hulu + LiveTV	4,000,000	4.92
Verizon FiOS	3,927,000	4.83
Cox Communications	3,650,000	4.49
AT&T U-Verse/AT&T TV	3,505,000	4.31
Altice USA Inc.	2,961,000	3.64
SlingTV	2,474,000	3.04
AT&T TV Now	656,000	0.81
Mediacom Communications Corp.	643,000	0.79
FuboTV	547,880	0.67
Frontier Communications Corp.	485,000	0.60
Atlantic Broadband	318,387	0.39
Cable One	261,000	0.32

Source: "Major Pay-TV Provider Lost About 5,120,000 Subscribers in 2020." [online] from https://www.leichtmanresearch.com/major-pay-tv-providers-lost-about-5120000-subscribers-in-2020/ [Press release March 4, 2021], from Leichtman Research Group.

★ 2632 ★
Pay Television
SIC: 4841; NAICS: 51521

Most-Watched Television Networks, 2020

Networks are ranked by thousands of viewers. Viewership covers December 30, 2019-December 6, 2020, live+7 and December 7, 2020-December 22, 2020, live+SD, Monday-Saturday 8 p.m.-11 p.m./Sun 7 p.m.-11 p.m., ad supported and premium pay networks.

CBS	5,603
NBC	5,025
ABC	4,522
Fox	4,157
Fox News Channel	3,596
MSNBC	2,135
CNN	1,790
ESPN	1,500
Univision	1,445
TLC	1,365
HGTV	1,360
Hallmark Channel	1,214

Source: *Variety*, December 28, 2020, p. NA, from Nielsen.

★ 2633 ★
Payment Cards
SIC: 6141; NAICS: 52221

Leading General Purpose Card Brands, 2020

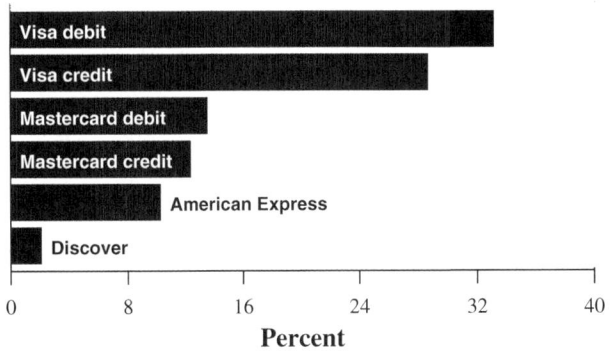

Consumer, business and commercial cards generated $6.74 trillion in purchase volume in 2020, up 0.8% over 2019.

	($ tril.)	Share
Visa debit	$ 2.23	33.14%
Visa credit	1.93	28.68
Mastercard debit	0.91	13.52
Mastercard credit	0.83	12.33
American Express	$ 0.69	10.25%
Discover	0.14	2.08

Source: *Nilson Report*, February 2021, p. 1, from *Nilson Report* research.

★ 2634 ★
Payment Cards
SIC: 6141; NAICS: 52221

Leading General Purpose Card Issuers in the Asia-Pacific Region, 2019

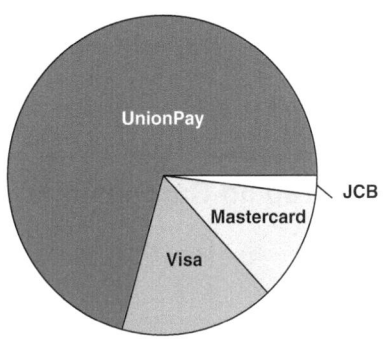

Market shares are shown in percent. The credit, debit, and prepaid cards through UnionPay, Visa, Mastercard, JCB, American Express and Diners Club generated $17.98 trillion in goods and services.

UnionPay	70.0%
Visa	16.0
Mastercard	11.0
JCB	2.0

Source: *Nilson Report*, July 2020, p. NA.

★ 2635 ★
Payment Cards
SIC: 6141; NAICS: 52221

Leading Payment Card Issuers Worldwide, 2020

Distribution is shown based on $35 trillion in purchase volume.

UnionPay	45.0%
Visa	27.0
Mastercard	18.0

Continued on next page.

★ 2635 ★
[Continued]
Payment Cards
SIC: 6141; NAICS: 52221

Leading Payment Card Issuers Worldwide, 2020

Distribution is shown based on $35 trillion in purchase volume.

Domestic	4.0%
Other	6.0

Source: "UnionPay Accounts for 45% of Global Cards Spending, but Only 1% Outside China." [online] from https://www.rbrlondon.com/press/ [Published November 5, 2020], from Global Payment Cards Data and Forecast to 2025 (RBR).

★ 2636 ★
Payment Cards
SIC: 6141; NAICS: 52221

Leading Prepaid Card Issuers, 2018-2019

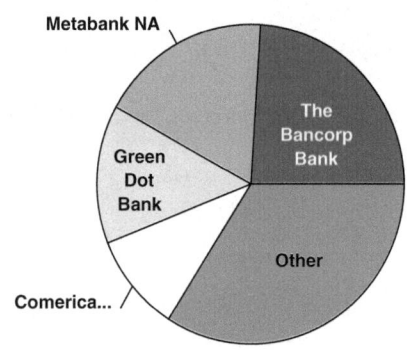

Market shares are shown based on payment volume of the top 25 providers. The top 25 largest Visa, Mastercard and Discover brand prepaid card issuers in the United States generated $198.97 billion in goods and services.

	2018	2019
The Bancorp Bank	21.36%	24.09%
Metabank NA	19.24	18.19
Green Dot Bank	13.25	13.57
Comerica Bank	9.97	10.34
Other	36.18	33.81

Source: *Nilson Report*, September 2020, p. 1.

★ 2637 ★
Payment Cards
SIC/NAICS: See frontmatter for explanation.

Open-Loop Prepaid Card Market, 2015-2024

Open-loop cards are payment cards that can be used anywhere that card brand is accepted. Data shows the amount loaded onto open-loop prepaid cards for flexible spending accounts, health savings accounts and health reimbursement arrangements in billions of dollars. Data for 2020-2024 are forecasts.

2015	$ 17.4
2016	21.9
2017	36.2
2018	40.2
2019	46.3
2020	46.9
2021	51.3
2022	55.6
2023	59.9
2024	64.3

Source: *Convenience Store Decisions*, March 2021, p. 97, from Mercator CustomerMonitor Survey Series, 2020 Payments Survey.

★ 2638 ★
Payment Cards
SIC: 6141; NAICS: 52221

Payment Card Spending, 2024

Data show projected spending on goods and services in billions of dollars. Spending on private label cards, credit cards, debit cards and prepaid cards should reach $10.718 trillion, up 35.7% over 2019.

	($ bil.)	Share
Visa	$ 5,623	52.98%
Mastercard	2,439	22.98
American Express	916	8.63
Domestic debit	883	8.32
Prepaid	410	3.86
Store	174	1.64
Discover	168	1.58

Source: *Nilson Report*, October 2020, p. 1.

★ 2639 ★
Payment Cards
SIC: 6141; NAICS: 52221

Payment Card Transactions Worldwide, 2020 and 2025

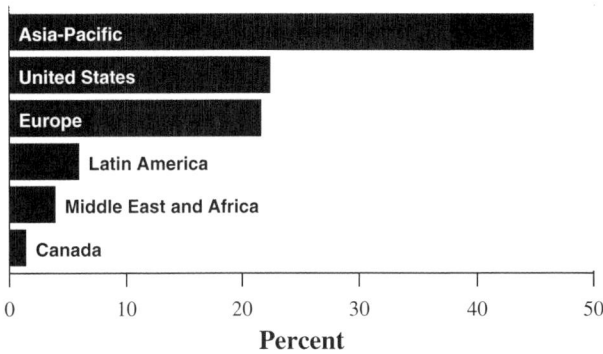

Data show projected transactions in billions of transactions.

	2020 (bil.)	2025 (bil.)	Share
Asia-Pacific	196	288	44.79%
United States	111	144	22.40
Europe	102	139	21.62
Latin America	26	38	5.91
Middle East and Africa	12	25	3.89
Canada	7	9	1.40

Source: *Nilson Report*, January 2021, p. 1.

★ 2640 ★
Payment Cards
SIC: 6141; NAICS: 52221

Top Credit Card Marketers, 2018-2019

Market shares are shown based on ad spending of $85.8 billion in 2018 and $85.4 billion in 2019.

	2018	2019
American Express Co.	20.5%	20.2%
JPMorgan Chase & Co.	20.1	20.4
Citigroup	11.1	11.2
Bank of America Corp.	9.8	9.6
Capital One Financial Corp.	9.2	9.3
U.S. Bancorp.	4.0	3.9
Discover Financial Services	3.8	3.7
Wells Fargo & Co.	3.7	3.5
Barclays	2.2	2.1
Synchrony Financial	1.5	1.4
Other	14.1	14.7

Source: *Leading National Advertisers 2020 Fact Book - A Supplement to Advertising Age*, July 13, 2020, p. 34, from Ad Age Datacenter and Kantar.

★ 2641 ★
Pearls
SIC: 3911; NAICS: 33991

Top Pearl Exporters Worldwide, 2019

Data show the major exporters of pearls and precious or semiprecious stones, unworked or worked. Exports reached $124.9 billion in 2019, a 14.4% decrease from 2018.

India	18.2%
United States	16.1
China, Hong Kong SAR	13.3
United Arab Emirates	9.6
Belgium	9.3
Israel	9.2
Botswana	3.8
Russian Federation	3.0
Thailand	2.3
Switzerland	2.2
Other	13.0

Source: "2019 International Trade Statistics Yearbook." [online] from https://comtrade.un.org/pb/ [Published December 2020], from U.N. Comtrade.

★ 2642 ★
Pearls
SIC: 3911; NAICS: 33991

Top Pearl Importers Worldwide, 2019

Data show the major importers of pearls and precious or semiprecious stones, unworked or worked. Imports reached $120.5 billion in 2019, a 15.2% decrease from 2018.

India	19.7%
United States	18.6
China, Hong Kong SAR	16.4
United Arab Emirates	9.3
Belgium	8.7
China	7.1
Israel	4.0
Switzerland	2.7
Thailand	2.0
United Kingdom	1.7
Other	9.8

Source: "2019 International Trade Statistics Yearbook." [online] from https://comtrade.un.org/pb/ [Published December 2020], from U.N. Comtrade.

★ 2643 ★
Peat
SIC: 1499; NAICS: 212399

Top Peat Producing Nations, 2020

Countries are ranked by production in thousands of metric tons. In the United States, 30 companies in 12 states harvest and process peat. About 93% was reed-sedge peat, followed by sphagnum moss at 3%. Peat is an important component of plant-growing media. In other countries, peat is used as fuel but because of climate change concerns, several countries plan to decrease or eliminate the use of peat. Peatland has the ability to act as a carbon sink. Several European countries including Belarus, Ireland and Sweden plan to implement peatland restoration projects to not only help combat climate change but to restore wildlife habitats also. Production data are estimated.

	(000)	Share
Finland	10,000	34.44%
Germany	4,000	13.77
Belarus	2,600	8.95
Sweden	2,500	8.61
Ireland	2,000	6.89
Latvia	1,900	6.54
Canada	1,300	4.48
Estonia	900	3.10
Russia	800	2.75
Poland	700	2.41
Ukraine	680	2.34
Lithuania	500	1.72
United States	430	1.48
Other	730	2.51

Source: "Mineral Commodity Summaries 2021." [online] from https://www.usgs.gov/centers/nmic/mineral-commodity-summaries [Published January 29, 2021], from U.S. Geological Survey.

★ 2644 ★
Pelts
SIC: 0271; NAICS: 11293

Mink Pelt Production, 2019

Data show number of pelts produced. Production reached 2.7 million pelts, down 15% from 2018. Wisconsin was the leading state with production of 1.02 million pelts, followed by Utah with production of 556,710 pelts.

	Pelts	Share
Black	1,404,600	51.94%
Mahogany	468,680	17.33
White	209,030	7.73
Sapphire	155,130	5.74
Blue Iris	118,540	4.38%
Demi/Wild	90,440	3.34
Pastel	84,340	3.12
Pearl	79,000	2.92
Violet	56,790	2.10
Lavender	25,790	0.95
Other	11,860	0.44

Source: "Mink." [online] from https://usda.library.cornell.edu/concern/publications/2227mp65f [Published July 23, 2020], from U.S. Department of Agriculture.

★ 2645 ★
Pensions
SIC: 6371; NAICS: 52511

Largest Pension Funds, 2020

Fund sponsors are ranked by total assets in millions of dollars as of September 30, 2020.

Federal Retirement Thrift	$ 651,124
California Public Employees	426,247
California State Teachers	259,246
New York States Common	226,400
New York City Retirement	225,450
Florida State Board	180,221
Texas Teachers	162,656
Boeing Co.	133,688
Washington State Board	128,897
AT&T	127,365
Wisconsin Investment Board	124,508
New York State Teachers	122,767
North Carolina Retirement System	120,727
IBM	109,027
Ohio Public Employees	104,307

Source: *Pensions & Investments*, February 8, 2021, p. 16.

★ 2646 ★
Pensions
SIC: 6371; NAICS: 52511

Largest Pension Markets in Europe, 2020

Countries are ranked by pension assets in billions of euros.

	(bil.)	Share
United Kingdom	€ 1,946.6	23.52%
Netherlands	1,454.4	17.57
Norway	1,149.7	13.89
Germany	720.8	8.71
Switzerland	709.0	8.56

Continued on next page.

★ 2646 ★
[Continued]
Pensions
SIC: 6371; NAICS: 52511

Largest Pension Markets in Europe, 2020

Countries are ranked by pension assets in billions of euros.

	(bil.)	Share
Denmark	€ 591.6	7.15%
Sweden	458.0	5.53
France	288.8	3.49
CEE	216.4	2.61
Finland	209.7	2.53
Other	533.1	6.44

Source: *Investment & Pensions Europe*, September 2020, p. 2, from *Investment & Pensions Europe* research.

★ 2647 ★
Pensions
SIC: 6371; NAICS: 52511

Largest Sovereign Pension Funds Worldwide, 2020

Sovereign pension funds are established by national authorities for the meeting of pension liabilities. Figures are in millions of dollars.

Government Pension Investment Fund (Japan)	$ 1,555,550
Government Pension Fund (Norway)	1,066,380
National Pension Fund (South Korea)	637,279
National Social Security Fund (China)	361,087
Central Provident Fund (Singapore)	315,857
Canada Pension (Canada)	315,344
Employees' Provident Fund (Malaysia)	226,101
Employees' Provident (India)	168,095
GEPF (South Africa)	129,914
National Wealth Fund (Russia)	125,302

Source: "P&I 300 2020 Release." [online] from https://www.thinkingaheadinstitute.org/news/article/pi-300-2020-press-release/ [Press release August 26, 2020], from Thinking Ahead Institute.

★ 2648 ★
Pensions
SIC: 6371; NAICS: 52511

Pension Fund Assets by Country, 2020

Shares are shown for the top 300 fund assets under management.

United States	38.0%
Japan	12.0
Netherlands	6.7
Canada	5.8
Norway	5.5
United Kingdom	4.3
Australia	4.1
South Korea	3.4
Denmark	2.1
Sweden	2.0
Other	16.1

Source: "P&I 300 2020 Release." [online] from https://www.thinkingaheadinstitute.org/news/article/pi-300-2020-press-release/ [Press release August 26, 2020], from Willis Towers Watson.

★ 2649 ★
Peppers, Pimentos and Olives
SIC: 2099; NAICS: 311991

Leading Pepper/Pimento/Olive Brands, 2020

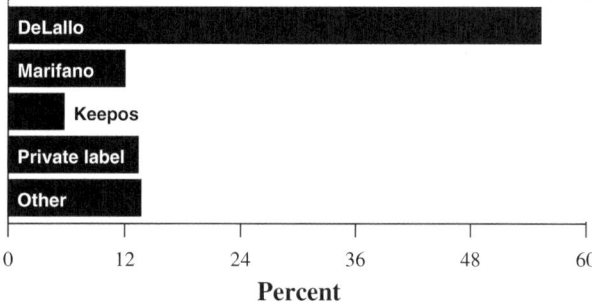

Brands are ranked based on sales at supermarkets, drug stores, mass merchandisers, military commissaries, and select club and dollar chains for the 12 weeks ended September 6, 2020.

	($ mil.)	Share
DeLallo	$ 5.62	55.26%
Marifano	1.22	12.00
Keepos	0.58	5.70
Private label	1.36	13.37
Other	1.39	13.67

Source: *Frozen & Refrigerated Buyer*, November 2020, p. 10, from IRI.

★ 2650 ★
Personal Care Products
SIC: 2844; NAICS: 32562

Beauty Product Sales in China, 2019

Retail sales of beauty products grew from 251.4 billion renminbi in 2017 to 271.8 billion renminbi in 2018 to 299.2 billion in renminbi in 2019. Beauty care sales suffered in the first several months of 2020 because of COVID-19. However, sales are expected to recover quickly, as men see beauty care products as a necessary expense.

Skin Care	54.0%
Cosmetics	10.0
Other	36.0

Source: "Beauty Sector Before and After COVID-19." [online] from https://daxueconsulting.com/how-millenials-and-low-tier-cities-are-shaping-chinas-jewelry-market/ [Published May 2020], from Daxue Consulting.

★ 2651 ★
Personal Care Products
SIC: 2844; NAICS: 32562

Largest Beauty Care Firms Worldwide, 2019

Companies are ranked by beauty sales in billions of dollars.

L'Oréal	$ 33.4
Unilever	24.5
The Estée Lauder Cos. Inc.	14.3
Colgate-Palmolive Co.	13.1
Procter & Gamble Co.	12.9
Shiseido Co.	10.8
LVMH	7.7
Beiersdorf AG	7.0
Johnson & Johnson Co.	6.3
Kao Corp.	5.9

Source: *Beauty Packaging*, October-November 2020, p. NA.

★ 2652 ★
Personal Care Products
SIC: 2844; NAICS: 32562

Leading Beauty and Personal Care Firms, 2016 and 2019

Market shares are shown in percent.

	2016	2019
L'Oréal	12.7%	12.4%
Procter & Gamble Co.	10.8	10.7
Estée Lauder Cos. Inc.	7.4	7.3
Private label	5.8	5.6
Other	63.3	64.0

Source: "U.S. Consumer Goods: Sector Overview, Credit Trends and Outlook." [online] from https://www.spglobal.com/_assets/documents/ratings/research/100049347.pdf [Published March 2021], from Euromonitor.

★ 2653 ★
Personal Care Products
SIC: 3421; NAICS: 332215

Leading Refillable Razor Makers Worldwide, 2019

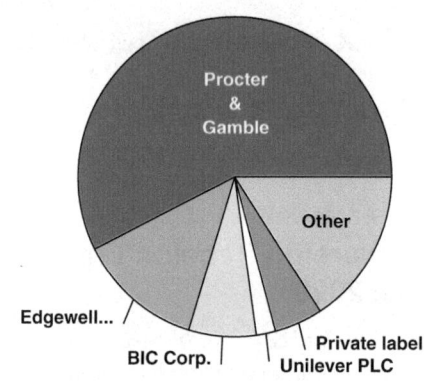

The industry was valued at €12 billion. Refillables claimed 58% of overall razor set sales, one-piece 39% and double-edge 3%.

Procter & Gamble Co.	58.0%
Edgewell Personal Care Co.	13.0
BIC Corp.	7.0
Unilever PLC	2.0
Private label	5.0
Other	16.0

Source: "BIC Group Presentation for Investors." [online] from http://www.bicworld.com [Published November 2020].

★ 2654 ★
Personal Care Products
SIC: 3999; NAICS: 326199

Top Bath/Body Scrubber/Massager Brands, 2020

Market shares are shown based on drug store sales for the 52 weeks ended April 19, 2020.

Axe Detailer	2.78%
Revlon	1.85
Clio Plum Beauty	1.05

Continued on next page.

★ 2654 ★
[Continued]
Personal Care Products
SIC: 3999; NAICS: 326199

Top Bath/Body Scrubber/Massager Brands, 2020

Market shares are shown based on drug store sales for the 52 weeks ended April 19, 2020.

Danielle Creations	0.91%
Sage	0.70
Dove Men+Care	0.64
Simple Pleasures	0.62
Back Buddie	0.47
Private label	86.09
Other	4.89

Source: DrugStore Management, Annual 2020-2021, p. 88, from IRI.

★ 2655 ★
Personal Care Products
SIC: 2844; NAICS: 32562

Top Deodorant Brands, 2020

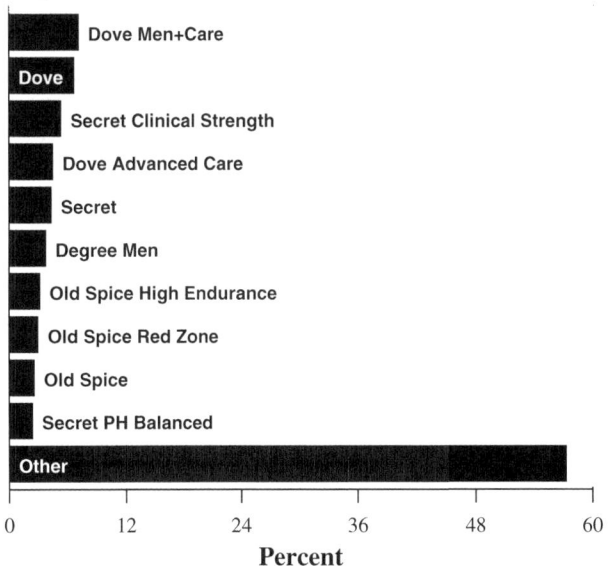

Market shares are shown based on drug store sales for the 52 weeks ended April 19, 2020.

Dove Men+Care	7.10%
Dove	6.64
Secret Clinical Strength	5.30
Dove Advanced Care	4.48
Secret	4.32
Degree Men	3.76
Old Spice High Endurance	3.17
Old Spice Red Zone	2.96
Old Spice	2.58
Secret PH Balanced	2.39%
Other	57.30

Source: DrugStore Management, Annual 2020-2021, p. 88, from IRI.

★ 2656 ★
Personal Care Products
SIC: 2844; NAICS: 32562

Top Deodorant Makers, 2020

Companies are ranked based on sales at supermarkets, drug stores, mass merchandisers, military commissaries, and select club and dollar chains for the 52 weeks ended October 4, 2020.

	($ mil.)	Share
Unilever PLC	$1,440.41	44.63%
Procter & Gamble Co.	1,189.03	36.84
The Dial Corp.	104.29	3.23
Colgate-Palmolive Co.	83.12	2.58
Native	75.64	2.34
Other	334.81	10.37

Source: Household and Personal Products Industry, November 2020, p. 52, from Market Advantage TSV and IRI Liquid Data.

★ 2657 ★
Personal Care Products
SIC: 3069; NAICS: 326299

Top Male Contraceptive Makers, 2020

Market shares are shown based on drug store sales for the 52 weeks ended April 19, 2020.

Church & Dwight Co. Inc.	69.61%
Reckitt Benckiser Inc.	15.01
Lifestyles Healthcare	14.70
Global Protection Corp.	0.53
Okamoto USA	0.12
Other	0.03

Source: DrugStore Management, Annual 2020-2021, p. 95, from IRI.

★ 2658 ★
Personal Care Products
SIC: 2844; NAICS: 32562

Top Personal Lubricant Makers, 2020

Market shares are shown based on drug store sales for the 52 weeks ended April 19, 2020.

Reckitt Benckiser Inc.	40.25%
Biofilm Inc.	19.33

Continued on next page.

★ 2658 ★
[Continued]
Personal Care Products
SIC: 2844; NAICS: 32562
Top Personal Lubricant Makers, 2020

Market shares are shown based on drug store sales for the 52 weeks ended April 19, 2020.

Church & Dwight Co. Inc.	9.04%
Trigg Labs	7.05
Private label	13.93
Other	10.40

Source: *DrugStore Management*, Annual 2020-2021, p. 98, from IRI.

★ 2659 ★
Personal Watercraft
SIC: 3799; NAICS: 336999
Personal Watercraft Market, 2020

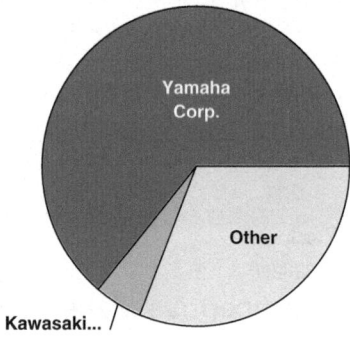

Average industry growth fell 2.8% from 2015 to 2020, when it reached $673.6 million.

Yamaha Corp.	64.0%
Kawasaki Motors Corp.	4.9
Other	31.1

Source: "Personal Watercraft Manufacturing Industry in the U.S." [online] from http://www.ibisworld.com [Published November 2020], from IBISWorld.

★ 2660 ★
Pest Control Industry
SIC: 3999; NAICS: 339999
Leading Outdoor Pest Control Device Makers Worldwide, 2019

Outdoor pest control devices emit high-frequency sound to repel rodents and insects. Market shares are shown based on revenue.

Woodstream Corp.	8.91%
Bird B Gone	2.96
Bell Labs	2.87%
Other	85.26

Source: "Global Outdoor Pest Control Devices Market Research Report 2020." [online] from http://www.qyresearch.com [Published March 2020], from QY Research.

★ 2661 ★
Pest Control Industry
SIC: 7342; NAICS: 56171
Leading Pest Control Firms in North America, 2019

Companies are ranked by pest control revenue in millions of dollars. Total professional pest control revenue reached $9.359 billion.

	($ mil.)	Share
Rollins Inc.	$ 2,015.0	21.53%
Terminix International	1,710.0	18.27
Rentokil Initial	950.0	10.15
Ecolab Inc.	557.9	5.96
Massey Services Inc.	261.2	2.79
Arrow Exterminators	253.4	2.71
Aptiv International	199.7	2.13
Anticimex	194.6	2.08
Cook's Pest Control	180.0	1.92
Terminix Service	133.0	1.42
Other	2,904.2	31.03

Source: *Pest Control Technology*, May 2020, p. NA, from Research and Markets.

★ 2662 ★
Pest Control Industry
SIC: 7342; NAICS: 56171
Leading Pest Control Firms Worldwide, 2018

Companies are ranked by pest control revenue in millions of dollars. Global pest control revenue was estimated to reach approximately $20 billion. North America claimed 58% of the total, Europe 19%, Asia 14%, and the Pacific Region and other regions 4.5% each.

	($ mil.)	Share
Rentokil Initial	$ 2,094	10.47%
Rollins Inc. (Orkin)	2,015	10.07
ServiceMaster Corp.	1,655	8.27
Ecolab Inc.	907	4.53
Anticimex	513	2.57
Other	12,816	64.08

Source: *Pest Control Technology*, May 2020, p. NA, from Research and Markets.

★ 2663 ★
Pet Food
SIC: 2047; NAICS: 311111

Cat and Dog Food Sales in Italy, 2019

There were 29.9 million fish, 12.9 million birds, 7.3 million cats, 7 million dogs, 1.8 million small animals and 1.4 million reptiles in the country. Cat and dog food sales at grocery stores, traditional pet shops, and chain pet shops generated turnover of €2.078 billion. The market for small animal pet food was worth €12.5 million. Birds claimed 39.2% of the total, rodents 30.2% and other small animals 30.6%.

Cats	52.6%
Dogs	47.4

Source: *Pet Food & Animal Feed Technology*, October 2020, p. 35, from Zoomark.

★ 2664 ★
Pet Food
SIC: 2047; NAICS: 311111

Largest Premium Pet Nutrition Markets Worldwide, 2019

Consumers are showing an increasing interest in high-quality pet food in order to ensure the health and wellbeing of their pets. The source notes that premium pet food sales began to take off in 2010, when Blue Buffalo urged consumers to take the "True Blue Test." Other vendors during this time also emphasized the natural ingredients used in their products. Market shares are shown in percent.

United States	43.6%
Japan	5.4
Germany	5.0
France	4.7
Italy	4.7
Australia	4.2
Canada	4.2
China	4.0
United Kingdom	3.2
Russia	2.3
Brazil	2.1
Mexico	1.2
Other	15.3

Source: "Solid Gold Investor Presentation." [online] from http://media.biostime.com/hhglobal/files [Published November 2020], from Euromonitor.

★ 2665 ★
Pet Food
SIC: 2047; NAICS: 311111

Leading Dog Food Makers in India, 2020

Market shares are shown in percent.

Mars International India Pvt Ltd.	29.0%
Royal Canin India Pvt Ltd.	19.6
Indian Broiler Group	13.9
Purina Pet Care India Pvt Ltd.	2.7
Cuddle Up Diet Products Pvt Ltd.	2.6
Other	32.0

Source: "The Packaged Dog Food Market in India." [online] from https://casereads.com/the-packaged-dog-food-market-in-india/ [Published December 22, 2020], from Euromonitor.

★ 2666 ★
Pet Food
SIC: 2047; NAICS: 311111

Leading Fresh Pet Food Makers Worldwide, 2019

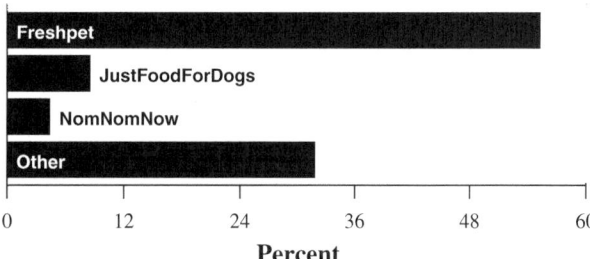

Fresh pet food uses fresh ingredients, is gently cooked without preservatives, and kept in the refrigerator. The industry was valued at $413 million in 2019. Market shares are shown based on revenue.

Freshpet	55.30%
JustFoodForDogs	8.50
NomNomNow	4.38
Other	31.82

Source: "Global Fresh Pet Market Research Report 2020." [online] from http://www.qyresearch.com [Published July 2020], from QY Research.

★ 2667 ★
Pet Food
SIC: 2047; NAICS: 311111

Pet Food and Treat Sales, 2013-2022

Sales are shown in millions of dollars. Figures are estimated for 2019-2022.

2013	$ 28.2
2014	28.9
2015	30.0
2016	31.5
2017	33.1
2018	34.6
2019	35.8
2020	37.0
2021	38.2
2022	39.4

Source: "Better Choice Company Investor Presentation." [online] from https://betterchoicecompany.com/wp-content/uploads/2020/08/bttr-Investor-presentation.pdf [Published August 4, 2020], from Packaged Facts.

★ 2668 ★
Pet Food
SIC: 2047; NAICS: 311111

Pet Food Sales by Category, 2020

Categories are ranked by sales in millions of dollars at supermarkets, drug stores, mass merchandisers, military commissaries, and select club and dollar chains for the 52 weeks ended August 9, 2020. All categories saw sales increase from the previous 52 week period except for refrigerated/frozen cat food which saw its sales decline by 12.6%.

	($ mil.)	Share
Dry dog food	$ 5,417.0	33.23%
Dog treats	2,955.0	18.13
Dry cat food	2,448.0	15.02
Wet cat food	2,390.0	14.66
Wet dog food	1,860.0	11.41
Cat treats	835.0	5.12
Refrigerated/frozen dog food	389.0	2.39
Refrigerated/frozen cat food	7.7	0.05

Source: *Pet Food Processing Resource Guide*, Annual 2020, p. 12, from IRI.

★ 2669 ★
Pet Food
SIC: 2047; NAICS: 311111

Sales of Animal-Based Pet Food Ingredients, 2019

Sales are shown in millions of dollars. Total value of animal-based ingredients reached $4.63 billion. By volume, the market reached 3.83 million tons. There were 8.65 million tons of food ingredients used in cat and dog food production, valued at $6.9 billion.

	($ mil.)	Share
Meat and poultry	$ 2,794.60	60.23%
Broth	834.25	17.98
By-product and organ meat	294.73	6.35
Poultry meal	276.74	5.96
Animal meal	211.34	4.56
Animal fat	125.00	2.69
Fish meal	74.49	1.61
Poultry fat	28.43	0.61

Source: *Oils & Fats International*, January 2021, p. 28, from Decision Innovation Solutions.

★ 2670 ★
Pet Food
SIC: 2047; NAICS: 311111

Top Cat Treat and Beverage Makers, 2020

Companies are ranked by sales in thousands of dollars at supermarkets, drug stores, mass merchandisers, military commissaries, and select club and dollar chains for the 52 weeks ended August 9, 2020. Ainsworth Pet Nutrition saw sales increase the most, 79.9%, from the previous 52 week period. Big Heart Pet Brands was the only firm to see its sales decrease.

	($ mil.)	Share
Mars Petcare	$ 467.46	55.96%
Nestlé Purina PetCare Co.	215.43	25.79
Hartz Mountain Corp.	89.21	10.68
Big Heart Pet Brands	17.40	2.08
Blue Buffalo Co. Ltd.	11.69	1.40
Worldwise Inc.	8.02	0.96
Ainsworth Pet Nutrition L.L.C.	6.23	0.75
Cosmic Pet L.L.C.	1.00	0.12
Private label	16.70	2.00
Other	2.28	0.27

Source: *Pet Food Processing Resource Guide*, Annual 2020, p. 16, from IRI.

★ 2671 ★
Pet Food
SIC: 2047; NAICS: 311111

Top Dog Biscuit, Treat and Beverage Makers, 2020

Companies are ranked by sales in thousands of dollars at supermarkets, drug stores, mass merchandisers, military commissaries, and select club and dollar chains for the 52 weeks ended August 9, 2020. Blue Buffalo saw sales increase the most, 57.0%, from the previous 52 week period. Waggin Train saw its sales decrease the most, 4.0%.

	($ mil.)	Share
Big Heart Pet Brands	$ 833.74	28.21%
Nestlé Purina PetCare Co.	436.29	14.76
Mars Petcare	288.00	9.74
Tyson Pet Products Inc.	194.62	6.58
Petmatrix L.L.C.	170.76	5.78
Blue Buffalo Co. Ltd.	108.39	3.67
Ainsworth Pet Nutrition L.L.C.	76.83	2.60
Spectrum Brands Inc.	58.57	1.98
Waggin Train	53.28	1.80
Private label	411.87	13.93
Other	323.40	10.94

Source: *Pet Food Processing Resource Guide*, Annual 2020, p. 16, from IRI.

★ 2672 ★
Pet Food
SIC: 2047; NAICS: 311111

Top Dog Biscuits/Treats/Beverage Brands, 2020

Brands are ranked by sales at supermarkets, drug stores, mass merchandisers, military commissaries, and select club and dollar chains for the 52 weeks ended July 12, 2020. Figures are in millions of dollars.

	($ mil.)	Share
Milk-Bone	$ 213.58	7.28%
Pup-Peroni	157.79	5.38
Purina Beggin' Strips	140.77	4.80
Canine Carry Outs	131.03	4.46
PetMatrix DreamBone	96.77	3.30
Pedigree DentaStix	95.68	3.26
Nudges Jerky Cuts	91.61	3.12
Greenies	65.84	2.24
Healthy Hide Good 'n' Fun	58.27	1.98
Private label	407.75	13.89
Other	1,476.44	50.30

Source: *2020 Sosland Publishing's Corporate Profiles State of the Industry Report*, October 2020, p. 53, from Information Resources Inc.

★ 2673 ★
Pet Food
SIC: 2047; NAICS: 311111

Top Dry Cat Food Brands, 2020

Brands are ranked by sales at supermarkets, drug stores, mass merchandisers, military commissaries, and select club and dollar chains for the 52 weeks ended July 12, 2020. Figures are in millions of dollars.

	($ mil.)	Share
Purina Kit & Kaboodle	$ 208.85	8.54%
Meow Mix Original Choice	202.75	8.29
Purina Cat Chow Complete	154.77	6.33
Meow Mix Tender Centers	119.92	4.90
Purina Cat Chow Naturals	111.41	4.56
Purina Friskies Seafood Sensations	86.70	3.55
Rachael Ray Nutrish	75.40	3.08
Iams ProActive Health	74.77	3.06
Meow Mix	73.76	3.02
Private label	205.64	8.41
Other	1,130.93	46.26

Source: *2020 Sosland Publishing's Corporate Profiles State of the Industry Report*, October 2020, p. 52, from Information Resources Inc.

★ 2674 ★
Pet Food
SIC: 2047; NAICS: 311111

Top Dry Cat Food Makers, 2020

Companies are ranked by sales in millions of dollars at supermarkets, drug stores, mass merchandisers, military commissaries, and select club and dollar chains for the 52 weeks ended August 9, 2020. Blue Buffalo sales jumped 61.9% from the previous 52 week period, the highest gain among all brands listed. Mars Inc. sales declined the most, 46.5%.

	($ mil.)	Share
Nestlé Purina PetCare Co.	$ 1,260.60	51.49%
Big Heart Pet Brands	576.29	23.54
Mars Petcare	187.19	7.65
Blue Buffalo Co. Ltd.	106.14	4.34
Ainsworth Pet Nutrition	78.10	3.19
Mars Inc.	7.62	0.31
I and love and you	4.57	0.19
Simmons Pet Food Inc.	4.57	0.19
Sunshine Mills Inc.	3.79	0.15
Private label	210.87	8.61
Other	8.36	0.34

Source: *Pet Food Processing Resource Guide*, Annual 2020, p. 14, from IRI.

★ 2675 ★
Pet Food
SIC: 2047; NAICS: 311111

Top Dry Dog Food Brands, 2020

Brands are ranked by sales at supermarkets, drug stores, mass merchandisers, military commissaries, and select club and dollar chains for the 52 weeks ended July 12, 2020. Figures are in millions of dollars.

	($ mil.)	Share
Pedigree	$ 640.76	11.77%
Purina Dog Chow	523.09	9.61
Purina One SmartBlend	457.80	8.41
Iams ProActive Health	306.05	5.62
Blue Life Protection Formula	273.71	5.03
Rachael Ray Nutrish	257.28	4.73
Kibbles 'n Bits	238.73	4.39
Purina One SmartBlend True Instinct	144.69	2.66
Purina Beneful	117.88	2.17
Private label	697.33	12.81
Other	1,786.66	32.82

Source: *2020 Sosland Publishing's Corporate Profiles State of the Industry Report*, October 2020, p. 52, from Information Resources Inc.

★ 2676 ★
Pet Food
SIC: 2047; NAICS: 311111

Top Dry Dog Food Makers, 2020

Companies are ranked by sales in millions of dollars at supermarkets, drug stores, mass merchandisers, military commissaries, and select club and dollar chains for the 52 weeks ended August 9, 2020. Blue Buffalo sales saw the largest gain from the previous 52 week period, 67.5%, while Mars Inc. saw its sales decline the most, 23.4%.

	($ mil.)	Share
Nestlé Purina PetCare Co.	$ 2,018.23	37.26%
Mars Petcare	1,290.20	23.82
Big Heart Pet Brands	484.37	8.94
Ainsworth Pet Nutrition	406.04	7.50
Blue Buffalo Co. Ltd.	394.71	7.29
Sunshine Mills Inc.	24.98	0.46
American Pet Nutrition Inc.	22.66	0.42
Mars Inc.	18.23	0.34
Gentle Giants	15.01	0.28
Private label	689.18	12.72
Other	53.50	0.99

Source: *Pet Food Processing Resource Guide*, Annual 2020, p. 14, from IRI.

★ 2677 ★
Pet Food
SIC: 2047; NAICS: 311111

Top Frozen/Refrigerated Cat Food Makers, 2020

Companies are ranked by sales at supermarkets, drug stores, mass merchandisers, military commissaries, and select club and dollar chains for the 52 weeks ended August 9, 2020.

	Sales	Share
Freshpet	$ 7,739,972	99.99%
Primal Pet Foods	1,012	0.01

Source: *Pet Food Processing Resource Guide*, Annual 2020, p. 15, from IRI.

★ 2678 ★
Pet Food
SIC: 2047; NAICS: 311111

Top Frozen/Refrigerated Dog Food Makers, 2020

Companies are ranked by sales in thousands of dollars at supermarkets, drug stores, mass merchandisers, military commissaries, and select club and dollar chains for the 52 weeks ended August 9, 2020. Yogi-Dog saw sales increase the most, 114.3%, from the previous 52 week period, followed by The Bear & The Rat with a 69.5% increase. The Barking Dog, whose sales decreased 58.4%, was the only company to see its sales fall over this time period.

	($ mil.)	Share
Freshpet	$ 342,992.09	88.09%
Nestlé Purina PetCare Co.	25,711.85	6.60
J&J Snack Foods Corp.	11,449.89	2.94
Bil-Jac	3,555.94	0.91
The Bear & The Rat	2,173.25	0.56
The Barking Dog	103.53	0.03
Yogi-Dog	136.02	0.03
Idahound	63.11	0.02
Pooch Cake	46.23	0.01
Private label	3,041.68	0.78
Other	91.41	0.02

Source: *Pet Food Processing Resource Guide*, Annual 2020, p. 15, from IRI.

★ 2679 ★
Pet Food
SIC: 2047; NAICS: 311111

Top Pet Food Makers in Australia, 2020

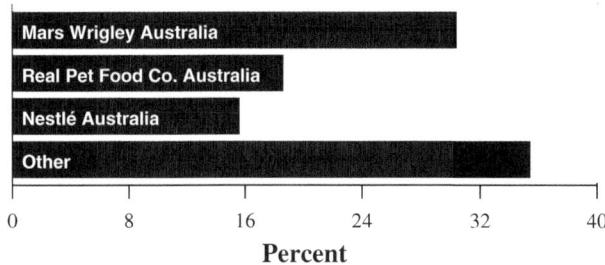

Australia has one of the highest pet ownership rates in the world, with approximately 60% of households owning a pet. The pet population consists of roughly 8.7 million fish, 4.8 million dogs, 4.2 million birds, 3.9 million cats, and a number of small animals. Market shares are shown in percent.

Mars Wrigley Australia	30.4%
Real Pet Food Co. Australia	18.6
Nestlé Australia	15.6
Other	35.4

Source: "Australian Pet Food Market Trend." [online] from http://www.news.kotra.or.kr [Published April 5, 2021], from IBISWorld.

★ 2680 ★
Pet Food
SIC: 2047; NAICS: 311111

Top Pet Food Makers in Japan, 2018

Companies are ranked by sales in millions of yen. Dog food claimed 50% of the market, cat food 45%, and other types 5%.

	(mil.)	Share
Mars Japan Ltd.	¥ 68,540	18.5%
Unicharm Corp.	39,100	10.6
Royal Canin Japan Inc.	31,820	8.6
Inaba-Petfood Co. Inc.	29,700	8.0
Nestlé Japan	29,150	7.9
Hills-Colgate Japan Ltd.	26,550	7.2
Doggyman Ha Co. Ltd.	13,200	3.6
Nisshin Pet Food Inc.	13,500	3.6
Nippon Pet Food Co. Ltd.	12,300	3.3
Petline	11,834	3.2
Other	49,887	25.5

Source: "Japan Pet Food Market Trend." [online] from http://news.kotra.or.kr [Published September 18, 2020], from Yano Economic Research Institute.

★ 2681 ★
Pet Food
SIC: 2047; NAICS: 311111

Top Pet Food Makers Worldwide, 2020

Companies are ranked by sales in millions of dollars. Shares are shown based on sales generated by the top 40 companies.

	($ mil.)	Share
Mars Petcare Inc.	$ 18,085.00	33.9%
Nestlé Purina PetCare Co.	13,955.00	26.1
The J.M. Smucker Co.	2,822.00	5.3
Hill's Pet Nutrition	2,388.00	4.5
Diamond Pet Foods	1,500.00	2.8
General Mills Inc.	1,430.00	2.7
Spectrum Brands/United Pet Group	870.20	1.6
Unicharm Corp.	748.59	1.4
Deuerer	721.10	1.4
Heristo AG	700.00	1.3
Simmons Pet Food Inc.	700.00	1.3
WellPet L.L.C.	700.00	1.3
Agrolimen SA	580.00	1.1
Thai Union Group	575.39	1.1
Jeil Feed	534.72	1.0
Other	7,107.10	13.3

Source: *Petfood Industry*, June 2020, p. 10, from WATT Global Media.

★ 2682 ★
Pet Food
SIC: 2047; NAICS: 311111

Top Wet Cat Food Makers, 2020

Companies are ranked by sales in millions of dollars at supermarkets, drug stores, mass merchandisers, military commissaries, and select club and dollar chains for the 52 weeks ended August 9, 2020. I and love and you sales jumped 107.6% from the previous 52 week period, the highest gain among all brands listed. Mars Inc. sales declined the most, 54.8%.

	($ mil.)	Share
Nestlé Purina PetCare Co.	$ 1,781.88	74.55%
Big Heart Pet Brands	201.72	8.44
Mars Petcare	183.83	7.69
Blue Buffalo Co. Ltd.	54.40	2.28
Ainsworth Pet Nutrition	19.55	0.82
I and love and you	4.84	0.20
Mars Inc.	2.91	0.12
MPM Products Ltd.	2.30	0.10
Simmons Pet Food Inc.	2.26	0.09

Continued on next page.

★ 2682 ★
[Continued]
Pet Food
SIC: 2047; NAICS: 311111
Top Wet Cat Food Makers, 2020

Companies are ranked by sales in millions of dollars at supermarkets, drug stores, mass merchandisers, military commissaries, and select club and dollar chains for the 52 weeks ended August 9, 2020. I and love and you sales jumped 107.6% from the previous 52 week period, the highest gain among all brands listed. Mars Inc. sales declined the most, 54.8%.

	($ mil.)	Share
Private label	$130.26	5.45%
Other	6.19	0.26

Source: *Pet Food Processing Resource Guide*, Annual 2020, p. 14, from IRI.

★ 2683 ★
Pet Food
SIC: 2047; NAICS: 311111
Top Wet Dog Food Makers, 2020

Companies are ranked by sales in millions of dollars at supermarkets, drug stores, mass merchandisers, military commissaries, and select club and dollar chains for the 52 weeks ended August 9, 2020. I and love and you saw sales increase the most, 79.1%, from the previous 52 week period, followed by Blue Buffalo with a 58.0% increase. Mars Inc. saw their sales decrease 51.5%, followed by Newman's Own Organics with a 36.0% decrease.

	($ mil.)	Share
Mars Petcare	$958.36	51.51%
Nestlé Purina PetCare Co.	529.51	28.46
Blue Buffalo Co. Ltd.	113.01	6.07
Ainsworth Pet Nutrition	47.42	2.55
Big Heart Pet Brands	43.17	2.32
Newman's Own Organics Inc.	5.35	0.29
I and love and you	2.66	0.14
Mars Inc.	2.28	0.12
Sunshine Mills Inc.	1.84	0.10
Private label	147.22	7.91
Other	9.70	0.52

Source: *Pet Food Processing Resource Guide*, Annual 2020, p. 15, from IRI.

★ 2684 ★
Pet Food
SIC: 2047; NAICS: 311111
Wild Bird Food Sales, 2020

Sales are shown for the previous 12 months in the independent hardware channel. The top 5 items represented 32.5% of unit sales, the top 10 items 45.4%, the top 20 items 59.7%, and top 30 items 67.4%.

Mixed seed blends	54.3%
Straight sunflower seed	18.1
Suets	11.4
Straight thistle/Nyjer seed	3.8
Hummingbird food	3.5
Pressed seed	3.3
Straight safflower seed	1.8
Dried mealworms	1.5
Other	2.1

Source: *The Hardware Connection*, Sept./Oct. 2020, p. 76, from Vista Information Services, division of Epicor Software Corp.

★ 2685 ★
Pet Products
SIC: 2399; NAICS: 314999
Top Dog Apparel Makers Worldwide, 2018

The industry generated revenue of $775 million in 2019. North America was the global leader with a 57.08% market share.

Weatherbeeta	2.01%
Ruffwear	1.87
Other	96.12

Source: "COVID-19 Impact on Global Dog Apparel Market Share Status and Forecast 2020-2026." [online] from http://reports.valuates.com [Published April 2020], from QY Research.

★ 2686 ★
Pet Services
SIC: 2834; NAICS: 325412
Leading Pet Care Firms, 2017 and 2019

Market shares are shown in percent.

	2017	2019
Nestlé S.A.	19.9%	19.3%
Mars Inc.	12.8	12.6
The J.M. Smucker Co.	5.8	6.6

Continued on next page.

★ 2686 ★
[Continued]
Pet Services
SIC: 2834; NAICS: 325412

Leading Pet Care Firms, 2017 and 2019

Market shares are shown in percent.

	2017	2019
Private label	11.8%	12.5%
Other	49.7	49.0

Source: "U.S. Consumer Goods: Sector Overview, Credit Trends and Outlook." [online] from https://www.spglobal.com/_assets/documents/ratings/research/100049347.pdf [Published March 2021], from Euromonitor.

★ 2687 ★
Pet Stores
SIC: 5999; NAICS: 45391

Largest Pet Store Retailers in North America, 2020

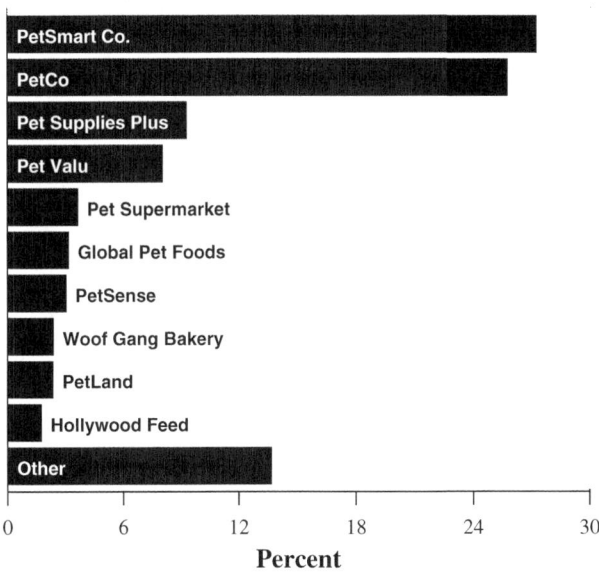

Companies are ranked by estimated number of outlets. Shares are shown based on the 6,063 stores operated by the top 25 firms. Figures are as of March 1, 2021.

	Stores	Share
PetSmart Co.	1,650	27.21%
PetCo	1,559	25.71
Pet Supplies Plus	561	9.25
Pet Valu	486	8.02
Pet Supermarket	219	3.61
Global Pet Foods	190	3.13
PetSense	182	3.00
Woof Gang Bakery	142	2.34
PetLand	141	2.33
Hollywood Feed	105	1.73%
Other	828	13.66

Source: *Pet Business*, March 2021, p. 67.

★ 2688 ★
Pet Stores
SIC: 5999; NAICS: 45391

Leading Online Pet Product Retailers, 2020

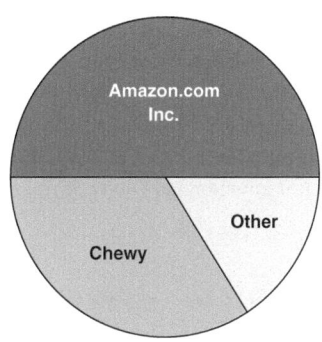

Market shares are shown in percent.

Amazon.com Inc.	50.0%
Chewy	34.0
Other	16.0

Source: *Atlanta Journal-Constitution*, January 1, 2021, p. NA, from 1010data.

★ 2689 ★
Pet Stores
SIC: 5999; NAICS: 45391

Premium Pet Nutrition Sales by Channel, 2019

Just as many consumers have turned away from processed foods, pet owners are looking past heavily processed pet food for healthier alternatives. Chilled pet food is seen as retaining its nutritional properties better than canned or dry food; raw food is thought to be closer to what animals eat in the wild. Premium pet food sales are shown by channel.

Food, drug, mass merchandisers	46.0%
E-commerce	22.0
Pet specialty	17.0
Vets	4.0

Continued on next page.

★ 2689 ★
[Continued]
Pet Stores
SIC: 5999; NAICS: 45391

Premium Pet Nutrition Sales by Channel, 2019

Just as many consumers have turned away from processed foods, pet owners are looking past heavily processed pet food for healthier alternatives. Chilled pet food is seen as retaining its nutritional properties better than canned or dry food; raw food is thought to be closer to what animals eat in the wild. Premium pet food sales are shown by channel.

Neighborhood pet stores	3.0%
Other	7.0

Source: "Solid Gold Investor Presentation." [online] from http://media.biostime.com/hhglobal/files [Published November 2020], from Euromonitor and Oliver Wyman estimates.

★ 2690 ★
Pet Stores
SIC: 5999; NAICS: 45391

Premium Pet Nutrition Sales by Channel in China, 2019

China agreed to lift a trade ban on certain U.S. poultry and other products in early 2020. This was good news for U.S. pet food makers. China's pet product industry is growing. The country was not one of the top 10 export markets for pet food from the United States in 2020; by 2021, it is expected to be second only to Canada. Premium pet foods are not widely available in China offline, but that is expected to soon change. Taoball and Tmall represent 75% of the e-commerce segment, which is the fastest growing. Market shares are shown in percent.

E-commerce	50.0%
Neighborhood pet stores	29.0
Food, drug, mass merchandisers	9.0
Vets	9.0
Pet specialty	2.0
Other	1.0

Source: "Solid Gold Investor Presentation." [online] from http://media.biostime.com/hhglobal/files [Published November 2020], from Euromonitor and Oliver Wyman estimates.

★ 2691 ★
Pets
SIC: 0279; NAICS: 112519

Aquarium Fish Population in Europe, 2019

Data show population in thousands.

	(000)	Share
Russia	3,800	24.45%
France	2,600	16.73
Germany	1,600	10.30
Italy	1,500	9.65
United Kingdom	1,200	7.72
Turkey	900	5.79
Spain	815	5.24
Netherlands	769	4.95
Poland	390	2.51
Denmark	350	2.25
Other	1,616	10.40

Source: "Facts & Figures 2019 European Review." [online] from https://fediaf.org/who-we-are/european-statistics.html [Accessed February 2, 2021], from European Pet Food Industry Federation.

★ 2692 ★
Pets
SIC: 0279; NAICS: 11299

Cat Population in Europe, 2019

Data show population in thousands.

	(000)	Share
Russia	22,800	21.42%
Germany	14,700	13.81
France	14,200	13.34
United Kingdom	7,500	7.05
Italy	7,290	6.85
Poland	6,600	6.20
Romania	4,300	4.04
Spain	3,795	3.57
Turkey	3,800	3.57
Netherlands	2,940	2.76
Other	18,499	17.38

Source: "Facts & Figures 2019 European Review." [online] from https://fediaf.org/who-we-are/european-statistics.html [Accessed February 2, 2021], from European Pet Food Industry Federation.

★ 2693 ★
Pets
SIC: 0279; NAICS: 11299

Dog Population in Europe, 2019

Data show population in thousands.

	(000)	Share
Russia	16,800	19.20%
Germany	10,100	11.54
United Kingdom	9,000	10.28
Poland	7,750	8.86
France	7,600	8.68
Italy	7,011	8.01
Spain	6,733	7.69
Romania	4,150	4.74
Belgium	1,320	1.51
Other	17,046	19.48

Source: "Facts & Figures 2019 European Review." [online] from https://fediaf.org/who-we-are/european-statistics.html [Accessed February 2, 2021], from European Pet Food Industry Federation.

★ 2694 ★
Pets
SIC: 0279; NAICS: 11299

Ornamental Bird Population in Europe, 2019

Data show population in thousands.

	(000)	Share
Italy	12,880	24.83%
Turkey	11,200	21.59
Spain	6,991	13.48
France	4,700	9.06
Germany	4,000	7.71
Russia	3,200	6.17
Netherlands	2,440	4.70
Poland	1,200	2.31
United Kingdom	1,000	1.93
Greece	970	1.87
Other	3,287	6.34

Source: "Facts & Figures 2019 European Review." [online] from https://fediaf.org/who-we-are/european-statistics.html [Accessed February 2, 2021], from European Pet Food Industry Federation.

★ 2695 ★
Pets
SIC: 2047; NAICS: 311111

Pet Ownership in China, 2019

According to the State Council of China, approximately 73.55 million households own a pet. The table shows share of overall pet population.

Dog	34.0%
Cat	20.0
Fish	15.0
Other	31.0

Source: "China Pet Food Market Growth, Trends, and Forecast (2020-2025)." [online] from http://www.mordorintelligence.com [Accessed January 5, 2021], from Mordor Intelligence and State Council of China.

★ 2696 ★
Pets
SIC/NAICS: See frontmatter for explanation.

Pet Population, 2019-2020

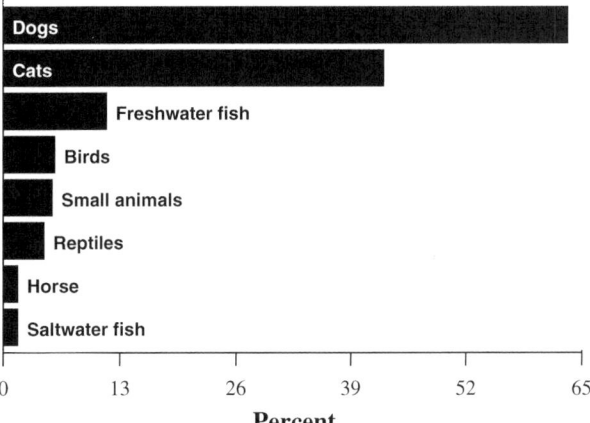

Data show the millions of households that own a pet. Pet spending is forecast to grow from $95.7 billion in 2019 to $99 billion in 2020. Pet food claimed $36.9 billion, or 38.55%, of the total in 2019; vet care $29.3 billion (30.6%); supplies, live animals, and OTC treatments $19.2 billion (20.06%); other categories, such as boarding, training, and insurance, the remaining $10.3 billion (10.7%).

Dogs	63.4
Cats	42.7
Freshwater fish	11.5
Birds	5.7
Small animals	5.4
Reptiles	4.5

Continued on next page.

★ 2696 ★
[Continued]
Pets
SIC/NAICS: See frontmatter for explanation.

Pet Population, 2019-2020

Data show the millions of households that own a pet. Pet spending is forecast to grow from $95.7 billion in 2019 to $99 billion in 2020. Pet food claimed $36.9 billion, or 38.55%, of the total in 2019; vet care $29.3 billion (30.6%); supplies, live animals, and OTC treatments $19.2 billion (20.06%); other categories, such as boarding, training, and insurance, the remaining $10.3 billion (10.7%).

Horse	1.6
Saltwater fish	1.6

Source: "Pet Industry Market Size & Ownership Statistics." [online] from https://www.americanpetproducts.org/press_industrytrends.asp [Accessed January 5, 2021], from *2019-2020 APPA National Pet Owners Survey*.

★ 2697 ★
Pets
SIC/NAICS: See frontmatter for explanation.

Pet Population in Europe, 2019

Data show the pet population. Europe refers to the member states of the Council of Europe. Approximately 85 million households are thought to own at least one pet.

	(mil.)	Share
Cats	106.42	43.01%
Dogs	87.51	35.36
Small animals	28.57	11.54
Aquaria	15.54	6.28
Reptiles	9.43	3.81

Source: *Petfood Industry*, October 2020, p. 12, from Statista.

★ 2698 ★
Pets
SIC/NAICS: See frontmatter for explanation.

Pet Population in Poland, 2019

Poland's pet care market reached $1.25 billion in 2019, making it a leader among Mid-Eastern European countries. Dog food sales have seen strong growth in recent years, and growth will continue but at a lower rate. Premium cat food sales have shown robust growth in recent years. Figures show population, in thousands.

Dogs	7,750
Cats	6,600
Birds	1,200
Small animals	1,150
Aquaria	390
Reptiles	250

Source: *PETS International*, October 2020, p. 56, from FEDIAF.

★ 2699 ★
Pets
SIC: 0279; NAICS: 11299

Small Mammal Pet Population in Europe, 2019

Data show population in thousands.

	(000)	Share
Russia	6,000	21.00%
Germany	5,200	18.20
France	3,800	13.30
United Kingdom	2,000	7.00
Italy	1,823	6.38
Spain	1,490	5.22
Poland	1,150	4.03
Netherlands	1,120	3.92
Turkey	800	2.80
Austria	510	1.79
Other	4,672	16.36

Source: "Facts & Figures 2019 European Review." [online] from https://fediaf.org/who-we-are/european-statistics.html [Accessed February 2, 2021], from European Pet Food Industry Federation.

★ 2700 ★
Pharmaceutical Refrigeration
SIC: 3585; NAICS: 333415

Pharmaceutical Refrigeration Market in India, 2020

Blue Star has 70-75% of the market.

Blue Star	70.0-75.0%
Other	25.0-30.0

Source: "COVID Vaccine Storage Won't Need Phenomenal Investment, Says Blue Star." [online] from https://www.bloombergquint.com/business/covid-vaccine-storage-transport-wont-need-phenomenal-investment-says-blue-star [Published December 16, 2020].

★ 2701 ★
Pharmacy Benefit Managers
SIC: 5912; NAICS: 44611

Leading Pharmacy Benefit Managers, 2020

Market shares are shown in percent. CVS' figure excludes estimates of double-counted network claims for mail choice filled at CV retail pharmacies. Cigna's figure includes Cigna claims that fully transitioned to Express Scripts claims at the end of 2020. Prime Therapeutics' figure includes estimates of 2020 claims for which Health Ascent Services handled rebate negotiations and pharmacy network contracting. "Other" includes cash pay prescriptions that use a discount card processed by one of the six PBMs shown in this entry.

CVS Health (Caremark)	32.0%
Cigna (Express Scripts + Ascent Health Services)	24.0
UnitedHealth (OptumRx)	21.0
Humana Pharmacy Solutions	8.0
Medimpact Healthcare Systems	6.0
Prime Therapeutics	4.0
Other PBMs and cash pay	4.0

Source: "The Top Pharmacy Benefit Managers of 2020: Vertical Integration Drives Consolidation." [online] from https://www.drugchannels.net/2021/04/the-top-pharmacy-benefit-managers-pbms.html [Published April 6, 2021], from Drug Channels Institute.

★ 2702 ★
Phosphate Rock
SIC: 1475; NAICS: 212392

Top Phosphate Rock Producing Nations, 2020

Countries are ranked by production in thousands of metric tons. Figures for China include large mines only, as reported by the National Bureau of Statistics of China. In the United States, phosphate rock ore was processed into 24 million tons of marketable product valued at $1.7 billion. More than 75% of total domestic output came from Florida and North Carolina, the remainder from Idaho and Utah. Production data are estimated.

	(000)	Share
China	90,000	40.35%
Morocco and Western Sahara	37,000	16.59
United States	24,000	10.76
Russia	13,000	5.83
Jordan	9,200	4.12
Saudi Arabia	6,500	2.91
Brazil	5,500	2.47%
Egypt	5,000	2.24
Vietnam	4,700	2.11
Peru	4,000	1.79
Tunisia	4,000	1.79
Senegal	3,500	1.57
Israel	2,800	1.26
Australia	2,700	1.21
South Africa	2,100	0.94
India	1,500	0.67
Kazakhstan	1,500	0.67
Algeria	1,300	0.58
Finland	1,000	0.45
Uzbekistan	900	0.40
Togo	800	0.36
Mexico	600	0.27
Syria	360	0.16
Other	1,100	0.49

Source: "Mineral Commodity Summaries 2021." [online] from https://www.usgs.gov/centers/nmic/mineral-commodity-summaries [Published January 29, 2021], from U.S. Geological Survey.

★ 2703 ★
Photo Printing
SIC: 2759; NAICS: 323111

Leading Photo Printing and Merchandise Firms Worldwide, 2019

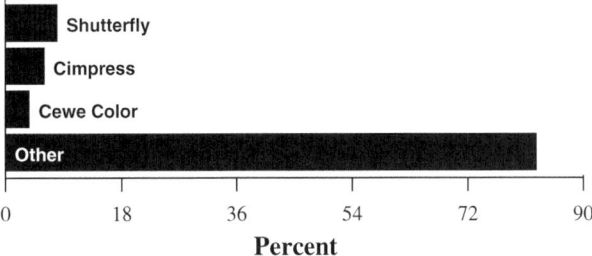

Photo printing and merchandise refers to personalized gifting and decorated products that use photographs. The market is forecast to grow from $19.33 billion in 2020 to $30.7 billion in 2026.

Shutterfly	7.86%
Cimpress	5.88
Cewe Color	3.61
Other	82.65

Source: "Global Photo Printing and Merchandise Market Size, Status and Forecast 2020-2026." [online] from http://www.qyresearch.com [Published September 2020], from QY Research.

★ 2704 ★
Photocontrols
SIC: 3643; NAICS: 335931

Photocontrol Sales by Style, 2020

According to Chapman Electric Supply, photocontrols are "light responsive switches that can be paired with traditional lighting solutions to provide illumination during periods of relative darkness." Distribution is shown based on style for the 12 months ended June 2020.

Twist-lock mount	67.0%
Stem & swivel mount	14.1
Fixed mounting	7.9
Stem mount	6.3
Daylighting	3.5
Other	1.2

Source: *The Electrical Distributor*, November 2020, p. 41, from Epicor's Industry Data Analytics.

★ 2705 ★
Photofinishing
SIC: 7384; NAICS: 812922

One-Hour Photofinishing, 2017

Total sales were valued at $28.04 million. The term "nec" stands for not elsewhere classified.

	($ 000)	Share
Photofinishing services	$ 21,368	79.44%
Passport photography services	1,347	5.01
General individual and group portrait photography services	1,282	4.77
Duplication and copying (except large-run) services for audiovisual works, digital and video	834	3.10
Retail sales of photographic equipment and supplies	767	2.85
School portrait services	322	1.20
Wedding still photography services	136	0.51
Commercial and industrial photography services	35	0.13
Maintenance and repair services for home audio and visual equipment	17	0.06
Other portrait photography services	439	1.63
Other service revenue, nec	350	1.30

Source: "Economic Census." [online] from https://www.census.gov/programs-surveys/economic-census/data/tables.html [Accessed December 2, 2020], from U.S. Census Bureau.

★ 2706 ★
Photofinishing
SIC: 7384; NAICS: 812922

One-Hour Photofinishing Leaders, 2017

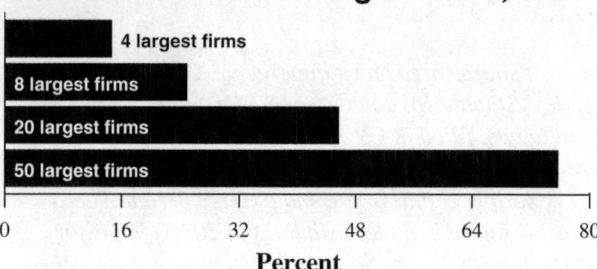

Data show the percent of industry sales held by the largest 4, 8, 20 and 50 firms in the sector. There are approximately 119 players operating in the industry generating employment for 365 people.

4 largest firms	14.6%
8 largest firms	24.8
20 largest firms	45.6
50 largest firms	75.7

Source: "Economic Census." [online] from https://www.census.gov/content/census/en/data/tables/2017/econ/economic-census/naics-sector-31-33.html [Accessed January 21, 2021], from U.S. Census Bureau.

★ 2707 ★
Photographic and Photocopying Equipment
SIC: 3861; NAICS: 333316

Photographic and Photocopying Equipment Manufacturing Leaders, 2017

Data show the percent of industry sales held by the largest 4, 8, 20 and 50 firms in the sector. There are approximately 186 players operating in the industry generating employment for 3,846 people. According to Kentley Insights, the industry generated sales of $1.6 billion in 2019.

4 largest firms	55.4%
8 largest firms	66.4
20 largest firms	79.0
50 largest firms	91.1

Source: "Economic Census." [online] from https://www.census.gov/content/census/en/data/tables/2017/econ/economic-census/naics-sector-31-33.html [Accessed January 21, 2021], from U.S. Census Bureau.

★ 2708 ★
Photographic Equipment Wholesalers
SIC: 5043; NAICS: 42341

Photographic Equipment and Supplies Merchant Wholesale Leaders, 2017

Data show the percent of industry sales held by the largest 4, 8, 20 and 50 firms in the sector. There are approximately 660 players operating in the industry generating employment for 10,766 people.

4 largest firms	57.6%
8 largest firms	69.6
20 largest firms	79.0
50 largest firms	88.0

Source: "Economic Census." [online] from https://www.census.gov/content/census/en/data/tables/2017/econ/economic-census/naics-sector-31-33.html [Accessed January 21, 2021], from U.S. Census Bureau.

★ 2709 ★
Photographic Film and Supplies
SIC: 3861; NAICS: 325992

Photographic Film, Paper, Plate, and Chemical Leaders, 2017

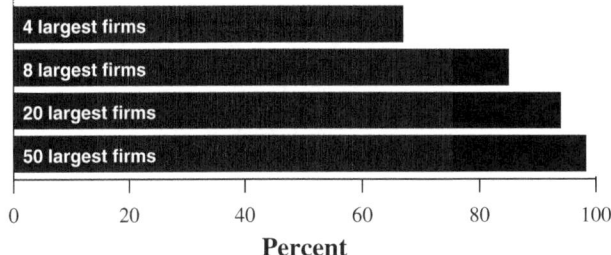

Data show the percent of industry sales held by the largest 4, 8, 20 and 50 firms in the sector. There are approximately 207 players operating in the industry generating employment for 9,083 people.

4 largest firms	66.9%
8 largest firms	85.0
20 largest firms	94.0
50 largest firms	98.3

Source: "Economic Census." [online] from https://www.census.gov/content/census/en/data/tables/2017/econ/economic-census/naics-sector-31-33.html [Accessed January 21, 2021], from U.S. Census Bureau.

★ 2710 ★
Photographic Film and Supplies
SIC: 3861; NAICS: 325992

Photographic Film, Paper, Plate, and Chemical Manufacturing, 2019

Total shipments were valued at $5.26 billion.

	($ 000)	Share
Photographic presensitized printing plates (unexposed), phototypesetting and imagesetting film, sensitized photographic paper and cloth, silver-halide-type (excluding X-ray)	$ 2,270,891	43.17%
Prepared photographic chemicals, office copy toners	1,159,504	22.04
Other	1,829,605	34.78

Source: "Annual Survey of Manufactures." [online] from https://www.census.gov/programs-surveys/asm/data/tables.html [Accessed March 18, 2021], from U.S. Department of Commerce.

★ 2711 ★
Photographic Film and Supplies
SIC: 3861; NAICS: 325992

Top Conventional Film Brands, 2020

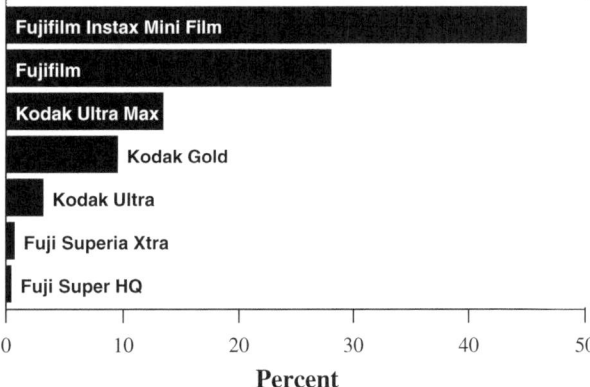

Market shares are shown based on supermarket sales for the 52 weeks ended April 19, 2020.

Fujifilm Instax Mini Film	44.91%
Fujifilm	27.99
Kodak Ultra Max	13.36
Kodak Gold	9.49
Kodak Ultra	3.13
Fuji Superia Xtra	0.70
Fuji Super HQ	0.42

Source: *Non-Foods Management*, Annual 2020-2021, p. 224, from IRI.

★ 2712 ★
Photography
SIC: 7335; NAICS: 541922

Commercial Photography, 2017

Total sales were valued at $2.13 billion. "Other services" includes special event photography, misc. portrait photography, and other services. The term "nec" stands for not elsewhere classified. IBISWorld estimates the photography industry, which includes commercial and portrait services, saw a decline in revenue of 12.4% for the five years leading up to 2020.

	($ 000)	Share
Commercial and industrial photography services	$ 1,828,405	87.98%
Convention and meeting photography services	35,641	1.71
General individual and group portrait photography services	31,846	1.53
Rental of commercial and service industry machinery and equipment, without operator	30,580	1.47
Licensing of rights to others to distribute audiovisual works protected by copyright	24,389	1.17
Licensing of rights to use intellectual property protected by copyright, excluding audiovisual works and musical compositions and recordings	23,440	1.13
Wedding still photography services	15,362	0.74
Licensing of rights to exhibit, broadcast, or rent audiovisual works protected by copyright	9,138	0.44
Wedding video photography services	4,628	0.22
Licensing of other rights to use audiovisual works protected by copyright, nec	3,074	0.15
School portrait services	2,836	0.14
Retail sales of other goods, nec	1,583	0.08
Maintenance and repair services for home audio and visual equipment	256	0.01
Other services	67,141	3.23

Source: "Economic Census." [online] from https://www.census.gov/programs-surveys/economic-census/data/tables.html [Accessed December 2, 2020], from U.S. Census Bureau.

★ 2713 ★
Photography
SIC: 7335; NAICS: 541922

Commercial Photography Leaders, 2017

Data show the percent of industry sales held by the largest 4, 8, 20 and 50 firms in the sector. There are approximately 4,229 players operating in the industry generating employment for 12,388 people. According to Kentley Insights, the industry generated sales of $1.8 billion in 2018. Over the previous three years, the industry saw an annual growth rate of 1.9%.

4 largest firms	8.5%
8 largest firms	12.1
20 largest firms	18.6
50 largest firms	27.7

Source: "Economic Census." [online] from https://www.census.gov/content/census/en/data/tables/2017/econ/economic-census/naics-sector-31-33.html [Accessed January 21, 2021], from U.S. Census Bureau.

★ 2714 ★
Photonics
SIC: 3827; NAICS: 333314

Photonics Industry Worldwide by Sector, 2018

Photonics is the physical science of generating, controlling and detecting light particles (photons). Figures are in billions of dollars.

	($ bil.)	Share
Information and communication technology	$ 135.3	24.0%
Displays	98.7	18.0
Lighting	86.4	16.0
Photovoltaics	55.9	10.0
Production technology	47.7	9.0
Medical technology and life science	39.2	7.0
Measurement and automated vision	33.6	6.0
Other	59.6	11.0

Source: "LightPath Investor Presentation." [online] from http://www.lightwave.com [Published May 2020], from MarketsandMarkets research and secondary research.

★ 2715 ★
Photovoltaics
SIC: 3433; NAICS: 333414

Leading Concentrator Photovoltaic Plant Operators Worldwide, 2020

Companies are ranked by active capacity in megawatts. Figures are as of July 2020.

Suncore Photovoltaic Technology Co.	110
Total S.A.	103
Soitec S.A.	92
Inner Mongolia Power (Group) Ltd.	32
Tianjin Zhonghuan Semiconductor Co. Ltd.	32
Hohhot Jinqiao City Development Co. Ltd.	25
Korea Electric Power Corp.	18
NextEra Energy Inc.	10
Valmont Industries Inc.	8
Axpo Holding AG	7

Source: *Future Power Technology*, August 2020, p. NA, from GlobalData's Power Intelligence Centre.

★ 2716 ★
Pipe
SIC: 3272; NAICS: 327332

Concrete Pipe Manufacturing, 2019

Total shipments were valued at $1.71 billion. The term "nec" stands for not elsewhere classified.

	($ 000)	Share
Concrete reinforced and nonreinforced culvert pipe	$ 522,354	30.76%
Precast concrete products, excluding burial vaults and boxes, concrete slabs and tile, and architectural wall panels	496,203	29.22
Concrete reinforced and nonreinforced storm sewer pipes	464,153	27.34
Concrete sanitary sewer pipes including other pipes such as concrete pressure, prestressed cylinder pressure, pretensioned cylinder, irrigation pipes, and drain tile	198,229	11.67
Wholesale sales of concrete, cement, sand, gravel, stone, brick, block, and tile	16,246	0.96
Mining of fire clay, including mined and/or basic preparation for transport	691	0.04
All other products and services, nec	135	0.01

Source: "Annual Survey of Manufacturers." [online] from https://www.census.gov/programs-surveys/asm/data/tables.html [Accessed March 18, 2021], from U.S. Department of Commerce.

★ 2717 ★
Pipe
SIC: 3272; NAICS: 327332

Concrete Pipe Manufacturing Leaders, 2017

Data show the percent of industry sales held by the largest 4, 8, 20 and 50 firms in the sector. There are approximately 221 players operating in the industry generating employment for 5,184 people. According to Kentley Insights, the industry generated sales of $7.1 billion in 2019.

4 largest firms	46.8%
8 largest firms	60.7
20 largest firms	83.7
50 largest firms	96.8

Source: "Economic Census." [online] from https://www.census.gov/content/census/en/data/tables/2017/econ/economic-census/naics-sector-31-33.html [Accessed January 21, 2021], from U.S. Census Bureau.

★ 2718 ★
Pipe
SIC/NAICS: See frontmatter for explanation.

Demand for Conduit Pipe, 2019

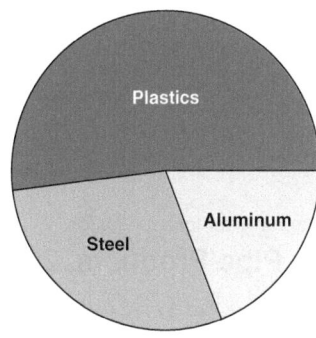

Revenue is forecast to see a CAGR of 2.3% from 2019-2024. The industry has benefited from the health of the overall construction market, as well as the push to install the 5G network, which requires conduit pipe for protection. Plastic has become a major material for conduit pipe in recent years.

Plastics	52.0%
Steel	29.0
Aluminum	19.0

Source: "Conduit Pipe." [online] from http://www.freedoniagroup.com [Published January 2021], from The Freedonia Group Inc.

★ 2719 ★
Pipe
SIC/NAICS: See frontmatter for explanation.
Demand for Drain, Waste and Vent Pipe, 2019

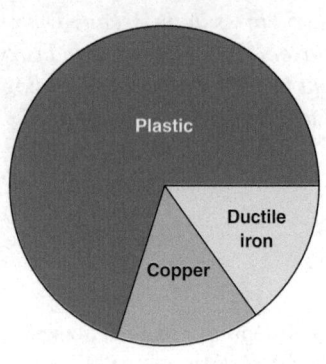

The industry was valued at $1.3 billion in 2019. Demand is forecast to see a CAGR of 3% from 2019-2024. Major players include Aliaxis, Charlotte Pipe & Foundry, Forterra, J.M. Eagle, Mueller Industries, and Otter Tail (Northern Pipe Products and Vinyltech).

Plastic	70.0%
Copper	15.0
Ductile iron	15.0

Source: "Drain, Waste and Vent Pipe." [online] from http://www.freedoniagroup.com [Published October 2020], from The Freedonia Group Inc.

★ 2720 ★
Pipe
SIC/NAICS: See frontmatter for explanation.
Demand for Pipe Products, 2019

The industry was valued at $41.1 billion in 2019. Demand is forecast to see a CAGR of 2.9% from 2019-2024. Major players include J.M. Eagle, Tenaris, Vallourec and Zekelman Industries.

Oil and natural gas	22.0%
Potable water	20.0
Storm and sanitary sewer	15.0
Other	43.0

Source: "Pipe Products & Markets." [online] from http://www.freedoniagroup.com [Published October 2020], from The Freedonia Group Inc.

★ 2721 ★
Pipe
SIC: 3084; NAICS: 326122
Leading CPVC Pipe Firms, 2019

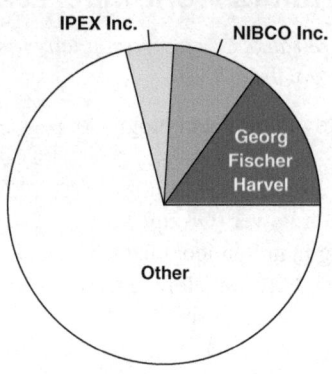

Chlorinated polyvinyl chloride (CPVC) is a white or yellow, non-toxic loose grain or powder. It is a thermoplastic produced by chlorination of polyvinyl chloride resin. The market was valued at $3.61 billion in 2021.

Georg Fischer Harvel L.L.C.	14.84%
NIBCO Inc.	8.94
IPEX Inc.	5.10
Other	71.12

Source: "CPVC Pipe and Fitting Market Size 2021-2026." [online] from https://www.marketwatch.com/press-release/cpvc-pipe-and-fitting-market-size-2021-2026-top-leading-countries-companies-consumption-drivers-trends-forces-analysis-revenue-challenges-and-forecast-2026-2021-03-04 [Published March 4, 2021], from QY Research.

★ 2722 ★
Pipe
SIC: 3084; NAICS: 326122
Plastics Pipe and Pipe Fitting Manufacturing, 2019

Total shipments were valued at $11.48 billion.

	($ 000)	Share
Plastics drain, waste, and vent pipe	$ 2,759,302	24.04%
Plastics pipe fittings and unions	2,065,085	17.99
Plastics water pipe	1,720,050	14.98
Plastics sewer, stormdrain, and water main pipe	1,569,809	13.67
Plastics oil and gas pipe	1,311,627	11.43

Continued on next page.

★ 2722 ★
[Continued]
Pipe
SIC: 3084; NAICS: 326122

Plastics Pipe and Pipe Fitting Manufacturing, 2019

Total shipments were valued at $11.48 billion.

	($ 000)	Share
Plastics industrial and mining pipe (including chemical processing, food processing)	$ 310,437	2.70%
Building and construction fabricated plastics products (excluding foam, plumbing fixtures, hardware, or reinforced plastics)	3,024	0.03
Other plastics pipe	1,512,073	13.17
Other	228,593	1.99

Source: "Annual Survey of Manufactures." [online] from https://www.census.gov/programs-surveys/asm/data/tables.html [Accessed March 18, 2021], from U.S. Department of Commerce.

★ 2723 ★
Pipe
SIC: 3317; NAICS: 33121

Steel Pipe Demand in China, 2019-2023

Figures are forecast in billions of renminbi. The market for SSAW (Spiral Submerged Arc-Welding) and ERW (Electric Resistance Welded) pipe saw CAGR of 0.7% and 0.8%, respectively, from 2013-2018. From 2018-2023, rates are forecast to reach 4.1% and 4.2%, respectively, because of increasing demand for steel pipe in underground urban electricity and telecom networks.

2019	¥ 345
2020	349
2021	355
2022	362
2023	372

Source: "Maike Tube Industry Holdings Ltd." [online] from https://www1.hkexnews.hk/listedco/listconews/sehk/2019/1129/2019112900019.pdf [Published November 29, 2019], from National Bureau of Statistics, China and Frost & Sullivan.

★ 2724 ★
Plastics
SIC: 2821; NAICS: 325211

Global Market for Blow Molded Plastics, 2018

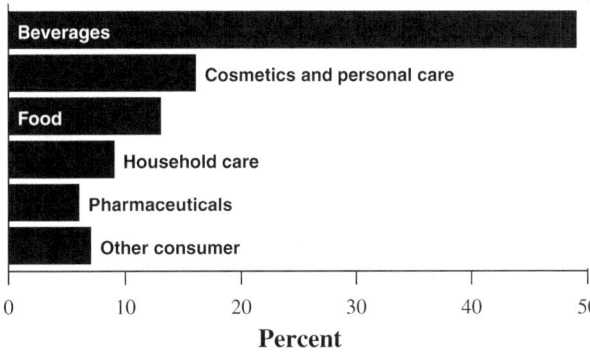

The market was valued at $82-83 billion in 2018, and it is forecast to grow at a CAGR of 4-5% to reach $102-103 billion in 2023.

Beverages	49.0%
Cosmetics and personal care	16.0
Food	13.0
Household care	9.0
Pharmaceuticals	6.0
Other consumer	7.0

Source: "Blow Molded Plastic Packaging Market Trends." [online] from http://www.beroeinc.com [Accessed October 2, 2020], from Beroe Inc.

★ 2725 ★
Plastics
SIC: 3089; NAICS: 326199

Leading Misc. Plastic Product Makers, 2019

Miscellaneous plastic products include housewares, building materials, motor vehicle parts, appliance parts and resilient flooring. It excludes plastic film, sheet, profile shapes, pipe, pipe fittings, laminates, foam products and bottles. A total of 6,341 businesses operated in this industry in 2019. Revenue is estimated to rise from $105.6 billion in 2019 to $107.9 billion in 2024. Exports represented 10% of industry revenue. California claimed 10.9% of businesses, Ohio 6.6%, Michigan 6.5% and other states 76%.

Saudi Basic Industries Corp.	2.5%
PolyOne Corp.	1.4
Armstrong Flooring Inc.	0.7
Other	95.4

Source: "Trade Market Intelligence: Special Report Hotspots in the United States." [online] from http://www.novascotiabusiness.com [Published September 2019], from IBISWorld.

★ 2726 ★
Plastics
SIC: 3089; NAICS: 326199

Leading Plastic Bin Makers Worldwide, 2015

The industry generated revenue of $278.8 billion in 2019.

Akro Mills	10.81%
Allit AG	10.10
Edsal Manufacturing Co.	9.34
Other	69.75

Source: "Global Plastic Bins Market Insights, Forecast to 2026." [online] from https://www.qyresearch.com [Published April 2020], from QY Research.

★ 2727 ★
Plastics
SIC: 3089; NAICS: 326121

Leading Plastic Blow Molding Firms, 2019

Companies are ranked by estimated blow molding sales in millions of dollars.

Amcor Rigid Plastics	$ 2,335
Graham Packaging Co. L.P.	1,924
Plastipak Packaging Inc.	1,900
Altium Packaging L.P.	1,525
Alpla Inc.	1,400
Plastic Omnium Auto Inergy Division	1,100
Kautex Textron GmbH & Co. KG	810
Silgan Plastics L.L.C.	611
Berry Global Inc.	541
Southeastern Container Inc.	530

Source: *Plastics News*, November 2020, p. 3.

★ 2728 ★
Plastics
SIC: 3081; NAICS: 326113

Leading Plastic Film and Sheet Firms, 2019

Companies are ranked by estimated film and sheet sales in millions of dollars.

Amcor Flexibles North America	$ 2,800
Berry Global Inc.	2,731
Inteplast Group	2,690
Sigma Plastics Group	2,100
Sealed Air Corp.	1,670
Novolex	1,400
DuPont Co.	1,250
Printpack Inc.	1,075
ProAmpac L.L.C.	$ 990
Winpak Ltd.	845

Source: *Plastics News*, September 2020, p. 3.

★ 2729 ★
Plastics
SIC: 3089; NAICS: 326121

Leading Plastic Injection Molders, 2019

Companies are ranked by estimated injection molding sales in millions of dollars.

Berry Global Inc.	1,700
International Automotive Components	1,475
Grupo Antolin North America Inc.	1,425
SRG Global Inc.	1,015
AptarGroup Inc.	915
U.S. Farathane L.L.C.	800
Jabil Healthcare	750
Mauser Packaging Solutions	650
ABC Group Inc.	625
Silgan Holdings Inc.	605

Source: *Plastics News*, June 2020, p. 3.

★ 2730 ★
Plastics
SIC: 3084; NAICS: 326122

Leading Plastic Pipe and Parts Makers, 2019

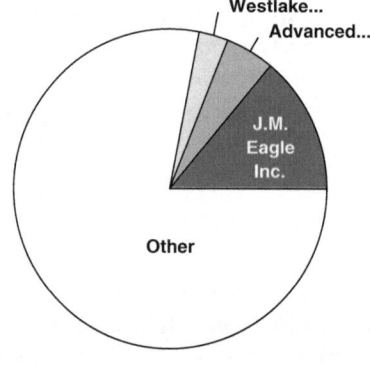

The 621 businesses in the industry generated revenue of $21.4 billion in 2019. Unlaminated plastic profile extrusions and shapes claimed 44% of the total, drain, waste and vent (DWV) pipes 12.2%, pipe fittings and unions 9.4%, and other sectors 34.4%.

J.M. Eagle Inc.	13.8%
Advanced Drainage Systems Inc.	5.3

Continued on next page.

★ 2730 ★
[Continued]
Plastics
SIC: 3084; NAICS: 326122

Leading Plastic Pipe and Parts Makers, 2019

The 621 businesses in the industry generated revenue of $21.4 billion in 2019. Unlaminated plastic profile extrusions and shapes claimed 44% of the total, drain, waste and vent (DWV) pipes 12.2%, pipe fittings and unions 9.4%, and other sectors 34.4%.

Westlake Chemical Corp.	3.1%
Other	77.8

Source: "Plastic Pipe & Parts Manufacturing in the U.S." [online] from http://www.ibisworld.com [Published October 2019], from IBISWorld.

★ 2731 ★
Plastics
SIC: 2821; NAICS: 325211

Leading Plastic Recyclers, 2019

Companies are ranked by plastics processed in millions of pounds.

KW Plastics Recycling	570.0
Green Line Polymers	499.0
B. Schoenberg & Co. Inc.	486.0
B&B Plastics Inc.	440.0
Waste Management Recycle America L.L.C.	426.0
Merlin Plastics Supply Inc.	370.0
Clean Tech Inc.	300.0
RJM International Inc.	280.5
Joe's Plastics Inc.	230.0
Greenpath Recovery Inc.	210.0

Source: *Plastics News*, May 2020, p. 3.

★ 2732 ★
Plastics
SIC: 2899; NAICS: 325998

Leading Polyamide 6.6 Firms in the EEA, 2018

Polyamide 6.6 is used in the production of plastics with heat resistance and durability. Market shares are shown based on volume. EEA stands for the European Economic Area, which consists of the European Union and Iceland, Liechtenstein and Norway. Figures reflect the merger of Domo with Solvay's polyamide business.

BASF Corp.	20.0-30.0%
Domo Chemicals	20.0-30.0
DowDupont Corp.	20.0-30.0
RadiciGroup	10.0-20.0%
EMS-Chemie	5.0-10.0
Lanxess Corp.	5.0-10.0
Albis	0.0-5.0
Ascend Performance Materials	0.0-5.0
Celanese Corp.	0.0-5.0
Royal DSM	0.0-5.0
Other	0.0-20.0

Source: "Domo Investment Group/Solvay Performance Polyamides Business in the EEA Regulation Merger Procedure." [online] from http://www.ec.europa.eu [Published November 26, 2019], from Form CO.

★ 2733 ★
Plastics
SIC: 2821; NAICS: 325211

Leading Superabsorbent Polymer Makers Worldwide, 2019

Companies are ranked by production capacity tons annually. The top 11 companies had capacity of 4.12 million tons each year.

Nippon Shokubai Co. Ltd.	710,000
BASF	595,000
Evonik Industries	506,000
Sumitomo Seika Chemicals	445,000
Dansonpack Industries	420,000
SDP Global	420,000
LG Chemical	400,000
Satellite Science & Technology	210,000
Taiwan Plastics	200,000
Quen Zhou Banglida Technology Industry	140,000
Shenghong Group	80,000

Source: *Nonwovens Industry*, January 2021, p. 24.

★ 2734 ★
Plastics
SIC: 3089; NAICS: 326199

Plastic Products Market in China, 2019

More than 81.8 million tons of plastic were produced in 2019, a 3.91% increase from 2018. Plastic film saw the strongest growth over the previous year, up 16.35%. Foam products saw the largest decline, down 16.16%.

Plastic film	19.48%
Household plastics	7.93
Synthetic leather	4.01
Foamed plastics	3.15
Other	65.42

Source: *China Chemical Reporter*, May 21, 2020, p. 19, from China Plastics Processing Association.

★ 2735 ★
Plastics
SIC: 3085; NAICS: 32616

Plastics Bottle Manufacturing, 2019

Total shipments were valued at $11.55 billion.

	($ 000)	Share
Manufacturing of plastics bottles	$ 11,257,914	97.47%
Manufacturing of plastics closure products	47,112	0.41
Other	244,974	2.12

Source: "Annual Survey of Manufactures." [online] from https://www.census.gov/programs-surveys/asm/data/tables.html [Accessed March 18, 2021], from U.S. Department of Commerce.

★ 2736 ★
Plastics
SIC: 3085; NAICS: 32616

Plastics Bottle Manufacturing Leaders, 2017

Data show the percent of industry sales held by the largest 4, 8, 20 and 50 firms in the sector. There are approximately 470 players operating in the industry generating employment for 31,030 people. According to Kentley Insights, the industry generated sales of $12.1 billion in 2019.

4 largest firms	51.7%
8 largest firms	65.6
20 largest firms	83.4
50 largest firms	92.8

Source: "Economic Census." [online] from https://www.census.gov/content/census/en/data/tables/2017/econ/economic-census/naics-sector-31-33.html [Accessed January 21, 2021], from U.S. Census Bureau.

★ 2737 ★
Plastics
SIC: 2821; NAICS: 325211

Polymer Consumption by the Automotive Industry, 2019

Passenger car sales fell from 80.6 million in 2018 to 77.5 million in 2019, according to Fitch Solutions. COVID-19 presented the industry with another challenge in 2020 as auto plants shut down to fight the virus and consumers stayed away from dealer showrooms. "Other" includes polystyrene, PMMA and nylons.

Polypropylene	35.0%
Polyurethane	19.0
Polyamides	11.0%
Polyvinyl chloride	9.0
ABS/SAN	8.0
Polycarbonate	4.0
Polyethylene	4.0
Other	10.0

Source: "Automotive - Impact on Chemicals." [online] from https://www.icis.com/explore/resources/news/2020/09/11/10541454/topic-page-automotive-impact-on-chemicals [Published September 11, 2020], from ICIS Analytics.

★ 2738 ★
Plastics
SIC: 2821; NAICS: 325211

Polypropylene Consumption in China, 2019

Market shares are shown based on consumption of 28.02 million tons, 37% of global polypropylene consumption. Sinopec claimed 26% of capacity in 2019. PetroChina was the second with an 18% share.

Yarn	37.0%
Injection	27.0
Film & sheet	24.0
Fiber	8.0
Pipe	4.0

Source: *China Chemical Reporter*, June 6, 2020, p. 17, from PetroChina Petrochemical Research Institute.

★ 2739 ★
Plastics
SIC: 2821; NAICS: 325211

Top End Markets for Propylene Worldwide, 2019

Market shares are shown in percent.

Polypropylene	68.0%
Propylene oxide	8.0
Acrylonitrile	5.0
Acrylic acids	4.0
Cumene	4.0
2-Ethyl Hexanol	3.0
Butanols	3.0
Isopropanel	1.0
Other	3.0

Source: *Adhesives & Sealants Industry*, November 2020, p. 23, from IHS Inc.

★ 2740 ★
Plastics

SIC: 2821; NAICS: 325211

Top Ethylene Polymer Exporters Worldwide, 2019

Data show the major exporters of ethylene polymers, in primary forms. Exports reached $77.1 billion in 2019, a 9.6% decrease from 2018.

United States	14.2%
Saudi Arabia	12.5
Singapore	7.3
Belgium	7.0
South Korea	5.4
Canada	5.0
Germany	4.4
Thailand	4.4
Netherlands	3.6
Iran	3.2
Other	33.0

Source: "2019 International Trade Statistics Yearbook." [online] from https://comtrade.un.org/pb/ [Published December 2020], from U.N. Comtrade.

★ 2741 ★
Plastics

SIC: 2821; NAICS: 325211

Top Ethylene Polymer Importers Worldwide, 2019

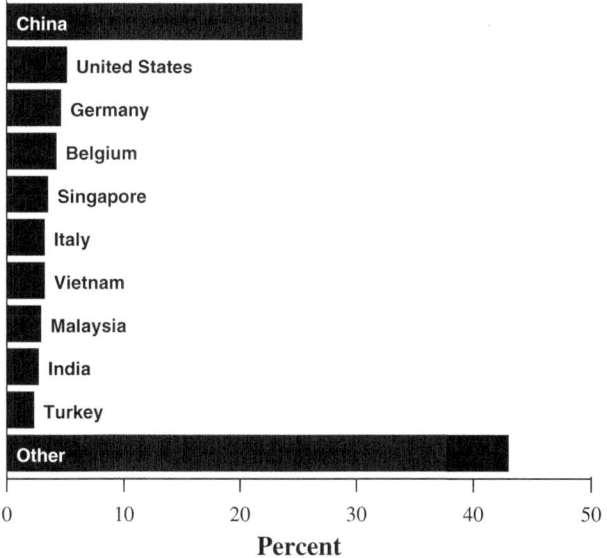

Data show the major importers of ethylene polymers, in primary forms. Imports reached $81.8 billion in 2019, a 7.2% decrease from 2018.

China	25.3%
United States	5.1
Germany	4.6%
Belgium	4.2
Singapore	3.5
Italy	3.2
Vietnam	3.2
Malaysia	2.9
India	2.7
Turkey	2.3
Other	43.0

Source: "2019 International Trade Statistics Yearbook." [online] from https://comtrade.un.org/pb/ [Published December 2020], from U.N. Comtrade.

★ 2742 ★
Plastics

SIC: 2821; NAICS: 325211

Top Styrene Polymer Exporters Worldwide, 2019

Data show the major exporters of styrene polymers, in primary forms. Exports reached $20.2 billion in 2019, a 16.7% decrease from 2018.

South Korea	16.9%
Belgium	7.7
China, Hong Kong SAR	7.0
United States	6.4
Netherlands	5.1
Malaysia	4.4
France	3.5
Germany	3.4
Japan	3.4
Thailand	2.9
Other	39.3

Source: "2019 International Trade Statistics Yearbook." [online] from https://comtrade.un.org/pb/ [Published December 2020], from U.N. Comtrade.

★ 2743 ★
Plastics

SIC: 2821; NAICS: 325211

Top Styrene Polymer Importers Worldwide, 2019

Data show the major importers of styrene polymers, in primary forms. Imports reached $22.8 billion in 2019, a 14.9% decrease from 2018.

China	27.5%
Germany	5.4
United States	5.3
China, Hong Kong SAR	4.6
Mexico	3.6

Continued on next page.

★ 2743 ★
[Continued]
Plastics
SIC: 2821; NAICS: 325211

Top Styrene Polymer Importers Worldwide, 2019

Data show the major importers of styrene polymers, in primary forms. Imports reached $22.8 billion in 2019, a 14.9% decrease from 2018.

Italy	3.4%
Poland	3.3
Vietnam	3.0
France	2.3
Turkey	2.3
Other	39.3

Source: "2019 International Trade Statistics Yearbook." [online] from https://comtrade.un.org/pb/ [Published December 2020], from U.N. Comtrade.

★ 2744 ★
Plastics
SIC: 2821; NAICS: 325211

Top Vinyl Chloride Polymer Exporters Worldwide, 2019

Data show the major exporters of polymers of vinyl chloride or of other halogenated olefins. Exports reached $18.4 billion in 2019, a 6.4% decrease from 2018.

United States	20.2%
Germany	9.9
Japan	7.6
China	6.7
Belgium	6.0
Netherlands	5.2
France	5.0
Italy	3.1
South Korea	2.8
Thailand	2.6
Other	30.9

Source: "2019 International Trade Statistics Yearbook." [online] from https://comtrade.un.org/pb/ [Published December 2020], from U.N. Comtrade.

★ 2745 ★
Plastics
SIC: 2821; NAICS: 325211

Top Vinyl Chloride Polymer Importers Worldwide, 2019

Data show the major importers of polymers of vinyl chloride or of other halogenated olefins. Imports reached $19.3 billion in 2019, a 6.9% decrease from 2018.

India	12.1%
China	6.9
Germany	5.8
United States	5.7
Italy	4.9
Belgium	4.4
Turkey	3.6
Mexico	3.3
Canada	3.0
Brazil	2.6
Vietnam	2.6
Other	45.1

Source: "2019 International Trade Statistics Yearbook." [online] from https://comtrade.un.org/pb/ [Published December 2020], from U.N. Comtrade.

★ 2746 ★
Plastics Machinery
SIC: 3559; NAICS: 333318

Injection Molding Machinery Industry in China, 2019

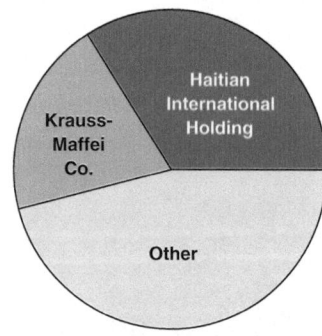

Injection molding machinery represents 40-50% of the output value of plastics processing. Market shares are estimated.

Haitian International Holding Ltd.	34.1%
Krauss-Maffei Co. Ltd.	20.4
Other	45.5

Source: "Global and China Injection Molding Machinery Industry Report 2020-2026." [online] from http://www.research-inchina.com [Published May 2020], from Research in China.

★ 2747 ★
Plastics Machinery
SIC: 3559; NAICS: 333249

Leading Injection Press Makers Worldwide, 2019

The industry generated revenue of $10.88 billion in 2019. Market shares are shown based on revenue.

Haitian International Holding Ltd.	13.64%
ENGEL Holding GmbH	12.71
Krauss-Maffei Co. Ltd.	9.73
Other	63.92

Source: "Global Plastic Injection Molding Industry Research Report 2020." [online] from http://www.qyresearch.com [Published November 2020], from QY Research.

★ 2748 ★
Plastics Wholesalers
SIC: 5162; NAICS: 42461

Plastics Materials and Basic Forms and Shapes Merchant Wholesale Leaders, 2017

Data show the percent of industry sales held by the largest 4, 8, 20 and 50 firms in the sector. There are approximately 2,955 players operating in the industry generating employment for 32,750 people.

4 largest firms	22.0%
8 largest firms	29.4
20 largest firms	45.0
50 largest firms	61.5

Source: "Economic Census." [online] from https://www.census.gov/content/census/en/data/tables/2017/econ/economic-census/naics-sector-31-33.html [Accessed January 21, 2021], from U.S. Census Bureau.

★ 2749 ★
Platinum
SIC: 1099; NAICS: 212299

Leading Platinum Consumers Worldwide, 2019

Consumption is shown by region. Exhaust treatment systems claimed 41% of consumption, jewelry 28%, chemical catalysts 11%, glass 6%, electronics 3% and other sectors 11%.

China	29.0%
Europe	26.0
Japan	13.0
North America	13.0%
Other	19.0

Source: "Nornickel Expanding the Horizons of Sustainable Growth." [online] from http://ar2019.nornickel.com [Accessed December 10, 2020], from company reports.

★ 2750 ★
Platinum
SIC: 1099; NAICS: 212299

Leading Platinum Producers Worldwide, 2019

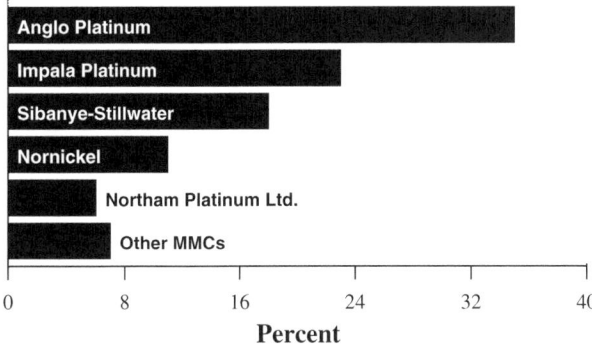

Market shares are shown based on production.

Anglo Platinum	35.0%
Impala Platinum	23.0
Sibanye-Stillwater	18.0
Nornickel	11.0
Northam Platinum Ltd.	6.0
Other MMCs	7.0

Source: "Nornickel Expanding the Horizons of Sustainable Growth." [online] from http://ar2019.nornickel.com [Accessed December 10, 2020], from company reports.

★ 2751 ★
Platinum
SIC: 1099; NAICS: 212299

Top Platinum Producing Nations, 2020

Countries are ranked by production in kilograms of platinum-group metal content. In the United States, one company produced about 18,000 kilograms of platinum-group metals valued at an estimated $1.1 billion. Production data are estimated.

	(kg.)	Share
South Africa	120,000	70.34%
Russia	21,000	12.31
Zimbabwe	14,000	8.21
Canada	7,800	4.57

Continued on next page.

★ 2751 ★
[Continued]
Platinum
SIC: 1099; NAICS: 212299
Top Platinum Producing Nations, 2020

Countries are ranked by production in kilograms of platinum-group metal content. In the United States, one company produced about 18,000 kilograms of platinum-group metals valued at an estimated $1.1 billion. Production data are estimated.

	(kg.)	Share
United States	4,000	2.34%
Other	3,800	2.23

Source: "Mineral Commodity Summaries 2021." [online] from https://www.usgs.gov/centers/nmic/mineral-commodity-summaries [Published January 29, 2021], from U.S. Geological Survey.

★ 2752 ★
Playground Equipment
SIC: 3999; NAICS: 339999
Leading Playground Equipment Makers Worldwide, 2019

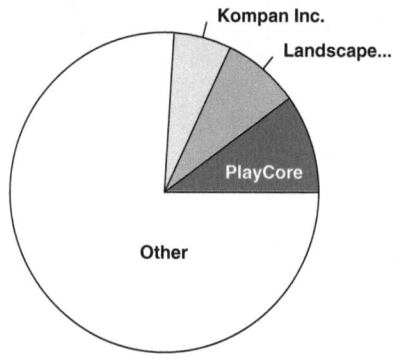

The industry generated revenue of $4.49 billion in 2019.

PlayCore	10.23%
Landscape Structures	7.97
Kompan Inc.	5.92
Other	75.88

Source: "Global Playground Equipment Market Size, Manufacturers, Supply Chain, Sales Channel and Clients 2020-2026." [online] from http://reports.valuates.com [Published April 2020], from QY Research.

★ 2753 ★
Plumbing Fixture Retailers
SIC: 5251; NAICS: 44413
Leading Plumbing Fixture Retailers, 2020

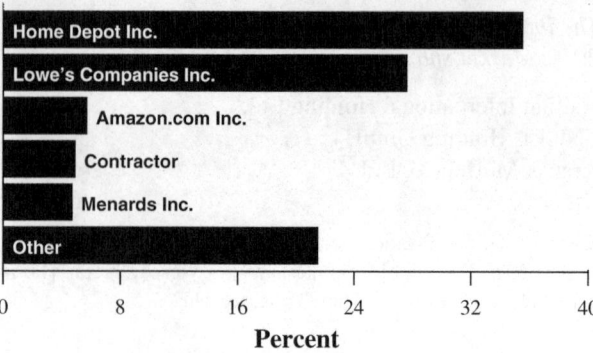

Market shares are shown based on dollar sales for full year 2020. Market shares by brand: Kohler 21.1%, Moën 14.4%, Delta 13.3%, American Standard 11.7%, Toto 3.3% and other 36.3%.

Home Depot Inc.	35.5%
Lowe's Companies Inc.	27.6
Amazon.com Inc.	5.7
Contractor	4.9
Menards Inc.	4.7
Other	21.5

Source: "Bathroom Fixture Market Infographic." [online] from http://www.traqline.com [Published January 25, 2021], from TraQline.

★ 2754 ★
Plumbing Fixtures
SIC: 3432; NAICS: 332913
Global Demand for Faucets and Taps, 2019

Revenue is forecast to see a CAGR of 3.6% from 2019-2024. The need for water and proper sanitation in developing nations will help drive this growth, as will the increase in home renovations and DIY projects.

Residential I&R	40.0%
New residential	25.0
Nonresidential I&R	18.0
New nonresidential	16.0

Source: "Global Faucets and Taps." [online] from http://www.freedoniagroup.com [Published January 2021], from The Freedonia Group Inc.

★ 2755 ★
Plumbing Fixtures
SIC: 3261; NAICS: 32711

Leading Plumbing Fixture Brands, 2020

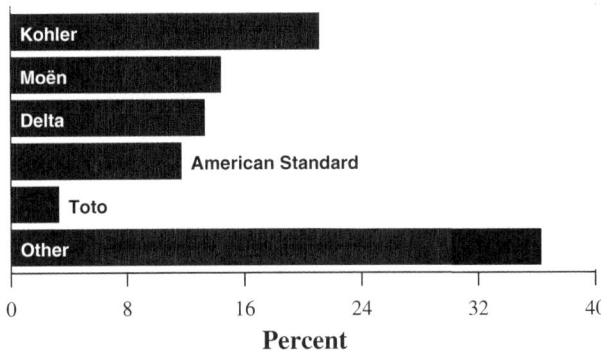

Market shares are shown for the full year.

Kohler	21.1%
Moën	14.4
Delta	13.3
American Standard	11.7
Toto	3.3
Other	36.3

Source: "Bathroom Fixtures Composite." [online] from https://www.traqline.com/newsroom/category/infographics/ [Published January 25, 2021], from TraQline.

★ 2756 ★
Plumbing Fixtures
SIC: 3431; NAICS: 332999

Leading Toilet Tank Fittings Makers Worldwide, 2019

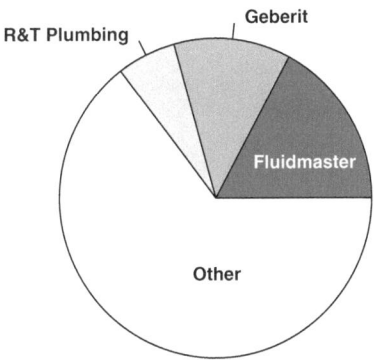

Toilet tank fittings include inlet valves, flush valves, push buttons, push levers, and similar components. The industry was valued at $1.88 billion in 2019. Market shares are shown based on revenue.

Fluidmaster	17.28%
Geberit	11.82
R&T Plumbing	6.45%
Other	64.45

Source: "Global Toilet Tank Fittings Market Insight, Forecast to 2026." [online] from http://www.qyresearch.com [Published April 2020], from QY Research.

★ 2757 ★
Plumbing Fixtures
SIC: 3088; NAICS: 326191

Plastics Plumbing Fixture Manufacturing Leaders, 2017

Data show the percent of industry sales held by the largest 4, 8, 20 and 50 firms in the sector. There are approximately 348 players operating in the industry generating employment for 17,716 people.

4 largest firms	32.8%
8 largest firms	45.6
20 largest firms	63.4
50 largest firms	83.4

Source: "Economic Census." [online] from https://www.census.gov/content/census/en/data/tables/2017/econ/economic-census/naics-sector-31-33.html [Accessed January 21, 2021], from U.S. Census Bureau.

★ 2758 ★
Plumbing Fixtures
SIC: 3431; NAICS: 332999

Toilet Repair Sales by Type, 2020

Sales are shown for the previous 12 months in the independent hardware channel. The top 5 items represented 21.3% of unit sales, the top 10 items 31.7%, the top 20 items 44.5%, and top 30 items 53.9%.

Tank flapper/tank ball	19.5%
Repair kits	19.0
Fill valve/ballcock	18.5
Tank flush lever	17.4
Toilet wax/install ring	14.4
Toilet waxless/install ring	4.1
Gaskets	4.0
Flush valve	1.6
Flush valve kit	1.1
Dual flush kit	0.2

Source: *The Hardware Connection*, July/August 2020, p. 59, from Vista Information Services, division of Epicor Software Corp.

★ 2759 ★
Plumbing Fixtures
SIC: 3432; NAICS: 332913

Top Linear Shower Drain Makers Worldwide, 2019

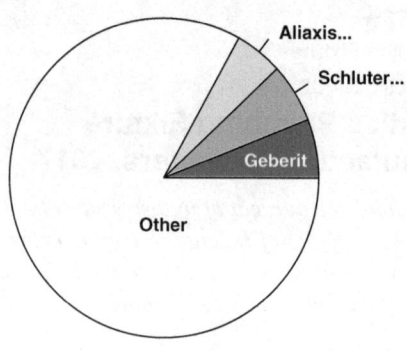

A linear shower drain is a generally rectangular plumbing fixture installed in the floor of a structure to drain away standing water. Market shares are shown based on revenues of $608.1 million.

Geberit	6.04%
Schluter-Systems	5.70
Aliaxis Group S.A.	4.85
Other	83.41

Source: "COVID-19 Impact on Global Linear Shower Drain Market Size, Status and Forecast 2020-2026." [online] from http://reports.valuates.com [Published April 2020], from QY Research.

★ 2760 ★
Pneumatic Cylinders
SIC: 3593; NAICS: 333995

Leading Pneumatic Cylinder Makers Worldwide, 2015

The industry is expected to climb from $1.04 billion in 2019 to $1.25 billion in 2024.

SMC Corp.	16.69%
Festo Corp.	12.01
IMI Norgren	6.90
Other	64.40

Source: "Global Pneumatic Cylinder Market Growth 2019-2024." [online] from https://www.absolutereports.com [Published February 2019], from Absolute Reports.

★ 2761 ★
Pneumatic Tubes and Fittings
SIC: 3492; NAICS: 332912

Pneumatic Tube and Fitting Consumption by Region, 2019

Regions are ranked by sales of pneumatic tubes and fittings consumed in the manufacturing and construction industries. Sales totaled $1.5 billion in 2019.

	($ mil.)	Share
Northeast Central	$ 375.02	24.55%
South Atlantic	235.35	15.41
Pacific Coast	184.78	12.10
Mid-Atlantic	171.76	11.24
Southwest Central	167.02	10.93
Northwest Central	151.40	9.91
Southeast Central	92.03	6.02
Mountain states	75.61	4.95
Northeast Coastal	74.65	4.89

Source: *Industrial Supply*, May/June 2020, p. 21, from MDM Analytics.

★ 2762 ★
Podcasting
SIC: 4832; NAICS: 515111, 515112

Leading Podcast Publishers, 2020

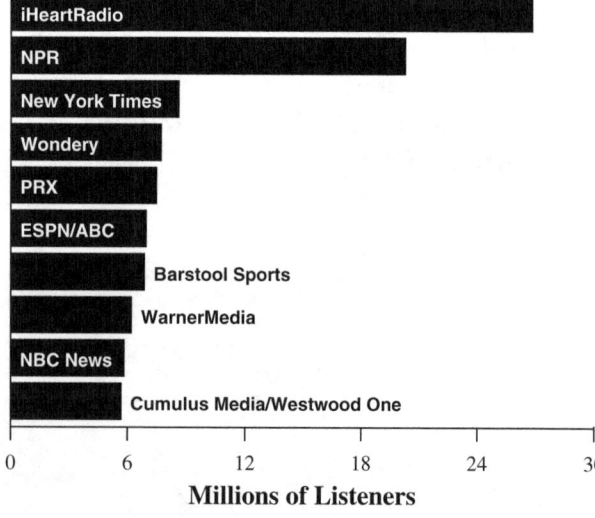

Publishers are ranked by millions of unique monthly listeners for December 2020. The most popular podcasts in December 2020 were, in order, The Daily, NPR News Now, Up First and The Ben Shapiro Show.

iHeartRadio	26.77
NPR	20.25

Continued on next page.

★ 2762 ★
[Continued]
Podcasting
SIC: 4832; NAICS: 515111, 515112

Leading Podcast Publishers, 2020

Publishers are ranked by millions of unique monthly listeners for December 2020. The most popular podcasts in December 2020 were, in order, The Daily, NPR News Now, Up First and The Ben Shapiro Show.

New York Times	8.57
Wondery	7.69
PRX	7.46
ESPN/ABC	6.94
Barstool Sports	6.85
WarnerMedia	6.19
NBC News	5.82
Cumulus Media/Westwood One	5.67

Source: "Top Publishers." [online] from http://analytics.podtrac.com/podcast-publisher-rankings [Accessed January 5, 2021], from Podtrac.

★ 2763 ★
Podcasting
SIC: 4832; NAICS: 515111, 515112

Monthly Podcast Listening, 2008-2020

Data show percent of U.S. population 12+ years of age that listened to a podcast in the previous month. Just 13% of the same group reported ever listening to a podcast in 2008; by 2020, 55% of the population, or approximately 155 million, had reported doing so. Data are estimated for 2020.

2008	9.0%
2009	11.0
2010	12.0
2011	12.0
2012	14.0
2013	12.0
2014	15.0
2015	17.0
2016	21.0
2017	24.0
2018	26.0
2019	32.0
2020	37.0

Source: "Infinite Deal 2020." [online] from https://www.podcastinsights.com/podcast-statistics/ [Accessed January 3, 2021], from Edison Research and Triton Digital.

★ 2764 ★
Podcasting
SIC: 4832; NAICS: 515111, 515112

Monthly Podcast Listening by Age Group, 2017-2020

Data show percent of U.S. population 12+ years of age that listened to a podcast in the previous month. Population figures for men: 27% in 2017, 27% in 2018, 36% in 2019, and 39% in 2020. Population for women: 21%, 24%, 29% and 36%, respectively. Data are estimated for 2020.

	2017	2018	2019	2020
12-34	27.0%	34.0%	42.0%	49.0%
35-54	31.0	29.0	36.0	40.0
55+	12.0	13.0	17.0	22.0

Source: "Infinite Deal 2020." [online] from https://www.podcastinsights.com/podcast-statistics/ [Accessed January 3, 2021], from Edison Research and Triton Digital.

★ 2765 ★
Podcasting
SIC: 7313; NAICS: 54184

Podcast Advertising Spending, 2018-2022

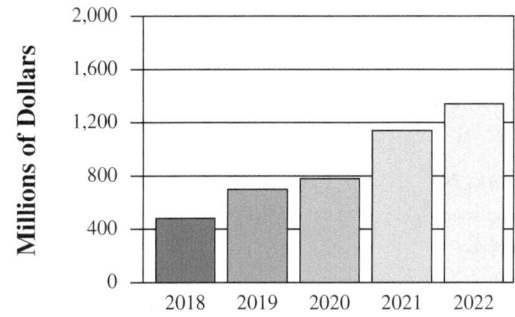

As podcasts have grown in popularity, spending on advertising has also increased. Figures are in millions of dollars. Figures refer to audio advertising within a podcast; includes all types of advertising on podcasts.

2018	$ 479.1
2019	708.1
2020	782.0
2021	1,132.9
2022	1,331.3

Source: "U.S. Podcast Ad Spending to Surpass $1 Billion Next Year." [online] from https://www.emarketer.com/content/us-podcast-ad-spending-surpass-1-billion-next-year [Published August 4, 2020], from eMarketer.

★ 2766 ★
Podcasting
SIC: 4832; NAICS: 515111, 515112

Podcast Listeners, 2019-2023

Data show millions of users.

2019	92.0
2020	105.6
2021	115.6
2022	124.3
2023	131.4

Source: "U.S. Podcast Ad Spending to Surpass $1 Billion Next Year." [online] from https://www.emarketer.com/content/us-podcast-ad-spending-surpass-1-billion-next-year [Published August 4, 2020], from eMarketer.

★ 2767 ★
Police
SIC: 9221; NAICS: 92212

Police Budgets by City, 2020

Spending is shown in millions of dollars. Police department funding is drawn from community discretionary spending. Most cities spend approximately 25-40% of their budgets on policing. Some analysts have discovered interesting discrepancies from this statistic. A Mother Jones article from September 2020 notes that Los Angeles spends about 25% of its budget on policing, while New York spends about 8%. However, New York's 8%, $5.2 billion, is nearly twice the spending of Los Angeles.

New York, NY	$ 5,600.0
Los Angeles, CA	1,730.0
Chicago, IL	1,680.0
Houston, TX	934.0
Baltimore, MD	536.4
Detroit, MI	330.0
Atlanta, GA	248.5
Minneapolis, MN	163.2

Source: "How Much Are U.S. Cities Spending on Policing in 2020?" [online] from https://www.forbes.com/sites/niallmccarthy/2020/06/12/how-much-are-us-cities-spending-on-policing-in-2020-infographic/?sh=4e559323751a [Published June 13, 2020], from The Center for Popular Democracy, Law for Black Lives and Black Youth Project 100.

★ 2768 ★
Ports
SIC: 4491; NAICS: 48831

Leading Ports by Palm Oil Imports, 2019

The United States is a leading global market for edible oils. Consumption reached 1.55 million metric tons in 2019. Market shares are shown based on imports.

New Orleans, LA	35.7%
Savannah, GA	30.6
New York, NY	14.3
Stockton, CA	6.7
Richmond, VA	5.6
Charleston, SC	3.9
Houston, TX	1.5
Long Beach, CA	0.5
Los Angeles, CA	0.4
Boston, MA	0.3

Source: *Oils & Fats International*, November/December 2020, p. 31, from http://www.datamyne.com.

★ 2769 ★
Ports
SIC: 4491; NAICS: 48831

Top Ports, 2020

Ports are ranked by shipments in twenty-foot equivalent units.

	TEUs	Share
Los Angeles, CA	4,999,403	17.1%
Newark, NJ	4,599,961	15.7
Long Beach, CA	4,288,103	14.7
Savannah, GA	2,430,103	8.3
Houston, TX	1,995,734	6.8
Seattle, WA	1,428,567	4.9
Tacoma, WA	1,315,826	4.5
Norfolk, VA	1,284,567	4.4
Charleston, SC	1,173,536	4.0
Oakland, CA	1,102,037	3.8

Source: "Top 30 Ports: Big Port Got Bigger in 2020." [online] from https://www.logisticsmgmt.com/article/top_30_u.s._ports_big_ports_got_bigger_in_2020 [Published May 5, 2021], from Panjiva.

★ 2770 ★
Ports
SIC: 4491; NAICS: 48831

Top Ports Worldwide, 2019

Ports are ranked by container throughput in millions of twenty-foot equivalent units.

Shanghai, China	43.30
Singapore	37.20
Ningbo-Zhoushan, China	27.54
Shenzhen, China	25.77
Guangzhou (Nansha)	23.24
Busan, South Korea	21.99
Qingdao, China	21.01
Hong Kong, China	18.36
Tianjin, China	17.30
Rotterdam, Netherlands	14.81

Source: *Journal of Commerce*, August 18, 2020, p. NA, from Alphaliner.

★ 2771 ★
POS Terminals
SIC: 3578; NAICS: 333318

Point-of-Sale Terminal Shipments Worldwide, 2019

Shipments reached 128.2 million in 2019, up 24.2% from 2018.

Asia-Pacific	67.0%
Latin America	15.0
Europe	7.0
Middle East and Africa	5.0
United States	5.0
Canada	< 1.0

Source: *Nilson Report*, August 2020, p. 1.

★ 2772 ★
Postal Service
SIC: 4311; NAICS: 49111

Postal Service Revenues Worldwide, 2013 and 2018

Mail revenues declined for nearly two-thirds of postal services around the world from 2013 to 2018. As a result, many postal services have diversified by investing in e-commerce logistics, expanding financial services, and improving retail networks.

	2013	2018
Financial services	38.2%	35.1%
Mail	35.2	32.5
Parcels and express mail	14.7	20.9
Logistics and freight	8.1%	8.8%
Other	3.8	2.7

Source: "Global Postal Industry Report 2019." [online] from https://www.ipc.be/services/markets-and-regulations/market-intelligence/global-postal-industry-report [Published December 2019], from International Post Corp.

★ 2773 ★
Postal Service
SIC: 4311; NAICS: 49111

Revenue Sources for the Post Office, 2018-2020

Data show revenue in millions of dollars for fiscal year. The number of pieces of mail fell from 146.4 million in 2018 to 142.5 million in 2019 to 129.7 million in 2020. The total number of business and residential delivery points increased from 158.5 million to 159.9 million to 161.3 million, respectively. Shipping and packages claimed 39% of the total, first-class mail 32.5%, marketing mail 19.2%, international mail 3.28%, periodicals 1.4% and other sectors 4.75%.

	2018 ($ mil.)	2019 ($ mil.)	2020 ($ mil.)
Shipping and packages	$ 21,467	$ 22,783	$ 28,537
First-class mail	24,948	24,431	23,778
Marketing mail	16,512	16,359	13,909
International mail	2,630	2,476	2,400
Periodicals	1,277	1,194	1,024
Other	3,788	3,895	3,475

Source: "United States Postal Service - FY 2020 Annual Report to Congress." [online] from https://about.usps.com/what/financials/ [Published December 11, 2020], from U.S. Postal Service.

★ 2774 ★
Potash
SIC: 1474; NAICS: 212391

Leading Potash Producers Worldwide, 2019

Sales slipped from 71.8 million tons in 2018 to 68.5 million tons in 2019.

Canadian Potash Exporters	29.0%
Belarusian Potash Company	16.0
Chinese companies	15.0
Uralkali	15.0
K+S Potash	9.0
Israel Chemicals Ltd.	7.0

Continued on next page.

★ 2774 ★
[Continued]
Potash
SIC: 1474; NAICS: 212391

Leading Potash Producers Worldwide, 2019

Sales slipped from 71.8 million tons in 2018 to 68.5 million tons in 2019.

Arab Potash Company	4.0%
Eurochem	2.0
SQM Ltd.	1.0
Other	3.0

Source: "K+S Compendium." [online] from https://www.kpluss.com/en-us/.pdf/investor-relations/2020/compendium-september-2020.pdf [Published September 2020], from International Fertilizer Association and K+S Potash.

★ 2775 ★
Potash
SIC: 1474; NAICS: 212391

Top Potash Producing Nations, 2020

Countries are ranked by production in thousands of metric tons of potash equivalent. In 2020, the estimated sales value of marketable potash, free on board mine, was $430 million, 10% higher than in 2019. In the United States, the fertilizer industry used about 85% of potash sales. Production data are estimated.

	(000)	Share
Canada	14,000	32.41%
Russia	7,600	17.60
Belarus	7,300	16.90
China	5,000	11.58
Germany	3,000	6.95
Israel	2,000	4.63
Jordan	1,500	3.47
Chile	900	2.08
Spain	470	1.09
United States	470	1.09
Laos	400	0.93
Brazil	250	0.58
Other	300	0.69

Source: "Mineral Commodity Summaries 2021." [online] from https://www.usgs.gov/centers/nmic/mineral-commodity-summaries [Published January 29, 2021], from U.S. Geological Survey.

★ 2776 ★
Potatoes
SIC: 0134; NAICS: 111219

Best-Selling Types of Potatoes, 2020

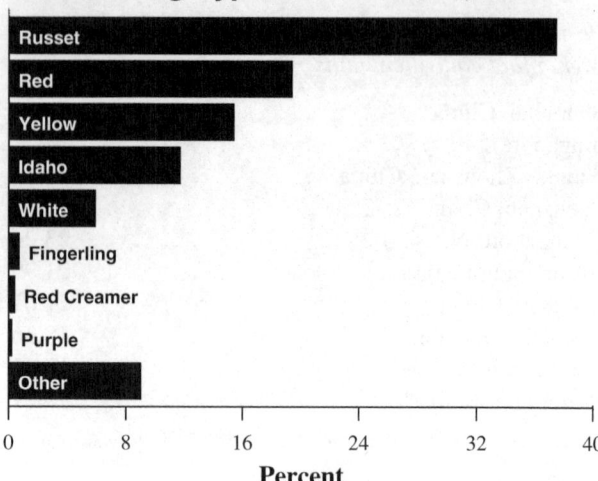

Market shares are shown based on multi-outlet dollar sales for the 52 weeks ended August 9, 2020. Sales reached $3.3 billion.

Russet	37.4%
Red	19.4
Yellow	15.4
Idaho	11.7
White	5.9
Fingerling	0.7
Red Creamer	0.4
Purple	0.2
Other	9.0

Source: *Produce News*, September 14-28, 2020, p. 8, from IRI/FreshLook.

★ 2777 ★
Potatoes
SIC: 0134; NAICS: 111211

Largest U.S. Potato Export Markets, 2019

Exports are in millions of dollars. Shares are shown for the group.

	($ mil.)	Share
Japan	$ 365	23.81%
Canada	335	21.85
Mexico	254	16.57
Philippines	123	8.02
South Korea	120	7.83
China	85	5.54
Taiwan	83	5.41
Malaysia	67	4.37

Continued on next page.

★ 2777 ★
[Continued]
Potatoes
SIC: 0134; NAICS: 111211

Largest U.S. Potato Export Markets, 2019

Exports are in millions of dollars. Shares are shown for the group.

	($ mil.)	Share
Saudi Arabia	$ 56	3.65%
Singapore	45	2.94

Source: "Annual Potato Yearbook." [online] from https://www.nationalpotatocouncil.org/files/8415/9231/8115/Annual_Potato_Yearbook_FNL.pdf [Accessed December 2, 2020].

★ 2778 ★
Potatoes
SIC: 0134; NAICS: 111211

Potato Industry by Category, 2020

Sales are shown in millions of dollars for July 2019-June 2020. By volume, potato chips claimed 37%, fresh 31%, frozen 17%, refrigerated 11%, dehydrated 2%, and deli prepared 1%.

	($ mil.)	Share
Potato chips	$ 6,300.25	48.35%
Fresh	3,285.60	25.22
Frozen	1,865.64	14.32
Refrigerated	628.39	4.82
Dehydrated	581.02	4.46
Deli - prepared sides	314.97	2.42
Canned	54.03	0.41

Source: "Total Potato Sales." [online] from https://potatoes-usa.com/wp-content/uploads/2020/07/FY20-Total-Potatoes-7.1.19_6.30.20.pdf [Accessed December 2, 2020], from U.S. Department of Agriculture.

★ 2779 ★
Potatoes
SIC: 0134; NAICS: 111211

Potato Production by State, 2019

Production is shown in thousand hundredweight.

	cwt (000)	Share
Idaho	130,900	30.84%
Wisconsin	28,700	6.76
Oregon	25,311	5.96
Michigan	20,370	4.80
Colorado	19,666	4.63
North Dakota	19,430	4.58
Minnesota	17,845	4.20%
California	16,842	3.97
Maine	16,738	3.94
Other	128,617	30.30

Source: "Potatoes 2019 Summary." [online] from http://www.nass.usda.gov [Published September 2020], from U.S. Department of Agriculture.

★ 2780 ★
Pottery
SIC: 3269; NAICS: 32711

Top Pottery Exporters Worldwide, 2019

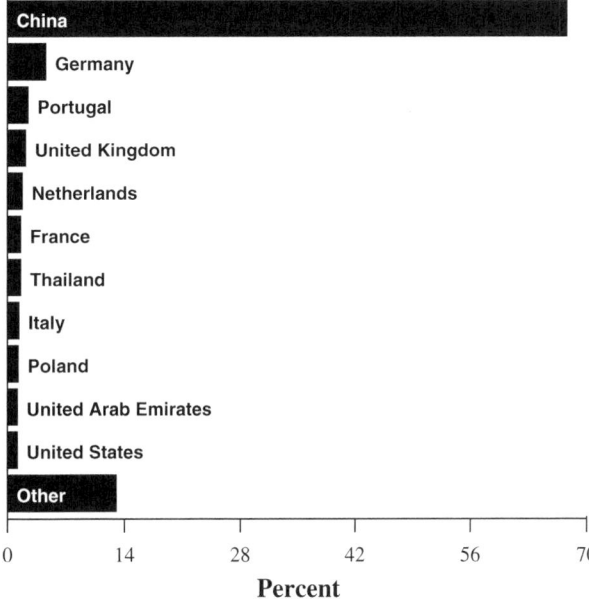

Data show the major exporters of pottery. Exports reached $12.9 billion in 2019, a 4.5% increase from 2018.

China	67.6%
Germany	4.6
Portugal	2.5
United Kingdom	2.2
Netherlands	1.8
France	1.6
Thailand	1.6
Italy	1.4
Poland	1.3
United Arab Emirates	1.2
United States	1.2
Other	13.0

Source: "2019 International Trade Statistics Yearbook." [online] from https://comtrade.un.org/pb/ [Published December 2020], from U.N. Comtrade.

★ 2781 ★
Pottery
SIC: 3269; NAICS: 32711

Top Pottery Importers Worldwide, 2019

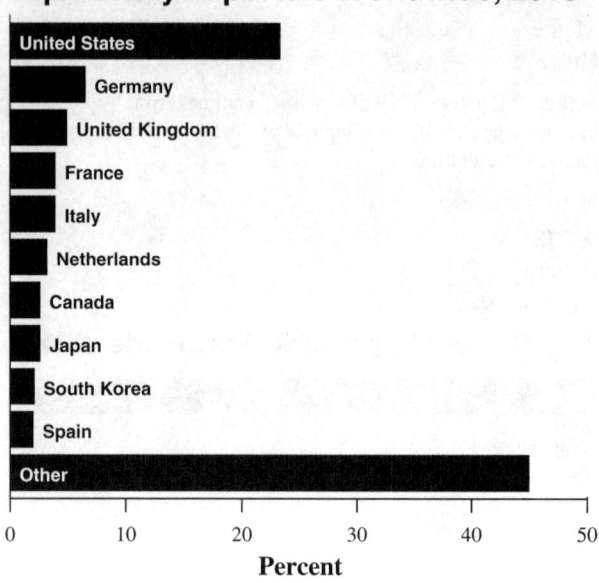

Data show the major importers of pottery. Imports reached $8.9 billion in 2019, a 0.7% decrease from 2018.

United States	23.3%
Germany	6.5
United Kingdom	4.9
France	3.9
Italy	3.9
Netherlands	3.2
Canada	2.6
Japan	2.6
South Korea	2.1
Spain	2.0
Other	45.0

Source: "2019 International Trade Statistics Yearbook." [online] from https://comtrade.un.org/pb/ [Published December 2020], from U.N. Comtrade.

★ 2782 ★
Power Distribution Blocks
SIC: 3612; NAICS: 335311

Power Distribution Block by Market, 2019

Market shares are shown based on dollar sales for the 12 months ended December 2019.

Aluminum	71.2%
Copper	17.3
Dual	10.1%
Other and unknown	1.3

Source: The Electrical Distributor, May 2020, p. 65, from Epicor's Industry Data Analytics.

★ 2783 ★
Power Infrastructure
SIC: 3612; NAICS: 335311

Leading Power Infrastructure Makers, 2019

Market shares are shown for the fourth quarter of 2019. Figures include UPS, PDU, surge protectors, rack mounts and chassis.

APC by Schneider Electric	38.9%
Cisco Systems Inc.	12.3
Tripp Lite	11.4
Eaton Corp.	7.6
Hewlett Packard Enterprise	6.2
Other	23.6

Source: CRN, March 5, 2020, p. NA.

★ 2784 ★
Powered Pressure Washers
SIC: 3589; NAICS: 333318

Leading Powered Pressure Washer Makers Worldwide, 2016

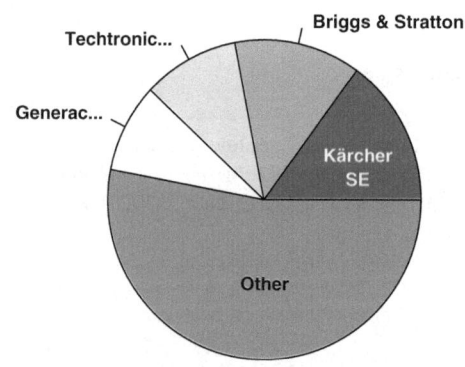

A powered pressure washer has an electric motor that powers a water pump. This pump is used to send water through a hose under high pressure. Market shares are shown based on revenue.

Kärcher SE	15.11%
Briggs & Stratton	12.64
Techtronic Industries Inc. (TTI)	9.75

Continued on next page.

★ 2784 ★
[Continued]
Powered Pressure Washers
SIC: 3589; NAICS: 333318

Leading Powered Pressure Washer Makers Worldwide, 2016

A powered pressure washer has an electric motor that powers a water pump. This pump is used to send water through a hose under high pressure. Market shares are shown based on revenue.

Generac Holdings Inc.	9.12%
Other	53.38

Source: "Global Powered Pressure Washer Market Insights, Forecast to 2026." [online] from http://www.qyresearch.com [Published April 2020], from QY Research.

★ 2785 ★
Prepared Salads, Fruit and Coleslaw
SIC: 2099; NAICS: 311991

Leading Prepared Salad/Fruit/Coleslaw Brands, 2020

Brands are ranked based on sales at supermarkets, drug stores, mass merchandisers, military commissaries, and select club and dollar chains for the 12 weeks ended August 9, 2020.

	($ mil.)	Share
Reser's Fine Foods	$ 48.85	14.39%
Del Monte Sun Fresh	12.39	3.65
Del Monte Fruit Naturals	12.21	3.60
Grandma's	5.38	1.58
Hans Kissle	3.80	1.12
Mrs. Gerry's	3.46	1.02
Yoder's	3.25	0.96
Reser's	1.85	0.54
Private label	220.80	65.03
Other	27.55	8.11

Source: *Frozen & Refrigerated Buyer*, October 2020, p. 18, from IRI.

★ 2786 ★
Printed Circuit Boards
SIC: 3672; NAICS: 334412

Bare Printed Circuit Board Manufacturing, 2017

Total shipments were valued at $4.32 billion. The term "nec" stands for not elsewhere classified.

	($ 000)	Share
Manufacturing of other printed circuit boards	$ 1,963,877	45.84%
Manufacturing of flex printed circuit boards	909,797	21.24
Manufacturing of glass printed circuit boards	750,266	17.51
Manufacturing printed circuit (wiring) boards for others on their materials	153,624	3.59
Manufacturing printed circuit assemblies, loaded boards, or modules for others on their materials	147,843	3.45
Manufacturing of printed circuit assemblies, loaded boards and modules (printed circuit boards with inserted electronic components)	41,594	0.97
Wholesale sales of materials and supplies for electronic and electrical equipment, appliances, and component manufacturing	33,726	0.79
Retail sales of other goods, nec	6,786	0.16
Other electronic and electrical contract manufacturing services	274,079	6.40
Other manufacturing revenue, nec	2,342	0.05

Source: "Economic Census." [online] from https://www.census.gov/programs-surveys/economic-census/data/tables.html [Accessed December 2, 2020], from U.S. Census Bureau.

★ 2787 ★
Printed Circuit Boards
SIC: 3672; NAICS: 334412

Circuit Board and Electronic Component Revenue, 2010-2024

A total of 2,598 business establishments operated in this industry in 2019. Operators have been moving domestic production to countries with lower labor costs for a number of years. Domestic production is concentrated in the West and Southwest. Figures are in billions of dollars.

Year	Revenue
2010	$ 49.07
2011	49.93
2012	47.23
2013	46.63
2014	45.09
2015	46.45
2016	42.88
2017	44.09
2018	43.79
2019	43.36
2020	43.10
2021	42.80
2022	42.51
2023	42.26
2024	41.98

Source: "Trade Market Intelligence: Special Report Hotspots in the United States." [online] from http://www.novascotiabusiness.com [Published September 2019], from IBISWorld.

★ 2788 ★
Printed Circuit Boards
SIC: 3672; NAICS: 334412

Global Market for Printed Circuit Boards, 2018

The market is forecast to grow from $60 billion in 2017 to $66 billion in 2020.

Business/retail/computers	30.0%
Communications/telecom	28.0
Consumer electronics	20.0
Automotive	10.0
Industrial/medical	9.0
Government/military/defense	3.0

Source: "Printed Circuit Boards (PCB) Market Overview." [online] from http://www.beroeinc.com [Accessed October 2, 2020], from Beroe Inc.

★ 2789 ★
Printed Circuit Boards
SIC: 3672; NAICS: 334412

Leading Circuit Board and Electronic Component Makers, 2019

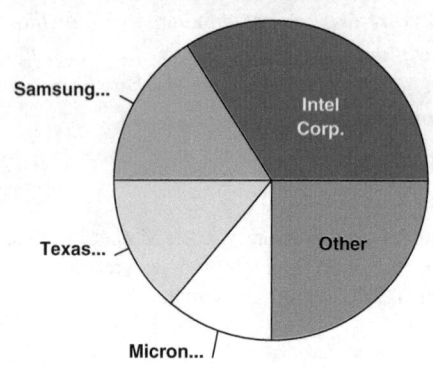

A total of 2,598 businesses operated in this industry in 2019. Revenue is estimated to slip from $43.36 billion in 2019 to $41.98 billion in 2024. Exports claimed 18.3% of the market.

Intel Corp.	33.9%
Samsung Electronics Co. Ltd.	16.1
Texas Instruments Inc.	14.1
Micron Technology Inc.	11.0
Other	24.9

Source: "Trade Market Intelligence: Special Report Hotspots in the United States." [online] from http://www.novascotiabusiness.com [Published September 2019], from IBISWorld.

★ 2790 ★
Printed Circuit Boards
SIC: 3672; NAICS: 334412

Leading Printed Circuit Board Makers Worldwide, 2019

Companies are ranked by revenue in millions of dollars. Shares are shown based on the $62.31 billion generated by the top 122 companies. Taiwan was the leader worldwide with 34% of production, China had 27.1%, Japan 18%, and other countries 20.9%.

	($ mil.)	Share
ZD Tech	$ 3,887	6.24%
TTM Technologies	2,689	4.32
Unimicron Tehnology Corp.	2,668	4.28

Continued on next page.

★ 2790 ★
[Continued]
Printed Circuit Boards
SIC: 3672; NAICS: 334412

Leading Printed Circuit Board Makers Worldwide, 2019

Companies are ranked by revenue in millions of dollars. Shares are shown based on the $62.31 billion generated by the top 122 companies. Taiwan was the leader worldwide with 34% of production, China had 27.1%, Japan 18%, and other countries 20.9%.

	($ mil.)	Share
Nippon Mektron Ltd.	$ 2,597	4.17%
M-Flex (Dongshan Precision)	2,115	3.39
Compeq Manufacturing Co.	1,816	2.91
Tripod Technology Corp.	1,760	2.82
Shennan Circuit Co. Ltd.	1,523	2.44
HannStar Display Corp.	1,395	2.24
Samsung Electro-Mechanical	1,386	2.22
KBC PCB Group	1,234	1.98
Ibiden Co. Ltd.	1,213	1.95
Wus Group	1,193	1.91
Young Poong Group	1,149	1.84
AT&S	1,119	1.80
Other	34,571	55.48

Source: *Printed Circuit Design & Fab/Circuits Assembly*, September 2020, p. 26.

★ 2791 ★
Printing
SIC: 2752; NAICS: 323111

Commercial Printing Leaders (except Screen and Books), 2017

Data show the percent of industry sales held by the largest 4, 8, 20 and 50 firms in the sector. There are approximately 18,203 players operating in the industry generating employment for 323,955 people. According to Kentley Insights, the industry generated sales of $68.6 billion in 2019.

4 largest firms	14.8%
8 largest firms	20.4
20 largest firms	29.5
50 largest firms	39.2

Source: "Economic Census." [online] from https://www.census.gov/content/census/en/data/tables/2017/econ/economic-census/naics-sector-31-33.html [Accessed January 21, 2021], from U.S. Census Bureau.

★ 2792 ★
Printing
SIC: 2759; NAICS: 323113

Commercial Screen Printing Leaders, 2017

Data show the percent of industry sales held by the largest 4, 8, 20 and 50 firms in the sector. There are approximately 5,165 players operating in the industry generating employment for 61,897 people. According to Kentley Insights, the industry generated sales of $9 billion in 2019.

4 largest firms	16.2%
8 largest firms	21.0
20 largest firms	30.7
50 largest firms	41.6

Source: "Economic Census." [online] from https://www.census.gov/content/census/en/data/tables/2017/econ/economic-census/naics-sector-31-33.html [Accessed January 21, 2021], from U.S. Census Bureau.

★ 2793 ★
Printing
SIC: 2759; NAICS: 323111

Leading Catalog Printers in North America, 2020

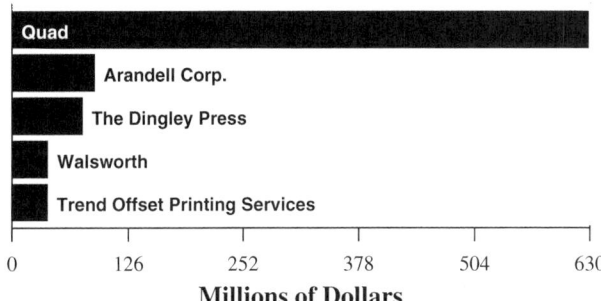

Companies are ranked by segment sales in millions of dollars. Figures are based on the source's top 400 list. Quad recently completed the divestiture of its book manufacturing platform in the United States. Taylor Corp. and CJK Group did not divulge their annual or book segment sales; the source notes both companies should appear in the top five. LSC Communications did not provide the source with segment sales and so does not appear in the ranking.

Quad	$ 627.68
Arandell Corp.	88.20
The Dingley Press	75.00
Walsworth	37.55
Trend Offset Printing Services	37.50

Source: *Printing Impressions*, Top 400, 2020, p. 14.

★ 2794 ★
Printing
SIC: 2754; NAICS: 323111

Leading Direct Mail Printers in North America, 2020

Companies are ranked by segment sales in millions of dollars. Figures are based on the source's top 400 list. Quad recently completed the divestiture of its book manufacturing platform in the United States. Taylor Corp. and CJK Group did not divulge their annual or book segment sales; the source notes both companies should appear in the top five. LSC Communications did not provide the source with segment sales and so does not appear in the ranking.

SG360, a Segerdahl Co.	$ 255.00
R.R. Donnelley	473.00
Quad	470.76
IWCO Direct	464.00
Cenveo Enterprises	340.00

Source: *Printing Impressions*, Top 400, 2020, p. 14.

★ 2795 ★
Printing
SIC: 2750; NAICS: 323111

Leading Printing Firms in North America, 2020

Companies are ranked by sales in millions of dollars.

R.R. Donnelley	$ 5,500.0
Quad	3,923.0
LSC Communications	2,845.0
Taylor Corp.	2,500.0
Cimpress	2,481.0
Transcontinental Inc.	2,285.0
Cenveo Enterprises	1,000.0
Donnelley Financial Solutions Inc.	874.7
CJK Group	664.0
Mondi North America	650.0
FastSigns International	545.0
Fort Dearborn	525.0
IWCO Direct	464.0
Minuteman Press Intl.	463.0
Alliance Franchise Brands	448.0

Source: *Printing Impressions*, Top 400, 2020, p. 3.

★ 2796 ★
Printing
SIC: 2754; NAICS: 323111

Leading Publication Printers in North America, 2020

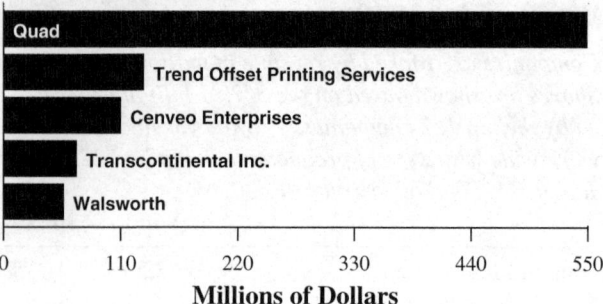

Companies are ranked by segment sales in millions of dollars. Figures are based on the source's top 400 list. Quad recently completed the divestiture of its book manufacturing platform in the United States. Taylor Corp. and CJK Group did not divulge their annual or book segment sales; the source notes both companies should appear in the top five. LSC Communications did not provide the source with segment sales and so does not appear in the ranking.

Quad	$ 549.22
Trend Offset Printing Services	131.25
Cenveo Enterprises	110.00
Transcontinental Inc.	68.57
Walsworth	56.33

Source: *Printing Impressions*, Top 400, 2020, p. 14.

★ 2797 ★
Printing
SIC: 2750; NAICS: 323111

Leading Small Commercial Printers, 2019

Companies are ranked by sales in millions of dollars. Shares are shown based on sales of $549.41 million for the top 100 printers.

	($ mil.)	Share
Firespring Print Inc.	$ 24.99	4.55%
I Color Printing & Mailing Inc.	24.58	4.47
HBP Inc.	23.07	4.20
Professional Printers	21.44	3.90
Allen Printing Company	17.00	3.09
Cedar Graphics Inc.	15.00	2.73
Allegra Asheville	14.57	2.65
Sir Speedy Printing	13.72	2.50
Alphagraphics	13.06	2.38

Continued on next page.

★ 2797 ★
[Continued]
Printing
SIC: 2750; NAICS: 323111

Leading Small Commercial Printers, 2019

Companies are ranked by sales in millions of dollars. Shares are shown based on sales of $549.41 million for the top 100 printers.

	($ mil.)	Share
Influence Graphics	$ 12.80	2.33%
Other	369.28	67.20

Source: *WhatTheyThink*, June-July 2020, p. 16.

★ 2798 ★
Prisons
SIC: 9223; NAICS: 92214

Leading Correctional Facility Managers, 2019

Companies are ranked by annual estimated sales in millions of dollars. The private prison market was valued at $5.8 billion.

The GEO Group Inc.	$ 2,200
CoreCivic	2,000
Management & Training Corp.	450

Source: "The Prison Industry - How it Started, How it Works, How it Harms." [online] from http://static1.squarespace.com [Published September 20, 2020], from annual reports.

★ 2799 ★
Prisons
SIC: 4813; NAICS: 517311

Leading Correctional Telecom Firms, 2019

Correctional telecom firms sign contracts with government agencies to control communication services within these organizations. Correctional telecom spending generates revenue of $1.4 billion annually. Global Tel Link (GTL) has service contracts in 479 counties and 23 prison systems that cover 930,000 people. Data are drawn from Worth Rises database, which did not specify year, so it was estimated.

GlobalTelLink (GTL)	43.0%
Securus	30.0
Securus (CenturyLink)	9.0
ICSolutions (CenturyLink)	5.0%
ICSolutions	4.0
Other	9.0

Source: "The Prison Industry - How it Started, How it Works, How it Harms." [online] from http://static1.squarespace.com [Published September 20, 2020], from Worth Rises.

★ 2800 ★
Prisons
SIC: 9223; NAICS: 92214

Prison Population, 2009-2019

The number of prisoners under state and federal jurisdiction stood at 1.43 million in 2019, a decline of 2.3% from 2018-2019, and a decline of 11.4% from 2009-2019. In 2019, 90% of all prisoners were male; 87% of prisoners were under state jurisdiction.

2009	1,615,487
2010	1,613,803
2011	1,598,968
2012	1,570,397
2013	1,576,950
2014	1,562,319
2015	1,526,603
2016	1,508,129
2017	1,489,189
2018	1,464,385
2019	1,430,805

Source: "Prisoners in 2019." [online] from https://www.bjs.gov/index.cfm?ty=pbdetail&iid=7106 [Published October 2020], from Bureau of Justice Statistics.

★ 2801 ★
Private Clubs
SIC: 7997; NAICS: 71391

Membership in Private Clubs in Florida, 2019

Clubs are a dues business, and many organizations set up various levels of membership at a variety of price points. Data show average membership level for clubs with common interest reality associations (CIRAs).

Boca Raton area	990
Southwest CIRAs	990
North and Central	910
Florida statewide	820
Yacht and beach clubs	750

Continued on next page.

★ 2801 ★
[Continued]
Private Clubs
SIC: 7997; NAICS: 71391

Membership in Private Clubs in Florida, 2019

Clubs are a dues business, and many organizations set up various levels of membership at a variety of price points. Data show average membership level for clubs with common interest reality associations (CIRAs).

Southwest without CIRAs	680
Southeast without Boca	630

Source: "2019-2020 Trends in Private Clubs." [online] from https://www.stoneybrook.net/files/2019-20%20trends%20in%20private%20clubs%20report.pdf [Accessed February 15, 2021].

★ 2802 ★
Private Label Industry
SIC/NAICS: See frontmatter for explanation.

Fastest-Growing Edible Private Brands, 2020

Consumers stockpiled items during the pandemic, occasionally resulting in shortages of some grocery products. This trend helped increase sales of some private label items. Data show dollar sales growth for edible private brands. Figures are based on MULO (drug stores, food/grocery stores, mass merchandisers, military commissaries, and select club and dollar chains) sales for the 52 weeks ended December 27, 2020.

Baby food	659.0%
Ham, refrigerated	467.0
Egg substitutes, shelf-stable	289.0
Salad dressing, refrigerated	125.0
Powdered milk	69.0
Wine	54.0
Pickles/relish, refrigerated	49.0
Asian food	47.0
Fruit, vegetable preservative/pectin	44.0
Pizza products	42.0

Source: *Store Brands*, March 2021, p. 27, from IRI.

★ 2803 ★
Private Label Industry
SIC/NAICS: See frontmatter for explanation.

Fastest-Growing Non-Edible Private Brands, 2020

Data show dollar sales growth for non-edible private brands. Figures are based on MULO sales (drug stores, food/grocery stores, mass merchandisers, military commissaries, and select club and dollar chains) for the 52 weeks ended December 27, 2020.

Shaving lotion/men's fragrances	170.0%
Personal thermometers	87.0
Hair conditioners	69.0
Baby gifts/toys/furniture	60.0
Household cleaner cloths	58.0
Home health care/kits	54.0
Candles	48.0
Household cleaners	44.0
Bleach	38.0
Cosmetics, lip	37.0

Source: *Store Brands*, March 2021, p. 28, from IRI.

★ 2804 ★
Private Mail Centers
SIC: 7389; NAICS: 561431

Private Mail Center Leaders, 2017

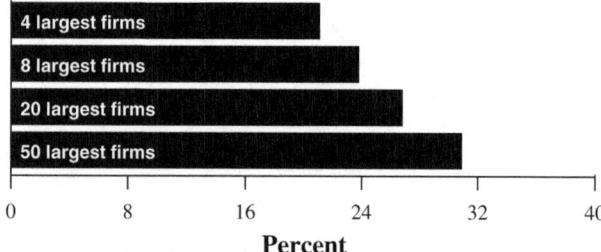

Data show the percent of industry sales held by the largest 4, 8, 20 and 50 firms in the sector. There are approximately 4,812 players operating in the industry generating employment for 26,272 people. According to Kentley Insights, the industry generated sales of $3.2 billion in 2019.

4 largest firms	21.1%
8 largest firms	23.8
20 largest firms	26.8
50 largest firms	30.9

Source: "Economic Census." [online] from https://www.census.gov/content/census/en/data/tables/2017/econ/economic-census/naics-sector-31-33.html [Accessed January 21, 2021], from U.S. Census Bureau.

★ 2805 ★
Private Mail Centers
SIC: 7389; NAICS: 561431

Private Mail Centers, 2017

Total sales were valued at $2.83 billion. The term "nec" stands for not elsewhere classified.

	($ 000)	Share
Mailroom services and mailbox rentals	$ 1,316,068	46.66%
Packaging and labeling services	970,469	34.41
Copying and reproduction services	77,180	2.74
Retail sales of other goods, nec	64,300	2.28
Mail presorting and address barcoding services	57,207	2.03
Quick printing	55,536	1.97
Document processing and editing services	54,476	1.93
Digital printing	51,867	1.84
Document finishing services	37,776	1.34
Typing services	3,622	0.13
Call support services	107	< 0.01
Inbound telemarketing services	59	< 0.01
Outbound telemarketing services, including fax broadcasting services	348	0.01
Other products and services, nec	86,589	3.07
Other service revenue, nec	44,935	1.59

Source: "Economic Census." [online] from https://www.census.gov/programs-surveys/economic-census/data/tables.html [Accessed December 2, 2020], from U.S. Census Bureau.

★ 2806 ★
Promotional Products
SIC/NAICS: See frontmatter for explanation.

Leading Promotional Product Suppliers in North America, 2019

Companies are ranked by sales in millions of dollars. T-shirts, drinkware and outerwear are some of the most popular items offered by promotional product companies. According to the Advertising Specialty Institute, sales in the United States reached a record high of $25.8 billion in 2019. The pandemic brought sales down to $16.8 billion in 2020.

SanMar	$ 2,400.0
Alphabroder	1,700.0
S&S Activewear	1,300.0
Polyconcept North America	818.2
Gildan Activewear Inc.	624.0
Hit Promotional Products	495.7
BIC Graphic	310.1
Next Level Apparel	$ 228.3
HPG	205.7
Staton Corporate and Casual	170.4
TSC Apparel	155.0
Magnet Group	121.4
Gemline	105.0
Sweda Co.	100.8
Logomark	98.5

Source: *Counselor*, September 2020, p. NA.

★ 2807 ★
Promotional Products
SIC/NAICS: See frontmatter for explanation.

Promotional Products Industry, 2019

The industry generated sales of $24.22 billion in 2019. Business services claimed 13.8% of the industry by category, education 11.5%, health care 7.3%, and other categories 67.4%.

Wearables	31.0%
Drinkware	11.1
Travel	7.6
Technology	6.6
Writing	5.6
Awards	3.8
Office	3.7
Desk	3.0
Event	3.0
Home decor	2.4
Health & beauty	2.0
Other	20.2

Source: "The 2019 Sales Volume Study Summary (Categories)." [online] from https://ppai.org/members/research/ [Accessed November 17, 2020], from Promotional Products Association International.

★ 2808 ★
Propane Retailers
SIC: 5984; NAICS: 45431

Leading Propane Retailers, 2020

Companies are ranked by retail sales volume in millions of gallons. Shares are shown based on retail sales for the top 40 firms.

	(mil.)	Share
AmeriGas Propane	1,078.00	27.40%
Ferrellgas	638.01	16.21
Suburban Propane Partners L.P.	402.90	10.24
Growmark Inc.	242.77	6.17
Superior Plus Propane	220.40	5.60
Thompson Gas L.L.C.	130.70	3.32

Continued on next page.

★ 2808 ★
[Continued]
Propane Retailers
SIC: 5984; NAICS: 45431

Leading Propane Retailers, 2020

Companies are ranked by retail sales volume in millions of gallons. Shares are shown based on retail sales for the top 40 firms.

	(mil.)	Share
Blossman Gas Inc.	106.00	2.69%
CHS Inc.	105.00	2.67
MFA Oil Co.	103.00	2.62
Energy Distribution Partners	96.50	2.45
Other	811.56	20.62

Source: *LP Gas*, February 2021, p. 28.

★ 2809 ★
Public Relations
SIC: 8743; NAICS: 54182

Largest Public Relations Firms, 2019

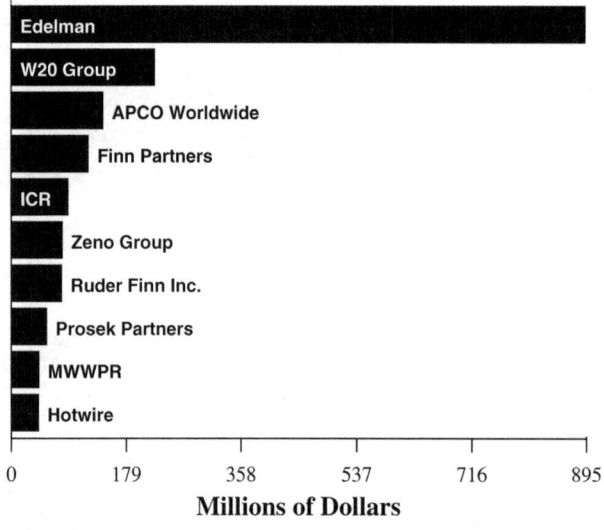

The largest firms in the United States are ranked by worldwide fees in millions of dollars.

Edelman	$ 892.0
W20 Group	222.8
APCO Worldwide	142.2
Finn Partners	119.3
ICR	88.2
Zeno Group	79.2
Ruder Finn Inc.	78.0
Prosek Partners	$ 54.7
MWWPR	42.7
Hotwire	42.1

Source: *O'Dwyer's*, June 2020, p. 48.

★ 2810 ★
Publishing
SIC: 2731; NAICS: 51113, 51223, 51913

Higher Education Publishing by Sector, 2013, 2016 and 2019

Figures are estimated in billions of dollars.

	2013 ($ bil.)	2016 ($ bil.)	2019 ($ bil.)	Share
Digital textbook content	6.7	10.1	12.0	37.97%
Print textbook content	15.8	13.2	11.0	34.81
Whole course solutions	3.7	5.8	8.6	27.22

Source: "K-12 and Higher Education Textbooks Market Size, Share and Forecast, 2019." [online] from http://www.outsell-inc.com [Published December 2019], from Outsell Inc.

★ 2811 ★
Publishing
SIC: 2700; NAICS: 51111, 51112, 51113

Top Publishers Worldwide, 2019

Companies are ranked by revenue in millions of dollars.

RELX Group	$ 5,636
Thomson Reuters	5,277
Pearson	5,084
Bertelsmann	4,156
Wolters Kluwer	3,976
Hachette Livre	2,675
Springer Nature	1,928
John Wiley & Sons Inc.	1,800
HarperCollins	1,754
Scholastic Corp.	1,654
Phoenix Publishing and Media	1,634
McGraw-Hill Education	1,571
Cengage Learning Holdings II	1,442
Holtzbrinck Publishing	1,398
Houghton Mifflin Harcourt	1,319

Source: *Publishers Weekly*, November 2, 2020, p. 33, from Livres Hebdo.

★ 2812 ★
Pudding, Mousse, Gelatin and Parfait
SIC: 2099; NAICS: 311991

Leading Pudding/Mousse/Gelatin/Parfait Brands, 2020

Brands are ranked based on sales at supermarkets, drug stores, mass merchandisers, military commissaries, and select club and dollar chains for the 12 weeks ended August 9, 2020.

	($ mil.)	Share
Jell-O	$67.12	34.17%
Kozy Shack	36.37	18.52
Raymundo's	10.97	5.58
Senor Rico	10.86	5.53
Winky	6.24	3.18
Patti's Gold Life	3.70	1.88
Kraft Heinz Hershey's	3.34	1.70
Jell-O Temptations	2.99	1.52
Kozy Shack Simply Well	2.00	1.02
Private label	24.39	12.42
Other	28.45	14.48

Source: *Frozen & Refrigerated Buyer*, October 2020, p. 20, from IRI.

★ 2813 ★
Pulp
SIC: 2611; NAICS: 32211

Global Pulp Demand, 2019

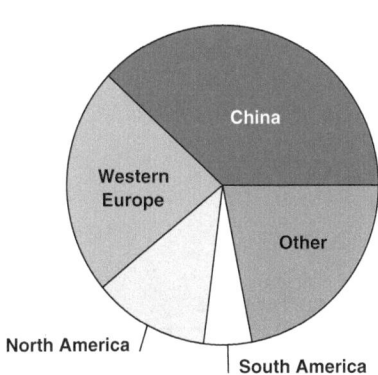

Figures are in millions of tons.

	(mil.)	Share
China	24	37.50%
Western Europe	15	23.44
North America	8	12.50
South America	3	4.69%
Other	14	21.88

Source: "Leaders in the Sustainable Use of Natural Resources." [online] from https://ence.es/wp-content/uploads/2020/09/09.20-Corporate-Presentation-ENG-1.pdf [Published September 2020], from PPPC G-100 and RISI.

★ 2814 ★
Pulp
SIC: 2611; NAICS: 32211

Leading Hardwood Pulp Makers Worldwide, 2018

Market shares are shown based on capacity.

Suzano Papel e Celuloso	29.0%
April Group	8.0
CMPC	8.0
Asia Pulp & Paper	7.0
Arauco	6.0
UPM Communications Paper	5.0
El Dorado Celulose	4.0
Other	33.0

Source: "Delivering Value Delivering Commitments." [online] from https://ence.es/wp-content/uploads/2020/03/03.20-Corporate-Presentation-ENG.pdf [Published March 2020], from RISI.

★ 2815 ★
Pulp
SIC: 2611; NAICS: 32211

Leading Pulp Producers Worldwide, 2019

Companies are ranked by hardwood and softwood pulp capacity in metric tons.

Suzano Papel e Celuloso	10.9
Asia Pulp & Paper + PE	3.8
CMPC	3.7
Arauco	3.1
April Group	2.8
Metsä Group	2.7
UPM Paper	2.6
Stora Enso	2.1
Mercer International Inc.	2.0
Ilim Group	1.8

Source: "Credit Suisse 2020 Latin American Conference." [online] from https://s1.q4cdn.com/987436133/files/doc_presentations/pt/2020.01.28-Credit-Suisse-2020-Latin-America-Investment-Conference.pdf [Published January 2020], from Hawkins-Wright, August 2019.

★ 2816 ★
Pulp
SIC: 2611; NAICS: 32211

Leading Softwood Pulp Makers Worldwide, 2018

Market shares are shown based on capacity.

International Paper Co.	12.0%
Koch Industries Inc.	8.0
Metsä Group	8.0
Arauco	6.0
Domtar Corp.	6.0
Mercer International	6.0
Södra Skogsägarma	6.0
Ilim Group	5.0
Paper Excellence	5.0
Stora Enso	4.0
Other	33.0

Source: "Delivering Value Delivering Commitments." [online] from https://ence.es/wp-content/uploads/2020/03/03.20-Corporate-Presentation-ENG.pdf [Published March 2020], from RISI.

★ 2817 ★
Pulp
SIC: 2611; NAICS: 32211

Top Pulp and Waste Paper Exporters Worldwide, 2019

Data show the major exporters of pulp and waste paper. Exports reached $46.5 billion in 2019, a 14.6% decrease from 2018.

United States	18.3%
Brazil	16.1
Canada	13.0
Indonesia	6.0
Chile	5.9
Sweden	5.9
Finland	5.7
Germany	2.8
Netherlands	2.8
Russian Federation	2.4
Other	21.1

Source: "2019 International Trade Statistics Yearbook." [online] from https://comtrade.un.org/pb/ [Published December 2020], from U.N. Comtrade.

★ 2818 ★
Pulp
SIC: 2611; NAICS: 32211

Top Pulp and Waste Paper Importers Worldwide, 2019

Data show the major importers of pulp and waste paper. Imports reached $53.5 billion in 2019, a 15.8% decrease from 2018.

China	35.9%
Germany	7.7
United States	6.7
India	4.6
Italy	4.4
South Korea	3.2
Indonesia	2.9
Netherlands	2.6
Japan	2.5
France	2.4
Other	27.1

Source: "2019 International Trade Statistics Yearbook." [online] from https://comtrade.un.org/pb/ [Published December 2020], from U.N. Comtrade.

★ 2819 ★
Pulp
SIC: 2611; NAICS: 32211

Top Pulp Producers in Europe, 2019

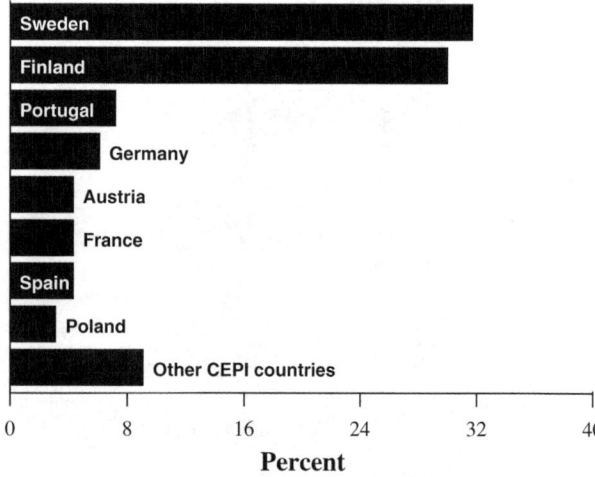

Production reached 38 million tons. Figures refer to market pulp and integrated pulp.

Sweden	31.7%
Finland	30.0
Portugal	7.2
Germany	6.1
Austria	4.3

Continued on next page.

★ 2819 ★
[Continued]
Pulp
SIC: 2611; NAICS: 32211

Top Pulp Producers in Europe, 2019

Production reached 38 million tons. Figures refer to market pulp and integrated pulp.

France	4.3%
Spain	4.3
Poland	3.1
Other CEPI countries	9.1

Source: "European Pulp & Paper Industry Key Statistics 2019." [online] from https://www.cepi.org/key-statistics-2019/ [Accessed December 2, 2020], from Confederation of European Paper Industries.

★ 2820 ★
Pumice
SIC: 1499; NAICS: 212399

Top Pumice Producing Nations, 2020

Countries are ranked by production in thousands of metric tons. Data for Algeria, Cameroon, Chile, Ecuador, France, Greece, Saudi Arabia, Syria and "Other" include pozzolan and/or volcanic tuff. Production data are estimated.

	(000)	Share
Turkey	7,800	37.46%
Ethiopia	2,400	11.53
Cameroon	1,000	4.80
Greece	1,000	4.80
Uganda	1,000	4.80
Algeria	900	4.32
Jordan	900	4.32
Chile	800	3.84
Indonesia	770	3.70
Ecuador	600	2.88
Guatemala	600	2.88
Saudi Arabia	550	2.64
United States	480	2.31
France	300	1.44
Tanzania	260	1.25
New Zealand	220	1.06
Guadeloupe	200	0.96
Spain	200	0.96
Syria	200	0.96
Other	640	3.07

Source: "Mineral Commodity Summaries 2021." [online] from https://www.usgs.gov/centers/nmic/mineral-commodity-summaries [Published January 29, 2021], from U.S. Geological Survey.

★ 2821 ★
Pumps
SIC: 3568; NAICS: 333613

Global Demand for Distributed Peristaltic Pumps, 2018

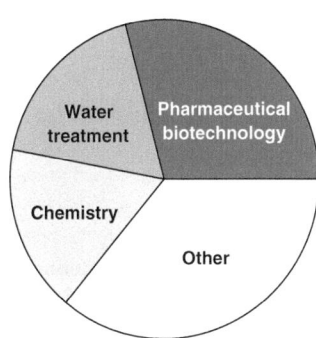

According to the source, "distributed peristaltic pumps are positive displacement pumps which use rotating rollers pressed against special flexible tubing to create a pressurized flow. The tubing isolates the fluid from the rest of the pump and environment, eliminating contamination and making it ideal for handling aggressive, corrosive, or abrasive media." The industry was valued at $597.2 million in 2018.

Pharmaceutical biotechnology	29.33%
Water treatment	17.80
Chemistry	17.17
Other	35.70

Source: "Global Distributed Peristaltic Pump Market Report, History and Forecast 2014-2025, Breakdown Data by Manufacturer Key Regions, Types and Applications." [online] from http://www.qyresearch.com [Published October 2020], from QY Research.

★ 2822 ★
Pumps
SIC: 3568; NAICS: 333613

Leading Pump and Compressor Makers, 2020

The industry generated revenue of $27.2 billion in 2020. Demand comes from the oil and gas industry with a 21.7% share, manufacturing with a 16.4%, chemicals 7.3%, construction 6.6%, public facilities 5%, and other sectors 43%.

Atlas Copco AB	4.7%
Flowserve Corp.	1.5

Continued on next page.

★ 2822 ★
[Continued]
Pumps
SIC: 3568; NAICS: 333613
Leading Pump and Compressor Makers, 2020

The industry generated revenue of $27.2 billion in 2020. Demand comes from the oil and gas industry with a 21.7% share, manufacturing with a 16.4%, chemicals 7.3%, construction 6.6%, public facilities 5%, and other sectors 43%.

Gardner Denver Holdings Inc.	1.2%
Other	92.6

Source: "Pump & Compressor Manufacturing in the U.S." [online] from http://www.ibisworld.com [Published December 2020], from IBISWorld.

★ 2823 ★
Pumps
SIC: 3568; NAICS: 333613
Top Booster Pump Makers Worldwide, 2019

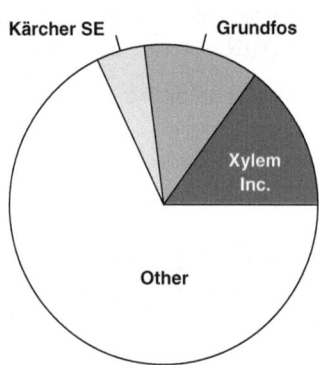

Booster pumps are designed to boost water pressure in municipal well water systems, rainwater collection systems, irrigation and gardens, and similar systems. The industry is forecast to see revenue grow from $2.48 billion in 2020 to $3.05 billion in 2026.

Xylem Inc.	15.26%
Grundfos	11.64
Kärcher SE	4.90
Other	68.20

Source: "Global Booster Pump Sales Market Report 2020." [online] from http://www.qyresearch.com [Published November 2020], from QY Research.

★ 2824 ★
Pumps
SIC: 3568; NAICS: 333613
Top Dewatering Pump Makers Worldwide, 2018

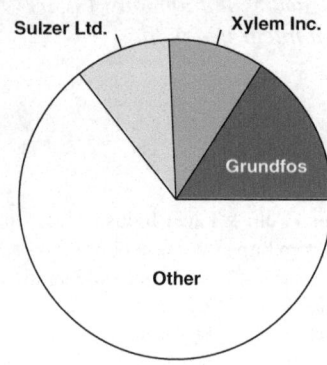

Dewatering pumps are centrifugal pumps installed in a building situated below the groundwater level to reduce the water level and maintain it at the current level. Market shares are shown based on revenue of $3.33 billion in 2019.

Grundfos	16.10%
Xylem Inc.	9.57
Sulzer Ltd.	9.53
Other	64.80

Source: "Global Dewatering Pump Sales Market Insights, Forecast to 2026." [online] from http://www.qyresearch.com [Published November 2020], from QY Research.

★ 2825 ★
Pumps
SIC: 3568; NAICS: 333613
Top Sealless Pump Makers Worldwide, 2018

Sealless pumps do not require a seal because the pump and the motor are contained separately. By eliminating the seal, sealless pumps are safer and more environmentally friendly. The industry is forecast to grow from $3.2 billion in 2020 to $4.16 billion in 2026. Market shares are shown based on revenue.

Nikkiso Co. Ltd.	6.85%
PSG Dover	6.10
IDEX Corp.	3.70
Other	83.35

Source: "Global Sealless Pump Sales Market Report 2020." [online] from http://www.qyresearch.com [Published November 2020], from QY Research.

R

★ 2826 ★
Racetracks
SIC: 7948; NAICS: 711212

Leading Racetrack Operators, 2020

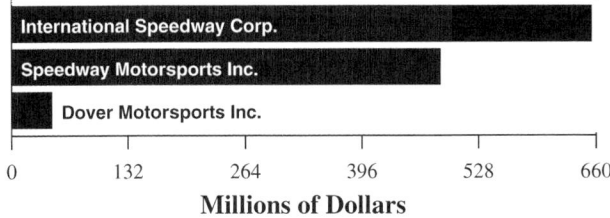

Millions of Dollars

Companies are ranked by revenue in millions of dollars. Figures are for 2020 or latest year available. Industry revenue fell from $8.6 billion in 2019 to $1.9 billion in 2020. Revenue is forecast to reach $2.53 billion in 2027.

International Speedway Corp.	$ 654.78
Speedway Motorsports Inc.	485.00
Dover Motorsports Inc.	45.95

Source: "Racetracks Industry (U.S.)." [online] from http://www.plunkettresearch.com [Published March 5, 2021], from Plunkett Research.

★ 2827 ★
Radio Broadcasting
SIC: 4832; NAICS: 515112

Leading Talk Radio Shows, 2020

Shows are ranked by millions of unique listeners in October 2020. Figures do not include popular hosts featured exclusively on SiriusXM Satellite Radio, which operates a closed subscriber system and does not make specific host audience numbers available.

Rush Limbaugh	15.50
Sean Hannity	15.00
Dave Ramsey	14.00
Mark Levin	11.00
George Noory	10.50
Glenn Beck	10.50
Mike Gallagher	8.50
Hugh Hewitt	8.00
Michael Savage	7.50
Dana Loesch	7.25

Source: "Top Talk Audiences." [online] from http://www.talkers.com/top-talk-audiences/ [Accessed November 3, 2020].

★ 2828 ★
Radio Broadcasting
SIC: 4832; NAICS: 515112

Top Radio Station Owners, 2020

Companies are ranked by net advertising revenue in millions of dollars as of October 27, 2020.

iHeartMedia Inc.	$ 2,328
Entercom Communications Corp.	1,294
Cumulus Media Inc.	602
Beasley Broadcast Inc.	263
Apollo Global Management	238
Hubbard Broadcasting Inc.	222
Townsquare Media Inc.	211
Univision Communications Inc.	206
Urban One Inc.	197
Salem Media Group Inc.	138

Source: *Radio World*, February 17, 2021, p. 29, from S&P Global, *Top Radio Station Owners*.

★ 2829 ★
Radios
SIC: 3663; NAICS: 33422

Leading Military Airborne Radio Makers, 2016-2018

Data show average market shares based on value for 2016-2018.

UTC Corp.	40.0-50.0%
Raytheon Corp.	20.0-30.0
Northrop Grumman Corp.	10.0-20.0
Rohde & Schwarz GmbH	5.0-10.0
Other	0.0-25.0

Source: "Case M.9434 - UTC/Raytheon." [online] from https://ec.europa.eu/competition/elojade/isef/case_details.cfm?proc_code=2_M_9434 [Published March 13, 2020], from Form CO, Annex A.5.44.

★ 2830 ★
Railings
SIC/NAICS: See frontmatter for explanation.

Railing Industry by Type, 2019

The industry was valued at 0.2 billion square feet.

Wood	67.0%
Composite and aluminum	16.0
Other	17.0

Source: "The Azek Company." [online] from https://www.sec.gov/Archives/edgar/data/1782754/000119312520028208/d776367ds1.htm [Published February 2020], from Principia.

★ 2831 ★
Railroad Equipment
SIC: 3743; NAICS: 33651

Electric Commuter-Train Market in Europe, 2018

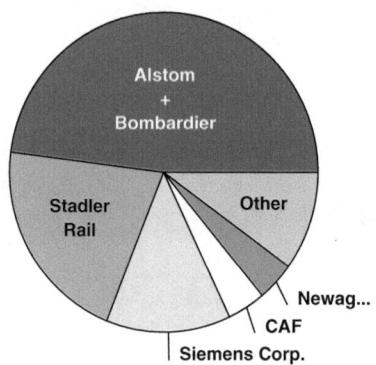

Market shares are shown in percent.

Alstom + Bombardier	48.0%
Stadler Rail	21.0
Siemens Corp.	13.0
CAF	4.0
Newag S.A.	4.0
Other	10.0

Source: "Alstom, Bombardier Seek to Avoid Path That Derailed Siemens Deal." [online] from https://www.bloomberg.com/news/articles/2020-02-19/alstom-bombardier-seek-to-avoid-path-that-derailed-siemens-deal [Published February 19, 2020], from Bloomberg Intelligence.

★ 2832 ★
Railroad Equipment
SIC: 3743; NAICS: 33651

HSR Control System Market Worldwide, 2015-2018

Market shares are shown in percent.

China Railway Signal & Communication Corp.	60.0%
China Railway and CRCC	40.0

Source: "China Railway System and Communication." [online] from https://pdf.dfcfw.com/pdf/H3_AP202006041382253833_1.pdf?1591264893000.pdf [Published June 3, 2020], from Frost & Sullivan and CICC Research.

★ 2833 ★
Railroad Equipment
SIC: 3743; NAICS: 33651

Leading Diesel Locomotive Makers Worldwide, 2015-2019

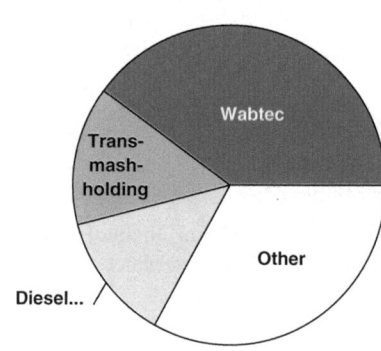

Approximately 8,300 diesel and alternative powered locomotives were delivered from 2015-2019.

Wabtec	40.0%
Transmashholding	14.0
Diesel Locomotive Works	13.0
Other	33.0

Source: "SCI Verkehr Forecasts 24% Drop in Diesel Locomotive Purchases." [online] from https://www.railjournal.com/fleet/sci-verkehr-forecasts-24-drop-in-diesel-locomotive-purchases/ [Published August 28, 2020], from SCI Verkehr.

★ 2834 ★
Railroad Equipment
SIC: 3743; NAICS: 33651

Leading Light Rail Vehicle Makers in North America, 2019

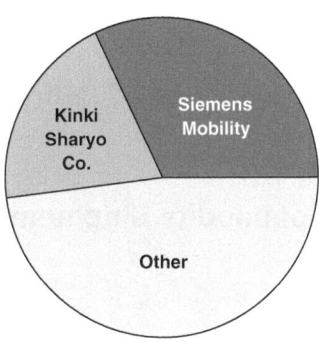

The total light rail vehicle fleet (excluding metro) was 3,200 units as of December 2019. Market shares are estimated.

Siemens Mobility	32.0%
Kinki Sharyo Co.	20.0
Other	48.0

Source: "Rolling Stock Market in North America 2020-2025." [online] from https://mobilityforesights.com/product/rolling-stock-market-in-north-america/ [Published January 2020], from Mobility Foresights.

★ 2835 ★
Railroad Equipment
SIC: 3743; NAICS: 33651

Leading Railway Track System Makers Worldwide, 2015-2019

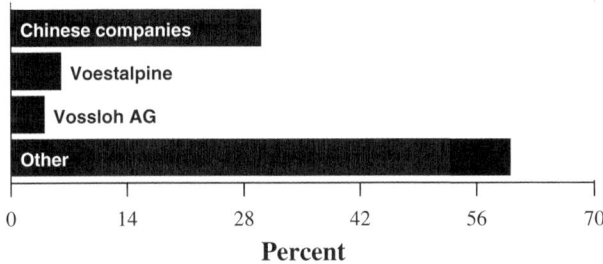

Market share are estimated based on production.

Chinese companies	30.0%
Voestalpine	6.0
Vossloh AG	4.0
Other	60.0

Source: "Rail Track System - Global Market Trends 2020." [online] from http://www.sci.de [Press release September 24, 2020], from SCI Verkehr.

★ 2836 ★
Railroad Equipment
SIC: 3743; NAICS: 33651

Rail Transit Signal System Market Worldwide, 2018

Market shares are shown in percent.

TCT	32.0%
Chinese-American Signal Co.	24.0
CRSC Rapid Transit	12.0
Nanjing Research Institute of Electronics Technology	12.0
Thales SEC Transport System	8.0
Bombardier NUG Signaling	4.0
CRRC Times Electric	4.0
UniTTEC Co. Ltd.	4.0

Source: "China Railway System and Communication." [online] from https://pdf.dfcfw.com/pdf/H3_AP202006041382253833_1.pdf?1591264893000.pdf [Published June 3, 2020], from corporate filings and CICC Research.

★ 2837 ★
Railroad Equipment
SIC: 3743; NAICS: 33651

Railcar Fleet by Type in North America, 2017-2019

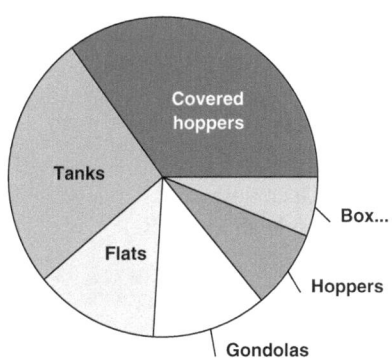

The total revenue-earning fleet was 1,639 in 2017, 1,650 in 2018 and 1,658 in 2019. The revenue-earning fleet is a subset of the North American fleet that is largely composed of freight cars that can be used in interchange service and against which an interline waybill can be placed.

	2017	2018	2019	Share
Covered hoppers	554	569	571	34.69%
Tanks	415	417	432	26.25
Flats	202	205	210	12.76
Gondolas	211	208	202	12.27

Continued on next page.

★ 2837 ★
[Continued]
Railroad Equipment
SIC: 3743; NAICS: 33651

Railcar Fleet by Type in North America, 2017-2019

The total revenue-earning fleet was 1,639 in 2017, 1,650 in 2018 and 1,658 in 2019. The revenue-earning fleet is a subset of the North American fleet that is largely composed of freight cars that can be used in interchange service and against which an interline waybill can be placed.

	2017	2018	2019	Share
Hoppers	135	131	126	7.65%
Box cars	108	107	105	6.38

Source: *Railway Age*, April 2020, p. 31, from Rail Inc.

★ 2838 ★
Railroads
SIC: 4011; NAICS: 482111

High-Speed Rail Worldwide, 2019

Data show the location of the approximately 6,000 high-speed trainsets worldwide. A total of 11,693 kilometers of high-speed lines are under construction.

	Trainsets	Share
China (China State Railway Group)	464.1	64.0%
Japan (JR Group)	99.6	14.0
France (SNCF)	50.5	7.0
Germany (DB AG)	27.2	4.0
Korea (Korail)	16.3	2.0
Spain (Renfe Operadora)	15.1	2.0
Taiwan (Taiwan High Speed Rail Corp.)	10.5	2.0
Italy (NTV) 2017	4.7	1.0
Italy (TrenItalia) 2017	9.6	1.0
Other	22.6	3.0

Source: "The Perpetual Growth of High-Speed Rail Development." [online] from https://www.globalrailwayreview.com/article/112553/perpetual-growth-high-speed-rail/ [Published November 3, 2020], from International Union of Railways.

★ 2839 ★
Railroads
SIC: 4011; NAICS: 482111

Leading Railroads, 2019

Companies are ranked by revenue in millions of dollars.

BNSF Railway	$ 23,133
Union Pacific	21,708
Canadian National	$ 14,917
CSX Transportation	11,937
Norfolk Southern	11,296
Canadian Pacific	7,792
Kansas City Southern	2,866

Source: "Class I Railroads." [online] from https://www.american-rails.com/class.html#gallery[pageGallery]/5/ [Accessed March 10, 2021], from company reports.

★ 2840 ★
Railroads
SIC: 4011; NAICS: 482111

Railroad Commodity Shipments, 2019-2020

Data show carloads by commodity for the five weeks ended January 2, 2021.

	Dec. 2019	Dec. 2020	Share
Coal	347,348	296,839	26.95%
Chemicals	155,436	161,200	14.64
Grain	100,664	128,759	11.69
Crushed stone, sand and metal	83,156	70,823	6.43
Motor vehicles and parts	67,604	68,658	6.23
Petroleum and petroleum products	65,844	55,458	5.04
Grain mill products	44,027	44,641	4.05
Primary metal products	40,770	38,035	3.45
Stone, clay and glass products	32,975	34,428	3.13
Other	206,166	202,483	18.39

Source: *Railway Age*, February 2021, p. 4, from Rail Time Indicators and Association of American Railroads.

★ 2841 ★
Rare Earths
SIC: 1499; NAICS: 212399

Leading End Markets for Rare Earths, 2020

Rare earths are used in the production of a variety of goods. China supplied 80% of rare-earth compounds to the United States in 2020, followed by Estonia with 5%, Japan 4%, Malaysia 4% and other countries 7%.

Catalysts	75.0%
Ceramics and glass	6.0
Polishing	5.0

Continued on next page.

★ 2841 ★
[Continued]
Rare Earths
SIC: 1499; NAICS: 212399

Leading End Markets for Rare Earths, 2020

Rare earths are used in the production of a variety of goods. China supplied 80% of rare-earth compounds to the United States in 2020, followed by Estonia with 5%, Japan 4%, Malaysia 4% and other countries 7%.

Metallurgical applications and alloys	4.0%
Other	10.0

Source: "Mineral Commodity Summaries 2021." [online] from https://www.usgs.gov/centers/nmic/mineral-commodity-summaries [Published January 29, 2021], from U.S. Geological Survey.

★ 2842 ★
Rare Earths
SIC: 1499; NAICS: 212399

Top Rare Earth Producing Nations, 2020

Countries are ranked by production in metric tons of rare-earth oxide equivalent content. In the United States, bastnaesite, a rare earth, was mined as a primary product at one mine in California. China's figure does not include undocumented production. Production data are estimated.

	MT	Share
China	140,000	57.54%
United States	38,000	15.62
Burma	30,000	12.33
Australia	17,000	6.99
Madagascar	8,000	3.29
India	3,000	1.23
Russia	2,700	1.11
Thailand	2,000	0.82
Brazil	1,000	0.41
Vietnam	1,000	0.41
Burundi	500	0.21
Other	100	0.04

Source: "Mineral Commodity Summaries 2021." [online] from https://www.usgs.gov/centers/nmic/mineral-commodity-summaries [Published January 29, 2021], from U.S. Geological Survey.

★ 2843 ★
Real Estate
SIC: 6531; NAICS: 53121

Largest Industrial Real Estate Brokers, 2020

Companies are ranked by value of deals in millions of dollars. Brokered deals reached $38.7 billion. Figures refer to deals of at least $25 million.

	($ mil.)	Share
CBRE	$ 14,561	37.61%
Jones Lang LaSalle (JLL)	7,477	19.31
Cushman & Wakefield	6,192	15.99
Eastdil Secured	4,632	11.96
Newmark Group Inc.	2,343	6.05
Colliers International	1,966	5.08
Bank of America Corp.	416	1.07
Transwestern	240	0.62
Avison Young	228	0.59
Savills PLC	155	0.40
Kidder Mathews	146	0.38
Other	357	0.92

Source: "Rankings Table." [online] from https://www.greenstreet.com/news/real-estate-alert?breakdownId=1 [Accessed February 15, 2021], from Real Estate Alert.

★ 2844 ★
Real Estate
SIC: 6531; NAICS: 53121

Largest Lodging Real Estate Brokers, 2020

Companies are ranked by value of deals in millions of dollars. Deals reached $4.7 billion. Figures refer to deals of at least $25 million.

	($ mil.)	Share
Jones Lang LaSalle (JLL)	$ 1,378	28.76%
Hodges Ward Elliott Inc.	1,338	27.92
CBRE	782	16.32
Eastdil Secured L.L.C.	703	14.67
Berkadia	144	3.01
Avison Young	140	2.92
Newmark Group Inc.	136	2.84
Hunter Hotel Advisors	123	2.57
Robert Douglas	120	2.50
Cushman & Wakefield PLC	39	0.81

Source: "Rankings Table." [online] from https://www.greenstreet.com/news/real-estate-alert?breakdownId=1 [Accessed February 15, 2021], from Real Estate Alert.

★ 2845 ★
Real Estate
SIC: 6531; NAICS: 53121

Largest Multifamily Real Estate Brokers, 2020

Companies are ranked by value of deals in millions of dollars. Brokered deals reached $80.9 billion. Figures refer to deals of at least $25 million.

	($ mil.)	Share
CBRE	$ 19,733	24.37%
Newmark Group Inc.	16,368	20.21
Jones Lang LaSalle (JLL)	13,858	17.11
Cushman & Wakefield	8,481	10.47
Marcus & Millichap IPA	4,633	5.72
Eastdil Secured	3,924	4.85
Berkadia	3,008	3.71
Colliers International	1,388	1.71
NorthMarq Capital L.L.C.	807	1.00
Other	8,779	10.84

Source: "Rankings Table." [online] from https://www.greenstreet.com/news/real-estate-alert?breakdownId=1 [Accessed February 15, 2021], from Real Estate Alert.

★ 2846 ★
Real Estate
SIC: 6531; NAICS: 53121

Largest Office Space Real Estate Brokers, 2020

Companies are ranked by value of deals in millions of dollars. Brokered deals reached $53.38 million. Figures refer to deals of at least $25 million.

	($ mil.)	Share
Eastdil Secured	$ 14,318	26.82%
Newmark Group Inc.	10,299	19.29
CBRE	10,090	18.90
Jones Lang LaSalle (JLL)	9,535	17.86
Cushman & Wakefield	6,804	12.75
Colliers International	1,268	2.38
Transwestern	222	0.42
Avison Young	137	0.26
Savills PLC	136	0.25
Hoffman Co.	106	0.20
Hodges Ward Elliott Inc.	100	0.19
Lee & Associates	84	0.16
Other	282	0.53

Source: "Rankings Table." [online] from https://www.greenstreet.com/news/real-estate-alert?breakdownId=1 [Accessed February 15, 2021], from Real Estate Alert.

★ 2847 ★
Real Estate
SIC: 6531; NAICS: 53121

Largest Real Estate Brokers, 2020

Companies are ranked by value of deals in millions of dollars. Brokered deals reached $80.08 billion. Figures refer to deals of at least $25 million and cover multi-family, office, industrial, retail and hotel markets.

	($ mil.)	Share
CBRE	$ 47,122	25.46%
Jones Lang LaSalle (JLL)	34,110	18.43
Newmark Group Inc.	30,157	16.29
Eastdil Secured L.L.C.	24,967	13.49
Cushman & Wakefield PLC	22,050	11.91
Walker & Dunlop Inc.	5,126	2.77
Marcus & Millichap IPA	4,963	2.68
Colliers International	4,721	2.55
Berkadia	3,152	1.70
Hodges Ward Elliott Inc.	1,438	0.78
Other	7,306	3.95

Source: "Rankings Table." [online] from https://www.greenstreet.com/news/real-estate-alert?breakdownId=1 [Accessed February 15, 2021], from Real Estate Alert.

★ 2848 ★
Real Estate
SIC: 6531; NAICS: 53121

Largest Real Estate Firms in Indianapolis, MD, 2019

Companies are ranked by value of residential home sales in millions of dollars.

F.C. Tucker Co. Inc.	$ 3,000.0
Century 21 Scheetz	1,500.0
Keller Williams Realty Greater Indianapolis	1,500.0
Carpenter Realtors	1,300.0
Berkshire Hathaway HomeServices Indiana Realty	867.9
Keller Williams Indianapolis Metro North/Carmel	541.1
RE/MAX Ability Plus	522.7
Coldwell Banker Kaiser	512.5
Highgarden Real Estate	300.2
RE/MAX Centerstone	299.4

Source: Indianapolis Business Journal, March 27, 2020, p. 18A, from agency reports.

★ 2849 ★
Real Estate
SIC: 6531; NAICS: 53121

Largest Real Estate Firms in Wilmington, NC, 2019

Companies are ranked by closed sales volume in millions of dollars.

Coldwell Banker Sea Coast Advantage	$ 1,401.0
Intracoastal Realty	1,076.8
Keller Williams Realty	534.2
Century 21 Swayer & Associates	358.0
RE/MAX Essential	266.3
BlueCoast Realty	197.6
Landmark Sotheby's International Realty	169.1
Margaret Rudd & Associates	112.6
Next Realty	108.1
RE/MAX at the Beach	99.2

Source: *Greater Wilmington Business Journal*, March 27-April 5, 2020, p. 5.

★ 2850 ★
Real Estate
SIC: 6531; NAICS: 53121

Largest Residential Real Estate Brokerages, 2020

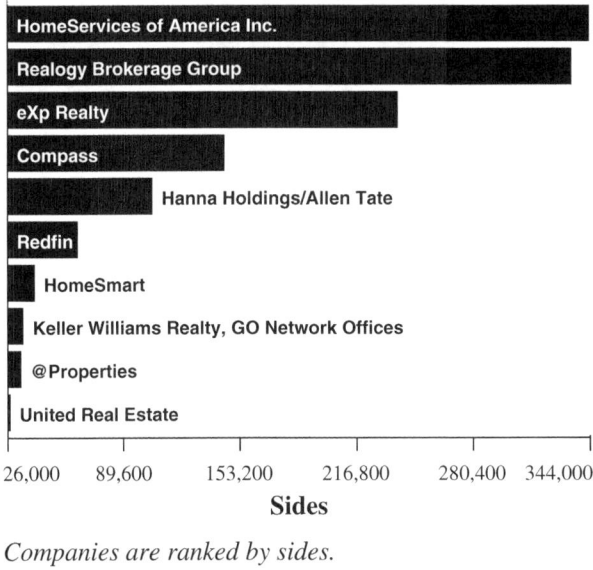

Sides

Companies are ranked by sides.

HomeServices of America Inc.	343,220
Realogy Brokerage Group	333,737
eXp Realty	238,981
Compass	144,784
Hanna Holdings/Allen Tate	105,455
Redfin	64,420
HomeSmart	40,809
Keller Williams Realty, GO Network Offices	34,463
@Properties	33,259
United Real Estate	27,292

Source: *Wall Street Journal*, March 26, 2021, p. M16, from Real Trends.

★ 2851 ★
Real Estate
SIC: 6531; NAICS: 53121

Largest Retail Real Estate Brokers, 2020

Companies are ranked by value of deals in millions of dollars. Deals reached $8 billion. Figures refer to deals of at least $25 million.

	($ mil.)	Share
Eastdil Secured	$ 1,611	24.2%
CBRE	1,498	22.5
JLL	1,413	21.3
Newmark Group Inc.	1,136	17.1
Cushman & Wakefield	535	8.0
Marcus & Millichap IPA	124	1.9
Mid-America	102	1.5
Colliers International	100	1.5
Kidder Mathews	61	0.9
Avison Young	55	0.8

Source: "Rankings Table." [online] from https://www.greenstreet.com/news/real-estate-alert?breakdownId=1 [Accessed February 15, 2021], from Real Estate Alert.

★ 2852 ★
Real Estate
SIC: 6531; NAICS: 53132

Offices of Real Estate Appraisers, 2017

Total sales were valued at $6.58 billion. The term "nec" stands for not elsewhere classified.

	($ 000)	Share
Urban real estate appraisal services	$ 5,124,946	$ 78.28
Rural real estate appraisal services	1,269,345	19.39
Real estate consulting services	50,599	0.77
Residential building property management	24,406	0.37
Nonresidential building property management	19,544	0.30
Agent and brokerage services, sale of residential real estate	18,037	0.28

Continued on next page.

★ 2852 ★
[Continued]
Real Estate
SIC: 6531; NAICS: 53132

Offices of Real Estate Appraisers, 2017

Total sales were valued at $6.58 billion. The term "nec" stands for not elsewhere classified.

	($ 000)	Share
Agent and brokerage services, sale of nonresidential real estate	$ 10,719	$ 0.16
Marketing research services	5,660	0.09
Agent and brokerage services, rental of residential real estate	2,692	0.04
Land property management	2,905	0.04
Agent and brokerage services, sale of land	2,123	0.03
Agent and brokerage services, rental of nonresidential real estate	954	0.01
Home, apartment, rooming house, and other residential space rental and leasing	410	0.01
Real estate listing services	587	0.01
Rental and leasing, office and professional space	357	0.01
Rental and leasing, commercial space	276	< 0.01
Retail sales of other goods, nec	195	< 0.01
Other products and services, nec	13,568	0.21

Source: "Economic Census." [online] from https://www.census.gov/programs-surveys/economic-census/data/tables.html [Accessed December 2, 2020], from U.S. Census Bureau.

★ 2853 ★
Real Estate
SIC: 6531; NAICS: 53132

Real Estate Appraiser Leaders, 2017

Data show the percent of industry sales held by the largest 4, 8, 20 and 50 firms in the sector. There are approximately 13,241 players operating in the industry generating employment for 35,144 people. According to Kentley Insights, the industry generated sales of $6.1 billion in 2019.

4 largest firms	17.3%
8 largest firms	22.7
20 largest firms	31.0
50 largest firms	40.1

Source: "Economic Census." [online] from https://www.census.gov/content/census/en/data/tables/2017/econ/economic-census/naics-sector-31-33.html [Accessed January 21, 2021], from U.S. Census Bureau.

★ 2854 ★
Receptacles
SIC: 3643; NAICS: 335931

Receptacle Sales by Designation/Grade, 2019

An electrical receptacle is designed to receive an electrical plug for lamps and other appliances. Market shares are shown based on dollar sales for the 12 months ended September 2019.

Straight blade	37.6%
Residential grade	24.1
Commercial grade	23.4
Locking	9.2
Hospital grade	5.6
Unknown	0.1

Source: The Electrical Distributor, August 2020, p. 39, from Epicor's Industry Data Analytics.

★ 2855 ★
Recording Media
SIC: 3695; NAICS: 334613

Blank Magnetic and Optical Recording Media Manufacturing Leaders, 2017

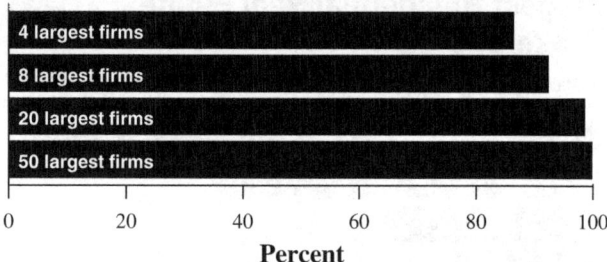

Data show the percent of industry sales held by the largest 4, 8, 20 and 50 firms in the sector. There are approximately 57 players operating in the industry generating employment for 520 people. According to IBISWorld, industry growth fell 16.4% from 2015 through 2020. The main reason for this decline is the move from physical media to new formats. However, there are those who feel that physical media is of superior quality to streaming formats. The industry was worth $1 billion in 2020.

4 largest firms	86.3%
8 largest firms	92.3
20 largest firms	98.5
50 largest firms	100.0

Source: "Economic Census." [online] from https://www.census.gov/content/census/en/data/tables/2017/econ/economic-census/naics-sector-31-33.html [Accessed January 21, 2021], from U.S. Census Bureau.

★ 2856 ★
Recreation Management
SIC: 7032; NAICS: 721214

Recreation, Sports and Fitness Facilities Industry, 2020

Data show the types of recreation, sports and fitness facilities managed by respondents to the source's annual survey. Respondents served an average population of 108,300. Average population size for other categories: recreation centers 109,200, parks 142,000, Ys 83,310, camps 79,500, colleges 55,550, health clubs 42,970, and schools 30,080.

Parks and recreation department	47.1%
Schools/school districts	10.5
Colleges and universities	9.5
Y, JCC, Boys & Girls Clubs	6.6
Recreation and sports centers	6.5
Camp facilities	5.7
Health/fitness clubs	2.8
Resorts/resort hotels	1.8
Water/amusement parks	1.1

Source: *Recreation Management*, State of the Industry 2020, p. NA.

★ 2857 ★
Recreational Goods Rental
SIC: 7999; NAICS: 532284

Number of Firms In Recreational Goods Rental, 1998-2019

Operators in this industry rent bicycles, canoes, motorcycles, sailboats and similar products. According to Kentley Insights, the industry generated sales of $1.7 billion in 2019.

1998	1,726
1999	1,739
2000	1,742
2001	1,768
2002	1,877
2003	1,771
2004	1,761
2005	1,768
2006	1,719
2007	1,823
2008	1,749
2009	1,777
2010	1,807
2011	1,866
2012	1,935
2013	1,951
2014	2,037
2015	2,162
2016	2,255
2017	2,341
2018	2,385
2019	2,435

Source: "County Business Patterns." [online] from https://www.census.gov/programs-surveys/cbp/data/datasets.html [Published April 22, 2021], from U.S. Census Bureau.

★ 2858 ★
Recreational Goods Rental
SIC: 7999; NAICS: 532284

Recreational Goods Rental Leaders, 2017

Data show the percent of industry sales held by the largest 4, 8, 20 and 50 firms in the sector. There are approximately 2,327 players operating in the industry generating employment for 11,870 people.

4 largest firms	16.3%
8 largest firms	19.6
20 largest firms	26.0
50 largest firms	35.3

Source: "Economic Census." [online] from https://www.census.gov/content/census/en/data/tables/2017/econ/economic-census/naics-sector-31-33.html [Accessed January 21, 2021], from U.S. Census Bureau.

★ 2859 ★
Recreational Vehicles
SIC: 3716; NAICS: 336213

Leading Class A Recreational Vehicle Makers, 2020

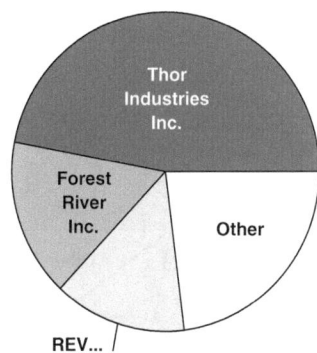

Market shares are shown based on 16,413 registrations.

Thor Industries Inc.	47.1%
Forest River Inc.	16.0

Continued on next page.

★ 2859 ★
[Continued]
Recreational Vehicles
SIC: 3716; NAICS: 336213

Leading Class A Recreational Vehicle Makers, 2020

Market shares are shown based on 16,413 registrations.

REV Recreation Group	14.2%
Other	22.7

Source: "Industry Eclipses 500,000 in Retail Sales for First Time Ever." [online] from https://rvbusiness.com/industry-eclipses-500000-in-retail-sales-for-first-time-ever/ [Published February 9, 2021], from Statistical Surveys.

★ 2860 ★
Recreational Vehicles
SIC: 3716; NAICS: 336213

Leading Class B Recreational Vehicle Makers, 2020

Market shares are shown based on 7,877 registrations.

Winnebago Motorized	49.9%
Thor Industries Inc.	13.9
Forest River Inc.	9.9
Other	26.3

Source: "Industry Eclipses 500,000 in Retail Sales for First Time Ever." [online] from https://rvbusiness.com/industry-eclipses-500000-in-retail-sales-for-first-time-ever/ [Published February 9, 2021], from Statistical Surveys.

★ 2861 ★
Recreational Vehicles
SIC: 3716; NAICS: 336213

Leading Class C Recreational Vehicle Makers, 2020

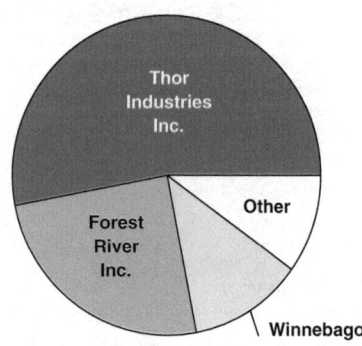

Market shares are shown based on 25,759 registrations.

Thor Industries Inc.	53.3%
Forest River Inc.	25.1
Winnebago Motorized	11.8%
Other	9.8

Source: "Industry Eclipses 500,000 in Retail Sales for First Time Ever." [online] from https://rvbusiness.com/industry-eclipses-500000-in-retail-sales-for-first-time-ever/ [Published February 9, 2021], from Statistical Surveys.

★ 2862 ★
Recreational Vehicles
SIC: 3716; NAICS: 336213

Leading Park Model Recreational Vehicle Makers, 2020

Market shares are shown based on 2,461 registrations.

Skyline Equipment	34.4%
Kropf Industries	16.5
Cavco Industries Inc.	15.6
Other	33.5

Source: "Industry Eclipses 500,000 in Retail Sales for First Time Ever." [online] from https://rvbusiness.com/industry-eclipses-500000-in-retail-sales-for-first-time-ever/ [Published February 9, 2021], from Statistical Surveys.

★ 2863 ★
Recreational Vehicles
SIC: 3792; NAICS: 336214

Wholesale Recreational Vehicle Shipments, 2019-2020

Data show unit shipments. Van campers (Type B) grew 70%, the largest increase. Conventional motorhomes (Type A) saw shipments fall 27.6%, the biggest decline.

	2019	2020
Travel trailers (all)	274,630	298,478
Travel trailers, 5th wheel	74,875	81,508
Mini (Type C)	25,961	21,685
Motorhomes, conventional type A	16,420	11,892
Folding camping trailers	6,534	6,255
Van campers (type B)	4,248	7,222
Truck campers	3,402	3,372

Source: "2020 RV Shipments Surpass 2019 By 6% With December Shipments Best on Record." [online] from https://www.rvia.org/news-insights/2020-rv-shipments-surpass-2019-6-december-shipments-best-record [Published December 2020], from Recreational Vehicle Industry Association.

★ 2864 ★
Refrigeration Equipment Wholesalers
SIC: 5078; NAICS: 42374

Refrigeration Equipment and Supplies Merchant Wholesalers, 2017

Data show the percent of industry sales held by the largest 4, 8, 20 and 50 firms in the sector. There are approximately 1,230 players operating in the industry generating employment for 14,248 people. According to IBISWorld, the industry generated sales of $5.6 billion in 2020.

4 largest firms	31.6%
8 largest firms	43.7
20 largest firms	58.2
50 largest firms	74.4

Source: "Economic Census." [online] from https://www.census.gov/content/census/en/data/tables/2017/econ/economic-census/naics-sector-31-33.html [Accessed January 21, 2021], from U.S. Census Bureau.

★ 2865 ★
Relays and Industrial Controls
SIC: 3625; NAICS: 335314

Relay and Industrial Control Manufacturing Leaders, 2017

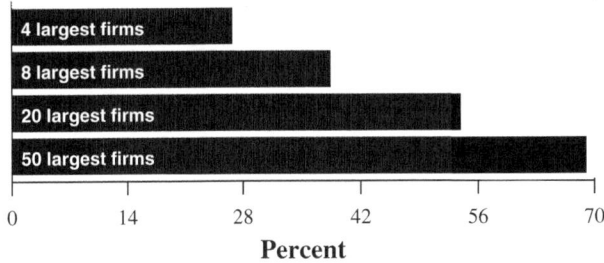

Data show the percent of industry sales held by the largest 4, 8, 20 and 50 firms in the sector. There are approximately 874 players operating in the industry generating employment for 33,319 people. According to Kentley Insights, the industry generated sales of $11.8 billion in 2020.

4 largest firms	26.7%
8 largest firms	38.4
20 largest firms	53.9
50 largest firms	69.0

Source: "Economic Census." [online] from https://www.census.gov/content/census/en/data/tables/2017/econ/economic-census/naics-sector-31-33.html [Accessed January 21, 2021], from U.S. Census Bureau.

★ 2866 ★
Religious Organizations
SIC: 8661; NAICS: 81311

Church Affiliation by Generation, 1998-2020

Church affiliation among Americans has been on the decline for some time. Membership dropped below 50% for the first time in 2020, when 47% of Americans said they belonged to a church, mosque or synagogue, down from 70% in 1999 and 50% in 2018. As the table shows, membership correlates closely with age, with older Americans much more likely to be attending services than their younger counterparts. Women were more likely to be a member of a church than men, 53% to 43%. Traditionalists (born pre-1946); Baby boomers (born 1946-1964); Generation X (born 1965-1980); Millennials (born 1981-1996).

	1998-2000	2008-2010	2018-2020
Traditionalists	77.0%	73.0%	66.0%
Baby boomers	67.0	63.0	58.0
Generation X	62.0	57.0	50.0
Millennials	0.0	51.0	36.0

Source: "U.S. Church Membership Falls Below Majority for First Time." [online] from https://news.gallup.com/poll/341963/church-membership-falls-below-majority-first-time.aspx [Published March 29, 2021], from Gallup.

★ 2867 ★
Religious Organizations
SIC: 8661; NAICS: 81311

Largest Churches, 2020

Churches are ranked by average attendance. According to the source, the fastest-growing church was the Destiny Church, located in Columbia, Maryland. Average attendance was 2,726, and it had an attendance increase of 1,261, a jump of 86%.

North Point Ministries (GA)	38,589
Gateway Church (TX)	31,690
Eagle Brook Church (MN)	25,340
Saddleback Church (CA)	23,494
Mount Zion Baptist Church (TN)	21,223
Second Baptist Church (TX)	20,871
New Life Church (AR)	17,877
Flatirons Community Church (CO)	16,364
LCBC Church (PA)	16,268
Community Bible Church (TX)	14,520

Source: *Outreach Magazine*, Annual 100, 2020, p. NA.

★ 2868 ★
Remediation Services
SIC: 4959; NAICS: 56291

Remediation Service Leaders, 2017

Data show the percent of industry sales held by the largest 4, 8, 20 and 50 firms in the sector. There are approximately 4,809 players operating in the industry generating employment for 85,402 people. According to IBISWorld, the remediation and environmental cleanup industry generated revenue of $20.1 billion in 2021.

4 largest firms	11.3%
8 largest firms	17.1
20 largest firms	27.9
50 largest firms	39.9

Source: "Economic Census." [online] from https://www.census.gov/content/census/en/data/tables/2017/econ/economic-census/naics-sector-31-33.html [Accessed January 21, 2021], from U.S. Census Bureau.

★ 2869 ★
Remittances
SIC: 6099; NAICS: 52232

Top Remittance Recipients Worldwide, 2020

Data show value in billions of dollars. The source expects that the money sent home by migrant workers is expected to fall 20% in 2020 because of the economic crisis brought on by COVID-19. According to the source, this will be the largest decline in recent history.

India	$ 76
China	60
Mexico	41
Philippines	33
Egypt, Arab Republic	24
Pakistan	24
Nigeria	21
Bangladesh	20
Vietnam	16
Ukraine	14

Source: "Phase II: COVID-19 Crisis Through a Migration Lens." [online] from https://www.knomad.org/publication/migration-and-development-brief-33 [Published October 2020], from World Bank, World Development Indicators and IMF Balance of Payments.

★ 2870 ★
Rental Industry
SIC: 7359; NAICS: 53221

Leading Consumer Appliance and Furniture Rental Providers, 2020

Companies are ranked by revenue in millions of dollars. Figures are for 2020 or latest year available. Industry revenue fell from $29.53 billion in 2019 to $28.53 billion in 2020. Revenue is forecast to reach $37.9 billion in 2027.

Aaron's Holdings Company Inc.	$ 3,947.65
Rent-A-Center Inc.	2,669.85
Apria Healthcare Group Inc.	1,423.00
Redbox Automated Retail L.L.C.	975.00
CORT Business Services Corp.	466.01
Family Video Movie Club Inc.	452.02
Bestway Inc.	294.36
Motivate International Inc.	110.25
FlexShopper Inc.	88.78
Boatsetter	29.91

Source: "Consumer Furniture and Appliance Rentals Industry (U.S.)." [online] from http://www.plunkettresearch.com [Published March 4, 2021], from Plunkett Research.

★ 2871 ★
Rental Industry
SIC: 7359; NAICS: 53231

Number of General Rental Centers, 1998-2019

Operators in this industry rent a variety of equipment, including consumer, commercial and industrial. According to Kentley Insights, sales reached $5.9 billion in 2019.

1998	6,246
1999	6,428
2000	6,358
2001	6,406
2002	6,737
2003	5,351
2004	5,169
2005	5,544
2006	5,569

Continued on next page.

★ 2871 ★
[Continued]
Rental Industry
SIC: 7359; NAICS: 53231

Number of General Rental Centers, 1998-2019

Operators in this industry rent a variety of equipment, including consumer, commercial and industrial. According to Kentley Insights, sales reached $5.9 billion in 2019.

Year	Number
2007	5,435
2008	4,566
2009	4,335
2010	4,228
2011	4,019
2012	3,600
2013	2,949
2014	2,890
2015	2,811
2016	2,768
2017	3,011
2018	3,045
2019	2,993

Source: "County Business Patterns." [online] from https://www.census.gov/programs-surveys/cbp/data/datasets.html [Published April 22, 2021], from U.S. Census Bureau.

★ 2872 ★
Repossession Services
SIC: 7389; NAICS: 561491

Number of Firms Engaged in Repossession Services, 1998-2019

Operators in this industry repossess appliances, autos, boats, furniture and similar products for creditors. According to Kentley Insights, the industry generated sales of $1 billion in 2019. The recent recession saw a rise in the number of repossessions, and some analysts expect this number to increase in 2021 because of the pandemic. Approximately 2.2 million cars are repossessed annually, by one estimate.

Year	Number
1998	1,133
1999	1,188
2000	1,263
2001	1,131
2002	955
2003	1,032
2004	1,064
2005	1,002
2006	970
2007	966
2008	1,012
2009	1,034
2010	1,052
2011	1,015
2012	955
2013	902
2014	844
2015	814
2016	835
2017	812
2018	776
2019	841

Source: "County Business Patterns." [online] from https://www.census.gov/programs-surveys/cbp/data/datasets.html [Published April 22, 2021], from U.S. Census Bureau.

★ 2873 ★
Repossession Services
SIC: 7389; NAICS: 561491

Repossession Service Leaders, 2017

Data show the percent of industry sales held by the largest 4, 8, 20 and 50 firms in the sector. There are approximately 816 players operating in the industry generating employment for 8,280 people.

4 largest firms	15.8%
8 largest firms	23.8
20 largest firms	36.3
50 largest firms	53.0

Source: "Economic Census." [online] from https://www.census.gov/content/census/en/data/tables/2017/econ/economic-census/naics-sector-31-33.html [Accessed January 21, 2021], from U.S. Census Bureau.

★ 2874 ★
Research
SIC: 8732; NAICS: 54172, 54191

Leading Market Research Firms, 2019

Companies are ranked by revenue in millions of dollars.

Nielsen	$ 3,875.0
IQVIA	2,220.0
Gartner Research	1,800.0
Kantar Group	950.0
Information Resources Inc. (IRI)	815.0
Ipsos	682.0
Westat	590.0
The NPD Group	339.5
comScore	336.1
GfK	320.0

Source: *Marketing News*, Fall 2020, p. NA, from American Marketing Association, ESOMAR and Global Research Business Network.

★ 2875 ★
Research
SIC: 8732; NAICS: 54191

Leading Research Markets Worldwide, 2019-2021

China has made significant investments in research and development. Spending reached $532.8 billion in 2019, $574.4 billion in 2020 and $621.5 billion in 2021. The United States, as well as many other countries, saw a funding decrease. Spending in the U.S. reached $596.6 billion, $580.2 billion and $598.7 billion, respectively. Total global spending by year: $2.37 trillion in 2019, $2.32 trillion in 2020 and $2.44 trillion in 2021.

	2019	2020	2021
China	22.5%	24.7%	25.5%
United States	25.2	25.0	24.5
South America	2.2	2.1	20.0
Europe	20.6	19.7	19.6
Russia/CIS	2.7	2.6	2.6
Middle East	2.4	2.3	2.3
Africa	0.9	0.8	0.8
Other	23.5	22.8	4.7

Source: *R&D Magazine*, Funding Forecast 2021, p. NA, from National Science Foundation.

★ 2876 ★
Research
SIC: 8733; NAICS: 541714

Top Clinical Trial Firms Worldwide, 2019

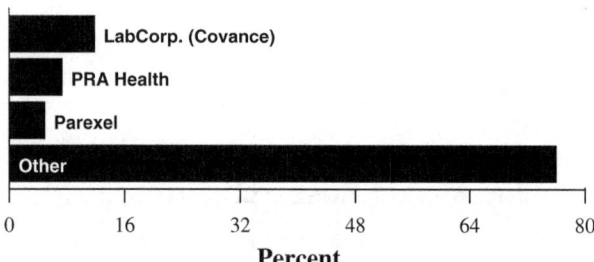

Clinical trials are experiments or observations done in clinical research. The goal of these processes is to note the reaction of study subjects to these new treatments and to see if further study is needed. Market shares are estimated based on revenue of $39.5 billion in 2019.

LabCorp. (Covance)	11.8%
PRA Health	7.3
Parexel	4.9%
Other	76.0

Source: "Global Clinical Trial Market Report, History and Forecast 2015-2026, Breakdown Data by Companies, Key Regions Types and Applications." [online] from http://www.qy-research.com [Published May 2020], from QY Research.

★ 2877 ★
Residential Intellectual Disability Care
SIC: 8051; NAICS: 62321

Residential Intellectual and Developmental Disability Facility Leaders, 2017

Data show the percent of industry sales held by the largest 4, 8, 20 and 50 firms in the sector. There are approximately 34,146 players operating in the industry generating employment for 580,691 people. According to the American Association on Intellectual and Developmental Disability, roughly 7.38 million people, or 2.28% of the population, are believed to have intellectual or developmental challenges. IBISWorld estimates this industry to be worth $31 billion in 2021, and that it faces certain challenges, such as rising costs and a decline in the number of residents because of COVID-19.

4 largest firms	9.3%
8 largest firms	12.0
20 largest firms	17.1
50 largest firms	24.6

Source: "Economic Census." [online] from https://www.census.gov/content/census/en/data/tables/2017/econ/economic-census/naics-sector-31-33.html [Accessed January 21, 2021], from U.S. Census Bureau.

★ 2878 ★
Restaurants
SIC: 5812; NAICS: 722513

Fast-Food Breakfast Visits, 2020-2021

Breakfasts have become a competitive part of the fast-food industry. McDonald's receives an estimated 30% of its sales during the morning period. However, a report from 2021 notes that because of COVID-19 breakfast visits have fallen dramatically. Market shares are shown based on number of visits on weekly mornings, 6 a.m.-11 a.m.

	Jan. 5 2021	March 6 2021
McDonald's Corp.	39.0%	42.0%
Starbucks Corp.	32.0	26.0

Continued on next page.

★ 2878 ★
[Continued]
Restaurants
SIC: 5812; NAICS: 722513
Fast-Food Breakfast Visits, 2020-2021

Breakfasts have become a competitive part of the fast-food industry. McDonald's receives an estimated 30% of its sales during the morning period. However, a report from 2021 notes that because of COVID-19 breakfast visits have fallen dramatically. Market shares are shown based on number of visits on weekly mornings, 6 a.m.-11 a.m.

	Jan. 5 2021	March 6 2021
Dunkin' Donuts	11.0%	13.0%
Wendy's	8.0	9.0
Burger King	5.0	6.0
Taco Bell	4.0	4.0

Source: "Breakfast, Back on the Menu." [online] from https://www.earnestresearch.com/data-bites/breakfast-back-on-the-menu/ [Published March 18, 2021], from Earnest Research.

★ 2879 ★
Restaurants
SIC: 5812; NAICS: 722513
Global Fast-Food Market, 2019

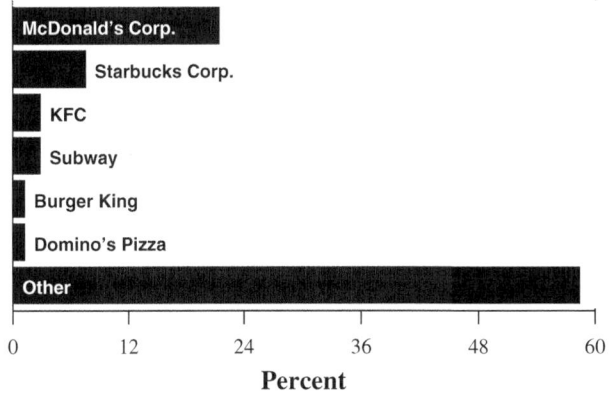

The market is forecast to see revenue rise from $611 billion in 2019 to $691 billion in 2022.

McDonald's Corp.	21.4%
Starbucks Corp.	7.5
KFC	2.8
Subway	2.8
Burger King	1.2
Domino's Pizza	1.2
Other	58.4

Source: "Fast-Food Market Share." [online] from https://www.t4.ai/industry/fast-food-market-share [Published August 16, 2020].

★ 2880 ★
Restaurants
SIC: 5812; NAICS: 722513
Global Market for Ghost Kitchens, 2020

According to the source, ghost kitchens are "cooking facilities that produce food only for delivery with no dine-in or customer facing areas." Food delivery services are expanding, becoming more reliable, and less expensive. Euromonitor predicts ghost kitchens could capture 50% of the drive-thru service ($75 billion), 50% of takeaway foodservice ($250 billion), 35% of ready meals ($40 billion), 30% of packaged cooking ingredients ($100 billion), 25% of dine-in foodservice ($450 billion), and 15% of packaged snacks ($125 billion). Data show estimated kitchens by country.

China	> 7,500
India	> 3,500
United States	1,500

Source: "Ghost Kitchens Could be a $1T Global Market by 2030, Says Euromonitor." [online] from https://www.restaurantdive.com/news/ghost-kitchens-global-market-euromonitor/581374/ [Published July 10, 2020], from Euromonitor.

★ 2881 ★
Restaurants
SIC: 5812; NAICS: 722513
Global Pizza Restaurant Sales, 2021

Data how sales in billions of dollars. Figures include all outlets that specialize in pizza, including fast-food pizza, pizza full-service restaurants, and pizza 100% home delivery/takeaway. Sales fell 18.51% in 2020 as a result of the pandemic; sales for 2021 are expected to grow 10.96% to $132.2 billion.

	($ bil.)	Share
Western Europe	$ 49.3	37.26%
North America	48.6	36.73
Latin America	12.5	9.45
Asia-Pacific	11.7	8.84
Eastern Europe	4.2	3.17
Middle East and Africa	4.1	3.10
Australasia	1.9	1.44

Source: *PMQ Pizza Magazine*, December 2020, p. 18, from Euromonitor.

★ 2882 ★
Restaurants
SIC: 5812; NAICS: 722513

Leading Bakery-Cafe Chains, 2019

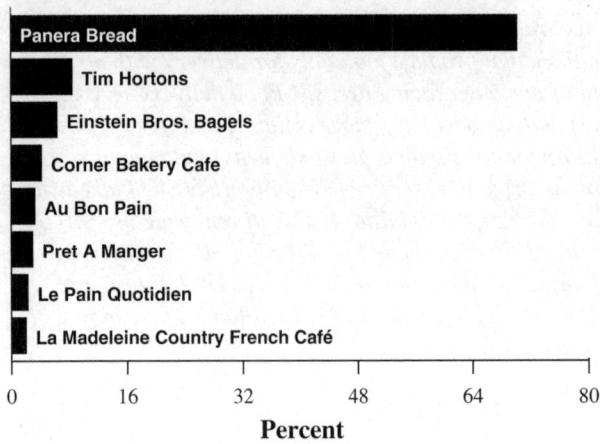

Percent

Market shares are shown based on segment sales in the source's list of top 200 chains. Sales reached $8.52 billion.

	($ mil.)	Share
Panera Bread	$5,980.3	70.17%
Tim Hortons	722.4	8.48
Einstein Bros. Bagels	544.1	6.38
Corner Bakery Cafe	361.1	4.24
Au Bon Pain	284.2	3.33
Pret A Manger	255.3	3.00
Le Pain Quotidien	198.8	2.33
La Madeleine Country French Café	176.8	2.07

Source: *Nation's Restaurant News*, July 13, 2020, p. 43, from *Nation's Restaurant News* research.

★ 2883 ★
Restaurants
SIC: 5812; NAICS: 722513

Leading Bakery-Snack Chains, 2019

Market shares are shown based on segment sales in the source's list of top 200 chains. Sales reached $36.54 billion.

	($ mil.)	Share
Starbucks Coffee Co.	$22,282.90	60.97%
Dunkin'	9,228.50	25.25
Krispy Kreme Doughnuts	900.70	2.46
Baskin-Robbins	608.00	1.66
Tropical Smoothie Cafe	576.80	1.58
Auntie Anne's	563.00	1.54
Jamba Juice	495.80	1.36
Smoothie King	461.60	1.26
Cold Stone Creamery	$388.20	1.06%
Peet's Coffee & Tea	365.50	1.00
Other	675.89	1.85

Source: *Nation's Restaurant News*, July 13, 2020, p. 34, from *Nation's Restaurant News* research.

★ 2884 ★
Restaurants
SIC: 5812; NAICS: 722513

Leading Casual Dining Chains, 2019

Market shares are shown based on segment sales in the source's list of top 200 chains. Sales reached $48.47 billion.

	($ mil.)	Share
Applebee's Neighborhood Grill & Bar	$4,085.5	8.43%
Olive Garden	4,017.5	8.29
Buffalo Wild Wings	3,669.6	7.57
Chili's Grill & Bar	3,100.1	6.39
Texas Roadhouse	3,018.9	6.23
Outback Steakhouse	2,635.8	5.44
Red Lobster	2,224.7	4.59
The Cheesecake Factory	2,162.9	4.46
Longhorn Steakhouse	1,731.2	3.57
Red Robin Gourmet Burgers and Brews	1,495.4	3.08
Other	20,336.0	41.95

Source: *Nation's Restaurant News*, July 13, 2020, p. 30, from *Nation's Restaurant News* research.

★ 2885 ★
Restaurants
SIC: 5812; NAICS: 722513

Leading Chicken Chains, 2019

Companies are ranked by sales in millions of dollars. Market shares are estimated.

	($ mil.)	Share
Chick-fil-A	$11,320.0	38.37%
KFC	4,546.0	15.41
Popeye's Louisiana Kitchen	3,812.0	12.92
Zaxby's	1,886.0	6.39
Raising Cane's Chicken Fingers	1,466.2	4.97
Wingstop	1,363.0	4.62
Bojangles	1,331.6	4.51
El Pollo Loco	894.5	3.03
Church's Chicken	716.0	2.43

Continued on next page.

★ 2885 ★
[Continued]
Restaurants
SIC: 5812; NAICS: 722513
Leading Chicken Chains, 2019

Companies are ranked by sales in millions of dollars. Market shares are estimated.

	($ mil.)	Share
Boston Market	$ 501.8	1.70%
Other	1,662.9	5.64

Source: *Restaurant Business*, May-June 2020, p. 40, from Technomic.

★ 2886 ★
Restaurants
SIC: 5812; NAICS: 722515
Leading Doughnut Vendors Worldwide, 2019

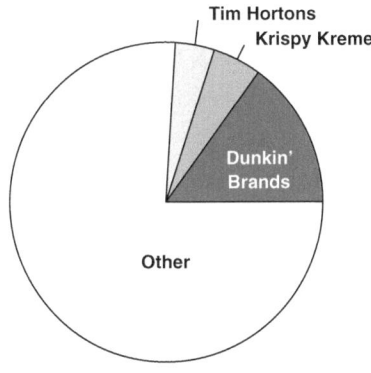

The industry is forecast to grow from $14.98 billion in 2019 to $18.6 billion in 2026. Market shares are shown based on revenue.

Dunkin' Brands	15.16%
Krispy Kreme	4.65
Tim Hortons	4.43
Other	75.76

Source: "Global Doughnuts Market Size, Manufacturers, Supply Chain, Sales Channel and Clients, 2020-2026." [online] from http://www.qyresearch.com [Published July 2020], from QY Research.

★ 2887 ★
Restaurants
SIC: 5812; NAICS: 722513
Leading Family Dining Chains, 2019

Market shares are shown based on segment sales in the source's list of top 200 chains.

IHOP	20.54%
Cracker Barrel Old Country Store	19.19
Denny's	17.42
Golden Corral	10.93
Waffle House	6.64
Bob Evans Restaurants	4.75
Perkins Restaurant & Bakery	3.48
First Watch	3.29
Big Boy/Frisch's Big Boy	2.19
Black Bear Diner	2.11
Other	9.46

Source: *Nation's Restaurant News*, June 15, 2020, p. 60, from *Nation's Restaurant News* research.

★ 2888 ★
Restaurants
SIC: 5812; NAICS: 722513
Leading Fast-Casual Chains, 2019

Companies are ranked by sales in millions of dollars.

Panera Bread	$ 5,890.0
Chipotle Mexican Grill	5,509.4
Panda Express	3,946.8
Jimmy John's Gourmet Sandwiches	2,105.2
Zaxby's	1,886.0
Five Guys Burgers and Fries	1,661.7
Raising Cane's Chicken Fingers	1,466.2
Wingstop	1,363.0
Jersey Mike's Subs	1,340.0
Qdoba Mexican Eats	901.2

Source: *Restaurant Business*, May-June 2020, p. 36, from Technomic.

★ 2889 ★
Restaurants
SIC: 5812; NAICS: 722513
Leading Fast-Food Chains, 2019

Companies are ranked by systemwide sales in millions of dollars. Shares are shown based on sales of $214.5 billion generated by the top 50 firms.

	($ mil.)	Share
McDonald's Corp.	$ 40,413	18.83%
Starbucks Corp.	21,550	10.04

Continued on next page.

★ 2889 ★
[Continued]
Restaurants
SIC: 5812; NAICS: 722513
Leading Fast-Food Chains, 2019

Companies are ranked by systemwide sales in millions of dollars. Shares are shown based on sales of $214.5 billion generated by the top 50 firms.

	($ mil.)	Share
Chick-fil-A	$ 11,000	5.13%
Taco Bell	11,000	5.13
Burger King	10,300	4.80
Subway	10,000	4.66
Wendy's	9,865	4.60
Dunkin'	9,220	4.30
Domino's	7,100	3.31
Panera Bread	5,925	2.76
Chipotle	5,520	2.57
Pizza Hut	5,380	2.51
Sonic Drive-In	4,687	2.18
KFC	4,280	1.99
Arby's	3,885	1.81
Other	54,473	25.38

Source: *QSR Magazine*, August 2020, p. NA.

★ 2890 ★
Restaurants
SIC: 5812; NAICS: 722513
Leading Fine-Dining Chains, 2019

Millions of Dollars

Companies are ranked by sales in millions of dollars.

Ruth's Chris Steak House	$ 703.4
The Capital Grille	461.4
Fleming's Prime Steakhouse & Wine Bar	307.2
Morton's The Steakhouse	266.0
Mastro's Restaurants	242.4

Source: *Restaurant Business*, May-June 2020, p. 38, from Technomic.

★ 2891 ★
Restaurants
SIC: 5812; NAICS: 72231
Leading Full-Service Restaurant Chains, 2019

Companies are ranked by sales in millions of dollars. Shares are shown based on sales generated by the top 50 companies.

	($ mil.)	Share
Olive Garden	$ 4,351	7.31%
Applebee's Neighborhood Grill & Bar	4,085	6.87
Buffalo Wild Wings	3,700	6.22
Chili's Grill & Bar	3,550	5.97
IHOP	3,300	5.55
Texas Roadhouse	2,886	4.85
Denny's	2,710	4.56
Outback Steakhouse	2,630	4.42
Cracker Barrel	2,525	4.24
Red Lobster	2,350	3.95
Other	27,401	46.06

Source: *FSR*, August 2020, p. NA.

★ 2892 ★
Restaurants
SIC: 5812; NAICS: 722513
Leading Hamburger Chains, 2019

Market shares are shown based on segment sales in the source's list of the top 200 chains.

McDonald's Corp.	45.53%
Burger King	11.50
Wendy's	11.00
Sonic Drive-In	5.28
Dairy Queen	3.95
Whataburger	2.88
Hardee's	2.30
Culver's	2.02
Five Guys Burgers and Fries	1.87
Carl's Jr.	1.66
In-N-Out Burger	1.10
Steak 'N Shake	0.71
White Castle	0.64
Other	9.56

Source: *Nation's Restaurant News*, June 15, 2020, p. 60, from *Nation's Restaurant News* research.

★ 2893 ★
Restaurants
SIC: 5812; NAICS: 722513
Leading In-Store Dining Chains, 2019

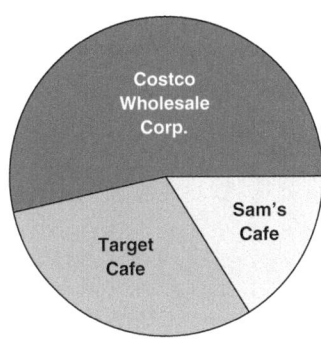

Market shares are shown based on segment sales in the source's list of the top 200 chains.

Costco Wholesale Corp.	53.44%
Target Cafe	30.17
Sam's Cafe	16.39

Source: *Nation's Restaurant News*, June 15, 2020, p. 62, from *Nation's Restaurant News* research.

★ 2894 ★
Restaurants
SIC: 5812; NAICS: 722513
Leading Mexican Chains, 2019

Market shares are shown based on segment sales in the source's list of the top 200 chains.

Taco Bell	54.60%
Chipotle Mexican Grill	26.63
Qdoba Mexican Eats	4.36
Del Taco	4.11
Moe's Southwest Grill	3.53
Taco John's	1.80
Taco Cabana	1.52
Cafe Rio Mexican Grill	1.28
Rubio's Coastal Grill	1.11
Fuzzy's Taco Shop	1.04
Other	0.02

Source: *Nation's Restaurant News*, June 15, 2020, p. 60, from *Nation's Restaurant News* research.

★ 2895 ★
Restaurants
SIC: 5812; NAICS: 722513
Leading Sandwich Chains, 2019

Companies are ranked by sales in millions of dollars. Market shares are estimated.

	($ mil.)	Share
Subway	$ 10,200.0	42.15%
Arby's	3,884.8	16.05
Jimmy John's Gourmet Sandwiches	2,105.2	8.70
Jersey Mike's Subs	1,340.0	5.54
Firehouse Subs	832.4	3.44
McAlister's Deli	725.5	3.00
Jason's Deli	647.4	2.68
Portillo's	505.0	2.09
Potbelly Sandwich Shop	446.2	1.84
Charley's Philly Steaks	435.2	1.80
Other	3,078.3	12.72

Source: *Restaurant Business*, May-June 2020, p. 40, from Technomic.

★ 2896 ★
Restaurants
SIC: 5812; NAICS: 722513
Leading Specialty Chains, 2019

Market shares are shown based on segment sales in the source's list of the top 200 chains.

Panda Express	51.61%
Captain D's Seafood Kitchen	7.35
Noodles & Company	6.96
Long John Silver's	5.01
Dickey's Barbecue Pit	4.55
Zoe's Kitchen	4.35
Pei Wei Asian Kitchen	3.99
Sarku Japan	3.71
Wienerschnitzel	3.67
Fazoli's	3.04
Sbarro	3.04
Other	2.72

Source: *Nation's Restaurant News*, June 15, 2020, p. 60, from *Nation's Restaurant News* research.

★ 2897 ★
Restaurants
SIC: 5812; NAICS: 722513

Leading Sports Bar Chains, 2019

Companies are ranked by sales in millions of dollars. Shares are shown for the group.

	($ mil.)	Share
Buffalo Wild Wings	$ 3,670	56.59%
Hooters	859	13.25
Dave & Buster's	572	8.82
Miller's Ale House	446	6.88
Twin Peaks	336	5.18
Beef 'O Brady's	171	2.64
Hurricane Grill & Wings	152	2.34
Duffy's Sports Grill	145	2.24
Walk-On's Sports Bistreaux	134	2.07

Source: *Restaurant Business Online*, May 13, 2020, p. NA, from Technomic.

★ 2898 ★
Restaurants
SIC: 5812; NAICS: 722513

Restaurant Industry Sales, 2020

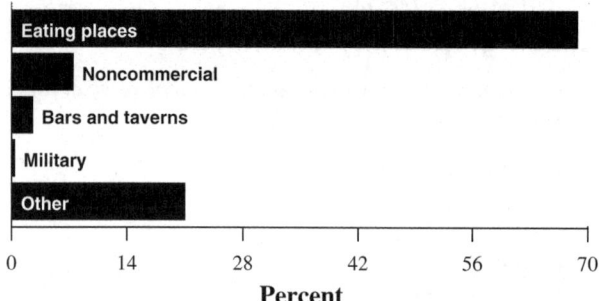

Restaurant sales reached $899 billion in 2020. "Other" includes managed services, lodging, retail, mobile, and vending services. Approximately 15.6 million people were employed in the industry in 2020; the source expects this number to reach 17.2 million in 2030.

	($ bil.)	Share
Eating places	$ 617.5	68.70%
Noncommercial	66.9	7.44
Bars and taverns	22.8	2.54
Military	3.0	0.33
Other	188.7	20.99

Source: "Restaurant Industry Facts at a Glance." [online] from https://restaurant.org/research/restaurant-statistics/restaurant-industry-facts-at-a-glance [Accessed December 2, 2020], from National Restaurant Industry Association.

★ 2899 ★
Retailing
SIC: 5300; NAICS: 45221, 452311, 452319

Planned Back-to-School College Spending, 2007-2020

Spending is shown in billions of dollars. College students and their families expected to spend an average of $1,059.20 in 2020.

2007	$ 31.7
2008	31.3
2009	41.2
2010	45.8
2011	46.0
2012	53.5
2013	45.8
2014	48.4
2015	43.1
2016	48.5
2017	54.1
2018	55.3
2019	54.5
2020	67.7

Source: "Coronavirus Could Push Back-to-School Spending to Record Level as Uncertain Families Gear Up for At-Home Learning." [online] from https://nrf.com/media-center/press-releases/coronavirus-could-push-back-school-spending-record-level-uncertain [Published July 15, 2020], from National Retail Federation 2020 Back-to-School/Spending Survey and Prosper Insights & Analytics.

★ 2900 ★
Retailing
SIC: 5300; NAICS: 45221, 452311, 452319

Planned Back-to-School K-12 Spending, 2007-2020

Spending is shown in billions of dollars. Parents with children in elementary and high school planned on spending an average of $789.49 in 2020.

2007	$ 18.4
2008	20.1
2009	17.4
2010	21.4
2011	22.8
2012	30.3
2013	26.7
2014	26.5
2015	24.9
2016	27.3
2017	29.5
2018	27.5

Continued on next page.

★ 2900 ★
[Continued]
Retailing
SIC: 5300; NAICS: 45221, 452311, 452319

Planned Back-to-School K-12 Spending, 2007-2020

Spending is shown in billions of dollars. Parents with children in elementary and high school planned on spending an average of $789.49 in 2020.

2019	$ 26.2
2020	33.9

Source: "Coronavirus Could Push Back-to-School Spending to Record Level as Uncertain Families Gear Up for At-Home Learning." [online] from https://nrf.com/media-center/press-releases/coronavirus-could-push-back-school-spending-record-level-uncertain [Published July 15, 2020], from National Retail Federation 2020 Back-to-School/Spending Survey and Prosper Insights & Analytics.

★ 2901 ★
Retailing
SIC: 5300; NAICS: 45221, 452311, 452319

Retail Spending in China and the United States, 2018-2023

The table compares retail spending in the United States and Mainland China. Spending is shown in billions of dollars. Figures are estimated for 2020-2023.

	U.S.	China
2018	$ 5.32	$ 5.11
2019	5.48	5.29
2020	5.58	5.47
2021	5.69	5.78
2022	5.83	6.09
2023	6.00	6.41

Source: "2020 China Marketing Trends." [online] from https://as-pacific.com/assets/presentations/2020-China-Report.pdf [Accessed January 10, 2021], from eMarketer.

★ 2902 ★
Retailing
SIC: 5300; NAICS: 45221, 452311, 452319

Top Chain Retailers in the Mid-Atlantic Region, 2020

Market shares are shown based on total sales of retail grocery, drugs, health and beauty care, general merchandise and tobacco products. Petroleum sales are not included. Sales totaled $50.04 billion.

Giant Food Stores L.L.C.	11.24%
Walmart Inc.	10.04
CVS Pharmacy	6.71%
Food Lion L.L.C.	5.73
The Giant Company (Martin's)	4.79
Safeway Inc.	4.67
Harris Teeter Supermarkets Inc.	4.20
7-Eleven Inc.	4.04
International Markets	3.50
Wegmans Food Markets Inc.	3.50
Walgreens Co.	3.37
Target Corp. (Super Target)	3.20
Costco Wholesale Corp.	3.17
Weis Markets Inc.	3.17
Kroger Co. (Marketplace)	2.45
Other	26.23

Source: *Food World*, June 2020, p. 10, from *Food World* research.

★ 2903 ★
Retailing
SIC: 5300; NAICS: 45221, 452311, 452319

Top Hypermarkets in China, 2019

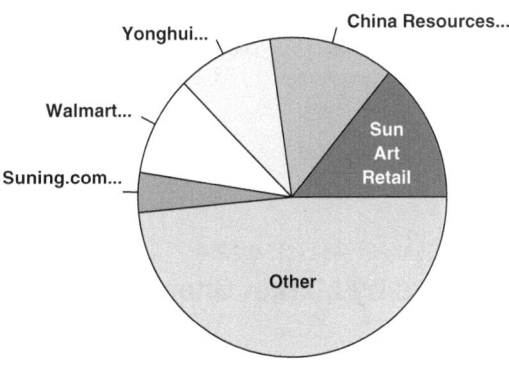

Market shares are shown in percent. In 2020, E-commerce giant Alibaba announced plans to spend $3.6 billion to take control of Sun Art, China's largest big box retailer and a major competitor of Walmart. Sun Art operates more than 480 supermarket-department stores.

Sun Art Retail Group	14.1%
China Resources Holdings Co. Ltd.	12.8
Yonghui Superstores	10.4
Walmart China	10.3
Suning.com Co. Ltd.	4.1
Other	48.3

Source: *Wall Street Journal*, October 20, 2020, p. B1, from Euromonitor.

★ 2904 ★
Retailing
SIC: 5300; NAICS: 45221, 452311, 452319
Top Retailers, 2019

Data show the leading companies with U.S. headquarters ranked by worldwide sales in billions of dollars.

Walmart Inc.	$ 523.96
Amazon.com Inc.	250.50
Costco Wholesale Corp.	152.70
Walgreens Boots Alliance	136.86
The Kroger Co.	122.28
7-Eleven Inc.	115.02
Home Depot Inc.	110.54
Aldi	107.20
McDonald's Corp.	100.18
CVS Health Corp.	88.51
Target Corp.	77.13
Ahold Delhaize USA	75.67
Lowe's Companies Inc.	72.15
Albertsons Companies	62.41
Apple Store/iTunes	61.34
Best Buy Co.	43.68

Source: "Top 100 Retailers 2020 List." [online] from https://nrf.com/resources/top-retailers/top-100-retailers/top-100-retailers-2020-list [Accessed August 10, 2020], from National Retail Federation.

★ 2905 ★
Retailing
SIC: 5300; NAICS: 45221, 452311, 452319
Top Retailers by Market Share, 2018-2019

Market shares are shown based on retail sales of $3.5 trillion in 2018 and $3.7 trillion in 2019.

	2018	2019
Walmart Inc.	10.8%	10.7%
Amazon.com Inc.	3.4	3.9
The Kroger Co.	3.4	3.3
Home Depot Inc.	2.8	2.7
Target Corp.	2.1	2.1
Lowe's Companies Inc.	1.9	1.8
Best Buy Inc.	1.1	1.1
Macy's Inc.	0.7	0.7
Kohl's Corp.	0.5	0.5
Wayfair Inc.	0.2	0.2
Other	73.1	73.0

Source: *Leading National Advertisers 2020 Fact Book - A Supplement to Advertising Age*, July 13, 2020, p. 27, from Ad Age Datacenter and Kantar.

★ 2906 ★
Retailing
SIC: 5300; NAICS: 45221, 452311, 452319
Top Retailers in China, 2019

Companies are ranked by net revenue in billions of dollars.

JD.com	$ 82.9
Suning.com Co. Ltd.	38.7
Sun Art Retail Group	13.7
VIP.com	13.4
YH Yonghui Superstores	12.2
Alibaba New Retail Initiatives	10.7
GOME Retail Holdings	8.5
Balian Group	7.2

Source: "J.D. Com Inc. Financial and Operational Highlights." [online] from https://ir.jd.com/static-files/177fd537-03c0-4f0b-954a-40f0be141ae4 [Published March 2021], from company reports.

★ 2907 ★
Retailing
SIC: 5300; NAICS: 45221, 452311, 452319
Top Retailers in CT-DE-NJ-NY-PA, 2020

Market shares are shown based on total sales of retail grocery, health and beauty care, general merchandising, pharmacy, floral and tobacco products. Petroleum sales are not included. Sales reached $101.4 billion.

ShopRite Supermarkets (Dearborn Market/Fresh Grocer/Price Rite/Gourmet Garage)	15.56%
Stop & Shop Supermarket Co.	7.90
CVS Pharmacy	5.95
The Giant Company (Martin's)	5.92
Walmart Inc. (Neighborhood Market/SuperCenter)	5.23
Walgreens Co. (Duane Reade)	5.06
Costco Wholesale Corp.	4.27
Krasdale Foods (AIM/Bravo/CTown/Market Fresh/Stop 1/Shop Smart)	4.08
Acme Markets Inc.	3.33
Wawa Inc.	3.22
BJ's Wholesale Club Holdings Inc.	3.14
Target Corp.	3.05
Key Food Stores Co-op Inc. (Key/Key Fresh/Food Dynasty/Food Emporium/Food Universe Marketplace/SuperFresh)	2.91
Rite Aid Corp.	2.72
Whole Foods Market Inc. (Amazon Go)	2.30
Other	25.36

Source: *Food Trade News*, June 2020, p. 24, from *Food Trade News* research.

★ 2908 ★
Retailing
SIC: 5300; NAICS: 45221, 452311, 452319

Top Retailers in the Asia-Pacific Region, 2019

Companies are ranked by sales in millions of dollars. Shares are shown based on sales generated by the top 100 retailers.

	($ mil.)	Share
Alibaba Group Holding Ltd.	$ 310.0	20.23%
JD.com	210.0	13.71
Seven & I Holdings Co. Ltd.	80.0	5.22
AEON Group	70.0	4.57
Suning.com Co. Ltd.	45.0	2.94
Amazon.com Inc.	40.0	2.61
Pinduoduo Inc.	40.0	2.61
Walmart Inc.	35.0	2.28
Lotte Group	30.0	1.96
Shinsegae Co. Ltd.	25.0	1.63
FamilyMart	20.0	1.31
Other	627.1	40.93

Source: "The Top 30 Retailers in Asia in 2020." [online] from https://blog.euromonitor.com/the-top-30-retailers-in-asia-in-2020/ [Published May 29, 2020], from Euromonitor.

★ 2909 ★
Retailing
SIC: 5300; NAICS: 45221, 452311, 452319

Top Retailers Worldwide, 2019

The largest public companies are ranked by share of overall retail sales.

Walmart Inc.	15.90%
Amazon.com Inc.	8.81
Apple Inc.	7.97
Costco Wholesale Corp.	4.71
The Kroger Co.	3.64
Home Depot Inc.	3.33
JD.com	2.55
Target Inc.	2.37
Lowe's Companies Inc.	2.20
Alibaba Corp.	2.10
Alimentation Couche-Tard	1.71
George Weston (Loblaw)	1.52
Best Buy Inc.	1.28
Nike Inc.	1.23
Other	40.68

Source: "Top 100 Retailers 2020." [online] from https://risnews.com/top-100-retailers-2020 [Published June 29, 2020], from Retail Info Systems.

★ 2910 ★
Retailing
SIC: 5300; NAICS: 45221, 452311, 452319

Top Retailers Worldwide, 2020

Companies are ranked by international revenue in millions of dollars. The source considers more than just sales for this list. Retailers had to have direct investment in at least three countries in order to be included. The source also considers retailers that operate outside of their local area, their participation in franchising and alliances, and their ability to sell online.

Walmart Inc.	$ 120.13
Shwarz Group	84.96
Aldi	84.89
Amazon.com Inc.	74.72
Ahold Delhaize	60.70
Ikea Corp.	44.00
Costco Wholesale Corp.	43.73
Carrefour	42.94
Alibaba Group	23.24

Source: "Top 50 Global Retailers 2021." [online] from https://nrf.com/resources/top-retailers/top-50-global-retailers/top-50-global-retailers-2021 [Accessed May 20, 2021], from Kantar.

★ 2911 ★
Reverse Vending Machines
SIC: 3581; NAICS: 333318

Reverse Vending Machine Market Worldwide, 2017

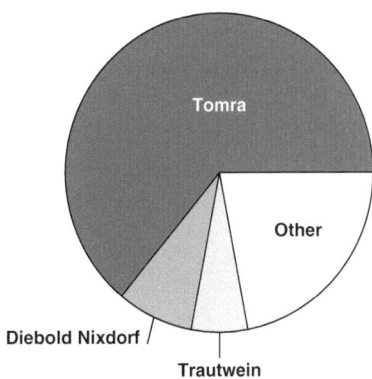

The market is forecast to grow from $314.46 million in 2017 to $527.18 million in 2022. Market shares are shown based on revenue.

Tomra	64.08%
Diebold Nixdorf	7.66

Continued on next page.

★ 2911 ★
[Continued]
Reverse Vending Machines
SIC: 3581; NAICS: 333318

Reverse Vending Machine Market Worldwide, 2017

The market is forecast to grow from $314.46 million in 2017 to $527.18 million in 2022. Market shares are shown based on revenue.

Trautwein	6.32%
Other	21.94

Source: "Global Reverse Vending Machine Market by Manufacturers, Regions, Type and Application, Forecast to 2025." [online] from http://www.radiantinsights.com [Published February 2020], from QY Research.

★ 2912 ★
Rice
SIC: 2044; NAICS: 311212

Rice Milling, 2019

Total shipments were valued at $3.93 billion.

	($ 000)	Share
Milled rice (including second heads, screenings, brewers, bran, sharps, rice flour, residues, and byproducts)	$ 2,161,633	55.00%
Rice, processed, without other ingredients	1,329,367	33.83
Head rice packaged with other ingredients	306,584	7.80
Other	132,416	3.37

Source: "Annual Survey of Manufactures." [online] from https://www.census.gov/programs-surveys/asm/data/tables.html [Accessed March 18, 2021], from U.S. Department of Commerce.

★ 2913 ★
Rice
SIC: 2044; NAICS: 311212

Rice Milling Leaders, 2017

Data show the percent of industry sales held by the largest 4, 8, 20 and 50 firms in the sector. There are approximately 80 players operating in the industry generating employment for 5,078 people. According to Kentley Insights, the industry generated sales of $3.9 billion in 2020.

4 largest firms	42.8%
8 largest firms	62.3
20 largest firms	90.8%
50 largest firms	99.9

Source: "Economic Census." [online] from https://www.census.gov/content/census/en/data/tables/2017/econ/economic-census/naics-sector-31-33.html [Accessed January 21, 2021], from U.S. Census Bureau.

★ 2914 ★
Rice
SIC: 0112; NAICS: 11116

Top Milled Rice Producers Worldwide, 2020-2021

Figures are in thousands of metric tons.

	(000)	Share
China	147,000	29.31%
India	120,000	23.93
Bangladesh	35,997	7.18
Indonesia	34,900	6.96
Vietnam	27,000	5.38
Thailand	18,600	3.71
Burma	12,900	2.57
Philippines	11,700	2.33
Pakistan	7,600	1.52
Brazil	7,480	1.49
United States	7,186	1.43
Other	71,110	14.18

Source: "Rice." [online] from https://apps.fas.usda.gov/psdonline/circulars/grain-rice.pdf [Published October 2020], from U.S. Department of Agriculture.

★ 2915 ★
Rice
SIC: 0112; NAICS: 11116

Top Rice Consumers Worldwide, 2020-2021

Figures are in thousands of metric tons. Data include consumption and residual.

	(000)	Share
China	146,300	29.29%
India	106,000	21.22
Bangladesh	36,100	7.23
Indonesia	35,400	7.09
Vietnam	21,200	4.24
Philippines	14,400	2.88
Thailand	12,000	2.40
Burma	10,500	2.10
Brazil	7,200	1.44

Continued on next page.

★ 2915 ★
[Continued]
Rice
SIC: 0112; NAICS: 11116

Top Rice Consumers Worldwide, 2020-2021

Figures are in thousands of metric tons. Data include consumption and residual.

	(000)	Share
United States	4,620	0.93%
Other	105,720	21.17

Source: "Rice." [online] from https://apps.fas.usda.gov/psdonline/circulars/grain-rice.pdf [Published October 2020], from U.S. Department of Agriculture.

★ 2916 ★
Rice
SIC: 0112; NAICS: 11116

Top Rice Exporters Worldwide, 2020-2021

Figures are in thousands of metric tons. Data refer to trade year.

	(000)	Share
India	12,500	28.27%
Thailand	7,000	15.83
Vietnam	6,300	14.25
Pakistan	4,100	9.27
United States	3,100	7.01
China	2,900	6.56
Burma	2,200	4.97
Cambodia	1,300	2.94
Other	4,823	10.91

Source: "Rice." [online] from https://apps.fas.usda.gov/psdonline/circulars/grain-rice.pdf [Published October 2020], from U.S. Department of Agriculture.

★ 2917 ★
Rice
SIC: 0112; NAICS: 11116

Top Rice Importers Worldwide, 2020-2021

Figures are in thousands of metric tons. Data refer to trade year.

	(000)	Share
Philippines	2,600	5.88%
European Union	2,350	5.31
China	2,200	4.97
Saudi Arabia	1,350	3.05%
Côte d'Ivoire	1,200	2.71
Iran	1,200	2.71
Nigeria	1,200	2.71
United Arab Emirates	1,200	2.71
United States	1,200	2.71
Senegal	1,175	2.66
Iraq	1,150	2.60
Other	27,398	61.95

Source: "Rice." [online] from https://apps.fas.usda.gov/psdonline/circulars/grain-rice.pdf [Published October 2020], from U.S. Department of Agriculture.

★ 2918 ★
Ride-Hailing
SIC: 4119; NAICS: 485999

Leading Ride-Hailing Firms, 2018-2021

Sales are shown in billions of dollars. Figures for 2020 and 2021 are projections. Uber figures do not include Uber Eats. Usage of ride-hailing services dropped dramatically in 2020 as state and local governments implemented stay-at-home orders to slow the spread of COVID-19. In 2021 Uber should claim 67%, Luft 29.3% and other companies 3.7%.

	2018	2019	2020	2021
Uber Technologies Inc.	$22.39	$28.88	$17.39	$29.59
Lyft Inc.	7.89	11.95	8.97	12.93
Other	2.91	2.80	1.39	1.60

Source: "Uber and Lyft Users and Sales Will Decline Dramatically in 2020 Before Rebounding in 2021." [online] from https://www.businessinsider.com/uber-lyft-sales-will-rebound-2021-after-declining-this-year-2020-9 [Published September 16, 2020], from eMarketer.

★ 2919 ★
Ride-Hailing
SIC: 4119; NAICS: 485999

Ride-Hailing Industry in China, 2016-2019

Market sizes are shown in billions of renminbi. There are about 360 million registered users and 30 million registered drivers operating in the country.

2016	¥ 128.8
2017	229.2

Continued on next page.

★ 2919 ★
[Continued]
Ride-Hailing
SIC: 4119; NAICS: 485999

Ride-Hailing Industry in China, 2016-2019

Market sizes are shown in billions of renminbi. There are about 360 million registered users and 30 million registered drivers operating in the country.

2018	¥ 294.3
2019	304.4

Source: "Mobility in China." [online] from https://daxueconsulting.com/ride-hailing-market-in-china/ [Published August 2020], from Analysys.

★ 2920 ★
Robotics
SIC: 3634; NAICS: 333249, 33522

Floor Care Cleaning Market, 2019

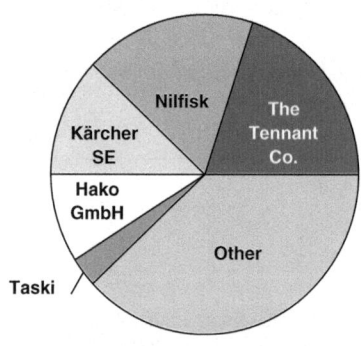

The industry was worth $5 billion in 2019. Tennant's brands include Tennant, IPC, Gaomei Nobles and Alfa. Nilfisk brands include Nilfisk, Advance, Clarke and Viper. Kärcher brands include Kärcher, Windsor, TecServ and ProChem. Hako's brands include Hako, Minuteman and PowerBoss. Taski brands include Taski.

The Tennant Co.	20.0%
Nilfisk	18.0
Kärcher SE & Co.	12.0
Hako GmbH	9.0
Taski (Diversey)	3.0
Other	38.0

Source: "Tennant Investor Presentation." [online] from https://investors.tennantco.com/news-and-events/Current-Investor-Presentation/default.aspx# [Published January 2021].

★ 2921 ★
Robotics
SIC: 3569; NAICS: 333999

Global Market for Industrial Robots, 2019

Countries are ranked by annual installations in thousands of units. Annual installations by year: 254,000 in 2015, 304,000 in 2016, 400,000 in 2017, 422,000 in 2018, and 373,000 in 2019.

	(000)	Share
China	140.5	37.67%
Japan	49.9	13.38
United States	33.3	8.93
South Korea	27.9	7.48
Germany	20.5	5.50
Italy	11.1	2.98
France	6.7	1.80
Chinese Taipei	6.4	1.72
Mexico	4.6	1.23
India	4.3	1.15
Spain	3.8	1.02
Canada	3.6	0.97
Thailand	2.9	0.78
Czech Republic	2.6	0.70
Poland	2.6	0.70
Other	52.3	14.02

Source: "Welcome to the IFR Press Conference." [online] from https://ifr.org/ifr-press-releases/news/record-2.7-million-robots-work-in-factories-around-the-globe [Published September 24 2020], from International Federation of Robotics and World Robotics 2020.

★ 2922 ★
Robotics
SIC: 3569; NAICS: 333999

Global Market for Industrial Robots by Industry, 2017-2019

Industries are ranked by annual installations in thousands of units. A record 2.7 million industrial robots were in operation worldwide. China was the largest market with 783,000 units; shipments rose 21% over the previous year. Japan rose 12% to 355,000 units, putting it in second place.

	2017 (000)	2018 (000)	2019 (000)	Share
Automotive	123	126	105	28.15%
Electrical/electronics	122	105	88	23.59
Unspecified	56	81	76	20.38
Metal and machinery	44	44	44	11.80

Continued on next page.

★ 2922 ★
[Continued]
Robotics
SIC: 3569; NAICS: 333999

Global Market for Industrial Robots by Industry, 2017-2019

Industries are ranked by annual installations in thousands of units. A record 2.7 million industrial robots were in operation worldwide. China was the largest market with 783,000 units; shipments rose 21% over the previous year. Japan rose 12% to 355,000 units, putting it in second place.

	2017 (000)	2018 (000)	2019 (000)	Share
Plastic and chemical products	21	20	19	5.09%
Food	9	12	11	2.95
Other	23	34	30	8.04

Source: "Welcome to the IFR Press Conference." [online] from https://ifr.org/ifr-press-releases/news/record-2.7-million-robots-work-in-factories-around-the-globe [Published September 24, 2020], from International Federation of Robotics and World Robotics 2020.

★ 2923 ★
Robotics
SIC: 3569; NAICS: 333999

Global Market for Service Robots by End Use, 2018-2020

Data are ranked by annual installations in thousands of units. Figures for 2020 are projections.

	2018 (000)	2019 (000)	2020 (000)	Share
Logistics	52.0	75.0	114.0	47.50%
Public environments	14.0	20.0	28.0	11.67
Defense applications	17.0	19.0	22.0	9.17
Professional cleaning	10.0	13.0	19.0	7.92
Inspection and maintenance	11.0	15.0	18.0	7.50
Field robots	10.0	10.0	12.0	5.00
Medical robots	7.0	9.0	12.0	5.00
Powered human exoskeletons	7.0	9.0	11.0	4.58
Construction and demolition	1.0	1.2	1.4	0.58
Other	1.7	2.2	2.6	1.08

Source: "Welcome to the IFR Press Conference." [online] from https://ifr.org/ifr-press-releases/news/record-2.7-million-robots-work-in-factories-around-the-globe [Published September 24 2020], from International Federation of Robotics and World Robotics 2020.

★ 2924 ★
Robotics
SIC: 3569; NAICS: 333999

Installed Base of Industrial Robots Worldwide, 2016-2021

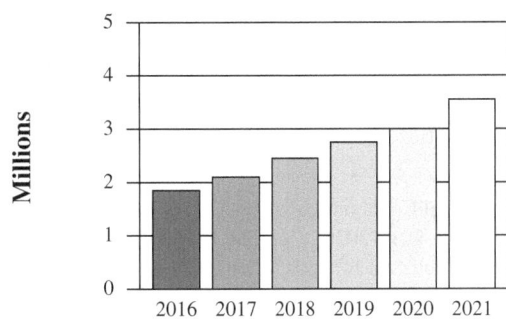

The installed base is shown in millions. Figures are estimated for 2019 and forecast for 2020-2021.

2016	1.83
2017	2.12
2018	2.44
2019	2.75
2020	3.00
2021	3.55

Source: "Technology, Media, and Telecommunications Predictions 2020." [online] from https://www2.deloitte.com/content/dam/Deloitte/at/Documents/technology-media-telecommunications/at-tmt-predictions-2020.pdf [Accessed January 20, 2021], from International Federation of Robotics.

★ 2925 ★
Robotics
SIC: 3569; NAICS: 333999

Robot Sales in China, 2019

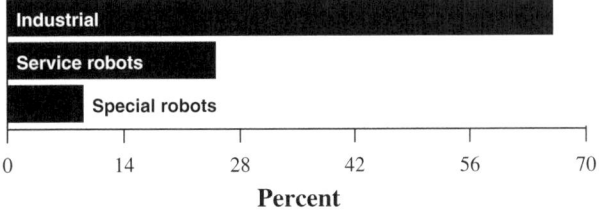

China is the largest market for industrial robots and also the fastest growing.

Industrial	66.0%
Service robots	25.0
Special robots	9.0

Source: "China's Industrial Robot Market is Growing." [online] from http://www.news.kotra.or.kr [Published August 13, 2020], from Qianzhan Industrial Research Institute.

★ 2926 ★
Robotics
SIC: 3569; NAICS: 333999

Top Collaborative Robot Firms Worldwide, 2016

Market shares are estimated based on revenue.

Universal Robot	47.60%
ABB Inc.	18.41
Rethink Robotics	12.30
Other	21.69

Source: "Global Collaborative Robots Market Report, History and Forecast, 2015-2026." [online] from http://www.qyresearch.com [Published July 2019], from QY Research.

★ 2927 ★
Robotics
SIC: 3569; NAICS: 333999

Top Collaborative Robot Sectors Worldwide, 2019

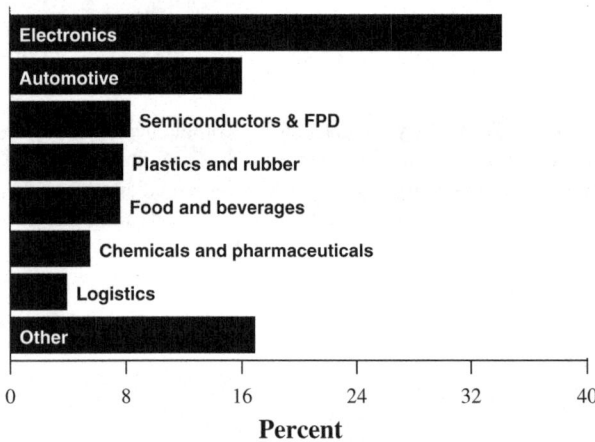

The collaborative market slowed in 2019 as the result of an overall slowdown in the global economies, especially in the Asian market.

Electronics	34.1%
Automotive	16.0
Semiconductors & FPD	8.3
Plastics and rubber	7.8
Food and beverages	7.6
Chemicals and pharmaceuticals	5.5
Logistics	3.9
Other	16.9

Source: "The Collaborative Robot Market 2021-28; Grounds for Optimism After a Turbulent Two Years." [online] from https://www.interactanalysis.com/the-collaborative-robot-market-2021-28-grounds-for-optimism-after-a-turbulent-two-years/ [Accessed February 10, 2021], from Interact Analysis.

★ 2928 ★
Robotics
SIC: 3569; NAICS: 333999

Top Markets Worldwide for B2B Floor Cleaning Robots, 2019

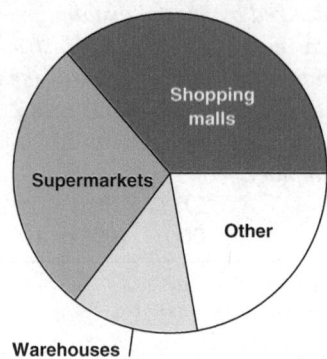

Business-to-business floor cleaning robots are used in the cleaning of commercial spaces. The market is shown by application. Tennant, Avidbots, Gaussian Robotics and Intellibot Robotics claimed 75.05% of the market.

Shopping malls	36.10%
Supermarkets	28.30
Warehouses	13.38
Other	22.22

Source: "Global B2B Floor Cleaning Robots Market Report History and Forecast 2015-2026." [online] from http://www.qyresearch.com [Published July 2020], from QY Research.

★ 2929 ★
Roofing
SIC/NAICS: See frontmatter for explanation.

Demand for Commercial Roofing, 2019

The industry reached 91.5 million square meters. Demand is forecast to see a CAGR of -0.6% from 2019-2024. Major players include Carlisle Construction Materials, Firestone Building Products, GAF Materials and Johns Manville.

Office, retail and lodging	54.0%
Industrial	23.0
Institutional	18.0
Transportation and other	6.0

Source: "Commercial Roofing." [online] from http://www.freedoniagroup.com [Published September 2020], from The Freedonia Group Inc.

★ 2930 ★
Roofing
SIC/NAICS: See frontmatter for explanation.

Demand for Low-Slope Roofing, 2019

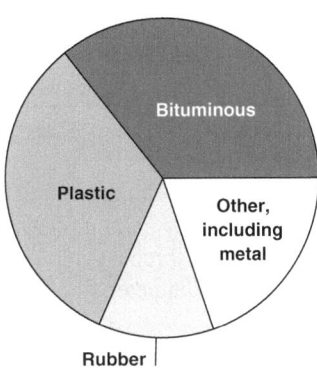

The industry reached 75.79 million square meters. Demand is forecast to see a CAGR of -0.6% from 2019-2024. Major players include Carlisle Construction Materials, Firestone Building Products, GAF Materials and Johns Manville.

Bituminous	36.0%
Plastic	33.0
Rubber	12.0
Other, including metal	20.0

Source: "Low-Slope Roofing." [online] from http://www.freedoniagroup.com [Published September 2020], from The Freedonia Group Inc.

★ 2931 ★
Roofing
SIC/NAICS: See frontmatter for explanation.

Demand for Residential Roofing, 2019

The market reached 127.78 million squares in 2019. Major players include CertainTeed, GAF and Owens Corning. The source expects demand to reach 253 million squares in 2024. The replacement market will fuel this demand, as will the expected recovery of the housing market after the COVID-19 pandemic.

Single family	87.0%
Multifamily	8.0
Manufactured housing	5.0

Source: "Residential Roofing." [online] from http://www.freedoniagroup.com [Published September 2020], from The Freedonia Group Inc.

★ 2932 ★
Rooming and Boarding Houses
SIC: 7021; NAICS: 72131

Rooming and Boarding Houses, Dormitories, and Workers' Camp Leaders, 2017

Data show the percent of industry sales held by the largest 4, 8, 20 and 50 firms in the sector. There are approximately 1,887 players operating in the industry generating employment for 9,658 people. According to Kentley Insights, the industry generated sales of $1.7 billion in 2019.

4 largest firms	27.0%
8 largest firms	36.0
20 largest firms	47.9
50 largest firms	56.4

Source: "Economic Census." [online] from https://www.census.gov/content/census/en/data/tables/2017/econ/economic-census/naics-sector-31-33.html [Accessed January 21, 2021], from U.S. Census Bureau.

★ 2933 ★
Rooming and Boarding Houses
SIC: 7021; NAICS: 72131

Rooming and Boarding Houses, Dormitories, and Workers' Camps, 2017

Total revenues were valued at $1.75 billion. The term "nec" stands for not elsewhere classified.

	($ 000)	Share
Home, apartment, rooming house, and other residential space rental and leasing	$ 1,553,055	88.75%
Meals, snacks, other food items, and nonalcoholic beverages, prepared and served or dispensed, for immediate consumption	110,563	6.32
Civic and social organization membership services	54,124	3.09
Room or unit accommodation for travelers, with maid service	6,041	0.35
Room or unit accommodation for travelers, without maid service	3,356	0.19
Shared-room accommodation for travelers	2,338	0.13
Meals, snacks, other food items, and beverages prepared for catered events	2,094	0.12

Continued on next page.

★ 2933 ★
[Continued]
Rooming and Boarding Houses
SIC: 7021; NAICS: 72131

Rooming and Boarding Houses, Dormitories, and Workers' Camps, 2017

Total revenues were valued at $1.75 billion. The term "nec" stands for not elsewhere classified.

	($ 000)	Share
Parking services	$ 1,913	0.11%
Short-term access to communications services	1,672	0.10
Rental and leasing of nonresidential space in buildings or other facilities, except hosting of coin-operated self-service gambling machines	1,474	0.08
Retail sales of candy, prepackaged cookies, and snack foods	1,378	0.08
Access to laundry machines	1,293	0.07
Rental of home audiovisual equipment (including cable program distribution equipment), components, and accessories, except computers and peripherals	375	0.02
Other products and services, nec	10,324	0.59

Source: "Economic Census." [online] from https://www.census.gov/programs-surveys/economic-census/data/tables.html [Accessed December 2, 2020], from U.S. Census Bureau.

★ 2934 ★
Rope, Cordage, Twine, Tire Cord, and Tire Fabric
SIC: 2298; NAICS: 314994

Rope, Cordage, Twine, Tire Cord, and Tire Fabric Leaders, 2017

Data show the percent of industry sales held by the largest 4, 8, 20 and 50 firms in the sector. There are approximately 143 players operating in the industry generating employment for 6,050 people. According to Kentley Insights, the industry generated sales of $1.6 billion in 2019.

4 largest firms	43.9%
8 largest firms	63.4
20 largest firms	84.5
50 largest firms	96.1

Source: "Economic Census." [online] from https://www.census.gov/content/census/en/data/tables/2017/econ/economic-census/naics-sector-31-33.html [Accessed January 21, 2021], from U.S. Census Bureau.

★ 2935 ★
Rope, Cordage, Twine, Tire Cord, and Tire Fabric
SIC: 2298; NAICS: 314994

Rope, Cordage, Twine, Tire Cord, and Tire Fabric Mills, 2019

Total shipments were valued at $1.72 billion. The term "nec" stands for not elsewhere classified.

	($ 000)	Share
Tire cord and tire fabrics	$ 860,573	52.90%
Fishing line and fish netting, manmade soft fiber, commercial and recreational	199,676	12.27
Rope, manmade soft fiber, three-sixteenths of an inch in diameter and larger	190,422	11.71
Cordage and twine, manmade soft fiber, all other types	155,474	9.56
Cordage and twine, hard fiber	122,270	7.52
Cordage and twine, cotton	33,546	2.06
Cordage and twine, soft fiber (including hemp, jute, and paper), excluding cotton and manmade fiber	25,817	1.59
Wholesale sales of packing and packaging materials and supplies	12,795	0.79
Wholesale sales of sporting and recreational equipment	6,550	0.40
Twine, manmade soft fiber, less than three-sixteenths of an inch in diameter, industrial and agriculture	5,603	0.34
Other textile contract manufacturing services	11,735	0.72
Other manufacturing revenue, nec	2,233	0.14

Source: "Annual Survey of Manufactures." [online] from https://www.census.gov/programs-surveys/asm/data/tables.html [Accessed March 18, 2021], from U.S. Department of Commerce.

★ 2936 ★
Rubber
SIC: 2822; NAICS: 325212

Leading Rubber Goods Makers in North America, 2019

Firms are ranked by sales in millions of dollars.

Bridgestone Americas Inc.	$ 10.70
Michelin North America Inc.	9.97
Goodyear Tire and Rubber Co.	6.98
Continental AG	5.01
Cooper Tire & Rubber Co.	2.28

Continued on next page.

★ 2936 ★
[Continued]
Rubber
SIC: 2822; NAICS: 325212

Leading Rubber Goods Makers in North America, 2019

Firms are ranked by sales in millions of dollars.

Parker-Hannifin Corp.	$ 1.90
Hankook Tire America Corp.	1.89
Toyo Tire (USA) Corp.	1.82
Yokohama Tire Corp.	1.60
Cooper Standard Automotive Inc.	1.56

Source: *Rubber & Plastics News*, July 9, 2020, p. NA.

S

★ 2937 ★
Salt
SIC: 1479; NAICS: 212393

Top Salt Producing Nations, 2020

Countries are ranked by production in thousands of metric tons. Production data are estimated.

	(000)	Share
China	60,000	22.17%
United States	39,000	14.41
India	28,000	10.35
Germany	14,000	5.17
Australia	12,000	4.43
Canada	10,000	3.70
Chile	10,000	3.70
Mexico	9,000	3.33
Brazil	7,200	2.66
Turkey	6,400	2.37
Russia	6,000	2.22
France	5,500	2.03
Netherlands	5,000	1.85
Italy	4,000	1.48
Poland	4,000	1.48
Spain	4,000	1.48
United Kingdom	4,000	1.48
Djibouti	3,500	1.29
Belarus	3,000	1.11
Iran	3,000	1.11
Pakistan	3,000	1.11
Other	30,000	11.09

Source: "Mineral Commodity Summaries 2021." [online] from https://www.usgs.gov/centers/nmic/mineral-commodity-summaries [Published January 29, 2021], from U.S. Geological Survey.

★ 2938 ★
Sand and Gravel
SIC: 1442; NAICS: 212321

Leading End Markets for Construction Sand and Gravel, 2020

In the United States, 960 million tons of construction sand and gravel valued at $9.2 billion was produced in 2020.

Portland cement concrete aggregates	46.0%
Road base and coverings and road stabilization	21.0
Construction fill	13.0
Asphaltic concrete aggregate and other bituminous mixtures	12.0
Other	8.0

Source: "Mineral Commodity Summaries 2021." [online] from https://www.usgs.gov/centers/nmic/mineral-commodity-summaries [Published January 29, 2021], from U.S. Geological Survey.

★ 2939 ★
Sand and Gravel
SIC: 1446; NAICS: 212322

Top Industrial Sand and Gravel Producing Nations, 2020

Countries are ranked by production in thousands of metric tons. In the United States, about 58% of tonnage was used as hydraulic-fracturing sand and well-packing and cementing sand, down from 73% a year earlier. Consumption of industrial sand and gravel was down 38% in 2020 due to decreased natural gas and petroleum well drilling and oil well completions in North America. The COVID-19 pandemic restrictions led to a decrease in petroleum product consumption which led to a decrease in demand for hydraulic-fracturing sand. Production data are estimated.

	(000)	Share
United States	71,000	26.76%
Netherlands	51,000	19.22
Spain	34,000	12.82
Italy	13,000	4.90
India	11,000	4.15

Continued on next page.

★ 2939 ★
[Continued]
Sand and Gravel
SIC: 1446; NAICS: 212322

Top Industrial Sand and Gravel Producing Nations, 2020

Countries are ranked by production in thousands of metric tons. In the United States, about 58% of tonnage was used as hydraulic-fracturing sand and well-packing and cementing sand, down from 73% a year earlier. Consumption of industrial sand and gravel was down 38% in 2020 due to decreased natural gas and petroleum well drilling and oil well completions in North America. The COVID-19 pandemic restrictions led to a decrease in petroleum product consumption which led to a decrease in demand for hydraulic-fracturing sand. Production data are estimated.

	(000)	Share
Malaysia	9,500	3.58%
France	8,800	3.32
Turkey	8,600	3.24
Bulgaria	7,300	2.75
Germany	7,100	2.68
Poland	4,800	1.81
United Kingdom	3,800	1.43
Australia	2,900	1.09
Canada	2,700	1.02
Indonesia	2,600	0.98
Mexico	2,300	0.87
Japan	2,200	0.83
South Africa	1,900	0.72
New Zealand	1,500	0.57
South Korea	1,300	0.49
Other	18,000	6.78

Source: "Mineral Commodity Summaries 2021." [online] from https://www.usgs.gov/centers/nmic/mineral-commodity-summaries [Published January 29, 2021], from U.S. Geological Survey.

★ 2940 ★
Sand Castings
SIC: 3369; NAICS: 331529

Top Markets for Sand Castings Worldwide, 2018

Sand casting is the process of metal casting using sand as the mold material. Market shares are estimated. China represented 45-47% of global production.

Automotive	42.0-45.0%
Machinery	20.0-22.0
Civil engineering	10.0-15.0
Energy	8.0-10.0%
Other	0.0-20.0

Source: "Global Market Outlook for Sand Casting." [online] from http://www.beroeinc.com [Accessed October 1, 2020], from Beroe Inc.

★ 2941 ★
Sanitary Paper Products
SIC: 2676; NAICS: 322291

Global Tissue Paper Capacity, 2019

Market shares are shown based on capacity. China, the United States and Japan were the leading producers.

Consumer bath	51.0%
Consumer facial	15.0
Consumer towel	13.0
Commercial bath	7.0
Commercial towel	5.0
Consumer napkins	4.0
Commercial facial	2.0
Other	3.0

Source: *Paper360°*, July/August 2020, p. 36, from FisherSolve.

★ 2942 ★
Sanitary Paper Products
SIC: 2676; NAICS: 322291

Largest Adult Incontinence Markets in Southeast Asia, 2023-2025

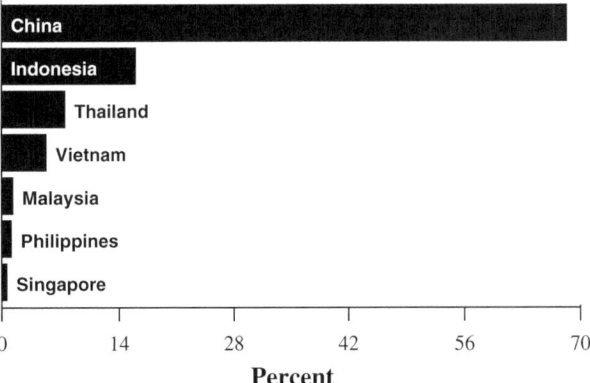

Retail sales are estimated in millions of dollars.

	2023 ($ mil.)	2024 ($ mil.)	2025 ($ mil.)	Share
China	$ 1,208.5	$ 1,420.2	$ 1,666.7	68.28%
Indonesia	259.1	319.0	389.6	15.96
Thailand	158.9	171.1	182.2	7.46
Vietnam	87.0	106.0	128.0	5.24
Malaysia	28.4	30.1	32.0	1.31

Continued on next page.

★ 2942 ★
[Continued]
Sanitary Paper Products
SIC: 2676; NAICS: 322291

Largest Adult Incontinence Markets in Southeast Asia, 2023-2025

Retail sales are estimated in millions of dollars.

	2023 ($ mil.)	2024 ($ mil.)	2025 ($ mil.)	Share
Philippines	$25.5	$26.5	$27.6	1.13%
Singapore	13.5	14.1	14.7	0.60

Source: *Nonwovens Industry*, Spring 2021, p. 22, from Euromonitor.

★ 2943 ★
Sanitary Paper Products
SIC: 2676; NAICS: 322291

Largest Sanitary Protection Markets in Southeast Asia, 2023-2025

Retail sales are estimated in millions of dollars. Shares are shown for the group.

	2023 ($ mil.)	2024 ($ mil.)	2025 ($ mil.)	Share
China	$13,415.3	$13,615.2	$13,803.6	88.01%
Vietnam	478.5	520.2	568.3	3.62
Indonesia	402.5	434.8	471.9	3.01
Thailand	297.9	306.5	315.4	2.01
Philippines	248.5	256.5	265.0	1.69
Malaysia	205.0	211.3	217.4	1.39
Singapore	41.3	42.2	43.0	0.27

Source: *Nonwovens Industry*, Spring 2021, p. 22, from Euromonitor.

★ 2944 ★
Sanitary Paper Products
SIC: 2676; NAICS: 322291

Leading Paper Towel Makers in Canada, 2020

Market shares are shown based on multi-outlet sales for the 52 weeks ended October 2, 2020.

Procter & Gamble Co.	34.2%
Kruger Products	22.0
Irving Tissue Co.	12.5
Other	31.3

Source: "KP Tissue Well Positioned for Growth." [online] from https://www.kptissueinc.com/en-CA/gpc/_media/Document/kpt-rbc-conference-december-2020-vf.pdf [Published December 2020], from Nielsen.

★ 2945 ★
Sanitary Paper Products
SIC: 2676; NAICS: 322291

Leading Sanitary Tissue Makers in Canada, 2017-2019

The industry generated revenue of C$634.8 million in 2019. Market shares are shown based on unit sales.

	2017	2018	2019
Procter & Gamble Co.	59.1%	58.4%	58.2%
Kimberly-Clark Corp.	11.9	11.8	11.8
Playtex Products Inc.	4.1	4.0	3.9
Reckitt Benckiser Group	2.5	2.5	2.6
The Clorox Co.	2.3	2.3	2.3
Johnson & Johnson Co.	1.1	1.1	1.2
Other	19.0	19.9	20.0

Source: "Canadian Sanitary Tissue Market Trend." [online] from http://www.news.kotra.or.kr [Published August 14, 2020], from Euromonitor.

★ 2946 ★
Sanitary Paper Products
SIC: 2676; NAICS: 322291

Leading Tissue and Hygiene Paper Makers, 2017 and 2019

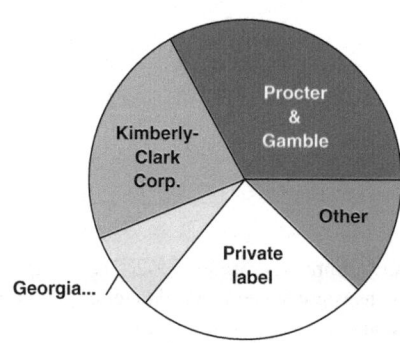

Market shares are shown in percent.

	2017	2019
Procter & Gamble Co.	32.4%	32.8%
Kimberly-Clark Corp.	23.8	23.2
Georgia-Pacific L.L.C.	8.6	8.0
Private label	22.9	23.5
Other	12.3	12.5

Source: "U.S. Consumer Goods: Sector Overview, Credit Trends and Outlook." [online] from https://www.spglobal.com/_assets/documents/ratings/research/100049347.pdf [Published March 2021], from Euromonitor.

★ 2947 ★
Sanitary Paper Products
SIC: 2676; NAICS: 322291

Leading Toilet Paper Makers in Canada, 2020

Market shares are shown based on multi-outlet sales for the 52 weeks ended October 2, 2020.

Kruger Products Inc.	36.4%
Irving Tissue Co.	18.9
Procter & Gamble Co.	10.1
Kimberly-Clark Corp.	1.3
Other	33.3

Source: "KP Tissue Well Positioned for Growth." [online] from https://www.kptissueinc.com/en-CA/gpc/_media/Document/kpt-rbc-conference-december-2020-vf.pdf [Published December 2020], from Nielsen.

★ 2948 ★
Sanitary Paper Products
SIC: 2676; NAICS: 322291

Leading Toilet Paper Makers Worldwide, 2019

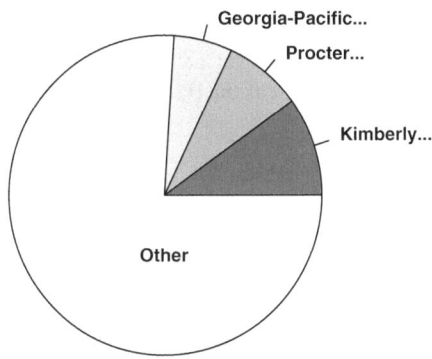

The industry generated revenue of $35.9 billion. Market shares are shown based on revenue.

Kimberly-Clark Corp.	10.0%
Procter & Gamble Co.	8.5
Georgia-Pacific L.L.C.	5.5
Other	76.0

Source: "Global Toilet Paper Market Research Report 2020." [online] from http://www.qyresearch.com [Published April 2020], from QY Research.

★ 2949 ★
Sanitary Paper Products
SIC: 2676; NAICS: 322291

Sales of Feminine Hygiene Products, 2022-2024

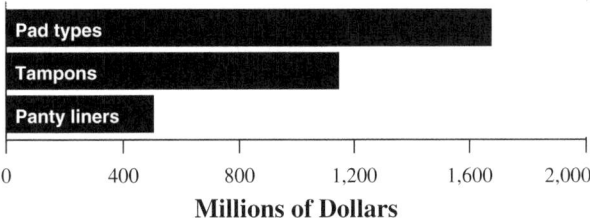

Millions of Dollars

Figures are estimated in millions of dollars. Sales in this industry have been stagnant in recent years. There has been slow growth in the female population, as well as high rates of birth control use by women of childbearing age. Pad types should claim 50.4% of the market in 2024, tampons 34.4% and panty liners 15.1%.

	2022	2023	2024
Pad types	$ 1,628.1	$ 1,649.1	$ 1,674.2
Tampons	1,148.4	1,147.7	1,145.0
Panty liners	482.9	493.8	502.5

Source: "U.S. Sanitary Napkin Market Trend." [online] from http://www.news.kotra.or.kr [Published August 13, 2020], from Euromonitor.

★ 2950 ★
Sanitary Paper Products
SIC: 2676; NAICS: 322291

Top Adult Incontinence Brands, 2020

Market shares are shown based on supermarket sales for the 52 weeks ended April 19, 2020.

Poise	32.96%
Depend Fit Flex	17.17
Always Discreet	16.71
Depend	5.64
Depend Night Defense	2.48
Tena Serenity	2.09
Tena	1.43
Always Discreet Boutique	1.24
Depend Silhouette	0.97
Private label	16.14
Other	3.17

Source: *Non-Foods Management*, Annual 2020-2021, p. 87, from IRI.

★ 2951 ★
Sanitary Paper Products
SIC: 2676; NAICS: 322291
Top Diaper Brands, 2019

Market shares are shown based on unit sales. Euromonitor places diaper sales in 2019 at $9.1 billion. The source points out several interesting trends. The number of newborns grew 0.09% in 2019, but this rate declined at an annual average rate of 0.2% over the previous five years. Also, consumers stockpiled diapers during the pandemic; this prompted diaper sales to increase 45% during the first six months in 2020 as compared to the same period in 2019.

Pampers	27.9%
Huggies	22.9
Luvs	9.0
Huggies Pull-Ups	8.0
Parent's Choice	6.6
Goodnites	3.7
Pampers Easy Ups	3.0
Kirkland Signature	2.5
Honest Diapers	2.4
Up & Up	1.9
Pure Protection	1.4
Kroger	1.0
Private label	3.8
Other	5.9

Source: "The U.S. Diaper Market Continues to Grow." [online] from http://news.kotra.or.kr [Published August 28, 2020], from Statista and Chicago Trade Center.

★ 2952 ★
Sanitary Paper Products
SIC: 2676; NAICS: 322291
Top Diaper Categories, 2020

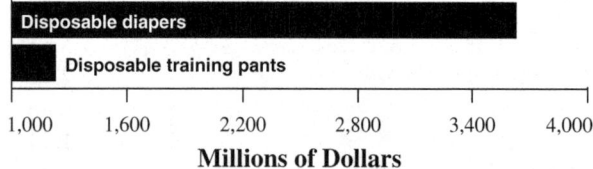

Millions of Dollars

Categories are ranked by sales in millions of dollars at supermarkets, drug stores, mass merchandisers, military commissaries, and select club and dollar chains for the 52 weeks ended October 4, 2020.

Disposable diapers	$ 3,630
Disposable training pants	1,230

Source: *MMR*, November 16, 2020, p. 36, from IRI.

★ 2953 ★
Sanitary Paper Products
SIC: 2676; NAICS: 322291
Top Diaper Makers Worldwide, 2019

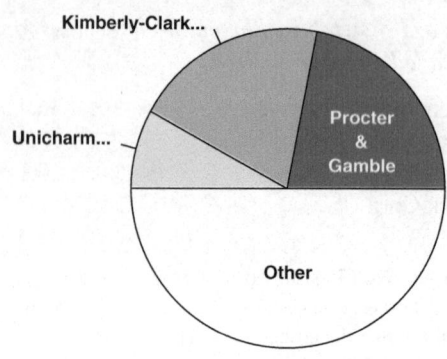

The industry is forecast to grow from $43.31 billion in 2019 to $52.48 billion in 2026. Market shares are shown based on revenue.

Procter & Gamble Co.	21.50%
Kimberly-Clark Corp.	19.70
Unicharm Corp.	8.35
Other	50.45

Source: "Global Diaper Market Size, Manufacturers, Supply Chain, Sales Channel and Clients, 2020-2026." [online] from http://www.qyresearch.com [Published July 2020], from QY Research.

★ 2954 ★
Sanitary Paper Products
SIC: 2676; NAICS: 322291
Top Diaper Markets in Southeast Asia, 2023-2025

Retail sales are estimated in millions of dollars.

	2023 ($ mil.)	2024 ($ mil.)	2025 ($ mil.)	Share
China	$ 11,877.4	$ 12,633.3	$ 13,507.5	71.80%
Indonesia	2,083.2	2,334.2	2,628.3	13.97
Vietnam	882.6	955.9	1,031.2	5.48
Thailand	640.8	674.0	705.5	3.75
Philippines	546.4	574.5	605.2	3.22
Malaysia	235.8	244.1	252.2	1.34
Singapore	78.0	80.3	82.6	0.44

Source: *Nonwovens Industry*, Spring 2021, p. 22, from Euromonitor.

★ 2955 ★
Sanitary Paper Products
SIC: 2676; NAICS: 322291

Top Sanitary Napkin/Liner Brands, 2020

Market shares are shown based on supermarket sales for the 52 weeks ended April 19, 2020.

Always	28.51%
Stayfree	6.46
Always Infinity	6.28
Always Radiant	6.04
Carefree Acti-Fresh	5.87
U by Kotex Security	4.39
Always Maxi	4.09
U by Kotex Clean Wear	3.23
Always Ultra Thin	3.03
Private label	10.91
Other	21.19

Source: *Non-Foods Management*, Annual 2020-2021, p. 108, from IRI.

★ 2956 ★
Sanitary Paper Products
SIC: 2676; NAICS: 322291

Top Tampon Brands, 2020

Market shares are shown based on supermarket sales for the 52 weeks ended April 19, 2020.

Tampax Pearl	31.71%
Playtex Sport	11.97
U by Kotex Click	10.98
Tampax Radiant	5.75
Tampax	5.46
U by Kotex Security	4.10
Tampax Pocket Pearl	3.67
o.b.	2.93
Kotex Natural Balance Security	2.54
Private label	5.45
Other	15.44

Source: *Non-Foods Management*, Annual 2020-2021, p. 110, from IRI.

★ 2957 ★
Sanitaryware
SIC: 3261; NAICS: 32711

Leading Sanitaryware Exporters Worldwide, 2018

Market shares are shown based on shipments of 2.69 billion tons.

China	53.2%
Mexico	11.9
India	6.3%
Turkey	5.4
Portugal	3.5
Thailand	3.3
Germany	2.8
Poland	2.7
Vietnam	2.6
Italy	1.9
Other	6.4

Source: *Tile International*, no. 1, 2020, p. 52, from Acimac, BSRIA and International Trade Commission.

★ 2958 ★
Sanitaryware
SIC: 3261; NAICS: 32711

Leading Sanitaryware Firms Worldwide, 2019

Companies are ranked by production in millions of pieces as of December 31, 2019. Lixil's production is from 7-8 million pieces. Cersanit ranked ninth on the list but its production was not available. Installed capacity was 8 million pieces.

Roca Group	33.6
Kohler Group	18.0
Gerberit Group	12.0
Toto Ltd.	12.0
Corona	9.9
Lixil Corp.	8.0
Huida Sanitaryware	7.6
Duratex	6.5
Ideal Standard	5.5
RAK Ceramics PJSC	4.8

Source: *Ceramic World Review*, no. 139, 2020, p. 62, from Acimac.

★ 2959 ★
Sanitaryware
SIC: 3261; NAICS: 32711

Leading Sanitaryware Importers Worldwide, 2018

Market shares are shown based on shipments of 1.77 billion tons.

United States	24.1%
Germany	4.7
South Korea	4.3
United Kingdom	4.1
France	3.7
Spain	3.2

Continued on next page.

★ 2959 ★
[Continued]
Sanitaryware
SIC: 3261; NAICS: 32711

Leading Sanitaryware Importers Worldwide, 2018

Market shares are shown based on shipments of 1.77 billion tons.

Canada	3.1%
Italy	2.0
Australia	1.9
Nigeria	1.7
Other	47.2

Source: *Tile International*, no. 1, 2020, p. 54, from Acimac, BSRIA and International Trade Commission.

★ 2960 ★
Satellites
SIC: 3663; NAICS: 33422

Global Market for Satellite Ground Industry, 2018-2028

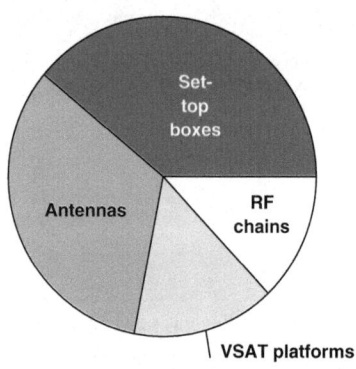

Market shares are shown based on revenue. The industry is forecast to grow 2.8% from 2018 to 2028.

Set-top boxes	39.0%
Antennas	33.0
VSAT platforms	15.0
RF chains	13.0

Source: "Commercial Satellite Ground Segment, 4th Edition." [online] from http://www.nsr.com [Published December 2019], from Northern Sky Research.

★ 2961 ★
Satellites
SIC: 3663; NAICS: 33422

Global Market for Satellite Manufacturing and Launches, 2019

The source notes a variety of factors affecting this market, including declining capacity prices, evolving industry KPI metrics, accelerating development of technology, increasing complexity, and rising diversification.

Science and technology	52.0%
Communications	17.1
Earth observation	15.2
SA	11.5
Navigation	2.0
Other	0.5

Source: "Global Satellite Manufacturing and Launch Markets, 10th Edition." [online] from http://www.nsr.com [Published June 2020], from Northern Sky Research.

★ 2962 ★
Satellites
SIC: 3663; NAICS: 33422

Global Satellite Industry, 2019

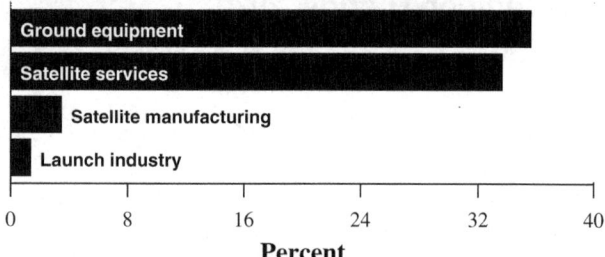

The industry generated revenue of $279 billion. "Satellite services" includes sectors such as telecommunications, remote sensing and science applications. The source notes that another $95 billion is spent on non-satellite industries, such as government space budgets and efforts connected to commercial human spaceflight. This brings the entire space economy to $366 billion.

	($ bil.)	Share
Ground equipment	$ 130.3	35.63%
Satellite services	123.0	33.63
Satellite manufacturing	12.5	3.42
Launch industry	4.9	1.34

Source: "State of the Satellite Report 2020." [online] from https://sia.org/news-resources/state-of-the-satellite-industry-report/ [Accessed November 10, 2020], from Satellite Industry Association.

★ 2963 ★
Satellites
SIC: 9661; NAICS: 92711

Global Space Activity, 2019

Spending is shown in billions of dollars. Total spending reached $423.8 billion in 2019, up from $245.08 billion in 2010.

	($ bil.)	Share
Commercial space products and services	$ 217.72	51.37%
Commercial infrastructure and support industries	119.17	28.12
U.S. government budgets	47.17	11.13
Non-U.S. government space budgets	39.74	9.38

Source: *Milsat Magazine*, September 2020, p. 34, from Space Foundation Database.

★ 2964 ★
Satellites
SIC: 3669; NAICS: 33429

LEO Satcom Market Worldwide, 2019

Distribution is shown based on total low-Earth orbit commercial satellite communications in tons. Low-Earth satellites orbit 500-2,000 kilometers above the Earth.

SpaceX	29.3%
Iridium	8.6
OneWeb Ltd.	0.9
Other	75.3

Source: "ESPI Yearbook 2019." [online] from https://espi.or.at/publications/espi-yearbook [Accessed February 15, 2021], from European Space Policy Institute.

★ 2965 ★
Satellites
SIC: 3663; NAICS: 33422

Satellite Launches by Country, 2020

Countries are ranked by number of orbital launch attempts. There were a total of 114 launches. More launches failed in 2020 than in any year since 1971.

	Launches	Share
United States	44	38.60%
China	39	34.21
Russia	14	12.28
Europe	8	7.02
Japan	4	3.51
India	2	1.75
Iran	2	1.75%
Israel	1	0.88

Source: *SatMagazine*, February 2021, p. 27, from *The Space Report*.

★ 2966 ★
Satellites
SIC: 3663; NAICS: 33422

Satellite Launches by Type, 2020

A total of 392 spacecraft were launched during the fourth quarter of 2020.

Communications	79.0%
Remote sensing	13.0
Development	3.0
Scientific	3.0
Crew and cargo transportation	1.0
Navigation	< 1.0
Other	1.0

Source: "Bryce Briefing Q4 2020." [online] from https://brycetech.com/briefing [Accessed March 22, 2021], from Bryce Space & Technology.

★ 2967 ★
Sauces, Dressings and Condiments
SIC: 2035; NAICS: 311941

Best-Selling Sauce, Dressing and Condiment Categories, 2018-2020

Sales are shown in millions of dollars.

	2018 ($ mil.)	2019 ($ mil.)	2020 ($ mil.)
Dipping sauces	$ 4,062.9	$ 4,195.3	$ 4,983.2
Herbs and spices	3,456.3	3,547.5	4,200.2
Salad dressings	2,635.7	2,648.0	3,090.8
Pickles	2,521.4	2,602.8	3,075.5
Pasta sauces	2,560.8	25,989.0	3,043.6
Broth	1,879.9	1,929.1	2,295.9
Mayonnaise	1,822.7	1,824.5	2,117.6
Ketchup	905.8	926.2	1,069.8
Soy sauces	862.2	892.2	1,030.8
Chili sauces	769.3	821.2	973.3
Dry source	785.5	803.4	939.7
Barbecue sauces	763.9	766.9	909.0
Cooking sauces	726.9	746.6	863.4
Tomato paste puree	609.2	633.1	718.7
Mustard	438.9	443.2	509.1

Continued on next page.

★ 2967 ★
[Continued]
Sauces, Dressings and Condiments
SIC: 2035; NAICS: 311941

Best-Selling Sauce, Dressing and Condiment Categories, 2018-2020

Sales are shown in millions of dollars.

	2018 ($ mil.)	2019 ($ mil.)	2020 ($ mil.)
Other table sauces	$693.3	$696.3	$779.9
Other	380.5	387.9	442.9

Source: "Use it as an Opportunity to Grow the U.S. Sauce Market and ex-Korean Sauces." [online] from http://www.news.kotra.or.kr [Published January 19, 2021], from Euromonitor.

★ 2968 ★
Sauces, Dressings and Condiments
SIC: 2035; NAICS: 311941

Best-Selling Sauce Categories in Canada, 2020

Sales are shown across all channels for the 52 weeks ended August 15, 2020. Figures are in Canadian dollars and exclude Newfoundland. Shares are shown for the group.

	($ mil.)	Share
Pasta sauces, cans and bottles	$356.77	34.50%
Sauce and gravy mixes	126.12	12.20
Meat and seafood sauces	125.45	12.13
Asian sauces	124.14	12.00
Baking and cooking sauces	92.90	8.98
Barbecue sauces	82.88	8.01
Tomato sauce	37.80	3.66
Pizza sauce	32.54	3.15
Chili sauces	30.97	2.99
Apple sauces	22.98	2.22
Dips, mixes	1.60	0.15

Source: *Canadian Grocer*, November 2020, p. 42, from Nielsen.

★ 2969 ★
Sauces, Dressings and Condiments
SIC: 2035; NAICS: 311941

Ketchup Market in Canada, 2020

Kraft Heinz announced plans to resume selling ketchup in Canada in 2020. The announcement came after Heinz shut down a production plant in Ontario in 2014, a move that eliminated 740 jobs and prompted some consumers to switch brands in retaliation.

Heinz	76.1%
French's	6.9
Primo	2.8
Aylmer	0.2
Private label	13.4
Other	0.7

Source: *Financial Post*, November 18, 2020, p. NA, from Euromonitor.

★ 2970 ★
Sauces, Dressings and Condiments
SIC: 2035; NAICS: 311941

Ketchup Market in North America, 2017-2019

Market shares are shown based on dollar sales.

	2017	2018	2019
Heinz	64.0%	65.0%	67.0%
Other	36.0	35.0	33.0

Source: "Kraft Heinz - A New Model for Growth." [online] from http://ir.kraftheinzcompany.com/overview [Published September 15, 2020], from Nielsen.

★ 2971 ★
Sauces, Dressings and Condiments
SIC: 2035; NAICS: 311941

Sales of Sauces, Seasonings and Condiments in China, 2019

Categories are ranked by sales in millions of yuan. Pasta sauce sales grew 18.6% over the year, making it the fastest-growing category. Shares are shown for the group.

	(mil.)	Share
Soy sauces	¥80,001.0	74.32%
Bouillon	8,844.0	8.22
Chili sauces	7,533.0	7.00
Oyster sauces	6,572.0	6.11
Ketchup	1,822.0	1.69
Herbs and spices	1,289.0	1.20

Continued on next page.

★ 2971 ★
[Continued]
Sauces, Dressings and Condiments
SIC: 2035; NAICS: 311941

Sales of Sauces, Seasonings and Condiments in China, 2019

Categories are ranked by sales in millions of yuan. Pasta sauce sales grew 18.6% over the year, making it the fastest-growing category. Shares are shown for the group.

	(mil.)	Share
Salad dressings	¥ 730.0	0.68%
Mayonnaise	684.0	0.64
Dry sauces	91.8	0.09
Pasta sauces	79.4	0.07

Source: "China's Growing Seasoning Market." [online] from http://news.kotra.or.kr [Published September 24, 2020], from Euromonitor and KOTRA Shenzhen Trade Center.

★ 2972 ★
Sauces, Dressings and Condiments
SIC: 2035; NAICS: 311941

Top Refrigerated Salad Dressing Brands, 2020

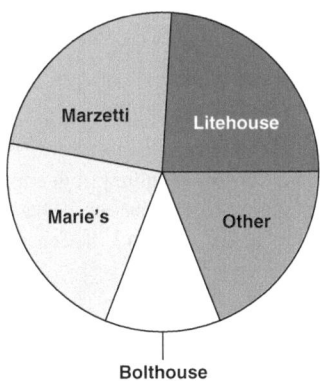

Market shares are shown based on multi-outlet sales for the 52 weeks ended June 28, 2020. Total sales reached $443.2 million.

Litehouse	24.1%
Marzetti	23.4
Marie's	21.5
Bolthouse	11.8
Other	19.2

Source: "Lancaster Colony Corporation." [online] from http://s21.q4cdn.com/151907755/files/doc_presentations/2020/09/LANC-Slide-Deck-CL-King-9-16-20.pdf [Published September 16, 2020], from IRI.

★ 2973 ★
Sauces, Dressings and Condiments
SIC: 2035; NAICS: 311941

Top Soy Sauce Brands in China, 2018

Market shares are shown based on sales of 745 million yuan.

Haiten	15.0%
Chuwoobang	3.0
Leekumkee	3.0
JiaJia	1.0
Other	78.0

Source: "Chinese Soy Sauce Market Trend." [online] from http://www.news.kotra.or.kr [Published April 2, 2020], from Hwajing Industry Institute.

★ 2974 ★
Saw Blades and Handtools
SIC: 3425; NAICS: 332216

Number of Firms In Saw Blade and Handtool Manufacturing, 1998-2019

According to Kentley Insights, the industry generated sales of $6.5 billion in 2019. Over the previous three years, the industry saw an annual growth rate of 0.9%.

1998	1,449
1999	1,434
2000	1,405
2001	1,365
2002	1,321
2003	1,325
2004	1,312
2005	1,322
2006	1,291
2007	1,273
2008	1,354
2009	1,236
2010	1,186
2011	1,171
2012	1,012
2013	985
2014	993
2015	980
2016	948
2017	930
2018	895
2019	874

Source: "County Business Patterns." [online] from https://www.census.gov/programs-surveys/cbp/data/datasets.html [Published April 22, 2021], from U.S. Census Bureau.

★ 2975 ★
Sawmill, Woodworking and Paper Machinery
SIC: 3553; NAICS: 333243

Leading Woodworking Machinery Producers, 2020

Market shares are shown based on revenue.

Globe Machine Manufacturing Co.	4.7%
Wood-Mizer L.L.C.	4.4
Other	90.9

Source: "The Growth of the Construction Market Drives the Growth of the U.S. Woodworking Machinery Industry." [online] from https://www.market-prospects.com/articles/construction-market-drives-the-growth-of-usa-woodworking [Published February 1, 2021], from IBISWorld.

★ 2976 ★
Sawmill, Woodworking and Paper Machinery
SIC: 3553; NAICS: 333243

Number of Firms In Sawmill, Woodworking, and Paper Machinery Manufacturing, 1998-2019

According to Kentley Insights, the industry generated sales of $3.4 billion in 2019.

1998	661
1999	678
2000	653
2001	621
2002	590
2003	599
2004	575
2005	568
2006	552
2007	551
2008	508
2009	467
2010	443
2011	432
2012	425
2013	410
2014	406
2015	404
2016	398
2017	371
2018	364
2019	367

Source: "County Business Patterns." [online] from https://www.census.gov/programs-surveys/cbp/data/datasets.html [Published April 22, 2021], from U.S. Census Bureau.

★ 2977 ★
Scales and Balances
SIC: 3596; NAICS: 333997

Scale and Balance Manufacturing, 2017

Total shipments were valued at $1.01 billion. The term "nec" stands for not elsewhere classified. Major players include Illinois Tool Works and Mettler-Toledo.

	($ 000)	Share
Motor truck scales	$ 364,041	42.01%
Wholesale sales of new industrial machinery and equipment, nec, including storage tanks, pumps and scales	172,172	19.87
Household, retail, and commercial scales, all types	51,398	5.93
Digital indicators for scales and balances	51,318	5.92
Industrial bench and portable scales	49,877	5.76
Parts for scales and balances	41,063	4.74
Industrial floor scales, dormant, pitless	36,197	4.18
Automatic checkweigher and bulkweigher scales	32,845	3.79
Industrial over-under (predetermined weight) and counting scales	28,668	3.31
Railroad track scales	6,997	0.81
Printers for scales and balances	4,307	0.50
Mailing and parcel post scales (including handheld scales)	1,075	0.12
Other accessories and attachments for scales and balances	26,587	3.07

Source: "Economic Census." [online] from https://www.census.gov/programs-surveys/economic-census/data/tables.html [Accessed December 2, 2020], from U.S. Census Bureau.

★ 2978 ★
Scales and Balances
SIC: 3596; NAICS: 333997

Scale and Balance Manufacturing Leaders, 2017

Data show the percent of industry sales held by the largest 4, 8, 20 and 50 firms in the sector. There are approximately 84 players operating in the industry generating employment for 3,106 people. The industry generated sales of $1.1 billion in 2018.

4 largest firms	66.5%
8 largest firms	78.3

Continued on next page.

★ 2978 ★
[Continued]
Scales and Balances
SIC: 3596; NAICS: 333997

Scale and Balance Manufacturing Leaders, 2017

Data show the percent of industry sales held by the largest 4, 8, 20 and 50 firms in the sector. There are approximately 84 players operating in the industry generating employment for 3,106 people. The industry generated sales of $1.1 billion in 2018.

20 largest firms	92.5%
50 largest firms	99.2

Source: "Economic Census." [online] from https://www.census.gov/content/census/en/data/tables/2017/econ/economic-census/naics-sector-31-33.html [Accessed January 21, 2021], from U.S. Census Bureau.

★ 2979 ★
School Buses
SIC: 4151; NAICS: 48541

Largest School Bus Operators, 2019

Companies are ranked by size of fleet in 2019.

First Student	42,000
National Express L.L.C.	21,000
Student Transportation Inc.	15,800
North American Central School Bus	3,092
Logan Bus Co & Affiliates	2,550
Krapf School Bus	2,400
Cook-Illinois Corp.	2,200
Sharp Bus Lines Ltd.	1,790
WE Transport Inc.	1,739
Apple Bus Co.	1,687

Source: *School Bus Fleet*, Fact Book 2020, p. 40.

★ 2980 ★
Schools
SIC: 8211; NAICS: 61111

Largest School Districts, 2018-2019

Districts are ranked by enrollment.

New York, NY	1,126,501
Los Angeles Unified, CA	607,723
Chicago, IL	363,954
Miami-Dade County, FL	350,456
Clark County, NV	335,333
Broward County, FL	270,978
Hillsborough County, FL	220,257
Houston, TX	209,772
Orange County, FL	209,144
Palm Beach County, FL	194,985

Source: *American School & University*, September 2020, p. 15, from U.S. Department of Education.

★ 2981 ★
Schools
SIC: 8222; NAICS: 61121

Number of Junior Colleges, 1998-2018

A junior college is an educational institution that offers courses in liberal arts, technological and vocational training. About 5.8 million students were enrolled in junior colleges in 2017.

1998	818
1999	816
2000	809
2001	848
2002	931
2003	909
2004	933
2005	861
2006	881
2007	862
2008	882
2009	916
2010	936
2011	958
2012	953
2013	1,006
2014	1,083
2015	1,041
2016	1,013
2017	806
2018	787

Source: "County Business Patterns." [online] from https://www.census.gov/programs-surveys/cbp/data/datasets.html [Accessed June 25, 2020], from U.S. Census Bureau.

★ 2982 ★
Seafood and Fish
SIC: 2091; NAICS: 31171

Canned Premium Sardine Market, 2019

Market shares are shown in percent.

King Oscar	63.5%
Other	36.5

Source: "Thai Union Investor Report 2019." [online] from http://www.investor.thaiunion.com [Accessed October 30, 2020], from Euromonitor.

★ 2983 ★
Seafood and Fish
SIC: 2092; NAICS: 31171

Cod Shipments, 2019-2021

Atlantic cod supply is expected to increase 11% in 2021 to 1,271,000 tons, but prices are slipping, according to the source. Figures are in thousands of metric tons. H& G stands for headed and gutted.

	2019 (000)	2020 (000)	2021 (000)	Share
Frozen H&G	355	350	390	31.2%
Frozen fillets	340	350	380	30.4
Fresh fish and fillets	250	250	280	22.4
Salted and dried	185	180	200	16.0

Source: *Intrafish*, November 2020, p. 31.

★ 2984 ★
Seafood and Fish
SIC: 2092; NAICS: 31171

Frozen Seafood by Category, 2020

Categories are ranked based on sales at supermarkets, drug stores, mass merchandisers, military commissaries, and select club and dollar chains for the 52 weeks ended September 6, 2020.

	($ mil.)	Share
Shrimp	$3,500.17	53.93%
Fish/seafood	2,990.00	46.07

Source: *The National Provisioner*, October 2020, p. 52, from IRI.

★ 2985 ★
Seafood and Fish
SIC: 2091; NAICS: 31171

Global Market for Fish and Seafood by Segment, 2017-2018 and 2022

Figures are in billions of dollars. Chilled products are expected to take 44.96% of the total in 2022, shelf-stable 38% and frozen 17%.

	2017 ($ bil.)	2018 ($ bil.)	2022 ($ bil.)	Share
Chilled	$38.4	$39.1	$41.5	44.96%
Shelf-stable	29.0	30.3	35.1	38.03
Frozen	13.3	14.0	15.7	17.01

Source: "Thai Union Investor Report 2019." [online] from http://www.investor.thaiunion.com [Accessed October 30, 2020], from Euromonitor.

★ 2986 ★
Seafood and Fish
SIC: 2092; NAICS: 31171

Leading Refrigerated Fish/Herring/Seafood Brands, 2020

Brands are ranked based on sales at supermarkets, drug stores, mass merchandisers, military commissaries, and select club and dollar chains for the 52 weeks ended September 6, 2020.

	($ mil.)	Share
Trans Ocean	$64.38	8.03%
Acme	31.80	3.97
Louis Kemp Crab Delights	28.14	3.51
Echo Falls	27.14	3.38
Vita	23.48	2.93
Ducktrap River	22.58	2.82
Latitude 45	21.42	2.67
Chicken of the Sea	21.18	2.64
Dockside Classics	20.98	2.62
Private label	149.95	18.70
Other	390.83	48.74

Source: *The National Provisioner*, October 2020, p. 52, from IRI.

★ 2987 ★
Seafood and Fish
SIC: 2092; NAICS: 31171

Retail Finfish Sales, 2019

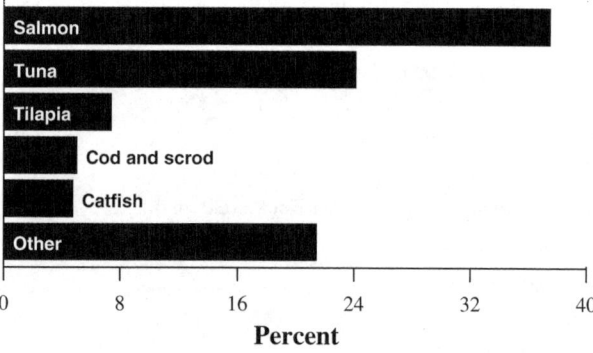

Sales are shown in millions of dollars based on sales at food stores, drug stores, mass merchandisers, military commissaries, select club and dollar chains, and Whole Foods stores for the 52 weeks ended December 31, 2019.

	($ mil.)	Share
Salmon	$2,800	37.46%
Tuna	1,800	24.08
Tilapia	551	7.37
Cod and scrod	372	4.98

Continued on next page.

★ 2987 ★
[Continued]
Seafood and Fish
SIC: 2092; NAICS: 31171

Retail Finfish Sales, 2019

Sales are shown in millions of dollars based on sales at food stores, drug stores, mass merchandisers, military commissaries, select club and dollar chains, and Whole Foods stores for the 52 weeks ended December 31, 2019.

	($ mil.)	Share
Catfish	$ 352	4.71%
Other	1,600	21.40

Source: "Opportunities in Alternative Seafood." [online] from https://gfi.org/images/uploads/2020/06/GFI_Opportunities_in_Alternative_Seafood.pdf [Published June 25, 2020], from Nielsen.

★ 2988 ★
Seafood and Fish
SIC: 2092; NAICS: 31171

Retail Sales of Seafood, 2020

Categories are ranked by multi-outlet sales in millions of dollars for the 52 weeks ended May 30, 2020. Crustaceans include crab, lobster and shrimp. Mollusks include clams, mussels, oysters and scallops. Meat shortages and price increases helped drive sales. Finfish sales grew 9.5% over the previous year, crustacean sales grew 12.5%, prepared seafood 6.5% and mollusks 1.2%.

	($ mil.)	Share
Finfish	$ 3,100.0	43.36%
Crustaceans	2,200.0	30.77
Prepared seafood (value added)	1,600.0	22.38
Mollusks	248.7	3.48

Source: *Supermarket News*, August 2020, p. 37, from Nielsen.

★ 2989 ★
Seafood and Fish
SIC: 5421; NAICS: 44522

Seafood and Fish Sales in China, 2017-2018

Data show sales by type of outlet. Retail sales grew from $28.03 billion in 2017 to $28.72 billion in 2018.

	2017 ($ mil.)	2018 ($ mil.)	Share
Accommodation	$ 125.3	$ 128.7	0.45%
Health care	95.2	98.8	0.35
Leisure	93.2	95.8	0.34
Education	$ 66.8	$ 68.5	0.24%
Pubs, clubs and bars	61.1	62.7	0.22
Travel	54.0	55.3	0.19
Workplace	44.6	45.7	0.16
Mobile operators	30.4	31.1	0.11
Welfare and services	31.7	32.4	0.11
Military and civil defense	27.5	28.2	0.10
Retail foodservice providers	17.1	17.5	0.06
Other	27,163.5	27,835.5	97.67

Source: "Sector Trend Analysis — Crustacean Trends in China." [online] from https://www.agr.gc.ca/eng/international-trade/market-intelligence/reports [Published February 2020], from GlobalData.

★ 2990 ★
Seafood and Fish
SIC: 2091; NAICS: 31171

Top Seafood and Fish Markets in Japan, 2018

Market shares are shown in percent. Hypermarkets and supermarkets claimed 79% of sales by channel, convenience stores 7.7%, department stores 6.4%, and other channels 7.1%.

Hagoromo Foods Corp.	8.5%
Nippon Suisan Kaisha Ltd. (Nissui)	8.3
Maruha Nichiro Corp.	2.3
Daiichi Co. Ltd.	1.3
Private label	5.5
Other	74.1

Source: "Sector Trend Analysis — Fish and Seafood Trends in Japan." [online] from https://www.agr.gc.ca/eng/international-trade/market-intelligence/reports/?id=1522931721523 [Published July 2020], from Global Trade Tracker.

★ 2991 ★
Seafood and Fish
SIC: 2091; NAICS: 31171

Top Seafood and Fish Markets Worldwide, 2018-2019

Markets are ranked by sales in millions of dollars.

	2018 ($ mil.)	2019 ($ mil.)	Share
United States	$ 23,992.40	$ 23,522.0	15.26%
China	14,745.20	18,413.6	11.95
Japan	15,771.90	15,562.7	10.10

Continued on next page.

★ 2991 ★
[Continued]
Seafood and Fish
SIC: 2091; NAICS: 31171

Top Seafood and Fish Markets Worldwide, 2018-2019

Markets are ranked by sales in millions of dollars.

	2018 ($ mil.)	2019 ($ mil.)	Share
Spain	$ 8,655.70	$ 8,104.6	5.26%
France	7,145.20	6,784.2	4.40
Italy	7,113.80	6,038.9	3.92
Germany	6,172.20	5,848.2	3.79
South Korea	6,060.30	5,717.9	3.71
Sweden	5,630.10	5,221.5	3.39
United Kingdom	4,540.90	4,718.9	3.06
Other	58,586.71	54,201.8	35.17

Source: "Sector Trend Analysis — Fish and Seafood Trends in Japan." [online] from https://www.agr.gc.ca/eng/international-trade/market-intelligence/reports/?id=1522931721523 [Published July 2020], from Global Trade Tracker.

★ 2992 ★
Search, Detection, and Navigation Apparatus
SIC: 3812; NAICS: 334511

Search, Detection, Navigation, Guidance, Aeronautical, and Nautical Apparatus Manufacturing Leaders, 2017

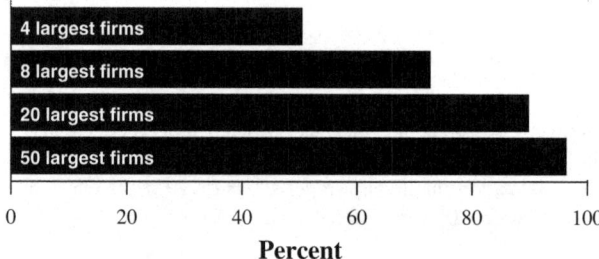

Data show the percent of industry sales held by the largest 4, 8, 20 and 50 firms in the sector. There are approximately 552 players operating in the industry generating employment for 124,780 people.

4 largest firms	50.4%
8 largest firms	72.7
20 largest firms	89.7
50 largest firms	96.3

Source: "Economic Census." [online] from https://www.census.gov/content/census/en/data/tables/2017/econ/economic-census/naics-sector-31-33.html [Accessed January 21, 2021], from U.S. Census Bureau.

★ 2993 ★
Seaweed
SIC: 0182; NAICS: 111419

Global Carrageenan Production, 2019

Data show the leading producers of carrageenan, an extract from red seaweed used in the food industry. Production reached an estimated 110,000 tons, according to most recent statistics.

FMC Corp.	27.0%
Shemberg Marketing Corp.	15.0
Hercules L.L.C.	13.0
SKW Trostberg	11.0
Gelymar S.A.	7.0
Ceamsa	3.0
Danisco A/S	3.0
Hispanagar S.A.	2.0
Quest	2.0
Other	17.0

Source: *Aquaculture Magazine*, October-November 2020, p. 12.

★ 2994 ★
Secondhand Apparel
SIC: 5932; NAICS: 45331

Secondhand Apparel Market, 2019 and 2029

The secondhand market consists of two sectors: the resale market and the thrift/donation market. Sales are expected to be worth $28 billion in 2019.

	2019	2029
Off-price	16.0%	19.0%
Secondhand	7.0	17.0
Mid-priced	20.0	13.0
Direct to consumer	8.0	12.0
Value chains	11.0	10.0
Fast fashion	9.0	9.0
Department stores	13.0	7.0
Amazon.com Inc.	2.0	4.0
Subscription	2.0	4.0
Other	12.0	7.0

Source: "ThredUp 2020 Resale Report." [online] from https://www.thredup.com/resale/static/thredup-resaleReport2020-42b42834f03ef2296d83a44f85a3e2b3.pdf [Published March 2020], from GlobalData.

★ 2995 ★
Security Equipment
SIC: 3669; NAICS: 33429

Demand for Safety and Security Alarms, 2018

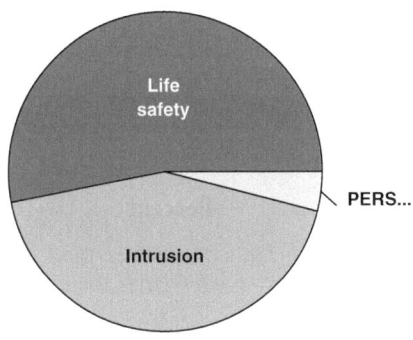

The market is forecast to see a CAGR of 4.8% from 2018-2023. Homeowners are moving towards smart equipment and multi-service operators. The market is also seeing expansion from baby boomers aging in place and millennials buying their first homes. Major players include Johnson Controls, Melrose Industries (Nortek), Siemens and United Technologies. PERS stands for personal emergency response system. M stands for mobile.

Life safety	53.0%
Intrusion	43.0
PERS and mPERS	4.0

Source: "Safety & Security Alarms." [online] from http://www.freedoniagroup.com [Published January 2020], from The Freedonia Group Inc.

★ 2996 ★
Security Equipment
SIC: 3669; NAICS: 33429

Leading Gas Alarm/Detector Makers Worldwide, 2016

The industry generated revenue of $6.38 billion in 2019.

Tyco International	12.15%
MSA Safety	11.96
Industrial Scientific	10.35
Other	65.54

Source: "COVID-19 Impact on Global Gas Alarm Market Size, Status and Forecast 2020-2026." [online] from http://reports.valuates.com [Published April 2020], from QY Research.

★ 2997 ★
Security Equipment
SIC: 3669; NAICS: 33429

Popular Access Control Brands, 2020

Data show the most popular brands among information integrators in the source's annual 100 Brand Analysis Survey. Respondents represent a small but influential section of the overall custom integrator market.

Control4	57.0%
Yale	40.0
Kwikset	34.0
Crestron	33.0
Savant	32.0

Source: *CE Pro*, June 2020, p. 42.

★ 2998 ★
Security Equipment
SIC: 3669; NAICS: 33429

Popular Smart Lock/Deadbolt Brands, 2020

Data show the most popular brands among information integrators in the source's annual 100 Brand Analysis Survey. Respondents represent a small but influential section of the overall custom integrator market.

Yale	69.0%
Black & Decker Kwikset	63.0
Schlage	39.0
Black & Decker Baldwin	22.0
August	14.0

Source: *CE Pro*, June 2020, p. 42.

★ 2999 ★
Security Industry
SIC/NAICS: See frontmatter for explanation.

Global Spending on Security/Risk Management, 2019-2020

Spending is shown in millions of dollars. The market is forecast to grow 2.4% to $123.8 billion in 2020. The move to cloud-based applications is making this market more resilient to a potential economic downturn. Cloud security grew 33.3%. Network security equipment fell 12.6%, the largest decline.

	2019 ($ mil.)	2020 ($ mil.)	Share
Security services	$61,979	$64,270	51.91%
Infrastructure protection	16,520	17,483	14.12

Continued on next page.

★ 2999 ★
[Continued]
Security Industry
SIC/NAICS: See frontmatter for explanation.

Global Spending on Security/Risk Management, 2019-2020

Spending is shown in millions of dollars. The market is forecast to grow 2.4% to $123.8 billion in 2020. The move to cloud-based applications is making this market more resilient to a potential economic downturn. Cloud security grew 33.3%. Network security equipment fell 12.6%, the largest decline.

	2019 ($ mil.)	2020 ($ mil.)	Share
Network security equipment	$ 13,387	$ 11,694	9.44%
Identity access management	9,837	10,409	8.41
Consumer security software	6,254	6,235	5.04
Integrated risk management	4,555	4,731	3.82
Application security	3,095	3,287	2.65
Data security	2,662	2,852	2.30
Cloud security	439	585	0.47
Other information security software	2,206	2,273	1.84

Source: "Gartner Forecasts Worldwide Security and Risk Management Spending Growth to Slow but Remain Positive in 2020." [online] from http://www.gartner.com [Press release June 17, 2020], from Gartner Inc.

★ 3000 ★
Security Industry
SIC: 7382; NAICS: 561621

Leading Guarding Firms in North America, 2019

Firms are ranked by revenue in millions of dollars.

Allied Universal	$ 8,000.00
Securitas North America	4,300.00
G4S Secure Solutions	2,411.00
SecurAmerica	1,000.00
Constellis	673.10
Paladin/PalAmerican Security	670.00
Walden Security	305.00
Summit Security Services	214.00
Prosegur USA	200.00
Andy Frain Services	131.75

Source: *Security*, December 2020, p. 19.

★ 3001 ★
Security Industry
SIC: 7382; NAICS: 561621

Leading Security Firms, 2019

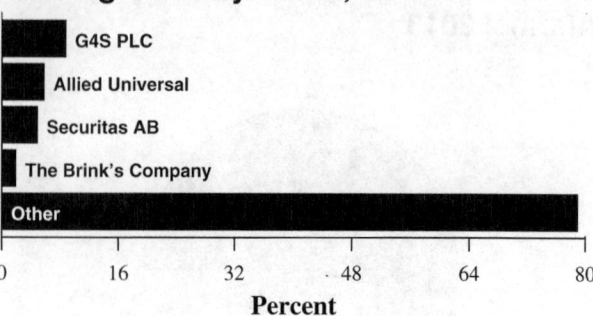

Companies in this industry might provide one of the following: investigative or detective services, guard and patrol services, or protected transportation of valuables. It excludes companies primarily involved in selling alarm systems. The industry generated revenue of $38.5 billion.

G4S PLC	8.7%
Allied Universal	5.7
Securitas AB	4.8
The Brink's Company	1.9
Other	78.9

Source: "Security Services in the U.S." [online] from http://www.ibisworld.com [Published October 2019], from IBISWorld.

★ 3002 ★
Security Industry
SIC: 7382; NAICS: 561621

Leading Security Service Firms, 2019

Companies are ranked by recurring monthly revenue in millions of dollars as of December 31, 2019. Monthly revenue was $661 million, up 1% from 2018.

	($ mil.)	Share
ADT	$ 336.00	50.83%
Vivint Smart Home	97.90	14.81
Brinks Home Security	38.30	5.79
Vector Security	19.14	2.90
Bay Alarm Company	12.99	1.97
Guardian Protection	12.68	1.92
Interface Security Systems Holdings Inc.	10.28	1.56
Securitas Electronic Security	10.10	1.53
CPI Security Systems Inc.	9.80	1.48
Alert 360	9.06	1.37
Other	104.75	15.85

Source: *SDM*, May 2020, p. 31.

★ 3003 ★
Seeds
SIC: 0161; NAICS: 111219

Demand for Lawn and Garden Seeds, 2019

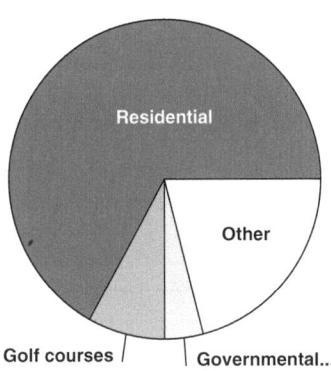

The packaged lawn and garden seed market was valued at $920 million in 2019. Revenue is forecast to see a CAGR of 3.3% from 2019-2024. Major companies include Bayer, Central Garden & Pet, Royal Barenburg and Scotts Miracle-Gro.

Residential	67.0%
Golf courses	8.0
Governmental and institutional	4.0
Other	21.0

Source: "Lawn & Garden Seeds." [online] from http://www.freedoniagroup.com [Published December 2020], from The Freedonia Group Inc.

★ 3004 ★
Seeds
SIC: 0161; NAICS: 111219

Leading Seed Makers Worldwide, 2017-2018

Tier 1 companies are ranked by sales in millions of dollars. Tier 1 companies have sales greater than $500 million. Monsanto had sales of $10.91 billion in 2017, DuPont Pioneer $6.8 billion and DowAgroSciences $1.45 billion; the source did not include 2018 sales.

	2017 ($ mil.)	2018 ($ mil.)
Bayer Crop Science	$ 10,835	$ 10,433
Corteva Inc.	8,056	7,842
Syngenta Corp.	2,829	3,204
BASF Corp.	1,694	1,800
Vilmorin	1,542	1,568
KWS SAAT	1,173	1,339
DLF Seeds	517	693
AgReliant Genetics	657	638
Kaneko Seeds Co.	531	542
Yuan Longping High-Tech Agriculture	473	541

Source: "Analysis of Sales and Profitability Within the Seed Sector." [online] from http://www.fao.org/3/ca6929en/ca6929-en.pdf [Published November 2019], from Phillips McDougall and IHS Markit.

★ 3005 ★
Self-Checkout Terminals
SIC: 3578; NAICS: 333318

Leading Self-Checkout Terminal Makers Worldwide, 2020

Market shares are shown based on shipments. According to the source, shipments rose 52% over 2018. NCR, the largest supplier, shipped 58,000 units, an increase of 50% over the previous year.

NCR	47.0%
Toshiba Corp.	24.0
CCL Technology	7.0
Diebold Nixdorf	7.0
Wintec System Co.	3.0
Fujitsu Inc.	2.0
ITAB Shop Concept	2.0
Sedpos	2.0
Other	5.0

Source: "NCR Leads Booming Global Self-Checkout Market." [online] from https://www.rbrlondon.com/press/ [Published August 17, 2020], from Global EPOS and Self-Checkout 2020 (RBR).

★ 3006 ★
Self-Storage Industry
SIC: 4225; NAICS: 53113

Largest Self-Storage Providers, 2020

Companies are ranked by millions of square feet under management.

Public Storage Inc.	183.00
Extra Storage Space	89.98
National Storage Affiliates	49.00
U-Haul International Inc.	43.39
Life Storage Inc.	40.39
CubeSmart	36.73
Prime Group Holdings L.L.C.	17.75
StorageMart	15.22
W.P. Carey Inc.	13.76
SmartStop Self Storage	12.00

Source: *Inside Self-Storage*, September 2020, p. NA.

★ 3007 ★
Semiconductor Machinery
SIC: 3559; NAICS: 333242

Leading Semiconductor WFE Firms Worldwide, 2020

Market shares are shown in percent. WFE stands for wafer fabrication equipment.

Applied Materials	16.4%
ASML	15.4
Tokyo Electron	12.3
Lam Research	10.8
KLA	6.2
Other	38.9

Source: "Applied Materials Will Regain Semiconductor Equipment Lead From ASML in 2020." [online] from https://semiwiki.com/semiconductor-services/information-network/293298-applied-materials-will-regain-semiconductor-equipment-lead-from-asml-in-2020/ [Published November 29, 2020], from The Information Network.

★ 3008 ★
Semiconductor Machinery
SIC: 3559; NAICS: 333242

Number of Firms In Semiconductor Machinery Manufacturing, 1998-2019

According to Kentley Insights, the industry generated sales of $9.3 billion in 2019.

1998	269
1999	269
2000	259
2001	257
2002	259
2003	285
2004	263
2005	244
2006	236
2007	222
2008	219
2009	204
2010	195
2011	197
2012	184
2013	189
2014	184
2015	177
2016	170
2017	157
2018	157
2019	168

Source: "County Business Patterns." [online] from https://www.census.gov/programs-surveys/cbp/data/datasets.html [Published April 22, 2021], from U.S. Census Bureau.

★ 3009 ★
Semiconductors
SIC: 3674; NAICS: 334413

Desktop CPU Market Worldwide, 2020

Market shares are shown for the third and fourth quarter 2020. Figures exclude Internet of Things.

	3Q 2020	4Q 2020
Intel Corp.	79.9%	80.7%
Advanced Micro Devices	20.1	19.3
VIA Technologies Inc.	0.1	0.1

Source: "AMD's CPU Share Skyrocketed in 2020 Along With Low-End PC Sales." [online] from https://www.pcworld.com/article/3606108/amds-cpu-share-skyrocketed-in-2020-along-with-low-end-pc-sales.html [Published February 3, 2021], from Mercury Research.

★ 3010 ★
Semiconductors
SIC: 3674; NAICS: 334413

Global Semiconductor Sales, 2020-2021

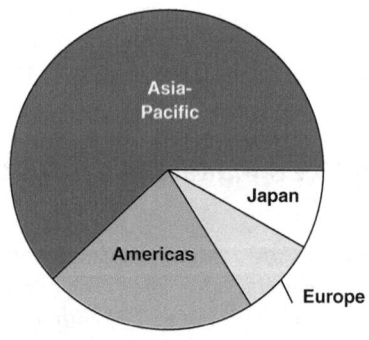

Sales are shown in millions of dollars. The market is forecast to grow from $433.1 billion in 2020 to $469.4 billion in 2021.

	2020 ($ mil.)	2021 ($ mil.)	Share
Asia-Pacific	$ 267,590	$ 290,854	61.96%
Americas	93,343	102,164	21.76

Continued on next page.

★ 3010 ★
[Continued]
Semiconductors
SIC: 3674; NAICS: 334413
Global Semiconductor Sales, 2020-2021

Sales are shown in millions of dollars. The market is forecast to grow from $433.1 billion in 2020 to $469.4 billion in 2021.

	2020 ($ mil.)	2021 ($ mil.)	Share
Europe	$ 36,452	$ 38,543	8.21%
Japan	35,759	37,841	8.06

Source: "The Worldwide Semiconductor Market is Expected to Increase 5.1 Percent in 2020, According to 8.4 Percent in 2021." [online] from http://www.wsts.org [Press release December 1, 2020], from World Semiconductor Trade Statistics.

★ 3011 ★
Semiconductors
SIC: 3674; NAICS: 334413
Leading 16-bit MCU Makers Worldwide, 2018

Market shares are estimated.

Renesas Electronics Corp.	20.0-30.0%
Infineon Technologies	10.0-20.0
NXP Semiconductors	10.0-20.0
Texas Instruments	10.0-20.0
Cypress Semiconductor Corp.	0.0-5.0
Other	0.0-50.0

Source: "Infineon/Cypress Regulation Merger Procedure." [online] from http://www.ec.europa.eu [Published October 16, 2019], from Form CO.

★ 3012 ★
Semiconductors
SIC: 3674; NAICS: 334413
Leading Gallium Arsenide Open Epiwafer Makers Worldwide, 2019

The industry generated revenue of $262 million.

IQE PLC	53.0%
Visual Photonics Epitaxy Co.	26.0
Sumitomo Chemicals	8.0
Intelligent Epitaxy Technology Inc.	4.0
II-IV Inc.	3.0
LandMark Optoelectronics Corp.	2.0
Other	4.0

Source: *Semiconductor Today*, June-July 2020, p. 59, from Yole.

★ 3013 ★
Semiconductors
SIC: 3674; NAICS: 334413
Leading NAND Flash-Memory Makers Worldwide, 2020

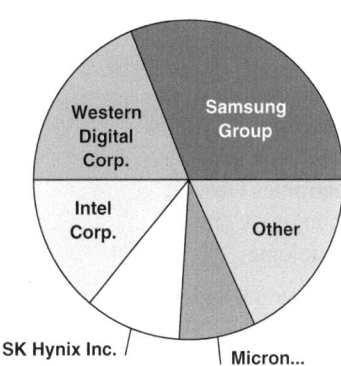

Shares are shown based on capacity shipped in the second quarter of 2020. In October 2020, Intel reached a deal to sell its NAND flash-memory business to SK Hynix for $9 billion. The sale, pending regulatory approval, would also include its solid-state drive business and its production facilities in China.

Samsung Group	31.1%
Western Digital Corp.	18.6
Intel Corp.	13.6
SK Hynix Inc.	10.1
Micron Technology Inc.	8.2
Other	18.4

Source: "Intel Looks to Shed Legacy Businesses by Selling NAND Flash-Memory Business to SK Hynix." [online] from https://www.businessinsider.com/what-intel-could-gain-by-selling-memory-business-sk-hynix-2020-10 [Published October 21, 2020], from TrendForce.

★ 3014 ★
Semiconductors
SIC: 3674; NAICS: 334413
Leading OSAT Firms Worldwide, 2020

Market shares are shown for the third quarter of 2020. OSAT stands for Outsourced Semiconductor Assembly and Test.

Advanced Semiconductor Engineering Inc. (ASE)	22.5%
Amkor Technology Inc.	20.0
JCET Group	14.5
Siliconware Precision Industries	13.3

Continued on next page.

★ 3014 ★
[Continued]
Semiconductors
SIC: 3674; NAICS: 334413

Leading OSAT Firms Worldwide, 2020

Market shares are shown for the third quarter of 2020. OSAT stands for Outsourced Semiconductor Assembly and Test.

Powertech Technology Inc.	9.6%
Tongfu Microelectronics Co. Ltd.	5.9
Tianshui Huatian Technology	4.7
King Yuan Electronics Group	3.7
Chipbond Technology Corp.	2.9
ChipMOS Technologies	2.9

Source: "Top 10 Largest OSAT Companies' Revenues Exceed U.S.$6.7 Billion, While Amkor Scores Highest YoY Growth, According to TrendForce." [online] from https://www.trendforce.com/presscenter/news/20201116-10553.html [Published November 16, 2020], from TrendForce.

★ 3015 ★
Semiconductors
SIC: 3674; NAICS: 334413

Leading Pure-Play Foundry Makers in China, 2018-2020

Sales grew from $10.72 billion in 2018 to $11.82 billion in 2019 to $14.86 billion in 2020. Data are forecast for 2020.

	2018	2019	2020
Taiwan Semiconductor Manufacturing Co.	55.0%	59.0%	61.0%
Semiconductor Manufacturing International Corp.	19.0	16.0	16.0
Huahong Group	8.0	8.0	8.0
United Microelectronics Corp.	7.0	7.0	7.0
GlobalFoundries	5.0	4.0	3.0
World Xinxin Semiconductor Manufacturing Co.	2.0	2.0	1.0
Other	5.0	4.0	4.0

Source: "China Forecast to Represent 22% of the Foundry Market in 2020." [online] from https://www.icinsights.com/news [Press release October 13, 2020], from company reports and IC Insights.

★ 3016 ★
Semiconductors
SIC: 3674; NAICS: 334413

Leading Semiconductor Buyers Worldwide, 2020

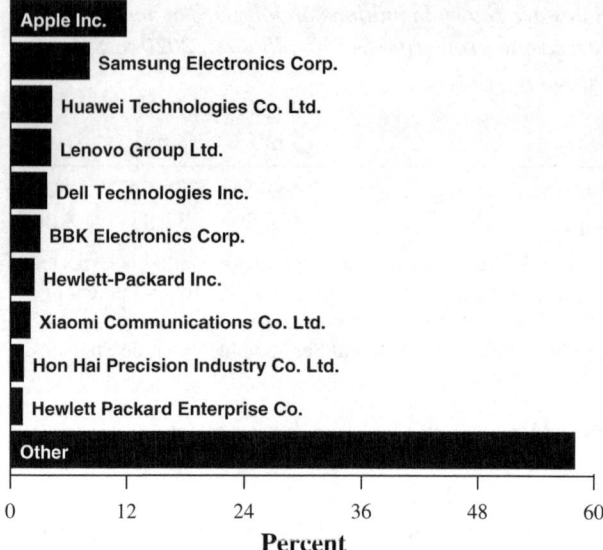

Companies are ranked by spending in millions of dollars. All but two companies in the top 10 spent more on semiconductors in 2020 than they did in 2019. The pandemic reduced demand for 5G smartphones and vehicle production, but increased demand for video games and mobile PCs. There was also increased investment in cloud data centers. In addition, a rise in memory prices caused spending to increase. Huawei's spending, however, was down 23.5% due to the U.S. government imposing trade restrictions which limited its ability to purchase semiconductors. Hon Hai Precision Industry also spent less on semiconductors, -1.5%, than they did in 2019.

	($ mil.)	Share
Apple Inc.	$ 53,616	11.9%
Samsung Electronics Corp.	36,416	8.1
Huawei Technologies Co. Ltd.	19,086	4.2
Lenovo Group Ltd.	18,555	4.1
Dell Technologies Inc.	16,581	3.7
BBK Electronics Corp.	13,393	3.0
Hewlett-Packard Inc.	10,992	2.4

Continued on next page.

★ 3016 ★
[Continued]
Semiconductors
SIC: 3674; NAICS: 334413

Leading Semiconductor Buyers Worldwide, 2020

Companies are ranked by spending in millions of dollars. All but two companies in the top 10 spent more on semiconductors in 2020 than they did in 2019. The pandemic reduced demand for 5G smartphones and vehicle production, but increased demand for video games and mobile PCs. There was also increased investment in cloud data centers. In addition, a rise in memory prices caused spending to increase. Huawei's spending, however, was down 23.5% due to the U.S. government imposing trade restrictions which limited its ability to purchase semiconductors. Hon Hai Precision Industry also spent less on semiconductors, -1.5%, than they did in 2019.

	($ mil.)	Share
Xiaomi Communications Co. Ltd.	$ 8,790	2.0%
Hon Hai Precision Industry Co. Ltd.	5,730	1.3
Hewlett Packard Enterprise Co.	5,570	1.2
Other	261,109	58.0

Source: "Gartner Says Apple and Samsung Extended Their Lead as Top Semiconductor Customers in 2020." [online] from https://www.gartner.com/en/newsroom/press-releases/2021-02-09-gartner-says-apple-and-samsung-extended-their-lead-as [Press release February 9, 2021], from Gartner Inc.

★ 3017 ★
Semiconductors
SIC: 3674; NAICS: 334413

Leading Semiconductor Makers Worldwide, 2020

Companies are ranked by revenue in millions of dollars. After falling 12% in 2019, semiconductor revenue grew 7.3% in 2020 to $449.8 billion. While demand for semiconductors in the automotive, industrial and some consumer sectors was down due to the pandemic, increased work and study from home caused rising demand for computer CPUs, NAND flash and DRAM. Memory accounted for 44% of the growth.

	($ mil.)	Share
Intel Corp.	$ 70,244	15.6%
Samsung Electronics Corp.	56,197	12.5
SK Hynix Inc.	25,271	5.6
Micron Technology Inc.	$ 22,098	4.9%
Qualcomm	17,906	4.0
Broadcom Inc.	15,695	3.5
Texas Instruments Inc.	13,074	2.9
MediaTek Inc.	11,008	2.4
Kioxia Holdings Corp.	10,208	2.3
Nvidia Corp.	10,095	2.2
Other	198,042	44.0

Source: "Gartner Says Worldwide Semiconductor Revenue Grew 7.3% in 2020." [online] from https://www.gartner.com/en/newsroom/press-releases/2021-01-14-gartner-says-worldwide-semiconductor-revenue-grew-7-percent-in-2020 [Press release January 14, 2021], from Gartner Inc.

★ 3018 ★
Semiconductors
SIC: 3674; NAICS: 334413

Leading Smartphone Chipset Makers Worldwide, 2019-2020

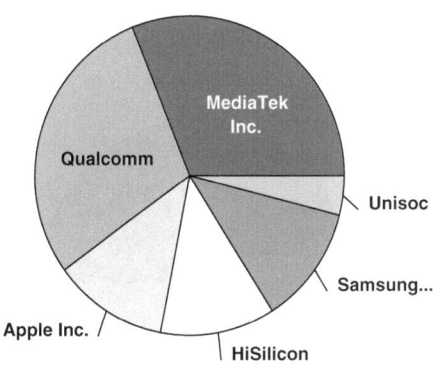

Market shares are shown for the third quarter of each year.

	3Q 2019	3Q 2020
MediaTek Inc.	26.0%	31.0%
Qualcomm	31.0	29.0
Apple Inc.	11.0	12.0
HiSilicon	12.0	12.0
Samsung Electronics Corp.	16.0	12.0
Unisoc	3.0	4.0

Source: "MediaTek Becomes Biggest Smartphone Chipset Vendor for First Time in Q3 2020." [online] from https://www.counterpointresearch.com/mediatek-biggest-smartphone-chipset-vendor-q3-2020/ [Press release December 24, 2020], from Counterpoint Research.

★ 3019 ★
Semiconductors
SIC: 3674; NAICS: 334413

Leading Smartphone DRAM Makers Worldwide, 2020

Market shares are shown based on revenue for the first half of 2020.

Samsung Memory	54.0%
SK Hynix Inc.	24.0
Micron Technology Inc.	20.0
Other	1.0

Source: "Strategy Analytics: Samsung Widens Its Lead in the Smartphone DRAM & NAND Market in H1 2020." [online] from https://www.businesswire.com/news/home/2020101400 5657/en/Strategy-Analytics-Samsung-Widens-its-Lead-in-the-Smartphone-DRAM-NAND-Market-in-H1-2020 [Published October 14, 2020], from Handset Component Technologies.

★ 3020 ★
Semiconductors
SIC: 3674; NAICS: 334413

Leading Smartphone NAND Flash Makers Worldwide, 2020

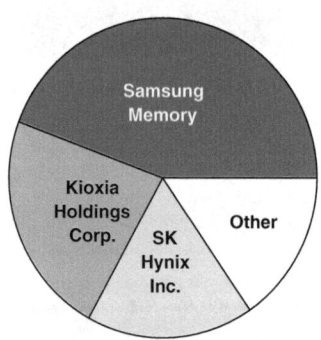

Market shares are shown based on revenue for the first half of 2020.

Samsung Memory	43.0%
Kioxia Holdings Corp.	22.0
SK Hynix Inc.	17.0
Other	15.0

Source: "Strategy Analytics: Samsung Widens Its Lead in the Smartphone DRAM & NAND Market in H1 2020." [online] from https://www.businesswire.com/news/home/2020101400 5657/en/Strategy-Analytics-Samsung-Widens-its-Lead-in-the-Smartphone-DRAM-NAND-Market-in-H1-2020 [Published October 14, 2020], from Handset Component Technologies.

★ 3021 ★
Semiconductors
SIC: 3674; NAICS: 334413

Leading SSD Module Makers Worldwide, 2019

Market shares are shown for channel-market SSDs.

Kingston Technology Corp.	26.0%
ADATA Technology Co.	8.0
Tigo Energy Inc.	6.0
Lenovo Group Ltd.	4.0
Maxsun Co. Ltd.	4.0
Teclast Electronics Co.	4.0
Colorful Co.	3.0
Lexar Media Inc.	3.0
Galaxy Microsystems Ltd.	2.0
Transcend Information Inc.	1.0
Other	39.0

Source: "Kingston, ADATA, Tigo Take Top Three Spots in 2019 Global Ranking of Top 10 SSD Module Makers, Says TrendForce." [online] from http://www.trendforce.com [Press release October 27, 2020], from TrendForce.

★ 3022 ★
Semiconductors
SIC: 3674; NAICS: 334413

Leading Tablet App Processor Makers Worldwide, 2020

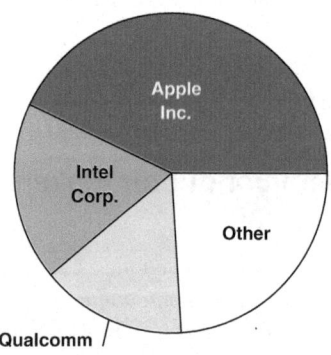

Market shares are shown based on second quarter revenue of $556 million.

Apple Inc.	43.0%
Intel Corp.	18.0

Continued on next page.

★ 3022 ★
[Continued]
Semiconductors
SIC: 3674; NAICS: 334413

Leading Tablet App Processor Makers Worldwide, 2020

Market shares are shown based on second quarter revenue of $556 million.

Qualcomm	15.0%
Other	24.0

Source: "Strategy Analytics: COVID-19 Drives Strong Growth in the Tablet Apps Processor Market in Q2 2020." [online] from https://www.businesswire.com/news/home/20201005005092/en/Strategy-Analytics-COVID-19-Drives-Strong-Growth-in-the-Tablet-Apps-Processor-Market-in-Q2-2020 [Published October 5, 2020], from Strategy Analytics.

★ 3023 ★
Semiconductors
SIC: 3674; NAICS: 334413

Mobile CPU Market Worldwide, 2020

Market shares are shown for the third and fourth quarter 2020. Figures exclude Internet of Things.

	3Q 2020	4Q 2020
Intel Corp.	79.8%	81.0%
Advanced Micro Devices	20.2	19.0

Source: "AMD's CPU Share Skyrocketed in 2020 Along With Low-End PC Sales." [online] from https://www.pcworld.com/article/3606108/amds-cpu-share-skyrocketed-in-2020-along-with-low-end-pc-sales.html [Published February 3, 2021], from Mercury Research.

★ 3024 ★
Semiconductors
SIC: 3674; NAICS: 334413

RF Front-End Component IDM Market Worldwide, 2020-2021

The market for RF front-end component integrated device manufacturers (IDMs) is shown by company. Revenues should reach $5.73 billion in 2020 and $6.09 billion in 2021. Figures are estimated for 2020 and forecast for 2021.

	2020	2021
Skyworks Solutions Inc.	42.3%	42.1%
Qorvo	38.5	38.9
Murata Manufacturing Co.	4.2%	4.2%
Analog Devices Inc.	4.0	3.5
MACOM Technology Solutions	3.6	3.5
Other	7.4	7.4

Source: *Semiconductor Today*, July/August 2020, p. 9, from TrendForce.

★ 3025 ★
Semiconductors
SIC: 3674; NAICS: 334413

Semiconductor Industry Worldwide by Sector, 2019

The industry was valued at $412.3 billion.

Communications	33.0%
Computers	28.5
Consumer	13.3
Automotive	12.2
Industrial	11.9
Government	1.3

Source: "Semiconductor Industry Factbook 2020." [online] from https://www.semiconductors.org/wp-content/uploads/2020/04/2020-SIA-Factbook-FINAL_reduced-size.pdf [Published April 2020], from World Semiconductor Trade Statistics.

★ 3026 ★
Semiconductors
SIC: 3674; NAICS: 334413

Semiconductor Industry Worldwide by Type, 2019

The industry was valued at $412.3 billion.

	($ bil.)	Share
Logic	$ 107	25.85%
Memory	106	25.60
Analog	54	13.04
MPU	48	11.59
Opto	42	10.14
Discretes	24	5.80
MCU	16	3.86
Sensor	14	3.38
DSP	3	0.72

Source: "Semiconductor Industry Factbook 2020." [online] from https://www.semiconductors.org/wp-content/uploads/2020/04/2020-SIA-Factbook-FINAL_reduced-size.pdf [Published April 2020], from Semiconductor Industry Association and World Semiconductor Trade Statistics.

★ 3027 ★
Semiconductors
SIC: 3674; NAICS: 334413
Semiconductor Production Market Worldwide, 2019

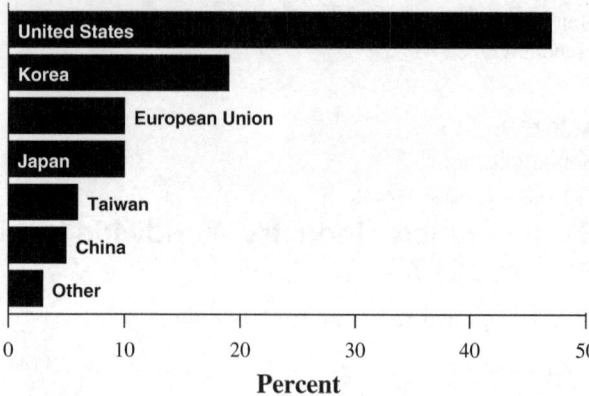

The United States lost global market share during the 1980s. It recovered over the next decade, and by 1997 it was back into a leadership position. The table shows the U.S.-based firms claimed 47% of the semiconductor industry.

United States	47.0%
Korea	19.0
European Union	10.0
Japan	10.0
Taiwan	6.0
China	5.0
Other	3.0

Source: "Semiconductor Industry Factbook 2020." [online] from https://www.semiconductors.org/wp-content/uploads/2020/04/2020-SIA-Factbook-FINAL_reduced-size.pdf [Published April 2020], from Semiconductor Industry Association, World Semiconductor Trade Statistics, IHS Global and PricewaterhouseCoopers.

★ 3028 ★
Semiconductors
SIC: 3674; NAICS: 334413
Server CPU Market Worldwide, 2020

Market shares are shown for the third and fourth quarter of 2020. Figures exclude Internet of Things.

	3Q 2020	4Q 2020
Intel Corp.	93.4%	92.9%
Other	6.6	7.1

Source: "Mercury Research Sees Resurgent Intel CPU Market Share." [online] from https://hexus.net/business/news/components/147376-mercury-research-sees-resurgent-intel-cpu-market-share/ [Published February 4, 2021], from Mercury Research.

★ 3029 ★
Semiconductors
SIC: 3674; NAICS: 334413
Top New Energy Vehicle IGBT Makers in China, 2019

IGBT (Insulated Gate Bipolar Transistor) is a fully controlled and voltage-driven power semiconductor device incorporating BJT and MOSFET. Market shares are estimated.

Infineon Technologies	49.2%
BYD Co. Ltd.	20.0
StarPower Semiconductor	16.6
Renesas Electronics Corp.	3.9
Denso Corp.	3.7
Fuji Electric Co. Ltd.	2.0
Mitsubishi Electric Corp.	1.3
Other	3.3

Source: "Automated IGBT Industry Report, 2020." [online] from http://www.researchinchina.com [Published July 2020], from Research in China.

★ 3030 ★
Semiconductors
SIC: 3674; NAICS: 334413
x86 CPU Market Worldwide, 2020

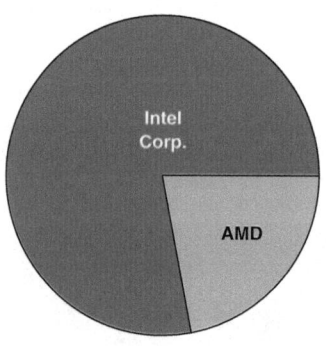

Market shares are shown for the third and fourth quarter 2020. Figures include Internet of Things and System on a Chip.

	3Q 2020	4Q 2020
Intel Corp.	77.6%	78.3%
AMD	22.4	21.7

Source: "AMD's CPU Share Skyrocketed in 2020 Along With Low-End PC Sales." [online] from https://www.pcworld.com/article/3606108/amds-cpu-share-skyrocketed-in-2020-along-with-low-end-pc-sales.html [Published February 3, 2021], from Mercury Research.

★ 3031 ★
Sensors
SIC: 3674; NAICS: 334413

Leading Image Sensor Makers Worldwide, 2019

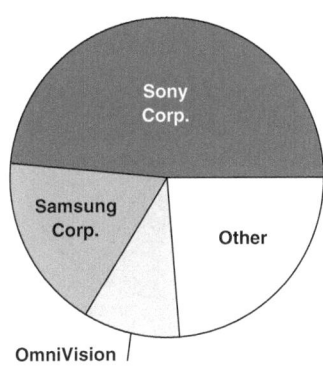

Market shares are shown in percent.

Sony Corp.	49.1%
Samsung Corp.	17.9
OmniVision	9.5
Other	23.5

Source: "Samsung Electric Uses Nonacell Tech to Upgrade World's Only 108-MP Image Sensor." [online] from https://pulsenews.co.kr/view.php?year=2020&no=149716 [Published February 17, 2020], from Techno Systems Research.

★ 3032 ★
Sensors
SIC: 3674; NAICS: 334413

Leading Smartphone Image Sensor Makers Worldwide, 2020

Market shares are shown based on revenue for the first six months of the year.

Sony Corp.	44.0%
Samsung LSI	32.0
OmniVision	9.0
Other	15.0

Source: "Strategy Analytics: Sony Led the Growing Smartphone Image Sensor Market in H1 2020." [online] from https://www.businesswire.com/news/home/20201007005124/en/ [Press release October 20, 2020], from Handset Component Technologies.

★ 3033 ★
Sensors
SIC: 3812; NAICS: 334511

Robot Sensor Market Worldwide, 2018

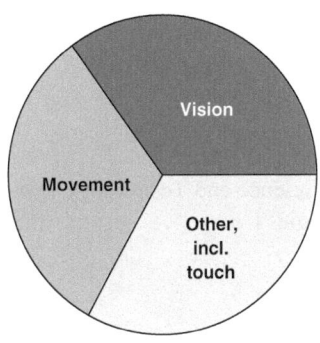

The robot sensor market is forecast to grow from $561.7 million in 2018 to $1.23 billion in 2025.

Vision	35.28%
Movement	31.65
Other, incl. touch and voice	33.08

Source: "Robot Sensors-Poised for Strong Global Growth." [online] from https://www.communicationstoday.co.in/robot-sensors-poised-for-strong-global-growth/ [Published October 8, 2020], from InForGrowth.

★ 3034 ★
Sensors
SIC: 3674; NAICS: 334413

Robotic Vehicle Sensor System Worldwide, 2024, 2028 and 2032

Revenues are estimated in millions of dollars. LiDAR is expected to claim 41.86% of the market in 2032, GNSS and IMUs 26.74%, cameras 22.67% and radar 8.72%.

	2024 ($ mil.)	2028 ($ mil.)	2032 ($ mil.)
LiDAR	$ 270	$ 1,600	$ 7,200
GNSS and IMU	250	970	4,600
Camera	160	700	3,900
Radar	60	270	1,500

Source: "MEMS Industry: The Headwinds from COVID-19 and the Way Forward." [online] from http://www.yole.fr/2020_press_releases.aspx [Press release July 15, 2020], from *Sensors for Robotics Mobility, 2020.*

★ 3035 ★
Servers
SIC: 3571; NAICS: 334111

Leading A.I. Server Makers in China, 2019

Market shares are shown in percent.

Inspur Group	50.8%
Huawei Technologies Corp.	18.4
Sugon	4.9
EngineTech	3.9
PowerLeader Science and Technology Group	3.9
H3C Technologies Co.	3.6
Dell Inc.	3.2
Lenovo Group	3.1
Other	8.2

Source: "IDC Releases 2019 Data for China's A.I. Server Market: Inspur Leads With a Share Over 50%." [online] from https://en.inspur.com/en/2490786/2508991/index.html [Published May 15, 2020], from IDC Infrastructure Data Tracker.

★ 3036 ★
Servers
SIC: 3571; NAICS: 334111

Leading Datacenter Server Providers Worldwide, 2018

A datacenter is a collection of servers that are connected by a network and used to process/compute workloads.

Dell EMC	20.0-30.0%
Hewlett Packard Enterprise	10.0-30.0
Self-build/ODM	10.0-20.0
Cisco Systems Inc.	5.0-10.0
Huawei Technologies Co.	5.0-10.0
IBM Corp.	5.0-10.0
Inspur Group	5.0-10.0
Lenovo Group	5.0-10.0
Fujitsu Ltd.	0.0-5.0
H3C Technologies Co.	0.0-5.0
Nvidia Corp.	0.0-5.0
Oracle Corp.	0.0-5.0
Sugon (Dawning Information)	0.0-5.0
Other	0.0-5.0

Source: "Nvidia/Mellanox Merger Procedure." [online] from https://ec.europa.eu/competition/mergers/cases/decisions/m9424_778_3.pdf [Published December 19, 2019], from Gartner Inc. and Nvidia.

★ 3037 ★
Servers
SIC: 3571; NAICS: 334111

Leading Server Makers in China, 2020

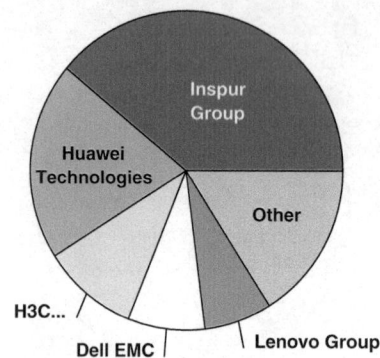

Market shares are shown based on revenues for the first quarter of 2020.

Inspur Group	39.0%
Huawei Technologies	20.0
H3C Technologies Co.	9.5
Dell EMC	8.5
Lenovo Group	7.0
Other	16.0

Source: "China Widens its Lead in China's Server Market." [online] from https://technology.informa.com/AboutUs/Press-Releases [Press release July 30, 2020], from Omdia.

★ 3038 ★
Servers
SIC: 3571; NAICS: 334111

Leading Server Makers Worldwide, 2020

Market shares are shown for the fourth quarter of 2020.

HPE/New H3C Group	16.0%
Dell Technologies	15.5
Inspur/Inspur Power Systems	8.0
IBM Corp.	7.0
Huawei Technologies Corp.	5.6
Lenovo Group	5.5
Other	42.4

Source: *CRN*, March 16, 2021, p. NA, from International Data Corp.

★ 3039 ★
Serviced Apartments
SIC: 7011; NAICS: 72111

Largest Serviced Apartment Operators Worldwide, 2020-2021

Companies are ranked by number of units. The number of serviced apartment units grew 14.75% to 1,174,012.

	Units	Share
Marriott (Worldwide)	153,318	13.06%
Hilton (Worldwide)	91,300	7.78
The Ascott Limited (Worldwide) Inc. Guest Apartment Hotels	86,926	7.40
Intercontinental Hotels Group (Worldwide)	70,353	5.99
Extended Stay America (U.S.)	69,381	5.91
Choice Hotels (USA)	39,860	3.40
Accor Hotels (Worldwide)	35,631	3.03
Oakwood Corp. Housing	35,000	2.98
Pierre & Vacancies (Europe)	24,156	2.06
Frasers Hospitality (Worldwide)	16,462	1.40
Other	551,625	46.99

Source: "The Global Serviced Apartments Industry Report 2020-2021." [online] from http://www.apartmentservice.com [Accessed December 10, 2020].

★ 3040 ★
Sewage Treatment
SIC: 4952; NAICS: 22132

Urban Sewage Treatment Industry in China, 2015-2024

Increased urbanization and industrial development help to drive growth in this market. Figures are in billions of cubic meters.

2015	446.7
2016	494.1
2017	561.9
2018	589.4
2019	616.9
2020	644.1
2021	671.2
2022	699.4
2023	726.8
2024	754.3

Source: "China Sewage Sludge Treatment Market Trends." [online] from http://news.kotra.or.kr [Published September 15, 2020], from China Industrial Information Network.

★ 3041 ★
Sheep and Goats
SIC: 0214; NAICS: 11241, 11242

Sheep and Goat Population by State, 2021

Inventory is shown in thousands of heads as of January 1, 2021. The inventory for sheep and goats fell from 5.2 million in 2020 to 5.17 million in 2021.

	(000)	Share
Texas	730	14.12%
California	555	10.74
Colorado	445	8.61
Wyoming	340	6.58
Utah	285	5.51
South Dakota	245	4.74
Idaho	230	4.45
Montana	200	3.87
Iowa	160	3.09
Oregon	155	3.00
Ohio	126	2.44
Other	1,699	32.86

Source: "Sheep and Goats." [online] from https://usda.library.cornell.edu/concern/publications/000000018?locale=en [Published January 29, 2021], from U.S. Department of Agriculture.

★ 3042 ★
Sheet Metal
SIC: 3444; NAICS: 332322

Sheet Metal Work Manufacturing Leaders, 2017

Data show the percent of industry sales held by the largest 4, 8, 20 and 50 firms in the sector. There are approximately 4,108 players operating in the industry generating employment for 104,797 people.

4 largest firms	8.2%
8 largest firms	12.4
20 largest firms	20.5
50 largest firms	32.0

Source: "Economic Census." [online] from https://www.census.gov/content/census/en/data/tables/2017/econ/economic-census/naics-sector-31-33.html [Accessed January 21, 2021], from U.S. Census Bureau.

★ 3043 ★
Shipping
SIC: 4210; NAICS: 48411, 484121

3PL Revenues by Fortune 1,000 Companies, 2019-2020

The table shows third-party logistics providers' revenues earned by domestic Fortune 1,000 companies.

	2019 ($ bil.)	2020 ($ bil.)	Share
Retailing	$ 40.1	$ 41.2	24.92%
Technological	38.2	36.8	22.26
Health care	15.2	16.0	9.68
Food, groceries	14.8	15.9	9.62
Automotive	16.0	13.5	8.17
Element	13.5	13.2	7.99
Industrial	13.4	13.0	7.86
Consumer goods	7.5	7.8	4.72
Other	8.1	7.9	4.78

Source: *Heavy Duty Trucking*, August 2020, p. 36, from Armstrong & Associates.

★ 3044 ★
Shipping
SIC: 4513; NAICS: 49211

Air Cargo Market by Region, 2019

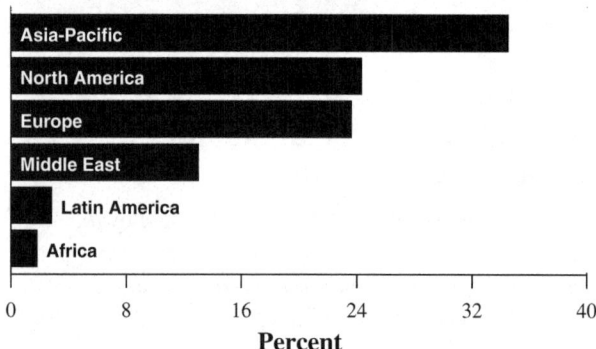

Distribution is shown based on cargo ton kilometers (CTKs). The source analyzes the state of the market in August 2020, when new COVID-19 outbreaks in key markets prompted the industry to shut down airline traffic that had only just started to recover. The overall industry fell 12.6% based on CTKs in August 2020 over August 2019. Latin America saw the largest decline, 27.3%.

Asia-Pacific	34.5%
North America	24.3
Europe	23.6
Middle East	13.0
Latin America	2.8%
Africa	1.8

Source: *Global Cargo Insight*, November-December 2020, p. 13, from International Air Transport Association.

★ 3045 ★
Shipping
SIC: 4432; NAICS: 483113

Cargo Shipping on the Great Lakes, 2019

The U.S.-flag sailing season beat the 5-year average by 4.6% and the 2018 total by 7.5%. Data show the types of cargo shipped on the Great Lakes by U.S.-flag vessels. Figures are in net tons. Sand saw the largest decline over 2018, down 16.2%. However, coal saw the largest decline over the 5-year average period, down 23%. Cement grew 12.8% over 2018, the largest increase; sand grew 12.8% over the 5-year average, the best performance over the same period.

	Net Tons	Share
Iron ore	49,683,474	55.20%
Limestone	24,086,722	26.76
Coal	11,318,946	12.58
Cement	3,288,509	3.65
Salt	923,476	1.03
Sand	413,040	0.46
Grain	289,728	0.32

Source: "2020 State of the Lakes." [online] from https://lca-ships.com/publications/state-of-the-lakes/ [Accessed October 28, 2020], from Lake Carriers' Association.

★ 3046 ★
Shipping
SIC: 4432; NAICS: 483113

Coastal and Great Lakes Freight Transportation Leaders, 2017

Data show the percent of industry sales held by the largest 4, 8, 20 and 50 firms in the sector. There are approximately 581 players operating in the industry generating employment for 17,641 people. According to Kentley Insights, the industry generated sales of $8.3 billion in 2019.

4 largest firms	26.7%
8 largest firms	45.5
20 largest firms	69.9
50 largest firms	89.6

Source: "Economic Census." [online] from https://www.census.gov/content/census/en/data/tables/2017/econ/economic-census/naics-sector-31-33.html [Accessed January 21, 2021], from U.S. Census Bureau.

★ 3047 ★
Shipping
SIC: 4491; NAICS: 48831

Global Fleet by Deadweight Carrying Capacity, 2020

Countries are ranked by deadweight carrying capacity in millions of tons. Figures are based on seagoing vessels of 1,000 gross tons and above, as of January 1, 2020.

	(mil.)	Share
Greece	363.85	24.73%
Japan	233.13	15.85
China	228.37	15.52
Singapore	137.29	9.33
Hong Kong	100.95	6.86
Germany	89.40	6.08
South Korea	80.58	5.48
Norway	63.93	4.35
Bermuda	60.41	4.11
United States	57.21	3.89
United Kingdom	53.19	3.62
Other	2.72	0.18

Source: "Review of Maritime Transport 2020." [online] from https://unctad.org/topic/transport-and-trade-logistics/review-of-maritime-transport [Published November 12, 2020], from United Nations Conference on Trade and Development and Clarksons Research.

★ 3048 ★
Shipping
SIC: 4412; NAICS: 483111

Largest Bulk Carriers Worldwide, 2020

Companies are ranked by kilotons (deadweight tons) transported as of January 1, 2020.

China COSCO Shipping Lines	31,977
NYK Line	15,989
K-Line	13,845
Fredriksen Group	13,529
China Merchants Group	12,922
Star Bulk Carriers Corp.	12,922
Mitsui O.S.K. Lines	11,277
Berge Bulk	11,041
Polaris Shipping Co.	9,120
Oldendorff Carriers	9,043

Source: "NYK Fact Book I 2020." [online] from https://www.nyk.com/english/ir/library/fact/ [Published May 25, 2020], from NYK Line and Clarksons Database.

★ 3049 ★
Shipping
SIC: 4412; NAICS: 483111

Largest Car Transport Operators Worldwide, 2019

Companies are ranked by car capacity as of December 31, 2019.

	Cars	Share
NYK Line	616,015	15.20%
Mitsui O.S.K. Lines	545,309	13.50
Halliburton Co.	524,790	13.00
K-Line	458,371	11.30
Hyundai Glovis Co. Ltd.	444,292	11.00
EUKOR	369,145	9.10
Wallenius Wilhelmsen Ocean	298,655	7.40
Grimaldi Group	269,137	6.70
Toyofuji Shipping Co. Ltd.	77,060	1.90
Sallaum Lines	68,625	1.70
Other	370,015	9.16

Source: "NYK Fact Book I 2020." [online] from https://www.nyk.com/english/ir/library/fact/ [Published May 25, 2020], from Hesnes Shipping AS and *The Car Carrier Market 2019*.

★ 3050 ★
Shipping
SIC: 4449; NAICS: 483211

Largest Inland Barge Operators, 2019

Companies are ranked by number of barges in operation.

	Barges	Share
Kirby Corp.	1,131	28.39%
American Commercial Lines L.L.C.	408	10.24
Canal Barge Company Inc.	339	8.51
MPLX L.P.	293	7.35
Ingram Barge Company	276	6.93
Florida Marine Transporters	270	6.78
Blessey Marine Services	174	4.37
Enterprise Products Partners	154	3.87
Westlake Vinyl PPG	102	2.56
Other	837	21.01

Source: "Kirby Corp. Investor Presentation." [online] from https://investors.kirbycorp.com/static-files/ac9a2956-de22-44fc-89ca-521650772256 [Published August 2020], from Informa Economics Barge Profile.

★ 3051 ★
Shipping
SIC: 4412; NAICS: 483111

Largest LNG Fleets Worldwide, 2020

Companies are ranked by number of vessels delivered by the end of March 2020. LNG stands for liquefied natural gas.

	Vessels	Share
Mitsui O.S.K. Lines	95	12.68%
NYK Line	78	10.41
Nakilat	65	8.68
K-Line	47	6.28
Teekay Shipping	47	6.28
Maran Gas Maritime Inc.	32	4.27
BW LNG	29	3.87
GasLog	29	3.87
MISC Group	29	3.87
Bonny Gas Transport (BGT)	23	3.07
Other	275	36.72

Source: "NYK Fact Book I 2020." [online] from https://www.nyk.com/english/ir/library/fact/ [Published May 25, 2020], from NYK Line.

★ 3052 ★
Shipping
SIC: 4789; NAICS: 488999

Largest Shuttle Tanker Operators Worldwide, 2019

Market shares are ranked by size of fleet, including existing order book.

Knutsen Group	37.0%
Altera Infrastructure	32.0
AET Tankers	17.0
Viken Mol AS	5.0
Other	9.0

Source: "Altera Investor Presentation." [online] from https://cms.alterainfra.com/wp-content/uploads/2020/08/Tap-Issue-AST02G-Investor-Presentation-August-2020-vF.pdf [Published August 2020].

★ 3053 ★
Shipping
SIC: 4412; NAICS: 483111

Largest Tanker Operators Worldwide, 2020

Companies are ranked by kilotons (deadweight tons) transported as of January 1, 2020.

China COSCO Shipping Lines	19,013
China Merchants Group	18,461
Euronav NV	17,490
Bahri	14,444
Angelicoussis Shipping Group Ltd.	14,285
National Iranian Tanker Co.	13,655
Mitsui O.S.K. Lines	12,350
SCF Group	11,720
NYK Line	10,712
Dynacom Tankers Management Ltd.	10,691

Source: "NYK Fact Book I 2020." [online] from https://www.nyk.com/english/ir/library/fact/ [Published May 25, 2020], from NYK Line and Clarksons Database.

★ 3054 ★
Shipping
SIC: 4513; NAICS: 49211

Leading Air Cargo Carriers Worldwide, 2019

Companies are ranked by shipments in millions of scheduled freight ton kilometers. Shares are shown based on sales for the top 25 firms.

	(mil.)	Share
Federal Express	17,503	10.36%
Qatar Airways Group	13,024	7.71
United Parcel Service	12,842	7.60
Emirates Airlines	12,052	7.13
Cathay Pacific Airways	10,930	6.47
Korean Air	7,412	4.39
Lufthansa AG	7,226	4.28
Cargolux Airlines	7,180	4.25
Turkish Airlines	7,029	4.16
China Southern Airlines	6,825	4.04
Other	66,948	39.62

Source: *Air Cargo News*, June 3, 2020, p. NA, from International Air Transport Association.

★ 3055 ★
Shipping
SIC: 4731; NAICS: 48851

Leading Air Freight Forwarders Worldwide, 2019

Companies are ranked by shipments in air metric tons. Shares are shown based on shipments for the top 25 firms.

	MT	Share
DHL Supply Chain & Global Forwarding	2,051,000	13.30%
Kuehne + Nagel	1,643,000	10.65
DB Schenker	1,186,000	7.69
DSV Panalpina	1,071,266	6.95

Continued on next page.

★ 3055 ★
[Continued]
Shipping
SIC: 4731; NAICS: 48851

Leading Air Freight Forwarders Worldwide, 2019

Companies are ranked by shipments in air metric tons. Shares are shown based on shipments for the top 25 firms.

	MT	Share
UPS Supply Chain Solutions	965,700	6.26%
Expeditors Intl.	955,391	6.20
Nippon Express	752,942	4.88
Bolloré Logistics	634,000	4.11
Hellmann Worldwide Logistics	586,670	3.80
Kinetsu World Express	566,814	3.68
Other	5,008,980	32.48

Source: *Air Cargo News*, July 2020, p. 13, from Armstrong & Associates.

★ 3056 ★
Shipping
SIC: 4491; NAICS: 48831

Leading Flags of Registration Worldwide, 2020

Countries are ranked by deadweight tonnage, in thousands. Figures are based on seagoing vessels of 100 gross tons and above, as of January 1, 2020.

	(000)	Share
Panama	328,950	15.95%
Liberia	274,786	13.33
Marshall Islands	261,806	12.70
Hong Kong	201,361	9.77
Singapore	140,333	6.81
Malta	115,879	5.62
China	100,086	4.85
Bahamas	77,869	3.78
Greece	68,632	3.33
Japan	40,323	1.96
Cyprus	34,533	1.67
Other	417,386	20.24

Source: "Review of Maritime Transport 2020." [online] from https://unctad.org/topic/transport-and-trade-logistics/review-of-maritime-transport [Published November 12, 2020], from United Nations Conference on Trade and Development and Clarksons Research.

★ 3057 ★
Shipping
SIC: 4731; NAICS: 48851

Leading Freight Brokerage Firms in North America, 2020

Companies are ranked by gross revenue in billions of dollars. Shares are shown based on revenue generated by the top 100 companies.

C.H. Robinson Worldwide	$ 11.31
Coyote Logistics	4.28
Total Quality Logistics	4.14
XPO Logistics	2.71
Mode Transportation	2.10
Landstar System	1.95
Echo Global Logistics	1.94
J.B. Hunt Integrated Capacity Solutions	1.66
GlobalTranz Enterprises	1.65
Worldwide Express	1.65
Other	125.41

Source: *Transport Topics*, Top 50 Annual, 2021, p. A16.

★ 3058 ★
Shipping
SIC: 4449; NAICS: 483211

Leading Inland Barge Fleet Operators, 2020

Companies are ranked by number of barges under operation.

	Barges	Share
Kirby Corp.	1,131	28.39%
American Commercial Lines L.L.C.	408	10.24
Canal Barge Company Inc.	339	8.51
MPLX L.P.	293	7.35
Ingram Barge Company	276	6.93
Florida Marine Transporters	270	6.78
Blessey Marine Services	174	4.37
Enterprise Products Partners	154	3.87
Westlake Vinyl PPG	102	2.56
Magnolia Marine Transport Co.	98	2.46
Other	739	18.55

Source: "Kirby Investor Presentation." [online] from https://investors.kirbycorp.com/events-and-presentations/presentations [Published August 2020], from Informa Economics.

★ 3059 ★
Shipping
SIC: 4731; NAICS: 48851

Leading Ocean Freight Firms Worldwide, 2020

Companies are ranked by shipments in millions of TEUs. Shares are shown based on shipments by the top 50 companies.

	(mil.)	Share
Kuehne + Nagel	4.52	11.60%
Sinotrans Ltd.	3.77	9.67
DHL Supply Chain & Global Forwarding	2.83	7.26
DSV Panalpina	2.20	5.65
DB Schenker	2.04	5.23
C.H. Robinson Worldwide	1.22	3.13
Ceva Logistics	1.05	2.69
Kerry Logistics	1.02	2.62
Expeditors International of Washington	1.01	2.59
Hellmann Worldwide Logistics	0.95	2.44
Other	18.36	47.11

Source: *Transport Topics*, Top 50 Annual, 2021, p. A20.

★ 3060 ★
Shipping
SIC: 4412; NAICS: 483111

Leading Shipping Alliances, 2020

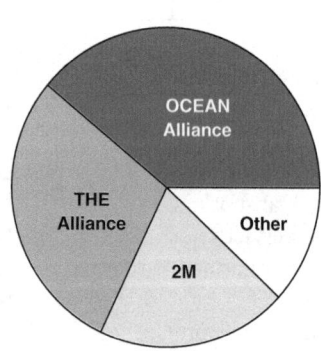

Data show the leading shipping alliances on U.S. shipping routes based on capacity as of June 2020.

OCEAN Alliance	39.0%
THE Alliance	29.0
2M	20.0
Other	12.0

Source: "COSCO Shipping Holding." [online] from http://pdf.dfcfw.com/pdf/H3_AP202008041396393109_1.pdf [Published August 4, 2020], from Alphaliner and CICC Research.

★ 3061 ★
Shipping
SIC: 4412; NAICS: 483111

Leading Shipping Alliances for Asia-Europe, 2019

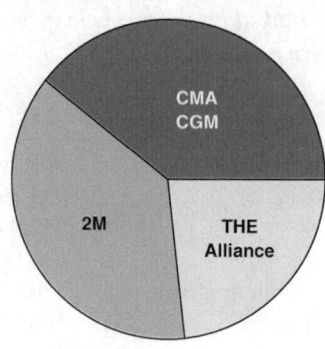

Market shares are shown based on capacity through October 2019.

CMA CGM	39.0%
2M	37.0
THE Alliance	23.0

Source: "News/Ocean Alliance Passes 2M to Take the Lead on Asia-Europe Market Share." [online] from https://theloadstar.com/ocean-alliance-passes-2m-to-take-the-lead-on-asia-europe-market-share/ [Published January 7, 2020].

★ 3062 ★
Shipping
SIC: 4412; NAICS: 483111

Leading Shipping Alliances in Europe, 2020

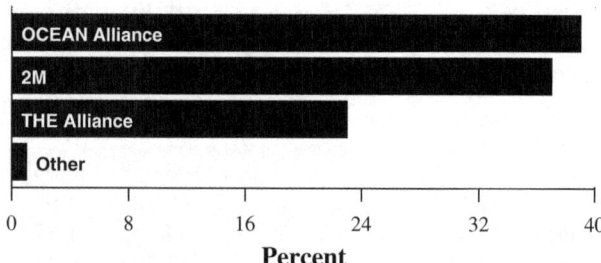

Data show the leading shipping alliances on European shipping routes as of June 2020.

OCEAN Alliance	39.0%
2M	37.0
THE Alliance	23.0
Other	1.0

Source: "COSCO Shipping Holding." [online] from http://pdf.dfcfw.com/pdf/H3_AP202008041396393109_1.pdf [Published August 4, 2020], from Alphaliner and CICC Research.

★ 3063 ★
Shipping
SIC: 4412; NAICS: 483111

Leading Shipping Alliances Worldwide, 2020

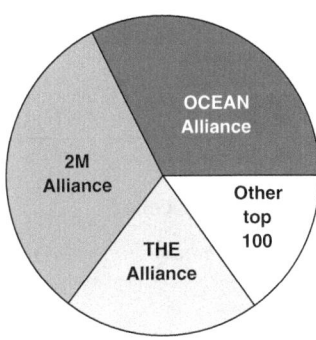

Market shares are shown based on TEUs.

OCEAN Alliance	32.5%
2M Alliance	32.4
THE Alliance	20.2
Other top 100	15.0

Source: "Global Ship Lease Investor Presentation April 2021." [online] from https://www.globalshiplease.com/static-files/a226750c-bb27-45e2-8017-a0183e07ad26 [Published April 2021].

★ 3064 ★
Shipping
SIC: 4491; NAICS: 48831

Leading Terminal Operators Worldwide, 2019

Companies are ranked by throughput capacity in millions of twenty-foot equivalent units.

	(mil.)	Share
COSCO Shipping Lines	141.6	15.64%
PSA International	117.0	12.92
Hutchinson Ports	113.0	12.48
APM Terminals	107.6	11.88
DP World	91.0	10.05
Terminal Investment Ltd.	72.8	8.04
China Merchants Port Holdings Co. Ltd.	44.2	4.88
CMA CGM	43.1	4.76
NYK Line	22.5	2.48
Eurogate GmbH	20.6	2.27
SSA Marine Inc.	20.5	2.26
International Container Terminal Services	20.0	2.21%
Other	91.7	10.13

Source: "Review of Maritime Transport 2020." [online] from https://unctad.org/topic/transport-and-trade-logistics/review-of-maritime-transport [Published November 12, 2020], from Drewery.

★ 3065 ★
Shipping
SIC: 4731; NAICS: 541614

Leading Third-Party Logistics Providers, 2020

Companies are ranked by gross logistics revenue in millions of dollars. Third-party logistics operators generated revenue of $231.5 billion in 2020 and an estimated $246 billion in 2021.

C.H. Robinson	$ 15,490
XPO Logistics	12,107
UPS Supply Chain Solutions	11,048
J.B. Hunt (JBI, DCS & ICS)	9,198
Expeditors Intl.	10,116
Kuehne + Nagel (Americas)	6,789
DHL Supply Chain North America	4,415
Transportation Insights	4,270
Hub Group	3,668
Total Quality Logistics	4,138

Source: *Logistics Management*, June 2021, p. 57, from Armstrong & Associates.

★ 3066 ★
Shipping
SIC: 4215; NAICS: 49211

Package Delivery in China, 2013-2021

Data show the millions of parcels delivered by year. Figures are estimated for 2021. Industry revenue grew from 144.2 billion renminbi in 2013 to 749.7 billion renminbi in 2019. Estimated revenues should reach 751.7 billion in 2020 and 841.3 billion in 2021.

2013	9.2
2014	14.0
2015	20.7
2016	31.3
2017	40.1
2018	50.7
2019	63.5

Continued on next page.

★ 3066 ★
[Continued]
Shipping
SIC: 4215; NAICS: 49211
Package Delivery in China, 2013-2021

Data show the millions of parcels delivered by year. Figures are estimated for 2021. Industry revenue grew from 144.2 billion renminbi in 2013 to 749.7 billion renminbi in 2019. Estimated revenues should reach 751.7 billion in 2020 and 841.3 billion in 2021.

2020	62.6
2021	70.5

Source: "Mobility in China." [online] from https://daxueconsulting.com/ride-hailing-market-in-china/ [Published August 2020], from The Chinese State Post Bureau.

★ 3067 ★
Shipping
SIC: 4215; NAICS: 49211
Package Delivery Leaders in China, 2019

The leading express package delivery firms are shown by market share for the first three quarters of 2019.

ZTO Express	19.2%
Yunda Express	15.8
YTO Express	14.0
Best Express	11.7
STO Express	11.5
SF Express	7.4
Other	20.4

Source: "CICC Yunda Holding." [online] from http://www.pdf.dfcfw.com [Published December 3, 2019], from State Post Bureau and CICC Research.

★ 3068 ★
Shipping
SIC: 4215; NAICS: 49211
Package Delivery Market, 2019

Market shares are shown based on package deliveries.

Federal Express	34.6%
United Parcel Service	26.3
U.S. Postal Service	17.3
Amazon.com Inc.	12.8
Other	8.9

Source: "Parcel Distribution: The Race to Own the Delivery Network." [online] from https://www.interactanalysis.com/parcel-distribution-the-race-to-own-the-delivery-network/ [Published November 11, 2020], from Bank of America Global Research, April 2020.

★ 3069 ★
Shipping
SIC: 4215; NAICS: 49211
Package Delivery Market (Holiday), 2019

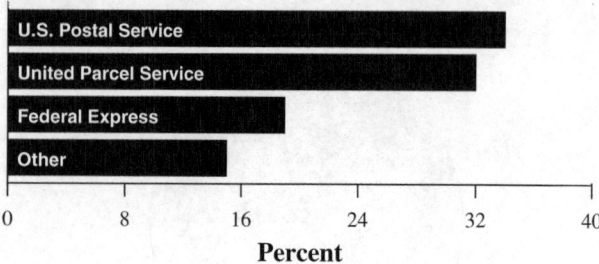

Market shares are shown based on volume of package deliveries.

U.S. Postal Service	34.0%
United Parcel Service	32.0
Federal Express	19.0
Other	15.0

Source: "U.S. Postal Service Adds First Surcharges Ahead of Holiday Rush." [online] from https://www.bloomberg.com/news/articles/2020-08-14/u-s-postal-service-adds-first-surcharges-ahead-of-holiday-rush [Published August 14, 2020], from S.J. Consulting Group.

★ 3070 ★
Shipping
SIC/NAICS: See frontmatter for explanation.
Shipments of Freight, 2012, 2018 and 2045

Figures are in millions of tons. "Multiple modes" includes mail. "Other" includes other, unknown, and imported crude oil with no domestic mode. In 2045 trucks should claim 64.4% of the market, pipelines 18.7%, rail 8.8%, water 3.7%, multiple modes 3.1%, air and truck-air 0.1%, and other modes 1%.

	2012	2018	2045
Truck	10,700	11,920	16,415
Pipeline	3,031	3,346	4,766
Rail	1,797	1,782	2,250
Water	658	838	942
Multiple modes	418	504	800
Air and truck-air	7	6	26
Other	342	221	273

Source: "Pocket Guide to Transportation 2020." [online] from http://www.bts.gov [Published June 2020], from U.S. Department of Transportation.

★ 3071 ★
Ships
SIC: 3731; NAICS: 336611

Largest Shipbuilders Worldwide, 2020

Companies are ranked by revenue in billions of dollars. Worldwide, the shipbuilding market was valued at $120.6 billion in 2019 and is expected to top $175 billion in 2025 due to increasing international trading, rapid industrialization and globalization. As well, advanced technology allowing for energy-saving ships and shipping services will contribute to growth over this time period. The Asia-Pacific region currently garners 82% of the market.

Hyundai Heavy Industries	$ 39.33
CSSC (China State Shipbuilding Corp.)	29.79
STX Offshore & Shipbuilding	16.96
DSME (Daewoo Shipbuilding & Marine Engineering Co. Ltd.)	12.76
Samsung Heavy Industries	8.58
Sumitomo Heavy Industries	6.59
Fincantieri	5.17
United Shipbuilding Corp.	5.10
Tsuneishi Shipbuilding	1.55
Sembcorp Marine Ltd.	1.18

Source: "Current State of the Top Shipbuilding Companies in the World." [online] from https://www.bizvibe.com/blog/top-shipbuilding-companies-world [Published September 22, 2020].

★ 3072 ★
Siding
SIC/NAICS: See frontmatter for explanation.

Global Demand for Siding, 2019

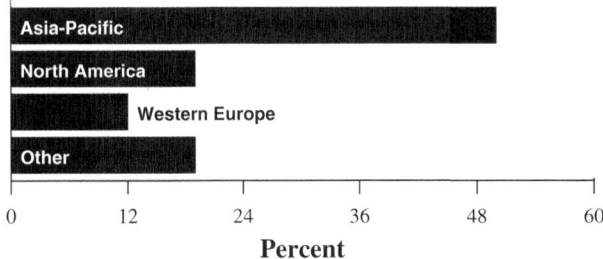

Demand is forecast to see a CAGR of 1.9% from 2019-2024. Growth in the nonresidential market is driving demand for brick, concrete and metal. The popularity of siding materials that imitate higher value materials while also providing additional advantages is also driving demand.

Asia-Pacific	50.0%
North America	19.0
Western Europe	12.0%
Other	19.0

Source: "Global Siding (Cladding)." [online] from http://www.freedoniagroup.com [Published October 2020], from The Freedonia Group Inc.

★ 3073 ★
Sightseeing
SIC: 4119; NAICS: 48711

Scenic and Sightseeing Transportation Leaders, Land, 2017

Data show the percent of industry sales held by the largest 4, 8, 20 and 50 firms in the sector. There are approximately 743 players operating in the industry generating employment for 11,844 people. According to Kentley Insights, the industry generated sales of $1.1 billion in 2018.

4 largest firms	22.6%
8 largest firms	32.9
20 largest firms	47.7
50 largest firms	64.2

Source: "Economic Census." [online] from https://www.census.gov/content/census/en/data/tables/2017/econ/economic-census/naics-sector-31-33.html [Accessed January 21, 2021], from U.S. Census Bureau.

★ 3074 ★
Sightseeing
SIC: 4489; NAICS: 48721

Scenic and Sightseeing Transportation Leaders, Water, 2017

Data show the percent of industry sales held by the largest 4, 8, 20 and 50 firms in the sector. There are approximately 1,863 players operating in the industry generating employment for 16,069 people. According to Kentley Insights, the industry generated sales of $1.9 billion in 2019.

4 largest firms	17.7%
8 largest firms	26.3
20 largest firms	38.0
50 largest firms	51.7

Source: "Economic Census." [online] from https://www.census.gov/content/census/en/data/tables/2017/econ/economic-census/naics-sector-31-33.html [Accessed January 21, 2021], from U.S. Census Bureau.

★ 3075 ★
Signs
SIC: 3996; NAICS: 326199

Methods Used in CAS/Commercial Signs, 2019-2020

Companies that sell CAS/commercial signs sell a variety of products. Most reported selling banners, 89% in 2019 and 85.4% in 2020. Many also sell vehicle graphics, window graphics, floor graphics, magnetic signs, and similar products.

	2019	2020
Vinyl	48.0%	43.0%
In-house digital imaging	38.0	42.0
Wholesale digital imaging	17.0	14.0
Hand-painting	9.0	9.0
Screenprinting	7.0	8.0
Other	20.0	25.0

Source: *Signs of the Times*, December 2020, p. 28.

★ 3076 ★
Signs
SIC: 3993; NAICS: 33995

Sign Manufacturing, 2019

Total shipments were valued at $13.26 billion. The term "nec" stands for not elsewhere classified.

	($000)	Share
Electric signs and displays, including counter, floor, and point-of-purchase displays, scoreboards, and custom trade show exhibits	$ 6,202,567	46.78%
Nonelectric signs and displays	5,450,162	41.10
Construction services for additions, renovations, and alterations to other nonresidential constructions, except buildings	371,539	2.80
Digital printing	232,061	1.75
Fixtures (bank, office, and store), excluding wood	116,856	0.88
Wholesale sales of nonelectric signs and coin-operated games	115,289	0.87
Wholesale sales of store equipment	113,446	0.86
Custom architectural woodwork, millwork, and wood fixtures (including custom wood and plastics laminated fixture tops) (excluding kitchen counters and cabinets and bathroom vanities and vanity tops)	75,784	0.57
Maintenance and repair services for other electronic and precision equipment	$ 55,347	0.42%
Wholesale sales of other goods, nec	55,777	0.42
Fixtures (bank, office, and store), wood, excluding custom	54,482	0.41
Construction services for maintenance and repair of all other nonresidential constructions, except buildings	45,887	0.35
Advertising printing, excluding direct mail (lithographic)	23,977	0.18
Advertising printing (screen), including point-of-purchase, counter, window, and floor display materials, posters, inserts, brochures, etc.	16,746	0.13
Retail sales of other goods, nec	10,849	0.08
Screen printing on garments, apparel accessories, and other fabric articles, excluding labels and banners	10,887	0.08
Wood custom kitchen cabinets and related cabinetwork for permanent installation, excluding those sold directly to the customer at retail	8,187	0.06
Other manufacturing revenue, nec	68,904	0.52
Other service revenue, nec	46,132	0.35
Other household furnishings	30,649	0.23
Other corrugated and solid fiber products, including containers, pallets, pads, partitions, point-of-purchase displays, etc.	20,692	0.16
Other contract manufacturing services, nec	19,121	0.14
Other fabricated metal products	13,853	0.10
Other consumer, institutional, and commercial plastics products, including plastics laboratory ware (petri dishes, flasks, funnels, etc.) (excluding foam and wire-coated)	8,550	0.06
Other	92,256	0.70

Source: "Annual Survey of Manufactures." [online] from https://www.census.gov/programs-surveys/asm/data/tables.html [Accessed March 18, 2021], from U.S. Department of Commerce.

★ 3077 ★
Signs
SIC: 3993; NAICS: 33995

Sign Manufacturing Leaders, 2017

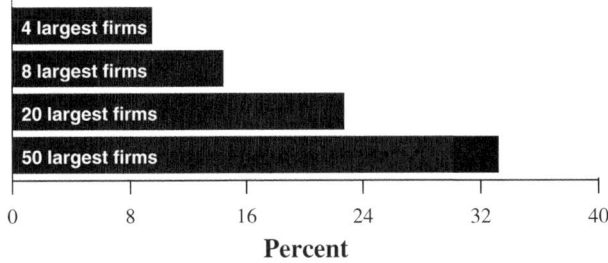

Percent

Data show the percent of industry sales held by the largest 4, 8, 20 and 50 firms in the sector. There are approximately 5,699 players operating in the industry generating employment for 75,195 people. According to Kentley Insights, the industry generated sales of $13.2 billion in 2019. Major sign and billboard producers include Daktronics Inc., Young Electric Sign Co., Brady Corp. and Visual Graphic Systems Inc.

4 largest firms	9.5%
8 largest firms	14.4
20 largest firms	22.7
50 largest firms	33.2

Source: "Economic Census." [online] from https://www.census.gov/content/census/en/data/tables/2017/econ/economic-census/naics-sector-31-33.html [Accessed January 21, 2021], from U.S. Census Bureau.

★ 3078 ★
Silicon
SIC: 3339; NAICS: 33141

Top Silicon Producing Nations, 2020

Countries are ranked by production in thousands of metric tons. In the United States, producers of aluminum alloys and the chemical industry were the main consumers of silicon. Production data are estimated.

	(000)	Share
China	5,400	67.87%
Russia	540	6.79
Brazil	340	4.27
Norway	330	4.15
United States	290	3.65
France	130	1.63
Malaysia	130	1.63
South Africa	96	1.21
Iceland	87	1.09
Bhutan	85	1.07
Spain	66	0.83
Ukraine	60	0.75%
Canada	57	0.72
India	55	0.69
Other	290	3.65

Source: "Mineral Commodity Summaries 2021." [online] from https://www.usgs.gov/centers/nmic/mineral-commodity-summaries [Published January 29, 2021], from U.S. Geological Survey.

★ 3079 ★
Silk
SIC: 0279; NAICS: 11299

Top Silk Exporters Worldwide, 2019

Data show the major exporters of silk. Exports reached $450.5 million in 2019, a 10.5% decrease from 2018.

China	57.8%
Uzbekistan	12.8
Vietnam	12.6
Italy	5.6
India	3.3
Germany	2.1
Romania	1.9
Other	3.9

Source: "2019 International Trade Statistics Yearbook." [online] from https://comtrade.un.org/pb/ [Published December 2020], from U.N. Comtrade.

★ 3080 ★
Silk
SIC: 0279; NAICS: 11299

Top Silk Importers Worldwide, 2019

Data show the major importers of silk. Imports reached $463.8 million in 2019, a 12.7% decrease from 2018.

India	35.4%
Romania	15.6
Italy	12.6
Vietnam	7.7
China	5.1
Japan	4.4
Iran	2.8
South Korea	2.6
Angola	2.4
Germany	2.3
Other	9.1

Source: "2019 International Trade Statistics Yearbook." [online] from https://comtrade.un.org/pb/ [Published December 2020], from U.N. Comtrade.

★ 3081 ★
Silver
SIC: 1044; NAICS: 212222

Industrial Silver Demand Worldwide, 2018-2019

Figures are in millions of ounces. The Silver Institute reports that COVID-19 had a negative effect on this sector during the first six months of 2020. Rising unemployment drove down demand for industrial silver end markets such as autos and consumer electronics.

	2018 (mil.)	2019 (mil.)	Share
China	121.3	121.3	23.74%
United States	124.9	120.8	23.64
Japan	93.6	99.1	19.40
India	40.2	37.8	7.40
Germany	31.2	31.0	6.07
South Korea	19.1	18.4	3.60
United Kingdom	16.6	17.7	3.46
France	9.1	9.3	1.82
Italy	9.1	9.2	1.80
Other	46.4	46.3	9.06

Source: "World Silver Survey 2020." [online] from http://www.silverinstitute.org [Accessed October 25, 2020], from Metals Focus and company reports.

★ 3082 ★
Silver
SIC: 1044; NAICS: 212222

Silver Demand by Application, 2019-2020

Demand is shown in millions of ounces. Data for 2020 are forecasts.

	2019 (mil.)	2020 (mil.)	Share
Industrial	510.9	475.4	49.34%
New physical investment	186.1	215.8	22.40
Jewelry	201.3	187.5	19.46
Silverware	59.8	54.3	5.64
Photography	33.7	30.5	3.17

Source: "World Silver Survey 2020." [online] from http://www.silverinstitute.org [Accessed October 25, 2020], from Metals Focus.

★ 3083 ★
Silver
SIC: 3911; NAICS: 33991

Top Silver Mines Worldwide, 2019

Mines are ranked by production in millions of ounces.

KGHM Polska Miedz (Poland)	40.2
Peñasquito (Mexico)	22.7
Dukat (Russia)	19.3
Saucito (Mexico)	18.3
Antamina (Peru)	16.0
Sindesar Khurd (India)	14.0
Fresnillo (Mexico)	13.0
San Julian (Mexico)	13.0
Cannington (Australia)	12.3
Chuquicamata (Chile)	10.9

Source: "World Silver Survey 2020." [online] from http://www.silverinstitute.org [Accessed October 25, 2020], from Metals Focus.

★ 3084 ★
Silver
SIC: 1044; NAICS: 212222

Top Silver Producing Firms Worldwide, 2018-2019

Companies are ranked by production in millions of ounces. Total production fell from 847.8 million ounces in 2018 to 836.5 million ounces. The top producing countries were, in order, Mexico, Peru and China.

	2018 (mil.)	2019 (mil.)	Share
Fresnillo PLC	58.1	51.8	6.19%
KGHM Polska Miedz	38.7	45.6	5.45
Glencore PLC	34.9	32.0	3.83
Pan American Silver Corp.	24.8	25.9	3.10
Polymetal International PLC	25.3	21.6	2.58
Hindustan Zinc Ltd.	21.2	20.4	2.44
Southern Copper Corp.	17.3	20.3	2.43
Buenaventura	26.3	20.1	2.40
Codelco	18.9	17.9	2.14
Hochschild Mining PLC	19.7	16.8	2.01
Other	562.6	564.1	67.44

Source: "World Silver Survey 2020." [online] from http://www.silverinstitute.org [Accessed October 25, 2020], from Metals Focus and company reports.

★ 3085 ★
Silver
SIC: 1044; NAICS: 212222

Top Silver Producing Nations, 2020

Countries are ranked by production in metric tons. Production data are estimated.

	MT	Share
Mexico	5,600	22.86%
Peru	3,400	13.88
China	3,200	13.06
Russia	1,800	7.35
Australia	1,300	5.31
Chile	1,300	5.31
Poland	1,300	5.31
Bolivia	1,100	4.49
Argentina	1,000	4.08
United States	1,000	4.08
Other	3,500	14.29

Source: "Mineral Commodity Summaries 2021." [online] from https://www.usgs.gov/centers/nmic/mineral-commodity-summaries [Published January 29, 2021], from U.S. Geological Survey.

★ 3086 ★
Silverware
SIC: 3914; NAICS: 33991

Global Silverware Fabrication Worldwide, 2019-2020

Figures are in millions of ounces. Data are forecast for 2020. Demand is expected to fall 9%, almost entirely from a decline in demand from India.

	2019 (mil.)	2020 (mil.)	Share
South Asia	44.9	44.1	76.96%
East Asia	5.0	4.0	6.98
Europe	3.9	3.6	6.28
Middle East	2.4	2.2	3.84
North America	1.9	1.8	3.14
CIS	1.0	1.0	1.75
Other	0.6	0.6	1.05

Source: "World Silver Survey 2020." [online] from http://www.silverinstitute.org [Accessed October 25, 2020], from Metals Focus and company reports.

★ 3087 ★
Skiing Facilities
SIC: 5942; NAICS: 451211

Leading Skiing Facility Operators, 2020

Companies are ranked by revenue in millions of dollars. Figures are for 2020 or latest year available. Industry revenue fell from $3.1 billion in 2019 to $1.9 billion in 2020. Revenue is forecast to reach $2.55 billion in 2027. Vail and Alterra merged in 2020.

Vail Resorts Inc.	$ 2,271.57
Alterra Mountain Company	565.00
Boyne Resorts	400.00
Booth Creek Ski Holdings Inc.	137.55

Source: "Skiing Facilities Industry (U.S.)." [online] from http://www.plunkettresearch.com [Published March 5, 2021], from Plunkett Research.

★ 3088 ★
Skin Care
SIC: 2844; NAICS: 32562

Best-Selling Body Care Brands, 2020

The table shows the leading brands by channel. The source notes that current industry practice is to measure market share using aggregated point-of-sale data. Numerator's TruView system calculates market share by measuring in-store sales, online sales, and emerging retail channels. Figures compare sales at food stores, mass merchandisers, drug stores and club stores with the full omnichannel from February 1, 2020 to January 31, 2021. Bath & Body Works had a point difference of 14.7%, the largest on the list.

	Food, Mass Drug, Club	Full Omnichannel
Gold Bond	10.1%	7.2%
Aveeno	9.1	6.2
Nivea	8.7	6.5
CeraVe	8.5	6.1
Jergens	7.7	5.5
Eucerin	6.4	4.6
Cetaphil	6.3	4.2
Vaseline	6.3	5.0
Bath & Body Works	0.1	14.8
Private label	5.2	3.6
Other	31.6	36.3

Source: "Numerator Launches Omnichannel Market Share Solution." [online] from https://www.prnewswire.com/news-releases/numerator-launches-omnichannel-market-share-solution-301278031.html [Press release April 27, 2021], from Numerator TruView.

★ 3089 ★
Skin Care
SIC: 2844; NAICS: 32562
Skin Care Sales in China, 2019

Skin care sales reached 244.41 billion yuan in 2019, up from 188.13 billion yuan in 2017 and 213.07 billion yuan in 2018. The market can be broken down into several main categories: body care, face care and hand care. Sales are shown in millions of yuan.

	(mil.)	Share
Face masks	¥ 29,028.0	11.88%
Facial cleaners	20,734.6	8.48
Toners	18,751.1	7.67
Mass skin care sets/kits	14,686.5	6.01
Premium skin care sets/kits	5,305.2	2.17
Mass hand care	5,013.6	2.05
General purpose body care	3,335.6	1.36
Lip care	1,996.5	0.82
Firming/anti-cellulite body care	1,820.6	0.74
Premium hand care	1,260.8	0.52
Acne treatments	1,032.0	0.42
Other	141,445.5	57.87

Source: "Chinese Foot Care Market Trend." [online] from http://www.news.kotra.or.kr [Published July 28, 2020], from Euromonitor.

★ 3090 ★
Skin Care
SIC: 2844; NAICS: 32562
Top Acne Treatment Brands, 2020

Market shares are shown based on drug store sales for the 52 weeks ended April 19, 2020.

Neutrogena	14.93%
Differin	11.65
Neutrogena Rapid Clear	6.50
Panoxyl	5.19
Clearasil	3.28
St. Ives	3.01
Aveeno Active Naturals Clear Complexion	2.93
Neutrogena Acne Stress Control	2.32
Neutrogena Clear Pore	2.08
Private label	10.70
Other	37.41

Source: *DrugStore Management*, Annual 2020-2021, p. 79, from IRI.

★ 3091 ★
Skin Care
SIC: 2844; NAICS: 32562
Top Facial Cleanser Brands, 2020

Brands are ranked based on sales at supermarkets, drug stores, mass merchandisers, military commissaries, and select club and dollar chains for the 12 weeks ended November 29, 2020.

	($ mil.)	Share
CeraVe	$ 41.0	11.88%
Cetaphil	25.2	7.30
Garnier Skinactive	18.8	5.45
Bioré	14.4	4.17
Neutrogena	12.9	3.74
Burt's Bees	9.5	2.75
Neutrogena Hydro	8.2	2.38
Thayers	7.2	2.09
Clean & Clear	7.1	2.06
Private label	26.7	7.73
Other	174.2	50.46

Source: *MMR*, January 22, 2021, p. 49, from IRI.

★ 3092 ★
Skin Care
SIC: 2844; NAICS: 32562
Top Facial Moisturizer Brands, 2020

Market shares are shown based on drug store sales for the 52 weeks ended April 19, 2020.

CeraVe	11.79%
Neutrogena Hydro Boost	11.30
Cetaphil	5.55
Aveeno Active Naturals Positively Radiant	4.86
Olay Regenerist Retinol24	4.85
Neutrogena Moisture	4.70
Olay Complete	4.24
Ponds	3.52
Olay Active Hydrating	2.05
Private label	11.15
Other	35.99

Source: *DrugStore Management*, Annual 2020-2021, p. 90, from IRI.

★ 3093 ★
Skin Care
SIC: 2844; NAICS: 32562

Top Hand and Body Lotion Brands, 2020

Brands are ranked based on sales at supermarkets, drug stores, mass merchandisers, military commissaries, and select club and dollar chains for the 12 weeks ended November 29, 2020.

	($ mil.)	Share
CeraVe	$ 41.0	8.53%
Gold Bond Ultimate	28.9	6.01
Cetaphil	22.9	4.76
Jergens	20.2	4.20
Jergens Ultra Healing	17.1	3.56
Nivea	16.1	3.35
Aveeno Active	13.8	2.87
Palmer's Cocoa Butter	12.3	2.56
Vaseline Total Moisture	11.4	2.37
Private label	28.9	6.01
Other	268.0	55.76

Source: *MMR*, January 22, 2021, p. 44, from IRI.

★ 3094 ★
Skin Care
SIC: 2844; NAICS: 32562

Top Skin Care Categories, 2020

Categories are ranked by sales in millions of dollars at supermarkets, drug stores, mass merchandisers, military commissaries, and select club and dollar chains for the 52 weeks ended October 4, 2020.

	($ mil.)	Share
Facial cleansers	$ 1,590.0	37.86%
Facial antiaging	1,090.0	25.95
Facial moisturizers	746.8	17.78
Acne treatments	558.8	13.30
Depilatories	160.9	3.83
Fade/bleach	49.4	1.18
Body antiaging	2.8	0.07
Other	1.3	0.03

Source: *MMR*, November 16, 2020, p. 38, from IRI.

★ 3095 ★
Skin Care
SIC: 2844; NAICS: 32562

Top Sun Care Product Makers, 2020

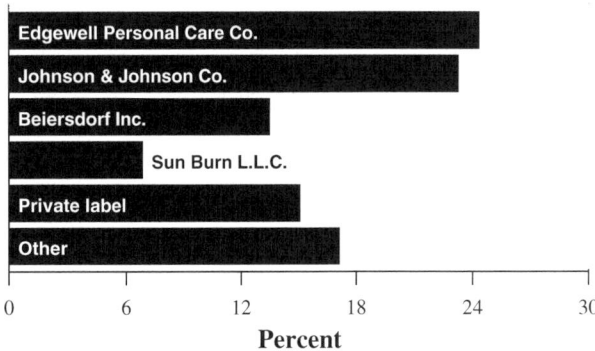

Companies are ranked by sales in millions of dollars at supermarkets, drug stores, mass merchandisers, military commissaries, and select club and dollar chains for the 52 weeks ended December 27, 2020.

	($ mil.)	Share
Edgewell Personal Care Co.	$ 286.44	24.32%
Johnson & Johnson Co.	273.91	23.25
Beiersdorf Inc.	158.60	13.46
Sun Burn L.L.C.	80.51	6.83
Private label	177.15	15.04
Other	201.41	17.10

Source: *Household and Personal Products Industry*, March 2021, p. 62, from Market Advantage TSV and IRI Liquid Data.

★ 3096 ★
Skin Care
SIC: 2844; NAICS: 32562

Top Suntan Lotion/Oil Brands, 2020

Brands are ranked by sales in millions of dollars at supermarkets, drug stores, mass merchandisers, military commissaries, and select club and dollar chains for the 12 weeks ended May 17, 2020.

	($ mil.)	Share
Neutrogena Ultra Sheer	$ 19.4	8.79%
Sun Bum	13.2	5.98
Coppertone Sport	11.6	5.25
Neutrogena Beach	7.7	3.49
Hawaiian Tropic	7.4	3.35
Banana Boat	6.5	2.94
Banana Boat Ultra	6.5	2.94
Private label	28.6	12.95
Other	119.9	54.30

Source: *MMR*, July 13, 2020, p. 30, from IRI.

★ 3097 ★
Sleep Industry
SIC/NAICS: See frontmatter for explanation.

Sleep Industry Sectors Worldwide, 2019

The sleep industry is worth $432 billion annually. Figures are in billions of dollars. "Airplane sleep accessories" refers to pillows and bedding.

	($ bil.)	Share
Bedroom furniture	$ 106	24.54%
Bedding	98	22.69
Mattresses	81	18.75
Pajamas	32	7.41
CPAP devices	25	5.79
Supplements	18	4.17
Medical diagnostic services and devices	15	3.47
Pillows	15	3.47
Sleep technology tracking and monitoring	15	3.47
Sleep services	11	2.55
Ambience optimization	9	2.08
Pet sleep (beds and medicine)	5	1.16
Airplane sleep accessories	1	0.23
Other	1	0.23

Source: "Casper." [online] from http://www.s24.q4cdn.com. CSPR-Investor-Presentation [Published June 2020], from Frost & Sullivan and Global Wellness Institute.

★ 3098 ★
Small Arms and Ordnance
SIC: 3489; NAICS: 332994

Small Arms, Ordnance, and Ordnance Accessories Leaders, 2017

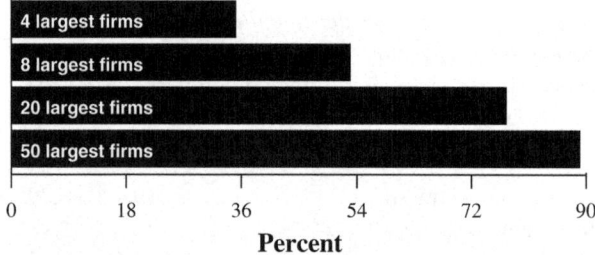

Percent

Data show the percent of industry sales held by the largest 4, 8, 20 and 50 firms in the sector. There are approximately 407 players operating in the industry generating employment for 18,426 people. According to Kentley Insightsl, the industry generated sales of $6.4 billion in 2019.

4 largest firms	35.1%
8 largest firms	52.9
20 largest firms	77.4%
50 largest firms	89.0

Source: "Economic Census." [online] from https://www.census.gov/content/census/en/data/tables/2017/econ/economic-census/naics-sector-31-33.html [Accessed January 21, 2021], from U.S. Census Bureau.

★ 3099 ★
Small Arms and Ordnance
SIC: 3489; NAICS: 332994

Small Arms, Ordnance, and Ordnance Accessories Manufacturing, 2019

Total shipments were valued at $6.65 billion.

	($ 000)	Share
Centerfire pistols and revolvers	$ 1,951,118	29.34%
Parts and attachments for small firearms	872,448	13.12
Machine guns (30 mm or less, 1.18 in. or less)	705,484	10.61
Guns, howitzers, mortars, turrets, parts, and all other miscellaneous ordnance, accessories and related equipment (more than 30 mm (1.18 in.)), including parts	657,930	9.89
Centerfire semiautomatic rifles	614,092	9.23
Rifles, excluding semiautomatic rifles	540,264	8.12
Single barrel shotguns and other small firearms	525,152	7.90
Rimfire pistols and revolvers	156,719	2.36
Electronic teaching machines, teaching aids, trainers, and simulators (including kits)	15,732	0.24
Other	611,061	9.19

Source: "Annual Survey of Manufactures." [online] from https://www.census.gov/programs-surveys/asm/data/tables.html [Accessed March 18, 2021], from U.S. Department of Commerce.

★ 3100 ★
Smart Technology
SIC: 3669; NAICS: 33429

Global Market for Smart Security and Video Security, 2019-2022

Revenue for security and video services are shown in billions of dollars. Figures include commercial and residential.

2019	$ 11
2020	14

Continued on next page.

★ 3100 ★
[Continued]
Smart Technology
SIC: 3669; NAICS: 33429

Global Market for Smart Security and Video Security, 2019-2022

Revenue for security and video services are shown in billions of dollars. Figures include commercial and residential.

2021	$ 17
2022	21

Source: "The Platform for the Connected Home and Business." [online] from http://www.alarm.com [Published August 2020], from IHS Markit.

★ 3101 ★
Smart Technology
SIC: 7389; NAICS: 561439

Self-Service Locker Market in China, 2019

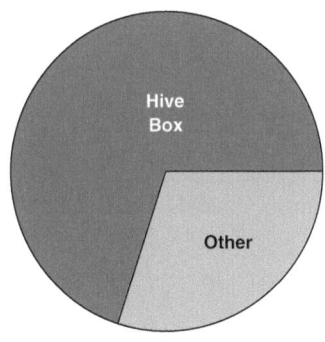

Hive Box is the largest express locker system in the world. The company has 150,000 lockers in China. It also announced its acquisition of China Post in May 2020. The merger gives Hive Box a nearly 70% share.

Hive Box	70.0%
Other	30.0

Source: "A Bumpy Week for China's Logistics Market." [online] from https://technode.com/2020/05/12/a-bumpy-week-for-chinas-logistics-market/ [Published May 12, 2020].

★ 3102 ★
Smart Technology
SIC: 3669; NAICS: 33429

Smart Doorbell Market, 2018

Smart doorbells are the fastest-growing sector of the surveillance camera industry. Amazon purchased Ring in February 2018 for $839 million.

Ring	68.0%
Other	32.0

Source: "Ring Doorbells and the Police: What to Do if Surveillance Has You Worried." [online] from https://www.cnet.com/how-to/ring-doorbells-and-the-police-what-to-do-if-surveillance-has-you-worried/ [Published December 1, 2019], from IHS Inc.

★ 3103 ★
Smart Technology
SIC: 7389; NAICS: 561431

Smart Mailbox Market in China, 2015-2020

In self-service mailboxes, also known as smart mailboxes, couriers log into a mailbox system and then place the delivered item into a suitable mailbox. The system then sends a message to the recipient with a password. The recipient enters the password into the mailbox to obtain the item. Data show thousands of smart mailboxes in China by year. Data are estimated for 2020.

2015	61
2016	102
2017	205
2018	331
2019	534
2020	769

Source: "Mobility in China." [online] from https://daxueconsulting.com/ride-hailing-market-in-china/ [Published August 2020], from http://www.chyxx.com.

★ 3104 ★
Smart Technology
SIC: 3812; NAICS: 334511

Top Smart Agricultural Technology Firms Worldwide, 2019

Market shares are estimated based on revenue. According to the source, smart agriculture "allows farmers to maximize yields using minimal resources such as water, fertilizer, and seeds. By deploying sensors and mapping fields, farmers can begin to understand their crops at a micro scale, conserve resources, and reduce impacts on the environment."

AGCO Corp.	11.00%
Texas Instruments	8.10
GEA Farm Technologies	2.67
Other	78.23

Source: "Global Smart Agriculture Market Report, History and Forecast 2015-2026." [online] from http://www.qyresearch.com [Published August 2020], from QY Research.

★ 3105 ★
Smart Technology
SIC: 3571; NAICS: 334111

Top Smart Home Vendors in Europe, 2020

Market shares are shown based on shipments for the second quarter of 2020. Video entertainment's share of the market is forecast to fall from 52.7% in 2020 to 39.8% in 2024. The smart speakers category will slip from 23.6% to 23.3%, respectively, while lighting will climb from 6.5% to 16.6%. Home monitoring/security will grow from 10.3% to 11.9%, thermostats from 2.6% to 3.3%, and other products 4.3% to 5.1%.

	(000)	Share
Amazon.com Inc.	3,937	19.4%
Google Inc.	3,486	17.2
Samsung Electronics Corp.	2,084	10.3
LG Electronics Corp.	1,736	8.6
Sony Corp.	867	4.3
Other	8,177	40.2

Source: "Despite a Decline in 2Q2020, the Smart Home Market is Expected to Rebound in the Second Half of the Year in EMEA, says IDC." [online] from http://www.idc.com [Press release October 12, 2020], from IDC Worldwide Quarterly Smart Home Tracker.

★ 3106 ★
Smart Technology
SIC: 3651; NAICS: 33431

Top Smart TV Brands, 2019-2020

Shares are shown based on sales.

	2019	2020
Samsung	31.0%	32.0%
Alcatel/TCL	10.0	14.0
Vizio	20.0	13.0
LG	11.0	12.0
Hisense	3.0	5.0
Insignia	3.0	5.0
Sharp	3.0	3.0
Sony	5.0	3.0
Other	14.0	13.0

Source: *Multichannel News*, September 28, 2020, p. 27, from Statista.

★ 3107 ★
Snacks
SIC: 2096; NAICS: 311919

Retail Snack Sales in Western Europe, 2020 and 2023

Retail sales are in millions of dollars. Figures are forecasts.

	2020 ($ mil.)	2023 ($ mil.)	Share
United Kingdom	$12,720.9	$14,372.9	28.11%
France	5,835.7	6,376.3	12.47
Italy	5,142.3	5,601.5	10.95
Spain	5,056.2	5,498.6	10.75
Germany	4,866.8	5,447.3	10.65
Netherlands	2,792.7	3,081.9	6.03
Belgium	1,861.6	1,995.8	3.90
Austria	1,351.6	1,468.9	2.87
Greece	1,298.2	1,438.1	2.81
Denmark	1,062.4	1,208.2	2.36
Sweden	1,056.9	1,205.8	2.36
Other	3,141.7	3,440.0	6.73

Source: "Healthy Snacks in France and Belgium." [online] from https://www.agr.gc.ca/eng/international-trade/market-intelligence/reports [Published May 2020], from Global Data Intelligence.

★ 3108 ★
Snacks
SIC: 2096; NAICS: 311919

Salty Snacks Market, 2020

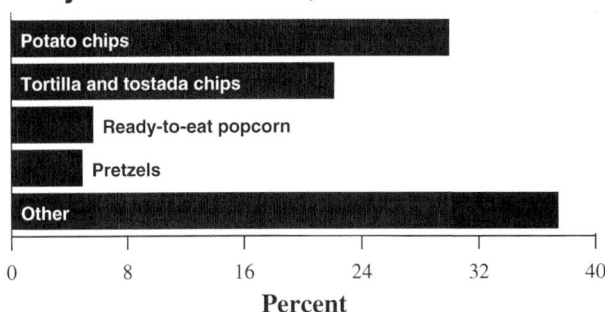

Sales are shown in billions of dollars for the 52 weeks ended May 17, 2020.

	($ bil.)	Share
Potato chips	$ 8.0	29.96%
Tortilla and tostada chips	5.9	22.10
Ready-to-eat popcorn	1.5	5.62
Pretzels	1.3	4.87
Other	10.0	37.45

Source: "Snacking Industry." [online] from https://www.bglco.com/wp-content/uploads/2021/04/BGL-Insider-Special-Report-Food-Beverage-Snacking-Industry-4.8.2021.pdf [Published April 2021], from Packaged Facts.

★ 3109 ★
Snacks
SIC: 2096; NAICS: 311919

Snack Sales in the Gulf Cooperation Council, 2017-2019

The Gulf Cooperation Council countries represent a small region geographically, but these countries are home to 57 million people. The region is linguistically and ethnically diverse, and also contains a significant expatriate population. Sales are shown in millions of dollars. Market share by country in 2019: Saudi Arabia 53.41%, United Arab Emirates 20.77%, Qatar 8.42%, Kuwait 7.39%, Oman 6.46% and Bahrain 3.56%.

	2017 ($ mil.)	2018 ($ mil.)	2019 ($ mil.)
Saudi Arabia	$ 1,793.1	$ 1,801.9	$ 1,831.9
United Arab Emirates	680.6	694.1	712.2
Qatar	271.4	279.1	288.9
Kuwait	$ 233.2	$ 246.6	$ 253.3
Oman	192.2	210.1	221.4
Bahrain	110.7	118.1	122.0

Source: "Opportunities for U.S. Snacks & Sweets in the GCC Region." [online] from https://www.fas.usda.gov/data/opportunities-us-snacks-sweets-gcc-region [Published January 2021], from Euromonitor.

★ 3110 ★
Snacks
SIC: 2096; NAICS: 311919

Top Apple Chip Brands, 2020

Brands are shown based on multi-outlet sales in millions of dollars for the 52 weeks ended June 14, 2020.

	($ mil.)	Share
Bare	$ 15.5	61.02%
Seneca	8.4	33.07
Private label	0.5	1.97
Other	1.0	3.94

Source: State of the Industry - A Supplement to Snac World, August 2020, p. 23, from IRI.

★ 3111 ★
Snacks
SIC: 2096; NAICS: 311919

Top Apple Chip Makers, 2020

Market shares are shown based on sales at supermarkets, drug stores, mass merchandisers, gas and convenience stores, military commissaries, and select club and dollar chains for the 52 weeks ended May 17, 2020. Sales totaled $28.09 million.

Bare Foods Co.	63.62%
Seneca Foods Corp.	31.26
Greene Town Foods L.L.C.	0.97
Martins Family Fruit Farm	0.79
Good Health Natural Products Inc.	0.56
Transnational Foods Inc.	0.34
Private label	1.80
Other	0.66

Source: Snack Food & Wholesale Bakery, July 2020, p. 22, from IRI.

★ 3112 ★
Snacks
SIC: 2068; NAICS: 311911

Top Cheese Snack Brands, 2020

Brands are shown based on multi-outlet sales in millions of dollars for the 52 weeks ended June 14, 2020.

	($ mil.)	Share
Cheetos	$1,329.1	63.61%
Chester's	103.0	4.93
Cheez-It Snap'd	95.8	4.58
Simply Cheetos	94.9	4.54
Utz	82.3	3.94
Whisps	48.7	2.33
Baked Cheetos	37.2	1.78
Wise Cheez Doodles	25.0	1.20
Private label	58.3	2.79
Other	215.2	10.30

Source: *State of the Industry - A Supplement to Snac World*, August 2020, p. 37, from IRI.

★ 3113 ★
Snacks
SIC: 2096; NAICS: 311919

Top Cheese Snack Makers, 2020

Market shares are shown based on sales at supermarkets, drug stores, mass merchandisers, gas and convenience stores, military commissaries, and select club and dollar chains for the 52 weeks ended May 17, 2020. Sales totaled $2.9 billion.

Frito-Lay Inc.	81.18%
The Kellogg Company	3.82
Utz Quality Foods	3.24
Schuman Cheese	1.69
Herr Foods Inc.	1.07
Wise Foods Inc.	1.03
That's How We Roll L.L.C.	0.73
Kraft Heinz Co.	0.57
Golden Flake Snack Foods Inc.	0.40
Private label	2.14
Other	4.13

Source: *Snack Food & Wholesale Bakery*, July 2020, p. 56, from IRI.

★ 3114 ★
Snacks
SIC: 2096; NAICS: 311919

Top Corn Snack Brands, 2020

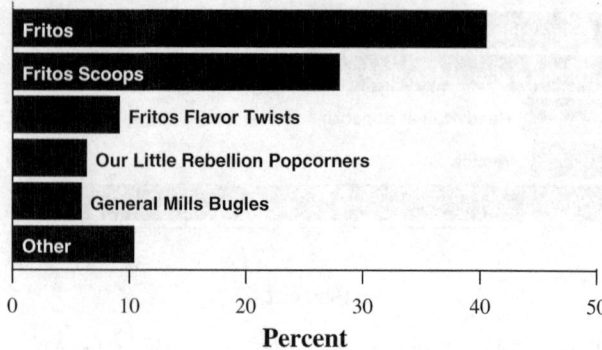

Brands are shown based on multi-outlet sales in millions of dollars for the 52 weeks ended June 14, 2020.

	($ mil.)	Share
Fritos	$369.2	40.47%
Fritos Scoops	255.2	27.97
Fritos Flavor Twists	82.9	9.09
Our Little Rebellion Popcorners	57.3	6.28
General Mills Bugles	53.2	5.83
Other	94.5	10.36

Source: *State of the Industry - A Supplement to Snac World*, August 2020, p. 24, from IRI.

★ 3115 ★
Snacks
SIC: 2096; NAICS: 311919

Top Corn Snack Makers (No Tortilla Chips), 2020

Market shares are shown based on sales at supermarkets, drug stores, mass merchandisers, gas and convenience stores, military commissaries, and select club and dollar chains for the 52 weeks ended May 17, 2020. Sales totaled $1.3 billion.

Frito-Lay Inc.	78.89%
General Mills Inc.	9.35
BFY Brands	4.90
Barcel USA L.L.C.	1.64
Snyder's-Lance Inc.	0.88
Private label	2.06
Other	2.28

Source: *Snack Food & Wholesale Bakery*, July 2020, p. 59, from IRI.

★ 3116 ★
Snacks
SIC: 2096; NAICS: 311919

Top Dried Fruit Chip Brands, 2020

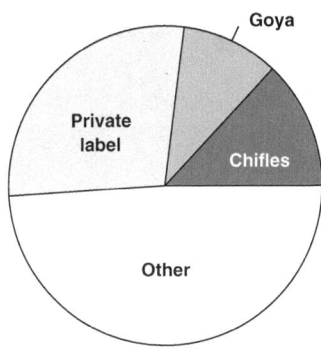

Brands are shown based on multi-outlet sales in millions of dollars for the 52 weeks ended June 14, 2020.

	($ mil.)	Share
Chifles	$ 13.4	13.4%
Goya	10.0	10.0
Private label	27.8	27.8
Other	48.8	48.8

Source: *State of the Industry - A Supplement to Snac World*, August 2020, p. 23, from IRI.

★ 3117 ★
Snacks
SIC: 2096; NAICS: 311919

Top Nutritional Snack Mix/Trail Mix Brands, 2020

Brands are shown based on multi-outlet sales in millions of dollars for the 52 weeks ended June 14, 2020.

	($ mil.)	Share
Kars Sweet N Salty Mix	$ 39.7	4.13%
Second Nature	24.2	2.52
Orchard Valley Harvest	21.7	2.26
Planters Nutrition	21.0	2.19
Private label	565.6	58.89
Other	288.3	30.02

Source: *State of the Industry - A Supplement to Snac World*, August 2020, p. 24, from IRI.

★ 3118 ★
Snacks
SIC: 2096; NAICS: 311919

Top Other Salted Snack Makers (No Nuts), 2020

Market shares are shown based on sales at supermarkets, drug stores, mass merchandisers, gas and convenience stores, military commissaries, and select club and dollar chains for the 52 weeks ended May 17, 2020. Sales in this category (puffed and extruded snacks) totaled $5.03 billion.

Frito-Lay Inc.	66.58%
General Mills Inc.	8.08
The Hain Celestial Group Inc.	4.28
Pirate Brands	1.92
Mondelez International Inc.	1.91
The Kellogg Company	1.78
Utz Quality Foods	1.39
Conagra Brands	1.14
Calbee North America L.L.C.	1.11
Private label	1.99
Other	9.82

Source: *Snack Food & Wholesale Bakery*, July 2020, p. 54, from IRI.

★ 3119 ★
Snacks
SIC: 2096; NAICS: 311919

Top Popcorn Makers (Shelf-Stable, Microwave), 2020

Market shares are shown based on sales at supermarkets, drug stores, mass merchandisers, gas and convenience stores, military commissaries, and select club and dollar chains for the 52 weeks ended May 17, 2020. Sales totaled $848 million.

Conagra Brands	47.67%
Snyder's-Lance Inc.	23.40
American Pop Corn Co.	4.94
SkinnyPop Popcorn L.L.C.	1.87
Angie's Artisan Treats L.L.C.	1.46
Weaver Popcorn Co.	1.34
Ramsey Popcorn Co. Inc.	1.10
Soller L.L.C.	0.64
Newman's Own Inc.	0.50
Private label	15.85
Other	1.23

Source: *Snack Food & Wholesale Bakery*, July 2020, p. 44, from IRI.

★ 3120 ★
Snacks
SIC: 2068; NAICS: 311911

Top Pork Rind Brands, 2020

Brands are shown based on multi-outlet sales in millions of dollars for the 52 weeks ended June 14, 2020.

	($ mil.)	Share
Mac's	$94.7	24.98%
Baken-ets	63.8	16.83
Golden Flake	37.2	9.81
Mission	11.3	2.98
Southern Recipe	8.6	2.27
Turkey Creek	7.7	2.03
Mambi	6.6	1.74
Brim's	6.3	1.66
4505	6.2	1.64
Private label	44.0	11.61
Other	92.7	24.45

Source: *State of the Industry - A Supplement to Snac World*, August 2020, p. 39, from IRI.

★ 3121 ★
Snacks
SIC: 2096; NAICS: 311919

Top Pork Rind Makers, 2020

Market shares are shown based on sales at supermarkets, drug stores, mass merchandisers, gas and convenience stores, military commissaries, and select club and dollar chains for the 52 weeks ended May 17, 2020. Sales totaled $596.9 million.

Frito-Lay Inc.	22.39%
Macs Snacks	16.76
Golden Flake Snack Foods Inc.	10.64
Snyder's-Lance Inc.	4.71
Turkey Creek Pork Skins Inc.	4.65
Rudolph Foods Co.	3.71
Brimhall Foods Co. Inc.	2.34
Carolina Country Manufacturing Inc.	2.02
Mission Foods Inc.	1.88
Private label	8.61
Other	22.29

Source: *Snack Food & Wholesale Bakery*, July 2020, p. 60, from IRI.

★ 3122 ★
Snacks
SIC: 2096; NAICS: 311919

Top Potato Chip Brands, 2020

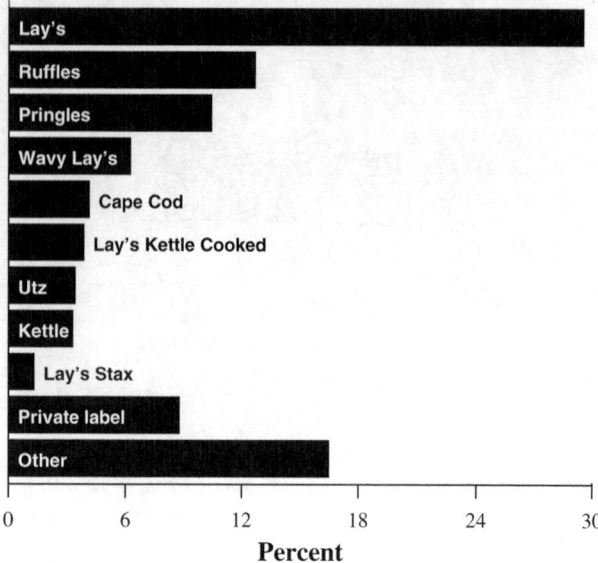

Brands are shown based on multi-outlet sales in millions of dollars for the 52 weeks ended June 14, 2020.

	($ mil.)	Share
Lay's	$1,871.4	29.51%
Ruffles	804.4	12.68
Pringles	660.6	10.42
Wavy Lay's	395.8	6.24
Cape Cod	261.6	4.12
Lay's Kettle Cooked	243.8	3.84
Utz	214.9	3.39
Kettle	206.5	3.26
Lay's Stax	81.9	1.29
Private label	556.2	8.77
Other	1,045.1	16.48

Source: *State of the Industry - A Supplement to Snac World*, August 2020, p. 19, from IRI.

★ 3123 ★
Snacks
SIC: 2096; NAICS: 311919

Top Potato Chip Makers, 2020

Market shares are shown based on sales at supermarkets, drug stores, mass merchandisers, gas and convenience stores, military commissaries, and select club and dollar chains for the 52 weeks ended May 17, 2020. Sales totaled $8.05 billion.

Frito-Lay Inc.	59.79%
The Kellogg Company	11.60

Continued on next page.

★ 3123 ★
[Continued]
Snacks
SIC: 2096; NAICS: 311919

Top Potato Chip Makers, 2020

Market shares are shown based on sales at supermarkets, drug stores, mass merchandisers, gas and convenience stores, military commissaries, and select club and dollar chains for the 52 weeks ended May 17, 2020. Sales totaled $8.05 billion.

Cape Cod	3.82%
Utz Quality Foods	3.72
Kettle Foods Inc.	2.92
Wise Foods	1.40
Herr Foods Inc.	1.39
Snyder's-Lance Inc.	0.80
Zappe Endeavors Inc.	0.77
Private label	7.52
Other	6.27

Source: *Snack Food & Wholesale Bakery*, July 2020, p. 20, from IRI.

★ 3124 ★
Snacks
SIC: 2096; NAICS: 311919

Top Pretzel Brands, 2020

Brands are shown based on multi-outlet sales in millions of dollars for the 52 weeks ended June 14, 2020.

	($ mil.)	Share
Snyder's of Hanover	$411.4	37.66%
Rold Gold	125.1	11.45
Utz	92.7	8.49
Dots Homestyle Pretzels	69.0	6.32
Combos	42.8	3.92
Snyder's of Hanover 100 Cal Pack	22.9	2.10
Utz Specials	17.9	1.64
Herr's	14.7	1.35
Unique Splits	12.0	1.10
Private label	177.6	16.26
Other	106.4	9.74

Source: *State of the Industry - A Supplement to Snac World*, August 2020, p. 24, from IRI.

★ 3125 ★
Snacks
SIC: 2096; NAICS: 311919

Top Pretzel Makers, 2020

Market shares are shown based on sales at supermarkets, drug stores, mass merchandisers, gas and convenience stores, military commissaries, and select club and dollar chains for the 52 weeks ended May 17, 2020. Sales totaled $1.3 billion.

Snyder's-Lance Inc.	36.06%
Frito-Lay Inc.	11.30
Mars Inc.	9.45
Utz Quality Foods	9.09
Dots Homestyle Pretzels	6.34
Herr Foods Inc.	1.56
Unique Pretzel Bakery	1.31
The Bachman Co.	1.06
Old Dutch Foods Inc.	0.94
Private label	17.51
Other	5.38

Source: *Snack Food & Wholesale Bakery*, July 2020, p. 48, from IRI.

★ 3126 ★
Snacks
SIC: 2096; NAICS: 311919

Top Salted Snack Brands (All Other), 2020

Brands are shown based on multi-outlet sales in millions of dollars for the 52 weeks ended June 14, 2020. The market covers "healthy" salted snacks and excludes potato chips, tortilla/tostada chips, cheese snacks, and similar types. Figures refer to puffed and extruded snacks.

	($ mil.)	Share
All Frito-Lay Products	$1,705.1	40.49%
Sunchips	266.7	6.33
Funyuns	241.0	5.72
Chester's	176.3	4.19
General Mills Chex Mix	176.0	4.18
Doritos & Cheetos	157.1	3.73
Sensible Portions Veggie Straw	123.9	2.94
Lay's Poppables	96.7	2.30
Pirate's Booty	94.5	2.24
Private label	97.6	2.32
Other	1,076.5	25.56

Source: *State of the Industry - A Supplement to Snac World*, August 2020, p. 17, from IRI.

★ 3127 ★
Snacks
SIC: 2096; NAICS: 311919

Top Salty Snack Food Makers in Convenience Stores, 2019

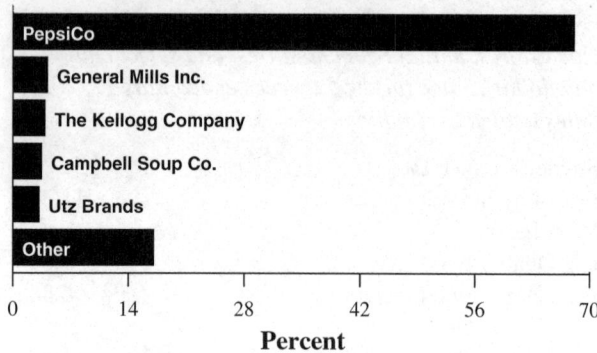

Market shares are shown based on convenience store sales for the 52 weeks ended January 26, 2019.

PepsiCo	68.1%
General Mills Inc.	4.2
The Kellogg Company	3.9
Campbell Soup Co.	3.5
Utz Brands	3.2
Other	17.1

Source: "Utz Brands Collier Creek." [online] from http://www.colliercreekholdings.com [Accessed August 25, 2020], from IRI.

★ 3128 ★
Snacks
SIC: 2096; NAICS: 311919

Top Salty Snack Food Makers in Food Stores, 2019

Market shares are shown based on food store sales for the 52 weeks ended January 26, 2019.

PepsiCo	56.9%
Campbell Soup Co.	7.3
Utz Brands	4.7
The Kellogg Company	3.6
The Hershey Co.	1.9
Other	25.6

Source: "Utz Brands Collier Creek." [online] from http://www.colliercreekholdings.com [Accessed August 25, 2020], from IRI.

★ 3129 ★
Snacks
SIC: 2096; NAICS: 311919

Top Salty Snack Food Makers in Mass Merchandisers, 2019

Market shares are shown based on mass merchandiser sales for the 52 weeks ended January 26, 2019.

PepsiCo	66.3%
The Kellogg Company	4.9
Campbell Soup Co.	3.1
Utz Brands	2.4
Grupo Bimbo	2.1
Other	21.2

Source: "Utz Brands Collier Creek." [online] from http://www.colliercreekholdings.com [Accessed August 25, 2020], from IRI.

★ 3130 ★
Snacks
SIC: 2096; NAICS: 311919

Top Salty Snack Food Makers in Warehouse Clubs, 2019

Market shares are shown based on warehouse club sales for the 52 weeks ended January 26, 2019.

PepsiCo	57.6%
The Hershey Co.	5.3
Utz Brands	4.3
The Kellogg Company	3.8
The Hain Celestial Group Inc.	3.6
Other	25.4

Source: "Utz Brands Collier Creek." [online] from http://www.colliercreekholdings.com [Accessed August 25, 2020], from IRI.

★ 3131 ★
Snacks
SIC: 2096; NAICS: 311919

Top Snack and Bakery Product Makers, 2018-2019

Companies are ranked by sales in billions of dollars. Shares are shown based on sales for the top 25 firms.

	2018 ($ bil.)	2019 ($ bil.)	Share
Nestlé S.A.	$90.8	$101.5	25.77%
PepsiCo	64.7	67.2	17.06
Mars Inc.	35.0	35.0	8.89
Mondelez International	25.9	25.9	6.58
Kraft Heinz Co.	26.3	25.0	6.35
General Mills Inc.	15.7	16.9	4.29

Continued on next page.

★ 3131 ★
[Continued]
Snacks
SIC: 2096; NAICS: 311919

Top Snack and Bakery Product Makers, 2018-2019

Companies are ranked by sales in billions of dollars. Shares are shown based on sales for the top 25 firms.

	2018 ($ bil.)	2019 ($ bil.)	Share
The Kellogg Company	$13.5	$13.6	3.45%
Ferrero S.p.A.	10.7	12.6	3.20
Grupo Bimbo S.A.B. de C.V.	15.0	12.1	3.07
Conagra Brands	7.9	9.5	2.41
Other	77.0	74.5	18.92

Source: *Snack Food & Wholesale Bakery*, December 2020, p. 17.

★ 3132 ★
Snacks
SIC: 2096; NAICS: 311919

Top Snack Food Brands in China, 2018

The industry was valued at 41.1 billion yuan.

Want Want	21.0%
Lay's (Frito-Lay)	16.0
Kirbiker	15.0
Orion	10.0
Oishi (Liwayway Holdings Co.)	7.0
Other	31.0

Source: "China Snack Food Market Trend." [online] from http://www.news.kotra.or.kr [Published May 28, 2020], from Chen Jjanwang.

★ 3133 ★
Snacks
SIC: 2068; NAICS: 311911

Top Snack Nut Brands, 2020

Brands are shown based on multi-outlet sales in millions of dollars for the 52 weeks ended June 14, 2020.

	($ mil.)	Share
Planters	$766.4	17.71%
Wonderful	652.1	15.07
Blue Diamond	489.4	11.31
Emerald	101.0	2.33
Private label	1,678.0	38.77
Other	641.0	14.81

Source: *State of the Industry - A Supplement to Snac World*, August 2020, p. 35, from IRI.

★ 3134 ★
Snacks
SIC: 2068; NAICS: 311911

Top Snack Nut Makers, 2020

Companies are ranked based on sales at supermarkets, drug stores, mass merchandisers, convenience stores, military commissaries, and select club and dollar chains for the 52 weeks ended December 27, 2020.

	($ mil.)	Share
Kraft Heinz Co.	$1,006.76	19.89%
Wonderful Pistachios & Almonds	783.04	15.47
Blue Diamond Growers	548.78	10.84
Frito-Lay Inc.	127.51	2.52
Snyder's-Lance Inc.	123.93	2.45
Hampton Farms Inc.	87.14	1.72
McCall Farms Inc.	51.33	1.01
Star Snacks Co. L.L.C.	27.15	0.54
Century Snacks L.L.C.	23.42	0.46
Private label	1,872.02	36.99
Other	409.39	8.09

Source: *The Manufacturing Confectioner*, February 2021, p. 17, from IRI.

★ 3135 ★
Snacks
SIC: 2068; NAICS: 311911

Top Snack Nut Makers in China, 2017

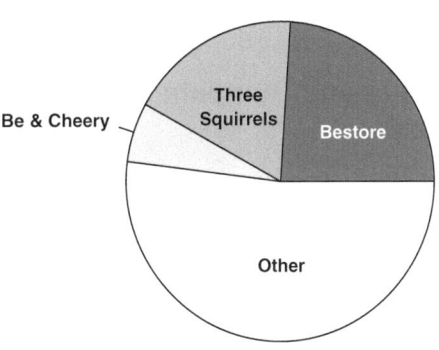

Market shares are shown in percent.

Bestore	23.6%
Three Squirrels	18.2
Be & Cheery	6.1
Other	52.1

Source: *just-food.com*, March 10, 2021, p. NA, from Zhongwei Intelligent.

★ 3136 ★
Snacks
SIC: 2068; NAICS: 311911

Top Sunflower and Pumpkin Seed Brands, 2020

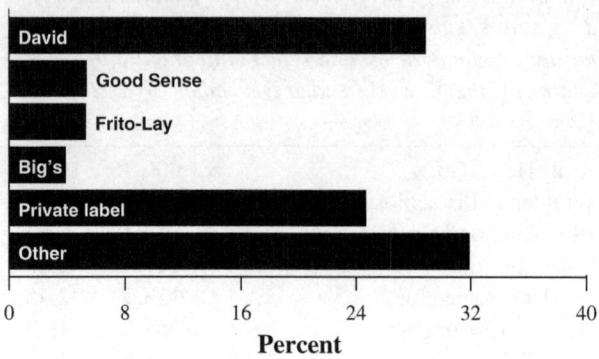

Brands are shown based on multi-outlet sales in millions of dollars for the 52 weeks ended June 14, 2020.

	($ mil.)	Share
David	$ 62.7	28.87%
Good Sense	11.6	5.34
Frito-Lay	11.5	5.29
Big's	8.5	3.91
Private label	53.6	24.68
Other	69.3	31.91

Source: *State of the Industry - A Supplement to Snac World*, August 2020, p. 35, from IRI.

★ 3137 ★
Snacks
SIC: 2068; NAICS: 311911

Top Sunflower and Pumpkin Seed Makers, 2020

Companies are ranked based on sales at supermarkets, drug stores, mass merchandisers, convenience stores, military commissaries, and select club and dollar chains for the 52 weeks ended December 27, 2020.

	($ mil.)	Share
Conagra Brands	$ 145.85	31.23%
Frito-Lay Inc.	97.08	20.78
Thanasi Foods L.L.C.	69.04	14.78
Giant Snacks Inc.	13.88	2.97
Waymouth Farms Inc.	12.60	2.70
International Foodsource L.L.C.	4.29	0.92
Snyder's-Lance Inc.	4.07	0.87
Kraft Heinz Co.	3.56	0.76
Johnvince Foods Ltd.	3.21	0.69
Private label	60.11	12.87
Other	53.38	11.43

Source: *The Manufacturing Confectioner*, February 2021, p. 17, from IRI.

★ 3138 ★
Snacks
SIC: 2096; NAICS: 311919

Top Tortilla/Tostada Chip Brands, 2020

Brands are shown based on multi-outlet sales in millions of dollars for the 52 weeks ended June 14, 2020.

	($ mil.)	Share
Doritos	$ 1,852.9	38.08%
Tostitos	712.0	14.63
Tostitos Scoops	499.9	10.27
Barcel Takis Fuego	294.8	6.06
On The Border	195.9	4.03
Santitas	186.7	3.84
Mission	85.9	1.77
Calidad	75.1	1.54
Late July Organic	60.4	1.24
Private label	311.1	6.39
Other	591.6	12.16

Source: *State of the Industry - A Supplement to Snac World*, August 2020, p. 19, from IRI.

★ 3139 ★
Snacks
SIC: 2096; NAICS: 311919

Top Tortilla/Tostada Chip Makers, 2020

Market shares are shown based on sales at supermarkets, drug stores, mass merchandisers, military commissaries, gas and convenience stores, and select club and dollar chains for the 52 weeks ended May 17, 2020. Sales totaled $5.97 billion.

Frito-Lay Inc.	71.16%
Barcel USA L.L.C.	7.86
Truco Enterprises	3.39
Clearview Foods	1.54
Mission Foods Inc.	1.51
Gruma Corp.	1.28
Dominguez Family	0.68
The Hain Celestial Group Inc.	0.67
Xochitl Inc.	0.46
Private label	5.49
Other	5.96

Source: *Snack Food & Wholesale Bakery*, August 2020, p. 32, from IRI.

★ 3140 ★
Soap
SIC: 2841; NAICS: 325611

Bath and Shower Product Sales, 2019-2021

Sales are shown in millions of dollars. Unilever Home & Personal Care was the leader in 2019 with a 23.2% share, Brand L 16.9% and Procter & Gamble 7.4%. Body wash/shower gel should claim 48.8% of the market in 2021, liquid soap 29.4% and solid soap 21.8%.

	2019 ($ mil.)	2020 ($ mil.)	2021 ($ mil.)
Body wash/shower gel	$3,446.0	$3,546.0	$3,617.0
Liquid	1,931.5	2,127.8	2,179.6
Solid	1,624.8	1,626.9	1,615.7

Source: "Soap and Detergent Market Trends." [online] from http://www.news.kotra.or.kr [Published October 14, 2020], from Euromonitor.

★ 3141 ★
Soap
SIC: 2841; NAICS: 325611

Body Shower Gel Market in China, 2012-2018

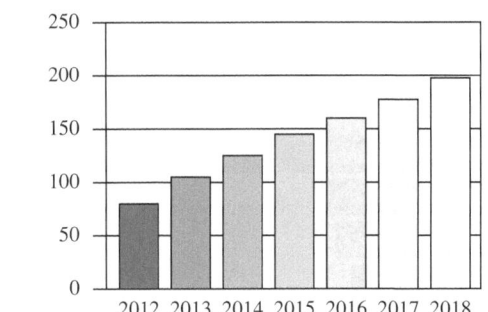

Figures are in billions of renminbi. The body soap market has been growing quickly in China. Safeguard was the leader in the market with a 16.1% share in 2018.

2012	¥ 79
2013	105
2014	126
2015	145
2016	160
2017	177
2018	198

Source: "China Body Shower Gel Market Trends." [online] from http://news.kotra.or.kr [Published September 15, 2020], from Sina.

★ 3142 ★
Soap
SIC: 2841; NAICS: 325611

Top Bath Fragrance/Bubble Bath Brands, 2020

Brands are ranked based on sales at supermarkets, drug stores, mass merchandisers, military commissaries, and select club and dollar chains for the 12 weeks ended November 29, 2020.

	($ mil.)	Share
Dr. Teals	$28.6	34.46%
Dr. Teals Relax & Relief	4.2	5.06
Mr. Bubble	3.6	4.34
Village Naturals Therapy	3.1	3.73
Dr. Teals Restore and Replenish	2.2	2.65
Crayola	1.8	2.17
Dove	1.7	2.05
Bodycology	1.1	1.33
Vicks Vapobath	1.1	1.33
Private label	6.4	7.71
Other	29.2	35.18

Source: *MMR*, January 22, 2021, p. 44, from IRI.

★ 3143 ★
Soap
SIC: 2841; NAICS: 325611

Top Body Wash Brands, 2020

Brands are ranked based on sales in millions of dollars at supermarkets, drug stores, mass merchandisers, military commissaries, and select club and dollar chains for the 12 weeks ended May 17, 2020.

	($ mil.)	Share
Dove	$11.0	3.90%
Cetaphil	3.9	1.38
Softsoap	3.4	1.21
Dove Men+Care	3.1	1.10
Olay	2.9	1.03
Olay Ultra Moisture	2.5	0.89
Dove Deep Moisture	2.4	0.85
Old Spice	2.3	0.82
Nivea	2.2	0.78
Private label	4.3	1.52
Other	244.0	86.52

Source: *Chain Drug Review*, August 10, 2020, p. 106, from IRI.

★ 3144 ★
Soap
SIC: 2841; NAICS: 325611
Top Hand Sanitizer Brands, 2020

Brands are ranked based on sales in millions of dollars at supermarkets, drug stores, mass merchandisers, military commissaries, and select club and dollar chains for the 12 weeks ended May 17, 2020. Sales climbed 119% from the same 12 weeks a year earlier. At drug stores alone, sales jumped 346%.

	($ mil.)	Share
Germ X	$ 9.6	2.01%
Wet Ones	3.6	0.75
Purell Advanced	2.3	0.48
Blumen	0.9	0.19
Purell	0.8	0.17
Soapbox	0.7	0.15
Sunmark	0.7	0.15
Nice N Clean	0.6	0.13
Oralabs Sanell	0.6	0.13
Private label	17.8	3.73
Other	439.3	92.12

Source: *Chain Drug Review*, August 10, 2020, p. 119, from IRI.

★ 3145 ★
Soap
SIC: 2841; NAICS: 325611
Top Liquid Hand Soap Brands, 2020

Brands are ranked based on sales in millions of dollars at supermarkets, drug stores, mass merchandisers, military commissaries, and select club and dollar chains for the 12 weeks ended May 17, 2020. Sales grew 118.5% from the same 12 weeks a year before. Drug store sales alone jumped 197.9%.

	($ mil.)	Share
Softsoap	$ 11.2	2.66%
Mrs. Meyer's Clean Day	5.1	1.21
Dial	4.2	1.00
Dial Complete	3.7	0.88
J R Watkins	2.4	0.57
Method	2.4	0.57
Dr. Bronner's Magic Soaps	2.0	0.48
Raw Sugar	1.4	0.33
Tom's of Maine	0.7	0.17
Private label	5.9	1.40
Other	381.4	90.72

Source: *Chain Drug Review*, August 10, 2020, p. 114, from IRI.

★ 3146 ★
Soap
SIC: 2841; NAICS: 325611
Top Nondeodorant Bar Soap Brands, 2020

Brands are ranked based on sales in millions of dollars at supermarkets, drug stores, mass merchandisers, military commissaries, and select club and dollar chains for the 12 weeks ended May 17, 2020.

	($ mil.)	Share
Dove	$ 9.6	2.99%
Cetaphil	1.7	0.53
Dove Men+Care	1.7	0.53
Dove Go Fresh Cool Moisture	1.4	0.44
Shea Moisture	1.3	0.41
Ivory	1.2	0.37
Dove Purely Pampering	1.1	0.34
Olay	1.0	0.31
Yardley London	0.9	0.28
Private label	0.7	0.22
Other	300.0	93.57

Source: *Chain Drug Review*, August 10, 2020, p. 119, from IRI.

★ 3147 ★
Soap
SIC: 2841; NAICS: 325611
Top Soap Categories, 2020

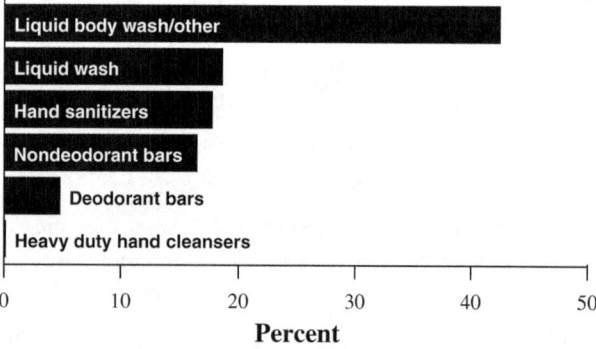

Categories are ranked by sales in millions of dollars at supermarkets, drug stores, mass merchandisers, military commissaries, and select club and dollar chains for the 52 weeks ended October 4, 2020.

	($ mil.)	Share
Liquid body wash/other	$ 2,970.0	42.43%
Liquid wash	1,300.0	18.57
Hand sanitizers	1,240.0	17.72
Nondeodorant bars	1,150.0	16.43

Continued on next page.

★ 3147 ★
[Continued]
Soap
SIC: 2841; NAICS: 325611

Top Soap Categories, 2020

Categories are ranked by sales in millions of dollars at supermarkets, drug stores, mass merchandisers, military commissaries, and select club and dollar chains for the 52 weeks ended October 4, 2020.

	($ mil.)	Share
Deodorant bars	$ 331.3	4.73%
Heavy duty hand cleansers	7.8	0.11

Source: *MMR*, November 16, 2020, p. 33, from IRI.

★ 3148 ★
Soda Ash
SIC: 1474; NAICS: 212391

Soda Ash Demand Worldwide, 2020

Shares are shown based on total world demand of 58.1 million metric tons, down from 61.9 million metric tons in 2019. Demand slowed during the height of the pandemic. The glass industry consumes about 50% of all soda ash. China is the largest flat glass manufacturer in the world. In total, China consumed 26.4 million metric tons of soda ash in 2020.

Flat glass	29.0%
Container glass	18.0
Soaps and detergents	12.0
Metals and mining	4.0
Sodium bicarbonate	4.0
Sodium triphosphate	2.0
Alumina	1.0
Lithium carbonate	1.0
Pulp and paper	1.0
Sodium dichromate	1.0
Sodium percarbonate	1.0
Other glass	5.0

Source: *Glass International*, September 2020, p. 85, from IHS Markit.

★ 3149 ★
Soda Ash
SIC: 1474; NAICS: 212391

Top Soda Ash Producing Nations, 2020

Countries are ranked by production in thousands of metric tons of natural soda ash. In the United States, glass claimed 48% of the end market, chemicals 28%, soap and detergents 6%, distributors 5%, flue gas desulfurization 3%, pulp and paper 1%, water treatment 1% and other uses 8%. Production data are estimated.

	(000)	Share
United States	9,700	69.29%
Turkey	3,400	24.29
Kenya	300	2.14
Botswana	250	1.79
Ethiopia	20	0.14
Other	330	2.36

Source: "Mineral Commodity Summaries 2021." [online] from https://www.usgs.gov/centers/nmic/mineral-commodity-summaries [Published January 29, 2021], from U.S. Geological Survey.

★ 3150 ★
Soft Drinks
SIC: 2086; NAICS: 312111

Leading Soft Drink Firms, 2016 and 2020

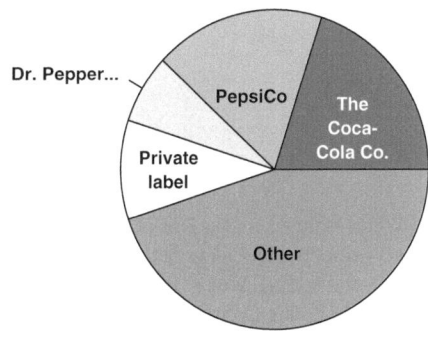

Market shares are shown in percent.

	2016	2020
The Coca-Cola Co.	21.6%	20.0%
PepsiCo	17.9	18.1
Dr. Pepper Snapple Group Inc.	8.5	7.4

Continued on next page.

★ 3150 ★
[Continued]
Soft Drinks
SIC: 2086; NAICS: 312111
Leading Soft Drink Firms, 2016 and 2020

Market shares are shown in percent.

	2016	2020
Private label	9.1%	9.9%
Other	42.9	44.6

Source: "U.S. Consumer Goods: Sector Overview, Credit Trends and Outlook." [online] from https://www.spglobal.com/_assets/documents/ratings/research/100049347.pdf [Published March 2021], from Euromonitor.

★ 3151 ★
Soft Drinks
SIC: 2086; NAICS: 312111
Soft Drink Consumption, 2006-2019

Consumption is shown in millions of gallons.

Year	
2006	15,022.72
2007	14,634.08
2008	14,186.37
2009	13,869.48
2010	13,746.51
2011	13,502.95
2012	13,257.16
2013	12,828.23
2014	12,703.49
2015	12,507.85
2016	12,406.32
2017	12,246.23
2018	12,172.75
2019	12,065.95

Source: "Bottled Water Volume Grows 3.6% Globally." [online] from https://www.foodbusinessnews.net/articles/16071-bottled-water-volume-grows-52-globally [Published May 20, 2020], from Beverage Marketing Corp.

★ 3152 ★
Soft Drinks
SIC: 2086; NAICS: 312111
Soft Drink Manufacturing, 2019

Total shipments were valued at $37.60 billion. The term "nec" stands for not elsewhere classified.

	($ 000)	Share
Soft drinks, carbonated	$ 23,824,042	63.36%
Soft drinks, non-carbonated, fruit drinks, cocktails, and ades, with or without some real juice or concentrates	7,291,708	19.39
Wholesale sales of other goods, nec	2,245,601	5.97
Soft drinks, non-carbonated, iced tea and other types, excluding fruit drinks, cocktails, and ades	2,139,502	5.69
Bottled water, non-carbonated, processed or pasteurized, excluding artificially carbonated and sterile	568,308	1.51
Wholesale sales of soft drinks, bottled water, juices, and nonalcoholic beverages	522,305	1.39
Soft drink flavoring syrup, sold in bulk	338,258	0.90
Canned and fresh fruit juices, nectars, and concentrates	43,843	0.12
Other manufacturing revenue, nec	53,593	0.14
Other	572,836	1.52

Source: "Annual Survey of Manufactures." [online] from https://www.census.gov/programs-surveys/asm/data/tables.html [Accessed March 18, 2021], from U.S. Department of Commerce.

★ 3153 ★
Software
SIC: 7372; NAICS: 334614, 51121

Augmented/Virtual Reality Users, 2019-2023

Data show millions of augmented reality and virtual reality users. Figures cover individuals of any age who experience VR content at least once per month over any device; AR users are individuals of any age who experience AR content at least once per month via any device. Virtual reality includes headset and non-headset users.

	AR	VR
2019	72.8	43.1
2020	83.7	50.2
2021	93.3	58.9
2022	101.6	64.0
2023	110.1	65.9

Source: "U.S. Virtual and Augmented Reality Users 2021." [online] from https://www.emarketer.com/content/us-virtual-augmented-reality-users-2021 [Published April 15, 2021], from eMarketer.

★ 3154 ★
Software
SIC: 7372; NAICS: 334614, 51121

Augmented/Virtual Reality Users by Age Worldwide, 2020

Data show the share of global users of augmented reality (AR) or virtual reality (VR) in the past year by age. Figures are based on a survey of 20,203 digital consumers. This industry is expected to grow as various technical, financial and ethical issues are resolved. Sales of AR headsets are expected to grow from 1 million in 2021 to 23.4 million units in 2025.

15-29	59.3%
30-44	54.5
45-59	33.4
60+	21.7

Source: *Wall Street Journal*, April 7, 2021, p. B4, from Euromonitor International.

★ 3155 ★
Software
SIC: 7372; NAICS: 334614, 51121

Browser Market, 2020

Market shares are shown across all platforms.

Chrome	46.93%
Safari	36.72
Firefox	4.07
Internet Explorer	2.65%
Edge	2.47
Edge Legacy	2.38
Samsung Internet	2.34
Android	0.96
Opera	0.60
Other	0.88

Source: "Browser Market Share United States of America - 2020." [online] from https://gs.statcounter.com/browser-market-share/all/united-states-of-america#yearly-2020-2020-bar [Accessed January 3, 2021], from StatCounter.

★ 3156 ★
Software
SIC: 7372; NAICS: 334614, 51121

Browser Market in China, 2020

Market shares are shown across all platforms.

Chrome	48.19%
UC Browser	13.62
QQ Browser	9.94
Safari	8.86
360 Safe Browser	7.09
Firefox	3.02
Internet Explorer	2.28
Android	1.81
Sogou Explorer	1.77
Other	3.41

Source: "Browser Market Share China - 2020." [online] from https://gs.statcounter.com/browser-market-share/all/china#yearly-2020-2020-bar [Accessed January 3, 2021], from StatCounter.

★ 3157 ★
Software
SIC: 7372; NAICS: 334614, 51121

Browser Market Worldwide, 2020

Market shares are shown across all platforms.

Chrome	64.60%
Safari	17.84
Firefox	4.22
Samsung Internet	3.35
Opera	1.99
UC Browser	1.74
Edge	1.45
Edge Legacy	1.38
Internet Explorer	1.35
Other	2.08

Source: "Browser Market Share Worldwide - 2020." [online] from https://gs.statcounter.com/browser-market-share#yearly-2020-2020-bar [Accessed January 3, 2021], from StatCounter.

★ 3158 ★
Software
SIC: 7372; NAICS: 334614, 51121
Comment System Software Market Worldwide, 2020

Sites are ranked by number of domains using the technology in the Datanyze Universe, which refers to the number of websites tracked by the source.

	Sites	Share
Facebook Comments	216,751	53.45%
Disqus	186,166	45.91
Livefyre	909	0.22
IntenseDebate	671	0.17
Vuukle	315	0.08
Viafoura	284	0.07
Spot.IM	208	0.05

Source: "Comment System." [online] from http://www.datanyze.com/market-share [Accessed November 10, 2020], from Datanyze.

★ 3159 ★
Software
SIC: 7372; NAICS: 334614, 51121
DIY Tax Software Market, 2019

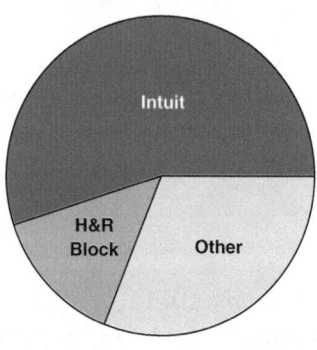

DIY tax preparation represents about 49% of the 136.5 million tax returns prepared during the year (assisted preparation claimed the remaining 51%).

Intuit	55.0%
H&R Block	14.0
Other	31.0

Source: "At-Home Tax Prep Trend Likely to Grow After Pandemic's Boost." [online] from https://news.bloombergtax.com/daily-tax-report/at-home-tax-prep-trend-likely-to-grow-after-pandemics-boost [Published July 10, 2020], from Bloomberg Intelligence.

★ 3160 ★
Software
SIC: 7372; NAICS: 334614, 51121
E-Commerce Software Market Worldwide, 2020

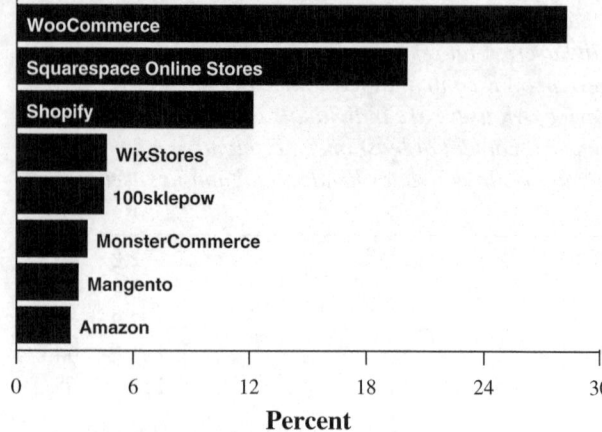

Sites are ranked by number of domains using the technology in the Datanyze Universe, which refers to the number of websites tracked by the source.

	Sites	Share
WooCommerce	620,743	28.21%
Squarespace Online Stores	440,524	20.02
Shopify	267,487	12.16
WixStores	100,962	4.59
100sklepow	98,079	4.46
MonsterCommerce	79,260	3.60
Mangento	68,960	3.13
Amazon	59,868	2.72

Source: "E-Commerce Platform." [online] from http://www.datanyze.com/market-share [Accessed November 10, 2020], from Datanyze.

★ 3161 ★
Software
SIC: 7372; NAICS: 334614, 51121
E-Mail Client Leaders Worldwide, 2021

Market shares are shown as of March 2021.

Apple iPhone	38.0%
Gmail	30.0
Apple Mail	11.0
Outlook	7.0
Yahoo! Mail	5.0
Google Android	2.0
Apple iPad	1.0
Outlook.com	1.0

Continued on next page.

★ 3161 ★
[Continued]
Software
SIC: 7372; NAICS: 334614, 51121

E-Mail Client Leaders Worldwide, 2021

Market shares are shown as of March 2021.

Samsung Mail	1.0%
Window Live Mail	< 1.0

Source: "Email Client Market Share." [online] from https://emailclientmarketshare.com/ [Accessed April 15, 2021], from Litmus Email Analytics.

★ 3162 ★
Software
SIC: 7372; NAICS: 334614, 51121

File Sharing Software Market Worldwide, 2020

Sites are ranked by number of domains using the technology in the Datanyze Universe, which refers to the number of websites tracked by the source.

	Domains	Share
Google Drive	8,833	34.40%
Dropbox	5,453	21.24
Microsoft OneDrive	3,120	12.15
Egnyte	1,746	6.80
Box	1,241	4.83
Jupyter	1,105	4.30
Microsoft Windows SharePoint Services	881	3.43
Huddle	787	3.07

Source: "File Sharing." [online] from http://www.datanyze.com/market-share [Accessed November 10, 2020], from Datanyze.

★ 3163 ★
Software
SIC: 7372; NAICS: 334614, 51121

Global A.I.-Based Medical Image Analysis Software by Application, 2023

Market shares are based on projected revenue of more than $2 billion in 2023.

Neurological imaging	23.0%
Cardiovascular imaging	21.0
Breast imaging	15.0
Lung imaging	14.0
Liver imaging	7.0%
Other	20.0

Source: "A.I. in Medical Imaging to Top $2 Billion by 2023." [online] from https://www.prnewswire.com/news-releases/ai-in-medical-imaging-to-top-2-billion-by-2023-300691229.html [Published August 2, 2018], from Signify Research.

★ 3164 ★
Software
SIC: 7372; NAICS: 334614, 51121

Leading Cloud Infrastructure Firms Worldwide, 2020

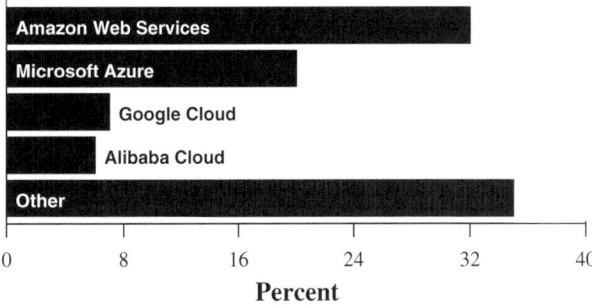

Market shares are shown for the fourth quarter 2020.

Amazon Web Services	32.0%
Microsoft Azure	20.0
Google Cloud	7.0
Alibaba Cloud	6.0
Other	35.0

Source: "Global Cloud Infrastructure Market Q4 2020." [online] from https://www.canalys.com/newsroom/global-cloud-market-q4-2020 [Press release February 2, 2021], from Canalys.

★ 3165 ★
Software
SIC: 7372; NAICS: 334614, 51121

Leading Cloud Infrastructure Service Firms in China, 2020

Fourth quarter spending increased by a record $2.2 billion over the same period in 2019. Market shares are shown for the fourth quarter.

Alibaba Cloud	40.3%
Huawei Cloud	17.4
Tencent Cloud	14.9
Baidu AI Cloud	8.4
Other	18.9

Source: "Record Breaking Spend Grows 62% in Q4 2020 to U.S.$5.8 Billion." [online] from https://canalys.com/newsroom/canalys-china-cloud-services-market-Q4-2020 [Press release March 24, 2021], from Canalys.

★ 3166 ★
Software
SIC: 7372; NAICS: 334614, 51121

Leading CRM Software Firms Worldwide, 2020

Shares of the CRM (customer relationship management) market are shown based on revenue for 2020.

Salesforce.com Inc.	19.5%
Oracle Corp.	4.8
SAP SE	4.8
Microsoft Corp.	4.0
Adobe Inc.	3.8
Other	63.1

Source: *Wall Street Journal*, May 27, 2021, p. A22, from IDC, Worldwide Semiannual Software Tracker.

★ 3167 ★
Software
SIC: 7372; NAICS: 334614, 51121

Leading Data Loss Prevention Software Firms in the EEA, 2018

Market shares are estimated in percent. EEA stands for the European Economic Area, which consists of the European Union and Iceland, Liechtenstein and Norway.

SESB	10.0-20.0%
McAfee L.L.C.	5.0-10.0
Broadcom Inc.	0.0-5.0
Digital Guardian	0.0-5.0
Fidelis Cybersecurity	0.0-5.0
Forcepoint	0.0-5.0
RSA Security L.L.C.	0.0-5.0
Stormshield	0.0-5.0
Venustech Inc.	0.0-5.0
Other	35.0-85.0

Source: "Broadcom/Symantec Enterprise Regulation Merger Procedure." [online] from http://www.ec.europa.eu [Published October 30, 2019], from Form CO and Gartner Inc.

★ 3168 ★
Software
SIC: 7372; NAICS: 334614, 51121

Leading Hyperconverged System Makers Worldwide, 2020

Companies are ranked by revenue in millions of dollars for the first quarter of 2020.

	($ mil.)	Share
VMware	$ 841.2	42.4%
Nutanix Inc.	561.7	28.3
Hewlett Packard Enterprise	$ 101.8	5.1%
Cisco Systems Inc.	85.1	4.3
Other	392.8	19.8

Source: "Worldwide Converged Systems Market Grows 4.5% Year Over Year During the First Quarter of 2020, According to IDC." [online] from http://www.idc.com [Press release June 18, 2020], from IDC Worldwide Quarterly Converged Systems Tracker.

★ 3169 ★
Software
SIC: 7372; NAICS: 334614, 51121

Leading IaaS and PaaS Firms in China, 2019

Market shares are shown in percent for July-December 2019.

Alibaba Cloud	42.0%
Tencent Cloud	12.0
Huawei Cloud	8.0
TianYi Cloud by China Telecom	8.0
Amazon Web Services	7.0
Other	23.0

Source: "Huawei Grabs a Quarter of China's Cloud Management Market in 2019." [online] from https://kr-asia.com/key-stat-huawei-controlled-a-quarter-of-chinas-cloud-management-market-in-2019 [Published June 3, 2020], from International Data Research and Forward Research.

★ 3170 ★
Software
SIC: 7372; NAICS: 334614, 51121

Leading POS Software Firms Worldwide, 2020

Market shares are shown based on 8.1 million installations. Figures are for June 2020.

NCR	16.0%
Proprietary	14.0
Oracle Corp.	12.0
Toshiba Corp.	12.0
Diebold Nixdorf	3.0
GK Software	3.0
Heading	3.0
Aptos Inc.	2.0
Other	35.0

Source: "NCR is the World's Largest Supplier of POS Software." [online] from https://www.rbrlondon.com/press/ [Published November 5, 2020], from Global POS Software 2020 (RBR).

★ 3171 ★
Software
SIC: 7372; NAICS: 334614, 51121
Leading Security Software Firms, 2019

Operators in this industry develop software to protect against spyware, viruses, keylogging, and other computer threats. The industry generated revenue of $17.9 billion.

Symantec Corp.	23.1%
McAfee L.L.C.	8.8
Check Point Software	2.8
Other	65.3

Source: "Security Software Publishing in the U.S." [online] from http://www.ibisworld.com [Published November 2019], from IBISWorld.

★ 3172 ★
Software
SIC: 7372; NAICS: 334614, 51121
Leading Tax Software Makers Worldwide, 2019

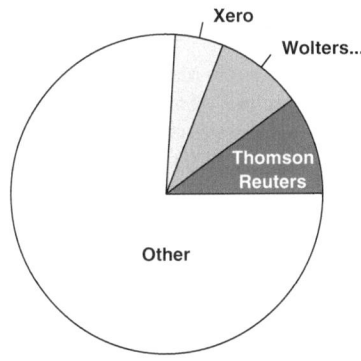

The industry is forecast to grow from $8.36 billion in 2020 to $14.13 billion in 2026. Market shares are shown based on revenue.

Thomson Reuters	10.12%
Wolters Kluwer	8.73
Xero	5.37
Other	75.78

Source: "Global Tax Software Market Research Report 2020." [online] from http://www.qyresearch.com [Published September 2020], from QY Research.

★ 3173 ★
Software
SIC: 7372; NAICS: 334614, 51121
Leading Virtual Data Room Providers, 2019

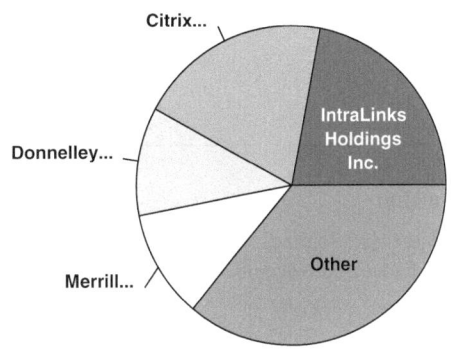

Virtual data rooms provide a secure online space for document sharing and storage solutions for the legal industry, merger and acquisitions, IPOs, bankruptcies, and other financial transactions. The industry generated revenue of $920.3 million in 2019. Revenue grew 7.6% annually during the five years leading up to 2019.

IntraLinks Holdings Inc.	22.1%
Citrix Systems Inc.	20.1
Donnelley Financial Solutions Inc.	11.2
Merrill Corp.	11.1
Other	35.5

Source: "Virtual Data Rooms in the U.S." [online] from http://www.ibisworld.com [Published October 2019], from IBISWorld.

★ 3174 ★
Software
SIC: 7372; NAICS: 334614, 51121
Live Blogging Software Market Worldwide, 2020

Sites are ranked by number of domains using the technology in the Datanyze Universe, which refers to the number of websites tracked by the source.

	Sites	Share
24Liveblog	325	25.71%
ScribbleLive Engage	270	21.36
Live Writer Support	221	17.48
Chatroll	188	14.87
CoveritLive	114	9.02
Liveblog	38	3.80

Continued on next page.

★ 3174 ★
[Continued]
Software
SIC: 7372; NAICS: 334614, 51121
Live Blogging Software Market Worldwide, 2020

Sites are ranked by number of domains using the technology in the Datanyze Universe, which refers to the number of websites tracked by the source.

	Sites	Share
Storify	31	2.45%
Livefyre StreamHub	20	1.58

Source: "Live Blogging." [online] from http://www.datanyze.com/market-share [Accessed November 10, 2020], from Datanyze.

★ 3175 ★
Software
SIC: 7372; NAICS: 334614, 51121
LMS Higher Education Market in North America, 2020

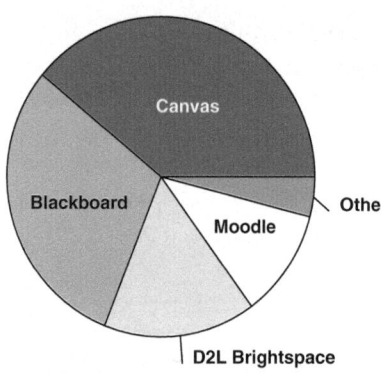

The table shows the leaders in the LMS (Learning Management System) higher education market. Market shares are shown based on enrollment. Based on institution count, however, Canvas claimed 31% of the total, Moodle 24%, Blackboard 23%, and D2L Brightspace 12%.

Canvas	39.0%
Blackboard	30.0
D2L Brightspace	16.0
Moodle	11.0
Other	4.0

Source: "State of Higher Ed LMS Market for U.S. and Canada: Mid-Year 2020 Edition." [online] from https://philonedtech.com/state-of-higher-ed-lms-market-for-us-and-canada-mid-year-2020-edition/ [Published August 12, 2020], from LISTedTECH LMS database.

★ 3176 ★
Software
SIC: 7372; NAICS: 334614, 51121
Operating System Market, 2020

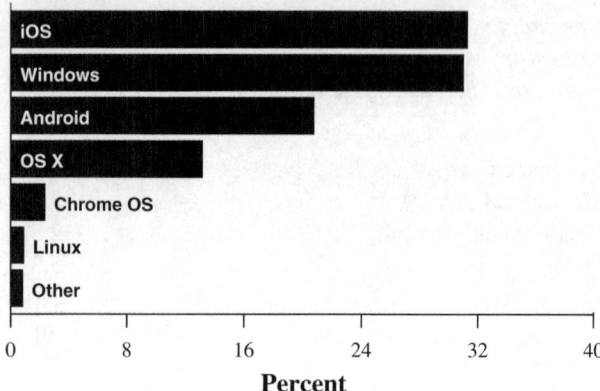

Market shares are shown across all platforms.

iOS	31.25%
Windows	30.98
Android	20.73
OS X	13.15
Chrome OS	2.33
Linux	0.88
Other	0.81

Source: "Operating System Market Share United States of America - 2020." [online] from https://gs.statcounter.com/os-market-share/all/united-states-of-america#yearly-2020-2020-bar [Accessed January 3, 2021], from StatCounter.

★ 3177 ★
Software
SIC: 7372; NAICS: 334614, 51121
Operating System Market in China, 2020

Market shares are shown across all platforms.

Android	49.12%
Windows	33.20
iOS	12.21
OS X	2.97
Unknown	2.17
Linux	0.32
Other	0.02

Source: "Operating System Market Share China - 2020." [online] from https://gs.statcounter.com/os-market-share/all/china#yearly-2020-2020-bar [Accessed January 3, 2021], from StatCounter.

★ 3178 ★
Software
SIC: 7372; NAICS: 334614, 51121

Operating System Market Worldwide, 2020

Market shares are shown across all platforms.

Android	38.80%
Windows	35.07
iOS	15.18
OS X	8.04
Unknown	1.20
Linux	0.81
Other	0.90

Source: "Operating System Market Share Worldwide - 2020." [online] from https://gs.statcounter.com/os-market-share#yearly-2020-2020-bar [Accessed January 3, 2021], from StatCounter.

★ 3179 ★
Software
SIC: 7372; NAICS: 334614, 51121

Operating Systems Worldwide, 2019-2020

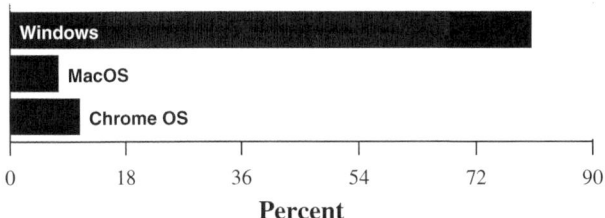

Market shares are based on desktops, laptops and workstations. Chromebooks outsold Macs for the first time in 2020.

	2019	2020
Windows	85.4%	80.5%
MacOS	6.7	7.5
Chrome OS	6.4	10.8

Source: "Chromebooks Outsold Macs Worldwide in 2020, Cutting into Windows Market Share." [online] from https://www.geekwire.com/2021/chromebooks-outsold-macs-worldwide-2020-cutting-windows-market-share/ [Published January 16, 2021], from International Data Corp.

★ 3180 ★
Software
SIC: 7372; NAICS: 334614, 51121

Pre-Employment Assessment Software Worldwide, 2020

Sites are ranked by number of domains using the technology in the Datanyze Universe, which refers to the number of websites tracked by the source.

	Sites	Share
Sterling	3,098	63.13%
eSkill	874	17.81
HackerRank	161	3.28
HireRight	94	1.92
Infor Talent Science	93	1.90
Checkr	68	1.39
SilkRoad RedCarpet	68	1.39
SkillSurvey	65	1.32

Source: "Pre-Employment Assessment." [online] from http://www.datanyze.com/market-share [Accessed November 10, 2020], from Datanyze.

★ 3181 ★
Software
SIC: 7372; NAICS: 334614, 51121

Project Management Software Market Worldwide, 2020

Sites are ranked by number of domains using the technology in the Datanyze Universe, which refers to the number of websites tracked by the source.

	Domains	Share
Jira	33,299	36.24%
Microsoft Project	18,143	19.74
Smartsheet	4,702	5.12
Airtable	4,613	5.02
Trello	2,522	2.74
Kanban	2,461	2.68
Azure DevOps Server	2,221	2.42
Asana	2,013	2.19

Source: "Project Management." [online] from http://www.datanyze.com/market-share [Accessed November 10, 2020], from Datanyze.

★ 3182 ★
Software
SIC: 7372; NAICS: 334614, 51121
Push Notification Software Market Worldwide, 2020

Sites are ranked by number of domains using the technology in the Datanyze Universe, which refers to the number of websites tracked by the source.

	Sites	Share
Onesignal	22,625	77.93%
PushCare	2,822	9.72
PushEngage	1,179	4.06
iZooto	907	3.12
Aimtell	560	1.93
WonderPush	150	0.52
Roost	140	0.48

Source: "Push Notification." [online] from http://www.datanyze.com/market-share [Accessed November 10, 2020], from Datanyze.

★ 3183 ★
Software
SIC: 7372; NAICS: 334614, 51121
Recurring Billing Software Worldwide, 2020

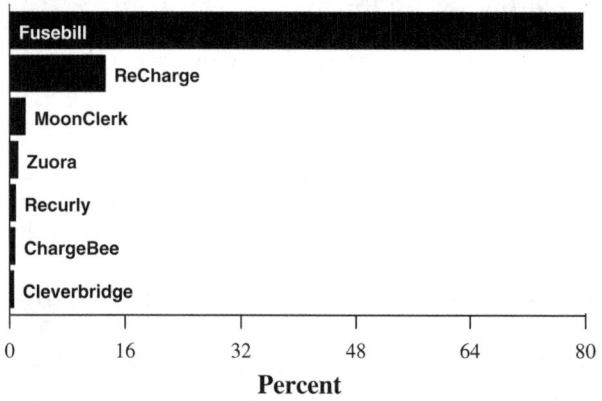

Sites are ranked by number of domains using the technology in the Datanyze Universe, which refers to the number of websites tracked by the source.

	Sites	Share
Fusebill	49,327	79.56%
ReCharge	8,177	13.19
MoonClerk	1,320	2.13
Zuora	691	1.11
Recurly	490	0.79
ChargeBee	443	0.71%
Cleverbridge	329	0.53

Source: "Recurring Billing." [online] from http://www.datanyze.com/market-share [Accessed November 10, 2020], from Datanyze.

★ 3184 ★
Software
SIC: 7372; NAICS: 334614, 51121
Search Engine Market, 2020

Market shares are shown across all platforms.

Google	88.00%
Bing	6.63
Yahoo!	3.40
DuckDuckGo	1.61
Ecosia	0.13
Other	0.23

Source: "Search Engine Market Share United States of America - 2020." [online] from https://gs.statcounter.com/search-engine-market-sharc/all/united-states-of-america#yearly-2020-2020-bar [Accessed January 3, 2021], from StatCounter.

★ 3185 ★
Software
SIC: 7372; NAICS: 334614, 51121
Search Engine Market in China, 2020

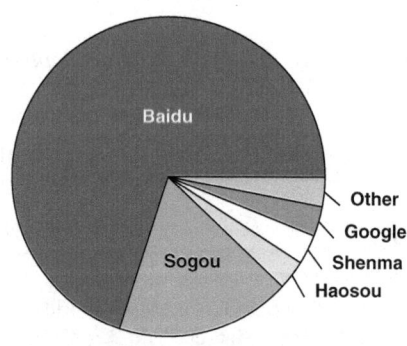

Market shares are shown across all platforms.

Baidu	69.93%
Sogou	18.15
Haosou	3.47
Shenma	3.09

Continued on next page.

★ 3185 ★
[Continued]
Software
SIC: 7372; NAICS: 334614, 51121
Search Engine Market in China, 2020

Market shares are shown across all platforms.

Google	2.83%
Other	2.52

Source: "Search Engine Market Share China - 2020." [online] from https://gs.statcounter.com/search-engine-market-share/all/china#yearly-2020-2020-bar [Accessed January 3, 2021], from StatCounter.

★ 3186 ★
Software
SIC: 7372; NAICS: 334614, 51121
Search Engine Market Worldwide, 2020

Market shares are shown across all platforms.

Google	92.08%
Bing	2.70
Yahoo!	1.63
Baidu	1.16
Yandex	0.60
Other	1.83

Source: "Search Engine Market Share Worldwide - 2020." [online] from https://gs.statcounter.com/search-engine-market-share#yearly-2020-2020-bar [Accessed January 3, 2021], from StatCounter.

★ 3187 ★
Software
SIC: 7372; NAICS: 334614, 51121
Spending on Public Cloud Services Worldwide, 2020-2022

Figures are in millions of dollars. Spending is forecast to reach $270.03 billion in 2020, $332.2 billion in 2021, and $397.4 billion in 2022. Cloud application services (SaaS) should claim 36.57% of the total in 2022, cloud system infrastructure services (IaaS) 26.87%, cloud application infrastructure services (Paa) 17.99%, cloud business process services (BPaaS) 13.36%, Cloud management and security services 4.53%, and desktop as a service (DaaS) 0.67%.

	2020 ($ mil.)	2021 ($ mil.)	2022 ($ mil.)
Cloud application services (SaaS)	$102,798	$122,633	$145,377
Cloud system infrastructure services (IaaS)	59,225	82,023	106,800
Cloud application infrastructure services (Paa)	46,335	59,451	71,525
Cloud business process services (BPaaS)	46,131	50,165	53,121
Cloud management and security services	14,323	16,029	18,006
Desktop as a service (DaaS)	1,220	2,046	2,667

Source: "Gartner Forecasts Worldwide Public Cloud End-User Spending to Grow 23% in 2021." [online] from https://www.gartner.com/en/newsroom [Press release April 21, 2021], from Gartner Inc.

★ 3188 ★
Software
SIC: 7372; NAICS: 334614, 51121
Stock Image Software Market Worldwide, 2020

Sites are ranked by number of domains using the technology in the Datanyze Universe, which refers to the number of websites tracked by the source.

	Sites	Share
Shutterstock	2,169,690	59.20%
iStock	96,526	21.19
Unsplash	16,550	3.63
Adobe Stock	16,153	3.55

Continued on next page.

★ 3188 ★
[Continued]
Software
SIC: 7372; NAICS: 334614, 51121

Stock Image Software Market Worldwide, 2020

Sites are ranked by number of domains using the technology in the Datanyze Universe, which refers to the number of websites tracked by the source.

	Sites	Share
Thinkstock	15,225	3.34%
Fotolia	8,225	1.81
Flickr	7,266	1.59
Stocksy	4,607	1.01

Source: "Stock Image." [online] from http://www.datanyze.com/market-share [Accessed November 10, 2020], from Datanyze.

★ 3189 ★
Software
SIC: 7372; NAICS: 334614, 51121

Strength and Personal Training Platform Market Worldwide, 2020

Tonal has more than 95% of the market for advanced strength and personal training platforms. It combines digital weight management, artificial intelligence and professional coaching. The company is thought to have benefited from the increased number of people exercising at home because of the pandemic.

Tonal	> 95.0%
Other	5.0

Source: "Tonal Announces $110M in New Capital, Building on Its Leadership in Connected Strength Training." [online] from https://www.tonal.com/press/tonal-announces-110-million-in-new-funding/ [Press release September 17, 2020].

★ 3190 ★
Software
SIC: 7372; NAICS: 334614, 51121

Top Acute Care/Health System Electronic Health Record Firms in the EMEA, 2019

EMEA stands for Europe, the Middle East and Africa. The market remains fragmented despite some consolidation in Europe. Most countries primarily have a mix of local and international firms.

Cerner Corp.	15.0%
Dedalus Healthcare Systems Group/Agfa HealthCare Corp.	13.0
Asseco Group	5.0%
CompuGroup Medical	4.0
TietoEVRY Oyj	4.0
Chipsoft B.V.	3.0
DXC Technology Corp.	3.0
InterSystems Corp.	3.0
Nexus Clinical L.L.C.	3.0
Engineering Ingegneria Informatica S.p.A.	2.0
Epic Systems Corp.	2.0
iMDsoft	2.0
System C	2.0
Systematic A/S	2.0
Telekom Healthcare Solutions	2.0
Other	36.0

Source: "EHR Supplier Base in EMEA Consolidates." [online] from https://www.prnewswire.com/news-releases/ehr-supplier-base-in-emea-consolidates-301211306.html [Published January 20, 2021], from Signify Research.

★ 3191 ★
Software
SIC: 7372; NAICS: 334614, 51121

Top Operating Systems Worldwide for Smartphones, 2021-2024

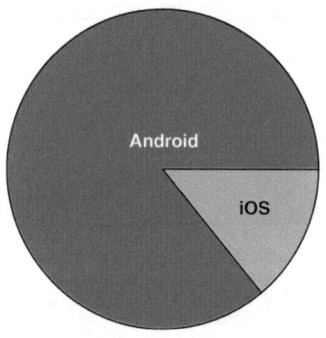

Market shares are shown in percent.

	2021	2022	2023	2024
Android	85.0%	85.3%	85.6%	85.7%
iOS	15.0	14.7	14.4	14.3

Source: "Smartphone Market Share." [online] from https://www.idc.com/promo/smartphone-market-share/os [Published December 15, 2020], from International Data Corp.

★ 3192 ★
Software
SIC: 7372; NAICS: 334614, 51121

Virtual Reality Industry in China, 2021

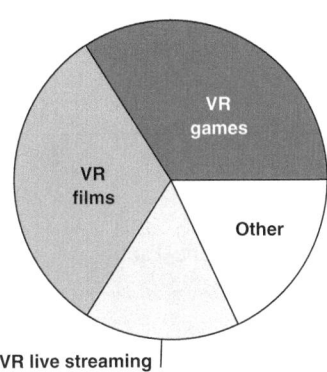

Market shares are forecast. Consumption of virtual reality products is forecast to grow from 3.03 billion yuan in 2018 to 25.13 billion in 2021 to 65.20 billion in 2023.

VR games	34.0%
VR films	32.0
VR live streaming	16.0
Other	18.0

Source: "The Virtual Reality Market in China." [online] from https://daxueconsulting.com/virtual-reality-market-in-china/ [Published April 13, 2020], from Qianzhan.

★ 3193 ★
Software
SIC: 7372; NAICS: 334614, 51121

Website Building Software Market Worldwide, 2020

Sites are ranked by number of domains using the technology in the Datanyze Universe, which refers to the number of websites tracked by the source.

	Sites	Share
Squarespace	491,037	23.43%
Wix	472,290	22.54
GoCentral	284,876	13.59
Weebly	225,374	10.76
Duda	101,409	4.84
Microsoft Frontpage	80,519	3.80

Source: "Website Builders." [online] from http://www.datanyze.com/market-share [Accessed November 10, 2020], from Datanyze.

★ 3194 ★
Sound Recording
SIC: 7389; NAICS: 51224

Sound Recording Studios, 2017

Data show the percent of industry sales held by the largest 4, 8, 20 and 50 firms in the sector. There are approximately 1,863 players operating in the industry generating employment for 5,421 people. According to IBISWorld, the industry generated revenue of $1 billion in 2020. Major players include Paramount Recording Studios and Sterling Sound Inc. No company in this industry has a market share greater than 5%.

4 largest firms	12.0%
8 largest firms	16.3
20 largest firms	25.5
50 largest firms	38.3

Source: "Economic Census." [online] from https://www.census.gov/content/census/en/data/tables/2017/econ/economic-census/naics-sector-31-33.html [Accessed January 21, 2021], from U.S. Census Bureau.

★ 3195 ★
Soup
SIC: 2032; NAICS: 311422

Top Organic Soup Firms, 2018

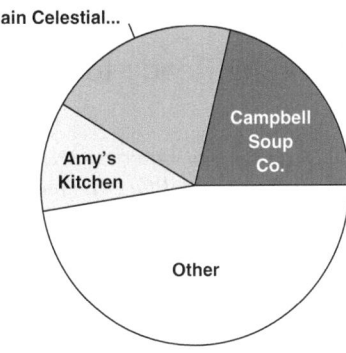

Market shares are shown in percent. Retail sales reached $567.5 million.

Campbell Soup Co.	21.4%
The Hain Celestial Group Inc.	20.1
Amy's Kitchen	11.4
Other	47.1

Source: "Sector Trend Analysis — Organic Market Trend of Corn, Soya, Beans and Wheat Between Canada and the United States." [online] from https://www.agr.gc.ca/eng/international-trade/market-intelligence/reports/?id=1522931721523 [Published July 2020], from GlobalData Intelligence Center.

★ 3196 ★
Soup
SIC: 2032; NAICS: 311422

Top Soup Brands (Condensed), 2020

Brands are ranked by sales at supermarkets, drug stores, mass merchandisers, military commissaries, and select club and dollar chains for the 52 weeks ended July 12, 2020. Figures are in millions of dollars.

	($ mil.)	Share
Campbell's	$1,112.54	69.27%
Campbell's Healthy Request	206.79	12.88
Campbell's Disney Princess	6.76	0.42
Campbell's Light	6.59	0.41
American Beauty	6.07	0.38
Pacific Foods	5.57	0.35
Amy's	5.43	0.34
Campbell's Disney Pixar Incredibles 2	5.48	0.34
Campbell's Disney Frozen	5.10	0.32
Private label	229.48	14.29
Other	16.30	1.01

Source: *2020 Sosland Publishing's Corporate Profiles State of the Industry Report*, October 2020, p. 31, from Information Resources Inc.

★ 3197 ★
Soup
SIC: 2032; NAICS: 311422

Top Soup Brands (Ready-to-Serve), 2020

Brands are ranked by sales at supermarkets, drug stores, mass merchandisers, military commissaries, and select club and dollar chains for the 52 weeks ended July 12, 2020. Figures are in millions of dollars.

	($ mil.)	Share
Campbell's Chunky	$456.31	24.06%
Progresso Traditional	292.63	15.43
Progresso Vegetable Classics	151.88	8.01
Progresso	117.50	6.20
Progresso Light	103.85	5.48
Campbell's Chunky Healthy Request	96.38	5.08
Progresso Rich & Hearty	88.30	4.66
Amy's	79.80	4.21
Campbell's	54.61	2.88
Private label	57.70	3.04
Other	397.46	20.96

Source: *2020 Sosland Publishing's Corporate Profiles State of the Industry Report*, October 2020, p. 30, from Information Resources Inc.

★ 3198 ★
Sour Cream
SIC: 2026; NAICS: 311511

Top Sour Cream Brands, 2020

Brands are ranked based on sales at supermarkets, drug stores, mass merchandisers, military commissaries, and select club and dollar chains for the 52 weeks ended September 6, 2020.

	($ mil.)	Share
Daisy Brand	$756.6	54.09%
Breakstone's	63.2	4.52
Knudsen	35.8	2.56
Mid-America Farms Top the Tater	13.0	0.93
Cacique	12.6	0.90
All Dean Foods brands	12.1	0.87
Hood	11.3	0.81
Kemps	8.4	0.60
Friendship	8.0	0.57
Private label	350.6	25.07
Other	127.1	9.09

Source: *Dairy Foods*, November 2020, p. 51, from IRI.

★ 3199 ★
Space Industry
SIC: 9661; NAICS: 92711

Space Budgets Worldwide, 2020

Figures are in billions of dollars.

	($ bil.)	Share
United States	$43.01	57.47%
China	8.16	10.90
Russia	3.37	4.50
France	3.30	4.41
Japan	3.30	4.41
Germany	2.21	2.95
India	1.94	2.59
Italy	1.13	1.51
United Kingdom	1.00	1.34
Spain	0.40	0.53
Other European Union	1.93	2.58
Other Europe	1.51	2.02
Other	3.58	4.78

Source: "ESPI Yearbook 2020." [online] from https://espi.or.at/publications/espi-yearbook [Accessed June 15, 2021], from European Space Policy Institute and Euroconsult.

★ 3200 ★
Spas
SIC: 7991; NAICS: 71394

Health and Wellness Spa Industry Revenue, 2020

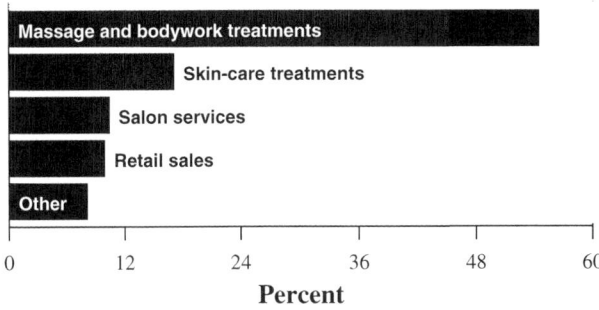

The industry generated revenue of $46.3 billion in 2020. Revenue grew 2.1% annually during the five years leading up to 2020. An estimated 190 million spa visits occurred in 2018, according to the International Spa Association.

Massage and bodywork treatments	54.5%
Skin-care treatments	17.1
Salon services	10.4
Retail sales	9.9
Other	8.1

Source: "Health and Wellness Spas in the U.S." [online] from http://www.ibisworld.com [Published February 2020], from IBISWorld.

★ 3201 ★
Special Die and Tools, Die Set, Jigs and Fixtures
SIC: 3544; NAICS: 333514

Special Die and Tool, Die Set, Jig and Fixture Manufacturing Leaders, 2017

Data show the percent of industry sales held by the largest 4, 8, 20 and 50 firms in the sector. There are approximately 2,343 players operating in the industry generating employment for 44,604 people. According to Kentley Insights, the industry generated sales of $9.4 billion in 2019.

4 largest firms	21.0%
8 largest firms	28.0
20 largest firms	37.4
50 largest firms	47.8

Source: "Economic Census." [online] from https://www.census.gov/content/census/en/data/tables/2017/econ/economic-census/naics-sector-31-33.html [Accessed January 21, 2021], from U.S. Census Bureau.

★ 3202 ★
Specialized Storage and Warehousing
SIC: 4226; NAICS: 49319

Specialized Storage and Warehousing Industry Revenue, 2019

Specialized storage and warehousing excludes general merchandise, refrigerated and farm product warehousing or storage. The industry generated revenue of $8.1 billion in 2019. Bulk petroleum and chemical storage claimed 71% of the total, bulk storage 13%, and other sectors 16%.

Kinder Morgan Inc.	25.4%
Iron Mountain Inc.	20.1
Sunoco Inc.	6.6
Apex Oil Company Inc.	5.6
Other	42.3

Source: "Specialized Storage and Warehousing in the U.S." [online] from http://www.ibisworld.com [Published December 2019], from IBISWorld.

★ 3203 ★
Spices and Extracts
SIC: 2099; NAICS: 311942

Spice and Extract Manufacturing, 2019

Total shipments were valued at $13.08 billion. The term "nec" stands for not elsewhere classified. "Smelting and refining materials" are owned by others on a toll basis. "Bread-type" includes rolls, croissants and English muffins. "Prepared sauces" includes mustard, Worcestershire, soy, horseradish, and other sauces to be used as a condiment to meat, vegetable, and seafood, but excludes tomato and meat-based sauces.

	($ 000)	Share
Flavoring extracts, emulsions, and other liquid flavors and food colorings (excluding synthetic)	$ 3,844,208	29.39%
Dry mix food preparations, nec, including dip, salad dressing, seasoning, frosting, gravy, and sauce dry mixes	3,588,638	27.44
Pepper, white and black, and other spices in consumer sizes (less than 1 lb)	3,458,739	26.44
Pepper, white and black, and other spices in commercial sizes (1 lb or more)	682,785	5.22
Flavoring powders, tablets, and paste (inc. dry mix cocktails)	423,050	3.23

Continued on next page.

★ 3203 ★
[Continued]
Spices and Extracts
SIC: 2099; NAICS: 311942

Spice and Extract Manufacturing, 2019

Total shipments were valued at $13.08 billion. The term "nec" stands for not elsewhere classified. "Smelting and refining materials" are owned by others on a toll basis. "Bread-type" includes rolls, croissants and English muffins. "Prepared sauces" includes mustard, Worcestershire, soy, horseradish, and other sauces to be used as a condiment to meat, vegetable, and seafood, but excludes tomato and meat-based sauces.

	($ 000)	Share
Wholesale sales of other goods, nec	$ 253,859	1.94%
Table salt	148,866	1.14
Prepared sauces	112,459	0.86
Wholesale sales of confectionery and snack foods	20,754	0.16
Bread (white, wheat, rye, etc.) and rolls, bread-type, including frozen	16,817	0.13
Smelting and refining materials	1,566	0.01
Other food and beverage contract manufacturing services	50,628	0.39
Other manufacturing revenue, nec	17,352	0.13
Other contract manufacturing services, nec	12,043	0.09
Other	448,236	3.43

Source: "Annual Survey of Manufactures." [online] from https://www.census.gov/programs-surveys/asm/data/tables.html [Accessed March 18, 2021], from U.S. Department of Commerce.

★ 3204 ★
Spices and Extracts
SIC: 2099; NAICS: 311942

Spice and Extract Manufacturing Leaders, 2017

Data show the percent of industry sales held by the largest 4, 8, 20 and 50 firms in the sector. There are approximately 420 players operating in the industry generating employment for 19,872 people. According to Kentley Insights, the industry generated sales of $12.6 billion in 2019.

4 largest firms	31.4%
8 largest firms	40.6
20 largest firms	58.5%
50 largest firms	79.6

Source: "Economic Census." [online] from https://www.census.gov/content/census/en/data/tables/2017/econ/economic-census/naics-sector-31-33.html [Accessed January 21, 2021], from U.S. Census Bureau.

★ 3205 ★
Sporting Goods
SIC: 3949; NAICS: 33992

Best-Selling Hardgoods at Specialty Outdoor Stores, 2020

Data show the best-selling hardgoods at specialty outdoor retailers. Figures are based on a survey. "Other" includes alpine ski, climbing, coolers, helmets, cross-country skis, and other categories.

Cycling	25.8%
Paddlesports	25.8
Backpacks	13.5
Camping	9.0
Backcountry ski	7.9
Other	18.0

Source: *The Voice*, Winter 2021, p. 24, from survey by source.

★ 3206 ★
Sporting Goods
SIC: 3949; NAICS: 33992

Best-Selling Softgoods at Specialty Outdoor Stores, 2020

Data show the best-selling softgoods at specialty outdoor retailers. Figures are based on a survey. "Other" includes accessories, gloves, hats, rain wear, socks, swimwear, and other categories.

Men's sportswear	17.5%
Footwear	11.3
Men's lifestyle	10.0
Outerwear	10.0
Women's sportswear	10.0
Other	41.2

Source: *The Voice*, Winter 2021, p. 24, from survey by source.

★ 3207 ★
Sporting Goods
SIC: 3949; NAICS: 33992

Leading Casting Fishing Rod Makers Worldwide, 2019

The industry is forecast to grow from $331.7 million in 2019 to $435.5 million in 2026. Market shares are shown based on revenue.

Daiwa Seiko Corp.	16.52%
Pure Fishing Inc.	13.84
Shimano Inc.	10.03
Other	59.61

Source: "Global Casting Fishing Rods Market Size, Manufacturers, Supply Chain, Sales Channel and Clients, 2020-2026." [online] from http://www.qyresearch.com [Published July 2020], from QY Research.

★ 3208 ★
Sporting Goods
SIC: 3949; NAICS: 33992

Leading Ski Touring Bindings Makers Worldwide, 2019

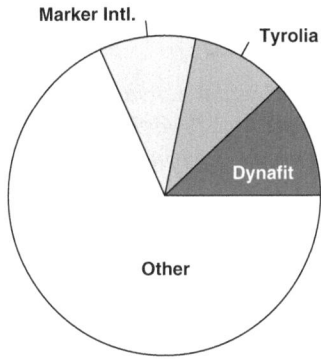

The market is forecast to climb from $103.2 million in 2019 to $117.9 million in 2026. Market shares are shown based on revenue.

Dynafit	11.80%
Tyrolia	9.74
Marker Intl.	9.72
Other	68.74

Source: "Global Ski Touring Binding Market Research Report 2020." [online] from http://www.qyresearch.com [Published September 2020], from QY Research.

★ 3209 ★
Sporting Goods
SIC: 3949; NAICS: 33992

Leading Sporting Goods Brands, 2020

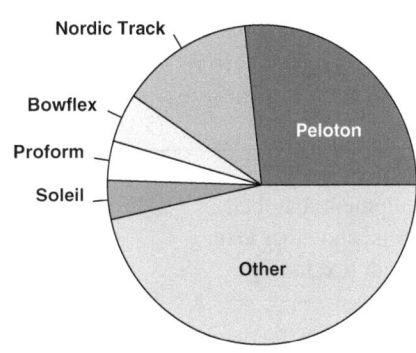

Market shares are shown for the full year. Market shares by vendor: Peloton 21.4%, Amazon.com Inc. 17.5%, internet 8.1%, Dick's 6.9%, Nordic Track 6.2% and other 39.9%.

Peloton	26.6%
Nordic Track	14.3
Bowflex	5.0
Proform	4.0
Soleil	3.5
Other	46.6

Source: "U.S. Sports Equipment." [online] from https://www.traqline.com/newsroom/category/infographics/ [Published February 8, 2021], from TraQline.

★ 3210 ★
Sporting Goods
SIC: 3949; NAICS: 33992

Sporting and Athletic Goods Manufacturing, 2019

Total shipments were valued at $10.71 billion. The term "nec" stands for not elsewhere classified.

	($ 000)	Share
Gymnasium and exercise equipment	$ 2,446,860	23.12%
Wholesale sales of sporting and recreational equipment	1,028,269	9.72
Playground equipment for other uses (including heavy-duty commercial and institutional)	769,370	7.27
Golf balls and clubs	663,028	6.26
Fishing tackle and equipment	615,680	5.82

Continued on next page.

★ 3210 ★
[Continued]
Sporting Goods
SIC: 3949; NAICS: 33992

Sporting and Athletic Goods Manufacturing, 2019

Total shipments were valued at $10.71 billion. The term "nec" stands for not elsewhere classified.

	($ 000)	Share
Team sports helmets, body protective equipment, baseball and softball bats, and other team sports equipment (excluding apparel and shoes)	$ 509,613	4.81%
Above-ground swimming pools, 15 feet or more in diameter, filtered, completely manufactured	157,854	1.49
Playground equipment for home use (including sandboxes, seesaws, slides, and swing sets)	97,839	0.92
Retail sales of other sporting goods and equipment, excluding sport vehicles	13,416	0.13
Warehousing and storage services	9,164	0.09
Retail sales of other goods, nec	2,072	0.02
Retail sales of hunting, fishing, hiking, and camping equipment	615	0.01
Other athletic goods	2,626,457	24.81
Other golf equipment (including golf bags, handcarts for golf bags, golf club shafts, tees, and training devices)	1,545,741	14.60
Other bowling equipment (excluding apparel and shoes)	75,707	0.72
Other manufacturing revenue, nec	12,018	0.11
Other contract manufacturing services, nec.	9,736	0.09
Other products and services, nec	749	0.01

Source: "Annual Survey of Manufactures." [online] from https://www.census.gov/programs-surveys/asm/data/tables.html [Accessed March 18, 2021], from U.S. Department of Commerce.

★ 3211 ★
Sporting Goods
SIC: 3949; NAICS: 33992

Sporting and Athletic Goods Manufacturing Leaders, 2017

Data show the percent of industry sales held by the largest 4, 8, 20 and 50 firms in the sector. There are approximately 1,632 players operating in the industry generating employment for 36,387 people. According to Kentley Insights, the industry generated sales of $10.5 billion in 2019.

4 largest firms	31.8%
8 largest firms	42.5
20 largest firms	56.0
50 largest firms	70.1

Source: "Economic Census." [online] from https://www.census.gov/content/census/en/data/tables/2017/econ/economic-census/naics-sector-31-33.html [Accessed January 21, 2021], from U.S. Census Bureau.

★ 3212 ★
Sporting Goods
SIC: 3949; NAICS: 33992

Tennis Racquet Sales at Specialty Stores, 2019-2020

According to the Physical Activity Council, tennis participation increased by 22% in 2020, with 21.64 million people hitting the courts during the year. About 2.96 million of these participants were playing for the first time, a 44% increase over 2019. The rise in players has meant an increase in racquet sales. Entry-level racquet sales were up 40% in 2020 over the previous year, according to the Tennis Industry Association. Spending is in millions of dollars.

	Units	Dollars
2019	602,680	$ 101.98
2020	588,538	93.34

Source: *Tennis Industry*, April 2021, p. 10, from Tennis Industry Association.

★ 3213 ★
Sporting Goods Retailers
SIC: 5941; NAICS: 45111

Leading Camping Goods Retailers, 2019

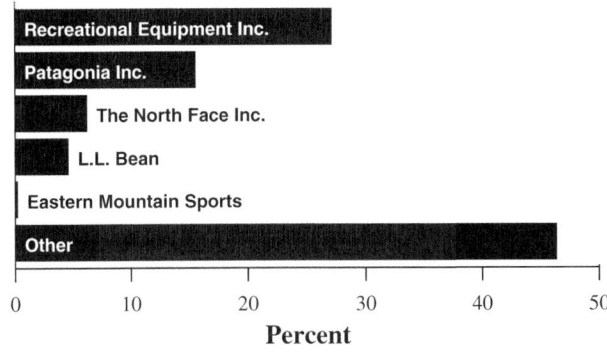

The market was valued at $8.1 billion. Camping clothes claimed 30%, camping equipment 26%, camping shoes 26%, and other sectors 18%. Market shares are shown based on units.

Recreational Equipment Inc.	27.1%
Patagonia Inc.	15.5
The North Face Inc.	6.2
L.L. Bean	4.6
Eastern Mountain Sports	0.2
Other	46.4

Source: "U.S. Camping Goods Market Trend." [online] from http://www.news.kotra.or.kr [Published July 7, 2020], from IBISWorld.

★ 3214 ★
Sporting Goods Retailers
SIC: 5941; NAICS: 45111

Leading Online Sporting Goods Retailers, 2017-2020

Market shares are shown in percent.

	2017	2018	2019	2020
Recreational Equipment Inc.	42.0%	44.0%	45.0%	36.0%
Dick's Sporting Goods	34.0	37.0	39.0	41.0
Academy Sports	7.0	8.0	8.0	12.0
Other	17.0	17.0	17.0	11.0

Source: "Academy Sports' COVID-Driven IPO." [online] from https://www.earnestresearch.com/academys-covid-driven-ipo/ [Published September 25, 2020], from Earnest Research.

★ 3215 ★
Sporting Goods Retailers
SIC: 5941; NAICS: 45111

Leading Sporting Goods Retailers, 2020

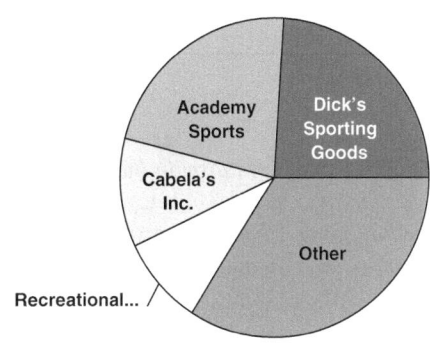

Market shares are shown for the first and second quarter of 2020.

	Q1	Q2
Dick's Sporting Goods	26.0%	24.0%
Academy Sports	20.0	22.0
Cabela's Inc.	10.0	11.0
Recreational Equipment Inc.	12.0	9.0
Other	32.0	34.0

Source: "Academy Sports' COVID-Driven IPO." [online] from https://www.earnestresearch.com/academys-covid-driven-ipo/ [Published September 25, 2020], from Earnest Research.

★ 3216 ★
Sports
SIC: 7941; NAICS: 711211

College Football Revenue, 2018-2019

Data show revenue in millions of dollars. COVID-19 has meant the delay or cancellation of a number of games for the 2020-2021 season. The virus has left teams with new rules around practices and scrambling to fill rosters. It also has meant games are played without fans in stands, leading to billions in lost revenue.

Big Ten	$ 781.5
Southeastern Conference	720.6
PAC-12	530.0
Atlantic Coast Conference	455.4
Big 12	439.0

Source: *The Denver Post*, November 15, 2020, p. A12.

★ 3217 ★
Sports
SIC: 7941; NAICS: 711211
Fantasy Sports Market in India, 2019

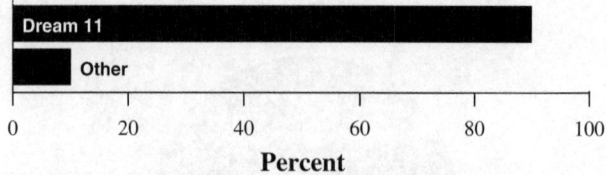

Dream 11 is a fantasy sports platform in India that allows users to play fantasy cricket, hockey, football, kabaddi and basketball games. The company was started in 2012 and has more than 30 million users.

Dream 11	90.0%
Other	10.0

Source: "Mad in Cricket: Dream 11 Business Model." [online] from https://timesofindia.indiatimes.com/readersblog/jordenskyupdates/mad-in-cricket-dream-11-business-model-27561/ [Published October 27, 2020].

★ 3218 ★
Sports
SIC: 7941; NAICS: 711211
Global Sports Sponsorship, 2018-2020

Sports sponsorship spending is shown in billions of dollars. Total spending is to grow from $44.3 billion in 2018 to $46.10 billion in 2019 and to a projected $28.90 billion. Projections are current as of May 15, 2020.

	2018 ($ bil.)	2019 ($ bil.)	2020 ($ bil.)
Financial services	$ 12.45	$ 12.58	$ 6.92
Technology	5.17	5.58	4.58
Automotive	5.76	5.93	2.67
Telecoms	3.02	3.14	2.55
Retailing	2.70	2.87	1.81
Soft drinks	2.29	2.33	1.42
Energy	1.60	1.76	0.99
Alcohol	0.75	0.76	0.62
Gaming	0.63	0.70	0.48
Airlines	0.79	0.83	0.33
Other	9.13	9.61	0.48

Source: *Advertising Age*, May 25, 2020, p. 13, from Two Circles.

★ 3219 ★
Sports
SIC: 7941; NAICS: 711211
Leading NFL Teams, 2020

Teams are ranked by total attendance. As a result of COVID-19 restrictions, the source notes that attendance barely cracked 1.1 million fans at the end of the 2020 season, one-tenth of the attendance from the 2019 season. Approximately 40% of stadiums hosted only cut-outs in their stadiums.

	2019	2020
Dallas Cowboys	727,432	197,313
Jacksonville Jaguars	504,686	127,355
Kansas City Chiefs	587,723	105,228
Tampa Bay	415,189	101,383
Miami Dolphins	504,540	98,352
Houston Texans	574,345	86,800
Tennessee Titans	516,074	84,527
Indianapolis Colts	488,886	79,560
Cleveland Browns	539,448	68,681
Cincinnati Bengals	377,432	66,965

Source: *Kansas City Business Journal*, February 5, 2020, p. NA, from ESPN.

★ 3220 ★
Sports
SIC/NAICS: See frontmatter for explanation.
Running Sports Industry in China, 2017-2020

Revenue in billions of yuan, by year: 272 billion in 2017, 324.2 billion in 2018, 363.1 billion in 2019, and 407 billion in 2020.

	2017	2018	2019	2020
Shoes and clothes	80.3%	73.2%	71.9%	70.6%
Smart devices	19.8	23.8	25.0	26.3
Sports service	1.5	1.6	1.6	1.6
Running events service	1.3	1.4	1.5	1.5

Source: "Revenue of Running Sports Industry is Estimated to Hit 360 Bn Yuan by the End of 2019." [online] from http://www.iresearchchina.com/content/details7_57483.html [Published September 25, 2019], from Chinese Athletics Association and National Bureau of State Statistics, China.

★ 3221 ★
Sports
SIC: 7941; NAICS: 711211

Sports Franchise Revenue, 2015-2024

Figures are in millions of dollars.

2015	$ 31,411.2
2016	33,506.5
2017	36,127.0
2018	37,115.1
2019	38,398.3
2020	29,690.8
2021	31,429.6
2022	32,441.6
2023	33,616.9
2024	34,723.1

Source: "The Media Report Media & Entertainment Data in America." [online] from https://digitalcommons.pepperdine.edu/cgi/viewcontent.cgi?article=1026&context=graziadiowps [Published September 2020], from IBISWorld.

★ 3222 ★
Sports Drinks
SIC: 2086; NAICS: 312111

Top Non-Aseptic Sports Drink Brands, 2020

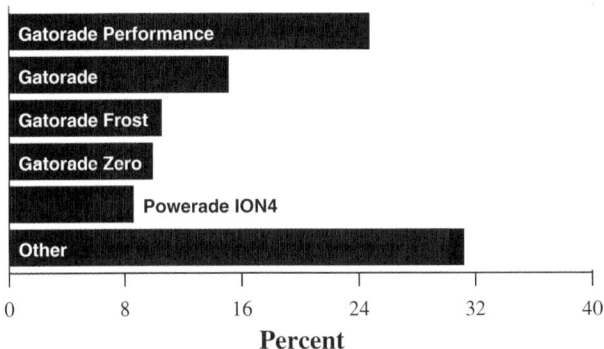

Brands are ranked based on sales at supermarkets, drug stores, mass merchandisers, military commissaries, and select club and dollar chains for the 52 weeks ended May 17, 2020. Most brands listed saw their sales drop from the previous year while Gatorade Zero and Gatorade sales increased by 202.1% and 14.0%, respectively.

	($ mil.)	Share
Gatorade Performance	$ 1,751.87	24.7%
Gatorade	1,071.84	15.1
Gatorade Frost	749.64	10.5
Gatorade Zero	703.82	9.9
Powerade ION4	612.70	8.6
Other	2,215.53	31.2

Source: *Beverage Industry*, July 2020, p. SOI-34, from IRI.

★ 3223 ★
Sports Drinks
SIC: 2086; NAICS: 312111

Top Sports Drink Mix Brands, 2020

Brands are ranked based on sales at supermarkets, drug stores, mass merchandisers, military commissaries, and select club and dollar chains for the 52 weeks ended May 17, 2020. Liquid I.V. saw a 216.6% increase in sales from the prior year. Nuun's sales increased by 76.7%.

	($ mil.)	Share
Gatorade Perform	$ 46.54	45.1%
Propel	33.65	32.6
Nuun	7.79	7.5
Liquid I.V.	6.06	5.9
Private label	5.90	5.7
Other	3.28	3.2

Source: *Beverage Industry*, July 2020, p. SOI-34, from IRI.

★ 3224 ★
Spreads and Syrups
SIC: 2099; NAICS: 311911

Best-Selling Seed and Nut Butters, 2019-2020

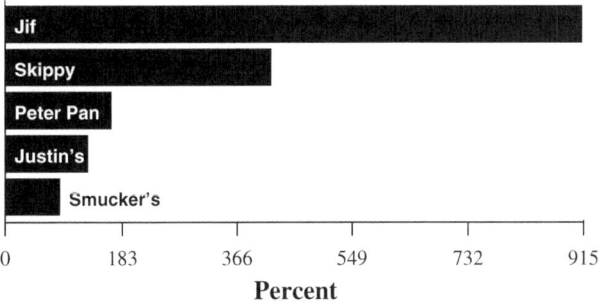

Retail sales are shown in millions of dollars. Sales rose 14% in 2020 to reach $2.7 billion. Based on this total, Jif claimed 33.75% of the total, Skippy 15.51%, Peter Pan 6.09%, Justin's 4.71% and Smucker's 3.1%.

	2019 ($ mil.)	2020 ($ mil.)
Jif	$ 803.8	$ 911.3
Skippy	370.6	418.9
Peter Pan	146.9	164.5
Justin's	111.3	127.3
Smucker's	73.7	83.8

Source: "U.S. Nut-Butter Demand Soars as PB&Js Fuel Pandemic Year." [online] from https://www.bloomberg.com/news/articles/2020-12-08/u-s-nut-butter-demand-soars-as-pb-js-fuel-pandemic-year-chart [Published December 8, 2020], from Euromonitor.

★ 3225 ★
Spreads and Syrups
SIC: 2035; NAICS: 311941

Top Organic Syrup and Spread Firms, 2018

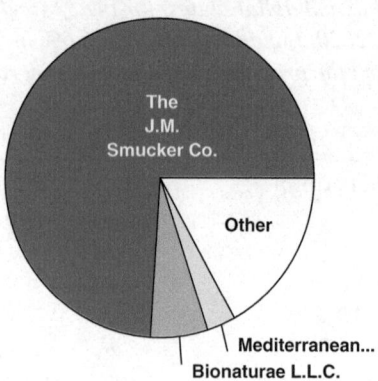

Market shares are shown in percent. Retail sales reached $428.4 million.

The J.M. Smucker Co.	73.7%
Bionaturae L.L.C.	5.8
Mediterranean Organics	3.4
Other	17.1

Source: "Sector Trend Analysis — Organic Market Trend of Corn, Soya, Beans and Wheat Between Canada and the United States." [online] from https://www.agr.gc.ca/eng/international-trade/market-intelligence/reports/?id=1522931721523 [Published July 2020], from GlobalData Intelligence Center.

★ 3226 ★
Springs
SIC: 3495; NAICS: 332613

Spring Manufacturing Leaders, 2017

Data show the percent of industry sales held by the largest 4, 8, 20 and 50 firms in the sector. There are approximately 376 players operating in the industry generating employment for 16,756 people. According to Kentley Insights, the industry generated sales of $4.4 billion in 2019. Major players include Leggett & Platt, Peterson Spring Co. and Barnes Group Inc.

4 largest firms	37.1%
8 largest firms	47.8
20 largest firms	63.1
50 largest firms	79.0

Source: "Economic Census." [online] from https://www.census.gov/content/census/en/data/tables/2017/econ/economic-census/naics-sector-31-33.html [Accessed January 21, 2021], from U.S. Census Bureau.

★ 3227 ★
Staffing Industry
SIC: 7363; NAICS: 56132

Largest STEM Staffing Markets Worldwide, 2018

Countries are ranked by temporary help and place & search revenues in billions of dollars. STEM stands for science, technology, engineering and mathematics.

United States	$ 148
Japan	65
United Kingdom	44
France	32
Germany	32
Netherlands	25
Italy	16
Australia	15
China	14
Switzerland	10

Source: "Bringing Skilled People Together to Build the Future." [online] from https://www.sthree.com/en/investors/financial-results/ [Published November 21, 2019], from Staffing Industry Analysts.

★ 3228 ★
Staffing Industry
SIC: 7363; NAICS: 56132

Leading Engineering Staffing Firms Worldwide, 2018

Companies are ranked by staffing industry revenue in millions of dollars. The top 20 firms generated revenue of $13.27 billion.

	($ mil.)	Share
Aerotek (Allegis)	$ 1,566.2	4.6%
The Adecco Group	1,175.1	3.5
NES Global Talent	1,128.0	3.3
Brunei International	1,080.1	3.2
Fircroft Inc.	1,063.3	3.1
Moron Group	1,026.9	3.0
Randstad Holding	925.9	2.7
Airswift Holdings Ltd.	858.0	2.5
Gattaca PLC	616.3	1.8
System One	526.3	1.5

Source: "Largest Global Engineering Staffing Firms." [online] from http://www2.staffingindustry.com [Press release October 24, 2019], from Staffing Industry Analysts.

★ 3229 ★
Staffing Industry
SIC: 7363; NAICS: 56132

Leading Health Care Staffing Firms, 2019

Companies are ranked by staffing industry revenue in millions of dollars.

	($ mil.)	Share
AMN Healthcare	$ 2,093	11.89%
CHG Healthcare Services	1,770	10.06
Jackson Healthcare	1,230	6.99
Medical Solutions	1,048	5.95
Cross Country Healthcare	807	4.59
Other	10,652	60.52

Source: "Largest Healthcare Staffing Firms in the U.S. Reach to $18 Billion in Combined Revenue." [online] from http://www2.staffingindustry.com [Press release October 28, 2020], from Staffing Industry Analysts.

★ 3230 ★
Staffing Industry
SIC: 7363; NAICS: 56132

Leading Staffing Firms, 2019

Companies are ranked by staffing industry revenue in millions of dollars.

	($ mil.)	Share
Allegis Group	$ 10,481	6.90%
Randstad Holding	4,763	3.14
The Adecco Group	4,300	2.83
Robert Half International	3,831	2.52
Kelly Services	3,481	2.29
Other	124,944	82.31

Source: "SIA Ranks Largest U.S. Staffing Firms." [online] from http://www2.staffingindustry.com [Press release October 26, 2020], from Staffing Industry Analysts.

★ 3231 ★
Staffing Industry
SIC: 7363; NAICS: 56132

Temporary Staffing Industry, 2018

Data show percentage of annual sales for the temporary employment industry. The overall staffing and recruiting industry generated sales of $167 billion in 2018; the temporary and contract industry claimed 83% of this total, while search and placement services claimed the remaining 17%.

Engineering, IT and scientific	26.0%
Industrial	23.0
Office-clerical and administrative	17.0%
Uncategorized	16.0
Health care	10.0
Professional-managerial	8.0

Source: *Staffing Success*, Special Issue, 2019, p. 32, from American Staffing Association and U.S. Census Bureau.

★ 3232 ★
Staffing Industry
SIC: 7363; NAICS: 56132

Temporary Staffing Industry Sectors, 2019-2021

Revenues are shown in billions of dollars. Figures for 2020-2021 are projections.

	2019 ($ bil.)	2020 ($ bil.)	2021 ($ bil.)	Share
Information technology	$ 32.3	$ 27.8	$ 32.5	23.83%
Industrial	34.9	26.2	30.9	22.65
Health care	17.6	17.8	17.9	13.12
Office/clerical	16.6	12.4	14.3	10.48
Direct hire	13.5	6.7	8.1	5.94
Finance/accounting	8.4	7.1	7.9	5.79
Engineering	8.8	6.7	7.7	5.65
Retained search	7.6	5.4	6.4	4.69
Life sciences	2.7	2.0	2.3	1.69
Marketing/creating	1.6	1.3	1.5	1.10
Education	1.3	1.1	1.3	0.95
Other	6.5	4.9	5.6	4.11

Source: "U.S. Staffing Industry Forecast." [online] from http://www.staffingindustry.com [Published April 2020], from Staffing Industry Analysts.

★ 3233 ★
Stainless Steel
SIC: 3312; NAICS: 33111

Leading Stainless Steel Markets, 2019

Production rose from 50.73 million tons in 2018 to 52.21 million tons in 2019. Asia claimed 71.42% of the total, Europe 13%, the Americas 4.9% and other regions 10.68%.

Metal products	37.5%
Mechanical engineering	29.1
Construction	12.2
Motor vehicles and parts	8.5

Continued on next page.

★ 3233 ★
[Continued]
Stainless Steel
SIC: 3312; NAICS: 33111

Leading Stainless Steel Markets, 2019

Production rose from 50.73 million tons in 2018 to 52.21 million tons in 2019. Asia claimed 71.42% of the total, Europe 13%, the Americas 4.9% and other regions 10.68%.

Electrical machinery	7.7%
Other transport	4.9

Source: "ISSF Stainless Steel in Figures 2020." [online] from http://www.worldstainless.org [Accessed March 30, 2021], from International Stainless Steel Federation.

★ 3234 ★
Stationery Products
SIC: 2678; NAICS: 32223

Leading Stationery Makers in China, 2016-2018

Market shares are shown in percent.

	2016	2017	2018
Shanghai M&G Stationery	16.5%	17.2%	17.8%
Lotus Stationery	4.5	3.9	3.3
Deli Group	3.9	4.0	4.0
Wenzhou Aihao Pen	2.8	2.8	2.7
Mont Blanc Commercial	2.3	2.5	2.7
Mitsubishi Pencil	2.2	2.2	2.2
Crayola Ltd.	2.0	2.1	2.2
Sunwood Holding Group	1.8	1.8	1.8
Guangdong Baoke Stationery	1.7	1.6	1.6
Pilot Corp.	1.3	1.4	1.5
Other	61.0	60.5	60.2

Source: "M&G Stationery Inc." [online] from http://www.chinastock.com.hk [Published August 4, 2020], from CGIS Research and Euromonitor.

★ 3235 ★
Stationery Products
SIC: 2678; NAICS: 32223

Who Uses Stationery, 2020

Data show stationery users by age group. Retail sales grew from $8.8 billion in 2010 to $10.5 billion in 2017. Sales then fell to $10.1 billion in 2018, $9.8 billion in 2019, and $9.7 billion in 2020.

18-24	13.0%
25-34	26.0
35-44	28.0
45-54	18.0%
55-64	15.0

Source: *Gifts & Decorative Accessories*, November 2020, p. 41, from Statista Global Consumer Survey.

★ 3236 ★
Steam and Air-Conditioning Supply
SIC: 4961; NAICS: 22133

Steam and Air-Conditioning Supply, 2017

Total revenues were valued at $1.31 billion. "nec" stands for not elsewhere classified. "Other" includes steam distribution services, including air-conditioning; electricity generation; other utilities or waste management operating revenue; and all other products and services, not elsewhere classified. The source withheld revenue data for each of these products and services individually to avoid disclosing data for individual companies.

	($ 000)	Share
Water supply, transmission, treatment, and distribution, including water supply through irrigation systems	$ 51,382	3.92%
Sewage treatment	24,447	1.87
Other service revenue, nec	156	0.01
Other	1,234,015	94.20

Source: "Economic Census." [online] from https://www.census.gov/programs-surveys/economic-census/data/tables.html [Accessed December 2, 2020], from U.S. Census Bureau.

★ 3237 ★
Steam and Air-Conditioning Supply
SIC: 4961; NAICS: 22133

Steam and Air-Conditioning Supply Leaders, 2017

Data show the percent of industry sales held by the largest 4, 8, 20 and 50 firms in the sector. There are approximately 125 players operating in the industry generating employment for 2,439 people. According to Kentley Insights, the industry generated sales of $1.7 billion in 2019. Major players include Clearway Energy, District Energy St. Paul Inc., Consolidated Edison Co. and Veolia Energy North America Holdings.

4 largest firms	55.0%
8 largest firms	76.1

Continued on next page.

★ 3237 ★
[Continued]
Steam and Air-Conditioning Supply
SIC: 4961; NAICS: 22133

Steam and Air-Conditioning Supply Leaders, 2017

Data show the percent of industry sales held by the largest 4, 8, 20 and 50 firms in the sector. There are approximately 125 players operating in the industry generating employment for 2,439 people. According to Kentley Insights, the industry generated sales of $1.7 billion in 2019. Major players include Clearway Energy, District Energy St. Paul Inc., Consolidated Edison Co. and Veolia Energy North America Holdings.

20 largest firms	94.8%
50 largest firms	100.0

Source: "Economic Census." [online] from https://www.census.gov/content/census/en/data/tables/2017/econ/economic-census/naics-sector-31-33.html [Accessed January 21, 2021], from U.S. Census Bureau.

★ 3238 ★
Steel
SIC: 3312; NAICS: 33111

Largest Steel Producers Worldwide, 2020

Companies are ranked by production in millions of tons. Production reached 1.87 billion tons.

	(mil.)	Share
China Baowu Group	115.29	6.14%
ArcelorMittal	78.46	4.18
HBIS Group	43.76	2.33
Nippon Steel Corp.	41.58	2.21
Shagang Group	41.59	2.21
POSCO	40.58	2.16
Ansteel Group	38.19	2.03
Jianlong Group	36.47	1.94
Shougang Group	34.00	1.81
Tata Steel Group	28.07	1.49
Other	1,380.01	73.48

Source: "World Steel Figures in 2021." [online] from https://www.worldsteel.org/steel-by-topic/statistics/World-Steel-in-Figures.html [Accessed June 20, 2021], from World Steel Association.

★ 3239 ★
Steel
SIC: 3312; NAICS: 33111

Leading Crude Steel Producing Nations, 2020

Production is estimated in metric tons.

	(mil.)	Share
China	1,053.0	56.49%
India	99.6	5.34
Japan	83.2	4.46
Russia	73.4	3.94
United States	72.7	3.90
South Korea	67.1	3.60
Germany	35.7	1.92
Turkey	35.8	1.92
Brazil	31.0	1.66
Iran	29.0	1.56
Other	283.5	15.21

Source: "Global Crude Steel Output Decreases by 0.9% in 2020." [online] from https://www.worldsteel.org/media-centre/press-releases/2021/Global-crude-steel-output-decreases-by-0.9—in-2020.html [Published January 26, 2021], from World Steel Association.

★ 3240 ★
Steel
SIC: 3312; NAICS: 33111

Leading Iron and Steel Exporters Worldwide, 2019

Exports reached $337 billion in 2019. China's figure include significant shipments through processing zones.

European Union	36.3%
China	13.3
Japan	6.8
South Korea	6.3
Russia	4.7
United States	3.2
India	2.9
Brazil	2.8
Turkey	2.7
Chinese Taipei	2.4
Other	18.6

Source: "World Trade Statistical Review 2020." [online] from https://www.wto.org/english/res_e/statis_e/wts2020_e/wts20_toc_e.htm [Accessed October 28, 2020], from World Trade Organization.

★ 3241 ★
Steel
SIC: 3312; NAICS: 33111

Leading Iron and Steel Importers Worldwide, 2019

Imports reached $288 billion in 2019. Figures for Russia, Canada and Mexico are valued f.o.b. Hong Kong figure is Secretariat estimate.

European Union	34.6%
United States	7.8
China	5.9
South Korea	3.5
Thailand	3.0
Indonesia	2.6
Mexico	2.6
Vietnam	2.4
India	2.3
Turkey	2.3
Other	33.0

Source: "World Trade Statistical Review 2020." [online] from https://www.wto.org/english/res_e/statis_e/wts2020_e/wts20_toc_e.htm [Accessed October 28, 2020], from World Trade Organization.

★ 3242 ★
Steel
SIC: 3312; NAICS: 33111

Leading Steel Consuming Countries, 2021-2022

Countries are ranked by consumption in millions of tons. Figures are forecasts.

	2021 (mil.)	2022 (mil.)	Share
China	1,024.9	1,035.1	53.78%
India	106.1	112.3	5.83
United States	86.5	90.2	4.69
Japan	56.0	58.8	3.06
South Korea	51.5	52.8	2.74
Russia	43.8	45.1	2.34
Turkey	35.0	37.0	1.92
Germany	34.0	35.8	1.86
Vietnam	24.5	26.3	1.37
Mexico	23.4	24.6	1.28
Other	388.3	406.6	21.13

Source: "Short Range Outlook." [online] from https://www.worldsteel.org/steel-by-topic/statistics/short-range-outlook.html [Published April 2021], from World Steel Association.

★ 3243 ★
Steel
SIC: 3312; NAICS: 33111

Leading Wear-Resistant Steel Makers Worldwide, 2019

Wear-resistant steel is stronger and more durable than conventional steel. The market is forecast to grow from $2.91 billion in 2020 to $3.76 billion in 2026.

SSAB AB	41.34%
JFE Steel Corp.	6.15
Other	52.51

Source: "Global Wear-Resistant Steel Sales Market Report 2020." [online] from https://www.360researchreports.com/global-wear-resistant-steel-sales-market-16616738 [Published October 2020].

★ 3244 ★
Steel
SIC: 3312; NAICS: 33111

Steel Bar Market in Russia, 2020

The industry suffered as a result of COVID-19 precautions. Demand fell 17% for steel beams, 7% for rebar, 14% for wire rod, and 21% for structural products.

EVRAZ	68.0%
Other	32.0

Source: "EVRAZ Investor Presentation." [online] from https://www.evraz.com/en/investors/reports-and-results/presentations/#2020 [Published August 6, 2020], from company reports.

★ 3245 ★
Steel
SIC: 3312; NAICS: 33111

Steel Imports by Product, 2019-2020

Steel mill products are ranked by thousands of net tons. Most products saw imports drop by double-digits between 2019 and 2020. Tin plate was the only product that saw an increase in imports, up 1.7%. Overall, steel imports were down 21.2%.

	2019	2020	Share
Ingots, billets and slabs	6,869.04	5,865.29	26.64%
Sheets and strip, galvanized hot dipped	2,437.21	2,194.71	9.97
Sheets, hot rolled	1,882.60	1,620.72	7.36

Continued on next page.

★ 3245 ★
[Continued]
Steel
SIC: 3312; NAICS: 33111

Steel Imports by Product, 2019-2020

Steel mill products are ranked by thousands of net tons. Most products saw imports drop by double-digits between 2019 and 2020. Tin plate was the only product that saw an increase in imports, up 1.7%. Overall, steel imports were down 21.2%.

	2019	2020	Share
Sheets, cold rolled	1,699.16	1,304.01	5.92%
Oil country goods	2,354.11	1,101.77	5.00
Bars, reinforcing	1,103.23	1,080.82	4.91
Plates in coils	1,155.65	801.79	3.64
Tin plate	755.96	768.46	3.49
Line pipe	1,820.40	710.66	3.23
Wire rods	943.88	708.47	3.22
Bars, hot rolled	901.41	681.19	3.09
Sheets and strip, other	692.71	679.71	3.09
Wire, drawn	685.62	654.09	2.97
Standard pipe	707.86	625.66	2.84
Mechanical tubing	583.30	483.34	2.20
Structural shapes, heavy	550.17	429.44	1.95
Structural pipe and tubing	416.78	393.38	1.79
Other	2,378.16	1,915.75	8.70

Source: "Steel Imports Declined 21.2% in 2020." [online] from https://www.steel.org/2021/01/december-2020-imports/ [Published January 27, 2021], from American Iron and Steel Institute and U.S. Census Bureau.

★ 3246 ★
Steel
SIC: 3312; NAICS: 33111

Top Pig Iron Producing Nations, 2020

Pig iron is produced by processing iron ore with coke in a blast furnace. Countries are ranked by production in millions of metric tons. Production data are estimated.

	(mil.)	Share
China	830	66.51%
Japan	61	4.89
India	56	4.49
Russia	49	3.93
South Korea	43	3.45
Brazil	23	1.84
Germany	21	1.68
Ukraine	19	1.52
United States	18	1.44%
Taiwan	14	1.12
Turkey	10	0.80
Vietnam	9	0.72
Italy	4	0.32
Iran	3	0.24
Mexico	3	0.24
Other	85	6.81

Source: "Mineral Commodity Summaries 2021." [online] from https://www.usgs.gov/centers/nmic/mineral-commodity-summaries [Published January 29, 2021], from U.S. Geological Survey.

★ 3247 ★
Stone, Sand and Gravel
SIC: 1442; NAICS: 212321

Top Stone, Sand and Gravel Exporters Worldwide, 2019

Data show the major exporters of stone, sand and gravel. Exports reached $10.6 billion in 2019, a 2.6% decrease from 2018.

Turkey	9.3%
India	9.1
United Arab Emirates	6.4
United States	6.0
Italy	5.4
Germany	5.1
China	4.3
Oman	4.1
Belgium	3.2
Norway	3.0
Other	44.1

Source: "2019 International Trade Statistics Yearbook." [online] from https://comtrade.un.org/pb/ [Published December 2020], from U.N. Comtrade.

★ 3248 ★
Stone, Sand and Gravel
SIC: 1442; NAICS: 212321

Top Stone, Sand and Gravel Importers Worldwide, 2019

Data show the major importers of stone, sand and gravel. Imports reached $13.3 billion in 2019, a 0.9% decrease from 2018.

China	21.6%
India	6.3
Netherlands	4.2

Continued on next page.

★ 3248 ★
[Continued]
Stone, Sand and Gravel
SIC: 1442; NAICS: 212321

Top Stone, Sand and Gravel Importers Worldwide, 2019

Data show the major importers of stone, sand and gravel. Imports reached $13.3 billion in 2019, a 0.9% decrease from 2018.

United States	3.9%
Germany	3.6
China, Hong Kong SAR	3.5
United Kingdom	3.1
Canada	2.7
Italy	2.7
Belgium	2.6
Other	45.8

Source: "2019 International Trade Statistics Yearbook." [online] from https://comtrade.un.org/pb/ [Published December 2020], from U.N. Comtrade.

★ 3249 ★
Storage Industry
SIC: 4225; NAICS: 49311, 53113

Leading Mobile Storage Firms, 2019

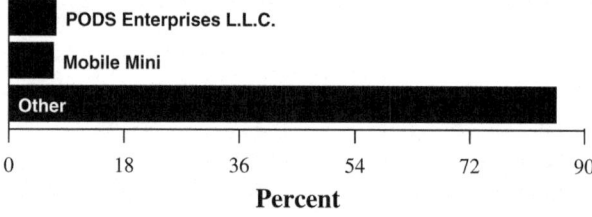

The industry generated revenue of $8.9 billion. Long-term residential customers claimed 41.7%, commercial clients 32.2%, short-term residential customers 13.7%, and other 12.4%.

PODS Enterprises L.L.C.	7.4%
Mobile Mini	7.0
Other	85.6

Source: "Benefits & Challenges to Entering the Storage Container Industry." [online] from https://www.360connect.com/supplier-blog/benefits-challenges-to-entering-the-storage-container-industry/ [Published June 2, 2020], from IBISWorld.

★ 3250 ★
Streaming Media Devices
SIC: 3663; NAICS: 33422

Leading Streaming Media Devices, 2020

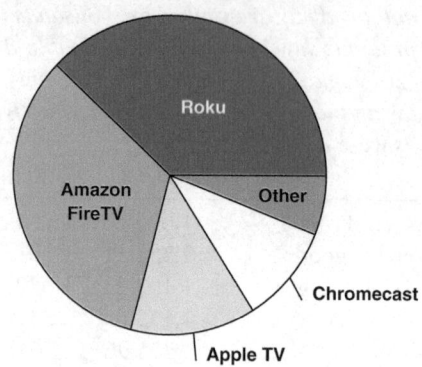

Market shares are shown for the third quarter of 2020. Figures are for devices connected to televisions; they exclude smart televisions.

Roku	38.0%
Amazon FireTV	33.0
Apple TV	13.0
Chromecast	10.0
Other	6.0

Source: *Wall Street Journal*, March 20-21, 2021, p. B9, from Parks Associates.

★ 3251 ★
Streaming Media Devices
SIC: 3663; NAICS: 33422

Top TV Streaming Device Brands Worldwide, 2020

Market shares are shown based on 1.14 billion devices in use in the first quarter of 2020.

Samsung	14.0%
Sony	12.0
LG	8.0
Amazon	5.0
Hisense	5.0
TCL	5.0
Microsoft	4.0
Nintendo	4.0
Google	3.0
Philips	3.0
Roku	3.0
Sharp	3.0
Skyworth	3.0
Vizio	3.0

Continued on next page.

★ 3251 ★
[Continued]
Streaming Media Devices
SIC: 3663; NAICS: 33422

Top TV Streaming Device Brands Worldwide, 2020

Market shares are shown based on 1.14 billion devices in use in the first quarter of 2020.

Xiaomi	3.0%
Other	22.0

Source: "Strategy Analytics: Apple TV Holds 2% Market Share in Fragmented Streaming Devices Industry." [online] from https://9to5mac.com/2020/09/02/apple-tv-market-share-report/ [Published September 2, 2020], from Strategy Analytics.

★ 3252 ★
Streaming Media Devices
SIC: 3663; NAICS: 33422

Top TV Streaming Device Platforms Worldwide, 2020

Market shares are shown based on 1.14 billion devices in use in the first quarter of 2020.

Tizen	11.0%
Sony PlayStation	7.0
WebOS	7.0
Fire OS	5.0
Roku TV OS	5.0
Android TV	4.0
Microsoft Xbox	4.0
Chromecast/Google Cast	3.0
Firefox OS	2.0
tvOS	2.0
Other	49.0

Source: "Strategy Analytics: Apple TV Holds 2% Market Share in Fragmented Streaming Devices Industry." [online] from https://9to5mac.com/2020/09/02/apple-tv-market-share-report/ [Published September 2, 2020], from Strategy Analytics.

★ 3253 ★
Sugar
SIC: 2063; NAICS: 311313

Beet Sugar Manufacturing, 2017

Total shipments were valued at $3.60 billion.

	($ 000)	Share
Refined granulated sugar, including cube and tablet sugar, shipped in bulk (rail cars, trucks, or bins)	$ 2,547,631	70.77%
Refined granulated sugar, including cube and tablet sugar, shipped in commercial units (bags and other containers greater than 25 lb)	387,912	10.78
Whole, straighthouse, or discard beet sugar molasses and molasses beet sugar pulp	114,021	3.17
Refined liquid sugar or sugar syrup, sucrose-type or invert- and/or partially-invert-type	105,698	2.94
Molasses beet sugar pulp, pelletized	95,297	2.65
Refined confectioners' powdered sugar and refined soft or brown sugar, shipped in consumer units (containers 10 lb or less)	56,123	1.56
Refined confectioners' powdered sugar and refined soft or brown sugar, shipped in commercial units (containers greater than 10 lb)	49,668	1.38
Pepper, white and black, and other spices in consumer sizes (less than 1 lb)	2,796	0.08
Other	240,854	6.69

Source: "Economic Census." [online] from https://www.census.gov/programs-surveys/economic-census/data/tables.html [Accessed December 2, 2020], from U.S. Census Bureau.

★ 3254 ★
Sugar
SIC: 2063; NAICS: 311313

Beet Sugar Manufacturing Leaders, 2017

Data show the percent of industry sales held by the largest 4, 8, 20 and 50 firms in the sector. There are approximately 29 players operating in the industry generating employment for 6,918 people. Beet sugar represents approximately 55-60% of sugar production in the United States, with sugarcane claiming the balance.

4 largest firms	79.5%
8 largest firms	98.5
20 largest firms	100.0
50 largest firms	100.0

Source: "Economic Census." [online] from https://www.census.gov/content/census/en/data/tables/2017/econ/economic-census/naics-sector-31-33.html [Accessed January 21, 2021], from U.S. Census Bureau.

★ 3255 ★
Sugar
SIC: 2062; NAICS: 311314

Cane Sugar Manufacturing, 2017

Total shipments were valued at $6.52 billion. "Other" includes manufacturing of dry and/or canned dairy product substitutes; pepper and other spices in consumer sizes (less than 1 lb); raw cane sugar, sugarcane molasses, syrup, and blackstrap and all other sugarcane mill products and byproducts without further processing; refined confectioners' powdered sugar and refined soft or brown sugar shipped in containers 10 lbs or less; chips and sticks excluding crackers, soft pretzels and nuts; and other manufacturing revenue not elsewhere classified. The source withheld shipment data for each of these products separately to avoid disclosing data for individual companies.

	($ 000)	Share
Refined granulated sugar, including cube and tablet sugar, shipped in bulk (rail cars, trucks, or bins)	$ 1,952,885	29.95%
Refined sugar, cube and tablet, shipped in small individual packets or consumer units	1,064,615	16.33
Refined granulated sugar, including cube and tablet sugar, shipped in commercial units (bags and other containers greater than 25 lb)	469,735	7.20
Refined liquid sugar or sugar syrup, sucrose-type or invert- and/or partially-invert-type	$ 414,267	6.35%
Refined confectioners' powdered sugar and refined soft or brown sugar, shipped in commercial units (containers greater than 10 lb)	8,663	0.13
Other	2,609,835	40.03

Source: "Economic Census." [online] from https://www.census.gov/programs-surveys/economic-census/data/tables.html [Accessed December 2, 2020], from U.S. Census Bureau.

★ 3256 ★
Sugar
SIC: 2062; NAICS: 311314

Cane Sugar Manufacturing Leaders, 2017

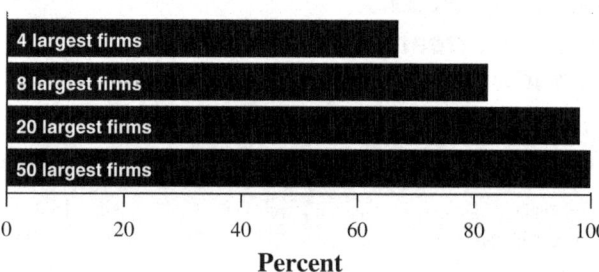

Data show the percent of industry sales held by the largest 4, 8, 20 and 50 firms in the sector. There are approximately 52 players operating in the industry generating employment for 7,155 people. According to Kentley Insights, the industry generated sales of $6.7 billion in 2019.

4 largest firms	66.8%
8 largest firms	82.1
20 largest firms	97.9
50 largest firms	100.0

Source: "Economic Census." [online] from https://www.census.gov/content/census/en/data/tables/2017/econ/economic-census/naics-sector-31-33.html [Accessed January 21, 2021], from U.S. Census Bureau.

★ 3257 ★
Sugar
SIC: 2061; NAICS: 311314

Leading Sugar Consuming Regions, 2020-2021

Data are in thousands of metric tons. Figures are as of October 2020.

	(000)	Share
India	28,500	16.03%
European Union	18,600	10.46
China	15,200	8.55
United States	11,000	6.19
Brazil	10,650	5.99
Indonesia	7,200	4.05
Russia	6,200	3.49
Pakistan	5,800	3.26
Mexico	4,388	2.47
Egypt	3,360	1.89
Other	66,897	37.63

Source: "World Centrifugal Sugar: Production and Consumption." [online] from https://apps.fas.usda.gov/psdonline/app/index.html#/app/downloads [Published May 2020], from U.S. Department of Agriculture.

★ 3258 ★
Sugar
SIC: 2061; NAICS: 311314

Leading Sugar Producing Regions, 2020-2021

Data are in thousands of metric tons. Figures are as of October 2020.

	(000)	Share
Brazil	39,480	20.99%
India	33,705	17.92
European Union	17,680	9.40
Thailand	12,900	6.86
China	10,700	5.69
United States	8,169	4.34
Russia	6,500	3.46
Mexico	6,466	3.44
Pakistan	5,900	3.14
Australia	4,500	2.39
Other	42,077	22.37

Source: "World Centrifugal Sugar: Production and Consumption." [online] from https://apps.fas.usda.gov/psdonline/app/index.html#/app/downloads [Published May 2020], from U.S. Department of Agriculture.

★ 3259 ★
Sugar Substitutes
SIC: 2061; NAICS: 311314

Sugar Substitute Sales by Year Worldwide, 2017-2025

Figures are in billions of dollars. High-intensity sweeteners are expected to see their market share drop from 44.2% in 2017 to 30.3% in 2025. High fructose syrup's share will grow from 28.8% to 36%. Low-intensity sweeteners will see a market share of 26.9% and 33.6%, respectively.

2017	$ 14.3
2018	15.6
2019	16.4
2020	17.2
2021	18.1
2022	19.1
2023	20.1
2024	21.1
2025	23.4

Source: *Perfumer & Flavorist*, October 2020, p. 9, from Statista.

★ 3260 ★
Sulfur
SIC: 1479; NAICS: 212393

Top Sulfur Producing Nations, 2020

Countries are ranked by production in thousands of metric tons. Production data are estimated.

	(000)	Share
China	17,000	21.78%
United States	8,100	10.38
Russia	7,500	9.61
Saudi Arabia	6,500	8.33
Canada	6,300	8.07
India	3,600	4.61
Kazakhstan	3,500	4.48
Japan	3,400	4.36
United Arab Emirates	3,300	4.23
South Korea	3,100	3.97
Iran	2,200	2.82
Qatar	1,800	2.31
Chile	1,500	1.92
Poland	1,200	1.54
Australia	900	1.15
Kuwait	850	1.09
Finland	770	0.99
Germany	670	0.86
Italy	550	0.70
Netherlands	510	0.65

Continued on next page.

★ 3260 ★
[Continued]
Sulfur
SIC: 1479; NAICS: 212393

Top Sulfur Producing Nations, 2020

Countries are ranked by production in thousands of metric tons. Production data are estimated.

	(000)	Share
Brazil	500	0.64%
Other	4,300	5.51

Source: "Mineral Commodity Summaries 2021." [online] from https://www.usgs.gov/centers/nmic/mineral-commodity-summaries [Published January 29, 2021], from U.S. Geological Survey.

★ 3261 ★
Sunglasses
SIC: 3851; NAICS: 339115

Sales of Sunglasses in China, 2016-2019

Sales are shown in millions of yuan. Analysts note that the sales of sunglasses have increased in recent years because of the influence of fashion trends and celebrity culture.

2016	¥ 9,371
2017	10,037
2018	10,769
2019	11,580

Source: "China Sunglasses Market Trend." [online] from http://www.news.kotra.or.kr [Published December 8, 2020], from Euromonitor.

★ 3262 ★
Superchargers
SIC: 3563; NAICS: 333912

Leading Supercharger Makers, 2015

A supercharger (also known as a blower) is an air compressor used to force air into the combustion chambers of an internal combustion engine at pressures higher than would otherwise be the case. Market shares are shown based on production.

Eaton Corp.	88.21%
Vortech Superchargers	0.92
Whipple Superchargers	0.78
Other	10.09

Source: "Global Supercharger Market Growth 2019-2024." [online] from https://www.absolutereports.com/global-supercharger-market-13855178 [Published February 2019].

★ 3263 ★
Supplements
SIC: 2833; NAICS: 325411

Best-Selling Categories of Dietary Supplements, 2020

Dietary supplements include vitamins, supplements, herbs and homeopathics. Categories are ranked by sales in millions of dollars at supermarkets, drug stores, mass merchandisers including Walmart, military commissaries, and select club and dollar chains for the 52 weeks ended November 29, 2020.

Cold and flu	$ 1,703.76
Digestive health	878.62
Energy support	845.34
Heart health	635.96
Sleep	603.69
Weight management	578.62
Bone health	545.48
Brain health	318.83
Eye health	316.26
Hair, skin and nails	286.27

Source: *Nutritional Outlook*, January/February 2021, p. 42, from IRI.

★ 3264 ★
Supplements
SIC: 2833; NAICS: 325411

Best-Selling Dietary Supplements, 2020

Dietary supplements include vitamins, supplements, herbs and homeopathics. Ingredients are ranked by sales in millions of dollars at supermarkets, drug stores, mass merchandisers including Walmart, military commissaries, and select club and dollar chains for the 52 weeks ended November 29, 2020.

Protein - animal and plant combo	$ 1,471.92
Probiotic supplements	759.18
Protein - animal (multi)	752.51
Vitamin C (not Ester-C)	575.56
Melatonin	573.41
Vitamin D	544.23
Protein - animal (general)	482.63
Specialty remedies (homeopathic)	479.71
Multivitamin (women)	473.59
Multivitamin (adult)	385.58
Multivitamin (children)	306.19
Protein - animal (whey)	269.27
Vitamin B12	266.47
Elderberry	265.80
Calcium	261.63

Source: *Nutritional Outlook*, January/February 2021, p. 39, from IRI.

★ 3265 ★
Supplements
SIC: 2833; NAICS: 325411

Best-Selling Dietary Supplements for Bone Health, 2020

Dietary supplements include vitamins, supplements, herbs and homeopathics. Categories are ranked by sales in millions of dollars at supermarkets, drug stores, mass merchandisers including Walmart, military commissaries, and select club and dollar chains for the 52 weeks ended November 29, 2020.

	($ mil.)	Share
Vitamin D	$ 291.76	53.48%
Calcium	149.75	27.45
Multivitamin (women)	40.57	7.44
Calcium/magnesium combo	39.54	7.25
Magnesium	18.03	3.30
Multivitamin (children)	1.47	0.27
Vitamin K	1.45	0.27
Vitamin A - D - K	1.01	0.19
Cranberry supplements	0.92	0.17
Fish oil concentrate	0.32	0.06
Other	0.76	0.14

Source: *Nutritional Outlook*, January/February 2021, p. 42, from IRI.

★ 3266 ★
Supplements
SIC: 2833; NAICS: 325411

Best-Selling Dietary Supplements for Brain Health, 2020

Dietary supplements include vitamins, supplements, herbs and homeopathics. Categories are ranked by sales in millions of dollars at supermarkets, drug stores, mass merchandisers including Walmart, military commissaries, and select club and dollar chains for the 52 weeks ended November 29, 2020.

	($ mil.)	Share
Phosphatidylserine	$ 54.09	17.60%
DMAE	10.13	3.30
Ginkgo biloba	10.02	3.26
Caprylic acid	4.85	1.58
Ginseng	3.10	1.01
L-theanine	2.85	0.93
Bacopa	2.42	0.79
Protein - plant	1.86	0.61
Multivitamin (women)	1.81	0.59
Other	216.23	70.35

Source: *Nutritional Outlook*, January/February 2021, p. 42, from IRI.

★ 3267 ★
Supplements
SIC: 2833; NAICS: 325411

Best-Selling Dietary Supplements for Cold and Flu, 2020

Dietary supplements include vitamins, supplements, herbs and homeopathics. Categories are ranked by sales in millions of dollars at supermarkets, drug stores, mass merchandisers including Walmart, military commissaries, and select club and dollar chains for the 52 weeks ended November 29, 2020.

	($ mil.)	Share
Vitamin C (not Ester-C)	$ 408.39	23.97%
Specialty remedies (homeopathic)	261.96	15.38
Elderberry	223.21	13.10
Vitamin C (Ester-C only)	213.39	12.52
Echinacea	179.69	10.55
Horehound	144.48	8.48
Chinese herbs	104.11	6.11
Zinc	32.33	1.90
Ivy leaf	27.14	1.59
Bee products (not propolis)	16.49	0.97
Other	92.57	5.43

Source: *Nutritional Outlook*, January/February 2021, p. 44, from IRI.

★ 3268 ★
Supplements
SIC: 2833; NAICS: 325411

Best-Selling Dietary Supplements for Digestive Health, 2020

Dietary supplements include vitamins, supplements, herbs and homeopathics. Categories are ranked by sales in millions of dollars at supermarkets, drug stores, mass merchandisers including Walmart, military commissaries, and select club and dollar chains for the 52 weeks ended November 29, 2020.

	($ mil.)	Share
Probiotic supplements	$ 552.09	62.84%
Fiber (other)	120.26	13.69
Psyllium	50.81	5.78
Lactase	40.79	4.64
Ginger	32.13	3.66
Digestive enzymes (other)	18.72	2.13
Fennel	9.77	1.11
Magnesium	7.43	0.85
Vegetable supplement oils	6.58	0.75

Continued on next page.

★ 3268 ★
[Continued]
Supplements
SIC: 2833; NAICS: 325411

Best-Selling Dietary Supplements for Digestive Health, 2020

Dietary supplements include vitamins, supplements, herbs and homeopathics. Categories are ranked by sales in millions of dollars at supermarkets, drug stores, mass merchandisers including Walmart, military commissaries, and select club and dollar chains for the 52 weeks ended November 29, 2020.

	($ mil.)	Share
Charcoal	$ 5.38	0.61%
Other	34.66	3.94

Source: *Nutritional Outlook*, January/February 2021, p. 44, from IRI.

★ 3269 ★
Supplements
SIC: 2833; NAICS: 325411

Best-Selling Dietary Supplements for Energy Support, 2020

Dietary supplements include vitamins, supplements, herbs and homeopathics. Categories are ranked by sales in millions of dollars at supermarkets, drug stores, mass merchandisers including Walmart, military commissaries, and select club and dollar chains for the 52 weeks ended November 29, 2020.

	($ mil.)	Share
Taurine	$ 224.81	26.59%
Vitamin B12	164.94	19.51
Caffeine	127.69	15.11
Vitamin B complex	52.62	6.22
Protein - animal (multi)	52.09	6.16
Tyrosine	29.86	3.53
Protein - animal and plant combo	27.59	3.26
Creatine	24.65	2.92
Multivitamin (women)	13.68	1.62
Phenylalanine	12.62	1.49
Other	114.79	13.58

Source: *Nutritional Outlook*, January/February 2021, p. 44, from IRI.

★ 3270 ★
Supplements
SIC: 2833; NAICS: 325411

Best-Selling Dietary Supplements for Eye Health, 2020

Dietary supplements include vitamins, supplements, herbs and homeopathics. Categories are ranked by sales in millions of dollars at supermarkets, drug stores, mass merchandisers including Walmart, military commissaries, and select club and dollar chains for the 52 weeks ended November 29, 2020.

	($ mil.)	Share
Eye health formulas	$ 108.24	34.23%
Lutein	98.91	31.27
Multivitamin (adult)	72.09	22.79
Specialty remedies (homeopathic)	30.67	9.70
Combination oils (supplements)	3.72	1.18
Vitamin A	1.26	0.40
Hyaluronic acid	0.59	0.19
Bilberry	0.37	0.12
Multivitamin (children)	0.15	0.05
Fish oil concentrate	0.07	0.02
Other	0.19	0.06

Source: *Nutritional Outlook*, January/February 2021, p. 45, from IRI.

★ 3271 ★
Supplements
SIC: 2833; NAICS: 325411

Best-Selling Dietary Supplements for Hair, Skin and Nails, 2020

Dietary supplements include vitamins, supplements, herbs and homeopathics. Categories are ranked by sales in millions of dollars at supermarkets, drug stores, mass merchandisers including Walmart, military commissaries, and select club and dollar chains for the 52 weeks ended November 29, 2020.

	($ mil.)	Share
Biotin	$ 146.00	51.00%
Collagen products	65.92	23.03
Alpha-lipoic acid	14.32	5.00
Specialty remedies (homeopathic)	11.25	3.93
Borage oil	7.49	2.62

Continued on next page.

★ 3271 ★
[Continued]
Supplements
SIC: 2833; NAICS: 325411

Best-Selling Dietary Supplements for Hair, Skin and Nails, 2020

Dietary supplements include vitamins, supplements, herbs and homeopathics. Categories are ranked by sales in millions of dollars at supermarkets, drug stores, mass merchandisers including Walmart, military commissaries, and select club and dollar chains for the 52 weeks ended November 29, 2020.

	($ mil.)	Share
Multivitamin (adult)	$ 6.72	2.35%
Shark cartilage	5.63	1.97
Zinc	3.68	1.29
MSM	2.72	0.95
Vitamin A	2.48	0.87
Other	20.06	7.01

Source: *Nutritional Outlook*, January/February 2021, p. 45, from IRI.

★ 3272 ★
Supplements
SIC: 2833; NAICS: 325411

Best-Selling Dietary Supplements for Heart Health, 2020

Dietary supplements include vitamins, supplements, herbs and homeopathics. Categories are ranked by sales in millions of dollars at supermarkets, drug stores, mass merchandisers including Walmart, military commissaries, and select club and dollar chains for the 52 weeks ended November 29, 2020.

	($ mil.)	Share
Psyllium	$ 180.06	28.31%
Fish oil concentrate	141.17	22.20
CoQ10	137.98	21.70
Krill oil	30.30	4.76
Vitamin E (not Ester-E)	26.37	4.15
Garlic	18.06	2.84
CoQ10 (Ubiquinol)	14.62	2.30
DHA products	10.90	1.71
Red yeast rice	9.23	1.45
Flaxseed and/or oil	8.39	1.32
Other	58.88	9.26

Source: *Nutritional Outlook*, January/February 2021, p. 46, from IRI.

★ 3273 ★
Supplements
SIC: 2833; NAICS: 325411

Best-Selling Dietary Supplements for Sleep, 2020

Dietary supplements include vitamins, supplements, herbs and homeopathics. Categories are ranked by sales in millions of dollars at supermarkets, drug stores, mass merchandisers including Walmart, military commissaries, and select club and dollar chains for the 52 weeks ended November 29, 2020.

	($ mil.)	Share
Melatonin	$ 535.68	88.73%
Specialty remedies (homeopathic)	16.63	2.75
Valerian	11.51	1.91
Ivy Leaf	5.61	0.93
Ashwagandha	4.53	0.75
5-HTP	2.44	0.40
L-theanine	2.41	0.40
Chamomile	2.19	0.36
Vitamin C (not Ester-C)	1.65	0.27
DHEA	1.36	0.23
Other	19.68	3.26

Source: *Nutritional Outlook*, January/February 2021, p. 46, from IRI.

★ 3274 ★
Supplements
SIC: 2833; NAICS: 325411

Best-Selling Dietary Supplements for Weight Management, 2020

Dietary supplements include vitamins, supplements, herbs and homeopathics. Categories are ranked by sales in millions of dollars at supermarkets, drug stores, mass merchandisers including Walmart, military commissaries, and select club and dollar chains for the 52 weeks ended November 29, 2020.

	($ mil.)	Share
Protein - animal (multi)	$ 120.58	20.84%
Protein - animal (general)	116.92	20.21
Protein - animal and plant combo	63.06	10.90
Caffeine	56.52	9.77
Protein - animal (casein)	28.85	4.99
Green teas and supplements	18.11	3.13
Glucomannan	17.08	2.95
Protein - animal (whey and casein)	16.90	2.92
MCT (medium-chain triglycerides)	15.61	2.70

Continued on next page.

★ 3274 ★
[Continued]
Supplements
SIC: 2833; NAICS: 325411

Best-Selling Dietary Supplements for Weight Management, 2020

Dietary supplements include vitamins, supplements, herbs and homeopathics. Categories are ranked by sales in millions of dollars at supermarkets, drug stores, mass merchandisers including Walmart, military commissaries, and select club and dollar chains for the 52 weeks ended November 29, 2020.

	($ mil.)	Share
Cider vinegar supplements	$ 15.18	2.62%
Other	109.81	18.98

Source: *Nutritional Outlook*, January/February 2021, p. 46, from IRI.

★ 3275 ★
Supplements
SIC: 2833; NAICS: 325411

Health Care Product Sales in China, 2019

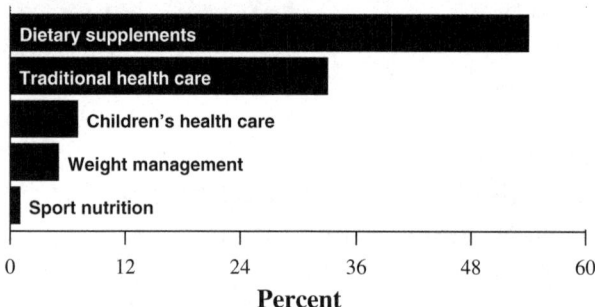

The industry was valued at 222.7 billion renminbi.

Dietary supplements	54.0%
Traditional health care	33.0
Children's health care	7.0
Weight management	5.0
Sport nutrition	1.0

Source: "Vitamin and Health Supplement in China." [online] from https://daxueconsulting.com/athleisure-market-in-china/ [Published July 2020], from http://www.chyxx.com.

★ 3276 ★
Supplements
SIC: 2833; NAICS: 325411

Leading Dietary Supplement Makers in India, 2019

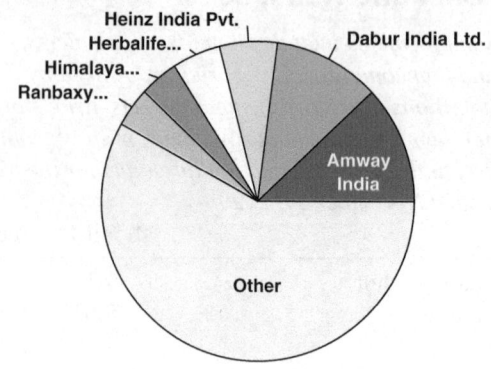

The industry was valued at $6 billion in 2019. Vitamins and minerals claimed 40% of the total, herbal supplements 30%, proteins 25% and other 5%.

Amway India	12.0%
Dabur India Ltd.	11.0
Heinz India Pvt.	6.0
Herbalife International India	5.0
The Himalaya Drug Co.	4.0
Ranbaxy Laboratories	4.0
Other	58.0

Source: "Opportunities in the Indian Nutraceutical and Wellness Sector." [online] from https://missp.ch/docs/1590652307Overview%20and%20Opportunities%20in%20the%20Indian%20Nutraceuticals%20and%20Wellness%20Sectors.pdf [Published May 2020], from Euromonitor.

★ 3277 ★
Supplements
SIC: 2833; NAICS: 325411

Leading Meal Replacement Brands, 2020

Meal replacement sales reached $2.9 billion.

	($ mil.)	Share
Atkins	$ 698.9	23.40%
Premier Protein	561.4	18.79
Herbalife Nutrition	385.9	12.92
Shakeology	360.6	12.07

Continued on next page.

★ 3277 ★
[Continued]
Supplements
SIC: 2833; NAICS: 325411

Leading Meal Replacement Brands, 2020

Meal replacement sales reached $2.9 billion.

	($ mil.)	Share
Kellogg's Special K	$ 302.4	10.12%
Slim Fast	227.3	7.61
Soylent	59.5	1.99
Huel	48.4	1.62
BodyKey by Nutrilite	30.4	1.02
Pharmanex	22.7	0.76
Other	289.7	9.70

Source: "Meal Replacement and Meal Replacement Drinks in Canada and the United States." [online] from https://www.agr.gc.ca/eng/international-trade/market-intelligence/reports/?id=1522931721523 [Accessed May 1, 2021], from Euromonitor.

★ 3278 ★
Supplements
SIC: 2833; NAICS: 325411

Leading Meal Replacement Makers, 2020

Meal replacement sales reached $2.9 billion.

	($ bil.)	Share
The Simply Good Foods Co.	$ 698.9	23.40%
BellRing Brands Inc.	561.4	18.79
Herbalife Nutrition Ltd.	385.9	12.92
Beachbody L.L.C.	360.6	12.07
The Kellogg Company	302.4	10.12
Glanbia PLC	227.3	7.61
Rosa Foods Inc.	59.5	1.99
Huel Ltd.	48.4	1.62
Amway Corp.	30.4	1.02
Nu Skin Enterprises Inc.	22.7	0.76
Other	289.7	9.70

Source: "Meal Replacement and Meal Replacement Drinks in Canada and the United States." [online] from https://www.agr.gc.ca/eng/international-trade/market-intelligence/reports/?id=1522931721523 [Accessed May 1, 2021], from Euromonitor.

★ 3279 ★
Supplements
SIC: 2833; NAICS: 325411

Meal Replacement Market, 2019

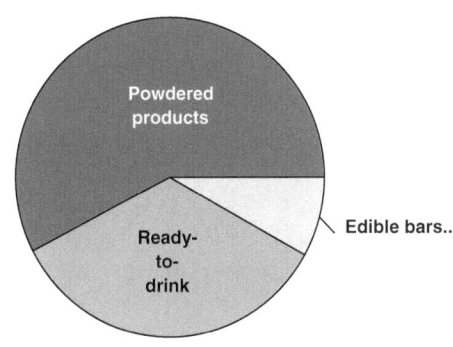

The industry is forecast to climb from $3.77 billion in 2019 to $4.39 billion in 2024. Distribution is shown based on unit sales.

Powdered products	57.4%
Ready-to-drink shakes	34.2
Edible bars and other	8.4

Source: "U.S. Meal Replacement Market Trend." [online] from http://news.kotra.or.kr [Published November 2, 2020], from IBISWorld.

★ 3280 ★
Supplements
SIC: 2836; NAICS: 325414

Omega Supplement Sales on Amazon, 2020

Data show sales of omega supplements by delivery method. There are 396 active brands in the category. However, the top 20 best-selling brands claimed approximately two-thirds of sales. Fish oil claimed two-thirds of sales, followed by krill and black seed.

Softgels	80.0%
Liquid	13.0
Capsules	5.0

Source: "Omega Supplements are Projected to Steadily Grow in 2021." [online] from https://clearcutanalytics.com/omega-supplements-are-projected-to-steadily-grow-in-2021/ [Published January 13, 2021], from ClearCut Analytics.

★ 3281 ★
Supplements
SIC: 2836; NAICS: 325414
Probiotic Sales on Amazon, 2020

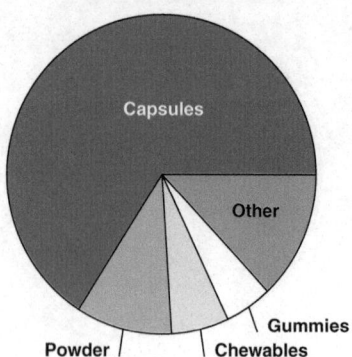

Probiotic sales reached nearly $400 million. Unit sales are shown by delivery method. Capsules claimed 66% of unit sales and 72% of revenue.

Capsules	66.0%
Powder	10.0
Chewables	6.0
Gummies	5.0
Other	13.0

Source: "Probiotics Category With Room to Innovate." [online] from https://clearcutanalytics.com/probiotics-rising-category-with-room-to-innovate/ [Published November 19, 2020], from ClearCut Analytics.

★ 3282 ★
Supplements
SIC: 2833; NAICS: 325411
Top Mineral Supplement Brands, 2020

Brands are ranked by sales in thousands of dollars at supermarkets, drug stores, mass merchandisers, military commissaries, and select club and dollar chains for the 12 weeks ended September 6, 2020.

	($ mil.)	Share
Nature Made	$ 78.8	8.02%
Nature's Bounty	71.9	7.32
Prevagen	65.5	6.67
Align	20.7	2.11
Qunol	19.7	2.00
Olly	17.4	1.77
Culturelle	16.8	1.71
Nature's Truth	15.7	1.60
Schiff Mega Red	12.6	1.28
Private label	281.2	28.62
Other	382.3	38.91

Source: *MMR*, October 12, 2020, p. 26, from IRI.

★ 3283 ★
Supplements
SIC: 2833; NAICS: 325411
Top Sports Nutrition Brands, 2019

Market shares are shown based on $13.1 billion retail sales RSP (retail selling price).

Clif	7.8%
Optimum Nutrition	7.5
BSN	5.1
Cellucor	4.5
Muscle Milk	4.5
Quest	3.6
RXBar	2.7
Cytosport	2.4
GNC	1.8
Nature Valley	1.4
Isopure	1.3
Pure Protein	1.3
ThinkThin	1.2
Other	54.9

Source: "U.S. Exercise Supplement Market Focused on Health." [online] from http://www.news.kotra.or.kr [Published March 3, 2020], from Euromonitor.

★ 3284 ★
Supplements
SIC: 2833; NAICS: 325411
Top Weight Control/Nutritional Drink Brands, 2020

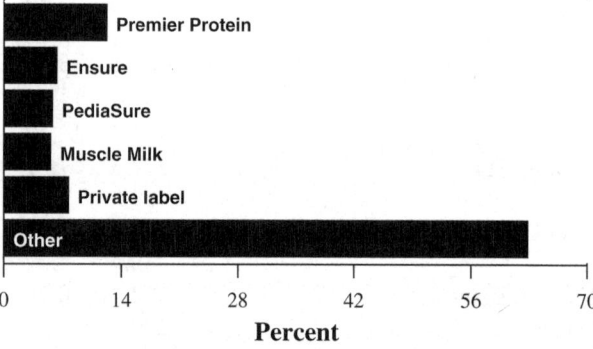

Brands are ranked based on sales at supermarkets, drug stores, mass merchandisers, military commissaries, and select club and dollar chains for the 52 weeks ended May 17, 2020.

	($ mil.)	Share
Premier Protein	$ 488.05	12.2%
Ensure	250.46	6.2
PediaSure	229.41	5.7
Muscle Milk	221.58	5.5

Continued on next page.

★ 3284 ★
[Continued]
Supplements
SIC: 2833; NAICS: 325411

Top Weight Control/Nutritional Drink Brands, 2020

Brands are ranked based on sales at supermarkets, drug stores, mass merchandisers, military commissaries, and select club and dollar chains for the 52 weeks ended May 17, 2020.

	($ mil.)	Share
Private label	$ 303.89	7.6%
Other	2,514.99	62.8

Source: *Beverage Industry*, July 2020, p. SOI-35, from IRI.

★ 3285 ★
Supplements
SIC: 2833; NAICS: 325411

Top Weight Control Product Categories, 2020

Categories are ranked by sales in millions of dollars at supermarkets, drug stores, mass merchandisers, military commissaries, and select club and dollar chains for the 52 weeks ended October 4, 2020.

	($ mil.)	Share
Nutritionals liquid/powder	$ 3,790.0	92.44%
Candy/tablets	211.7	5.16
Refrigerated/nutritional liquid/powder	94.0	2.29
Other	4.3	0.10

Source: *MMR*, November 16, 2020, p. 38, from IRI.

★ 3286 ★
Surge Protectors
SIC: 3643; NAICS: 335931

Surge Protector Sales by Mounting/Use, 2020

Market shares are shown based on sales for the 12 months ended March 2020. "Other" includes ethernet/coax, data and component.

Panel mount	74.8%
DIN-Rail	22.4
Other	2.8

Source: *The Electrical Distributor*, June 2020, p. 65, from Epicor's Industry Data.

★ 3287 ★
Swimming Pools
SIC: 3089; NAICS: 326199

Leading Fiberglass Swimming Pool Makers Worldwide, 2019

The industry is forecast to grow from $1.56 billion in 2019 to $2.26 billion in 2026. Market shares are shown based on revenue.

Latham Pool	5.45%
Compass Pools	4.08
Leisure Pools	1.80
Other	88.67

Source: "Global Fiberglass Swimming Pool Market Research Report 2020." [online] from http://www.qyresearch.com [Published July 2020], from QY Research.

★ 3288 ★
Switches
SIC: 3613; NAICS: 335313

Disconnect Switches by Type, 2018

Market shares are shown based on dollar sales for the 12 months ended December 2018.

Motor disconnects	56.7%
UL98 fusible and nonfusible disconnects	27.7
UL508 fusible and nonfusible disconnects	10.9
Elevator disconnects	4.4
DC disconnects	0.3

Source: *The Electrical Distributor*, May 2019, p. 60, from Epicor's Industry Data Analytics.

★ 3289 ★
Systems Integrators
SIC: 7379; NAICS: 51821, 541512, 541519

Leading Systems Integrators, 2018-2020

Companies are ranked by average revenue from commercial AV systems installations in millions of dollars from 2018-2020.

AVI-SPL	$ 1,114.0
Diversified Systems	855.0
Kinly	277.0
AVI Systems	260.0
Avidex	152.7
Solutionz Inc.	150.0
CCS Presentation Systems	146.1
Ford Audio-Video	136.7
Solotech Inc.	132.8
SKC Communications	108.0

Source: *Systems Contractor News*, December 2020, p. 2.

★ 3290 ★
T&D Equipment
SIC: 3612; NAICS: 335311

Leading Transmission and Distribution Equipment Firms Worldwide, 2020

Companies are ranked by revenue in millions of dollars. Figures are as of September 2020.

Siemens AG	$ 93,623
Hitachi Ltd.	84,538
Mitsubishi Heavy Industries Ltd.	37,094
Toshiba Corp.	35,621
ABB Inc.	34,312
Schneider Electric SE	27,895
GE Power	26,827
Kawasaki Heavy Industries Ltd.	14,205
Korea Shipbuilding & Offshore Engineering Co.	13,706
Shanghai Electric Group Co. Ltd.	11,770

Source: *Future Power Technology*, October 2020, p. NA, from GlobalData's Power Intelligence Centre.

★ 3291 ★
Tank Terminals
SIC: 5171; NAICS: 42471, 45431

Largest Tank Terminal Operators Worldwide, 2019

Companies are ranked by capacity in millions of cubic meters. The top 10 firms claimed 21% of total capacity. The regions with the most terminals: the United States with 1,447, Europe with 1,125 and Asia with 1,057.

China Petroleum & Chemical Corp. (Sinopec)	44.1
Vopak N.V.	33.1
China National Petroleum Corp.	25.7
Kinder Morgan Inc.	21.7
PetroChina	19.8
Buckeye Partners	18.1
Oiltanking	17.6
Marathon Oil Corp.	16.7
Enterprise Products Partners	13.2
Magellan Midstream Partners	13.1

Source: "Who are the Biggest Players in the Tank Terminal Market?" [online] from https://www.insights-global.com/who-are-the-biggest-players-in-the-tank-terminal-market/ [Accessed August 25, 2020].

★ 3292 ★
Tank Trucks
SIC: 4213; NAICS: 48423

Tank Truck Market, 2018

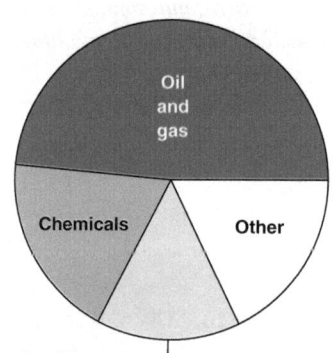

A tank truck, gas truck, fuel truck, or tanker truck, is a motor vehicle designed to carry liquefied loads or gases on roads. Major players include EnTrans International, MAC Trailer, Amthor, Seneca Tank, Tremcar, Oilmens, Westmor, Burch Tank & Truck.

Oil and gas	48.59%
Chemicals	18.97
Food and beverages	14.76
Other	17.68

Source: "Global Tank Truck Market Research Reports 2020." [online] from https://www.marketinsightsreports.com [Published January 2020], from QY Research.

★ 3293 ★
Tape
SIC: 2672; NAICS: 32222
Tape Sales by Type, 2019

Market shares are shown based on dollar sales for the 12 months ended March 2019. Figures are based on sales made by a representative sample of full-line electrical distributors located throughout the United States.

Electrical vinyl tape	52.4%
Rubber/insulating tape	18.3
Duct tape	8.2
Special purpose tape	6.5
Barricade tape	5.6
Glass tape	3.3
Arc/fire-proofing tape	3.2
Mastic tape	1.8
Other	0.6

Source: *The Electrical Distributor*, June 2019, p. 72, from Epicor's Industry Data Analytics.

★ 3294 ★
Tape
SIC: 2672; NAICS: 32222
Top Household Tape Brands, 2020

Market shares are shown based on drug store sales for the 52 weeks ended April 19, 2020.

Scotch	46.40%
Scotch Magic	17.87
Flex Tape	2.82
Gorilla	1.92
Gorilla Tape	1.73
Duck EZ Start	1.30
3M Scotch	1.15
Scotch Sure Start	1.13
Duck	1.00
Private label	20.10
Other	4.58

Source: *DrugStore Management*, Annual 2020-2021, p. 230, from IRI.

★ 3295 ★
Tape Measures
SIC: 3829; NAICS: 334519
Leading Tape Measure Makers Worldwide, 2019

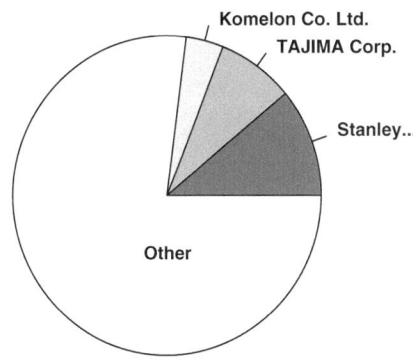

Market shares are shown based on revenue of $1.25 billion. The Asia-Pacific region claimed the largest share worldwide with a 42.43% share.

Stanley Black & Decker Corp.	11.40%
TAJIMA Corp.	7.71
Komelon Co. Ltd.	3.85
Other	77.04

Source: "COVID-19 Impact on Global Tape Measures Market Size Status and Forecast 2020-2026." [online] from http://reports.valuates.com [Published April 2020], from QY Research.

★ 3296 ★
Tattoos
SIC: 7299; NAICS: 81299
Tattoo Artist Industry Revenue, 2019

The industry generated revenue of $1.7 billion in 2019. Revenue grew 6.1% annually from 2014-2019. Mario Barth Tattoo was the only company listed by the source to have more than a 5% market share.

Custom-designed tattoos	59.5%
Predesigned tattoos	19.8
Body piercing	14.3
Other	6.4

Source: "Tattoo Artists in the U.S." [online] from http://www.ibisworld.com [Published April 2019], from IBISWorld.

★ 3297 ★
Tattoos
SIC: 7299; NAICS: 81299

Top Temporary Tattoo Makers Worldwide, 2019

Market shares are shown based on revenue of $827.3 million.

Inkbox	6.35%
TM International	4.64
Temporary Tattoos	3.22
Other	85.79

Source: "Global Temporary Tattoo Market Report, History and Forecast 2015-2026, Breakdown by Manufacturers, Key Regions, Types and Applications." [online] from http://www.qyresearch.com [Published May 2020], from QY Research.

★ 3298 ★
Tax Preparation
SIC: 7291; NAICS: 541213

How Tax Returns Were Prepared, 2019

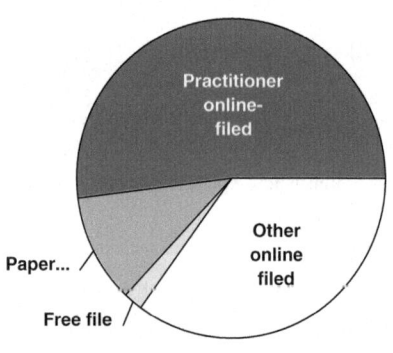

Distribution is shown based on the 154.1 million returns filed October 1, 2018-September 30, 2019.

	(mil.)	Share
Practitioner online-filed	79.9	51.85%
Paper filed	16.9	10.97
Free file	2.8	1.82
Other online filed	54.5	35.37

Source: "2019 Internal Revenue Service Data Book." [online] from https://www.irs.gov/statistics/soi-tax-stats-irs-data-book [Accessed April 20, 2021], from Internal Revenue Service.

★ 3299 ★
Tax Preparation
SIC: 7291; NAICS: 541213

Leading Tax Preparation Firms, 2020

Companies are ranked by revenue in millions of dollars. Figures are for 2020 or latest year available. Industry revenue fell from $8.0 billion in 2019 to $7.77 billion in 2020. Revenue is forecast to reach $10.2 billion in 2027.

H&R Block	$ 3,094.88
Jackson Hewitt Tax Service Inc.	240.00
Gilman Ciocia Inc.	85.00

Source: "Tax Preparation Industry (U.S.)." [online] from http://www.plunkettresearch.com [Published March 4, 2021], from Plunkett Research.

★ 3300 ★
Tax Preparation
SIC: 7291; NAICS: 541213

Tax Return Preparation Industry, 2019

Operators in this industry offer tax return preparation services. They do not offer accounting, bookkeeping or payroll services. The offices of CPAs are excluded. Revenue reached $11 billion. Basic returns are limited to basic IRS forms such as the 1040; standard returns are more complicated and require more forms. Full-service returns are filed by users with special circumstances, such as the self-employed or those with income from rental properties. The source cites Intuit as the leader in the market through its TurboTax product.

Standard tax preparation	55.4%
Basic tax preparation	23.1
Full-service tax preparation	13.8
Tax-related financial	7.7

Source: "Tax Preparation Services in the U.S." [online] from http://www.ibisworld.com [Published August 2019], from IBISWorld.

★ 3301 ★
Tea
SIC: 2099; NAICS: 31192

Tea and Infusion Sales in Europe, 2019 and 2022

Retail sales are shown in millions of dollars.

	2019 ($ mil.)	2022 ($ mil.)	Share
Russia	$ 3,631.0	$ 4,004.0	41.51%
Germany	1,486.1	1,667.1	17.28
United Kingdom	830.9	989.2	10.25

Continued on next page.

★ 3301 ★
[Continued]
Tea
SIC: 2099; NAICS: 31192

Tea and Infusion Sales in Europe, 2019 and 2022

Retail sales are shown in millions of dollars.

	2019 ($ mil.)	2022 ($ mil.)	Share
Turkey	$746.8	$670.2	6.95%
France	598.8	655.5	6.80
Poland	354.0	376.0	3.90
Italy	339.8	368.4	3.82
Spain	213.8	236.4	2.45
Netherlands	189.8	196.7	2.04
Switzerland	89.4	96.5	1.00
Other	359.0	386.4	4.01

Source: "Non-Alcoholic Fermented and Cold Pressed Juice Trends in the United States and Europe." [online] from https://www.agr.gc.ca/eng/international-trade/market-intelligence/reports/?id=1522931721523 [Published April 2021], from Mintel.

★ 3302 ★
Tea
SIC: 2099; NAICS: 31192

Tea Sales by Channel in China, 2018

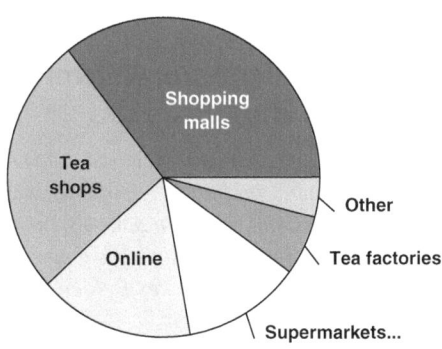

China is the largest tea producer in the world. Tea sales reached 240 billion renminbi in 2018; sales were expected to reach 284 billion renminbi in 2019.

Shopping malls	34.9%
Tea shops/tea houses	26.5
Online	15.6
Supermarkets/convenience stores	12.5
Tea factories	6.5%
Other	4.0

Source: "Tea Market in China." [online] from https://www.slideshare.net/DaxueConsulting/the-tea-market-in-china-report-by-daxue-consulting [Published April 2020], from China Tea Industry Economic Research.

★ 3303 ★
Tea
SIC: 2099; NAICS: 31192

Top Canned/Bottled Tea Brands, 2020

Brands are ranked based on sales at supermarkets, drug stores, mass merchandisers, military commissaries, and select club and dollar chains for the 52 weeks ended May 17, 2020.

	($ mil.)	Share
Lipton Pure Leaf	$788.51	20.0%
AriZona	578.89	14.7
Gold Peak	425.18	10.8
Lipton Brisk	362.81	9.2
Lipton	298.89	7.6
Other	1,490.70	37.7

Source: *Beverage Industry*, July 2020, p. SOI-26, from IRI.

★ 3304 ★
Tea
SIC: 2099; NAICS: 31192

Top Matcha Tea Makers Worldwide, 2016

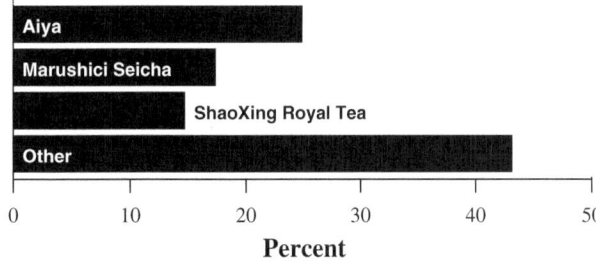

Matcha tea is a type of green tea rich in antioxidants. The industry is forecast to grow from $1.39 billion in 2018 to $1.97 billion in 2025. Market shares are shown based on revenue.

Aiya	24.84%
Marushici Seicha	17.33
ShaoXing Royal Tea	14.68
Other	43.15

Source: "Global Matcha Tea Market Report, History and Forecast 2014-2025, Breakdown by Manufacturers, Key Regions, Types and Applications." [online] from http://www.qyresearch.com [Published April 2020], from QY Research.

★ 3305 ★
Tea
SIC: 2099; NAICS: 31192

Top Refrigerated Tea Brands, 2020

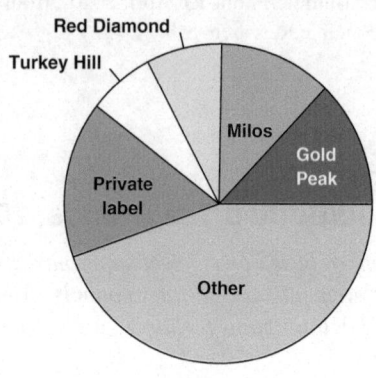

Brands are ranked based on sales at supermarkets, drug stores, mass merchandisers, military commissaries, and select club and dollar chains for the 52 weeks ended May 17, 2020.

	($ mil.)	Share
Gold Peak	$ 221.70	12.9%
Milos	198.08	11.5
Red Diamond	136.17	7.9
Turkey Hill	117.86	6.9
Private label	266.11	15.5
Other	779.81	45.3

Source: *Beverage Industry*, July 2020, p. SOI-27, from IRI.

★ 3306 ★
Telecommunications Equipment
SIC: 3669; NAICS: 33429

Leading Telecommunications Equipment Makers Worldwide, 2017-2019

Market shares are shown in percent.

	2017	2018	2019
Huawei Technologies Co.	26.0%	28.0%	28.0%
Nokia Corp.	16.0	17.0	16.0
Ericsson Corp.	13.0	14.0	14.0
ZTE Corp.	10.0	8.0	10.0
Cisco Systems Inc.	8.0	8.0	7.0
Other	27.0	25.0	25.0

Source: "How a Potential Nokia Takeover Would Impact the Network Equipment Market." [online] from https://www.businessinsider.com/taking-over-nokia-would-be-met-with-regulatory-scrutiny-2020-4 [Published April 20, 2020], from Dell'Oro Group.

★ 3307 ★
Telecommunications Equipment
SIC: 3669; NAICS: 33429

Leading Telecommunications Equipment Makers Worldwide, 2020

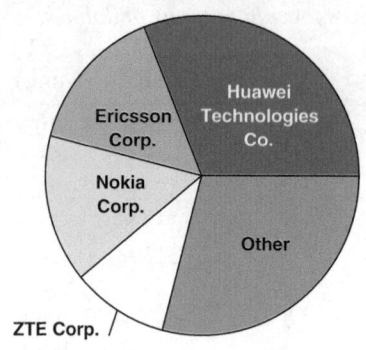

Market shares are shown in percent.

Huawei Technologies Co.	31.0%
Ericsson Corp.	15.0
Nokia Corp.	15.0
ZTE Corp.	10.0
Other	29.0

Source: *Wall Street Journal*, March 17, 2021, p. B3, from Dell'Oro Group.

★ 3308 ★
Telecommunications Equipment
SIC: 3669; NAICS: 33429

Telecommunications Networking Equipment Market, 2019

Operators produce wired (voice and data) telecommunications equipment, including telephone switching systems, telephones, answering machines, modems and gateways. A total of 206 businesses generated revenue of $6.1 billion. The source cites Belden and Plantronics as major players.

Carrier line equipment and non-consumer modems	41.1%
Wireline voice and data network equipment	31.1
Telephone switching and switchboard equipment	27.8

Source: "Telecommunications Networking Equipment Manufacturing in the U.S." [online] from http://www.ibisworld.com [Published July 2019], from IBISWorld.

★ 3309 ★
Telecommunications Equipment
SIC: 3661; NAICS: 33421

Telephone Apparatus Manufacturing, 2019

Total shipments were valued at $4.47 billion. The term "nec" stands for not elsewhere classified.

	($ 000)	Share
Data communications equipment, including LAN/WAN switches, routers, and other networking equipment	$ 3,585,148	80.20%
Carrier line equipment and non-consumer modems	269,413	6.03
Parts, components, and subassemblies for wireline voice and data network equipment	182,141	4.07
Telephone switching and switchboard equipment	138,627	3.10
Other electronic and electrical contract manufacturing services	91,577	2.05
Other service revenue, nec	7,743	0.17
Other manufacturing revenue, nec	2,033	0.05
Other	193,318	4.32

Source: "Annual Survey of Manufactures." [online] from https://www.census.gov/programs-surveys/asm/data/tables.html [Accessed March 18, 2021], from U.S. Department of Commerce.

★ 3310 ★
Telecommunications Services
SIC: 4813; NAICS: 517311

Telecom Tower Infrastructure Market in China, 2019

More than 200 companies providing telecommunication tower infrastructure services operate in China. However, fewer than 10 companies have more than 1,000 sites. China Telecom has more than 97% of the market.

China Telecom	> 97.0%
Other	3.0

Source: "Leading 5G Infrastructure Provider, Initiate With Accumulate." [online] from http://www.gtja.com.hk [Published March 6, 2020].

★ 3311 ★
Teleproduction and Postproduction Services
SIC: 7819; NAICS: 512191

Number of Firms In Teleproduction and Other Postproduction Services, 1998-2019

According to Kentley Insights, the industry generated sales of $6.8 billion in 2019. Over the previous three years, the industry saw an annual growth rate of 15.5%.

1998	2,990
1999	2,851
2000	2,816
2001	2,702
2002	2,594
2003	1,786
2004	1,784
2005	1,804
2006	1,841
2007	2,128
2008	2,183
2009	2,147
2010	2,126
2011	2,162
2012	2,302
2013	2,306
2014	2,371
2015	2,408
2016	2,468
2017	2,608
2018	2,714
2019	2,882

Source: "County Business Patterns." [online] from https://www.census.gov/programs-surveys/cbp/data/datasets.html [Published April 22, 2021], from U.S. Census Bureau.

★ 3312 ★
Teleproduction and Postproduction Services
SIC: 7819; NAICS: 512191

Teleproduction and Other Postproduction Service Leaders, 2017

Data show the percent of industry sales held by the largest 4, 8, 20 and 50 firms in the sector. There are approximately 2,576 players operating in the industry generating employment for 28,529 people.

4 largest firms	30.5%
8 largest firms	37.3

Continued on next page.

★ 3312 ★
[Continued]
Teleproduction and Postproduction Services
SIC: 7819; NAICS: 512191

Teleproduction and Other Postproduction Service Leaders, 2017

Data show the percent of industry sales held by the largest 4, 8, 20 and 50 firms in the sector. There are approximately 2,576 players operating in the industry generating employment for 28,529 people.

20 largest firms	48.0%
50 largest firms	60.8

Source: "Economic Census." [online] from https://www.census.gov/content/census/en/data/tables/2017/econ/economic-census/naics-sector-31-33.html [Accessed January 21, 2021], from U.S. Census Bureau.

★ 3313 ★
Telescopes
SIC: 3827; NAICS: 333314

Astronomical Telescope Market Worldwide, 2017

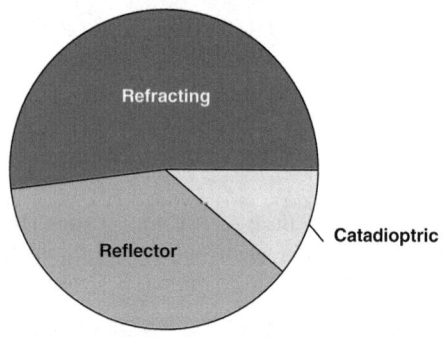

The market is forecast to grow from $191.15 million in 2017 to $251.26 million in 2022. North America claimed 45.35% of the overall market, followed by Europe with 29.93%. The market consists of three major categories, shown in the table below. Synta produces the top three brands (Celestron, Meade and Sky Watcher), as well as a number of OEM brands. It claims 60% of the global market.

Refracting	51.68%
Reflector	37.45
Catadioptric	10.86

Source: "Global Astronomical Telescope Market 2020-2026, With Breakdown Data of Capacity, Sales, Revenue, Price, Cost and Gross Profit." [online] from http://www.radiantinsights.com [Published February 2020], from XYZ Reports.

★ 3314 ★
Television Broadcasting
SIC: 4833; NAICS: 51512

Largest Markets for Antenna TV-Watching, 2020

Data show the estimated millions of people that watch television through the use of an antenna. The source estimates a market of 1.6 billion, based a survey of 83 countries and 6.6 billion people.

	(mil.)	Share
Indonesia	251	15.69%
India	130	8.13
Nigeria	127	7.94
Japan	121	7.56
Philippines	75	4.69
Brazil	66	4.13
Mexico	66	4.13
Pakistan	48	3.00
Vietnam	44	2.75
Egypt	42	2.63
Italy	42	2.63
United States	41	2.56
Other	547	34.19

Source: "Technology, Media, and Telecommunications Predictions 2020." [online] from https://www2.deloitte.com/content/dam/Deloitte/at/Documents/technology-media-telecommunications/at-tmt-predictions-2020.pdf [Accessed January 20, 2021], from Deloitte estimates.

★ 3315 ★
Television Broadcasting
SIC: 4833; NAICS: 51512

Largest Television Groups in Europe, 2020

Market shares are shown based on revenue.

Comcast Corp.	12.0%
Netflix Inc.	6.1
ARD	5.7
BBC	4.2
Canal+ Group	3.2
France Televisions	2.8
Vodafone	2.7
RTL Group	2.6
Deutsche Telekom	2.4
Liberty Global	2.4
Other	55.9

Source: "Netflix Becomes the Second Largest TV Group in Europe." [online] from https://www.ampereanalysis.com/insight/netflix-becomes-the-second-largest-tv-group-in-europe [Published January 14, 2021], from Ampere Analysis.

★ 3316 ★
Television Broadcasting
SIC: 7812; NAICS: 51211

Leading Morning Shows, 2019-2020

Morning shows are ranked by millions of viewers from December 30, 2019 through December 20, 2020.

	2019	2020
Good Morning America	3.9	3.7
Today	3.8	3.6
CBS This Morning	3.0	2.8

Source: *USA Today*, January 12, 2021, p. NA, from Nielsen.

★ 3317 ★
Television Broadcasting
SIC: 7812; NAICS: 51211

Leading Television News Shows, 2019-2020

News shows are ranked by millions of viewers from December 30, 2019 through December 20, 2020.

	2019	2020
ABC World News Tonight With David Muir	8.6	9.6
NBC Nightly News With Lester Holt	7.8	8.3
CBS Evening News With Norah O'Donnell	5.7	5.9
Tucker Carlson Tonight (Fox News)	3.1	4.5
Hannity (Fox News)	3.4	4.4
Ingraham Angle (Fox News)	2.7	3.6
Rachel Maddow (MSNBC)	2.9	3.4
Last Word-Lawrence O'Donnell (MSNBC)	2.2	2.5
All In With Chris Hayes (MSNBC)	1.8	2.1
Cuomo Prime Time (CNN)	1.1	2.0
Anderson Cooper 360 (CNN)	1.1	1.8
CNN Tonight With Don Lemon (CNN)	1.0	1.6

Source: *USA Today*, January 12, 2021, p. NA, from Nielsen.

★ 3318 ★
Television Broadcasting
SIC: 4833; NAICS: 51512

Leading Television Providers in Finland, 2018

Market shares are estimated based on free-to-air broadcasting. Finland's overall media market was valued at approximately 3.9 billion euros; the television industry represents about on-third of this total.

Yle	40.0-50.0%
Bonnier Broadcasting	20.0-30.0
Sanoma/Nelonen	10.0-20.0
Discovery Channel	5.0-10.0%
Disney	5.0-10.0
MTG/NENT	0.0-5.0
Telia	0.0-5.0
Other	0.0-20.0

Source: "Telia Company/Bonnier Broadcasting Holding." [online] from https://ec.europa.eu/competition/mergers/cases/decisions/m9064_3542_7.pdf [Published November 12, 2019], from Form CO, Annex 7.

★ 3319 ★
Television Broadcasting
SIC: 4833; NAICS: 51512

Leading Television Station Groups, 2020

Television groups are ranked by share of television households reached as of October 27, 2020.

ION Television	69.5%
Nexstar Media Group	62.1
Univision	45.5
Fox Broadcasting Co.	39.2
TEGNA Inc.	39.0
ViacomCBS	38.4
Sinclair Broadcast Corp.	38.3
Comcast Communications	37.5
E.W. Scripps	31.4
WRNN-TV Associates	25.3
Gray Television Inc.	24.0
Disney	22.7

Source: "2020 Communications Marketplace Report." [online] from https://www.fcc.gov/document/fcc-releases-2020-communications-marketplace-report [Published December 2020], from S&P Global, *Top TV Station Owners* (Oct. 2020) and Nielsen, *DMA Universe Estimates, 2019-2020*.

★ 3320 ★
Television Broadcasting
SIC: 7812; NAICS: 51211

Most-Streamed Acquired Television Series, 2020

Shows are ranked by estimated millions of minutes of streamed content. The source covers Netflix, Amazon Prime, Disney+ and Hulu. Figures cover U.S. viewing through television by persons 2+ years of age. Total minutes cover viewing in 2020 (December 30, 2019 through December 27, 2020).

The Office	57,127
Grey's Anatomy	39,405
Criminal Minds	35,414

Continued on next page.

★ 3320 ★
[Continued]
Television Broadcasting
SIC: 7812; NAICS: 51211

Most-Streamed Acquired Television Series, 2020

Shows are ranked by estimated millions of minutes of streamed content. The source covers Netflix, Amazon Prime, Disney+ and Hulu. Figures cover U.S. viewing through television by persons 2+ years of age. Total minutes cover viewing in 2020 (December 30, 2019 through December 27, 2020).

NCIS	28,134
Schitt's Creek	23,785
Supernatural	20,336
Shameless	18,218
New Girl	14,545
The Blacklist	14,480
Vampire Diaries	14,091

Source: *Variety*, January 12, 2021, p. NA, from Nielsen SVOD Content Ratings.

★ 3321 ★
Television Broadcasting
SIC: 7812; NAICS: 51211

Most-Streamed Original Television Series, 2020

Shows are ranked by estimated millions of minutes of streamed content. The source covers Netflix, Amazon Prime, Disney+ and Hulu. Figures cover U.S. viewing through television by persons 2+ years of age. Total minutes cover viewing in 2020 (December 30, 2019 through December 27, 2020).

Ozark	30,462
Lucifer	18,975
The Crown	16,275
Tiger King	15,611
The Mandalorian	14,519
The Umbrella Academy	13,470
The Great British Baking Show	13,279
Boss Baby: Back in Business	12,625
Longmire	11,382
You	10,965

Source: *Variety*, January 12, 2021, p. NA, from Nielsen SVOD Content Ratings.

★ 3322 ★
Television Broadcasting
SIC: 7812; NAICS: 51211

Television Production Revenue, 2013-2023

Figures are in billions of dollars. Documentary and news shows claimed 40% of production revenue in 2018, dramas 22.8%, reality shows 12%, sitcoms 10.5%, sports 10% and talk shows 4.7%.

2013	$ 29.9
2014	30.5
2015	32.6
2016	32.1
2017	35.4
2018	36.8
2019	38.9
2020	40.6
2021	42.4
2022	44.2
2023	46.0

Source: "eOne Annual Reports and Accounts 2018." [online] from http://investor.hasbro.com [Accessed November 17, 2020], from IBISWorld.

★ 3323 ★
Television Broadcasting
SIC: 7812; NAICS: 51211

Top Regularly Scheduled Television Programs, 2020

Programs are ranked by thousands of average viewers. Figures include broadcast and cable from January 1 through November 15, 2020, live +7, broadcast prime P2+. It excludes breakouts, specials, repeats and duration < 5 min, sustainers, and programs with fewer than four telecasts. Manually excluded pre-kick/post gun sports programming. Sample minimums applied.

NBC Sunday Night Football	16,286
NCIS	15,415
FBI	12,890
Fox and NFL Thursday Night Football	12,859
Blue Bloods	12,163
Chicago Fire	11,992
Chicago PD	11,519
Young Sheldon	11,407
Chicago Med	11,363
This is Us	11,254

Source: "Tops of 2020: Television." [online] from https://www.nielsen.com/us/en/insights/article/2020/tops-of-2020-television/ [Published December 14, 2020], from Nielsen.

★ 3324 ★
Television Broadcasting
SIC: 7812; NAICS: 51211

Top Time-Shifted Television Programs, 2020

Programs are ranked by percentage increase in thousands of average viewers. Figures include broadcast and cable from January 1 through November 15, 2020, live +7, broadcast prime P2+. Percent increase is based on absolute difference between live and live+7 projected (000). It excludes breakouts, specials, repeats and duration < 5 min, sustainers, and programs with fewer than four telecasts. Manually excluded pre-kick/post gun sports programming. Sample minimums applied.

Yellowstone	214.8%
Emergence	191.7
Stumptown	170.7
Manifest	157.6
The Resident	152.6
New Amsterdam	152.3
Walking Dead	148.4
Will & Grace	144.0
Million Little Things	143.9
Good Girls	142.7

Source: "Tops of 2020: Television." [online] from https://www.nielsen.com/us/en/insights/article/2020/tops-of-2020-television/ [Published December 14, 2020], from Nielsen.

★ 3325 ★
Tents, Awnings and Canvas
SIC: 2394; NAICS: 31491

Leading Tent, Awning and Canvas Makers, 2020

The industry generated revenue of $3 billion in 2020. Major distribution channels by outlet: retail locations 19.6%, transportation and warehousing 17.7%, sporting goods wholesalers 11.3%, government and military 8.9%, and other sectors 42.5%.

Outdoor Venture Corp.	1.2%
Eide Industries	0.8
Thomas Sign	0.2
Other	97.8

Source: "Tent, Awning & Canvas Manufacturing in the U.S." [online] from http://www.ibisworld.com [Published July 2020], from IBISWorld.

★ 3326 ★
Testing Instruments
SIC: 3825; NAICS: 334515

Instrument Manufacturing For Measuring and Testing Electricity and Electrical Systems, 2017

Data show the percent of industry sales held by the largest 4, 8, 20 and 50 firms in the sector. There are approximately 751 players operating in the industry generating employment for 30,104 people. According to Kentley Insights, the industry generated sales of $12 billion in 2019.

4 largest firms	25.1%
8 largest firms	34.1
20 largest firms	52.9
50 largest firms	71.6

Source: "Economic Census." [online] from https://www.census.gov/content/census/en/data/tables/2017/econ/economic-census/naics-sector-31-33.html [Accessed January 21, 2021], from U.S. Census Bureau.

★ 3327 ★
Textile Machinery
SIC: 3552; NAICS: 333249

Global Shipments of Textile Machinery, 2019

Shipments are shown in thousands of units. Short-staple spindle shipments fell 1.7 million units from 2018 to 2019. Long-staple wool spindle shipments fell from 120,000 in 2018 to nearly 40,000 in 2019. Single heater draw-texturing spindle shipments grew from 22,800 to 25,500 in 2019. Double heater draw-texturing spindle shipments decreased 5% during the year to 464,000. Shuttle-less loom shipments decreased 0.6% over the year. Water-jet looms increased 12%. Large circular knitting machines fell 1.2%.

Short-staple spindles	6,960.0
Open-end rotors	563.6
Double heater draw-texturing spindles	464.0
Shuttle-less looms	133.2
Water-jet looms	78.0
Long-staple wool spindles	> 40.0
Large circular knitting machines	26.4
Single heater draw-texturing spindles	25.5

Source: *Tecoya Trend*, July 7, 2020, p. 1, from International Textile Manufacturers Federation.

★ 3328 ★
Textile Rental Services
SIC: 7213; NAICS: 812331

Leading Textile Rental Firms, 2019

The industry was valued at $39 billion in 2019. Figures include uniform rental, uniform sales, ancillary services and linen services.

Cintas Corp.	14.0%
Aramark Corp.	7.0
UniFirst Corp.	5.0
Other	74.0

Source: "UniFirst Investing to Compete With Cintas." [online] from https://seekingalpha.com/article/4417968-unifirst-investing-to-compete-with-cintas [Published April 7, 2021], from Form 10-K filings.

★ 3329 ★
Textile Rental Services
SIC: 7213; NAICS: 812331

Leading Uniform Rental and Dust Control Firms, 2019

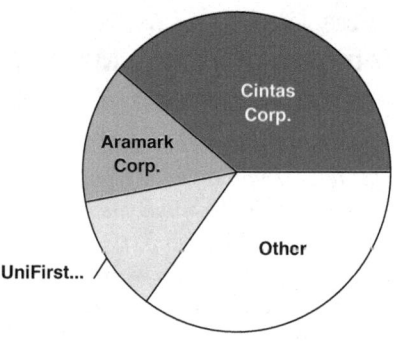

The industry was estimated at $10.3 billion in 2019.

Cintas Corp.	39.0%
Aramark Corp.	14.0
UniFirst Corp.	12.0
Other	35.0

Source: "UniFirst Investing to Compete With Cintas." [online] from https://seekingalpha.com/article/4417968-unifirst-investing-to-compete-with-cintas [Published April 7, 2021], from Robert W. Baird & Co.

★ 3330 ★
Textiles
SIC: 2200; NAICS: 31311, 31321, 31322

Leading Textile Exporters Worldwide, 2019

Exports reached $262 billion in 2019. China's include significant shipments through processing zones. Vietnam figure is a Secretariat estimate.

China	39.2%
European Union	21.7
India	5.6
United States	4.4
Turkey	3.9
South Korea	3.0
Vietnam	2.9
Chinese Taipei	2.8
Pakistan	2.3
Other	14.2

Source: "World Trade Statistical Review 2020." [online] from https://www.wto.org/english/res_e/statis_e/wts2020_e/wts20_toc_e.htm [Accessed October 28, 2020], from World Trade Organization.

★ 3331 ★
Textiles
SIC: 2200; NAICS: 31321, 31322, 31323

Leading Textile Importers Worldwide, 2019

Imports reached $168 billion in 2019. China and Mexico figures include significant shipments through processing zones. Vietnam, Bangladesh and Hong Kong figures are Secretariat estimates.

European Union	21.3%
United States	10.0
Vietnam	5.2
China	5.0
Bangladesh	3.1
Japan	2.8
United Kingdom	2.3
Indonesia	2.1
Other	48.2

Source: "World Trade Statistical Review 2020." [online] from https://www.wto.org/english/res_e/statis_e/wts2020_e/wts20_toc_e.htm [Accessed October 28, 2020], from World Trade Organization.

★ 3332 ★
Textiles
SIC: 2200; NAICS: 31321, 31323, 31324

Textile Industry in Russia, 2019

Figures are in billions of square meters. COVID-19 is expected to reduce fabric production by about 7.6% in 2020. The industry is expected to then return to growth for 2021-2024.

2015	2.43
2016	2.46
2017	2.50
2018	2.61
2019	2.64

Source: "Russia Textile Market Trends." [online] from http://news.kotra.or.kr [Published September 25, 2020], from http://businessstat.ru/catalog/id8923.

★ 3333 ★
Theater Companies and Dinner Theaters
SIC: 7922; NAICS: 71111

Theater Company and Dinner Theater Leaders, 2017

Data show the percent of industry sales held by the largest 4, 8, 20 and 50 firms in the sector. There are approximately 3,244 players operating in the industry generating employment for 66,566 people. According to Kentley Insights, the industry generated sales of $9.3 billion in 2019.

4 largest firms	10.4%
8 largest firms	17.0
20 largest firms	29.3
50 largest firms	44.8

Source: "Economic Census." [online] from https://www.census.gov/content/census/en/data/tables/2017/econ/economic-census/naics-sector-31-33.html [Accessed January 21, 2021], from U.S. Census Bureau.

★ 3334 ★
Theaters
SIC: 7922; NAICS: 71131, 71132

Leading Theater Venues Worldwide, 2020

Venues are ranked by tickets sold for November 21, 2019-November 18, 2020.

Radio City Music Hall (NY)	988,712
Hulu Theater/Madison Square Garden (NY)	201,665
Auditorio Nacional (Mexico)	184,802
Dreyfoos Hall (FL)	180,700
Fox Theatre (MI)	171,692
Chicago Theatre (IL)	170,318
DPAC/Durham Performing Arts Center (NC)	169,296
Fox Theatre (GA)	168,530
Paramount Theatre (WA)	149,810
Auditorio Telmex (Mexico)	148,134

Source: *Pollstar*, December 14, 2020, p. 22.

★ 3335 ★
3D Printing
SIC: 3577; NAICS: 334118

3D Printing Market Worldwide, 2020, 2022 and 2024

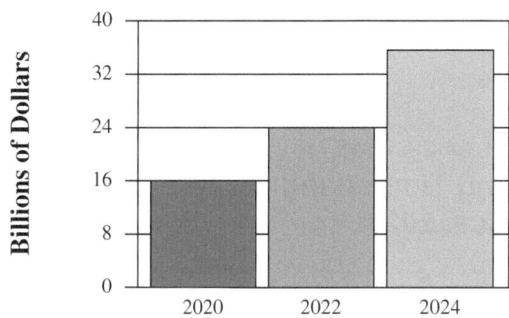

Figures are in billions of dollars.

2020	$ 15.8
2022	23.9
2024	35.6

Source: *Radiology Business Journal*, February/March 2020, p. 11, from Wohlers Report.

★ 3336 ★
Timber
SIC: 0811; NAICS: 11311

Leading Timberland Managers in North America, 2020

Companies are ranked by thousands of acres under management.

American Forest Management	5,698
Hancock (HTRG/HNRG)	3,654
Wagner Forest Management	2,640
The Forestland Group	2,594
LandVest Timberlands	2,460
Resource Management Service	2,247
Forest Resource Consultants	2,200
Forest Investment Associates	2,111

Continued on next page.

★ 3336 ★
[Continued]
Timber
SIC: 0811; NAICS: 11311

Leading Timberland Managers in North America, 2020

Companies are ranked by thousands of acres under management.

Molpus Woodlands Group	1,905
F&W Forestry Services	1,695

Source: "North America's Top Timberland Owners and Managers, 2020 Update." [online] from https://forisk.com/blog/2020/05/21/north-americas-top-timberland-owners-and-managers-2020-update/ [Published May 21, 2020], from Forisk North American Timberland Owner List.

★ 3337 ★
Timber
SIC: 0811; NAICS: 11311

Leading Timberland Owners in North America, 2020

Companies are ranked by thousands of acres under ownership.

Weyerhaeuser	11,100
J.D. Irving	3,177
Sierra Pacific Industries	2,058
Rayonier Inc.	2,052
PotlatchDeltic	1,859
Green Diamond Resource Company	1,676
Tall Timbers Trust	1,236
Triple T Timberlands J.V.	1,108
The Nature Conservancy	1,080
Acadian Timber/Katahdin Forest Management	1,061

Source: "North America's Top Timberland Owners and Managers, 2020 Update." [online] from https://forisk.com/blog/2020/05/21/north-americas-top-timberland-owners-and-managers-2020-update/ [Published May 21, 2020], from Forisk North American Timberland Owner List.

★ 3338 ★
Tin
SIC: 1099; NAICS: 212299

Leading End Uses for Tin Worldwide, 2019

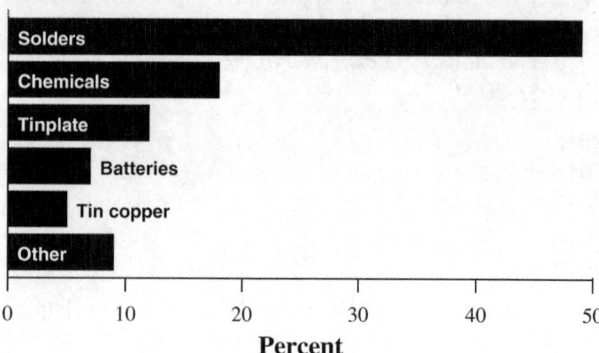

Shares are shown based on 359,200 tons of refined tin used.

Solders	49.0%
Chemicals	18.0
Tinplate	12.0
Batteries	7.0
Tin copper	5.0
Other	9.0

Source: "Pandemic Not All Bad News For Tin." [online] from https://www.internationaltin.org/pandemic-not-all-bad-news-for-tin/ [Press release October 20, 2020], from International Tin Association.

★ 3339 ★
Tin
SIC: 1099; NAICS: 212299

Top Tin Exporters Worldwide, 2019

Data show the major exporters of tin. Exports reached $4.5 billion in 2019, a 11.6% decrease from 2018.

Indonesia	28.5%
Malaysia	10.2
Peru	8.6
Bolivia	7.0
Singapore	6.6
Belgium	4.7
China, Hong Kong SAR	4.2
Brazil	3.8
Thailand	3.3
United States	2.9
Other	20.2

Source: "2019 International Trade Statistics Yearbook." [online] from https://comtrade.un.org/pb/ [Published December 2020], from U.N. Comtrade.

★ 3340 ★
Tin
SIC: 1099; NAICS: 212299
Top Tin Importers Worldwide, 2019

Data show the major importers of tin. Imports reached $4.6 billion in 2019, a 11.9% decrease from 2018.

United States	15.5%
Japan	10.7
Singapore	8.7
Germany	8.5
South Korea	5.5
India	4.7
Malaysia	3.4
Spain	2.9
Belgium	2.8
China	2.8
Other	34.5

Source: "2019 International Trade Statistics Yearbook." [online] from https://comtrade.un.org/pb/ [Published December 2020], from U.N. Comtrade.

★ 3341 ★
Tin
SIC: 1099; NAICS: 212299
Top Tin Producers Worldwide, 2019

Companies are ranked by refined tin production in tons. In 2019, 334,400 tons of refined tin were produced, down 6.6% from 2018. More than 75% was produced by the top 10 companies. The top 10 companies produced 14% more refined tin in 2019 than 2018 due to the 128.7% increase in PT Timah's production.

	Tons	Share
PT Timah	76,400	22.85%
Yunnan Tin Group Co.	72,000	21.53
Malaysia Smelting Corp.	24,300	7.27
Minsur	19,600	5.86
Yunnan Chengfeng Nonferrous Metals	19,100	5.71
Empresa Metalúrgica Vinto	11,500	3.44
Thaisarco Smelting and Refining	10,900	3.26
Metallo	9,300	2.78
Guangxi China Tin Group Co.	8,200	2.45
Gejiu Zi-Li Mining & Smelting	8,000	2.39
Other	75,100	22.46

Source: "PT Timah Becomes Top Tin Producer." [online] from https://www.internationaltin.org/pt-timah-top-tin-producer/ [Published February 14, 2020], from International Tin Association.

★ 3342 ★
Tin
SIC: 1099; NAICS: 212299
Top Tin Producing Nations, 2020

Countries are ranked by production in metric tons of tin content. In the United States, 25 firms accounted for more than 90% of the tin consumed in 2020. Tinplate claimed 21% of the total; chemicals 18%; solder 15%; alloys 10%; babbit, brass, bronze and tinning 10% and other uses 26%. Production data are estimated.

	MT	Share
China	81,000	30.08%
Indonesia	66,000	24.51
Burma	33,000	12.25
Peru	18,000	6.68
Congo (Kinshasa)	17,000	6.31
Bolivia	15,000	5.57
Brazil	13,000	4.83
Australia	6,800	2.53
Nigeria	6,000	2.23
Vietnam	4,900	1.82
Malaysia	3,300	1.23
Russia	2,500	0.93
Laos	1,200	0.45
Rwanda	1,200	0.45
Other	400	0.15

Source: "Mineral Commodity Summaries 2021." [online] from https://www.usgs.gov/centers/nmic/mineral-commodity-summaries [Published January 29, 2021], from U.S. Geological Survey.

★ 3343 ★
Tire Retailers
SIC: 5531; NAICS: 44132
Largest Tire Dealerships in North America, 2020

Companies are ranked based on sales of tires and related automotive services at company owned outlets in millions of dollars. Shares are shown based on sales generated by the top 26 dealerships.

	($ mil.)	Share
Discount Tire/America's Tire	$ 5,172	17.23%
Bridgestone Americas Inc.	4,500	14.99
Walmart Inc.	3,250	10.83
Icahn Automotive/Pep Boys	2,670	8.89
TBC Corp.	2,000	6.66
Les Schwab Tire Centers	1,610	5.36

Continued on next page.

★ 3343 ★
[Continued]
Tire Retailers
SIC: 5531; NAICS: 44132

Largest Tire Dealerships in North America, 2020

Companies are ranked based on sales of tires and related automotive services at company owned outlets in millions of dollars. Shares are shown based on sales generated by the top 26 dealerships.

	($ mil.)	Share
Monro Inc.	$ 1,257	4.19%
Midas International	1,050	3.50
Big O Tires network	950	3.16
Costco Wholesale Corp.	925	3.08
Other	6,637	22.11

Source: *Tire Business*, February 15, 2021, p. 14.

★ 3344 ★
Tire Retailers
SIC: 5531; NAICS: 44132

Tire Purchases by Outlet, 2018-2020

Retail sales are shown by channel. Walmart Auto Care Centers briefly closed during 2020 because of the pandemic.

	2018	2019	2020
Independent tire dealers	62.5%	63.0%	65.5%
Mass merchandisers	10.5	10.5	8.0
Warehouse clubs	8.5	8.5	8.0
Auto dealerships	6.5	6.5	6.5
Tire company-owned stores	6.5	6.0	6.0
Other	2.5	2.5	3.0

Source: *Modern Tire Dealer*, January 2021, p. 42, from *Modern Tire Dealer* research.

★ 3345 ★
Tire Retreading
SIC: 7534; NAICS: 326212

Leading Tire Retreaders in North America (Medium and Heavy Truck), 2019

Companies are ranked by amount of tread rubber used during 2019 in millions of pounds per year.

Southern Tire Mart L.L.C.	33.0
Goodyear Commercial Tire Systems L.L.C.	31.0
Snider Fleet Solutions	21.0
Pomp's Tire & Auto Service Inc.	17.7
Best One Tire & Service	16.5
McCarthy Tire Service Co. Inc.	13.0
GCR Tires & Service	12.0
Les Schwab Tire Centers	11.1
Kal Tire	9.8
Service Tire Truck Centers Inc.	8.5

Source: *Tire Business*, December 21, 2020, p. 36.

★ 3346 ★
Tire Retreading
SIC: 7534; NAICS: 326212

Leading Tire Retreaders in North America (Off-the-Road), 2019

Companies are ranked by amount of tread rubber used during 2019 in millions of pounds per year.

Purcell Tire & Rubber Co.	9.0
RDH Tire Co.	5.0
H&H Industries Inc.	4.8
B.R. Retreading Inc.	4.0
Kal Tire	3.0
Goodyear Canada Inc.	2.5
Community Tire Co. Inc.	2.0
Craft Tire Inc.	1.7
Lan OTR Inc./Pneus	1.0
Les Schwab Tire Centers Inc.	0.6

Source: *Tire Business*, December 21, 2020, p. 37.

★ 3347 ★
Tire Retreading
SIC: 7534; NAICS: 326212

Leading Tire Retreaders in North America (Passenger and Light Truck), 2019

Companies are ranked by amount of tread rubber used during 2019 in millions of pounds per year.

Tread Wright Inc.	2.40
Eastern Tire Service Ltd.	1.50
Techno Pneu Inc.	1.50
Pomp's Tire & Auto Service Inc.	0.75
Purcell Tire & Rubber Co.	0.55

Source: *Tire Business*, December 21, 2020, p. 37.

★ 3348 ★
Tires
SIC: 3011; NAICS: 326211

Global Market for Pneumatic Tires for Industrial Trucks, 2015

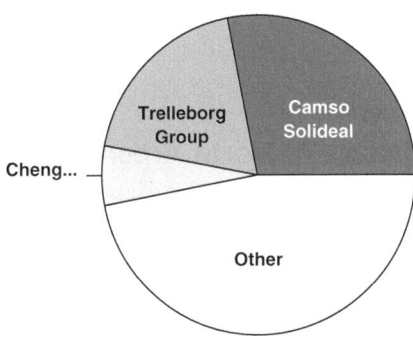

The industry is forecast to be worth $1.31 billion in 2020.

Camso Solideal	27.99%
Trelleborg Group	19.15
Cheng Shin Tire (CST)	5.62
Other	47.24

Source: "Global Pneumatic Tires for Industrial Truck (Forklift) Sales Market Report 2020." [online] from http://www.qy-research.com [Published November 2020], from QY Research.

★ 3349 ★
Tires
SIC: 3011; NAICS: 326211

Performance and Specialty Equipment Tire Market, 2019

The market for performance and specialty tires grew from $2.22 billion in 2016 to $2.54 billion in 2019. "Other" includes vans, sports cars, classic cars, alternative power vehicles, as well as other types.

Midrange cars and pickups	19.0%
Sports cars	16.0
SUVs	14.0
CUVs	11.0
Other	40.0

Source: "Wheel and Tire Market Trends." [online] from https://www.sema.org/news-media/magazine/2021/02/wheel-and-tire-market-trends-0 [Published February 2021], from Specialty Equipment Manufacturers Association.

★ 3350 ★
Tires
SIC: 3011; NAICS: 326211

Performance OE Tire Market by Speed Rating, 2019

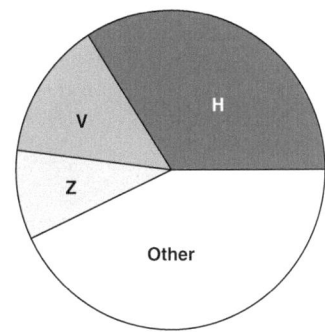

Market shares are shown for the OE market. In the replacement tire market, H claimed 25%, V 13%, Z 8%, and other speeds 54%.

H	34.0%
V	14.0
Z	9.0
Other	43.0

Source: *Rubber & Plastics News*, July 27, 2020, p. 4, from U.S. Tire Manufacturers Association and *Tire Business* research.

★ 3351 ★
Tires
SIC: 3011; NAICS: 326211

Replacement Light Truck Tire Market, 2020

Market shares are shown based on estimated sales of 30.4 million units.

Goodyear	10.0%
BFGoodrich	7.5
Firestone	6.5
Bridgestone	6.0
Cooper	5.5
General	5.5
Toyo	5.0
Yokohama	5.0
Falken	4.0
Hankook	3.5
Other	41.5

Source: *Modern Tire Dealer*, January 2021, p. 32, from *Modern Tire Dealer* research.

★ 3352 ★
Tires
SIC: 3011; NAICS: 326211

Replacement Passenger Tire Market, 2020

Market shares are shown based on estimated sales of 202.6 million units.

Goodyear	11.0%
Michelin	9.0
Firestone	7.0
Bridgestone	6.5
Falken	5.0
Continental	4.5
Cooper	4.5
BFGoodrich	4.0
Yokohama	3.5
General	3.0
Hamkook	3.0
Kumho	3.0
Other	36.0

Source: *Modern Tire Dealer*, January 2021, p. 32, from *Modern Tire Dealer* research.

★ 3353 ★
Tires
SIC: 3011; NAICS: 326211

Specialty Tire Market in Asia, 2025

The tire market in Asia was placed at 1.3 billion units in 2020, worth $97.4 billion. The rise of vehicle ownership in the region has helped boost the replacement market.

PC/LGV high performance/premium tires	43.9%
T&B premium tires	36.0
Motorcycle premium tires	20.0

Source: *Tire Review*, August 2020, p. 45.

★ 3354 ★
Tires
SIC: 3011; NAICS: 326211

Tire Shipments by Type, 2019-2020

Shipments are shown in millions of units. Figures for 2020 are forecasts.

	2019 (mil.)	2020 (mil.)	Share
Passenger, replacement	223.6	188.7	67.56%
Passenger, OEM	46.3	34.9	12.50
Light truck, replacement	32.5	28.7	10.28
Truck	18.9	18.0	6.44
Light truck, OEM	5.9	4.6	1.65%
Truck, OEM	6.5	4.4	1.58

Source: *Rubber World*, August 2020, p. 10, from U.S. Tire Manufacturers Association.

★ 3355 ★
Tires
SIC: 3011; NAICS: 326211

Top Tire Makers in North America, 2020

Shares are shown based on sales of $43 billion.

Michelin North America Inc.	19.2%
Bridgestone Americas Inc.	18.7
Goodyear Tire and Rubber Co.	11.9
Continental Tire the Americas	6.7
Cooper Tire & Rubber Co.	4.8
Toyo Tire (USA) Corp.	3.5
Hankook Tire America Corp.	3.3
Sumitomo Rubber Industries Ltd.	3.2
Yokohama Tire Corp.	2.8
Pirelli Tire North America	2.2
Other	37.4

Source: *Tire Business*, February 15, 2021, p. 16.

★ 3356 ★
Tires
SIC: 3011; NAICS: 326211

Top Tire Makers Worldwide, 2019

Companies are ranked by sales in millions of dollars. Due to the COVID-19 economic slowdown, the top dozen publicly traded tire makers reported declining operating income and sales between 16 and 32 percent through the first half of 2020. While the market was affected by the stay-at-home orders to stop the spread of COVID-19 in the first half of the year, sales in the second half of the year are expected to be affected by the economic recession that followed.

	($ mil.)	Share
Group Michelin	$25,000.0	14.97%
Bridgestone Corp.	24,325.0	14.57
Goodyear Tire and Rubber Co.	13,690.0	8.20
Continental AG	11,275.0	6.75
Sumitomo Rubber Industries Ltd.	7,060.0	4.23
Pirelli & C. S.p.A.	5,935.0	3.55
Hankook Tire & Technology Co. Ltd.	5,725.0	3.43

Continued on next page.

★ 3356 ★
[Continued]
Tires
SIC: 3011; NAICS: 326211

Top Tire Makers Worldwide, 2019

Companies are ranked by sales in millions of dollars. Due to the COVID-19 economic slowdown, the top dozen publicly traded tire makers reported declining operating income and sales between 16 and 32 percent through the first half of 2020. While the market was affected by the stay-at-home orders to stop the spread of COVID-19 in the first half of the year, sales in the second half of the year are expected to be affected by the economic recession that followed.

	($ mil.)	Share
Yokohama Rubber Co. Ltd.	$ 4,810.0	2.88%
Maxxis International/Cheng Shin Rubber	3,908.1	2.34
Zhongce Rubber Group Co. Ltd.	3,585.0	2.15
Giti Tire PTE Ltd.	3,100.0	1.86
Toyo Tire Corp.	3,060.0	1.83
Cooper Tire & Rubber Co.	2,750.0	1.65
Linglong Group Co. Ltd.	2,400.4	1.44
Apollo Tyres Ltd.	2,267.2	1.36
Other	48,109.3	28.81

Source: *Rubber & Plastics News*, September 7, 2020, p. 16.

★ 3357 ★
Titanium
SIC: 1099; NAICS: 212299

Global Demand for Titanium, 2019

Market shares are estimated in percent. Russia, China and Japan represent more than three quarters of output. There is a high degree of downstream integration into the production of milled products.

Aerospace	42.0%
Industrial	34.0
Military	11.0
Consumer/other	5.0
Medical	3.0

Source: *Titanium Today*, Second Quarter, 2019, p. 30.

★ 3358 ★
Tobacco and Tobacco Products
SIC: 2121; NAICS: 31223

Leading Cigar Brands, 2020

Market shares are shown based on convenience store sales for the 52 weeks ended June 13, 2020. Sales reached $2.5 billion.

Black & Mild	32.0%
Swisher Sweets	22.0
Backwoods	11.0
Game	9.0
White Owl	5.0
Dutch Masters	4.0
Jackpot	2.0
Cheyenne	1.0
Optimo	1.0
Pom Pom	1.0
Other	12.0

Source: *Guide to Tobacco - A Supplement to Convenience Store News*, August 2020, p. 22, from Management Science Associates.

★ 3359 ★
Tobacco and Tobacco Products
SIC: 2121; NAICS: 31223

Leading Cigar Makers, 2020

Market shares are shown based on convenience store sales for the 52 weeks ended June 13, 2020. Sales reached $2.5 billion.

Altria Group	31.9%
Swisher International	25.5
ITG Brands L.L.C.	17.0
Swedish Match	16.5
Good Times Tobacco	1.6
Cheyenne International	1.4
Kretek International	1.3
JTI-Japan Tobacco International	0.9
National Honey Almond Inc.	0.8
Intercontinental Cigar Co.	0.6
Other	2.5

Source: *Guide to Tobacco - A Supplement to Convenience Store News*, August 2020, p. 22, from Management Science Associates.

★ 3360 ★
Tobacco and Tobacco Products
SIC: 2111; NAICS: 31223
Leading Cigarette Brands, 2020

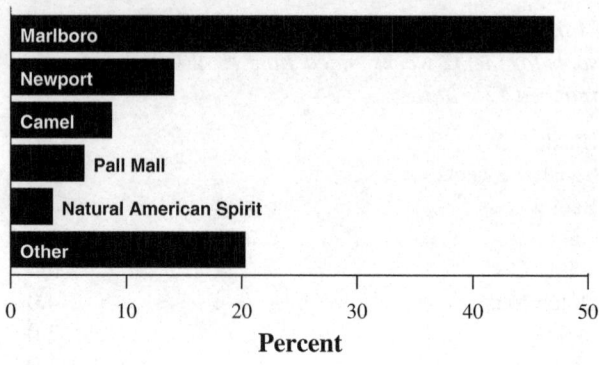

Market shares are shown as of June 13, 2020.

Marlboro	47.00%
Newport	14.10
Camel	8.70
Pall Mall	6.31
Natural American Spirit	3.60
Other	20.29

Source: *Winston-Salem Journal*, June 25, 2020, p. NA, from Goldman Sachs.

★ 3361 ★
Tobacco and Tobacco Products
SIC: 2111; NAICS: 31223
Leading Cigarette Makers Worldwide, 2019

Market shares are shown in percent.

China National Tobacco Corp.	44.0%
Philip Morris Intl.	14.0
British American Tobacco	12.0
Japan Tobacco Inc.	8.5
Imperial Tobacco	3.5
Other	18.0

Source: "Marketing in Regulated Industry." [online] from http://www.theseus.fl/handle/10024/346377 [Published October 2020], from Statista.

★ 3362 ★
Tobacco and Tobacco Products
SIC: 2131; NAICS: 31223
Leading Modern Oral Nicotine Product Brands, 2020

Market shares are shown based on convenience store sales for the 52 weeks ended June 13, 2020. Sales reached $508.4 million, a 178.1% increase from the same period a year ago. Modern oral nicotine products are nicotine pouches meant to be placed between the gum and upper lip. In addition to nicotine, they may also contain flavorings, fibers and sweeteners. Not all modern oral nicotine products contain tobacco.

ZYN	89.87%
VELO	8.61
ON!	1.09
DRYFT	0.41
REVEL	0.01

Source: *Guide to Tobacco - A Supplement to Convenience Store News*, August 2020, p. 21, from Management Science Associates.

★ 3363 ★
Tobacco and Tobacco Products
SIC: 2131; NAICS: 31223
Leading Modern Oral Nicotine Product Makers, 2020

Market shares are shown based on convenience store sales for the 52 weeks ended June 13, 2020. Sales reached $508.4 million, a 178.1% increase from the same period a year ago. Modern oral nicotine products are nicotine pouches meant to be placed between the gum and upper lip. In addition to nicotine, they may also contain flavorings, fibers and sweeteners. Not all modern oral nicotine products contain tobacco.

Swedish Match	89.87%
Reynolds American Inc.	8.62
Helix Innovations L.L.C.	1.09
Kretek International	0.41

Source: *Guide to Tobacco - A Supplement to Convenience Store News*, August 2020, p. 21, from Management Science Associates.

★ 3364 ★
Tobacco and Tobacco Products
SIC: 2131; NAICS: 31223

Leading Moist Tobacco Brands, 2020

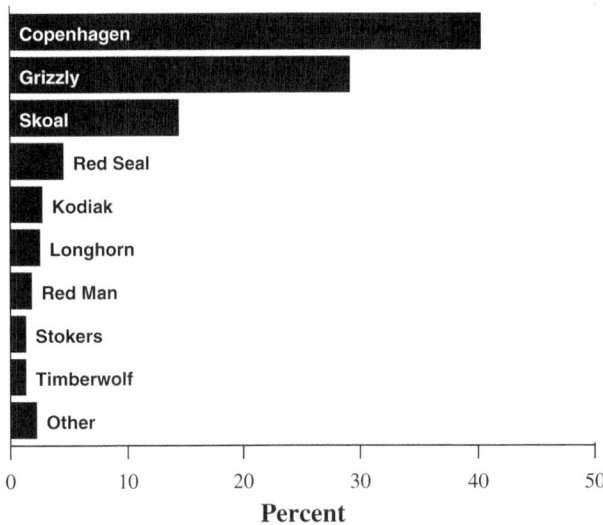

Market shares are shown based on convenience store sales for the 52 weeks ended June 13, 2020. Sales reached $7.7 billion.

Copenhagen	40.2%
Grizzly	29.1
Skoal	14.4
Red Seal	4.5
Kodiak	2.7
Longhorn	2.5
Red Man	1.8
Stokers	1.3
Timberwolf	1.3
Other	2.2

Source: *Guide to Tobacco - A Supplement to Convenience Store News*, August 2020, p. 20, from Management Science Associates.

★ 3365 ★
Tobacco and Tobacco Products
SIC: 2131; NAICS: 31223

Leading Moist Tobacco Makers, 2020

Market shares are shown based on convenience store sales for the 52 weeks ended June 13, 2020. Sales reached $7.7 billion.

Altria Group	59.51%
Reynolds American Inc.	32.68
Swedish Match	5.67
National Tobacco Co.	1.31
Swisher International	0.70
Smokey Mountain Chew Inc.	0.12

Cheyenne International	0.02%
Grand River Enterprises	< 0.01

Source: *Guide to Tobacco - A Supplement to Convenience Store News*, August 2020, p. 20, from Management Science Associates.

★ 3366 ★
Tobacco and Tobacco Products
SIC: 2131; NAICS: 31223

Leading Pipe/Cigarette Tobacco Brands, 2020

Market shares are shown based on convenience store sales for the 52 weeks ended June 13, 2020. Sales reached $276.3 million.

Natural American Spirit	23.0%
Gambler	11.0
Bugler	9.0
Good Stuff	9.0
Largo	7.0
Criss Cross	5.0
Golden Harvest	4.0
4 Aces	3.0
Ohm	3.0
Top	3.0
Other	23.0

Source: *Guide to Tobacco - A Supplement to Convenience Store News*, August 2020, p. 25, from Management Science Associates.

★ 3367 ★
Tobacco and Tobacco Products
SIC: 2131; NAICS: 31223

Leading Pipe/Cigarette Tobacco Makers, 2020

Market shares are shown based on convenience store sales for the 52 weeks ended June 13, 2020. Sales reached $276.3 million.

Republic Tobacco	30.6%
Reynolds American Inc.	22.7
Scandinavian Tobacco Group	11.5
RSB Tobacco	9.4
SX Brands	5.7
Rouseco Inc.	5.2
Inter Continental Trading USA Inc.	3.3
Farmers Tobacco Co.	2.0
XCaliber International Ltd.	1.7
Other	7.8

Source: *Guide to Tobacco - A Supplement to Convenience Store News*, August 2020, p. 25, from Management Science Associates.

★ 3368 ★
Tobacco and Tobacco Products
SIC: 2131; NAICS: 31223

Leading Smokeless Tobacco Brands, 2020

Market shares are shown based on convenience store sales for the 52 weeks ended June 13, 2020. Sales reached $8.4 billion.

Copenhagen	36.0%
Grizzly	26.0
Skoal	13.0
ZYN	5.0
Red Seal	4.0
Camel Snus	3.0
Kodiak	2.0
Longhorn	2.0
Red Man	2.0
Stokers	1.0
Other	6.0

Source: *Guide to Tobacco - A Supplement to Convenience Store News*, August 2020, p. 19, from Management Science Associates.

★ 3369 ★
Tobacco and Tobacco Products
SIC: 2131; NAICS: 31223

Leading Smokeless Tobacco Makers, 2020

Market shares are shown based on convenience store sales for the 52 weeks ended June 13, 2020. Sales reached $8.4 billion.

Altria Group	54.0%
Reynolds American Inc.	32.9
Swedish Match	10.6%
National Tobacco Co.	1.4
Swisher International	0.9
Smokey Mountain Chew Inc.	0.1
Other	0.2

Source: *Guide to Tobacco - A Supplement to Convenience Store News*, August 2020, p. 19, from Management Science Associates.

★ 3370 ★
Tobacco and Tobacco Products
SIC: 2621; NAICS: 322121

Leading Tobacco Paper Brands, 2020

Market shares are shown based on convenience store sales for the 52 weeks ended June 13, 2020. Sales reached $227.2 million.

Zig-Zag	41.6%
Job	14.4
Gambler	12.3
Top	6.7
Golden Harvest	3.3
Premier	2.5
Bugler	2.3
OCB	1.8
Raw	1.7
Other	2.9

Source: *Guide to Tobacco - A Supplement to Convenience Store News*, August 2020, p. 26, from Management Science Associates.

★ 3371 ★
Tobacco and Tobacco Products
SIC: 2621; NAICS: 322121

Leading Tobacco Paper Makers, 2020

Market shares are shown based on convenience store sales for the 52 weeks ended June 13, 2020. Sales reached $227.2 million.

National Tobacco Co.	42.0%
Republic Tobacco	41.0
HBI International	3.0
Rouseco Inc.	3.0
New Image Global	2.0
Scandinavian Tobacco Group	2.0
Other	7.0

Source: *Guide to Tobacco - A Supplement to Convenience Store News*, August 2020, p. 26, from Management Science Associates.

★ 3372 ★
Tobacco and Tobacco Products
SIC: 2131; NAICS: 31223

Nicotine Pouch Market, 2019

Market shares are shown in percent.

Swedish Match	84.0%
Other	16.0

Source: "Swedish Match Investor Presentation." [online] from https://www.swedishmatch.com/Investors/Presentations/ [Accessed January 13, 2021], from Nielsen Co.

★ 3373 ★
Tobacco and Tobacco Products
SIC: 2100; NAICS: 31223

Tobacco Product Sales at Convenience Stores, 2020

Market shares are shown based on wholesale sales at convenience stores for the first three quarters of 2020.

Cigarettes	79.0%
Moist smokeless	7.3
Vapor	5.3
Paper, tubes, wraps	3.4
Large cigars	1.9
Little filtered cigars	1.1
Modern oral	0.7
Snus	0.3
Pipe tobacco	< 0.1
Roll-your-own	< 0.1

Source: *CSP*, March 2021, p. 51, from MSA.

★ 3374 ★
Tobacco and Tobacco Products
SIC: 0132; NAICS: 11191

Tobacco Production by State, 2019-2020

Production is shown in thousands of pounds. Production fell from 467.9 million pounds in 2019 to 387.58 million in 2020.

	2019 (000)	2020 (000)	Share
North Carolina	234,700	184,095	47.50%
Kentucky	123,390	108,210	27.92
Tennessee	30,490	30,180	7.79
Virginia	30,406	26,290	6.78
Georgia	18,900	16,560	4.27
Pennsylvania	14,300	12,650	3.26%
South Carolina	15,770	9,600	2.48

Source: "Crop Production." [online] from https://www.nass.usda.gov/Publications/Todays_Reports/reports/crop1020.pdf [Published October 9, 2020], from U.S. Department of Agriculture.

★ 3375 ★
Tobacco Stores
SIC: 5993; NAICS: 453991

Tobacco Stores, 2017

Data show the percent of industry sales held by the largest 4, 8, 20 and 50 firms in the sector. There are approximately 10,415 players operating in the industry generating employment for 40,239 people. According to Kentley Insights, the industry generated sales of $48.9 billion in 2019.

4 largest firms	4.3%
8 largest firms	6.9
20 largest firms	12.5
50 largest firms	20.3

Source: "Economic Census." [online] from https://www.census.gov/content/census/en/data/tables/2017/econ/economic-census/naics-sector-31-33.html [Accessed January 21, 2021], from U.S. Census Bureau.

★ 3376 ★
Toll Roads
SIC: 4785; NAICS: 48849

Bridge and Tunnel Toll Road Travel in New York, 2020

Data show the methods of payment for bridge and tunnel travel for year-to-date 2020. E-Z Pass had a 95.4% share for cars and 96.5% for trucks. Verrazzano-Narrows Bridge tolls are only collected in the westbound direction. These transactions are doubled to provide traffic statistics that are consistent with other bridge and tunnel facilities. Average traffic excludes holidays.

	YTD (mil.)	Share
E-Z Pass	175.90	94.94%
Tolls by Mail	9.37	5.06

Source: "MTA Bridges and Tunnels Report on Operations September 2020." from [online] from http://www.new.mta.info [Published September 2020], from Metropolitan Transit Authority.

★ 3377 ★
Toll Roads
SIC: 4785; NAICS: 48849

Toll Road Operations in Indonesia, 2020

Private corporations are moving into the market for toll road operation as the government prepares to launch a number of projects over the next five years.

Jasa Marga	60.0%
PT Hutama Karya	11.0
PT Waskita Karya	11.0
PT Astra Tol Nusantara	1.0
PT Citra Marga Nusaphala Persada	1.0
PT Nusantara Infrastruktur	1.0
Other	1.0

Source: "Toll Road Project: Private Companies Ready to Take Over Market." [online] from https://www.pwc.com/id/en/media-centre/infrastructure-news/march-2020/toll-road-project-private-companies-ready-to-take-over-market.html [Published March 9, 2020].

★ 3378 ★
Toll Roads
SIC: 4785; NAICS: 48849

Toll Road Revenue in Europe, 2018

Member countries are ranked by toll road revenue in millions of euros as of December 31, 2018. Figures exclude VAT and other taxes.

	(mil.)	Share
France	€ 10,603.24	31.88%
Germany	7,144.30	21.48
Italy	5,016.95	15.08
Austria	2,238.61	6.73
Portugal	1,205.48	3.62
Hungary	855.51	2.57
Greece	687.34	2.07
Denmark	587.00	1.76
Croatia	425.74	1.28
Czech Republic	419.00	1.26
Slovak Republic	300.40	0.90
Other	3,780.40	11.36

Source: "Member Statistics." [online] from http://www.asecap.com/members-statistics.html [Accessed January 2, 2021], from European Association of Operators of Toll Road Infrastructures.

★ 3379 ★
Tools
SIC: 3429; NAICS: 33251

Adjustable Wrench Sales by Type, 2020

Sales are shown for the previous 12 months in the independent hardware channel. The top 5 items represented 35.4% of unit sales, the top 10 items 51.1%, the top 20 items 67.7%, and top 30 items 77.4%.

Wrenches	95.0%
Wrench sets	5.0

Source: *The Hardware Connection*, March 2020, p. 47, from Vista Information Services, division of Epicor Software Corp.

★ 3380 ★
Tools
SIC: 3546; NAICS: 333991

Consumption of Power Tools by Region, 2019

Total consumption reached $1.39 billion. Figures are in millions of dollars.

	($ mil.)	Share
South Atlantic	$ 324.69	23.36%
Pacific Coast	219.74	15.81
Southwest Central	186.10	13.39
Northeast Central	158.95	11.43
Mid-Atlantic	150.84	10.85
Mountain states	112.35	8.08
Northwest Central	99.75	7.18
Southeast Central	71.43	5.14
Northeast Coastal	66.28	4.77

Source: *Industrial Supply*, March-April 2020, p. 43, from MDM Analytics.

★ 3381 ★
Tools
SIC: 3546; NAICS: 333991

Demand for Power Tools Worldwide, 2019

The industry was valued at $32.1 billion in 2019. Revenue is forecast to see a CAGR of 3.4% from 2019-2024. Major producers include Bosch, Hilti, Makita, Stanley Black & Decker and Techtronic Industries.

Plug-in electric tools	38.0%
Cordless electric tools	30.0

Continued on next page.

★ 3381 ★
[Continued]
Tools
SIC: 3546; NAICS: 333991

Demand for Power Tools Worldwide, 2019

The industry was valued at $32.1 billion in 2019. Revenue is forecast to see a CAGR of 3.4% from 2019-2024. Major producers include Bosch, Hilti, Makita, Stanley Black & Decker and Techtronic Industries.

Pneumatic tool	22.0%
Other power	10.0

Source: ''Power Tools.'' [online] from http://www.freedoniagroup.com [Published January 2021], from The Freedonia Group Inc.

★ 3382 ★
Tools
SIC: 3546; NAICS: 333991

Demand for Professional Power Tools Worldwide, 2019

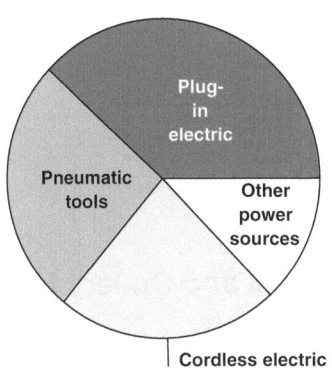

The industry was valued at $23.1 billion in 2019. Revenue is forecast to see a CAGR of 3.7% from 2019-2024. Major players include Bosch, Hilti, Makita, Stanley Black & Decker and Techtronic Industries.

Plug-in electric tools	38.0%
Pneumatic tools	26.0
Cordless electric tools	23.0
Other power sources	13.0

Source: ''Global Professional Power Tools.'' [online] from http://www.freedoniagroup.com [Published January 2021], from The Freedonia Group Inc.

★ 3383 ★
Tools
SIC/NAICS: See frontmatter for explanation.

Global Tool and Storage Market, 2018

North America is expected to be the largest market for 2019-2024, as a result of its DIY culture and lower population density. Transition to cordless power tools has been accelerated by lighter and less expensive lithium batteries.

Hand tools and storage	26.0%
Professional power tools	22.0
Power tool accessories	17.0
Consumer power tools	13.0
Outdoor tools	6.0
Other	16.0

Source: ''Cordless Power Tool Leader Driven by Technological Innovations, Initiate With Accumulate.'' [online] from http://wwww.gtja.com [Published November 12, 2020], from SBD and Guotai Junan International.

★ 3384 ★
Tools
SIC: 3546; NAICS: 333991

Leading Industrial Power Tool Makers Worldwide, 2017

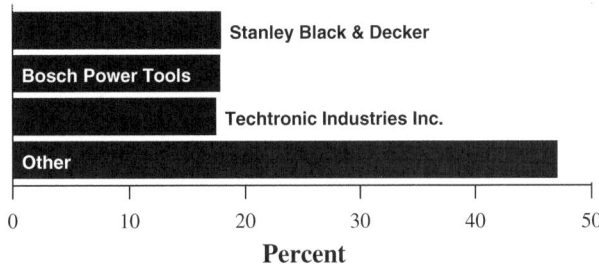

The source estimates that the probable effect of COVID-19 is to drive the revenue from $2.63 billion in 2019 to $2.56 billion in 2020. By 2020, the industry is forecast to see a CAGR of 5.31% from 2020 to 2026 to reach $3.49 billion.

Stanley Black & Decker	17.83%
Bosch Power Tools	17.76
Techtronic Industries Inc.	17.40
Other	47.01

Source: ''Global Industrial Power Tools Market Research Report 2020.'' [online] from https://www.marketstudyreport.com/reports/global-industrial-power-tools-market-research-report-2020 [Published June 2020].

★ 3385 ★
Tools
SIC: 3546; NAICS: 333991

Leading Power Tool Makers Worldwide, 2019

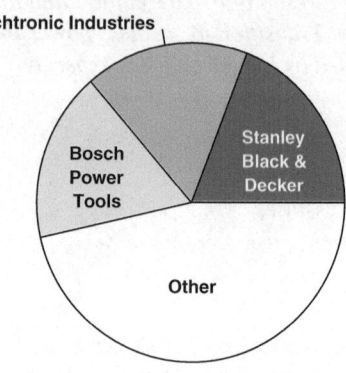

Market shares are shown based on revenue. The industry is forecast to grow from $26.39 billion in 2019 to $36.44 billion in 2026.

Stanley Black & Decker	19.25%
Techtronic Industries	17.49
Bosch Power Tools	17.19
Other	46.07

Source: "Global Power Tools Market Size, Manufacturers, Supply Chain, Sales Channel and Clients, 2020-2026." [online] from http://www.qyresearch.com [Published September 2020], from QY Research.

★ 3386 ★
Tools
SIC: 3546; NAICS: 333991

Oscillating Tool Accessory Sales, 2020

Sales are shown for the previous 12 months in the independent hardware channel. The top 5 items represented 18.7% of unit sales, the top 10 items 31.4%, the top 20 items 48.7%, and top 30 items 58.8%.

End/cut plunge blades	84.2%
Segment blades	6.4
Grout removal blades	2.4
Mixed product accessory kit	2.3
Sanding sheets	2.1
Other	2.7

Source: *The Hardware Connection*, March 2021, p. 60, from Vista Information Services, division of Epicor Software Corp.

★ 3387 ★
Tools
SIC: 3546; NAICS: 333991

Selected Power Tool Sales, 2019

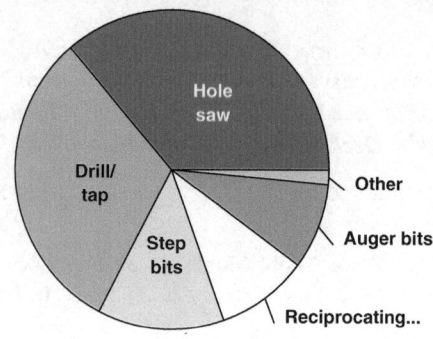

Market shares are shown based on dollar sales for the 12 months ended June 2019.

Hole saw	49.9%
Drill/tap	43.0
Step bits	18.2
Reciprocating saw blades	13.0
Auger bits	12.0
Other	2.4

Source: *The Electrical Distributor*, September 2019, p. 66, from Epicor's Industry Data Analytics.

★ 3388 ★
Tools
SIC: 3421; NAICS: 332216

Top Hand Tool and Cutlery Makers, 2019

The industry generated revenue of $10.1 billion in 2019. Razor blades and blades claimed 27.1%, edge tools, saws, blades and handsaws 18.2%, precision cutting tools 15.6%, and other categories 39.1%. Revenue declined 1.2% annually from 2014-2019.

Stanley Black & Decker Inc.	11.2%
Snap-On Inc.	11.1
Procter & Gamble Co.	8.0
Edgewell Personal Care Co.	5.0
Other	64.7

Source: "Hand Tool & Cutlery Manufacturing in the U.S." [online] from http://www.ibisworld.com [Published December 2019], from IBISWorld.

★ 3389 ★
Tools
SIC: 3423; NAICS: 332216

Top Pipe Wrench Makers Worldwide, 2016

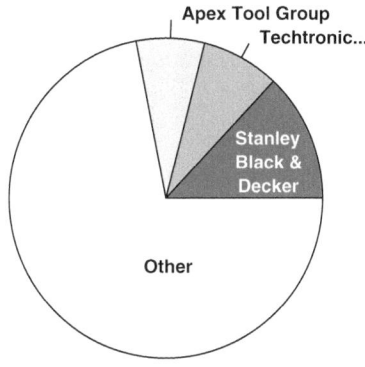

Pipe wrenches are used for turning soft iron pipes and fittings with a rounded surface. Market shares are shown based on revenues of $713.2 million.

Stanley Black & Decker	12.68%
Techtronic Industries	8.18
Apex Tool Group	7.37
Other	71.77

Source: "COVID-19 Impact on Global Pipe Wrenches Market Size, Status and Forecast 2020-2026." [online] from http://reports.valuates.com [Published April 2020], from QY Research.

★ 3390 ★
Tortillas and Taco Kits
SIC: 2099; NAICS: 31183

Top Hard/Soft Tortilla and Taco Kit Makers, 2020

Market shares are shown based on sales at supermarkets, drug stores, mass merchandisers, gas and convenience stores, military commissaries, and select club and dollar chains for the 52 weeks ended April 19, 2020.

Mission Foods Inc.	34.34%
Gruma Corp.	14.77
General Mills Inc.	11.81
Ole Mexican Foods Inc.	11.37
El Milagro	1.98
B&G Foods Inc.	1.95
La Tortilla Factory	1.49
Megamex Foods	1.42
Kraft Heinz Co.	0.97
Private label	7.17
Other	12.73

Source: *Snack Food & Wholesale Bakery*, June 2020, p. 86, from IRI.

★ 3391 ★
Tortillas and Taco Kits
SIC: 2099; NAICS: 31183

Top Refrigerated Tortilla Makers, 2020

Market shares are shown based on sales at supermarkets, drug stores, mass merchandisers, gas and convenience stores, military commissaries, and select club and dollar chains for the 52 weeks ended April 19, 2020.

Circle Foods L.L.C.	37.43%
Azteca Foods Baja Trading Inc.	13.02
La Abuela Mexican Foods	9.14
Siete Family Foods	5.27
Exquisita Tortillas Inc.	5.13
San Diego Tortilla	2.08
Cacique USA	1.76
Harvest States Foods	1.65
Franco Whole Foods	1.33
Private label	5.65
Other	17.54

Source: *Snack Food & Wholesale Bakery*, June 2020, p. 87, from IRI.

★ 3392 ★
Tourism
SIC: 4720; NAICS: 56151, 56152

Global Tourism Arrivals, 2019-2020

International tourist arrivals fell from 1.5 billion in 2019 to 301 million in 2020, a 74% decline. The decline in travel resulted in an estimated $1.3 trillion loss in tourism receipts. Countries that rely heavily on tourism saw devastating declines in receipts. For example, Macau and the Cook Islands both saw tourism receipts fall 85%. The Bahamas saw receipts fall 78% and Grenada's receipts fell 78%.

	2019 (mil.)	2020 (mil.)	Share
Europe	746	221	58.01%
Americas	219	69	18.11
Asia-Pacific	360	57	14.96

Continued on next page.

★ 3392 ★
[Continued]
Tourism
SIC: 4720; NAICS: 56151, 56152
Global Tourism Arrivals, 2019-2020

International tourist arrivals fell from 1.5 billion in 2019 to 301 million in 2020, a 74% decline. The decline in travel resulted in an estimated $1.3 trillion loss in tourism receipts. Countries that rely heavily on tourism saw devastating declines in receipts. For example, Macau and the Cook Islands both saw tourism receipts fall 85%. The Bahamas saw receipts fall 78% and Grenada's receipts fell 78%.

	2019 (mil.)	2020 (mil.)	Share
Africa	70	18	4.72%
Middle East	65	16	4.20

Source: "2020: A Year in Review." [online] from https://www.unwto.org/covid-19-and-tourism-2020 [Accessed March 7, 2020], from United Nations World Tourism Organization.

★ 3393 ★
Toy and Hobby Goods Wholesalers
SIC: 5092; NAICS: 42392
Toy and Hobby Goods and Supplies Merchant Wholesalers, 2017

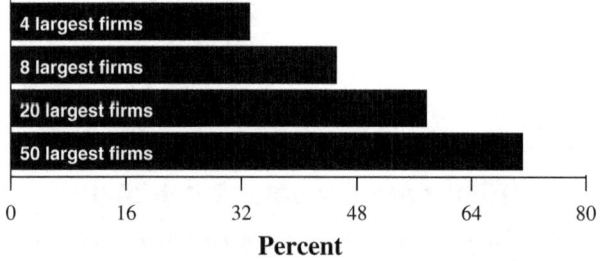

Data show the percent of industry sales held by the largest 4, 8, 20 and 50 firms in the sector. There are approximately 2,149 players operating in the industry generating employment for 35,346 people. According to IBISWorld, the industry is forecast to see revenue of $43.6 billion in 2021.

4 largest firms	33.1%
8 largest firms	45.1
20 largest firms	57.7
50 largest firms	71.1

Source: "Economic Census." [online] from https://www.census.gov/content/census/en/data/tables/2017/econ/economic-census/naics-sector-31-33.html [Accessed January 21, 2021], from U.S. Census Bureau.

★ 3394 ★
Toys and Games
SIC: 3944; NAICS: 33993
Designer Toy Market in China, 2020

The designer toy market started in Hong Kong in the 1990s, and it has grown in popularity since then. POP MART is the leader in the market for designer toy market with a 75% share. It is known for its blind boxes, small boxes identical on the outside with unique figurines on the inside.

POP MART	75.0%
Other	25.0

Source: "POP MART: Blind Box Toys Show the Designer Toy Market in China is Booming." [online] from https://daxueconsulting.com/pop-mart-designer-toy-market-in-china/ [Published February 4, 2021], from Daxue Consulting.

★ 3395 ★
Toys and Games
SIC: 3944; NAICS: 33993
Largest Toy and Game Markets in Europe, 2020

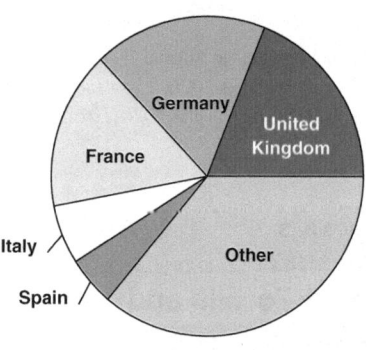

The toy and game market in Europe was valued at approximately €20 billion. Markets are ranked by value in millions of euros. There are 80 million children in the region under 14 years of age.

	(mil.)	Share
United Kingdom	€ 3,800	19.00%
Germany	3,600	18.00
France	3,300	16.50
Italy	1,200	6.00
Spain	930	4.65
Other	7,170	35.85

Source: "The European Toy Market 2020 and Digital Trends 2021." [online] from https://globaltoynews.com/2021/02/05/the-european-toy-market-2020-and-digital-trends-2021/ [Published February 5, 2021], from European Toy Association.

★ 3396 ★
Toys and Games
SIC: 3944; NAICS: 33993

Leading Go-Kart Makers Worldwide, 2019

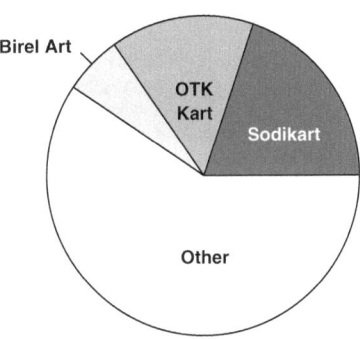

The industry is forecast to grow from $149.5 million in 2019 to $186.2 million in 2026. Market shares are shown based on revenue.

Sodikart	19.99%
OTK Kart	14.52
Birel Art	5.72
Other	59.77

Source: "Global Go-Kart Market Research Report 2020." [online] from http://www.qyresearch.com [Published July 2020], from QY Research.

★ 3397 ★
Toys and Games
SIC: 3944; NAICS: 33993

Leading Role-Playing Games on Roll20, 2020

Roll20 is a website that consists of tools for playing tabletop role-playing games. The company reported eight million users during the fourth quarter of 2020. Data show the types of campaigns during the fourth quarter.

D&D 5E	52.90%
Uncategorized	14.96
Call of Cthulhu (any edition)	10.30
Pathfinder	3.69
Pathfinder Second Edition	1.58
Warhammer	1.28
World of Darkness	1.14
D&D 3.5	1.02
Star Wars (any edition)	0.72
Starfinder	0.66
Other	11.73

Source: "The Orr Group Industry Report Q4 2020: 8 Million Users Edition." [online] from https://blog.roll20.net/posts/the-orr-group-industry-report-q4-2020-8-million-users-edition/ [Published February 8, 2021], from Orr Group.

★ 3398 ★
Toys and Games
SIC: 3944; NAICS: 33993

Leading Toy and Game Makers in India, 2019

The toy market is largely unorganized, with its size estimated at $1.2-1.5 billion. Hasbro officially launched operations in 2017, although its products were available before this through Funskool. Some analysts expect to see a jump in board game and other toy sales in 2020 and 2021 as consumers, stuck at home during COVID-19 shutdowns, look for sources of entertainment.

Funskool Ltd.	30.0%
Mattel Inc.	20.0
Hasbro Inc.	9.0
Other	41.0

Source: "An Indian Toy Story That Isn't Ending Well for Small Businesses." [online] from https://www.bloombergquint.com/bq-blue-exclusive/an-indian-toy-story-that-isnt-ending-well-for-small-businesses [Published December 17, 2020], from National Productivity Council Report.

★ 3399 ★
Toys and Games
SIC: 3942; NAICS: 33993

Market for Playset Dolls and Accessories, 2020

Market shares are shown based on dollar sales for the year-to-date August 2020. MGA claims to be the largest privately held toy company in the world. It is also the fastest growing.

MGA	49.0%
Other	51.0

Source: "MGA Entertainment Dominates August Doll and Toy Sales, Setting Stage for Exciting Holiday Season." [online] from https://www.mgae.com/press/mgae-dominates-august-doll-and-toy-sales-exciting-holiday-season [Published September 14, 2020], from NPD Group Inc./Retail Tracking Service.

★ 3400 ★
Toys and Games
SIC: 3944; NAICS: 33993

Top Educational Toy Makers Worldwide, 2018

The educational toy market is forecast to climb from $26.7 billion in 2020 to $45.7 billion in 2026. The source defines this market as a toy that teaches a child "something good" and be beneficial at some later date. Market shares are shown based on revenue.

Lego Group	22.0%
Mattel Inc.	8.0
Hasbro Inc.	6.0
Other	64.0

Source: "Global Educational Toy Market Research Report 2020." [online] from http://www.qyresearch.com [Published January 2020], from QY Research.

★ 3401 ★
Toys and Games
SIC: 3944; NAICS: 33993

Toy Sales by Segment, 2019-2020

Sales are shown in billions of dollars. Figures cover 78% of the market.

	2019 ($ bil.)	2020 ($ bil.)	Share
Outdoor and sports toys	$4.16	$5.35	21.28%
Dolls	3.29	3.64	14.48
Infant/toddler/preschool toys	3.00	3.27	13.01
Games/puzzles	2.21	2.93	11.65
Building sets	1.82	2.29	9.11
Action figures and accessories	1.72	1.66	6.60
Explorative and other toys	1.39	1.56	6.21
Vehicles	1.34	1.55	6.17
Plush	1.20	1.25	4.97
Arts and crafts	1.05	1.17	4.65
Youth electronics	0.46	0.47	1.87

Source: "U.S. Sales Data." [online] from https://www.toyassociation.org/ta/research/data/u-s-sales-data/toys/research-and-data/data/us-sales-data.aspx [Accessed February 15, 2021], from NPD Group Inc./Retail Tracking Service.

★ 3402 ★
Toys and Games Retailers
SIC: 5945; NAICS: 45112

Leading Toy Retailers, 2020

The source discusses how retailers are planning for the holiday season in light of the pandemic. Toys are expected to be a major sales category as in past years, and online sales will be especially important. More toys are expected to be shipped to fulfillment centers. Market shares are estimated. Target has about 15-20% of sales.

Walmart Inc.	25.0%
Amazon.com Inc.	20.0
Target Inc.	20.0
Other	35.0

Source: "Walmart Gets Creative, Goes Virtual as it Plans for Holiday Toy Shopping." [online] from https://www.cnbc.com/2020/09/03/walmart-gets-creative-goes-virtual-as-it-plans-for-holiday-toy-shopping.html [Published September 2, 2020], from Jeffries Group estimates.

★ 3403 ★
Trailers
SIC: 3792; NAICS: 336214

Leading Camping Trailer Makers, 2020

Market shares are shown based on 8,276 registrations.

Forest River Inc.	71.6%
Aliner	12.9
Purple Liner L.L.C.	4.9
Other	10.6

Source: "Industry Eclipses 500,000 in Retail Sales for First Time Ever." [online] from https://rvbusiness.com/industry-eclipses-500000-in-retail-sales-for-first-time-ever/ [Published February 9, 2021], from Statistical Surveys.

★ 3404 ★
Trailers
SIC: 3792; NAICS: 336214

Leading Fifth Wheel Trailer Makers, 2020

Market shares are shown based on 5,553 registrations.

Thor Industries Inc.	47.1%
Forest River Inc.	28.2
Grand Design RV Co.	17.9
Other	6.8

Source: "Industry Eclipses 500,000 in Retail Sales for First Time Ever." [online] from https://rvbusiness.com/industry-eclipses-500000-in-retail-sales-for-first-time-ever/ [Published February 9, 2021], from Statistical Surveys.

★ 3405 ★
Trailers
SIC: 3792; NAICS: 336214

Leading Towable Trailer Makers, 2020

Market shares are shown based on 515,819 registrations.

Thor Industries Inc.	41.2%
Forest River Inc.	39.1
Grand Design RV Co.	8.7
Other	11.0

Source: "Industry Eclipses 500,000 in Retail Sales for First Time Ever." [online] from https://rvbusiness.com/industry-eclipses-500000-in-retail-sales-for-first-time-ever/ [Published February 9, 2021], from Statistical Surveys.

★ 3406 ★
Trailers
SIC: 3792; NAICS: 336214

Leading Travel Trailer Makers, 2020

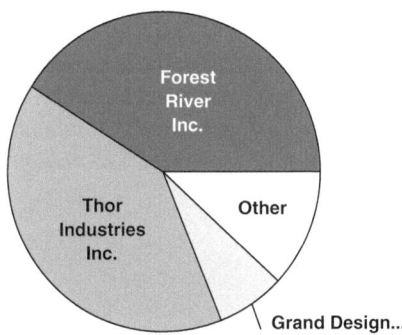

Market shares are shown based on 16,838 registrations.

Forest River Inc.	41.2%
Thor Industries Inc.	40.0
Grand Design RV Co.	6.7%
Other	12.1

Source: "Industry Eclipses 500,000 in Retail Sales for First Time Ever." [online] from https://rvbusiness.com/industry-eclipses-500000-in-retail-sales-for-first-time-ever/ [Published February 9, 2021], from Statistical Surveys.

★ 3407 ★
Trailers
SIC: 3715; NAICS: 336212

Leading Truck Trailer OEMs in North America, 2019-2020

Companies are ranked by production. Shares are shown based on production of the top 25 firms of 322,574 in 2019 and 211,807 in 2020.

	2019	2020	Share
Wabash National Corp.	55,700	36,400	17.19%
Hyundai Translead	66,097	34,739	16.40
Great Dane	50,500	34,500	16.29
Utility Trailer Manufacturing	51,911	33,850	15.98
Vanguard National	17,010	12,013	5.67
Stoughton Trailers	16,750	11,000	5.19
MANAC	8,200	7,000	3.30
EnTrans International	7,760	6,053	2.86
Pitts Enterprises	4,865	4,435	2.09
MAC Trailer	6,284	4,170	1.97
Other	37,497	27,647	13.05

Source: *Trailer Body Builders*, February 2021, p. 24.

★ 3408 ★
Training
SIC: 8299; NAICS: 61143

Corporate Training Industry, 2018

The market is forecast to reach $30 billion in 2022. Before COVID-19, corporate training was about a $30 billion market, with online training representing about 20% of the total. Demand for online services is increasing as a result of job losses and remote working.

	($ bil.)	Share
Instructor led	$ 14.5	48.5%
Blended	9.2	30.5
Online	6.3	21.0

Source: "Education and Training Market Analysis: Immediate and Systemic Impact on COVID-19." [online] from http://www.williamblair.com [Published May 2020], from Technavio.

★ 3409 ★
Training
SIC: 8299; NAICS: 61143

Training Spending by Year, 2015-2020

Data show training expenditures in billions of dollars. Figures include budgets, technology spending, and staff salaries. The average budget was $6.47 million. Average training budget by type of organization: associations $1.06 million, education $1.15 million, government/military $1.62 million, manufacturer/distributor $2.43 million, nonprofit $834,538, retail/wholesale $13.8 million, and services $10.4 million.

2015	$ 70.6
2016	70.6
2017	93.6
2018	87.6
2019	83.0
2020	82.5

Source: *Training*, November-December 2020, p. 23.

★ 3410 ★
Transformer Monitoring Systems
SIC: 3612; NAICS: 335311

Leading Transformer Monitoring System Makers Worldwide, 2019

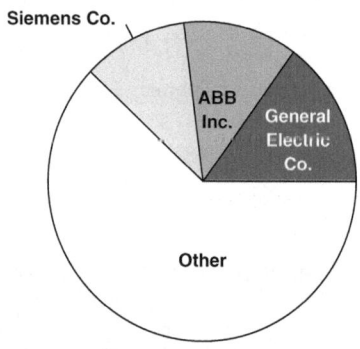

Transformer monitoring systems are used to ensure the continuous and safe transmission of electricity in real time from power plant to end user. The industry is forecast to see revenue grow from $2.11 billion in 2019 to $2.69 billion in 2026. Market shares are shown by revenue.

General Electric Co.	15.42%
ABB Inc.	12.13
Siemens Co.	10.71
Other	61.74

Source: "Global Transformer Monitoring System Sales Market Report 2020." [online] from http://www.qyresearch.com [Published November 2020], from QY Research.

★ 3411 ★
Translation Services
SIC: 7389; NAICS: 54193

Leading Translation Service Providers Worldwide, 2020

Companies are ranked by revenue in millions of dollars. The industry is forecast to grow from $55 billion in 2020 to $73.6 billion in 2025.

	($ mil.)	Share
TransPerfect Translations	$ 852.4	1.55%
Lionsbridge Techologies	739.0	1.34
LanguageLine Solutions	618.0	1.12
SDL	480.7	0.87
RWS Group	456.7	0.83
Keywords Studios	425.3	0.77
Appen Ltd.	413.2	0.75
Acolad Group	285.1	0.52
Welocalize	256.5	0.47
SDI Media	191.0	0.35
Other	50,282.1	91.42

Source: "The 201 Nimdzi: The Ranking of Top 100 Largest Language Service Providers." [online] from https://www.nimdzi.com/nimdzi-100-top-lsp/ [Published March 1, 2021], from Nimdzi.

★ 3412 ★
Transponders
SIC: 3699; NAICS: 333318

Leading AIS Transponder Makers Worldwide, 2019

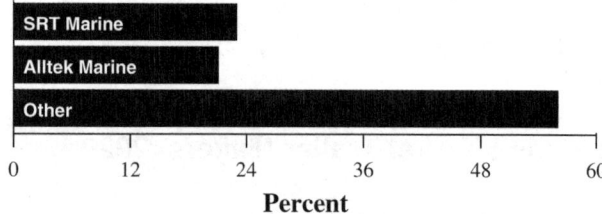

An Automatic Identification System transponder is designed to enable two-way communication between various vessels and onshore-based coastal authorities. The market is forecast to grow from $48 million in 2020 to $70 million in 2026.

SRT Marine	22.95%
Alltek Marine	21.07
Other	55.98

Source: "Global AIS Transponder Market Report, History and Forecast 2015-2026, Breakdown Data by Manufacturers, Key Regions, Types and Applications." [online] from http://www.qyresearch.com [Published July 2020], from QY Research.

★ 3413 ★
Travel
SIC: 4720; NAICS: 56151, 56152

Largest Travel Firms Worldwide, 2019

Companies are ranked by travel sales in millions of dollars. CWT was formerly known as Carlson Wagonlit Travel. Internova Travel Group was formerly known as Travel Leaders Group.

Expedia Group	$ 107.90
Booking Holdings Inc.	96.40
American Express Global Business Travel	34.10
BCD Travel	27.50
CWT	24.80
Flight Centre Travel Group The Americas	16.00
Internova Travel Group	7.48
American Express Travel	6.93
Direct Travel Inc.	5.80
Fareportal	5.34
Corporate Travel Management (CTM)	5.00
American Automobile Association (AAA)	4.10
Travel and Transport	3.53
Frosch	2.40
Ovation Travel Group	1.60
Omega World Travel Inc.	1.49
World Travel Holdings	1.47
World Travel Inc.	1.33
International Cruise & Excursions	1.09
AllStars Travel Group (ATG)	0.86

Source: *Travel Weekly*, Power List 2020, p. NA.

★ 3414 ★
Travel
SIC: 4720; NAICS: 56151, 56152

Leading Business Travel Firms, 2019

Companies are ranked by U.S.-booked air spending in millions of dollars. Shares are shown based on the $11.8 billion in spending generated by the top 100 companies.

	($ mil.)	Share
Deloitte	$ 583.1	4.94%
Amazon.com Inc.	500.0	4.24
IBM Corp.	415.0	3.52
Google Inc.	400.0	3.39
EY	346.8	2.94
PricewaterhouseCoopers	325.0	2.75
Apple Inc.	299.0	2.53
Microsoft Corp.	275.0	2.33
McKinsey & Co.	265.0	2.25
Accenture	260.0	2.20
Lockheed Martin Corp.	216.1	1.83
Boeing Co.	$ 214.2	1.82%
Other	7,700.8	65.26

Source: *Business Travel News*, October 2020, p. 49.

★ 3415 ★
Travel
SIC: 4720; NAICS: 56151, 56152

Leading Business Travel Firms in the United Kingdom, 2019

Companies are ranked by spending in millions of British pounds sterling.

	(mil.)	Share
Global Business Travel	£ 2,300.0	20.00%
CWT	1,253.0	10.90
FCM Travel Solutions	831.1	7.23
BCD Travel	694.0	6.03
Corporate Travel Management (CTM)	645.0	5.61
Travel Leaders Group U.K.	610.0	5.30
Capital Travel and Events	595.0	5.17
Egencia	594.3	5.17
Reed & Mackay	588.5	5.12
Clarity	450.0	3.91
Other	2,939.1	25.56

Source: *BTN Europe*, May-June 2020, p. 49.

★ 3416 ★
Travel
SIC: 4725; NAICS: 56152

Leading Tour Operators, 2019

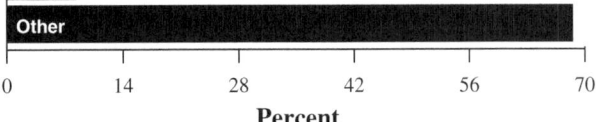

Companies in this industry assemble and sell tour packages; this industry also includes travel and wholesale tour operators that arrange travel and accommodations within the package of their provided tours. Companies that primarily provide accommodations are not included. Industry revenue reached $7.8 billion in 2019.

Apple Leisure Group	12.8%
The Travel Corp.	10.5

Continued on next page.

★ 3416 ★
[Continued]
Travel
SIC: 4725; NAICS: 56152
Leading Tour Operators, 2019

Companies in this industry assemble and sell tour packages; this industry also includes travel and wholesale tour operators that arrange travel and accommodations within the package of their provided tours. Companies that primarily provide accommodations are not included. Industry revenue reached $7.8 billion in 2019.

Flight Centre Travel Group Ltd.	8.2%
Other	68.5

Source: "Tour Operators in the United States." [online] from http://www.ibisworld.com [Published July 2019], from IBISWorld.

★ 3417 ★
Travel
SIC: 4724; NAICS: 56151
Leading Travel Agencies, 2019

Market shares are shown in percent. IBISWorld estimates the travel agency industry to be worth $32.1 billion in 2021, with the revenue growing 65.1% in 2020 because of pent-up demand due to the pandemic.

Booking Holdings Inc.	66.0%
Trip.com	18.0
Expedia Group	14.0
TripAdvisor	3.0

Source: "Expedia Inc." [online] from https://www.biz.uiowa.edu/henry/download/f20_EXPE.pdf [Published November 13, 2020], from FactSet.

★ 3418 ★
Travel
SIC: 4822; NAICS: 517311
Online Travel Arrangement Market, 2020

In 2019, Airbnb claimed about 40% of the online travel market. With the arrival of COVID, many travelers have turned to Airbnb as a safer option for lodging over a traditional hotel.

	Jan.	April	Oct.
Airbnb	42.0%	55.0%	54.0%
HomeAway (Expedia)	20.0	30.0	22.0
Expedia	16.0	6.0	8.0
Hotels.com (Expedia)	9.0	4.0	6.0
Expedia, other	8.0%	3.0%	4.0%
Booking-Priceline	4.0	3.0	6.0

Source: "Airbnb: A COVID Threat or Opportunity." [online] from https://www.earnestresearch.com/airbnbs-s-1-a-covid-threat-or-opportunity/ [Published November 30, 2020], from Earnest Research.

★ 3419 ★
Travel Retail
SIC: 5999; NAICS: 453998
Largest Travel Retailers Worldwide, 2019

Companies are ranked by sales in millions of euros.

Dufry Group	€ 8,138
Lotte Duty Free	7,665
The Shilla Duty Free	7,049
China Duty Free Group	6,065
Lagardère Travel Retail	4,500
DFS Group	4,010
GEBR Heinemann	3,900
Shinsegae Duty Free	2,837
King Power International Group (Thailand)	2,670
Ever Rich Duty Free Shop	1,932
Dubai Duty Free	1,808
Duty Free Americas	1,700
Aer Rianta International	1,192
WHSmith	965
Japan Airport Terminal Co.	964

Source: *The Moodie Davitt Report*, July-August 2020, p. 19.

★ 3420 ★
Trim
SIC/NAICS: See frontmatter for explanation.
Trim Industry by Type, 2019

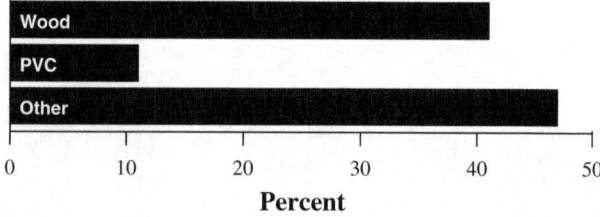

The industry was valued at 2.0 billion square feet.

Wood	41.0%
PVC	11.0
Other	47.0

Source: "The Azek Company." [online] from https://www.sec.gov/Archives/edgar/data/1782754/000119312520028208/d776367ds1.htm [Published February 2020], from Principia.

★ 3421 ★
Trucking
SIC: 4213; NAICS: 484121

Largest Bulk/Tank Carriers in North America, 2018-2019

Companies are ranked by revenues in millions of dollars.

	2018 ($ mil.)	2019 ($ mil.)
Kenan Advantage Group	$ 1,759	$ 1,730
Quality Distribution	789	822
Trimac	610	529
Foodliner/Quest Liner	334	314
A&R Transport	276	285
Superior Bulk Logistics	269	277
Groendyke Transport	273	245
Dupre Logistics	225	242
Schneider National Bank	194	200
Ruan Corp.	169	165

Source: *Journal of Commerce*, August 14, 2020, p. NA, from S.J. Consulting Group and company reports.

★ 3422 ★
Trucking
SIC: 4213; NAICS: 484121

Largest Flatbed Carriers in North America, 2018-2019

Companies are ranked by revenues in millions of dollars.

	2018 ($ mil.)	2019 ($ mil.)
Landstar System	$ 1,296	$ 1,386
Daseke Inc.	1,395	1,304
PS Logistics	702	617
Mercer Transportation	541	603
Universal Truckload Services	439	492
TMC/Annett Holdings	450	464
Anderson Trucking Services	358	406
Maverick Transportation	291	302
Melton Truck Lines Inc.	298	293
PGT Holdings	273	278

Source: *Journal of Commerce*, August 14, 2020, p. NA, from S.J. Consulting Group and company reports.

★ 3423 ★
Trucking
SIC: 4210; NAICS: 484121, 484122

Largest Green Trucking Fleets, 2020

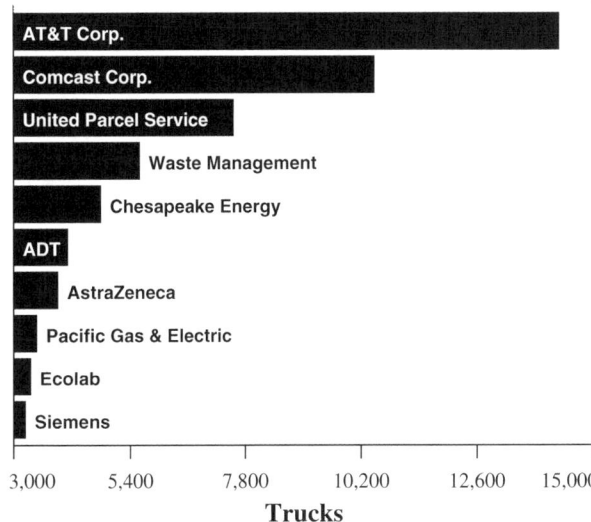

Companies are ranked by size of green trucking fleet. Figures include propane autogas, flex fuel, electric vehicles, hybrids, biodiesel and liquefied natural gas.

AT&T Corp.	14,296
Comcast Corp.	10,469
United Parcel Service	7,547
Waste Management	5,589
Chesapeake Energy	4,777
ADT	4,100
AstraZeneca	3,900
Pacific Gas & Electric	3,473
Ecolab	3,348
Siemens	3,240

Source: *Automotive Fleet*, Annual 2021, p. 28.

★ 3424 ★
Trucking
SIC: 4210; NAICS: 484121, 484122

Largest Household Goods Firms by Size of Fleet, 2020

Companies are ranked by number of trucks, tractors and trailers.

UniGroup Inc.	5,784
Sirva Inc.	3,038
Atlas Van Lines Inc.	2,759
Wheaton Worldwide Moving	1,067
The Suddath Companies	411
Volume Transportation Inc.	359
Hilldrup Moving & Storage	350

Continued on next page.

★ 3424 ★
[Continued]
Trucking
SIC: 4210; NAICS: 484121, 484122

Largest Household Goods Firms by Size of Fleet, 2020

Companies are ranked by number of trucks, tractors and trailers.

National Van Lines Inc.	337
Covan World-Wine Moving Inc.	274
New World Van Lines Inc.	217

Source: *Fleet Owner*, February 2021, p. 33.

★ 3425 ★
Trucking
SIC: 4213; NAICS: 484122

Largest Less-Than-Truckload Carriers in North America, 2019-2020

Companies are ranked by revenue in millions of dollars. Shares are shown based on revenue of $42.9 billion in 2019 and $42.1 billion in 2020.

	2019 ($ mil.)	2020 ($ mil.)	Share
FedEx Freight	$ 7,454	$ 7,115	16.90%
Old Dominion Freight Line	4,055	3,961	9.41
XPO Logistics	3,841	3,575	8.49
YRC Freight	3,049	3,055	7.26
Estes Express Lines	2,818	2,898	6.88
UPS Freight	2,679	2,844	6.75
ABF Freight System	2,094	2,036	4.84
R+L Carriers	1,848	1,973	4.69
Saia Motor Freight Line	1,787	1,822	4.33
Southeastern Freight Lines	1,242	1,256	2.98
Other	12,132	11,570	27.48

Source: *Logistics Management*, April 2021, p. 48, from S.J. Consulting Group and company reports.

★ 3426 ★
Trucking
SIC: 4213; NAICS: 48423

Largest Motor Vehicle Shipping Firms by Size of Fleet, 2020

Companies are ranked by number of trucks, tractors and trailers.

United Road Service	2,470
Jack Cooper Transport Co. Inc.	1,424
TruckMovers	1,400
Horizon Transport Inc.	1,383
Quality Drive Away Inc.	1,268
Hanen & Adkins Auto Transport Inc.	1,117
Cassens Transport Co.	909
JHT Holdings Inc.	855
Spirit Miller Trucking L.L.C.	630
U.S. AutoLogistics	467

Source: *Fleet Owner*, February 2021, p. 34.

★ 3427 ★
Trucking
SIC: 4213; NAICS: 48423

Largest Refrigerated Carriers in North America, 2018-2019

Companies are ranked by revenues in millions of dollars.

	2018 ($ mil.)	2019 ($ mil.)
Knight-Swift Transportation	$ 4,290.2	$ 3,952.8
New Prime Inc.	1,562.2	1,706.3
C.R. England Inc.	1,636.3	1,545.1
KLLM Transport Services L.L.C.	917.0	936.0
Marten Transport Ltd.	787.5	843.2
Stevens Transport Inc.	719.8	737.2
Hirschbach Motor Lines Inc.	454.4	550.5
John Christner Trucking L.L.C.	294.7	338.8
Shaffer Trucking	265.8	285.4
K&B Transportation Inc.	185.0	187.2

Source: *Refrigerated Transporter*, May 2020, p. NA, from S.J. Consulting Group and company reports.

★ 3428 ★
Trucking
SIC: 4210; NAICS: 484121, 484122

Largest Trucking Firms by Size of Fleet, 2020

Companies are ranked by number of trucks, tractors and trailers. The top 500 operate a fleet of 871,871 vehicles.

	Fleet	Share
United Parcel Service	133,931	15.36%
Federal Express Corp.	127,706	14.65
Penske Truck	43,151	4.95
Knight-Swift Transportation Holdings	20,868	2.39
J.B. Hunt Transport Services	18,314	2.10
TransForce Inc.	14,384	1.65

Continued on next page.

★ 3428 ★
[Continued]
Trucking
SIC: 4210; NAICS: 484121, 484122

Largest Trucking Firms by Size of Fleet, 2020

Companies are ranked by number of trucks, tractors and trailers. The top 500 operate a fleet of 871,871 vehicles.

	Fleet	Share
YRC Worldwide Inc.	14,350	1.65%
R.L. Carriers	12,431	1.43
Schneider National Carriers	11,985	1.37
XPO Logistics L.L.C.	11,733	1.35
Other	463,018	53.11

Source: *Fleet Owner*, February 2021, p. 17.

★ 3429 ★
Trucking
SIC: 4213; NAICS: 484121

Largest Truckload Carriers in North America, 2019-2020

Companies are ranked by revenue in millions of dollars. Figures exclude fuel surcharges. Shares are shown based on revenue of $31.77 billion in 2019 and $30.86 billion in 2020 generated by the top 25 firms.

	2019 ($ mil.)	2020 ($ mil.)	Share
Knight-Swift Transportation	$ 3,953	$ 3,786	12.27%
J.B. Hunt Transport Services	2,518	2,659	8.62
Prime	2,107	2,088	6.77
Schneider National	2,397	2,066	6.69
Landstar System	2,057	2,033	6.59
Werner Enterprises	1,887	1,826	5.92
U.S. Xpress Enterprises	1,521	1,513	4.90
CRST International	1,469	1,388	4.50
Daseke Inc.	1,395	1,182	3.83
Crete Carrier Corp.	1,151	1,171	3.79
Other	11,317	11,150	36.13

Source: *Logistics Management*, April 2021, p. 50, from S.J. Consulting Group.

★ 3430 ★
Trucking
SIC: 4212; NAICS: 484121, 484122

Leading Contract Logistics Firms Worldwide, 2019

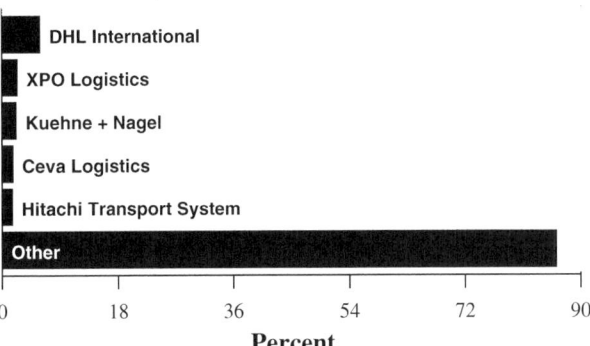

Market shares are shown based on divisional revenue.

DHL International	5.9%
XPO Logistics	2.4
Kuehne + Nagel	2.2
Ceva Logistics	1.7
Hitachi Transport System	1.6
Other	86.2

Source: "Deutsche Post DHL Group 2021 Business Profile." [online] from https://www.dpdhl.com/content/dam/dpdhl/de/media-center/investors/documents/business-profiles/DPDHL-Business-Profile-2021.pdf [Published March 2021], from Transport Intelligence and company estimates.

★ 3431 ★
Trucking
SIC: 4213; NAICS: 484121

Leading Dedicated Contract Carrier Firms in North America, 2020

Companies are ranked by number of power units. Shares are shown based on the top 51 companies.

	Units	Share
J.B. Hunt Dedicated Contract Services	9,911	12.11%
Penske Logistics	6,718	8.21
Ryder Supply Chain Solutions	6,000	7.33
Knight-Swift Transportation	5,099	6.23
Werner Logistics	4,945	6.04
NFI Transportation	4,500	5.50
Schneider National	3,940	4.81
Ruan Transportation	3,556	4.34
Cardinal Logistics	3,400	4.15
Marten Transport Ltd.	3,238	3.96
Other	30,547	37.32

Source: *Transport Topics*, Top 50 Annual, 2021, p. A19.

★ 3432 ★
Trucks
SIC: 3713; NAICS: 336211

Class 5 Truck Market, 2020

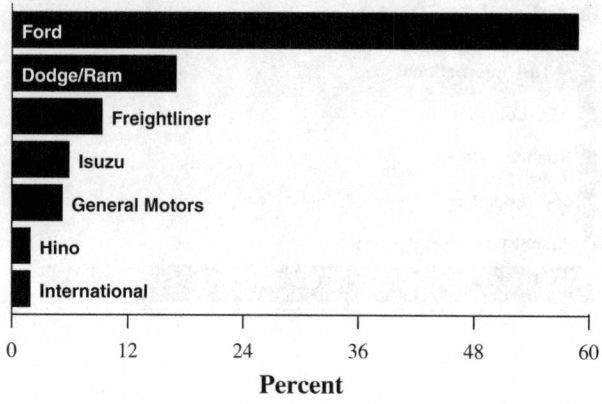

Market shares are shown based on 93,081 registrations.

Ford	58.8%
Dodge/Ram	17.0
Freightliner	9.3
Isuzu	5.9
General Motors	5.2
Hino	1.9
International	1.9

Source: *Today's Trucking*, March 2021, p. 16, from WardsAuto.

★ 3433 ★
Trucks
SIC: 3713; NAICS: 336211

Class 6 Truck Market, 2020

Market shares are shown based on 52,213 registrations.

Ford	32.0%
Freightliner	25.8
International	20.3
Hino	10.1
Kenworth	5.8
General Motors	3.5
Isuzu	2.3
Mack	0.1
Peterbilt	0.1

Source: *Today's Trucking*, March 2021, p. 16, from WardsAuto.

★ 3434 ★
Trucks
SIC: 3713; NAICS: 336211

Class 7 Truck Market, 2020

Market shares are shown based on 50,676 registrations.

Freightliner	39.6%
International	29.8
Peterbilt	14.9
Kenworth	10.4
Ford	3.3
Hino	2.2

Source: *Today's Trucking*, March 2021, p. 16, from WardsAuto.

★ 3435 ★
Trucks
SIC: 3713; NAICS: 336211

Class 8 Truck Market, 2020

Market shares are shown based on 191,900 registrations.

Freightliner	37.4%
Kenworth	15.7
Peterbilt	14.7
International	12.1
Volvo Truck	9.7
Mack	7.5
Western Star	2.9

Source: *Today's Trucking*, March 2021, p. 16, from WardsAuto.

★ 3436 ★
Trucks
SIC: 3713; NAICS: 336211

Heavy-Duty Truck Manufacturing, 2019

Total shipments were valued at $33.79 billion. The term "nec" stands for not elsewhere classified.

	($ 000)	Share
Heavy-duty trucks, including heavy-duty truck, tractor, and bus chassis	$ 24,318,912	71.97%
Buses, complete, including military (excluding trolley buses)	6,919,793	20.48

Continued on next page.

★ 3436 ★
[Continued]
Trucks
SIC: 3713; NAICS: 336211

Heavy-Duty Truck Manufacturing, 2019

Total shipments were valued at $33.79 billion. The term "nec" stands for not elsewhere classified.

	($ 000)	Share
Firefighting vehicles and other heavy trucks, complete	$ 2,270,352	6.72%
Wholesale sales of other goods, nec	904	< 0.01
Other	280,040	0.83

Source: "Annual Survey of Manufactures." [online] from https://www.census.gov/programs-surveys/asm/data/tables.html [Accessed March 18, 2021], from U.S. Department of Commerce.

★ 3437 ★
Trucks
SIC: 3713; NAICS: 336211

Leading Commercial Vehicle Markets Worldwide, 2019-2020

Sales fell from 23,264,445 in 2019 to 21,590,167 in 2020.

	2019	2020	Share
United States	12,317,378	11,051,054	51.19%
China	4,324,839	5,133,338	23.78
Japan	894,125	788,634	3.65
India	854,743	505,189	2.34
France	541,448	449,932	2.08
Mexico	595,709	444,276	2.06
Brazil	525,781	442,495	2.05
Germany	409,801	350,544	1.62
United Kingdom	425,778	333,708	1.55
Russia	211,092	197,207	0.91
Other	2,163,752	1,893,788	8.77

Source: "2020 Sales Statistics." [online] from https://www.oica.net/category/production-statistics/2020-statistics/ [Accessed April 10, 2021], from International Organization of Motor Vehicle Manufacturers.

★ 3438 ★
Trucks
SIC: 3713; NAICS: 336211

Leading Heavy Duty Truck Brands in China, 2020

Brands are ranked by January-October 2020 unit sales.

	Sales	Share
FAW Jiefang	351,800	25.77%
Dongfeng	259,800	19.03
Sinotruk Group	218,700	16.02
Shacman	190,400	13.95
Foton	131,200	9.61
Hongyan	64,937	4.76
JAC	46,245	3.39
Dayun	28,897	2.12
XCMG	22,454	1.64
CAMC	18,901	1.38
Other	31,800	2.33

Source: "China Recorded 1209,000 Heavy-Duty Truck Sales in October." [online] from http://m.chinaspv.com/statistics/3792.html [Published November 27, 2020].

★ 3439 ★
Trucks
SIC: 3713; NAICS: 336211

Leading Heavy Truck Producing Regions, 2019-2020

Production rose from 4,152,408 in 2019 to 4,361,421 in 2020. Some countries were not included because figures were confidential.

	2019	2020	Share
China	2,217,847	2,976,459	68.25%
Japan	506,541	405,541	9.30
United States	345,067	235,011	5.39
Europe	287,129	225,470	5.17
Mexico	195,421	133,314	3.06
South Korea	64,758	55,583	1.27
Indonesia	91,757	53,219	1.22
South Africa	27,872	22,567	0.52
Canada	23,311	14,719	0.34
Iran	9,600	10,301	0.24
Other	383,105	229,237	5.26

Source: "2020 Production Statistics." [online] from https://www.oica.net/category/production-statistics/2020-statistics/ [Accessed April 10, 2021], from International Organization of Motor Vehicle Manufacturers.

Trucks

★ 3440 ★
Trucks
SIC: 3713; NAICS: 336211

New Commercial Trucks by Fuel Type in the EU, 2019

Distribution is shown in percent. Data for Bulgaria, Croatia, Malta and Lithuania not available. Figures refer to commercial vehicles over 3.5 tons. "Electrically-chargeable" includes battery electric vehicles, fuel-cell electric vehicles, extended-range and plug-in hybrid electric vehicles. "Hybrids" include full and mild hybrids. "Alternative fuels" includes LPG, natural gas and ethanol vehicles.

Diesel	97.9%
Alternative fuels	1.7
Electrically-chargeable	0.2
Hybrids	0.1
Petrol	0.1

Source: "The Automobile Industry Pocket Guide 2020-2021." [online] from http://www.acea.be/publications/article/acea-pocket-guide [Accessed April 12, 2021], from European Automobile Manufacturers' Association.

★ 3441 ★
Tungsten
SIC: 1061; NAICS: 212299

Top Tungsten Producing Nations, 2020

Countries are ranked by production in metric tons of tungsten content. The source notes that while the United States has significant tungsten resources, no domestic commercial production of tungsten concentrates has taken place there since 2015. Production data are estimated.

	MT	Share
China	69,000	82.47%
Vietnam	4,300	5.14
Russia	2,200	2.63
Mongolia	1,900	2.27
Bolivia	1,400	1.67
Rwanda	1,000	1.20
Austria	890	1.06
Spain	800	0.96
Portugal	680	0.81
Korea, North	500	0.60
Other	1,000	1.20

Source: "Mineral Commodity Summaries 2021." [online] from https://www.usgs.gov/centers/nmic/mineral-commodity-summaries [Published January 29, 2021], from U.S. Geological Survey.

★ 3442 ★
Turbines
SIC: 3511; NAICS: 333611

Gas Electrical Power Turbine Production Worldwide, 2020-2029

Figures are in millions of dollars.

2020	$ 8,015.29
2021	8,145.40
2022	8,782.56
2023	8,930.00
2024	9,878.50
2025	10,474.62
2026	11,158.28
2027	11,812.17
2028	12,212.04
2029	12,920.58

Source: *Turbomachinery International*, November 2020, p. NA, from Forecast International.

★ 3443 ★
Turbines
SIC: 3511; NAICS: 333611

Leading Gas Electrical Power Turbine Makers Worldwide, 2020-2029

Market shares are shown based on estimated value of $12.92 billion in production.

GE Energy	29.83%
Siemens Corp.	21.88
Solar Turbines	20.18
Mitsubishi Heavy Power Systems	6.67
Other	21.44

Source: *Turbomachinery International*, November 2020, p. NA, from Forecast International.

★ 3444 ★
Turbines
SIC: 3511; NAICS: 333611

Leading Online Wind Turbine Makers in India, 2020

India added approximately 1.1 GW of capacity in 2020, the slowest pace of new build in a decade. Siemens Gamesa retained its lead position in spite of the slowdown. Market shares are shown based on capacity.

Siemens Gamesa	48.0%
General Electric Co.	21.0
Suzlon Energy Ltd.	12.0
Inox Wind Ltd.	11.0

Continued on next page.

★ 3444 ★
[Continued]
Turbines
SIC: 3511; NAICS: 333611
Leading Online Wind Turbine Makers in India, 2020

India added approximately 1.1 GW of capacity in 2020, the slowest pace of new build in a decade. Siemens Gamesa retained its lead position in spite of the slowdown. Market shares are shown based on capacity.

Vestas Wind Systems	7.0%
Other	1.0

Source: "Siemens Gamesa Retains Top Spot in India as Wind Turbine Market Set to Rebound." [online] from https://about.bnef.com/blog/siemens-gamesa-retains-top-spot-in-india-as-wind-turbine-market-set-to-rebound/ [Press release March 8, 2021], from BloombergNEF.

★ 3445 ★
Turbines
SIC: 3511; NAICS: 333611
Leading Onshore Wind Turbine Makers Worldwide, 2020

Companies are ranked by capacity in gigawatts.

	GW	Share
General Electric Co.	13.53	15.00%
Goldwind Science & Technology	12.75	14.14
Vestas Wind Systems	12.16	13.48
Envision Energy	9.48	10.51
Siemens Gamesa	5.74	6.36
Mingyang Wind Power	4.76	5.28
Windey Co. Ltd.	3.98	4.41
CRRC Wind Power (Shandong) Co.	3.84	4.26
Sany Heavy Industry Co.	3.72	4.12
Shanghai Electric Wind Power Group	3.52	3.90
Other	16.72	18.54

Source: "Global Wind Industry Had a Record, Near 100GW, Year as GE, Goldwind Took Lead from Vestas." [online] from https://about.bnef.com/blog/global-wind-industry-had-a-record-near-100gw-year-as-ge-goldwind-took-lead-from-vestas/ [Press release March 10, 2021], from BloombergNEF.

★ 3446 ★
Turbines
SIC: 3511; NAICS: 333611
Leading Wind Turbine Makers, 2020

The leading OEMs are ranked by capacity installations in 2020.

	GW	Share
General Electric Co.	8,777	53.0%
Vestas Wind Systems	5,803	35.0
Siemens Gamesa Renewable Energy	1,680	10.0
Nordex SE	451	3.0
Goldwind Science & Technology	202	1.0

Source: "ACP Market Report Fourth Quarter 2020." [online] from https://cleanpower.org/resources/american-clean-power-market-report-q4-2020/ [Accessed April 11, 2021], from American Clean Power.

★ 3447 ★
Turbines
SIC: 3511; NAICS: 333611
Leading Wind Turbine Makers Worldwide, 2020

Companies are ranked by capacity in gigawatts.

	GW	Share
General Electric Co.	13.53	14.05%
Goldwind Science & Technology	13.06	13.56
Vestas Wind Systems	12.40	12.88
Envision Energy	10.35	10.75
Siemens Gamesa	7.65	7.94
Mingyang Wind Power	5.64	5.86
Shanghai Electric Wind Power Group	5.07	5.26
Zhejiang Windey Co. Ltd.	3.98	4.13
CRRC Wind Power (Shandong) Co.	3.84	3.99
Sany Heavy Industry	3.72	3.86
Other	17.06	17.72

Source: "Global Wind Industry Had a Record, Near 100GW, Year as GE, Goldwind Took Lead from Vestas." [online] from https://about.bnef.com/blog/global-wind-industry-had-a-record-near-100gw-year-as-ge-goldwind-took-lead-from-vestas/ [Press release March 10, 2021], from BloombergNEF.

★ 3448 ★
Turbines
SIC: 3511; NAICS: 333611

Top Industrial and Marine Turbine Makers Worldwide, 2020-2034

Market shares are shown based on the value of production. Figures include gas and steam.

GE Energy	39.41%
Siemens AG	21.67
Mitsubishi Power Ltd.	12.00
Solar Turbines	6.00
Ansaldo Energia	4.56
Skoda Holding	2.86
Mitsubishi Heavy Industries Ltd.	2.39
Other	11.11

Source: "Industrial & Marine Gas and Steam Turbines." [online] from http://www.fi-powerweb.com/Industrial-Marine-Gas-Steam-Turbines.html [Accessed September 16, 2020], from Platinum Forecast System.

★ 3449 ★
Tutoring and Test Preparation
SIC: 8299; NAICS: 61171

After-School Tutoring in China, 2018-2022

Figures are in billions of renminbi. Data are projected from 2017, when this industry was just beginning to develop. Various factors helped this industry develop. The government showed an increasing interest in education programs, and it relaxed its One Child policy in 2016. There was a greater emphasis in China on academic performance, as well as tutoring services to help students perform well on tests. A strong economy raised funds for new education businesses.

2018	¥ 433
2019	475
2020	518
2021	564
2022	611

Source: "OneSmart Education OMO the New Era of Online Education." [online] from http://www.onesmart.investorroom.com [Published March 2020], from Frost & Sullivan.

★ 3450 ★
Tutoring and Test Preparation
SIC: 8299; NAICS: 611691

Leading Tutoring and Test Preparation Firms, 2019

The 2,944 businesses in this industry generated revenue of $1.1 billion in 2019. Schools and colleges are not excluded, as are organizations that provide driving, language and sports instruction. Educate Inc. owns Sylvan Learning Inc.

Kumon North America	13.3%
Educate Inc.	4.2
Huntington Learning Center	2.3
Other	80.2

Source: "Tutoring & Test Preparation Franchises in the United States." [online] from http://www.ibisworld.com [Published March 2019], from IBISWorld.

U-V

★ 3451 ★
Unions
SIC: 8631; NAICS: 81393

Number of Labor Unions and Similar Labor Organizations, 1998-2018

In 2020, 7.2 million workers in the public sector and 7.1 workers in the private sector belonged to unions. Private sector membership fell by 428,000 over 2019; the level in the public sector was mostly unchanged. Men had a higher union membership rate than women, 11% to 10.5%.

Year	Number
1998	18,695
1999	18,197
2000	17,811
2001	17,476
2002	17,520
2003	17,116
2004	16,169
2005	16,144
2006	15,627
2007	15,873
2008	15,351
2009	15,260
2010	15,018
2011	14,832
2012	14,555
2013	14,508
2014	14,312
2015	14,203
2016	14,015
2017	13,923
2018	13,665

Source: "County Business Patterns." [online] from https://www.census.gov/programs-surveys/cbp/data/datasets.html [Accessed June 25, 2020], from U.S. Census Bureau.

★ 3452 ★
Unions
SIC: 8631; NAICS: 81393

Union Membership by State, 2020

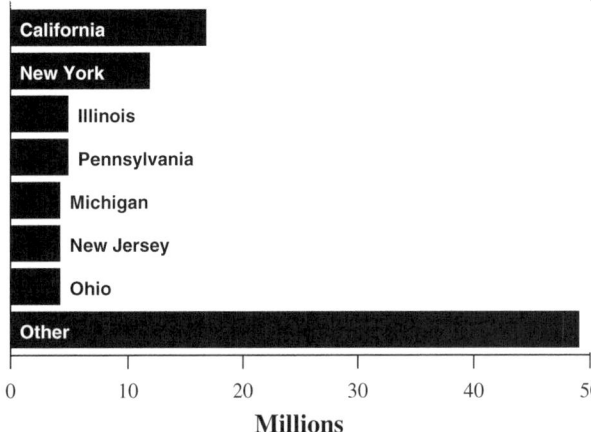

In 2020, the percent of wage and salary workers who were members of unions was 10.8%, up by 0.5% from 2019. The number of wage and salary workers belonging to unions fell by 321,000 to reach 14.3 million. The union membership rate of public-sector workers was 34.8%, significantly higher than the rate for private-sector workers at 6.3%.

	(mil.)	Share
California	2.40	16.75%
New York	1.70	11.86
Illinois	0.70	4.88
Pennsylvania	0.70	4.88
Michigan	0.60	4.19
New Jersey	0.60	4.19
Ohio	0.60	4.19
Other	7.03	49.06

Source: "Union Members Summary." [online] from https://www.bls.gov/news.release/union2.nr0.htm [Published January 22, 2021], from U.S. Bureau of Labor.

★ 3453 ★
Unmanned Aerial Vehicles
SIC: 3721; NAICS: 336411
Global Demand for eVTOLs, 2025-2040

Data show the forecast market for electric vertical take-off and landing vehicles. Figures are in billions of dollars.

2025	$ 3.4
2030	5.7
2035	6.8
2040	17.7

Source: "U.S. Flying Car Pays Attention in the eVTOL Market." [online] from http://news.kotra.or.kr [Published September 22, 2020], from Deloitte.

★ 3454 ★
Unmanned Aerial Vehicles
SIC: 8713; NAICS: 54136
Leading Drone Surveillance Firms Worldwide, 2019

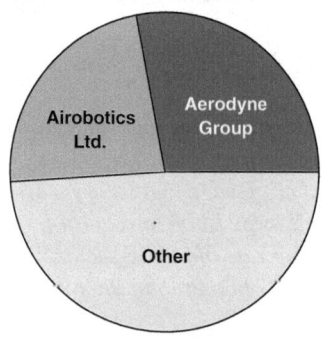

According to the source, drone surveillance is the "use of unmanned aerial vehicles to capture still images and video to gather information on specific targets." Market shares are shown based on revenue.

Aerodyne Group	28.07%
Airobotics Ltd.	23.03
Other	48.90

Source: "Global Drone Surveillance Research Report 2020." [online] from http://www.qyresearch.com [Published April 2020], from QY Research.

★ 3455 ★
Unmanned Aerial Vehicles
SIC: 3728; NAICS: 336411
Top Drone Makers, 2019

Market shares are shown as of registrations as of March 2019.

DJI Technology Co.	76.1%
Intel Corp.	4.1
Yuneec International	2.6
Parrot	2.5
Autel Robotics	0.6
3D Robotics Inc.	0.6
Skydio Inc.	0.3
SenseFly	0.2
AeroVironment	0.1
Kespry Inc.	0.1
Other	12.8

Source: "Drone Market Shares in the USA After China-U.S. Disputes." [online] from https://droneii.com/drone-market-shares-usa-after-china-usa-disputes [Published March 2, 2021], from Federal Aviation Authority.

★ 3456 ★
Uranium
SIC: 1094; NAICS: 212291
Leading Uranium Producers Worldwide, 2019

Market shares are shown in percent. The leading producers of uranium in 2019 were Kazakhstan with a 42% share of production, followed by Canada with a 13% share, and Australia with a 12% share. Other countries claimed the remaining 33%.

Kazatomprom	24.0%
China General Nuclear Power/China National Nuclear Corp.	13.0
Orano TN	12.0
Cameco Corp.	8.0
Uranium One	8.0
ARMZ Uranium Holding	6.0
BHP	6.0
Other	23.0

Source: "Kazatomprom #1 Global Uranium Producer." [online] from https://uraniumstockinvesting.com/uranium-producers/kazatomprom/ [Accessed March 22, 2021].

★ 3457 ★
Uranium
SIC: 1094; NAICS: 212291

Top Uranium Producing Nations, 2019

Production is shown in thousands of uranium-content tons.

	Tons	Share
Kazakhstan	22,808	35.33%
Canada	6,938	10.75
Australia	6,613	10.24
Namibia	5,476	8.48
Uzbekistan	3,500	5.42
Niger	2,983	4.62
Russia	2,911	4.51
China	1,885	2.92
Ukraine	801	1.24
South Africa	346	0.54
Other	10,305	15.96

Source: "World Uranium Mining Production." [online] from https://world-nuclear.org/information-library/nuclear-fuel-cycle/mining-of-uranium/world-uranium-mining-production.asp [Published December 2020], from World Nuclear Association.

★ 3458 ★
Utilities
SIC: 4911; NAICS: 221112, 221113, 221114

Largest Utilities by Customers, 2019

Companies are ranked by millions of residential and commercial customers.

Southern California Gas Company	5.72
Pacific Gas & Electric	4.07
Atmos Energy Corp.	3.19
Southwest Gas Corp.	2.05
Centerpoint Energy Entex	1.99
Nicor Gas	1.95
Consumers Energy Co.	1.77
Public Service Electric & Gas Co.	1.76
Pub Service Co. of Colorado	1.41
Spire Missouri Inc.	1.17

Source: "Top 50 Total Sales Customers." [online] from https://www.aga.org/research/data/utility-rankings/ [Accessed January 25, 2021], from American Gas Association Statistics Database.

★ 3459 ★
Vaccines
SIC: 2833; NAICS: 325411

COVID-19 Vaccine Production, 2020-2021

Producers are ranked by millions of doses produced in 2020 or promised for 2021. As of February 5, 2021, there were 1,056 drugs and vaccines aimed at COVID-19.

AstraZeneca-Oxford University (AZD1222)	3,000
Novanax (NVX-CoV2373)	2,100
Pfizer-BioNTech (Tozinmeran)	1,400
Sinopharm (BBiBP-CorV)	1,300
Gamaleya Centre (Sputnik V)	1,000
Johnson & Johnson Co. (JNJ-78436735)	1,000
Sinovac Biotech (CornoVac)	900
Moderna (mRNA-1273)	770
Bharat Biotech-ICMR	720
CureVac (CV nCOV)	300

Source: *The Economist*, January 9, 2021, p. 19, from Regulatory Affairs Professional Society and The Economist Intelligence Unit.

★ 3460 ★
Vaccines
SIC: 2836; NAICS: 325414

Global Shipments of COVID-19 Vaccines, 2020

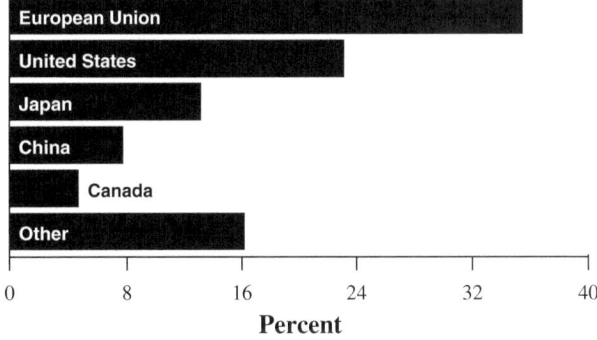

Pfizer and Moderna received FDA approval for the emergency use of their vaccines to treat COVID-19 in December 2020. Data show the initial shipments in millions of doses.

	(mil.)	Share
European Union	460	35.38%
United States	300	23.08
Japan	170	13.08
China	100	7.69

Continued on next page.

★ 3460 ★
[Continued]
Vaccines
SIC: 2836; NAICS: 325414

Global Shipments of COVID-19 Vaccines, 2020

Pfizer and Moderna received FDA approval for the emergency use of their vaccines to treat COVID-19 in December 2020. Data show the initial shipments in millions of doses.

	(mil.)	Share
Canada	60	4.62%
Other	210	16.15

Source: *Wall Street Journal*, December 19-20, 2020, p. A6, from Duke Global Health Innovation Center.

★ 3461 ★
Vaccines
SIC: 2836; NAICS: 325414

Leading Fish Vaccine Makers Worldwide, 2019

The industry is forecast to grow from $283.5 million in 2019 to $525.7 million in 2026. Market shares are shown based on revenue.

Zoetis	52.92%
Merck & Co. Inc.	34.85
Other	12.23

Source: "Global Fish Vaccine Market Size, Manufacturers, Supply Chain, Sales Channel and Clients, 2020-2026." [online] from http://www.qyresearch.com [Published July 2020], from QY Research.

★ 3462 ★
Vaccines
SIC: 2836; NAICS: 325414

Leading Flu Vaccine Makers Worldwide, 2019

The industry is forecast to grow from $4.71 billion in 2019 to $6.83 billion in 2026. Market shares are shown based on revenue.

Sanofi Pasteur	44.94%
CSL Behring	25.37
GlaxoSmithKline	14.70
Other	14.99

Source: "Global Flu Vaccine Market Size, Manufacturers, Supply Chain, Sales Channel and Clients, 2020-2026." [online] from http://www.qyresearch.com [Published July 2020], from QY Research.

★ 3463 ★
Vaccines
SIC: 2836; NAICS: 325414

Leading Varicella Vaccine Makers Worldwide, 2015

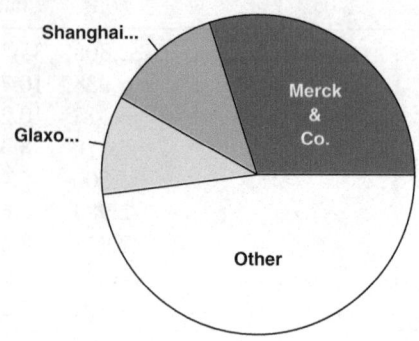

The varicella vaccine, also known as the chickenpox vaccine, generated revenue of $3.57 billion in 2019.

Merck & Co.	30.40%
Shanghai Institute	11.60
GlaxoSmithKline	10.04
Other	47.96

Source: "COVID-19 Impact on Global Varicella Vaccine Market Insights, Forecast to 2026." [online] from http://www.qyresearch.com [Published May 2020], from QY Research.

★ 3464 ★
Vaccines
SIC: 2836; NAICS: 325414

Top Vaccine Makers in China, 2019

The source notes that the market is ripe for concentration, as it is seeing overcapacity and homogenous products. The animal vaccine market saw a CAGR of 8% from 2013 to 2017, but then declined as a result of the African Swine fever outbreak of 2018. The market declined again to reach 11.2 billion renminbi in 2019. Market shares are estimated.

Jinyu Bio-technology	15.6%
China Animal Husbandry Industry Co. Ltd.	10.6
Qingdao Yebio Biological Engineering	10.2
Tecon Biology	6.3
Keqian Biology	6.1
Ringpu Bio-technology	5.2
Pulike Biological Engineering	3.4
Shanghai Shen Lian Biomedical	2.3

Continued on next page.

★ 3464 ★
[Continued]
Vaccines
SIC: 2836; NAICS: 325414

Top Vaccine Makers in China, 2019

The source notes that the market is ripe for concentration, as it is seeing overcapacity and homogenous products. The animal vaccine market saw a CAGR of 8% from 2013 to 2017, but then declined as a result of the African Swine fever outbreak of 2018. The market declined again to reach 11.2 billion renminbi in 2019. Market shares are estimated.

Hile Bio-Technology	1.8%
Other	38.5

Source: "China Animal Vaccine Industry Report, 2019-2025." [online] from http://www.researchinchina.com [Published February 2020], from Research in China.

★ 3465 ★
Valves
SIC: 3491; NAICS: 332911

Industrial Valve Sales by End Market, 2019

Shares are shown based on revenues in the United States for 2019.

Petroleum refining	12.0%
Chemical production	10.0
Oil and gas extraction	10.0
Power generation	10.0
Wastewater	9.0
Oil and gas transmission	8.0
Petrochemical production	8.0
Pulp and paper production	7.0
Water	6.0
Metals	5.0
Pharmaceutical production	5.0
Food production	3.0
Mining	1.0
Other	6.0

Source: *Valve World Americas*, May 2020, p. 21, from McIlvaine Co.

★ 3466 ★
Valves
SIC: 3491; NAICS: 332911

Industrial Valve Shipments by Type, 2019

Data show shipments in millions of dollars.

	($ mil.)	Share
Automated	$ 1,453.3	31.09%
Ball	865.5	18.51
Gate, globe and check	691.1	14.78
Industrial butterfly	440.2	9.42
Plug	313.8	6.71
Pressure-relief	270.2	5.78
Other	640.8	13.71

Source: "VMA Statistical Reports." [online] from https://www.vma.org/page/StatisticalReports [Accessed November 16, 2020], from Valve Manufacturers Association.

★ 3467 ★
Vans
SIC: 3713; NAICS: 336211

Best-Selling Commercial Vans, 2020

Commercial van sales fell 15% in 2020, from 496,491 in 2019 to 422,366 in 2020.

	Sales	Share
Ford Transit	131,556	31.15%
Chevrolet Express	55,131	13.05
Ram ProMaster	50,556	11.97
Mercedes-Benz Sprinter	41,930	9.93
Ford E-series	37,001	8.76
Ford Transit Connect	34,596	8.19
Nissan NV200	17,126	4.05
Nissan NV Van	15,247	3.61
GMC Savana	15,108	3.58
Ram ProMaster City	10,409	2.46
Other	13,706	3.25

Source: "U.S. Car Sales Analysis 2020 - Commercial Vans." [online] from https://carsalesbase.com/us-car-sales-analysis-2020-commercial-vans/ [Accessed April 21, 2021], from manufacturer reports.

★ 3468 ★
Vans
SIC: 3713; NAICS: 336211

New Vans by Fuel Type in the EU, 2019

Distribution is shown in percent. Data for Bulgaria, Croatia, Malta and Lithuania not available. Figures refer to commercial vehicles over 3.5 tons. "Electrically-chargeable" includes battery electric vehicle, fuel-cell electric vehicles, extended-range and plug-in hybrid electric vehicles. "Hybrids" include full and mild hybrids. "Alternative fuels" includes LPG, natural gas and ethanol vehicles.

Diesel	92.8%
Petrol	4.4
Alternative fuels	1.3
Electrically-chargeable	1.2
Hybrid	0.2

Source: "The Automobile Industry Pocket Guide 2020-2021." [online] from http://www.acea.be/publications/article/acea-pocket-guide [Accessed April 12, 2021], from European Automobile Manufacturers' Association.

★ 3469 ★
Vegetarians
SIC: 2099; NAICS: 311991, 311999

Largest Markets Worldwide for Vegetarians, 2019

Data show the countries with the largest population of vegetarians in millions.

India	390.0
Indonesia	66.9
Nigeria	58.1
China	51.9
Pakistan	33.2

Source: "China's Centuries-old Plant Based Meat Industry Set for Growth." [online] from https://ld-investments.com/china-alternative-meat/ [Published October 21, 2020], from Euromonitor.

★ 3470 ★
Vending Machines
SIC: 5962; NAICS: 45421

Micro Markets by Location, 2019

Micro markets are small, self-contained stores with self-checkout kiosks and no employees. There were 26,094 active micro markets in 2019, up from 25,339 a year earlier.

Manufacturing	25.0%
Offices	23.9
Retail sites	9.3%
Hospitals and nursing homes	8.4
Universities and colleges	8.3
Military bases	7.0
Hotels and motels	6.0
Restaurants, bars and clubs	5.8
Elementary, middle and high schools	5.6
Correctional facilities	0.9

Source: *Automatic Merchandiser*, June/July 2020, p. 11.

★ 3471 ★
Vending Machines
SIC: 5962; NAICS: 45421

Top Micro Market Product Categories, 2019

Data are shown in percent. "Other" includes cooperative service vending, condoms, toll passes, repair services, rental equipment, chips and crackers.

Cold beverages	25.9%
Food	17.4
Snacks	14.8
Candy	12.7
Confectionery	9.0
Healthy	6.8
Ice cream/frozen	4.6
Hot beverages	4.5
Other	4.3

Source: *Automatic Merchandiser*, June/July 2020, p. 17.

★ 3472 ★
Vending Machines
SIC: 5962; NAICS: 45421

Top Vending Machine Product Categories, 2019

Data are shown in percent. "Other" includes non-edible items. Industry revenue grew from $23.5 billion in 2018 to $24.2 billion in 2019. Consumers are moving away from carbonated soft drinks and salty snacks and to healthier options. Suppliers have had to diversify their offerings to respond to this trend. The closing of offices and retail establishments because of the pandemic is expected to have a negative effect on this market in 2020.

Cold beverages	22.8%
Snacks	14.1
Candy	13.2
Confectionery	9.1
Healthy	7.0

Continued on next page.

★ 3472 ★
[Continued]
Vending Machines
SIC: 5962; NAICS: 45421

Top Vending Machine Product Categories, 2019

Data are shown in percent. "Other" includes non-edible items. Industry revenue grew from $23.5 billion in 2018 to $24.2 billion in 2019. Consumers are moving away from carbonated soft drinks and salty snacks and to healthier options. Suppliers have had to diversify their offerings to respond to this trend. The closing of offices and retail establishments because of the pandemic is expected to have a negative effect on this market in 2020.

Hot beverages	4.4%
Food	4.3
Ice cream/frozen	2.4
Other	22.8

Source: *Automatic Merchandiser*, June/July 2020, p. 17.

★ 3473 ★
Vending Machines
SIC: 5962; NAICS: 45421

Vending Machines by Location, 2019

The vending and micro market industry generated revenues of $24.2 billion in 2019. There were an estimated 2.18 million vending machines in use in 2019 up slightly from 2.08 million 2018, but down from 3.5 million in 2016.

Manufacturing	22.1%
Offices	22.1
Retail sites	13.5
Elementary, middle and high schools	9.8
Hospitals and nursing homes	7.4
Hotels and motels	7.4
Universities and colleges	6.5
Military bases	4.5
Restaurants, bars and clubs	4.4
Correctional facilities	2.4

Source: *Automatic Merchandiser*, June/July 2020, p. 11.

★ 3474 ★
Veterinary Patient Monitoring Equipment
SIC: 3842; NAICS: 339113

Leading Veterinary Patient Monitoring Equipment Makers Worldwide, 2019

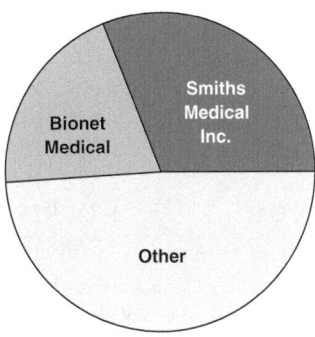

Market shares are shown based on revenue.

Smiths Medical Inc.	30.91%
Bionet Medical	19.71
Other	49.38

Source: "Global Veterinary Patient Monitoring Equipment Market Research Report 2020." [online] from http://www.qyresearch.com [Published March 2020], from QY Research.

★ 3475 ★
Veterinary Services
SIC: 0742; NAICS: 54194

Leading Veterinary Operators, 2018

There are 28,000-32,000 vet practices in the United States, of which only approximately 3,500 are company owned.

VCA Inc.	5.9%
IDEXX Laboratories	2.9
National Veterinary Associates Inc.	0.7
Other	90.5

Source: "Covetrus." [online] from milclub.org/wp-content/uploads/2020/08/CVET-UIC/-VF.pdf [Published October 18, 2019].

★ 3476 ★
Video Game Industry
SIC: 3944; NAICS: 33993

Best-Selling Video Game Consoles, 2020-2021

Data show annual sales for the year ended January 1.

	Jan. 1 2020	Jan. 1 2021
Nintendo Switch	9,367,556	1,513,262
PlayStation 5	1,940,361	751,870
Microsoft Xbox S	1,525,675	569,421
PlayStation 4	2,372,519	148,798
Microsoft Xbox One	1,758,975	134,417
Nintendo 3DS	279,847	3,413

Source: "Yearly Hardware Comparisons - USA." [online] from https://www.vgchartz.com/tools/hw_date.php?reg=USA&ending=Yearly [Accessed March 28, 2021], from VGChartz.

★ 3477 ★
Video Game Industry
SIC: 3944; NAICS: 33993

Best-Selling Video Game Consoles in China, 2020

Video game consoles are ranked by estimated lifetime sales. Figures are in millions of units and cover legal and gray channels. The Nintendo Switch sold more than 1.3 million units in 2020.

Nintendo Switch	3.95
PlayStation 4	3.52
Xbox One	1.24

Source: "China is Nintendo's Secret Weapon in War With PlayStation, Xbox." [online] from https://finance.yahoo.com/news/china-nintendo-secret-weapon-war-210000850.html [Published December 9, 2020], from Niko Partners.

★ 3478 ★
Video Game Industry
SIC: 3944; NAICS: 33993

Best-Selling Video Game Consoles Worldwide, 2020-2021

Data show annual sales for the year ended January 1.

	Jan. 1 2020	Jan. 1 2021
Nintendo Switch	28,293,919	4,645,361
PlayStation 5	4,390,029	2,113,446
Microsoft Xbox S	3,031,468	1,111,382
PlayStation 4	8,596,987	587,913
Microsoft Xbox One	3,146,542	235,795
Nintendo 3DS	460,537	16,023

Source: "Yearly Hardware Comparisons - USA." [online] from https://www.vgchartz.com/tools/hw_date.php?reg=USA&ending=Yearly [Accessed March 28, 2021], from VGChartz.

★ 3479 ★
Video Game Industry
SIC: 7372; NAICS: 334614, 51121

Leading Video Game Firms, 2019

The leading companies in the video game industry are shown by estimated market share. Nintendo Co. Ltd. has 8-9% of the market, Activision 6-7%, GameStop 4-6% and Electronic Arts 2-4%.

Microsoft Corp.	9.8%
Nintendo Co. Ltd.	> 8.0
Activision Blizzard Inc.	< 7.0
GameStop	< 6.0
Sony Corp.	4.5
Electronic Arts	< 4.0
Other	60.7

Source: "Tech Disruption (Part 1) - Video Game Streaming Services." [online] from https://www.ibisworld.com/industry-insider/analyst-insights/tech-disruption-part-1-video-game-streaming-services-in-the-us/ [Published October 1, 2019], from IBISWorld.

★ 3480 ★
Video Game Industry
SIC: 7372; NAICS: 334614, 51121

Leading Video Game Markets in Central and South America, 2019

Countries are ranked by sales in millions of dollars. Mexico was the largest market in the region in 2019 and was the twelfth largest worldwide.

Mexico	$ 1,577
Brazil	1,452
Argentina	448
Colombia	322
Chile	234
Peru	152
Ecuador	75
Puerto Rico	67

Continued on next page.

★ 3480 ★
[Continued]
Video Game Industry
SIC: 7372; NAICS: 334614, 51121

Leading Video Game Markets in Central and South America, 2019

Countries are ranked by sales in millions of dollars. Mexico was the largest market in the region in 2019 and was the twelfth largest worldwide.

Dominican Republic	$ 58
Uruguay	47

Source: "Mexican Game Industry and Consumption Trends." [online] from http://news.kotra.or.kr [Published September 17, 2020], from Statista.

★ 3481 ★
Video Game Industry
SIC: 3944; NAICS: 33993

Lifetime Video Game Consoles Worldwide, 2020

Data show estimated lifetime sales in millions of units. There were 2.7 billion gamers worldwide in 2020.

Sony PlayStation 2	157.7
Sony PlayStation 4	112.1
Sony PlayStation	102.5
Nintendo Wii	101.6
Sony PlayStation 3	87.4
Microsoft Xbox 360	85.5
Nintendo NES	61.9
Nintendo Switch	61.4
Nintendo Super NES	49.1
Microsoft Xbox One	48.4
Nintendo N64	32.9
Sega Genesis	29.5

Source: "The State of the Multi-Billion Dollar Console Gaming Market." [online] from https://www.visualcapitalist.com/multi-billion-dollar-console-gaming-market/ [Published November 9, 2020], from Statista.

★ 3482 ★
Video Game Industry
SIC: 5945; NAICS: 45112

Retail Sales of Video Games in Russia, 2019

The market grew 15% over the year to reach 129.5 billion rubles (about $2 billion). Free games represented 99 billion rubles, while paid games generated 20.5 billion rubles. The PS4 was the most popular game console. There are more than 150 companies active in this market.

E-commerce	86.8%
Electronics and appliance specialist retailers	8.8
Leisure and personal goods specialist retailers	2.6
Modern grocery retailers	1.2
Other	0.6

Source: "Russian Video Game Market Trends." [online] from http://www.news.kotra.or.kr [Published August 19, 2020], from Euromonitor.

★ 3483 ★
Video Game Industry
SIC: 7372; NAICS: 334614, 51121

Strategy Subgenre iOS Revenue, 2020

Revenues are shown in millions of dollars for the second quarter of 2020. The best-selling games, based on revenue in millions of dollars: Clash of Clans $23.67 million, Rise of Kingdoms $12.51 million and Game of Thrones: Conquest $11.16 million.

	($ mil.)	Share
4X strategy	$ 124.0	67.98%
Build and battle	36.5	20.01
Tactical battler	12.8	7.02
Multiplayer battle arena	9.1	4.99

Source: "Game Refinery Strategy Genre Snapshot." [online] from https://www.gamerefinery.com/strategy-genre-snapshot-report-september-2020/ [Published September 2020], from Game Refinery Saas Dashboard.

★ 3484 ★
Video Game Industry
SIC: 3944; NAICS: 33993

Top Video Game Platforms Worldwide, 2020

Platforms are ranked by estimated sales of games in billions of dollars. The coronavirus pandemic has increased demand for video games and consoles as consumers shift their spending from vacations and live experiences to home entertainment. Both Microsoft and Sony released new consoles in November. Although the number of console game players (0.8 billion) are about one third of mobile players (2.6 billion), revenues for console games are more than half of that of mobile. Video games are no longer device-specific and gamers frequently play on more than one platform. To capitalize on that, both Microsoft and Sony offer monthly subscription services that allow users access to hundreds of games on their consoles and PCs. Microsoft's service, Xbox Game Pass, has users download games while Sony's service, PS Now, is a streaming service.

	($ bil.)	Share
Mobile	$ 77.2	48.46%
Console	45.2	28.37
PC	36.9	23.16

Source: *Variety*, October 20, 2020, pp. 7-8, from Newzoo.

★ 3485 ★
Video Game Industry
SIC: 7372; NAICS: 334614, 51121

Video Game Streaming Market Worldwide, 2018-2019

Market shares are shown based on hours watched by platform. Twitch saw its streaming platform hours increase from 7.77 billion in 2018 to 9.34 billion in 2019.

	2018	2019
Twitch	75.0%	73.0%
YouTube Gaming	22.0	21.0
Facebook Gaming	1.0	3.0
Mixer	1.0	3.0

Source: "Microsoft's Mixer Grows Audience, but Amazon's Twitch Continues to Dominate Streaming Market." [online] from https://www.geekwire.com/2019/microsofts-mixer-grows-audience-amazons-twitch-continues-dominate-streaming-market/ [Published December 26, 2019], from StreamElements.

★ 3486 ★
Virtual Events
SIC: 7389; NAICS: 56192

Virtual Events Market Worldwide, 2019-2026

The virtual events market is growing annually by 20%. The industry reached $58.11 billion in 2020. The United States claimed 47% of the global market. Figures are in billions of dollars.

2019	$ 25.56
2020	30.77
2021	37.05
2022	44.61
2023	53.71
2024	64.67
2025	77.86
2026	93.74

Source: "Overview of the Virtual Events Market." [online] from https://mhojhosresearch.com/2020/05/01/global-virtual-event-market-is-growing-annually-by-22/ [Published May 1, 2020], from Mhojhos Research.

★ 3487 ★
Vitamin and Supplement Retailers
SIC: 5499; NAICS: 446191

Retail Sales of Vitamins and Supplements, 2018-2020

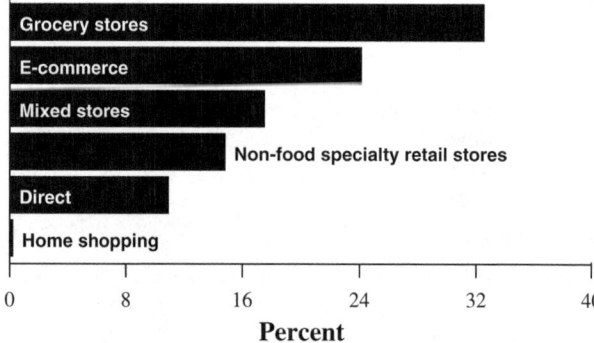

Market shares are shown based on channel. Sales are forecast to grow from $33.47 billion in 2020 to $39.1 billion in 2025.

	2018	2019	2020
Grocery stores	33.5%	32.9%	32.5%
E-commerce	18.1	19.3	24.1
Mixed stores	18.2	18.1	17.5

Continued on next page.

★ 3487 ★
[Continued]
Vitamin and Supplement Retailers
SIC: 5499; NAICS: 446191

Retail Sales of Vitamins and Supplements, 2018-2020

Market shares are shown based on channel. Sales are forecast to grow from $33.47 billion in 2020 to $39.1 billion in 2025.

	2018	2019	2020
Non-food specialty retail stores	18.3%	17.6%	14.8%
Direct	11.8	11.8	10.9
Home shopping	0.2	0.2	0.2

Source: "U.S. Vitamin and Health Supplement Market Exploded Through the Let's Raise the Immunity Pandemic." [online] from http://www.news.kotra.or.kr [Published March 29, 2021], from Euromonitor.

★ 3488 ★
Vitamins
SIC: 2833; NAICS: 325411

Top 1 & 2 Letter Vitamin Brands, 2020

Market shares are shown based on drug store sales for the 52 weeks ended April 19, 2020.

Nature Made	33.30%
Nature's Bounty	17.80
Nature's Bounty Optimal Solutions	4.25
Emergen C	2.58
Nature's Truth	1.33
Sundown	1.27
Ester-C	1.22
Vitafusion	1.03
Vitafusion Power C	0.78
Private label	29.26
Other	7.18

Source: *DrugStore Management*, Annual 2020-2021, p. 100, from IRI.

★ 3489 ★
Vitamins
SIC: 2833; NAICS: 325411

Top Multivitamin Brands, 2020

Brands are ranked by sales in millions of dollars at supermarkets, drug stores, mass merchandisers, military commissaries, and select club and dollar chains for the 12 weeks ended May 17, 2020.

	($ mil.)	Share
Airborne	$ 26.7	4.16%
Bausch + Lomb Preservision	21.0	3.27
Centrum Silver	$ 13.8	2.15%
Airborne Original	8.7	1.35
Nature Made	7.0	1.09
Vitafusion	6.0	0.93
Centrum	5.6	0.87
Nature's Way Alive	5.4	0.84
Centrum Multigummies	4.8	0.75
Private label	25.4	3.96
Other	517.7	80.63

Source: *Chain Drug Review*, August 10, 2020, p. 110, from IRI.

★ 3490 ★
Vitamins
SIC: 2833; NAICS: 325411

Top Vitamin Categories, 2020

Categories are ranked by sales in millions of dollars at supermarkets, drug stores, mass merchandisers, military commissaries, and select club and dollar chains for the 52 weeks ended October 4, 2020.

	($ mil.)	Share
Mineral supplements	$ 4,140.0	47.25%
Multivitamins	2,230.0	25.45
1 and 2 letter vitamins	1,600.0	18.26
Liquid/minerals	792.8	9.05

Source: *MMR*, November 16, 2020, p. 30, from IRI.

★ 3491 ★
Vitamins
SIC: 2833; NAICS: 325411

Vitamin Production in China, 2019-2020

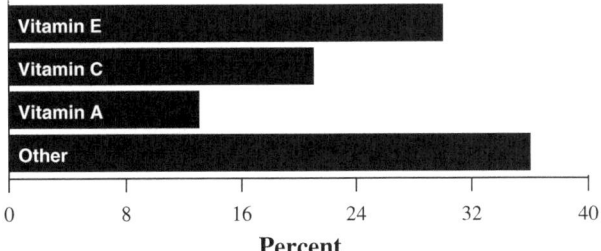

Vitamin sales reached 14.5 billion renminbi in 2016, 16.6 billion renminbi in 2017 and 24.8 billion renminbi in 2018. Vitamin C saw a rise in sales in 2020 as consumers looked for ways to boost their immune systems.

Vitamin E	30.0%
Vitamin C	21.0

Continued on next page.

★ 3491 ★
[Continued]
Vitamins
SIC: 2833; NAICS: 325411

Vitamin Production in China, 2019-2020

Vitamin sales reached 14.5 billion renminbi in 2016, 16.6 billion renminbi in 2017 and 24.8 billion renminbi in 2018. Vitamin C saw a rise in sales in 2020 as consumers looked for ways to boost their immune systems.

Vitamin A	13.0%
Other	36.0

Source: "China Industry Information." [online] from http://www.news.kotra.or.kr [Published June 5, 2020], from China Industrial Information Network.

★ 3492 ★
Voting Machines
SIC: 3578; NAICS: 333318

Voting Machine Market, 2020

Companies are ranked by number of registered voters. State and local governments conduct elections using Direct Record Electronic (DRE) voting machines, optical scan ballot readers, and ballot marking devices to conduct elections. Companies tend to sell software, hardware, service and support as part of a package; the source notes this makes it difficult for new companies to break into the market.

	(mil.)	Share
Election Systems & Software	90.31	43.67%
All Dominion Voting Systems	68.03	32.90
Hart InterCivic	25.60	12.38
Hand-counted paper ballots	0.82	0.40
Other	22.48	10.87

Source: "Cybersecurity and U.S. Election Infrastructure." [online] from https://foreignpolicy.com/2020/10/27/election-cybersecurity-cyberattack-critical-infrastructure-voting/ [Published October 27, 2020], from VerifiedVoting.org.

W-Z

★ 3493 ★
Wallboard
SIC: 3275; NAICS: 32742

Leading Gypsum Wallboard Makers Worldwide, 2019

Companies are ranked by capacity in millions of square meters.

	(mil.)	Share
Knauf Gips KG	2,913	21.33%
Saint-Gobain S.A.	2,525	18.49
Beijing New Building Materials Public Ltd.	2,263	16.57
National Gypsum	793	5.81
Georgia-Pacific Corp.	677	4.96
Etex Group	654	4.79
Yoshino Gypsum	616	4.51
USG Boral	359	2.63
American Gypsum	300	2.20
KCC Corp.	263	1.93
Boral Ltd.	205	1.50
Chiyoda-Ute	194	1.42
PABCO Gypsum	147	1.08
Jason Plasterboard	135	0.99
Panel Rey	86	0.63
Volma Corp.	85	0.62
CSR Gyprock	80	0.59
Other	1,363	9.98

Source: *Global Gypsum Magazine*, July 2020, p. 12.

★ 3494 ★
Wallpaper
SIC: 2679; NAICS: 322299

Leading Wallpaper Makers Worldwide, 2016

The industry is expected to climb from $26.9 billion in 2019 to $30.6 billion in 2024.

York Wallcoverings	8.50%
Sangetsu Co. Ltd.	5.67
A.S. Création	4.38%
Other	81.45

Source: "Global Wallpaper Market Growth 2019-2024." [online] from https://www.absolutereports.com/global-wallpaper-market-13877835 [Published February 2019], from Absolute Reports.

★ 3495 ★
Warehouse Clubs
SIC: 5331; NAICS: 452319

Leading Warehouse Club Operators, 2019

The industry generated revenue of $505.6 billion in 2019. Walmart includes supercenters and Sam's Club.

Walmart Inc.	70.7%
Costco Wholesale Corp.	19.3
BJ's	2.6
Other	7.4

Source: *Beverage Industry*, August 2019, p. 24, from IBISWorld.

★ 3496 ★
Warehousing
SIC: 4213; NAICS: 48423

Cold Chain Logistics in China, 2011-2020

Data are in billions of renminbi. Data for 2017-2020 are forecasts. The top 10 cold storage operators claim approximately 21% of total capacity.

2011	¥ 81
2013	109

Continued on next page.

★ 3496 ★
[Continued]
Warehousing
SIC: 4213; NAICS: 48423

Cold Chain Logistics in China, 2011-2020

Data are in billions of renminbi. Data for 2017-2020 are forecasts. The top 10 cold storage operators claim approximately 21% of total capacity.

2015	¥ 181
2017	236
2019	368
2020	470

Source: "Bright Prospects for China's Cold Chain Logistics Sector." [online] from https://ld-investments.com/author/ld_investments/ [Accessed August 25, 2020], from L.E.K. Consulting.

★ 3497 ★
Warehousing
SIC: 4222; NAICS: 49312

Commodities Held in Cold Storage, 2019 and 2020

Data show stocks held in all warehouses in thousands of pounds. Total commodities slipped from 9.95 billion pounds in 2019 to 9.69 billion in 2020.

	Dec. 31, 2019	Dec. 31, 2020
Vegetables	2,354,632	2,486,744
Natural cheese	1,322,014	1,397,941
Potatoes	1,155,930	1,121,376
Chicken	977,622	863,077
Beef	480,116	534,297
Pork	580,464	408,361
Butter	189,655	273,390
Blueberries	246,625	237,060
Turkey	232,652	223,637
Strawberries	157,388	150,580
Pecans, in-shell	75,123	132,616
Raspberries, red	62,654	54,205
Pecans, shelled	52,466	45,479
Eggs, frozen	40,771	31,696
Blackberries	21,741	18,794
Ducks	2,647	2,855

Source: "Cold Storage." [online] from https://www.nass.usda.gov/Surveys/Guide_to_NASS_Surveys/Cold_Storage/index.php [Published January 25, 2021], from U.S. Department of Agriculture.

★ 3498 ★
Warehousing
SIC: 4221; NAICS: 49313

Farm Product Warehousing and Storage Leaders, 2017

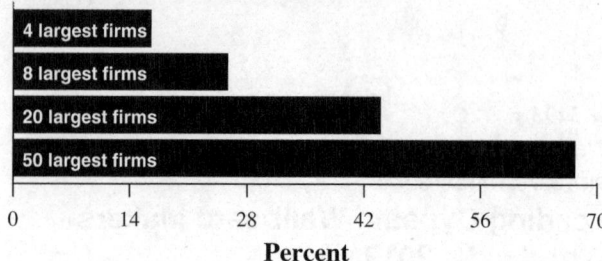

Data show the percent of industry sales held by the largest 4, 8, 20 and 50 firms in the sector. There are approximately 561 players operating in the industry generating employment for 5,155 people. According to Kentley Insights, the industry generated sales of $1 billion in 2019.

4 largest firms	16.5%
8 largest firms	25.6
20 largest firms	43.9
50 largest firms	67.3

Source: "Economic Census." [online] from https://www.census.gov/content/census/en/data/tables/2017/econ/economic-census/naics-sector-31-33.html [Accessed January 21, 2021], from U.S. Census Bureau.

★ 3499 ★
Warehousing
SIC: 4222; NAICS: 49312

Leading Cold Storage Firms in India, 2019

Data show the leading providers with 10,000+ pallet capacity. India has an approximately 500,000 pallet capacity; players with 10,000+ capacity constitute about 60% of the market.

Snowman Logistics	104,343
Coldman Logistics	66,799
Coldrush Logistics	28,200
Western Logistics	24,000
JWL Cold Store	20,000
MJ Logistics	20,000
Stellar Value Chain	20,000
Schedulers Logistics	13,000

Source: "Acquisition of Snowman Logistics Limited (Snowman) by Adani Logistics Limited." [online] from https://www.adaniports.com/-/media/Project/Ports/Investor/Investor-Downloads/Investors-Presentation/Snowman-Acquisition.pdf [Published December 27, 2019].

★ 3500 ★
Warehousing
SIC: 4225; NAICS: 49311

Leading Dry Warehousing Firms in North America, 2020

Companies are ranked by millions of square feet of storage space. Shares are shown based on the top 105 companies.

	(mil.)	Share
DHL Supply Chain North America	139.6	13.30%
XPO Logistics	101.0	9.62
Ryder Supply Chain Solutions	64.0	6.10
NFI Industries	53.0	5.05
Geodis North America	52.2	4.97
FedEx Logistics	30.7	2.92
Kenco Logistics Services	30.0	2.86
Penske Logistics	26.5	2.52
Saddle Creek Logistics Services	26.2	2.50
CJ Logistics North America	23.9	2.28
Other	502.9	47.90

Source: *Transport Topics*, Top 50 Annual, 2021, p. A18.

★ 3501 ★
Warehousing
SIC: 4222; NAICS: 49312

Leading Refrigerated Warehouse Operators in North America, 2020

Companies are ranked by capacity in millions of cubic meters. Shares are shown based on a total of 98.69 million cubic meters operated by the top 25 firms.

	(mil.)	Share
Lineage Logistics	39.41	39.93%
Americold Logistics	29.22	29.61
United States Cold Storage	10.59	10.73
VersaCold Logistics Services	3.48	3.53
AGRO Merchants Group	3.36	3.40
Interstate Warehousing	3.27	3.31
Frialsa Frigorificos	2.89	2.93
Burris Logistics	2.12	2.15
Congebec Logistics Inc.	1.63	1.65
Conestoga Cold Storage	1.60	1.62
Other	1.12	1.13

Source: "IARW North America Top 25 List of Refrigerated Warehousing and Logistics Providers." [online] from https://www.gcca.org/about/resources/about-industry/technical-publications/surveys-market-research/iarw-north-american [Accessed May 20, 2021], from International Association of Refrigerated Warehouses.

★ 3502 ★
Warehousing
SIC: 4222; NAICS: 49312

Leading Refrigerated Warehouse Operators Worldwide, 2020

Companies are ranked by capacity in millions of cubic meters. Shares are shown based on a total of 145.63 million cubic meters of the top 25 firms.

	(mil.)	Share
Lineage Logistics	50.66	34.79%
Americold Logistics	31.42	21.58
United States Cold Storage	10.59	7.27
AGRO Merchants Group L.L.C.	6.86	4.71
NewCold Advanced	5.51	3.78
Nichirei Logistics Group Inc.	5.18	3.56
Kloosterboer	4.84	3.32
VersaCold Logistics Services	3.48	2.39
Interstate Warehousing	3.27	2.25
Frialsa Frigorificos	2.89	1.98
Other	20.93	14.37

Source: "IARW Global Top 25 List of Refrigerated Warehousing and Logistics Providers." [online] from https://www.gcca.org/about/resources/about-industry/technical-publications/surveys-market-research/iarw-global-top-25 [Accessed May 20, 2021], from International Association of Refrigerated Warehouses.

★ 3503 ★
Warehousing
SIC: 4225; NAICS: 49311

Third-Party Logistics Warehousing in North America, 2020

Companies are ranked by millions of square feet of warehousing space.

DHL Supply Chain North America	139.0
XPO Logistics	90.0
Ryder Supply Chain Solutions	56.4
NFI Industries	49.6
Geodis North America	44.0
Americold Logistics L.L.C.	42.7
Lineage Logistics L.L.C.	37.0
FedEx Logistics	30.7
Kenco Logistics Services	26.0
CJ Logistics North America	24.9

Source: *Modern Materials Handling*, December 2020, p. 38, from Armstrong & Associates.

★ 3504 ★
Waste Removal
SIC: 4953; NAICS: 562212

Leading Waste Removal Firms in North America, 2019

Firms are ranked by revenue in millions of dollars. Shares are shown based on revenue generated by the top 50 firms.

	($ bil.)	Share
Waste Management Inc.	$ 15.46	29.34%
Republic Services Inc.	10.30	19.54
Waste Connections	5.38	10.21
Clean Harbors Inc.	3.41	6.47
Stericycle Inc.	3.31	6.28
GFL Environmental Inc.	2.53	4.80
Covanta Energy	1.87	3.55
Advanced Disposal Services Inc.	1.62	3.07
Recology	1.30	2.47
U.S. Ecology	1.05	1.99
Other	6.47	12.28

Source: *Waste Today*, July-August 2020, p. NA.

★ 3505 ★
Watches
SIC: 3873; NAICS: 334519

Top Swiss Watch Brands Worldwide, 2020

Shipments of Swiss watches fell from 20.5 billion Swiss francs in 2019 to 16.1 billion Swiss francs in 2020.

Rolex	24.9%
Omega	8.8
Cartier Watches	6.7
Longines	6.2
Patek Philippe	5.8
Audemars Piguet	4.3
TAG Heuer	3.0
IWC	2.7
Richard Mille	2.5
Breitling	2.4
Other	32.7

Source: "The Top 50 Swiss Watch Brands of 2020...And the Invincible Hegemony of Rolex." [online] from https://monochrome-watches.com/top-50-swiss-watch-brands-2020-market-share-sales-editorial/ [Published March 9, 2021].

★ 3506 ★
Watches
SIC: 3873; NAICS: 334519

Top Swiss Watch Export Markets Worldwide, 2019-2020

Markets are ranked by sales in millions of Swiss francs. Spending fell from 21.71 billion Swiss francs in 2019 to 16.98 billion Swiss francs in 2020.

	2019 (mil.)	2020 (mil.)	Share
China	1,994.2	2,394.0	14.10%
United States	2,409.4	1,986.7	11.70
Hong Kong	2,691.0	1,696.7	9.99
Japan	1,608.6	1,189.5	7.00
United Kingdom	1,366.2	1,030.2	6.07
Singapore	1,269.0	933.6	5.50
Germany	1,127.3	886.4	5.22
United Arab Emirates	935.3	758.5	4.47
France	1,073.7	667.2	3.93
Italy	970.8	647.6	3.81
Other	6,272.2	4,793.7	28.22

Source: "Watch Distribution of Swiss Watch Exports." [online] from https://www.fhs.swiss/eng/statistics.html [Accessed January 25, 2021], from Federation of the Swiss Watch Industry.

★ 3507 ★
Watches
SIC: 3873; NAICS: 334519

Top Swiss Watch Makers Worldwide, 2020

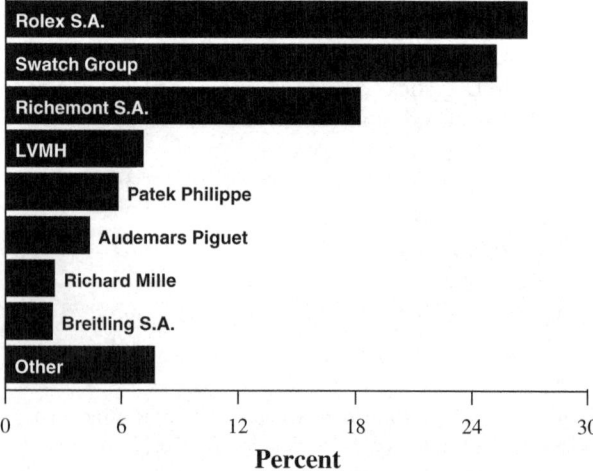

The Swiss watch industry saw its largest decline since 2009, with exports dropping 21.8% by value.

Rolex S.A.	26.8%
Swatch Group	25.2

Continued on next page.

★ 3507 ★
[Continued]
Watches
SIC: 3873; NAICS: 334519

Top Swiss Watch Makers Worldwide, 2020

The Swiss watch industry saw its largest decline since 2009, with exports dropping 21.8% by value.

Richemont S.A.	18.2%
LVMH	7.1
Patek Philippe	5.8
Audemars Piguet	4.3
Richard Mille	2.5
Breitling S.A.	2.4
Other	7.7

Source: "The Top 50 Swiss Watch Brands of 2020...And the Invincible Hegemony of Rolex." [online] from https://monochrome-watches.com/top-50-swiss-watch-brands-2020-market-share-sales-editorial/ [Published March 9, 2021].

★ 3508 ★
Water Filtration
SIC: 3564; NAICS: 333413

Consumer Water Filtration, 2019

The industry was valued at $795 million in 2019. Interest in water quality has helped drive growth in this category. Demand has also increased as consumers stayed home because of the pandemic.

Under-the-sink	37.0%
Point-of-entry	18.0
Countertop	16.0
Faucet-mounted	16.0
Flow-through	9.0

Source: "Consumer Water Filtration." [online] from http://www.freedoniagroup.com [Published April 2021], from The Freedonia Group Inc.

★ 3509 ★
Water Industry
SIC: 4941; NAICS: 22131

Largest Water Firms Worldwide, 2019

Companies are ranked by estimated annual revenue in billions of dollars.

Veolia Environnement S.A.	$ 12.2
Suez Water	11.2
Ecolab Inc.	5.5
Xylem Inc.	5.2
Sabesp	4.5
Grundfos	4.1
American Water	$ 3.6
Beijing Enterprises Water Group	3.6
Orbia	3.4
Pentair PLC	3.0

Source: *GWI*, August 2020, p. NA, from GWI WaterData.

★ 3510 ★
Water Parks
SIC: 7996; NAICS: 71311

Largest Water Parks Worldwide, 2019

Parks are ranked by millions of attendees. The top 25 parks saw attendance of 31.1 million.

Chimelong Water Park	3.01
Typhoon Lagoon at Disney World	2.24
Blizzard Beach at Disney World	1.98
Therme Erding	1.85
Thermas Dos Laranjais	1.84
Bahama Aquaventure Water Park	1.81
Volcano Bay	1.81
Aquatica	1.53
Hot Park Rio Quente	1.46
Wuhu Fanta Wild Water Park	1.34

Source: "Theme Index Museum Index 2019." [online] from https://www.teaconnect.org/index.cfm [Accessed November 4, 2020], from Themed Entertainment Association.

★ 3511 ★
Water Transportation
SIC: 4482; NAICS: 483114

Coastal and Great Lakes Freight Transportation, 2017

Total shipments were valued at $7.56 billion. The term "nec" stands for not elsewhere classified.

	($ 000)	Share
Transportation of bulk liquids and gases in intermodal tank by water	$ 1,479,893	19.58%
Transportation of other goods by water	1,081,432	14.30
Transportation of dry bulks, except in intermodal containers, by water	925,663	12.24
Transportation of other intermodal containers, not climate-controlled, nec., by water	892,126	11.80
Transportation of bulk liquids and gases, except in intermodal tank containers, by water	725,931	9.60

Continued on next page.

★ 3511 ★
[Continued]
Water Transportation
SIC: 4482; NAICS: 483114

Coastal and Great Lakes Freight Transportation, 2017

Total shipments were valued at $7.56 billion. The term "nec" stands for not elsewhere classified.

	($ 000)	Share
Transportation of climate-controlled intermodal containers, nec., by water	$ 455,284	6.02%
Towing services by water	365,544	4.84
Transportation of automobiles and light trucks by water	264,842	3.50
Tugboat services	112,987	1.49
Transportation of climate-controlled boxed, palletized, and other packed goods, except in intermodal containers, by water	46,714	0.62
Marine facility services	35,117	0.46
Transportation of boxed, palletized, and other packed goods, not climate-controlled and not in intermodal containers, by water	26,016	0.34
Transportation of waste by water	12,754	0.17
Transportation of livestock by water	395	0.01
Other water transportation support services, nec	1,010,473	13.37
Other products and services, nec	124,829	1.65
Transportation of automobiles and light trucks by water	$ 6,826	1.18%
Transportation of other goods by water	2,791	0.48
Other	36,247	6.28

Source: "Economic Census." [online] from https://www.census.gov/programs-surveys/economic-census/data/tables.html [Accessed December 2, 2020], from U.S. Census Bureau.

★ 3512 ★
Water Transportation
SIC: 4481; NAICS: 483114

Coastal and Great Lakes Passenger Transportation, 2017

Total shipments were valued at $576.83 million. "nec" stands for not elsewhere classified.

	($ 000)	Share
Coastal and Great Lakes fixed-route, passenger transportation by water	$ 284,639	49.35%
Cruises	232,276	40.27
Local passenger transportation by water	14,051	2.44

★ 3513 ★
Water Treatment
SIC: 4952; NAICS: 22132

Leading Wastewater Treatment Firms Worldwide, 2019

Companies are ranked by sector revenue in millions of dollars.

	($ mil.)	Share
Jacobs	$ 781.7	6.63%
AECOM	740.7	6.28
MWH Constructors Inc.	541.2	4.59
Aegion Corp.	512.8	4.35
Stantec Inc.	454.8	3.85
Sundt Construction Inc.	406.8	3.45
Kiewit Corp.	394.8	3.35
Webuild S.p.A.	351.2	2.98
Garney Holding Co.	343.8	2.91
Black & Veatch Corp.	343.7	2.91
Other	6,927.3	58.71

Source: *ENR*, July 20-27, 2020, p. 42.

★ 3514 ★
Water Treatment
SIC: 4952; NAICS: 22132

Leading Water Treatment/Supply Firms Worldwide, 2019

Companies are ranked by sector revenue in millions of dollars.

	($ mil.)	Share
Tetra Tech Inc.	$ 1,602.0	13.99%
Jacobs	862.9	7.53
Suez North America	770.0	6.72
Garney Holding Co.	765.1	6.68
AECOM	609.4	5.32
Stantec Inc.	478.7	4.18
Kiewit Corp.	444.3	3.88
CDM Smith Inc.	415.5	3.63
Black & Veatch Corp.	381.1	3.33

Continued on next page.

★ 3514 ★
[Continued]
Water Treatment
SIC: 4952; NAICS: 22132

Leading Water Treatment/Supply Firms Worldwide, 2019

Companies are ranked by sector revenue in millions of dollars.

	($ mil.)	Share
The Walsh Group	$ 336.7	2.94%
Other	4,786.7	41.80

Source: *ENR*, July 20-27, 2020, p. 42.

★ 3515 ★
Wearable Devices
SIC: 3571; NAICS: 334111

Leading Wearable Brands Worldwide, 2020

Market shares are shown for the third quarter of 2020. Earware claimed 52%, wristwear 41%, bodywear and eyewear 3% each, and skinwear 1%.

Apple	29.0%
Xiaomi	13.0
JBL	5.0
Samsung	5.0
Jabra	3.0
JLAB	3.0
QCY	3.0
Edifier	2.0
Realme	2.0
Sony	2.0
Other	33.0

Source: "TWS Drives 2020 Wearables Growth; Smartwatches to Add Momentum From 2021." [online] from https://www.counterpointresearch.com/tws-drives-2020-wearables-growth-smartwatches-add-momentum-2021/ [Press release January 14, 2021], from Counterpoint Research.

★ 3516 ★
Wearable Devices
SIC: 3571; NAICS: 334111

Smartwatch Ownership, 2013-2020

Data show ownership by percent of U.S. population 12+ years of age. Data are estimated for 2020.

2017	9.0%
2018	9.0
2019	17.0%
2020	17.0

Source: "Infinite Deal 2020." [online] from https://www.podcastinsights.com/podcast-statistics/ [Accessed January 3, 2021], from Edison Research and Triton Digital.

★ 3517 ★
Wearable Devices
SIC: 3571; NAICS: 334111

Spending on Wearable Devices Worldwide, 2020-2022

Spending is shown in millions of dollars. The market grew 18.1% from 2020 to 2021. Factors driving this growth include the rise of remote work and health concerns as a result of COVID-19. In 2022, ear-worn devices are expected to claim a market share of 47.05%, smartwatches 33.39%, smart patches 7.62%, head-mounted displays 4.87%, wristbands 4.77%, and smart clothing 2.77%.

	2020 ($ mil.)	2021 ($ mil.)	2022 ($ mil.)
Ear-worn	$ 32,724	$ 39,220	$ 44,160
Smartwatches	21,758	25,827	31,337
Smart patches	4,690	5,963	7,150
Head-mounted display	3,414	4,054	4,573
Wristbands	4,987	4,906	4,477
Smart clothing	1,411	1,529	2,160

Source: "Gartner Forecasts Global Spending on Wearable Devices to Total $81.5 Billion in 2021." [online] from http://www.gartner.com [Press release January 12, 2021], from Gartner Inc.

★ 3518 ★
Wearable Devices
SIC: 3571; NAICS: 334111

Top Kids' Smartwatch Brands Worldwide, 2018-2019

Market shares are shown based on shipments.

	2018	2019
Imoo	24.0%	26.0%
Huawei	8.0	9.0
360	6.0	6.0
Aberdeen	5.0	6.0
Jet	4.0	3.0
MI	4.0	4.0
Vtech	3.0	2.0

Continued on next page.

★ 3518 ★
[Continued]
Wearable Devices
SIC: 3571; NAICS: 334111

Top Kids' Smartwatch Brands Worldwide, 2018-2019

Market shares are shown based on shipments.

	2018	2019
Mimi	2.0%	2.0%
Khonka	1.0	1.0
Verizon	1.0	1.0
Other	42.0	37.0

Source: "Imoo Leads the Global Kids' Smartwatch Market With 26% Market Share." [online] from https://www.counterpointresearch.com/category/press-release/ [Press release April 7, 2020], from Global Smartwatch Shipment by Model Tracker.

★ 3519 ★
Wearable Devices
SIC: 3571; NAICS: 334111

Top Smart Personal Audio Makers Worldwide, 2020

Companies are ranked by shipments in millions of units. Apple includes Beats. Samsung includes Harman.

	(mil.)	Share
Apple Inc.	108.9	25.2%
Samsung Electronics Corp.	38.3	8.9
Xiaomi Corp.	25.4	5.9
Sony Corp.	15.1	3.5
Edifier	12.3	2.8
Other	232.1	53.7

Source: "TWS and Watches Became Smartphone Companion Devices in Q4 2020." [online] from https://www.canalys.com/newsroom/canalys-tws-and-wearables-q4-2020 [Press release March 30, 2021], from Canalys.

★ 3520 ★
Wearable Devices
SIC: 3571; NAICS: 334111

Top Smart Wearable Band Makers Worldwide, 2020

Companies are ranked by shipments in millions of units.

	(mil.)	Share
Xiaomi Corp.	37.7	20.3%
Apple Inc.	35.2	19.0
Huawei Technologies Corp.	32.2	17.4
Fitbit Inc.	13.4	7.2
Samsung Electronics Corp.	9.6	5.2%
Other	57.1	30.8

Source: "TWS and Watches Became Smartphone Companion Devices in Q4 2020." [online] from https://www.canalys.com/newsroom/canalys-tws-and-wearables-q4-2020 [Press release March 30, 2021], from Canalys.

★ 3521 ★
Wearable Devices
SIC: 3571; NAICS: 334111

Top Smartwatch Brands Worldwide, 2019-2020

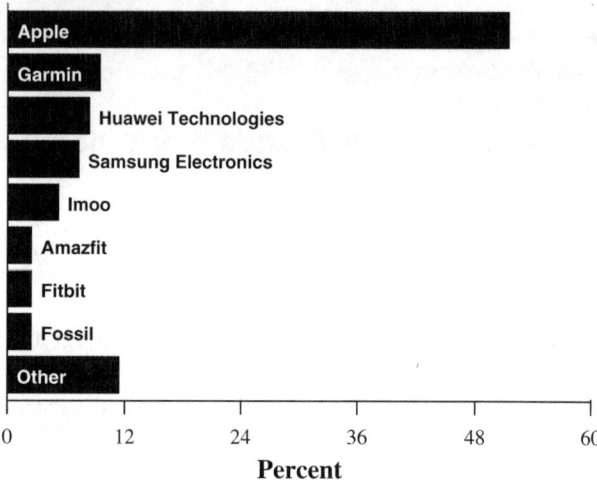

Market shares are shown based on shipments for the first half of 2019 and 2020.

	2019	2020
Apple	43.2%	51.4%
Garmin	8.9	9.4
Huawei Technologies	5.5	8.3
Samsung Electronics	9.3	7.2
Imoo	5.3	5.1
Amazfit	2.0	2.4
Fitbit	3.4	2.4
Fossil	2.6	2.4
Other	19.8	11.4

Source: "Global Smartwatch Market Revenue Up 20% in H1 2020, Led by Apple, Garmin & Huawei." [online] from http://www.counterpointresearch.com [Press release August 20, 2020], from Counterpoint Technology Market Research.

★ 3522 ★
Weather Forecasting
SIC: 8999; NAICS: 54169

Leading Weather Forecasting Firms Worldwide, 2019

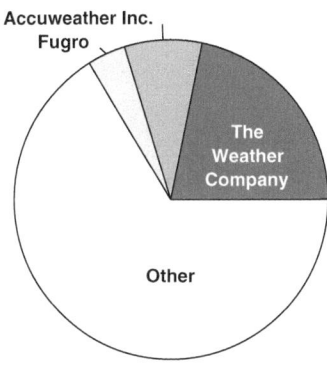

The source defines this market as "the application of science and technology to predict the condition of the atmosphere for a given time and location." Market shares are shown based on revenue of $2.2 billion.

The Weather Company	21.8%
Accuweather Inc.	7.6
Fugro	3.5
Other	67.0

Source: "COVID-19 Impact on Global Weather Forecasting Services Market Size Status and Forecast 2020-2026." [online] from http://reports.valuates.com [Published April 2020], from QY Research.

★ 3523 ★
Weatherproof Boxes
SIC: 3644; NAICS: 335932

Weatherproof Box Sales by Material, 2019

Market shares are shown based on dollar sales for the 12 months ended September 2019.

Aluminum	55.6%
Plastics	27.1
Polycarbonate	14.6
Steel	1.0
Zinc	1.0
Other	0.7

Source: *The Electrical Distributor*, December 2019, p. 59, from Epicor's Industry Data Analytics.

★ 3524 ★
Weddings
SIC/NAICS: See frontmatter for explanation.

Wedding Planner Industry in China, 2017-2021

Figures are in billions of yuan. China reached an 11-year low in the marriage rate in 2018. This occurred even as the cost of the average marriage is on the rise. The wedding planner market is increasingly rapidly, and the source attributes this growth to the shift in how marriages are viewed. It has moved from an event focused on the bride, groom and family to an event that many people gather together to enjoy.

2017	¥ 14,639
2018	18,350
2019	22,694
2020	28,110
2021	34,000

Source: "Wedding Consumption Trends in China." [online] from http://www.news.kotra.or.kr [Published May 27, 2020], from China Industry Information.

★ 3525 ★
Welding Industry
SIC: 3548; NAICS: 333992

Leading Structural Welding Consumables Firms in India, 2019

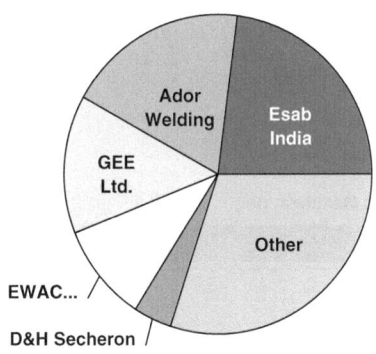

The market for welding consumables include sticks, wires/fluxes, cutting equipment, automation equipment, and welding equipment. The industry is worth 3,150 crore and is split between a 700 crore reclamation welding and 2,450 crore structural welding. Roughly half of the structural market consists of unorganized players. Market shares are estimated for the organized sector.

Esab India	23.0%
Ador Welding	19.0

Continued on next page.

★ 3525 ★
[Continued]
Welding Industry
SIC: 3548; NAICS: 333992

Leading Structural Welding Consumables Firms in India, 2019

The market for welding consumables include sticks, wires/fluxes, cutting equipment, automation equipment, and welding equipment. The industry is worth 3,150 crore and is split between a 700 crore reclamation welding and 2,450 crore structural welding. Roughly half of the structural market consists of unorganized players. Market shares are estimated for the organized sector.

GEE Ltd.	14.0%
EWAC Alloys	10.0
D&H Secheron	4.0
Other	30.0

Source: "Leading Player in Domestic Welding Market." [online] from https://www.icicidirect.com/mailimages/IDirect_EsabIndia_StockTales.pdf [Published January 8, 2021], from ICICI Direct Research and company reports.

★ 3526 ★
Welding Industry
SIC: 3548; NAICS: 333992

Leading Welding Equipment Makers Worldwide, 2019

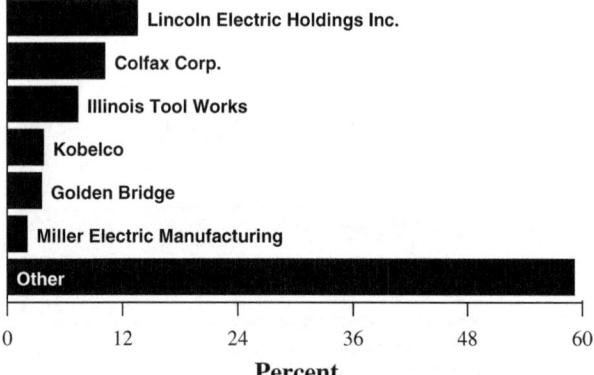

The market for arc welding, brazing and cutting equipment reached $22 billion.

Lincoln Electric Holdings Inc.	13.6%
Colfax Corp.	10.2
Illinois Tool Works	7.4
Kobelco	3.8
Golden Bridge	3.6
Miller Electric Manufacturing	2.1%
Other	59.2

Source: "Leading Player in Domestic Welding Market." [online] from https://www.icicidirect.com/mailimages/IDirect_EsabIndia_StockTales.pdf [Published January 8, 2021], from ICICI Direct Research and company reports.

★ 3527 ★
Welding Industry
SIC: 3548; NAICS: 333992

Welding and Soldering Equipment Manufacturing, 2017

Total shipments were valued at $5.49 billion. The term "nec" stands for not elsewhere classified. "Other products and services, nec" also includes wholesale sales of specialized industrial machinery and equipment.

	($ 000)	Share
Arc welding machines, components, and accessories, excluding electrodes and stud welding equipment	$ 2,986,449	54.40%
Arc welding metal electrodes	805,821	14.68
Resistance welders, components, accessories, and electrodes	669,525	12.20
Tips for gas welding and cutting equipment	136,583	2.49
Pressure regulators for gas welding and cutting equipment	128,797	2.35
Gas welding and cutting torches (including gas air torches)	48,422	0.88
Machine shop job work and job order repairs	30,605	0.56
Maintenance and repair services for industrial machinery and equipment	8,561	0.16
Maintenance and repair services for other commercial and service industry machinery and equipment, nec	8,749	0.16
Laser systems and equipment, all other types	5,974	0.11
Wholesale sales of other industrial materials and supplies, including abrasives and welding supplies	4,144	0.08
Parts for all other miscellaneous general industrial machinery and equipment	3,041	0.06

Continued on next page.

★ 3527 ★
[Continued]
Welding Industry
SIC: 3548; NAICS: 333992

Welding and Soldering Equipment Manufacturing, 2017

Total shipments were valued at $5.49 billion. The term "nec" stands for not elsewhere classified. "Other products and services, nec" also includes wholesale sales of specialized industrial machinery and equipment.

	($ 000)	Share
Metal coating, engraving (excluding jewelry and silverware), and allied services to manufacturers	$ 1,908	0.03%
Manufacturing of all other miscellaneous machinery products, excluding electrical	649	0.01
Other welding equipment, components, and accessories (excluding arc, resistance, and gas welding equipment)	506,829	9.23
Other spare parts, accessories, attachments, adaptors, etc., for gas welding and cutting equipment	50,010	0.91
Other gas welding and cutting equipment, excluding pressure containers	9,532	0.17
Other products and services, nec	84,401	1.54

Source: "Economic Census." [online] from https://www.census.gov/programs-surveys/economic-census/data/tables.html [Accessed December 2, 2020], from U.S. Census Bureau.

★ 3528 ★
Wet Corn
SIC: 2046; NAICS: 311221

Wet Corn Milling, 2017

Total shipments were valued at $9.78 billion. The term "nec" stands for not elsewhere classified. "Other" includes manufacturing of starch, including corn, potato, rice and wheat starch and dextrin; crude corn oil; vinegar; sweetening syrups and molasses not made from sugarcane; dry mix food preparations; and fuel ethanol and other biodiesel fuels. "Other" also includes the wholesale sales of baking ingredients and nonperishable canned and packaged food. The source withheld shipment data for each of these separately to avoid disclosing data for individual companies.

	($ 000)	Share
Corn sweeteners	$ 4,257,128	43.53%
Wet process corn byproducts	1,039,777	10.63
Fully-refined corn oil, including margarine oil	778,315	7.96
Partially hydrogenated soybean cooking or salad oil, fully refined and deodorized, edible	7,377	0.08
Mixtures of vegetable cooking or salad oil, fully refined and deodorized, edible	6,976	0.07
Baking or frying fats (shortening), 100 percent vegetable oil, edible	1,257	0.01
Other fully refined shortening and cooking oils, edible, including oils used for margarine	81,626	0.83
Other manufacturing revenue, nec	20,375	0.21
Other	3,587,169	36.68

Source: "Economic Census." [online] from https://www.census.gov/programs-surveys/economic-census/data/tables.html [Accessed December 2, 2020], from U.S. Census Bureau.

★ 3529 ★
Wet Corn
SIC: 2046; NAICS: 311221

Wet Corn Milling Leaders, 2017

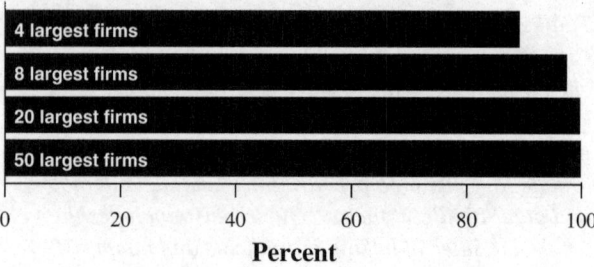

Data show the percent of industry sales held by the largest 4, 8, 20 and 50 firms in the sector. There are approximately 74 players operating in the industry generating employment for 6,288 people. According to Kentley Insights, the industry generated sales of $10 billion in 2019.

4 largest firms	89.2%
8 largest firms	97.4
20 largest firms	99.7
50 largest firms	100.0

Source: "Economic Census." [online] from https://www.census.gov/content/census/en/data/tables/2017/econ/economic-census/naics-sector-31-33.html [Accessed January 21, 2021], from U.S. Census Bureau.

★ 3530 ★
Wheat
SIC: 0111; NAICS: 11114

Top Wheat Consumers Worldwide, 2020-2021

Figures are in thousands of metric tons. Data refer to local marketing year.

	(000)	Share
China	130,000	17.31%
European Union	117,500	15.65
India	99,500	13.25
Russia	41,000	5.46
United States	30,510	4.06
Pakistan	25,800	3.44
Egypt	20,800	2.77
Turkey	20,200	2.69
Brazil	12,200	1.62
Algeria	11,050	1.47
Other	242,466	32.28

Source: "Wheat." [online] from https://apps.fas.usda.gov/psd-online/circulars/grain-wheat.pdf [Published October 2020], from U.S. Department of Agriculture.

★ 3531 ★
Wheat
SIC: 0111; NAICS: 11114

Top Wheat Exporters Worldwide, 2020-2021

Figures are in thousands of metric tons. Data refer to trade year.

	(000)	Share
Russia	39,000	20.57%
United States	27,000	14.24
European Union	25,500	13.45
Canada	25,000	13.19
Australia	18,000	9.49
Ukraine	17,500	9.23
Argentina	13,000	6.86
Turkey	6,600	3.48
Kazakhstan	6,500	3.43
Other	11,486	6.06

Source: "Wheat." [online] from https://apps.fas.usda.gov/psd-online/circulars/grain-wheat.pdf [Published October 2020], from U.S. Department of Agriculture.

★ 3532 ★
Wheat
SIC: 0111; NAICS: 11114

Top Wheat Importers Worldwide, 2020-2021

Figures are in thousands of metric tons. Data refer to trade year.

	(000)	Share
Egypt	13,000	6.86%
Indonesia	10,800	5.70
China	7,500	3.96
Algeria	7,000	3.69
Philippines	7,000	3.69
Brazil	6,700	3.53
Bangladesh	6,600	3.48
Morocco	6,500	3.43
Japan	5,600	2.95
European Union	5,500	2.90
Other	113,386	59.81

Source: "Wheat." [online] from https://apps.fas.usda.gov/psd-online/circulars/grain-wheat.pdf [Published October 2020], from U.S. Department of Agriculture.

★ 3533 ★
Wheat
SIC: 0111; NAICS: 11114

Top Wheat Producers Worldwide, 2020-2021

Figures are in thousands of metric tons. Data refer to local marketing year.

	(000)	Share
European Union	136,750	17.69%
China	136,000	17.59
India	107,592	13.92
Russia	83,000	10.74
United States	49,691	6.43
Canada	35,000	4.53
Australia	28,500	3.69
Pakistan	25,700	3.32
Ukraine	25,500	3.30
Argentina	19,000	2.46
Other	126,349	16.34

Source: "Wheat." [online] from https://apps.fas.usda.gov/psdonline/circulars/grain-wheat.pdf [Published October 2020], from U.S. Department of Agriculture.

★ 3534 ★
Whipped Toppings
SIC: 2023; NAICS: 311514

Leading Non-Aerosol Whipped Topping Brands, 2020

Brands are ranked based on sales at supermarkets, drug stores, mass merchandisers, military commissaries, and select club and dollar chains for the 12 weeks ended September 6, 2020.

	($ mil.)	Share
Horizon Organic	$ 10.99	6.12%
WhiteWave Land O'Lakes	9.12	5.08
Organic Valley	5.29	2.95
Dairy Pure Multiple Brands	5.12	2.85
Kemps Select	3.03	1.69
Hiland	2.79	1.55
Prairie Farms	2.33	1.30
Darigold	2.32	1.29
Knudsen	2.08	1.16
Private label	119.97	66.80
Other	16.55	9.22

Source: *Frozen & Refrigerated Buyer*, November 2020, p. 11, from IRI.

★ 3535 ★
Whipped Toppings
SIC: 2023; NAICS: 311514

Leading Whipped Topping Brands, 2020

Brands are ranked based on sales at supermarkets, drug stores, mass merchandisers, military commissaries, and select club and dollar chains for the 12 weeks ended August 9, 2020.

	Sales	Share
Cool Whip	$ 58,835,118	67.21%
So Delicious Cocowhip	1,527,974	1.75
Truwhip	917,219	1.05
Cool Whip Mix Ins	276,111	0.32
Private label	22,235,547	25.40
Other	3,748,680	4.28

Source: *Frozen & Refrigerated Buyer*, October 2020, p. 10, from IRI.

★ 3536 ★
Windows and Doors
SIC/NAICS: See frontmatter for explanation.

Best-Selling Window and Door Brands, 2020

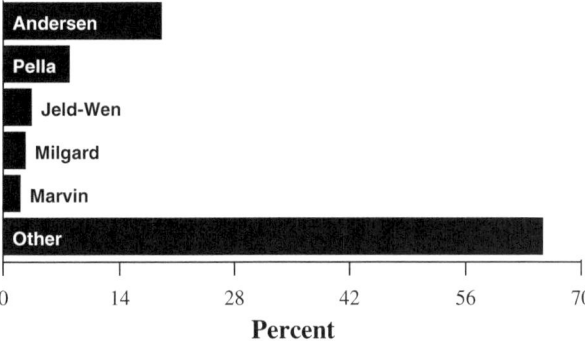

Market shares are shown for the year ended second quarter 2020. Salesmen represented 24.3% of sales, window/millwork specialty stores 23.8%, contractors 19.7%, Home Depot 10.8%, Lowe's 9.8%, and other channels 12.2%.

Andersen	19.0%
Pella	7.8
Jeld-Wen	3.3
Milgard	2.6
Marvin	2.0
Other	65.3

Source: "U.S. Windows/Doors Infographic." [online] from https://stevensoncompany.com/category/infographics/ [Published August 3, 2020], from TraQline.

★ 3537 ★
Windows and Doors
SIC/NAICS: See frontmatter for explanation.

Energy Star Window Market by Climate Zone, 2018

Energy Star is a government program that promotes energy efficiency. Windows and skylights were added to this program in 1998. Data show overall window sales and Energy Star window sales in millions of units.

	All Windows	ES Windows	Market Share
Northern Zone	20.45	18.35	90.0%
South Central Zone	14.33	12.45	87.0
North Central Zone	11.03	8.81	80.0
Southern Zone	6.33	4.52	71.0

Source: "Energy Star Windows, Doors, and Skylights Response to Comments." [online] from https://www.energystar.gov/partner_resources/products_partner_resources/public_notices [Published September 2020], from DuckerFrontier.

★ 3538 ★
Windows and Doors
SIC/NAICS: See frontmatter for explanation.

Manual Entry Door Market, 2018, 2023 and 2028

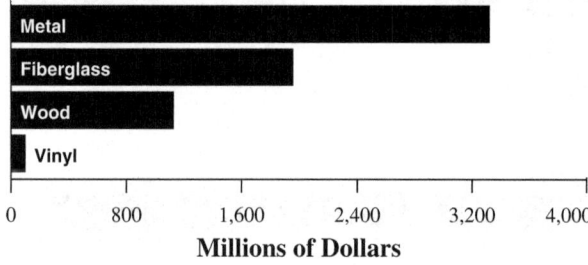

Sales are shown in millions of dollars. In 2028, metal should claim 51.1% of sales, fiberglass 30%, wood 17.3% and vinyl 1.4%.

	2018 ($ mil.)	2023 ($ mil.)	2028 ($ mil.)
Metal	$ 2,576	$ 2,910	$ 3,318
Fiberglass	1,297	1,612	1,954
Wood	863	969	1,125
Vinyl	64	75	96

Source: *Door & Window*, Jan.-Feb. 2020, p. 56, from The Freedonia Group Inc.

★ 3539 ★
Windows and Doors
SIC: 3442; NAICS: 332321

Metal Window and Door Manufacturing, 2017

Total shipments were valued at $12.53 billion. The term "nec" stands for not elsewhere classified. Overhead, residential, sliding, swing, and all other commercial and institutional iron and steel doors exclude shower doors, tub enclosures and storm doors. Sliding residential aluminum doors exclude shower, tub and storm doors. "Other products and services, nec" also includes wholesale sales of millwork; electrical, communication, and lighting system products; bolts, nuts, rivets, and other fasteners, except nails; other construction materials and supplies; and household furnishings, except artificial flowers, plants, and trees.

	($ 000)	Share
Overhead, sliding, swing, and all other commercial and institutional iron and steel doors	$ 1,262,297	10.07%
Residential iron, steel and composite doors	1,222,417	9.76
Overhead and sliding commercial and institutional aluminum doors	1,152,925	9.20
Metal window and door screens (excluding combination) and metal weather strip	747,224	5.96
Swing and all other commercial, institutional, and industrial aluminum doors	692,183	5.52
Overhead, swing, and all other industrial iron and steel doors (including sliding)	625,991	5.00
Metal combination screen, storm sash, and storm doors	571,099	4.56
Swinging residential aluminum doors	456,339	3.64
Aluminum and steel door frames, including trim sold as an integral part of the door frame (excluding storm door frames)	453,462	3.62
Shower doors and tub enclosures (all metals), and other metal doors not made of aluminum or steel	283,044	2.26
Sliding residential aluminum doors (glass, patio-type)	155,829	1.24

Continued on next page.

★ 3539 ★
[Continued]
Windows and Doors
SIC: 3442; NAICS: 332321

Metal Window and Door Manufacturing, 2017

Total shipments were valued at $12.53 billion. The term "nec" stands for not elsewhere classified. Overhead, residential, sliding, swing, and all other commercial and institutional iron and steel doors exclude shower doors, tub enclosures and storm doors. Sliding residential aluminum doors exclude shower, tub and storm doors. "Other products and services, nec" also includes wholesale sales of millwork; electrical, communication, and lighting system products; bolts, nuts, rivets, and other fasteners, except nails; other construction materials and supplies; and household furnishings, except artificial flowers, plants, and trees.

	($ 000)	Share
Other metal window awning, skylights, sash, and frames, including jalousie, single-and double-hung frames (excluding storm sash)	$ 1,877,038	14.98%
Other metal molding, trim, store fronts and curtain walls (including combination of metal)	513,638	4.10
Other residential aluminum doors, including garage and closet doors	492,887	3.93
Other products and services, nec	2,023,627	16.15

Source: "Economic Census." [online] from https://www.census.gov/programs-surveys/economic-census/data/tables.html [Accessed December 2, 2020], from U.S. Census Bureau.

★ 3540 ★
Windows and Doors
SIC: 3442; NAICS: 332321

Metal Window and Door Manufacturing Leaders, 2017

Data show the percent of industry sales held by the largest 4, 8, 20 and 50 firms in the sector. There are approximately 1,045 players operating in the industry generating employment for 51,197 people. According to Kentley Insights, the industry generated sales of $13 billion in 2019.

4 largest firms	20.4%
8 largest firms	32.3
20 largest firms	49.3%
50 largest firms	65.9

Source: "Economic Census." [online] from https://www.census.gov/content/census/en/data/tables/2017/econ/economic-census/naics-sector-31-33.html [Accessed January 21, 2021], from U.S. Census Bureau.

★ 3541 ★
Windows and Doors
SIC/NAICS: See frontmatter for explanation.

Residential Window Market by Material, 2019

Unit shipments are shown by year: 48.7 million in 2019, 45.35 million in 2020, 49.76 million in 2021 and 54.99 million in 2022. Figures are forecast for 2021 and 2022.

Vinyl	65.6%
Wood/wood cladding	21.8
Composite	7.7
Aluminum	2.9
Fiberglass	1.0

Source: "WDMA 2020 U.S. Industry Market Study Products Trend." [online] from https://www.openuptoperformance.com/wdma-2020-u-s-industry-market-study-product-trends/ [Accessed December 5, 2020], from Window & Door Manufacturers Association.

★ 3542 ★
Windows and Doors
SIC/NAICS: See frontmatter for explanation.

Window and Door Demand in North America, 2020

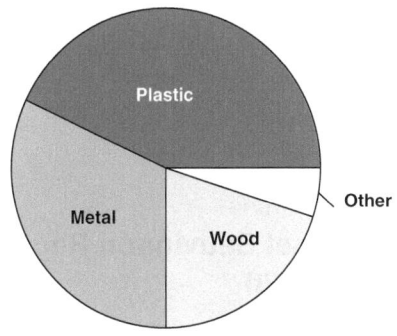

Market shares are shown in percent. The residential market represents approximately 75% of demand.

Plastic	43.0%
Metal	32.0

Continued on next page.

★ 3542 ★
[Continued]
Windows and Doors
SIC/NAICS: See frontmatter for explanation.

Window and Door Demand in North America, 2020

Market shares are shown in percent. The residential market represents approximately 75% of demand.

Wood	20.0%
Other	5.0

Source: "North America Doors and Windows Market Outlook and Forecast Report 2021-2026." [online] from https://www.globenewswire.com/en/news-release/2021/02/25/2182161/28124/en/North-America-Doors-and-Windows-Market [Published February 25, 2021].

★ 3543 ★
Wine
SIC: 2084; NAICS: 31213

Number of Wineries by State, 2021

States are ranked by total number of wineries as of February 2021.

	Wineries	Share
California	4,745	43.10%
Oregon	844	7.67
Washington	843	7.66
Texas	466	4.23
New York	431	3.91
Pennsylvania	353	3.21
Virginia	310	2.82
Ohio	302	2.74
Michigan	222	2.02
North Carolina	189	1.72
Other	2,304	20.93

Source: *Wine Business Monthly*, February 2021, p. 78, from Wines Vines Analytics database.

★ 3544 ★
Wine
SIC: 2084; NAICS: 31213

Top Cabernet Sauvignon Regions in Australia, 2020

Shares are shown based on a total crush of 223,942 tons. Domestic off-trade sales of Cabernet Sauvignon totaled $540 million in the 12 months ended July 5, 2020. Single variety claimed about two-thirds of revenue, Merlot less than a quarter, and other Cabernet blends nearly 15%.

Riverland	36.0%
Murray Darling - Swan Hill	25.0
Riverina	11.0%
Coonawarra	7.0
Langhorne Creek	3.0
McLaren Vale	3.0
Barossa Valley	2.0
Margaret River	2.0
Padthaway	2.0
Wrattonbully	2.0
Other	7.0

Source: *National Liquor News*, October 2020, p. 24, from Wine Australia.

★ 3545 ★
Wine
SIC: 2084; NAICS: 31213

Top Sparkling Wine Brands (Domestic), 2017-2019

Brands are ranked by sales in thousands of 9-liter cases. Figures for 2019 are preliminary. Andre's claimed an estimated 24.85% of the market in 2019, Cook's 16.39%, Korbel 12.48% and other brands 46.28%.

	2017	2018	2019
Andre	3,024	2,890	2,857
Cook's	2,050	1,973	1,885
Korbel	1,473	1,446	1,435
Barefoot Bubbly	1,270	1,275	1,330
J. Roget	1,000	1,020	930
Domaine Chandon	484	457	455
Ballatore	395	370	368
Mumm Napa	333	353	351
Wycliff Sparkling	186	214	250
Michelle	170	165	160
Other	1,225	1,363	1,477

Source: *Cheers*, August/September 2020, p. 21, from Beverage Information and Insights Group.

★ 3546 ★
Wine
SIC: 2084; NAICS: 31213

Top Sparkling Wine Brands (Imported), 2017-2019

Brands are ranked by sales in thousands of 9-liter cases. Figures for 2019 are preliminary. La Marca Prosecco claimed an estimated 13.86% of the market, Verdi Spumante 10.14%, Mionetto 6.63% and other brands 69.37%.

	2017	2018	2019
La Marca Prosecco	1,380	1,550	1,755
Verdi Spumante	1,145	1,177	1,284

Continued on next page.

★ 3546 ★
[Continued]
Wine
SIC: 2084; NAICS: 31213

Top Sparkling Wine Brands (Imported), 2017-2019

Brands are ranked by sales in thousands of 9-liter cases. Figures for 2019 are preliminary. La Marca Prosecco claimed an estimated 13.86% of the market, Verdi Spumante 10.14%, Mionetto 6.63% and other brands 69.37%.

	2017	2018	2019
Mionetto	690	750	840
Cupcake Sparkling	635	620	600
Ruffino Prosecco	440	540	595
Zonin	440	495	571
Freixenet	575	559	559
Veuve Clicquot/La Grande Dame	500	520	540
Cristalino Cava	450	465	490
Martini & Rossi Asti	504	467	456
Other	4,323	4,625	4,973

Source: *Cheers*, August/September 2020, p. 21, from Beverage Information and Insights Group.

★ 3547 ★
Wine
SIC: 2085; NAICS: 31213

Top White Wine Firms in China, 2017 and 2019

Market shares are shown based on sales. According to a 2019 report, white wine represents only about 15% of the market. The market is seeing some growth in consumption, primarily among young drinkers.

	2017	2019
Cultural Revolution/10 (CR/10)	26.6%	40.0%
Kweichow Moutai Company	10.3	15.2
Wuliangye Yibin Co. Ltd.	5.3	8.9
Yanghe Distillery	3.5	4.1
Luzhou Laojiao	1.8	2.8
Shanxi Fen Wine	1.1	2.1
Anhui Gujing Distillery Co.	1.2	1.9
Shunxin Agriculture	1.1	1.8
Lang Jiu Group Co.	0.9	1.5
Jiangsu King's Luck Brewery	0.5	0.9
Kouzi Distillery	0.6	0.8
Other	47.1	20.0

Source: "China Beer and White Wine Sector." [online] from https://www.cmbi.com/upload/202011/20201109416735.pdf [Published November 9, 2020], from Lanjiu prospectus.

★ 3548 ★
Wine
SIC: 2084; NAICS: 31213

Top Wine Brands Worldwide, 2019

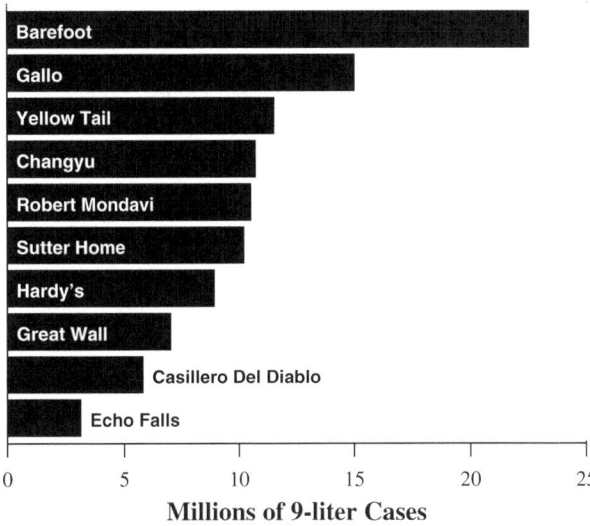

Brands are ranked by estimated sales in millions of 9-liter cases.

Barefoot	22.5
Gallo	15.0
Yellow Tail	11.5
Changyu	10.7
Robert Mondavi	10.5
Sutter Home	10.2
Hardy's	8.9
Great Wall	7.0
Casillero Del Diablo	5.8
Echo Falls	3.1

Source: *The Drinks Business*, July 7, 2020, p. NA.

★ 3549 ★
Wine
SIC: 2084; NAICS: 31213

Top Wine Makers, 2020

Companies are ranked by sales in millions of cases. Shares are shown based on the top 50 companies. More than 90% of the domestic wine sold by volume was produced by the top 50 companies.

	(mil.)	Share
E. & J. Gallo Winery Inc.	88.00	30.62%
The Wine Group Inc.	51.00	17.75
Constellation Brands Inc.	28.00	9.74
Trinchero Family Estates	20.00	6.96
Delicato Family Wines	16.00	5.57
Treasury Wine Estates Americas Co.	15.00	5.22

Continued on next page.

★ 3549 ★
[Continued]
Wine
SIC: 2084; NAICS: 31213

Top Wine Makers, 2020

Companies are ranked by sales in millions of cases. Shares are shown based on the top 50 companies. More than 90% of the domestic wine sold by volume was produced by the top 50 companies.

	(mil.)	Share
Bronco Wine Co.	10.00	3.48%
Ste. Michelle Wine Estates	8.20	2.85
Jackson Family Wines	6.00	2.09
Deutsch Family Wine & Spirits (Josh Cellars)	4.30	1.50
Other	40.89	14.23

Source: *Wine Business Monthly*, February 2021, p. 28.

★ 3550 ★
Wine
SIC: 2084; NAICS: 31213

Top Wine Producing Regions, 2019

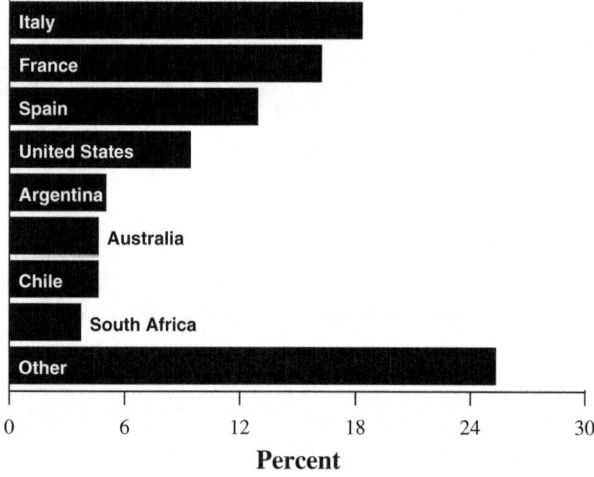

Market shares are shown in percent. The wine industry suffered in 2020 as COVID-19 forced the cancellation of a number of wine events. Sales have also been curtailed as result of shutdowns in the hotel, travel and restaurant industries.

Italy	18.3%
France	16.2
Spain	12.9
United States	9.4
Argentina	5.0
Australia	4.6
Chile	4.6
South Africa	3.7%
Other	25.3

Source: *Wall Street Journal*, August 24, 2020, p. B3, from International Organization of Vine and Wine.

★ 3551 ★
Wine Distribution
SIC: 5182; NAICS: 42482

Top Wine Distributors, 2020

Companies in the top 10 are listed based on market size, number of wineries represented and other factors based on proprietary data from Wines Vines Analytics' Distributor Market Service. Distributors are ranked here based on number of wineries represented. The wholesale market continues to be impacted by the COVID-19 pandemic as on-premise restaurant sales of wine is a fraction of what it was before the pandemic. Wholesalers are using technology to deal with the challenges, in some cases adopting e-commerce and home delivery options and in others using artificial intelligence to implement automation and efficiencies. There were 1,126 distributors nationwide, a 4% decrease from the prior year.

Southern Glazer's Wine and Spirits	1,102
Republic National Distributing Co./Young's Market Co.	1,027
Breakthru Beverage Group	661
Winebow Group	617
Empire Distributors	584
Johnson Brothers Liquor Co.	432
Horizon Beverage Co.	262
Opici Family Distributing	201
Heidelberg Distributing Co.	90
Wine Warehouse	72

Source: *Wine Business Monthly*, February 2021, p. 70, from Wines Vines Analytics' Distributor Market Service.

★ 3552 ★
Wipes
SIC: 2297; NAICS: 31323

Largest Personal Care Wipe Markets in Southeast Asia, 2023-2025

Retail sales are estimated in millions of dollars.

	2023 ($ mil.)	2024 ($ mil.)	2025 ($ mil.)	Share
China	$ 2,171.8	$ 2,344.0	$ 2,501.3	85.37%
Indonesia	234.0	268.0	307.9	10.51

Continued on next page.

★ 3552 ★
[Continued]
Wipes
SIC: 2297; NAICS: 31323

Largest Personal Care Wipe Markets in Southeast Asia, 2023-2025

Retail sales are estimated in millions of dollars.

	2023 ($ mil.)	2024 ($ mil.)	2025 ($ mil.)	Share
Thailand	$56.0	$60.7	$64.7	2.21%
Singapore	23.9	24.2	24.5	0.84
Vietnam	12.2	14.0	16.3	0.56
Malaysia	10.7	11.2	11.6	0.40
Philippines	3.3	3.5	3.8	0.13

Source: *Nonwovens Industry*, Spring 2021, p. 22, from Euromonitor.

★ 3553 ★
Wipes
SIC: 2676; NAICS: 322291

Leading Wipe Makers in Brazil, 2019

Retail sales reached $300 million in 2019. Wipes include baby wipes, personal wipes, moist wipes and home care wipes.

Kimberly-Clark Corp.	36.0%
Johnson & Johnson Co.	23.0
Procter & Gamble Co.	6.0
Eurofral Industria	5.0
Ever Green Industria	5.0
Clin Off	3.0
Natura & Co.	3.0
Ontex bvba	3.0
Beiersdorf AG	2.0
Private label	3.0
Other	11.0

Source: "Suominen One Sweeping Turn." [online] from https://pankki.evli.com/hubfs/ERP/Raportit/Suominen/Suominen%20200924%20Company%20report.pdf [Published September 24, 2020], from Euromonitor.

★ 3554 ★
Wipes
SIC: 2676; NAICS: 322291

Leading Wipe Makers in Europe, 2019

Retail sales reached $3.9 billion in 2019. Wipes include baby wipes, personal wipes, moist wipes and home care wipes.

Procter & Gamble Co.	19.0%
Johnson & Johnson Co.	6.0
Kimberly-Clark Corp.	5.0
Beiersdorf AG	4.0
Essity Corp.	4.0
Unilever Corp.	2.0
Private label	29.0
Other	31.0

Source: "Suominen One Sweeping Turn." [online] from https://pankki.evli.com/hubfs/ERP/Raportit/Suominen/Suominen%20200924%20Company%20report.pdf [Published September 24, 2020], from Euromonitor.

★ 3555 ★
Wipes
SIC: 2676; NAICS: 322291

Leading Wipe Makers in North America, 2019

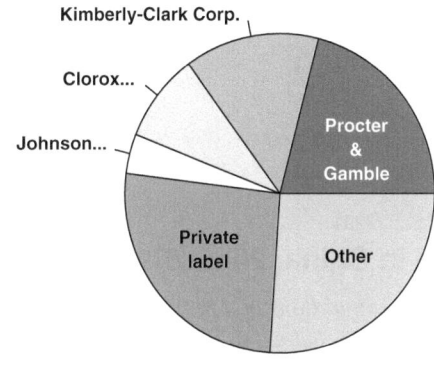

Retail sales reached $5.4 billion in 2019. Wipes include baby wipes, personal wipes, moist wipes and home care wipes.

Procter & Gamble Co.	21.0%
Kimberly-Clark Corp.	14.0
Clorox Corp.	9.0
Johnson & Johnson Co.	4.0
Private label	26.0
Other	26.0

Source: "Suominen One Sweeping Turn." [online] from https://pankki.evli.com/hubfs/ERP/Raportit/Suominen/Suominen%20200924%20Company%20report.pdf [Published September 24, 2020], from Euromonitor.

★ 3556 ★
Wipes
SIC: 2297; NAICS: 31323

Top Baby Wipe Brands, 2020

Market shares are shown based on supermarket sales for the 52 weeks ended April 19, 2020.

Huggies Natural Care	18.34%
Pampers Sensitive	15.42
Huggies Simply Clean Disney Mickey Mouse & Friends	12.88
Pampers	8.46
Huggies Refreshing Clean	5.75
Pampers Aqua Pure	2.17
Water Wipes	2.17
Seventh Generation	1.48
The Honest Co.	1.45
Private label	24.80
Other	7.08

Source: *Non-Foods Management*, Annual 2020-2021, p. 89, from IRI.

★ 3557 ★
Wipes
SIC: 2676; NAICS: 322291

Wipe Sales in China, 2015-2019

Data show revenue in billions of dollars. The booming e-commerce market has helped this market expand from offline to online sales. Baby wipes claim the largest share of sales; it claimed 56.4% of sales in 2017.

2015	$ 3.0
2016	3.9
2017	4.7
2018	5.6
2019	7.0

Source: "China's Baby Wipes Market is Driven by Consumption Upgrade." [online] from https://daxueconsulting.com/chinas-baby-wipes-market/ [Published October 28, 2020], from Daxue Consulting.

★ 3558 ★
Wire and Cable
SIC: 3315; NAICS: 331222

Top Wire Exporters Worldwide, 2019

Data show the major exporters of wire made of iron or steel. Exports reached $11.7 billion in 2019, a 7.4% decrease from 2018.

China	21.5%
South Korea	7.6
Germany	6.6%
Italy	6.2
Czechia	5.1
Japan	4.9
France	3.0
India	2.9
Turkey	2.8
United States	2.7
Other	36.7

Source: "2019 International Trade Statistics Yearbook." [online] from https://comtrade.un.org/pb/ [Published December 2020], from U.N. Comtrade.

★ 3559 ★
Wire and Cable
SIC: 3315; NAICS: 331222

Top Wire Importers Worldwide, 2019

Data show the major importers of wire made of iron or steel. Imports reached $11.6 billion in 2019, a 9.2% decrease from 2018.

Germany	8.4%
United States	8.3
France	4.1
Japan	4.0
Poland	3.9
China	3.8
Italy	3.0
South Korea	2.9
Thailand	2.7
Vietnam	2.7
Other	56.2

Source: "2019 International Trade Statistics Yearbook." [online] from https://comtrade.un.org/pb/ [Published December 2020], from U.N. Comtrade.

★ 3560 ★
Wireless Services
SIC: 4812; NAICS: 517312

5G Fixed Wireless Access Worldwide, 2020 and 2030

The number of 5G fixed wireless access subscribers is forecast to grow from 10.3 million in 2020 to 459.1 million in 2030.

	2020	2030
Europe	20.0%	31.0%
Asia-Pacific	36.0	20.0
Middle East and Africa	5.0	18.0

Continued on next page.

★ 3560 ★
[Continued]
Wireless Services
SIC: 4812; NAICS: 517312

5G Fixed Wireless Access Worldwide, 2020 and 2030

The number of 5G fixed wireless access subscribers is forecast to grow from 10.3 million in 2020 to 459.1 million in 2030.

	2020	2030
Latin America	20.0%	17.0%
North America	39.0	14.0

Source: "Global Household Fixed Wireless Access Subscribers to Cross Half a Billion Market by 2030." [online] from https://www.counterpointresearch.com/category/press-release/ [Press release August 6, 2020], from Counterpoint Research Broadband Subscribers Tracker.

★ 3561 ★
Wireless Services
SIC: 4812; NAICS: 517312

Leading Wireless Service Firms, 2018-2019

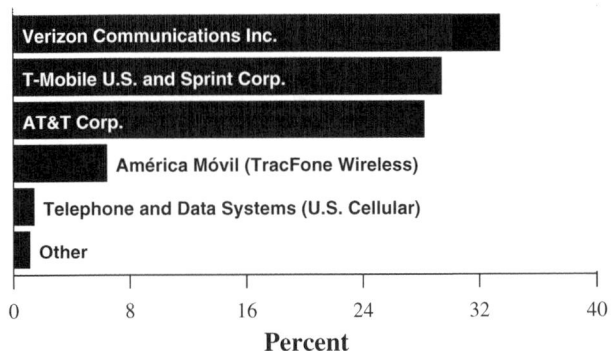

Percent

Market shares are shown based on ad spending of $4.38 billion in 2018 and $4.45 billion in 2019.

	2018	2019
Verizon Communications Inc.	32.9%	33.4%
T-Mobile U.S. and Sprint Corp.	27.3	29.4
AT&T Corp.	30.1	28.2
América Móvil (TracFone Wireless)	7.0	6.4
Telephone and Data Systems (U.S. Cellular)	1.4	1.4
Other	1.2	1.1

Source: *Leading National Advertisers 2020 Fact Book - A Supplement to Advertising Age*, July 13, 2020, p. 33, from Ad Age Datacenter and Kantar.

★ 3562 ★
Wireless Services
SIC: 4812; NAICS: 517312

Leading Wireless Service Firms, 2020-2023

Shares are shown based on estimated number of post-paid phone subscribers.

	2020	2021	2022	2023
Verizon Communications Inc.	41.0%	40.0%	39.0%	39.0%
T-Mobile	29.0	29.0	30.0	30.0
AT&T Corp.	28.0	27.0	26.0	26.0
Cable	2.0	3.0	5.0	6.0

Source: "US Wireless Snapshot: Subscribers, Market Share and Q3 Estimates." [online] from https://www.lightreading.com/4g3gwifi/us-wireless-snapshot-subscribers-market-share-and-q3-estimates/d/d-id/764688 [Published October 16, 2020], from Evercore ISI Research and company data.

★ 3563 ★
Wireless Services
SIC: 4812; NAICS: 517312

Leading Wireless Service Firms in Brazil, 2020

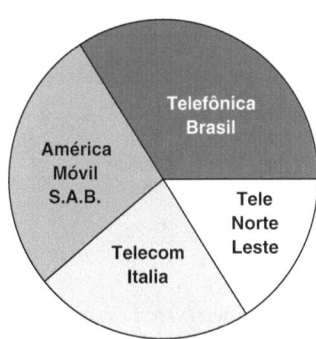

Market shares are shown based on number of subscribers.

Telefônica Brasil	34.0%
América Móvil S.A.B. de C.V.	27.0
Telecom Italia	23.0
Tele Norte Leste Participacoes S.A.	16.0

Source: "American Tower Corporation: International Market Overview Fourth Quarter 2020." [online] from https://www.americantower.com/investor-relations/investor-presentations/ [Accessed April 1, 2021], from American Tower research and analysis, Altman Solon research and analysis, BAML Global Wireless Matrix, RCR and press releases.

★ 3564 ★
Wireless Services
SIC: 4812; NAICS: 517312

Leading Wireless Service Firms in Burkina Faso, 2020

Market shares are shown based on number of subscribers.

Orange	44.0%
Onatel S.A.	42.0
Telecel Faso	14.0

Source: "American Tower Corporation: International Market Overview Fourth Quarter 2020." [online] from https://www.americantower.com/investor-relations/investor-presentations/ [Accessed April 1, 2021], from American Tower research and analysis, Altman Solon research and analysis and ARCEP BF.

★ 3565 ★
Wireless Services
SIC: 4812; NAICS: 517312

Leading Wireless Service Firms in Canada, 2020

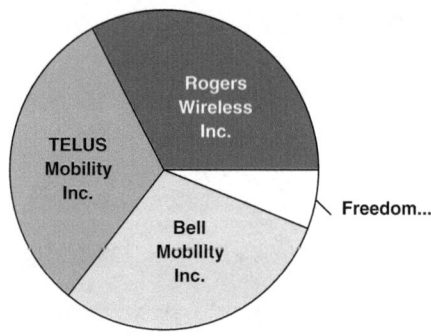

Market shares are shown based on number of subscribers.

Rogers Wireless Inc.	33.0%
TELUS Mobility Inc.	32.0
Bell Mobility Inc.	30.0
Freedom Mobile Inc.	6.0

Source: "American Tower Corporation: International Market Overview Fourth Quarter 2020." [online] from https://www.americantower.com/investor-relations/investor-presentations/ [Accessed April 1, 2021], from American Tower research and analysis, Altman Solon research and analysis, BAML Global Wireless Matrix and company annual reports, press releases and news articles.

★ 3566 ★
Wireless Services
SIC: 4812; NAICS: 517312

Leading Wireless Service Firms in France, 2020

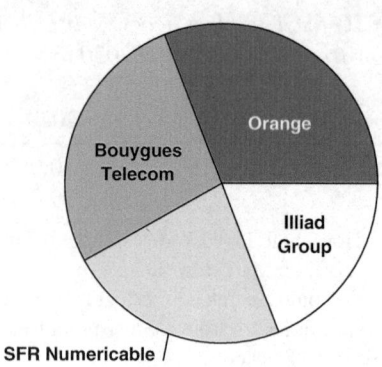

Market shares are shown based on number of subscribers.

Orange	31.0%
Bouygues Telecom	27.0
SFR Numericable	23.0
Illiad Group	19.0

Source: "American Tower Corporation: International Market Overview Fourth Quarter 2020." [online] from https://www.americantower.com/investor-relations/investor-presentations/ [Accessed April 1, 2021], from American Tower research and analysis, Altman Solon research and analysis, BAML Global Wireless Matrix, ARCEP, Tefficient and company annual reports, press releases and news articles.

★ 3567 ★
Wireless Services
SIC: 4812; NAICS: 517312

Leading Wireless Service Firms in Ghana, 2020

Market shares are shown based on number of subscribers.

MTN Group	57.0%
Vodafone Ghana	21.0
AirtelTigo	20.0

Source: "American Tower Corporation: International Market Overview Fourth Quarter 2020." [online] from https://www.americantower.com/investor-relations/investor-presentations/ [Accessed April 1, 2021], from American Tower research and analysis, Altman Solon research and analysis, BuddeComm, NCA Report 1Q20, Pulse Ghana, NCA, MTN Investor reports and Commsupdate.

★ 3568 ★
Wireless Services
SIC: 4812; NAICS: 517312

Leading Wireless Service Firms in India, 2020

Market shares are shown based on number of subscribers.

Reliance Jio Infocomm Ltd.	35.0%
Bharti Airtel Ltd., Singtel	29.0
Vodafone Idea Ltd.	25.0

Source: "American Tower Corporation: International Market Overview Fourth Quarter 2020." [online] from https://www.americantower.com/investor-relations/investor-presentations/ [Accessed April 1, 2021], from American Tower research and analysis, Altman Solon research and analysis, BAML Global Wireless Matrix, TRAI and Commsupdate.

★ 3569 ★
Wireless Services
SIC: 4812; NAICS: 517312

Leading Wireless Service Firms in Mexico, 2020

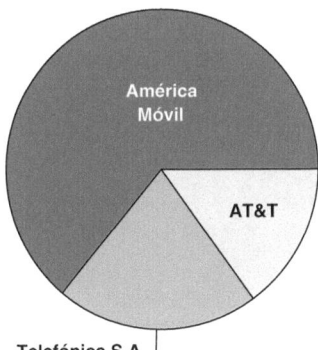

Market shares are shown based on number of subscribers.

América Móvil	64.0%
Telefónica S.A.	21.0
AT&T	15.0

Source: "American Tower Corporation: International Market Overview Fourth Quarter 2020." [online] from https://www.americantower.com/investor-relations/investor-presentations/ [Accessed April 1, 2021], from American Tower research and analysis, Altman Solon research and analysis, BAML Global Wireless Matrix, news and press releases.

★ 3570 ★
Wireless Services
SIC: 4812; NAICS: 517312

Leading Wireless Service Firms in Nigeria, 2020

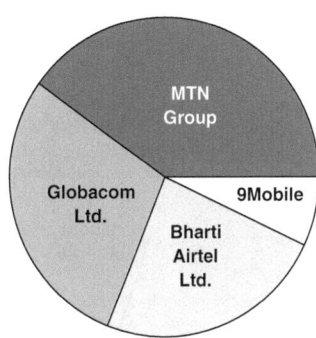

Market shares are shown based on number of subscribers.

MTN Group	40.0%
Globacom Ltd.	29.0
Bharti Airtel Ltd.	24.0
9Mobile	7.0

Source: "American Tower Corporation: International Market Overview Fourth Quarter 2020." [online] from https://www.americantower.com/investor-relations/investor-presentations/ [Accessed April 1, 2021], from American Tower research and analysis, Altman Solon research and analysis, BAML Global Wireless Matrix, Nigerian Communications Commission and GSMA.

★ 3571 ★
Wireless Services
SIC: 4812; NAICS: 517312

Leading Wireless Service Firms in Peru, 2020

Market shares are shown based on number of subscribers.

América Móvil	30.0%
Telefónica	30.0
Entel Perú S.A.	23.0
Viettel Perú S.A.C.	18.0

Source: "American Tower Corporation: International Market Overview Fourth Quarter 2020." [online] from https://www.americantower.com/investor-relations/investor-presentations/ [Accessed April 1, 2021], from American Tower research and analysis, Altman Solon research and analysis, BAML Global Wireless Matrix, Gartner Mobile Services Forecast 1Q15 and TeleGeography.

★ 3572 ★
Wireless Services
SIC: 4812; NAICS: 517312

Leading Wireless Service Firms in Poland, 2020

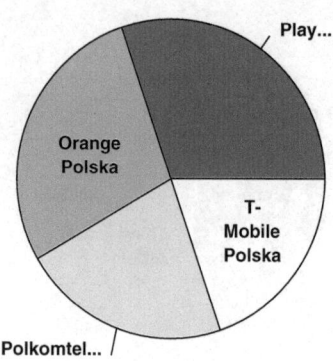

Market shares are shown based on number of subscribers.

Play Communications S.A.	29.0%
Orange Polska	27.0
Polkomtel Sp. z.o.o.	21.0
T-Mobile Polska S.A.	19.0

Source: "American Tower Corporation: International Market Overview Fourth Quarter 2020." [online] from https://www.americantower.com/investor-relations/investor-presentations/ [Accessed April 1, 2021], from American Tower research and analysis, Altman Solon research and analysis, OEC, CMS and company annual reports, press releases and news articles.

★ 3573 ★
Wireless Towers
SIC: 4899; NAICS: 517312

Largest Wireless Tower Companies, 2020

Companies are ranked by towers under ownership. Shares are shown based on the 128,686 under ownership by the top 130 companies.

	Towers	Share
American Tower	40,586	31.54%
Crown Castle	40,567	31.52
SBA Communications	16,401	12.74
Vertical Bridge	5,089	3.95
U.S. Cellular Co.	4,207	3.27
Melody Wireless Infrastructure	1,682	1.31
Insite Wireless Group	1,196	0.93
Peppertree Capital	1,023	0.79
BNSF Railway	941	0.73

	Towers	Share
Tillman Infrastructure L.L.C.	809	0.63%
Other	16,185	12.58

Source: "The 100 Tower Companies in the U.S." [online] from http://wirelessestimator.com/top-100-us-tower-companies-list/ [Published February 2, 2021].

★ 3574 ★
Wireless Towers
SIC: 3663; NAICS: 33422

Largest Wireless Tower Markets in Sub-Saharan Africa, 2019

Data show the estimated number of wireless towers by country. Major independent operators are IHS Towers, American Tower, Helio Towers and Eaton Towers.

	Towers	Share
Nigeria	30,540	22.37%
South Africa	30,183	22.10
Tanzania	8,278	6.06
Ethiopia	8,000	5.86
Kenya	7,591	5.56
Ghana	6,605	4.84
Mozambique	4,400	3.22
Congo	4,293	3.14
Côte d'Ivoire	4,271	3.13
Senegal	3,925	2.87
Other	28,458	20.84

Source: "TowerXchange Africa 2019 Dossier." [online] from http://www.towerxchange.com [Published August 2020], from TowerXchange.

★ 3575 ★
Wiring Ducts
SIC: 3351; NAICS: 33142

Leading Wiring Duct Makers in North America, 2017

Wiring ducts are rigid trays typically used as raceways for cables and wires within electrical enclosures. Wiring ducts, along with conduit, wireways, and cable carriers, are often used as basic components of a cable management system. Market shares are shown based on production.

ABB Inc.	19.12%
Panduit	18.86
Phoenix Conduit	12.44
Other	49.58

Source: "Global Wiring Duct Market Report." [online] from https://www.absolutereports.com/global-wiring-duct-market-16127117 [Published August 2020].

★ 3576 ★
Wood
SIC: 2491; NAICS: 321114

Crosstie Sales, 2003-2018

Data show tie purchases in thousands of units.

Year	Units
2003	16,645
2004	17,966
2005	18,967
2006	20,809
2007	20,584
2008	21,025
2009	19,464
2010	19,685
2011	21,968
2012	23,087
2013	24,462
2014	22,678
2015	24,385
2016	24,319
2017	23,329
2018	21,361

Source: *Crossties*, January-February 2020, p. 10, from *Hardwood Market Report*.

★ 3577 ★
Wood
SIC: 2426; NAICS: 321113, 321912

Hardwood Consumption by Sector, 2020

Shares are shown for mid-year 2020.

Pallets	41.0%
Railway ties	13.0
Exports - Rest of world	12.0
Flooring	7.0
Board road/mat timbers	6.0
Exports - China	6.0
Millwork	6.0
Furniture	5.0
Cabinets	4.0

Source: *Panels & Furniture Asia*, July/August 2020, p. 18, from *Hardwood Market Report*.

★ 3578 ★
Wood
SIC: 2500; NAICS: 337121, 337212, 337214

Leading Furniture and Other Wood Product Makers, 2020

Companies are ranked by estimated sales of furniture, cabinets and other wood products in billions of dollars. The top 300 companies generated sales of $57.883 billion in 2020, up 1.25% from 2019.

	($ bil.)	Share
Ashley Furniture Industries Inc.	$ 6.44	11.13%
Steelcase Inc.	3.72	6.43
Andersen Corp.	2.50	4.32
Herman Miller Inc.	2.49	4.30
Jeld-Wen Inc.	2.48	4.28
MasterBrand Cabinets	2.42	4.18
Haworth Inc.	2.25	3.89
ACProducts Inc.	1.80	3.11
American Woodmark Corp.	1.65	2.85
Masonite International Corp.	1.58	2.73
Other	30.55	52.78

Source: *FDM+C*, February 2021, p. 28.

★ 3579 ★
Wood
SIC: 2435; NAICS: 321211

Leading Industrial Roundwood Consumers in Europe, 2019

Countries are ranked by consumption in thousands of cubic meters.

	(000)	Share
Sweden	76,430	17.99%
Finland	60,828	14.32
Germany	52,138	12.27
Poland	35,833	8.43
France	23,041	5.42
Austria	22,929	5.40
Turkey	22,691	5.34
Spain	14,578	3.43
Portugal	14,522	3.42
Czechia	11,372	2.68
Romania	11,216	2.64
Other	79,335	18.67

Source: "UNECE Forest Products Annual Market Review 2019-2020." [online] from https://unece.org/forests/fpamr-2020 [Accessed December 10, 2020], from FAOSTAT, UNECE/FAO database and TDM database.

★ 3580 ★
Wood
SIC: 2435; NAICS: 321211

Leading Industrial Roundwood Exporters Worldwide, 2019

Countries are ranked by exports in thousands of cubic meters. Total consumption of roundwood (logs for industrial uses and fuel) in the UNECE region was estimated at 1.4 billion cubic meters, the first decline in six years. China was the largest importer; it imported four times more than the other nine countries of the top 10 importers combined.

New Zealand	21,721
Russia	18,857
Czechia	15,297
Germany	8,558
Uruguay	8,178
United States	7,801
Canada	7,548
Australia	4,361
Poland	4,175
France	3,877

Source: "UNECE Forest Products Annual Market Review 2019-2020." [online] from https://unece.org/forests/fpamr-2020 [Accessed December 10, 2020], from FAOSTAT, UNECE/FAO database and TDM database.

★ 3581 ★
Wood
SIC: 2493; NAICS: 321219

Leading Oriented Strand Board Makers in Europe, 2019

Market shares are shown based on capacity of 12 billion square feet as of December 31, 2019. Figures exclude siding.

Kronospan	41.0%
SwissKrono	16.0
Norbord	10.0
Egger	8.0
Smartply	4.0
Sonae Arauco	4.0
Other	16.0

Source: "Norbord Investor Presentation." [online] from https://www.norbord.com/investors/presentations [Published November 10, 2020], from company reports and other filings.

★ 3582 ★
Wood
SIC: 2493; NAICS: 321219

Leading Oriented Strand Board Makers in North America, 2019

Market shares are shown based on capacity of 27 billion square feet as of December 31, 2019. Figures exclude siding.

Norbord	29.0%
Louisiana-Pacific Corp.	17.0
Georgia-Pacific L.L.C.	15.0
Weyerhaeuser	11.0
J.M. Huber Corp.	8.0
Tolko Industries Ltd.	8.0
Martco L.L.C.	6.0
Other	6.0

Source: "Norbord Investor Presentation." [online] from https://www.norbord.com/investors/presentations [Published November 10, 2020], from company reports and other filings.

★ 3583 ★
Wood
SIC: 2493; NAICS: 321219

Leading Particleboard Consumers in Europe, 2019

Countries are ranked by apparent consumption in thousands of cubic meters.

	(000)	Share
Poland	6,613	17.84%
Germany	5,845	15.76
Italy	3,665	9.88
Turkey	3,564	9.61
United Kingdom	2,791	7.53
France	2,530	6.82
Spain	1,640	4.42
Lithuania	1,134	3.06
Romania	1,002	2.70
Sweden	972	2.62
Portugal	747	2.01
Bulgaria	615	1.66
Other	5,960	16.07

Source: "UNECE Forest Products Annual Market Review 2019-2020." [online] from https://unece.org/forests/fpamr-2020 [Accessed December 10, 2020], from UNECE/FAO database.

★ 3584 ★
Wood

SIC: 2493; NAICS: 321219

Leading Plywood Consumers in Europe, 2019

Countries are ranked by apparent consumption in thousands of cubic meters.

	(000)	Share
Germany	1,207	13.59%
Netherlands	573	6.45
Poland	548	6.17
Italy	418	4.71
Slovakia	395	4.45
Belgium	378	4.26
Spain	361	4.06
Sweden	308	3.47
Finland	290	3.27
Israel	277	3.12
Denmark	235	2.65
Switzerland	202	2.27
Other	3,690	41.54

Source: "UNECE Forest Products Annual Market Review 2019-2020." [online] from https://unece.org/forests/fpamr-2020 [Accessed December 10, 2020], from UNECE/FAO database.

★ 3585 ★
Wood

SIC: 2435; NAICS: 321211

Leading Sawn Hardwood Consumers in Europe, 2019

Countries are ranked by apparent consumption in thousands of cubic meters.

	(000)	Share
Turkey	2,425	15.86%
Bosnia and Herzegovina	1,184	7.74
Italy	1,134	7.41
France	1,009	6.60
Germany	908	5.94
Netherlands	859	5.62
Denmark	827	5.41
Poland	698	4.56
United Kingdom	627	4.10
Spain	595	3.89
Czechia	408	2.67
Lithuania	400	2.62
Croatia	386	2.52
Slovakia	314	2.05%
Other	3,520	23.02

Source: "UNECE Forest Products Annual Market Review 2019-2020." [online] from https://unece.org/forests/fpamr-2020 [Accessed December 10, 2020], from UNECE/FAO database.

★ 3586 ★
Wood

SIC: 2436; NAICS: 321212

Leading Sawn Softwood Consumers in Europe, 2019

Countries are ranked by apparent consumption in thousands of cubic meters.

	(000)	Share
Germany	19,317	19.89%
United Kingdom	9,652	9.94
France	8,097	8.34
Sweden	6,498	6.69
Turkey	6,232	6.42
Austria	6,039	6.22
Poland	4,615	4.75
Italy	4,437	4.57
Romania	3,184	3.28
Spain	3,039	3.13
Finland	2,967	3.06
Norway	2,915	3.00
Netherlands	2,810	2.89
Other	17,297	17.81

Source: "UNECE Forest Products Annual Market Review 2019-2020." [online] from https://unece.org/forests/fpamr-2020 [Accessed December 10, 2020], from UNECE/FAO database.

★ 3587 ★
Wood

SIC: 2493; NAICS: 321219

Leading Wood-Based Panel Consumers in Europe, 2019

Countries are ranked by apparent consumption in thousands of cubic meters.

	(000)	Share
Germany	12,088	15.83%
Poland	11,617	15.21

Continued on next page.

★ 3587 ★
[Continued]
Wood
SIC: 2493; NAICS: 321219
Leading Wood-Based Panel Consumers in Europe, 2019

Countries are ranked by apparent consumption in thousands of cubic meters.

	(000)	Share
Turkey	8,455	11.07%
United Kingdom	6,453	8.45
Italy	6,179	8.09
France	4,934	6.46
Spain	3,228	4.23
Romania	2,315	3.03
Belgium	1,929	2.53
Netherlands	1,656	2.17
Sweden	1,659	2.17
Lithuania	1,567	2.05
Other	14,298	18.72

Source: "UNECE Forest Products Annual Market Review 2019-2020." [online] from https://uncce.org/forests/fpamr-2020 [Accessed December 10, 2020], from UNECE/FAO database.

★ 3588 ★
Wood
SIC: 2435; NAICS: 321211
Top Plywood Producers in North America, 2019

Market shares are shown based on production capacity.

Georgia-Pacific L.L.C.	23.0%
Boise Cascade Co.	18.0
Roseburg Forest Products Co.	7.0
West Fraser Timber Co.	6.0
Weyerhaeuser Co.	5.0
Martco L.L.C.	4.0
Other	37.0

Source: "Boise Cascade Company Investor Presentation." [online] from https://www.bc.com/portal/investor-relations/presentations/ [Published November 2020], from Boise Cascade Company estimates, Forest Economic Advisors and APA-The Engineered Wood Association.

★ 3589 ★
Wood
SIC: 2449; NAICS: 32192
Wood Barrel Market in the EU, 2019

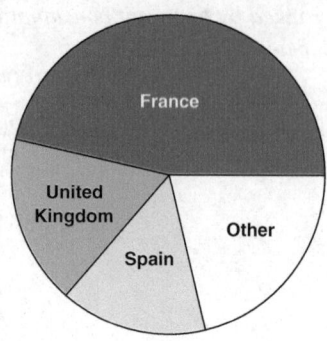

Production of casks, barrels, vats, tubs and cooper products of wood reached 155 million in 2019, the first time since 2016.

	(mil.)	Share
France	72	46.45%
United Kingdom	27	17.42
Spain	23	14.84
Other	33	21.29

Source: "The European Wood Barrel Market Bounced Back to $1.2B." [online] from https://www.indexbox.io/blog/wood-barrel-market-in-the-eu-key-insights-2020/ [Published October 8, 2020], from IndexBox.

★ 3590 ★
Wood
SIC: 2421; NAICS: 321113
Wood Consumption in Europe, 2019

Consumption reached 152.8 million square meters.

Spruce	36.7%
Pine	34.4
Birch	14.8
Eucalyptus	8.3
Beech	2.6
Aspen	1.5
Other hardwood	1.6
Other softwood	0.1

Source: "European Pulp & Paper Industry Key Statistics 2019." [online] from https://www.cepi.org/key-statistics-2019/ [Accessed December 2, 2020], from Confederation of European Paper Industries.

★ 3591 ★
Wood
SIC: 2499; NAICS: 321999

Wood Pellet Production by Country, 2018

Countries are ranked by production capacity in tons. Total capacity was 79.49 million tons; actual production was 55.7 million tons.

	(mil.)	Share
China	34.05	42.84%
United States	11.99	15.08
Canada	4.16	5.23
Denmark	3.75	4.72
Sweden	2.30	2.89
Russia	2.17	2.73
Latvia	1.95	2.45
France	1.80	2.26
Spain	1.76	2.21
Austria	1.63	2.05
Estonia	1.61	2.03
Brazil	1.21	1.52
Other	11.11	13.98

Source: "Bioenergy Europe Statistical Report 2019." [online] from https://bioenergyeurope.org/statistical-report.html [Accessed October 10, 2020], from European Pellet Council and FutureMetrics.

★ 3592 ★
Wool
SIC: 0214; NAICS: 11241

Top Wool Exporters Worldwide, 2019

Data show the major exporters of wool and other animal hair (including wool tops). Exports reached $6.0 billion in 2019, an 18.1% decrease from 2018.

Australia	36.9%
China	13.6
Mongolia	6.2
South Africa	6.0
New Zealand	5.7
Czechia	3.8
Italy	3.6
Argentina	3.5
Uruguay	3.1
Germany	2.6
Other	15.0

Source: "2019 International Trade Statistics Yearbook." [online] from https://comtrade.un.org/pb/ [Published December 2020], from U.N. Comtrade.

★ 3593 ★
Wool
SIC: 0214; NAICS: 11241

Top Wool Importers Worldwide, 2019

Data show the major importers of wool and other animal hair (including wool tops). Imports reached $6.3 billion in 2019, an 18.6% decrease from 2018.

China	42.5%
Italy	15.9
Czechia	4.7
India	4.0
Germany	3.8
South Korea	3.0
Bulgaria	2.5
United Kingdom	2.5
Japan	2.4
Romania	2.4
Other	16.3

Source: "2019 International Trade Statistics Yearbook." [online] from https://comtrade.un.org/pb/ [Published December 2020], from U.N. Comtrade.

★ 3594 ★
Writing Instruments
SIC: 3952; NAICS: 33994

Leading Writing Instrument Makers Worldwide, 2019

The industry was valued at €19 billion. Ballpoint pens claimed 22%, marking products 17%, roller and gel pens 15%, coloring 13%, and other products 33%.

BIC Corp.	9.0%
Newell Brands Inc.	9.0
Pilot Corp.	6.0
Faber-Castell Corp.	4.0
M&G Stationery Inc.	4.0
Other	69.0

Source: "Bic Group Presentation for Investors." [online] from http://www.bicworld.com [Published November 2020].

★ 3595 ★
Writing Instruments
SIC: 3951; NAICS: 33994

Top Pen Brands, 2020

Market shares are shown based on drug store sales for the 52 weeks ended April 19, 2020.

Pilot G2	18.29%
Paper Mate Inkjoy	14.48

Continued on next page.

★ 3595 ★
[Continued]
Writing Instruments
SIC: 3951; NAICS: 33994

Top Pen Brands, 2020

Market shares are shown based on drug store sales for the 52 weeks ended April 19, 2020.

Paper Mate Profile	3.32%
Sanford Sharpie	2.76
BIC Cristal	2.69
Zebra F301	2.62
BIC BU3	2.55
BIC Gel-ocity	2.45
Paper Mate Flair	2.42
Private label	8.58
Other	39.84

Source: *DrugStore Management*, Annual 2020-2021, p. 231, from IRI.

★ 3596 ★
Yarn
SIC: 2281; NAICS: 31311

Filament and Spun Yarn Production, 2018

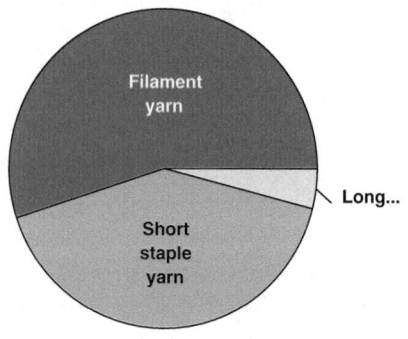

Production reached 87 million tons. China, India and Pakistan were the leading producers.

Filament yarn	55.0%
Short staple yarn	41.0
Long staple yarn	4.0

Source: *International Fiber Journal*, November/December 2019, p. 30.

★ 3597 ★
Yarn
SIC: 2281; NAICS: 31311

Top Textile Yarn Exporters Worldwide, 2019

Data show the major exporters of textile yarn. Exports reached $51.4 billion in 2019, a 7.2% decrease from 2018.

China	25.9%
India	9.6
Vietnam	7.8
United States	6.4
Indonesia	4.3
Italy	4.0
Turkey	3.6
South Korea	2.7
Germany	2.6
China, Hong Kong SAR	2.5
Other	30.6

Source: "2019 International Trade Statistics Yearbook." [online] from https://comtrade.un.org/pb/ [Published December 2020], from U.N. Comtrade.

★ 3598 ★
Yarn
SIC: 2281; NAICS: 31311

Top Textile Yarn Importers Worldwide, 2019

Data show the major importers of textile yarn. Imports reached $49.8 billion in 2019, a 9.2% decrease from 2018.

China	14.5%
Turkey	6.5
United States	4.8
Italy	4.7
Germany	4.3
Vietnam	4.2
Bangladesh	4.1
South Korea	3.9
India	2.8
Brazil	2.6
China, Hong Kong SAR	2.6
Egypt	2.6
Japan	2.6
Other	39.8

Source: "2019 International Trade Statistics Yearbook." [online] from https://comtrade.un.org/pb/ [Published December 2020], from U.N. Comtrade.

★ 3599 ★
Yogurt
SIC: 2026; NAICS: 311511

Top Chilled Yogurt Makers in China, 2017

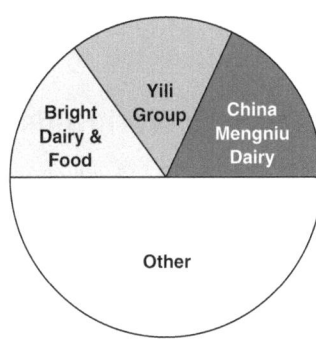

In the ambient yogurt category, Ambpoeial claimed 45.3% of sales while Just Yogurt claimed 26.1% of sales.

China Mengniu Dairy Co.	18.2%
Yili Group	17.1
Bright Dairy & Food Co.	14.6
Other	50.1

Source: *just-food.com*, March 10, 2021, p. NA, from Frost & Sullivan.

★ 3600 ★
Yogurt
SIC: 2026; NAICS: 311511

Top Greek Yogurt Brands in Greece, 2019

Market share shown based on sales for the year ended December 31, 2019. Figures do not include traditional yogurt sales.

	Volume	Value
FAGE	22.3%	22.6%
Vivartia (formerly Delta)	12.2	16.8
Kri Kri	14.9	14.0
Olympos	8.6	10.0
Mevgal	5.7	5.9
Dodoni	7.4	5.8
Danone	3.2	4.6
Friesland/Campina	3.0	2.9
Farma Koukaki	2.5	2.4
Private label	12.7	7.7
Other	7.5	7.3

Source: "Analysis of Kri Kri Milk Industry." [online] from https://smallcapseurope.com/2020/12/04/analysis-of-kri-kri-milk-industry/ [Published December 4, 2020], from IRI.

★ 3601 ★
Zinc
SIC: 3339; NAICS: 33141

Largest Refined Zinc Producers Worldwide, 2019

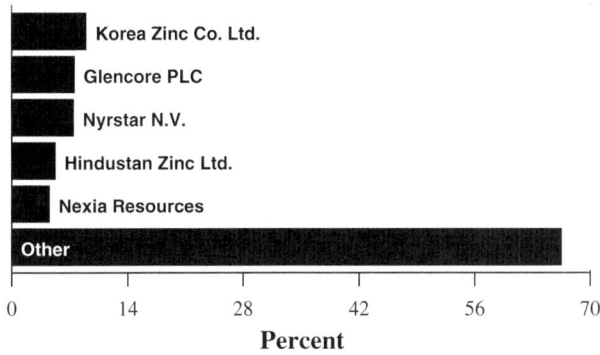

Zinc smelter production grew from 13.2 million in 2018 to 13.4 million in 2019.

Korea Zinc Co. Ltd.	8.9%
Glencore PLC	7.5
Nyrstar N.V.	7.4
Hindustan Zinc Ltd.	5.2
Nexia Resources	4.5
Other	66.5

Source: "Vedanta Resources Ltd." [online] from https://links.sgx.com/FileOpen/Vedanta%20Holdings%20Mauritius%20II%20Limited_OC%20dtd%2017%20Aug%202020.ashx?App=Prospectus&FileID=46149 [Published August 17, 2020], from Wood Mackenzie Metals Market Service Report.

★ 3602 ★
Zinc
SIC: 3339; NAICS: 33141

Largest Refined Zinc Producing Regions, 2017-2019

Zinc smelter production grew from 13.2 million in 2018 to 13.4 million in 2019.

	2017	2018	2019
China	44.4%	42.6%	44.2%
Europe	16.0	16.9	16.3
North America	7.8	8.4	8.6
India	6.1	5.7	5.5
Latin America	4.3	4.6	4.6
Russia and Caspian	4.8	4.8	4.2
Oceania	3.4	3.7	3.4
Africa	0.7	0.6	0.6
Other Asia	12.5	12.7	12.6

Source: "Vedanta Resources Ltd." [online] from https://links.sgx.com/FileOpen/Vedanta%20Holdings%20Mauritius%20II%20Limited_OC%20dtd%2017%20Aug%202020.ashx?App=Prospectus&FileID=46149 [Published August 17, 2020], from Wood Mackenzie Metals Market Service Report.

★ 3603 ★
Zinc
SIC: 3356; NAICS: 331491

Top End Markets for Zinc Worldwide, 2019

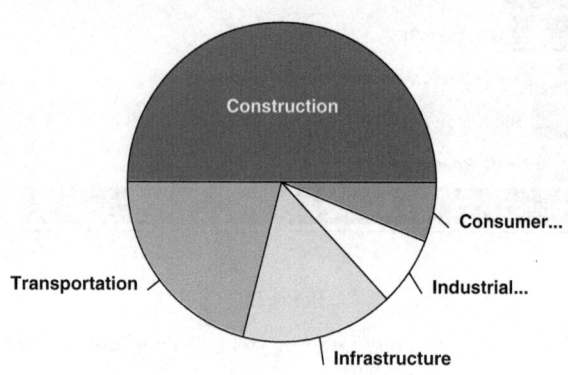

Zinc prices were volatile in 2019. Prices slipped in early 2020 because of COVID-19, but they recovered during the second half of the year. Some analysts were optimistic about zinc in 2021, with strong demand coming from China. Demand for zinc is forecast to grow 1.5% annually from 2021-2030.

Construction	50.0%
Transportation	21.0
Infrastructure	16.0
Industrial machinery	7.0
Consumer products	6.0

Source: "New Century Resources March 2020 Quarter Results Presentation." [online] from http://www.newcenturyresources.com [Published March 2020], from Wood Mackenzie.

★ 3604 ★
Zinc
SIC: 1031; NAICS: 21223

Top Zinc Exporters Worldwide, 2019

Data show the major exporters of zinc. Exports reached $14.8 billion in 2019, a 11.9% decrease from 2018.

Canada	10.3%
South Korea	10.3
Spain	9.8
Belgium	8.4
Australia	6.7
Netherlands	6.6
Peru	5.3
Finland	4.4
India	3.7
Norway	3.6%
Other	30.9

Source: "2019 International Trade Statistics Yearbook." [online] from https://comtrade.un.org/pb/ [Published December 2020], from U.N. Comtrade.

★ 3605 ★
Zinc
SIC: 1031; NAICS: 21223

Top Zinc Importers Worldwide, 2019

Data show the major importers of zinc. Imports reached $16.2 billion in 2019, a 14.2% decrease from 2018.

United States	13.2%
China	11.9
Germany	7.8
Netherlands	5.8
Belgium	4.7
Turkey	4.4
Italy	3.9
France	3.7
India	2.9
Vietnam	2.9
Other	38.8

Source: "2019 International Trade Statistics Yearbook." [online] from https://comtrade.un.org/pb/ [Published December 2020], from U.N. Comtrade.

★ 3606 ★
Zinc
SIC: 1031; NAICS: 21223

Top Zinc Mines Worldwide, 2019

Mines are ranked by output in kilotons.

Red Dog (Teck)	552
Rampura Agucha (Hindustan Zinc)	447
Mt Isa (Glencore)	326
Antamina (multiple owners)	303
MacArthur River (Glencore)	271
San Cristobal (Sumitomo)	255
Dugald River (MMG)	170
Sindesar Khurd (Vedanta)	160
Vazante (Nexa Resources)	139
Century (New Century Resources)	138

Source: "New Century Resources March 2020 Quarter Results Presentation." [online] from http://www.newcenturyresources.com [Published March 2020], from Wood Mackenzie.

★ 3607 ★
Zinc
SIC: 1031; NAICS: 21223

Top Zinc Producing Nations, 2020

Countries are ranked by production in thousands of metric tons of zinc content. Global mine production was 12 million tons, a 6.0% decrease from 2019. Global refined zinc production was 13.60 million tons, a slight increase from 2019; consumption was 12.98 million tons, a 5% decrease from 2019. Production data are estimated.

	(000)	Share
China	4,200	34.48%
Australia	1,400	11.49
Peru	1,200	9.85
India	720	5.91
United States	670	5.50
Mexico	600	4.93
Bolivia	330	2.71
Kazakhstan	300	2.46
Canada	280	2.30
Russia	260	2.13
Sweden	220	1.81
Other	2,000	16.42

Source: ''Mineral Commodity Summaries 2021.'' [online] from https://www.usgs.gov/centers/nmic/mineral-commodity-summaries [Published January 29, 2021], from U.S. Geological Survey.

★ 3608 ★
Zoos and Botanical Gardens
SIC: 8422; NAICS: 71213

Zoos and Botanical Gardens, 2017

Data show the percent of industry sales held by the largest 4, 8, 20 and 50 firms in the sector. There are approximately 646 players operating in the industry generating employment for 39,987 people. Zoos and aquariums closed for a time in 2020 as a result of the pandemic. These closures helped drive down industry revenue; average annual growth was -2.6% for the five years leading up to 2021. According to IBISWorld, the industry generated revenue of $2 billion in 2021.

4 largest firms	16.6%
8 largest firms	24.5
20 largest firms	40.7
50 largest firms	64.2

Source: ''Economic Census.'' [online] from https://www.census.gov/content/census/en/data/tables/2017/econ/economic-census/naics-sector-31-33.html [Accessed January 21, 2021], from U.S. Census Bureau.

SOURCE INDEX

This index is divided into *secondary sources* and *primary sources*. Secondary sources are the publications which quote market share data from a primary source. Primary sources are either the publications from which a particular market share is taken when no other source has been quoted or are the sources cited by a secondary source. Numbers following the sources are entry numbers, arranged sequentially; the first number refers to the first appearance of the source in *Market Share Reporter*. All told, 2,433 organizations are listed. Roman numerals indicate volume number.

Secondary Sources

"The #1 Wireless Hauling Specialist Positioned to Lead in a Growing Market." [online] from http://www.ceragon.com [Published May 2020], II-2421

"19% Plug-In Vehicle Market Share in France in December!" [online] from https://cleantechnica.com/2021/01/17/19-plugin-vehicle-market-share-in-france-in-december-2020/ [Published January 17, 2021], I-334

"1H2020 Financial Results Autogrill Group." [online] from https://www.autogrill.com/en/investors [Published July 30, 2020], I-1417

20/20 Magazine, II-2525

"2007 Economic Census." [online] from http://www.census.gov/econ/concentration.html [Accessed August 12, 2011], I-1893

"The 201 Nimdzi: The Ranking of Top 100 Largest Language Service Providers." [online] from https://www.nimdzi.com/nimdzi-100-top-lsp/ [Published March 1, 2021], II-3411

"2019-2024 U.S. Equipment Rental Forecast." [online] from https://www.businessdisputeclinic.com/2019-2024-us-equipment-rental-forecast/ [Accessed May 20, 2021], I-1770

"2019 Annual Report of the U.S. Fluid Power Industry." [online] from http://www.nfpa.com [Accessed February 15, 2021], I-1379-1380

"2019 Eye Banking Statistical Report." [online] from https://restoresight.org/what-we-do/publications/statistical-report/ [Accessed March 10, 2021], II-2259

"2019 Internal Revenue Service Data Book." [online] from https://www.irs.gov/statistics/soi-tax-stats-irs-data-book [Accessed April 20, 2021], II-3298

"2019 International Trade Statistics Yearbook." [online] from https://comtrade.un.org/pb/ [Published December 2020], I-164-165, 171-172, 947-948, 955, 957, 963-964, 1263-1264, 1269-1270, 1321-1322, 1538-1539, 1630-1633, 2039-2040, 2050-2051, II-2284-2285, 2435-2436, 2489-2490, 2641-2642, 2740-2745, 2780-2781, 2817-2818, 3079-3080, 3247-3248, 3339-3340, 3558-3559, 3592-3593, 3597-3598, 3604-3605

"2019 Market Share Reports." [online] from http://content.naic.org [Accessed January 10, 2021], I-1921-1922, 1927-1928, 1930-1936, 1938, 1943-1945, 1947-1949, 1952-1953

"The 2019 Sales Volume Study Summary (Categories)." [online] from https://ppai.org/members/research/ [Accessed November 17, 2020], II-2807

"2019 Top 100 Listing for Pesticide Formulations Sales in China." [online] from http://news.agropages.com/News/NewsDetail---35759.htm [Published June 30, 2020], I-710

"2019 Water Heating Market Review." [online] from https://www.bsria.com/us/news/article/2019_water_heating_market_review/ [Published May 2020], I-233

"2020: A Year in Review." [online] from https://www.unwto.org/covid-19-and-tourism-2020 [Accessed March 7, 2020], II-3392

2020 ASHA 50 - A Supplement to Seniors Housing Business, I-1861

"2020 China Marketing Trends." [online] from https://as-pacific.com/assets/presentations/2020-China-Report.pdf [Accessed January 10, 2021], II-2901

"2020 China's Game Livestreaming Industry Report." [online] from http://www.iresearchchina.com/content/details7_63591.html [Published August 18, 2020], I-2099

"2020 Communications Marketplace Report." [online] from https://www.fcc.gov/document/fcc-releases-2020-communications-marketplace-report [Published December 2020], II-3319

"2020 Economic Briefing." [online] from https://www.distilledspirits.org/data-economic-impact/ [Published January 2021], I-2087

"2020 Facts and Figures Aerospace and Defense." [online] from https://www.aia-aerospace.org/report/2020-facts-figures/ [Accessed December 1, 2020], I-1045

"2020 Global Leasing Report." [online] from https://pages.whiteclarkegroup.com/rs/187-PFS-866/

images/WCG%20Global%20Leasing%20Report_2020.pdf [Accessed March 26, 2021], I-2045

"2020 Insurance Fact Book." [online] from http://www.iii.org [Accessed January 20, 2021], I-1913

"2020 Preferred Fiber and Materials Market Report." [online] from https://textileexchange.org/2020-preferred-fiber-and-materials-market-report-pfmr-released/ [Published June 2020], I-1319

"2020 Production Statistics." [online] from https://www.oica.net/category/production-statistics/2020-statistics/ [Accessed April 10, 2021], I-350, 567, II-3439

"2020 Public Transportation Fact Book." [online] from https://www.apta.com/wp-content/uploads/APTA-2020-Fact-Book.pdf [Published March 2020], II-2150-2162

"2020 RV Shipments Surpass 2019 By 6% With December Shipments Best on Record." [online] from https://www.rvia.org/news-insights/2020-rv-shipments-surpass-2019-6-december-shipments-best-record [Published December 2020], II-2863

"2020 Sales Statistics." [online] from https://www.oica.net/category/production-statistics/2020-statistics/ [Accessed April 10, 2021], II-3437

2020 Sosland Publishing's Corporate Profiles State of the Industry Report, I-386-387, 539, 661-662, 674, 758, 1005, 1007, 1238, 1487-1488, 1490-1493, 1873, 1875, 2012, II-2672-2673, 2675, 3196-3197

"2020 State of the Lakes." [online] from https://lcaships.com/publications/state-of-the-lakes/ [Accessed October 28, 2020], II-3045

"2020 Theme Trends." [online] from https://www.motionpictures.org/wp-content/uploads/2021/03/MPA-2020-THEME-Report.pdf [Published March 2021], I-1248-1249, II-2355, 2365, 2376, 2383, 2385

"2020 Top 100 Home Healthcare Providers." [online] from https://risk.lexisnexis.com/-/media/files/healthcare/research/2020-top-100-hospice-and-home-health-report%20pdf.pdf [Accessed February 22, 2021], I-1748

"2020 Top 100 Hospice Providers." [online] from https://risk.lexisnexis.com/-/media/files/healthcare/research/2020-top-100-hospice-and-home-health-report%20pdf.pdf [Accessed February 22, 2021], I-1749

"2020 U.S. Electric Vehicle Sales Report." [online] from https://cleantechnica.com/2021/02/08/2020-us-electric-vehicle-sales-report/ [Published February 8, 2021], I-329

"3-Year European Market Forecast: App Spending to Surpass $23 Billion in 2022 as Non-Gaming Surges." [online] from https://sensortower.com/blog/sensor-tower-europe-app-market-forecast-2022 [Published February 24, 2020], I-251

"361 Degrees International Limited." [online] from http://ir.361sport.com/html/share_presentation.php [Published August 2020], I-204

"4Q19 HME Oxygen, Sleep, And Complex Rehab Survey." [online] from https://cdn2.hubspot.net/hubfs/5670140/4Q19%20HME%20Sleep-Oxygen-Rehab%20Survey%2001-27-20.pdf [Published January 27, 2020], II-2235, 2251-2252

"5 Takeaways from Sensor Tower's New Mobile App Industry Trends Report." [online] from https://sensortower.com/blog/mobile-industry-trends-report-2021 [Published January 28, 2021], II-2340

"5-Year Market Forecast: App Spending Will Climb to $270 Billion by 2025." [online] from https://sensortower.com/blog/sensor-tower-app-market-forecast-2025 [Published February 22, 2021], I-255

"5G Connected Cars to Grab 40% of China Market by 2025." [online] from https://www.counterpointresearch.com/5g-connected-cars-to-grab-china-market-by-2025/ [Press release December 18, 2020], I-339, 342

5thWave, I-764-768, 770-771

"6 Things to Know About the Metal Stamping & Forging Industry." [online] from https://teamcoact.com/learning-center/metal-stamping-forging-industry/ [Accessed February 15, 2021], II-2298

"72% Plug-In Vehicle Market Share in the Netherlands." [online] from https://cleantechnica.com/2021/01/17/19-plugin-vehicle-market-share-in-france-in-december-2020/ [Published January 9, 2021], I-335

"A Dozen Facts About Medicare Advantage in 2020." [online] from https://www.kff.org/medicare/issue-brief/a-dozen-facts-about-medicare-advantage-in-2020/ [Published April 22, 2020], I-1919-1920

"A Tale of Two Chains: Walgreens Exits Pharmacy Clinics While CVS Reinvents In-Store Care." [online] from http://www.drugchannels.net [Published November 7, 2019], I-1744

"A United Voice for Banana Workers in Africa." [online] from https://www.bananalink.org.uk/wp-content/uploads/2020/06/FES Towards-A-United-Voice-for-Banana-Workers-ENG-FINAL.pdf [Published March 2020], I-1515

"A Virtual Hit: JibJab's Quarantine Birthday Card Gives E-Greeting Company a Boost." [online] from https://www.uschamber.com/co/good-company/the-leap/jibjab-quarantine-greeting-ecards [Published November 23, 2020], I-1677

"AAP StatShot: U.S. Trade Book Sales up 9.7 Percent for 2020." [online] from https://publishingperspectives.com/2021/02/aap-statshot-sees-us-trade-book-sales-up-9-7-percent-for-2020-covid19/ [Published February 25, 2021], I-526

"AbbVie/Allergan Regulation Merger Procedure." [online] from https://ec.europa.eu/competition/mergers/cases/decisions/m9461_

1187_3.pdf [Published January 10, 2020], I-1119-1121, 1139-1140

"Academy Sports' COVID-Driven IPO." [online] from https://www.earnestresearch.com/academys-covid-driven-ipo/ [Published September 25, 2020], II-3214-3215

"Acadia Investor Presentation." [online] from https://www.acadiahealthcare.com/investors/presentations/ [Published March 2020], I-1761

"Accounting Services in the U.S." [online] from http://www.ibisworld.com [Published August 2019], I-4

"ACI World Data Reveals COVID-19 Impact on World's Busiest Airports." [online] from https://aci.aero/news/2021/04/22/aci-world-data-reveals-covid-19s-impact-on-worlds-busiest-airports/ [Press release April 22, 2021], I-97-98

"ACP Market Report Fourth Quarter 2020." [online] from https://cleanpower.org/resources/american-clean-power-market-report-q4-2020/ [Accessed April 11, 2021], I-1234, II-3446

Adhesives & Sealants Industry, I-12, II-2739

"ADMA Biologics." [online] from http://d1io3yog0ouxcloudfront.net/admabiologicvs.pdf [Published March 2020], I-1877

Advertising Age, I-24-25, II-3218

"Affected by the Pandemic, The Global Curtain Market to Lose Growth Momentum." [online] from https://www.globaltrademag.com/affected-by-the-pandemic-the-global-curtain-market-to-lose-growth-momentum/ [Published August 14, 2020], I-1795

"African SVOD Subs to More than Quadruple." [online] from http://www.digitaltvresearch.com/products [Press release October 2020], II-2539

Aggregates Business Europe, I-51

"Agricultural Fencing." [online] from http://www.freedoniagroup.com [Published September 2020], I-1303

"Agriculture, Crops, Fruits and Vegetable Growing (Farming) Industry (U.S.)." [online] from http://www.plunkettresearch.com [Published December 30, 2019], I-1291

Agropages, I-688-689

"AHRI Releases September 2020 U.S. Heating and Cooling Equipment Shipment Data." [online] from http://www.ahrinet.org [Press release November 13, 2020], I-1769

"A.I. in Medical Imaging to Top $2 Billion by 2023." [online] from https://www.prnewswire.com/news-releases/ai-in-medical-imaging-to-top-2-billion-by-2023-300691229.html [Published August 2, 2018], II-3163

Air Cargo News, II-3054-3055

"Airbnb: A COVID Threat or Opportunity." [online] from https://www.earnestresearch.com/airbnbs-s-1-a-covid-threat-or-opportunity/ [Published November 30, 2020], II-3418

"Airbus Helicopters Market Share Down to 48% in 2020." [online] from https://www.helicopterinvestor.com/articles/airbus-helicopters-market-share-down-to-48-in-2020-111/ [Accessed January 27, 2021], I-62

Airline Business, I-75-77, 80

"Airline Domestic Market Share March 2020-February 2021." [online] from https://www.transtats.bts.gov/ [Accessed May 20, 2021], I-86-96

"Alipay Retains Leadership Position with 55% in China's Mobile Payments Market." [online] from https://www.businesstoday.com.my/2020/07/09/alipay-retains-leadership-position-with-55-market-share-in-chinas [Published July 9, 2020], I-1186

"Allianz Holdings/Legal and General Insurance Regulation Merger Procedure." [online] from http://www.ec.europa.eu [Published September 26, 2019], I-1918

"AlphaWise Survey: 5G Consumer Demand Bigger Than You Think." [online] from http://www.advisor.morganstanley.com [Published November 29, 2020], I-609

"Alstom, Bombardier Seek to Avoid Path That Derailed Siemens Deal." [online] from https://www.bloomberg.com/news/articles/2020-02-19/alstom-bombardier-seek-to-avoid-path-that-derailed-siemens-deal [Published February 19, 2020], II-2831

"Alternative Fueling Station Counts by State." [online] from https://afdc.energy.gov/stations/states [Published January 15, 2021], I-104-153

"Always Room for Dessert." [online] from https://www.nomura.com/europe/resources/upload/Alwaysroomfordessert.pdf [Published December 31, 2020], I-1214

"Amazon Echo & Alexa Stats." [online] from https://voicebot.ai/amazon-echo-alexa-stats/ [Published April 2020], I-894

"Amazon Prime Day 2020 Sees Another Record Year, with Online Spend Up 36% Year Over Year." [online] from https://trends.edison.tech/research/amazon-prime-day-sales-2020.html [Published October 23, 2020], I-1168

"Amazon's Share of the U.S. Digital Ad Market Surpassed 10% in 2020." [online] from https://www.emarketer.com/content/amazon-s-share-of-us-digital-ad-market-surpassed-10-2020 [Published April 6, 2021], I-17

"AMD's CPU Share Skyrocketed in 2020 Along With Low-End PC Sales." [online] from https://www.pcworld.com/article/3606108/amds-cpu-share-skyrocketed-in-2020-along-with-low-end-pc-sales.html [Published February 3, 2021], II-3009, 3023, 3030

American Ceramic Society Bulletin, I-11, 654, 1626, 2076

"American Online Hobbies and Crafts Market Booming After Corona 19." [online] from http://news.kotra.or.kr [Published October 20, 2020], I-1780

American School & University, II-2980

"American Staple Food, Bread Consumption Trends Change." [online] from http://www.news.kotra.or.kr [Published June 15, 2020], I-547

"American Tower Corporation: International Market Overview Fourth Quarter 2020." [online] from https://www.americantower.com/investor-relations/investor-presentations/ [Accessed April 1, 2021], II-3563-3572

American Vegetable Grower, I-1292, 1531

"An Indian Toy Story That Isn't Ending Well for Small Businesses." [online] from https://www.bloombergquint.com/bq-blue-exclusive/an-indian-toy-story-that-isnt-ending-well-for-small-businesses [Published December 17, 2020], II-3398

"Analysis of AMF Data Reveals Largest ELP SI Market Shares in France." [online] from https://www.thetradenews.com/analysis-of-amf-data-reveals-largest-elp-si-market-shares-in-france/ [Published June 17, 2020], I-1979

"Analysis of Kri Kri Milk Industry." [online] from https://smallcapseuropc.com/2020/12/04/analysis-of-kri-kri-milk-industry/ [Published December 4, 2020], II-3600

"Analysis of Sales and Profitability Within the Seed Sector." [online] from http://www.fao.org/3/ca6929en/ca6929en.pdf [Published November 2019], II-3004

"Analysis of the Digitalization Process of the E-Commerce Industry." [online] from http://www.analysyschina.com [Published August 14, 2020], I-1170

"Annual Energy Outlook 2021." [online] from https://www.eia.gov/outlooks/aeo/ [Published February 3, 2021], I-1215, 1227-1228

"Annual Report on Nationally Recognized Statistical Rating Organizations." [online] from http://www.sec.gov [Published December 2020], I-1017

"Annual Survey of Manufactures." [online] from https://www.census.gov/programs-surveys/asm/data/tables.html [Accessed March 18, 2021], I-176, 187, 470, 561, 583, 605, 617, 684, 1099, 1207, 1300, 1317, 1337, 1546, 1621, 1708, 1724, 1766, 1866, 1868, 1887, 1894, 1901, 1988, 1997, II-2326, 2610, 2710, 2716, 2722, 2735, 2912, 2935, 3076, 3099, 3152, 3203, 3210, 3309, 3436

"APAC Smart Personal Audio Device Shipments Q1 2020." [online] from https://www.canalys.com/newsroom/Canalys-smart-personal-audio-device-shipments-Q1-2020 [Press release July 15, 2020], I-285, 287-291

"Apple Shipped Record iPhones in Q4 2020, Global Smartphone Market Continues to Recover." [online] from https://www.counterpointresearch.com/apple-shipped-record-iphones-q4-2020-global-smartphone-market-continues-recover/ [Press release January 28, 2021], I-641

"Applied Materials Will Regain Semiconductor Equipment Lead From ASML in 2020." [online] from https://semiwiki.com/semiconductor-services/information-network/293298-applied-materials-will-regain-semiconductor-equipment-lead-from-asml-in-2020/ [Published November 29, 2020], II-3007

"AquaBounty Investor Presentation." [online] from https://www.aquabounty.com/wp-content/uploads/2020/02/February-2020-Investor-Deck.pdf [Published February 2020], I-1326

"Architectural Services in the U.S." [online] from http://www.ibisworld.com [Published July 2019], I-260

"Arconic Second Quarter 2020 Earnings Call." [online] from https://www.arconic.com/investors/ [Published August 4, 2020], I-161

"Argentina 2020. Honda Dominates Ahead of Local Manufacturers." [online] from https://www.motorcyclesdata.com/2021/01/18/argentine-motorcycles-market/ [Published January 18, 2021], II-2369

"Art Attack: Pandemic Will Have Lasting Effects on Creative Markets." [online] from https://www.arabnews.com/node/1797186/business-economy [Published January 23, 2021], I-265

"Art Market in 2020." [online] from http://www.artbasel.com [Accessed November 10, 2020], I-266-272

"Ashtead Group PLC Annual Report & Accounts 2020." [online] from https://www.ashtead-group.com/investors/results-centre/annual-reports/ [Published June 15, 2020], I-1771-1772, 1774

Asia Food & Beverages Report, I-481

"Asia Pacific Spending on IoT Expected to Reach U.S.$ 288.6 Billion in 2021, IDC Reports." [online] from http://www.idc.com [Press release February 16, 2021], I-1963

Asian Ceramics, I-2014

"At-Home Tax Prep Trend Likely to Grow After Pandemic's Boost." [online] from https://news.bloombergtax.com/daily-tax-report/at-home-tax-prep-trend-likely-to-grow-after-pandemics-boost [Published July 10, 2020], II-3159

Atlanta Journal-Constitution, II-2688

The Atlantic, I-529

"Aurobindo Investor Presentation." [online] from http://www.aurobindo.com [Published August 2019], I-1129

"Aurora Cannabis Leads Canada in Market Share Decline While Smaller Companies Gain, Report Says." [online] from https://mjbizdaily.com/aurora-cannabis-leads-canada-in-market-share-decline-while-smaller-companies-gain/ [Published April 13, 2021], I-601

"Australian Pet Food Market Trend." [online] from http://www.news.kotra.or.kr [Published April 5, 2021], II-2679

"Auto Parts." [online] from http://www.chinastock.com.hk/en/NC/CA/index.aspx [Published January 8, 2021], I-462

Autocar, I-355

"Automated IGBT Industry Report, 2020." [online] from http://www.researchinchina.com [Published July 2020], II-3029

"The Automobile Industry Pocket Guide 2020-2021." [online] from http://www.acea.be/publications/article/acea-pocket-guide [Accessed April 12, 2021], I-358, 569, II-3440, 3468

"Automotive Coatings." [online] from https://www.freedoniagroup.com [Published May 2021], II-2583

"Automotive Dealers (New) Industry (U.S.)." [online] from http://www.plunkettresearch.com [Published March 4, 2021], I-296

Automotive Fleet, I-298

"Automotive - Impact on Chemicals." [online] from https://www.icis.com/explore/resources/news/2020/09/11/10541454/topic-page-automotive-impact-on-chemicals [Published September 11, 2020], II-2737

"Aviation Gas Turbines." [online] from http://www.fi-powerweb.com/Aviation-Gas-Turbines.html [Accessed September 16, 2020], I-78

Aviation Week & Space Technology, I-65-66, 68-70, 73-74

"The Azek Company." [online] from https://www.sec.gov/Archives/edgar/data/1782754/000119312520028208/d776367ds1.htm [Published February 2020], I-1042, II-2830, 3420

"Baby Food Has Too Much Sugar and is Marketed Wrongly." [online] from https://www.bloomberg.com/news/articles/2019-07-15/baby-food-has-too-much-sugar-and-is-marketed-wrongly-who-says [Published July 15, 2019], I-376

Baking & Snack, I-384

Baltimore Business Journal, II-2347

Barron's, I-1114

"Bars and Nightclubs." [online] from http://www.sdcnet.org/small-business-research-reports/bar-business-nightclub [Published June 2020], II-2438

"Bathroom Fixture Market Infographic." [online] from http://www.traqline.com [Published January 25, 2021], II-2753

"Bathroom Fixtures Composite." [online] from https://www.traqline.com/newsroom/category/infographics/ [Published January 25, 2021], II-2755

"Battery Market Size, Share & Trends Analysis Report by Product (Lead Acid, Li-ion, Nickel Metal Hydride, Ni-cd)." [online] from https://www.grandviewresearch.com/industry-analysis/battery-market [Published July 2020], I-463

"Beauty Sector Before and After COVID-19." [online] from https://daxueconsulting.com/how-millenials-and-low-tier-cities-are-shaping-chinas-jewelry-market/ [Published May 2020], II-2650

Bedding Yearbook - A Supplement to Furniture Today, I-1801

"Beer, Wine & Liquor Stores in the U.S." [online] from http://www.ibisworld.com [Published October 2019], I-101

"Beer and Wine Labels: Market Highlight Beer Market." [online] from https://labels.network/content/beer-and-wine-labels-market-highlights-part-1-the-beer-market/ [Published June 7, 2020], I-2018

"Benefits & Challenges to Entering the Storage Container Industry." [online] from https://www.360connect.com/supplier-blog/benefits-challenges-to-entering-the-storage-container-industry/ [Published June 2, 2020], II-3249

Best's Review, I-1788, 1915, 1923-1926, 1929, 1937, 1939, 1941-1942, 1946

"Better Choice Company Investor Presentation." [online] from https://betterchoicecompany.com/wp-content/uploads/2020/08/bttr-Investor-presentation.pdf [Published August 4, 2020], II-2667

Beverage Dynamics, I-2096-2097

Beverage Industry, I-478-480, 484, 541, 757, 759-760, 1239-1240, 1336, 1739, 2010-2011, II-2320, 2322, 3222-3223, 3284, 3303, 3305, 3495

BevNet Magazine, I-542, 2005-2007, II-2321

Bicycle Retailer & Industry News, I-491

"Big Banks Still Dominate Mortgage Market Share." [online] from https://www.canadianmortgagetrends.com/2020/09/big-banks-still-dominate-mortgage-market-share-says-cmhc/ [Published September 14, 2020], II-2352

"Bigger Fleet. Bigger Challenges." [online] from http://www.oliverwyman.com [Published February 2020], II-2386

Bike & E-Bike Market Update, I-492-493

"Billion Board Foot Club Ranking: 2019." [online] from https://getfea.com/wp-content/uploads/2020/04/Billion-Board-Foot-Club-20-04-27.pdf [Published April 27, 2020], I-2127

"Billionaire Rides Cooking Oil Dominance to Record China IPO." [online] from https://www.bloomberg.com/news/articles/2020-10-14/billionaire-rides-cooking-oil-dominance-to-record-chinese-ipo [Published October 15, 2020], I-1294

Biodiesel Magazine, I-497

"Bioenergy Europe Statistical Report 2019." [online] from https://bioenergyeurope.org/statistical-report.html [Accessed October 10, 2020], II-3591

"Biofuels Annual." [online] from https://apps.fas.usda.gov/newgainapi/api/Report/DownloadReportByFileName?fileName=Biofuels%20Annual_The%20Hague_European%20Union_06-29-2020 [Published June 29, 2020], I-498, 500

"Biofuels Annual." [online] from https://www.fas.usda.gov/data/china-biofuels-annual-6 [Published July 31, 2020], I-499

"Bioplastics Market Data." [online] from https://www.european-bioplastics.org/market/ [Accessed September 16, 2020], I-502

"Biotechnology in Europe." [online] from http://www.globaldata.com [Published December 2019], I-503

Birmingham Business Journal, II-2348

"Blow Molded Plastic Packaging Market Trends." [online] from http://www.beroeinc.com [Accessed October 2, 2020], II-2724

"BofA: Auto Parts Retailers Have Strong Margin in $300B Market." [online] from https://www.benzinga.com/analyst-ratings/analyst-color/20/09/17702804/bofa-auto-parts-retailers-have-strong-margins-in-300b-market [Published September 29, 2020], I-310

"Boise Cascade Company Investor Presentation." [online] from https://www.bc.com/portal/investor-relations/presentations/ [Published November 2020], I-1241, II-3588

"Book Stores Industry (U.S.)." [online] from http://www.plunkettresearch.com [Published March 4, 2021], I-518

The Boston Globe, I-769

"Bottled Water Market in China." [online] from https://daxueconsulting.com/bottled-water-market-in-china/ [Published May 30, 2020], I-538

"Bottled Water Volume Grows 3.6% Globally." [online] from https://www.foodbusinessnews.net/articles/16071-bottled-water-volume-grows-52-globally [Published May 20, 2020], I-535, 2003, II-3151

"BPGIC Investor Presentation." [online] from https://sec.report/Document/0001213900-19-024529/ [Published November 2019], II-2494

"Breakfast, Back on the Menu." [online] from https://www.earnestresearch.com/data-bites/breakfast-back-on-the-menu/ [Published March 18, 2021], II-2878

"Brief Consumer: The Online Fashion Wars: Rakuten Takes on Zozo and More." [online] from https://www.smartkarma.com/home/daily-briefs/brief-consumer-the-online-fashion-wars-rakuten-takes-on-zzozo-and-more/ [Published Nov. 19, 2019], I-215

"Brief Industrials: Weichai Power, Engine Power Retained and More." [online] from https://www.smartkarma.com/home/daily-briefs/brief-industrials-weichai-power-2338-hk-engine-power-regained-and-more/ [Published February 17, 2020], I-308

"Bright Prospects for China's Cold Chain Logistics Sector." [online] from https://ld-investments.com/author/ld_investments/ [Accessed August 25, 2020], II-3496

"Bringing Skilled People Together to Build the Future." [online] from https://www.sthree.com/en/investors/financial-results/ [Published November 21, 2019], II-3227

"Broadcom/Symantec Enterprise Regulation Merger Procedure." [online] from http://www.ec.europa.eu [Published October 30, 2019], II-3167

"Browser Market Share China - 2020." [online] from https://gs.statcounter.com/browser-market-share/all/china#yearly-2020-2020-bar [Accessed January 3, 2021], II-3156

"Browser Market Share United States of America - 2020." [online] from https://gs.statcounter.com/browser-market-share/all/united-states-of-america#yearly-2020-2020-bar [Accessed January 3, 2021], II-3155

"Browser Market Share Worldwide - 2020." [online] from https://gs.statcounter.com/browser-market-share#yearly-2020-2020-bar [Accessed January 3, 2021], II-3157

"Bryce Briefing Q4 2020." [online] from https://brycetech.com/briefing [Accessed March 22, 2021], II-2966

"Bubble Packaging." [online] from http://www.freedoniagroup.com [Published July 2020], II-2557

Building Design + Construction, I-863, 865-868

Business Insurance, I-1909-1912, 1914, 1951

Business Standard, I-223, 899

"Butter Production and Consumption: Summary for Selected Countries." [online] from https://apps.fas.usda.gov/psdonline/app/index.html#/app/downloads [Published July 2020], I-577, 580

"BYD - A Hidden Giant in the Cave." [online] from https://www.cmbi.com/article/4526.html?lang=en [Published July 23, 2020], I-349, 467

"Cabinets." [online] from http://www.freedoniagroup.com [Published February 2020], I-582

"California Auto Outlook." [online] from https://www.cncda.org/news/?category=auto-outlook [Published February 2021], I-364

"Cameras and Computing for Surveillance and Security." [online] from http://www.yole.fr [Press release September 2020], I-593

"Can Brickworks Succeed in the North American Brick Market?" [online] from https://www.capitalisticman.com/can-brickworks-succeed-in-the-north-american-brick-market/ [Published November 28, 2019], I-560

"Can the American Casket Monopoly Be Disrupted?" [online] from https://thehustle.co/casket-industry-monopoly-batesville/ [Published December 2019], I-618

"Canada's Health Functional Food Market Rising With Corona 19." [online] from http://www.news.kotra.or.kr [Published April 13, 2021], I-1386

Canadian Grocer, II-2968

"Canadian Hue Cosmetic Market Trend." [online] from http://www.news.kotra.or.kr [Published July 7, 2020], I-977

"Canadian Sanitary Tissue Market Trend." [online] from http://www.news.kotra.or.kr [Published August 14, 2020], II-2945

"Canalys: Tablets and Chromebooks Set All-Time High Shipment Records in Q4 2020." [online] from https://www.canalys.com/newsroom/tablets-chromebooks-q4-2020 [Press release January 28, 2021], I-795-796, 799

"Canalys: TWS Shipments to Exceed 200 Million in 2020." [online] from https://www.canalys.com/newsroom/canalys-tws-smart-audio-shipments-Q1-2020 [Press release June 18, 2020], I-284

"Candy & Snack Food Pouches." [online] from http://www.freedoniagroup.com [Published November 2020], II-2558

Candy Industry, I-835-837, 851-852, 1712

Car Dealer, I-338

"Car Sales in India for the Year 2020. Maruti Manages to Grab 50% Market Share." [online] from https://www.autopunditz.com/car-sales-in-india-for-the-year-2020-maruti-manages-to-grab-50-market-share/ [Published January 12, 2021], I-366

Car Wash Magazine, I-614

"Carbon Fiber and Graphene Manufacturing in the U.S." [online] from http://www.ibisworld.com [Published October 2019], I-612

"Cardboard Box and Container Manufacturing." [online] from http://www.ibisworld.com [Published June 2020], I-546

"Carded Nonwovens." [online] from http://www.freedoniagroup.com [Published November 2020], II-2439

"Carrier Intelligence Report." [online] from https://www.ipc.be/sector-data/reports-library/cir [Published March 2020], I-1182

"Case M.9434 - UTC/Raytheon." [online] from https://ec.europa.eu/competition/elojade/isef/case_details.cfm?proc_code=2_M_9434 [Published March 13, 2020], I-1667-1668, II-2829

"Casper." [online] from http://www.s24.q4cdn.com.CSPR-Investor-Presentation [Published June 2020], II-3097

"Casper's S-1 Investor Relations." [online] from https://www.earnestresearch.com/caspers-s-1-investor-insomnia/ [Published February 3, 2020], I-1543

Casual Living, I-1564

"Cattle." [online] from https://usda.library.cornell.edu/concern/publications/h702q636h?locale=en [Published January 29, 2021], I-620

"Cattle on Feed." [online] from https://usda.library.cornell.edu/concern/publications/m326m174z?locale=en [Published January 2021], I-624

"Cell Phone 4 Quarters Ending Q3 2020." [online] from http://www.traqline.com [Published November 3, 2020], I-628

"Cellular Connected Industrial Machine Shipments to Grow 43% CAGR till 2025." [online] from http://www.counterpointresearch.com [Press release April 22, 2019], I-642

Ceramic World Review, I-655-657, II-2958

Chain Drug Review, I-1113, 1149, II-3143-3146, 3489

"Chain Link Fencing." [online] from http://www.freedoniagroup.com [Published July 2020], I-1304

"The Charging Service Industry Hasn't Formed a Steady Market Structure in China." [online] from http://www.iresearchchina.com/content/details7_58008.html [Published October 16, 2019], I-155

Charlotte Business Journal, I-1683

"Chart: The P&I Thinking Ahead Institute World 500 Largest Money Managers." [online] from https://www.pionline.com/specialreports/worlds-largest-asset-managers [Published August 19, 2020], I-1981

"Chart: Top CBD Sales Channels in 2020." [online] from https://hemp-industrydaily.com/chart-top-cbd-sales-channels/ [Published March 15, 2021], I-598

Cheers, I-2090-2091, II-3545-3546

"Cheese Production and Consumption: Summary for Selected Countries." [online] from https://apps.fas.usda.gov/psdonline/app/index.html#/app/downloads [Published July 2020], I-678-679

"Chemical Wholesaling in the U.S." [online] from http://www.ibisworld.com [Published December 2019], I-682

"Chicken Meat Production - Top Countries Summary." [online] from https://apps.fas.usda.gov/psdonline/app/index.html#/app/downloads [Published October 2020], II-2188-2190, 2192

"China - 9.4% Plug-In Vehicle Share in Another Record Month." [online] from https://cleantechnica.com/2021/01/24/china-9-4-plugin-vehicle-share-in-another-record-month/ [Published January 24, 2021], I-333

"China Animal Vaccine Industry Report, 2019-2025." [online] from http://www.researchinchina.com [Published February 2020], II-3464

"China Apparel Market Series." [online] from https://www.fbic-group.com/sites/default/files/CAMS_Issue01.pdf [Published December 2020], I-207

"China Beer and White Wine Sector." [online] from https://www.cmbi.com/upload/202011/20201109416735.pdf [Published November 9, 2020], II-3547

"China Body Shower Gel Market Trends." [online] from http://news.kotra.or.kr [Published September 15, 2020], II-3141

China Chemical Reporter, II-2734, 2738

"China Cosmetics Industry." [online] from http://www.news.kotra.or.kr [Published August 13, 2020], I-970

"China Dairy and Beverages: A Hungry Thirst." [online] from https://www.spglobal.com/_assets/documents/ratings/research/100049639.pdf [Published March 18, 2021], I-1032

"China Electric Oven Market Trend." [online] from http://www.news.kotra.or.kr [Published October 16, 2020], I-236

China Fastener World, I-1882

"China Food Processing Equipment Market Trends." [online] from http://www.news.kotra.or.kr [Published September 15, 2020], I-245

"China Forecast to Represent 22% of the Foundry Market in 2020." [online] from https://www.icinsights.com/news [Press release October 13, 2020], II-3015

"China GM Report 2020." [online] from https://static1.squarespace.com/static/583cff1a59cc68a8c3ce896f/t/5f8feca46239e53ac2dcb420/1603267846724/2020+China+GA+Report+EN_Final_Web2.pdf [Accessed February 11, 2021], I-57, 60, 71-72

"China Industry Information." [online] from http://www.news.kotra.or.kr [Published June 5, 2020], II-3491

"China is Nintendo's Secret Weapon in War With PlayStation, Xbox." [online] from https://finance.yahoo.com/news/china-nintendo-secret-weapon-war-210000850.html [Published December 9, 2020], II-3477

"China Pet Food Market Growth, Trends, and Forecast (2020-2025)." [online] from http://www.mordorintelligence.com [Accessed January 5, 2021], II-2695

"China Pharma Forecast 2019-2023." [online] from https://pharmaboardroom.com/facts/china-pharma-forecast-2019-2023/ [Published July 2019], I-1118

"China Portable Gas Range Market Trends." [online] from http://www.news.kotra.or.kr [Published August 28, 2020], I-247

"China Printer Market Trend." [online] from http://www.news.kotra.or.kr [Published November 18, 2020], I-787

"China Railway System and Communication." [online] from https://pdf.dfcfw.com/pdf/H3_AP202006041382253833_1.pdf?1591264893000.pdf [Published June 3, 2020], II-2832, 2836

"China Retail Highlights & Insights." [online] from http://www.fbicgroup.com/sites/default/files/ChinaRetailInsights_04Aug2020.pdf [Published August 4, 2020], I-220

"China Sewage Sludge Treatment Market Trends." [online] from http://news.kotra.or.kr [Published September 15, 2020], II-3040

"China Snack Food Market Trend." [online] from http://www.news.kotra.or.kr [Published May 28, 2020], II-3132

"China Sunglasses Market Trend." [online] from http://www.news.kotra.or.kr [Published December 8, 2020], II-3261

"China Ventilator Market Trend." [online] from http://www.news.kotra.or.kr [Published December 15, 2020], II-2256

"China Widens its Lead in China's Server Market." [online] from https://technology.informa.com/AboutUs/PressReleases [Press release July 30, 2020], II-3037

"China's Baby Wipes Market is Driven by Consumption Upgrade." [online] from https://daxueconsulting.com/chinas-baby-wipes-market/ [Published October 28, 2020], II-3557

"China's Catering Market: Key Facts and Trends." [online] from http:/www.fbicgroup.com/sites/default/files/QuickTake-catering.pdf [Published February 2020], I-1416

"China's Centuries-old Plant Based Meat Industry Set for Growth." [online] from https://ld-investments.com/china-alternative-meat/ [Published October 21, 2020], II-3469

"China's Growing Seasoning Market." [online] from http://news.kotra.or.kr [Published September 24, 2020], II-2971

"China's Industrial Robot Market is Growing." [online] from http://www.news.kotra.or.kr [Published August 13, 2020], II-2925

"China's Love for Lipstick." [online] from https://graphics.reuters.com/CHINA-COSMETICS/yxmvjnlydvr/ [Accessed May 5, 2021], I-985

"China's Online K-12 Tutor Zuoyebang Collects USD 750 Million in Series E Round." [online] from https://kr-asia.com/key-stat-chinas-online-k-12-tutor-zuoyebang-collects-usd-750-million-in-series-e-round [Published June 3, 2020], I-257

"China's Outdoor Advertising Revenue is Estimated to Reach 71.15 Bn Yuan by 2021." [online] from http://www.iresearchchina.com/content/details7_56939.html [Published August 23, 2019], I-31

"China's Pharmaceutical Industry Will be the World's Largest in Under 10 Years." [online] from https://daxueconsulting.com/pharmaceutical-industry-china/ [Published February 9, 2021], I-1122

"China's Psychological Counseling Service Market Rises After Coronavirus." [online] from http://news.kotra.or.kr [Published September 22, 2020], I-1754

"China's Smartphone Market in 2020 Logs Sharpest Decline in 3 Years." [online] from https://www.counterpointresearch.com/chinas-smartphone-market-in-2020/ [Press release January 29, 2021], I-638

"China's Top eCommerce Players Increase Their Market Share in Disruptive Year for Retail." [online] from https://www.furninfo.com/Furniture%20Industry%20News/11926 [Published June 17, 2020], I-1179

"Chinese Bakery Industry Market Status." [online] from http://www.news.kotra.or.kr [Published February 5, 2021], I-382

"The Chinese Beverage Market: How Health Trends Shape Drink Preferences." [online] from https://daxueconsulting.com/beverage-market-in-china/ [Published March 9, 2021], I-489, 1236

"Chinese Convenience Food Market Trend." [online] from http://www.news.kotra.or.kr [Published August 7, 2020], I-1384

"Chinese Dishwashing Liquid Market Trend." [online] from http://www.news.kotra.or.kr [Published June 2, 2020], I-1063

"Chinese Escape Room Café Trends." [online] from http://www.news.kotra.or.kr [Published March 15, 2021], I-1254

"Chinese Foot Care Market Trend." [online] from http://www.news.kotra.or.kr [Published July 28, 2020], II-3089

"Chinese Market Undergoing Drastic Change Through Coronavirus Crisis." [online] from https://www.seafoodsource.com/news/foodservice-retail/chinese-market-undergoing-drastic-change-through-coronavirus-crisis [Published June 11, 2020], I-1468

"Chinese Panel Makers Expected to Occupy More Than 50% Share in Monitor Panel Market in 2021 Through Production Capacity Advantages, Says TrendForce." [online] from https://www.trendforce.com/presscenter/news/20201015-10511.html [Press release October 15, 2020], II-2600-2601

"Chinese Sneakers Market Trend." [online] from http://www.news.kotra.or.kr [Published July 15, 2020], I-1430

"Chinese Soy Sauce Market Trend." [online] from http://www.news.kotra.or.kr [Published April 2, 2020], II-2973

"Chinese Suppliers Take Top Three Spots in TV Panel Shipment Ranking, With Combined Shipment of More Than 50% of All Suppliers, Says TrendForce." [online] from https://www.trendforce.com/presscenter/news/20210409-10747.html [Press release April 9, 2021], II-2602

"Chinese Women's Wear Market Trend." [online] from http://www.news.kotra.or.kr [Published December 1, 2020], I-212

"Chromebooks Outsold Macs Worldwide in 2020, Cutting into Windows Market Share." [online] from https://www.geekwire.com/2021/chromebooks-outsold-macs-worldwide-2020-cutting-windows-market-share/ [Published January 16, 2021], II-3179

"CICC Yunda Holding." [online] from http://www.pdf.dfcfw.com [Published December 3, 2019], II-3067

Cincinnati Business Courier, I-1685

"Citrus: World Markets and Trade." [online] from https://apps.fas.usda.gov/psdonline/circulars/citrus.pdf [Published July 2020], I-1521-1524, 2008-2009

"Class I Railroads." [online] from https://www.american-rails.com/class.html#gallery[pageGallery]/5/ [Accessed March 10, 2021], II-2839

"Clean Vehicle Market Share Trends." [online] from https://energycenter.org/thought-leadership/research-and-reports/clean-vehicle-market-share-trends-report [Accessed December 10, 2020], I-368

Club Business International, I-1722

"CMI Shipments Report 2018-2019." [online] from https://www.cancentral.com/media/publications/2019-cmi-annual-and-can-shipments-report [Published December 10, 2020], II-2281

"Coal 2020." [online] from https://www.iea.org/reports/coal-2020 [Published December 2020], I-742-743, 748

Coatings World, I-10

CoatingsTech, II-2587, 2590, 2592

"Coconut Water Hype Fades Away as U.S. Consumer Tastes Change." [online] from https://www.bloomberg.com/news/articles/2020-11-13/coconut-water-hype-fades-away-as-u-s-consumer-tastes-change [Published November 13, 2020], I-537

"Coffee: World Markets and Trade." [online] from https://apps.fas.usda.gov/psdonline/app/index.html#/app/downloads [Published June 2020], I-752, 756

"Cold Storage." [online] from https://www.nass.usda.gov/Surveys/Guide_to_NASS_Surveys/Cold_Storage/index.php [Published January 25, 2021], II-3497

"The Collaborative Robot Market 2021-28; Grounds for Optimism After a Turbulent Two Years." [online] from https://www.interactanalysis.com/the-collaborative-robot-market-2021-28-grounds-for-optimism-after-a-turbulent-two-years/ [Accessed February 10, 2021], II-2927

The College Store Magazine, I-516-517

"Colorado Ranks Seventh Among States With Most Energy Production." [online] from https://www.eia.gov/todayinenergy/detail.php?id=44476 [Published July 23, 2020], I-1233

Columbus Business First, I-1682

"Comment System." [online] from http://www.datanyze.com/marketshare [Accessed November 10, 2020], II-3158

Commercial Baking, I-383

"Commercial Market Outlook 2020-2039." [online] from https://www.boeing.com/commercial/market/commercial-market-outlook/ [Accessed October 22, 2020], I-58-59

"Commercial Roofing." [online] from http://www.freedoniagroup.com [Published September 2020], II-2929

"Commercial Satellite Ground Segment, 4th Edition." [online] from http://www.nsr.com [Published December 2019], II-2960

"Comparing Bitcoin's Market Cap to Other Cryptocurrencies." [online] from https://www.visualcapitalist.com/bitcoin-market-cap-compared-to-crypto/ [Published January 13, 2021], I-1028

Composites Manufacturing, I-611

"Computer Peripheral Manufacturing in the U.S." [online] from http://www.ibisworld.com [Published May 2020], I-788

"Conduit Pipe." [online] from http://www.freedoniagroup.com [Published January 2021], II-2718

"Connected Car Shipments for Europe Hit the Expressway." [online] from https://www.counterpointresearch.com/connected-car-shipments-for-europe-hit-expressway/ [Published November 20, 2020], I-340

"Consolidation in the Dairy Farming Industry." [online] from https://www.ers.usda.gov/publications/pub-details/?pubid=98900 [Published July 2020], I-1288

"Construction Machinery Manufacturing in the U.S." [online] from http://www.ibisworld.com [Published February 2020], I-856

"Consumer Electronics Infographic." [online] from http://www.traqline.com [Published November 3, 2020], I-883

"Consumer Electronics Stores in the U.S." [online] from http://www.ibisworld.com [Published July 2019], I-901

"Consumer Furniture and Appliance Rentals Industry (U.S.)." [online] from http://www.plunkettresearch.com [Published March 4, 2021], II-2870

"Consumer Product Pouches." [online] from http://www.freedoniagroup.com [Published November 2020], II-2559

"Consumer Water Filtration." [online] from http://www.freedoniagroup.com [Published April 2021], II-3508

Contact Lens Spectrum, I-903

Control, I-322

Convenience Store Decisions, II-2637

Convenience Store News, I-933, 935

Converting Quarterly, I-2019

"Conveyancing Services in the U.S." [online] from http://www.ibisworld.com [Published July 2019], I-944

"CooperCompanies Investor Presentation." [online] from https://investor.coopercos.com/static-files/ef18c70e-45e9-4ee6-a49a-a284abc5d624 [Published March 4, 2021], I-904

"Cordless Power Tool Leader Driven by Technological Innovations, Initiate With Accumulate." [online] from http://wwww.gtja.com [Published November 12, 2020], II-3383

"Cornerstone Building Brands Investor Presentation." [online] from https://investors.cornerstonebuildingbrands.com/investor-home/default.aspx [Published November 2020], I-566, 1860

"Corona 19 Accelerates U.S. Mobile Game Market Growth." [online] from http://www.news.kotra.or.kr [Published February 10, 2021], II-2332

"Coronavirus Could Push Back-to-School Spending to Record Level as Uncertain Families Gear Up for At-Home Learning." [online] from https://nrf.com/media-center/press-releases/coronavirus-could-push-back-school-spending-record-level-uncertain [Published July 15, 2020], II-2899-2900

"Coronavirus to Increase Pressure on China's Already Vulnerable Travel Sector." [online] from https://equalocean.com/analysis/2020012813468 [Published January 28, 2020], II-2521

"COSCO Shipping Holding." [online] from http://pdf.dfcfw.com/pdf/H3_AP202008041396393109_1.pdf [Published August 4, 2020], II-3060, 3062

"Cotton: World Markets and Trade." [online] from https://apps.fas.usda.gov/psdonline/circulars/cotton.pdf [Published October 2020], I-992-995

"Cotton Ginnings." [online] from https://usda.library.cornell.edu/concern/publications/6108vb275 [Published March 2021], I-991

"Countertops." [online] from http://www.freedoniagroup.com [Published February 2020], I-997

Countertops & Architectural Surfaces, I-996

"The Countries Most Reliant on Cash in 2021." [online] from https://merchantmachine.co.uk/most-reliant-on-cash/ [Published February 2, 2021], I-1184

"County Business Patterns." [online] from https://www.census.gov/programs-surveys/cbp/data/datasets.html [Published April 22, 2021], I-1161, 1558, 1762, 2058, II-2857, 2871-2872, 2974, 2976, 2981, 3008, 3311, 3451

"COVID-19 Impact on Global Cooling Fan Market Size Status and Forecast 2020-2026." [online] from http://reports.valuates.com [Published April 2020], I-1276

"COVID-19 Impact on Global Dog Apparel Market Share Status and Forecast 2020-2026." [online] from http:/reports.valuates.com [Published April 2020], II-2685

"COVID-19 Impact on Global Gas Alarm Market Size, Status and Forecast 2020-2026." [online] from http://reports.valuates.com [Published April 2020], II-2996

"COVID-19 Impact on Global Gift Cards Market Size, Status and Forecast 2020-2026." [online] from http://www.qyresearch.com [Published April 2020], I-1618

"COVID-19 Impact on Global In-Flight Entertainment (IFE) Market Size, Status and Forecast 2020-2026." [online] from https://reports.valuates.com [Published April 2020], I-1878

"COVID-19 Impact on Global Indoor Air Quality (IAQ) Market Size, Status and Forecast 2020-2026." [online] from http://reports.valuates.com [Published April 2020], I-1879

"COVID-19 Impact on Global KVM Switches Market Size, Status and Forecast 2020-2026." [online] from http://reports.valuates.com [Published April 2020], II-2428

"COVID-19 Impact on Global Linear Shower Drain Market Size, Status and Forecast 2020-2026." [online] from http://reports.valuates.com [Published April 2020], II-2759

"COVID-19 Impact on Global Manhole Covers Market Size Status and Forecast 2020-2026." [online] from http://reports.valuates.com [Published April 2020], II-2144

"COVID-19 Impact on Global Outboard Electric Motor Market Insights, Forecast to 2026." [online] from http://reports.valuates.com [Published May 2020], I-1242

"COVID-19 Impact on Global Pipe Wrenches Market Size, Status and Forecast 2020-2026." [online] from http://reports.valuates.com [Published April 2020], II-3389

"COVID-19 Impact on Global Sports Footwear Market Size, Status and Forecast 2020-2026." [online] from http://reports.valuates.com [Published April 2020], I-1429

"COVID-19 Impact on Global Storage System Market Size, Status and Forecast 2020-2026." [online] from http://reports.valuates.com [Published April 2020], I-1587

"COVID-19 Impact on Global Tape Measures Market Size Status and Forecast 2020-2026." [online] from http://reports.valuates.com [Published April 2020], II-3295

"COVID-19 Impact on Global Varicella Vaccine Market Insights, Forecast to 2026." [online] from http://www.qyresearch.com [Published May 2020], II-3463

"COVID-19 Impact on Global Voice and Flight Data Recorder Market Size, Status and Forecast 2020-2026." [online] from http://reports.valuates.com [Published April 2020], I-81

"COVID-19 Impact on Global Weather Forecasting Services Market Size Status and Forecast 2020-2026." [online] from http://reports.valuates.com [Published April 2020], II-3522

"COVID-19 Impact on Global Wedding Dress Market Share Status and Forecast 2020-2026." [online] from http://reports.valuates.com [Published August 2020], I-209

"Covid and Convenience-Confirming Opportunities in E-Retail Market." [online] from https://www.fas.usda.gov/data/taiwan-covid-and-convenience-confirming-opportunities-e-retail-market [Published April 10, 2021], I-1181

"CPVC Pipe and Fitting Market Size 2021-2026." [online] from https://www.marketwatch.com/press-release/cpvc-pipe-and-fitting-market-size-2021-2026-top-leading-countries-companies-consumption-drivers-trends-forces-analysis-revenue-challenges-and-forcast-2026-2021-03-04 [Published March 4, 2021], II-2721

"Credit Suisse 2020 Latin American Conference." [online] from https://s1.q4cdn.com/987436133/files/doc_presentations/pt/2020.01.28-Credit-Suisse-2020-Latin-America-Investment-Conference.pdf [Published January 2020], II-2815

CRN, II-3038

"Crop Production." [online] from https://www.nass.usda.gov/Publications/Todays_Reports/reports/crop1020.pdf [Published October 9, 2020], II-3374

Crossties, II-3576

"Crowdfunding Statistics Worldwide: Market Development, Country Volumes, and Industry Trends." [online] from https://p2pmarketdata.com/crowdfunding-statistics-worldwide/ [Published May 16, 2020], I-1022

CSI Magazine, II-2629

CSP, I-477, 485, II-3373

Culinology, I-600

"Culp Investor Overview." [online] from https://culpinc.gcs-web.com/static-files/e30b2693-26da-4983-9a16-4cf9aeabcf2d [Published September 2020], I-1552

"Cybersecurity and U.S. Election Infrastructure." [online] from https://foreignpolicy.com/2020/10/27/election-cybersecurity-cyberattack-critical-infrastructure-voting/ [Published October 27, 2020], II-3492

"Dairy: World Markets and Trade." [online] from https://apps.fas.usda.gov/psdonline/circulars/dairy.pdf [Published July 2020], I-578-579, 669-670, II-2312-2313

Dairy Foods, I-576, 673, 680, 1872, 1874, II-2315-2316, 3198

"Data Center Colocation Market." [online] from https://www.t4.ai/industry/data-center-colocation-market [Published February 18, 2020], I-772

"Dating App Revenue and Usage Statistics (2021)." [online] from https://www.businessofapps.com/data/dating-app-market/ [Published March 10, 2021], I-253-254

"dbAccess Berlin Conference 2020." [online] from https://www.infineon.com/dgdl/2020-06-03+dbAccess+Berlin+Conference.pdf?fileId=5546d461724f4ecc01727554b6ca001d [Published June 2020], I-1958-1961

Dealerscope, I-902

"Debt Collection Agencies in the U.S." [online] from http://www.ibisworld.com [Published June 2019], I-1041

"Decarbonizing The U.S.'s Yellow School Bus Fleet: A Policy Worth Pursuing?" [online] from https://www.interactanalysis.com/decarbonising-the-us-yellow-school-bus-fleet-a-policy-worth-pursuing/ [Published November 19, 2020], I-301

Defense News, I-274, 1048

"DEG: 2020 Consumer Spending on Home Entertainment Up to 21% to $30 Billion." [online] from https://www.degonline.org/deg-year-end-report-consumer-spending-on-digital-sales-rentals-rises-

30-billion-2020-2/ [Press release January 27, 2021], I-1247

"Delivering Value Delivering Commitments." [online] from https://ence.es/wp-content/uploads/2020/03/03.20-Corporate-Presentation-ENG.pdf [Published March 2020], II-2814, 2816

"Denmark Exporter Guide." [online] from https://gain.fas.usda.gov [Published March 16, 2020], I-1688

"Denver-area Grocery Stores, Ranked by 2020 Market Share." [online] from https://www.bizjournals.com/denver/news/2020/10/22/denver-area-grocery-stores-market-share.html#g/472799/1 [Published October 22, 2020], I-1689

"Department Stores (Except Discount Department Stores Industry (U.S.)." [online] from http://www.plunkettresearch.com [Published March 4, 2021], I-1056

"Deposit Market Share Report." [online] from https://www7.fdic.gov/sod/sodMarketBank.asp?barItem=2 [Accessed September 24, 2020], I-404-459

"Designer Brands Inc. Corporate Update." [online] from https://www.sec.gov/Archives/edgar/data/1319947/000131994720000057/designerbrandsinccorpora.htm [Published July 2020], I-1431-1432, 1434

"Despite a Decline in 2Q2020, the Smart Home Market is Expected to Rebound in the Second Half of the Year in EMEA, says IDC." [online] from http://www.idc.com [Press release October 12, 2020], II-3105

"Detroit Casinos: Monthly Statistics." [online] from http://gaming.unlv.edu [Published February 2021], I-1568

"Deutsche Post DHL Group 2021 Business Profile." [online] from https://www.dpdhl.com/content/dam/dpdhl/de/media-center/investors/documents/business-profiles/DPDHL-Business-Profile-2021.pdf [Published March 2021], II-3430

"The Diamond Insight Report 2020." [online] from https://www.debeersgroup.com/reports/insights/the-diamond-insight-report-2020/value-chain/upstream [Accessed February 15, 2021], I-1073

"Differential Thermal Analysis (DTA) Market 2020: Top Countries Data, Market Size, Share Analysis to 2026." [online] from https://www.marketwatch.com/press-release/differential-thermal-analysis-dta-market-2020-top-countries-data-market-size-share-analysis [Press release August 18, 2020], I-1077

"Digital Ad Spending 2021." [online] from https://www.emarketer.com/content/china-digital-ad-spending-2021-forecast [Accessed April 16, 2021], I-20

"Digital Cameras Market Share: Canon is King, Fujifilm Stable 4th, Nikon is Falling. Olympus is Out." [online] from http://ww.fujirumors.com/tag/nikon [Published August 14, 2020], I-595

"Direct Mail." [online] from https://www.rab.com/whyradio/mfdetailsUpdate.cfm?theCat=Direct%20Mail [Accessed March 3, 2021], I-22

"Direct Selling Companies in the United States." [online] from http://www.ibisworld.com [Published June 2019], I-1080

Direct Selling News, I-1082

"Directory & Database Publishers in the United States." [online] from http://www.ibisworld.com [Published March 2019], I-1085

"Disney+ to Add 112 Million Subscribers." [online] from http://www.digitaltvresearch.com/products [Press release November 2020], II-2553

"Document Management Services in the U.S." [online] from http://www.ibisworld.com [Published August 2019], I-1090

"Documentary Increases Stably in China." [online] from http://www.iresearchchina.com/content/details7_57986.html [Published October 15, 2019], II-2354

"Doing Business in Europe." [online] from https://www.ubs.com/global/en/wealth-management/chief-investment-office/life-goals/executives-and-entrepreneurs/2020/doing-business-in-europe-opportunities.html [Published July 9, 2020], I-323-324

"Dollar General: Local Monopoly Generates Big Returns." [online] from https://seekingalpha.com/article/4377768-dollar-general-local-monopoly-generates-big-returns [Published October 6, 2020], I-1091

"Domestic Box Office for 2020." [online] from https://www.boxofficemojo.com/year/2020/?ref_=bo_lnav_hm_shrt [Accessed January 5, 2021], II-2359

"Domo Investment Group/Solvay Performance Polyamides Business in the EEA Regulation Merger Procedure." [online] from http://www.ec.europa.eu [Published November 26, 2019], II-2732

Door & Window, II-3538

"DraftKings Investor Presentation." [online] from http://eagleinvestmentpartners.com/wp-content/uploads/2020/01/DK-Investor-Presentation-13-Jan-2020.pdf [Published January 2020], I-1571, 1580

"Drain, Waste and Vent Pipe." [online] from http://www.freedoniagroup.com [Published October 2020], II-2719

"Drone Market Shares in the USA After China-U.S. Disputes." [online] from https://droneii.com/drone-market-shares-usa-after-china-usa-disputes [Published March 2, 2021], II-3455

DrugStore Management, I-374, 468, 663, 709, 973-974, 976, 980, 982, 984, 1146-1148, 1153-1154, 1157, 1734, 1736, II-2272, 2529, 2654-2655, 2657-2658, 3090, 3092, 3294, 3488, 3595

"E-Commerce Platform." [online] from http://www.datanyze.com/market-share [Accessed November 10, 2020], II-3160

"The E-sports Hotel Market in China Has Tremendous Potential: 5-fold Growth from 2019 to 2020." [online] from https://daxueconsulting.

com/e-sports-hotel-market-in-china/ [Published April 6, 2021], I-1826

"Eastern Europe to Add 16 Million SVOD Subs." [online] from http://www.digitaltvresearch.com/products [Press release September 2020], II-2542

"Ecommerce Growth in 202: Global Digital Shopping Performance Report." [online] from https://www.semrush.com/blog/2020-global-digital-shopping-performance-report/ [Published January 27, 2021], I-256

"Economic Census." [online] from https://www.census.gov/content/census/en/data/tables/2017/econ/economic-census/naics-sector-31-33.html [Accessed January 21, 2021], I-1, 8, 50, 158, 173, 175, 177, 186, 263, 279, 281, 313-316, 381, 460, 471, 474-475, 505, 515, 543, 562, 574-575, 683, 733, 775-777, 779-780, 784, 804-807, 859, 876, 937, 946, 950, 999, 1026-1027, 1035-1036, 1055, 1065-1066, 1084, 1098, 1160, 1205, 1208, 1210, 1250, 1259, 1262, 1266, 1268, 1271, 1274-1275, 1277, 1301, 1318, 1325, 1445, 1447, 1455, 1494-1495, 1547, 1554, 1559, 1591, 1622-1623, 1625, 1707, 1709, 1738, 1740, 1755-1760, 1767, 1778, 1794, 1867, 1880, 1888, 1892, 1895, 1902, 1976, 1995, 2013, 2023, 2031, 2049, 2053, 2057, 2066, 2080, 2082, 2112, II-2148, 2232, 2257, 2280, 2283, 2287, 2293, 2300, 2323, 2328, 2345, 2366, 2377, 2532, 2576, 2580-2581, 2593, 2616, 2618, 2706-2709, 2713, 2717, 2736, 2748, 2757, 2791-2792, 2804, 2853, 2855, 2858, 2864-2865, 2868, 2873, 2877, 2913, 2932, 2934, 2978, 2992, 3042, 3046, 3073-3074, 3077, 3098, 3194, 3201, 3204, 3211, 3226, 3237, 3254, 3256, 3312, 3326, 3333, 3375, 3393, 3498, 3529, 3540, 3608

"Economic Census." [online] from https://www.census.gov/programs-surveys/economic-census/data/tables.html [Accessed December 2, 2020], I-157, 174, 217, 278, 280, 506, 778, 949, 1000, 1030, 1054, 1076, 1083, 1211, 1267, 1368, 1444, 1446, 1553, 1675, 1777, 1881, 1891, 1977, 2022, 2032, 2048, 2056, 2079, 2083, II-2279, 2282, 2286, 2292, 2299, 2329, 2344, 2378, 2388, 2533, 2621, 2705, 2712, 2786, 2805, 2852, 2933, 2977, 3236, 3253, 3255, 3511-3512, 3527-3528, 3539

The Economist, II-3459

Editor & Publisher, I-259

"Education and Training Market Analysis: Immediate and Systemic Impact on COVID-19." [online] from http://www.williamblair.com [Published May 2020], I-1187, II-3408

"Egg Cartons." [online] from http://www.freedoniagroup.com [Published July 2020], II-2561

"EHR Supplier Base in EMEA Consolidates." [online] from https://www.prnewswire.com/news-releases/ehr-supplier-base-in-emea-consolidates-301211306.html [Published January 20, 2021], II-3190

"Electric Power Annual 2019." [online] from http://www.eia.gov [Published October 2020], I-1212, 1231

"Electric Wheelchair Market." [online] from https://centaurrobotics.com/wp-content/uploads/2020/07/Report_Global-Electric-Wheelchair-Market_Coherent-Market-Insights.pdf [Accessed April 21, 2021], II-2233

The Electrical Distributor, I-1261, 1566, II-2290, 2704, 2782, 2854, 3286, 3288, 3293, 3387, 3523

"Electricians in the U.S." [online] from http://www.ibisworld.com [Published July 2019], I-906

"Electricians in the United States." [online] from http://www.ibisworld.com [Published July 2019], I-914

"Elevators and Escalators." [online] from http://www.freedoniagroup.com [Published June 2020], I-1206

"Email Client Market Share." [online] from https://emailclientmarketshare.com/ [Accessed April 15, 2021], II-3161

"Emerald Holding." [online] from https://investor.emeraldx.com/Overview/default.aspx [Published December 2020], I-941

"Energy Star Windows, Doors, and Skylights Response to Comments." [online] from https://www.energystar.gov/partner_resources/products_partner_resources/public_notices [Published September 2020], II-3537

"Engineered Stone Countertops." [online] from http://www.freedoniagroup.com [Published May 2020], I-998

"Entertainment Industry Market Update." [online] from https://hl.com/about-us/insights/insights-article/?id=17179871911 [Published Summer 2020], II-2556

"eOne Annual Reports and Accounts 2018." [online] from http://investor.hasbro.com [Accessed November 17, 2020], II-3322

"ESPI Yearbook 2019." [online] from https://espi.or.at/publications/espi-yearbook [Accessed February 15, 2021], II-2964

"ESPI Yearbook 2020." [online] from https://espi.or.at/publications/espi-yearbook [Accessed June 15, 2021], II-3199

"EssilorLuxottica 2019 Universal Registration Document." [online] from http://www.essilorluxottica.com [Published April 2020], II-2523

"E.U. & U.K. Cinema Attendance Down by 70.7% in 2020 Amid Global Pandemic." [online] from https://www.obs.coe.int/en/web/observatoire/home [Published February 25, 2021], II-2384

Eurofish, I-1330

Eurofresh Distribution, I-1497, 1529

"Europcar Mobility Group Financial Restructuring Project." [online] from https://investors.europcar-group.com/static-files/bcdfd0b9-

dcca-4541-8de2-7c77d09a832d [Published December 28, 2020], I-312

"The European Brassiere, Girdle and Corset Market Peaked at $3.2B." [online] from https://www.indexbox.io/blog/brassiere-girdle-and-corset-market-in-the-eu-key-insights-2020/ [Published September 24, 2020], I-195

"European Fitness Market Continues to Grow." [online] from https://www.fibo.com/en/Business/European-fitness-market-continues-to-grow/n866/ [Published April 8, 2020], I-1721

"The European Medical Technology Industry in Figures 2020." [online] from https://www.medtecheurope.org/wp-content/uploads/2020/05/The-European-Medical-Technology-Industry-in-figures-2020.pdf [Accessed September 16, 2020], I-1067, II-2255

"European Pulp & Paper Industry Key Statistics 2019." [online] from https://www.cepi.org/key-statistics-2019/ [Accessed December 2, 2020], II-2613, 2819, 3590

"European Smartphone Market Down 14% YoY in 2020; Xiaomi Gains While Huawei and Samsung Lose." [online] from https://www.counterpointresearch.com/european-smartphone-market-2020/ [Published February 26, 2021], I-635

"The European Toy Market 2020 and Digital Trends 2021." [online] from https://globaltoynews.com/2021/02/05/the-european-toy-market-2020-and-digital-trends-2021/ [Published February 5, 2021], II-3395

"The European Wood Barrel Market Bounced Back to $1.2B." [online] from https://www.indexbox.io/blog/wood-barrel-market-in-the-eu-key-insights-2020/ [Published October 8, 2020], II-3589

"Evaluate Vantage 2021 Preview." [online] from https://www.evaluate.com/thought-leadership/vantage/evaluate-vantage-2021-preview [Published December 2020], I-1117

"EVRAZ Investor Presentation." [online] from https://www.evraz.com/en/investors/reports-and-results/presentations/#2020 [Published August 6, 2020], II-3244

"Exhibition Industry - Key Figures." [online] from https://www.auma.de/en/facts-and-figures/trade-fair-sector-key-figures [Accessed January 10, 2021], I-942

"Expedia Inc." [online] from https://www.biz.uiowa.edu/henry/download/f20_EXPE.pdf [Published November 13, 2020], II-3417

"Expert Witness Consulting Services in the U.S." [online] from http://www.ibisworld.com [Published July 2019], I-1260

"Facebook and YouTube Account for 49% of Online Video Ad Revenue in 2020." [online] from https://omdia.tech.informa.com/pr/pr-listing [Published February 11, 2021], I-30

"Facebook Takes Top Spot in AppsFlyer's Performance App Marketing Ranking." [online] from https://www.businessinsider.com/facebook-ranked-number-one-by-appsflyers-performance-index-2020 [Published October 16, 2020], I-28

"Facts & Figures 2019 European Review." [online] from https://fediaf.org/who-we-are/european-statistics.html [Accessed February 2, 2021], II-2691-2694, 2699

"Facts from IQVIA." [online] from http://www.iqvia.com [Accessed March 30, 2021], I-1134-1136

"Family Clothing Stores in the U.S." [online] from http://www.ibisworld.com [Published August 2019], I-213

F&L Magazine, I-154, 2118

"Farm Animal Feed Production in the U.S." [online] from http://www.ibisworld.com [Published March 2020], I-1884

Farm Equipment, I-1285

"Farms and Land in Farms 2020 Summary." [online] from http://www.nass.usda.gov/Publications/Todays_Reports/reports/fnlo0221.pdf [Published February 2021], I-1289

FDM+C, I-1544

Federal Computer Week, I-1665

Feed Strategy, I-1883,

"Fewer Guards, More Black Brands: Sephora's Plan to Win Back Shoppers." [online] from https://www.bloomberg.com/news/articles/2021-01-13/fewer-guards-more-black-brands-sephora-s-plan-to-win-back-shoppers [Published January 13, 2021], I-990

"Fiber Optic Cable Manufacturing in the U.S." [online] from http://www.ibisworld.com [Published October 2020], I-584

"File Sharing." [online] from http://www.datanyze.com/market-share [Accessed November 10, 2020], II-3162

"Filtration Nonwovens." [online] from http://www.freedoniagroup.com [Published November 2020], II-2440

"Finance Market Report Q2 2020." [online] from http://www.experian.com [Accessed December 1, 2020], I-353, 2100, 2102-2103, 2106-2107

Financial Express, II-2544

Financial Post, II-2969

Financial Times, I-1982

"Fingerprint Biometrics Machine Market 2021." [online] from http://www.qyresearch.com [Published February 2021], I-501

"Firearm and Ammunition Industry Economic Impact Report 2021." [online] from http://www.nssf.org/government-relations/impact [Accessed April 1, 2021], I-1714

"Fleece Jackets & Vests Market 2021." [online] from https://www.360researchreports.com/global-fleece-jackets-vests-market-15075693 [Published January 2020], I-184

Flight International, I-82, 1046-1047, 1049-1050, 1053

Floor Covering News, I-1340-1341, 1343, 1345, 1349-1350, 1353-1354, 1363-1365

Floor Covering Weekly, I-1342, 1346-1348, 1352

"Flooring Wood Panels." [online] from http://www.freedoniagroup.com [Published December 2020], I-1344

"Floriculture Crops 2019 Summary." [online] from http://www.nass.usda.gov [Published December 2020], I-1375-1378

"Florida Casinos: Monthly Slot Revenues." [online] from https://gaming.unlv.edu/reports.html [Published January 2021], I-1581

"FMI's North American Engineering and Construction Outlook." [online] from https://www.fminet.com/wp-content/uploads/2020/06/FMI_Q2_Outlook_2020.pdf [Accessed September 1, 2020], I-872-873, 875

"Focusing in on the Geared Motors and Solo Gearbox Market." [online] from https://www.interactanalysis.com/focusing-in-on-the-geared-motors-and-solo-gearbox-market/ [Published December 16, 2020], I-1594

Food Business News, I-1391

"Food Service - Hotel Restaurant International." [online] from https://www.fas.usda.gov [Published September 28, 2020], I-1418

Food Trade News, I-1704-1705, II-2907

"Food Trucks in the U.S." [online] from http://www.ibisworld.com [Published March 2020], II-2330

Food World, I-1703, 1706, II-2902

"Foodservice Single-Use Products." [online] from http://www.freedoniagroup.com [Published February 2020], II-2572

"Forecast International Sees New Perspective on Boeing and Airbus Competition." [online] from https://dsm.forecastinternational.com/wordpress/2020/04/10/forecast-international-sees-new-perspective-on-boeing-and-airbus-competition/ [Published April 10, 2020], I-67

"Former Pipe Factory Worker Becomes a Budget Store Billionaire." [online] from https://www.bloomberg.com/news/articles/2020-10-16/budget-retail-billionaire-emerges-as-virus-hits-global-spending [Published October 15, 2020], I-936

"Foundry Revenue Expected to Reach New High in 2021 with Close to 6% YoY Growth as Capacities Remain Scarce." [online] from https://www.trendforce.com/presscenter/news/20201229-10617.html [Press release December 29, 2020], I-1448

"Four Companies Made Up More Than 95% of Digital Restaurant Sales in 2020." [online] from https://www.emarketer.com/content/four-companies-made-up-more-than-95-of-digital-restaurant-sales [Published March 23, 2021], I-1402

"Fresh Food Sales in China." [online] from http://www.iresearchchina.com [Published November 16, 2020], I-1385

"Fresh Peaches and Cherries: World Markets and Trade." [online] from https://apps.fas.usda.gov/psdonline/circulars/StoneFruit.pdf [Published September 2020], I-1525-1526

Frozen & Refrigerated Buyer, I-378, 389-390, 548, 581, 671-672, 675-677, 1092-1096, 1190-1191, 1201, 1457-1467, 1469-1477, 1479-1482, 1486, 1869-1871, 2085, II-2147, 2186, 2230, 2309, 2311, 2317, 2626, 2649, 2785, 2812, 3534-3535

"Frozen Food Packaging." [online] from http://www.freedoniagroup.com [Published February 2021], II-2562

"Frozen Food Tubs, Cups & Bowls." [online] from http://www.freedoniagroup.com [Published February 2021], II-2563

"Frozen Specialty Food Packaging." [online] from http://www.freedoniagroup.com [Published February 2021], II-2564

"Fuel Forecourt Retail Market." [online] from https://assets.kpmg/content/dam/kpmg/ie/pdf/2020/09/ie-fuel-forecourt-retail-market.pdf [Published September 2020], I-1437-1443

"Funeral Homes, Cemeteries and Crematoriums Industry (U.S.)." [online] from http://www.plunkettresearch.com [Published March 5, 2021], I-1040

Furniture Today, I-1565, 1796, 1802

Future Power Technology, II-2715, 3290

"Future Retail." [online] from https://links.sgx.com/1.0.0/prospectus-circulars/37304 [Published January 14, 2020], I-1678

"Gallery: Engine OEM Market Share in 2021." [online] from https://aviationweek.com/mro/gallery-engine-oem-market-share-2021 [Accessed February 17, 2021], I-79

"Game Refinery Strategy Genre Snapshot." [online] from https://www.gamerefinery.com/strategy-genre-snapshot-report-september-2020/ [Published September 2020], II-3483

Games & Parks Industry, I-1188

"Gartner Forecasts Global Devices Installed Base to Reach 6.2 Billion Units in 2021." [online] from https://www.gartner.com/en/newsroom [Press release April 1, 2021], I-1064

"Gartner Forecasts Global Government IT Spending to Decline 0.6% in 2020." [online] from http://www.gartner.com [Press release August 5, 2020], I-1897

"Gartner Forecasts Global Spending on Wearable Devices to Total $81.5 Billion in 2021." [online] from http://www.gartner.com [Press release January 12, 2021], II-3517

"Gartner Forecasts Worldwide Banking and Securities IT Spending to Decline 4.7% in 2020 Before 2021 Rebound." [online] from http://www.gartner.com [Press release August 12, 2020], I-1896

"Gartner Forecasts Worldwide Public Cloud End-User Spending to Grow 23% in 2021." [online] from https://www.gartner.com/en/newsroom [Press release April 21, 2021], II-3187

"Gartner Forecasts Worldwide Security and Risk Management Spending Growth to Slow but Remain Positive in 2020." [online] from http://www.gartner.com [Press release June 17, 2020], II-2999

"Gartner Says Apple and Samsung Extended Their Lead as Top Semiconductor Customers in 2020." [online] from https://www.gartner.com/en/newsroom/press-releases/2021-02-09-gartner-says-apple-and-samsung-extended-their-lead-as [Press release February 9, 2021], II-3016

"Gartner Says Worldwide IT Spending to Grow 4% in 2021." [online] from https://www.gartner.com/en/newsroom [Press release October 20, 2020], I-1898

"Gartner Says Worldwide PC Shipments Grew 10.7% in Fourth Quarter of 2020 and 4.8% for the Year." [online] from https://www.gartner.com/en/newsroom/press-releases/2021-01-11-gartner-says-worldwide-pc-shipments-grew-10-point-7-percent-in-the-fourth-quarter-of-2020-and-4-point-8-percent-for-the-year [Press release January 11, 2021], I-798

"Gartner Says Worldwide Semiconductor Revenue Grew 7.3% in 2020." [online] from https://www.gartner.com/en/newsroom/press-releases/2021-01-14-gartner-says-worldwide-semiconductor-revenue-grew-7-percent-in-2020 [Press release January 14, 2021], II-3017

"Gartner Says Worldwide Smartphone Sales to Grow 11% in 2021." [online] from https://www.gartner.com/en/newsroom/press-releases/2021-02-03-gartner-says-worldwide-smartphone-sales-to-grow-11-percent-in-2021 [Press release February 3, 2021], I-632

"GATX Company Overview 2021." [online] from https://ir.gatx.com/events-and-presentations/presentations [Accessed May 5, 2021], I-2042-2044

"General Aviation Aircraft Shipment Report 2020 Year-End." [online] from https://gama.aero/news-and-events/press-releases/gama-announces-2020-year-end-aircraft-billing-and-shipment-numbers-2/ [Press release February 24, 2021], I-61

"Genius Sports Group." [online] from https://news.geniussports.com/wp-content/uploads/2020/10/GSG-Investor-Presentation.pdf [Published October 27, 2020], I-1585

"Genomma Labs Investor Presentation." [online] from https://inversionistas.genommalab.com/wp-content/uploads/2019/11/GENOMMALAB-Corporate-Presentation-November-2019.pdf [Published November 2019], I-373

"German EV Market Reaches Escape Velocity." [online] from https://cleantechnica.com/2021/01/08/german-ev-market-reaches-escape-velocity-record-27-share-in-december/ [Published January 9, 2021], I-326

"Ghost Kitchens Could be a $1T Global Market by 2030, Says Euromonitor." [online] from https://www.restaurantdive.com/news/ghost-kitchens-global-market-euromonitor/581374/ [Published July 10, 2020], II-2880

Gifts & Decorative Accessories, II-3235

"Giving USA 2020: Charitable Giving Showed Solid Growth, Climbing to $449.64 Billion in 2019, One of the Highest Years for Giving on Record." [online] from https://givingusa.org/giving-usa-2020-charitable-giving-showed-solid-growth-climbing-to-449-64-billion-in-2019-one-of-the-highest-years-for-giving-on-record/ [Published June 16, 2020], I-664

Glass International, II-3148

"Global 3-Terminal Capacitor Market Research Report 2020." [online] from http://www.qyresearch.com [Published April 2020], I-608

"Global Acoustic Insulation." [online] from http://www.freedoniagroup.com [Published May 2019], I-1904

"Global Adhesives for Wearable Medical Device Market Size, Status and Forecast 2020-2026." [online] from https://www.qyresearch.com [Published April 2020], I-9

"Global Advanced Audio Market Research Report 2020." [online] from http://www.qyresearch.com [Published March 2020], I-882

"Global Agricultural Equipment." [online] from http://www.freedoniagroup.com [Published October 2020], I-1278

"Global AIS Transponder Market Report, History and Forecast 2015-2026, Breakdown Data by Manufacturers, Key Regions, Types and Applications." [online] from http://www.qyresearch.com [Published July 2020], II-3412

"Global and China Aluminum Electrolytic Capacitor Industry Report 2019-2025." [online] from http://www.researchinchina.com [Published August 2019], I-607

"Global and China Injection Molding Machinery Industry Report 2020-2026." [online] from http://www.researchinchina.com [Published May 2020], II-2746

"Global and China Jewelry Industry Report 2020-2026." [online] from http://www.researchinchina.com [Published July 2020], I-1998

"Global and China Laser Processing Equipment Industry Report 2020-2026." [online] from http://www.researchinchina.com [Published June 2020], I-2029

"Global and China Sweet Potato Fries Market Insights, Forecast to 2026." [online] from https://www.360researchreports.com/global-sweet-potato-fries-sales-market-16698297 [Published October 2020], I-1484

"Global & European Paints & Coatings Market Highlights: 2020." [online] from https://www.akiresearch.com/post/global-european-paints-coatings-market-highlights-2020 [Published January 14, 2021], II-2586

"Global and United States Automated Parking Systems Market Insights, Forecast to 2026." [online] from http://www.qyresearch.com [Published September 2020], I-320

"Global and United States Online Baby Products Retailing Market Size, Manufacturers, Supply Chain, Sales Channel and Clients, 2020-2026." [online] from http://www.qyresearch.com [Published September 2020], I-369

"Global Antifreeze and Coolants Market Size, Manufacturers, Supply Chain, Sales Channel and Clients, 2020-2026." [online] from http://www.qyresearch.com [Published July 2020], I-690

"Global Astronomical Telescope Market 2020-2026, With Breakdown Data of Capacity, Sales, Revenue, Price, Cost and Gross Profit." [online] from http://www.radiantinsights.com [Published February 2020], II-3313

"Global Autoclaved Aerated Concrete Market Growth 2019-2024." [online] from https://www.absolute-reports.com/global-autoclaved-aerated-concrete-aac-market-13827735 [Published February 2019], I-319

"Global Automatic Soldering Machine Market Report, History and Forecast, 2020-2026." [online] from http://www.qyresearch.com [Published April 2020], I-321

"Global Automotive 2020 Color Popularity Report." [online] from https://www.axalta.com/content/dam/New%20Axalta%20Corporate%20Website/Documents/Brochures/axalta-2020-global-automotive-color-popularity-report.pdf [Published December 2020], II-2589

"Global Automotive Driving Simulator Industry Research Report, Growth Trends and Competitive Analysis 2020-2026." [online] from http://www.qyresearch.com [Published April 2020], I-1101

"Global Automotive Exhaust Manifold Gasket Industry Research Report, Growth Trends and Competitive Analysis 2020-2026." [online] from http://www.qyresearch.com [Published February 2020], I-1590

"Global Automotive Laser Lighting Market." [online] from https://mobilityforesights.com/product/automotive-laser-lights-market/ [Published May 2020], I-2067

"Global Automotive LED Revenue Projected to Reach Nearly U.S. $3 Billion in 2021 Owing to High Demand for Headlights and Display Panels, Says TrendForce." [online] from https://www.trendforce.com/presscenter/news/20210325-10734.html [Press release March 25, 2021], I-2069

"Global Automotive Lighting Industry Research Report, Growth Trends and Competitive Analysis 2020-2026." [online] from http://www.qyresearch.com [Published July 2020], I-2070

"Global Automotive Oil Pump Market Research Report 2020." [online] from http://www.qyresearch.com [Published April 2020], I-299

"Global Automotive Rear View Mirror Market." [online] from https://mobilityforesights.com/product/automotive-rear-view-mirror-market/ [Published March 2021], I-303

"Global Automotive Rubber Seal Market Research Report 2020." [online] from http://www.qyresearch.com [Published April 2020], I-1592

"Global Automotive Shock Absorber Market Research Report 2020." [online] from http://www.qyresearch.com [Published April 2020], I-309

"Global Automotive Transmission Filter Industry Research Report, Growth Trends and Competitive Analysis 2020-2026." [online] from http://www.qyresearch.com [Published February 2020], I-302

"Global B2B Floor Cleaning Robots Market Report History and Forecast 2015-2026." [online] from http://www.qyresearch.com [Published July 2020], II-2928

"Global Binders for Lithium Ion Batteries Industry Research Report 2020-2026." [online] from http://www.qyresearch.com [Published August 2020], I-469

"Global Booster Pump Sales Market Report 2020." [online] from http://www.qyresearch.com [Published November 2020], II-2823

"Global Bromine Disinfectant Tablet Market Insight, Forecast to 2026." [online] from https://www.absolutereports.com/global-bromine-disinfectant-tablet-market-15572164 [Published April 17, 2020], I-691

"Global Canned Goods Industry Research Report, Growth Trends and Competitive Analysis 2020-2026." [online] from http://www.qyresearch.com [Published April 2020], I-606

"Global Caps & Closures." [online] from http://www.freedoniagroup.com [Published February 2021], I-610

"Global Cardan Shaft Market Research Report 2020." [online] from http://www.qyresearch.com [Published January 2020], I-300

Global Cargo Insight, II-3044

"Global Casting Fishing Rods Market Size, Manufacturers, Supply Chain, Sales Channel and Clients, 2020-2026." [online] from http://www.qyresearch.com [Published July 2020], II-3207

"Global Ceiling Grid System Market Size, Manufacturers, Supply Chain, Sales Channel and Clients, 2020-2026." [online] from http://www.qyresearch.com [Published July 2020], I-626

"Global Cellophane Industry Research Report, Growth Trends and Competitive Analysis 2020-2026." [online] from http://www.qyresearch.com [Published February 2020], I-627

"Global Cement and Aggregate Market Size, Manufacturers, Supply Chain, Sales Channel and Clients 2020-2026." [online] from https://www.marketreportsworld.com/

global-cement-and-aggregate-market-15954685 [Published July 2020], I-652

Global Cement Magazine, I-643-644, 647-648, 650-651

"Global Cinema Lens Research Report 2020." [online] from http://www.qyresearch.com [Published July 2020], I-2054

"Global Circuit Breakers Sales Market Report 2020." [online] from http://www.qyresearch.com [Published November 2020], I-731

"Global Clad Plate Research Report 2020." [online] from http://www.qyresearch.com [Published April 2020], I-732

"Global Cleaners and Degreasers Market Report." [online] from http:/reports.valuates.com [Published April 2020], I-739

"Global Clinical Trial Market Report, History and Forecast 2015-2026, Breakdown Data by Companies, Key Regions Types and Applications." [online] from http://www.qyresearch.com [Published May 2020], II-2876

"Global Cloud Infrastructure Market Q4 2020." [online] from https://www.canalys.com/newsroom/global-cloud-market-q4-2020 [Press release February 2, 2021], II-3164

"Global Coffee Roaster Market Size, Manufacturers, Supply Chain, Sales Channel and Clients, 2020-2026." [online] from http://www.qyresearch.com [Published July 2020], I-762

"Global Collaborative Robots Market Report, History and Forecast, 2015-2026." [online] from http://www.qyresearch.com [Published July 2019], II-2926

"Global Commercial Refrigeration and Freezing Equipment Sales Market Report 2020." [online] from http://www.qyresearch.com [Published November 2020], I-1765

"Global Commercial Refrigeration Equipment: Food Retail Market." [online] from http://www.freedoniagroup.com [Published February 2021], I-1764

"Global Computer Mice Market Research Report 2020." [online] from http://www.qyresearch.com [Published July 2020], I-786

"Global Concessions Catering Market Report, History and Forecast 2014-2025." [online] from http://www.qyresearch.com [Published April 2020], I-1424

"Global Conveyor and Drive Belt Market Report, History and Forecast 2015-2026, Breakdown by Manufacturers, Key Regions, Types and Applications." [online] from http://www.qyresearch.com [Published May 2020], I-945

"Global Corrugated Boxes." [online] from http://www.freedoniagroup.com [Published February 2020], I-544

"Global Crude Steel Output Decreases by 0.9% in 2020." [online] from https://www.worldsteel.org/media-centre/press-releases/2021/Global-crude-steel-output-decreases-by-0.9--in-2020.html [Published January 26, 2021], II-3239

"Global Curved Glass Sales Market Report 2020." [online] from http://www.qyresearch.com [Published November 2020], I-1627

"Global Cutting Tools Market Research Report 2020." [online] from https://www.360marketupdates.com/global-cutting-tools-market-14837730 [Published January 2020], II-2289

"Global Decorative Laminates." [online] from http://www.freedoniagroup.com [Published March 2021], I-2026

"Global Demands and Trends Analysis on Soluble Fibers in North America and Europe in 2020." [online] from https://www.agr.gc.ca/eng/international-trade/market-intelligence/reports/?id=1522931721523 [Published July 2020], I-1393

"Global Dewatering Pump Sales Market Insights, Forecast to 2026." [online] from http://www.qyresearch.com [Published November 2020], II-2824

"Global Diaper Market Size, Manufacturers, Supply Chain, Sales Channel and Clients, 2020-2026." [online] from http://www.qyresearch.com [Published July 2020], II-2953

"Global Distributed Peristaltic Pump Market Report, History and Forecast 2014-2025, Breakdown Data by Manufacturer Key Regions, Types and Applications." [online] from http://www.qyresearch.com [Published October 2020], II-2821

"Global Doughnuts Market Size, Manufacturers, Supply Chain, Sales Channel and Clients, 2020-2026." [online] from http://www.qyresearch.com [Published July 2020], II-2886

"Global Drone Surveillance Research Report 2020." [online] from http://www.qyresearch.com [Published April 2020], II-3454

"Global Dry Fruit Market Report, History and Forecast 2015-2026, Breakdown Data by Manufacturers, Key Regions, Types and Application." [online] from http://www.qyresearch.com [Published April 2020], I-1100

"Global Dry Ice Pelletizing Market Research Report 2020." [online] from http://www.qyresearch.com [Published July 2020], I-1159

"Global E-Commerce Update 2021." [online] from https://www.emarketer.com/content/global-ecommerce-update-2021 [Published January 13, 2021], I-1177

"Global Earthing Lightning Protection System Market Insights, Forecast to 2026." [online] from http://www.qyresearch.com [Published May 2020], I-1189

"Global Educational Furniture Market Insights and Forecast to 2026." [online] from http://www.qyresearch.com [Published September 2020], I-1548

"Global Educational Toy Market Research Report 2020." [online] from http://www.qyresearch.com [Published January 2020], II-3400

"Global Electric Hoist Market Size, Manufacturers, Supply Chain, Sales Channel and Clients 2020-2026." [online] from http://www.qyresearch.com [Published May 2020], I-1787

"Global Electric Vehicle Top 20 EV Sales Report." [online] from https://cleantechnica.com/2021/02/04/global-electric-vehicle-top-20-ev-sales-report/ [Published February 4, 2021], I-331, 336

"Global Electronic Shelf Label Market Report, History and Market Forecast 2014-2025." [online] from http://www.qyresearch.com [Published December 2020], I-1203

"Global Elevator Market Size, Manufacturers, Supply Chain Sales Channel and Clients, 2020-2026." [online] from http://www.qyresearch.com [Published July 2020], I-1209

"Global Encrypted USB Flash Drives Market Size, Manufacturers, Supply Chain, Sales Channel and Clients, 2020-2026." [online] from http:/reports.valuates.com [Published July 2020], I-783

"Global EV Outlook 2020."[online] from http://www.iae.org [Accessed September 21, 2020], I-156, 325, 354, 359, 362

"Global Evaporated Milk Market Insights and Forecast to 2026." [online] from http://www.qyresearch.com [Published September 2020], II-2310

"Global Events Market Size, Status and Forecast 2020-2026." [online] from http://www.qyresearch.com [Published April 2020], I-1256

"Global Face Recognition Device Market Insights, Forecast to 2025." [online] from http://www.marketinsightsreports.com [Published April 2020], I-1272

"Global Farm Tractors." [online] from http://www.freedoniagroup.com [Published October 2020], I-1279

"Global Fast Fashion Market Research Report 2020." [online] from http://www.qyresearch.com [Published March 2020], I-214

"Global Faucets and Taps." [online] from http://www.freedoniagroup.com [Published January 2021], II-2754

"Global Fiberglass Insulation." [online] from http://www.freedoniagroup.com [Published November 2020], I-1905

"Global Fiberglass Market Research Report." [online] from https://www.industryresearch.co/global-fiberglass-market-16396457 [Published September 2020], I-1624

"Global Fiberglass Swimming Pool Market Research Report 2020." [online] from http://www.qyresearch.com [Published July 2020], II-3287

"Global Fish Vaccine Market Size, Manufacturers, Supply Chain, Sales Channel and Clients, 2020-2026." [online] from http://www.qyresearch.com [Published July 2020], II-3461

"Global Flu Vaccine Market Size, Manufacturers, Supply Chain, Sales Channel and Clients, 2020-2026." [online] from http://www.qyresearch.com [Published July 2020], II-3462

"Global Fresh Pet Market Research Report 2020." [online] from http://www.qyresearch.com [Published July 2020], II-2666

"Global Frozen Potatoes Market Size, Manufacturers, Supply Chain, Sales Channel and Clients, 2020-2026." [online] from http://www.qyresearch.com [Published July 2020], I-1478

"Global Fruit Concentrates Market Research Report 2020." [online] from http://www.qyresearch.com [Published July 2020], I-1496

"Global Game Revenues Up an Extra $15 Billion Engagement Skyrockets." [online] from https://newzoo.com/insights/articles/game-engagement-during-covid-pandemic-adds-15-billion-to-global-games-market-revenue-forecast/ [Published November 4, 2020], I-1570

Global Gaming Business, I-1582-1583

"Global Garage Door Market Size, Manufacturers, Supply Chain, Sales Channel and Clients 2020-2026." [online] from http://www.qyresearch.com [Published July 2020], I-1586

"Global Garbage Can Market Size, Manufacturers, Supply Chain, Sales Channel and Clients 2020-2026." [online] from http://www.qyresearch.com [Published July 2020], I-1588

"Global Geosynthetics." [online] from http://www.freedoniagroup.com [Published June 2020], I-1617

"Global Go-Kart Market Research Report 2020." [online] from http://www.qyresearch.com [Published July 2020], II-3396

"Global Golf GPS Market Growth 2019-2024." [online] from https://www.absolutereports.com/global-golf-gps-market-13909354 [Published February 2019], I-1666

"Global Graphing Calculator Market Size, Status and Forecast 2020-2026." [online] from http://www.qyresearch.com [Published April 2020], I-589

Global Gypsum Magazine, I-1725-1728, 1908

"Global High Early Strength Concrete Market Size, Manufacturers, Supply Chain, Sales Channel and Clients, 2020-2026." [online] from http://www.qyresearch.com [Published July 2020], I-803

"Global Honey Food Industry Research Growth Trends and Competitive Analysis, 2020-2026." [online] from http://www.qyresearch.com [Published April 2020], I-1824

"Global Horticultural LED Industry Research Report, Growth Trends and Competitive Analysis 2020-2026." [online] from http://www.qyresearch.com [Published July 2020], I-2071

"Global Household Fixed Wireless Access Subscribers to Cross Half a Billion Market by 2030." [online] from https://www.counterpointresearch.com/category/press-release/ [Press release August 6, 2020], II-3560

"Global Humidifier Manufacturers Profiles, Market Size and Market Share." [online] from http://www.qyresearch.com [Published February 2020], I-237

"Global Hummus Market Size, Manufacturers, Supply Chain, Sales Channel and Clients, 2020-2026." [online] from http://www.qyresearch.com [Published July 2020], I-1078

"Global Insulation." [online] from http://www.freedoniagroup.com [Published November 2020], I-1906

"Global Jaundice Market Research Report 2020." [online] from http://www.qyresearch.com [Published January 2020], I-1070

"Global Kegs Market Insights, Forecast to 2025." [online] from http://www.qyresearch.com [Published May 2019], I-2016

"Global Ladder Market by Manufacturers, Regions, Types and Applications." [online] from https://www.360researchreports.com/global-ladder-market-14557759 [Published August 2019], I-2025

"Global Laser Marker Market Research Report 2020." [online] from http://www.qyresearch.com [Published March 2020], I-2028

"Global Leather Goods Market Size, Manufacturer, Supply Chain, Sales Channel and Clients, 2020-2026." [online] from http://www.qyresearch.com [Published July 2020], I-2046

"Global LED Stage Illumination Market Research Report 2020." [online] from http://www.qyresearch.com [Published January 2020], I-2072

"Global LED Video Display Market Recovers by 23.5% Quarter-on-Quarter." [online] from https://omdia.tech.informa.com/pr/pr-listing [Published March 16, 2021], I-1087

"Global LED Video Wall Driver IC Revenue for 2021 Projected to Reach U.S. $360 Million, a 13% Increase YoY, Says TrendForce." [online] from https://www.trendforce.com/presscenter/news/20210415-10756.html [Press release April 15, 2021], I-1957

"Global Lifeboat Report, History and Forecast 2015-2026, Breakdown Data by Manufacturers, Key Regions, Types and Applications." [online] from http://www.qyresearch.com [Published July 2020], I-509

"Global Low-Voltage Power Distribution Sales Market Report 2020." [online] from http://www.qyresearch.com [Published September 2020], I-2113

"Global Luxury Outdoor Furniture Market Research Report 2020." [online] from http://www.qyresearch.com [Published July 2020], I-1549

"Global Makeup Brushes Sales Market Report 2020." [online] from http://www.qyresearch.com [Published September 2020], I-986

"Global Mannequin Market Size, Manufacturers, Supply Chain, Sales Channel and Clients, 2020-2026." [online] from http://www.qyresearch.com [Published July 2020], II-2145

"Global Market Outlook for Sand Casting." [online] from http://www.beroeinc.com [Accessed October 1, 2020], II-2940

"Global Matcha Tea Market Report, History and Forecast 2014-2025, Breakdown by Manufacturers, Key Regions, Types and Applications." [online] from http://www.qyresearch.com [Published April 2020], II-3304

"Global Microgrid Market Size, Status and Forecast 2020-2026." [online] from http://www.qyresearch.com [Published February 2020], II-2305

"Global Microswitch Market Insights, Forecast to 2025." [online] from https://www.qyresearch.com [Published March 2019], II-2306

"Global Modular Gripper Market Research Report 2020." [online] from http://www.qyresearch.com [Published September 2020], II-2342

"Global Needle Roller Bearing Sales Market Report 2020." [online] from http://www.qyresearch.com [Published November 2020], I-473

"Global Nickel Alloy Wires Market Report, History and Forecast 2015-2026." [online] from http://www.qyresearch.com [Published July 2020], II-2434

"Global Nylon String Trimmer Line Market 2020: Top Countries Data, Revenue Growth Development with COVID-19 Impact Analysis and Emerging Technologies with Forecasts to 2024." [online] from http://www.marketwatch.com [Press release August 11, 2020], II-2457

"Global Off-Road Engines Market Insights, Forecast to 2026." [online] from http://reports.valuates.com [Published April 2020], I-1244

"Global Open Gear Lubricants Market Research Report 2020." [online] from http://www.qyresearch.com [Published March 2020], I-2119

"Global Orally Disintegrating Tablet Market Research Report 2020." [online] from http://www.qyresearch.com [Published August 2020], I-1132

"Global Outdoor Pest Control Devices Market Research Report 2020." [online] from http://www.qyresearch.com [Published March 2020], II-2660

"Global Ovulation Test Market Growth 2019-2024." [online] from https://www.absolutereports.com/global-ovulation-test-market-13851692 [Published February 2019], I-1071

"Global Pallet Pooling (Rental) Market Size, Status and Forecast." [online] from http://www.qyre-search.com [Published July 2020], II-2598

"Global Pallets." [online] from http://www.freedoniagroup.com [Published May 2020], II-2597

"Global Paper Cutting Machine Market Share 2026." [online] from http://www.qyresearch.com [Published September 2020], II-2617

"Global Parcel Sorting System Sales Market Report 2020." [online] from http://www.qyresearch.com [Published November 2020], II-2619

"Global Pay TV Revenues Down, Subscriptions Up." [online] from http://www.digitaltvresearch.com [Press release September 2020], II-2630

"Global Personal Protective Equipment Market 2020-2025." [online] from https://mobilityforesights.com/product/personal-protective-equipment-market/ [Published May 2020], II-2268

"Global Photo Printing and Merchandise Market Size, Status and Forecast 2020-2026." [online] from http://www.qyresearch.com [Published September 2020], II-2703

"Global Plain Bearings." [online] from http://www.freedoniagroup.com [Published May 2021], I-472

"Global Plastic Bins Market Insights, Forecast to 2026." [online] from https://www.qyresearch.com [Published April 2020], II-2726

"Global Plastic Injection Molding Industry Research Report 2020." [online] from http://www.qyresearch.com [Published November 2020], II-2747

"Global Playground Equipment Market Size, Manufacturers, Supply Chain, Sales Channel and Clients 2020-2026." [online] from http://reports.valuates.com [Published April 2020], II-2752

"Global Pneumatic Cylinder Market Growth 2019-2024." [online] from https://www.absolutereports.com [Published February 2019], II-2760

"Global Pneumatic Tires for Industrial Truck (Forklift) Sales Market Report 2020." [online] from http://www.qyresearch.com [Published November 2020], II-3348

"Global Postal Industry Report 2019." [online] from https://www.ipc.be/services/markets-and-regulations/market-intelligence/global-postal-industry-report [Published December 2019], II-2772

"Global Posture Corrector Market Research Report 2020." [online] from http://www.qyresearch.com [Published July 2020], II-2245

"Global Power Tools Market Size, Manufacturers, Supply Chain, Sales Channel and Clients, 2020-2026." [online] from http://www.qyresearch.com [Published September 2020], II-3385

"Global Powered Pressure Washer Market Insights, Forecast to 2026." [online] from http://www.qyresearch.com [Published April 2020], II-2784

"Global Powers of Luxury Goods 2020." [online] from http://www2.deloitte.com [Accessed January 7, 2021], I-192, 971, 2130-2134

"Global Prefabricated Housing." [online] from http://www.freedoniagroup.com [Published January 2021], I-1838

"Global Press Machine Sales Market Report 2020." [online] from http://www.qyresearch.com [Published November 2020], II-2137

"Global Primary Battery Market Size, Manufacturers, Supply Chain, Sales Channel and Clients 2020-2026." [online] from http://www.qyresearch.com [Published July 2020], I-465

"Global Professional Power Tools." [online] from http://www.freedoniagroup.com [Published January 2021], II-3382

"Global PVA Brush Market Research Report." [online] from http://www.qyresearch.com [Published March 2020], I-563

"Global Real Time Clock (RTC) Industry Research Report." [online] from http://www.qyresearch.com [Published September 2020], I-741

"Global Residential Generators Market Insights, Forecast to 2026." [online] from http://www.qyresearch.com [Published April 2020], I-1616

"Global Residential Insulation." [online] from http://www.freedoniagroup.com [Published November 2020], I-1907

"Global Reverse Vending Machine Market by Manufacturers, Regions, Type and Application, Forecast to 2025." [online] from http://www.radiantinsights.com [Published February 2020], II-2911

"Global Road Bikes Market Size, Manufacturers, Supply Chain, Sales Channel and Clients 2020-2026." [online] from http://www.qyresearch.com [Published July 2020], I-496

"Global Sales Statistics 2020." [online] from https://www.oica.net/category/sales-statistics/ [Accessed April 20, 2021], I-351

"Global Satellite Manufacturing and Launch Markets, 10th Edition." [online] from http://www.nsr.com [Published June 2020], II-2961

"Global Scouring Pad Research Report 2020." [online] from http://www.qyresearch.com [Published April 2020], I-738

"Global Sealless Pump Sales Market Report 2020." [online] from http://www.qyresearch.com [Published November 2020], II-2825

"Global Seamless Copper Tubes Market Size, Manufacturers, Supply Chain, Sales Channel and Clients 2020-2026." [online] from http://reports.valuates.com [Published July 2020], I-954

"Global Siding (Cladding)." [online] from http://www.freedoniagroup.com [Published October 2020], II-3072

"Global Simulator Market Insights, Forecast to 2026." [online] from http://www.qyresearch.com [Published April 2020], I-1338

"Global Ski Touring Binding Market Research Report 2020." [online] from http://www.qyresearch.com [Published September 2020], II-3208

"Global Smart Agriculture Market Report, History and Forecast 2015-

2026." [online] from http://www.qyresearch.com [Published August 2020], II-3104

"Global Smart TV Market 2020-2025." [online] from https://mobilityforesights.com/product/smart-tv-market/ [Published August 2020], I-900

"Global Smartphone Production Expected to Reach 1.38 Billion Units in 2021 as Huawei Drops Out of Top-Six Ranking, Says TrendForce." [online] from https://www.trendforce.com/presscenter/news [Press release January 5, 2021], I-629

"Global Smartwatch Market Revenue Up 20% in H1 2020, Led by Apple, Garmin & Huawei." [online] from http://www.counterpoint-research.com [Press release August 20, 2020], II-3521

"Global Spent Fuel Overview." [online] from https://cdn.ymaws.com/inmm.org/resource/resmgr/docs/events/spentfuel2020/proceedings/greene_uxc_political_landsca.pdf [Published January 28, 2020], II-2443-2444, 2446

"Global Sterilization Equipment Market Research Report 2020." [online] from http://www.qyrcsearch.com [Published May 2020], II-2249

"Global Tank Truck Market Research Reports 2020." [online] from https://www.marketinsightsreports.com [Published January 2020], II-3292

"Global Tattoo Aftercare Products Market Size, Manufacturer, Supply Chain, Sales Channel and Clients, 2020-2026." [online] from http://www.qyresearch.com [Published July 2020], II-2264

"Global Tax Software Market Research Report 2020." [online] from http://www.qyresearch.com [Published September 2020], II-3172

"Global Temporary Tattoo Market Report, History and Forecast 2015-2026, Breakdown by Manufacturers, Key Regions, Types and Applications." [online] from http://www.qyresearch.com [Published May 2020], II-3297

"Global Textile Chemicals Market Research Report 2020." [online] from http://www.qyresearch.com [Published May 2020], I-697

"Global Tissue Market Outlook." [online] from http://eventsrisiinfo.com [Published October 2020], II-2603

"Global Toilet Paper Market Research Report 2020." [online] from http://www.qyresearch.com [Published April 2020], II-2948

"Global Toilet Tank Fittings Market Insight, Forecast to 2026." [online] from http://www.qyresearch.com [Published April 2020], II-2756

"Global Tower Crane Market Report, History and Forecast 2015-2026, Breakdown Data by Manufacturers, Key Regions, Types and Applications." [online] from http://www.qyresearch.com [Published May 2020], I-1016

"Global Transformer Monitoring System Sales Market Report 2020." [online] from http://www.qyresearch.com [Published November 2020], II-3410

"Global USB Car Charger Market 2019." [online] from https://www.absolutereports.com/global-usb-car-chargers-market-16072370 [Published August 2020], I-885

"Global USB Portable Battery Market 2019." [online] from https://www.absolutereports.com [Published March 2019], I-466

"Global Veterinary Patient Monitoring Equipment Market Research Report 2020." [online] from http://www.qyresearch.com [Published March 2020], II-3474

"Global Wall Hanging Furnace Market Size Manufacturers, Supply Chain, Sales Channel and Clients 2020-2026." [online] from http://www.qyresearch.com [Published July 2020], I-1768

"Global Wallpaper Market Growth 2019-2024." [online] from https://www.absolutereports.com/global-wallpaper-market-13877835 [Published February 2019], II-3494

"Global Wind Industry Had a Record, Near 100GW, Year as GE, Goldwind Took Lead from Vestas." [online] from https://about.bnef.com/blog/global-wind-industry-had-a-record-near-100gw-year-as-ge-goldwind-took-lead-from-vestas/ [Press release March 10, 2021], II-3445, 3447

"Global Wind Report 2021." [online] from https://gwec.net/global-wind-report-2021/ [Accessed May 20, 2021], I-1220-1223

"Global Wine Glass Sales Market Report 2020." [online] from http://www.qyresearch.com [Published November 2020], I-1634

"Global Workwear Market Insights, Forecast to 2026." [online] from http://www.qyresearch.com [Published April 2020], I-194

"Gold Focus 2020." [online] from http://www.metalsfocus.com [Accessed December 10, 2020], I-1636-1641, 1996

"Golden Nugget Online Gaming." [online] from https://www.sec.gov/Archives/edgar/data/1768012/000110465920077710/tm2023623d3_ex99-2.htm [Published June 29, 2020], I-1572

"Goodfood Investor Presentation." [online] from https://www.makegoodfood.ca/en/investisseurs/evenements [Published January 2021], II-2165

"Google Collects More Than Half of All Search Ad Revenue." [online] from https://www.emarketer.com/content/google-collects-more-than-half-of-all-us-search-ad-revenue [Published April 12, 2021], I-42

"Graphic Packaging Holding Co." [online] from https://www.theowlfund.com/s/Graphic-Packaging-Holding-Co-GPK_Initiating-Coverage-Report-13-Nov-2020-2.pdf [Published November 13, 2020], II-2607-2609

"Greatview Aseptic: 10% Dividend for A Growing Company

in an Industry With High Barriers to Entry." [online] from https://seek-ingalpha.com/article/4353191-great-view-aseptic-10-dividend-for-grow-ing-company-in-industry-high-bar-riers-to-entry [Published June 10, 2020], II-2574

The Griffin Report Northeast Market Review, I-1687, 1694, 1697

The Grocer, I-1679

"Grocery Market Share." [online] from https://www.kantarworldpanel.com/global/grocery-market-share/china-national [Accessed June 19, 2021], I-1684

"Growing Alternative Meat Market." [online] from http://news.kotra.or.kr [Published July 15, 2020], II-2228

"The Growth of the Construction Market Drives the Growth of the U.S. Woodworking Machinery Industry." [online] from https://www.market-prospects.com/articles/construction-market-drives-the-growth-of-usa-woodworking [Published February 1, 2021], II-2975

"Growth of the U.S. Legal Cannabis Industry." [online] from https://newfrontierdata.com/cannabis-insights/legal-cannabis-industry-growth/ [Published October 13, 2020], I-604

The Guardian, II-2430

Guide to Tobacco - A Supplement to Convenience Store News, I-1164-1167, II-3358-3359, 3362-3371

"Guru Investor Presentation." [online] from https://investors.guruenergy.com/ [Published November 2020], I-1237

"Gutters & Downspouts." [online] from http://www.freedoniagroup.com [Published March 2021], I-1720

"GVC Investor Pack." [online] from https://gvc-plc.com/wp-content/uploads/2020/06/GVC-Investor-Pack-May20-Final.pdf [Published May 2020], I-1578

"GWEC: China Blows Past Global Wind Power Records, Doubling Annual Installations in 2020." [online] from https://gwec.net/china-blows-past-global-wind-power-records-doubling-annual-installations-in-2020 [Published March 18, 2021], I-1219

GWI, II-3509

"Gymshark's New Customer Acquisition is Devouring the Competition." [online] from https://secondmeasure.com/datapoints/gymsharks-new-customer-acquisition-is-devouring-the-competition/ [Published October 1, 2020], I-193

"Haier Smart Home Co." [online] from https://www1.hkexnews.hk/listedco/listconews/sehk/2020/1116/2020111600153.pdf [Published November 16, 2020], I-218, 224-231

"Hair & Nail Salons in the U.S." [online] from http://www.ibisworld.com [Published February 2019], I-1730

"Hand Tool & Cutlery Manufacturing in the U.S." [online] from http://www.ibisworld.com [Published December 2019], II-3388

"Handheld Surgical Instrument Market 2020-2026." [online] from http://www.qyresearch.com [Published February 2020], II-2234

"Hanger Investor Presentation." [online] from https://investor.hanger.com/home/default.aspx [Published August 2020], I-1751

Hardware + Building Supply Dealer, I-1789

The Hardware Connection, I-686, 2068, 2073, 2111, II-2585, 2588, 2684, 2758, 3379, 3386

Hardware Retailing, I-1790

Hardwood Floors, I-1361

"Harris Williams Physical Therapy Market Overview." [online] from https://www.harriswilliams.com/system/files/industry_update/hw_pt_market_overview_august_2020_0.pdf [Published August 2020], I-1752

"Has China's Coffee Market Already Reached Its Full Potential?" [online] from https://daxueconsulting.com/coffee-market-in-china-2/ [Published March 22, 2021], I-751

"Haymaker Acquisition Investor Presentation." [online] from http://www.haymakeracquisition.com [Published July 2020], I-934

"Health and Wellness Spas in the U.S." [online] from http://www.ibisworld.com [Published February 2020], II-3200

"The Health Food Market in China." [online] from https://www.flandersinvestmentandtrade.com/export/sites/trade/files/market_studies/The%20health%20food%20market%20in%20China_0.pdf [Published December 2020], I-1387

"Healthcare Consultants in the U.S." [online] from http://www.ibisworld.com [Published August 2019], I-877

"Healthy Snacks in France and Belgium." [online] from https://www.agr.gc.ca/eng/international-trade/market-intelligence/reports [Published May 2020], II-3107

The Hearing Review, II-2262

"Heating & Air-Conditioning Contracting Work in the U.S." [online] from http://www.ibisworld.com [Published July 2019], I-930

Heavy Duty Trucking, I-1243, II-3043

"Here are the Top 10 U.S. E-Commerce Companies for 2021." [online] from https://www.emarketer.com/content/top-10-us-ecommerce-companies-2021-plus-6-key-takeaways-our-latest-forecast [Published February 2021], I-1178

HFN, I-1367, 1561-1563, 1797, 1804, 1810, 1816, 1835-1836

"High-End TV Display Expect to be 30% of all TV Displays in 2025." [online] from https://omdia.tech.informa.com/pr/2021-jan/high-end-tv-display-expect-to-be-30-percent-of-all-tv-display-in-2025 [Published January 28, 2021], I-1089

"Higher Education Retail Market Facts & Figures." [online] from https://www.nacs.org/newpage [Accessed April 11, 2021], I-520

"Himax Investor Presentation." [online] from https://www.himax.com.

tw/investors/presentations/ [Published November 2020], I-1955

The Hollywood Reporter, II-2358, 2364

Home Accents Today, I-1806, 1809, 1811-1813, 1819

Home Furnishings Business, I-1557, 1793

"Home Organization Products." [online] from http://www.freedoniagroup.com [Published June 2020], I-1791

Home Textiles Today, I-1798-1800, 1803, 1805, 1807-1808, 1814-1815, 1817-1818, 1820-1821

HomeWorld Business, I-241, 1834

"Honey." [online] from https://usda.library.cornell.edu/concern/publications/hd76s004z [Published March 18, 2021], I-1823

Household and Personal Products Industry, I-53-55, 597, 735-736, 979, 981, 988, 1060-1062, 1449-1452, 1732-1733, II-2531, 2656, 3095

"How a Potential Nokia Takeover Would Impact the Network Equipment Market." [online] from https://www.businessinsider.com/taking-over-nokia-would-be-met-with-regulatory-scrutiny-2020-4 [Published April 20, 2020], II 3306

"How Have the Market Shares in the Spine Market Changed After 2020 with COVID-19." [online] from http://thespinemarketgroup.com/how-have-the-market-shares-in-the-spine-market-changed-after-2020-with-covid-19/ [Accessed March 2, 2021], II-2247

"How Might a Pernod Ricard & Brown-Forman Merger Shift the Industry Landscape?" [online] from https://www.theiwsr.com/how-might-a-pernod-ricard-brown-forman-merger-shift-the-industry-landscape/ [Accessed May 31, 2021], I-2086

"How Much Are U.S. Cities Spending on Policing in 2020?" [online] from https://www.forbes.com/sites/niallmccarthy/2020/06/12/how-much-are-us-cities-spending-on-policing-in-2020-infographic/?sh=4e559323751a [Published June 13, 2020], II-2767

"How Our Ad Spending Outlook Has Changed for the U.S., China and the Rest of the World." [online] from https://www.emarketer.com/content/how-our-ad-spending-outlook-has-changed-us-china-rest-of-world [Published July 28, 2020], I-35

"Huawei Grabs a Quarter of China's Cloud Management Market in 2019." [online] from https://kr-asia.com/key-stat-huawei-controlled-a-quarter-of-chinas-cloud-management-market-in-2019 [Published June 3, 2020], II-3169

"Hydrogen and Fuel Cells Market 2020." [online] from https://thedailychronicle.in/news/975228/hydrogen-and-fuel-cells-market-2020-latest-global-industry-trends-and-forecast-analysis-to-2025/ [Press release September 9, 2020], I-1865

"IAB Brand Disruption 2021." [online] from https://www.iab.com/insights/brand-disruption-2021/ [Published November 2020], I-1175

"IARW Global Top 25 List of Refrigerated Warehousing and Logistics Providers." [online] from https://www.gcca.org/about/resources/about-industry/technical-publications/surveys-market-research/iarw-global-top-25 [Accessed May 20, 2021], II-3502

"IARW North America Top 25 List of Refrigerated Warehousing and Logistics Providers." [online] from https://www.gcca.org/about/resources/about-industry/technical-publications/surveys-market-research/iarw-north-american [Accessed May 20, 2021], II-3501

IBD Weekly, II-2265

"ICCA Statistical Report 2019." [online] from http://www.iccaworld.org [Accessed February 3, 2021], I-943

"Ice Cream & Frozen Dessert Packaging." [online] from http://www.freedoniagroup.com [Published February 2021], II-2565

"IDC Releases 2019 Data for China's A.I. Server Market: Inspur Leads With a Share Over 50%." [online] from https://en.inspur.com/en/2490 786/2508991/index.html [Pub-lished May 15, 2020], II-3035

"IFCN World Dairy." [online] from https://ifcndairy.org/wp-content/uploads/2020/07/World-Dairy-Map-2020_presentation.pdf [Published July 2, 2020], I-1290

"IFPI Global Music Report 2020 - The Industry in 2019." [online] from https://www.ifpi.org/ifpi-issues-annual-global-music-report/ [Published May 4, 2020], II-2407

"Imoo Leads the Global Kids' Smartwatch Market With 26% Market Share." [online] from https://www.counterpointresearch.com/category/press-release/ [Press release April 7, 2020], II-3518

"The Impact of the Coronavirus on the Global Consulting Industry." [online] from https://www.consultancy.org/news/162/the-impact-of-the-coronavirus-on-the-global-consulting-industry [Published March 23, 2020], I-878

"In-Car Listening Shows Americans Increasingly on the Move." [online] from https://www.edisonresearch.com/in-car-listening-shows-americans-increasingly-on-the-move/ [Published October 20, 2020], I-283

"Increasing Demand for Aviation Drives Continues Growth of MRO Industry." [online] from http://www.williamblair.com [Accessed November 10, 2020], I-83

"Independent Study on Packaging Products Market in Southeast Asia." [online] from http://ww2.frost.com [Published August 2020], II-2605-2606

"India Networking Market Showed a 9.6% YoY Decline in 2Q20." [online] from https://www.eetindia.co.in/india-networking-market-showed-a-9-6-yoy-decline-in-2q20/ [Published September 26, 2020], II-2424-2425, 2427

"India Smartphone Market Clocks Highest-Ever Shipments in a Single Quarter, Samsung Recovers Top Spot." [online] from http://www.counterpointresearch.com [Press release October 28, 2020], I-633, 639

"Indian Luggage Industry Sector Report: Bagging the Growth Story." [online] https://i.marketsmojo.com/pdf/research-report/202001/VIP.Ind_Axis_27012020.pdf [Published January 27, 2020], I-2122-2123

Indianapolis Business Journal, II-2848

"Industrial & Marine Gas and Steam Turbines." [online] from http://www.fi-powerweb.com/Industrial-Marine-Gas-Steam-Turbines.html [Accessed September 16, 2020], II-3448

"Industrial Building Construction in the U.S." [online] from http://www.ibisworld.com [Published October 2019], I-861

Industrial Supply, I-2, 564, 1786, II-2267, 2288, 2761, 3380

"Industry Eclipses 500,000 in Retail Sales for First Time Ever." [online] from https://rvbusiness.com/industry-eclipses-500000-in-retail-sales-for-first-time-ever/ [Published February 9, 2021], II-2859-2862, 3403-3406

"Industry Fast Facts." [online] from https://www.nbwa.org/resources/industry-fast-facts [Accessed June 1, 2021], I-482

"Industry Overview." [online] from https://www1.hkexnews.hk/listedco/listconews/sehk/2020/0323/9198226/sehk20030200063.pdf [Published March 23, 2020], I-1123

"Industry Overview." [online] from https://www1.hkexnews.hk/app/sehk/2021/103148/a107477/sehk21012901518.pdf [Accessed April 19, 2021], II-2261

"Industry Overview." [online] from https://www1.hkexnews.hk/app/sehk/2021/103312/a108111/sehk21032800441.pdf [Published March 2021], I-29

"Industry Overview." [online] from https://www1.hkexnews.hk/listedco/listconews/sehk/2020/0922/9448339/sehk20091000145.pdf [Published September 2020], I-1827, 1830

"Industry Overview Car Wash and Auto Detailing Services." [online] from https://davcapadvisors.com/wp-content/uploads/2020/11/carwash-auto-detailing-report-final.pdf [Accessed April 28, 2021], I-613

"Infineon/Cypress Regulation Merger Procedure." [online] from http://www.ec.europa.eu [Published October 16, 2019], II-3011

"Infinite Deal 2020." [online] from https://www.podcastinsights.com/podcast-statistics/ [Accessed January 3, 2021], I-631, 793, 897, 1169, 1964, II-2763-2764, 3516

Innovation & Tech Today, I-790-791, 794

Inside Unmanned Systems, I-1899

"Instacart Dominates Delivery, While Top Grocers See Little Shift in Market Share." [online] from https://secondmeasure.com/datapoints/grocery-spending-delivery-trends/ [Published August 13, 2020], II-2517

"Insulated Packaging Containers & Shippers." [online] from http://www.freedoniagroup.com [Published July 2020], II-2566

Insurance Journal, I-1940, 1954

"Intel Looks to Shed Legacy Businesses by Selling NAND Flash-Memory Business to SK Hynix." [online] from https://www.businessinsider.com/what-intel-could-gain-by-selling-memory-business-sk-hynix-2020-10 [Published October 21, 2020], II-3013

International Boat Industry, I-511

International Fiber Journal, I-1320

"International Society of Hair Restoration Surgery." [online] from https://ishrs.org/media/statistics-research/ [Published May 2020], I-1737

Investment & Pensions Europe, II-2646

Investor's Business Daily, I-667

"iPhone 11 the World's Most Shipped Smartphone in 2020-Shipping 64m Devices." [online] from https://omdia.tech.informa.com/pr/pr-listing [Published February 11, 2021], I-630

"Isotropic Graphite Market 2020 is Expected to See Magnificent Spike in CAGR with Global Industry Brief Analysis by Top Countries Data Which Includes Driving Factors by Manufacturers Growth and Forecast 2024." [online] from http://www.marketwatch.com [Press release August 6, 2020], I-1994

"ISSF Stainless Steel in Figures 2020." [online] from http://www.worldstainless.org [Accessed March 30, 2021], II-3233

"Italy 2020. Honda Was Market Leader in a Market -5%. Ducati Lost 25%." [online] from https://www.motorcyclesdata.com/2021/01/14/italian-motorcycles/ [Published January 14, 2021], II-2372

"Japan Pet Food Market Trend." [online] from http://news.kotra.or.kr [Published September 18, 2020], II-2680

"Japanese Automotive Lamp Market Trends." [online] from http://www.news.kotra.or.kr [Published July 16, 2020], I-2077

"Japanese Corrugated Cardboard Market Trend." [online] from http://news.kotra.or.kr [Published October 2, 2020], II-2612

"Japanese Dental Floss Market Trend." [online] from http://www.news.kotra.or.kr [Published April 23, 2020], II-2528

"Japanese Toothbrush Market Trend." [online] from http://news.kotra.or.kr [Published October 2, 2020], II-2530

"The Japanese Watch & Clock Industry in 2019." [online] from https://www.jcwa.or.jp/en/data/industry/ [Accessed September 3, 2020], I-740

"Japan's Yearly Manga and Light Novel Rankings for 2020." [online]

from https://myanimelist.net/news/61260265 [Published November 29, 2020], II-2142

"J.D. Com Inc. Financial and Operational Highlights." [online] from https://ir.jd.com/static-files/177fd537-03c0-4f0b-954a-40f0be141ae4 [Published March 2021], II-2906

"JDE Peet's A Global Coffee & Tea Champion." [online] from https://www.jdepeets.com/investors/financial-reports/results-publications/ [Published June 24, 2020], I-487

"Job Boards." [online] from http://www.datanyze.com/market-share [Accessed November 10, 2020], I-1974

Journal of Commerce, II-2770, 3421-3422

"Jubilant Life Sciences Limited." [online] from https://www.jubl.com/pdf/JLL-Investor-Presentation-Feb-2020.pdf [Published February 2020], I-1124-1125

just-food.com, II-3135, 3599

"K-12 and Higher Education Textbooks Market Size, Share and Forecast, 2019." [online] from http://www.outsellinc.com [Published December 2019], II-2810

"K+S Compendium." [online] from https://www.kpluss.com/en-us/.pdf/investor-relations/2020/compendium-september-2020.pdf [Published September 2020], II-2774

Kansas City Business Journal, II-3219

"Kingston, ADATA, Tigo Take Top Three Spots in 2019 Global Ranking of Top 10 SSD Module Makers, Says TrendForce." [online] from http://www.trendforce.com [Press release October 27, 2020], II-3021

"Kirby Corp. Investor Presentation." [online] from https://investors.kirbycorp.com/static-files/ac9a2956-de22-44fc-89ca-521650772256 [Published August 2020], II-3050, 3058

"Korea EV Battery Materials." [online] from http://www.skc.co.kr/upload/ir/20191216/20191216134813349290.pdf [Published December 5, 2019], I-956

"Korrun: The Rise and Rise of China's Luggage Giant." [online] from http://pdf.dfcfw.com/pdf/H3_AP202003241376867456_1.pdf [Published March 24, 2020], I-2121

"KP Tissue Well Positioned for Growth." [online] from https://www.kptissueinc.com/en-CA/gpc/_media/Document/kpt-rbc-conference-december-2020-vf.pdf [Published December 2020], II-2944, 2947

"Kraft Heinz - A New Model for Growth." [online] from http://ir.kraftheinzcompany.com/overview [Published September 15, 2020], II-2970

"Kuke Music Holding Ltd." [online] from https://www.sec.gov/Archives/edgar/data/1809158/000104746920005717/a2242706zf-1.htm [Published December 18, 2020], II-2404

"La Fleur's Fiscal 2020 Report Released." [online] from https://lafleurs.com/news/2020/10/19/lafleurs-fiscal-2020-report/ [Accessed December 20, 2020], I-1574

Labels & Labeling, I-2020

"Laboratory Fume Hood Manufacturing in the U.S." [online] from http://www.ibisworld.com [Published June 2019], I-2024

"Lancaster Colony Corporation." [online] from http://s21.q4cdn.com/151907755/files/doc_presentations/2020/09/LANC-Slide-Deck-CL-King-9-16-20.pdf [Published September 16, 2020], I-553-554, 1021, 1079, II-2972

Landscape Architect and Specifier News, I-1837, 1858

"Large Education Rollout Continue Driving the Tablet Market in EMEA." [online] from http://www.idc.com [Press release February 15, 2021], I-792

"Largest Global Engineering Staffing Firms." [online] from http://www2.staffingindustry.com [Press release October 24, 2019], II-3228

"Largest Healthcare Staffing Firms in the U.S. Reach to $18 Billion in Combined Revenue." [online] from http://www2.staffingindustry.com [Press release October 28, 2020], II-3229

Laser Focus World, I-2030

"LATAM Smartphone Shipments Fall 36% YoY in Q2 2020 on COVID-19." [online] from http://www.counterpointresearch.com [Press release August 31, 2020], I-640

"Latin America to Add 63 Million SVOD Subscriptions." [online] from http://www.digitaltvresearch.com/products [Press release March 2021], II-2547

"Lawn & Garden Consumables." [online] from http://www.freedoniagroup.com [Published December 2020], I-2033

"Lawn & Garden Growing Media." [online] from http://www.freedoniagroup.com [Published December 2020], I-2034

"Lawn & Garden Mulch." [online] from http://www.freedoniagroup.com [Published December 2020], I-2035

"Lawn & Garden Seeds." [online] from http://www.freedoniagroup.com [Published December 2020], II-3003

"Leaders in the Sustainable Use of Natural Resources." [online] from https://ence.es/wp-content/uploads/2020/09/09.20-Corporate-Presentation-ENG-1.pdf [Published September 2020], II-2813

Leading National Advertisers 2020 Fact Book - A Supplement to Advertising Age, I-15, 26-27, 32-34, 36-38, 40-41, 344, 346, II-2640, 2905, 3561

"Leading Player in Domestic Welding Market." [online] from https://www.icicidirect.com/mailimages/IDirect_EsabIndia_StockTales.pdf [Published January 8, 2021], II-3525-3526

"Leisure Business Market Research Handbook 2021-2022." [online] from http://www.rkma.com [Accessed March 8, 2021], I-1643

Licensing Letter, I-2060, 2062

"LightPath Investor Presentation." [online] from http://www.lightwave.com [Published May 2020], II-2714

"Lion's Share." [online] from https://twitter.com/thekenweb/status/1283329913412481024 [Published July 15, 2020], I-1692

"Lithium Battery Manufacturing in the U.S." [online] from http://www.ibisworld.com [Published December 2020], I-464

"Live Blogging." [online] from http://www.datanyze.com/market-share [Accessed November 10, 2020], II-3174

"Livestock and Poultry: World Markets and Trade." [online] from https://apps.fas.usda.gov/psdonline/circulars/livestock_poultry.pdf [Published October 9, 2020], I-621-622, 1784-1785, II-2173-2174, 2187, 2191, 2212

"Loan Brokers in the U.S." [online] from http://www.ibisworld.com [Published May 2019], I-2101

Logging & Sawmilling Journal, I-2128

Logistics Management, II-3065, 3425, 3429

"Low-Slope Roofing." [online] from http://www.freedoniagroup.com [Published September 2020], II-2930

Lubes 'n Greases, I-461, 2117

"Magazine Media Factbook 2020." [online] from https://mpa.pressreader.com/magazine-media-factbook-2020/20200629 [Accessed August 18, 2020], II-2140

"Magazine Media - Search Results." [online] from https://abcas3.auditedmedia.com/ecirc/magtitlesearch.asp [Accessed January 21, 2021], II-2138

"Maike Tube Industry Holdings Ltd." [online] from https://www1.hkexnews.hk/listedco/listconews/sehk/2019/1129/2019112900019.pdf [Published November 29, 2019], II-2723

"Major Oilseeds: World Supply and Distribution." [online] from https://apps.fas.usda.gov/psdonline/app/index.html#/app/downloads [Published October 2020], II-2496-2498

"Major Pay-TV Provider Lost About 5,120,000 Subscribers in 2020." [online] from https://www.leichtmanresearch.com/major-pay-tv-providers-lost-about-5120000-subscribers-in-2020/ [Press release March 4, 2021], II-2631

"Major Vegetable Oils: World Supply and Distribution." [online] from https://apps.fas.usda.gov/psdonline/app/index.html#/app/downloads [Published October 2020], I-1295-1298, II-2500-2501, 2507

"The Majority of Time Spend Viewing OTT Streaming Video Occurs on CTV Device." [online] from https://www.emarketer.com/content/majority-of-time-spent-viewing-ott-streaming-video-occurs-on-ctv-devices [Published December 29, 2020], II-2536

"Male Beauty Market in China." [online] from https://daxueconsulting.com/pesticide-market-in-china/ [Published September 2020], I-972

"Man Wah Holdings Limited." [online] from http://manwah.todayir.com/html/ir_presentations.php [Published May 15, 2020], I-1550-1551

"M&G Stationery Inc." [online] from http://www.chinastock.com.hk [Published August 4, 2020], II-3234

"Mango TV to Become China's Third Largest SVOD Service in 2021." [online] from https://www.ampereanalysis.com/insight/mango-tv-to-become-chinas-third-largest-svod-service-in-2021 [Published April 27, 2021], II-2540

The Manufacturing Confectioner, I-718-727, 810-811, 814, 816-826, 828-834, 838, 841-846, 848-850, 1002-1004, 1009, 1011, 1710-1711, 1713, II-3134, 3137

"Market Overview." [online] from https://www.european-aluminium.eu/activity-report-2019-2020/market-overview/ [Accessed December 7, 2020], I-163

"The Market Power of Agrobusiness." [online] from http://www.fairer-agrarhandel.de [Published April 2020], I-711, 1280, 1282-1284

"Market Share of LTPS Smartphone Panels in 2021 Likely to Be Constrained by Increasing AMOLED Panel Capacities and High a-Si Panel Demand, Says Trendforce." [online] from http://www.trendforce.com [Press release November 5, 2020], I-1086

"Marketing Consultants in the U.S." [online] from http://www.ibisworld.com [Published August 2019], I-879

"Marketing in Regulated Industry." [online] from http://www.theseus.fi/handle/10024/346377 [Published October 2020], II-3361

Marketing News, II-2874

"Meal Delivery and Fast Food Will Struggle to Deliver in 2021." [online] from https://www.ibisworld.com/industry-insider/press-releases/ [Press release January 17, 2021], I-1415

"Meal Replacement and Meal Replacement Drinks in Canada and the United States." [online] from https://www.agr.gc.ca/eng/international-trade/market-intelligence/reports/?id=1522931721523 [Accessed May 1, 2021], II-3277-3278

"Meat Markets in the United States." [online] from http://www.ibisworld.com [Published December 2019], II-2231

"Meat Snacks in China: Meat Rose from 14% to 21% of Country's Snack Consumption in 2020." [online] from https://daxueconsulting.com/meat-snacks-in-china/ [Published March 2, 2021], II-2175

Media Play News, I-1163

"The Media Report Media & Entertainment Data in America." [online] from https://digitalcommons.pepperdine.edu/cgi/viewcontent.cgi?article=1026&context=graziadiowps [Published September 2020], I-525, II-2139, 2431, 3221

"MediaTek Becomes Biggest Smartphone Chipset Vendor for First Time in Q3 2020." [online] from https://www.counterpointresearch.com/mediatek-biggest-smartphone-chipset-vendor-q3-2020/ [Press release December 24, 2020], II-3018

"Medical Imaging: Semiconductor Technology is a Key Enabler for Truly Dedicated Solutions." [online] from http://www.yole.fr/MedicalImaging_Equipment_Detectors_Overview.aspx [Accessed May 1, 2021], II-2241

Medical Marketing & Media, I-23

"Medical Nonwovens." [online] from http://www.freedoniagroup.com [Published November 2020], II-2441

"Meeting Consumer Demand for Eco-Friendly and Circular Solutions." [online] from https://www.storaenso.com/en/investors/reports-and-presentations [Published November 2020], II-2567

"Member Statistics." [online] from http://www.asecap.com/members-statistics.html [Accessed January 2, 2021], II-3378

"MEMS Industry: The Headwinds from COVID-19 and the Way Forward." [online] from http://www.yole.fr/2020_press_releases.aspx [Press release July 15, 2020], II-3034

"MENA SVOD Subs to Grow by 148%." [online] from http://www.digitaltvresearch.com/products [Press release September 2020], II-2550

"Mercury Research Sees Resurgent Intel CPU Market Share." [online] from https://hexus.net/business/news/components/147376-mercury-research-sees-resurgent-intel-cpu-market-share/ [Published February 4, 2021], II-3028

"Merger Magic: How M&A is Shaking Up Category Leaders in Mobile Games." [online] from https://sensortower.com/blog/mobile-gaming-market-share-q4-2020 [Published October 30, 2020], II-2335-2336, 2338-2339

"Meten EdTech Investor Presentation." [online] from https://investor.metenedu-edtechx.com/investor-relations [Published February 2020], I-1245

"Mexican Blueberries Gain U.S. Market Share." [online] from https://www.producebluebook.com/2021/01/18/mexican-blueberries-gain-u-s-market-share/ [Published January 18, 2021], I-1516

"Mexican Game Industry and Consumption Trends." [online] from http://news.kotra.or.kr [Published September 17, 2020], II-3480

"MGA Entertainment Dominates August Doll and Toy Sales, Setting Stage for Exciting Holiday Season." [online] from https://www.mgae.com/press/mgae-dominates-august-doll-and-toy-sales-exciting-holiday-season [Published September 14, 2020], II-3399

MHInsider, I-1851

"Microdisplay Industry: An Explosive Ecosystem Mining Technical Innovations, Strategy and Attractive Applications." [online] from http://www.yole.fr/iso_upload/News/2020/PR_MICRODISPLAYS_MarketUpdate_YOLE_Oct2020.pdf [Press release October 1, 2020], II-2304

"Microsoft Scientific Corp." [online] from http://www.chinastock.com.hk/en/NC/CA/index.aspx [Published August 10, 2020], II-2244, 2263

"Microsoft's Mixer Grows Audience, but Amazon's Twitch Continues to Dominate Streaming Market." [online] from https://www.geekwire.com/2019/microsofts-mixer-grows-audience-amazons-twitch-continues-dominate-streaming-market/ [Published December 26, 2019], II-3485

"Milk Alternative Beverages in the United States and Canada." [online] from https://www.agr.gc.ca/eng/international-trade/market-intelligence/reports/?id=1522931721523 [Published May 2021], II-2318

"The Milk Market in China: Consumers' Perception of Nutrition Has Sustained the Growth of This Sector." [online] from https://daxueconsulting.com/report-on-dairy-milk-market-in-china/ [Published July 24, 2020], II-2314

Milling & Baking News, I-551-552, 1371

Milsat Magazine, II-2963

Milwaukee Business Journal, I-1695

Mine, II-2324-2325

"Mineral Commodity Summaries 2021." [online] from https://www.usgs.gov/centers/nmic/mineral-commodity-summaries [Published January 29, 2021], I-3, 160, 167, 183, 264, 277, 534, 588, 653, 693-694, 729, 749, 959, 1074-1075, 1302, 1316, 1381, 1567, 1589, 1642, 1673, 1729, 1890, 1987, 1993, 2015, 2041, 2081, 2098, II-2141, 2143, 2276, 2303, 2343, 2437, 2596, 2643, 2702, 2751, 2775, 2820, 2841-2842, 2937-2939, 3078, 3085, 3149, 3246, 3260, 3342, 3441, 3607

"Mink." [online] from https://usda.library.cornell.edu/concern/publications/2227mp65f [Published July 23, 2020], II-2644

MMR, I-370, 983, 987, 989, 1031, 1150-1152, 1156, 1158, 1265, 1601, 1604, 1606, 1731, 1735, II-2271, 2527, 2952, 3091, 3093-3094, 3096, 3142, 3147, 3282, 3285, 3490

"Mobile Games Market Spotlight: Japan Accounted for Nearly a Quarter of Global Revenue in First Nine Months of 2020." [online] from https://sensortower.com/blog/japan-mobile-games-market-spotlight [Published October 16, 2020], II-2334

"Mobility in China." [online] from https://daxueconsulting.com/ride-hailing-market-in-china/ [Published August 2020], I-1414, II-2919, 3066, 3103

Modern Machine Shop, II-2136

Modern Materials Handling, I-2064, II-3503

Modern Tire Dealer, II-3344, 3351-3352

"Moody's Corp." [online] from https://www.biz.uiowa.edu/henry/research/ [Published October 21, 2020], I-1018

"More Than Half of Internet Users Have Purchased Groceries Online." [online] from https://www.emarketer.com/content/nearly-half-of-internet-users-have-purchased-groceries-online [Published August 20, 2020], II-2516

"Morgan Stanley: Aggressive Growth Strategy With Major Acquisitions." [online] from https://seekingalpha.com/article/4412794-morgan-stanley-major-acquisitions [Published March 10, 2021], I-1985

"Motorcycle Apparel Market Research Report 2020-2026." [online] from http://www.qyresearch.com [Published February 2020], I-185

"Motorcycles." [online] from http://www.freedoniagroup.com [Published May 2020], II-2367

"Mountain Bike Electric Bikes and Growth Expectations." [online] from http://www.news.kotra.or.kr [Published June 15, 2020], I-494

"MRC Data Year-End Report U.S. 2020." [online] from http://www.billboard.com [Accessed January 10, 2021], II-2390-2397, 2405

"MTA Bridges and Tunnels Report on Operations September 2020." from [online] from http://www.new.mta.info [Published September 2020], II-3376

Multi-Unit Franchisee, I-1454

Multichannel News, II-3106

Music & Sound Retailer, II-2412, 2414

Music Week, II-2399-2402

Musical Merchandise Review, II-2411

"NADA Market Beat." [online] from https://www.nada.org/nadamarketbeat/ [Accessed December 2020], I-348

National Fisherman, I-1331

National Liquor News, II-3544

National Oil & Lube News, I-2114-2116

The National Provisioner, II-2166, 2168, 2193-2203, 2205-2207, 2209-2210, 2218-2223, 2226, 2229, 2984, 2986

National Underwriter, I-1950

Nation's Restaurant News, II-2882-2884, 2887, 2892-2894, 2896

"Nation's Stock of Second Homes." [online] from http://eyeonhousing.org/2020/10/nations-stock-of-second-homes-2 [Published October 16, 2020], I-1859

Natural Foods Merchandiser, II-2418-2419

"NCA Sweet Insights State of Treaty 2021." [online] from https://candyusa.com/sweet-insights-state-of-treating-2021 [Accessed April 8, 2021], I-715, 809, 813

"NCR is the World's Largest Supplier of POS Software." [online] from https://www.rbrlondon.com/press/ [Published November 5, 2020], II-3170

"NCR Leads Booming Global Self-Checkout Market." [online] from https://www.rbrlondon.com/press/ [Published August 17, 2020], II-3005

"NCUA Releases Q4 2020 Credit Union System Performance Data." [online] from https://www.ncua.gov/newsroom/press-release/2021/ncua-releases-q4-2020-credit-union-system-performance-data [Press release March 4, 2021], I-1019

"Nestlé Introduces Plant-based Milk Brand to Rival Oatly, Alpro." [online] from https://www.bloomberg.com/news/articles/2021-05-04/nestle-introduces-plant-based-milk-brand-to-rival-oatly-alpro [Published May 4, 2021], II-2319

"Netflix Becomes the Second Largest TV Group in Europe." [online] from https://www.ampereanalysis.com/insight/netflix-becomes-the-second-largest-tv-group-in-europe [Published January 14, 2021], II-3315

"Nevada Gaming Revenues, 1984-2020." [online] from https://gaming.unlv.edu/reports.html [Published February 2021], I-1569

"New Century Resources March 2020 Quarter Results Presentation." [online] from http://www.newcenturyresources.com [Published March 2020], II-3603, 3606

"New Commercial Vehicle Registrations European Union." [online] from https://www.acea.be/press-releases/article/commercial-vehicle-registrations-18.9-in-2020-4.2-in-december [Press release January 26, 2021], I-356-357, 568

"New Honor Expected to Capture 2% Smartphone Market Share in 2021 Due to Limited Foundry Capacity, Says TrendForce." [online] from https://www.trendforce.com/presscenter/news/20201124-10565.html [Press release November 24, 2020], I-634

"New Kid on the Block?" [online] from https://home.kpmg/de/en/home/insights/2020/11/cbd-in-consumer-health.html [Published November 2020], I-599

"New Passenger Car Registrations European Union." [online] from https://www.acea.be/press-releases/article/passenger-car-registrations-23.7-in-2020-3.3-in-december [Press release January 19, 2021], I-365, 367

"New Wind in the Chinese Fan Market Brought About by Technological Innovation." [online] from http://www.news.kotra.or.kr [Published June 23, 2020], I-234

"NFI Group Q2 2020 Earnings Presentation." [online] from https://www.nfigroup.com/investor-relations/events-presentations/ [Published August 6, 2020], I-573

"Nike Will Continue to Run After Lockdown But It's Still Pricey." [online] from https://seekingalpha.com/article/4347600-nike-will-continue-to-run-after-lockdown-still-pricey [Published May 14, 2020], I-1425

Nilson Report, II-2633

"Non-Alcoholic Fermented and Cold Pressed Juice Trends in the United States and Europe." [online] from https://www.agr.gc.ca/eng/international-trade/market-intelligence/reports/?id=1522931721523 [Published April 2021], I-2004, II-3301

Non-Foods Management, I-13, 170, 208, 273, 371-372, 596, 1142-1145, 1155, 1324, 2017, 2078, II-2270, 2711, 2950, 2955-2956, 3556

Nonwovens Industry, II-2942-2943, 2954, 3552

"Norbord Investor Presentation." [online] from https://www.norbord.com/investors/presentations [Published November 10, 2020], II-3581-3582

"Normad Foods Investor Presentation." [online] from https://www.nomadfoods.com/investors/presentations/ [Published February 19, 2020], I-1489

"Nornickel Expanding the Horizons of Sustainable Growth." [online] from http://ar2019.nornickel.com [Accessed December 10, 2020], II-2432-2433, 2594-2595, 2749-2750

"North American OTT TV Revenues to Double." [online] from http://www.digitaltvresearch.com/products [Press release September 2020], II-2555

"North America's Top Timberland Owners and Managers, 2020 Update." [online] from https://forisk.com/blog/2020/05/21/north-americas-top-timberland-owners-and-managers-2020-update/ [Published May 21, 2020], II-3336-3337

Northeast Dairy, II-2308

"Norway Hits Record 87% Plug-In EV Share & 66% Pure Electrics in December." [online] from https://cleantechnica.com/2021/01/06/norway-hits-record-87-plug-in-ev-share-66-pure-electrics-in-december [Published January 6, 2021], I-327

"Not All Products Are Created Equal: Thermometers." [online] from https://www.traqline.com/newsroom/blog/not-all-products-are-created-equal-thermometers/ [Published January 13, 2021], II-2269

"NPD: As Comfort Drove Apparel Decisions, Sales of Men's Underwear Increased in the Second Half of 2020." [online] from https://www.prweb.com/releases/npd_as_comfort_drove_apparel_decisions_sales_of_mens_underwear_increased_in_the_second_half_of_2020 [Press release March 25, 2021], I-200

"Numerator Launches Omnichannel Market Share Solution." [online] from https://www.prnewswire.com/news-releases/numerator-launches-omnichannel-market-share-solution-301278031.html [Press release April 27, 2021], II-3088

Nutfruit Magazine, I-1517-1520, 1527-1528, II-2447-2456

"Nutrien Fact Book 2020." [online] from http://www.nutrien.com [Accessed November 4, 2020], I-1307-1312

Nutritional Outlook, II-3263-3274

"Nvidia/Mellanox Merger Procedure." [online] from https://ec.europa.eu/competition/mergers/cases/decisions/m9424_778_3.pdf [Published December 19, 2019], II-3036

"NYK Fact Book I 2020." [online] from https://www.nyk.com/english/ir/library/fact/ [Published May 25, 2020], II-3048-3049, 3051, 3053

Octane, I-1593

"Oculus Captures Half of XR Headset Market in 2020." [online] from https://www.counterpointresearch.com/oculus-captures-half-xr-headset-market-2020/ [Published March 10, 2021], I-1743

"Of Cars and Cans: U.S. Aluminum and the Pandemic." [online] from https://www.spglobal.com/en/research-insights/articles/of-cars-and-cans-us-aluminum-and-the-pandemic [Published July 2020], I-168

Offshore Technology Focus, I-696, II-2466, 2484, 2495

OGV Energy, II-2481, 2483, 2493

Oils & Fats International, II-2669, 2768

"Oilseeds: World Markets and Trade." [online] from https://www.fas.usda.gov/data/oilseeds-world-markets-and-trade [Published February 2021], II-2499, 2502-2506, 2508-2514

"Omdia: The $5bn Ripple Effect of Private LTE and 5G Networks." [online] from https://omdia.tech.informa.com/pr/2021-feb/omdia---the-5bn-usd-ripple-effect-of-lte-and-5g [Published February 9, 2021], II-2423

"Omega Supplements are Projected to Steadily Grow in 2021." [online] from https://clearcutanalytics.com/omega-supplements-are-projected-to-steadily-grow-in-2021/ [Published January 13, 2021], II-3280

"OneSmart Education OMO the New Era of Online Education." [online] from http://www.onesmart.investorroom.com [Published March 2020], II-3449

"Onewater Investor Presentation." [online] from http://investor.onewatermarine.com [Published May 2020], I-507

"Online Channels Grab Record 50% of Indonesia Smartphone Sales in Q4 2020." [online] from https://www.counterpointresearch.com/online-channels-indonesia-smartphone-sales-q4-2020/ [Published March 22, 2021], I-636

"Online Grocery to More Than Double Market Share by 2025." [online] from https://www.supermarketnews.com/online-retail/online-grocery-more-double-market-share-2025 [Published September 18, 2020], II-2520

"Online Hotel Accommodation Market Will Maintain Growing Momentum in China." [online] from http://www.iresearchchina.com/content/details7_57335.html [Published September 16, 2019], I-1831

"Operating System Market Share China - 2020." [online] from https://gs.statcounter.com/os-market-share/all/china#yearly-2020-2020-bar [Accessed January 3, 2021], II-3177

"Operating System Market Share United States of America - 2020." [online] from https://gs.statcounter.com/os-market-share/all/united-states-of-america#yearly-2020-2020-bar [Accessed January 3, 2021], II-3176

"Operating System Market Share Worldwide - 2020." [online] from https://gs.statcounter.com/os-market-share#yearly-2020-2020-bar [Accessed January 3, 2021], II-3178

"Opportunities for U.S. Snacks & Sweets in the GCC Region." [online] from https://www.fas.usda.gov/data/opportunities-us-snacks-sweets-gcc-region [Published January 2021], II-3109

"Opportunities in Alternative Seafood." [online] from https://gfi.org/images/uploads/2020/06/GFI_Opportunities_in_Alternative_Seafood.pdf [Published June 25, 2020], II-2987

"Opportunities in the Indian Nutraceutical and Wellness Sector." [online] from https://missp.ch/docs/1590652307Overview%20and%20Opportunities%20in%20the%20Indian%20Nutraceuticals%20and%20Wellness%20Sectors.pdf [Published May 2020], I-1390, II-3276

"The Optical Transceivers Market Will More Than Double by 2025 Driven by Heavy Investments in Data Centers." [online] from http://www.yole.fr [Accessed November 29, 2020], II-2526

"Organic Produce Sales Up 14 Percent in 2020, Topping $8.5 Billion." [online] from https://www.organic-producenetwork.com/article/1253/organic-produce-sales-up-14-percent-in-2020-topping-85-billion [Published January 21, 2021], I-1398

Orlando Business Journal, II-2349

"The Orr Group Industry Report Q4 2020: 8 Million Users Edition." [online] from https://blog.roll20.net/posts/the-orr-group-industry-report-q4-2020-8-million-users-edition/ [Published February 8, 2021], II-3397

"Orthopedic Outlook: COVID-19's Impact on Industry Growth and Trends." [online] from https://www.bonezonepub.com/2710-orthopedic-outlook-covid-19-s-impact-on-industry-growth-and-trends [Published June 19, 2020], II-2242-2243

"OUT Investor Presentation." [online] from https://investor.outfrontmedia.com/overview/default.aspx [Published December 2020], I-39

"Outdoor Kitchens." [online] from http://www.freedoniagroup.com [Published April 2020], II-2534

"Outdoor Living." [online] from http://www.freedoniagroup.com [Published March 2020], II-2535

"Overview of the Virtual Events Market." [online] from https://mhojhosresearch.com/2020/05/01/global-virtual-event-market-is-growing-annually-by-22/ [Published May 1, 2020], II-3486

"Owens Corning 4Q 2020 Focused on Shareholder Value." [online] from https://investor.owenscorning.com/investors/overview/default.aspx [Accessed February 20, 2021], I-282

"The Packaged Dog Food Market in India." [online] from https://casereads.com/the-packaged-dog-food-market-in-india/ [Published December 22, 2020], II-2665

"Packaging & Labeling in the U.S." [online] from http://www.ibisworld.com [Published May 2019], II-2575

Packaging Strategies, II-2577, 2579

The Packer, I-1681, 1686, 1690, 1700

Paint & Coatings Industry, I-685

"Pakistan 2020. Two & Three Wheeler Market Lost 8.9%" [online] from https://www.motorcyclesdata.com/2021/01/20/pakistan-motorcycles/ [Published January 20, 2021], II-2373

"Pandemic Not All Bad News For Tin." [online] from https://www.internationaltin.org/pandemic-not-all-bad-news-for-tin/ [Press release October 20, 2020], II-3338

"P&I 300 2020 Release." [online] from https://www.thinkingaheadinstitute.org/news/article/pi-300-2020-press-release/ [Press release August 26, 2020], II-2647-2648

Panels & Furniture Asia, I-2126, II-3577

Paper360°, II-2568, 2941

"Parcel Distribution: The Race to Own the Delivery Network." [online] from https://www.interactanalysis.com/parcel-distribution-the-race-to-own-the-delivery-network/ [Published November 11, 2020], II-3068

"Pasta and Pasta Sauces Market in Europe: a 24 Country Analysis." [online] from https://www.globenewswire.com/news-release/2020/06/12/2047322/0/en/Pasta-and-Pasta-Sauces-Market-in-Europe-A-24-Country-Analysis.html [Published June 12, 2020], II-2625

"Paul Singer Got Coronavirus Right But May Still Lose." [online] from https://www.bloomberg.com/opinion/articles/2020-04-16/coronavirus-paul-singer-saw-lockdowns-coming-but-may-still-lose [Published April 16, 2020], I-1635

"PC Sales Remain on Fire as Fourth Quarter Shipments Grow 26.1% Over the Previous Year, According to IDC." [online] from http://www.idc.com [Press release January 11, 2021], I-797

"Peak Aluminum Looms for China as Xi Pushes New Green Mission." [online] from https://www.bloomberg.com/news/articles/2021-03-07/peak-aluminum-looms-for-china-as-xi-pushes-new-green-mission [Published March 7, 2021], I-162

"Peer-to-Peer Loan Platforms in the U.S." [online] from http://www.ibisworld.com [Published November 2019], I-2104

Perfumer & Flavorist, I-695, II-3259

"The Perpetual Growth of High-Speed Rail Development." [online] from https://www.globalrailwayreview.com/article/112553/perpetual-growth-high-speed-rail/ [Published November 3, 2020], II-2838

"Personal Watercraft Manufacturing Industry in the U.S." [online] from http://www.ibisworld.com [Published November 2020], II-2659

Pest Control Technology, II-2661-2662

"The Pesticide Market in China Under Environmental Regulations and Industrial Restructuring Amid COVID-19." [online] from https://daxueconsulting.com/pesticide-market-in-china/ [Published December 7, 2020], I-712

Pet Food & Animal Feed Technology, II-2663

Pet Food Processing Resource Guide, II-2668, 2670-2671, 2674, 2676-2678, 2682-2683

"Pet Industry Market Size & Ownership Statistics." [online] from https://www.americanpetproducts.org/press_industrytrends.asp [Accessed January 5, 2021], II-2696

Petfood Industry, II-2681, 2697

PETS International, II-2698

"Phase II: COVID-19 Crisis Through a Migration Lens." [online] from https://www.knomad.org/publication/migration-and-development-brief-33 [Published October 2020], II-2869

Phoenix Business Journal, I-1698

"Piling Rigs Market 2020 Share, Size." [online] from https://thedailychronicle.in/tag/piling-rigs-market-report/ [Press release September 10, 2020], I-858

"Pipe Products & Markets." [online] from http://www.freedoniagroup.com [Published October 2020], II-2720

Pittsburgh Business Journal, II-2350

"Plastic Fencing." [online] from http://www.freedoniagroup.com [Published July 2020], I-1305

"Plastic Pipe & Parts Manufacturing in the U.S." [online] from http://www.ibisworld.com [Published October 2019], II-2730

"The Platform for the Connected Home and Business." [online] from http://www.alarm.com [Published August 2020], II-3100

"Plumbers in the U.S." [online] from http://www.ibisworld.com [Published December 2019], I-931

PMG Producemarketguide.com, I-1510-1513

PMQ Pizza Magazine, II-2881

"Pocket Guide to Transportation 2020." [online] from http://www.bts.gov [Published June 2020], II-2149, 3070

"Pokémon GO Hits $1 Billion in 2020 as Lifetime Revenue Surpasses $4 Billion." [online] from https://sensortower.com/blog/pokemon-go-one-billion-revenue-2020 [Published November 3, 2020], II-2337

"Pollard Banknote Ltd." [online] from http://www.pollardbanknote.com [Published March 11, 2020], I-1577

"POP MART: Blind Box Toys Show the Designer Toy Market in China is Booming." [online] from https://daxueconsulting.com/pop-mart-designer-toy-market-in-china/ [Published February 4, 2021], II-3394

"Pork Production - Top Countries Summary." [online] from https://apps.fas.usda.gov/psdonline/app/index.html#/app/downloads [Published October 2020], II-2213-2214, 2216

"Potatoes 2019 Summary." [online] from http://www.nass.usda.gov [Published September 2020], II-2779

"Pouches." [online] from http://www.freedoniagroup.com [Published November 2020], II-2569

"Poultry and Products Annual." [online] from https://www.fas.usda.gov/data/russia-poultry-and-products-annual-3 [Published September 21, 2020], II-2208

Poultry International, I-1192-1200, II-2177-2185

"Powell's Books Has Had Enough of Amazon." [online] from https://www.retaildive.com/news/powells-books-has-had-enough-of-amazon/585161/ [Published October 1, 2020], I-519

"Power Lawn & Garden Equipment." [online] from http://www.freedoniagroup.com [Published January 2021], I-2036

"Power Tools." [online] from http://www.freedoniagroup.com [Published January 2021], II-3381

PowerSports Business, II-2368

"Pre-Employment Assessment." [online] from http://www.datanyze.com/market-share [Accessed November 10, 2020], II-3180

"Presentation at Nomura Investment Forum 2020." [online] from https://www.nomuraholdings.com/investor/presentation/data/2020_1201_prem.pdf [Published November 1, 2020], I-1983

"Pressure-Sensitive Labels — New AWA Market Study." [online] from https://www.printingnews.com/labels-packaging/press-release/21132434/awa-alexander-watson-associates-pressuresensitive-labels-new-awa-market-study [Published May 8, 2020], I-2021

"Printed Circuit Boards (PCB) Market Overview." [online] from http://www.beroeinc.com [Accessed October 2, 2020], II-2788

"The Prison Industry - How it Started, How it Works, How it Harms." [online] from http://static1.squarespace.com [Published September 20, 2020], I-1421, 1746, II-2798-2799

"Prisoners in 2019." [online] from https://www.bjs.gov/index.cfm?ty=pbdetail&iid=7106 [Published October 2020], II-2800

"Private Detective Services in the U.S." [online] from http://www.ibisworld.com [Published June 2019], I-1978

"Private Student Lending." [online] from https://protectborrowers.org/category/reports/page/2/ [Published April 2020], I-2105

"Probiotics Category With Room to Innovate." [online] from https://clearcutanalytics.com/probiotics-rising-category-with-room-to-innovate/ [Published November 19, 2020], II-3281

"Processed Food Pouches." [online] from http://www.freedoniagroup.com [Published November 2020], II-2570

Produce Blueprints Supplement, I-1696

Produce News, I-1499-1509, II-2389, 2776

"Production, Shipment of Digital Still Cameras." [online] from http://www.cipa.jp/stats/dc_e.html [Accessed February 15, 2021], I-590

"Production Quantities of Cocoa, Beans by Country." [online] from http://www.fao.org/faostat/en/#data/QC/visualize [Accessed February 4, 2021], I-750

Professional Pasta, II-2624

ProFood World, I-102, 1396

Progressive Dairy, I-1034

Progressive Grocer, I-486, 734, 1382

"Project Management." [online] from http://www.datanyze.com/market-share [Accessed November 10, 2020], II-3181

"Protective Mailers." [online] from http://www.freedoniagroup.com [Published July 2020], II-2571

"Pruning Continues as Loss-Making Lloyd's Syndicates Strive for Profit." [online] from https://www.spglobal.com/marketintelligence/en/news-insights/latest-news-headlines/pruning-continues-as-loss-making-lloyd-s-syndicates-strive-for-profit-58165477 [Published May 7, 2020], I-1916-1917

"PT Timah Becomes Top Tin Producer." [online] from https://www.internationaltin.org/pt-timah-top-tin-producer/ [Published February 14, 2020], II-3341

"Public Libraries in the United States." [online] from https://www.imls.gov/sites/default/files/publications/documents/publiclibrariesintheunitedstatessurveyfiscalyear-2017volume1.pdf [Published June 2020], I-2059

"Publisher Market Shares: September 2020." [online] from https://www.previewsworld.com/Article/246764-Publisher-Market-Shares-September-2020 [Published October 21, 2020], I-774

Publishers Weekly, I-521-524, 527, 530-533, II-2811

"Pump & Compressor Manufacturing in the U.S." [online] from http://www.ibisworld.com [Published December 2020], II-2822

"PureGym Investor Presentation." [online] from http://corporate.puregym.com [Published April 2020], I-1723

"Push Notification." [online] from http://www.datanyze.com/market-share [Accessed November 10, 2020], II-3182

"PVH Investor Update Summer 2020." [online] from https://www.pvh.com/investor-relations/reports [Accessed January 10, 2021], I-189, 198

"Q3 2020 IPOs: Auditor Market Share and Stats." [online] from https://blog.auditanalytics.com/q3-2020-ipos-auditor-market-share-and-stats/ [Published October 21, 2020], I-7

Qualified Remodeler, I-874

"Quarterly Hogs and Pigs." [online] from https://usda.library.cornell.edu/concern/publications/rj430453j?locale=en [Published December 23, 2020], I-1781

"Quectel Widens Gap with Competition in Global Cellular IoT Module Market During Covid-Hit Q2 2020." [online] from https://www.counterpointresearch.com/quectel-widens-gap-with-competition-in-global-cellular-iot-module-market-during-q2-2020/ [Published October 28, 2020], II-2422

"QY Research Expects Global Manuka Honey Market Size to Reach Above U.S.$676.1 mn by 2026." [online] from http://www.qyresearch.com [Press release July 20, 2020], I-1825

"RAC Sales Cool Off in Summer." [online] from https://www.edelweiss.in/research/sector-specific-reports-2/consumer-durable-sector-up-date [Published May 11, 2020], I-242

"Racetracks Industry (U.S.)." [online] from http://www.plunkettresearch.com [Published March 5, 2021], II-2826

Radio World, II-2828

Radiology Business Journal, II-3335

"Rail Track System - Global Market Trends 2020." [online] from http://www.sci.de [Press release September 24, 2020], II-2835

Railway Age, II-2837, 2840

Railway Pro, II-2163

R&D Magazine, II-2875

"Rankings Table." [online] from https://www.greenstreet.com/news/real-estate-alert?breakdownId=1 [Accessed February 15, 2021], II-2843-2847, 2851

"Raymond Corporate Overview." [online] from http://www.raymond.ir [Published July 2020], I-196

"The Real Story About the Supply and the Price of Christmas Tree in 2019." [online] from https://realchristmastrees.org/2020/04/06/the-real-story-about-the-price-of-christmas-trees-in-2019/ [Accessed December 2, 2020], I-728

"Realty Income Investor Presentation." [online] from https://www.realtyincome.com/investors/investor-presentation/default.aspx?LanguageId=1 [Published May 2021], I-1680

"Recent Trends in U.S. Services Trade: 2020 Annual Report." [online] from https://www.wita.org/atp-research/trends-in-u-s-services-trade/ [Published July 2020], I-400, 1258, 1984

"ReCon Remarket B2B Digital Platform." [online] from https://img1.wsimg.com/blobby/go/c1799350-4e18-4103-a000-74d35ba69fff/ReconRemarket_Pitch_Deck_v12_info-0004.pdf [Accessed April 13, 2021], I-294

"Record Breaking Spend Grows 62% in Q4 2020 to U.S.$5.8 Billion." [online] from https://canalys.com/newsroom/canalys-china-cloud-services-market-Q4-2020 [Press release March 24, 2021], II-3165

"Record Sales of Forwarders in Sweden 2020." [online] from https://www.forestry.com/editorial/record-sales-forwarders-sweden-2020/ [Published January 25, 2021], I-854

"Recurring Billing." [online] from http://www.datanyze.com/market-share [Accessed November 10, 2020], II-3183

Redbook - A Supplement to Bake Magazine, I-380, 385, 388, 393-399, 549, 555-559, 827

"Refrigerated & Frozen Display Cases." [online] from http://www.freedoniagroup.com [Published July 2020], I-1763

Refrigerated & Frozen Foods, I-1392, 1483

Refrigerated Transporter, II-3427

"Regional Energy: China Refining & Petrochemical Sector." [online] from https://www.dbs.id/id/corporate-id/aics/pdfController.page?pdfpath=/content/article/pdf/AIO/032020/200303_insights_reg_energy.pdf [Published March 3, 2020], II-2468

"The Remarkable Expansion of the Custom Built Market." [online] from https://agbproducts.com/news/the-remarkable-expansion-of-the-custom-built-market/ [Published January 28, 2020], II-2291

Render, I-1293, 1299

"Renewable Capacity Statistics 2020." [online] from http://www.irena.org [Accessed January 2, 2021], I-1229

"Renewables 2020 Global Status Report." [online] from http://www.ren21.net [Published June 2020], I-1216, 1218, 1226, 1230, 1232, 1235

"Report: DIY Camera Market to Experience Exponential Growth." [online] from https://www.security-infowatch.com/video-surveillance/cameras/news/21128925/report-diy-camera-market-to-experience-exponential-growth [Published March 9, 2020], I-591

"Residential Roofing." [online] from http://www.freedoniagroup.com [Published September 2020], II-2931

Restaurant Business, I-763, II-2885, 2888, 2890, 2895, 2897

"Restaurant Industry Facts at a Glance." [online] from https://restaurant.org/research/restaurant-statistics/restaurant-industry-facts-at-a-glance [Accessed December 2, 2020], II-2898

Retail News, I-1693

"Reusable Transport Packaging State of the Industry Report 2020." [online] from http://www.reusables.org [Accessed January 25, 2021], II-2578

"Revenue of Running Sports Industry is Estimated to Hit 360 Bn Yuan by the End of 2019." [online] from http://www.iresearchchina.com/content/details7_57483.html [Published September 25, 2019], II-3220

"Revenue of Top 10 IC Design (Fabless) Companies for 2020 Undergoes 26.4% Increase YoY Due to High Demand for Notebooks and Networking Products, Says TrendForce." [online] from https://www.trendforce.com/presscenter/news/20210325-10735.html [Press release March 25, 2021], I-1956

"Review of 2019 Commercial Boilers Market." [online] from https://www.bsria.com/us/news/article/review_of_2019_commercial_boilers_market/ [Published June 2020], I-512-514

"Review of Maritime Transport 2020." [online] from https://unctad.org/topic/transport-and-trade-logistics/review-of-maritime-transport [Published November 12, 2020], I-745-746, 1669-1670, 1990-1991, II-3047, 3056, 3064

"Reynolds Consumer Products." [online] from https://www.sec.gov/Archives/edgar/data/1786431/000119312520021414/d769843d424b4.htm [Published January 30, 2020], I-169, II-2614-2615

"Rice." [online] from https://apps.fas.usda.gov/psdonline/circulars/grain-rice.pdf [Published October 2020], II-2914-2917

"Ring Doorbells and the Police: What to Do if Surveillance Has You Worried." [online] from https://www.cnet.com/how-to/ring-doorbells-and-the-police-what-to-do-if-surveillance-has-you-worried/ [Published December 1, 2019], II-3102

"Road & Highway Contractors in the U.S." [online] from http://www.ibisworld.com [Published October 2019], I-860

"Robot Sensors-Poised for Strong Global Growth." [online] from https://www.communicationstoday.co.in/robot-sensors-poised-for-strong-global-growth/ [Published October 8, 2020], II-3033

"Rocket Mortgage." [online] from https://www.ml.com/content/dam/ML/ipo/equity_new_issues/Rocket-Companies.pdf [Published July 28, 2020], II-2353

"Rolling Stock Market in North America 2020-2025." [online] from https://mobilityforesights.com/product/rolling-stock-market-in-north-america/ [Published January 2020], II-2834

Rubber & Plastics News, I-708, II-3350

Rubber World, II-3354

"Rugged Data Drives Rugged Toppers." [online] from https://ruggedtoppers.com/blogs/news/rugged-data-drove-rugged-toppers [Published July 30, 2020], I-103

RugNews.com, I-1560

"Rush Street Interactive." [online] from https://www.dmytechnology.com/wp-content/uploads/2021/03/RSIInvestorPresentation15-Oct-2020_vF.pdf [Published October 2020], I-1579

"Russia Textile Market Trends." [online] from http://news.kotra.or.kr [Published September 25, 2020], II-3332

"Russian Video Game Market Trends." [online] from http://www.news.kotra.or.kr [Published August 19, 2020], II-3482

Sacramento Business Journal, II-2351

"Safety & Security Alarms." [online] from http://www.freedoniagroup.com [Published January 2020], II-2995

"Samsung Electric Uses Nonacell Tech to Upgrade World's Only 108-MP Image Sensor." [online] from https://pulsenews.co.kr/view.php?year=2020&no=149716 [Published February 17, 2020], II-3031

"Samsung Surpasses Huawei to Lead Russia Smartphone Market in Q3 2020." [online] from https://www.counterpointresearch.com/russia-smartphone-market-q3-2020/ [Press release November 25, 2020], I-637

"S&P's Plant to Buy IHS May Draw Antitrust Scrutiny from Biden Administration." [online] from https://www.dealstreetasia.com/stories/sp-ihs-218042/ [Published December 1, 2020], I-1323

"Sany Heavy Industry." [online] from https://pdf.dfcfw.com/pdf/H3_AP202101111449519837_1.pdf?1610358391000.pdf [Published January 11, 2021], I-857

SatMagazine, II-2965

"Saudi E-Commerce Industry Exploded With COVID-19 as an Opportunity." [online] from http://www.news.kotra.or.kr [Published May 3, 2021], I-1180

SBC Magazine, I-1857

"Scented American Life, the U.S. Home Fragrance Market." [online] from http://www.news.kotra.or.kr [Published July 20, 2020], I-56

"SCI Verkehr Forecasts 24% Drop in Diesel Locomotive Purchases." [online] from https://www.railjournal.com/fleet/sci-verkehr-forecasts-24-drop-in-diesel-locomotive-purchases/ [Published August 28, 2020], II-2833

"Search Engine Market Share China - 2020." [online] from https://gs.statcounter.com/search-engine-market-share/all/china#yearly-2020-2020-bar [Accessed January 3, 2021], II-3185

"Search Engine Market Share United States of America - 2020." [online] from https://gs.statcounter.com/search-engine-market-share/all/united-states-of-america#yearly-2020-2020-bar [Accessed January 3, 2021], II-3184

"Search Engine Market Share Worldwide - 2020." [online] from https://gs.statcounter.com/search-en-gine-market-share#yearly-2020-2020-bar [Accessed January 3, 2021], II-3186

"Sector Trend Analysis — Crustacean Trends in China." [online] from https://www.agr.gc.ca/eng/international-trade/market-intelligence/reports [Published February 2020], II-2989

"Sector Trend Analysis — Fish and Seafood Trends in Japan." [online] from https://www.agr.gc.ca/eng/international-trade/market-intelligence/reports/?id=1522931721523 [Published July 2020], II-2990-2991

"Sector Trend Analysis — Organic Market Trend of Corn, Soya, Beans and Wheat Between Canada and the United States." [online] from https://www.agr.gc.ca/eng/international-trade/market-intelligence/reports/?id=1522931721523 [Published July 2020], I-392, 490, 840, 1397, 1876, II-2211, 2627, 3195, 3225

"Security Services in the U.S." [online] from http://www.ibisworld.com [Published October 2019], II-3001

"Security Software Publishing in the U.S." [online] from http://www.ibisworld.com [Published November 2019], II-3171

"Semiconductor Industry Factbook 2020." [online] from https://www.semiconductors.org/wp-content/uploads/2020/04/2020-SIA-Factbook-FINAL_reduced-size.pdf [Published April 2020], II-3025-3027

Semiconductor Today, II-3012, 3024

"Seoul's Angels: South Korea Food Delivery Giants Rev Up Rider Race Amid Coronavirus Boom." [online] from https://www.reuters.com/article/health-coronavirus-southkorea-jobs-idUSKBN26Z083 [Published October 13, 2020], I-1413

"Shaft Drive Bike Market 2020." [online] from https://thedailychronicle.in/news/619797/global-shaft-drive-bike-market-size-2020-top-countries-outlook-and-manufacturers-with-impact-of-domestic-and-global-market-industry-outlook-in-depth-analysis-business-opportunities-and-demand-f/ [Press release August 13, 2020], I-495

"Share of K12 in Online Education Market Rose to 20.7% in H1 2019." [online] from http://www.iresearchchina.com/content/details7_58124.html [Published October 22, 2019], II-2515

"Sheep and Goats." [online] from https://usda.library.cornell.edu/concern/publications/000000018?locale=en [Published January 29, 2021], II-3041

"Sherwin-Williams Investor Presentation." [online] from https://s2.q4cdn.com/918177852/files/doc_presentations/2020/2020-Sherwin-Williams-Investor-Presentation.pdf [Accessed August 13, 2020], II-2582

"Sherwin-Williams Investor Presentation 2020." [online] from https://investors.sherwin-williams.com/events-and-presentations/default.aspx [Accessed October 30, 2020], II-2584

"Shipments Reports." [online] from https://www.gpi.org/shipment-reports [Accessed January 10, 2021], I-1628

"Shoe & Footwear Manufacturing in the U.S." [online] from http://www.ibisworld.com [Published March 2020], I-1426

"Shoe & Footwear Wholesaling in the U.S." [online] from http://www.ibisworld.com [Published May 2020], I-1436

"Shoe Stores Industry (U.S.)." [online] from http://www.plunkettresearch.com [Published March 4, 2021], I-1433

"Short Range Outlook." [online] from https://www.worldsteel.org/steel-by-topic/statistics/short-range-outlook.html [Published April 2021], II-3242

"The Show Must Go On." [online] from http://www.goldmansachs.com [Published May 14, 2020], II-2410

"SIA Ranks Largest U.S. Staffing Firms." [online] from http://www2.staffingindustry.com [Press release October 26, 2020], II-3230

"Siemens Gamesa Retains Top Spot in India as Wind Turbine Market Set to Rebound." [online] from https://about.bnef.com/blog/siemens-gamesa-retains-top-spot-in-india-as-wind-turbine-market-set-to-rebound/ [Press release March 8, 2021], II-3444

"SIPRI Yearbook 2020." [online] from https://www.sipri.org/sites/default/files/2020-06/yb20_summary_en_v2.pdf [Accessed May 31, 2021], I-1051-1052

"Skiing Facilities Industry (U.S.)." [online] from http://www.plunkettresearch.com [Published March 5, 2021], II-3087

"Small Appliance Infographic." [online] from http://www.traqline.com [Published November 3, 2020], I-221, 239

"Smart Heat Industry Report 2020-2026." [online] from http://www.researchinchina.com [Published May 2020], II-2302

"Smart Speaker Shipments Cross Record 1 Mn in 2020, Apple Widens the Choice for Consumers." [online] from https://techarc.net/category/press-release/ [Press release February 17, 2021], I-895

"SmarTech Analysis: Over 1.4 Million Kg of AM Copper Powders to Ship by 2029." [online] from https://3dprint.com/267539/smartech-analysis-over-1-4-million-kg-of-am-copper-powders-to-ship-by-2029/ [Published May 19, 2020], II-2294

"Smartphone Market Share." [online] from https://www.idc.com/promo/smartphone-market-share/os [Published December 15, 2020], II-3191

"Smith+Nephew Investor Presentation." [online] from https://www.smith-nephew.com/investor-centre/reporting/presentations-and-site-visits/ [Published October-December 2020], II-2236, 2240, 2248

Snack Food & Wholesale Bakery, I-379, 391, 550, 815, 839, 847, 1006, 1008, 1010, 1012, 1097, 1400, 1485, II-2599, 3111, 3113, 3115, 3118-3119, 3121, 3123, 3125, 3139, 3390-3391

"Snacking Industry." [online] from https://www.bglco.com/wp-content/uploads/2021/04/BGL-Insider-Special-Report-Food-Beverage-Snacking-Industry-4.8.2021.pdf [Published April 2021], II-3108

"Soap and Detergent Market Trends." [online] from http://www.news.kotra.or.kr [Published October 14, 2020], II-3140

"Social Media Stats China - 2020." [online] from https://gs.statcounter.com/social-media-stats/all/china#yearly-2020-2020-bar [Accessed January 3, 2021], I-1968

"Social Media Stats United States of America - 2020." [online] from https://gs.statcounter.com/social-media-stats/all/united-states-of-america#yearly-2020-2020-bar [Accessed January 3, 2021], I-1967

"Social Media Stats Worldwide - 2020." [online] from https://gs.statcounter.com/social-media-stats#yearly-2020-2020-bar [Accessed January 3, 2021], I-1969

"SoFi Has Attained Preliminary Approval from the OCC for a National Bank Charter." [online] from https://www.businessinsider.com/sofi-secured-preliminary-us-bank-charter-approval-2020-10 [Published October 30, 2020], I-402

"Solid Gold Investor Presentation." [online] from http://media.biostime.com/hhglobal/files [Published November 2020], II-2664, 2689-2690

Soundings, I-508

South China Morning Post, II-2172

"South Korea: A Front Runner in E-Commerce." [online] from https://www.businessfinland.fi/49f3ab/globalassets/food/south-korea-mh-v1.pdf [Published June 12, 2020], II-2519

"Spain Retail Foods." [online] from https://gain.fas.usda.gov [Published June 30, 2020], I-1701

"Specialized Storage and Warehousing in the U.S." [online] from http://www.ibisworld.com [Published December 2019], II-3202

"Spirit Data by Category." [online] from https://www.distilledspirits.org/spirit-data-by-category/ [Accessed February 16, 2021], I-2084

"Sporting Goods 2021." [online] from https://wfsgi.org/wp-content/uploads/2021/01/Sporting-Goods-2021.pdf [Accessed January 20, 2021], I-203

Spotlight, II-2237-2239, 2246

Spray Technology & Marketing, I-43-49

"Sri Trang Gloves (Thailand) Public Company Limited Opportunity Day." [online] from https://www.sritranggloves.com/en/investor-relations/downloads/presentations-webcasts [Published September 16, 2020], II-2273

Staffing Success, II-3231

"Starling Gains Ground on Neobank Competitors in the U.K." [online] from https://www.businessinsider.com/starling-gaining-ground-on-larger-uk-neobank-competitors-2021-3 [Published March 18, 2021], I-403

"State of Higher Ed LMS Market for U.S. and Canada: Mid-Year 2020 Edition." [online] from https://philonedtech.com/state-of-higher-ed-lms-market-for-us-and-canada-mid-year-2020-edition/ [Published August 12, 2020], II-3175

State of the Industry - A Supplement to Snac World, II-3110, 3112, 3114, 3116-3117, 3120, 3122, 3124, 3126, 3133, 3136, 3138

"The State of the Multi-Billion Dollar Console Gaming Market." [online] from https://www.visualcapitalist.com/multi-billion-dollar-console-gaming-market/ [Published November 9, 2020], II-3481

"State of the PM Industry in North America - 2020." [online] from https://www.mpif.org/Resources/StateofthePMIndustry.aspx [Published July 2020], II-2296

"State of the Satellite Report 2020." [online] from https://sia.org/news-resources/state-of-the-satellite-industry-report/ [Accessed November 10, 2020], II-2962

"State of the States 2020." [online] from https://www.americangaming.org/resources/state-of-the-states-2020/ [Published June 2020], I-1575

"State of the U.S. Online Gambling and Sports Betting Industry 2021." [online] from https://readthejoe.com/reports/state-of-the-online-gambling-and-sports-betting-industry-2021/ [Published December 11, 2021], I-1573

"The State of World Fisheries and Aquaculture 2020." [online] from http://www.fao.org/3/ca9229en/CA9229EN.pdf [Accessed August 25, 2020], I-1332-1335

"Steel Imports Declined 21.2% in 2020." [online] from https://www.steel.org/2021/01/december-2020-imports/ [Published January 27, 2021], II-3245

"Stock Image." [online] from http://www.datanyze.com/market-share [Accessed November 10, 2020], II-3188

"Stock Tales." [online] from http://www.bsmedia.business-standard.com [Published April 21, 2020], I-211

"Stone Mor Inc." [online] from https://www.sec.gov/Archives/edgar/data/1753886/000156459020015753/ston-10k_20191231.htm [Published December 31, 2019], I-1038-1039

Stone World, I-1671, II-2146

"Stora Enso Investor Kit." [online] from https://www.storaenso.com/en/investors/reports-and-presentations [Published October 2020], II-2560

Store Brands, II-2802-2803

"Strategy Analytics: Apple TV Holds 2% Market Share in Fragmented Streaming Devices Industry." [online] from https://9to5mac.com/2020/09/02/apple-tv-market-share-report/ [Published September 2, 2020], II-3251-3252

"Strategy Analytics: COVID-19 Drives Strong Growth in the Tablet Apps Processor Market in Q2 2020." [online] from https://www.businesswire.com/news/home/20201005005092/en/Strategy-Analytics-COVID-19-Drives-Strong-Growth-in-the-Tablet-Apps-Processor-Market-in-Q2-2020 [Published October 5, 2020], II-3022

"Strategy Analytics: Global Smart Speaker Sales Rose 6% to 30 Million Units in Q2 2020." [online] from https://www.businesswire.com/news/home/20200811005706/en/Strategy-Analytics-Global-Smart-Speaker-Sales [Press release August 11, 2020], I-896

"Strategy Analytics: Samsung Display Captures 50% Revenue Share to Lead the Smartphone Display Panel Market in H1 2020." [online] from https://www.businesswire.com/news/home/20201008005167/en/Strategy-Analytics-Samsung-Display-Captures-50-Revenue-Share-to-Lead-the-Smartphone-Display-Panel-Market-in-H1-2020 [Published October 8, 2020], I-1088

"Strategy Analytics: Samsung Widens Its Lead in the Smartphone DRAM & NAND Market in H1 2020." [online] from https://www.businesswire.com/news/home/20201014005657/en/Strategy-Analytics-Samsung-Widens-its-Lead-in-the-Smartphone-DRAM-NAND-Market-in-H1-2020 [Published October 14, 2020], II-3019-3020

"Strategy Analytics: Sony Led the Growing Smartphone Image Sensor Market in H1 2020." [online] from https://www.businesswire.com/news/home/20201007005124/en/ [Press release October 20, 2020], II-3032

"Streaming Services Spend Heavily on Marketing amid Pandemic." [online] from https://www.emarketer.com/content/top-10-us-ecommerce-companies-2021-plus-6-key-takeaways-our-latest-forecast [Published October 21, 2020], II-2537

"Strong 3Q20 Sales Growth, Expected to Carry On in 4Q." [online] from http://www.gijas.com.hk [Published October 14, 2020], I-361

"Strong Treatment Growth for Seed Treatments and Coatings by Biologicals." [online] from https://ihsmarkit.com/research-analysis/strong-market-growth-for-seed-treatments-and-coatings-boo.html [Published June 1, 2020], I-698

"SunPharma Investor Presentation." [online] from https://www.aurobindo.com/investors/results-reports-presentations/investor-presentations/ [Published February 2020], I-1130

"Suominen One Sweeping Turn." [online] from https://pankki.evli.com/hubfs/ERP/Raportit/Suominen/Suominen%20200924%20Company%20report.pdf [Published September 24, 2020], II-3553-3555

Supermarket News, I-1383, II-2988

"Supreme in China: Behind the Iconic Streetwear Brand and the Battle with Counterfeiters." [online] from https://daxueconsulting.com/supreme-in-china/ [Published December 23, 2020], I-197

"SVOD to Generate $100 Billion." [online] from http://www.digitaltv-research.com/products [Press release September 2020], II-2554

"Swedish Cosmetics Market From Buyers." [online] from http://www.news.kotra.or.kr [Published November 6, 2020], I-978

"Swedish Match Investor Presentation." [online] from https://www.swedishmatch.com/Investors/Presentations/ [Accessed January 13, 2021], II-3372

"Table 10: Major U.S. Coal Producers, 2019." [online] from http://www.eia.gov [Accessed December 10, 2020], I-747

"Table 5: Refiners' Total Operable Atmospheric Crude Oil Distillation Capacity as of January 1, 2020." [online] from https://www.eia.gov/petroleum/refinerycapacity/table5.pdf [Accessed August 25, 2020], II-2467

"Tactical & Service Clothing Manufacturing in the U.S." [online] from http://www.ibisworld.com [Published October 2019], I-206

"Taking Stock With Teens." [online] from http://www.pipersandler.com [Published Fall 2020], I-201-202, 1427-1428

"Tattoo Artists in the U.S." [online] from http://www.ibisworld.com [Published April 2019], II-3296

"Tattooed Chef Investor Presentation." [online] from https://www.sec.gov/Archives/edgar/data/1741231/000121390020014761/ea122992-defa14a_forummerge2.htm [Published September 2020], I-1456

"Tax Preparation Industry (U.S.)." [online] from http://www.plunkettresearch.com [Published March 4, 2021], II-3299

"Tax Preparation Services in the U.S." [online] from http://www.ibisworld.com [Published August 2019], II-3300

"TDR/BCA Regulation Merger Procedure." [online] from http://www.ec.europa.eu [Published October 22, 2019], I-292-293, 295

Tea & Coffee Trade Journal, I-755

"Tea Market in China." [online] from https://www.slideshare.net/DaxueConsulting/the-tea-market-in-china-report-by-daxue-consulting [Published April 2020], II-3302

"Tech Disruption (Part 1) - Video Game Streaming Services." [online] from https://www.ibisworld.com/industry-insider/analyst-insights/tech-disruption-part-1-video-game-streaming-services-in-the-us/ [Published October 1, 2019], II-3479

"Technology, Media, and Telecommunications Predictions 2020." [online] from https://www2.deloitte.com/content/dam/Deloitte/at/Documents/technology-media-telecommunications/at-tmt-predictions-2020.pdf [Accessed January 20, 2021], II-2924, 3314

Tecoya Trend, II-3327

"Telecommunications Networking Equipment Manufacturing in the U.S." [online] from http://www.ibisworld.com [Published July 2019], II-3308

"Telia Company/Bonnier Broadcasting Holding." [online] from https://ec.europa.eu/competition/mergers/cases/decisions/m9064_3542_7.pdf [Published November 12, 2019], II-3318

Tennis Industry, II-3212

"Tent, Awning & Canvas Manufacturing in the U.S." [online] from http://www.ibisworld.com [Published July 2020], II-3325

"Tesla Boom Supercharges Stock of World's Biggest EV Battery Firm." [online] from https://www.bloomberg.com/news/articles/2020-07-19/tesla-boom-supercharges-stock-of-world-s-biggest-ev-battery-firm [Published July 19, 2020], I-307

"Tesla Takes Leadership Position in BEV Market While European Automakers Dominate Top Four PHEV in 2020, Says TrendForce." [online] from https://www.trendforce.com/presscenter/news/20201215-10604.html [Published December 15, 2020], I-332, 347

"Thai Union Investor Report 2019." [online] from http://www.investor.thaiunion.com [Accessed October 30, 2020], II-2982, 2985

"Theme Index Museum Index 2019." [online] from https://www.teaconnect.org/index.cfm [Accessed November 4, 2020], I-178-182, II-3510

"These Were the Best-Selling Cars, SUVs and Pickups of 2020." [online] from https://www.forbes.com/wheels/news/best-selling-cars-suvs-pickups-2020/ [Published January 6, 2021], I-337

"Third Quarter PC Monitor Volume Hits an 8-Year High; Pandemic-Driven Demand Expected to Last Several More Quarters, According to IDC." [online] from http://www.idc.com [Press release December 8, 2020], I-785

"ThredUp 2020 Resale Report." [online] from https://www.thredup.com/resale/static/thredup-resaleReport2020-42b42834f03ef2296d83a44f85a3e2b3.pdf [Published March 2020], II-2994

"Three-Quarters of All New Cars to be Connected in Five Years." [online] from https://www.counterpointresearch.com/three-quarters-new-cars-connected-five-years/ [Published November 11, 2020], I-341

Tile International, I 659-660, II-2957, 2959

The Times, I-1435

Tire Review, I-352, 360

TissueMag, II-2611

Today's Trucking, II-3432-3435

"Top 10 Beauty Websites Among U.S. Internet Users, Ranked by Market Share of Visits, Dec. 2019." [online] from http://www.emarketer.com [Published January 2020], I-1971

"Top 10 Cement Companies in 2020." [online] from https://datis-inc.com/blog/top-10-cement-companies-in-india-2020/ [Published July 19, 2020], I-646

"Top 10 Chinese Pharma Companies 2020." [online] from https://pharmaboardroom.com/facts/top-10-chinese-pharma-companies-2020/ [Accessed March 29, 2021], I-1133

"Top 10 Countries/Markets by Game Revenues." [online] from https://newzoo.com/insights/rankings/top-10-countries-by-game-revenues/ [Accessed January 5, 2021], I-1576

"Top 10 Home Appliance Brands in China." [online] from https://equalocean.com/analysis/2020071214225 [Published July 12, 2020], I-243-244, 248-249

"Top 10 House and Garden Websites Among U.S. Internet Users, Ranked by Market Share of Visits, Dec. 2019." [online] from http://www.emarketer.com [Published January 2020], I-1973

"Top 10 Largest Health Systems in the U.S." [online] from https://blog.definitivehc.com/top-10-largest-health-systems [Published July 23, 2020], I-1747

"Top 10 Largest OSAT Companies' Revenues Exceed U.S.$6.7 Billion, While Amkor Scores Highest YoY Growth, According to TrendForce." [online] from https://www.trendforce.com/presscenter/news/20201116-10553.html [Published November 16, 2020], II-3014

"Top 10 Pharmaceutical Markets Worldwide 2019." [online] from https://www.iqvia.com/-/media/iqvia/pdfs/canada/2019-trends/top10-worldwidesales_en_19.pdf?la=en&hash=5B6D9922E053B42D9F2A1FD7A1883A87 [Accessed April 20, 2021], I-1126

"Top 10 U.S. Lumber Producers in 2020." [online] from https://forisk.com/blog/2021/01/12/top-10-u-s-lumber-producers-in-2020/ [Published January 12, 2021], I-2129

"Top 100 Contractors Reports." [online] from https://beta.sam.gov/reports/awards/static [Accessed April 26, 2021], I-1645-1664

"Top 100 Retailers 2020." [online] from https://risnews.com/top-100-retailers-2020 [Published June 29, 2020], II-2909

"Top 100 Retailers 2020 List." [online] from https://nrf.com/resources/top-retailers/top-100-retailers/top-100-retailers-2020-list [Accessed August 10, 2020], II-2904

"Top 15 Specialty Pharmacies of 2019." [online] from http://www.drugchannels.net [Published July 22, 2020], I-1116

"The Top 15 U.S. Pharmacies of 2020: Market Shares and Revenues at the Biggest Companies." [online] from https://www.drugchannels.net/2021/03/the-top-15-us-pharmacies-of-2020-market.html#more [Published March 9, 2021], I-1115

"Top 30 Ports: Big Port Got Bigger in 2020." [online] from https://www.logisticsmgmt.com/article/top_30_u.s._ports_big_ports_got_bigger_in_2020 [Published May 5, 2021], II-2769

"The Top 30 Retailers in Asia in 2020." [online] from https://blog.euromonitor.com/the-top-30-retailers-in-asia-in-2020/ [Published May 29, 2020], II-2908

"Top 50 Global Retailers 2021." [online] from https://nrf.com/resources/top-retailers/top-50-global-retailers/top-50-global-retailers-2021 [Accessed May 20, 2021], II-2910

"Top 50 Multi-Platform Properties." [online] from https://www.comscore.com/Insights/Rankings [Accessed February 15, 2021], I-1975

"Top 50 Total Sales Customers." [online] from https://www.aga.org/research/data/utility-rankings/ [Accessed January 25, 2021], II-3458

"Top 50 U.S. Patent Assignees." [online] from https://www.ificlaims.com/rankings-top-50-2020.htm [Accessed April 20, 2021], II-2628

"Top E-Commerce Ranking Platform Rankings by Market Share." [online] from https://www.cloudways.com/blog/top-ecommerce-platforms/ [Published April 1, 2021], I-1173

"Top Lobbying Firms." [online] from https://www.opensecrets.org/federal-lobbying/top-lobbying-firms [Accessed February 1, 2021], I-2109

"The Top Pharmacy Benefit Managers of 2020: Vertical Integration Drives Consolidation." [online] from https://www.drugchannels.net/2021/04/the-top-pharmacy-benefit-managers-pbms.html [Published April 6, 2021], II-2701

"Top Publishers." [online] from http://analytics.podtrac.com/podcast-publisher-rankings [Accessed January 5, 2021], II-2762

"Top-Selling Video Titles in the United States 2020." [online] from https://www.the-numbers.com/home-market/packaged-media-sales/2020 [Accessed January 5, 2021], I-1162

"Top Urgent Care Centers in the U.S." [online] from https://www.scrapehero.com/top-urgent-care-centers-in-the-us/ [Published November 20, 2020], I-1753

"Tops of 2020: Television." [online] from https://www.nielsen.com/us/en/insights/article/2020/tops-of-2020-television/ [Published December 14, 2020], II-3323-3324

"Total Coffee Exports." [online] from https://apps.fas.usda.gov/psd-online/app/index.html#/app/downloads [Published December 2020], I-753

"Total Coffee Imports." [online] from https://apps.fas.usda.gov/psd-online/app/index.html#/app/downloads [Published December 2020], I-754

"Total Core Home Appliances." [online] from https://www.traqline.com/newsroom/category/infographics/ [Published April 12, 2021], I-222, 246

"Total Potato Sales." [online] from https://potatoesusa.com/wp-content/uploads/2020/07/FY20-Total-Potatoes-7.1.19_6.30.20.pdf [Accessed December 2, 2020], II-2778

"Tour Operators in the United States." [online] from http://www.ibisworld.com [Published July 2019], II-3416

"TowerXchange Africa 2019 Dossier." [online] from http://www.towerxchange.com [Published August 2020], II-3574

"Tractor and Agricultural Machinery Manufacturing in the U.S." [online] from http://www.ibisworld.com [Published October 2020], I-1281

"The Trade Desk's Q2 Earnings Show That CTV is Still a Silver Lining in Programmatic Advertising During the Pandemic." [online] from https://www.businessinsider.com/ctv-spending-sees-growth-amid-broader-revenue-decline-2020 [Published August 10, 2020], I-16

"Trade Market Intelligence: Special Report Hotspots in the United States." [online] from http://www.novascotiabusiness.com [Published September 2019], II-2420, 2725, 2787, 2789

"TransAlta Power the Future." [online] from https://www.transalta.com/wp-content/uploads/2021/04/Investor-Presentation-April-2021-Powering-the-Future.pdf [Published April 12, 2021], I-1225

Travel Retail Business, I-100

"TrendForce: Driven by Shrinking Pixel Pitch, Video Wall LED Market Revenue Still Projected to Grow 3.7%, YoY in 2020." [online] from https://www.ledinside.com/intelligence/2020/5/tf_video_wall_2020 [Published May 12, 2020], I-2052

"Trends in Japan's Telecommunications Equipment." [online] from https://workinjapan.today/hightech/trends-in-japans-telecommunications-equipment/ [Published January 21, 2020], II-2426

"Trends in the VOD Market in EU-28." [online] from https://rm.coe.int/trends-in-the-vod-market-in-eu28-final-version/1680a1511a [Published January 2021], II-2541, 2543, 2545-2546, 2548-2549, 2551

"The Trends That Will Shape the Data Centre Market in 2020." [online] from https://www.am.miraeasset.com.hk/insight/the-trends-that-will-shape-the-data-centre-market-in-2020/ [Accessed November 30, 2020], I-1037

"Trendyol Seeks Over $1 Billion to be Largest Turkish Startup." [online] from https://www.bloomberg.com/news/articles/2021-04-26/alibaba-backed-trendyol-seeks-over-1-billion-to-fund-growth [Published April 26, 2021], I-1183

"Trex Company Long Thesis." [online] from https://seekingalpha.com/instablog/51271678-james-weston/5444157-trex-company-long-thesis-written-10th-march-2020-when-shares-worth-93 [Published May 17, 2020], I-1043-1044

Triad Business Journal, I-1691, 1702

"Triton Investor Presentation." [online] from https://www.tritoninternational.com/investors/news-and-events/events [Published November 9, 2020], I-905

"Trout Production." [online] from https://www.nass.usda.gov/Surveys/Guide_to_NASS_Surveys/Trout_Production/index.php [Published February 25, 2021], I-1329

Turbomachinery International, II-3442-3443

"Turkeys Raised." [online] from https://usda.library.cornell.edu/concern/publications/0g354f23n?locale=en [Published September 24, 2020], II-2225

"Turning Point Brands Investor Presentation." [online] from https://www.turningpointbrands.com [Published Spring 2020], I-730

"Tutoring & Test Preparation Franchises in the United States." [online] from http://www.ibisworld.com [Published March 2019], II-3450

"TV Market Share." [online] from https://www.t4.ai/industry/tv-market-share [Published January 23, 2021], I-898

TV Veopar Journal, I-881

"Twitter: Most Followers." [online] from https://friendorfollow.com/twitter/most-followers/ [Accessed December 9, 2020], I-1970

"Two World's Largest Security Camera Companies Added to the U.S. Sanctions List." [online] from http://image-sensors-world.blogspot.com/2019/10/two-worlds-largest-security-camera.html [Published October 12, 2019], I-592

"TWS and Watches Became Smartphone Companion Devices in Q4 2020." [online] from https://www.canalys.com/newsroom/canalys-tws-and-wearables-q4-2020 [Press release March 30, 2021], II-3519-3520

"TWS Drives 2020 Wearables Growth; Smartwatches to Add Momentum From 2021." [online] from https://www.counterpointresearch.com/tws-drives-2020-wearables-growth-smartwatches-add-momentum-2021/ [Press release January 14, 2021], II-3515

"Uber and Lyft Users and Sales Will Decline Dramatically in 2020 Before Rebounding in 2021." [online] from https://www.businessinsider.com/uber-lyft-sales-will-rebound-2021-after-declining-this-year-2020-9 [Published September 16, 2020], II-2918

"Ultra-Large TVs Set to Join Mainstream, Led by Samsung, LG." [online] from https://pulsenews.co.kr/view.php?year=2020&no=1000557 [Published September 28, 2020], I-880

"Underestimated User Value, Initiate with Buy." [online] from http://www.pdf.dfcfw.com [Published October 7, 2020], II-2333

"UNECE Forest Products Annual Market Review 2019-2020." [online] from https://unece.org/forests/fpamr2020 [Accessed December 10, 2020], II-3579-3580, 3583-3587

"UniFirst Investing to Compete With Cintas." [online] from https://seekingalpha.com/article/4417968-unifirst-investing-to-compete-with-cintas [Published April 7, 2021], II-3328-3329

"Union Members Summary." [online] from https://www.bls.gov/

news.release/union2.nr0.htm [Published January 22, 2021], II-3452

"UnionPay Accounts for 45% of Global Cards Spending, but Only 1% Outside China." [online] from https://www.rbrlondon.com/press/ [Published November 5, 2020], II-2635

"U.S. AG Tractor and Combine Reports." [online] from https://www.aem.org/market-share-statistics/us-ag-tractor-and-combine-reports [Accessed January 18, 2021], I-1287

"U.S. Airbnb Usage Will Drop 60% This Year." [online] from https://www.emarketer.com/content/airbnb-usage-will-drop-60-percent-this-year [Published August 28, 2020], I-1792

"U.S. Artificial Marble Market Trend." [online] from http://www.news.kotra.or.kr [Published July 7, 2020], I-276

"U.S. Birth Rate Declines Due to Corona 19, Baby Products Industry Dark Clouds." [online] from http://www.news.kotra.or.kr [Published November 25, 2020], I-375

"U.S. Bottled Water Market." [online] from https://bottledwater.org/bottled-water-market/ [Accessed January 20, 2021], I-536

"U.S. Camping Goods Market Trend." [online] from http://www.news.kotra.or.kr [Published July 7, 2020], II-3213

"U.S. Car Sales Analysis 2020 - Commercial Vans." [online] from https://carsalesbase.com/us-car-sales-analysis-2020-commercial-vans/ [Accessed April 21, 2021], II-3467

"U.S. CBD Market Report." [online] from https://content.brightfieldgroup.com/2020-us-cbd-market-report [Published July 2020], I-603

"U.S. Church Membership Falls Below Majority for First Time." [online] from https://news.gallup.com/poll/341963/church-membership-falls-below-majority-first-time.aspx [Published March 29, 2021], II-2866

"U.S. Click and Collect in 2020 and 2021." [online] from https://www.emarketer.com/content/us-click-collect-2020-2021 [Published March 24, 2021], I-1171

"U.S. Computer Infographic." [online] from https://stevensoncompany.com/category/infographics/ [Published August 3, 2020], I-789

"U.S. Consumer Goods: Sector Overview, Credit Trends and Outlook." [online] from https://www.spglobal.com/_assets/documents/ratings/research/100049347.pdf [Published March 2021], I-235, 488, 737, 1141, 1399, II-2652, 2686, 2946, 3150

"U.S. Court Reporting Market Overview." [online] from https://verbit.ai/wp-content/uploads/2020/07/Status-Update-The-Legal-Market-Existing-Gaps-Presentation.pdf [Published July 2020], I-1001

"The U.S. Diaper Market Continues to Grow." [online] from http://news.kotra.or.kr [Published August 28, 2020], II-2951

"U.S. Digital Out-of-Home Ad Spending 2020." [online] from http://www.emarketer.com [Published August 2020], I-21

"U.S. Door Lock Market Record." [online] from http://www.news.kotra.or.kr [Published August 14, 2020], I-2110

"U.S. E-Commerce by Category 2021." [online] from https://www.emarketer.com/content/top-10-us-ecommerce-companies-2021-plus-6-key-takeaways-our-latest-forecast [Published April 27, 2021], I-1176

"U.S. Exercise Supplement Market Focused on Health." [online] from http://www.news.kotra.or.kr [Published March 3, 2020], II-3283

"U.S. Fish and Wildlife Service National Hunting License Data." [online] from https://www.fws.gov/wsfrprograms/subpages/licenseinfo/hunting.htm [Accessed January 20, 2021], I-1863-1864

"U.S. Flying Car Pays Attention in the eVTOL Market." [online] from http://news.kotra.or.kr [Published September 22, 2020], II-3453

"U.S. Furniture Sales Surge in the Era When Houses Become Companies, Schools, and Vacations." [online] from http://www.news.kotra.or.kr [Published July 15, 2020], I-1542

"U.S. Laundry Detergent Market Trend." [online] from http://www.news.kotra.or.kr [Published November 16, 2020], I-1059

"U.S. Meal Replacement Market Trend." [online] from http://news.kotra.or.kr [Published November 2, 2020], II-3279

"U.S. Medical Device Industry Trends." [online] from http://www.news.kotra.or.kr [Published December 2, 2020], II-2253

"U.S. Mobile Ad Spending Will Manage to Grow in 2020." [online] from https://www.emarketer.com/content/us-mobile-ad-spending-will-manage-grow-2020 [Published August 6, 2020], I-19

"U.S. Nut-Butter Demand Soars as PB&Js Fuel Pandemic Year." [online] from https://www.bloomberg.com/news/articles/2020-12-08/u-s-nut-butter-demand-soars-as-pb-js-fuel-pandemic-year-chart [Published December 8, 2020], II-3224

"U.S. Paper Box Market Trend." [online] from http://www.news.kotra.or.kr [Published June 15, 2020], I-545

"U.S. Payment Users Will Surpass 100 Million This Year." [online] from https://www.emarketer.com/content/us-payment-users-will-surpass-100-million-this-year [Published March 30, 2021], II-2341

"U.S. Pharmaceutical Trends, Issues, and Outlook for NACDS." [online] from https://regional.nacds.org/wp-content/uploads/Pharmaceutical-Trends-Issues-and-Forecasts.pdf [Published February 9, 2021], I-1128

"U.S. Podcast Ad Spending to Surpass $1 Billion Next Year." [online] from https://www.emarketer.com/content/us-podcast-ad-spending-surpass-1-billion-next-year [Published August 4, 2020], II-2765-2766

"U.S. Postal Service Adds First Surcharges Ahead of Holiday Rush." [online] from https://www.bloomberg.com/news/articles/2020-08-14/u-s-postal-service-adds-first-surcharges-ahead-of-holiday-rush [Published August 14, 2020], II-3069

"United States Postal Service - FY 2020 Annual Report to Congress." [online] from https://about.usps.com/what/financials/ [Published December 11, 2020], II-2773

"U.S. Sales Data." [online] from https://www.toyassociation.org/ta/research/data/u-s-sales-data/toys-research-and-data/data/us-sales-data.aspx [Accessed February 15, 2021], II-3401

"U.S. Sanitary Napkin Market Trend." [online] from http://www.news.kotra.or.kr [Published August 13, 2020], II-2949

"United States Sports Betting." [online] from http://gaming.unlv.edu [Published February 2021], I-1584

"U.S. Sports Betting App Download Growth Remains Strong." [online] from https://www.casinojournal.com/articles/93510-us-sports-betting-app-download-growth-remains-strong [Published March 5, 2020], I-258

"U.S. Sports Equipment." [online] from https://www.traqline.com/newsroom/category/infographics/ [Published February 8, 2021], II-3209

"U.S. Sportswear Market Expects a New Leap Forward." [online] from http://www.news.kotra.or.kr [Published March 9, 2021], I-205

"U.S. Staffing Industry Forecast." [online] from http://www.staffingindustry.com [Published April 2020], II-3232

"U.S. to Reach 317 Million SVOD Subscriptions." [online] from http://www.digitaltvresearch.com/products [Press release September 2020], II-2538

"U.S. Virtual and Augmented Reality Users 2021." [online] from https://www.emarketer.com/content/us-virtual-augmented-reality-us-ers-2021 [Published April 15, 2021], II-3153

"U.S. Vitamin and Health Supplement Market Exploded Through the Let's Raise the Immunity Pandemic." [online] from http://www.news.kotra.or.kr [Published March 29, 2021], II-3487

"U.S. Windows/Doors Infographic." [online] from https://stevensoncompany.com/category/infographics/ [Published August 3, 2020], II-3536

"US Wireless Snapshot: Subscribers, Market Share and Q3 Estimates." [online] from https://www.lightreading.com/4g3gwifi/us-wireless-snapshot-subscribers-market-share-and-q3-estimates/d/d-id/764688 [Published October 16, 2020], II-3562

USA Today, II-3316-3317

"Use it as an Opportunity to Grow the U.S. Sauce Market and ex-Korean Sauces." [online] from http://www.news.kotra.or.kr [Published January 19, 2021], II-2967

"Used Car Dealers in the U.S." [online] from http://www.ibisworld.com [Published July 2019], I-297

"Using Marketing to Accelerate Growth at Jackie Mason." [online] from https://gorogue.net/wp-content/uploads/2019/09/Jack-Mason-Pitch-Deck-_-Digital-Strategy.pdf [Published January 2018], I-2002

"Utz Brands Collier Creek." [online] from http://www.colliercreek-holdings.com [Accessed August 25, 2020], II-3127-3130

"Uzbek Leather and Footwear Industry." [online] from http://www.news.kotra.or.kr [Published September 19, 2019], I-2047

"Vacuum Skin Packaging." [online] from http://www.freedoniagroup.com [Published July 2020], II-2573

"Valentine's Day Disrupted: Venture-Backed Flower Firms Blossoms as Incumbents Wither." [online] from https://www.earnestresearch.com/valentines-day-disrupted-venture-backed-flower-firms-blossom-as-incumbents-wither/ [Published February 11, 2021], I-1369-1370

Valve World Americas, II-3465

"Vanguard Surpasses BlackRock in ETF Inflows During First Half." [online] from https://www.investmentnews.com/vanguard-surpasses-blackrock-in-etf-inflows-during-first-half-194862 [Published July 7, 2020], I-1980

Variety, II-2632, 3320-3321, 3484

"Vedanta Resources Ltd." [online] from https://links.sgx.com/FileOpen/Vedanta%20Holdings%20Mauritius%20II%20Limited_OC%20dtd%2017%20Aug%202020.ashx?App=Prospectus&FileID=46149 [Published August 17, 2020], I-159, 166, 958, 960-962, 1989, II-3601-3602

"Vegetables 2020 Summary." [online] from https://downloads.usda.library.cornell.edu/usdaesmis/files/02870v86p/j6731x86f/9306tr664/vegean21.pdf [Published February 2021], I-1498, 1514, 1530, 1532, 1534-1536, 1540-1541

"Verified Opera Statistics." [online] from https://www.operabase.com/statistics/en [Accessed April 26, 2021], I-1246

"Verijet Investor Presentation." [online] from https://genevalentino.com/wp-content/uploads/2020/10/Series-A-Presentation-October-2020-v11.pdf [Published October 2020], I-85

"View." [online] from https://www.cantor.com/wp-content/uploads/2020/11/View-Investor-Presentation.pdf [Published November 30, 2020], I-1619

"VIPKid." [online] from https://ld-investments.com/author/ld_investments/ [Accessed August 25, 2020], I-1966

"Virtual Data Rooms in the U.S." [online] from http://www.ibisworld.com [Published October 2019], II-3173

"The Virtual Reality Market in China." [online] from https://daxueconsulting.com/virtual-reality-market-in-china/ [Published April 13, 2020], II-3192

Vision Monday, II-2524

"Visitation Numbers." [online] from https://www.nps.gov/aboutus/visitation-numbers.htm [Published February 25, 2021], II-2622-2623

"Vitamin and Health Supplement in China." [online] from https://daxueconsulting.com/athleisure-market-in-china/ [Published July 2020], II-3275

"VMA Statistical Reports." [online] from https://www.vma.org/page/StatisticalReports [Accessed November 16, 2020], II-3466

The Voice, II-3205-3206

Wall Street Journal, I-343, 540, 1257, 1672, 1832, 1972, 2108, 2135, II-2277, 2346, 2850, 2903, 3154, 3166, 3250, 3307, 3460, 3550

"Walmart and Facebook are Taking Social Commerce Cues From China." [online] from https://www.businessinsider.com/walmart-and-facebook-are-following-chinas-social-commerce-trends-2020 [Published August 31, 2020], I-1185

"Walmart Gets Creative, Goes Virtual as it Plans for Holiday Toy Shopping." [online] from https://www.cnbc.com/2020/09/03/walmart-gets-creative-goes-virtual-as-it-plans-for-holiday-toy-shopping.html [Published September 2, 2020], II-3402

"Watch Distribution of Swiss Watch Exports." [online] from https://www.fhs.swiss/eng/statistics.html [Accessed January 25, 2021], II-3506

WATTPoultry USA, II-2224

"WDMA 2020 U.S. Industry Market Study Products Trend." [online] from https://www.openuptoperformance.com/wdma-2020-u-s-industry-market-study-product-trends/ [Accessed December 5, 2020], II-3541

"We Now Have a Better Outlook for Digital Advertising Spending: U.S. Spending to Grow by 21.1% in 2021, eMarketer Reports." [online] from https://whatsnewinpublishing.com/we-now-have-a-better-outlook-for-digital-ad-spending-us-spend-to-grow-by-21-1-in-2021-emarketer-reports/ [Accessed April 15, 2021], I-18

"Wealth Management Under the Development Mode of Asset-Liability Dual Engines." [online] from https://www.newchinalife.com/sen/info/50947 [Published December 2020], I-1986

"Website Builders." [online] from http://www.datanyze.com/market-share [Accessed November 10, 2020], II-3193

"Wedding Consumption Trends in China." [online] from http://www.news.kotra.or.kr [Published May 27, 2020], II-3524

"Weighing in on the Year 2020." [online] from https://www.jetnet.com/uploads/iq-pulse/JETNET%20iQ%20Pulse%20-%20January%2028%202021.pdf [Published January 21, 2021], I-63

"Welcome to the IFR Press Conference." [online] from https://ifr.org/ifr-press-releases/news/record-2.7-million-robots-work-in-factories-around-the-globe [Published September 24, 2020], II-2922

"Welcome to the IFR Press Conference." [online] from https://ifr.org/ifr-press-releases/news/record-2.7-million-robots-work-in-factories-around-the-globe [Published September 24 2020], II-2921, 2923

"West Fraser Investor Presentation." [online] from https://www.westfraser.com/sites/default/files/presentations/pdfs/Investor%20Presentation%20%28Jan-21%29.pdf [Published January 2021], I-2124

"Western Europe to Add 101 Million SVOD Subs." [online] from http://www.digitaltvresearch.com/products [Press release September 2020], II-2552

"What's Next for the Grocery Market in China After the Stay-at-Home Economy Slows?" [online] from https://daxueconsulting.com/online-grocery-market-in-china/ [Published April 23, 2021], II-2518

"Wheat." [online] from https://apps.fas.usda.gov/psdonline/circulars/grain-wheat.pdf [Published October 2020], II-3530-3533

"Wheel and Tire Market Trends." [online] from https://www.sema.org/news-media/magazine/2021/02/wheel-and-tire-market-trends-0 [Published February 2021], II-3349

"Which Company is Winning the Restaurant Food Delivery War?" [online] from https://secondmeasure.com/datapoints/food-delivery-services-grubhub-uber-eats-doordash-postmates/ [Published August 20, 2020], I-1403-1412

"Who Audits Public Companies - United Kingdom." [online] from https://blog.auditanalytics.com/who-audits-public-companies-united-kingdom/ [Published March 16, 2021], I-6

"Why Hanes Should Be on Your Shopping List." [online] from https://www.morningstar.com/articles/987983/why-hanes-should-be-on-your-shopping-list [Published June 11, 2020], I-199, 210

"Will COVID-19 Change the Parking Business?" [online] from https://thehustle.co/covid-19-business-of-parking-lots/ [Published April 26, 2020], II-2620

"Wind Energy in Europe 2020." [online] from https://windeurope.org/intelligence-platform/product/wind-energy-in-europe-in-2020-trends-and-statistics/ [Published February 2021], I-1224

"The Wind of Change in the U.S. Women's Clothing Market." [online] from http://www.news.kotra.or.ok [Published September 18, 2020], I-216

Wine Business Monthly, II-3543, 3551

Winsight Grocery Business, I-969, 1029, 1058, 1401, II-2167, 2169, 2171, 2204, 2217, 2227

Winston-Salem Journal, II-3360

"Wood Fencing." [online] from http://www.freedoniagroup.com [Published July 2020], I-1306

"World Centrifugal Sugar: Production and Consumption." [online] from https://apps.fas.usda.gov/psdonline/app/index.html#/app/downloads [Published May 2020], II-3257-3258

"The World Copper Factbook 2020." [online] from http://www.icsg.org [Accessed December 15, 2020], I-951-953

"World Corn Production - Top Countries Summary." [online] from https://apps.fas.usda.gov/psdonline/app/index.html#/app/downloads [Published October 2020], I-965-968

"World Energy Outlook 2020." [online] from https://www.iea.org/reports/world-energy-outlook-2020 [Accessed December 10, 2020], I-1217

"World Fertilizer Trends and Outlook to 2022." [online] from http://www.fao.org [Accessed November 4, 2020], I-1313-1315

"World Fertilizer Trends and Outlook to 2022." [online] from http://www.fao.org/3/ca6746en/ca6746en.pdf [Accessed November 4, 2020], I-681

World Furniture - International Markets Review, I-232, 2074

World Grain, I-1373-1374

"World Oats Production, Consumption and Stocks." [online] from https://apps.fas.usda.gov/psdonline/app/index.html#/app/downloads [Published October 2020], II-2458-2459

"World Preview 2020, Outlook to 2026." [online] from http://www.evaluate.com [Published July 2020], I-1137-1138

"World Silver Survey 2020." [online] from http://www.silverinstitute.org [Accessed October 25, 2020], I-1999, II-3081-3084, 3086

"World Steel Figures in 2021." [online] from https://www.worldsteel.org/steel-by-topic/statistics/World-Steel-in-Figures.html [Accessed June 20, 2021], II-3238

"World Trade Statistical Review 2020." [online] from https://www.wto.org/english/res_e/statis_e/wts2020_e/wts20_toc_e.htm [Accessed October 28, 2020], I-188, 190, 705, 707, 1388-1389, II-2460-2461, 3240-3241, 3330-3331

"World Uranium Mining Production." [online] from https://world-nuclear.org/information-library/nuclear-fuel-cycle/mining-of-uranium/world-uranium-mining-production.asp [Published December 2020], II-3457

"Worldwide Converged Systems Market Grows 4.5% Year Over Year During the First Quarter of 2020, According to IDC." [online] from http://www.idc.com [Press release June 18, 2020], II-3168

"Worldwide Enterprise External OEM Storage Systems Market Revenue Declined 1.4% During the Third Quarter of 2020, According to IDC." [online] from http://www.idc.com [Press release December 8, 2020], I-781

"Worldwide Enterprise WLAN Market Rebounds With 7.4% Growth in the Third Quarter of 2020, According to IDC." [online] from http://www.idc.com [Press release December 8, 2020], I-782

"The Worldwide Semiconductor Market is Expected to Increase 5.1 Percent in 2020, According to 8.4 Percent in 2021." [online] from http://www.wsts.org [Press release December 1, 2020], II-3010

"Worldwide Spending on Artificial Intelligence is Expected to Double in Four Years, Reaching $110 Billion in 2024, According to New IDC Spending Guide." [online] from http://www.idc.com [Press release August 25, 2020], I-275

"Worldwide Tablet Shipments Return to Growth in 2020, Fueled by Unprecedented Demand, According to IDC." [online] from http://www.idc.com [Press release February 1, 2021], I-800

"WPC & Plastic Lumber." [online] from http://www.freedoniagroup.com [Published September 2020], I-2125

"XPO Investor Presentation." [online] from https://www.xpo.com/investor-presentation/ [Published November 2020], I-1174

"Year-End 2020 RIAA Revenue Statistics." [online] from https://www.riaa.com/reports/2020-year-end-music-industry-revenue-report [Accessed March 26, 2021], II-2406

"Year-End Report U.S. 2020." [online] from https://www.billboard.com/p/u-s-music-year-end-report-2020 [Accessed January 10, 2021], II-2403

"Yearly Hardware Comparisons - USA." [online] from https://www.vgchartz.com/tools/hw_date.php?reg=USA&ending=Yearly [Accessed March 28, 2021], II-3476, 3478

Primary Sources

"The 100 Tower Companies in the U.S." [online] from http://wireless-estimator.com/top-100-us-tower-companies-list/ [Published February 2, 2021], II-3573

1010data, I-1560, II-2688

2017 Global Infrastructure Outlook, Oxford Economics, I-1899

2018 Fractionation Report, I-1877

2019-2020 APPA National Pet Owners Survey, II-2696

"2019-2020 Trends in Private Clubs." [online] from https://www.stoneybrook.net/files/2019-20%20trends

%20in%20private%20clubs%20report.pdf [Accessed February 15, 2021], II-2801

"2020 Insights on the Global & Chinese Jewelry Market to 2026." [online] from https://www.globenewswire.com/news-release/2020/08/05/2073121/0/en/2020-Insights-on-the-Global-Chinese-Jewelry-Market-to-2026.html [Published August 5, 2020], I-2001

"2020 is History — How Did Light Aircraft Fare in this Year of Fear?" [online] from https://www.bydanjohnson.com/2020-is-history-how-did-light-aircraft-fare-in-this-year-of-fear/ [Published January 31, 2021], I-64

2020 NOLN Fast Lube Operator Survey, I-2114-2116

2020 Organic Produce Performance Report, I-1398

"2020 Outlook: Dialysis Clinics and ESRD." [online] from https://healthcareappraisers.com/2020-outlook-dialysis-clinics-and-esrd/ [Published March 6, 2020], I-1745

2020 Sports Eyewear MarketPlus Survey, II-2525

"2020 Top Fairs." [online] from https://carnivalwarehouse.com/top-50-fairs [Accessed April 13, 2021], I-1273

"2021 Global Order Book." [online] from https://www.boatinternational.com/yacht-market-intelligence/luxury-yachts-on-order/2021-global-order-book [Published December 15, 2020], I-510

"2021 Worldwide Cruise Line Market Share." [online] from https://cruisemarketwatch.com/market-share/ [Accessed December 2, 2020], I-1025

"A Bumpy Week for China's Logistics Market." [online] from https://technode.com/2020/05/12/a-bumpy-week-for-chinas-logistics-market/ [Published May 12, 2020], II-3101

ABI, I-1918

Absolute Reports, I-319, 466, 691, 885, 1071, 1666, II-2760, 3494

Access, Lift & Handlers, I-1776

Acimac Research Department, I-655-657, II-2957-2959

"Acquisition of Snowman Logistics Limited (Snowman) by Adani Logistics Limited." [online] from https://www.adaniports.com/-/media/Project/Ports/Investor/Investor-Downloads/Investors-Presentation/Snowman-Acquisition.pdf [Published December 27, 2019], II-3499

Ad Age Datacenter, I-15, 24-27, 32-34, 36-38, 40-41, 344, 346, II-2640, 2905, 3561

ADMA Biologics, I-1877

Aegean Exporters' Association, I-1518, 1520, 1528

AEOFRUSE and DESCALMENDRA, Aegean Exporters' Association, Greek Nuts and Fruits Trade Association, II-2447

Aerosol Industry Association of Japan, I-47

The Aerosol Manufacturers' Association, I-48

Aerospace Industries Association, I-1045

Agrarheute, I-1280

Agriland, I-1282-1283

Agropages, I-687, 692

AgTools, I-1516

AIOCD Pharmasofttech, I-1130

Air-Conditioning, Heating & Refrigeration Institute, I-1769

"Air Products: Compounding Profitable Position." [online] from https://seekingalpha.com/article/4337681-air-products-compounding-profitable-growth [Published April 15, 2020], I-1889

Airbus, I-62

Airline Business, I-84

Airnow, I-254

Airports Council International, I-97-98

AKI Research & Consulting, II-2586

Alexander Watson Associates, I-2019-2020, II-2613

All Pakistan Cement Manufacturers Association, I-648

Allegra Coffee Cup Portal, I-764-768, 770-771

Alliance for Audited Media, II-2138

Allied Market Research, II-2578

Almond Board of Australia, II-2447

Almond Board of California, II-2447

Alphaliner, II-2770, 3060, 3062

"Alrosa Annual Report 2019." [online] from http://www.alrosa.ru [Accessed February 15, 2021], I-1072

"Altera Investor Presentation." [online] from https://cms.alterainfra.com/wp-content/uploads/2020/08/Tap-Issue-AST02G-Investor-Presentation-August-2020-vF.pdf [Published August 2020], II-3052

Alternative Fuels Data Center, I-104-153

Altman Solon research and analysis, II-3563-3572

The Aluminum Association, I-168

American Board for Certification, I-1751

American Clean Power, I-1234, II-3446

American Coatings Association, II-2582

American Cranes & Transport, I-1013-1014

American Gas Association Statistics Database, II-3458

American Iron and Steel Institute, II-3245

American Marketing Association, II-2874

American Pecan Council, II-2453

American Public Transportation Association, II-2150-2162

American Seniors Housing Association, I-1861

American Staffing Association, II-3231

American Tower research and analysis, II-3563-3572

Ampere Analysis, II-2540-2541, 2543, 2545-2546, 2548-2549, 2551, 3315

AMR International, I-941

Amtrak Fact Sheet, II-2149

"Analysis of the Color Cosmetics Market in China." [online] from http://www.news.kotra.or.kr [Published February 10, 2021], I-975

Analysys, I-257, 1170, 1414, II-2919

Anime News Network, II-2142

"Annual Potato Yearbook." [online] from https://www.nationalpotatocouncil.org/files/8415/9231/8115/

Annual_Potato_Yearbook_FNL.pdf [Accessed December 2, 2020], II-2777

"A.O. Smith Autumn 2020 Analyst Presentation." [online] from https://investor.aosmith.com/events-and-presentations [Published October 12, 2020], I-238

APA-The Engineered Wood Association, I-1241, II-3588

Apptopia, I-256, 403

Aquaculture Magazine, II-2993

ARCEP, II-3564, 3566

Architectural Record, I-261

Argentine Chamber of Peanuts, II-2452

Argus, I-85

Armstrong & Associates, II-3043, 3055, 3065, 3503

Art Economics, I-266-272

The Art Newspaper, II-2387

Artisan Gateway, II-2358, 2364

Artory, I-268, 270-272

ArtTactic, I-265

Ashapura Minchem, I-2014

Asian Sky Research, I-57, 60, 71-72

Asphalt Roofing Manufacturers Association, I-282

Association of American Publishers, I-526

Association of American Railroads, II-2840

Association of the German Trade Fair Industry, I-942

A.T. Kearney, II-2172

ATB Capital Markets, I-601

Audit Analytics, I-6-7

Australia Pistachio Growers' Association, II-2455

Australian Macadamia Society, II-2451

Auto Punditz, I-366

Auto Rental News, I-311

AutoCount data from Experian, I-364

Automatic Merchandiser, I-1423, II-3470-3473

Automotive Fleet, I-298, II-3423

Automotive News, I-304-306

Autorité des Marchés Financiers, I-1979

Aviation Week & Space Technology Military Fleet & MRO Forecast, I-65-66, 68-70, 79

AWA Alexander Watson Associates, I-2018, 2021

Axalta Coating Systems, II-2589

Axis Securities, I-2122-2123

Baltimore Business Journal, I-1840

BAML Global Wireless Matrix, II-3563, 3565-3566, 3568-3571

Banana Link, I-1515

Bank of America, I-310, II-3068

Barclays Research, I-1680

"BarthHaas Report: Hops 2019/2020." [online] from https://www.barthhaas.com/en/downloads/berichte-broschueren [Published October 2020], I-476, 483

BBI International, I-497

BCC Research, I-11, 1626

Beauty Packaging, II-2651

Becquerel Institute, I-1226, 1232

Beef, I-623

Beer Marketer's Insights, I-482

Benchmark Mineral Intelligence, I-1672

Bernstein Research, I-2135

Beroe Inc., II-2724, 2788, 2940

BestLink, I-1788, 1915, 1923-1926, 1929, 1937, 1939, 1941-1942, 1946, 1951

Beverage Dynamics, I-2088-2089, 2092-2095

Beverage Information and Insights Group, I-2096-2097, II-3545-3546

Beverage Information Group 2020 Liquor Handbook, I-2090-2091

Beverage Marketing Corp., I-535-536, 2003, II-3151,

"Bic Group Presentation for Investors." [online] from http://www.bicworld.com [Published November 2020], I-2065, II-2653, 3594

Black Youth Project 100, II-2767

Bloomberg Intelligence, I-1980, II-2831, 3159

BloombergNEF, II-3444-3445, 3447

The Blue Book of Medical Device Industry in China, 2019, II-2244, 2263

The Boeing Company, I-58-59

Boise Cascade Company, I-1241, II-3588

"Boomer Essentials." [online] from http://www.lythampartners.com [Published October 2020], II-2260

Box Office Mojo, II-2359

BoxOffice Pro, II-2379

Brazilian Agricultural Research Corporation, II-2453

Brazilian Association of Nuts and Chestnuts, II-2453

Brickworks' U.S. Brick Market Overview Presentation, I-560

Brightfield Group, I-600, 603

"Brink's to Acquire Bulk of G4S Cash Operations for $860 Million." [online] from https://cmspi.com/eur/news/brinks-g4s-cash/ [Published March 2, 2020], I-616

British Association for Screen International, I-1163

Bryce Space & Technology, II-2966

BSRIA, I-233, 512-514, 660, II-2957, 2959

BTN Europe, II-3415

BuddeComm, II-3567,

Builder, I-1839, 1841-1849

Building Design + Construction, I-863, 865-868, 870-871

Burton-Taylor, I-1323

Business Aviation Review, I-85

Business Communications Co., I-654, 2076

The Business Research Co., I-1985

Business Travel News, II-3414

California Fig Advisory Board, I-1520

California Prune Board, I-1527

California Walnut Board and Commission, II-2456

Camara Argentina del Aerosol, I-44

Camera & Imaging Products Association, I-590

Can Manufacturers Institute, II-2281

Canaccord Genuity, II-2265

Canada Mortgage and Housing Corp., II-2352

Canalys, I-284-285, 287-291, 795-796, 799, II-3164-3165, 3519-3520

Candy Industry, I-808, 812

Caobisco Statistical Bulletin, I-724-725, 810-811

The Car Carrier Market 2019, II-3049

CarbConsult GmbH, I-611

Casting Source, II-2301

Catalina Research Inc., I-1342, 1346-1348, 1352

CDK Global Lightspeed, II-2368,

CE Pro, I-240, 587, 594, 886-893, 1556, 1741, 2075, II-2997-2998
CEIC Data, I-1214
Center for Gaming Research, I-1569, 1581
The Center for Popular Democracy, II-2767
"Central Garden & Pet 2020 Investor Day." [online] from https://ir.central.com/investors/events-and-presentations/presentations/default.aspx [Published December 3, 2020], I-2038
Ceramic World Review, I-658
CERR.UZ, I-2047
CGIS Research, I-462, II-3234,
Chain Store Guide, I-1682-1683, 1685, 1689, 1691, 1695, 1698, 1702
Cheese Reporter - Dairy Production Extra, I-668
Chemical & Engineering News, I-706
The ChemQuest Group, I-685, II-2587, 2590, 2592
Chen Jjanwang, II-3132
Chen Zan Industry Research Institute, I-245
Chicago Sun-Times, I-363
Chicago Trade Center, II-2951
Chile Prunes Association, I-1527
China Academy of Information and Communications Technology, I-1037
China Association of Automobile Manufacturers, I-361
China Business Research Institute, I-538
China Chamber of Commerce for Import and Export Foodstuffs, II-2452, 2454
China Commerce Industry Research Institute, II-2256
China Construction Machinery Association, I-857
China Crop Protection Industry Association, I-710
China Economic Information Network, I-247, 1754, II-3040, 3491, 3524
China Home Electronic Appliance Research Institute, I-220
China Industry Research Institute, I-197, 1384

"China Office Furniture Market Analytics Definitive Guide and Case Study." [online] from https://www.bokefurniture.com/china-office-furniture-market-analytics-definitive-guide-and-case-study [Accessed March 29, 2021], I-1555
China Plastics Processing Association, II-2734
"China Recorded 1209,000 Heavy-Duty Truck Sales in October." [online] from http://m.chinaspv.com/statistics/3792.html [Published November 27, 2020], II-3438
"China Sold 150,637 Units Buses & Coaches in 2020." [online] from http://www.chinabuses.org/analyst/2021/0115/article_12287.html [Published January 15, 2021], I-571
"China Sold 334,400 Light Buses in 2020." [online] from http://www.chinabuses.org/analyst/2021/0119/article_12290.html [Published January 19, 2021], I-572
China Statistical Yearbook, I-1385
China Tea Industry Economic Research, II-3302
Chinese Athletics Association, II-3220
"Chinese Mobile Games Market 2020 vs. 2019." [online] from https://www.gamerefinery.com/chinese-mobile-games-market-2019-2020/ [Published October 13, 2020], II-2331
The Chinese State Post Bureau, II-3066
"Chocolate Industry Market Share." [online] from https://www.t4.ai/industry/chocolate-industry-market-share [Published August 16, 2020], I-717
"The Chocolate Market in China." [online] from https://www.flandersinvestmentandtrade.com/export/sites/trade/files/market_studies/The%20chocolate%20market%20in%20China_1.pdf [Published July 2020], I-716
CICC Research, I-2121, II-2832, 2836, 3060, 3062, 3067
"Cinemark Investor Presentation 2Q 2020." [online] from https://ir.cinemark.com/company-information/presentations [Published August 18, 2020], II-2380-2382

Cirium, I-75-77, 80, 82, 1046-1047, 1049-1050, 1053
Clarksons Research, I-745-746, 1669-1670, 1990-1991, II-3047-3048, 3053, 3056
Clean Technica, I-329
ClearCut Analytics, II-3280-3281
CMBIS Research, I-349, 467
CMS, II-3572
Coal Age, I-744
Codex, I-519
Coherent Market Insights, II-2233
Coin Market Cap, I-1028
"Comic Book Market 2020." [online] from https://www.marketwatch.com/press-release/comic-book-market-2020-global-industry-analysis-by-top-countries-data-share-market-size-share-demand-key-players-profiles-future-prospects-and-forecasts-to-2026-2020-12-02, I-773
Commsupdate, II-3567-3568
comScore, I-1248, 1975, II-2355, 2364, 2383
Confederation of European Paper Industries, II-2613, 2819, 3590
Congressional Research Service, I-274
Consultancy.org, I-878
Consumer Electronics and Appliances Manufacturers Association, I-223, 899
Control/ARC Top 50, I-322
Convenience Store News, I-933
Conviva, II-2536
Council on Tall Buildings and Urban Habitat, I-874
Counselor, II-2806
Counterpoint Channel Tracker, I-636
Counterpoint Research, I-339-342, 633, 635, 637-642, II-2422, 3018, 3515, 3560
Counterpoint Technology Market Research, II-3521
Counterpoint's Global XR Model Tracker, I-1743
Country Aircheck, II-2408
"Covetrus." [online] from milclub.org/wp-content/uploads/2020/08/CVET-UIC/-VF.pdf [Published October 18, 2019], II-3475

"COVID Vaccine Storage Won't Need Phenomenal Investment, Says Blue Star." [online] from https://www.bloombergquint.com/business/covid-vaccine-storage-transport-wont-need-phenomenal-investment-says-blue-star [Published December 16, 2020], II-2700

Crain's Detroit Business, I-666, 1750

CRN, II-2783

CropLife, I-52,

CRU, I-1307, 1309, 1311

Cruise Industry News, I-1023-1024

"Cruise Missile Market Size Growth Opportunities, Driving Factors by Manufacturers, Regions, Type and Application." [online] from https://www.wicz.com/story/43544912/cruise-missile-market-size-growth-opportunities-driving-factors-by-manufacturer [Press, II-2327

CSIL, I-232, 2074

"Current State of the Top Shipbuilding Companies in the World." [online] from https://www.bizvibe.com/blog/top-shipbuilding-companies-world [Published September 22, 2020], II-3071

Curvo Labs, II-2237-2239, 2246

CVWorld, I-308

Dairy Foods, I-1033

Dairy Marketing Institute, II-2308

Datanyze, I-1974, II-3158, 3160, 3162, 3174, 3180-3183, 3188, 3193

Daxue Consulting, I-1826, II-2518, 2650, 3394, 3557

DBS Bank, II-2468

DBusiness, I-1020

De Beers, I-1073

Dealogic, II-2277

Decision Innovation Solutions, II-2669

Definitive Healthcare's Hospitals & IDNs database, I-1747

Dell'Oro Group, II-3306-3307

Deloitte Touche Tohmatsu Ltd., I-192, 881, 971, 2130-2134, II-3314, 3453

Demolition & Recycling International, I-911

"Denim Jeans Market 2021 Analysis, Demand, Products and Suppliers Forecast to 2027." [online] from https://www.marketwatch.com/press-release/denim-jeans-market-2021-analysis-by-trends-demand-products [Press release February 7, 2021], I-191

The Denver Post, II-3216

Department for Promotion of Industry and Trade, India, I-646

Deutsche Bank, I-1043-1044

Diamond Comics, I-774

Die Industrie-Gemeinschaft Aerosole e.V., I-46

Digital Entertainment Group, I-1247-1249,

"Digital Printer Ink Market Share Analysis." [online] from https://www.marketwatch.com/press-release/digital-printer-ink-market-share-analysis-with-demand-status-2021-latest-technological-advancement-industry-trends-explosive-factors-of-revenue-by-key-v, I-1900

Digital TV Research, II-2538-2539, 2542, 2547, 2550, 2552-2555, 2630

Direct Selling News, I-1081

Directions - A Supplement to National Cattlemen, I-625

Distilled Spirits Council of the United States, I-2084, 2087

Documentary Center, II-2354

Dodge Data & Analytics, II-2582

Drewery, II-3064

Drewery Container Census & Lease Industry Annual Report 2020-2021, I-905

Dried Fruits Australia, 2019 International Seedless Grape Producing Countries Conference, I-1528

The Drinks Business, II-3548

Drug Channels Institute, I-1115-1116, 1744, II-2701

Dry Bulk Trade Outlook, I-745-746, 1669-1670

DSR, I-254

DuckerFrontier, II-3537

Duke Global Health Innovation Center, II-3460

Dun & Bradstreet, I-507

Dutch Aerosol Association, I-49

Earnest Research, I-1369-1370, 1543, II-2878, 3214-3215, 3418

The Economist Intelligence Unit, I-1688, II-3459

Edelweiss Professional Investor Research, I-242

Edison Research, I-283, 631, 793, 897, 1169, 1964, II-2763-2764, 3516

Edison Trends, I-1168

Egg Industry, I-1202

Eilers & Krejcik, I-1571-1573, 1579, 1583

Eilers-Fantini Central Game Performance Database, I-1582

Electrical Construction & Maintenance, I-913

Electronics Sourcing North America, I-1204

eMarketer, I-16-21, 28, 35, 42, 402, 1171, 1175-1179, 1185, 1402, 1792, II-2341, 2516, 2765-2766, 2901, 2918, 3153

ENGINE, II-2385

Engineering and Mining Journal, I-1992

ENR, I-907-910, 915-917, 919-921, 923, 927, 1057, 1251-1253, 1742, II-2445, 3513-3514

Epicor's Industry Data Analytics, I-1261, 1566, II-2290, 2704, 2782, 2854, 3286, 3288, 3293, 3387, 3523

EQ International, I-1213

EqualOcean, I-243-244, 248-249, II-2521

ESOMAR, II-2874

ESPN, II-3219

EssilorLuxottica estimates, II-2523

Euroconsult, II-3199

Eurofresh Distribution, I-1533, 1537

Euromonitor, I-56, 102, 199, 203-205, 207, 210, 212, 216, 218, 224-231, 235, 276, 312, 373, 375-376, 382, 487-488, 537, 540, 737, 755, 787, 936, 977, 985, 990, 1032, 1059, 1063, 1141, 1180-1183, 1390, 1396, 1399, 1413, 1417, 1430, 1437-1443, 1489, 1544, 1688, 1701, 2110, 2121, II-2314, 2318-2319, 2353, 2523, 2574, 2652, 2664-2665, 2686, 2689-2690, 2880-2881, 2903, 2908, 2942-2943, 2945-2946, 2949, 2954, 2967, 2969, 2971, 2982, 2985, 3089, 3109, 3140, 3150, 3154, 3224, 3234, 3261, 3276-3278, 3283, 3469, 3482, 3487, 3552-3555

European Aerosol Foundation, I-45
European Aluminum Association, I-163
European Association of Operators of Toll Road Infrastructures, II-3378
European Audiovisual Observatory, II-2384
European Automobile Manufacturers' Association, I-356-358, 568-569, II-3440, 3468
European Bioplastics, I-502
European Health & Fitness Report, I-1721, 1723
European Pellet Council, II-3591
European Pet Food Industry Federation, II-2691-2694, 2698-2699
"European Sales 2020 EV and PHEV." [online] from https://carsalesbase.com/european-sales-2020-ev-phev/ [Accessed April 19, 2021], I-330
European Space Policy Institute, II-2964, 3199
European Toy Association, II-3395
European Union Foreign Agricultural Service, I-498, 500
Eurostat, I-1688, 1701
EV Volumes, I-331, 333-336
EvaluatePharma, I-1117, 1137-1138
Evercore ISI Research, II-3562
Exchange, I-714
Experian, I-353, 2100, 2102-2103, 2106-2107
Eye Bank Association of America, II-2259
FactSet, I-189, 1018, 1091, II-3417
FAOSTAT, I-1320, II-3579-3580
Farm Equipment & WEDA North American Inventory Study, I-1285
FAS Moscow estimate based on data from Union of Poultry producers, II-2208
Fast Company, I-1595
"Fast-Food Market Share." [online] from https://www.t4.ai/industry/fast-food-market-share [Published August 16, 2020], II-2879
Fastmarkets, II-2568, 2611
fDa (The Aggregates Foundation), I-51
FDM+C, II-3578
Federal Aviation Authority, II-3455

Federal Data Procurement Systems, I-1665
Federal Deposit Insurance Corp., I-404-459
Federation of American Scientists, I-274
Federation of the Swiss Watch Industry, II-3506
FEFAC (European Compound Feed Manufacturers' Federation), I-1883
FisherSolve, II-2941
Fishery and Agricultural Organization, I-1330
Fitch Solutions, II-2255
Fleet Owner, II-3424, 3426, 3428
Flight International, I-1339
Floor Covering News, I-1340-1341, 1343, 1345, 1349-1350, 1353-1354, 1363-1365
Floor Covering Weekly, I-1362
Floor Focus, I-1351, 1355-1360, 1366
Food and Agriculture Organization, I-681, 750, 1313-1315, 1332-1335
Food Management, I-1420, 1422
Food Processing, I-1394
Food Trade News, I-1704-1705, II-2907
Food World, I-1703, 1706, II-2902
Foodservice Equipment & Supplies, I-1419
"For Application Equipment in 2020, Bigger Was Better." [online] from https://www.croplife.com/croplife-top-100/for-application-equipment-in-2020-bigger-was-better/ [Published December 21, 2020], I-1286
Forecast International, II-3442-3443
Foreign Intelligence Advisory Board, I-1701
Forest Economic Advisors, I-1241, 2124, 2127-2128, II-3588
Forisk Consulting, I-2129, II-3336-3337
Fortune, I-1133
Forward Research, II-3169
"France 2020. Piaggio Gains the Second Place in a Market Down 4%." [online] from https://www.motorcyclesdata.com/2021/01/13/french-motorcycles/ [Published January 13, 2021], II-2370
Franchise Times, I-1453
FRANdata, I-1454,

The Freedonia Group Inc., I-10, 472, 544, 582, 610, 996-998, 1206, 1278-1279, 1303-1306, 1344, 1617, 1720, 1763-1764, 1791, 1838, 1904-1907, 2026, 2033-2036, 2125, II-2367, 2439-2441, 2534-2535, 2557-2559, 2561-2566, 2569-2573, 2577, 2579, 2583, 2597, 2718-2720, 2754, 2929-2931, 2995, 3003, 3072, 3381-3382, 3508, 3538
Frost & Sullivan, I-29, 223, 899, 1123-1125, 1245, 1827, 1830, II-2261, 2404, 2605-2606, 2723, 2832, 3097, 3449, 3599
FSR, II-2891
Fuji Economy, II-2530
FutureMetrics, II-3591
Futuresource Consulting, I-1163
Gallup, II-2866
Gambling Compliance, I-1575
Game Refinery Saas Dashboard, II-3483
Gardner Intelligence, II-2136
Gartner Inc., I-632, 798, 1064, 1896-1898, II-2999, 3016-3017, 3036, 3167, 3187, 3517, 3571
General Aviation Manufacturers Association, I-61, 63
General Services Administration, I-1645-1664
"Germany 2020. December Sales Boomed 309% Ending a Memorable Year." [online] from https://www.motorcyclesdata.com/2021/01/17/germany-motorcycles/ [Published January 17, 2021], II-2371
Giving USA, I-664, 667
Glass Magazine, I-1629
Glass Packaging Institute, I-1628
Global Cashew Council, II-2449
Global Cement Directory, 2020, I-643
Global Cement Directory, 2021, I-644, 647, 650-651
Global Cement Magazine, I-645, 649
"Global Coffee Cup Market 2019." [online] from https://www.absolutereports.com/global-coffee-cup-market-14112997 [Published April 2019], I-761
Global Containerboard Outlook, II-2568
Global Data Intelligence, II-3107

"Global Electronic Special Gases Market Research Report." [online] from https://www.marketstudyreport.com/reports/global-electronic-special-gases-market-research-report-2020 [Published April 2020], I-1886

Global EPOS and Self-Checkout, 2020 (RBR), II-3005

Global EVs and Battery Shipment Tracker, I-307

"Global Flexible Flat Cable (FCC) Industry Research Report, Growth Trends and Competitive Analysis 2018-2025." [online] from https://www.qyresearch.com [Published September 2018], I-585

Global Gypsum Directory, 2020, I-1725-1728

Global Gypsum Magazine, II-3493

"Global In Vitro Diagnostics Market Report 2020-2026." [online] from https://www.globalmonitor.us/product/global-in-vitro-diagnostis-market-report [Accessed January 5, 2021], I-1068

"Global Industrial Power Tools Market Research Report 2020." [online] from https://www.marketstudyreport.com/reports/global-industrial-power-tools-market-research-report-2020 [Published June 2020], II-3384

"Global Infectious Diseases Rapid Diagnostic Testing Market Report 2020-2026." [online] from https://www.globalmonitor.us/product/global-infectious-diseases-rapid-diagnostic-testing-market-report [Accessed January 5, 2021], I-1069

"Global Instant Adhesive Market 2020." [online] from https://www.thecowboychannel.com/story/43803888/global-instant-adhesive-market-2020-industry-size-outlook-share-demand-manufacturers-and-2024-forecast-researchs [Published May 3, 2021], I-14

Global Insulation Directory, 2020, I-1908

Global Payment Cards Data and Forecast to 2025 (RBR), II-2635

Global POS Software, 2020 (RBR), II-3170

"Global Pro Audio Equipment Market Insights, Forecast to 2025." [online] from https://www.industryresearch.com/global-pro-audio-equipment-market-14847221 [Published October 2019], I-884

"Global PV Metallization Silver Paste Market Insights, Forecast to 2025." [online] from https://www.marketinsightsreports.com/reports/04081177834/global-pv-metallization-silver-paste-market-insights-forecast-to-2025 [Published April 2019], I-377

Global Research Business Network, I-878, II-2874

"The Global Serviced Apartments Industry Report 2020-2021." [online] from http://www.apartmentservice.com [Accessed December 10, 2020], II-3039

"Global Ship Lease Investor Presentation April 2021." [online] from https://www.globalshiplease.com/static-files/a226750c-bb27-45e2-8017-a0183e07ad26 [Published April 2021], II-3063

Global Smartwatch Shipment by Model Tracker, II-3518

"Global Sodium Chlorate Market Report." [online] from https://www.360researchreports.com/global-sodium-chlorate-market-15945263 [Published July 2020], I-713

"Global Supercharger Market Growth 2019-2024." [online] from https://www.absolutereports.com/global-supercharger-market-13855178 [Published February 2019], II-3262

"Global Surgical Microscope Market Insights, Forecast to 2026." [online] from https://www.marketreportsworld.com/global-surgical-microscope-market-15561647 [Published October 2019], II-2250

Global Trade Tracker, II-2990-2991

"Global Wear-Resistant Steel Sales Market Report 2020." [online] from https://www.360researchreports.com/global-wear-resistant-steel-sales-market-16616738 [Published October 2020], II-3243

Global Wellness Institute, II-3097

Global Wind Energy Council, I-1219-1223, 1235

"Global Wiring Duct Market Report." [online] from https://www.absolutereports.com/global-wiring-duct-market-16127117 [Published August 2020], II-3575

GlobalData, I-392, 490, 503, 696, 840, 1393, 1397, 1435, 1876, II-2211, 2324-2325, 2466, 2495, 2627, 2715, 2989, 2994, 3195, 3225, 3290

GNOG management, I-1572

"Go-Ahead Moving Communities Today Towards a Greener Tomorrow." [online] from https://gog-11615-s3.s3.eu-west-2.amazonaws.com/live/4016/0092/6016/The_Go_Ahead_Group_plc_Annual_Report_and_Accounts_2020.pdf [Published June 27, 2020], II-2164

Goldman Sachs, II-2410, 3360

Golf Inc., I-1644

Grand View Research, I-463, 599

"Great Lakes Dredge & Dock Investor Presentation." [online] from https://investor.gldd.com/static-files/387c8193-9467-4319-a157-cbda78e4b1e2 [Published August 2020], I-912

Greater Wilmington Business Journal, II-2849

Greek Nuts & Fruits Trade Association, I-1520, II-2455

Greenhouse Grower, I-1674

Greenwich Associates, I-1983

"Greeting Cards Market to Eyewitness Massive Growth by 2026." [online] from https://thedailychronicle.in/news/1919960/greeting-cards-market-to-eyewitness-massive-growth-by-2026-hallmark-cards-american-greetings-card-factory/ [Published September 20, 2020], I-1676

GSMA, II-3570

Guotai Junan International, I-361, II-2333, 3383

GWI WaterData, II-3509

H2 Gambling Capital, I-1585

Handset Component Technologies, I-1088, II-3019-3020, 3032

Harbor Aluminum, I-161

Hardlines 2020 Retail Report, I-1790
Hardware + Building Supply Dealer, I-1789
Hardwood Market Report, I-2126, II-3576-3577
Hawkins-Wright, II-2815
HDFC Securities, I-1692,
"The Health Food Market in China." [online] from https://www.flandersinvestmentandtrade.com/export/sites/trade/files/market_studies/The%20health%20food%20market%20in%20China_0.pdf [Published December 2020], I-1172
Healthcare Sales & Marketing, I-504
Hearing Industries Association, II-2262
Hesnes Shipping AS, II-3049
Hitwise, I-1971, 1973
"HOA Statistics." [online] from https://ipropertymanagement.com/research/hoa-statistics [Accessed December 2, 2020], I-1822
Home Accents Today, I-1800, 1806, 1809, 1811-1813, 1819
Home Textiles Today, I-1803
HomeWorld Business research, I-241
Hoover, II-2253
Hotel & Motel Management, I-1829
Hotels, I-1828, 1833
Houlihan Lokey, II-2556
Household & Commercial Products Association, I-43
HTF Market Intelligence, I-1421
http://businessstat.ru/catalog/id8923, II-3332
http://voicebot.ai, I-894
http://www.builtwith.com, I-1173
http://www.chyxx.com, I-243-244, 248-249, 489, 1236, II-3103, 3275
http://www.datamyne.com, II-2768
http://www.mops.twse.com.tw, I-1882
http://www.mortgagedataweb.com, II-2347-2351
http://www.oaaa.org, I-39
http://www.t4.ai, I-772, 898
https://www.iyiou.com, I-1986
Huajing Information Network, I-236
Hwajing Industry Institute, II-2973
IBISWorld, I-4, 22, 85, 101, 206, 213, 260, 297, 400, 464, 494, 525, 545-547, 584, 612-613, 618, 682, 788, 856, 860-861, 877, 879, 901, 906, 914, 930-931, 944, 1038-1039, 1041, 1080, 1085, 1090, 1122, 1260, 1281, 1386, 1415, 1426, 1436, 1542, 1677, 1730, 1761, 1770, 1780, 1884, 1978, 2002, 2024, 2101, 2104, II-2139, 2231, 2291, 2298, 2330, 2420, 2430-2431, 2438, 2575, 2620, 2659, 2679, 2725, 2730, 2787, 2789, 2822, 2975, 3001, 3171, 3173, 3200, 3202, 3213, 3221, 3249, 3279, 3296, 3300, 3308, 3322, 3325, 3388, 3416, 3450, 3479, 3495
"iBuyer Market Share Set to Drop by Half in 2020: DelPrete." [online] from https://www.inman.com/2020/11/19/ibuyer-market-share-set-to-drop-by-half-in-2020-delprete/ [Published November 19, 2020], I-1965
IC Insights, II-3015
ICEX, I-1284
ICICI Direct Research, I-211, II-3525-3526
ICIS Analytics, II-2737
ICIS Chemical Business, I-699-704
IFI Claims Patent Office, II-2628
IFPI Global Music Report 2020, II-2410
IHS Markit, I-352, 360, 368, 592, 698, 1243, 1619, 1771-1772, 1774, II-2484, 2494, 2739, 3004, 3027, 3100, 3102, 3148
iiMedia, I-1254
IMF Balance of Payments, II-2869
Impact Consulting Services Inc's FurnitureCore industry model, I-1793
Incisiv, II-2520
IndexBox, I-195, 1795, II-3589
"Industrial Lenses Market Size and Growth Share 2021." [online] from https://www.marketwatch.com/press-release/industrial-lenses-market-size-and-growth-share-2021-global-share-by-manufacturers-sales-revenue-key-strategies-development-history-and-future-, I-2055
IndustryARC, I-1280
InForGrowth, II-3033
Informa Economics, II-3050, 3058
The Information Network, II-3007
Information Resources Inc., I-386-387, 539, 661-662, 674, 758, 1005, 1007, 1238, 1487-1488, 1490-1493, 1873, 1875, 2012, II-2672-2673, 2675, 3196-3197
Informity Multiscreen Index, II-2629
Ink World, I-1903
Inside Mortgage Finance, II-2346
Inside Public Accounting, I-5
Inside Self-Storage, II-3006
Institute of Museum and Library Services, I-2059
Interact Analysis, I-301, 1594, II-2927
Interior Design, I-1962
Internal Correspondence, I-1779
Internal Revenue Service, II-3298
International Air Transport Association, II-3044, 3054
International Association of Refrigerated Warehouses, II-3501-3502
International Carwash Association, I-614
International Congress and Convention Association, I-943
International Construction, I-853, 855, 864
International Copper Study Group, I-951-953
International Data Corp., I-275, 781-782, 785, 792, 797, 800, 1963, II-2424-2425, 2427, 3035, 3038, 3105, 3166, 3168, 3179, 3191
International Data Research, II-3169
International Energy Agency, I-154, 156, 325, 354, 359, 362, 742-743, 748, 1216-1217, 1226, 1232
International Farm Comparison Network, I-1290
International Federation of Robotics, II-2921-2924
International Federation of the Phonographic Industry, II-2407
International Fertilizer Association, I-1307-1312, II-2774
International Fiber Journal, II-3596
International Grains Council, I-1373-1374
International Health, Racquet & Sportsclub Association, I-1722
International Hydropower Association, I-1218

International Nut and Dried Fruit Council, I-1517-1520, 1527-1528, II-2447-2456
International Organization of Motor Vehicle Manufacturers, I-350-351, 567, II-3437, 3439
International Organization of Vine and Wine, II-3550
International Post Corp., I-1182, II-2772
International Renewable Energy Agency, I-1229-1230
International Rental News, I-1773, 1775
International Sleep Products Association, I-1552
International Society of Hair Restoration Surgery, I-1737
International Stainless Steel Federation, II-3233
International Textile Manufacturers Federation, II-3327
International Tin Association, II-3338, 3341
International Trade Commission, I-1529, II-2957, 2959
International Union of Railways, II-2838
Intrafish, II-2983
Investment & Pensions Europe, II-2646
Investment Computer Fact Book, 2019, I-1258
IQVIA, I-1118, 1126, 1128-1129, 1134-1136
Iran Dried Fruit Exporters Association, I-1518, 1520, 1528
Iran Pistachio Association, II-2455
iResearch, I-31, 155, 1186, 1831, 2099, II-2333, 2354, 2515
IRG Rail, II-2163
IRI, I-13, 53-55, 170, 208, 273, 370-372, 374, 378-379, 383-384, 389-391, 468, 477-480, 484-486, 541-542, 548, 550-554, 576, 581, 596-597, 663, 671-673, 675-677, 680, 709, 718-723, 726-727, 734-736, 757, 759-760, 814-826, 828-839, 841-852, 969, 973-974, 976, 980, 982-984, 987, 989, 1002-1004, 1006, 1008-1012, 1021, 1029, 1031, 1058, 1060-1062, 1079, 1092-1097, 1142-1158, 1190-1191, 1201, 1239-1240, 1265, 1324, 1336, 1382-1383, 1391-1392, 1400-1401, 1457-1467, 1469-1477, 1479-1483, 1485-1486, 1601, 1604, 1606, 1710-1713, 1731, 1734-1736, 1739, 1869-1872, 1874, 2005-2007, 2010-2011, 2017, 2078, 2085, II-2147, 2166, 2168, 2186, 2193-2203, 2205-2207, 2209-2210, 2218-2223, 2226, 2229-2230, 2270-2272, 2309, 2311, 2315-2317, 2320-2322, 2527, 2529, 2599, 2626, 2649, 2654-2655, 2657-2658, 2668, 2670-2671, 2674, 2676-2678, 2682-2683, 2711, 2785, 2802-2803, 2812, 2950, 2952, 2955-2956, 2972, 2984, 2986, 3090-3094, 3096, 3110-3130, 3133-3134, 3136-3139, 3142-3147, 3198, 3222-3223, 3263-3274, 3282, 3284-3285, 3294, 3303, 3305, 3390-3391, 3488-3490, 3534-3535, 3556, 3595, 3600
IRI/FreshLook, I-1499-1509, II-2389, 2776
IRI Liquid Data, I-380, 385, 388, 393-399, 549, 555-559, 827, 979, 981, 988, 1449-1452, 1732-1733, II-2531, 2656, 3095
IRI Syndicated Integrated Fresh database, II-2167, 2169, 2171, 2204, 2217, 2227
iSpot.tv, II-2537
IWSR, I-2086
Japan Automobile Parts Manufacturers Association, I-2077
Japan Inc. Consulting estimates, I-215
Japan Watch & Clock Industry, I-740
Jeffries Group estimates, II-3402
John Burns Real Estate Consulting, I-874
John Durham and Associates, I-1714
K+S Potash, II-2774
Kantar, I-27, 32-34, 36-38, 40-41, 344, 346, 1163, 1684, II-2640, 2905, 2910, 3561
KAR Investor Relations, I-294
"Kazatomprom #1 Global Uranium Producer." [online] from https://uraniumstockinvesting.com/uranium-producers/kazatomprom/ [Accessed March 22, 2021], II-3456
Kent Report, I-1593

KFF analysis of CMS Medicare Advantage Enrollment files, I-1919-1920
Kleffman Group, I-712, 972
Kline & Co., I-2117
KNG Research, II-2584
Kontali Salmon World, 2019, I-1326
Korea Herald, I-252
KOTRA Chicago Trade Center, I-216, 494, 546-547
KOTRA Dallas Trade Center, II-2253
KOTRA Shenzhen Trade Center, II-2971
Kraftfahrt-Bundesmart, I-326
"Kuke Music Holding Ltd." [online] from https://www.sec.gov/Archives/edgar/data/1809158/000104746920005717/a2242706zf-1.htm [Published December 18, 2020], II-2398
La Fleur's, I-1574, 1577
Lake Carriers' Association, II-3045
The Land Report, I-2027
Lanjiu prospectus, II-3547
"The Largest Bank in the World 2020." [online] from https://www.advratings.com/banking/top-banks-in-the-world [Accessed January 20, 2021], I-401
Laser Focus World, I-2030
Law for Black Lives, II-2767,
"Leading 5G Infrastructure Provider, Initiate With Accumulate." [online] from http://www.gtja.com.hk [Published March 6, 2020], II-3310
Leaseurope, I-2045
Leffingwell & Associates, I-695
Leichtman Research Group, II-2631
"Leisure Business Market Research Handbook 2021-2022." [online] from http://www.rkma.com [Accessed March 8, 2021], I-938-939
L.E.K. Consulting, II-3496
LexisNexis MarketView, I-1748-1749
License Global, I-2061
Licensing Letter, I-2060, 2062
LISTedTECH LMS database, II-3175
Litmus Email Analytics, II-3161
Livres Hebdo, II-2811
LP Gas, II-2808
Macadamia Council, II-2451

Macadamias South Africa, II-2451
Macquarie Research, I-956
"Mad in Cricket: Dream 11 Business Model." [online] from https://timesofindia.indiatimes.com/readers-blog/jordenskyupdates/mad-in-cricket-dream-11-business-model-27561/ [Published October 27, 2020], II-3217
Management Science Associates, I-1164-1167, II-3358-3359, 3362-3371
Manufacturing & Supply Chain, I-1395
Marijuana Business Magazine, I-602
Market Advantage TSV, I-380, 385, 388, 393-399, 549, 555-559, 735-736, 827, 979, 981, 988, 1449-1452, 1732-1733, II-2531, 2656, 3095
Market Insights L.L.C., I-1361
"Market Share for Each Distributor in 2020." [online] from https://www.the-numbers.com/market/2020/summary [Accessed January 5, 2021], II-2356-2357
Marketing Information Services Inc., II-2412, 2414
Marketing Research Bureau, I-1877
MarketsandMarkets research, II-2714
McIlvaine Co., II-3465
McKnight's Senior Living, I-1862,
MDM Analytics, I-2, 564, 1786, II-2267, 2288, 2761, 3380
Media Play News, I-1162
Medical Design & Outsourcing, II-2254
MedTech Europe, I-1067
Mercator CustomerMonitor Survey Series, II-2637
Mercatus, II-2520
Merchant Marine, I-1184
Mercury Research, II-3009, 3023, 3028, 3030
Metal Center News, II-2297
Metal Construction News, II-2278
Metal Powder Industries Federation, II-2296
Metals Focus, I-1636-1641, 1996, 1999, II-3081-3084, 3086
Metro Magazine, I-573
Metro Market Studies, I-1696

Metropolitan Transit Authority, II-3376
Mhojhos Research, II-3486
Michigan Gaming Control Board, I-1568
"Mineral Insulated Cable Market Report 2020: Rising Impressive Business Opportunities Analysis with Top Countries Data Forecast By 2026." [online] from http://www.marketwatch.compress-release/mineral-insulated-cable-market-report-2020 [Press release Aug, I-586
Ministry of Coal, I-748
Mintel, I-1237, 1468, 2004, II-3301
Mixpanel, I-254
MMR, I-1102-1112, 1596-1600, 1602-1603, 1605, 1607-1615
Mobility Foresights, I-303, 900, 2067, II-2268, 2834
MobTech, II-2175
Modern Casting, I-619
Modern Materials Handling, I-2063
Modern Tire Dealer, II-3344, 3351-3352
The Moodie Davitt Report, II-3419
Mordor Intelligence, II-2695
Morgan Stanley, I-258, 609
Morningstar, I-1982
Mortgage Bankers Association, II-2353
Motion Picture Association, II-2385
Motor Intelligence, I-343
Motor Intelligence U.S. Market New Vehicle Deliveries Report, I-337
MotorCycles Data, II-2369, 2372-2373
MRC Data, II-2390-2397, 2403, 2405
MSA, II-3373
MSA 2020 Market Share Offer Control Report, I-1225
MSAi, I-730
MTN Investor reports, II-3567
Multifamily Executive, I-1852-1854
"Music Streaming Market Share." [online] from https://www.t4.ai/industry/music-streaming-market-share [Published August 16, 2020], II-2409
Music Trades, II-2415
Musical Merchandise Review, II-2413, 2416-2417

NACS OnCampus Research, I-516-517
National Agricultural Statistics Service, I-1293, 1299, 1371
National Association of College Book Stores, I-520
National Association of Convenience Stores, I-934
National Association of Home Builders, I-1859
National Association of Insurance Commissioners, I-1909-1911, 1914, 1921-1922, 1927-1928, 1930-1936, 1938, 1940, 1943-1945, 1947-1950, 1952-1954
National Association of Theatre Owners, II-2383
National Bureau of Statistics, China, I-970, 1416, II-2723, 3220
National Christmas Tree Association, I-728
National Confectioners Association, I-715, 809, 813
National Credit Union Administration, I-1019
National Fluid Power Association, I-1379-1380
National Golf Foundation, I-1643
National Hog Farmer, II-2215
National Jeweler, I-2000
National Leasing Association, I-2045
National Marine Manufacturers Association, I-511
National Ocean and Atmospheric Administration, I-1331
National Oil & Lube News, I-317, 2120
National Park Service, II-2622-2623
National Productivity Council Report, II-3398
National Restaurant Industry Association, II-2898
National Retail Federation, II-2904
National Retail Federation 2020 Back-to-School/Spending Survey, II-2899-2900
National Science Foundation, II-2875
Nation's Restaurant News, II-2882-2884, 2887, 2892-2894, 2896
Natural Foods Merchandiser's Market Overview, 2020, II-2418-2419,
Needham & Company, II-2235, 2251-2252

New Frontier Data, I-604
News Corp., I-529
"News Deserts and Ghost Newspapers: Will Local News Survive?" [online] from https://www.usnewsdeserts.com/reports/news-deserts-and-ghost-newspapers-will-local-news-survive/the-news-landscape-in-2020-transformed-and-diminished/the-new-media-giants/ [Published June 2020], II-2429
"News/Ocean Alliance Passes 2M to Take the Lead on Asia-Europe Market Share." [online] from https://theloadstar.com/ocean-alliance-passes-2m-to-take-the-lead-on-asia-europe-market-share/ [Published January 7, 2020], II-3061
Newzoo, I-1188, 1570, 1576, II-3484
Nielsen, I-23, 169, 598, 935, 1456, 1510-1513, 1679, II-2365, 2614-2615, 2632, 2944, 2947, 2968, 2970, 2987-2988, 3316-3317, 3319-3321, 3323-3324, 3372
"Nigeria Furniture Market Trend." [online] from http://news.kotra.or.kr [Published September 21, 2020], I-1545
Nigerian Communications Commission, II-3570
Nikkei XTech, II-2426
Niko Partners, II-3477
Nilson Report, II-2274-2275, 2633-2634, 2636, 2638-2639, 2771
Nimdzi, II-3411
NLC India Ltd., I-748
NLGI Grease Production Survey, I-2118
Nomisma, II-2624
Nomura estimates, I-1214
The NonProfit Times, I-665
Nonwovens Industry, II-2442, 2733
"North America Doors and Windows Market Outlook and Forecast Report 2021-2026." [online] from https://www.globenewswire.com/en/news-release/2021/02/25/2182161/28124/en/North-America-Doors-and-Windows-Market [Published February 25, 2021], II-3542
Northern Sky Research, II-2960-2961
Notch Consulting, I-708

"Novo Nordisk A Focused Healthcare Company." [online] from https://www.novonordisk.com/content/dam/nncorp/global/en/investors/irmaterial/investor_presentations/2020/20201030_Q3%202020-conference-call-presentation.pdf [Accessed April 13, 2021], I-1131
NPD BookScan, I-521-524, 527, 530-533
NPD Group Inc., I-198, 200, 1425, 1431-1432, 1434, 1834, II-3399, 3401
Numerator TruView, II-3088
Nursery Retailer, I-2037
Nut Processors Association of Kenya, China Chamber of Commerce for Import and Export of Foodstuffs, Brazilian Macadamia Association, Vietnam Macadamia Association, II-2451
Nutrition Business Journal, II-2419
Nvidia, II-3036
NYK Line, II-3048, 3051, 3053
O'Dwyer's, II-2809
OEC, II-3572
The Official Charts Company, I-1163, II-2399-2402
OFV, I-327
Oil & Gas Journal, II-2462-2465, 2469-2480, 2485-2488
Oliver Wyman, II-2386, 2689-2690
Omdia, I-30, 591, 630, 880, 1087, 1089, 1247, 1249, 1955, 1958-1961, II-2355, 2376, 2423, 3037
On-Site Magazine, I-862
Open Secrets, I-2109
Operabase, I-1246
Oregon Hazelnut Industry Office, II-2450
Orr Group, II-3397
Orthoworld, II-2242-2243
Outreach Magazine, II-2867
Outsell Inc., II-2810,
Ovum, II-2544,
Owens Corning research, I-282
P2P MarketData, I-1022
Packaged Facts, II-2667, 3108
Paint & Coatings Industry, II-2591
Panjiva, II-2769
Paper360°, II-2604
Parks Associates, II-3250
Pensions & Investments, II-2645
Pet Business, II-2687

Peter Backman Foodservice, I-1418
PetroChina Petrochemical Research Institute, II-2738
Phillips McDougall, I-688-689, 712, 972, II-3004
Pipeline & Gas Journal, II-2491-2492
Piper Jaffray, I-202
Piper Sandler, I-201, 1427-1428,
Plastics News, II-2727-2729, 2731
Platinum Forecast System, I-67, 78, II-3448
Plunkett Research, I-296, 518, 1040, 1056, 1291, 1433, II-2826, 2870, 3087, 3299
Podtrac, II-2762
Pollstar, I-262, 801-802, II-3334
Pool & Spa News, I-928
Poultry Trends, I-1885
Powder Metallurgy Review, II-2295
PPF Magazine, I-318
PricewaterhouseCoopers, I-1001, II-3027
Principia Consulting, I-1042, II-2830, 3420
Printed Circuit Design & Fab/Circuits Assembly, II-2790
Printing Impressions, I-528, II-2793-2796
Professional Carwashing & Detailing, I-615
Promotional Products Association International, II-2807
ProSales Magazine, I-565
Prosper Insights & Analytics, II-2899-2900
Qianzhan, I-751, 1387, II-2925, 3192
QSR Magazine, II-2889
Qualified Remodeler, I-869
QY Research, I-9, 81, 184-185, 194, 209, 214, 237, 299-300, 302, 309, 320-321, 369, 465, 469, 473, 495-496, 501, 509, 563, 589, 606, 608, 626-627, 652, 690, 697, 731-732, 738-739, 741, 762, 783, 786, 803, 858, 882, 945, 954, 986, 1016, 1070, 1077-1078, 1100-1101, 1132, 1159, 1189, 1203, 1209, 1242, 1244, 1256, 1272, 1276, 1338, 1424, 1429, 1478, 1484, 1496, 1548-1549, 1586-1588, 1590, 1592, 1616, 1618, 1624, 1627, 1634, 1765, 1768, 1787, 1824-1825, 1865, 1878-1879, 1994, 2016,

2025, 2028, 2046, 2054, 2070-2072, 2113, 2119, II-2137, 2144-2145, 2234, 2245, 2249, 2264, 2289, 2305-2306, 2310, 2342, 2428, 2434, 2457, 2598, 2617, 2619, 2660, 2666, 2685, 2703, 2721, 2726, 2747, 2752, 2756, 2759, 2784, 2821, 2823-2825, 2876, 2886, 2911, 2926, 2928, 2948, 2953, 2996, 3104, 3172, 3207-3208, 3287, 3292, 3295, 3297, 3304, 3348, 3385, 3389, 3396, 3400, 3410, 3412, 3454, 3461-3463, 3474, 3522

Rabobank, I-1034

RAI Vereniging, I-335

Rail Inc., II-2837

Rail Time Indicators, II-2840

Raisins South Africa, Greek Nuts & Fruits Trade Association, U.S. Department of Agriculture, I-1528

RCR, II-3563

Real Estate Alert, II-2843-2847, 2851

Real Trends, II-2850

Recording Industry Association of America, II-2406

Recreation Management, II-2856

Recreational Vehicle Industry Association, II-2863

Refinitiv, Global Investment Banking Review, I-1984

Regulatory Affairs Professional Society, II-3459

Religaire, I-711

"Resale Snapshot." [online] from http://www.ebmpubs.com/ECN/ecn_curis.asp [Accessed January 5, 2021], II-2307

Research and Markets, II-2247, 2625, 2661-2662

Research in China, I-607, 1998, 2029, II-2302, 2746, 3029, 3464

Retail Info Systems, II-2909

RISI, II-2603, 2813-2814, 2816

Robert W. Baird & Co., I-903, II-3329

Roofing Contractor, I-922

Rosenblatt Securities, I-1257

Rubber & Plastics News, II-2936, 3356

"Russian Federation Retail Foods." [online] from https://gain.fas.usda.gov [Published August 6, 2020], I-1699

Rystad Analytics, II-2481, 2483, 2493

"Salmon Farming Industry Handbook." [online] from https://mowi.com/it/wp-content/uploads/sites/16/2020/06/Mowi-Salmon-Farming-Industry-Handbook-2020.pdf [Accessed August 20, 2020], I-1327-1328

Samir "Mr. Magazine" Husni Launch Monitor, II-2140

S&P Global Market Intelligence, I-1912, 1916-1917, II-2828, 3319

Satellite Industry Association, II-2962

SBD, II-3383

Schlepper-Bundesliga, I-1282-1283

School Bus Fleet, II-2979

School Transportation News, I-570

SCI Verkehr, II-2833, 2835

ScrapeHero research, I-1753,

Screen Daily, II-2360,

SDM, II-3002

Second Measure, I-193, 769, 1403-1412, II-2517

Security, II-3000

Semiconductor Industry Association, II-3026-3027

Sensor Tower, I-251, 255, II-2334-2340

Sensors for Robotics Mobility, 2020, II-3034

Shanghai Metals Market, I-162

Shelby Market Data, I-1686

Shelby Report, I-1681, 1690, 1700

Shenzhen Gaogong Industry Research Co., I-349

Shooting Industry, I-1715-1719,

SIG Combibloc Group, II-2574

Signify Research, II-3163, 3190

Signs of the Times, II-3075

Similar Web, II-2165

Sina Finance, I-1387, II-3141

Sinolink Securities Co., I-1294

Sinopec, II-2468

S.J. Consulting Group, II-3069, 3421-3422, 3425, 3427, 3429

Sky Light Research, II-2421

Smart Research Insights, I-481

SmarTech Analysis, II-2294

Snack Food & Wholesale Bakery, II-3131

SNE Research, I-307

Snow Magazine, I-932

Society of Motor Manufacturers and Traders, I-338, 355

Solar Power World, I-924-926

"Sony and Pioneer Are Helping Drive Mobile Audio Market." [online] from https://www.traqline.com/newsroom/blog/sony-and-pioneer-are-helping-drive-mobile-audio-market/ [Published April 13, 2021], I-286

Space Foundation Database, II-2963

The Space Report, II-2965

"Spain 2020. Motorcycles Industry Hit More Than Other Top EU Markets (-12.6%)." [online] from https://www.motorcyclesdata.com/2021/01/15/spanish-motorcycles/ [Published January 15, 2021], II-2374

Special Events, I-1255

Specialty Equipment Manufacturers Association, II-3349

Spotlight, II-2258, 2266

Staffing Industry Analysts, II-3227-3230, 3232

Standard & Poor's, I-1635

StatCounter, I-1967-1969, II-3155-3157, 3176-3178, 3184-3186

State Council of China, II-2695

State Gaming Regulatory Agencies, I-1575

"The State of Online Travel Agencies 2020." [online] from https://medium.com/traveltechmedia/the-state-of-online-travel-agencies-2020-f6acc899aca2 [Published July 24, 2020], II-2522

State of the Vegetable Industry, I-1531

State Post Bureau, II-3067

Statista, I-103, 253, 259, 481, 790-791, 794, 978, 1114, II-2228, 2332, 2519, 2697, 2951, 3106, 3235, 3259, 3361, 3480-3481

Statistical Surveys, I-508, 1851, II-2859-2862, 3403-3406

Stephens Inc., II-2607-2609

Stockholm International Peace Research Institute, I-274, 1048, 1051-1052

Stora Enso, II-2567
StoreFUEL, II-2443-2444, 2446
STR, I-1832
Strategic Insights, I-1367, 1561-1565, 1796-1799, 1801-1820, 1835-1836
Strategy Analytics, I-896, II-3022, 3251-3252
Strategy&, I-1001
StreamElements, II-3485
Student Borrower Protection Center, I-2105
Student Housing Business, I-1855-1856
Successful Farming, I-1782-1783
Sullivan, I-1550-1551,
Suning Yigou, I-245,
Sustainable Ecommerce Packaging, II-2560
Swedish Transport Agency, I-854
Swiss Re, I-1913
Systems Contractor News, II-3289
TDM database, II-3579-3580,
Teal Group, I-73-74
TechARC, I-895
Technavio, I-83, 1187, II-3408
Techno Systems Research, I-595, II-3031
Technomic, I-763, II-2885, 2888, 2890, 2895, 2897
Technopak, I-196, 211, 1678, 1692
TeleGeography, II-3571
"Tennant Investor Presentation." [online] from https://investors.tennantco.com/news-and-events/Current-Investor-Presentation/default.aspx# [Published January 2021], II-2920
Tennis Industry Association, II-3212
Textile Exchange, I-1319
"Thailand 2020. Two-Wheeler Market Lost 9.7%" [online] from https://www.motorcyclesdata.com/2021/01/19/thailand-motorcycles/ [Published January 19, 2021], II-2375
Themed Entertainment Association, I-178-182, II-3510
Thinking Ahead Institute, I-1981, II-2647
Tile Council of North America, I-660
Tire Business, II-3343, 3345-3347, 3350, 3355

Tire Review, II-3353
Titanium Today, II-3357
Tmall, I-245
Today's Motor Vehicles, I-345
"Toll Road Project: Private Companies Ready to Take Over Market." [online] from https://www.pwc.com/id/en/media-centre/infrastructure-news/march-2020/toll-road-project-private-companies-ready-to-take-over-market.html [Published March 9, 2020], II-3377
"Tonal Announces $110M in New Capital, Building on Its Leadership in Connected Strength Training." [online] from https://www.tonal.com/press/tonal-announces-110-million-in-new-funding/ [Press release September 17, 2020], II-3189
"Top 20 Animal Health Companies Based on 2019 Revenue." [online] from https://pharmashots.com/52031/top-20-animal-health-companies-based-on-2019-revenue/ [Published November 20, 2020], I-1127
"The Top 50 Swiss Watch Brands of 2020...And the Invincible Hegemony of Rolex." [online] from https://monochrome-watches.com/top-50-swiss-watch-brands-2020-market-share-sales-editorial/ [Published March 9, 2021], II-3505, 3507
"Top Talk Audiences." [online] from http://www.talkers.com/top-talk-audiences/ [Accessed November 3, 2020], II-2827
TowerXchange, II-3574
Trade Data Monitor, I-1688, 1701
Trade Show Executive, I-940
TRAI, II-3568
Trailer Body Builders, II-3407
Training, II-3409,
Transport Intelligence, II-3430
Transport Topics, II-3057, 3059, 3431, 3500
TraQline, I-221-222, 239, 246, 628, 789, 883, II-2269, 2753, 2755, 3209, 3536
Travel Weekly, II-3413

TrendForce, I-332, 347, 629, 634, 1086, 1448, 1956-1957, 2052, 2069, II-2600-2602, 3013-3014, 3021, 3024
Trends in Biotechnology, II-2170
Triton Digital, I-897, 1169, 1964, II-2763-2764, 3516
Trustdata, I-1966
TV Veopar Journal, I-250
Twice, I-219
Twitter, I-1970
Two Circles, II-3218
UBS, I-323-324, 373
Ukrainian Walnut Association, II-2456
UMLER, I-2042-2044
U.N. Comtrade, I-164-165, 171-172, 947-948, 955, 957, 963-964, 1263-1264, 1269-1270, 1321-1322, 1538-1539, 1630-1633, 2039-2040, 2050-2051, II-2284-2285, 2435-2436, 2489-2490, 2641-2642, 2740-2745, 2780-2781, 2817-2818, 3079-3080, 3247-3248, 3339-3340, 3558-3559, 3592-3593, 3597-3598, 3604-3605
Underground Construction, II-2482
UNECE/FAO database, II-3579-3580, 3583-3587
United Nations Conference on Trade and Development, I-745-746, 1669-1670, 1990-1991, II-3047, 3056
U.S. Association of Equipment Manufacturers, I-1287
U.S. Bureau of Justice Statistics, II-2800
U.S. Bureau of Labor, II-3452
U.S. Bureau of Transportation, I-86-96
"U.S. Car Sales Analysis - Sports Cars." [online] from https://carsalesbase.com/us-car-sales-analysis-2020-sports-cars/ [Accessed April 21, 2021], I-328
U.S. Census Bureau, I-1, 8, 50, 157-158, 173-175, 177, 186, 217, 263, 278-281, 313-316, 381, 460, 471, 474-475, 505-506, 515, 543, 562, 574-575, 683, 733, 775-780, 784, 804-807, 859, 874, 876, 937, 946, 949-950, 999-1000, 1026-1027, 1030, 1035-1036, 1054-1055, 1065-1066, 1076, 1083-1084, 1098, 1113, 1160-1161, 1205,

1208, 1210-1211, 1250, 1259, 1262, 1266-1268, 1271, 1274-1275, 1277, 1301, 1318, 1325, 1368, 1444-1447, 1455, 1494-1495, 1547, 1553-1554, 1557-1559, 1591, 1622-1623, 1625, 1675, 1707, 1709, 1738, 1740, 1755-1760, 1762, 1767, 1777-1778, 1794, 1857, 1860, 1867, 1880-1881, 1888, 1891-1893, 1895, 1902, 1976-1977, 1995, 2013, 2022-2023, 2031-2032, 2048-2049, 2053, 2056-2058, 2066, 2079-2080, 2082-2083, 2112, II-2148, 2232, 2257, 2279-2280, 2282-2283, 2286-2287, 2292-2293, 2299-2300, 2323, 2328-2329, 2344-2345, 2366, 2377-2378, 2388, 2532-2533, 2576, 2580-2581, 2593, 2616, 2618, 2621, 2705-2709, 2712-2713, 2717, 2736, 2748, 2757, 2786, 2791-2792, 2804-2805, 2852-2853, 2855, 2857-2858, 2864-2865, 2868, 2871-2873, 2877, 2913, 2932-2934, 2974, 2976-2978, 2981, 2992, 3008, 3042, 3046, 3073-3074, 3077, 3098, 3194, 3201, 3204, 3211, 3226, 3231, 3236-3237, 3245, 3253-3256, 3311-3312, 3326, 3333, 3375, 3393, 3451, 3498, 3511-3512, 3527-3529, 3539-3540, 3608

U.S. Department of Agriculture, I-498-500, 577-580, 620-622, 624, 669-670, 678-679, 752-754, 756, 965-968, 991-995, 1288-1289, 1292, 1295-1298, 1329, 1375-1378, 1498, 1514, 1521-1526, 1530, 1532, 1534-1536, 1540-1541, 1781, 1784-1785, 1823, 2008-2009, II-2173-2174, 2187-2192, 2212-2214, 2216, 2225, 2312-2313, 2447, 2452, 2458-2459, 2496-2514, 2644, 2778-2779, 2914-2917, 3041, 3257-3258, 3374, 3497, 3530-3533

U.S. Department of Commerce, I-176, 187, 470, 491, 561, 583, 605, 617, 660, 684, 872-873, 875, 1099, 1207, 1300, 1317, 1337, 1546, 1621, 1671, 1708, 1724, 1766, 1837, 1858, 1866, 1868, 1887, 1894, 1901, 1988, 1997, II-2146, 2326, 2582, 2610, 2710, 2716, 2722, 2735, 2912, 2935, 3076, 3099, 3152, 3203, 3210, 3309, 3436

U.S. Department of Education, II-2980

U.S. Department of Energy, II-2467

U.S. Department of Labor, Mine Safety and Health Administration, I-747

U.S. Department of Transportation, II-2149, 3070

U.S. Energy Information Administration, I-461, 1212, 1215, 1227-1228, 1231, 1233

U.S. Fish and Wildlife Service, I-1863-1864

U.S. Foreign Trade, I-1557

U.S. Geological Survey, I-3, 160, 167, 183, 264, 277, 534, 588, 653, 693-694, 729, 749, 959, 1074-1075, 1302, 1316, 1381, 1567, 1589, 1642, 1673, 1729, 1890, 1987, 1993, 2015, 2041, 2081, 2098, II-2141, 2143, 2276, 2303, 2343, 2437, 2596, 2643, 2702, 2751, 2775, 2820, 2841-2842, 2937-2939, 3078, 3085, 3149, 3246, 3260, 3342, 3441, 3607

U.S. International Trade Commission, I-1361

U.S. Postal Service, II-2773

U.S. Securities and Exchange Commission, I-1017

U.S. Senate, I-2108

U.S. Tire Manufacturers Association, II-3350, 3354

University of Nevada Las Vegas Center for Gaming Research, I-1568, 1584

US Glass Metal & Grazing, I-918

Valve Manufacturers Association, II-3466

Variety, II-2361-2363

VerifiedVoting.org, II-3492

Verto, I-253

VGChartz, II-3476, 3478

"View." [online] from https://www.cantor.com/wp-content/uploads/2020/11/View-Investor-Presentation.pdf [Published November 30, 2020], I-1620

Vision Monday, II-2524

Vista Information Services, division of Epicor Software Corp., I-686, 2068, 2073, 2111, II-2585, 2588, 2684, 2758, 3379, 3386

Wall Street Research, I-1174, II-2556

Walls & Ceilings, I-929

Wards Intelligence, I-348

WardsAuto, II-3432-3435

Washington Business Journal, I-1850

Washington Technology, I-1665

Waste Today, II-3504

WATT Global Media, I-1192-1200, II-2177-2185, 2224, 2681

WATTPoultry USA, II-2176

We Are Social, I-1972

WhatTheyThink, II-2797

"Who are the Biggest Players in the Tank Terminal Market?" [online] from https://www.insights-global.com/who-are-the-biggest-players-in-the-tank-terminal-market/ [Accessed August 25, 2020], II-3291

"Will John Menzies Put Itself Up for Sale?" [online] from https://www.nasdaq.com/articles/will-john-menzies-put-itself-up-for-sale-2019-09-18 [Published September 18, 2019], I-99

Willis Towers Watson, II-2648

WindEurope Intelligence Platform, I-1224

Window & Door Manufacturers Association, II-3541

Wine Australia, II-3544

Wine Business Monthly, II-3549

Wines Vines Analytics, II-3543, 3551

Wohlers Report, II-3335

Wood Mackenzie, I-159, 166, 958, 960-962, 1989, II-3601-3603, 3606

World Agricultural Supply and Demand estimates, II-2166, 2168, 2205, 2226

World Apple and Pear Association, I-1497

World Bank, I-1258, II-2869

World Cargo News, I-1015

World Development Indicators, II-2869

World Federation of Direct Selling Associations, I-1082

World Grain, I-1372

World Industrial Truck Statistics, I-2064

World Nuclear Association, II-3457

World Robotics 2020, II-2921-2923
World Semiconductor Trade Statistics, II-3010, 3025-3027
World Steel Association, I-1990-1991, II-3238-3239, 3242
World Tourism Organization, II-3392
World Trade Organization, I-188, 190, 705, 707, 1388-1389, II-2460-2461, 3240-3241, 3330-3331
Worldpanel, I-1693
Worth Rises, II-2799
XYZ Reports, II-3313
Yano Economic Research Institute, II-2528, 2612, 2680
Ycharts, I-1028
Yole Développement, I-593, II-2241, 2304, 2526, 3012
ZDC Research Center, I-234
Zelman & Associates Research, II-2353
Zhong Yikang, I-245
Zhongwei Intelligent, II-3135
Zoomark, II-2663
Zweirad-Verband e.V., I-492-493

PLACE NAMES INDEX

This index shows countries, political entities, states, and provinces, regions within countries, parks, airports, and cities. For items in the index that refer to a large number of entries, a subject subheading is provided to make it as easy as possible to access entries of interest. The numbers that follow the place name, or one of its subheadings, are entry numbers; they are arranged sequentially so that the first mention of a place is listed first. The Roman numerals indicate the volume number. This index provides references for 545 places.

Acadia National Park, ME, II-2622
Afghanistan, I-1374, 1518, 1520, 1528, II-2454-2455
Africa
  Agriculture - Crops, I-1670
  Agriculture - Livestock, I-1192, II-2177
  Business Services, I-30
  Chemicals and Allied Products, I-681, 1313-1315
  Communications, II-2539, 3560
  Depository Institutions, I-400
  Eating and Drinking Places, I-1417, II-2881
  Electric/Gas/Sanitary Services, I-1213
  Electronic/Electric Equip., I-226-228, 230
  Engineering/Management Services, II-2875
  Heavy Construction, I-1899
  Industry Machinery/Equip., I-225, 792, 2064, II-2771
  Instruments and Related, II-2233
  Metal Mining, I-1989
  Misc. Manufacturing Industries, I-1996
  Motion Pictures, II-2376
  Nondepository Institutions, II-2639
  Oil and Gas Extraction, II-2469
  Paper and Allied Products, I-627, II-2603
  Personal Services, I-1737
  Primary Metal Industries, I-951, 962, II-3602
  Printing and Publishing, I-2018, 2020
  Transportation by Air, I-82, II-3044
  Transportation Equipment, I-58
  Transportation Services, II-3392
  Wholesale Trade - Nondurables, I-703
Alabama, I-104, 404, 531, 991, 1863-1864
Alaska, I-97, 105, 405
Albania, II-2476
Albany-Rensselaer, NY, II-2149
Alberta, Canada, I-602, 1225
Alexandria, VA, I-1113
Algeria, I-754, 967, 1052, 1316, 1517, 1729, 1890, II-2469, 2475, 2489, 2505, 2702, 2820, 3530, 3532
Alpharetta, GA, I-1839
Americas, I-233, 590, 681, 951, 1899, 2064, II-3010, 3392
Anaheim, CA, I-1604
Anaheim Convention Center, CA, I-940
Anchorage, AK, I-97
Andalusia, Spain, I-51
Angola, I-1074, II-2469, 2475, 3080
Antamina, Peru, I-952, II-3083, 3606
Aragon, Spain, I-51
Argentina
  Agriculture - Crops, I-965-966, 968, 1525-1526, 1669, II-2452, 2456, 2458-2459, 2500-2502, 2507, 3531, 3533
  Agriculture - Livestock, I-621-622, II-3592
  Business Services, I-44, II-3480
  Chemicals and Allied Products, I-1309
  Food and Kindred Products, I-578, 679, 1296, 1298, 1373, 1388, 1527-1528, II-2173-2174, 2187-2189, 2192, 2213, 2313, 2496-2499, 2503-2504, 2506, 3550
  Metal Mining, I-1642, II-2276, 3085
  Motion Pictures, II-2380
  Nonmetallic Minerals, I-534
  Oil and Gas Extraction, II-2473, 2479
  Stone/Clay/Glass Products, I-3
  Transportation Equipment, II-2369
Arizona, I-106, 406, 624, 1110, 1534, 1541, 1608, 1681, 1698, 1822, 1848, 1864
Arkansas, I-107, 407, 991, 1584, II-2225
Arlington, TX, I-1104, 1113, 1601, 1843
Arlington, VA, I-1113
Armenia, I-2047, II-2343
Asia-Pacific
  Agriculture - Crops, I-1670
  Agriculture - Livestock, I-1193, 1326, II-2178
  Amusement and Recreation, I-180, 1585
  Apparel and Textile Products, I-184
  Business Services, I-30
  Chemicals and Allied Products, I-681, 1313-1315
  Communications, II-3560
  Depository Institutions, I-400
  Eating and Drinking Places, I-1417, II-2881
  Electric/Gas/Sanitary Services, I-1219
  Electronic/Electric Equip., I-226-228, 230, 233, 632, 2076, II-3010
  Fabricated Metal Products, I-514
  General Merchandise Stores, II-2908
  Industry Machinery/Equip., I-225, 2064, II-2771

1023

Instruments and Related, II-2233
Motion Pictures, II-2376
Nondepository Institutions, II-2634, 2639
Oil and Gas Extraction, II-2471
Paper and Allied Products, I-627, II-2603
Personal Services, I-1737
Primary Metal Industries, I-951
Printing and Publishing, I-773, 2018, 2020
Rubber and Misc. Plastics, II-3353
Transportation by Air, I-82, II-3044
Transportation Equipment, I-58
Transportation Services, II-3392
Water Transportation, I-1024, II-3061
Wholesale Trade - Nondurables, I-702
Asturias, Spain, I-51
Atlanta, GA, I-98, 531, 1102, 1403, 1839, II-2767
Atlantic City, NJ, I-1575
Aurora, CO, I-1602
Australasia, II-2881
Australia
  Agriculture - Crops, I-993, 1669, II-2447, 2451, 2453, 2455-2456, 2458-2459, 3531, 3533
  Agriculture - Livestock, I-621-622, II-3592
  Automotive Dealers, I-1438
  Business Services, I-35, 2045, II-3227
  Chemicals and Allied Products, I-160, 1264, 1309, 1316, 1890
  Coal Mining, I-743, 745
  Electric/Gas/Sanitary Services, I-1219, 1221, 1226
  Electronic/Electric Equip., I-226-228, 230
  Food and Kindred Products, I-578-579, 678-679, 754, 1387, 1527-1528, 2008-2009, II-2174, 2213-2214, 2497, 2664, 2679, 3258, 3550
  Industry Machinery/Equip., I-225
  Insurance Carriers, II-2648
  Lumber and Wood Products, II-3580
  Metal Mining, I-171, 183, 749, 959, 1642, 1990, 1993, 2039, 2041, II-2437, 3085, 3342, 3457, 3604, 3607

Motion Pictures, II-2355
Nat. Security and Interntl. Affairs, I-1048-1049, 1052
Nonmetallic Minerals, I-1074-1075, 1589, II-2702, 2842, 2937, 2939, 3260
Oil and Gas Extraction, II-2471, 2477
Personal Services, I-1737
Primary Metal Industries, I-167, II-2143
Printing and Publishing, II-2430
Security and Commodity Brokers, I-1258
Stone/Clay/Glass Products, I-2081, II-2959
Trucking and Warehousing, I-1413, 1415
Austria
  Agriculture - Livestock, II-2699
  Chemicals and Allied Products, I-500, 1067
  Food and Kindred Products, I-724-725, 811, II-3107
  Instruments and Related, II-2255
  Lumber and Wood Products, II-3579, 3586, 3591
  Metal Mining, II-3441
  Miscellaneous Retail, I-270-271
  Motion Pictures, II-2384
  Nonmetallic Minerals, I-1673
  Oil and Gas Extraction, II-2474, 2480
  Paper and Allied Products, II-2611, 2613
  Stone/Clay/Glass Products, I-645
  Textile Mill Products, I-1269
  Transportation Equipment, I-356-357, 367
  Transportation Services, II-3378
Azerbaijan, I-1529, 1987, II-2450, 2470
Bahamas, II-3056
Bahrain, I-167, 172, 643, II-3109
Balearic Islands, I-51
Baltimore, MD, I-1575, 1703, 1840, II-2149, 2347, 2767
Bangladesh, I-188, 992, 994, 1270, 1297, 1332, 1334, II-2498, 2502-2503, 2505, 2869, 2914-2915, 3331, 3532, 3598
Barnstable County, MA, I-1859
Barossa Valley, Australia, II-3544
Basque Country, Spain, I-51

Baton Rouge, LA, I-1596
Baytown, TX, I-1113
Beijing, China, I-98, 100
Belarus, I-578, 679, 1312, 2047, II-2189, 2312, 2476, 2643, 2775, 2937
Belgium
  Agriculture - Crops, I-1529
  Agriculture - Livestock, II-2693
  Chemicals and Allied Products, I-500, 1067, 1321-1322, II-2740-2742, 2744-2745
  Electric/Gas/Sanitary Services, I-1220, 1222
  Fabricated Metal Products, I-947, II-2285
  Food and Kindred Products, I-725, 811, 1883, II-2624, 3107
  Instruments and Related, II-2255
  Lumber and Wood Products, II-3584, 3587
  Metal Mining, I-955, 2039, II-3339-3340, 3604-3605
  Misc. Manufacturing Industries, II-2641-2642
  Motion Pictures, II-2384
  Nonmetallic Minerals, I-264, II-3247-3248
  Paper and Allied Products, II-2611
  Stone/Clay/Glass Products, I-1630, 1633, 2081
  Transportation Equipment, I-356-357, 367
Bellevue, WA, I-1613
Benin, I-993, II-2449
Berlin, Germany, I-2074
Bermuda, II-3047
Bhutan, II-3078
Big Easy, FL, I-1581
Birmingham, AL, II-2348
Blue Ridge Parkway, NC, II-2623
Boddington, Australia, I-1640
Boise City, ID, I-1597, 1841
Bolivia, I-183, 264, 534, 2041, II-2448, 2473, 2504, 3085, 3339, 3342, 3441, 3607
Bosnia, II-3585
Boston, MA, I-531, 769, 1113, 1404, 1598, II-2149, 2768
Botswana, I-1074-1075, II-2641, 3149
Boulder Strip, NV, I-1569

Brazil
  Agriculture - Crops, I-965-966, 968, 993, 995, 1523-1526, 1669, II-2448-2449, 2451-2453, 2458-2459, 2500-2501, 2507, 2914-2915, 3530, 3532
  Agriculture - Livestock, I-621-622, 1784-1785
  Business Services, I-35, II-3480
  Chemicals and Allied Products, I-160, 707, 1126, 1307, 1309-1311, II-2745
  Communications, I-1972, II-2410, 3314, 3563
  Electric/Gas/Sanitary Services, I-1218, 1221, 1223, 1229
  Food and Kindred Products, I-476, 678-679, 716, 750, 752-753, 756, 1295, 1298, 1374, 1388, 2008-2009, II-2173-2174, 2187-2189, 2191-2192, 2212-2213, 2216, 2312-2313, 2496-2497, 2499, 2503-2504, 2506, 2664, 3257-3258
  Leather and Leather Products, I-2050
  Lumber and Wood Products, I-1361, II-3591
  Metal Mining, I-171, 1642, 1990, 1993, II-2437, 3339, 3342
  Miscellaneous Retail, I-1082
  Motion Pictures, II-2381
  Nat. Security and Interntl. Affairs, I-1049
  Nonmetallic Minerals, I-277, 1074, 1671, 1673, 1729, 2015, II-2702, 2775, 2842, 2937, 3260
  Oil and Gas Extraction, II-2473, 2479
  Paper and Allied Products, II-2817, 3553
  Primary Metal Industries, I-619, II-2143, 3078, 3239-3240, 3246
  Stone/Clay/Glass Products, I-3, 653, 655-656, 660, 1302, 2081
  Textile Mill Products, II-3598
  Transportation Equipment, I-350-351, II-3437
  Trucking and Warehousing, I-1413
Brazzaville, Congo, II-2469, 2475
British Columbia, I-602
Broward County, FL, I-1859, II-2980
Brunei, II-2471
Buenavista del Cobre, Mexico, I-952

Bulgaria, I-2039, 2081, II-2939, 3583, 3593
Burkina Faso, II-2449, 3564
Burma, I-183, 1381, II-2143, 2842, 2914-2916, 3342
Burundi, II-2842
Busan, South Korea, II-2770
C. Valenciana, Spain, I-51
Cadia Valley, Australia, I-1640
Calder, FL, I-1581
California
  Agricultural Services, I-991
  Agriculture - Crops, I-1289, 1292, 1375-1376, 1378, 1498, 1514, 1516, 1530, 1532, 1534-1536, 1541, II-2779
  Agriculture - Livestock, I-620, 624, 1823, II-2225, 3041
  Amusement and Recreation, I-1643
  Depository Institutions, I-408
  Educational Services, II-2980
  Electric/Gas/Sanitary Services, I-1231
  Fabricated Metal Products, I-1714
  Fishing, Hunting, and Trapping, I-1863
  Food and Kindred Products, I-1371, II-3543
  General Merchandise Stores, I-1604
  Membership Organizations, I-1822, II-3452
  Miscellaneous Retail, I-108, 1108
  Transportation by Air, I-97
  Transportation Equipment, I-364, 368
  Water Transportation, II-2769
Cambodia, I-188, 1270, 1334, 1361, II-2449, 2916
Cambridge, MA, I-1113, 1598
Camden, NJ, I-1113
Cameroon, I-750, II-2469, 2820
Canada
  Agriculture - Crops, I-965, 968, 1516, 1521, 1529, 1669, II-2458-2459, 2501, 2507, 2777, 3531, 3533
  Agriculture - Livestock, I-621-622, 1783-1785
  Amusement and Recreation, I-1576
  Apparel and Textile Products, I-190

Automotive Dealers, I-1439, 1593
Building Materials, I-1790
Business Services, I-35, 1772, 2045
Chemicals and Allied Products, I-160, 601-602, 705, 707, 977, 1126, 1263-1264, 1307-1309, 1312, 1316, 1890, II-2740, 2745, 3460
Coal Mining, I-745
Communications, I-1177, II-2630, 3565
Eating and Drinking Places, I-764
Electric/Gas/Sanitary Services, I-1218, 1223, 1225, 1229
Fabricated Metal Products, I-948, II-2285
Food and Kindred Products, I-577, 579, 678-679, 752, 754, 1296, 1386, 1388-1389, 1519, 2008, II-2173, 2213-2214, 2216, 2497, 2664, 2968-2969
Furniture and Fixtures, I-1557
Furniture Stores, I-902
General Building Contractors, I-862
Industry Machinery/Equip., II-2771, 2921
Insurance Carriers, I-1913, II-2648
Lumber and Wood Products, I-1361, 2128, II-3580
Metal Mining, I-172, 749, 959, 1642, 1990, 1993, 2039, II-2343, 2435, 2437, 2596, 2751, 3457, 3604, 3607
Miscellaneous Retail, I-156
Nondepository Institutions, II-2352, 2639
Nonmetallic Minerals, I-1074, 1381, 1671, 1673, 1729, II-2146, 2303, 2643, 2775, 2937, 2939, 3248, 3260
Oil and Gas Extraction, II-2473, 2479, 2489
Paper and Allied Products, II-2817, 2944-2945, 2947
Personal Services, I-1737
Primary Metal Industries, I-164, 167, 588, II-3078
Security and Commodity Brokers, I-1258
Stone/Clay/Glass Products, I-1631, 1633, 1726, 2081, II-2781, 2959

Transportation Equipment, I-325, 359, 362, II-3439
Trucking and Warehousing, II-2165
Canary Islands, I-51
Cannington, Australia, II-3083
Cantabria, Spain, I-51
Cape Cod National Seashore, MA, II-2623
Caribbean, I-30, 1198, 1313, 1315, II-2183
Carmel, IN, I-1106
Caspian region, II-3602
Castille, Spain, I-51
Castille La Mancha, Spain, I-51
Catalonia, Spain, I-51
CEE, II-2646
Central America, I-1198, 1737, 1996, II-2183, 3480
Cerro Verde II, Peru, I-952
Chad, II-2475
Chandler, AZ, I-1848
Charleston, SC, II-2768-2769
Charlotte, NC, I-1599, 1683, 1842
Chengdu, China, I-98
Chesapeake and Ohio Canal National Historic Park, DC-MD-WV, II-2623
Chicago, IL, I-531, 1103, 1113, 1405, 1600, II-2149, 2767, 2980
Chicago O'Hare International, IL, I-87
Chicagoland, IL, I-1575
Chile
  Agriculture - Crops, I-1516, 1526, II-2447, 2450, 2456, 2458-2459
  Business Services, II-3480
  Chemicals and Allied Products, I-1312, 1987
  Fishing, Hunting, and Trapping, I-1333, 1335
  Food and Kindred Products, I-1519, 1527-1528, II-2189, 2213-2214, 3550
  Lumber and Wood Products, I-964
  Metal Mining, I-955, 959, 1993, II-2343, 3085
  Motion Pictures, II-2382
  Nonmetallic Minerals, I-534, II-2775, 2820, 2937, 3260
  Oil and Gas Extraction, II-2473
  Paper and Allied Products, II-2817

China, I-2130, 2135, II-3220, 3524
  Admin. of Economic Programs, II-3199
  Agriculture - Crops, I-967-968, 992, 994-995, 1521-1526, 1538-1539, II-2450-2456, 2458-2459, 2500, 2502, 2507, 2777, 2914-2917, 3530, 3532-3533
  Agriculture - Livestock, I-621-622, 1784-1785, II-3079-3080, 3592-3593
  Amusement and Recreation, I-1254, 1576
  Apparel and Textile Products, I-188, 190, 197, 203-204, 207, 212, 1795
  Automotive Dealers, I-1440
  Business Services, I-20, 29, 31, 35, 257, 274, 941, 943, 1037, 2045, II-3101, 3103, 3156, 3165, 3169, 3177, 3185, 3192, 3227
  Chemicals and Allied Products, I-160, 499, 687, 707, 710, 712, 970, 972, 975, 985, 1063, 1118, 1122, 1126, 1133, 1263-1264, 1307-1312, 1316, 1321-1322, II-2583, 2650, 2738, 2741, 2743-2745, 3089, 3141, 3275, 3460, 3464, 3491
  Coal Mining, I-742-743, 746
  Communications, I-1170, 1172, 1177, 1179, 1185-1186, II-2410, 2540, 2554, 2630, 3310
  Depository Institutions, II-2869
  Eating and Drinking Places, I-765, 1416, II-2880
  Educational Services, I-1245, II-2515, 3449
  Electric/Gas/Sanitary Services, I-1214, 1218-1223, 1226, 1229, II-3040
  Electronic/Electric Equip., I-154, 234, 236, 245, 247-249, 467, 607, 632, 634, 638, II-2398, 2404, 2600-2601, 2965, 3015, 3027, 3029
  Engineering/Management Services, II-2875
  Fabricated Metal Products, I-947, II-2284-2285
  Fishing, Hunting, and Trapping, I-1332-1335
  Food and Kindred Products, I-382, 476, 481, 489, 538, 540, 577, 579, 670, 678, 716, 751-752, 754, 1032, 1236, 1294-1295, 1297-1298, 1384-1385, 1387-1389, 1468, 1518, 1528, 2008-2009, II-2173-2175, 2187-2192, 2212-2214, 2216, 2312, 2314, 2496, 2498-2499, 2503, 2505-2506, 2664, 2695, 2971, 2973, 2991, 3132, 3135, 3257-3258, 3469, 3547, 3599
  Food Stores, I-1684, II-2518, 2989
  Furniture and Fixtures, I-1555, 1557
  Furniture Stores, I-220
  General Merchandise Stores, I-936, II-2901, 2903, 2906
  Health Services, I-1754
  Hotels and Lodging Places, I-1826, 1830
  Industry Machinery/Equip., I-224, 243, 787, 853, 857, 2029, II-2136, 2460-2461, 2746, 2921, 2925, 3035, 3037
  Instruments and Related, I-590, 592, II-2244, 2263, 2302, 3261, 3506
  Insurance Carriers, I-1913
  Leather and Leather Products, I-2050-2051
  Local and Passenger Transit, II-2919
  Lumber and Wood Products, I-963, 1361, II-3591
  Metal Mining, I-172, 183, 749, 955, 957, 959, 1636-1637, 1642, 1989, 1991, 1993, 2040-2041, II-2276, 2343, 2435-2437, 2749, 3081, 3085, 3340, 3342, 3441, 3457, 3605, 3607
  Misc. Manufacturing Industries, I-1639, 1996, 1998, II-2642, 3394, 3477
  Miscellaneous Retail, I-155-156, 267-268, 270-272, 1082, 2001, II-2690
  Motion Pictures, II-2354-2355, 2358, 2360
  Nat. Security and Interntl. Affairs, I-1046-1049, 1051-1053
  Nonmetallic Minerals, I-264, 277, 534, 1381, 1567, 1589, 1671-

1673, 1729, 2015, II-2146, 2303, 2702, 2775, 2842, 2937, 3247-3248, 3260
  Oil and Gas Extraction, II-2471, 2477, 2490
  Paper and Allied Products, II-2603, 2813, 2818, 2942-2943, 2954, 3234, 3557
  Petroleum and Coal Products, II-2468
  Primary Metal Industries, I-162, 164, 167, 588, 619, 951, 962, II-2143, 2723, 3078, 3239-3242, 3246, 3558-3559, 3602
  Printing and Publishing, I-1966, 1968, 2099, II-2331, 2333-2334
  Railroad Transportation, II-2838
  Rubber and Misc. Plastics, I-1430, II-2734
  Security and Commodity Brokers, I-1258, 1986
  Stone/Clay/Glass Products, I-3, 653, 655-656, 660, 1302, 1624, 1630-1633, 2081, II-2780, 2957
  Textile Mill Products, I-1269-1270, II-3330-3331, 3552, 3597-3598
  Transportation by Air, I-97-98
  Transportation Equipment, I-57, 60, 71-72, 308, 325, 333, 339, 342, 349-351, 354, 359, 361-362, 567, 571-572, II-3437-3439
  Transportation Services, I-1831, II-2521
  Trucking and Warehousing, I-1413-1414, II-3066-3067, 3496
  Water Transportation, II-3047, 3056
Chinese Taipei, II-2460-2461, 2921, 3240, 3330
Chongqing, China, I-98
Chuquicamata, Chile, II-3083
Cincinnati, OH, I-1685
CIS, I-1989, 1999, II-3086
Clark County, NV, II-2980
Collahuasi, Chile, I-952
Collier County, FL, I-1859
Colombia, I-476, 745, 750, 753, 756, 967, 1538, II-2451, 2479, 2505, 3480
Colorado, I-98, 109, 409, 620, 624, 1233, 1329, 1376, 1530, 1584, 1602, 1863, II-2779, 3041
Concord, NC, I-1599, 1842

Congo (Kinshasa), I-749, 959, 1074-1075, 1640, II-3342
Connecticut, I-110, 410, 531, 1375, II-2907
Coonawarra, Australia, II-3544
Copenhagen, Denmark, I-2074
Costa Rica, I-1216
Côte d'Ivoire, I-750, II-2143, 2449, 2452, 2917
Croatia, II-2470, 3378, 3585
Cuba, I-749, II-2437
Cuyahoga Valley National Park, OH, II-2622
Cyprus, II-3056
Czech Republic, I-350, II-2921, 3378
Czechia, I-947, 1263, 1302, 1632, 2015, 2040, II-2284, 3558, 3579-3580, 3585, 3592-3593
Dallas, TX, I-1104, 1843
Dallas-Fort Worth, TX, I-98, 531, 1113, 1406, 1601
Dallas-Fort Worth Airport, TX, I-88
Dania Beach, FL, I-1581
Davidson, TN, I-1846
Dearborn, MI, I-1603, 1844
Delaware, I-411, 531, 1579, 1584, 1686-1687, II-2907
Delaware Water Gap National Recreation Area, NJ-PA, II-2623
Denmark, I-810-811, 1538, 1688, 1883, II-2474, 2480, 2541, 2611, 2646, 2648, 2691, 3107, 3378, 3584-3585, 3591
Denver, CO, I-98, 1602, 1689
Denver International Airport, CO, I-89
Detroit, MI, I-1020, 1568, 1575, 1603, 1844, II-2767
Detroit Metro Wayne County Airport, MI, I-90
Detroit-Warren-Livonia, MI, I-1105, 1113
Djibouti, II-2937
Doha, Qatar, I-97
Dominican Republic, I-750, II-2437, 3480
Dubai International, I-100
Dugald River, II-3606
Dukat, Russia, II-3083
Eastern Asia, I-1999, II-3086
Eastern Europe, I-30, 632, II-2470, 2476, 2542, 2603, 2881
Ecuador, I-750, 1332, II-2479, 2820, 3480

EFTA, I-356-357, 568
Egypt
  Agriculture - Crops, I-1523-1524, II-2500, 2502, 3530, 3532
  Chemicals and Allied Products, I-1308, 1316
  Communications, II-3314
  Depository Institutions, II-2869
  Fishing, Hunting, and Trapping, I-1333-1334
  Food and Kindred Products, I-1297, 1517, II-2498, 2503, 2505, 3257
  Nat. Security and Interntl. Affairs, I-1046, 1052-1053
  Nonmetallic Minerals, II-2702
  Oil and Gas Extraction, II-2469, 2475
  Stone/Clay/Glass Products, I-653, 655-656, 1302
  Textile Mill Products, II-3598
El Teniente, Chile, I-952
Elgin, IL, I-1600
EMEA, I-792, II-2376, 3190
Escondida, Chile, I-952
Estonia, II-2643, 3591
Ethiopia, I-752-753, 756, II-2820, 3149
EU-28, I-951, II-2549
Eurasia, I-632
Europe, I-2135, II-2697
  Agriculture - Livestock, I-1194, II-2179, 2691-2694, 2699
  Amusement and Recreation, I-1585, 1721, 1723
  Apparel and Textile Products, I-184
  Business Services, I-45, 251, 1773
  Chemicals and Allied Products, I-503, 681, 1067, 1313-1315, II-2586
  Communications, II-2629, 3315, 3560
  Depository Institutions, I-400
  Eating and Drinking Places, I-1417
  Electric/Gas/Sanitary Services, I-1224
  Electronic/Electric Equip., I-226-228, 230, 233, 635, 2076, II-2965, 3010
  Engineering/Management Services, II-2875
  Fabricated Metal Products, I-512

Food and Kindred Products, I-724,
810-811, 1883, 2004, II-2625,
3301
Heavy Construction, I-1899
Industry Machinery/Equip., I-225,
792, 2064, II-2771, 3105
Instruments and Related, I-590,
II-2233, 2255
Local and Passenger Transit,
II-2163
Lumber and Wood Products,
II-3579, 3581, 3583-3584, 3586-
3587, 3590
Metal Mining, I-1989, 1991,
II-2749
Misc. Manufacturing Industries,
I-1999, II-3086, 3395
Motion Pictures, II-2376, 2384
Nondepository Institutions, II-2639
Nonmetallic Minerals, I-1672
Paper and Allied Products, I-627,
II-2613, 2819, 3554
Personal Services, I-1737
Primary Metal Industries, I-163,
962, II-3602
Printing and Publishing, I-773,
2018, 2020
Stone/Clay/Glass Products, I-1624
Transportation by Air, I-82, II-3044
Transportation Equipment, I-58,
304, 330, 340, 342, 356-357, 365,
567-568, II-2831, 3439
Transportation Services, II-3378,
3392
Water Transportation, II-3061-3062
Wholesale Trade - Nondurables,
I-699
European Economic Area, I-1668,
II-2732, 3167
European Union
Admin. of Economic Programs,
II-3199
Agriculture - Crops, I-965-968,
1497, 1521-1526, 1669-1670,
II-2458-2459, 2500, 2502, 2917,
3530-3533
Agriculture - Livestock, I-621-622,
1326, 1784-1785
Apparel and Textile Products,
I-188, 190, 195
Chemicals and Allied Products,
I-498, 500, 705, 707, II-3460
Coal Mining, I-742-743, 746
Electronic/Electric Equip., II-3027

Food and Kindred Products, I-577-
580, 678-679, 752, 754, 1295-
1298, 1373, 1388-1389, 2008-
2009, II-2173-2174, 2187-2192,
2212-2213, 2216, 2312-2313,
2496, 2498, 2503-2506, 3257-
3258
Industry Machinery/Equip.,
II-2460-2461
Lumber and Wood Products,
II-3589
Primary Metal Industries, II-3240-
3241
Stone/Clay/Glass Products, I-1908
Textile Mill Products, II-3330-3331
Transportation Equipment, I-358,
569, II-3440, 3468
Extremadura, Spain, I-51
Faroe Islands, I-1326
Federated States of Micronesia,
I-450
Finland, I-359, 729, II-2303, 2435,
2613, 2643, 2646, 2702, 2817,
3260, 3318, 3579, 3584, 3586,
3604
Flagler, FL, I-1581
Florida, I-97, 111, 412, 1231, 1375,
1378, 1536, 1541, 1581, 1605,
1643, 1714, 1822-1823, 1847,
1863, II-2349, 2801, 2980
Fort Lauderdale, FL, I-1113, 1605
Fort Worth, TX, I-1104, 1601, 1843
France
Admin. of Economic Programs,
II-3199
Agriculture - Crops, I-1529, 1538-
1539, II-2450, 2456
Agriculture - Livestock, II-2691-
2694, 2699
Amusement and Recreation,
I-1576, 1721
Apparel and Textile Products, I-195
Automotive Dealers, I-292
Business Services, I-35, 45, 941,
943, 2045, II-3227
Chemicals and Allied Products,
I-498, 500, 1067, 1119, 1126,
1139, 1263-1264, 1307, II-2742-
2744
Communications, I-1177, II-2410,
2543, 2554, 3566
Eating and Drinking Places, I-766
Electric/Gas/Sanitary Services,
I-1218, 1221, 1223-1224, 1229

Electronic/Electric Equip., I-154
Fabricated Metal Products, I-948,
II-2285
Food and Kindred Products,
I-716, 724-725, 810-811, 1527,
1883, 2004, II-2624, 2664, 2991,
3107, 3301, 3550
Industry Machinery/Equip., I-1282,
II-2921
Instruments and Related, II-2255,
3506
Insurance Carriers, I-1913, II-2646
Leather and Leather Products,
I-2050-2051
Lumber and Wood Products, I-963-
964, II-3579-3580, 3583, 3585-
3587, 3589, 3591
Metal Mining, I-957, II-2436,
3081, 3605
Misc. Manufacturing Industries,
II-3395
Miscellaneous Retail, I-156, 267-
268, 270-272, 1082
Motion Pictures, II-2361, 2384
Nat. Security and Interntl. Affairs,
I-1047-1051
Nonmetallic Minerals, I-1729,
II-2303, 2820, 2937, 2939
Oil and Gas Extraction, II-2474,
2480, 2490
Paper and Allied Products, II-2611,
2613, 2818
Primary Metal Industries, I-164-
165, 619, II-3078, 3558-3559
Railroad Transportation, II-2838
Security and Commodity Brokers,
I-1979
Stone/Clay/Glass Products, I-3,
657, 1630-1633, 2081, II-2780-
2781, 2959
Transportation Equipment, I-325,
334, 351, 354, 356-357, 359, 362,
367, 568, II-2370, 3437
Transportation Services, II-3378
Frankfurt, Germany, I-2074
Franklin, TN, I-1846
Fresnillo, Mexico, II-3083
Fujairah, UAE, II-2494
Gabon, II-2143, 2475
Galicia, Spain, I-51
Gastonia, NC, I-1599, 1842
Gateway National Recreation Area,
NJ-NY, II-2623

George Washington Memorial Parkway, VA, II-2623
Georgia
 Agricultural Services, I-991
 Agriculture - Crops, I-1516, 1530, 1536, 1541, II-2450, 2456, 3374
 Agriculture - Livestock, I-1329
 Depository Institutions, I-413
 Electric/Gas/Sanitary Services, I-1231
 Fishing, Hunting, and Trapping, I-1863-1864
 Food Stores, I-1690
 General Building Contractors, I-1839
 Membership Organizations, I-1822
 Miscellaneous Retail, I-112, 1102
 Primary Metal Industries, II-2143
 Transportation by Air, I-98
 Trucking and Warehousing, I-1403
Georgia World Convention Center Authority, GA, I-940
Germany
 Admin. of Economic Programs, II-3199
 Agriculture - Crops, I-1538-1539
 Agriculture - Livestock, II-2691-2694, 2699, 3079-3080, 3592-3593
 Amusement and Recreation, I-1576, 1721
 Apparel and Textile Products, I-195, 203
 Automotive Dealers, I-293, 1441
 Business Services, I-35, 45-46, 941, 943, 2045, II-3227
 Chemicals and Allied Products, I-498, 500, 1067, 1120, 1126, 1140, 1263-1264, 1312, 1316, 1322, II-2740-2745
 Communications, I-1177, II-2410, 2554
 Eating and Drinking Places, I-767
 Electric/Gas/Sanitary Services, I-1220-1224, 1226, 1229
 Electronic/Electric Equip., I-154
 Fabricated Metal Products, I-947-948, II-2284-2285
 Food and Kindred Products, I-476, 716, 724-725, 810-811, 1883, 2004, II-2624, 2664, 2991, 3107, 3301
 Industry Machinery/Equip., I-1283, II-2136, 2921

 Instruments and Related, II-2255, 3506
 Insurance Carriers, I-1913, II-2646
 Leather and Leather Products, I-2050-2051
 Lumber and Wood Products, I-963-964, II-3579-3580, 3583-3587
 Metal Mining, I-171, 955, 957, 1636-1637, 2039-2040, II-2435-2436, 3081, 3340, 3605
 Misc. Manufacturing Industries, II-3395
 Miscellaneous Retail, I-156, 267, 270-272, 1082
 Motion Pictures, II-2355, 2384
 Nat. Security and Interntl. Affairs, I-1047-1051
 Nonmetallic Minerals, I-534, 1381, 1673, 1729, 2015, II-2643, 2775, 2937, 2939, 3247-3248, 3260
 Oil and Gas Extraction, II-2474
 Paper and Allied Products, II-2611, 2613, 2817-2818
 Primary Metal Industries, I-164-165, 619, II-3239, 3242, 3246, 3558-3559
 Railroad Transportation, II-2838
 Security and Commodity Brokers, I-1258
 Stone/Clay/Glass Products, I-3, 657, 1302, 1630-1633, 2081, II-2780-2781, 2957, 2959
 Textile Mill Products, I-1269, II-3597-3598
 Transportation Equipment, I-325-326, 350-351, 354, 356-357, 359, 362, 367, 492-493, 510, 568, II-2371, 3437
 Transportation Services, II-3378
 Trucking and Warehousing, I-1413
 Water Transportation, II-3047
Ghana, I-750, 1642, II-2143, 2452, 3567
Golden Gate National Recreation Area, CA, II-2623
Grand Canyon National Park, AZ, II-2622
Grand Teton National Park, WY, II-2622
Grasberg, Indonesia, I-952, 1640
Great Lakes, II-3045-3046, 3511-3512
Great Smoky Mountains National Park, NC-TN, II-2622-2623

Greece, I-993, 1520, 1528, II-2146, 2447, 2455, 2480, 2694, 2820, 3047, 3056, 3107, 3378, 3600
Greenspoint-High Point, NC, I-1691
Guadeloupe, II-2820
Guam, I-414
Guangzhou, China, I-98, II-2770
Guatemala, I-753, II-2451, 2820
Guinea, I-160, 171, 1074, II-2449, 2469
Gulf Coast, MS, I-1575
Gulf Cooperation Council, I-643, II-3109
Gulfstream, FL, I-1581
Hartsfield Jackson Airport, GA, I-91
Hawaii, I-113, 415
Henan, China, I-162
Herzegovina, II-3585
Hialeah Park, FL, I-1581
Hillsboro, OR-WA, I-1610
Hillsborough County, FL, II-2980
Honduras, I-753, 756
Hong Kong
 Chemicals and Allied Products, II-2742-2743
 Food and Kindred Products, I-1389, II-2190, 2214
 Instruments and Related, II-3506
 Leather and Leather Products, I-2050-2051
 Metal Mining, I-1636, II-3339
 Misc. Manufacturing Industries, I-1996, II-2641-2642
 Miscellaneous Retail, I-265
 Nonmetallic Minerals, II-3248
 Security and Commodity Brokers, I-1258
 Stone/Clay/Glass Products, I-1630-1631
 Textile Mill Products, I-1269-1270, II-3597-3598
 Transportation by Air, I-97
 Water Transportation, II-2770, 3047, 3056
Hong Kong International Airport, Hong Kong, I-100
Houston, TX, I-1113, 1407, 1845, II-2767-2769, 2980
Hungary, I-500, 810-811, II-2456, 3378
Iceland, I-167, 172, 1326, II-3078
Idaho, I-114, 416, 624, 1371, 1530, 1597, 1714, 1841, II-2779, 3041

Illinois, I-115, 417, 744, 1103, 1289, 1371, 1405, 1532, 1536, 1600, 1781, 1822, II-2980, 3452
Incheon, South Korea, I-97
India
　Admin. of Economic Programs, II-3199
　Agriculture - Crops, I-965, 968, 992-995, 1538, II-2449, 2452, 2456, 2500, 2507, 2914-2916, 3530, 3533
　Agriculture - Livestock, I-621-622, II-3079-3080, 3593
　Amusement and Recreation, II-3217
　Apparel and Textile Products, I-188, 196, 211
　Chemicals and Allied Products, I-160, 688, 705, 707, 711, 1130, 1307-1311, 1316, 1321-1322, II-2741, 2745, 3276
　Coal Mining, I-742-743, 746, 748
　Communications, I-1177, 1972, II-2410, 2544, 2630, 3314, 3568
　Depository Institutions, I-400, II-2869
　Eating and Drinking Places, II-2880
　Electric/Gas/Sanitary Services, I-1218-1219, 1221, 1223, 1226, 1229
　Electronic/Electric Equip., I-250, 285, 633, 639, 895, 899, II-2425, 2427, 2965
　Fishing, Hunting, and Trapping, I-1332, 1334-1335
　Food and Kindred Products, I-476, 577-578, 580, 753, 756, 1295, 1297, 1388, 1390, 1528, II-2173-2174, 2187-2188, 2191-2192, 2312-2313, 2496, 2499, 2503, 2505-2506, 2665, 3257-3258, 3469
　Food Stores, I-1678, 1692
　Industry Machinery/Equip., I-223, 242, 853, II-2136, 2700, 2921, 3444, 3525
　Leather and Leather Products, I-2050-2051, 2123
　Metal Mining, I-171-172, 729, 957, 1637, 1989-1990, 1993, 2039-2041, II-2436, 3081, 3340, 3604-3605, 3607
　Misc. Manufacturing Industries, I-1639, 1996, II-2641-2642, 3398
　Motion Pictures, II-2355
　Nat. Security and Interntl. Affairs, I-1046-1049, 1052-1053
　Nonmetallic Minerals, I-1589, 1671, 1673, 1729, 2014-2015, II-2303, 2702, 2842, 2937, 2939, 3247-3248, 3260
　Oil and Gas Extraction, II-2471, 2477, 2490
　Paper and Allied Products, II-2818
　Primary Metal Industries, I-164, 167, 619, 951, 962, II-2143, 3078, 3239-3242, 3246, 3558, 3602
　Security and Commodity Brokers, I-1258
　Stone/Clay/Glass Products, I-3, 646, 653, 655-656, 660, 1302, 2081, II-2957
　Textile Mill Products, I-1269, II-3330, 3597-3598
　Transportation Equipment, I-350-351, 366, 567, II-3437
　Trucking and Warehousing, I-1413, II-3499
Indiana, I-116, 418, 744, 1103, 1371, 1532, 1541, 1575, 1584, 1781, II-2225
Indianapolis, MD, II-2848
Indianapolis-Carmel, IN, I-1106
Indonesia
　Agriculture - Crops, I-994, II-2452, 2914-2915, 3532
　Apparel and Textile Products, I-188
　Chemicals and Allied Products, I-160, 1264, 1307-1309, 1311, 1316, 1321-1322, 1987
　Coal Mining, I-743, 745
　Communications, I-1972, II-3314
　Electric/Gas/Sanitary Services, I-1216
　Electronic/Electric Equip., I-287, 636
　Fishing, Hunting, and Trapping, I-1332-1335
　Food and Kindred Products, I-716, 750, 752-753, 756, 1295-1296, 1298, 1388, II-2498, 3257, 3469
　Leather and Leather Products, I-2051
　Lumber and Wood Products, I-1361
　Metal Mining, I-171, 1642, II-2437, 3339, 3342
　Misc. Manufacturing Industries, I-1639, 1996
　Nonmetallic Minerals, II-2820, 2939
　Oil and Gas Extraction, II-2471, 2477, 2490
　Paper and Allied Products, II-2605, 2817-2818, 2942-2943, 2954
　Primary Metal Industries, II-3241
　Stone/Clay/Glass Products, I-653, 655, 657
　Textile Mill Products, I-1270, II-3331, 3552, 3597
　Transportation Equipment, II-3439
　Transportation Services, II-3377
International Exposition Center, OH, I-940
Iowa, I-117, 419, 620, 624, 1289, 1584, 1781, II-2225, 3041
Iran
　Agriculture - Crops, I-967, II-2447, 2450, 2455-2456, 2917
　Agriculture - Livestock, II-3080
　Chemicals and Allied Products, I-1308, 1316, II-2740
　Electronic/Electric Equip., II-2965
　Food and Kindred Products, I-1297, 1517-1518, 1520, 1528
　Metal Mining, I-183, 1993, II-2343
　Nonmetallic Minerals, I-1381, 1729, 2015, II-2937, 3260
　Oil and Gas Extraction, II-2472, 2478, 2489
　Primary Metal Industries, II-3239, 3246
　Stone/Clay/Glass Products, I-653, 655-656, 1302, 2081
　Transportation Equipment, II-3439
Iraq, I-657, 1052, 1374, 1517, II-2190, 2472, 2478, 2917
Ireland, I-171, 1395, 1693, 1883, II-2363, 2474, 2545, 2643
Israel, I-657, 1050-1051, 1312, 1517, 1522, II-2472, 2641-2642, 2702, 2775, 2965, 3584
Istanbul Ataturk Airport, Turkey, I-100
Italy
　Admin. of Economic Programs, II-3199
　Agriculture - Crops, I-1538-1539, II-2447, 2450, 2454-2456

Agriculture - Livestock, II-2691-2694, 2699, 3079-3080, 3592-3593

Amusement and Recreation, I-1576, 1721

Business Services, I-45, 943, 2045, II-3227

Chemicals and Allied Products, I-498, 1067, 1126, 1264, 1322, II-2741, 2743-2745

Communications, II-2546, 3314

Electric/Gas/Sanitary Services, I-1223

Fabricated Metal Products, II-2284

Food and Kindred Products, I-716, 724-725, 810-811, 1520, 1527, 1883, 2004, II-2624, 2663-2664, 2991, 3107, 3301, 3550

Industry Machinery/Equip., II-2136, 2921

Instruments and Related, II-2255, 3506

Insurance Carriers, I-1913

Leather and Leather Products, I-2050-2051

Lumber and Wood Products, I-963-964, II-3583-3587

Metal Mining, I-957, 1637, II-2436, 3081, 3605

Misc. Manufacturing Industries, I-1639, II-3395

Miscellaneous Retail, I-272

Motion Pictures, II-2355

Nat. Security and Interntl. Affairs, I-1047-1048, 1050-1051

Nonmetallic Minerals, I-1671, II-2146, 2937, 2939, 3247-3248, 3260

Oil and Gas Extraction, II-2474

Paper and Allied Products, II-2611, 2613, 2818

Primary Metal Industries, I-164-165, 619, II-3246, 3558-3559

Railroad Transportation, II-2838

Stone/Clay/Glass Products, I-656, 658, 660, 1302, 1630, 1632-1633, 2081, II-2780-2781, 2957, 2959

Textile Mill Products, I-1269-1270, II-3597-3598

Transportation Equipment, I-351, 356-357, 367, 510, 568, II-2372

Transportation Services, II-3378

Jamaica, I-160, 171

Japan, I-2135

Admin. of Economic Programs, II-3199

Agriculture - Crops, I-965, 1521, 1539, II-2502, 2777, 3532

Agriculture - Livestock, I-1784-1785, II-3080, 3593

Amusement and Recreation, I-1576

Apparel and Accessory Stores, I-215

Apparel and Textile Products, I-190, 203

Business Services, I-35, 47, 943, 2045, II-3227

Chemicals and Allied Products, I-705, 707, 1126, 1264, 1321, 1987, II-2528, 2583, 2742, 2744, 3460

Coal Mining, I-742, 746

Communications, I-1177, II-2410, 3314

Electric/Gas/Sanitary Services, I-1216, 1218-1219, 1226, 1229

Electronic/Electric Equip., I-154, 632, 2077, II-2426, 2601, 2965, 3010, 3027

Fabricated Metal Products, I-947-948

Fishing, Hunting, and Trapping, I-1333, 1335

Food and Kindred Products, I-476, 579, 670, 678, 716, 752, 754, 1387, 1389, 2008, II-2187-2188, 2190, 2212, 2214, 2216, 2312, 2498, 2624, 2664, 2680, 2990-2991

Industry Machinery/Equip., I-853, II-2136, 2461, 2921

Instruments and Related, I-740, II-3506

Insurance Carriers, I-1913, II-2648

Metal Mining, I-955, 1636-1637, 1991, II-2435-2436, 2749, 3081, 3340

Misc. Manufacturing Industries, II-2530

Miscellaneous Retail, I-156, 1082

Motion Pictures, II-2355

Nat. Security and Interntl. Affairs, I-1047-1049, 1053

Nonmetallic Minerals, I-264, 1567, 1729, II-2939, 3260

Oil and Gas Extraction, II-2477, 2490

Paper and Allied Products, II-2603, 2612, 2818

Primary Metal Industries, I-165, 588, 619, II-3239-3240, 3242, 3246, 3558-3559

Printing and Publishing, II-2142, 2334

Railroad Transportation, II-2838

Security and Commodity Brokers, I-1258

Stone/Clay/Glass Products, I-3, 653, 660, 1630-1632, 2081, II-2781

Textile Mill Products, I-1269, II-3331, 3598

Transportation Equipment, I-325, 342, 350-351, 354, 362, 567, II-3437, 3439

Water Transportation, II-3047, 3056

Joliet, IL, I-1103, 1113

Jordan, I-1310, 1312, II-2702, 2775, 2820

Joshua Tree National Park, CA, II-2622

Kansas, I-118, 420, 620, 624, 1371, 1615, 1781

Kazakhstan

Agriculture - Crops, II-3531

Chemicals and Allied Products, I-160

Electric/Gas/Sanitary Services, I-1219

Fishing, Hunting, and Trapping, I-1330

Food and Kindred Products, I-1373

Leather and Leather Products, I-2047

Metal Mining, I-183, 729, 959, 1642, 1993, 2041, II-3457, 3607

Nonmetallic Minerals, I-277, 1381, II-2702, 3260

Oil and Gas Extraction, II-2470, 2476

Primary Metal Industries, I-588, II-2143

Kentucky, I-97, 119, 421, 744, 1289, 1864, II-3374

Kentucky Exposition Center, KY, I-940

Kenya, I-1216, II-2451, 3149

Kissimmee, FL, I-1847

Kunming, China, I-98

Kuwait, I-643, II-2472, 2478, 2489, 3109, 3260
Kyrgyzstan, I-1134, 2047, II-2276
La Rioja, Spain, I-51
Lake Mead National Recreation Area, NV-AZ, II-2623
Lakewood, CO, I-1602
Langhome Creek, Australia, II-3544
Laos, II-2775, 3342
Las Bambas, Peru, I-952
Las Vegas, NV, I-1107, 1569, 1575
Las Vegas Convention Center, NV, I-940
Latin America
  Agriculture - Livestock, I-1326
  Amusement and Recreation, I-178
  Business Services, I-30
  Chemicals and Allied Products, I-1313-1315
  Communications, II-2547, 3560
  Eating and Drinking Places, I-1417, II-2881
  Electronic/Electric Equip., I-226-228, 230, 632, 640
  Industry Machinery/Equip., I-225, II-2771
  Instruments and Related, II-2233
  Motion Pictures, II-2376
  Nondepository Institutions, II-2275, 2639
  Paper and Allied Products, I-627, II-2603
  Primary Metal Industries, I-962, II-3602
  Transportation by Air, I-82, II-3044
  Transportation Equipment, I-58
  Wholesale Trade - Nondurables, I-700
Latvia, II-2643, 3591
Lee County, FL, I-1859
Leon, Spain, I-51
Lesotho, I-1074
Liberia, II-3056
Libya, I-1517, II-2469, 2475
Lithuania, II-2643, 3583, 3585, 3587
Livonia, MI, I-1105, 1113
Logan International Airport, MA, I-92
London, U.K., I-2074
London Heathrow Airport, U.K., I-100
Long Beach, CA, I-1108, 1604, II-2768-2769
Long Island, NY, I-1109, 1113

Los Angeles, CA, I-97, 531, 1108, 1408, II-2149, 2767-2769, 2980
Los Angeles International Airport, CA, I-93
Los Angeles-Long Beach, CA, I-1113, 1604
Louisiana, I-120, 422, 991, 1233, 1596, 1863-1864
Louisville, KY, I-97
Loulo-Gounkoto, Mali, I-1640
MacArthur River, II-3606
Madagascar, I-749, 1673, II-2303, 2842
Madrid, Spain, I-51, 2074
Maine, I-121, 423, II-2779
Malawi, II-2451
Malaysia
  Agriculture - Crops, II-2777
  Chemicals and Allied Products, I-1321, II-2741-2742
  Coal Mining, I-746
  Electronic/Electric Equip., I-288
  Food and Kindred Products, I-753, 1295-1297, II-2187-2188, 2192
  Industry Machinery/Equip., II-2460
  Metal Mining, I-172, 957, 2039, II-3339-3340, 3342
  Misc. Manufacturing Industries, I-1639
  Miscellaneous Retail, I-1082
  Nonmetallic Minerals, II-2939
  Oil and Gas Extraction, II-2471, 2477
  Paper and Allied Products, II-2942-2943, 2954
  Primary Metal Industries, II-2143, 3078
  Stone/Clay/Glass Products, I-1302, 2081
  Textile Mill Products, II-3552
Mali, I-1642
Malta, II-3056
Malyasia, I-1298, 1311
Mandalay Bay Resort Convention Center, NV, I-940
Manitoba, Canada, I-602
Margaret River, Australia, II-3544
Maricopa County, AZ, I-1859
Marietta, GA, I-1102
Marshall Islands, II-3056
Maryland, I-122, 424, 531, 1575, 1686, 1714, II-2347, 2848

Massachusetts, I-123, 425, 769, 1404, 1598, 1694, 1822
McCormick Place, IL, I-940
McLaren Vale, Australia, II-3544
Memphis, TN, I-97
Mesa, AZ, I-1110, 1608, 1848
Mexico
  Agriculture - Crops, I-965, 967-968, 1516, 1521-1526, 1529, II-2452-2453, 2500, 2502, 2777
  Agriculture - Livestock, I-621-622, 1784-1785
  Business Services, II-3480
  Chemicals and Allied Products, I-1263-1264, 1310, II-2743, 2745
  Communications, I-1972, II-2410, 3314, 3569
  Depository Institutions, II-2869
  Electric/Gas/Sanitary Services, I-1216
  Fabricated Metal Products, I-947-948, II-2285
  Fishing, Hunting, and Trapping, I-1332
  Food and Kindred Products, I-373, 476, 577-580, 670, 678-679, 753, 756, 1388-1389, 2009, II-2173-2174, 2187-2188, 2190-2192, 2212-2214, 2216, 2312-2313, 2498, 2503, 2506, 2664, 3257-3258
  Furniture and Fixtures, I-1544, 1557
  Industry Machinery/Equip., II-2136, 2460-2461, 2921
  Leather and Leather Products, I-2051
  Lumber and Wood Products, I-964
  Metal Mining, I-183, 959, 1642, 2039, 2041, II-2276, 2343, 3085, 3607
  Miscellaneous Retail, I-156, 1082
  Motion Pictures, II-2355
  Nonmetallic Minerals, I-1381, 1673, 1729, 2015, II-2146, 2702, 2937, 2939
  Oil and Gas Extraction, II-2473, 2479, 2490
  Personal Services, I-1737
  Primary Metal Industries, I-165, 588, 619, II-2143, 3241-3242, 3246

Stone/Clay/Glass Products, I-3, 655, 660, 1302, 1631-1632, 1727, II-2957
Transportation Equipment, I-350, 567, II-3437, 3439
Miami, FL, I-97, 1409
Miami-Dade County, FL, I-1859, II-2980
Miami-Fort Lauderdale, FL, I-1113, 1605
Michigan
  Agriculture - Crops, I-1375, 1378, 1498, 1516, 1532, 1535, II-2779
  Agriculture - Livestock, I-1329, 1823, II-2225
  Amusement and Recreation, I-1575, 1584, 1643
  Depository Institutions, I-426
  Fabricated Metal Products, I-1714
  Fishing, Hunting, and Trapping, I-1863-1864
  Food and Kindred Products, II-3543
  General Building Contractors, I-1844
  General Merchandise Stores, I-1603
  Health Services, I-1750
  Miscellaneous Retail, I-124, 1103, 1105
  Social Services, I-666
Mid-Atlantic states, U.S., I-2, 564, 1786, II-2267, 2288, 2761, 2902, 3380
Middle East
  Agriculture - Livestock, I-1199, II-2184
  Business Services, I-30
  Communications, II-2550, 3560
  Depository Institutions, I-400
  Eating and Drinking Places, I-1417, II-2881
  Electronic/Electric Equip., I-226-228, 230, 233, 632
  Engineering/Management Services, II-2875
  Industry Machinery/Equip., I-225, 792, II-2771
  Instruments and Related, II-2233
  Misc. Manufacturing Industries, I-1999, II-3086
  Motion Pictures, II-2376
  Nondepository Institutions, II-2639
  Oil and Gas Extraction, II-2472, 2478
  Paper and Allied Products, I-627, II-2603
  Personal Services, I-1737
  Primary Metal Industries, I-951
  Printing and Publishing, I-2018
  Transportation by Air, I-82, II-3044
  Transportation Equipment, I-58
  Transportation Services, II-3392
  Wholesale Trade - Nondurables, I-703
Midwest states, U.S., I-1510
Milan, Italy, I-2074
Milwaukee, WI, I-1695
Minneapolis, MN, II-2767
Minnesota, I-125, 427, 624, 1289, 1371, 1536, 1781, 1823, 1863-1864, II-2225, 2779
Mississippi, I-126, 428, 991, 1575, 1584
Missouri, I-127, 429, 620, 991, 1289, 1371, 1781, 1863-1864, II-2225
Moldova, II-2456
Mongolia, I-162, 1381, II-2343, 3441, 3592
Montana, I-128, 430, 744, 1371, 1823, II-3041
Morenci mine, AZ, I-952
Morocco, I-264, 749, 1310, 1381, 1517, 1523-1524, 1529, II-2447, 2490, 2505, 2702, 3532
Mount Isa mine, Australia, II-3606
Mountain states U.S., I-2, 564, 1786, II-2267, 2288, 2761, 3380
Mozambique, I-1673, II-2469
Munich, Germany, I-2074
Murcia, Spain, I-51
Murfreesboro, TN, I-1846
Murray Darling - Swan Hill, Australia, II-3544
Muruntau, Uzbekistan, I-1640
Myanmar, I-1334, II-2471
Namibia, I-1074, II-3457
Naperville, IL, I-1103, 1113, 1600
Nashville, TN, I-1846
Natchez Trace Parkway, TN-MS, II-2623
Navarre, Spain, I-51
Nebraska, I-129, 431, 620, 624, 1781
Netherlands
  Agriculture - Crops, I-1529, 1538-1539
  Agriculture - Livestock, II-2691-2692, 2694, 2699
  Business Services, I-45, 49, 943, II-3227
  Chemicals and Allied Products, I-498, 500, 1067, 1316, II-2740, 2742, 2744
  Communications, I-1182
  Electric/Gas/Sanitary Services, I-1220, 1222, 1224
  Electronic/Electric Equip., I-154
  Fabricated Metal Products, I-947-948, II-2284-2285
  Food and Kindred Products, I-476, 725, 810-811, 1883, 2004, II-3107, 3301
  Instruments and Related, II-2255
  Insurance Carriers, II-2646, 2648
  Lumber and Wood Products, II-3584-3587
  Metal Mining, II-2435-2436, 3604-3605
  Motion Pictures, II-2355, 2384
  Nonmetallic Minerals, II-2937, 2939, 3248, 3260
  Oil and Gas Extraction, II-2474, 2480, 2489-2490
  Paper and Allied Products, II-2611, 2817-2818
  Primary Metal Industries, I-165, 588
  Stone/Clay/Glass Products, II-2780-2781
  Transportation Equipment, I-325, 335, 354, 356-357, 362, 367, 510
Nevada, I-130, 432, 1107, 1569, 1584, 1640, II-2980
New Braunfels, TX, I-1849
New Brunswick, I-602
New Caledonia, II-2437
New Carolina, I-1375
New England, I-1231
New Hampshire, I-131, 433, 1584
New Haven Union Station, CT, II-2149
New Jersey, I-132, 434, 531, 1109, 1113, 1375, 1378, 1498, 1516, 1534-1535, 1572, 1575, 1579, 1584, II-2769, 2907
New Jersey City, NJ, I-1606

New Mexico, I-133, 435, 1233, 1530, 1714
New Orleans, LA, II-2768
New Orleans Ernest Memorial Convention Center, LA, I-940
New York
  Agriculture - Crops, I-1292, 1378, 1530, 1532, 1535-1536
  Agriculture - Livestock, I-1823
  Amusement and Recreation, I-1575, 1584, 1643
  Depository Institutions, I-436
  Electric/Gas/Sanitary Services, I-1231
  Fabricated Metal Products, I-1714
  Fishing, Hunting, and Trapping, I-1863-1864
  Food and Kindred Products, II-3543
  General Merchandise Stores, I-1606, II-2907
  Membership Organizations, I-1822, II-3452
  Miscellaneous Retail, I-134, 1109
  Transportation Services, II-3376
New York, NY, I-265, 531, 1109, 1113, 1410, 1575, 1704, II-2767-2768, 2980
New York Penn Station, NY, II-2149
New Zealand, I-225-228, 230, 577-578, 580, 622, 679, 1219, II-2313, 2820, 2939, 3580, 3592
Newark, NJ, I-1606, II-2769
Newfoundland and Labrador, Canada, I-602
Newton, MA, I-1598
Nicaragua, II-2452
Niger, II-3457
Nigeria, I-750, 1334, 1633, II-2449, 2452, 2469, 2475, 2869, 2917, 2959, 3314, 3342, 3469, 3570
Ningbo-Zhoushan, China, II-2770
Norfolk, VA, II-2769
North Africa, I-233, 632, 951, II-2550, 2603
North America, I-566, 2062, II-2568, 2806, 3542
  Agriculture - Crops, I-1670
  Agriculture - Livestock, I-1195, 1326-1327, II-2180
  Amusement and Recreation, I-179
  Apparel and Textile Products, I-184, 199, 210

Auto Repair/Services/Parking, II-3345-3347
Automotive Dealers, I-294, II-3343
Building Materials, I-2037
Business Services, I-30, 1776, II-2661, 3000, 3175
Chemicals and Allied Products, I-1125, 1313-1315, II-2591, 2936
Communications, II-2555, 3560
Depository Institutions, I-400
Eating and Drinking Places, I-1417, 1420, II-2881
Electric/Gas/Sanitary Services, II-3504
Electronic/Electric Equip., I-226-228, 230, 466, 632, 2076
Fabricated Metal Products, I-513, II-2295-2296
Food and Kindred Products, I-1033, 1394, II-2970
Forestry, II-3336-3337
General Merchandise Stores, I-935
Industry Machinery/Equip., I-225, 853, 1013-1014, 2063, II-2617
Instruments and Related, II-2233
Insurance Carriers, I-1915
Lumber and Wood Products, I-1241, 2124, II-3582, 3588
Metal Mining, I-1989, II-2749
Misc. Manufacturing Industries, I-1779, 1999, II-3086
Miscellaneous Retail, I-2000, II-2687
Motion Pictures, II-2356-2357, 2379, 2383
Paper and Allied Products, I-627, II-2603, 2813, 3555
Primary Metal Industries, I-161, 962, II-3575, 3602
Printing and Publishing, I-528, 773, 2018, 2020, II-2793-2796
Rubber and Misc. Plastics, II-3355
Social Services, I-714
Stone/Clay/Glass Products, I-1624
Transportation by Air, I-82, II-3044
Transportation Equipment, I-58, 301, 305, 573, II-2834, 2837, 3407
Transportation Services, I-2042-2044, II-3057
Trucking and Warehousing, II-3421-3422, 3425, 3427, 3429, 3431, 3500-3501, 3503
Water Transportation, I-1023

Wholesale Trade - Durables, I-1204
Wholesale Trade - Nondurables, I-701
North Carolina
  Agricultural Services, I-991
  Agriculture - Crops, I-1378, 1516, 1532, 1535, 1541, II-3374
  Agriculture - Livestock, I-1329, 1781, II-2225
  Depository Institutions, I-437
  Electric/Gas/Sanitary Services, I-1231
  Fishing, Hunting, and Trapping, I-1863-1864
  Food and Kindred Products, II-3543
  Food Stores, I-1683, 1691, 1702
  General Building Contractors, I-1842
  General Merchandise Stores, I-1599
  Membership Organizations, I-1822
  Miscellaneous Retail, I-135
North Central, U.S., II-3537
North Dakota, I-136, 438, 744, 1233, 1371, 1823, II-2779
North Korea, I-1046, 1673, II-2454, 3441
Northeast Central U.S., I-2, 564, 1511, 1786, II-2267, 2288, 2761, 3380
Northeast Coastal U.S., I-2, 564, II-2267, 2288, 2761, 3380
Northern Europe, I-647
Northern Mariana Islands, I-451
Northern Zone, U.S., II-3537
Northwest Central U.S., I-2, 564, 1786, II-2267, 2288, 2761, 3380
Norway
  Agriculture - Livestock, I-1326, 1328
  Chemicals and Allied Products, I-1121, 1264
  Electric/Gas/Sanitary Services, I-1218, 1221, 1224
  Electronic/Electric Equip., I-154
  Fishing, Hunting, and Trapping, I-1333, 1335
  Food and Kindred Products, I-724
  Insurance Carriers, II-2646, 2648
  Lumber and Wood Products, II-3586
  Metal Mining, I-172, II-2276, 2435, 3604

Miscellaneous Retail, I-156
Nonmetallic Minerals, I-1673, II-3247
Oil and Gas Extraction, II-2474, 2480, 2489
Primary Metal Industries, I-164, 167, II-3078
Stone/Clay/Glass Products, I-3
Transportation Equipment, I-325, 327, 354, 359, 362, 510
Water Transportation, II-3047
Nova Scotia, I-602
NRG Park, TX, I-940
Oakland, CA, I-531, II-2769
Oceania, I-400, 681, 951, 1196, 1313-1315, 1326, 1899, 1989, 2064, II-2181, 2603, 3602
Odessa, TX, I-1696
Ohio, I-137, 439, 1231, 1233, 1289, 1371, 1375, 1378, 1532, 1614, 1682, 1781, 1863, II-2225, 3041, 3452, 3543
Oklahoma, I-138, 440, 620, 624, 1233, 1289, 1607, 1714, 1781, 1863-1864
Oklahoma City, OK, I-1607
Olimpiada, Russia, I-1640
Olympic National Park, WA, II-2622
Oman, I-643, 1316, 1517, 1729, II-2472, 2478, 3109, 3247
Ontario, Canada, I-602
Orange County, FL, II-2980
Orange County Convention Center, FL, I-940
Oregon, I-139, 441, 1371, 1376, 1516, 1530, 1532, 1535-1536, 1584, II-2779, 3041, 3543
Orlando, FL, I-1847
Pacific Coast U.S., I-2, 564, 1786, II-2267, 2288, 2761, 3380
Padthaway, Australia, II-3544
Pakistan
  Agriculture - Crops, I-992, 994-995, II-2454, 2914, 2916, 3530, 3533
  Chemicals and Allied Products, I-1307, 1309, 1316
  Communications, II-3314
  Depository Institutions, II-2869
  Electric/Gas/Sanitary Services, I-1219
  Food and Kindred Products, I-1295, 1297, 1517, II-2173-2174, 3257-3258, 3469

Nat. Security and Interntl. Affairs, I-1046, 1053
  Nonmetallic Minerals, I-1381, 1673, 1729, II-2937
  Oil and Gas Extraction, II-2471, 2477
  Stone/Clay/Glass Products, I-648
  Textile Mill Products, I-1269, II-3330
  Transportation Equipment, II-2373
Palau, I-442
Palm Beach County, FL, I-1859, II-2980
Panama, II-3056
Papua New Guinea, I-749, 1640, 1642, II-2471, 2477
Paradiso, NV, I-1107
Paraguay, I-966, II-2497, 2500-2501, 2504, 2507
Paris, France, I-2074
Paris Charles de Gaulle Airport, France, I-100
Peñasquito, Mexico, II-3083
Pennsylvania
  Agriculture - Crops, I-1292, 1376, 1532, II-3374
  Agriculture - Livestock, I-1329, II-2225
  Amusement and Recreation, I-1575, 1579, 1584
  Coal Mining, I-744
  Depository Institutions, I-443
  Electric/Gas/Sanitary Services, I-1231, 1233
  Fabricated Metal Products, I-1714
  Fishing, Hunting, and Trapping, I-1863-1864
  Food and Kindred Products, II-3543
  Food Stores, I-1697
  General Merchandise Stores, I-1609, II-2907
  Membership Organizations, II-3452
  Miscellaneous Retail, I-140, 1109, 1111
  Printing and Publishing, I-531
  Trucking and Warehousing, I-1411
Peru
  Agriculture - Crops, I-1516, II-2448
  Business Services, II-3480
  Communications, II-3571

Fishing, Hunting, and Trapping, I-1335
  Food and Kindred Products, I-750, 753, 756, II-2505
  Metal Mining, I-959, 1642, 1993, 2041, II-2276, 2343, 3085, 3339, 3342, 3604, 3607
  Nonmetallic Minerals, I-534, II-2702
  Oil and Gas Extraction, II-2473, 2479
  Primary Metal Industries, I-588
  Stone/Clay/Glass Products, I-660
Philadelphia, PA, I-531, 1113, 1411, 1575, 1705
Philadelphia Gray 30th Street Station, PA, II-2149
Philadelphia International Airport, PA, I-94
Philippines
  Agriculture - Crops, II-2777, 2914-2915, 2917, 3532
  Communications, II-3314
  Depository Institutions, II-2869
  Electronic/Electric Equip., I-291
  Fishing, Hunting, and Trapping, I-1332-1333, 1335
  Food and Kindred Products, I-752, 754, 1297, II-2190, 2214, 2216
  Metal Mining, I-749, II-2437
  Paper and Allied Products, II-2942-2943, 2954
  Stone/Clay/Glass Products, I-657
  Textile Mill Products, II-3552
Phoenix, AZ, I-1110, 1608, 1698, 1848
Pinellas County, FL, I-1859
Pittsburgh, PA, I-1111, 1609, II-2350
The Poconos, PA, I-1575
Poland, II-2698
  Agriculture - Livestock, II-2691-2694, 2699
  Business Services, I-2045
  Chemicals and Allied Products, I-498, 500, 1067, 1311, 1316, 1890, II-2743
  Communications, II-3572
  Fabricated Metal Products, I-947-948, II-2284
  Food and Kindred Products, I-476, 724-725, 811, 1883, 2004, II-3301

Industry Machinery/Equip., II-2921
Instruments and Related, II-2255
Lumber and Wood Products,
  II-3579-3580, 3583-3587
Metal Mining, I-955, 959, II-3085
Motion Pictures, II-2384
Nonmetallic Minerals, II-2643,
  2937, 2939, 3260
Oil and Gas Extraction, II-2470,
  2476
Paper and Allied Products, II-2613
Primary Metal Industries, II-3559
Stone/Clay/Glass Products, I-656,
  1630, 1632, 2081, II-2780, 2957
Transportation Equipment, I-356-
  357, 367, 568
Polar Division mine, Russia, I-952
Pompano Beach, FL, I-1113, 1581
Portland International Airport, OR,
  I-95
Portland-Vancouver-Hillsboro, OR-
  WA, I-1610
Portugal, I-51, 660, 943, 963-964,
  1671, II-2146, 2384, 2454, 2611,
  2780, 2957, 3378, 3441, 3579,
  3583
Prince Edward Island, Canada, I-602
Providence-Warwick, RI-WA, I-1611
Pueblo Viejo mine, Dominican Republic, I-1640
Puerto Rico, I-444, II-3480
Qatar, I-97, 643, 1052, 1316, 1890,
  II-2472, 2478, 3109, 3260
Qingdao, China, II-2770
Quebec, Canada, I-602
Quincy, MA, I-1113
Rampura Agucha mine, India,
  II-3606
Red Dog mine, AK, II-3606
Rhode Island, I-141, 445, 1584
Richmond, VA, I-1112, 1612,
  II-2768
Riverina, Australia, II-3544
Riverland, Australia, II-3544
Riverside County, CA, I-1859
Rocky Mountain National Park, CO,
  II-2622
Romania, I-810, 2081, II-2456,
  2470, 2476, 2692-2693, 3079-3080,
  3579, 3583, 3586-3587, 3593
Rotterdam, Netherlands, II-2770

Russia
  Admin. of Economic Programs,
    II-3199
  Agriculture - Crops, I-966, 968,
    1521, 1525, 1539, 1669, II-2454,
    2458-2459, 2500, 3530-3531,
    3533
  Agriculture - Livestock, I-621-622,
    1326, 1784-1785, II-2208, 2691-
    2694, 2699
  Apparel and Textile Products, I-190
  Chemicals and Allied Products,
    I-160, 1135, 1263, 1307-1312,
    1316, 1890, 1987
  Coal Mining, I-742-743, 745
  Communications, II-2410
  Electric/Gas/Sanitary Services,
    I-1218, 1229
  Electronic/Electric Equip., I-637,
    II-2965
  Engineering/Management Services, II-2875
  Fabricated Metal Products, I-948
  Fishing, Hunting, and Trapping,
    I-1334-1335
  Food and Kindred Products, I-476,
    579-580, 670, 678-679, 716, 752,
    754, 1295-1296, 1389, 2004,
    II-2173-2174, 2187-2189, 2191-
    2192, 2212-2213, 2216, 2313,
    2496, 2504, 2664, 3257-3258,
    3301
  Food Stores, I-1699
  Industry Machinery/Equip., II-2136
  Leather and Leather Products,
    I-2047
  Lumber and Wood Products, I-964,
    II-3580, 3591
  Metal Mining, I-172, 183, 749,
    955, 959, 1642, 1993, 2041,
    II-2343, 2435, 2437, 2596, 2751,
    3085, 3342, 3441, 3457, 3607
  Misc. Manufacturing Industries,
    I-1639, 1996, II-2641
  Miscellaneous Retail, II-3482
  Motion Pictures, II-2355
  Nat. Security and Interntl. Affairs,
    I-1046-1051, 1053
  Nonmetallic Minerals, I-264, 277,
    534, 1074-1075, 1567, 1673,
    1729, II-2643, 2702, 2775, 2842,
    2937, 3260
  Oil and Gas Extraction, II-2470,
    2476, 2489

Paper and Allied Products, II-2817
Primary Metal Industries, I-164,
  167, 588, 619, 962, II-3078,
  3239-3240, 3242, 3244, 3246,
  3602
Stone/Clay/Glass Products, I-653,
  655, 1302, 2081
Textile Mill Products, II-3332
Transportation Equipment, I-58,
  350-351, 567, II-3437
Trucking and Warehousing,
  I-1413
Rwanda, II-3342, 3441
Sacramento, CA, II-2149, 2351
St. Louis, MO, I-1575
San Antonio-New Braunfels, TX,
  I-1849
San Cristobal mine, Bolivia,
  II-3606
San Francisco, CA, I-531
San Jose, CA, I-531
San Julian mine, Mexico, II-3083
Sandy Springs, GA, I-1102, 1839
Sanford, FL, I-1847
Sans Expo & Convention Center,
  NV, I-940
Santa Ana, CA, I-1108
Saskatchewan, Canada, I-602
Saucito mine, Mexico, II-3083
Saudi Arabia
  Agriculture - Crops, I-967,
    II-2777, 2917
  Chemicals and Allied Products,
    I-160, 1308, 1310, 1316, II-2740
  Communications, I-1180
  Food and Kindred Products, I-1517,
    II-2190, 3109
  Misc. Manufacturing Industries,
    I-1639, 1996
  Nat. Security and Interntl. Affairs,
    I-1046, 1048, 1050, 1052
  Nonmetallic Minerals, I-1729,
    II-2702, 2820, 3260
  Oil and Gas Extraction, II-2472,
    2478
  Stone/Clay/Glass Products, I-643,
    657, 1302
Savannah, GA, II-2768-2769
Scandinavia, I-951
Scottsdale, AZ, I-1110, 1608
Seattle, WA, I-531, 1613, II-2769
Seattle/Tacoma International Airport, WA, I-96
Senegal, II-2452, 2702, 2917

Seoul Incheon Airport, South Korea, I-100
Serbia, I-966, 1527, II-2470, 2476
Shandong, China, I-162
Shanghai, China, I-97-98, II-2770
Shanghai Pudong International Airport, China, I-100
Shenzhen, China, I-98, II-2770
Sierra Leone, I-1074
Sindesar Khurd mine, India, II-3083, 3606
Singapore
 Agriculture - Crops, II-2777
 Chemicals and Allied Products, I-705, II-2740-2741
 Electronic/Electric Equip., I-289
 Industry Machinery/Equip., II-2460-2461
 Instruments and Related, II-3506
 Metal Mining, I-1636, II-2436, 3339-3340
 Nat. Security and Interntl. Affairs, I-1050
 Paper and Allied Products, II-2942-2943, 2954
 Stone/Clay/Glass Products, I-1633
 Textile Mill Products, II-3552
 Water Transportation, II-2770, 3047, 3056
Singapore Changi Airport, Singapore, I-100
Slovakia, II-3378, 3584-3585
Slovenia, I-2081
South Africa
 Agriculture - Crops, I-966, 968, 1522, 1524-1526, II-2451-2453
 Agriculture - Livestock, II-3592
 Business Services, I-48
 Chemicals and Allied Products, I-1263
 Food and Kindred Products, I-476, 1518, 1527-1528, 2009, II-2190, 2213, 3550
 Metal Mining, I-729, 749, 1642, 1990, 1993, II-2596, 2751, 3457
 Nonmetallic Minerals, I-1074-1075, 1381, 1589, II-2702, 2939
 Primary Metal Industries, II-2143, 3078
 Stone/Clay/Glass Products, I-2081
 Transportation Equipment, II-3439
South America, I-400, 1197, 1670, 1737, 1989, 1996, 2018, 2020, II-2182, 2813, 2875, 3480

South Atlantic U.S., I-2, 564, 1786, II-2267, 2288, 2761, 3380
South Carolina, I-142, 446, 1541, 1842, II-2769, 3374
South Central Zone, U.S., II-3537
South Dakota, I-143, 447, 620, 624, 1781, 1823, II-2225, 3041
South Florida, I-1700
South Korea
 Agriculture - Crops, II-2777
 Agriculture - Livestock, I-1784-1785, II-3080, 3593
 Amusement and Recreation, I-1576
 Apparel and Textile Products, I-190
 Business Services, I-35
 Chemicals and Allied Products, I-705, 707, 1321, II-2740, 2742, 2744
 Coal Mining, I-746
 Communications, I-1177
 Eating and Drinking Places, I-768
 Electric/Gas/Sanitary Services, I-1219, 1226
 Electronic/Electric Equip., II-2600-2601, 3027
 Fabricated Metal Products, II-2284-2285
 Food and Kindred Products, I-670, 754, 1387, 1389, II-2212, 2214, 2216, 2505, 2991
 Furniture Stores, I-252
 Industry Machinery/Equip., II-2136, 2460-2461, 2921
 Insurance Carriers, I-1913, II-2648
 Metal Mining, I-955, 957, 1636, 1991, 2039-2040, II-2436, 3081, 3340, 3604
 Miscellaneous Retail, I-1082
 Motion Pictures, II-2355
 Nat. Security and Interntl. Affairs, I-1046-1049, 1051-1053
 Nonmetallic Minerals, I-1567, II-2303, 2939, 3260
 Oil and Gas Extraction, II-2490
 Paper and Allied Products, II-2818
 Primary Metal Industries, I-165, 588, 619, II-3239-3242, 3246, 3558-3559
 Printing and Publishing, II-2334
 Railroad Transportation, II-2838
 Security and Commodity Brokers, I-1258

Stone/Clay/Glass Products, I-653, 657, 1302, 1630-1631, 2081, II-2781, 2959
Textile Mill Products, II-3330, 3597-3598
Transportation by Air, I-97
Transportation Equipment, I-325, 342, 351, 354, 567, II-3439
Trucking and Warehousing, I-1413, II-2519
Water Transportation, II-3047
Southeast Asia, I-400, 649, 742, 951, II-2942-2943, 2954, 3552
Southeast Central U.S., I-2, 564, 1786, II-2267, 2288, 2761, 3380
Southern Asia, I-1999, II-3086
Southern states, U.S., I-1512
Southern Zone, U.S., II-3537
Southwest Central U.S., I-2, 564, 1786, II-2267, 2288, 2761, 3380
Spain
 Admin. of Economic Programs, II-3199
 Agriculture - Crops, I-1529, 1538-1539, II-2447, 2450, 2454-2455
 Agriculture - Livestock, II-2691-2694, 2699
 Amusement and Recreation, I-1576, 1721
 Business Services, I-45, 943
 Chemicals and Allied Products, I-498, 500, 1067, 1126, 1263, 1322
 Communications, I-1177, II-2548
 Electric/Gas/Sanitary Services, I-1221, 1223-1224, 1226
 Fabricated Metal Products, II-2284
 Food and Kindred Products, I-476, 724-725, 810-811, 1520, 1883, 2004, II-2624, 2991, 3107, 3301, 3550
 Food Stores, I-1701
 Industry Machinery/Equip., I-1284, II-2921
 Instruments and Related, II-2255
 Leather and Leather Products, I-2050-2051
 Lumber and Wood Products, I-963-964, II-3579, 3583-3587, 3589, 3591
 Metal Mining, I-2040, II-3340, 3441, 3604
 Misc. Manufacturing Industries, II-3395

Miscellaneous Retail, I-267
Motion Pictures, II-2355, 2362, 2384
Nat. Security and Interntl. Affairs, I-1050-1051
Nonmetallic Minerals, I-1381, 1671, 1729, 2015, II-2775, 2820, 2937, 2939
Oil and Gas Extraction, II-2480
Paper and Allied Products, II-2611, 2613
Primary Metal Industries, I-619, II-3078
Railroad Transportation, II-2838
Stone/Clay/Glass Products, I-650, 656, 660, 1302, 1633, 2081, II-2781, 2959
Textile Mill Products, I-1269
Transportation Equipment, I-350-351, 356-357, 367, 568, II-2374
Sri Lanka, I-1219, 1270, 1673
Stockholm, Sweden, I-2074
Stockton, CA, II-2768
Sub-Saharan Africa, I-632, II-3574
Sudan, I-1517, 1642, II-2469, 2475
Suffolk County, NY, I-1859
Sugar Land, TX, I-1113, 1845
Sweden
  Chemicals and Allied Products, I-498, 978
  Electric/Gas/Sanitary Services, I-1224
  Food and Kindred Products, I-724, 810, 2004, II-2624, 2991, 3107
  Industry Machinery/Equip., I-854
  Insurance Carriers, II-2646, 2648
  Lumber and Wood Products, II-3579, 3583-3584, 3586-3587, 3591
  Metal Mining, I-1990, 1993, 2041, II-3607
  Miscellaneous Retail, I-156
  Motion Pictures, II-2384
  Nonmetallic Minerals, II-2643
  Paper and Allied Products, II-2611, 2613, 2817
  Transportation Equipment, I-354, 359, 362, 367, 568
Switzerland
  Apparel and Textile Products, I-190
  Business Services, II-3227
  Chemicals and Allied Products, I-705, 707, 1067

Food and Kindred Products, I-724-725, 754, II-3301
Instruments and Related, II-2255
Insurance Carriers, II-2646
Lumber and Wood Products, II-3584
Metal Mining, I-1636
Misc. Manufacturing Industries, I-1639, II-2641-2642
Miscellaneous Retail, I-267
Paper and Allied Products, II-2611
Primary Metal Industries, I-951
Security and Commodity Brokers, I-1258
Stone/Clay/Glass Products, I-645
Syria, II-2455, 2472, 2702, 2820
Tacoma, WA, I-1613, II-2769
Taipei, Taiwan, I-97
Taiwan, I-97, 579, 619, 746, 1046, 1082, 1181, 1219, 1636, 1882, 1913, II-2136, 2502, 2600-2601, 2777, 2838, 3027, 3246
Tajikistan, I-183, 2041, II-2276
Tanzania, I-1074, 1334, 1673, II-2449, 2820
Tennessee, I-97, 144, 448, 991, 1289, 1846, 1863-1864, II-3374
Texas
  Agricultural Services, I-991
  Agriculture - Crops, I-1289, 1375, 1378, 1530, 1534, 1541
  Agriculture - Livestock, I-620, 624, 1823, II-3041
  Amusement and Recreation, I-1643
  Coal Mining, I-744
  Depository Institutions, I-449
  Educational Services, II-2980
  Electric/Gas/Sanitary Services, I-1231, 1233
  Fabricated Metal Products, I-1714
  Fishing, Hunting, and Trapping, I-1863-1864
  Food and Kindred Products, I-1371, II-3543
  Food Stores, I-1696
  General Building Contractors, I-1843, 1845, 1849
  General Merchandise Stores, I-1601
  Membership Organizations, I-1822
  Miscellaneous Retail, I-145, 1104
  Transportation by Air, I-88, 98

Trucking and Warehousing, I-1406-1407
Water Transportation, II-2769
Thailand
  Agriculture - Crops, II-2502, 2914-2916
  Chemicals and Allied Products, I-1311, 1321, II-2740, 2742, 2744
  Electronic/Electric Equip., I-290
  Fishing, Hunting, and Trapping, I-1332
  Food and Kindred Products, I-1295, 1388, II-2187-2189, 2191-2192, 2498, 3258
  Industry Machinery/Equip., II-2921
  Leather and Leather Products, I-2050
  Metal Mining, I-957, II-3339
  Misc. Manufacturing Industries, II-2641-2642
  Nonmetallic Minerals, I-1729, II-2842
  Oil and Gas Extraction, II-2477
  Paper and Allied Products, II-2606, 2942-2943, 2954
  Primary Metal Industries, II-3241, 3559
  Stone/Clay/Glass Products, I-657, 1302, II-2780, 2957
  Textile Mill Products, II-3552
  Transportation Equipment, I-359, II-2375
  Trucking and Warehousing, I-1413
Tianjin, China, II-2770
Togo, II-2702
Tokyo Narita, I-100
Toledo, OH, I-1614
Trinidad and Tobago, I-1308, 1316, II-2473, 2479
Tunisia, I-1270, 1310, 1517, II-2447, 2702
Turkey
  Agriculture - Crops, I-992, 994-995, 1521-1526, 1529, II-2447, 2450, 2454-2456, 2502, 3530-3531
  Agriculture - Livestock, II-2691-2692, 2694, 2699
  Apparel and Textile Products, I-188
  Chemicals and Allied Products, I-1322, II-2741, 2743, 2745
  Communications, I-1183
  Electric/Gas/Sanitary Services, I-1216, 1218, 1221, 1224, 1229

Fishing, Hunting, and Trapping, I-1333
Food and Kindred Products, I-1373, 1518, 1520, 1528, 2004, II-2189, 2191-2192, 2498, 3301
Lumber and Wood Products, II-3579, 3583, 3585-3587
Metal Mining, I-183, 729, 957, 1993, 2040-2041, II-2343, 3605
Misc. Manufacturing Industries, I-1639, 1996
Nat. Security and Interntl. Affairs, I-1047, 1053
Nonmetallic Minerals, I-534, 1673, 1729, 2015, II-2146, 2303, 2820, 2937, 2939, 3149, 3247
Oil and Gas Extraction, II-2474, 2480
Primary Metal Industries, I-165, 619, II-3239-3242, 3246, 3558
Stone/Clay/Glass Products, I-653, 656, 660, 1302, 2081, II-2957
Textile Mill Products, I-1269, II-3330, 3597-3598
Transportation Equipment, I-510
Turkmenistan, I-1312, 1987, II-2470, 2476
Uganda, I-753, 756, 1334, II-2475, 2820
Ukraine
 Agriculture - Crops, I-1521, 1669, II-2456, 3531, 3533
 Agriculture - Livestock, I-1785
 Chemicals and Allied Products, I-1307, 1316
 Depository Institutions, II-2869
 Electric/Gas/Sanitary Services, I-1226
 Food and Kindred Products, I-578-579, 1296, 1373, II-2189, 2312-2313, 2496-2497
 Metal Mining, I-171, 1993, II-3457
 Nonmetallic Minerals, I-1673, 2015, II-2643
 Oil and Gas Extraction, II-2470, 2476
 Primary Metal Industries, I-619, II-2143, 3078, 3246
 Stone/Clay/Glass Products, I-2081
United Arab Emirates
 Agriculture - Crops, II-2917
 Food and Kindred Products, I-1517, II-2190, 3109
 Instruments and Related, II-3506

Lumber and Wood Products, I-963
Metal Mining, I-172, 957
Misc. Manufacturing Industries, II-2641-2642
Nat. Security and Interntl. Affairs, I-1052
Nonmetallic Minerals, II-3247, 3260
Oil and Gas Extraction, II-2472, 2478, 2489
Primary Metal Industries, I-164, 167
Stone/Clay/Glass Products, I-643, 656, II-2780
United Kingdom
 Admin. of Economic Programs, II-3199
 Agriculture - Crops, I-1539
 Agriculture - Livestock, II-2691-2694, 2699, 3593
 Amusement and Recreation, I-1576, 1721
 Apparel and Accessory Stores, I-1435
 Apparel and Textile Products, I-188, 190, 195, 203, 1795
 Automotive Dealers, I-295, 1442
 Business Services, I-35, 45, 941, 943, 1774, 2045, II-3227
 Chemicals and Allied Products, I-498, 500, 705, 707, 1067, 1126, 1322
 Communications, I-1177, II-2410, 2551, 2554, 2630
 Depository Institutions, I-403
 Eating and Drinking Places, I-770, 1418
 Electric/Gas/Sanitary Services, I-1220, 1222-1223
 Electronic/Electric Equip., I-154
 Engineering/Management Services, I-6
 Fabricated Metal Products, I-948, II-2284-2285
 Fishing, Hunting, and Trapping, I-1333
 Food and Kindred Products, I-476, 716, 724-725, 810-811, 1387, 1389, 1395, 1883, 2004, II-2624, 2664, 2991, 3107, 3301
 Food Stores, I-1679
 Instruments and Related, II-2255, 3506

Insurance Carriers, I-1913, 1918, II-2646, 2648
Local and Passenger Transit, II-2164
Lumber and Wood Products, I-964, II-3583, 3585-3587, 3589
Metal Mining, I-2039-2040, II-2435-2436, 3081
Misc. Manufacturing Industries, II-2642, 3395
Miscellaneous Retail, I-156, 267-268, 270-272
Motion Pictures, I-1163, II-2355, 2363, 2384
Nat. Security and Interntl. Affairs, I-1048, 1050-1051, 1053
Nonmetallic Minerals, II-2937, 2939, 3248
Oil and Gas Extraction, II-2474, 2480, 2489
Paper and Allied Products, II-2611
Primary Metal Industries, I-165
Stone/Clay/Glass Products, I-1631, 1633, 1728, 2081, II-2780-2781, 2959
Textile Mill Products, II-3331
Transportation Equipment, I-325, 338, 351, 354-357, 359, 362, 367, 568, II-3437
Transportation Services, II-3415
Trucking and Warehousing, I-1413
Water Transportation, II-3047
United States, I-370, 728, 734, 996-997, 1029, 1042, 1044, 1303, 1343, 1345, 1357, 1383, 1397-1398, 1650, 1656-1657, 1662, 1664, 1791, 2027, 2033, 2038, 2131, 2135, II-2534-2535, 2561-2565, 2572, 2577, 2637, 2696, 2718-2720, 2802-2803, 2807, 2830, 2929-2931, 3070, 3420, 3536-3538, 3541
 Admin. of Economic Programs, I-1645-1649, 1651-1653, 1661, 1663, 1665, II-3199
 Agricultural Services, I-623, 991, II-3475
 Agriculture - Crops, I-965-966, 968, 993, 995, 1289, 1291-1292, 1375-1378, 1499-1509, 1521-1526, 1529, 1531, 1534, 1538-1540, 1669, 1674, II-2389, 2447, 2450-2453, 2455-2456, 2458-

2459, 2500-2501, 2507, 2776-2779, 2914-2917, 3003, 3374, 3530-3531, 3533

Agriculture - Livestock, I-620-622, 624-625, 1201-1202, 1288, 1329, 1781-1782, 1784-1785, II-2168, 2176, 2224, 2226, 2644

Amusement and Recreation, I-50, 543, 1035, 1246, 1273, 1573-1574, 1576, 1579, 1582-1585, 1643-1644, II-2826, 2857-2858, 3200, 3216, 3219, 3221, 3333

Apparel and Accessory Stores, I-213, 216, 1431-1434

Apparel and Textile Products, I-190, 193, 198, 200-203, 205-206, 208, 1794-1797, 1799-1800, II-3325

Auto Repair/Services/Parking, I-298, 311, 313-318, 353, 613-615, II-2366, 2620-2621

Automotive Dealers, I-296-297, 310, 507, 1437, II-3344

Building Materials, I-1789, II-2593, 2753

Business Services, I-15-19, 21-23, 25-28, 32-43, 253, 256, 258-259, 274, 780, 784, 937-939, 941, 943, 999-1001, 1017-1018, 1036, 1041, 1090, 1098, 1255, 1770-1771, 1880-1881, 1962, 1976-1978, 1995, 2045, II-2341, 2575-2576, 2705-2706, 2712-2713, 2765, 2804-2805, 2870-2873, 3001-3002, 3153, 3155, 3159, 3171, 3173, 3176, 3184, 3194, 3227, 3229-3232, 3289, 3479, 3483

Chemicals and Allied Products, I-8, 10, 13, 53-56, 157-158, 160, 371-372, 599-600, 603-604, 663, 683-684, 686, 692-694, 698, 705, 707, 709, 735-737, 969, 973-974, 976, 979-984, 987-989, 1058-1062, 1066, 1117, 1126, 1128-1129, 1141-1153, 1155-1158, 1262-1265, 1307-1312, 1316-1318, 1321-1322, 1449-1452, 1731-1736, 1877, 1887-1888, 1890, 1901-1902, II-2527, 2529, 2531, 2582-2583, 2585, 2587-2588, 2590, 2652, 2655-2656, 2658, 2686, 2731, 2737, 2740-2745, 3088, 3090-3096, 3140, 3142-3147, 3263-3274, 3277-3285, 3460, 3488-3490

Coal Mining, I-742-745, 747

Communications, I-283, 1168-1169, 1171, 1173-1178, 1185, 1972, II-2277, 2410, 2537-2538, 2554, 2556, 2630-2632, 2762-2764, 2766, 2799, 2827-2828, 3314, 3319, 3418, 3561-3562, 3573

Depository Institutions, I-402, 1019, II-2344-2345

Eating and Drinking Places, I-763, 1421-1423, II-2330, 2438, 2878, 2880, 2882-2885, 2887-2898

Educational Services, I-574, 1187, 2056-2059, II-2980-2981, 3408-3409, 3450

Electric/Gas/Sanitary Services, I-932, 1212, 1215-1216, 1218, 1221, 1223, 1226-1229, 1233-1234, II-2492, 2868, 3236-3237, 3458

Electronic/Electric Equip., I-154, 235, 238-241, 246, 286, 464, 468, 612, 631, 883, 886-894, 897, 1261, 1566, 2066, 2068, 2073, 2075, 2078, II-2390-2397, 2399-2403, 2405-2406, 2408, 2704, 2782-2783, 2786-2787, 2789, 2829, 2854-2855, 2865, 2965-2966, 2995, 2997-2998, 3027, 3102, 3106, 3250, 3286, 3288, 3308-3309, 3523

Engineering/Management Services, I-4-5, 7, 260-261, 876-877, 879, 1259-1260, II-2809, 2874-2875

Environmental Quality, I-1654, 1659

Fabricated Metal Products, I-175-177, 515, 946-949, 1205, 1271, 1304, 1714-1720, 1740-1741, 1766-1767, 2110-2111, II-2278-2287, 2290-2291, 2298-2300, 2532-2533, 2758, 2974, 3042, 3098-3099, 3226, 3379, 3388, 3465-3466, 3539-3540

Finance/Taxation/Monetary Policy, I-1660

Fishing, Hunting, and Trapping, I-1331, 1335, 1864

Food and Kindred Products, I-375, 378-380, 383-399, 476-480, 482, 484-486, 488, 490, 535-537, 539, 541-542, 547-559, 576-581, 605, 661-662, 668, 670-680, 715-716, 718-723, 726-727, 752, 754, 757-760, 808-809, 813-852, 1002-1012, 1021, 1031, 1079, 1092-1097, 1099, 1190-1191, 1237-1240, 1293, 1295, 1297-1301, 1336-1337, 1371-1372, 1382, 1387-1389, 1391-1393, 1399-1400, 1456-1467, 1469-1477, 1479-1483, 1485-1488, 1490-1493, 1517-1520, 1527-1528, 1710-1713, 1739, 1866-1876, 1884, 2003, 2005-2012, 2084-2085, 2087-2097, II-2147, 2166-2167, 2169-2171, 2173-2174, 2186-2207, 2209-2214, 2216-2223, 2227, 2229-2230, 2308-2309, 2311-2313, 2315-2318, 2320-2322, 2496-2497, 2499, 2503-2504, 2506, 2599, 2624, 2626-2627, 2649, 2664, 2667-2678, 2682-2684, 2785, 2812, 2912-2913, 2967, 2972, 2982-2984, 2986-2988, 2991, 3108, 3110-3131, 3133-3134, 3136-3139, 3150-3152, 3195-3198, 3203-3204, 3222-3225, 3253-3258, 3302-3303, 3305, 3390-3391, 3528-3529, 3534-3535, 3545-3546, 3549-3550

Food Stores, I-381, 598, 806, 1494, 1533, 1680, 1762, II-2231, 2516-2517, 2520, 3487

Furniture and Fixtures, I-1542-1543, 1546-1547, 1550, 1552-1554, 1556, 1793, II-3578

Furniture Stores, I-219, 221-222, 628, 789, 901-902, 1364-1367, 1560-1565, 1798, 1801-1820, 1834-1836, II-2411

General Building Contractors, I-861, 863, 865-871, 873-875, 907, 915, 1837, 1852-1854, 1858, 1860

General Merchandise Stores, I-934, 1056, 1091, II-2899-2901, 2904-2905, 3495

Health Services, I-505-506, 1054-1055, 1065, 1274, 1744-1749, 1751-1753, 1755-1761, 1861-1862, II-2259, 2877

Heavy Construction, I-860, 872, 912

Hotels and Lodging Places, I-475, 1792, 1829, 1832, II-2856, 2932-2933

Industry Machinery/Equip., I-470-471, 778-779, 788, 793-794, 856, 1206-1208, 1243, 1275, 1281, 1285-1287, 1379-1380, 1763, 1769, 1786, 1894-1895, 2036, II-2136, 2460-2461, 2580, 2771, 2822, 2921, 2975-2978, 3008, 3201, 3262, 3386-3387, 3446, 3492, 3508, 3516, 3527

Instruments and Related, I-591, 594, 596, 903, 1667, 2022-2024, II-2235, 2237-2239, 2246, 2251-2253, 2256, 2258, 2260, 2262, 2264-2265, 2269-2272, 2420, 2707, 2709-2711, 2992, 3326, 3506

Insurance Agents and Brokers, I-1909

Insurance Carriers, I-1910-1914, 1919-1950, 1952-1954, II-2645, 2648

Investment Offices, I-1454, 1788, 1855-1856, II-2628

Justice/Public Order/Safety, I-1655, II-2767, 2798, 2800

Leather and Leather Products, I-192, 1426-1428, 1738, 2048-2051

Legal Services, I-944, 2053

Local and Passenger Transit, I-173-174, 2082-2083, II-2148-2155, 2157-2162, 2918, 2979, 3073

Lumber and Wood Products, I-582, 963-964, 1306, 1324, 1344, 1346-1347, 1358, 1361, 1851, 1857, 2034-2035, 2126, 2129, II-3576-3577, 3580, 3591

Membership Organizations, I-575, 1250, 1822, 2108-2109, II-2866-2867, 3451-3452

Metal Mining, I-749, 955, 957, 959, 1636-1637, 1642, 1993, 2040-2041, II-2343, 2435-2437, 2596, 2751, 3081, 3085, 3339-3340, 3605, 3607

Misc. Manufacturing Industries, I-273, 374, 561-562, 597, 617-618, 1164-1167, 1348-1354, 1639, 1996-1997, II-2412-2414, 2416-2417, 2641-2642, 2654, 3075-3077, 3205-3206, 3209-3212, 3397, 3399, 3401, 3476, 3595

Misc. Repair Services, I-217, 1558-1559, 2112

Miscellaneous Retail, I-101, 156, 267-268, 270-272, 516-520, 990, 1080, 1082, 1114-1116, 1369-1370, 1780, 2002, II-2307, 2328-2329, 2418-2419, 2524-2525, 2688-2689, 2701, 2808, 2994, 3087, 3213-3215, 3375, 3402, 3470-3473

Motion Pictures, I-1161-1162, 1247-1248, II-2355, 2359, 2365, 2376-2378, 2385, 3311-3312, 3316-3317, 3320-3324

Museums/Botanical/Gardens, I-1777-1778, II-2388, 3608

Nat. Security and Interntl. Affairs, I-1046-1051, 1053, 1658

Nondepository Institutions, I-2100-2107, II-2346, 2353, 2633, 2636, 2638-2640

Nonmetallic Minerals, I-733, 859, 1026-1027, 1073, 1589, 1617, 1672, 1729, 2013, 2015, II-2303, 2643, 2702, 2775, 2820, 2841-2842, 2937-2939, 3149, 3247-3248, 3260

Oil and Gas Extraction, II-2462, 2464, 2473, 2479, 2485, 2487, 2489-2490

Paper and Allied Products, I-545-546, 730, 1401, II-2558-2559, 2569-2571, 2610, 2614-2616, 2817-2818, 2946, 2949-2952, 2955-2956, 3235, 3293-3294, 3370-3371

Personal Services, I-460, 474, 1038-1040, 1076, 1160, 1444-1445, 1730, 1737, 1891-1892, 2031-2032, II-3296, 3298-3300, 3328-3329

Petroleum and Coal Products, I-278-282, 461, 2114-2116, 2120, II-2467

Pipelines, II-2491

Postal Service, II-2773

Primary Metal Industries, I-164-165, 167-170, 583-584, 587, 619, 950, 1446-1447, 1988, II-2141, 2292-2293, 2301, 3078, 3239-3242, 3245-3246, 3558-3559

Printing and Publishing, I-521-527, 529-530, 532-533, 774, 1083-1085, 1675, 1677, 1964-1965, 1967, 1971, 1973, 1975, II-2138-2140, 2332, 2334-2336, 2338-2340, 2429, 2431, 2791-2792, 2797, 2810

Railroad Transportation, II-2839-2840

Real Estate, II-2843-2847, 2850-2853

Rubber and Misc. Plastics, I-1043, 1305, 1359, 1425, 1591, 2017, 2125, II-2557, 2566, 2573, 2657, 2722, 2725, 2727-2730, 2735-2736, 2757, 3349-3352, 3354

Security and Commodity Brokers, I-775-776, 1257-1258, 1323, 1980, 1982

Social Services, I-664-665, 667, 777, 1210-1211

Special Trade Contractors, I-906, 908, 910, 913-914, 916-931

Stone/Clay/Glass Products, I-1, 3, 276, 560, 644, 653, 655, 657, 804-805, 1030, 1302, 1342, 1356, 1621-1623, 1625, 1628-1633, 1708-1709, 1724-1725, 2079-2081, II-2323, 2716-2717, 2755, 2780-2781, 2959

Textile Mill Products, I-186-187, 1266-1270, 1340-1341, 1355, 1360, II-2439-2441, 2934-2935, 3330-3331, 3556, 3596-3598

Tobacco Products, II-3358-3360, 3362-3369, 3372-3373

Transportation by Air, I-85-86

Transportation Equipment, I-59, 64, 263, 325, 328-329, 337, 342-346, 348, 350-352, 354, 359-360, 362-363, 491, 494, 508, 511, 570, 1045, II-2326, 2368, 2659, 2859-2863, 3403-3406, 3432-3437, 3439, 3453, 3455, 3467

Transportation Services, I-1635, II-3065, 3414, 3416-3417

Trucking and Warehousing, I-1402, 1413, II-3006, 3043, 3068-3069, 3202, 3249, 3292, 3423-3424, 3426, 3428, 3497-3498
Water Transportation, I-1025, II-2156, 2769, 3046-3047, 3050, 3058, 3060, 3074, 3511-3512
Wholesale Trade - Durables, I-565, 1277, 1362-1363, 1821, 1893, II-2257, 2297, 2708, 2864, 3393
Wholesale Trade - Nondurables, I-52, 682, 807, 933, 1325, 1368, 1419, 1436, 1455, 1495, 1707, II-2232, 2581, 2618, 2748, 3551

Uruguay, I-621, II-3480, 3580, 3592
Utah, I-146, 452, 744, 1329, 1371, II-2644, 3041
Uzbekistan, I-992, 995, 1136, 1316, 1374, 1518, 1525-1526, 1528, 1642, 1673, 2015, 2047, II-2343, 2470, 2476, 2702, 3079, 3457
Vancouver-Hillsboro, OR-WA, I-1610
Vazante mine, Brazil, II-3606
Venezuela, I-3, II-2473, 2479
Vermont, I-147, 453, 531
Vietnam
  Agriculture - Crops, I-965, 967, 992, 994, 1523, II-2449, 2451-2452, 2914-2916
  Agriculture - Livestock, II-3079-3080
  Apparel and Textile Products, I-188
  Chemicals and Allied Products, I-160, 1311, 1316, 1321-1322, II-2741, 2743, 2745
  Communications, II-3314
  Depository Institutions, II-2869
  Eating and Drinking Places, I-771
  Electric/Gas/Sanitary Services, I-1219, 1226
  Fabricated Metal Products, I-947
  Fishing, Hunting, and Trapping, I-1332-1333, 1335
  Food and Kindred Products, I-476, 753, 756, II-2212, 2214, 2216
  Furniture and Fixtures, I-1557
  Industry Machinery/Equip., II-2460-2461
  Leather and Leather Products, I-2051
  Lumber and Wood Products, I-1361
  Metal Mining, I-171, 183, 2040, II-3342, 3441, 3605
  Nonmetallic Minerals, I-1381, 1673, II-2702, 2842
  Oil and Gas Extraction, II-2471, 2477
  Paper and Allied Products, II-2943, 2954
  Primary Metal Industries, II-2143, 3241-3242, 3246, 3559
  Stone/Clay/Glass Products, I-653, 655, 1632, II-2957
  Textile Mill Products, I-1270, II-3330-3331, 3552, 3597-3598
Virginia, I-148, 454, 1112, 1329, 1375, 1378, 1532, 1612, 1686, II-2225, 2769, 3374, 3543
Warren, MI, I-1105, 1113, 1603, 1844
Warsaw, Poland, I-2074
Washington, I-149, 455, 624, 1292, 1371, 1376, 1498, 1514, 1530, 1532, 1536, 1613, 1822-1823, II-2769, 3543
Washington D.C., I-150, 456, 531, 1113, 1412, 1584, 1686, 1706, 1850, II-2149
Washoe County, NV, I-1569
West Palm Beach, FL, I-1605
West Virginia, I-151, 457, 744, 1233, 1329, 1579-1580, 1584, II-2225
Western Asia, I-1670
Western Europe, I-30, 312, 632, 853, II-2319, 2474, 2480, 2552, 2603, 2611, 2813, 2881, 3107
Western Hemisphere, II-2473, 2479
Western Sahara, II-2702
Western U.S., I-1513
Wichita, KS, I-1615
Wilmington, NC, I-1113, II-2849
Winston-Salem, NC, I-1702
Wisconsin, I-152, 458, 620, 1289, 1292, 1329, 1371, 1514, 1536, 1863-1864, II-2644, 2779
The Woodlands, TX, I-1845
World, I-1064, 1618, 1963, 1970, 2060-2061, 2132, 2135, II-2305, 2560, 2567, 2574, 2578, 2999, 3072, 3097, 3383
  Admin. of Economic Programs, II-2963
  Agriculture - Crops, I-965-968, 992-995, 1515-1516, 1521-1525, 1529, 1537-1539, 1669-1670, II-2458-2459, 2500-2502, 2507, 2915, 2917, 2993, 3004, 3532-3533
  Agriculture - Livestock, I-621-622, 1200, 1290, 1784-1785, II-2185, 3079-3080, 3592-3593
  Amusement and Recreation, I-181-182, 262, 801-802, 1188, 1570-1571, 1576-1578, 1585, 1722, II-3218, 3334, 3510
  Apparel and Accessory Stores, I-214
  Apparel and Textile Products, I-184-185, 188-191, 194, 203, 209, 1795, II-2685
  Auto Repair/Services/Parking, I-320
  Automotive Dealers, I-1443
  Business Services, I-24, 30, 35, 80, 254, 275, 616, 772, 905, 941-943, 1203, 1256, 1775, 1896-1898, II-2598, 2662, 3154, 3157-3158, 3160-3164, 3166, 3168, 3170, 3172, 3174, 3178-3183, 3186-3189, 3191, 3193, 3227-3228, 3411, 3485-3486
  Chemicals and Allied Products, I-9, 11-12, 14, 159-160, 502, 504, 681, 685, 689-691, 695-696, 705-708, 713, 739, 971, 1068-1071, 1123-1124, 1126-1127, 1131-1132, 1137-1138, 1263-1264, 1307-1316, 1319-1322, 1595, 1886, 1889-1890, 1900, 1903, 1987, 2098, II-2583-2584, 2589, 2592, 2651, 2724, 2733, 2739-2745, 3459, 3461-3463
  Coal Mining, I-745-746
  Communications, I-369, 1177, 1972, II-2409-2410, 2536, 2553-2554, 2630, 3314, 3560
  Depository Institutions, I-400-401, 1028
  Eating and Drinking Places, I-1417, 1424, II-2879, 2881, 2886
  Electric/Gas/Sanitary Services, I-1217, 1220-1223, 1226, 1229-1230, 1232, 1235, 1742, II-2445, 3509, 3513-3514
  Electronic/Electric Equip., I-226-233, 237, 244, 284, 462-463, 465, 469, 608-609, 611, 629-630, 632, 641, 731, 783, 880-882, 884-885, 896, 898, 900, 1086-1089, 1101,

1189, 1272, 1616, 1666, 1743, 1865, 1878, 1955-1961, 2028, 2030, 2067, 2069-2072, 2074, 2113, II-2304, 2306, 2407, 2421-2424, 2428, 2526, 2600-2602, 2788, 2790, 2920, 2960-2962, 2964-2965, 2996, 3009-3014, 3016-3028, 3030-3032, 3034, 3100, 3251-3252, 3290, 3306-3307, 3410, 3412

Engineering/Management Services, I-878, 1057, II-2876, 3454

Fabricated Metal Products, I-610, 732, 947-948, 956, 1586, 1768, 2025, II-2284-2285, 2294, 2653, 2715, 2754, 2756, 2759, 3389

Fishing, Hunting, and Trapping, I-1332-1335

Food and Kindred Products, I-102, 376, 483, 487, 578-580, 606, 669-670, 679, 716-717, 750, 752-756, 812, 1034, 1078, 1100, 1295-1298, 1387-1389, 1396, 1478, 1484, 1489, 1496, 1825, 1885, 2008-2009, 2086, II-2172-2174, 2187-2192, 2212-2216, 2228, 2310, 2312-2313, 2496-2499, 2503-2506, 2508-2514, 2664, 2666, 2681, 2985, 2991, 3257-3259, 3304, 3469, 3548, 3550

Furniture and Fixtures, I-1545, 1548-1549, 1551

Furniture Stores, I-218, 255

General Building Contractors, I-864

General Merchandise Stores, II-2909-2910

Heavy Construction, I-909, 1899

Hotels and Lodging Places, I-1827-1828, 1833, II-3039

Industry Machinery/Equip., I-225, 321, 472-473, 501, 589, 762, 781-782, 785-786, 790-791, 795-800, 855, 858, 945, 1015-1016, 1159, 1209, 1242, 1244, 1276, 1278-1280, 1594, 1764-1765, 1787, 1824, II-2136-2137, 2289, 2324-2325, 2460-2461, 2579, 2619, 2747, 2760, 2771, 2784, 2821, 2823-2825, 2911, 2921-2924, 2926-2928, 3005, 3007, 3036, 3038, 3327, 3335, 3381-3382, 3384-3385, 3442-3443, 3445, 3447-3448, 3515, 3517-3521, 3526

Instruments and Related, I-322-324, 590, 593, 595, 642, 741, 904, 1077, 1338-1339, 1879, 2054-2055, II-2233-2234, 2236, 2240-2243, 2245, 2247-2250, 2254, 2261, 2266, 2268, 2273, 2523, 2714, 3033, 3104, 3295, 3313, 3474, 3505-3507

Insurance Agents and Brokers, I-1916-1917, 1951

Insurance Carriers, II-2647-2648

Investment Offices, I-1453, 1981

Leather and Leather Products, I-2046, 2050-2051, 2121-2122, 2133

Lumber and Wood Products, I-963-964, 1361, 1838, 2016, 2127, II-2597

Membership Organizations, I-1022

Metal Mining, I-171-172, 183, 729, 749, 952, 955, 957-959, 1636-1638, 1641-1642, 1989-1993, 2039-2041, II-2276, 2343, 2433, 2435-2437, 2594-2596, 2750-2751, 3081-3082, 3084-3085, 3338-3342, 3357, 3441, 3456-3457, 3604-3607

Misc. Manufacturing Industries, I-563, 986, 1587-1588, 1996, 1999, 2052, 2065, 2134, II-2145, 2415, 2641-2642, 2660, 2752, 3083, 3086, 3207-3208, 3396, 3400, 3478, 3481, 3484, 3594

Miscellaneous Retail, I-265-271, 1081-1082, II-3419

Motion Pictures, I-1249, II-2355, 2364, 2376

Museums/Botanical/Gardens, II-2387

Nat. Security and Interntl. Affairs, I-1046-1053

Nondepository Institutions, I-1184, II-2274, 2635, 2639

Nonmetallic Minerals, I-264, 277, 534, 1072, 1074-1075, 1381, 1567, 1589, 1671, 1673, 1729, 2015, II-2146, 2303, 2643, 2702, 2774-2775, 2820, 2842, 2937, 2939, 3148-3149, 3247-3248, 3260

Oil and Gas Extraction, II-2463, 2465, 2471, 2481-2484, 2486, 2488-2490, 2493, 2495

Paper and Allied Products, I-544, 627, II-2603-2604, 2607-2609, 2813-2816, 2818, 2941, 2948, 2953, 3494

Personal Services, I-1737, II-3297

Petroleum and Coal Products, I-497, 2117-2119, II-2466

Postal Service, II-2772

Primary Metal Industries, I-164-167, 377, 585-586, 588, 619, 951, 953-954, 960-962, 1448, II-2143-2144, 2432, 2434, 2940, 3078, 3233, 3238-3239, 3241-3243, 3246, 3558-3559, 3601-3603

Printing and Publishing, I-1676, 1969, 1974, 2018-2019, 2021, II-2334, 2337, 2703, 2811

Railroad Transportation, II-2838

Rubber and Misc. Plastics, I-1429, 1590, 1592, 2026, II-2342, 2457, 2721, 2726, 3287, 3348, 3356

Security and Commodity Brokers, I-1258, 1983-1985

Services, NEC, II-3522

Special Trade Contractors, I-911, 1251-1253

Stone/Clay/Glass Products, I-3, 303, 319, 626, 651-654, 659-660, 738, 761, 803, 998, 1302, 1619-1620, 1624, 1626-1627, 1630-1632, 1634, 1904-1907, 1994, 2081, II-2443-2444, 2446, 2780-2781, 2958-2959, 3493

Textile Mill Products, I-697, 1269-1270, II-2442, 3330-3331, 3598

Tobacco Products, II-3361

Transportation by Air, I-83-84, 97, 99, II-2386, 3044, 3054

Transportation Equipment, I-61-63, 65-70, 73-79, 81, 103, 299-300, 302, 306-307, 309, 331-332, 336, 341-342, 347, 350-351, 359, 362, 495-496, 509, 567, II-2327, 2367, 2832-2833, 2835-2836, 3071, 3437, 3439

Transportation Services, II-2522, 3052, 3055, 3059, 3392, 3413

Trucking and Warehousing, I-1413, II-3430, 3502

Water Transportation, II-2770, 3048-3049, 3051, 3053, 3056, 3063-3064
Wholesale Trade - Nondurables, I-704, II-3291
Wrattonbully, Australia, II-3544
Wyoming, I-153, 459, 744, 1233, II-3041
Xinjiang, China, I-162
Yellowstone National Park, ID-MT-WY, II-2622
Yemen, I-1374, II-2472, 2478
Zambia, I-955, 959
Zimbabwe, I-277, 1074-1075, II-2596, 2751
Zion National Park, UT, II-2622

PRODUCTS, SERVICES, NAMES, AND ISSUES INDEX

This index shows, in alphabetical order, references to products, services, personal names, and issues covered in *Market Share Reporter, 32nd Edition*. More than 3,020 terms are included. Terms include subjects not readily categorized as products and services, including such subjects as aerospace and churches. The numbers that follow each term refer to entry numbers and are arranged sequentially so that the first mention is listed first. Roman numerals indicate volume number.

2-Ethyl Hexanol, II-2739
3D printing, II-3335
3D screens, II-2376
5-HTP (5-hydroxytryptophan), II-3273
5G technology, I-629, II-3560
8K technology, I-881
A-Kon convention, I-938
a-Si/IGZO technology, I-1086
Abrasives, I-1-3, II-3527
ABS/SAN resins, II-2737
Access control technology, II-2997
Accounting services, I-4-7
Acetate, I-1317
Acetylene, I-1887
Acne treatments, II-3089-3090, 3094
Acrow equipment, I-1774
Acrylic acids, II-2739
Acrylics, I-11
Acrylonitrile, II-2739
Action figures, II-3401
Activewear, I-196
Acute care, II-3190
Adhesives and sealants, I-8-14, 682
Adult incontinence products, II-2942, 2950
Advanced wound management, II-2236
Advertising, I-15-42, 1083, 1085, 1881, II-2378, 2537
Advertising, cable, I-34
Advertising, digital, I-17-20, 30
Advertising, direct mail, I-15, 22
Advertising, drug, I-23
Advertising, internet, I-15, 36-37, 42
Advertising, magazines, I-23, 38
Advertising, mobile, I-28-29
Advertising, newspapers, I-15, 23
Advertising, outdoor, I-15, 21, 23, 31, 35, 39-40

Advertising, podcasts, II-2765
Advertising, radio, I-15, 23, 35, 41
Advertising, search, I-42
Advertising, television, I-15-16, 23, 32-33, 35
Advertising, video on demand, II-2555
Aerial work platforms, I-1771-1772, 1774
Aeronautics, I-1045
Aerosols, I-43-49
Aerospace and defense, I-472, 611, 654, 1045, 1626, II-2294, 3357
Aftermarket accessories, I-511
Agents and managers, I-50, II-2852
Aggregate, I-51, 652, 1708
Agricultural markets, I-52, 698, 1260, 1303, 1305-1306, 1368, 1379
Agrochemicals, I-687-689
Air ambulances, I-174
Air care, I-53-56, 737
Air cargo, II-3044, 3054
Air conditioners, I-223-225, 228-229, 232, 242-243, 930, 1769, II-2533
Air fresheners, I-44, 46, 54, 56, 734
Air quality, I-1251, 1275, 1879
Aircraft, I-57-71, 77, 80-81, 1053, 1916, 1921, II-2386, 3097
Aircraft engines, I-72-79
Airline catering, I-1417
Airlines, I-82-96, II-3218
Airports, I-97-100, 863, II-2619-2620
Alarm companies, II-3002
Alarms, II-2995
Alcoholic beverage retailers, I-101
Alcoholic beverages, I-102, 476-485, 1336, 1739, 1777, 2084-2097,

II-2329, 2388, 2933, 3218, 3543-3551 *See also*: Beer; Liquor; Wine
Ale, II-2329
Alkalis, I-682
All-purpose cleaners, I-735-736
All-terrain vehicles, I-103
Allergy remedies, I-1141, 1146-1147
Almond milk, II-2320
Almonds, II-2447
Alpha-lipoic acids, II-3271
Alternative fueling stations, I-104-156
Alternative fuels, I-358, 569, II-3440, 3468
Alumina, I-157-160, II-3148
Aluminum, I-157, 161-168, 1261, 1446, II-2141, 2290, 2296, 2718, 3523, 3541
Aluminum foil, I-169-170
Aluminum ore, I-171-172
Aluminum oxide, I-157
Amazon Prime Day, I-1168
Ambulance services, I-173-174
American Whiskey, I-2084
Ammonia, I-681, 736
Ammunition, I-175-177, 1714, II-2299
AMOLED technology, I-1086
Amplifiers, I-882, II-3539
Amusement parks, I-178-182, 873, II-2378, 2388, 2856
Analgesics, I-599, 1142-1143, 1152
Analysis instruments, I-2022
Analytical instruments, I-2022
Andrea Bocelli, I-802
Animal fat, II-2669
Animal health, I-1127
Anime, I-938
Antacids, I-1151
Antennas, II-2960

Anti-aging products, II-3094
Anti-cellulite treatments, II-3089
Anti-rheumatics, I-1137
Anti-smoking treatments, I-1144-1145
Anti-virals, I-1137
Antibacterials, I-1128
Antifreeze, I-690
Antihypertensives, I-1128
Antimony, I-183
Antiperspirants, I-44
Antiseptics, I-1150
Apartments, I-868, 875, 1030, 1852-1854
App stores, I-255
Apparel, I-184-212, 215, 369, 1175-1176, 1444, 2062, II-2268, 2575, 3220
Apparel, children's, I-187, 207
Apparel, girl's, I-201
Apparel, men's, I-187, 196-200, 202, 207
Apparel, tactical, I-206
Apparel, winter, I-196, 211
Apparel, women's, I-187, 207, 209-212, 216, II-3206
Apparel, work, I-194
Apparel accessories, I-1368, 2133
Apparel repair, I-217, 1891
Apparel retailers, I-213-216
Apparel storage services, I-2032
Appetizers, I-1457
Apple chips, II-3110-3111
Apple sauces, II-2968
Apples, I-1398, 1497, 1499, 1510-1513
Appliance rental, II-2870
Appliance repair and maintenance, I-217
Appliance retailers, I-218-222
Appliances, I-217, 219-250, 901, 2062, II-2786
Application software, I-1963, II-2999
Appraisal services, II-2852
Apps, I-251-259, II-3022
Apricots, I-1518
Aprons, I-1798
Aquaculture, I-1329
Aquatic products, I-1385, II-2697
Arc welding, II-3527
Architectural services, I-260-261

Architectural work, II-2286, 2533, 2587, 3539
Archives, I-2056-2058
Arenas, I-262
Argon, I-1887
Ariana Grande, I-1970
Armored car services, I-616
Armored vehicles and tank parts, I-263
Arsenic trioxide, I-264
Art, I-265-273, 664, 1675, 2060, 2062, II-3401
Artificial intelligence, I-274-275, II-3035, 3163
Artificial marble, I-276
Artificial nails, I-973, 988
Artificial plants, I-1368
Artificial teeth, I-1054
Asbestos, I-277
Aseptic packaging, II-2574
Ashwagandha, II-3273
Asian food, II-2330, 2802, 2896, 2968
Asp (fish), I-1330
Asparagus, I-1498
Asphalt paving mixtures and blocks, I-278-279
Asphalt shingles and coatings, I-280-282
Asphaltic concrete aggregate, II-2938
Astronomy, II-3313
Athleisure, I-193, 205
Athletes, I-50
Atlantic Coast Conference, II-3216
Auctions, I-265
Audiologists, I-1758
Audiovisual equipment, I-283-291, 884, 886, 901, 1770, II-2712
Auditing services, I-4, 6-7
Augmented reality, II-2304, 3153-3154
Auto auctions, I-292-295
Auto bodies, I-313
Auto dealerships, I-296-297, II-3344
Auto detailing, I-613
Auto leasing, I-298, 353
Auto lighting, I-2069, 2077
Auto parts, I-44, 299-309, 313, 315, 1175, 2070, II-2300, 2533
Auto parts retailers, I-310
Auto rental, I-311-312
Auto repair, I-313-316
Autoclaved aerated concrete, I-319

Automated clearing house services, II-2344
Automated customer service agents, I-275
Automated guideway transit, II-2158
Automated parking systems, I-320
Automated threat intelligence, I-275
Automatic identification system transponders, II-3412
Automation equipment, I-322-324
Automotive markets, I-18, 43, 48-49, 168, 607, 611, 682, 1176, 1379-1380, 2021, 2062, 2106-2107, 2110, II-2294-2295, 2583, 2590, 2788, 2922, 2927, 2940, 3025, 3043, 3218, 3511-3512
Autos and trucks, I-325-368, II-3049, 3426 See also: Electric vehicles; Hybrids; Motor vehicles; Plug-ins
Avocados, I-1398, 1500, 1533
AVOD (advertising-based video on demand), II-2555
Awnings, II-2533, 3325, 3539
B2B commerce, I-23
Baby boomers, II-2368
Baby care, I-369-374, II-2803, 2954, 3556
Baby food, I-375-376, II-2802
Back side silver paste, I-377
Back-to-school spending, II-2899-2900
Backpacks, I-2122-2123
Bacon, II-2204, 2206-2207
Bacopa, II-3266
Bagels and bialys, I-378-380, 383, 547
Bakeries, I-381
Bakery-cafe chains, II-2882
Bakery products, I-382-399, 1393, II-2329, 2562-2563 See also: Bread and rolls
Bakeware, I-1029, 1835
Baking ingredients, I-718-719, II-2968, 3528
Baking needs, I-1383
Balances, II-2977-2978
Ball bearings, I-470
Bananas, I-1398, 1515, 1537
Bandages, II-2271
Bank wealth management, I-1986
Banking, I-22, 400-459, 1896, 1986, 2100, 2102, 2106, II-2352
Bar furniture, I-1546
Barack Obama, I-522, 1970

Barbecue sauces, II-2967-2968
Barber shops, I-460
Barges, II-3050, 3058
Barrels, II-2578, 3589
Barricade tape, II-3293
Bars and taverns, I-1418, II-2438, 2898, 3470
Base fluids, I-2118
Base oils, I-461
Baskets, I-1791
Bass straps, II-2413
Bath/body scrubbers/massagers, II-2654
Bath products, I-1807, II-3140, 3142
Bath tub/tile cleaners, I-736
Bathrooms, I-997-998, II-2941, 2957-2959
Batteries, I-301, 307, 462-469, 2098, II-3338
Beach clubs, II-2801
Beans, I-1458, 1476, 1531
Bearings, I-470-473
Beauty care, I-972, 975, 1175-1176, 1971, II-2652
Beauty salons, I-474
Beck, Glenn, II-2827
Bed-and-breakfasts, I-475
Bedding, I-1793, 1796, 1801-1802, II-3097
Bedrooms, I-1542, 1544-1545, 1553, 1561, II-3097
Bedspreads, I-1817
Bee products, II-3267
Beef, II-2166-2167, 2170-2171, 2173-2174, 3497
Beer, I-101-102, 476-485, 1628, 2018, II-2329
Beet sugar, II-3253-3254
Benches, I-21
Benefits brokers, I-1909
Bequests, I-667
Berries, I-1398
Best-of-breed equipment, II-2421
Beverages, I-477, 486-490, 544, 610, 1175-1176, 1337, 1394-1395, 1417, 1628, 1678, 1777, 2021, 2032, II-2329, 2378, 2388, 2575, 2579, 2724, 2927, 2933, 3292, 3471-3472 *See also*: Individual categories
Bialys, I-378-380, 383
Bicycles, I-491-496
Big 12 Conference, II-3216
Big Ten Conference, II-3216
Bilberry, II-3270

Billboards, I-21, 31, 39
Binance Coin, I-1028
Bindings, I-1368
Bingo, I-1571
Bins, I-1791, II-2578
Bio-based fluids, I-2118
Biodiesel, I-104, 106-113, 115-117, 119-125, 127, 129-142, 144-150, 152, 497
Biofuels, I-497-500, 682
Biomass, I-1227-1228, 1230
Biometrics, I-501
Bioplastics, I-502
Biotechnology, I-503-504, II-2821
Biotin, II-3271
Bird seed, II-2684
Birds, I-2038, II-2694, 2696
Biscuits, I-548, 1092
Bitcoin, I-1028
Bitumen membranes, I-280
Blackberries, I-1501, II-3497
Blankets, I-1800, 1818
Bleach, I-734, II-2803
Blind boxes, II-3394
Blister packaging, II-2577
Blood, I-506
Blood and organ banks, I-505-506
Blood clot treatments, II-2265
Blood glucose monitoring, I-1068
Blouses, I-211-212, 216
Blow molding, II-2724, 2727
Blowers, I-1275
Blu-ray technology, I-887, 1162-1163
Blueberries, I-1501, 1516, II-3497
Blush, I-974, 981
Board games, II-2333, 3395, 3398, 3401-3402
Boat dealers, I-507
Boat maintenance and repair, I-217
Boat trailers, I-511
Boats, I-508-511, 1242
Body care, I-981, 1452, II-3088, 3093-3094, 3140-3141, 3143, 3147
Body modification services, I-1076, 2032
Body piercing, II-3296
Bodyguard services, I-1977
Boilers, I-512-514, 1766
Bolts, I-515, II-3539
Bone health, II-3263, 3265
Book printing, I-528
Book retailers, I-516-520

Books, I-521-533, 1083, 1175-1176, 2062
Booster pumps, II-2823
Booster seats, I-370
Borage oil, II-3271
Boron, I-534
Botanical gardens, I-1777, II-2388, 3608
Bottled water, I-486, 489, 535-542
Bouillon, I-1099, II-2971
Bowling centers, I-543, 1546
Bowls (packaging), II-2563
Bowriders, I-508
Box cars, II-2837
Boxboard, II-2568
Boxer briefs, I-200
Boxer shorts, I-200
Boxes, I-544-546
Brad Kelley, I-2027
Brain health, II-3263, 3266
Braised meat, II-2175
Brandy, I-2084
Bras, I-195
Brazil nuts, II-2448
Bread and rolls, I-382-383, 547-559, 1094, II-3203 *See also*: Bakery products
Breadsticks, I-1002-1003
Breakfast/cereal/snack bars, I-814-815
Breakfasts, I-1382, 1467, II-2204, 2878
Breast imaging technology, II-3163
Breast implants, II-2258
Breath fresheners, I-816-817
Bricks, I-278, 560, 1030, 1368, II-2716
Bridges, I-906, 1054, II-3376
Brisket, II-2167
Broadcast spots, I-33
Broadwoven fabrics, I-2048
Broccoli, I-1460, 1476, 1483, 1540
Broilers, II-2168, 2176-2185
Brokerages, I-1444, II-2852
Bromine disinfectants, I-691
Bronchodilators, I-1137
Bronzers, I-981
Brooms, brushes and mops, I-561-564, 734
Broth, II-2669, 2967
Brownies, I-1093, 1097
Browsers, II-3155-3157
Bubble bath, II-3142
Bubble packaging, II-2557

Buck, Peter, I-2027
Building Materials See: Construction materials and supplies
Building sets, II-3401
Buildings, I-163, 168, 260, 861, 909, 1057
Bulk carriers, II-3048, 3421
Bulk storage, II-3202
Buns, I-383, 552
Burglaries, I-1928
Bus services, II-2148, 2150-2151, 2154, 2164
Buses, I-297, 301, 567-573, 708, II-3436
Business associations, I-575
Business jets, I-57, 65
Business process management services, II-2621
Business schools, I-574
Business travel, II-3414-3415
Butane, II-2489-2490
Butanols, II-2739
Butter, I-576-581, 1031-1032, II-3497
Buttermilk, II-2311
Buttons, I-1368
Butyl, I-11
Buy here, pay here policies, I-2106
Buy now, pay later policies, I-256
Cabbage, I-1531, 1540
Cabinets, I-582, 1030, 1553, 2126, II-2534, 3577-3578
Cable, I-583-587, II-3562
Cable cars, II-2152
Cable television, I-22, 34, II-2631
Cadmium, I-588
Cafeterias, I-1422, 1546
Caffeine, II-3269, 3274
Cakes, I-382, 385, 395, 547, 1392
Calciferous tufa, I-2079
Calcium, II-3264-3265
Calculators, I-589
Calendars, I-1675
Call support services, II-2805
Cameras, I-590-596, 901, II-3034
Camping equipment, II-3213
Camping facilities, II-2856
Camping trailers, II-2299, 3403
Campus book stores, I-517
Canadian Whisky, I-2084
Candles, I-56, 597, II-2803
Candy, I-715-717, 720-727, 810-813, 828, 830-831, 834, 836-837, 849-852, 2032, II-2329, 2378, 2558, 2569, 2933, 3471-3472
Candy corn, I-808
Candy stores, I-806
Cannabidiol, I-598-600, 603
Cannabis, I-601-602, 604
Canned food, I-605-606, 1383, II-2778, 2982
Canopies, II-2533
Cans, I-161, II-2279, 2282
Canvas, II-3325
Capacitors, I-607-609
Caprylic acid, II-3266
Caps and closures, I-610
Captive financing, I-2100, 2102, 2106
Car air fresheners, I-56
Car seat strollers, I-370
Car seats, I-1553
Car shipping, II-3049
Car stereos, I-882
Caramel corn, I-843-844
Caramel/taffy apple kits, I-813, 818-819
Carbide cutting tools, II-2288
Carbon black, I-708
Carbon dioxide, I-1887
Carbon fiber, I-611-612
Carbonated beverages, I-486, 489
Card games, II-2333
Cardan shafts, I-300
Cardboard, I-545
Cardiac rhythm management, II-2237
Cardiovascular imaging, II-3163
Cargo transport, II-3044, 3046, 3055, 3057, 3070, 3512
Carob/yogurt-coated snacks, I-820-821
Carpets, I-1340-1341, 1343, 1345, 1355, 1357
Carports, II-2533
Carrageenan, II-2993
Carrier line equipment, II-3308-3309
Carrots, I-1476, 1502, 1514, 1540
Cars See: Autos and trucks
Cartons, I-545
Carts, I-1553, II-2578
Carwashes, I-613-615
Cash handling, I-616, 1977, II-2344
Cashews, II-2449
Casinos, I-1568, 1571, 1575
Caskets, I-617-618
Casks, II-3589
Caspian roach, I-1330
Castings, I-619, II-2141, 2286, 2299
Casual dining chains, II-2884
Cat food, II-2663, 2666-2668, 2670, 2673-2674, 2677, 2679-2682
Cat treats, II-2668, 2670
Catalogs, I-22, 1367, 1675, II-2793
Catalysts, II-2594, 2749, 2841
Catering, I-1416
Catfish, I-1330, II-2987
Cats, II-2692, 2695-2697
Catsup, I-605
Cattle, I-620-623, 1884
Cattle feedlots, I-624-625
Cattle on feed, I-624
Ceiling contractors, I-929
Ceiling grids, I-626
Celine Dion, I-802
Cell towers, II-3310
Cellophane, I-627
Cellphone boosters, I-888
Cellphone retailers, I-628
Cellphones, I-628-641, 901, 1708, II-2536
Cellular-connected industrial machines, I-642
Cellulose, I-1908
Cellulosic fibers, I-1319
Cement, I-278, 280, 643-653, 1030, 1368, 1708, 2014, 2079, II-3045
Cement concrete aggregates, II-2938
Cemeteries, I-618, 1038, 1040
Central Florida Fair, I-1273
Ceramic tiles, I-655-657, 1342, 1356-1357
Ceramics, I-654-660, 693, 1343, 2014, 2098, II-2841
Cereal, I-392, 661-662, 1383, 1393
Cereal bars, I-814-815
Chainlink, I-1028
Chair pads, I-1798
Chairs, I-1545, 1548, 1553
Chamomile, II-3273
Charcoal, I-663, II-3268
Charging stations, I-154-156
Charities, I-664-667, 1211
Charlie Mackesy, I-522
Charter buses, II-2148
Charter flights, I-85
Cheddar cheese, I-668
Cheese, I-668-680, 1032, II-2573
Cheese snacks, II-3112-3113
Cheesecakes, I-389, 396, 1392, 1461
Chemical distributors, I-699-704

Chemicals and allied products, I-681-696, 698-713, 1380, 1626, II-2282, 2286, 2579, 2710, 2822, 2922, 2927, 3202, 3292, 3338, 3465
Chemistry, II-2821
Cherries, I-1503
Chewy candies, I-813, 834
Chicken, II-2169, 2171, 2187-2192, 2196, 2200, 3497
Chicken restaurants, II-2885
Chicken substitutes, II-2196, 2200
Chickenpox vaccines, II-3463
Child care, I-714
Children's programs, I-1777, II-2388
Chili sauces, II-2967-2968, 2971
Chimney cleaner/soot removers, I-736
Chipsets, II-3018
Chiropractors, I-1755
Chlorinated polyvinyl chloride, II-2721
Chlorine, I-682
Chocolate, I-715-727, 823, 835 *See also*: Confectionery products
Choice white grease, I-1299
Choose-and-cut farms, I-728
Christmas trees, I-728, 1368
Chromatic instruments, I-2022
Chromebooks, I-795
Chromium, I-729
Churches, II-2867
Cider, I-477
Cider vinegar supplements, II-3274
Cigar wraps, I-730
Cigarette paper, II-3370-3371
Cigarettes, I-933, II-3360-3361, 3366-3367, 3373
Cigars, II-3358-3359, 3373
Cinema lenses, I-2054
Circuit assemblies, II-2786
Circuit boards, II-2786-2787, 2789
Circuit breakers, I-731
Civil engineering, II-2940
Clarinet ligatures, II-2416
Classical music, II-2398, 2403
Clays, I-733, 1030, 1708
Clean rooms, I-1891, 2032
Cleaning products, I-44, 47, 685, 734-739, 1835, 2032, II-2559, 2803
Cleaning services, I-217, 2032, II-2621
Click-and-collect sales, I-1171
Clinical trials, II-2876

Clocks, I-740-741
Closures, II-2286
Clothing *See*: Apparel
Cloths for cleaning, I-734
Cloud computing, II-2999, 3164-3165, 3169, 3187
Clubs, II-3470
Coaches (bus), I-567-568, 571-572
Coal, I-742-748, 1212-1214, 1217, 1227-1228, II-3045
Coal tar, I-684
Coated bleached kraft, II-2608
Coated recycled board, II-2607
Coatings, I-47, 280-281, II-2282, 2586
Coats, I-212, 216
Cobalt, I-749
Cockpit voice recorders, I-81
Cocktail and bar centers, II-2534
Cocktail mixes, I-2085
Cocoa beans, I-750
Coconut candies, I-849-850
Coconut oil, II-2511-2514
Coconut water, I-537
Cod, II-2983, 2987
Coffee, I-486-489, 751-760, 1383, 1423, II-2281
Coffee, RTD, I-751, 759, 1628
Coffee cakes, I-393, 397
Coffee cups, I-761
Coffee roasters, I-762
Coffee shops, I-763-771
Cognac, I-2084
Coins, I-1997
Cold remedies, I-1146-1147, II-3263, 3267
Cold sore medication, I-1148
Cold storage, II-3496, 3499
Coleslaw, I-1392, II-2785
Collagen products, II-3271
Collateral recovery and repossession services, I-1000
College book stores, I-516, 520
Colleges, I-260, 517, 2062, II-2856, 2899, 3470
Collins, Suzanne, I-522
Colocation services, I-772
Colognes, I-47, 1452
Coloring products, II-2282, 2286, 2292, 3594
Combat aircraft, I-1046
Combines, I-1285, 1287
Comedies, II-2357
Comforters, I-1817

Comic books, I-773-774
Comic cons, I-939
Comment systems, II-3158
Commercial display cases, I-1763, 1765
Commercial replacement flooring, I-1342, 1346-1347, 1352
Commercial screen printing, II-2792
Commercial vehicles, I-356-357
Commodity contracts, I-775-776
Communications, I-873, 1896, 1898, 2030, II-2788, 2933, 2961, 2966, 3025, 3539
Community food services, I-777
Commuter rail, II-2153, 2831
Composites, I-1043, II-2830, 3541
Compressed natural gas, I-104-112, 114-117, 119-125, 127, 129-142, 144-153
Compressors, I-778-779, II-2822
Computer and office machine repair and maintenance, I-780
Computer data storage, I-781-783
Computer facilities management services, I-784
Computer peripherals, I-785-788, 901
Computer retailers, I-789
Computers, I-18, 607, 790-800, 1064, 1175-1176, 1570, II-2536, 2788, 3009, 3025
Concealers, I-976, 981
Concentrates, I-605, 1337
Concerts, I-801-802, II-2404
Concessions industry, I-1417, 1424
Concrete, I-278, 693, 803-804, 908, 1030, 1368, II-2533, 2717
Concrete blocks, I-805, II-2716
Concrete bricks, II-2716
Concrete pipes, II-2716
Condensers, II-2533
Conditioners, I-1735, II-2803
Condominiums, I-1852-1854
Condoms, II-2657
Confectionery products, I-382, 715-727, 806-852, 1393, II-2558, 3471-3472 *See also*: Chocolate; Gum
Connected cars, I-339-342
Connected televisions, I-16, II-2536
Conservation, I-872, 1250, 1777, II-2388
Consoles, video game, I-1570, II-3477, 3484

Construction, I-10, 168, 217, 278, 282, 582, 611, 860-875, 930, 961, 1030, 1304-1306, 1342, 1346, 1352, 1626, 1860, 1904-1905, 2032, II-2282, 2325, 2533, 2754, 2822, 2898, 2938, 3233, 3539, 3603 *See also*: Contracting work
Construction machinery, I-853-858, 1379
Construction materials and supplies, I-565-566, 693, 1368, 1724, II-2533, 3539
Construction sand and gravel, I-859
Consulting services, I-876-879, 1881, 1977, II-2852
Consumer electronics, I-18, 607, 880-900, 902, 1175-1176, II-2788, 3100
Consumer electronics retailers, I-902
Contact lens solutions, I-1265
Contact lenses, I-903-904, II-2523
Containerboard, II-2568, 2605-2606
Continuous casting mold flux powders, I-2098
Contraceptives, II-2657
Contract logistics, II-3430
Contract management, I-1420
Contract manufacturing services, I-278, 280, 949, 1054, 1124, 1553, 1881, 2022, 2032, II-2279, 2282, 2286, 2292, 2299, 2533, 2786
Contracting work, I-906-932, 1363-1364, II-2753, 3536 *See also*: Construction
Convectors, I-1766
Convenience foods, I-1384
Convenience store wholesalers, I-933
Convenience stores, I-477, 485, 934-936, 1437-1443, II-2990, 3127, 3302
Conventions and trade shows, I-937-943, II-2712
Conveyancing services, I-944
Conveyors and drive belts, I-945
Cookies, I-386-387, 1093, 1097, 1390, 1485, 2032, II-2329, 2378, 2933
Cooking equipment, I-232, 949
Cooking ingredients, II-2880
Cooking oil, I-1293, II-3528
Cooking sauces, I-1679, II-2968
Cookware, utensils, cutlery, and flatware, I-946-949, 1029, 1835
Cooper products, II-3589

Copings, II-2533
Copper, I-950-962, 1261, II-2294, 2296
Copra, II-2508-2510
Copying and reproduction services, I-1000, II-2805
Copying services, II-2705
CoQ10, II-3272
Cordage mills, II-2934-2935
Cordials, I-2084, 2090-2091
Cork, I-963-964
Corn, I-965-968, 1462-1463, 1476, 1536, 1540
Corn oil, II-3528
Corn on the cob, I-1483
Corn snacks, II-3114-3115
Corn sweeteners, II-3528
Corneal transplants, II-2259
Cornices, II-2533
Cornish game hens, II-2169
Corrals, II-2533
Corrugated paper and pulp, I-546, II-2560, 2597, 2612
Corsets, I-195
Cosmetics, I-969-989, 1076, II-2575, 2651, 2724, 2803 *See also*: Personal care products
Cosmetics and personal care retailers, I-990
Costume jewelry, I-1997
Costume rental, I-1444-1445
Cottage cheese, I-680
Cotton, I-991-995, 1300, 1319-1320, II-2413
Cotton pads, II-2271
Cottonseed, I-1300, II-2508-2514
Cough remedies, I-1141
Countertops, I-996-998, 1030
Country music, II-2391, 2403, 2408
Court reporting and stenotype, I-999-1001
Courts, I-1001
Covered hoppers, II-2837
COVID-19, I-283, II-3459-3460
CPAP devices, II-3097
CPUs, II-3009, 3023
Crackers, I-1002-1012
Craft and fabric stores, I-1806, 1809, 1811, 1813
Crafts, I-477, 1780
Cranberries, I-1501, 1519, II-3265
Cranes, I-856, 1013-1016
Crates, II-2578
Crawler dozers, I-853

Crayons, I-273
Cream, I-1031, 1382, II-2309
Cream cheese, I-668, 677, 1031
Cream cheese spreads, I-1031
Creatine, II-3269
Credit cards, II-2633, 2639
Credit markets, II-2344
Credit reporting agencies, I-1017-1018
Credit unions, I-1019-1020, 2100, 2102, 2105-2106, II-2352
Crematoriums, I-1040
Crew and cargo transportation, II-2966
Cribs, I-1553
Cricket, II-3217
CRISPR, I-1595
Cristiano Ronaldo, I-1970
Crohn's disease, I-1119-1121
Croissants, I-547, 552, 558
Crop insurance, I-1947
Crop protection, I-692
Cross utility vehicles, II-3349
Crossbody bags, I-2122
Crossovers, I-348
Crossties, II-3576
Croutons, I-1021
Crowdfunding, I-1022
Crowns, I-1054
Crude vegetable material, I-1538-1539
Cruise lines, I-1023-1025, II-3512
Crushed and broken stone, I-1026-1027, 1708
Crustaceans, I-1332, II-2988
Cryptocurrencies, I-1028
Cucumbers, I-1531
Culinary products, I-1029
Cultural institutions, I-1777, II-2388
Cultured meat, II-2170, 2172
Cumene, II-2739
Cups (packaging), II-2563
Curbs, I-278
Currants, I-1528
Curtain walls, II-2533, 3539
Curtains, I-1794-1795
Customer relationship management, II-3166
Cut cultivated greens, I-1377
Cut flowers, I-1377
Cutlery, I-946-949, 1835, II-3388
Cutting accessories, II-3527
Cyber security, I-1045, 1910-1911

Cyclic crude, intermediate, and gum and wood chemicals, I-683-684
Cyclic intermediates, I-684
Cyprinids nei, I-1330
Dairy industry, I-1031-1034, 1390, 1393, 1397, II-3255
Dana Loesch, II-2827
Dance companies, I-1035
Dance music, II-2392, 2403
Dandruff treatments, I-1735
Danishes, I-393, 397
Data centers, I-1037, 1896-1898, II-3036
Data plotting, printing, conversion, and migration services, I-1881
Data processing and hosting, I-1036
Data security, II-2999, 3167
Databases, I-1083, 1085
Dates, I-1517
Dating apps, I-253-254
Dav Pilkey, I-522
Dave Ramsey, II-2827
DC disconnects, II-3288
Dead & Company, I-802
Deadbolts, II-2998
Death care industry, I-1038-1040
Debit cards, II-2633, 2638-2639
Debt recovery and collection services, I-1000, 1041, II-2805
Decking, I-1042-1044, 2125
Dedicated contract carriers, II-3431
Deep subprime loans, I-2103, 2107
Defense, I-1045-1053, 1626, II-2295, 2788
Defibrillators, II-2238
Degreasers, I-739
Dehydrated food, I-1099, II-2778
Dehydropiandrosterone (DHEA), II-3273
Deli food, I-1393, II-2778
Delia Owen, I-522
Demand response systems, II-2155
Demolition work, I-910-911
Denim, I-196, 211
Dental laboratories, I-1054-1055
Dental supplies, I-1054, II-2257, 2295, 2527, 2594
Dentists, I-1756
Dentures, I-1054
Deodorants, I-44, 46-48, II-2655-2656
Deodorizers, I-736

Department stores, I-1056, 1367, 1798-1799, 1802, 1806-1820, II-2990, 2994
Depilatories, II-3094
Deposit boxes, I-1553, II-2533
Depositions, I-1001
Dermatologicals, I-1137
Dermatology, I-599
Design industry, I-1057, 1881
Designer toys, II-3394
Designers, I-1367, 1562-1563
Desks, I-1548, II-2807
Desktop advertising, I-36-37
Desktop as a service (DaaS), II-3187
Desserts, I-547, 1456, II-2330
Desulfurization processes, II-2141
Detergents, I-27, 682, 1058-1063
Developmental disabilities, II-2877
Dewatering pumps, II-2824
DHA products, II-3272
DHEA (dehydropiandrosterone), II-3273
Diabetes treatments, I-1128, 1137
Diagnostic imaging centers, I-1065
Diagnostics, I-1066-1071
Dialysis treatments, I-1745
Diamond cutting centers, I-1073
Diamonds, I-1072-1075
DiAngelo, Robin, I-522
Diapers, I-369, II-2946, 2951-2954
Diaries and time schedulers, I-1675
Diarrhea remedies, I-1151
Dies, II-2286, 2299
Diesel engines, I-1243
Diesel fuel, I-355, 358, 569, 2120, II-3440, 3468
Diet and weight loss centers, I-1076
Differential thermal analyzers, I-1077
Digestive health, I-1141, 1393, II-3263, 3268
Digital banking, I-402-403
Digital cameras, I-590, 595
Digital coursework/textbooks, II-2810
Digital printing, I-1000, 1083, 1675, II-2282, 2805
Digital wallets, I-1184
Dimension stone, I-1030
Dining rooms, I-1542, 1544, 1561, 1564, 1797
Dinner sausage, I-1382, II-2204
Dinner theaters, II-3333
Dinners, shelf-stable, I-1383

Dinnerware, I-1816, 1836
Diorite, I-1030
Dips, I-1078-1079, II-2967-2968
Direct hire, II-3232
Direct mail, I-15, 22, II-2794, 3487
Direct selling, I-1080-1082
Direct-to-consumer markets, I-1564, 1798-1799, 1806-1809, 1811-1815, 1817-1820, II-2994
Direct-to-own video, II-2555
Directories and mailing lists, I-15, 35, 1083-1085
Discount stores, I-1367, 1562-1564, 1798-1799, 1802, 1806-1820, II-2994
Discretes, II-3026
Dishcloths, I-1798
Dishwashers, I-222, 228, 232, 246
Dishwashing detergents, I-734, 737, 1063
Disinfectants, I-44, 736
Display cases, I-1763
Display drivers, I-1955
Displays, I-1086-1089, 1553, 1886, II-2282, 2714, 3076
Disposable cameras, I-596
Disposable food containers, I-545
Disposable training pants, II-2952
Distance conferencing services, I-1000, II-2805
Distributed peristaltic pumps, II-2821
DMAE, II-3266
Do-it-yourself industry, II-2582
Doctors, I-1755-1756, 1758, 1760
Document finishing services, I-1000, II-2805
Document management, I-1090
Document processing and editing services, I-1000, II-2805
Documentaries, II-2354, 2357, 3322
Dog apparel, II-2685
Dog food, II-2663, 2665-2668, 2671-2672, 2675-2676, 2678-2681, 2683
Dog treats, II-2668, 2671
Dogs, II-2693, 2695-2697
Dollar stores, I-1091
Dollies, II-2578
Dolls, II-3399, 3401
Dolomite, I-2079
Domes, II-2533
Donald J. Trump, I-1970
Door frames, II-3539
Doorbells, II-3102

Doorlocks, I-2110-2111, II-2286, 3539
Doors, I-1030, II-2533, 3536, 3539-3540, 3542
Dormitories, I-1548, 1855-1856, II-2932-2933
Double-heater draw-texturing spindles, II-3327
Dough, I-1092-1097
Doughnut shops, II-2886
Doughnuts, I-388, 399
Downspouts, I-1720
Dozers, I-856
Drafting services, I-1098
Draglines, I-856
Dragon* Con, I-938
Drain cleaners, I-736
Drains, II-2719, 2730
DRAMs, II-3019
Dredging, I-912
Dresses, I-212, 216
Dressings, I-1393, II-3225
Dried food, I-1099-1100, II-2193-2194, 2198, 2329, 2570, 3116
Drinkware, II-2807
Drive belts, I-945
Drive-in theaters, II-2377-2378
Driveways, I-860
Driving simulators, I-1101
Drones, II-3454-3455
Drug stores and pharmacies, I-1102-1116, II-2689-2690
Drugs, I-23, 1117-1140, II-2577
Drugs, over-the-counter, I-1141-1158
Drums, II-2578
Dry-cleaning machines, I-2032
Dry-cleaning services, I-1160, 1891, 2031-2032, II-2933
Dry ice pellet machinery, I-1159
Dryers, I-222, 227, 246
Drying machines, I-1891, 2032
Ducks, II-3497
Duct tape, II-3293
Dumplings, I-1095
Dunnage and cargo protection, II-2578
Dust control, I-1891, 2032, II-3329
Dusters, I-561
Duty-free industry, I-100, II-3419
Duvet covers, I-1817
DVD players, I-887
DVDs, I-1161-1163, 1248-1249
Dynamic glass, I-1620
E-bikes, I-492-493

E-books, I-530
E-cigarettes, I-1164-1167
E-commerce, I-193, 215, 218, 256, 369, 519, 544, 1168-1186, 1367, 1560, 1677, 1780, 1805, 2002, II-2419, 2557, 2560, 2566, 2571, 2619, 2688-2690, 3160, 3209, 3214, 3482, 3487
E-learning, I-1187
E-mail, II-3161
E-sports, I-1188, 1826
E85, I-104, 106-117, 119-120, 122-125, 127, 129-130, 132-140, 142-146, 148-153
Eagles, I-802
Ear drops, I-1149
Earbuds, I-285, 287-291, II-3517
Earphones, I-285
Earth moving equipment, I-1771-1772
Earth observation, II-2961
Earthing lightning protection, I-1189
Earthquakes, I-1932
Echinacea, II-3267
Economic experts, I-1260
Edible oils, I-1294, II-2768
Edible tallow, I-1299
Education, I-664, 873, 1418, 1548, 1629, 1966, II-2423, 3175, 3232, 3400
Egg cartons, II-2561
Egg rolls and wonton wrappers, I-1190
Egg substitutes, I-1191, 1392, II-2802
Eggnog, II-2311
Eggs, I-1031, 1192-1202, 1382, 1385, 1392, 1679, II-3497
Elderberry, II-3264, 3267
Electric charging stations, I-104-117, 119-125, 127, 129-153
Electric vehicles, I-154, 307, 325-327, 329-336, 343, 347-349, 354, 358-359, 362, 368, 569, II-3440, 3468
Electrical tape, II-3293
Electrical work, I-913
Electricity, I-607, 906, 914, 1212-1213, 1215, 1231, 2022, II-2482, 2783, 3236, 3326, 3465
Electrochemical instruments, I-2022
Electrodes, II-3527
Electronic components, II-2286, 2787, 2789

Electronic control systems, I-906, 914
Electronic health records, II-3190
Electronic liquidity provider systematic internalisers, I-1979
Electronic shelf labels, I-1203
Electronic special gases, I-1886
Electronics, I-168, 961, 1204, 1626, 1636, II-2286, 2295, 2575, 2594, 2749, 2786-2787, 2789, 2922, 2927, 3233, 3539
Electronics and appliance retailers, I-218, 901, II-3482
Electroplating, I-1205, II-2282, 2286, 2292
Electrotherapy devices, II-2271
Elevators and escalators, I-1206-1209, II-3288
Ellen DeGeneres, I-1970
Elton John, I-802
Emergency services, I-174, 1210-1211
Emmerson Family, I-2027
Endoscopy, II-2241
Energy, I-1212-1235, 1260, 1626, II-2294, 2423, 2940, 3218
Energy drinks, I-486, 489, 1236-1239
Energy shots, I-1240
Energy Star programs, II-3537
Energy support supplements, II-3263, 3269
Engineered stone, I-996, 998
Engineered wood, I-1241
Engineering, II-2786, 3228, 3231-3232
Engines, I-78, 368, 1242-1244
English-language training, I-1245, 1966
English muffins, I-383, 549, 559, II-3203
Engraving services, II-2282, 2286, 2292, 2299, 2533, 3527
Enterprise software, I-1896, 1898
Entertainment, I-18, 50, 251, 915, 1246-1249, 1777, 2030, 2060, 2062, II-2388, 2933, 3105
Entrées, I-1486-1488, 1490-1491, II-2564
Entry doors, II-3538
Environment and animal organizations, I-664
Environmental controls, I-2022

Environmental services, I-503, 876, 1250-1253, II-2868
Epoxy, I-11
EPS foam, II-2561
Equities trading, I-1257
Escalators and moving walks, I-1206-1207
Escape rooms, I-1254
Espresso machines, I-241
Estates, I-2062
Ethanol, I-498-500, II-3528
Ethereum, I-1028
Ethernet switches, II-2424
Ethnic wear, I-211
Ethyl glucuronide, I-1583
Ethylene polymers, II-2740-2741
Eucalyptus, II-3590
European perch, I-1330
Evaporated milk, II-2310
Events and exhibitions, I-1255-1256, II-2807
eVTOLs, II-3453
Excavation work, I-916
Excavators, I-857
Exchange-traded funds, I-1980
Exchanges, I-1257-1258
Executive search firms, I-1259
Exercise equipment, II-3210
Exhaust systems, I-314, II-2299, 2594, 2749
Exhibitions, I-940, 942
Expanded polystyrene, I-1908
Expert witness consulting services, I-1260
Explosion-proof control stations, I-1261
Explosives, I-1262-1264
Express delivery services, II-3066-3069
Extended reality, I-1743
External OEM storage systems, I-781
Extremities (orthopedics), II-2242
Extruded polystyrene, I-1908
Extruded snacks, II-3118, 3126
Eye care, I-903-904, 1265, II-2268, 3263, 3270
Eye makeup, I-969, 977, 979-980
Eyewear, II-2524-2525
Fabric mills, I-1266-1270, 1780
Fabric softeners, I-27, 734
Fabric treatments, I-734
Fabricated metal products, I-1271, II-2282, 2286, 2292, 2299, 2533

Face makeup, I-969, 977, 981
Face masks, I-1076, II-2260, 3089
Facial cleansers, II-3089, 3091, 3094
Facial moisturizers, II-3092, 3094
Facial recognition, I-1272
Facial tissue, II-2941, 2945-2946
Factory (discrete) automation, I-323
Fading/bleach products, II-3094
Fairs, I-1273
Family clothing retailers, I-213
Family dining chains, II-2887
Family planning centers, I-1274
Fans and blowers, I-234, 1275-1276
Fantasy sports, II-3217
Farm and garden machinery wholesalers, I-1277
Farm machinery, I-1278-1287, 1368, II-2533
Farms, I-1288-1292, 1884, II-3498
Fascia, II-2533
Fast-casual chains, II-2888
Fast fashion, I-214, II-2994
Fast-food industry, II-2878-2879, 2881, 2885, 2889, 2894, 2896
Fasteners, II-2292, 3539
Fats and oils, I-1293-1301, II-2768, 3528
Faucets, II-2534, 2754
Feedlots, I-624-625
Feldspar, I-1302
Felts, I-280
Feminine hygiene products, II-2943, 2955-2956
Feminine pain relievers, I-1152
Fencing, I-1303-1306, 2125, II-2533, 3539
Fennel, II-3268
Ferroalloys, I-1261
Fertilizers, I-1278, 1307-1316, 1368, 2038
Fiber optics, I-583-584
Fiberglass, I-1907, II-3538, 3541
Fibers and filaments, I-1317-1322, II-2738, 3268
Fifth wheel trailers, II-3404
Fighter attack aircraft, I-68
Figs, I-1520
Filaments, I-1317
File cabinets, I-1555
File sharing, II-3162
Filters, transmission, I-302

Financial services, I-18, 22, 297, 877, 1041, 1323, 2100, 2102, 2106, 2109, II-2772, 3218, 3232
Financial statements, I-4
Fine-dining chains, II-2890
Fine pixel pitch LED Displays, I-1087
Finfish, I-1333, II-2988
Fire and security systems, I-906, 914, 917
Fire escapes, II-2533
Firearms, II-2295
Firelogs, I-1324
First aid products, I-174, 1150, II-2271
Fish and seafood, I-1393, 1483, II-2695-2696, 2983, 2985-2986, 2988, 2990-2991
Fish and seafood wholesalers, I-1325
Fish (aquarium), II-2691
Fish farming, I-1326-1328
Fish meal, II-2669
Fish oil concentrates, II-3265, 3270, 3272
Fish vaccines, II-3461
Fishing, I-217, 1330-1335, 1863, II-3207, 3210
Fixtures, II-2282, 2286, 2299, 2534
Flatbed carriers, II-3422
Flatware, I-946, 949, 1029, 1836
Flatwork and full dry linens supply, I-1891, 2032
Flavored malt beverages, I-477, 1336
Flavoring syrups and similar products, I-695, 1337, II-3203
Flax, I-1320
Flaxseed, II-3272
Flaxseed oil, II-3272
Fleece, I-184
Flexible click luxury vinyl tile, I-1349-1350
Flexible flat cable, I-585
Flight data recorders, I-81
Flight simulators, I-1338-1339
Floodlights, I-2073
Floods, I-1938, 1948
Floor care equipment, II-2920, 2928
Floor covering stores, I-1363, 1367
Flooring, I-1030, 1340-1363, 2126, II-2533, 3577 *See also*: Individual categories
Flooring retailers, I-1364-1367
Florida State Fair, I-1273

Florida Strawberry Festival, I-1273
Florist and nursery supply wholesalers, I-1368
Florists, I-1368-1370
Flour, I-1371-1374
Flowers and other plants, I-1368, 1375-1378
Flu treatments, II-3267
Flu vaccines, II-3462
Fluid power, I-1379-1380
Flumes, I-1553
Fluorocarbon gases, I-1887
Fluorspar, I-1381
Foamed plastics, I-1907, II-2734
Folding camping trailers, II-2863
Folding cartons, I-546
Folding trays, I-1553
Food, I-43-44, 48, 375, 503, 544, 610, 1175-1176, 1380, 1382-1396, 1399-1400, 1628, 2021, 2062, II-2281, 2314, 2569, 2575, 2579, 2724, 2922, 2927, 3043, 3292, 3465, 3471-3472, 3528
Food delivery, I-1402-1415, II-2880
Food pantries, I-1211
Food storage bags, I-1401
Food trucks, II-2328-2330
Food waste appliances, I-245
Foodservice, I-933, 1416-1424, II-2880
Football, II-3216
Footwear, I-192, 205, 1425-1430, 1432, 1434, 1444, 2047, II-3206, 3213, 3220
Footwear, athletic, I-1425, 1429-1431
Footwear retailers, I-1431-1435
Footwear wholesalers, I-1436
Forecourt retailers, I-1437-1443
Forestry equipment, I-854
Forgings, II-2286, 2299
Forklifts, I-1771-1772, 1774
Formal wear and costume rental, I-1444-1445
Fort Worth Stock Show & Rodeo, I-1273
Forwarders (forestry), I-854
Forwarding services, II-3055
Foundation work, I-916, 981
Foundations, I-664, 666-667
Foundries, I-693, 1446-1448, II-2533, 2576, 2679, 2750, 2989, 2994, 3039
Fragrance dispensers, I-53

Fragrances, I-971, 1076, 1449-1452, II-2927
Franchising, I-1453-1454
Frankfurters, I-1483, II-2204
Fraud analysis, I-275
Freezer bags, I-1401
Freezer liner paper, II-2614
Freezers, I-222, 246, 1765
Freight cars, I-2042
Freight elevators, I-1206
Freight transportation, II-3044, 3046, 3055, 3057, 3070, 3511-3512
Freighters, I-59
French fries, I-1475
Frozen desserts, I-1868, 1871, II-2562-2563, 3472
Frozen dinners, I-1486-1488, II-2564
Frozen drink concentrates, I-1464
Frozen foods, I-378, 390, 553-554, 1455-1493, II-2195, 2229, 2329, 2562-2564, 2570, 2778, 2984-2985
Frozen novelties, I-1872-1873, II-2565
Frozen pizza, I-1492-1493, II-2564
Frozen yogurt, I-1869, II-2565
Fruit and vegetable markets, I-1494
Fruit and vegetable wholesalers, I-1495
Fruit beverages, I-2003, 2005
Fruit chips, II-3116
Fruit concentrates, I-605, 1496
Fruit salad, II-2785
Fruit snacks, I-824-825
Fruits and vegetables, I-605, 1100, 1291, 1385, 1392, 1456, 1465, 1483, 1497-1541, II-2281, 2802
Fuel cells, I-368, 1865
Fume hoods, I-2024
Functional clothing, I-205
Funeral homes, I-618, 1039-1040
Furnaces, I-1766, 1768-1769, II-3527
Furniture, I-1175-1176, 1542-1557, 1560-1565, 2126, II-2533, 3577-3578
Furniture, institutional, I-1546-1547, 1557
Furniture, metal, I-1554
Furniture, office, I-1555
Furniture, outdoor, I-1544, 1549
Furniture, upholstered, I-1557
Furniture rental, II-2870
Furniture repair services, I-1001, 1039, 1558-1559

Furniture retailers, I-1560-1565, 1802, 1806, 1809, 1811-1813, 1819
Furniture waxes and polishes, I-46, 735
Furs, I-2048
Fuses, I-1566
Gallagher, Mike, II-2827
Gallium, I-1567
Gallium arsenide open epiwafers, II-3012
Gambling, I-1568-1569, 1571-1573, 1575-1577, 1579-1582, 1584-1585
Gaming, I-1568-1585, II-2536, 3218
Garage door openers, II-3539
Garage doors, I-1586
Garage storage systems, I-1587
Garbage bags, I-1401
Garbage cans, I-1588
Gardening, I-1368, 1973, II-2535
Garlic, II-3272
Garlic bread, I-553
Garment alteration services, I-217, 1891, 2032
Garments supply, I-1891, 2032
Garnets, I-1589
Gas cookers, I-247
Gas cutting machines, II-3527
Gas cylinders, II-2291
Gas detectors, I-2022, II-2996
Gas stations, I-1437-1443, 1593
Gaskets, packing, and sealing devices, I-1590-1592
Gasoline, II-2468
Gastrointestinal products, I-1151
Gates, II-2533, 3539
Gauze, II-2271
Gearboxes, I-1594
Gelatin, II-2812
Gene editing, I-1595
General merchandise, I-1596-1615
Generation X, II-2368
Generators, I-731, 1616
Geogrids, I-1617
Geomembranes, I-1617
Geonets, I-1617
George Noory, II-2827
Geosynthetics, I-1617
Geotextiles, I-1617
Geothermal power, I-1212, 1216, 1227-1228, 1230
Ghost kitchens, II-2880
Giblets, II-2169, 2227
Gift boxes, I-715, 726-727
Gift cards, I-1618

Gift stores, I-1811, 1813
Gifts, I-174, 506, 1211, 1777, 2056, II-2388
Gin, I-2084
Ginger, II-3268
Ginkgo biloba, II-3266
Ginseng, II-3266
Girdles, I-195
Glass, I-47, 693, 1619-1631, 1708, 2098, II-2749, 2841, 3293, 3539
Glass cleaners, I-735-736
Glass containers, I-1623, 1628
Glass fibers, I-1624
Glass wool, I-1908
Glassware, I-949, 1632-1634, 1816, 1836
Glazing work, I-918
Glenn Beck, II-2827
Glennon Doyle, I-522
Global distribution systems, I-1635
Global navigation satellite systems, II-3034
Gloves, I-185, II-2273
Gloves, disposable, II-2261, 2270
Glucomannan, II-3274
Glue, I-13-14
Glue down luxury vinyl tile, I-1349-1350
Gneiss, I-1030
Gnocchi, I-1466
Go-Karts, II-3396
Goats, II-3041
Gold, I-1636-1642, 1998
Golf, I-1666, II-3210
Golf courses, I-1643-1644, 2033-2036, II-3003
Gondolas, II-2837
Gospel music, II-2403
Government, I-206, 865, 1041, 1629, 1777, 1897, 2033, 2036, II-2388, 2423, 2788, 2963, 3003, 3025, 3325
Government contracting, I-1645-1665
GPS, I-1666-1668
Graham crackers, I-1009-1010
Grains, I-1669-1670, II-3045
Granite, I-996, 1030, 1671
Granola bars, I-826-827, 847
Grants, I-174, 506, 1211, 1777, 2056, II-2388
Grapefruit, I-1521-1522
Grapes, I-1398, 1504
Graphic design services, I-1881

Graphite, I-1672-1673
Grass, I-2038
Grated cheese, I-1392
Gravel, I-278, 1030, 1368, II-3247-3248
Gravies, II-2968
Greasy wool, I-1320
Green industry, I-907, 1251, II-3423
Green tea, II-3274
Greenhouses, I-1674
Greeting cards, I-1675-1677
Grills, I-1368, II-2533
Grocery retailers, I-1678-1706, II-2689-2690, 3128, 3482, 3487
Grocery wholesalers, I-1707
Ground beef, II-2167
Ground handling equipment, I-99
Ground or treated mineral and earth, I-1708-1709
Grout removal, II-3386
Growing media, I-2034, 2038
Guarding industry, II-3000
Guardrails, I-278
Guitar straps, II-2413
Guitars, II-2412, 2414
Gum, I-1710-1713
Guns and ammunition, I-1714-1719
Gutters and downspouts, I-1720
Gymnasium equipment, II-3210
Gyms, I-1721-1723
Gypsum, I-1724-1729, II-3493
Hair and nail care salons, I-1730
Hair care, I-44, 46-48, 949, 1731-1736, II-3263, 3271
Hair removal services, I-1076, II-3250
Hair restoration, I-1737
Half and half, I-1392, II-2317
Halogen, I-2067-2068
Ham, II-2186, 2204, 2218, 2802
Hamburger rolls, I-555
Hamburgers, II-2892
Hand care, II-2268, 3089, 3093, 3144, 3147
Hand tools, II-3383
Handbags, I-1738, 2122-2123, 2133
Handguns, I-1716
Handsaws, II-3388
Hanging storage, I-1791
Hannity, Sean, II-2827
Hard candies, I-813, 828-829
Hard cider, I-1739
Hardware, I-1740-1741, 2062, II-2286, 2575, 3539

Hardwood, I-1344, 1357-1358, 2126, II-2814-2815, 3577, 3585
Hashbrowns, I-1475
Hazardous waste, I-1057, 1742
Hazelnuts, II-2450
HDMI cables, I-587
Head lamps, I-2077
Head-mounted displays, II-3517
Head-up displays, II-2304
Headlights, I-2067, 2070
Headphones, I-284-285
Headsets, I-1743
Health care, I-18, 39, 506, 654, 664, 873, 877, 1041, 1175-1176, 1418, 1629, 1744-1761, 2021, 2109, II-2423, 2807, 2856, 3043, 3229, 3231-3232, 3275
Health food, I-1387, II-3471-3472
Health food stores, I-1762
Hearing aids, II-2262
Heart health supplements, II-3263, 3272
Heat exchangers, II-2533
Heat/ice packs, II-2271
Heat pumps, I-1769
Heat treating of metal, II-2282, 2292
Heating and cooling, I-225, 233, 1763-1769
Heavy-duty motor oil, I-2117
Heavy equipment rental, I-1770-1776
Helicopters, I-60, 62, 1047, 1053, 1338
Helium, I-1890
Helmets, I-185
Hemp, I-1320
Henequen, I-1320
Herbalists, II-2418
Herbs and spices, I-1398, II-2967, 2971, 3267
Herring, II-2986
Hewitt, Hugh, II-2827
HID (high intensity discharge), I-2067-2068
Hides, I-2048
High early strength concrete, I-803
High-pressure laminates, I-2026
High schools, I-260
High-speed rail, II-2832
Higher education, I-526, 1187, II-2515, 2810
Highways, I-278, 860, 872, 906
Hip implants, II-2240, 2242
Historical sites, I-1777-1778, II-2388

Hobbies, I-1176, 1779-1780, II-3393
Hogs and pigs, I-1781-1785, 1884
Hoists, I-1776, 1786-1787
Holding companies, I-1788
Hole saws, II-3387
Holidays, II-3069
Hollowware, I-1997
Home accent/gift stores, I-1809, 1811-1813, 1819
Home care, I-43, 49, 734, 737, 1080, 1835, 2021, II-2724, 2803
Home equity, I-2101
Home health care, I-1748, II-2235, 2803
Home improvement centers, I-1367, 1563-1564, 1789-1790, 1806, 1809, 1811-1813, 1819-1820
Home organization products, I-1791
Home repair supply stores, I-2110
Home-sharing industry, I-1792
Home shopping, II-3487
Home specialty retailers, I-218
Home textiles, I-1797, 1803, 1810
Home theaters, I-1556
Home video industry, I-1248
Homefurnishings, I-1175-1176, 1368, 1553, 1793-1800, 1804, II-2533, 2807, 3539
Homefurnishings retailers, I-1801-1803, 1805-1820
Homefurnishings wholesalers, I-1821
Homeopathics, II-3264, 3267, 3270-3271, 3273
Homeowners associations, I-1822
Honey, I-1823-1825
Hoppers, II-2837
Horehound, II-3267
Horizontal directional drilling, II-2482
Horror movies, II-2357
Horses, II-2170, 2696
Horticultural products, I-2071
Hosiery, I-186-187
Hospices, I-1749
Hospitals, I-260, 1747, 1750, II-2257, 3470, 3473
Hot beverages, I-488, II-3471-3472
Hot chocolate, I-488
Hot dog buns, I-555
Hot dogs, II-2222-2223
Hotels, I-866, 1418, 1629, 1826-1833, II-2620, 2844, 3470, 3473
House boats, I-508

Household goods moving, II-3424
Housewares, I-239, 241, 1836
Housewares retailers, I-1834-1836
Housing, I-874-875, 1837-1862, 1965, 1973, II-2850, 2931
Houston Livestock Show & Rodeo, I-1273
Hugh Hewitt, II-2827
Human reproductive and stem cell bank services, I-506
Human resources and benefits, I-877
Humidifiers, I-237
Hummingbird food, II-2684
Hummus, I-1078
Hunting and fishing, I-1863-1864
HVAC equipment, I-930, 1904-1905
Hyaluronic acid, II-3270
Hybrid vehicles, I-154, 332, 348-349, 358-359, 362, 368, 569, II-3440, 3468
Hydraulic power, I-1379
Hydroelectric power, I-1212-1214, 1218, 1227-1228, 1230
Hydrogen, I-106, 108-110, 113, 123-124, 134, 137, 142, 149, 1865
Hyper-casual games, II-2335
Hyperconverged systems, II-3168
Hypermarkets, I-218, II-2903, 2990
iBuyers, I-1965
Ice, I-1866-1867
Ice cream and frozen desserts, I-1031, 1393, 1868-1870-1876, II-2562-2563, 2565, 3471-3472
Ice makers, I-1765
Identity access management, II-2999
iGaming, I-1572-1573
iGen/Generation Z, II-2368
Image sensors, II-3031-3032
Immunoassays, I-1068
Immunoglobulins, I-1877
Immunosuppressants, I-1137
Impressionism, I-268
In-flight entertainment, I-1878
In-store dining chains, II-2893
In-store health care, I-1744
In vitro diagnostics, I-1066-1068
Industrial coatings, I-693
Industrial design services, I-1880-1881
Industrial fasteners, I-1882
Industrial feed, I-693, 1368, 1883-1885

Industrial garments supply, I-1891, 2032
Industrial gases, I-682, 1886-1890
Industrial launderers, I-1891-1892
Industrial machinery, I-168, 472, 778, 961, 1893, 2022, II-2286, 2294, 2299, 2922, 2940, 2977, 3527, 3603
Industrial machinery rental, I-1770
Industrial markets, I-43-44, 47, 49, 861, 909, 1215, 1637-1638, 1770, 1904-1905, 1963, 2021, 2029, 2033-2035, II-2568, 2590, 2788, 2843, 2929, 3025, 3043, 3231-3232, 3357, 3527
Industrial mats, I-1891, 2032
Industrial molds, I-1894-1895
Industrial trucks, II-3348
Industrial wiping cloths, I-1891, 2032
Inedible tallow, I-1299
Inertial measurement units, II-3034
Infant formula, I-373
Infant/toddler/preschool toys, II-3401
Infectious diseases, I-1069
Influenza, II-3462
Information and document transformation services, I-1881
Information technology, I-275, 877, 1896-1898, 2056, II-2714, 3231-3232
Infrastructure, I-1899, II-2963, 2999, 3603
Infrastucture as a service, II-3169
Injection molding, I-611, II-2729, 2746
Ink, I-685, 1900-1903
Innerwear, I-196, 211
Insecticides, I-43-44, 46, 48, 686, 709, 2038
Instant coffee, I-751
Instant tickets, I-1574, 1577
Instructional programs, I-1076, 1777, II-2388
Insulated containers and shippers, II-2566
Insulated gate bipolar transistors, II-3029
Insulation, I-280, 1904-1908
Insulin, I-1131
Insurance, I-22, 1909-1954, 1978, 1986, 2109
Insurance, aircraft, I-1916, 1921

Insurance, allied, I-1922, 1937
Insurance, auto, I-1923-1926, 1929
Insurance, benefits, I-1909
Insurance, boiler, I-1927
Insurance, burglary, I-1928
Insurance, casualty, I-1940, 1950
Insurance, credit, I-1931
Insurance, cyber security, I-1910-1911
Insurance, directors, I-1912
Insurance, earthquake, I-1932
Insurance, farmowners multiple peril, I-1934
Insurance, fidelity, I-1935
Insurance, financial guaranty, I-1936
Insurance, fire, I-1937
Insurance, flood, I-1938, 1948
Insurance, health, I-1919-1920, 1942
Insurance, homeowners, I-1939
Insurance, liability, I-1912, 1949
Insurance, life, I-1942
Insurance, machinery, I-1927
Insurance, marine, I-1916, 1941, 1946
Insurance, medical professional, I-1943
Insurance, mortgage guaranty, I-1944
Insurance, multiple peril, I-1930, 1945
Insurance, office, I-1912
Insurance, pet, I-1918
Insurance, private crop, I-1947
Insurance, property, I-1940, 1950
Insurance, surety, I-1952
Insurance, theft, I-1928
Insurance, third party, I-1917
Insurance, warranty, I-1953
Insurance, workers' compensation, I-1933, 1954
Integrated circuits, I-1886, 1955-1961
Integrated risk management, II-2999
Intercoms, I-889
Interior designers, I-1806, 1809, 1811-1813, 1819, 1881, 1962
Intermediate bulk containers, II-2578
Internet, I-15, 23, 39, 215, 598, 728, 1415, 1562-1563, 1810, 1816, 1964-1975, II-2515, 2525, 2631, 3155-3157, 3184, 3302 *See also*: E-commerce
Internet of things, I-1963, II-2422
Intrinsic health bars, I-839

Investigation services, I-1976-1978, II-2805
Investment banking, I-1979-1986
Iodine, I-1987
IPOs, I-7
Irish whiskey, I-2084
Iron and steel, I-1261, 1988, II-2296, 2533, 3240-3241
Iron ore, I-1989-1993, II-3045
Irrigation pipes, I-1553
Irving Family, I-2027
Islands (furniture), II-2534
Isopropanel, II-2739
Isotropic graphite, I-1994
Jackets, I-212
Jade, I-1998
Jams, I-605
Janitorial services, I-1995
Jaundice meters, I-1070
Jazz, II-2403
Jeans, I-191, 212
Jeff Kinney, I-522
Jellies, I-605
Jerky, II-2198-2199
Jet boats, I-508
Jet fuel, II-2468
Jet transports, I-67
Jets, I-59
Jewelry, I-1368, 1444, 1638, 1996-1999, 2134, II-2594, 2749
Jewelry and watch retailers, I-1997, 2000-2002
Jigs, II-2282, 2286, 2299
Job boards, I-1974
Job stampings, II-2282, 2286, 2292, 2299, 3539
John Malone, I-2027
Jonas Brothers, I-802
Juices, I-486, 489, 605, 1382, 2003-2012, II-2563
Jumpers, I-212
Junior colleges, II-2981
Justin Bieber, I-1970
Jute, I-1320
K-12 education, I-526, 1187, 1422, II-2515, 2900
Kangaroo, II-2170
Kaolin and ball clays, I-2013-2015
Kapok, I-1320
Katy Perry, I-1970
Kegs, I-2016
Kelley, Brad, I-2027
Kenaf, I-1320
Keno, I-1583

Ketchup, II-2967, 2969-2971
Kilns, II-3527
Kinney, Jeff, I-522
Kit-built aircraft, I-64
Kitchens, I-224, 226, 228-229, 949, 997-998, 1544, 1797-1798, 1815, 1835, 2017, II-2534
Kitchenware, I-1029
Kiwi, I-1505
Knee implants, II-2240, 2242
Krill oil, II-3272
Kroenke, Stan, I-2027
KVM Switches, II-2428
L-theanine, II-3266, 3273
Labeling services, I-1000, II-2575, 2805
Labels, I-10, 2018-2021
Laboratory instruments, I-2022-2024
Lace, I-1368
Lactase, II-3268
Ladders, I-2025, II-2533
Lady Gaga, I-1970
Laminates, I-996, 1343, 1345, 1347, 1357, 1359, 2026
Lamp and lighting stores, I-1563, 1811-1812, 1819
Lamps, I-1563, 1811, 2066, 2068, 2077
Land and sea systems, I-1045
Landscape lighting, I-2075
Landscaping establishments, I-2036
Lapidary work, I-1997
Laptops, I-791, 796, 1064, II-2536
Lard, I-1299
Large circular knitting machines, II-3327
Laser equipment, I-2028-2030, II-3527
Latin music, II-2393, 2403
Launch industry, II-2962
Laundries, I-1205, 1267, 1891, 2031-2032, II-2933
Laundry care, I-734, 737
Laundry detergents, I-27, 734, 1058-1062
Laundry equipment, I-47, 224, 227-229, 249-250, 1891, 2032, II-2933
Lavatories, I-1030
Lawn and garden industry, I-1368, 1379, 1401, 2033-2038, II-2535, 2559, 3003
Lawn sprinkler installation, I-931
Laxatives, I-1151, 1153-1154
LCD technology, II-2600-2601

Products, Services, Names, and Issues Index

Lead, I-1446, 2039-2041
Learning management systems, II-3175
Leasing, I-298, 353, 905, 2042-2045, II-2852, 2933
Leather, I-2046-2051, II-2413, 2734
LEDs, I-1087, 1886, 1957, 2052, 2067-2068, 2072-2073
Legal services, I-1977-1978, 2053
Leggings, I-212
Lemonade, I-1483, 2006, 2010
Lenses, I-1265, 2054-2055, II-2523
Less-than-truckload services, II-3425
Lettuce, I-1540
Levin, Mark, II-2827
Libraries and archives, I-1083, 2056-2059
Lice treatments, I-1155
Licensing, I-1083-1084, 1675, 2056, 2060-2062, II-2712
Licorice, I-813, 830-831
LiDAR, II-3034
Life sciences, I-1626, II-3232
Lifeboats, I-509
Lifestyle stores, I-251, 1806, 1809, 1811-1813, 1819
Lift trucks, I-2063-2064
Light bulbs, I-2066, 2078
Light fixtures, I-2073
Light rail, II-2153, 2157, 2163, 2834
Light trucks, I-337-338, 344-346, 348, 352, 364, II-3351, 3354
Lighters, I-2065
Lighting, I-906, 1553, 1563, 1812, 2066-2078, II-2714, 3105, 3539
Limbaugh, Rush, II-2827
Lime, I-2079-2081
Lime/rust removers, I-736
Limeade, I-1483
Limestone, I-278, 1030, 2079, II-3045
Limousine services, I-2082-2083
Linens, I-1794, 1891, 2032, II-3328
Lingerie, I-210
Linoleum, I-1353-1354
Lip care, I-982-983, II-3089
Lip makeup, I-969, 977
Lipid regulators, I-1128
Lipstick, I-984-985
Liquefied natural gas, I-104, 106, 108, 111-113, 115-116, 119-120, 123, 127, 129, 133, 135, 137, 139-140, 142, 144-145, 149, 152
Liqueurs, I-2084, 2090-2091

Liquor, I-101-102, 1628, 2084-2097, II-2329
Listing services, II-2852
Litecoin, I-1028
Lithium, I-2098
Lithium carbonate, II-3148
Livestock, I-1278, II-3511
Livestreaming, I-2099
Living rooms, I-1542, 1544
LNG fleets, II-3051
Loans, I-2100-2107, II-2344, 2346-2347, 2350-2353
Lobbying industry, I-2108-2109
Lockers, I-1555, II-3101
Locks, I-1977, 2110-2111, II-2286, 3539
Locksmiths, I-2112
Lodging industry, I-873, II-2844, 2929
Loesch, Dave, II-2827
Logistics, II-2619, 2772, 2927, 3065, 3430, 3503
Long guns, I-1717
Long-staple wool spindles, II-3327
Loose lay luxury vinyl tile, I-1349-1350
Lotteries, I-1571, 1577
Loudspeakers, I-882
Low-pressure film and foils, I-2026
Low-pressure laminate papers, I-2026
Low-voltage power distribution, I-2113
Lubricants, I-43, 2098, 2114-2120
Luggage and bags, I-1553, 2121-2123
Lumber, I-2124-2129
Lunch kits, II-2230
Lunchmeat, I-1382, II-2202, 2204
Lutein, II-3270
Luxury industry, I-192, 348, 971, 1549, 2130-2135
Luxury vinyl tile, I-1348, 1353-1354
Lyocell, I-1317
Macadamia nuts, II-2451
Macaroni, I-1099
Machine guns, II-3099
Machine shop job work, I-1446, II-2282, 2286, 2292, 2299, 2533, 3527, 3539
Machine tools, I-1379-1380, II-2136-2137
Mackesy, Charlie, I-522

Magazines, I-15, 23, 38, II-2138-2140, 2773, 2796
Magnesium, I-1446, II-2141, 3265, 3268
Mail, II-2772, 2805
Mail order/direct response, II-2419
Mail services, II-2804-2805
Mailbox rentals, I-1000, II-2805
Mailers, II-2560
Mailing lists, I-1083-1084
Mailroom services, I-1000, II-2805
Maintenance and repair services, I-217, 778, 1030, 1891, 2022, 2032, II-2292, 2533, 2705, 2712, 2786, 2977, 3511, 3527
Mall stands, II-2418
Malone, John, I-2027
Malt beverages, II-2329
Management services, I-1977, II-2344, 2621, 2852
Managers, I-50, 1916-1917
Manga, II-2142
Manganese, II-2143
Manhole covers, II-2144
Mannequins, II-2145
Manufactured housing, I-1342, 1346, 1352, 1851, 1857, II-2931
Marble, I-996, 1030, II-2146
Margarine, I-581
Marinated vegetables and fruits, II-2147
Marine facility services, II-3511
Marine machinery, II-3511
Marine salvage services, II-3511
Mark Levin, II-2827
Markers, I-949, 1553, II-3594
Marketing, I-879, II-2419, 2773, 2852, 2874, 3232
Marshmallows, I-832-833
Mary L. Trump, I-522
Mascara, I-979, 987
Masks, II-2260
Masonry work, I-919
Mass spectroscopy instruments, I-2022
Mass transit, II-2149-2164
Massage and bodywork treatments, I-1076, II-3200
Masts, I-1776
Mat timbers, I-2126
Matcha tea, II-3304
Materials handling (incl. conveying), I-1379-1380
Mats, I-1798

Mattresses, I-1543, 1545, 1552-1553, 1561, 1797, 1800-1801, II-3097
Mayonnaise, II-2967, 2971
Meal kits, II-2165
Meal replacements, II-2172, 3277-3279
Mealworms, II-2684
Measuring equipment, I-2022
Meat, I-1299, 1382, 1385, 1393, 1456, II-2166-2207, 2209-2227, 2232, 2562, 2573, 2669 *See also*: Individual categories
Meat alternatives, II-2228-2229
Meat/cheese/cracker/desserts, II-2230
Meat markets, II-2231
Meat wholesalers, II-2232
Mechanical engineering, II-3233
Mechanical pencils, I-949, 1553
Mechanical work, I-920
Media monitoring and analysis services, I-2056
Media rights, I-1188
Medical and safety experts, I-1260
Medical equipment, I-1054, 1380, II-2233-2256
Medical equipment rental, I-1770
Medical equipment wholesalers, II-2257, 2298
Medical imaging, II-3163
Medical markets, I-503, 2029-2030, II-2294-2295, 2569, 2714, 2788, 2923, 3097, 3357
Medical products, II-2258-2273, 2441, 2575
Medicare Advantage program, I-1919-1920
Medicine cabinets, I-1553
Medium-chain triglycerides, II-3274
Megacarrier alliances, II-3060-3063
MegaCon, I-938
Melatonin, II-3264, 3273
Melons, I-1385
Membership services, I-1777, II-2388, 2933
Memory aids, II-3026
Memory foam, II-2413
Mental health, I-599, 1128, 1754, 1757, 1759, 1761
Mental retardation, II-2877
Merchant acquirers, II-2274-2275
Mercury, II-2276
Mergers and acquisitions, I-1983, II-2277

Metal bars, II-3245
Metal buildings, II-2278
Metal cans, II-2279-2281
Metal cleaners, I-735
Metal coatings, II-2282-2283, 2292, 2299, 2533, 3527
Metal coins, I-1997
Metal containers, II-2284-2285
Metal cutting tools, II-2288-2289
Metal framing, II-2290
Metal fuel tanks, II-2291
Metal heat treating, II-2292-2293
Metal injection molding, II-2295
Metal machining centers, I-1446
Metal powders, II-2294-2296
Metal scrap, I-1446, II-2279, 2282, 2292, 2299, 2533
Metal service centers, II-2297
Metal stampings, II-2282, 2286-2287, 2292, 2298-2300, 3539
Metal structural products, II-2282, 2533
Metals, I-1303, 1379-1380, II-2299, 2301, 2841, 2922, 3148, 3233, 3465, 3538, 3542
Meters, II-2302
Methylsulfonylmethane, II-3271
Mexican food, I-1383, 1469, II-2894
Meyer, Stephanie, I-522
Mica, II-2303
Michael Savage, II-2827
Micro markets, II-3470
Microcontroller units, I-1958
Microdisplays, II-2304
Microgrids, II-2305
Microprocessors, II-3011
Microscopes, II-2250
Microswitches, II-2306
Mike Gallagher, II-2827
Military bases, II-3470, 3473
Military exchanges, II-2307
Military markets, I-1045-1053, 1339, 1667-1668, II-2788, 2898, 3325, 3357
Military transports, I-69
Milk, I-1031-1032, 1382, 1385, II-2308-2316
Milk alternatives, II-2317-2322
Milk formula, I-1032
Millennials, II-2368
Millwork, I-1030, 2126, II-3539, 3577
Mineral wool, I-1907-1908, II-2323

Mining, I-1260, 1368, 1379, II-2324-2325, 2533, 3465
Mints, I-813, 841-842
Missiles, II-2326-2327
Mississippi State Fair, I-1273
MLCC capacitors, I-609
Mobile devices, II-3023
Mobile fleets, I-1013
Mobile food services, II-2328-2330
Mobile gaming, I-1570, 1576, II-2331-2340, 3484
Mobile marketing, I-29
Mobile payments, I-1184, 1186, II-2341
Mobile storage, II-3249
Model design services, I-1881
Model fabrication services, I-1881
Models, I-2062
Modems, II-3308-3309
Modern Art, I-270
Modern oral nicotine products, II-3362-3363, 3373
Modular grippers, II-2342
Moist smokeless, II-3373
Moist tobacco, II-3364-3365
Molasses, II-3253, 3255, 3528
Molasses beet sugar pulp, II-3253
Moldings, I-2125, II-2533, 3539
Molecular imaging, II-2241
Mollusks, II-2988
Molybdenum, II-2296, 2343
Monetary authorities, II-2344-2345
Money management, I-1981
Monitors, I-785, II-2600
Monorail, II-2158
Monumental stone, I-1030
Mopeds, II-2367
Mops, I-561, 734
Morning shows, II-3316
Mortgages, I-1944, 2101, II-2346-2353
Motels, II-2844
Motion pictures, I-1248-1249, 1777, II-2354-2365, 2378, 2388, 2710
Motion recliners, I-1550
Motion sofas, I-1561
Motion swing rockers, I-370
Motor disconnects, II-3288
Motor oil, I-2114-2116
Motor vehicles, I-472, 2062, II-2299-2300, 2366, 3233, 3401, 3426 *See also*: Autos and trucks
Motorbikes, II-2367

Motorcycles, I-185, 472, II-2367-2375, 3353
Motorhomes, II-2863
Mousse, I-1733, II-2812
Mouthwash, II-2529
Movie rental industry, I-1161, 1247-1249, 1770, II-2555
Movie theaters, I-23, 1248-1249, II-2376-2385
Moving companies, II-3424
Moving stairways, I-1207
Mozart, I-1246
Mozzarella, I-668
MRIs, II-2241
MRO industry, I-83, II-2386
Muffins, I-391
Mulch, I-2035, 2038
Multifamily housing, I-868, 875, 1629, 1852-1854, II-2845, 2931
Multiplayer online battle arena games, II-2333
Multiple sclerosis, I-1137
Multivitamins, II-3264-3266, 3269-3271, 3489-3490
Muscle support devices, II-2271-2272
Museums, I-1777, II-2387-2388
Mushrooms, II-2389
Music, I-251, 2062, II-2390-2408
Music festivals, II-2404
Music streaming, II-2409-2410
Musical instruments and product retailers, II-2411
Musical instruments and supplies, II-2412-2417
Musicals, II-2404, 3328-3329
Mustard, II-2967
Mutual funds, I-1982
Nail care, I-969, 973, 988, 1730, II-3271
Nails, II-2533
NAND flash, II-3013, 3020
Napkin rings, I-1799
Napkins, I-1799, II-2941, 2946
Nasal strips, I-1156-1157
National Endowment for the Arts, I-1777, II-2388
Nationally recognized statistical rating organizations, I-1017
Natural cheese, I-1031, 1382, 1392, II-3497
Natural fibers, I-1320

Natural gas, I-1212-1213, 1217, 1227-1228, 1379-1380, II-2462-2465, 2469-2474, 2482, 2492-2495
Natural gas liquids, I-1228, II-2485-2488
Natural products retailers, II-2418-2419
Natural stone, I-996
Navigational equipment, I-2022, II-2420, 2961, 2966, 3511
Neckwear, I-198
Nectarines, I-1525-1526
Nectars, I-605
Nervous system disorders, I-1128
Networking equipment, II-2421-2428, 2999, 3308-3309
Neufchâtel cheese, I-668
Neurological imaging, II-3163
New energy vehicles, I-349
News, I-259, II-3317
Newspapers, I-15, 23, 35, 1083, II-2429-2431
Nickel, I-1446, II-2296, 2432-2437
Nicotine pouches, II-3372
Nightclubs, II-2438
Nightwear, I-212
Nitrogen, I-1887
Nonferrous metals, I-1446
Nonprofits, I-22, 728
Nonwovens, II-2439-2442
Noodles, I-1099, 1393, II-2626-2627
Noory, George, II-2827
NOR Flash, I-1959
Northern pike, I-1330
Novelty candy, I-715, 813, 835-837
Nuclear power, I-1212, 1214, 1217, 1227-1228
Nuclear waste disposal, II-2443-2446
Nurseries, I-728, 1368, 2037
Nursing/feeding accessories, I-370, 374
Nursing homes, II-3470
Nut butters, I-1383
Nutritional supplements, I-838-839, 1386, II-3284-3285
Nuts, II-2447-2456, 3133-3135, 3539
Nuts (hardware), I-515
Nylon, I-1317, 1340, II-2413
Nylon string trimmer line, II-2457
Nylons, I-208
Oats, II-2458-2459
Obama, Barack, I-522

Occasional furniture, I-1561
Occupational therapists, I-1758
Ocean freight, II-3059
Off-price retailers, I-1806, 1809, 1811-1813, 1819, II-2994
Offal, II-2167, 2217
Office-clerical and administrative services, II-3231-3232
Office coffee services, I-1423
Office equipment, I-1175-1176, 1555, II-2460-2461, 2533
Office products, I-1544
Offices, I-260, 873, 1629, 2021, II-2620, 2807, 2846, 2929, 3470, 3473
Oil and gas, I-685, 1217, 1228, II-2294, 2462-2480, 2491, 2720, 2822, 3292, 3528
Oil and gas drilling, II-2481-2484, 2493
Oil and gas extraction, II-3465
Oil and gas liquids, II-2485-2490
Oil and gas machinery, I-1379-1380
Oil and gas refining, II-2466
Oil and gas rigs, II-2484
Oil and gas services, II-2493
Oil and gas storage, II-2494-2495
Oil and gas transmission, II-2482, 3465
Oil change shops, I-317, 2120
Oil country goods, II-3245
Oil pumps, automotive, I-299
Oilseeds, II-2496-2514
Olive oil, II-2511-2514
Olives, II-2649
Omega supplements, II-3280
Oncology, I-1123, 1137
One-hour photofinishing, II-2705-2706
Onion rings, I-1471
Onions, I-1476, 1483, 1530-1531, 1540
Online education, I-257, 1966, II-2515
Online gaming, I-1578-1580
Online grocers, II-2516-2520
Online travel, II-2521-2522, 3418
Online video, I-30
Open-end rotors, II-3327
Open-loop cards, II-2637
Operas, I-1246
Operating systems, II-3176-3179, 3191

Optical coherence tomagraphy, II-2241
Optical goods, II-2523
Optical goods retailers, II-2524-2525
Optical transceivers, II-2526
Optoelectronics, I-654, 1626
Oral care, II-2527-2531
Orange juice, I-1483, 2008-2009, 2011-2012
Oranges, I-1506, 1523-1524
Ordnance, II-3098-3099
Organ banks, I-505-506
Organic food, I-392, 490, 840, 1292, 1397-1398, 1876, II-2211, 3195, 3225
Oriented strand board, I-1344, II-3581-3582
Ornamental work, II-2532-2533, 3539
Orthobiologics, II-2242
Orthodontic appliances, I-1054
Orthopedics, II-2236, 2240, 2243-2244, 2247-2248
Orthotics, I-1751
Oscillating tools, II-3386
Outboard engines, I-511
Outdoor industry, I-205, 1549, 1561, 1564, II-2535, 3383, 3401
Outsourced semiconductor assembly and test, II-3014
Oven bags, II-2615
Oven cleaners, I-46, 48, 736
Ovens, I-226, 236, II-3527
Ovenware, I-1029
Over-the-top media, II-2536-2556
Ovulation Test kits, I-1071
Owen, Delia, I-522
Oxygen, I-1887
Oyster sauces, II-2971
PAC-12 Conference, II-3216
Pacemakers, II-2239, 2246
Package delivery, II-2773, 3066-3069
Packaging, I-10, 163, 168, 544-545, 1000, II-2557-2578, 2605, 2805
Packaging machinery, I-1380, II-2579-2580
Pain relievers, I-1128, 1141-1143
Paint, varnish and supplies wholesalers, II-2581
Paint and coatings, I-48, 313, 693, II-2582-2585, 2587-2592
Paint and wallpaper stores, II-2593

Paint protection film dealers, I-318
Painting work, I-921
Paints and coatings, I-43-44, 49, 685, 694, 2014, II-2586, 2590
Pajamas, II-3097
Palladium, II-2594-2596
Pallets, I-1368, 2126, II-2533, 2578, 2597-2598, 3577
Palm kernel oil, II-2508-2514
Palm oil, II-2511-2514
Pancake/french toast/waffle mixes, II-2599
Panels, II-2600-2602
Pants, I-196, 212, 216
Panty liners, II-2949
Pantyhose, I-187, 208
Paper and paperboard, I-694, 2014, II-2581, 2603-2613, 2618, 3298, 3373
Paper bags, and coated and treated paper, I-1401, II-2614-2616
Paper cups, I-1423
Paper machinery, II-2617, 2976
Paper towels, I-27, II-2941, 2944
Parasite treatments, I-1155
Parcel sorting machines, II-2619
Parenteral containers, II-2577
Parfaits, II-2812
Parking, I-860, 1777, II-2388, 2620-2621, 2933
Parks, I-1777, II-2388, 2622-2623, 2856
Particleboard, II-3583
Parties, I-1777, II-2388
Partitions, II-3539
Party string, I-44
Passenger cars, I-337, 340, 344-346, 348, 350-351, 354-355, 358, 360-361, 364-367, 708, II-3352, 3354
Passport photography services, II-2705, 2712
Pasta and noodles, I-1383, 1393, 1456, II-2624-2627
Pasta sauces, II-2967-2968, 2971
Pastries, I-393, 397, 1094-1095, 1473
Patents, II-2628
Patios, II-2533
Patrol services, I-1977
Pay television, II-2629-2632
Payment cards, II-2633-2640 See also: Credit cards; Debit cards
PC games, I-1570, II-3484
Peaches, I-1507, 1525-1526

Peanut oil, II-2508-2514
Peanuts, II-2452
Pearls, II-2641-2642
Pears, I-1508
Peas, I-1472, 1476
Peat, I-1368, II-2643
Pecans, II-2453, 3497
Peer-to-peer industry, I-2104
Pellets, II-3591
Pelts, I-2048, II-2644
Pens, I-949, 1553, II-3594-3595
Pensacola Interstate Fair, I-1273
Pensions, II-2645-2648
Pepper, II-3253, 3255
Peppers, I-1531, II-2649
Performance rights, II-2407
Perfumes, I-47, 1452
Periodicals, I-1083
Permanent botanicals, I-1813
Personal background checks, I-1977
Personal care products, I-43, 49, 969-990, 1076, 1080, 1157, 1175-1176, 1450, 1731-1736, 1835, 1971, II-2527-2530, 2575, 2579, 2650-2658, 3090-3091, 3093-3094, 3096, 3140-3147, 3552 See also: Cosmetics
Personal emergency response systems, II-2995
Personal goods specialist retailers, II-3482
Personal lubricants, II-2658
Personal protective equipment, II-2267
Personal training, II-3189
Personal watercraft, I-508, II-2659
Pest control industry, II-2660-2662
Pesticides, I-710-712, 2014
Pet food, II-2281, 2663-2684, 2690 See also: Cat food; Dog food
Pet products, II-2685, 3097
Pet services, I-1918, II-2686
Pet stores, II-2687-2690
Peter Buck, I-2027
Petrochemicals, I-696, II-3465
Petroleum, I-278, 355, 358, 569, 909, 1057, 1212, 1227, II-2466-2468, 3202, 3440, 3465, 3468
Pets, II-2691-2699
Petticoats, I-211
Pharmaceutical refrigeration, II-2700
Pharmaceuticals, I-18, 39, 44, 47-49, 610, 2021-2022, II-2569, 2575, 2579, 2724, 2927, 3465

Pharmacies, I-1102-1116
Pharmacy benefit managers, II-2701
Phenylalanine, II-3269
Phosphate rock, II-2702
Phosphatidylserine, II-3266
Photo cells, I-2073
Photo printing, II-2703
Photocontrols, II-2704
Photocopying equipment, II-2707
Photofinishing, II-2705-2706, 2712
Photographic equipment wholesalers, II-2708
Photographic film and supplies, I-901, II-2705, 2707, 2709-2711
Photography, II-2705, 2712-2713
Photonics, II-2714
Photovoltaics, I-1226, II-2714-2715
Physical therapy, I-1752
Pickles, I-605, 1383, II-2802, 2967
Pickups, I-348
Pie shells, I-1473
Piece goods, I-1267
Pies, I-390, 394, 398, 547
Pig iron, II-3246
Pigs, I-1781-1785, 1884
Piling rigs, I-858
Pilkey, Dav, I-522
Pillows, I-1797, 1800-1801, 1818, II-3097
Pimentos, II-2649
Pine nuts, II-2454
Pipe, I-1988, II-2716-2722, 2730, 2738, 3245
Pipe fittings, II-2722, 2730
Pipe hangers, II-2533
Pipe tobacco, II-3366-3367, 3373
Pipe wrenches, II-3389
Pipelines, II-2491-2492
Pistachios, II-2455
Pistols, I-1718
Pita bread, I-556
Pizza, I-1400, 1456, 1474, II-2802, 2881
Pizza crust, I-1096
Pizza kits, I-1392, 1400
Pizza sauce, II-2968
Placemats, I-1799
Plants, I-1368, 1375, 1377-1378
Plasma collection, I-506
Plastic bottles, II-2577, 2735
Plastic boxes, II-2578
Plastic film, II-2728, 2734, 2738
Plastic lumber, I-2125
Plastic sheet, II-2728

Plastics, I-693-694, 1303, II-2533, 2597, 2718, 2722, 2724-2745, 2748, 2757, 2922, 2927, 2930, 3523, 3542
Plastics machinery, II-2746-2747
Platform as a service, II-3169
Platinum, II-2749-2751
Playground equipment, II-2752, 3210
Playgrounds, I-1553
Playpens, I-1553
Plug-ins, I-331-336, 348-349, 359, 362, 368
Plumbers, I-931
Plumbing fixtures, I-1030, II-2533, 2753-2759, 2957-2958
Plush toys, II-3401
Plywood, I-545, II-3584, 3588
Pneumatic power, I-1380, II-2760-2761, 3381-3382
Podcasting, II-2762-2766
Point-of-sale software, II-3170
Police, II-2767
Police cars, I-363
Polishes, I-44, 47-48, 737
Polkadot, I-1028
Polyamide 6.6, II-2732
Polyamide fibers, I-1317
Polyamides, I-502, 1319, II-2737
Polybutylene adipate terephthalate, I-502
Polybutylene succinate, I-502
Polycarbonate, II-2737, 3523
Polyester, I-1317, 1319, 1340, II-2413
Polyethylene, I-502, II-2737
Polyethylene terephthalate, I-502
Polymers, I-996, 2098
Polyolefin, I-1317
Polypropylene, I-1340, II-2737-2739
Polystyrene foam, I-1368
Polysulfide, I-11
Polyurethane, I-11, 1908, II-2737
Polyurethane foam, I-1368, II-3539
Polyvinyl, I-11
Polyvinyl acetate, I-563
Polyvinyl chloride, II-2737, 3420
Pontoons, I-508
Popcorn, I-843-844, II-3108, 3119, 3255
Popcorn cakes, I-845-846
Pork, II-2170-2171, 2212-2217, 3497
Pork rinds, II-3120-3121

Portable buildings, II-3539
Portrait photography services, II-2705, 2712
Ports, II-2768-2770
POS terminals, II-2771
Post-Impressionism, I-268
Post Malone, I-802
Post-War and Contemporary Art, I-272
Postal service, II-2772-2773
Postcards, I-1675
Posters, I-1675
Postproduction services, II-2705, 3312
Posture correctors, II-2245
Pot pies, I-1477
Potash, II-2774-2775
Potato chips, II-2778, 3108, 3122-3123
Potatoes, I-1398, 1475, 1478, II-2776-2779, 3497
Potholders/mitts, I-1798
Potpourri, I-55
Pottery, II-2780-2781
Pouches, II-2569-2570
Poultry, I-1385, 1884, II-2168, 2170, 2177-2185, 2187-2192, 2205, 2208, 2562, 2573
Poultry fat, I-1293, 1299, II-2669
Poultry meal, I-1299, II-2669
Powdered milk, II-2802
Power distribution blocks, II-2782
Power tools, I-462, II-3381-3383
Powerboats, I-511
Powered milk, I-375
Pre-employment assessments, I-1978, II-3180
Precious stones, II-2641-2642
Precision turned products, II-2292, 2299, 2533, 3388, 3527
Prefabricated buildings, I-1838, II-3539
Prepaid cards, II-2636, 2638
Prepared foods, I-1393, 1456, II-2204, 2329
Preserves, I-605
Press machines, II-2137
Pressing and ironing services, I-1891
Pressure cookers, I-1446
Pressure regulators, II-3527
Pressure washers, II-2784
Pretzels, I-1480, II-3108, 3124-3125, 3255

Printed circuit boards, II-2786, 2788, 2790
Printers, I-787, II-2977
Printing, I-1000, 1083, 1675, 1881, II-2791-2797, 2805
Printing machinery, I-1380
Prisons, I-1421, 1746, II-2798-2800, 3470, 3473
Private clubs, II-2801
Private detectives, I-1978
Probiotic supplements, II-3264, 3268, 3281
Process automation, I-324
Processed cheese, I-1031
Project management, II-3181
Promotional products, II-2806-2807
Propane, I-104-117, 119-125, 127, 129-149, 151-153, II-2489-2490, 2808
Property management services, II-2621, 2852
Propulsion units, II-2326
Propylene, II-2739
Propylene oxide, II-2739
Prosthetics, I-1751
Protective mailers, II-2571
Protein supplements, II-3264, 3266, 3269, 3274
Prototypes, I-1446, 1881, II-2286, 2299
Proximity payments, II-2341
Prunes, I-1527
Psychiatric hospitals, I-1761
Psychiatrists, I-1757
Psychological counseling services, I-1754
Psyllium, II-3268, 3272
Public relations, II-2809
Public safety, I-873
Public-society benefit organizations, I-664
Publishing, I-517, II-2810-2811
Pudding, II-2812
Puffed snacks, II-3118, 3126
Pulp, II-2561, 2813-2819, 3148, 3465
Pumice, II-2820
Pumpkin seeds, II-3136-3137
Pumpkins, I-1531-1532
Pumps, I-778, 1771-1772, 1774, II-2821-2825
Pure-play foundries, II-3015
Purses, I-1738, 2133
Push notifications, II-3182

Puzzles, II-2333, 2336, 3401
PVA brushes, I-563
Pyrotechnic products, I-1263-1264
Quarrying, I-278, 583, 956, 1030, 1291, 2079
Quartz, I-1030
Queen and Adam Lambert, I-802
Quick-service restaurants, II-2572
Quicklime, I-2079
Racetracks, II-2826, 3220
Racing, II-2333
Racks, II-2578
Radar, II-3034
Radiators, I-1766
Radio broadcasting, I-15, 23, 35, 41, II-2827-2828
Radiopharmaceuticals, I-1125
Radios, II-2829
Rail car leasing, I-2043
Rail transit signal system, II-2836
Railings, II-2830
Railroad equipment, I-2126, II-2832-2837, 3577
Railroads, II-2620, 2831, 2838-2840
Raisins, I-1528
Ramie, I-1320
Ramsey, Dave, II-2827
R&B music, II-2394, 2403
Ranges, I-222, 246
Rap music, II-2395
Rapeseed oil, II-2508-2514
Rare earths, II-2841-2842
Raspberries, I-1501, II-3497
Rayon, I-1317
Razor blades, I-949, II-2653, 3388
Readers, II-2523
Ready meals, II-2880
Ready-mix concrete, I-278, 804
Real estate, I-1965, 2109, II-2843-2853
Reality shows, II-3322
Rearview mirrors, I-303
Receptacles, II-2854
Recliners, I-1561
Recording media, II-2855
Recreation management, II-2856
Recreation/sports centers, II-2856
Recreational goods rental, II-2857-2858
Recreational vehicle sites, I-1777, 1880, 1894-1895
Recreational vehicles, II-2859-2863
Recurring billing, II-3183
Recycling, II-2731

Red yeast rice, II-3272
Reed Family, I-2027
Refrigerated food, I-1382, 1392, II-2668, 2778, 3285
Refrigerated trucking, II-3427
Refrigerated warehousing, II-3497, 3499, 3501-3502
Refrigeration equipment, I-222, 224, 228-230, 232, 246, 248, 930, 1763-1765, II-2534
Refrigeration equipment wholesalers, II-2864
Registers, II-2533
Reinforcement mesh, II-2533
Reinsurance, I-1951
Relays and industrial controls, II-2865
Religious organizations, I-526, 664, 873, II-2866-2867
Remediation services, II-2868
Remittances, II-2869
Remodeling, I-282, 869, 874
Remote sensing, II-2966
Renewables, I-497, 1216-1224, 1226-1230, 1232, 1235
Rental and leasing, I-217, 1076, 1444, 1562, 1770, 1773, 1775, 1777, 1891, 2022, II-2378, 2388, 2533, 2598, 2621, 2712, 2786, 2852, 2870-2871, 2933
Repossession services, II-2872-2873
Reptiles, II-2696-2697
Research, II-2874-2876
Residential construction, I-582, 1215, 1304-1306, 1342, 1346-1347, 1352, 1629, 1720, 1837, 1839-1850, 1852-1854, 1858, 1860, 1904-1905, 2033-2036, 2110, II-3003
Residential intellectual disability care, II-2877
Residential replacement flooring, I-1342, 1346-1347, 1352
Resilient flooring, I-1345, 1351-1352, 1354, 1357
Resorts, II-2856
Respiratory needs, I-1128, II-2260, 2268
Restaurants, I-260, 1418, 1546, 2062, II-2572, 2620, 2878-2898, 3470, 3473
Retail clinics, I-1744

Retailing, I-18, 22, 39, 174, 217, 260, 278, 728, 778, 870, 1000, 1030, 1041, 1083, 1367-1368, 1444, 1562-1565, 1596-1615, 1629, 1675, 1770, 1777, 1881, 1891, 2021-2022, 2056, 2079, 2083, II-2329, 2378, 2388, 2411, 2419, 2423, 2533, 2557, 2566, 2572, 2621, 2705, 2712, 2786, 2788, 2805, 2851-2852, 2899-2910, 2929, 2933, 3043, 3200, 3218, 3470, 3473, 3512
Retained searches, II-3232
Reupholstery, I-1558-1559
Reverse vending machines, II-2911
Revolvers, I-1719
Ribbons, I-1368
Ribeyes, II-2167
Ribs, II-2167, 2217
Rice, II-2912-2917
Rice cakes, I-845-846
Ricotta cheese, I-676
Ride-hailing, II-2918-2919
Rihanna, I-1970
Risk management, II-2999
Rivets, I-515, II-3539
Road bikes, I-496
Road oil, I-278
Roads, I-860, II-2938
Robin DiAngelo, I-522
Robotics, II-2920-2928, 3033-3034
Rock music, II-2396, 2403
Rodent control, I-709
Role-playing games, II-2333, 2338, 3397
Roll-your-own tobacco, II-3373
Roller bearings, I-470
Rolls, I-383, 547-548, 552, 554, 558, II-3203
Roof ventilators, I-280, II-2533
Roofing, I-280, 922, II-2929-2931
Room fresheners, I-47
Rooming and boarding houses, II-2932-2933
Rope, cordage, twine, tire cord, and tire fabric, II-2934-2935
Rotorcraft, I-70
Roundwood, II-3579-3580
Routers, II-2425-2426
Rubber, I-708, 1343, 1345, 1357, 2014, II-2273, 2927, 2930, 2936
Rug/upholstery cleaners, I-734
Rugs, I-1340, 1345, 1357, 1360, 1367, 1807

Rum, I-2084
Runners, I-1799
Runways, I-860
Rush Limbaugh, II-2827
Rust removal, I-736
Rye, I-2084
Sachets, I-55
Safes, I-1553, 1622, II-2287, 2533
Safety experts, I-1260
Sailboats, I-511
Salad dressings, II-2802, 2967, 2971-2972, 3528
Salads, I-1392, 1398, II-2785
Sales assistance, I-275, 879, II-2525
Salmon, I-1326-1328, II-2987
Salon services, II-3200
Salt, II-2937, 3045, 3203, 3253
Saltines, I-1011-1012
Saltwater fish, II-2696
San Antonio Stock Show & Rodeo, I-1273
Sand, I-278-281, 286, 294, 321, 1030, 1368, II-2938-2939, 3045, 3247-3248, 3526
Sandstone, I-1030
Sandwich bags, I-1401
Sandwich shops, II-2895
Sanitary napkins/liners, II-2943, 2955
Sanitary paper products, II-2941-2956
Sanitaryware, II-2957-2959
Sardines, II-2982
Saree, I-211
Sashes, II-3539
Satellite broadcasting, II-2631
Satellites, II-2960-2962, 2964-2966
Sauces, dressings and condiments, II-2570, 2967-2973, 3225
Sausage, II-2209-2210, 2218-2221
Savage, Michael, II-2827
Saw blades, II-2974, 3387
Sawmill, woodworking and paper machinery, II-2975-2976
Saws, II-3388
Scaffolding, I-1771, II-2533
Scales and balances, II-2977-2978
School buses, I-570, II-2979
School lunches, I-1422
Schools, I-162, 867, 1258, 1546, 1548, 1777, II-2388, 2856, 2900, 2980-2981, 3307, 3470, 3473
Science and technology, I-2022, 2030, II-2961, 3231

Scissors, I-949
Scooters, II-2367
Scotch, I-2084
Scouring cleaners, I-735
Scouring pads, I-738
Screens, II-2533, 3539
Screws, I-515
Scrod, II-2987
Seafood, I-1325, 1383, 1393, 1456, II-2170, 2562, 2573, 2896, 2982-2991
Sealants, I-8, 10-14, 1592
Sean Hannity, II-2827
Search, detection, and navigation apparatus, II-2992
Search engines, I-42, II-3184-3186
Seating, I-1544, 1553
Seaweed, II-2993
Second homes, I-1859
Secondhand apparel, II-2994
Secretarial schools, I-574
Securities trading, I-174, 506, 1211, 1777, 1896, II-2344, 2388
Security equipment, I-906, 1977, 2073, II-2995-2998
Security services, I-1977, II-2999-3002, 3100, 3171
Seeds, I-698, II-3003-3004
Seeds (snacks), II-3136-3137
Seedstock, I-623
Seismic services, II-2493
Self-checkout terminals, II-3005
Self-propelled sprayers, I-1286
Self-storage industry, II-3006
Semiconductor machinery, II-3007-3008
Semiconductors, I-1380, II-2786, 2927, 3009-3030
Semiprecious stones, II-2641-2642
Senior housing, I-1861-1862
Sensors, I-654, II-3026, 3031-3034
Servers, II-3028, 3035-3038
Serviced apartments, II-3039
Set-top boxes, II-2960
Sewage treatment, I-872, II-3040, 3236
Sewers, II-2482, 2720
Sewing accessories, I-1368
Shaft-driven bicycles, I-495
Shakes, II-3279
Shampoo, I-1734-1735
Shark cartilage, II-3271
Shaving needs, I-44, 46-48, 1450, II-2803

Shears, I-949
Sheep and goats, II-3041
Sheet metal work, I-923, 1553, II-2533, 3042, 3539
Sheets, I-1794, 1797, 1814
Shelving, I-1791
Sherbets, I-1871, II-2565
Shingles, I-280-281
Shipping, II-2773, 3043-3070
Ships, II-3071
Shirts, I-196, 211-212, 216
Shock absorbers, I-309
Shoe and leather care products, I-46, 48
Shoes, I-1427, II-9000
Shoplights, I-2073
Shopping malls, II-2620, 2928, 3302
Short-staple spindles, II-3327
Shortening, I-1383, II-3528
Shorts, I-212
Shovels, I-856
Shower doors, I-1030, II-3539
Shower drains, II-2759
Shrimp, I-1483, II-2984
Shutters, II-2533
Shuttle-less looms, II-3327
Shuttle tankers, II-3052
Sidewalks, I-932
Siding, I-280, II-3072
Sightseeing, II-3073-3074
Signs, I-1553, II-2617, 3075-3077
Silicates, I-1908
Silicon, II-3078
Silicon carbide, I-3
Silicone, I-11
Silk, I-1320, II-3079-3080
Silver, II-3081-3085
Silverware, I-1997, II-3086
Silyl modified polymers, I-11
Single heater draw-texturing spindles, II-3327
Single-use foodservice products, II-2572
Single-web rolls, II-2616
Singleton Family, I-2027
Sinks, I-1030, II-2534, 2957-2958
Sinus remedies, I-1146-1147
Sioux Empire Fair, I-1273
Sisal, I-1320
Sitcoms, II-3322
Skids, I-1368, II-2533
Skiing facilities, II-3087
Skin care, I-1076, II-2650, 3088-3096, 3200, 3271

Skins, I-2048
Skirts, I-212
Skylights, II-3539
Slate, I-1030
Sleep aids, I-599, 1158, 1553, II-3097, 3263, 3273
Sleep masks, II-2252
Sleeve labeling, I-2019
Slot machines, I-1571, 1581-1583
Small animals, II-2696-2697
Small arms and ordnance, I-176-177, II-3098-3099
Smart technology, I-240, 285, 339, 342, 894-898, 900, 1620, II-2302, 2536, 2998, 3100-3106, 3220, 3517, 3519
Smartphones, I-629-632, 634-641, 1064, 1086, 1088, 1570, II-3018-3020, 3032, 3191
Smartwatches, II-3516-3518, 3520-3521
Smelters, I-960
Smokeless tobacco, II-3368-3369
Snack bars, I-814-815, 847-848
Snacks, I-384, 399, 715, 1390, 1393, 1457, 1777, II-2175, 2193-2194, 2198-2199, 2329, 2378, 2388, 2558, 2883, 2933, 3107-3139, 3255, 3471-3472
Snowplowing, I-932
Snus, II-3373
Soap, I-682, II-2559, 3140-3148
Social assistance services, I-1211
Social commerce, I-1185
Social media, I-251, 1964, 1967-1969, 1972
Socks, I-186-187
Soda ash, II-3148-3149
Sodium bicarbonate, II-3148
Sodium chlorate, I-713
Sodium dichromate, II-3148
Sodium percarbonate, II-3148
Sodium triphosphate, II-3148
Sofas, I-1551
Soffits, II-2533
Soft drinks, I-1337, II-2329, 3150-3152, 3218
Software, I-901, 1897, 2022, II-2736, 2999, 3153-3193
Softwood, I-1344, 2127-2129, II-2815-2816, 3586
Solar power, I-924-926, 1212, 1227-1228, 1230, 1232, 1886, II-2482
Soldering machines, I-321

Solid bleached sulfate, II-2609
Solid surface materials, I-996
Solvents, I-685
Soot removers, I-736
Soothing accessories, I-370
Sorbets, I-1871, II-2565
Soup, I-1099, 1383, 1393, II-2281, 3195-3197
Sour cream, II-3198
South Florida Fair, I-1273
Southeastern Conference, II-3216
Souveniers, I-1368
Soy food, I-1393, 1397, II-2318, 2967, 2971, 2973
Soybean oil, I-1300, II-2503-2506, 2509, 2511, 2513-2514
Soybeans, I-1300-1301, II-2500-2502, 2507-2508, 2510, 2512
Space industry, I-1045, II-2326, 2963, 3199
Spaghetti sauces, I-1383
Sparkling water, I-542
Sparkling wine, II-3545-3546
Spas, II-3200
Speakers, I-893
Special die and tools, die set, jigs, and fixtures, II-3201
Specialized storage and warehousing, II-3202
Specialty blacks, I-708
Specialty stores, I-598, 1364-1365, 1367, 1562-1565, 1798-1799, 1807-1808, 1810, 1814-1818, 1820
Spectacle frames, II-2523
Spectrophotometric instruments, I-2022
Speech therapists, I-1758
Spices and extracts, II-3203-3204
Spinach, I-1476, 1483, 1534
Spinal implants, II-2242, 2244, 2247
Spirits *See*: Liquor
Sponsorships, I-1188
Sport utility vehicles, I-337, 348, II-3349
Sporting goods, I-611, 778, 2062, II-2525, 3205-3212, 3401
Sporting goods retailers, II-3213-3215
Sporting goods wholesalers, II-3325
Sports, I-2060, 2062, II-3216-3221, 3322
Sports betting, I-258, 1571, 1578, 1584-1585
Sports cars, I-328, II-3349

Sports drinks, I-486, II-3222-3223
Sports medicine, II-2242, 2248
Sports nutrition, I-599, II-2897, 3275, 3283
Sportswear, I-203-205, 1435, II-3206
Spraying equipment, I-778
Spreads and syrups, II-3224-3225
Springs, II-3226
Sprinklers, I-917, 931
Spruce, II-3590
Squash, I-1476, 1481, 1535
SSD modules, II-3021
Staff catering, I-1418
Staffing industry, II-2329, 3227-3232
Stainless steel, II-2290, 2296, 3233
Stairs, II-2533
Stalls, II-2533
Stan Kroenke, I-2027
Standard LCD TV, I-1089
Starch, II-3528
Stationery products, II-3234-3235
Steam and air-conditioning supply, II-3236-3237
Steam distribution services, II-3236
Steamfitting and piping services, I-931
Steel, I-1708, II-2533, 2718, 2723, 3238-3246, 3523
Steel erection, I-927
STEM, II-3227
Stenographic services, I-999-1000
Stents, II-2263
Stephanie Meyer, I-522
Stereos, I-882
Sterilization equipment, II-2249
Stock images, II-3188
Stocks, I-1986
Stokers, I-1766
Stomach pain remedies, I-1151
Stone, sand and gravel, I-1030, 1368, II-3247-3248
Stools and benches, II-2417
Storage industry, II-3249
Store cards, II-2638
Storms, I-282
Stoves, I-226, 1766
Strategic management, I-877, 879
Strategy games, II-2339
Strawberries, I-1501, II-3497
Streaming media devices, II-3250-3252
Streaming services, I-1188, II-2406-2407, 2410, 2536-2556
Street furniture, I-21

Streetcars, II-2159
Streets, I-860, 906
Strength training, II-3189
Structural shapes, heavy, II-3245
Student housing, I-1855-1856
Studs, II-2533
Styling gel, I-1733
Styrene polymers, II-2742-2743
Subprime loans, I-2103, 2107
Subsea services, II-2493
Subwoofers, I-890
Suets, II-2684
Sugar, II-3253-3259
Sugar syrup, II-3253, 3255
Suits, I-196, 212, 216
Sulfur, II-3260
Sultanas, I-1528
Sun care, II-3095-3096
Sunflower seeds, II-2684, 3136-3137
Sunflowerseed oil, II-2508-2514
Sunglasses, II-2523, 3261
Super prime loans, I-2103, 2107
Superabsorbent polymers, II-2733
Supercenters, I-1798-1799
Superchargers, II-3262
Supermarkets, I-218, 1533, 1680-1706, II-2314, 2928, 3302
Superyachts, I-510
Supplements, I-599, 1076, 1386, II-3097, 3263-3285, 3487, 3490
Surge protectors, II-3286
Surgical forceps, II-2234
Surgical masks, II-2260
Surgical scissors, II-2234
Surveillance cameras, I-593
Suzanne Collins, I-522
SVOD, I-1247, II-2538-2556
Sweet corn, I-1531, 1536
Sweet potato fries, I-1484
Sweet potatoes, I-1540
Swimming pools, I-928, 1368, II-3287
Swiss cheese, I-668
Switchboard equipment, II-3308
Switches, II-3288
Syenite, I-1030
Synchronization royalties, II-2406
Syrup, II-3255, 3528
T-shirts, I-196, 211
Table linens, I-1799, 1815
Tablecloths, I-1799
Tables, I-1553

Tablets, I-792-794, 796, 799-800, 892, 1064, 1152, 1570, II-2536, 3022
Tableware, I-949, 1816
Taco kits, II-3390
Taffy apple kits, I-818-819
Taillights, I-2070
Talk radio, II-2827
Talk shows, II-3322
Tallow, I-1293
Tampons, II-2949, 2956
T&D equipment, II-3290
Tangerines, I-1509
Tank carriers, II-3421
Tank cars, I-2044
Tank terminals, II-3291
Tank trucks, II-3292
Tankers, I-1050, II-3053
Tanks, II-2291, 2533, 2578, 2837
Tanks (military), I-263
Tanning services, I-1076
Tape, I-10, II-3293-3294
Tape measures, II-3295
Tape (medical), II-2271
Tar, I-280, 684
Tattoos, I-1076, II-2264, 3296-3297
Taurine, II-3269
Tax preparation, I-4, II-3159, 3172, 3298-3300
Taxi services, I-2083
Taylor Swift, I-1970
Tea, I-486-489, II 3301-3305
Tea shops, II-3302
Technical tallow, I-1299
Ted Turner, I-2027
Teenagers, I-201-202
Telecommunications, I-18, 22, 906, 914, 1041, 1897, II-2460-2461, 2482, 2788, 2799, 3218, 3306-3308, 3310
Telemarketing services, I-1000, II-2805
Telephone answering and messaging services, I-1000, II-2805
Telephone switching equipment, II-3308-3309
Telephones, I-889, 901, II-2799, 3309
Teleproduction and postproduction services, II-3311-3312
Telescopes, II-3313
Television broadcasting, I-15, 23, 32-33, 35, II-2632, 3314-3324
Television mounts, I-1741

Television shows, II-3323-3324
Televisions, I-880-881, 898-901, 1089, II-3314
Temp agencies, II-2329, 3232
Tennis, II-3212
Tennis racquets, II-3212
Tent sites, I-1777
Tents, awnings and canvas, II-3325
Tequila, I-2084
Terminal operations, II-3064
Test Preparation, II-3450
Tether, I-1028
Textbook rentals, I-516
Textbooks, I-516-517, II-2810
Textile machinery, II-3327
Textile rental services, II-3328-3329
Textiles, I-697, 1268, II-2575, 3330-3332
Theaters, II-3333-3334
Thefts, I-1928
Therapeutic massage services, I-1076
Thermal analysis instruments, I-2022
Thermometers, II-2269, 2803
Thermostats, II-3105
Third-party management, I-1829
Thistle/Nyjer seed, II-2684
Throws, I-1800, 1818
Thyroid, anti-thyroid and iodine preps, I-1128
Ties, I-198
Tilapia, II-2987
Tile, I-996, 1030, 1345, 1368
Tile cleaners, I-736
Timber, II-3336-3337
Tin, I-1446, II-3245, 3338-3342
Tinware, I-949, II-2279
Tire cord mills, II-2935
Tire fabric mills, II-2934-2935
Tire retailers, II-3343-3344
Tire retreading, II-3345-3347
Tires, II-3343, 3348-3356
Tissue bank services, I-506
Tissue paper, II-2603, 2611, 2941
Titanium, II-3357
Tobacco and tobacco products, I-933, II-3358-3374
Tobacco paper, II-3370-3371
Tobacco stores, II-3375
Tofu, I-1869
Toilet bowl cleaners, I-736
Toilet tank fittings, II-2756
Toilet tissue, II-2945-2948

Toiletries *See*: Personal care products
Toilets, II-2957-2959
Toll roads, II-3376-3378
Tomato paste, II-2967
Tomato sauces, I-605, II-2968
Tomatoes, I-1398, 1529, 1531, 1540
Toners, II-3089
Tools, I-1368, 2062, II-2527, 3379-3389
Toothbrushes, II-2527, 2530
Toothpaste, II-2531
Top-of-bed industry, I-1797, 1817
Torches, II-3527
Tortilla and tostada chips, II-3108, 3138-3139
Tortillas and taco kits, I-383, II-3390-3391
Totes, I-1791, II-2578
Tour operators, I-1777, II-2388, 3416
Tourism, II-3073-3074, 3392, 3413, 3417
Towable trailers, II-3405
Towels, I-1794, 1797, 1808
Tower cranes, I-1016
Towing services, II-3511
Toy and hobby goods wholesalers, II-3393
Toys and games, I-369, 1175-1176, II-3394-3401
Toys and games retailers, II-3402
Tractor shovel loaders, I-856
Tractors, I-856, 1279-1284, 1287, II-3426, 3436, 3527
Trade shows, I-941-942, II-2525
Trademarks, I-2060
Traffic needs, I-1774, II-2590
Trail mixes, II-3117
Trailers, I-217, II-2533, 3403-3407, 3426, 3511
Training, I-1076, 1977, II-3408-3409
Tramways, II-2152
Trans-Siberian Orchestra, I-802
Transformer monitoring systems, II-3410
Transit buses, I-573
Transit vanpools, II-2160
Translation services, II-3411
Transmissions, I-302, 316-318, 2067, 2077
Transparent ceramics, I-654
Transponders, II-3412
Transportation, I-10, 163, 174, 873, 909, 961, 1057, 1215, 1342, 1346, 1352, 1446, 1626, 1629, 1891,

1904, 1916, 2021, 2083, II-2286, 2299, 2329, 2423, 2621, 2929, 3325, 3511-3512, 3603
Trap rock, I-1030
Trash bags, I-1401
Trauma recovery, II-2242, 2244
Travel, I-18, 22, II-2807, 3392, 3413-3418
Travel arrangement, II-3417-3418
Travel retail, II-3419
Travel trailers, II-2863, 3406
Travertine, I-2079
Trays, II-2578
Trees, I-1368
Triexta, I-1340
Trim, I-2125, II-2533, 3420, 3539
Trolleybuses, II-2161
Truck trailers, II-3407, 3511
Trucking, II-3421-3431
Truckload carriers, II-3429
Trucks, I-297, 308, 708, II-2863, 3354, 3432-3440, 3511-3512, 3527
True wireless stereo, I-284, 287-291
Trump, Mary L., I-522
Trusts, I-1986
Tub enclosures, I-1030, II-3539
Tubes, I-1988, II-2533
Tubs (packaging), II-2563
Tugboat services, II-3511
Tuna, II-2987
Tungsten, II-2296, 3441
Tungsten carbide, II-2296
Tunnels, II-3376
Turbines, I-1220-1224, II-3442-3448
Turboprops, I-63, 71, 85
Turkey, II-2171, 2197, 2201, 2224-2227, 3497
Turkey substitutes, I-1483, II-2201
Turn signals, I-2077
Turner, Ted, I-2027
Turntables, I-891
Tutoring, II-3449-3450
Twine mills, II-2934-2935
Typing services, I-1000, II-2805
Tyrosine, II-3269
U2, I-802
Ubiquinol, II-3272
Ulcerative Colitis, I-1139-1140
Ultrasounds, II-2241
Underwear, I-199-200, 210, 212
Uniform rental, I-1891, II-3328-3329
Uniforms, I-194, 206
Unions, II-3451-3452
Universal remotes, I-892

Universities, I-260, 871, II-2856, 3470, 3473
University presses, I-526
Unmanned aerial vehicles, II-3453-3455
Uranium, II-3456-3457
Urgent care centers, I-1753
USB car chargers, I-885
USB drives, I-783
Used vehicles, I-297
Utensils, I-946, 949
Utilities, I-1041, 2083, II-3236, 3458, 3509
Utility bedding, I-1800, 1818
Vaccines, I-1137, II-3459-3464
Valentine's Day, I-1370
Valerian, II-3273
Valet parking services, II-2621
Valves, I-778, II-3465-3466
Van campers, II-2863
Vanity tops, I-1030
Vanpool and carpool coordination services, I-2083
Vans, I-297, 348, II-3467-3468
Vaping products, I-1164-1167
Varicella vaccines, II-3463
Varnishes, I-44
Vats, II-3589
Vaults, I-1553, II-2533
Veal, II-2173-2174
Vegetable dips, I-1079
Vegetable juices, I-605
Vegetable mill products, I-1300
Vegetable oil, I-1295-1298, 1300, 1390, II-2511-2514, 3268
Vegetables, I-605, 1291, 1383, 1385, 1456, 1459, 1470, 1479, 1481, 1529, 1531-1532, 1534-1536, 1538-1540, II-2281, 2563, 3497
Vegetarians, II-3469
Vending machines, I-232, II-3470-3473
Ventilators, I-280, II-2256, 2533
Vents, II-2719
Veterinarians, II-2689-2690, 3475
Veterinary products, I-44, 49, 1054, II-3474
Video game industry, I-1576, II-3476-3485
Video poker, I-1583
Vinegar, II-3528
Vinyl, I-1343, II-3538, 3541
Vinyl chloride polymers, II-2744-2745

Vinyl composite tile, I-1353
Vinyl records, II-2397
Virtual data rooms, II-3173
Virtual events, II-3486
Virtual reality, II-3153-3154, 3192
Vitamin A, II-3265, 3270-3271, 3491
Vitamin and supplement retailers, II-3487
Vitamin B complex, II-3269
Vitamin B12, II-3264, 3269
Vitamin C, II-3264, 3267, 3273, 3491
Vitamin D, II-3264-3265
Vitamin E, II-3272, 3491
Vitamin K, II-3265
Vitamins, I-599, 1076, 1386, II-3264-3267, 3269-3270, 3272-3273, 3276, 3488-3491
Vocal performance, II-2404
Vocational training, II-2515
VOD, I-1247
Vodka, I-2084, 2096-2097
Voting machines, II-3492
VSAT platforms, II-2960
Wafer fabrication equipment, II-3007
Waffles, I-1482
Wall contractors, I-929
Wall décor, I-1819
Wall hung non-condensing boilers, I-514
Wallboard, II-3493
Wallpaper, II-3494
Walnuts, II-2456
Warehouse clubs, I-1365, 1533, 1562, 1564, 1802, 1806-1809, 1811-1814, 1817-1819, II-2928, 3130, 3344, 3495
Warehousing, I-778, 1446, II-3325, 3496-3503
Warranties, I-1953
Washing machines, I-222, 227-228, 232, 246, 249-250, 515, 1891
Waste management, I-2083, II-3236, 3504, 3511
Waste paper, II-2817-2818
Watches, I-2000, 2002, 2134, II-3505-3507
Water, II-3465, 3513
Water heaters, I-231, 233, 238, 1769
Water-jet looms, II-3327
Water parks, II-2856, 3510
Water supply and treatment, I-872, 909, 1553, II-2482, 2720, 2821, 3236, 3465, 3508-3509, 3513-3514

Water transportation, II-3074, 3511-3512
Watermelons, I-1540-1541
Waxes, I-44, 47
Wear-resistant steel, II-3243
Wearable devices, I-9, II-2807, 3515-3521
Weather forecasting, II-3522
Weatherproof boxes, II-3523
Web site design and development, I-1881, II-3193
Wedding dresses, I-209
Wedding planners, II-3524
Weddings, II-3524
Weight management, I-599, 1076, II-3263, 3274-3275, 3284-3285
Welding industry, I-1233, II-2292, 2533, 3525-3527
Wellness industry, I-1080, II-3200
Wet corn, II-3528-3529
Wet machine board, II-2610
Wheat, II-3530-3533
Wheelchairs, II-2233, 2251
Wheels, II-2533
Whey, II-3264, 3274
Whipped toppings, I-1031, 1392, II-3534-3535
Whiskey, I-2088-2089, 2095
Whisky, I-2092-2094
White grease, I-1293
Whole course solutions, II-2810
Wholesaling, I 280, 778, 949, 1000, 1030, 1054, 1083, 1267, 1368, 1444, 1446, 1553, 1675, 1881, 2022, 2048, II-2279, 2292, 2533, 2712, 2786, 2805, 2977, 3511, 3528, 3539
Wi-Fi standalone IC suppliers, I-1961
Wind energy, I-611, 1212, 1219-1224, 1227-1228, 1230, 1234-1235, II-2482, 3444, 3446-3447
Window treatments, I-1820, II-3536
Windows and doors, I-1619-1620, II-3536-3542
Windshields, I-315
Wine, I-101-102, 1628, II-2329, 2802, 3543-3551
Wine glasses, I-1634
Winter, I-932, II-3543
Winter squash, I-1531
Wipes, II-2559, 3552-3557
Wire and cable, II-2533, 3245, 3558-3559

Wireless LANs, I-782, II-2427
Wireless services, II-3560-3572
Wireless towers, II-3310, 3573-3574
Wireline voice equipment, II-3308-3309
Wiring ducts, II-3575
Wonton wrappers, I-1190
Wood, I-684, 1030, 1044, 1212, 1303, 1343-1345, 1361, II-2597, 2830, 3420, 3538, 3541-3542, 3576-3591
Wood-plastic composites, I-1044, 1303, 1349-1350, 1353-1354, 2125
Woodworking, I-1030, II-2976
Wool, II-3592-3593
Worcestshire sauce, II-3203
Workers' camps, II-2932-2933
Worklights, I-2073
World music, II-2403
Wraparounds, I-2073
Wrapping paper, II-2568
Wrecking work, I-910
Wrench sets, II-3379
Wrenches, II-3379
Wristbands, II-3517, 3520
Writing instruments, II-2807, 3594-3595
X-ray machines, II-2241
Yacht and beach clubs, II-2801
Yachts, I-508
Yarn, I-1267, II-2738, 3596-3598
Yellow grease, I-1293, 1299
Yogurt, I-1031-1032, 1382, II-3599-3600
Young adults, I-526
Zinc, I-1261, 1446, II-3267, 3271, 3523, 3601-3607
Zippers, I-1368
Zoos and botanical gardens, II-2388, 3608
Zucchini, I-1476, 1481, 1531

COMPANY INDEX

The more than 6,680 companies and institutions in this book are indexed here in alphabetical order. Numbers following the terms are entry numbers. They are arranged sequentially; the first entry number refers to the first mention of the company in *Market Share Reporter, 32nd Edition*. Although most organizations appear only once, some entities are referred to under abbreviations in the sources and these have not always been expanded. Roman numerals indicate volume numbers.

@Properties, II-2850
1-800-Flowers, I-1369-1370
101 Studios, II-2356
1st Source Bank, I-418
2 Sisters Food Group, II-2179
20th Century Fox, II-2356
20th Century Studios, II-2356
21st Century Museum of Contemporary Art, II-2387
21Vianet Group, I-1037
24 Hour Fitness USA Inc., I-1722
2M Alliance, II-3060-3063
3D Robotics Inc., II-3455
3M Cogent, I-501
The 3M Company, I-8-9, 12, 14, 739, II-2236
44 Farms, I-623
51Talk, I-1966
631 Coatings, I-318
7 Days Inn, I-1833
7-Eleven Inc., I-935, 1453, 1593, II-2902, 2904
7X Energy Inc., I-924-925
84 Lumber Co., I-565, 1789
888 Holdings PLC, I-1578
9Mobile, II-3570
A123 Systems, I-464
AAA (American Automobile Association), II-3413
AAMCO Transmissions, I-316
A&R Transport, II-3421
AAR Corp., I-1657
AARD Mining Equipment (Pty) Ltd., II-2325
Aaron's Holdings Company Inc., II-2870
Abalioglu Group, I-1199, II-2184
ABB Inc., I-322-324, 586, 642, 731, II-2305, 2926, 3290, 3410, 3575
Abbott HealthCare, II-2254

Abbott Laboratories, I-1068-1069, 1130, 1136, II-2237, 2253, 2263
Abbott Nutrition, I-373, 376
AbbVie Inc., I-23, 32, 34, 38, 504, 1119-1121, 1138-1140, II-2258
ABC, II-2632, 2762
ABC Group Inc., II-2729
ABC Mannequins, II-2145
ABC Supply Co. Inc., I-565, 1789
ABF Freight System, II-3425
ABK Group, I-658
ABM Industries Inc., II-2620
ABP Food Group, I-1395
Absen Inc., I-2052
Abt Electronics and Appliances Inc., I-219
Acacia Communications Inc., II-2526
Academy Lines Inc., II-2154
Academy Sports+Outdoors, II-3214-3215
Acadian Timber Corp., II-3337
ACC Ltd., I-646
Accelink Technologies Co., II-2526
AccentCare Inc., I-1748
Accenture Public Ltd., I-877-878, 1645-1646, 1650, 1657, 1659-1660, II-3414
Accenture's Accenture Interactive, I-24
Accident Insurance Fund of America, I-1954
ACCO Engineered Systems, I-920
Accor Hotels, I-1828, II-3039
Accord Healthcare, I-1129
Accordia Golf Co. Ltd., I-1644
Accredo, I-1116
Accuweather Inc., II-3522
ACE American Insurance Co., I-1954
Ace Hardware Corp., I-1453

ACE Parking, II-2620
ACE Rent A Car, I-311
ACE Solar L.L.C., I-926
Acer Group Inc., I-795, 797-798
Acme Brick Company, I-560
Acme Markets Inc., I-1687, 1697, 1705, II-2907
Acolad Group, II-3411
ACProducts Inc., I-582, II-3578
Acrisure L.L.C., I-1940
ACS, I-864, 909
Activision Blizzard Inc., II-3479
Adama Agricultural Solutions Ltd., I-687, 689
Adams and Associates Inc., I-1656
Adams Publishing Group, II-2429
Adams Syrup Co. Inc., I-819
ADATA Technology Co., II-3021
The Adecco Group, II-3228, 3230
Ademar Kerckhoff, I-1197
Adesa Auctions, I-293-294
Adidas, I-1425, 1429, 1435-1436
Adient PLC, I-305-306
ADM Milling Co., I-1372
ADMA Biologics, I-1877
ADNOC Drilling, II-2484
Adobe Inc., II-3166
Adolfson & Peterson Construction, I-867
Ador Welding, II-3525
ADT, II-3002, 3423
Advance Auto Parts Inc., I-310
Advanced Disposal Services Inc., II-3504
Advanced Drainage Systems Inc., II-2730
Advanced Micro Devices, I-1956, II-3009, 3023, 3030
Advanced Semiconductor Engineering Inc., II-3014
Advancepierre Foods Inc., I-397

AECOM, I-261, 863, 866, 868, 870, 907, 1057, 1251-1253, 1651, 1742, 1962, II-2445, 3513-3514
Aecon Group Inc., I-862
AEG Presents, I-801
Aegion Corp., II-3513
AEON Group, II-2908
Aer Rianta International, II-3419
AerCap, I-80
Aercon AAC, I-319
Aerodyne Group, II-3454
Aerojet Rocketdyne Holdings Inc., I-1648
The Aerospace Corp., I-1649
Aerotek, II-3228
AeroVironment, II-3455
AET Tankers, II-3052
AF Gruppen, I-911
Affirm, I-256
Affirmed L.L.C., I-973
Affy Tapple L.L.C., I-819
AFL Telecommunications, I-584
Afognak Native Corp., I-1656
Afriglobal Commodities DMCC, I-703
Afterpay, I-256
Aftershock Comics, I-774
AGC Inc., I-1627
AGCO Corp., I-1278, 1280-1284, II-3104
Agfa HealthCare Corp., II-3190
Aggreko PLC, I-1775
Agnico Eagle Mines, I-1641
The Agrana Group, I-1496
AgReliant Genetics, II-3004
Agricultural Bank of China, I-401
AGRO Merchants Group L.L.C., I-1279, II-3501-3502
Agroindustrial Wilse CXA, I-1198
Agrokomplex, II-2208
Agrolimen SA, II-2681
Agropecuaria Río Bravo, I-1197
Agropur, I-1033
Agrosuper, II-2182
AGS L.L.C., I-1582
Ahern Rentals, I-1771
AHF Pharmacy, I-1116
AHF Products, I-1357-1358
Ahlstrom-Munksjö, II-2440-2442
Ahold Delhaize, I-1115, 1182, II-2904, 2910
AHORRAMAS, I-1701
Aida, II-2137
Aidells Sausage Co., II-2221

AIG Life & Retirement Group, I-1942
Aimbridge Hospitality, I-1828-1829
Ainsworth Game Technologies, I-1582
Ainsworth Pet Nutrition L.L.C., II-2670-2671, 2674, 2676, 2682-2683
Aion Co. Ltd., I-563
Air Brook Limousine, I-2082
Air Canada, I-84
Air China, I-84
Air France-KLM Group, I-84
Air Lease Corp., I-80
Air Liquide S.A., I-706, 1889
Air Medical Group Holdings Inc., I-173
Air Products & Chemicals Inc., I-1889
Airbnb, II-3418
Airbus SE, I-57, 60-62, 66-67, 69
Airmatik, I-237
Airobotics Ltd., II-3454
Airswift Holdings Ltd., II-3228
AirtelTigo, II-3567
Aisin Seiki Co. Ltd., I-299, 306
Aisin World Corp. of America, I-305
Aiya, II-3304
AJB Group, I-1943
Ajinomoto Foods North America, I-1488, 1491
AJ's Fine Foods, I-1698
Aker Solutions, II-2493
Akin, Gump Strauss Hauer & Feld L.L.P., I-2109
Akmenés Cementas, I-647
Akro Mills, II-2726
Aktio Corp., I-1775
AkzoNobel, I-713, II-2586, 2592
Al-Fakieh Poultry Farms, I-1199, II-2184
Al Shams Agro Group, I-1496
Al-Watania Poultry, I-1199, II-2184
Alameda-Contra Costa Transit District, II-2154
Alamo Drafthouse Cinemas, II-2379
Alaska Airlines, I-86, 95-96
Albertsons Companies, I-1115, 1681, 1698, II-2904
Albis, II-2732
Alcoa Inc., I-159
Alcon Inc., I-904
Alcopa Auction, I-292

Aldi, I-1679, 1682-1683, 1685, 1688, 1693, 1695, 1697, 1705-1706, II-2904, 2910
Alert 360 Home Security, II-3002
Alerus Financial NA, I-438
Alf Sahel S.A.R.L., II-2177
Algeco Scotsman Group, I-1773, 1775
Aliaxis Group S.A., II-2719, 2759
Alibaba Cloud, II-3164-3165, 3169
Alibaba Group Holding Ltd., I-1179, II-2908-2910
Alibaba New Retail Initiatives, II-2906
Alico Inc., I-1291
Aligned Ag Distributors L.L.C., I-692
Alimentation Couche-Tard Inc., I-935, 1437, 1439, 1443, 1593, II-2909
Aliner, II-3403
Alion Science and Technology Corp., I-1663
Alipay, I-1184, 1186
Alkem Laboratories, I-1130
All Dominion Voting Systems, II-3492
ALL Family of Companies, I-1013-1014
All State Investigations Inc., I-1978
All Tile/Carpet Cushions & Supplies, I-1362
All Twisted Pretzel Seven Brothers L.L.C., I-558
Alleghany Group, I-1948
Allegheny Technologies Inc., II-2298
Allegiance Retail Services L.L.C., I-1704
Allegion PLC, I-2110
Allegis Group, II-3230
Allegra Asheville, II-2797
Allen Edmonds Shoe Corp., I-1426
Allen Printing Company, II-2797
Allergan PLC, I-504, II-2258
Allete Inc., I-1234
Alliance Franchise Brands, II-2795
Alliance Residential, I-1852, 1854
Alliance Resources Partners L.P., I-747
THE Alliance, II-3060-3063
AllianceRx Walgreens Prime, I-1116
Alliant Credit Union, I-1019
Alliant Energy, I-1234

Alliant Insurance Services Inc., I-1909, 1940
Allianz Insurance Group, I-1921, 1931, 1941, 1946, 1948-1949, 1981
Allianz SE, I-1918
Allied Electronics & Automation/ RS Components, I-1204
Allied Experiential, I-1255
Allied Telesis, II-2426
Allied Universal, II-3000-3001
Allit AG, II-2726
AllStars Travel Group, II-3413
The Allstate Corp., I-1788, 1914-1915, 1923-1926, 1929, 1938-1939, 1950
Alltek Marine, II-3412
Ally Bank, I-402, 452
Ally Insurance Holdings Group, I-1953
Almarai Co., I-1290, II-2184
Alorica Corp., I-1041
Alphabet Inc., I-26
Alphabroder, II-2806
Alphagraphics, II-2797
Alpine Bank, I-409
Alpla Inc., II-2727
Alps Electric Co., II-2306
Alro Steel Corp., II-2297
Alrosa, I-1072-1073
Alsaker Fjordbruk A/S, I-1328
Alstom S.A., II-2831
ALT Balaji, II-2544
Alta Drywall Solutions Inc., I-929
Altana AG, I-1903
Altera Infrastructure L.P., II-3052
Alterra Mountain Company, II-3087
Altice USA Inc., II-2631
Altium Packaging L.P., II-2727
Altman Plants, I-1674
Altria Group, II-3359, 3365, 3369
Alturas Construction, I-1841
Aluminum Corp. of China Ltd., I-159
Amadeus IT Group, I-1635
Amadori, II-2179
Amalgamated Bank, I-456
Amarillo Copper Refinery, I-953
Amazon Pay, I-1184
Amazon Prime, I-1169, II-2537-2539, 2542-2553
Amazon Web Services, II-3164, 3169
Amazon.cn, I-1170, 1172

Amazon.com Inc., I-17, 26, 28, 32, 34, 36-37, 40, 42, 215, 219, 221-222, 516-517, 519, 789, 799-800, 894-896, 902, 1168, 1178, 1180, 1431-1432, 1434-1435, 1560, 1618, 1680, 1780, 1789, 1801, 1803-1805, 1834, 2000, 2002, 2108, II-2277, 2409, 2688, 2753, 2904-2905, 2908-2910, 2994, 3068, 3105, 3209, 3280-3281, 3402, 3414
AMB Credit Consultants, I-1017
Ambac Assurance Corp. Group, I-1936
Ambuja Cements Ltd., I-646
AMC Theatres, II-2379
AMCON Distributing Co., I-933
Amcor Flexibles North America, II-2728
Amcor PLC, II-2558, 2564, 2573
Amcor Rigid Plastics, II-2727
AmcorGroup Inc., II-2562, 2570
Amedisys Inc., I-1748-1749
America First Credit Union, I-1019
América Móvil, II-3561, 3563, 3569, 3571
American Airlines, I-84, 86-96
American Axle & Manufacturing Holdings Inc., I-305
American Bank Center, I-438
American Bicycle Group, I-494
American Blue Ribbon Holdings L.L.C., I-394
American Campus Communities, I-1855-1856
American Commercial Lines L.L.C., II-3050, 3058
American Crew Inc., I-1733
American Eagle Outfitters, I-216
American Express Co., I-26, II-2638, 2640
American Express Global Business Travel, II-3413
American Express National Bank, I-452
American Express Travel, II-3413
American Family Care, I-1753
American Family Insurance Group, I-1923-1926, 1934, 1938-1939
American Financial Group, I-1931, 1935, 1945, 1947, 1949
American Forest Management, II-3336
American Golf Corp., I-1644

American Greetings Corp., I-1676-1677
American Gypsum, I-1725, II-3493
American Home Star, I-1851
American International Group, I-973, 1788, 1911-1912, 1915, 1921-1922, 1927-1928, 1932, 1935, 1937, 1941, 1946-1950
American Licorice Co., I-831
American Medical Response, I-173
American National Bank, I-431
American National Financial Group, I-1931
American Pet Nutrition Inc., II-2676
American Pop Corn Co., II-3119
American Red Cross, I-505, 665
American Renal Associates, I-1745
American Road Insurance Co., I-1953
American Savings Bank FSB, I-415
American Signature, I-1565
American Tower, II-3573-3574
American Water, II-3509
American Woodmark Corp., I-582, II-3578
American Zurich Insurance Co., I-1954
America's Auto Auctions, I-294
Americas Best Value Inn, I-1832
Americold Logistics L.L.C., II-3501-3503
AmeriGas Propane, II-2808
Ameriprise Bank FSB, I-427
Ameris Bank, I-413
Ametek EIG, I-322
Amgen Inc., I-504, 2108
Amigear Ventures (PTY) Ltd., I-1192
Amkor Technology Inc., II-3014
AMN Healthcare Services Inc., II-3229
Amneal Pharmaceuticals Inc., I-1129
AMPCO Contracting Inc., I-910
Amthor Intl., II-3292
Amtrak, II-2149
Amtrust Financial Services Group, I-1953
Amundi, I-1981
AMVC Management Services, I-1782
Amway Corp., I-1080-1081, II-3276, 3278
Amy's Kitchen Inc., I-1488, 1491, 1493, II-3195

ANA Holdings Inc., I-84
Analog Devices Inc., II-3024
Analytic Services Inc., I-1658
Ananda Hemp Inc., I-603
ANB Bank, I-459
Andersen Corp., II-3578
Anderson Trucking Services, II-3422
Andrej's European Pastry, I-397
Andy Frain Services, II-3000
Angelicoussis Shipping Group Ltd., II-3053
Angénieux, I-2054
Angie's Artisan Treats L.L.C., I-844, II-3119
Anglo American PLC, I-1992
Anglo Platinum Ltd., II-2595, 2750
AngloGold Ashanti Ltd., I-1641
Anheuser-Busch InBev NV, I-102, 481-483, 1394
Anhui Conch Cement Co., I-651
Anhui Forklift Truck, I-2063
Anhui Gujing Distillery Co., II-3547
Anhui Korrun Co., I-2121
Animal Friends Insurance, I-1918
Anker Innovations Technology, I-466, 885
Ann Taylor, I-216
Annie's Homegrown Inc., I-825, 827, 1010, 1097
ANR Pipeline, II-2492
Ansaldo Energia S.p.A., II-3448
Ansteel Group, II-3238
Antea Group N.V., I-1252
Antero Resources Corp., II-2462-2465, 2485-2486
Anthem Inc., I-1788, 1915
Anticimex, II-2661-2662
Antler Luggage, I-2121
Anytime Fitness, I-1722
ANZ Guam Inc., I-414
A.O. Smith Corp., I-238
Aon PLC, I-1909
Apache Corp., II-2488
Apartment Management Consultants L.L.C., I-1854
APC by Schneider Electric, II-2783
APCO Worldwide, II-2809
Apex Oil Company Inc., II-3202
Apex Tool Group, II-3389
Aphria, I-601
API Group, I-917, 920
APM Terminals, II-3064
Apogee Enterprises Inc., I-566
Apollo Distributing Co., I-1362

Apollo Global Management, II-2828
Apollo Mechanical Contractors, I-920
Apollo Tyres Ltd., II-3356
Apotex Inc., I-1129
Appen Ltd., II-3411
Apple App Store, I-252, 255, 1180, II-2334
Apple Bus Co., II-2979
Apple Inc., I-32, 40, 284, 287-291, 628, 638, 641, 789, 792, 796-800, 894-895, 902, 1178, 1182, II-2628, 2909, 3016, 3018, 3022, 3161, 3414, 3519-3520
Apple Leisure Group, II-3416
Apple Mail, II-3161
Apple Music, II-2409
Apple Pay, I-1184, II-2341
Apple Store/iTunes, II-2904
Apple TV+, II-2537, 2539, 2542-2543, 2545, 2547-2550, 2552-2553
Applebee's Neighborhood Grill & Bar, II-2884, 2891
Applegate Farms Inc., II-2210
Applied Home Healthcare, II-2235
Applied Materials, II-3007
AppLovin, II-2335, 2339
Apria Healthcare Group Inc., II-2870
April Group, II-2814-2815
AptarGroup Inc., I-610, II-2729
Aptim Corp., II-2445
Aptiv PLC, I-305, II-2661
Aptos Inc., II-3170
Aquatica, II-3510
Arab Company for Livestock Development, I-1199-1200, II-2184
Arab Potash Company, II-2774
Arab Poultry Breeders Co., II-2177
Aramark Corp., I-1420-1421, 1454, II-3328-3329
Arandell Corp., II-2793
Arauco, II-2814-2816
Arby's, II-2889, 2895
ARC International, I-1634
Arcadis N.V., I-1252, 1742
ArcelorMittal S.A., I-1992, II-3238
Arch Insurance Group, I-1931, 1933, 1944, 1948
Arch Resources Inc., I-747
Archer Daniels Midland Co., I-1884
Architectural Glass & Aluminum, I-918
ArchKey Solutions, I-913
Archroma, I-697

Arcis Golf, I-1644
ARCO Construction, I-870
Arconic Inc., I-515
Arctic Cat, I-103
Arctic Glacier Inc., I-1867
Arctic Slope Mission Services Inc., I-1647
ARD, II-3315
Ardent Mills L.L.C., I-1372
Arena Ciudad De Mexico, I-262
Arena Monterrey, I-262
ARGO Group U.S. Insurance, I-1949, 1952
ARI, I-298
Aristocrat Technologies Inc., I-1582
Arkema S.A., I-12
Arla Foods, I-1034, 1395, II-2310
Arlo Technologies, I-591
Armour Eckrich Meats L.L.C., II-2221
Armstrong Flooring Inc., II-2725
Armstrong Garden Centers & Pike Nurseries, I-2037
Armstrong Industries, I-626, 1351, 1357
Army & Air Force Exchange Services, I-1454, II-2307
ARMZ Uranium Holding, II-3456
Arriva PLC, II-2164
Arrow Electronics, I-1204
Arrow Exterminators, II-2661
Art Van Furniture Inc., I-1565, 1802
Arthrex Corp., II-2243, 2248
Arthur J. Gallagher & Co., I-1909
Artisan Design Group, I-1366
Artists Writers & Artisans Inc., I-774
Artuso Pastry Foods Corp., I-397
Arvest Bank, I-407, 440
Aryzta L.L.C., I-391, 551, 1400
A.S. Création, II-3494
Asahi Group Holdings Ltd., I-102, 483
Asahi Kasei Corp., I-1838
Asbury Automotive Group Inc., I-296
Ascend, II-2732
Ascension Health, I-1747, 1750, 1753
Ascher Brothers Co. Inc., I-921
ASCO Group, I-1159
The Ascott Limited (Worldwide) Inc. Guest Apartment Hotels, II-3039
Asda, I-1679

ASG Stores, I-1704
Ashfield Meetings and Events, I-1255
Ashley Furniture Industries, I-1550-1551, 1796, II-3578
Ashley HomeStore, I-1565, 1802, 1804
Ashtead Group, I-1775
Ashton Woods Homes, I-1839, 1847-1848
Asia Kraft Paper, II-2606
Asia Pulp & Paper, II-2814-2815
Asian Paints Ltd., II-2592
Asian Player, I-2065
ASML Holding, II-3007
Aspiration Bank, I-402
ASRC Industrial, I-921
Assa Abloy, I-2110
Asseco Group, II-3190
Asset Living, I-1855
Associated Bank NA, I-458
Associated British Foods, I-1395
Assurant Group, I-1922, 1937-1938, 1941, 1948
Assured Guaranty Group, I-1936
AssuredPartners Inc., I-1940
Aston Barclay, I-295
Astral Foods Ltd., II-2177
AstraZeneca PLC, I-1138, II-3423, 3459
AsusTek Computer Inc., I-798
AT&S, II-2790
AT&T Corp., I-26, 32-34, 37, 40-41, 628, 1654, 2108, II-2537, 2631, 2645, 3423, 3561-3562, 3569
Aten, II-2428
Athleta, I-213
Athletico Physical Therapy, I-1752
ATI Physical Therapy, I-1752
ATI Restoration, I-869
Atkinson Candy Co., I-850
Atlantic Broadband, II-2631
Atlantic Union Bank, I-454
Atlas Copco AB, I-779, II-2324-2325, 2822
Atlas Technical Consultants, I-1252
Atlas Van Lines Inc., II-3424
Atmos Energy Corp., II-3458
Atomy, I-1081
ATR Corp., I-66
Atradius Trade Credit Insurance Co., I-1931
Atria Senior Living Inc., I-1861

Atyab Investments, I-1199
Au Bon Pain, II-2882
AU Optronics, II-2602
Auchan, I-1699, 1701
Audemars Piguet, II-3507
Audi AG, I-331
Audible, II-2277
Auditorio Nacional, II-3334
Auditorio Telmex, II-3334
August Storck KG, I-812
AUI Partners L.L.C., I-925
Aunt Millie's Bakeries Inc., I-549-551, 555
Auntie Anne's, II-2883
Aurobindo Pharma Ltd., I-1129
Aurora Alimentos, II-2182
Aurora Cannabis Inc., I-601
Aurora Computer Services, I-1272
Aurora Urgent Care, I-1753
Aurubis AG, I-960
Austin Foods Co., I-1008
Austin Industries, I-863, 865
Austin Powder Co., I-1262
Australian Community Media, II-2430
Austro Engine, I-72
Autel Robotics, II-3455
Authentic Brands Group, I-2061
Authenticity Co. Ltd., I-247
Auto 1, I-292-293
Auto-Owners Insurance Group, I-1929-1930, 1939
Autobell Car Wash, I-615
Autobid, I-293
Autogrill, I-1424
Automotive Appearance Pros, I-318
Automotive Elegance L.L.C., I-318
AutoNation Inc., I-296
AutoNuvo Inc., I-318
Autorola, I-293
AutoZone Inc., I-310
Auxly Cannabis Group, I-601
AV Simulation, I-1101
AvalonBay Communities Inc., I-1853
Avalotis Corp., I-921
Avangardco, I-1194
Avery Dennison Corp., I-12
Avgol Industries, II-2442
AVI Foodsystems Inc., I-1420
AVI-SPL, II-3289
AVI Systems, II-3289
Avia International, I-1441
Aviat Networks, II-2421

Aviation Capital Group, I-80
Aviation Industry Corporation of China, I-60
AVIC Aircraft Corp., I-71
Avícola El Ciprés, I-1198
Avícola La Calera, I-1197
Avícola Rosanda, I-1198
Avicultores de Mixco S.A., I-1198
Avidbots, II-2928
Avidesa, II-2182
Avidex, II-3289
Avis Budget Group, I-311-312
Avison Young, II-2843-2844, 2846, 2851
Aviva PLC, I-1918
Avnet Inc., I-1204
Avocent, II-2428
Avolon Aerospace Leasing, I-80
Avon Products, I-1080
Avril Group, I-1194
AXA Insurance Group, I-1911, 1921, 1927-1928, 1932, 1948
AXA S.A., I-1912, 1916-1917
Axalta Coating Systems, II-2586, 2591-2592
Axia Capital Holdings Ltd., I-1911
Axiom Corp., I-1180
Axis Capital Holdings Ltd., I-1910, 1935
Axis Communications, I-593
Axpo Holding AG, II-2715
Azek Building Products, I-1043-1044, 2125
Azelis S.A., I-699, 701
Azteca Foods Baja Trading Inc., II-3391
Azure, I-1582
B. Green & Co. Inc., I-1703
B. Schoenberg & Co. Inc., II-2731
b1BANK, I-422
Babaka, II-2245
Baby Gap, I-213
The Bachman Co., II-3125
BackJoy Orthotics L.L.C., II-2245
Badcock Home Furniture, I-1802
Badoo, I-254
BAE Systems PLC, I-1658, 1664
Baggit, I-2123
Bahama Aquaventure Water Park, II-3510
Bahri, II-3053
Baiada Poultry, II-2181
BAIC Group, I-349, 572
Baidu AI Cloud, II-3165

Baidu Inc., I-896
Bailian Group, I-1684
Bain & Company, I-878
BAK Battery Co. Ltd., I-467
Baker Builders L.L.C., II-2278
Baker Construction Enterprises, I-908
Baker Electric Inc., I-924
Baker Hughes Co., II-2493
Baker Mills Inc., I-1010, II-2599
Baker Roofing, I-922
Baker's Perfection Inc., I-397
BakerTriangle, I-929
Bakkavör, I-1078
Balfour Beatty U.S., I-867-868, 870
Balian Group, II-2906
Balich Worldwide Shows, I-1255
Ballard Partners, I-2109
Banana Republic, I-213
BancFirst, I-440
Banco Popular de Puerto Rico, I-444
Banco Santander Puerto Rico, I-444
The Bancorp Bank, I-411, II-2636
BancorpSouth Bank, I-407, 428
Bandai Namco Entertainment Inc., II-2338
B&B Italia S.p.A., I-1549
B&B Plastics Inc., II-2731
B&B Theatres, II-2379
B&G Foods Inc., I-850, 1006, II-3390
Banesco USA, I-444
Bangor Savings Bank, I-423
Bank First NA, I-458
Bank of America Merrill Lynch, I-1984-1985
Bank of America Mortgage, II-2349
Bank of America NA, I-401, 406-410, 412-413, 416-417, 420, 423-427, 429, 432-437, 440-441, 443, 445-446, 448-449, 454-456, 1983, II-2274, 2640, 2843
Bank of China, I-401
Bank of Colorado, I-409
The Bank of Commerce, I-416
Bank of Guam, I-414, 442, 450-451
Bank of Hawaii, I-414-415, 442, 451
Bank of Jackson Hole, I-459
Bank of New Hampshire, I-433
The Bank of New York Mellon, I-436, 443
Bank of the Federated States of Micronesia, I-450

Bank of the West, I-408-409, 431, 435, 441, 459
Bank OZK, I-407, 413
Bank Rhode Island, I-445
Bankers Trust Co., I-419
BankMobile, I-402
BankNewport, I-445
BankPacific Ltd., I-414, 442, 451
BankPlus, I-428
BankUnited NA, I-412
Banner Bank, I-441, 455
Banvit, II-2184
Baogai New Material, II-2144
Bar Harbor Bank & Trust, I-423
Bar-S Foods Co., II-2223
Barcel USA L.L.C., I-835, II-3115, 3139
Barclays Bank Delaware, I-411
Barclays Center, I-262
Barclays PLC, I-1984-1985, II-2640
Bare Foods Co., II-3111
Barely Bread, I-558
Barcntz International B.V., I-699
Bargreen Ellingson Inc., I-1419
Barilla, II-2625, 2627
The Barking Dog, II-2678
Barnard Construction, I-1251
Barnes & Noble Education Inc., I-518
Barnes & Noble Inc., I-518
Barnes Group Inc., II-3226
Barnhart Crane & Rigging, I-1013
Barrette Outdoor Living, I-1305-1306
Barrick Gold, I-1641
Barstool Sports, II-2762
Bartlett Milling Co., I-1372
Basden Steel, I-927
BASF, I-304, 689, 706, 710-711, II-2586, 2592, 2732-2733, 3004
Basha's, I-1698
Basic-Fit International, I-1722-1723
Baskin-Robbins, II-2883
Bath & Body Works, I-990, 1971
Battelle, I-1651, II-2445
Bauducco Foods Inc., I-385
Baxter International, II-2254
Bay Alarm Company, II-3002
Bay State Milling Co., I-1372
Bayada Home Healthcare, I-1748
Bayer AG, I-1127, 1141, 2033, II-3003
Bayer Crop Science, I-689, 711, II-3004

Bayer Healthcare, I-1135
Bays English Muffin Corp., I-559
BBAM L.L.C., I-80
BBC, II-3315
BBDO Worldwide, I-25
BBK Electronics Corp., II-3016
BBVA, I-404, 406, 449, II-2275
BCD Travel, II-3413, 3415
BCS Insurance Co., I-1910-1911
BDO U.K., I-6
BDO USA L.L.P., I-5, 7
Be & Cheery, II-3135
Beachbody L.L.C., II-3278
Beacon Building Products, I-565
Beacon Intermodal Leasing, I-905
Beacon Roofing Supply Inc., I-1789
Beal Bank USA, I-432
The Bear & The Rat, II-2678
Bear Naked Inc., I-662, 825
Beasley Broadcast Inc., II-2828
Beaumont Health, I-1750
Beaver Excavating Co., I-916
Beazer Homes, I-1840, 1843, 1846
Beazley Insurance Co. Inc., I-1911
Beazley PLC, I-1916-1917
Bechtel Corp., I-1251, 1742, II-2445
Becton Dickinson, I-1068
Bed Bath & Beyond, I-1803-1804, 1834
Beechcraft, I-63
Beef 'O Brady's, II-2897
Beelen Sloopwerken, I-911
Behn Meyer Group, I-702
Behr Process Corp., II-2591
Beiersdorf AG, II-2651, 3095, 3553-3554
Beijing Dequingyuan Agriculture Technology, I-1193
Beijing Edifier Technology Co., II-3519
Beijing Enterprises Water Group Ltd., II-3509
Beijing New Building Materials Public Ltd., II-3493
Beijing Sinnet Technology Co., I-1037
Beijing Yanjing Brewery Co. Ltd., I-102, 481, 483
Bekaert Corp., I-1303
Bel Brands USA, I-1008
Belarusian Potash Company, II-2774
BelAZ, II-2324
The Belden Brick Co., I-560
Belfor Holdings Inc., I-869

BelGioioso Cheese Inc., I-674
Belgrankorm, II-2208
Belimed AG, II-2249
Belk Inc., I-1056
Belkin, I-885
The Belknap-White Group, I-1362
Bell Bank, I-427, 438
Bell Boeing, I-70
Bell Boeing Joint Project Office, I-1664
Bell Helicopter, I-62
Bell Labs, II-2660
Bell Mobility Inc., II-3565
Bell Nursery USA, I-1674
Bell Textron Inc., I-60
Bellisio Foods, I-1488
BellRing Brands Inc., II-3278
BEML Ltd., I-853, II-2324
Ben & Jerry's Homemade Inc., I-1875
Benjamin Moore, II-2591
Benson Industries, I-918
Beretta Boilers, I-1768
Beretta USA Corp., I-1718
Berge Bulk, II-3048
Bericap, I-610
Berkadia, II-2844-2845, 2847
Berkel & Company Contractors, I-916
Berkshire Bank, I-425
Berkshire Hathaway Inc., I-26, 32-34, 36, 38, 40-41, 296, 1234, 1565, 1660, 1788, 1802, 1910, 1912, 1914-1915, 1921, 1923-1926, 1929, 1943, 1946, 1950-1951, II-2848
Bernatello's Foods Inc., I-1493
Berry Global Inc., I-12, 610, II-2440-2442, 2562-2565, 2570, 2727-2729
Bertelsmann, II-2811
Bertelsmann Music Group, II-2399-2402, 2408
Bespoke Paint Protection, I-318
Best Buy Inc., I-219, 221-222, 628, 789, 902, 1168, 1178, 1834, II-2904-2905, 2909
BEST Contracting Services Inc., I-922
Best Express, II-3067
Best One Tire & Service, II-3345
Best Western, I-1828, 1833
Bestore, II-3135
Bestway Cement Ltd., I-648
Bestway Inc., II-2870
Bet365, I-1578

Betfair, I-1579
Beto Carrero World, I-178
Betsson AB, I-1578
Better Bites Bakery, I-399
Beypiliç, I-1199, II-2184
BFBC L.L.C., I-1658
BFY Brands, II-3115
BG Fuels, I-1593
BGI/Groupe Castel, I-483
BGR Group, I-2109
BH Management L.L.C., I-1854
BH Media, II-2429
Bharat Biotech-ICMR, II-3459
Bharat Group, I-688
Bharti Airtel Ltd., II-3568, 3570
BHP, I-958, 1992, II-2432-2433, 3456
BIC S.A., I-2065, II-2653, 2806, 3594
Bierlein Companies Inc., I-910
Biesterfeld AG, I-699, 704
Big Boy/Frisch's Big Boy, II-2887
Big D Builders Inc., II-2278
Big Heart Pet Brands, II-2670-2671, 2674, 2676, 2682-2683
Big Lots Inc., I-1091, 1565, 1802-1803
Big Loud, II-2408
Big O Tires, II-3343
Bigge Crane and Rigging Company, I-1013-1014
Bil-Jac Foods Inc., II-2678
Bilka markets, I-1688
Billy Casper Golf, I-1644
BillyBey Ferry Co., II-2156
Bimbo Bakeries USA Inc., I-380, 387
Binswanger Glass, I-918
Bio Ritmo Group, I-1722
Biochem Pharmaceuticals Industries, I-1130
Biofilm Inc., II-2658
Biogen Inc., I-504
bioMérieux, I-1068-1069
Bionaturae L.L.C., II-3225
Bionet Medical, II-3474
Bionutritional Research, I-839
Biotronik, II-2237
Birch Bemnders, II-2599
Bird B Gone, II-2660
Bird Construction, I-862
Birel Art, II-3396
Birla Copper, I-953
Birla Corp., I-646

Bissell Inc., I-1059
BJ's Wholesale Club Holdings Inc., I-1598, 1605-1606, II-2524, 2907, 3495
B.L. Harbert Holdings L.L.C., I-865, 1657
Black & Veatch Corp., I-924, 1057, 1251, II-3513-3514
Black Bear Diner, II-2887
Blackboard, II-3175
Blackrock Homes, I-1841
BlackRock Inc., I-1981-1982
Blattner Energy Inc., I-924
Blaze Grills, II-2534
Blefa Gmbh, I-2016
Blenz Coffee, I-764
Blessey Marine Services, II-3050, 3058
Blizzard Beach at Disney World, II-3510
Bloom Nation, I-1369
Bloomberg, I-1323
Bloomfield Homes, I-1843
Blossman Gas Inc., II-2808
Blount International, II-2457
Blue Bell Creameries, I-1873, 1875
Blue Buffalo Co. Ltd., II-2670-2671, 2674, 2676, 2682-2683
Blue Cross Blue Shield, I-1919
Blue Diamond Growers, I-1006, II-2318, 3134
Blue Green Group Saur Group, I-1644
Blue Marble Ice Cream, I-1876
Blue Nile Inc., I-2000, 2002
Blue Star L.L.C., II-2700
BlueCoast Realty, II-2849
BlueFocus Communication Group, I-24
Bluestar Alliance, I-2061
BMC Stock Holdings Inc., I-565, 1789
BMO Harris Bank NA, I-406, 417-418, 427, 458
BMR Group, I-1790
BMW Group, I-331-332, 339-340, 365
BNP Paribas, I-401
BNSF Railway, II-2839, 3573
BNY Mellon NA, I-443, 1981
Boatsetter, II-2870
Bob Evans Farms Inc., II-2219
Bob Evans Restaurants, II-2887

Bob's Discount Furniture, I-1565, 1802
Bob's Red Mills Natural Foods, II-2599
BOC Aviation, I-80
BoComm Leasing, I-80
The Body Shop, I-990
BOE Display Technology Co. Ltd., I-1088, 1203, II-2602
Boehringer Ingelheim, I-1127
Boeing Co., I-57, 66-70, 1339, 1648-1649, 1658, 1664-1665, 2108, II-2645, 3414
Boeing Employees Credit Union, I-1019
Boels Rental, I-1773
Boels Verhurr, I-1775
The Boetler Companies, I-1419
Bohr Poultry, I-1194
Boise Cascade Co., I-1241, II-3588
Boise Hunter Homes, I-1841
Bojangles, II-2885
BOKF NA, I-409, 435, 440
Bolloré Logistics, II-3055
Bombardier Inc., I-57, 61, 65, II-2831
Bombardier NUG Signaling, II-2836
Bon Appetit Danish Inc., I-391
Bonland Industries Inc., I-923
Bonnier Broadcasting, II-3318
Bonny Gas Transport, II-3051
Booking Holdings Inc., I-37, II-2522, 3413, 3417-3418
Books A Million Inc., I-518
Boom! Studios, I-774
Boone Newspapers, II-2429
Boot Barn Holdings, I-1433
Booth Creek Ski Holdings Inc., II-3087
Booz Allen Hamilton Holding Corp., I-878, 1647, 1656, 1659-1660, 1662-1663, 1665
Boparan Holdings Ltd., I-1395
Boral Ltd., I-566, II-3493
Borr Drilling, II-2484
Borrego Solar Systems, I-925
Bosch GmbH, II-3381-3382, 3384-3385
Bosch Rexroth AG, I-323
Bosch Security Systems, I-593
Bosch Thermotechnology Corp., I-1768
Boscovs Inc., I-1056
Bose Corp., I-882

Boston Beer Co., I-482
Boston Capital, I-1862
Boston Consulting Group, I-878
Boston Market Corp., II-2885
Boston Scientific Corp., II-2237, 2254, 2263, 2265
Boulangerie Neuhauser, I-1485
Boulder Brands Inc., I-821
The Bouqs Company, I-1369-1370
Bouygues' Construction Divisions, I-864, 909
Bouygues Telecom, II-3566
Bowlero Corp., I-543
Boyd Sleep, I-1796
Boyne Resorts, II-3087
Boys & Girls Clubs of America, I-665, II-2856
BP Firearms Co., I-1717
BP North America, I-935
BP PLC, I-696, II-2467
BPGIC, II-2494
BPI, I-1362
B.R. Funsten & Co., I-1362
B.R. Retreading Inc., II-3346
Brach's, I-808
Bracing Systems, I-1776
Bradford White, I-238
Brady Corp., II-3077
Brambles Ltd., II-2598
Brampton Brick, I-560
Brand L Embroidery & Screenprinting, II-3140
Brandenburg Industrial Service Co., I-910-911
BrandSafway, I-908, 921, 1775-1776
BrandsMart USA, I-219
Bread Srsly L.L.C., I-558
Breakthru Beverage Group, II-3551
Breitling S.A., II-3507
Bremer Bank NA, I-427, 438
Brenntag AG, I-699-702, 704
Brentwood Home, I-1801
BRF S.A., I-1489, 1885, II-2182, 2185, 2215
Bridgestone Americas Inc., II-2936, 3343, 3355
Bridgestone Corp., II-3356
Bridgestone Retail Operations, I-317
Bridgewater Bank, I-427
Bridgford Foods Inc., II-2199
Briggs & Stratton, I-1616, II-2784
Bright Dairy & Food Co., II-3599
Bright Horizons, I-714
Brighton Corp., I-1841

BrightSpring Health Services, I-1115
Brimhall Foods Co. Inc., II-3121
The Brink's Company, I-616, II-3001
Brinks Home Security, II-3002
Bristol-Myers Squibb Co., I-1138
Britannia Industries, I-1390
British American Tobacco, II-3361
British Gypsum, I-1728
British Museum, II-2387
British Petroleum Co. PLC, I-1438, 1440-1441, 1443
Broadcom Inc., I-1956, 1961, II-3017, 3167
BroadStreet Partners Inc., I-1940
Broadview Holding, I-2026
Brodie Contractors Inc., I-919
Broken Bow Records, II-2408
Bronco Wine Co., II-3549
Brook Mays Music Co., II-2411
Brookdale Senior Living, I-1748, 1861-1862
Brookside Foods Ltd., I-721
Brother Corp., II-2617
Broward County Public Schools, I-1422
Brown & Brown Inc., I-1909
Brown Jordan, I-1549
Browning Arms Co., I-1716, 1718
Brownstein, Hyatt Farber Schreck, I-2109
Brunei International, II-3228
BTG Hotels Group Co., I-1828
Buana Megah Paper Mills, II-2605
Bubugao Group, I-1684
Bucherer Group U.K. Ltd., I-2000
Buckeye Partners, II-3291
Bud's Best Cookies Inc., I-1012
Buffalo Technology, II-2426
Buffalo Wild Wings, II-2884, 2891, 2897
Build American Mutual Assurance Co., I-1936
Builders FirstSource Inc., I-565, 1789
Bumble, I-253-254
Bumble Bee Seafoods, II-2211
Bunn-O-Matic Corp., I-1423
Burberry, I-189
Burch Tank & Truck, II-3292
Burger King, I-1453, II-2878-2879, 2889, 2892
Burlington Stores, I-1803
Burly Corp., I-1303
Burns & McDonnell, I-1057

Burris Logistics, II-3501
Bushnell Corp., I-1666
Butterball L.L.C., II-2211, 2224
Buzzi Unicem, I-644
BW LNG, II-3051
BWH Hotel Group, I-1828
BYD Co. Ltd., I-301, 307, 331, 347, 349, 467, II-3029
Byrdie.com, I-1971
C Vale - Cooperativa Agroindustrial, II-2182
Cabela's Inc., II-3215
Cable One, II-2631
Cabot Creamery Inc., I-674
Cabot Gypsum ULC, I-1726
Cabot Oil & Gas Corp., II-2462-2465
Cachet Pharmaceuticals, I-1130
CACI International Inc., I-1663
Cacique USA, II-3391
Cactus Feeders, I-625
Caddell Construction Co., I-1653
Cadence Bank NA, I-404
CAE Inc., I-1338-1339
Caesar Stone, I-276
Caesars Casino, I-1572
CAF, II-2831
Cafe Rio Mexican Grill, II-2894
Café Valley Bakery, I-385, 391
Cafection, I-1423
Caffè Nero, I-770
CAI International Inc., I-905
Cairo Poultry Co., II-2177
Cal-Maine Foods, I-1195, 1200, 1202
CALB USA Inc., I-467
Calbee North America L.L.C., II-3118
Caleres Inc., I-1433
Califia Farms L.P., II-2318
California, State of (contracting), I-1651
California Dairies Inc., I-1033
California Drywall Co., I-929
California Institute of Technology, I-1648
California Pools and Landscape, I-928
California Public Employees, II-2645
California State Lottery, I-1577
California State Teachers, II-2645
California Vanpool Authority, II-2160

Calise & Sons Bakery Inc., I-550
Callan Marine Ltd., I-1659
Callaway Golf, I-1666
Calloway's Nursery, I-2037
Caltex Australia Ltd., I-1438
Cambria, I-276
The Camden National Bank, I-423
Cameco Corp., II-3456
Camel Games, II-2339
Camino Real Foods Inc., I-1491
Campbell Soup Co., I-379, 550-552, 555, 606, II-2318, 3127-3129, 3195
Campus Advantage, I-1855-1856
Campus Apartments, I-1856
Camso Solideal, II-3348
Can-Am Motorcycles, I-103
Canada Pension, II-2647
Canadian National Railway, II-2839
Canadian Pacific Railway, II-2839
Canadian Potash Exporters, II-2774
Canadian Tire, I-1593, 1790
Canal Barge Company Inc., II-3050, 3058
Canal+France, II-2629
Canal+Group, II-3315
Candyrific, I-835
Canfor Corp., I-2127-2129
Canon Inc., I-595, II-2241, 2628
Canopy, I-601
Cantsink Manufacturing Inc., I-925
Canvas, II-3175
Cape Cod, II-3123
Capilano Honey, I-1824
Capital Grille, II-2890
Capital Group, I-1981
Capital One Financial Corp., II-2640
Capital One NA, I-411, 422, 424, 454
Capital Power, I-1225
Capital Senior Living Corp., I-1861
Capital Travel and Events, II-3415
Capitol Federal Savings Bank, I-420
Capitol Music Group, II-2408
Capri Holdings Ltd., I-189
Capstone On-Campus Management, I-1855
Captain D's Seafood Kitchen, II-2896
Card Factory, I-1676
Cardem, I-911
Cardif Pinnacle, I-1918
Cardinal Group Management, I-1855
Cardinal Health Inc., II-2254
Cardinal Logistics, II-3431

Carey International Inc., I-2082
Cargill Inc., I-1390, 1394, 1884-1885, II-2180, 2224
Cargill Proteína Latinoamérica, II-2183
Cargolux Airlines, II-3054
Carhartt Inc., I-194
Caribbean Cinemas, II-2379
Caribbean Produce Exchange L.L.C., I-1645
Carl Zeiss AG, I-2054, II-2250
Carlisle Companies, I-566
Carlisle Construction Materials, II-2929-2930
Carl's Jr., II-2892
Carlsberg A/S, I-102, 483
Carlsberg Group, I-481
Carnival Corp., I-1024-1025
Carolina Country Manufacturing Inc., II-3121
Carolina Foods Inc., I-388
Carpenter Realtors, II-2848
Carrefour, II-2910
Carriage Services Inc., I-1040
Carrier Global, I-1764
Carrington Mortgage Services L.L.C., I-1654
Carrols Group, I-1454
Carrs Foods Intl., I-550, 1006
CarsontheWeb, I-293
Carter-Jones Lumber, I-565
Carthage System, I-1782
Casa Del Gelato, I-1485
Casalgrande Padana, I-658
Case Construction Equipment, I-853
Casey's General Stores Inc., I-935, 1437
Cash & Carry, I-1678
Cashman Dredging & Marine Contracting Co., I-912
Casio Computer Co., I-589
Casper Sleep, I-1543, 1801
Cassens Transport Co., II-3426
Castel Groupe, I-102
Castle Building Centers, I-1790
Caterpillar Inc., I-853, 855-857, 1244, II-2324-2325
Cathay Pacific Airways, II-3054
Catholic Charities USA, I-665
Caulipower, I-1493
Cavco Industries Inc., I-1851, II-2862
CBD American Shaman, I-603
CBD Aviation, I-80

CBDfx, I-603
CBG Building Company L.L.C., I-1852
CBH Homes, I-1841
CBIZ Inc., I-5
CBRE, II-2843-2847, 2851
CBS, II-2632
CBS All Access, II-2537-2538
CCL Technology, II-3005
CCS Presentation Systems, II-3289
CDM Smith Inc., I-1647, II-3514
CDW Corp., I-902, 1646, 1661
Ceamsa, II-2993
CEC Huada Electronic Design Co., I-1960
Ceco Construction Group, I-908
Cedar Fair Entertainment Company, I-182
Cedar Graphics Inc., II-2797
Celanese Corp., II-2732
Celgene Corp., I-504
Celltrion Inc., I-1121
Cementir, I-647
Cementos Cosmos, I-650
Cementos Portland Valderrivas, I-650
Cementos Tudela Veguin, I-650
Cemex España, I-650
Cemex S.A.B. de C.V., I-644, 651
Cengage Learning Holdings II, II-2811
Centene Corp., I-1115, 1788, 1915, 1919
Centennial Bank, I-407
Center Fresh Group, I-1202
Centerpoint Energy Entex, II-3458
CentiMark Corp., I-922
Central Bank & Trust Co., I-421
Central Florida Regional Transportation Authority, II-2151
Central Garden & Pet, I-2033, II-3003
Central Pacific Bank, I-415
Central Provident Fund, II-2647
Central Puget Sound Regional Transit Authority, II-2154, 2157, 2159
Central Research Inc., I-1650
Central Wire Industries, II-2434
Central Wrap L.L.C., I-1008
Centrepointstores.com, I-1180
Centreville Bank, I-445
Centurion Health, I-1746
Century 21 Scheetz, II-2848
Century 21 Swayer & Associates, II-2849

Century Communities, I-1839, 1842
Century Snacks L.L.C., II-3134
CenturyLink, II-2799
Cenveo Enterprises, II-2794-2796
Ceragon Networks Ltd., II-2421
Ceramica Carmelo Fior, I-659
Ceramiche Gresmalt Group, I-658
Cerbelli Creative, I-1255
Cermaq, I-1327-1328
Cerner Corp., I-1662, II-3190
Cersanit, II-2958
CertainTeed, I-281, 1305, 1725-1726, 2125, II-2931
Cessna Aircraft Co., I-63
Ceva Logistics, II-3059, 3430
Cewe Color, II-2703
CFM International, I-74, 76, 78-79
CGB Insurance Co., I-1937, 1945, 1947
CGC Inc., I-1726
CGI Inc., I-1655, 1657, 1659
C.H. Robinson Worldwide, II-3057, 3059, 3065
Champion Foods L.L.C., I-1400
Champion Painting Specialty Services Group, I-921
Champion Window Manufacturing & Supply Co. L.L.C., I-869
Chanel Ltd., I-2132
Chang Chun Group Corp., I-956
Chang'an Automobile Co. Ltd., I-339
Chang'an Bus Manufacturing Co., I-572
Changsha Jinlong Foundry Industry, II-2144
Chapters Health System, I-1749
Charles Schwab, I-432, 449, 1982
Charley's Philly Steaks, II-2895
Charlotte Pipe & Foundry, II-2719
Charlotte's Web, I-603
Charms L.L.C., I-829
Charoen Pokphand Foods PCL, I-1783, II-2215
Charoen Pokphand Group, I-1200, 1885, II-2185
Charter Arms, I-1719
Charter Communications Inc., I-26, 33, 2108, II-2631
Chattanooga Area Regional Transportation Authority, II-2152
Chattem Inc., I-1452
Check Point Software, II-3171
The Cheesecake Factory, II-2884

Chef Bob Brand Inc., I-846
Chegg, I-516-517
Chem Nut Inc., I-692
Chemtura Corp., I-691
Cheng Shin Rubber Co., II-3348, 3356
Chengdu Aircraft Industry Group, I-68
Cherkizovo Group, II-2179, 2208
Cherokee Brick, I-560
Chery Automobile Co., I-349
Cheryl's (Cheryl & Co.), I-1485
Chesapeake Energy Corp., II-2462, 2464-2465, 3423
Chevron Corp., I-696, 935, 2119, II-2463, 2465, 2467, 2485-2488
Chewy, II-2688
Cheyenne International, II-3359, 3365
CHG Healthcare Services, II-3229
Chicago Board Options Exchange, I-1257
Chicago Public Schools, I-1422
Chicago Theatre, II-3334
Chicago Transit Authority, II-2150, 2162
Chick-fil-A, I-1453, II-2885, 2889
Chico's FAS, I-216
Childcare Network, I-714
Chili's Grill & Bar, II-2884, 2891
Chime, I-402
Chimelong Group, I 182
Chimelong Ocean Kingdom, I-180-181
Chimelong Water Park, II-3510
China Animal Husbandry Industry Co. Ltd., II-3464
China Baowu Steel Group Corp., II-3238
China Biopharmaceutical Co. Ltd., I-1133
China Communications Construction Group, I-864, 909
China Construction Bank, I-401
China COSCO Shipping Lines, II-3048, 3053
China Duty Free Group, II-3419
China Eastern Airlines, I-84
China General Nuclear Power Group, II-3456
China Guardian Auctions Co., I-269
China Hongqiao Group, I-159, 166
China Huishan Dairy Holdings, I-1290

China Mengniu Dairy Co. Ltd., I-1032, 1034, 1396, II-3599
China Merchants Group, II-3048, 3053
China Merchants Port Holdings Co. Ltd., II-3064
China Mobile Ltd., I-1037
China Modern Dairy Holdings, I-1290
China National Building Material Co., I-651-652
China National Chemical Corp., I-2033
China National Nuclear Corp., II-3456
China National Offshore Oil Corp., II-2468
China National Petroleum Corp., I-696, 1440, II-2466, 2495, 3291
China National Pharmaceutical & Health Industry Co. Ltd., I-1133
China National Tobacco Corp., II-3361
China Oilfield Services Ltd., II-2484
China Petrochemical Corp., II-2466
China Petroleum & Chemical Corp., I-696, 1440, II-2468, 2495, 3291
China Railway Construction Corp., I-864, 909, II-2832
China Railway Signal & Communication Corp., II-2832
China Reinsurance (Group) Corp., I-1951
China Resources Beverage Holdings Co. Ltd., I-102, 481, 538, 540
China Resources Cement Holdings Co. Ltd., I-651
China Resources Holdings Co. Ltd., II-2903
China Resources Pharmaceutical Group Co. Ltd., I-1133
China Resources Snow Breweries Ltd., I-483
China Shengmu Organic Milk Ltd., I-1290
China Southern Airlines Co., I-84, II-3054
China Star Optoelectronics Corp., II-2602
China State Construction Engineering Corp., I-864, 909
China State Railway Group, I-864, II-2832, 2838

China State Shipbuilding Corp., II-3071
China Telecom, I-772, 1037, II-3310
China Unicom, I-1037
Chinese-American Signal Co., II-2836
Chip One Stop Inc., I-1957
Chipbond Technology Corp., II-3014
ChipMOS Technologies, II-3014
Chipotle Mexican Grill, II-2888-2889, 2894
Chipsoft B.V., II-3190
Chiquita Brands International, I-1515
Chiyoda-Ute, II-3493
Choice Financial Group, I-438
Choice Foods, I-1097
Choice Hotels, I-1828, II-3039
Chongqing Polycom International Corp., I-1624
Chow Sang Sang Holdings Intl., I-2130
Chow Tai Fook, I-1998, 2001, 2130, 2132, 2134
CHR, I-803
Christensen Farms, I-1782
Christie's, I-269
Chronos Solutions L.L.C., I-1654
CHS Inc., I-52, 692, 1884, II-2808
Chubb Group, I-1910, 1912, 1914, 1922, 1927-1930, 1932-1933, 1935, 1937, 1939, 1941, 1945-1947, 1949-1950, 1952
Chuckanut Bay Foods, I-396
Chugach Alaska Corp., I-1656
Chun Yu Works & Go, I-1882
Church & Dwight Co. Inc., I-1059-1062, II-2531, 2657-2658
Church's Chicken, II-2885
CIBC Bank USA, I-417
CIC Intl., I-379
Cielo, II-2275
Cigna, I-1114-1115, 1919, II-2701
Cimpress, II-2703, 2795
CinArt Lumière, II-2380
Cincinnati Bengals, II-3219
Cincinnati Financial Corp., I-1910, 1930
Cincinnati Insurance Group, I-1928
Cine Araújo, II-2381
Cinemacenter, II-2380
Cinemark Holdings Inc., II-2379-2382
Cineplanet, II-2382

Cineplex Entertainment, II-2379
Cinépolis, II-2379-2382
Cingular Wireless, I-628
Cintas Corp., II-3328-3329
Cipla Ltd., I-1130
Circle Foods L.L.C., II-3391
Circle K, I-1453
Cirrus Aircraft, I-61, 71
Cisco Systems Inc., I-782, II-2424-2427, 2526, 2783, 3036, 3168, 3306
CIT Bank NA, I-408
CIT Group Inc., I-2042-2044
Citadel Securities, I-1979
CITGO Petroleum Corp., I-935
Citibank NA, I-408, 410, 412, 417, 424, 436, 444, 447, 456
Citigroup, I-1984-1985, II-2640
Citizens Bank NA, I-410, 425-426, 433, 439, 443, 445, 453
Citizens Bank of Pennsylvania, II-2350
Citizens Financial Group Inc., I-2105
The Citizens National Bank of Meridian, I-428
Citrix Systems Inc., II-3173
Citrus World Inc., I-2012
City National Bank, I-408, 432
City National Bank of West Virginia, I-457
City of Portland, II-2152, 2159
City of Seattle-Seattle Center Monorail Transit, II-2158
City of Tucson, II-2159
CJ Logistics North America, II-3500, 3503
CJK Group, II-2795
CKF, II-2561
CLA, I-5
Claas Corp., I-1280, 1283
Claffey Pools, I-928
Clarion Events/Comet Bidco, I-942
Clarity, II-3415
Clark Associates Inc., I-1419
Clark Construction L.L.C., I-1655
Clark County (NV) School District, I-1422
Clark Group, I-863, 865, 868, 907
Clark Material Handling International Inc., I-2063
Claro Video, II-2547
Classic Brands, I-1796
Classic Foods Inc., I-1400
Claxton Bakery Inc., I-395

Clay Paky, I-2072
Clayco Inc., I-907
Clayton Homes, I-1838, 1851
Clean Harbors Inc., II-3504
Clean Tech Inc., II-2731
Clear Bra Indy, I-318
Clear Bra Ohio, I-318
Clear Channel Outdoor Holdings Inc., I-39
Clearview Foods, I-823, 1006, II-3139
Clearview Homes, I-1844
Clearway Energy, II-3237
Cleveland Browns, II-3219
Clever Fit, I-1723
Clif Bar & Co., I-825, 839, 847
Clin Off, II-3553
The Clorox Co., I-1059, II-2945
Clorox Corp., II-3555
ClosetMaid, I-1587
Cloudwalk Software, I-1272
ClubCorp, I-1644
Clyde's Delicious Doughnuts, I-388
CMA CGM, II-3061, 3064
CMPC, II-2814-2815
CMX Cinemas, II-2379
CNA Financial Corp., I-1910, 1912
CNA Insurance, I-1927-1928, 1935, 1941, 1943, 1946, 1952
CNH Industrial, I-1278-1284
CNHI L.L.C., II-2429
CNN, II-2632
CNX Resources Corp., II-2462-2464
The Co-operative Group Ltd., I-1442
Coal India Ltd., I-748
Coast Guard Exchange, II-2307
Coast Professional Inc., I-1650
Coast to Coast Pools, I-928
Coastal Greenhouses, I-1674
Coave SRL, II-2183
Cobham Ltd., I-1667
Coca-Cola China, I-540
The Coca-Cola Co., I-539, 1394, 1396, 2012, II-3150
Coco Coffee, I-765
Coco International Inc., I-846
Codelco, I-958, II-3084
Codman Neurosurgery, II-2266
Cody Pools, I-928
Coface North American Insurance Co., I-1931
COFCO, I-1294
COFCO Biochemical, I-499
COFCO Bioenergy, I-499

Coffee Fellow, I-767
Cofrad Mannequins, II-2145
Coins 'n Things, I-1660
Cold Jet, I-1159
Cold Stone Creamery, II-2883
Coldman Logistics, II-3499
Coldrush Logistics, II-3499
Coldwell Banker Kaiser, II-2848
Coldwell Banker Sea Coast Advantage, II-2849
Coleen's Better Than Breadsticks, I-1003
Coles Group Ltd., I-1438
Colfax Corp., II-3526
Colgate-Palmolive Co., I-1059, II-2531, 2651, 2656
The Collier Companies, I-1856
Colliers International, II-2843, 2845-2847, 2851
Colony Capital, I-1862
Colorful Co., II-3021
Colourpop.com, I-1971
Colt's Manufacturing Co., I-1719
Columbia Gas Transmission, II-2492
Columbia Sportswear, II-2408
Columbia State Bank, I-441, 455
Columbus Café & Co., I-766
Comcast Corp., I-26, 33-34, 36, 40-41, 2108, II-2631, 3315, 3319, 3423
Comerica Bank, I-426, II-2636
Comfort Systems USA Inc., I-920
Command Cos., I-528
Commerce Bank, I-420, 429
The Commercial Aircraft Corporation of China, I-66-67
CommonSpirit Health, I-1747
Commonwealth of Pennysylvania, I-1650
CommScope, I-782
Community Bank NA, I-453
Community Bank of Mississippi, I-428
Community Bible Church, II-2867
Community Choice Credit Union, I-1020
Community Financial Credit Inc., I-1020
Community Foundation for Southeast Michigan, I-666
Community Media Group, II-2429
Community National Bank, I-453
Community Tire Co. Inc., II-3346
Community Trust Bank Inc., I-421

Compagnie Financière Richemont S.A., I-2000, 2132
Compagnie Fruitière, I-1515
Compañia de Minas Buenaventura, II-3084
Compass Group North America, I-1420
Compass International, II-2356
Compass Pools, II-3287
Compass (real estate), II-2850
Compassus, I-1749
Compeq Manufacturing Co., II-2790
CompuGroup Medical, II-3190
Computar, I-2055
comScore, II-2874
Comstock Resources Inc., II-2462
Comvita Ltd., I-1824-1825
Conagra Brands, I-379, 606, 1033, 1394, 1485, 1488-1489, II-2194, 2210, 2219, 2223, 3118-3119, 3131, 3137
Conair Corp., I-235
Concentra Inc., I-1753
Concord Confections Inc., I-1711
Concord Foods Inc., I-819
Conestoga Cold Storage, II-3501
Confie Co., I-1940
Congebec Logistics Inc., II-3501
Connealy Angus, I-623
Connecticut Department of Transportation, II-2151
Connie's Products Development Inc., I-1400
Conn's Inc., I-219
Conoco Resources Inc., II-2487
ConocoPhillips, I-935, 1441, II-2463, 2465, 2485-2488
CONSOL Energy Inc., I-747
Consolidated Edison Co., II-3237
Consolidated Nuclear Security L.L.C., I-1651
Constellation Brands Inc., I-102, 482, II-3549
Constellis, II-3000
Consulting & Investigations Inc., I-1978
Consum S. Coop, I-1701
Consumers Energy Co., II-3458
Contemporary Amperex Technology Co., I-307, 467
Continental Aerospace Technologies, I-72
Continental AG, I-304, 306, II-2936, 3356

Continental Automotive Systems U.S. Inc., I-305
Continental Mills Inc., II-2599
Continental Resources Inc., II-2462
Continental Tire the Americas, II-3355
ContiTech AG, I-945
Contura Energy Inc., I-747
Convatec, II-2236
The Converse County Bank, I-459
Cook-Illinois Corp., II-2979
Cooke Aquaculture, I-1327
Cooke Optics Ltd., I-2054
The Cookie Dough Cafe, I-1097
Cook's Pest Control, II-2661
Coolblue, I-1182
Coop. Ceramica Imola Group, I-658
Cooper-Booth Wholesale Co., I-933
Cooper Farms, II-2224
Cooper Standard Automotive Inc., I-1592, II-2936
Cooper Tire & Rubber Co., II-2936, 3355-3356
Copacol, II-2182
Cordialsa USA Inc., I-1012
CORE Construction Group, I-867
Core-Mark Holding Co. Inc., I-933
CoreCivic Inc., I-1655, II-2798
Corizon Health, I-1746
Corner Bakery Cafe, II-2882
Cornerstone Bank, I-431
Cornerstone Building Brands, I-566, 1720, 2125
Cornerstone Government Affairs, I-2109
Corning Inc., I-584
Coromandel International, I-688
Corona S.A., II-2958
Corporate Travel Management, II-3413, 3415
Corsicana Mattress Company, I-1796
CORT Business Services Corp., II-2870
Corteva Inc., I-689, II-3004
COSCO Shipping Lines, II-3064
Cosmic Pet L.L.C., II-2670
Costa Coffee Co., I-770
Costa Cruises, I-1024-1025
Costa Farms Inc., I-1674
Costco Wholesale Corp., I-219, 221, 902, 1115, 1178, 1560, 1597-1600, 1602-1606, 1608-1613, 1680, 1683, 1685, 1689, 1691, 1695, 1698, 1702, 1802, 1804, 1834, 2000, II-2524, 2893, 2902, 2904, 2907, 2909-2910, 3343, 3495

Coty Inc., I-977, 1449-1452
Country Bird Holdings Ltd., II-2177
Country Insurance & Financial Services Group, I-1934
Country Style, I-764
Countryside Lefse Co., I-557
Coupang, II-2519
Courtesy Insurance Co., I-1953
Courtyard by Marriott, I-1833
Covan World-Wine Moving Inc., II-3424
Covanta Energy, II-3504
Covenant HealthCare, I-1750
Coverys Group, I-1943
Covetrus, I-1127
Coway Co., I-1081
Cox Communications, II-2631
Coyote Logistics, II-3057
CP Foods, I-1193, II-2178, 2215
CP Standart Gida Sanayi Ve Ticaret, I-1199
CPI Security Systems Inc., II-3002
CR/10 (Cultural Revolution/10), II-3547
C.R. England Inc., II-3427
Cracker Barrel Old Country Store, II-2887, 2891
Craft Tire Inc., II-3346
Crane Co., I-1660
Crane Merchandising Systems, I-1423
CraneWorks Inc., I-1013
Crate and Barrel, I-1565
Crayola Ltd., II-3234
Crazy Labs, II-2335
Creative Artists Agency, I-50
Creative Lifting Services, I-1014
Creative Snacks Co., I-821
Credit Agricole Group, I-401
Credit Suisse, I-1984-1985
Credit Union One, I-1020
CREE Inc., I-2069
Crescent Hotels & Resorts, I-1829
Crete Carrier Corp., II-3429
CRH PLC, I-566, 644-645, 647, 651
Cricut, II-2617
CRISPR Therapeutics, I-1595
Cromology, II-2586
Cronos Group, I-601
Cross Country Healthcare, II-3229
Crossfirst Bank, I-420

Crossland Construction Co. Inc., I-866, 915, II-2278
Crossmatch, I-501
Crossroads Hospice & Palliative Care, I-1749
Crossroads Strategies, I-2109
Crossville Inc., I-1356
Crowe L.L.P., I-5-6
Crown Castle, II-3573
Crown Corr Inc., I-918, 923
Crown Equipment Co., I-2063
Crown Holdings Inc., I-610
CRRC Times Electric, II-2836
CRRC Wind Power (Shandong) Co., II-3445, 3447
CRSC Rapid Transit, II-2836
CRST International, II-3429
Crunch Fitness, I-1722
Crunchmaster & TH Foods Inc., I-1006
Crystal Farms, I-380, 559, 674
CSL Behring, II-3462
CSL Ltd., I-1877
CSM Bakery Products North America, I-385
CSM Tech, I-1242
CSN Mining, I-1992
CSPC Group Co. Ltd., I-1133
CSR Gyprock, II-3493
CSX Transportation, II-2839
Ctrip, II-2522
CubeSmart, II-3006
Cuddle Up Diet Products Pvt Ltd., II-2665
Culver's, II-2892
Cummins Filtration Inc., I-302
Cummins Inc., I-1244
Cumulus Media Inc., II-2762, 2828
CUNA Mutual Group, I-1935
Cupertino Electric Inc., I-913
CureVac, II-3459
Curtiss-Wright, I-81
Cushman & Wakefield, II-2843-2847, 2851
CV Sciences, I-603
CVI, I-904
CVS Corp., I-1102-1112, 1114-1116, 1744, 1919, II-2701, 2902, 2904, 2907
CWS High River, I-497
CWT, II-3413, 3415
Cyfrowy Polsat, II-2629
Cypress Semiconductor Corp., II-3011

Cyrus O'Leary Pies, I-398
CZ-USA Inc., I-1719
D. L. Evans Bank, I-416
D-Link Corp., II-2427
D Mart, I-1678
D2L Brightspace, II-3175
Da Milano Leathers Pvt Ltd., I-2123
Dabur India Ltd., I-1824, II-3276
DAC/Heilind, I-1204
Dacotah Bank, I-447
DaDa English, I-1966
DAE Capital, I-80
Daewoo Shipbuilding & Marine Engineering Co. Ltd., II-3071
Dagli'Brugsen, I-1688
Daher (Socata), I-63
Dahua Technology, I-593
Daiichi Co. Ltd., II-2990
Daikin Industries, I-1764
Daimler AG, I-340-341, 365
Dairy Farmers of America, I-674, 1033-1034
Dairy Fresh Foods Inc., I-380
Dairy Queen, II-2892
Daiwa House, I-1838
Daiwa Seiko Corp., II-3207
Daktronics Inc., I-2052, II-3077
Dal-Tile, I-1356
Dalian Shipbuilding, I-732
Dallas Area Rapid Transit, II-2157
Dallas Cowboys, II-3219
Dallas Johnson Greenhouses, I-1674
Dalmia Bharat Ltd., I-646
Dalo Group, II-2612
Dan Ryan Builders, I-1850
Dana Corp., I-300, 1590
Danaher Corp., I-1068, II-2253-2254
D&H Secheron, II-3525
Danfoss, I-323
Dangdang.com, I-1170, 1179
Danisco A/S, II-2993
Danone, I-376, 540, 1033-1034, 1396-1397, II-2318
Dansonpack Industries, II-2733
Daojia.jd.com, II-2518
DAREU, I-786
Dark Horse Comics, I-774
Darko Farms, I-1192
Darrell Lea Confectionery Co., I-831
Daseke Inc., II-3422, 3429
Dassault Aviation S.A., I-57, 61, 65, 68
Dav El/Boston Coach Chauffered Transportation, I-2082

Dave & Buster's, II-2897
David Lloyd Clubs, I-1723
David Weekley Homes, I-1843
Davidson Hotels & Resorts, I-1829
Davita Kidney Care, I-1745
DAW SE, II-2586
Dawn Foods Products Inc., I-395
The Day & Zimmermann Group Inc., I-1657
Daybreak Farms, I-1202, II-2177
Daybreak Foods, I-1195, 1200
Daye Co., I-953
Dayoo Group, II-2178
Days Inn, I-1832
DAZN, II-2549
DB Schenker, II-3055, 3059
DD's Discounts, I-213
De Beers Group, I-1072-1073
DEACERO, I-1303
Dechra Pharmaceuticals PLC, I-1127
Dedalus Healthcare Systems Group, II-3190
Dee Brown Inc., I-919
Deere & Co., I-103, 853-856, 1278-1284, 2036
Deezer, II-2409
Defense Commissary Exchange, II-2307
DEHN USA, I-1189
Del Conca Group, I-658
Del Monte Pacific, I-606
Del Taco, II-2894
Delaware North Cos., I-1420
Delete Group, I-911
Deli Group, II-3234
Delicato Family Wines, II-3549
Delice Global Inc., I-846
Deliveroo Australia, I-1415
Delizza Patisserie, I-1485
Dell Inc., I-781, 785, 788-789, 795-798, 902, 1662, II-2424, 3016, 3035-3038
Deloitte, I-5-7, 25, 878, II-3414
Deloitte Touche Tohmatsu L.L.C., I-877
Deloitte's Deloitte Digital, I-24
Delsey, I-2121
Delta Air Lines, I-84, 86, 90-96
Delta Group, I-1276
DeMet's Candy Co., I-727, 823
Denali State Bank, I-405
DenMat Holdings L.L.C., I-1055
Denny's, II-2887, 2891
Denso Corp., I-306, II-3029

Denso International America Inc., I-305
DentalPro, II-2530
Dentsply Sirona, II-2241
Dentsu Group, I-24
Denver Regional Transportation District, II-2153, 2157
Departments & Stores Europe AB, I-978
DePuy Synthes, II-2240, 2243, 2248
Designer Brands Inc., I-1431-1434
Dessert Holdings (The Original Cakerie Ltd.), I-385, 395
The Detroit People Mover, II-2158
Detroit Transportation Corp., II-2158
Deuerer, II-2681
Deutsch Family Wine & Spirits (Josh Cellars), II-3549
Deutsche Bahn, II-2838
Deutsche Bank, I-1984-1985
Deutsche Messe, I-942
Deutsche Telekom, II-3315
Devon Energy Corp., II-2487-2488
Dex Media, I-1085
D.F. Stauffer Biscuit Co., I-387
DFCU Financial, I-1020
DFS Group, II-3419
DG Khan Cement, I-648
DGG Re Investments L.L.C., I-1654
D.H. Griffin Wrecking Co. Inc., I-910-911
Dhanani Group, I-1454
Dhanuka Agritech, I-711
DHL International, II-3430
DHL Supply Chain & Global Forwarding, II-3055, 3059
DHL Supply Chain North America, II-3065, 3500, 3503
DIA Retail, I-1701
Diageo PLC, I-102, 1395, 2086
The Dial Corp., I-54, 1059-1061, II-2656
Dialog Semiconductor, I-1956
Dialysis Clinic Inc., I-1745
Diamond Aircraft Industries, I-71
Diamond Bedding Ltd., I-1796
Diamond Green Diesel, I-497
Diamond Pet Foods, II-2681
Diamondback Energy Inc., II-2486-2488
DiamondEnergy Resources Inc., II-2485
DIC Corp., I-1903
Dickey's Barbecue Pit, II-2896

Dick's Sporting Goods, I-1431, II-3209, 3214-3215
Diebold Nixdorf, II-2911, 3005, 3170
Diedrich Coffee, I-762
Diesel Locomotive Works, II-2833
Diesel S.p.A., I-191
Digi-Key Electronics, I-1204
Digital First Media, II-2429
Digital Guardian, II-3167
Digital Realty, I-772
Dillards Inc., I-1056
Dimare Brothers Inc., I-1645
The Dingley Press, II-2793
Diplomat Pharmacy, I-1116
Direct Line Insurance Group, I-1918
Direct Travel Inc., II-3413
Directional Services Inc., I-924
DirecTV, II-2631
Discount Tire/America's Tire, II-3343
Discover Bank, I-411
Discover Financial Services, I-2105, II-2638, 2640
Discovery, II-3318
DishTV, II-2631
Disney California Adventure Park, I-179
Disney Cruise Line, I-1025
Disney+, II-2537-2539, 2542, 2547, 2549-2553
Disneyland Park, I-179, 181
Disney's Animal Kingdom at Walt Disney World, I-179, 181
Disney's Hollywood Studios at Walt Disney World, I-179, 181
District De La Rosa S.A. de C.V., I-850
District Energy St. Paul Inc., II-3237
Diversified Healthcare Trust, I-1862
Diversified Systems, II-3289
Division Industial Pecuaria, II-2183
The Dixie Group, I-1355, 1357
Dixy, I-1699
DJI Technology Co., II-3455
DKSH Holding, I-702
DLF Seeds, II-3004
DMart, I-1692
DMH Services, I-925
dnata (Dubai National Air Travel Agency), I-99
Doctors Co. Group, I-1943
Doggyman Ha Co. Ltd., II-2680

Dolcissimo Group Solo Italia Srl, I-399
Dolco Packaging, II-2561
Dollar Bank FSB, II-2350
Dollar General, I-1091, 1680, 1685, 1691, 1702, 1834
Dollar Tree, I-1091, 1685, 1689, 1691, 1803
Dominant Opto Electronics, I-2069
Dominguez Family, II-3139
Dominion Energy Transmission, II-2492
Domino's Pizza, I-1453, II-2879, 2889
Domo Chemicals, II-2732
Domtar Corp., II-2816
Dongfeng Motor Group, I-308
Donlen Corp., I-298
Donnelley Financial Solutions Inc., II-2795, 3173
DoorDash, I-1402-1412
Doosan Industrial Vehicle America Corp., I-2063
Doosan Infracore, I-855
Dormakaba Holding AG, I-2110
Dossen International Group, I-1828
Dots Homestyle Pretzels, II-3125
Doubletree by Hilton, I-1833
Doumak Inc., I-833
Dovel Technologies Group Inc., I-1659
Dover Motorsports Inc., II-2826
Dow Inc., I-8-9, 706
DowDupont, II-2732
DP World, II-3064
DPR Construction, I-866, 871
D.R. Horton, I-1839-1840, 1842-1843, 1845-1849
Dr. Oetker, I-1489
Dr. Pepper Snapple Group Inc., I-490, II-3150
Draft Kings, I-258, 1572-1573, 1579-1580
Dräger, I-1070
Dream 11, II-3217
Dream Cruises, I-1024-1025
Dreamstyle Remodeling, I-869
Dreyer's Grand Ice Cream Co., I-1873, 1875
Dreyfoos Hall, II-3334
Drill Tech Drilling & Shoring Inc., I-916
Driven Brands Inc., I-317
DS Smith PLC, II-2604

DSV Panalpina, II-3055, 3059
Dubai Duty Free, II-3419
Duffy's Sports Grill, II-2897
Dufry Group, II-3419
Dun & Bradstreet, I-1017
Dunkin', I-763, 769, II-2878, 2883, 2886, 2889
Dunkley Lumber, I-2128
Dunlop Mastclimbers, I-1776
Dunnes, I-1693
DuPont Inc., I-12, 377, 706, 997, 1900, II-2441-2442, 2728
Dupre Logistics, II-3421
Duracell Inc., I-465
Duratex, II-2958
Durham Performing Arts Center, II-3334
Dürr, I-642
Dutch Bros. Coffee, I-763
Dutch Farms Inc., I-380, 559, 674
Dutch Maid Bakery Inc., I-395
The Dutra Group, I-912
Duty Free Americas, II-3419
DXC Technology Corp., II-3190
Dynacom Tankers Management Ltd., II-3053
Dynafit, II-3208
Dynamic Bicycles, I-495
Dynamite Entertainment, I-774
E-Alternative Solutions, I-1167
E. & J. Gallo Winery Inc., II-3549
E-mart mall, II-2519
E*TRADE Bank, I-454
EA Engineering, Science and Technology Inc., I-1647
EA Fragrance Co., I-1449
Eable Creek, I-2121
Eacom Timber Corp., I-2128
Eagle Brook Church, II-2867
Eagle Cement, I-649
Eagle Materials, I-644
Eaglebank, I-424, 456
Eaglepak, I-2121
E&L Insurance, I-1918
Earthbound Farm L.L.C., I-1291
East & West Gourmet Afghan Food, I-557
East Kansas Agri-Energy, I-497
Eastdil Secured L.L.C., II-2843-2847, 2851
Eastern Bank, I-425
Eastern Mountain Sports, II-3213
Eastern Research Group, I-1647

Eastern Shipbuilding Group Inc., I-1653
Eastern Tire Service Ltd., II-3347
Eastern Wholesale Fence, I-1306
Eaton Corp., I-2113, II-2783, 3262
Eaton Towers, II-3574
eBay, I-1178, 1183
EBC Inc., I-862
Ebis Cosmetics, II-2530
EBM-Papst, I-1276
Ebro Foods, II-2625
Eby-Brown Co., I-933
ECA Group, I-1101
ECC, I-1742
Echo Global Logistics, II-3057
ECHO-USA, II-2457
Eckroth Music Co., II-2411
Eclipse Mattress, I-1796
Eclipse Window Tinting, I-318
Eco Log, I-854
Ecolab Inc., I-739, II-2661-2662, 3423, 3509
Econo Lodge, I-1832
Edda's Cale Co., I-399
Edelman, II-2809
Edgewell Personal Care Co., II-2653, 3095, 3388
Editas Medicine, I-1595
Ediya Coffee, I-768
Edsal Manufacturing Co., II-2726
Educate Inc., II-3450
Edward Don & Co., I-1419
Edward Marc Chocolatier, I-823
Edward Rose Building Enterprise, I-1853
Edwards Lifesciences, II-2263
EF (English First), I-1245
Efes Group, I-483
EG America, I-935
Egan Jones Rating Co., I-1017
Egencia, II-3415
Egger, II-3581
Eide Industries, II-3325
Eimco Elecon (India) Ltd., II-2325
Einstein Bros. Bagels, II-2882
EkoNiva-APK-Holding, I-1290
El Corte Ingles Alimentacion, I-1701
El Dorado Celulose, II-2814
El Granjero, I-1198
El Latino Foods Inc., I-557
El Milagro, II-3390
El Paso Natural Gas, II-2492
El Pollo Loco, II-2885
Elanco Animal Health, I-1127

Elara Caring, I-1748
Election Systems & Software, II-3492
Electronic Arts Inc., II-2338, 3479
Element Fleet Management, I-298
Elemental Technologies, II-2277
Eli Lilly & Co., I-1131
Elior Group, I-1424
Elior North America, I-1420
Eli's Chicago Finest Inc., I-396
Elite Kraft Paper, II-2606
Elizabeth Arden Inc., I-1451-1452
EllisDon, I-862
Elmer's Candy Co., I-727
ElringKlinger AG, I-1590
Embraer S.A., I-57, 61, 65-66, 69
EMCOR Group Inc., I-917, 920
Emergent Biosolutions Inc., I-1652
Emerson Corp., I-322, 324
Emerson Electric Co., I-586
Emirates Airlines, II-3054
Emirates Global Aluminum, I-166
Emirates Group, I-84
Emkay Inc., I-298
Empire Co. Ltd., I-1439
Empire Distributors, II-3551
Empire Roofing, I-922
Employees' Provident Fund (India), II-2647
Employees' Provident Fund (Malaysia), II-2647
Empresa Metalûrgica Vinto, II-3341
Empresas Guadalupe, I-1195
Emprise Bank, I-420
EMS-Chemie, II-2732
Enbridge Energy Inc., II-2491, 2495
Enclos Corp., I-918
Encompass Home Health & Hospice, I-1748
Encore Capital Group Inc., I-1041
Endeavor Airlines, I-50, 90-91
Endless Horizons Inc., I-1656
Endress+Hauser, I-324
ENEOS Corp., II-2495
Energizer Holdings Inc., I-465
Energy Distribution Partners, II-2808
EnerSys, I-464
ENGEL Holding GmbH, II-2747
Engie S.A., I-1234
Engineered Floors L.L.C., I-1355, 1357
Engineering Ingegneria Informatica S.p.A., II-3190
EngineTech, II-3035

Englander Sleep Products, I-1796
ENI S.p.A., I-1441
Enjoy Life Natural Brands L.L.C., I-719
Enlivant, I-1861
Enmax Corp., I-1225
Ennis-Flint Inc., II-2591
Enstrom Helicopter Corp., I-60
Entel Perú S.A., II-3571
Entercom Communications Corp., II-2828
Enterprise Bank & Trust, I-429, 435
Enterprise Crude Pipeline, II-2491
Enterprise Events Group, I-1255
Enterprise Fleet Management, I-298
Enterprise Holdings, I-311-312
Enterprise Products Partners, II-3050, 3058, 3291
Enterprise Rent-A-Car, I-295
EnTrans International, II-3292, 3407
Environmental Protection Agency, I-1647
Environmental Restoration L.L.C., I-1647
Envision Energy, II-3445, 3447
Envoy Air, I-86-88
EOG Resources Inc., II-2464, 2485-2488
Eonsmoke L.L.C., I-1167
Epcot at Walt Disney World, I-179, 181
EPIC Insurance, I-1940
Epic Systems Corp., II-3190
Epiroc AB, I-855
EQT Corp., II-2462-2465
Equinix Inc., I-772
Equity Residential, I-1853-1854
ERCO Worldwide, I-713
Erich Netzsch GmbH, I-1077
Erickson Living, I-1861
Ericsson Corp., II-2421, 3306-3307
Erith Contractors, I-911
ERM, I-1252
Ernst & Young, I-5-7, 878, II-3414
Eros Now, II-2544
Erpiliç, II-2184
E.S. Kluft, I-1796
Esab India, II-3525
ESPN, II-2632, 2762
ESPN+, II-2537
Essent Group, I-1944
Essex Property Trust Inc., I-1853
EssilorLuxottica S.A., I-2132-2133, II-2254

Essity Corp., II-3554
The Estée Lauder Companies Inc., I-971, 977, 986, 2131-2132, II-2651-2652
Estes Express Lines, II-3425
Esther's Price Candies Corp., I-727
Etailing India, I-1678
ETC (Electronic Theatre Controls Inc.), I-2072
Etex Group, II-3493
Etsy Inc., I-2002
EUKOR, II-3049
Eureden Group, I-1194
Euro Pool Group, II-2598
Eurochem, II-2774
Eurofighter Corp., I-68
Eurofral Industria, II-3553
Eurogate GmbH, II-3064
Euronav NV, II-3053
Europcar Mobility Group, I-312
EVE Energy Co. Ltd., I-467
Eventim Live, I-801
Ever Green Industria, II-3553
Ever Rich Duty Free Shop, II-3419
Everi Holding Corp., I-1582
Everland, I-180
Everlight Electronics Co., I-2069, 2071
Evol Foods, I-1488
Evonik Industries, II-2733
Évora S.A., II-2441
EVRAZ, II-3244
E.W. Scripps, II-3319
EWAC Alloys, II-3525
eXp Realty, I-1081, II-2850
Expedia Group, I-37, II-2522, 3413, 3417-3418
Expeditors Intl., II-3055, 3059, 3065
Experian PLC, I-37
Express Lane, I-317
Express Ranches, I-623
Exquisita Tortillas Inc., II-3391
Extended Stay America, I-1832, II-3039
Extra Storage Space, II-3006
Extrastores.com, I-1180
ExxonMobil Corp., I-690, 696, 706, 935, 1441, 2119, II-2462-2467, 2485-2488, 2495
ExxonMobil Pipeline, II-2491
Ezaki Glico Co. Ltd., I-717, 812
Faber-Castell Corp., II-3594
Faber Halbertsma, II-2598
Fábrica de Jabón, I-1059, 1062

Fabtex Inc., I-1794
Facebook Inc., I-17, 28, 1964, 1968, 1972, 2108
Fairfax Financial Holdings Ltd., I-1911-1912, 1917
Fairfax Insurance Group, I-1947, 1952
Fairway Independent Mortgage Corp., II-2348
Fairway Market, I-1704
Faith Technologies Inc., I-913
Fakta (chain store), I-1688
Family Dollar, I-1689
Family Video Movie Club Inc., II-2870
FamilyMart, II-2908
Famous Brands Intl., I-1097
Famur Group, II-2325
FanDuel, I-258, 1572, 1580
F&W Forestry Services, II-3336
Fantasialandia, I-178
Fantawild Group, I-182
Fanuc, I-323, 642
Farass Energy, I-467
Farbest Foods, II-2224
Fareportal, II-3413
Faria Brothers, I-1290
Farmak Kiev, I-1136
Farmers Insurance Group, I-1914, 1922-1926, 1930, 1938-1939, 1950
Farmers Mutual Hail Insurance Group, I-1947
Farmers Mutual Insurance Co. of Nebraska, I-1934
Farmers Tobacco Co., II-3367
Farmgirl Flowers, I-1369
Fast Retailing, I-214
Fast Track Erectors L.L.C., II-2278
FastMed, I-1753
FastSigns International, II-2795
The Fathers Table, I-396
Faurecia Corp., I-304-306
FAW Group, I-308
Fazoli's, II-2896
F.C. Tucker Co. Inc., II-2848
FCA Group, I-365
FCM Travel Solutions, II-3415
FCN Inc., I-1660
Federal Express Corp., I-84, II-3054, 3068-3069, 3425, 3428, 3500, 3503
Federal-Mogul Corp., I-1590
Federal Retirement Thrift Investment Board, II-2645
Federated Cooperatives Ltd., I-1593

Feeding America, I-665
Fehr Foods Inc., I-1012
Feld Entertainment, I-801
Fender Musical Instruments, II-2415
Ferrara Candy Co., I-825, 829, 835, 837, 842, 850
Ferrellgas Partners L.P., II-2808
Ferrero S.p.A., I-717, 812, 1396, II-3131
Ferrero USA Inc., I-721, 723, 727, 817, 850, 1008
Ferrovial S.A., I-909
Festo Corp., II-2760
FGF Brands Inc., I-557
FHIA Holdings L.L.C., I-869
Fiat Chrysler Automobiles, I-33, 41, 344
Fiberon L.L.C., I-1043-1044
Fibertex, II-2441
Fibocom Wireless, II-2422
Fidelis Cybersecurity, II-3167
Fidelity Bank NA, I-420
Fidelity Investments, I-1981-1982
Fidelity National Financial Inc., I-944
Fidentia Fortuna Holdings Ltd., I-1916
Fiera Foods, I-395
Fifth Third Bank NA, I-417-418, 421, 426, 437, 439, 448
Filmmaster Group S.p.A., I-1255
Finance Factors Ltd., I-415
Finance of America, II-2351
Fincantieri, II-3071
Finfloor Group, I-658
Finisar Corp., II-2526
The Finish Line, I-1433
Finn Partners, II-2809
Fircroft Inc., II-3228
Firecraft Studios, II-2336
Firehouse Subs, II-2895
Firespring Print Inc., II-2797
Firestone Building Products, II-2929-2930
Firmenich S.A., I-695
The First, A National Banking Association, I-428
First American Bank, I-435
First American Financial Corp., I-944
First Bank, I-405, 437
First Bank & Trust, I-447
First-Citizens Bank & Trust Co., I-437, 446

First Community Bank, I-457
First Dakota National Bank, I-447
First Financial Bank, I-418, 439
First Foundation Bank, I-415
First Hawaiian Bank, I-414-415, 451
First Home Mortgage Corp., II-2347
First Horizon Bank, I-448
First International Bank & Trust, I-438
First Interstate Bank, I-416, 430, 459
First Merchants Bank, I-418
First Midwest Bank, I-417
First National Bank, I-407, 423
First National Bank Alaska, I-405
First National Bank in Sioux Falls, I-447
First National Bank of Omaha, I-431
First National Bank of Pennsylvania, I-437, 443
First Premier Bank, I-447
First Republic Bank, I-408, 425
First Security Bank, I-407
First Student, II-2979
First Tech Credit Union, I-1019
First Texas Homes, I-1843
First Trust, I-1982
First United Bank and Trust Co., I-440
First Watch, II-2887
Firstbank, I-409, 448
FirstBank Mortgage Partners, II-2348
Firstbank Puerto Rico, I-444
Firstgroup, II-2164
FIS (Worldpay), II-2274
Fiserv (First Data), II-2274
Fish House Dressing, I-819
Fisher & Paykel Appliances, II-2252, 2534
Fisher Sand & Gravel Co., I-1653, 1658
Fitbit Inc., II-3520
Fitch Ratings Inc., I-1017
Fitesa S.A., II-2441-2442
Fitipower Integrated Technology, I-1955
Fitness World, I-1723
Fitx (Creative Edge Nutrition), I-1723
Five Guys Burgers and Fries, II-2888, 2892
Five Points Bank, I-431
Five Rivers Cattle Feeding L.L.C., I-625

Five Star Senior Living Inc., I-1861
Flagstar Bank FSB, I-426
Flamagas S.A., I-2065
Flatirons Community Church, II-2867
Fleming's Prime Steakhouse & Wine Bar, II-2890
Flex-N-Gate Corp., I-305
FlexShopper Inc., II-2870
Fliggy, II-2521
Flight Centre Travel Group, II-3413, 3416
FlightSafety International, I-1338-1339
Flint Group, I-1903
FLIR Systems, I-593
Floor & Decor, I-1366
Flora Classique Inc., I-55
Florens Container Holdings, I-905
Florida Lottery, I-1577
Florida Marine Transporters, II-3050, 3058
Florida State Board, II-2645
Florida Tile, I-1356
Florim USA, I-1356
Flowers Foods, I-379, 384, 388, 391, 393, 549-552, 555
Flowserve Corp., II-2822
Fluidmaster, II-2756
Fluke Corp., I-1879
Fluor Corp., I-1651, 1664-1665
Flutter Entertainment, I-1573, 1578
Flynn Group of Cos., I-862, 922-923
Flynn Restaurant Group, I-1454
FM Global Group, I-1922, 1927, 1937, 1941
FMC Corp., I-689, II-2993
F.N.B. Corp., II-2350
FocalTech Systems Co., I-1955
Focus Features, II-2356
The Folger Coffee Co., I-758
Fontem US Inc., I-1165, 1167
Fonterra Co-operative Group, I-1034
Food Bazaar Supermarket, I-1704
Food City, I-1681, 1698
Food Depot, I-1690
Food for Life Baking Co. Inc., I-549
Food Lion L.L.C., I-1683, 1686-1687, 1691, 1702-1703, 1706, II-2902
Foodliner/Quest Liner, II-3421
Foot Locker Inc., I-1431-1433, 1435
Footasylum, I-1435
Foote Cattle Co., I-625

Forcepoint, II-3167
Ford Audio-Video Systems, II-3289
Ford Gum & Machine Co., I-1711
Ford Motor Co., I-341, 344-345, 365-366, 1663
The Foreign Candy Co. Inc., I-831
Foreo AB, I-978
Forest Investment Associates, II-3336
Forest Resource Consultants, II-3336
Forest River Inc., II-2859-2861, 3403-3406
The Forestland Group, II-3336
ForFarmers N.V., I-1885
Formica Corp., I-997
Formosa Plastics Corp., I-706
Fort Dearborn, II-2795
Forterra Inc., II-2719
Fortescue Metals Group Ltd., I-1992
Fortive Corp., I-322
Fortune Brands, I-566, 582, 2110, 2125
The Forum (CA), I-262
Foshan Net Deogu Jyaming Gas Appliances Co., I-247
Foshan TDJDC Bicycle Science and Technology Co., I-495
Foster Farms, I-1491
Fotex (supermarkets), I-1688
Foundation Building Materials, I-565
Four Points Technology L.L.C., I-1662
Fox Broadcasting Co., II-2632, 3319
Fox Brother's Piggly Wiggly, I-1695
Fox Nation, II-2537
Fox News Channel, II-2632
Fox Rent A Car, I-311
Fox Theatre (GA), II-3334
Fox Theatre (MI), II-3334
Foxconn International Technology, II-2526
FPI Management Inc., I-1854
Fraco Products Ltd., I-1776
Fragrantica, I-1971
France Televisions, II-3315
Franco Whole Foods, II-3391
Frank A Zurro Inc., I-1003
Frank Roth Co. Inc., I-1719
Frankford Candy L.L.C., I-835
Franklin Corp., I-1550-1551
Franklin Synergy Bank, I-448
Fraser and Neave, II-2310
Frasers Hospitality (Worldwide), II-3039

The Fred A. & Barbara M. Erb Family Foundation, I-666
Fred Meyer, I-1597, 1610, 1613, II-2524
Fredriksen Group, II-3048
Free, II-2629
Freedom Fertility Pharmacy, I-1116
Freedom Forever L.L.C., I-926
Freedom Mobile Inc., II-3565
The Freeman Company, I-1256
Freeport-McMoran, I-958
Freestate Electrical Cos., I-917
Freimuth Abbruch und Recycling, I-911
The French Patisserie, I-1485
Fresenius Medical Care, I-1745
Fresh Del Monte Produce, I-1515
Fresh Thyme, I-1682
FreshDirect, II-2517
Freshippo, II-2518
Freshpet, II-2666, 2677-2678
Fresnillo PLC, II-3084
The Freudenberg Group, II-2440
Freudenberg Performance Materials, II-2442
Freudenberg Sealing Technologies, I-1592
Frialsa Frigorificos, II-3501-3502
Friendly's Ice Cream L.L.C., I-1875
FriendTimes Inc., II-2331
FrieslandCampina, I-1034
Friona Industries L.P., I-625
FRISA (Areca), II-2183
Fristads Kansas Group, I-194
Frito-Lay Inc., I-823, 844, 1008, II-3113, 3115, 3118, 3121, 3123, 3125, 3134, 3137, 3139
Fritz Egger GmbH, I-2026
Frontier Airlines, I-86, 89, 94
Frontier Communications Corp., II-2631
Frontier Food Co. Ltd., I-1395
Frontier Touring Company, I-801
Frosch, II-3413
Frost Bank, I-449
Fruit of the Loom, I-199
Fry's Food & Drug Store, I-1681, 1698
Fry's Marketplace, I-1608, 1698
FTD, I-1369-1370
FuboTV, II-2631
FuelCell Energy Inc., I-1865
Fugro, II-3522

Fujairah Oil Terminal, II-2494
Fuji Electric Co. Ltd., II-3029
Fujian Sunner Development Co. Ltd., II-2178
Fujifilm Holdings Corp., I-595, 2055
Fujifilm North America Corp., I-1903
Fujitsu Ltd., II-2426, 3005, 3036
Fujitu Optical Components, II-2526
Fulton Homes, I-1848
FunPlus, II-2339
Funskool, II-3398
Furukawa Electric Co., I-956
Future Electronics Inc., I-1204
Future Retail Ltd., I-1678, 1692
Fuzzy's Taco Shop, II-2894
Fyffes PLC, I-1515
FYM (HeidelbergCement), I-650
G-III Apparel Group, I-189
G4S, I-616, II-3000-3001
G.A. Food Services of Pinellas County Inc., I-1645
GAF Materials, I-281, II-2929-2931
Galaxy Desserts, I-1485
Galaxy Microsystems Ltd., II-3021
Galleher L.L.C., I-1362
Gamaleya Centre, II-3459
GameStop, I-902, II-3479
Gamesys Group, I-1578
Gamevil, II-2338
Gannett Co., II-2429
GAP Hire Solutions, I-1774
Gap Inc., I-213, 216
GAP Resurs, II-2208
GapKids, I-213
GarageTek, I-1587
GardaWorld Corp., I-616
Garden of Life, I-603
Gardiner Angus Ranch, I-623
Gardner Denver Holdings Inc., II-2822
Garmin Ltd., I-1666
Garney Holding Co., II-3513-3514
Garnier Inc., I-1732-1733
Gartner Research, II-2874
GasLog, II-3051
Gate City Bank, I-438
GateHouse Media, II-2429
Gates Corp., I-945
Gateway Church, II-2867
Gattaca PLC, II-3228
GATX Corp., I-2042-2044
Gaussian Robotics, II-2928
GCR Tires & Service, II-3345

GDS Holdings Ltd., I-1037
GE Aviation, I-78-79
GE Capital Aviation Services, I-80
GE Energy, II-3443, 3448
GE Healthcare, II-2241, 2254
GE Power, II-3290
GEA Farm Technologies, II-3104
Geberit, II-2756, 2759
GEBR Heinemann, II-3419
Gedeon Richter PLC, I-1134, 1136
GEE Ltd., II-3525
Geely Holding, I-349
Geisha Tokyo Entertainment Inc., II-2335
Gejiu Zi-Li Mining & Smelting, II-3341
Gelymar S.A., II-2993
Gemline, II-2806
Generac Holdings Inc., I-1616, II-2784
General Dynamics Corp., I-1646-1647, 1652-1653, 1657-1659, 1661, 1663-1665
General Electric Co., I-73, 75-77, 324, 1649, 1664, II-2253, 2305, 3410, 3444-3447
General Mills Inc., I-662, 812, 815, 823, 825, 827, 839, 1097, 1372, 1394, 1396, 1468, 1489, 1493, II-2599, 2681, 3115, 3118, 3127, 3131, 3390
General Motors Co., I-26, 32-33, 38, 339, 341, 344-345, 2061
General Services Administration, I-1663
General Shale, I-560
Genisys Credit Union, I-1020
Gensler, I-261, 1057, 1962
Gentle Giants, II-2676
Genuine Parts/NAPA, I-310
Genworth Financial Group, I-1944
The Geo Group Inc., I-1653, 1655, II-2798
Geodis North America, II-3500, 3503
Georg Fischer Harvel L.L.C., II-2721
George E. Masker Inc., I-921
George P. Johnson Experience Marketing, I-1255
George Weston Ltd., I-394, II-2909
George's Inc., II-2176, 2180
Georgia Lottery Corp., I-1577

Georgia-Pacific L.L.C., I-545, 1344, 1725-1726, 2127, 2129, II-2562, 2564, 2946, 2948, 3493, 3582, 3588
Geovera Holdings Inc. Group, I-1932
GEPF Pensions, II-2647
Gerberit Group, II-2958
Gestamp, I-304
Getinge, II-2249
GetNet, II-2275
GfK, II-2874
GFL Environmental Inc., II-3504
Gharda Group, I-688
GHD, I-1253, 1742
Ghirardelli Chocolate Co., I-719, 721
Gia Brands Inc., I-558
Giant Eagle, I-1111, 1682, 1697
Giant Food Stores L.L.C., I-1686-1687, 1697, 1703, 1705-1706, II-2902, 2907
Giant Manufacturing Co., I-496
Giant Snacks Inc., II-3137
Gibraltar Industries, I-1720
Gibson Guitars, II-2415
Giga Solar Materials Corp., I-377
GigaDevice Semiconductor, I-1959
Gilbane Building Co., I-865-868, 871, 907, 915
Gildan Activewear Inc., II-2806
Gilead Sciences Inc., I-504
Gilman Ciocia Inc., II-3299
Ginza Stefany Cosmetics Co., II-2530
Giovanni Rana AG, II-2625
Giti Tire PTE Ltd., II-3356
GittGidiyor (eBay), I-1183
Givaudan Flavors and Fragrances, I-695
Give & Go Prepared Foods Corp., I-391, 393
GK Software, II-3170
GKN Automotive, I-300
GL Events, I-942
Glaceau Water Co. Inc., I-539
Glacier Bank, I-416, 430, 459
Gladiator, I-1587
Glanbia PLC, I-1033, II-3278
Glatfelter, II-2442
GlaxoSmithKline, I-1130, 1135, 1138, 1652, II-2530-2531, 3462-3463
Glen-Gery Corp., I-560
Glencore PLC, I-958, 960, II-2432-2433, 2595, 3084, 3601

GlideWell Dental Laboratories, I-1055
Globacom Ltd., II-3570
Global Business Travel, II-3415
Global Eagle Entertainment Inc., I-1878
Global Infrastructure Partners, I-1234
Global Medical Response Inc., I-1653
Global Payments, II-2274
Global Pet Foods, II-2687
Global Protection Corp., II-2657
Global Tel Link (GTL), II-2799
Global Widget, I-603
GlobalFoundries, I-1448, II-3015
GlobalTranz Enterprises, II-3057
Globe Machine Manufacturing Co., II-2975
Globus Medical Inc., II-2247
Glock Inc., I-1715-1716, 1718
Gloster, I-1549
Gmarket, II-2519
GNC Holdings Inc., II-2418
Go-Ahead, II-2164
Goddard Systems Inc., I-714
Godiva Chocolatier, I-727
Gogo Inc., I-1878
Gold Fields, I-1641
Gold Metal Bakery Inc., I-549
Gold Peak Industries, II-2415
The Golden 1 Credit Union, I-1019
Golden Bridge, II-3526
The Golden Cockerel Group, II-2181
Golden Corral, II-2887
Golden Flake Snack Foods Inc., II-3113, 3121
Golden Gate Bridge, Highway and Transportation District, II-2156
Golden Lady Co., I-186
Golden Nozzle CarWash, I-615
Golden Nugget Online Gaming, I-1572-1573, 1579
Golder Associates Inc., I-1252
Goldman Sachs & Co., I-1981, 1983-1985
Goldman Sachs Bank USA, I-436, 452
Goldwind Science & Technology, II-3445-3447
GolfPipeline Corp., I-36
GOME, I-220, 1170, 1179, II-2906
Good Food, II-2165
Good Groceries Co. Inc., I-846

Good Health Natural Products Inc., II-3111
Good Humor/Breyers, I-1873, 1875
Good Job, II-2335
Good Times Tobacco, II-3359
Goodall Homes, I-1846
Goodman Food Products Inc., I-1645
Goodwill Industries International, I-665
Goodyear Canada Inc., II-3346
Goodyear Commercial Tire Systems L.L.C., II-3345
Goodyear Tire and Rubber Co., II-2936, 3355-3356
Goodyear Tire and Service Network Outlets, I-317
Google Inc., I-17, 28, 42, 252, 255, 894-896, 1184, II-2334, 2341, 2409, 3105, 3161, 3164, 3414
Gorham Savings Bank, I-423
Gottsch Cattle Co., I-625
Government Pension Fund (Norway), II-2647
Government Pension Investment Fund (Japan), II-2647
GPM Investments L.L.C., I-935
GPS Chemical Services, II-2494
Graham Group Ltd., I-862
Graham Packaging Co. L.P., II-2727
Grain Craft Inc., I-1372
Grand Design RV Co., II-3404-3406
Grand River Enterprises, II-3365
Grand Traverse Pie Co., I-394
Granite Construction Inc., I-924
Granja Almeida, I-1197
Granja Catalana, I-1198
Granja Faria, I-1197
Granja Mantiqueira, I-1197
Granja Tres Arroyos, II-2182
Granja Yabuta, I-1197
Grant Thornton, I-5
Graphic Packaging, II-2564, 2607-2609
Gravotech Group, I-2028
Gray Construction, I-870
Gray Television Inc., II-3319
Graydaze Contracting Inc., I-921
Great Clips, I-1730, 1971
Great Dane, II-3407
Great Lakes Dredge & Dock Corp., I-912
Great Lakes Insurance, I-1918
Great Southern Bank, I-429
Great West Lifeco, I-1951

Great Western Bank, I-419, 431, 447
Greater Cleveland Regional Transit Authority, II-2151
Greater Dayton Regional Transit Authority, II-2161
Greatview Aseptic Packaging Co., II-2574
Greektown Casino, I-1568
Green Brick Partners, I-1839, 1843
Green Circle Growers, I-1674
Green Diamond Resource Company, II-3337
Green Dot Bank, II-2636
Green Line Polymers, II-2731
Green Plains Cattle Company L.L.C., I-625
Green Roads, I-603
Greene Town Foods L.L.C., II-3111
Greenpath Recovery Inc., II-2731
Greenpoint AG, I-52
GreenTree Hospitality Group, I-1828
GreenTree Inn, I-1833
Greenwood Industries Inc., I-922
Greggs, I-770
Greig Seafood, I-1327
Gremo AB, I-854
Greystar Real Estate Partners, I-1852-1856
Grieg Seafood, I-1328
Grifols S.A., I-1877
Grimaldi Group, II-3049
Grindr, I-253-254
Groendyke Transport, II-3421
Groundworks, I-869
Group 1 Automotive Inc., I-296
Group Marcelle, I-977
Group Michelin, II-3356
Groupe Filgo-Sonic, I-1593
Growmark Inc., I-52, II-2808
GrubHub, I-1402-1412
Gruma Corp., II-3139, 3390
Grundfos, II-2823-2824, 3509
Grupo Agroamérica, I-1515
Grupo Agropecuario Don Julio, I-1198
Grupo Antolin North America Inc., II-2729
Grupo Bimbo S.A.B. de C.V., I-379, 384-385, 388, 391, 393, 549-552, 555-556, 1396, II-3129, 3131
Grupo Carrefour, I-1701
Grupo Cedasa/Incopisos, I-659
Grupo Cocentino, I-276
Grupo El Tunal, I-1197

Grupo Eroski, I-1701
Grupo Fragnani, I-659
Grupo Gloria, II-2310
Grupo HAME, I-1515
Grupo LALA, I-1033
Grupo Lamosa, I-659
Grupo Melo, I-1198, II-2183
Grupo Samesa S.A., I-1012
Grupo SuperAlba, II-2183
Gruppo Veronesi, II-2179
GSC Enterprises Inc., I-933
GSN Games, II-2336
GT, I-6
GTM Holdings S.A., I-700
Guangdong Baoke Stationery, II-3234
Guangxi China Tin Group Co., II-3341
Guangxi Jinchuan Non-Ferrous Metal Co., I-953
Guangxi Tianyuan Biochemistry Co. Ltd., I-710
Guangzhou Douyi Network Technology Co., II-2331
Guangzhou Hongreu Gas Appliance Co. Ltd., I-247
Guangzhou Pearl River Piano Group, II-2415
Guanxi LiuGong Machinery Co., I-857
Guardian Protection, II-3002
Guess, I-189
Guild Mortgage Co., II-2351
Guitar Center Inc., II-2411
Guittard Chocolate Co., I-719
Guixi Smelter, I-953
Gujarat Corp., I-1390
Gulf Coast Bank and Trust Co., I-422
Gulf Petrochem Group, II-2494
Gulf South Pipeline, II-2492
Gulfport Energy Corp., II-2464
Gulfstream Aerospace Corp., I-57, 61, 65
Guoxuan H-Tech Co. Ltd., I-467
GVC Holdings, I-1578
The Gym - Find Your Fit, I-1723
Gypsum Management & Supplies Inc., I-565
H-E-B Grocery, I-1115, 1696, 1744
H. Ikeuchi & Co., I-237
H2Ocean, II-2264
H3C Technologies Co., II-3035-3037
Haas Corp., II-2486

Habitat for Humanity International, I-665
Hachette Book Group, I-532-533
Hachette Livre, II-2811
Hagedorn Unternehmensgruppe, I-911
Hagoromo Foods Corp., II-2990
Haid Group, I-1885
Haier Group, I-1764
Hail Merry L.L.C., I-397
The Hain Celestial Group Inc., II-2318, 2627, 3118, 3130, 3139, 3195
Haines, I-1362
Haitian International Holding Ltd., II-2746-2747
Hako GmbH, II-2920
Halliburton Co., II-2493, 3049
Hallmark Cards, I-1676-1677
Hallmark Channel, II-2632
Hamilton Homebuilders, I-1851
Hamilton Laboratory Solutions L.L.C., I-2024
Hampton Affiliates Inc., I-2129
Hampton by Hilton, I-1833
Hampton Farms Inc., II-3134
Hancock Prospecting Pty Ltd., I-1992
Hancock Timber Resource Group, II-3336
Hancock Whitney Bank, I-422, 428
H&E Equipment Services, I-1771
H&H Industries Inc., II-3346
H+H International A.S., I-319
H&H Music Co., II-2411
H&M Group, I-214
H&M Sverige AB, I-978
H&R Block, II-3159, 3299
H&S Bakery, I-550-551
Hanen & Adkins Auto Transport Inc., II-3426
Hanesbrands Inc., I-189, 199, 210, 216
Hangcha Group Co. Ltd., I-2063
Hanger Clinic, I-1751
HangTing Hotel, I-1833
The Hangzhou Wahaha Group Co., I-540
Hankook Tire America Corp., II-2936, 3355
Hankook Tire & Technology Co. Ltd., II-3356
Hanna Holdings/Allen Tate, II-2850
Hannaford Supermarket, I-1694

Hannover Rück SE, I-1951
HannStar Display Corp., II-2790
Han's Laser Technology Co., I-2028
Hanwha Group, I-593
Happn, I-254
Happy Apple Inc., I-819
Harbor Freight Tools, I-1789
Harborone Bank, I-445
Hardee's, II-2892
Harder Mechanical Contractors Inc., I-920
Hargrove L.L.C., I-1255
Haribo GmbH & Co., I-812
Harim Group, II-2178
Harkins Theatres, II-2379
Harman International, I-882
Harman Professional Solutions, II-2415
Harmon, I-918
Harnois Énergies, I-1593
HarperCollins Publishers L.L.C., I-532-533, II-2811
Harris Company, I-920
Harris Teeter Supermarkets Inc., I-1683, 1686, 1691, 1702-1703, 1706, II-2902
Harrison Contracting Co. Inc., I-921
Harrison Street Real Estate Capital, I-1856, 1862
Harsco Environmental, I-1742
Hart InterCivic, II-3492
Hartalega Holdings Bhd., II-2273
The Hartford Financial Services Group, I-1950
Hartford Fire & Casualty Group, I-1910, 1935, 1938, 1952
Hartford Insurance Group, I-1946
Hartford Marine Holdings Inc. Group, I-1930
Hartmann A/S, II-2561
Hartz Mountain Corp., II-2670
Harvest States Foods, II-3391
Hasbro Inc., I-2061, II-3398, 3400
Hawaii National Bank, I-415
Hawkins Inc., I-701
Haworth Inc., II-3578
Hayden Homes, I-1841
Hazeldene's, II-2181
H.B. Fuller Co., I-8, 12
HBA (Hirsch Bedner Associates), I-1962
HBI International, II-3371
HBIS Group, II-3238
HBO, II-2542, 2549

HBO Max, II-2547, 2552-2553
HBO Now, II-2538
HBP Inc., II-2797
HCA Healthcare, I-1747
HCR Manorcare, I-1749
HD Supply Holdings Inc., I-1789
HDR, I-261, 1057, 1253
He Hui Electronics, I-585
Heading, II-3170
Healthpeak Properties, I-1862
Healthsmart Foods Inc., I-852
Heartland, I-1225
Heartland Automotive Service, I-1454
Heathcare Services Group Inc., I-1420
Hebei Yangyuan Zhihui Beverage Co., II-2314
HEI Hotels & Resorts, I-1829
Heidelberg Baking Co., I-557
Heidelberg Distributing Co., II-3551
HeidelbergCement, I-646-647, 649, 651-652
Heineken, I-102, 482-483
Heinz India Pvt., II-3276
Helena Agri-Enterprises, I-52
Helena Corp., I-692
Helio Towers, II-3574
Helix Innovations L.L.C., II-3363
Hellmann Worldwide Logistics, II-3055, 3059
Hello Fresh, II-2165
Helm AG, I-704
Helzberg Diamond Shops Inc., I-2000
Hempel Group, II-2586
Henan Jinxing Brewery Group, I-481
Henan Tianguan Group Co., I-499
Hendrick Automotive Group, I-296
Henkel AG & Co., I-8, 12, 14, 737, II-2586
Henkel Norden AB, I-978
Henkels & McCoy Group Inc., I-913
Henry Ford Health System, I-1750
Henry Repeating Arms Co., I-1715, 1717
Hensel Phelps, I-863, 865, 871, 907
Hepsiburada, I-1183
Heraeus, I-377
Herbalife International India, II-3276
Herbalife Nutrition Ltd., I-1080-1081, II-3278
Herbruck's Poultry Ranch, I-1202
Herc Rentals Inc., I-1771, 1775

Hercules L.L.C., II-2993
Heristo AG, II-2681
Heritage Auctions, I-269
Heritage Manufacturing Inc., I-1716, 1719
Herman Miller Inc., II-3578
Hermès India, I-2123
Herr Foods Inc., II-3113, 3123, 3125
The Hershey Co., I-717, 719, 721, 723, 812, 817, 823, 829, 831, 840, 850, 852, 1711-1712, II-3128, 3130
The Hertz Corp., I-311-312
Hestan Home L.L.C., II-2534
Hewlett Packard Enterprise, I-781-782, II-2424-2425, 2427, 2783, 3016, 3036, 3038, 3168
Hewlett-Packard Inc., I-589, 785, 788, 795-798, 902, II-3016
Hexcel Corp., I-612
Hexo Corp., I-601
HG Genuine Optics Tech Co., II-2526
HGTV, II-2632
HHM (Hersha Hospitality Management), I-1829
Hicks Nurseries, I-2037
Hidesign, I-2123
High Performance Beverage, I-1238
High Ridge Brands Co., I-1732
The Higher Taste, I-557
Highgarden Real Estate, II-2848
Highgate, I-1829
Highland Homes, I-1843
Highland Packaging Solutions, II-2561
Highlands Coffee, I-771
Highview Capital L.L.C., I-1645
Hikvision, I-592-593
Hile Bio-Technology, II-3464
Hill Mechanical Corp., I-917, 923
Hillandale Farms, I-1195, 1200, 1202
Hilldrup Moving & Storage, II-3424
Hills Bank and Trust Co., I-419
Hills-Colgate Japan Ltd., II-2680
Hill's Pet Nutrition, II-2681
Hillsborough County (PA) Public Schools, I-1422
Hillshire Brands Co., I-1491, II-2210, 2219, 2221, 2223
Hilltop National Bank, I-459
Hilti Corp., II-3381-3382
Hilton Hotels & Resorts, I-1833

Hilton Worldwide Holdings, I-1828, II-3039
The Himalaya Drug Co., II-3276
Himatsingka Seide Ltd., I-1821
Himax Technologies Inc., I-1955
Hindustan Aeronautics Ltd., I-68
Hindustan Zinc Ltd., II-3084, 3601
Hinge, I-253-254
Hirschbach Motor Lines Inc., II-3427
Hiscox Insurance Group, I-1928
Hiscox Ltd., I-1917
Hisense Group, I-880
HiSilicon, II-3018
Hispanagar S.A., II-2993
Hit Promotional Products, II-2806
Hitachi Ltd., I-781, 855, II-2241, 2324, 3290
Hitachi Transport System, II-3430
Hive Box, II-3101
HKC Overseas Ltd., II-2602
HKS, I-261
HLB, I-509
HMSHost, I-1420
Hobby Lobby Stores Inc., I-1780
Hochschild Mining PLC, II-3084
Hochtief Aktiengesellschaft, I-864, 909
Hodges Ward Elliott Inc., II-2844, 2846-2847
Hoffman Co., II-2846
Hohhot Jinqiao City Development Co. Ltd., II-2715
HOK, I-261, 1962
Holder Construction, I-863
Holiday Inn, I-1833
Holiday Inn Express, I-1833
Holiday Retirement, I-1861
Holland America, I-1025
Holland & Knight, I-2109
Hollander Sleep Products, I-1821
HollyFrontier Corp., II-2467
Hollywood Feed, II-2687
Hologic Inc., II-2241
Holtec International, II-2443-2444, 2446
Holtzbrinck Publishing, II-2811
Home Bank NA, I-422
Home City Ice Holdings Inc., I-1867
Home Depot Canada, I-1790
Home Depot Inc., I-41, 219, 222, 1178, 1365-1366, 1560, 1771, 1775, 1789, 1804-1805, 1834, II-2753, 2904-2905, 2909, 3536

Home Hardware Stores, I-1790
Home Run Inn, I-1493
HomeAway, II-3418
HomeGoods, I-213, 1803-1804
Homeinns, I-1833
Homeland Vinyl Products, I-1305
Homeplus mall, II-2519
HomeServices of America Inc., II-2850
HomeSmart, II-2850
Homestreet Bank, I-415
Hometown Food Co., I-385, II-2599
Hon Hai Precision Industry Co. Ltd., II-3016
Honda Aircraft Co., I-57, 61
Honda Motor Co., I-103, 339, 344-345, 366
Honda Power Equipment, I-1616
Honey Baked Ham Company, II-2231
Honeywell Analytics, I-1879
Honeywell International Inc., I-78, 81, 322, 324, 1651, II-2420
Hong Kong Disneyland, I-180
Hongli Zhihui Group Co., I-2069
Hongzhan Group, I-499
Hooters, II-2897
Horizon Air, I-95-96
Horizon Beverage Co., II-3551
Horizon Transport Inc., II-3426
Hormann, I-1586
Hormel Foods Corp., I-1394
Hormel Foods L.L.C., I-815
Horne Brothers Construction Inc., I-924
Hoshizaki, I-1764
Hospice of the Valley, I-1749
Hospitality Mints L.L.C., I-842
Hostess Brands L.L.C., I-384, 388, 391, 393
Hot Park Rio Quente, II-3510
Hotel Equities, I-1829
Hotels.com, II-3418
Hotstar Premium, II-2544
Hotwire, II-2809
Houdini Inc., I-727
Houghton Mifflin Harcourt, II-2811
House of Raeford Farms Inc., II-2176
Houston Independent School District, I-1422
Houston Texans, II-3219
Hovnanian Enterprises, I-1845
HPG Brands, II-2806

HR Ratings, I-1017
HSBC Bank USA NA, I-436, 456
HSBC Holdings, I-401
HSN Inc., I-2000
HSS Hire Service Group PLC, I-1774
H.T. Hackney Co., I-933
Huada Semiconductor Corp., I-1958
Huadong Pharmaceutical Co. Ltd., I-1133
Huahong Group, II-3015
Huawei Cloud, II-3165, 3169
Huawei Technologies, I-284, 638, 640-641, 781-782, 792, 799-800, II-2421, 2424-2425, 2628, 3016, 3035-3038, 3306-3307, 3520
Huazhu Group Ltd., I-1828
Hub Group, II-3065
Hub International Ltd., I-1909, 1940
Hubbard Broadcasting Inc., II-2828
Hubble Homes, I-1841
Hubei Co., I-953
Hubei Xingfa Chemicals Group Co., I-687
Hubergroup, I-1903
Hubert Co., I-1419
Hudson River Trading, I-1979
Hudson Transit Lines Inc., II-2154
Hudson-Webber Foundation, I-666
Huel Ltd., II-3278
Hugo Boss, I-189, 192
Huhtamäki Oyj, II-2561-2563, 2565
Huida Sanitaryware, II-2958
Huizhong Instrumentation Co. Ltd., II-2302
Huizhou Sino-Quick Chemcial Co. Ltd., I-710
Hulu, II-2537-2538, 2631
Hulu Theater, II-3334
Humana Inc., I-1788, 1915, 1919
Humana Pharmacy Solutions, I-1115-1116, II-2701
Hunter Douglas, I-1794
Hunter Hotel Advisors, II-2844
Hunter Pasteur Homes, I-1844
Huntington Ingalls Industries Inc., I-1664
Huntington Learning Center, II-3450
The Huntington National Bank, I-426, 439, 457
Huntsman Corp., I-12, 697, 1900
Hurricane Grill & Wings, II-2897
Husky Energy Inc., I-1439, 1593
Husqvarna Group, I-2036

Hustle Butter, II-2264
Hutchinson Ports, II-3064
Hyatt Hotels Corp., I-1828
Hydrite Chemical Co., I-701
HyLife Ltd., I-1783
Hyster-Yale Materials Handling Inc., I-2063
Hyundai Glovis Co. Ltd., II-3049
Hyundai Group, I-365
Hyundai Heavy Industries, II-3071
Hyundai Living & Culture, I-276
Hyundai Mobis, I-305-306
Hyundai Motor Co., I-345, 366
Hyundai Translead, II-3407
I and love and you, II-2674, 2682-2683
I Color Printing & Mailing Inc., II-2797
I-O Data Device, II-2426
IA Interior Architects, I-1962
IAC, I-37, 42
IAI, II-2342
IAT Reinsurance Co. Group, I-1952
Iberiabank, I-404, 407, 422
Ibiden Co. Ltd., II-2790
Ibis, I-1833
IBM Corp., I-781, II-2628, 2645, 3036, 3038, 3414
IBM Corp.'s IBM iX, I-24
Ibon Mart, I-1181
Icahn Automotive/Pep Boys, II-3343
ICBC Leasing, I-80
ICC Chemical Corp., I-702-703
ICF International Inc., I-1251, 1253, 1647
ICL-IP, I-691
ICM Partners, I-50
Iconix Brand Group, I-2061
ICR, II-2809
ICSolutions, II-2799
Idaho Forest Group, I-2129
Idahound, II-2678
Ideal Standard, II-2958
Idemitsu Kosan Co. Ltd., I-1438
IDEX Corp., II-2825
IDEXX Laboratories, I-1127, II-3475
IDW Publishing, I-774
IES Holdings Inc., I-913
IFA Rotorion, I-300
IGA, II-2165
IGG Inc., II-2339
iHeartMedia Inc., I-41, II-2828
iHeartRadio, II-2762

IHI Parking System, I-320
IHOP, II-2887, 2891
IHS Markit, I-1018
IHS Towers, II-3574
II-IV Inc., II-3012
II-VI Inc., II-2526
Ikea Corp., I-1560, 1565, 1803-1804, II-2910
Ilijin Materials Co., I-956
Ilim Group, II-2815-2816
Illiad Group, II-3566
Illinois Tool Works, I-12, 515, II-2977, 3526
Image Comics, I-774
IMCD, I-699, 701-702, 704
iMDsoft, II-3190
IMI Norgren, II-2760
Immaculate Baking Co., I-1097
Immediate Credit Recovery Inc., I-1650
Impala Platinum, II-2750
Imperial Super Regional Distributor, I-933
Imperial Tobacco, II-3361
Implata Platinum, II-2595
IMS Masonry Inc., I-919
In-N-Out Burger, II-2892
Inaba-Petfood Co. Inc., II-2680
Inari Medical, II-2265
Inavih (Inversiones Avícolas de Honduras), I-1198
Incitec Pivot, I-1262
Incredible Technologies, I-1582
Incubadora Santander, I-1197
Indchemie Health Specialties, I-1130
Independence Bank, I-430
Independence Bank of Kentucky, I-421
Independence Excavating Inc., I-910
Independent Bank, I-426
Independent Lumber Dealers Cooperative, I-1790
Index Creative Village, I-1255
India Cements Ltd., I-646
Indian Broiler Group, II-2665
Indianapolis Colts, II-3219
Inditex, I-214
Indiva, I-601
Indo Count Industries Ltd., I-1821
Indofil Industries Ltd., I-688
Industrial & Commercial Bank of China, I-401
Industrial Scientific, II-2996

Industrias Bachoco, I-1195, II-2180, 2185
Ineos Corp., I-706
Infineon Technologies, I-1958-1961, II-3011, 3029
Infinity Homes, I-1844
Influence Graphics, II-2797
Informa, I-942, 1256
Information International Associates Inc., I-1646
Information Resources Inc. (IRI), II-2874
Inghams Enterprises PTY Ltd., II-2181
Ingles Markets Inc., I-1690
Ingram Barge Company, II-3050, 3058
Inkbox, II-3297
InMusic, II-2415
Inner Mongolia Power (Group) Ltd., II-2715
Inner Mongolia Saikexing Reproductive Biotechnology Co., I-1290
Inner Mongolia Yili Industrial Group Co. Ltd., I-1032, 1396
Innolight Technology Corp., II-2526
Innolux Corp., II-2602
Innotion Enterprises Inc., I-1654
InnovAsian Cuisine Enterprises Inc., I-1488
Innovative Ag Performance Group, I-692
Innovative Chemical Products Group, II-2591
Innovative Livestock Services Inc., I-625
Inogen, II-2235
Inox Wind Ltd., II-3444
Insecticide India, I-711
Insigma Group, I-1272
Insite Wireless Group, II-3573
Inspur Group, II-3035-3038
Instacart, II-2165, 2517
Insurance Company of the West, I-1954
Insurgent Brands L.L.C., I-839
Intact Financial Group, I-1931, 1952
Intai Technology, I-1882
Intas Pharmaceuticals, I-1130
Integra LifeSciences, II-2266
Intel Corp., II-2628, 2789, 3009, 3013, 3017, 3022-3023, 3028, 3030, 3455
Intellia Therapeutics, I-1595

Intellibot Robotics, II-2928
Intelligent Epitaxy Technology Inc., II-3012
IntelliSkin, II-2245
Inteplast Group, II-2728
Inter Continental Trading USA Inc., II-3367
Intercontinental Cigar Co., II-3359
Intercontinental Hotels Group, I-1828, II-3039
Interface Inc., I-1355, 1357
Interface Security Systems Holdings Inc., II-3002
Interfor Corp., I-2127-2129
Interim Healthcare, I-1748
Interior Logic Group, I-1366
International Aero Engines, I-79
International Airlines Group, I-84
International Automotive Components, II-2729
International Brand Management and Licensing, I-2061
International Car Wash Group, I-615
International Container Terminal Services, II-3064
International Cruise & Excursions, II-3413
International Flavors & Fragrances, I-695
International Foodsource L.L.C., I-821, II-3137
International Game Technology, I-1582
International Markets, I-1703, 1706, II-2902
International Paper Co., I-545, II-2562, 2564, 2604, 2816
International Speedway Corp., II-2826
Internationale Spar Centrale BV, I-1441-1442
Internova Travel Group, II-3413
Interpublic Group of Cos., I-24
Interstate Warehousing Inc., II-3501-3502
InterSystems Corp., II-3190
InTown Suites, I-1832
Intracoastal Realty, II-2849
Intracom Holdings, II-2421
IntraLinks Holdings Inc., II-3173
Intrust Bank NA, I-420
Intuit, II-3159
Invacare Corp., II-2235, 2251
Investors Bank, I-434

Investors Exchange, I-1257
Invision Communications, I-1255
INVNT, I-1255
ION Solar L.L.C., I-926
ION Television, II-3319
Iowa Farm Bureau Group, I-1934
Iowa Select Farms, I-1782
IPEX Inc., II-2721
IPLA, II-2549
Ipsos, II-2874
Ipsy, I-1971
IPTF Terminals, II-2494
IQE PLC, II-3012
IQIYI, II-2540
IQVIA, II-2874
Iridium, II-2964
Iris Ceramica Group, I-658
iRoko, II-2539
Iron Mountain Inc., I-1090, II-3202
Irsik & Doll Feed Services Inc., I-625
The Irvine Company, I-1853
Irvine's Zimbabwe, I-1192
Irving Tissue Co., II-2944, 2947
Irving Wallboard, I-1726
Irwin Naturals, I-603
Iscar Ltd., II-2289
Ise Inc., I-1193, 1200
iShares, I-1980
Island Hospitality Management, I-1829
Israel Chemicals Ltd., II-2774
ITAB Shop Concept, II-3005
Italcer Group, I-658
Itel Mobile, I-633
ITG Brands L.L.C., II-3359
ITOCHU, I-1306
iTunes, I-1618
ITW EAE, I-321
ITW Rippey, I-563
Iwatani Co. Ltd., I-247
IWCO Direct, II-2794-2795
J. Derenzo Co., I-916
J. Sainsbury PLC, I-1442
JAB Holding Johann A. Benckiser, I-388
Jabil Healthcare, II-2729
Jack Cooper Transport Co. Inc., II-3426
Jack Morton Worldwide, I-1255
Jackson Family Wines, II-3549
Jackson Furniture Industries, I-1550-1551
Jackson Healthcare, II-3229

Jackson Hewitt Tax Service Inc., II-3299
Jacksonville Jaguars, II-3219
Jacobs Douwe Egberts, I-755
Jacobs Engineering Group, I-261, 1057, 1251-1253, 1647-1648, 1653, 1742, 1962, II-2445, 3513-3514
Jam City Inc., II-2336
JAM Industries, II-2415
Jamaica Broilers Group Ltd., II-2183
Jamba Juice, II-2883
James Hardie, I-566
The James Skinner Baking Co., I-393
J&E Companies, I-919
J&J Snack Foods Corp., I-1873, II-2678
Jane Street, I-1979
JanSport, I-2121
Japan Airport Terminal Co., II-3419
Japan Credit Rating Agency, I-1017
Japan Railways Group, II-2838
Japan Tobacco Intl., I-1165, II-3359, 3361
Japfa Ltd., II-2178
Jasa Marga, II-3377
Jason Plasterboard, II-3493
Jason's Deli, II-2895
J.B. Hunt Dedicated Contract Services, II-3431
J.B. Hunt Integrated Capacity Solutions, II-3057, 3065
J.B. Hunt Transport Services, II-3428-3429
JBS, I-1394, 1782, II-2182, 2185
J.C. Penney Co. Inc., I-1056, 1803, 1805, 2000
JCB, I-855, II-2634
JCC, II-2856
JCDeceaux, I-39
JCET Group, II-3014
J.D. Irving, I-2128, II-3337
J.D. Long Masonry, I-1776
JD Sports Fashion, I-1435
JDC Demolition Co. Inc., I-910
JD.com, I-220, 1170, 1172, 1179, II-2906, 2908-2909
JDE Peet's, I-487
J.E. Dunn Construction, I-865, 915
Jebsen & Jessen Group, I-702
Jeil Feed, II-2681
Jeld-Wen Inc., I-566, II-3578
Jennie-O Turkey Store, II-2224
Jerry Thompson & Sons, I-921

Jersey Mike's Subs, II-2888, 2895
Jessie Lord Bakery L.L.C., I-394, 398
JetBlue, I-86, 92
Jewel-Osco, I-1103
Jewelry Television, I-2000
Jewish Federation of Metropolitan Detroit, I-666
J.F. Ahern Co., I-917, 923
JFE Steel Corp., II-3243
J.H. Fletcher & Co., II-2325
JHT Holdings Inc., II-3426
Jianglang Motors Co., I-572
Jiangsu Delong Nickel Industry Co., II-2433
Jiangsu King's Luck Brewery, II-3547
Jiangsu Lianhai Biotechnology, I-499
Jiangsu Lihua Animal Husbandry, II-2178
Jiangsu Yangnong Chemical Group Co., I-687, 689
Jiangu Hengrui Pharmaceutical Co. Ltd., I-1133
Jiangxi Copper Co., I-960
Jiangxi Yufan Agricultural Development, I-499
Jiangxi Zhengbang Biochemical Co. Ltd., I-710
Jianlong Group, II-3238
Jiffy International, I-2034
Jiffy Lube, I-317
Jilin Boda Biochemistry, I-499
Jimmy John's Gourmet Sandwiches, II-2888, 2895
Jin Jiang International Holdings Co. Ltd., I-1828
Jinchuan Group, I-953, II-2432-2433
Jinmailang Foods Co., I-540
Jinyu Bio-technology Co. Ltd., II-3464
J.M. Eagle Inc., II-2719-2720, 2730
J.M. Huber Corp., II-3582
The J.M. Smucker Co., I-487-488, 758, 827, 1491, II-2681, 2686, 3225
The J.M. Smucker's Co., I-1423
Jo-Ann Stores Inc., I-1780
Jockey International Inc., I-199
Joeris General Contractors, I-867
Joe's Plastics Inc., II-2731
John Christner Trucking L.L.C., II-3427

John Lewis Partnership, I-1442
John Smith Masonry, I-919
John Wiley & Sons Inc., II-2811
Johns Manville, I-1905, II-2440, 2442, 2929-2930
Johnson & Johnson Co., I-38, 817, 904, 1119-1120, 1135, 1138-1141, 1652, II-2247, 2254, 2258, 2528, 2651, 2945, 3095, 3459, 3553-3555
Johnson Bank, I-458
Johnson Brothers Liquor Co., II-3551
Johnson Controls, II-2995
Johnson Electric, I-585, II-2306
Johnsonville Sausage L.L.C., II-2219, 2221
Johnvince Foods Ltd., I-821, II-3137
JollyChic.com, I-1180
The Jones Co. of Tennessee, I-1846
Jones Dairy Farm, II-2210
Jones Lang LaSalle, II-2843-2847, 2851
Jorgensen Land & Cattle, I-623
The Jotun Group, II-2586, 2592
Joyva Corp., I-847
JPMorgan Chase & Co., I-26, 1981-1985, II-2274, 2346, 2640
JPMorgan Chase Bank NA, I-401, 406, 408-410, 412-413, 416-418, 421-422, 426, 432, 434, 436, 439-441, 449, 452, 455, 457-458
The J.R. Simplot Co., I-625, 692, 1484, 2033
The JSC Sukhoi Co., I-68
JSW Group, I-732
JTEKT Corp., I-471
Juhayna Food Industries, I-1496
Julian Pie Co., I-394
Junge Bäckerei, I-767
Jungheinrich AG, I-2063
Jungle Jim's, I-1685
Junior's, I-396
Juniper Networks, II-2425-2426
Jushi Group, I-1624
Just Born Inc., I-837
Just Eat, I-1415
JustFoodForDogs, II-2666
Juul Labs Inc., I-1165, 1167
JW Medical Corp., II-2263
J.W. Pepper & Son Inc., II-2411
JWL Cold Store, II-3499
JXTG Group, I-960
K. Hovnanian Homes, I-1840
K-Line, II-3048-3049, 3051

Kaiser Permanente, I-1747, 1919
Kaiser Permanente Northern California, I-1747
Kaiser Permanente Southern California, I-1747
Kajaria Ceramics, I-659
Kal Tire, II-3345-3346
Kalkreuth Roofing & Sheet Metal, I-922
Kamps Bäckerei, I-767
Kanamoto Co. Ltd., I-1775
K&B Transportation Inc., II-3427
K&K Café, I-767
K+S Potash, II-2774
Kaneko Seeds Co., II-3004
Kanguru Solutions, I-783
Kansai Paint Co. Ltd., II-2592
Kansas City, City of Missouri, II-2159
Kansas City Area Transportation Authority, II-2151
Kansas City Chiefs, II-3219
Kansas City Southern, II-2839
Kantar Group, II-2874
Kao Corp., II-2530, 2651
Kaola, I-1172
Kärcher SE, I-1159, II-2784, 2823, 2920
Karl Storz SE & Co., II-2241
Kashi Co., I-662, 815, 827
Katahdin Forest Management, II-3337
Katerra Inc., I-1852
Kautex Textron GmbH & Co. KG, II-2727
Kawai Musical Instruments Mfg. Co., II-2415
Kawasaki Heavy Industries Ltd., II-3290
Kawasaki Motors Corp., I-103, II-2659
Kawasaki Robotics, I-642
Kazatomprom, II-3456
Kazi Farms Group, I-1193
KB Home, I-1845, 1847-1849
KBC PCB Group, II-2790
KBP Foods, I-1454
KBR Inc., I-1057, 1648
KCC Corp., II-3493
KCF Technologies, I-956
The Keebler Co., I-387
Keeco L.L.C., I-1821
Keith Zars Pools, I-928
Keller Inc., II-2278

Keller North America, I-916
Keller Williams Indianapolis Metro North/Carmel, II-2848
Keller Williams Realty, II-2848-2850
The Kellogg Company, I-662, 812, 815, 1006, 1008, 1010, 1012, 1390, 1396, II-3113, 3118, 3123, 3127-3131, 3278
Kelly-Moore Paint Co., II-2591
Kelly Services, II-3230
Keltbray Group, I-911
KelTec Weapons, I-1717
Kemira Oyj, I-713
KemperSports, I-1644
Kenan Advantage Group, II-3421
Kenco Logistics Services, II-3500, 3503
Kennametal, II-2289
Kenny's Great Pies Inc., I-398-399
Kent Building Materials, I-1790
Kent Cos. Inc., I-908
Keqian Biology, II-3464
Kering S.A., I-2046, 2123, 2132
Kerry Group PLC, I-695, 1395
Kerry Logistics, II-3059
Kesai Agrochem Co. Ltd., I-710
Keskinoglu, I-1199, II-2184
Kespry Inc., II-3455
Kettle Foods Inc., II-3123
Keurig Dr. Pepper Inc., I-487, 755
Keurig S.A., I-1423
Kewaunee Scientific Corp., I-2024
Key Food Stores Co-op Inc., I-1704, II-2907
Keybank NA, I-405, 409-410, 416, 418, 423, 439, 441, 453, 455
Keystone Concrete, I-908
Keystone Sporting Arms, I-1717
Keywords Studios, II-3411
KFC, I-1453, II-2879, 2885, 2889
KGHM Polska Miedz, II-3084
KHS&S Contractors, I-929
Kia Motors Corp., I-332, 344-345, 366
Kicks AB, I-978
Kidder Mathews, II-2843, 2851
Kiddie Academy, I-714
Kids R Kids, I-714
Kiewit Canada Group, I-862
Kiewit Corp., I-915, II-3513-3514
Kiewit Peter Sons' Inc., I-747
Kiloutou S.A.S., I-1773
Kimber Manufacturing Inc., I-1715-1716, 1718-1719

Kimberly-Clark Corp., II-2441-2442, 2945-2948, 2953, 3553-3555
Kind L.L.C., I-662, 815, 827, 839
Kinder Morgan Inc., II-3202, 3291
KinderCare Learning Centers, I-714
Kindred Group PLC, I-1578
Kindred Healthcare, I-1748-1749
Kinetsu World Express, II-3055
King Arthur Flour Co., II-2599
King County Department of Transportation, II-2150, 2159-2162
King Koil, I-1796
King Ltd., II-2336
King Power International Group, II-3419
King Ranch Inc., I-2027
King Soopers Marketplace, I-1689
King Yuan Electronics Group, II-3014
King's Hawaiian Bakery West Inc., I-550, 552, 555
Kingsdown Inc., I-1796
Kingspan Group, I-1906
Kingston Technology Corp., I-783, II-3021
Kinki Sharyo Co., II-2834
Kinly, II-3289
Kinnikinnick Foods Inc., I-1010
Kinoplex, II-2381
Kinross Gold, I-1641
Kiokia Holdings Corp., II-3017
KION Group AG, I-2063
Kioxia Holdings Corp., II-3020
Kirby Corp., II-3050, 3058
Kirin Holdings Co. Ltd., I-102
Kiss Products Inc., I-973
Kito Group, I-1787
Kiva Systems, II-2277
KLA, II-3007
Klarna, I-256
Klimer Platforms Inc., I-1776
KLLM Transport Services L.L.C., II-3427
Kloeckner Metals Corp., II-2297
Kloosterboer, II-3502
Knauf, I-626, 1728, 1905-1906, II-3493
Knight Homes, I-1839
Knight-Swift Transportation, II-3427-3429, 3431
Knutsen Group, II-3052
Kobayashi Pharmaceutical, II-2528
Kobelco Construction Machinery America, II-3526

Koch Foods Inc., II-2176, 2180, 2185
Koch Industries Inc., II-2467, 2816
Koelnmesse Inc., I-942
Kohat Cement Co., I-648
Kohlberg, Kravis Roberts & Co., I-173
Kohler Group, II-2958
Kohl's Corp., I-1803, 1805, 1834, II-2905
Koito Manufacturing Co., I-2070, 2077
The Kokosing Group of Cos., I-915
Kolmar Group AG, I-699, 701-704
Komatsu Ltd., I-853-856, II-2137, 2324-2325
Komelon Co. Ltd., II-3295
Kompan Inc., II-2752
Konami Holdings Corp., I-1582
Kone Corp., I-1208
Koninklijke Philips N.V., I-1652
Kontoor, I-189
Kontos Foods Inc., I-556
Korail (The Korea Railroad Co.), II-2838
Korea Aerospace Industries, I-68
Korea Electric Power Corp., II-2715
Korea National Oil Corp., II-2495
Korea Shipbuilding & Offshore Engineering Co., II-3290
Korea Zinc Co. Ltd., II-3601
Korean Air, II-3054
Kossan Rubber Industries Bhd., II-2273
Kouzi Distillery, II-3547
Kowa Lenses, I-2055
KPMG L.L.P., I-5-7, 878
Kraft Heinz Co., I-38, 396, 487-488, 674, 719, 758, 833, 1033, 1394, 1396, 1399, 1488-1489, II-2223-2224, 3113, 3131, 3134, 3137, 3390
Krapf School Bus, II-2979
Krasdale Foods, I-1704, II-2907
Krauss-Maffei Co. Ltd., II-2746-2747
The Kresge Foundation, I-666
Kretek International, II-3359, 3363
Krishi Rasayan Group, I-688
Krispy Kreme Doughnuts, I-770, II-2883, 2886
KRKA d.d. Novo Mesto, I-1134, 1136

The Kroger Co., I-1115, 1178, 1680, 1682, 1685, 1690, 1744, II-2902, 2904-2905, 2909
Kroger Specialty Pharmacy, I-1116
Kroll Bond Rating Agency, I-1017
Kronos Food Corp., I-397
Kronospan, I-1359, II-3581
Kropf Industries, II-2862
Kruger Products Inc., II-2944, 2947
Kubota Corp., I-103, 1244, 1278-1280, 1284
Kuehne + Nagel, II-3055, 3059, 3065, 3430
Kuka, I-642
Kumon North America, II-3450
Kureha Corp., I-469
Kurt Weiss Greenhouses, I-1674
Kurtz Ersa Corp., I-321
Kvickly, I-1688
KW Plastics Recycling, II-2731
Kweichow Moutai Company, II-3547
KWS SAAT, II-3004
KYB Corp., I-309
Kyocera Corp., I-608
L Brands, I-216
L3Harris Technologies, I-81, 1339, 1649, 1661, 1665, 1667-1668
La Abuela Mexican Foods, II-3391
La Croissanterie, I-766
La Feria De Chapultepec, I-178
La Francaise des Jeux, I-1577
La Madeleine Country French Café, II-2882
La Tortilla Factory, II-3390
La-Z-Boy Furniture Galleries, I-1565
La-Z-Boy Inc., I-1550-1551
Labconco, I-2024
LabCorp., II-2876
Lactalis, I-1034, 1396
LafargeHolcim, I-644-645, 649-652, 803
Lagardère Travel Retail, II-3419
Lam Research, II-3007
Lamar Advertising Co., I-39
Lamb Weston, I-1478, 1484
Laminam, I-658
Lampson International, I-1013
Lan OTR Inc./Pneus, II-3346
Lanco Paints & Coatings, II-2591
Land O'Lakes Inc., I-1033, 1885
L&G Insurance, I-1918
Landmark Cinemas of Canada, II-2379

Landmark Media Enterprises, II-2429
LandMark Optoelectronics Corp., II-3012
Landmark Properties, I-1855-1856
Landmark Sotheby's International Realty, II-2849
Landscape Structures, II-2752
Landstar System, II-3057, 3422, 3429
LandVest Timberlands, II-3336
Lane Transit District, II-2151
Lang Jiu Group Co., II-3547
LanguageLine Solutions, II-3411
Lanxess Arena, I-262
Lanxess Corp., II-2732
Lao Feng Xiang, I-2001, 2130
Lar Cooperativa Agroindustrial, II-2182
Largo Concrete Inc., I-908
Larry H. Miller Group of Companies, I-296
Larry's Hi Lo Bakery, I-558
Las Delicias, I-1198
Latham Pool, II-3287
Lavazza S.p.A., I-487
Lawrence Livermore National Security L.L.C., I-1651
Lay Hong Bhd., I-1193
Layal's Gourmet Sweets, I-397
LAZ Parking Market, II-2620
Lazarus Naturals, I-603
LCBC Church, II-2867
LCS, I-1861
LDC, II-2179
Le Gouessant, I-1194
Le Pain Quotidien, II-2882
Leachman of Colorado, I-623
Leaf Home Solutions, I-1720
Leaffilter Gutter Protection, I-869
Lear Corp., I-304-306
Learning Care Group, I-714
The Learning Experience, I-714
LeasePlan Corp., I-298
Leavitt Cranes, I-1014
Ledcor Group, I-862
Lee & Associates, II-2846
Lee & Man Paper Manufacturing Ltd., II-2604
Lee Enterprises, II-2429
Legacy Homes, I-1851
Legal & General America Group, I-1942
Legen Hospitality, I-1420

Legend Homes, I-1849
Leggett & Platt Inc., II-3226
Lego Group, II-3400
Leica Microsystems, II-2250
Leidos Holdings Inc., I-1252, 1648, 1652-1655, 1661-1663, 1665, II-2445
Leisure Pools, II-3287
LendingClub, I-2104
LendingTree, I-37
Lendlease, I-865, 868
Lennar Corp., I-1839-1840, 1842-1843, 1845-1850
Lenovo Group, I-641, 785, 792, 795-800, 902, II-3016, 3021, 3035-3038
Leonardo S.p.A., I-60, 62
Leong Hup Holdings Bhd., I-1193
Leprino Foods Co., I-1033
Lepu Medical Technology (Beijing) Co. Ltd., II-2263
Leroy Seafood, I-1328
Les Schwab Tire Centers, II-3343, 3345-3346
L'Estis Desserts, I-397
Level 5 Inc., I-929
Levi Strauss & Co., I-189, 191
Lewis Bakeries Inc., I-549, 551, 555
Lexar Media Inc., II-3021
Leyard Optoelectronic, I-2052
LG Chemical Ltd., I-307, 462, 464, 706, II-2733
LG Electronics Corp., I-640-641, 880, 900, II-2602, 2628, 3105
LG Haus Ltd., I-276
LGI Homes, I-1842-1843, 1845, 1849
LHC Group Inc., I-1748
LHSC Inc., I-1794
Lianyungang Liben Crop Science and Technology Co., I-687
Liaoyuan Jufeng Biochemical Science & Technology, I-499
Libbey, I-1634
Liberty Bank, I-410
Liberty Global, II-3315
Liberty Mutual Group, I-1922-1927, 1929-1930, 1933-1934, 1937, 1939, 1941, 1943, 1948-1950, 1952
Liberty Mutual Holding Co. Inc., I-1788, 1910-1911, 1914
Liberty Power Corp., I-1234
Liberty Steel & Wire, I-1303
Lidl, I-1683, 1693, 1701-1702
Lieber Chocolate & Food, I-846

The Liebherr Group, I-853, 855, 858, 1015-1016, II-2324
Lier Chemical Co. Ltd., I-687
Life Storage Inc., II-3006
Lifestyles Healthcare, II-2657
LifeWay Christian Resources, I-518
Lilith Games, II-2338-2339
Lily's Sweets L.L.C., I-719, 852
Limbach Holdings L.L.C., I-920
Limoneira Co., I-1291
Lincoln Electric Holdings Inc., II-3526
Lincoln Financial Group, I-1942
Lincoln Property Company, I-1854
Linde PLC, I-706, 1889
Lindex Sverige AB, I-978
Lindt & Sprüngli AG, I-717, 721, 727, 812
Lineage Logistics L.L.C., II-3501-3503
Lingbao Jinyuan Zhaohui Copper Co., I-956
Linglong Group Co. Ltd., II-3356
Lingxi Games Inc., II-2331
Link Snacks Inc., II-2194, 2199
LinkedIn, I-1968
Lion Corp., II-2528, 2530
The Lion Electric Co., I-301
Lionsbridge Techologies, II-3411
Lionsgate, II-2356
Lipari Foods Inc., I-559
Litehouse Inc., I-819
Lithia Motors Inc., I-296
Lithko Contracting L.L.C., I-908
Little Angel Foods Inc., I-396
Little Giant Ladders, I-2025
Little Red Book, I-1172
LiuGong Dressta Machinery Sp. z.o.o., I-853
LiuGong Machinery Co., I-855
Live Nation, I-801
Live Oak Banking Co., I-437
Lixil Corp., II-2958
L.L. Bean, II-3213
L.L. Flooring, I-1366
Lloyd's of London, I-1951
llstate Arena, I-262
Loblaws, II-2165
LOCAP L.L.C., II-2491
Lockhart Fine Foods, I-847
Lockheed Martin Corp., I-68-69, 1648-1649, 1658, 1664-1665, 2108, II-2327, 3414
Lockton Companies, I-1909, 1940

Lofthouse Foods, I-387
Logan Bus Co & Affiliates, II-2979
Logitech, I-786
Logomark, II-2806
Lombardo Homes, I-1844
Lone Creek Farm, I-623
Long Fence, I-1306
Long John Silver's, II-2896
Long Lake Ltd., I-1845
Long Tech Network Ltd., II-2339
Longhorn Steakhouse, II-2884
Lonza Group, I-691
Loomis, I-616
Lord Abbett & Co., I-1982
L'Oréal, I-26, 38, 971, 977-978, 986, 2132, II-2651-2652
Los Angeles County Metropolitan Transportation Authority, II-2150-2151, 2157, 2160, 2162
Los Angeles Unified School District, I-1422
Lotte Duty Free, II-3419
Lotte Group, II-2908
Lotte World, I-180
Lottomatica S.p.A., I-1577
Lotus Stationery, II-3234
Louisiana-Pacific Corp., I-566, 1241, 1344, II-3582
Louisville Ladder, I-2025
Low & Bonar, II-2442
Lowe's Companies Inc., I-219, 222, 1365-1366, 1789-1790, 1804, 1834, II-2753, 2904-2905, 2909, 3536
Lowes Foods, I-1691, 1702
Loxam S.A.S., I-1773, 1775
LPR Construction Co., I-927
LS Technologies L.L.C., I-1661
LSC Communications, II-2795
Luckin Coffee, I-765
Lucky Cement, I-648
Lucky Country Inc., I-831
Lucky Strike Entertainment L.L.C., I-543
Lufthansa, I-84, II-3054
Lululemon Athletica, I-216
Lumber Liquidators Inc., I-1365
Lumentum Holdings, II-2526
Lumileds Holding B.V., I-2069
Lundberg Family Farms, I-846
Lupin Ltd., I-1129-1130
Luxury Brand Holdings Inc., I-2000
Luzhou Laojiao Company, II-3547

LVMH Moët Hennessy-Louis Vuitton SE, I-38, 2046, 2121, 2123, 2132, II-2651, 3507
Lycoming Engines, I-72
Lydall Inc., II-2440, 2442
Lyft Inc., II-2918
LyondellBassell Industries, I-706
M-1 Rail, II-2159
M Bar C Construction, I-925
M-Flex (Dongshan Precision), II-2790
M/I Homes, I-1842, 1844, 1847, 1849
M S International Inc., I-1362
MAA, I-1853-1854
MAC Trailer, II-3292, 3407
Machias Savings Bank, I-423
Macmillan Publishers Ltd., I-532-533
MACOM Technology Solutions, II-3024
Macroblock Inc., I-1957
Macronix International, I-1959
Macs Snacks, II-3121
Macy's Inc., I-1056, 1434, 1560, 1802-1803, 2000, II-2905
Madison Square Garden, I-262
Maersk Drilling, II-2484
Magellan Midstream Partners, II-3291
Magento, I-1173
Magic Kingdom Theme Park at Walt Disney World Resort, I-179, 181
MagMutual Insurance Co., I-1943
Magna International Inc., I-299, 304-306
MagnaChip, I-1955
Magnet Group, II-2806
Magneti Marelli S.p.A., I-304, 306, 2070
Magnolia Marine Transport Co., II-3058
Mahachai Kraft Paper Co., II-2606
Mahindra & Mahindra, I-366
Mahle Group, I-302, 304
Mahoney's Garden Centers, I-2037
Makita Corp., II-3381-3382
MAKRO, I-1701
Malaysia Smelting Corp., II-3341
Malco Theatres Inc., II-2379
Malcolm Drilling Co. Inc., I-916
Mammoet Americas, I-1013
Mammoth Holdings, I-615

Man Wah Holdings Ltd., I-1550-1551
MANAC, II-3407
Management & Training Corp., I-1656, II-2798
Mandalay Bay Resort & Casino, I-940
M&G Stationery Inc., II-3594
Mane S.A., I-695
Mango TV, II-2540
Manheim Auctions, I-294-295
Manitowoc, I-1016
Mankind Pharma, I-1130
Mann-Hummel, I-302
Mannington Mills Inc., I-1351, 1355, 1357, 1359
Manson Construction Co., I-912
Mantech International Corp., I-1663
Manuchar NV, I-700, 703
Manufacturers and Traders Trust Co., I-411, 424, 436, 456
Manuka Health, I-1825
Manulife Financial Corp., I-1915
Maple Donuts Inc., I-388
Maple Leaf Agri-Farms, I-1783
Maple Leaf Cement Factory, Pakistan, I-648
Maples Industries Inc., I-1357, 1360
Maran Gas Maritime Inc., II-3051
Marathon Oil Corp., I-1437, II-2485, 2487-2488, 3291
Marathon Petroleum Corp., I-935, II-2466-2467, 2495
Marathon Pipe Line, II-2491
Marcum, I-7
Marcus & Millichap IPA, II-2845, 2847, 2851
Marcus Theatres, II-2379
Margaret Rudd & Associates, II-2849
Mariani Packing Co., I-821
Marie Blachère, I-766
Marine Corps. Exchange, II-2307
MarineMax, I-507
Mario Barth Tattoo, II-3296
Mark Anthony Brands, I-482
Marker Intl., II-3208
Market Basket, I-1694
Market Corp. Group, I-1946
Marks & Spencer PLC, I-1442
Marmon Crane Services, I-1013
Maroon Group, I-701
Marquis Book Printing, I-528

Marriott International, I-1828, 1833, II-3039
Mars Inc., I-717, 837, 1008, 1097, 1394, 1396, 1423, 1873, II-2674, 2676, 2682-2683, 2686, 3125, 3131
Mars International India Pvt Ltd., II-2665
Mars Japan Ltd., II-2680
Mars Oil Pipeline, II-2491
Mars Petcare, II-2670-2671, 2674, 2676, 2681-2683
Mars Wrigley Australia, II-2679
Mars Wrigley Confectionery, I-719, 721, 723, 812, 850
Marsh & McLennan Cos. inc., I-1909
Marshalls, I-213, 1803-1804
Martco L.L.C., II-3582, 3588
Marten Transport Ltd., II-3427, 3431
Martha's Vineyard and Nantucket Steamship, II-2156
Martins Family Fruit Farm, II-3111
Martin's Famous Pastry Shoppe Inc., I-551, 555
Marubeni Group, II-2612
Marubeni Nisshin Feed Co., I-1193
Maruha Nichiro Corp., II-2990
Marushici Seicha Co. Ltd., II-3304
Maruti Suzuki, I-366
Marvel Comics, I-774
Marvell Technology Group, I-1956
Maryland Transit Administration, II-2153-2155
The Maschhoffs, I-1782
Masco Corp., I-582, II-2592
Mascoma Bank, I-433, 453
Masonite International Corp., II-3578
Massachusetts Bay Transportation Authority, II-2150-2151, 2153, 2155-2157, 2161
Massachusetts Institute of Technology, I-1649
Massachusetts Metropolitan Area Transit Authority, II-2162
Massachusetts Mutual Life Group, I-1942
Massachusetts State Lottery, I-1577
Massey Services Inc., II-2661
Massey's Plate Glass & Aluminum Inc., I-918
Mastclimbers L.L.C., II-1776
Mastec Inc., I-916
Mastemacher Gmbh, I-557

Master Electronics, I-1204
Master Halco, I-1304
MasterBrand Cabinets, II-3578
Mastercard, II-2634-2635, 2638
Mastro's Restaurants, II-2890
MAT Holdings, I-1303
Match.com, I-253
Matli, I-1199
Mattamy Homes, I-1842, 1847
Mattel Inc., II-3398, 3400
Mattress Firm, I-1543, 1565, 1801-1802
Mattress Warehouse, I-1802
Mauser Packaging Solutions, II-2729
Maverick Arms Inc., I-1715, 1717
Maverick Transportation, II-3422
Max M. & Marjorie S. Fisher Foundation, I-666
Max Wild GmbH, I-911
Maxi Canada, II-2165
Maxim Crane Works, I-1013-1014, 1775
Maximus Inc., I-1646, 1650
Maxun Co. Ltd., II-3021
Maxxis International, II-3356
Mayer Berkshire Corp., I-186
Mayflower Communications, I-1667
MBIA Group, I-1936
M.C. Dean Inc., I-913
MCA Records, II-2408
McAfee L.L.C., II-3167, 3171
McAlister's Deli, II-2895
MCassab Group, I-700
MCC (Metallurgical Corporation of China), I-864
McCafé, I-766-767
McCain Foods Ltd., I-1478, 1484-1485, 1489
McCall Farms Inc., II-3134
McCann, I-25
McCarthy Building Cos., I-915
McCarthy Holdings, I-866-867, 871, 1251
McCarthy Tire Service Co. Inc., II-3345
McDonald's Corp., I-40, 769, 1453, II-2878-2879, 2889, 2892, 2904
The McDougall Family of Cos., I-923
McFit, I-1723
McGee Group, I-911
McGraw-Hill Education, II-2811
McGregor Fund, I-666
MCH Group, I-942

MCIC Vermont A Reciprocating Retention Group, I-1943
McKee Foods Corp., I-384, 387-388, 391, 393, 827
McKesson Corp., I-1662
McKinsey & Co., I-878, II-3414
McKinstry, I-917
McLane Co. Inc., I-933
McLaren Health Care Corp., I-1750
MCM Management Corp., I-910
The McShane Companies, I-867, 1852
M.D.C. Holdings, I-1848
MDU Construction Services Group, I-913, 917
Meadow Farms Nursery & Landscape, I-2037
MedExpress, I-1753
Mediacom Communications Corp., II-2631
MediaTek Inc., I-1955-1956, 1961, II-3017-3018
Medical Solutions, II-3229
Medimpact Healthcare Systems, II-2701
Mediterranean Organics, II-3225
Medline Industries Inc., II-2254
Medterra, I-603
Medtronic PLC, II-2237, 2243, 2247, 2253-2254, 2263, 2266
Megamex Foods, II-3390
Mehlman, Castagnetti et al, I-2109
Meijer Inc., I-1603, 1614, 1682, 1685, 1695
Meiji Co. Ltd., I-812
Meiji Holdings Co., I-717
Meituan-Dianping, II-2521
Mekabox, II-2605
Mellace Family Brands Inc., I-1010
Melody Wireless Infrastructure, II-3573
MelON, II-2409
Melrose Industries, II-2995
Melton Truck Lines Inc., II-3422
Menards Inc., I-219, 1365, 1789, II-2753
The Menarini Group, I-1134, 1136
Menchey Music Service, II-2411
Mengniu Dairy, II-2314
The Mennel Milling Co., I-1372
Mentor Worldwide L.L.C., II-2258
Meny, I-1688
Menzies Aviation, I-99
Mercadona, I-1701

Mercedes-Benz, I-331-332, 339
Mercer (consulting), I-878
Mercer International Inc., II-2815-2816
Mercer Transportation, II-3422
Merchants Bank of Indiana, I-418
Merchants Fleet Management, I-298
Merchants Metals, I-1304
Merck & Co., I-38, 1132, 1138, 1652, II-3461, 3463
Merck KGAA, I-504
Merck Sharp Dohme, I-1135
Meredith Corp., I-2061
Meredith Village Savings Bank, I-433
Merida Industry Co., I-496
Meridian Brick, I-560
Meritage Homes, I-1839, 1845-1849
Merlin Entertainments Group, I-182
Merlin Plastics Supply Inc., II-2731
Merrill Corp., II-3173
Merrimack County Savings Bank, I-433
Mersen, I-1994
Mesa Airlines, I-88
Messe Düsseldorf, I-942
Messe Frankfurt, I-942
Messe München, I-942
Messer Construction Co., I-915
Messina Touring Group, I-801
Metabank NA, I-447, II-2636
Metallo, II-3341
Metalloinvest Management Co. L.L.C., I-1992
Meten, I-1245
MetLife Inc., I-1788, 1915
Metro Cash & Carry, I-1692, 1699
Metro Inc., II-2165
Metro Mobility, II-2155
Metro Transit, II-2157
Metrolina Greenhouses, I-1674
Metropolitan Detail, I-318
Metropolitan Museum of Art, II-2387
Metropolitan Security Services Inc., I-1655
Metropolitan Transit Authority of Harris County, Texas, II-2154-2155, 2160
Metsä Group, II-2815-2816
Metso Outotec Oyj, I-855
Mettler-Toledo, I-1077, II-2977
MFA Inc., I-52
MFA Oil Co., II-2808

M.G. McGrath Inc., I-923
MGIC Group, I-1944
MGM, II-2277
MGM Grand Detroit, I-1568
MGM Resorts, I-1572-1573
MHA MacIntyre Hudson, I-6
MHP (Myronivsky Hliboproduct), II-2179
Miami-Dade County Public Schools, I-1422
Miami-Dade Transit, II-2155, 2158
Miami Dolphins, II-3219
Miami Jai-Alai casino, I-1581
Michael Foods, I-1195, 1200, 1202
Michael T. Costello, I-747
Michael's, I-1780
Michelin North America Inc., II-2936, 3355
Michigan Education Credit Inc., I-1020
Michigan First Credit Union, I-1020
Michigan Health Endowment Fund, I-666
Michigan Medicine, I-1750
Michigan Schools and Government Credit Union, I-1020
Michigan Turkey Producers, II-2224
Microchip Technology Inc., I-1958
Micron Technology Inc., I-1959, II-2789, 3013, 3017, 3019
MicroPort, II-2263
Microsoft Azure, II-3164
Microsoft Corp., I-42, 792, II-3166, 3414, 3476, 3479
Microsoft Technology Licensing, II-2628
Microvention, II-2266
Mid-America Real Estate Group, II-2851
Mid-Continental Restoration Co., I-919
Midas International, II-3343
Middle East Bakery, I-556
Middleby, II-2534
Midfirst Bank, I-406, 440
MidMichigan Health, I-1750
Midwest Steel Inc., I-927
Midwestone Bank, I-419
Migalito's Supermercado, I-558
Migros InJoy, I-1723
Mike Albert Fleet Solutions, I-298
Mil Moscow Helicopter Plant, I-70
Milano Coffee, I-771
Milgro Nursery, I-1674

Mill Creek Residential, I-1852
Miller Electric Manufacturing, II-3526
Miller Milling Co., I-1372
Miller's Ale House, II-2897
Minact Inc., I-1656
Minburn Technology Group L.L.C., I-1654
Mingyang Wind Power, II-3445, 3447
Miniso, I-936
Minn Kota, I-1242
Minsur, II-3341
Minuteman Press Intl., II-2795
Miratorg, II-2208
MISC Group, II-3051
MissFresh, II-2518
Mission Foods Inc., II-3121, 3139, 3390
Mister Car Wash, I-615
The Mitre Corp., I-1661
Mitsubishi Chemical Holdings Ltd., I-706
Mitsubishi Corp., I-696, 1327-1328
Mitsubishi Electric Corp., I-322-324, 642, II-3029
Mitsubishi Heavy Industries Ltd., II-3290, 3448
Mitsubishi Heavy Power Systems, II-3443
Mitsubishi Logisnext Co. Ltd., I-2063
Mitsubishi Pencil, II-3234
Mitsubishi Power Ltd., II-3448
Mitsubishi UFJ Financial Group, I-401
Mitsui Engineering & Shipbuilding Group, I-1015
Mitsui O.S.K. Lines, II-3048-3049, 3051, 3053
Mizuho Financial Group, I-1984
MJ Logistics, II-3499
MJC Cos., I-1844
MMC Contractors, I-923
Mobike, I-495
Mobile Mini, II-3249
Mode Transportation, II-3057
Modern Dental Laboratory, I-1055
Modern Poultry Farms, I-1199
Moderna Inc., I-1652, II-3459-3460
Moe's Southwest Grill, II-2894
Mogujie, I-1179
Mohawk Home, I-1821

Mohawk Industries Inc., I-659, 1351, 1355, 1357-1360
Molnlycke, II-2236
Molpus Woodlands Group, II-3336
Molson Coors Brewing Co., I-102, 482-483, 1394
Momentum Solar, I-926
Momo Shop, I-1181
Mondelez International, I-387, 717, 723, 812, 840, 1006, 1008, 1010, 1012, 1396, 1711-1712, II-3118, 3131
Mondi North America, II-2795
Mondrian Properties, I-1844
Monro Inc., II-3343
Monro Muffler Brake & Service, I-317
Monster Beverage Corp., I-1238
Mont Blanc Commercial, II-3234
Monzo Bank Ltd., I-403
Moodle, II-3175
Moody's Investor Service, I-1017-1018
More Retail Ltd., I-1692
Morgan Properties, I-1853
Morgan Stanley, I-436, 452, 1983-1985
Morningstar Inc., I-1018
Moron Group, II-3228
Morris Garage, I-366
Morrisons, I-1679
Morrow Equipment Company, I-1014
Mortensen Inc., I-1251
Mortenson Co., I-924
MortgageBanc, II-2348
Morton's The Steakhouse, II-2890
Motel 6, I-1832
Motiva Enterprises L.L.C., I-935
Motivate International Inc., II-2870
Motley Fool, I-36
MotorCity Casino Hotel, I-1568
Motorlease Corp., I-298
Motorola Mobilty, I-640
Mott Macdonald, II-2445
Mt. McKinley Bank, I-405
Mount Zion Baptist Church, II-2867
Mountaire Farms Inc., II-2176, 2180
Mouser Electronics, I-1204
Mowi ASA, I-1327-1328
Moy Park Ltd., II-2179
Moyer Farms, I-819
MPLX L.P., II-3050, 3058

MPM Products Ltd., II-2682
MPS Egg Farms, I-1202
Mr. Roof/ABLE Roofing, I-922
Mrs. Gerry's Kitchen Inc., I-558
MSA Safety, II-2996
MSC Cruises, I-1024-1025
MSD Animal Health, I-1127
MSNBC, II-2632
MTA Bus Co., II-2150, 2162
MTA Long Island Rail Road, II-2153
MTA Metro-North Commuter Railroad, II-2153
MTA New York City Transit, II-2150-2151, 2154-2155, 2162
MTD Products, I-2036
MTG AB, II-3318
MTN Group, II-3567, 3570
Mueller Industries Co., II-2719
Mueller Streamline Co., I-954
The Muffin Mam Inc., I-391
MUFG Union Bank NA, I-406, 408
Muji variety stores, I-936
Mullican Flooring L.P., I-1358
MULTIVAC Inc., II-2573
Mundo Petapa, I-178
Munich Re Group, I-1916, 1921, 1927, 1951
Murata Manufacturing Co., I-462, 608-609, II-3024
Murphy Company, I-1241
Murphy USA Inc., I-1437
Murray Energy Corp., I-747
Musée de Louvre, II-2387
Museo Reina Sofia, II-2387
Music Go Round, II-2411
Music Tribe, II-2415
MUY Brands, I-1454
Muyuan Foodstuffs Co. Ltd., II-2215
MVB Bank Inc., I-457
MVP Group Inc., I-597
MWH Constructors Inc., II-3513
MWWPR, II-2809
Mylan N.V., I-1129, 1132
MYR Group Inc., I-913
MZB (Massimo Zanetti Beverage USA), I-1423
n11.com, I-1183
N26, I-403
Nabholz Corp., I-867
NAC International, II-2444, 2446
NACCO Industries Inc., I-747
NAFCO, I-1882
Nagashima Spa Land, I-180
Nakilat, II-3051

Namshi, I-1180
Nana Regional Corporation Inc., I-1655
Nanhui Xinyuan Helmets, I-185
Nanjing Iveco Motor Co., I-572
Nanjing Red Sun Co. Ltd., I-687
Nanjing Research Institute of Electronics Technology, II-2836
NaphCare Inc., I-1655, 1746
Nardone Brothers Baking Co., I-1400
Nasco Gourmet Foods, I-557
Nasdaq, I-1257
Natco Home Fashions Inc., I-1360, 1821
National Aeronautics and Space Administration, I-1648
National Amusements Inc., II-2379-2380
National Convenience Distributors L.L.C., I-933
National Dentex Corp., I-1055
National Express L.L.C., II-2164, 2979
National Football League, I-2061
National Gallery, II-2387
National General Group, I-1938, 1948
National Gypsum, I-1725, II-3493
National Health Investors, I-1862
National Honey Almond Inc., II-3359
National Iranian Tanker Co., II-3053
National Museum of China, II-2387
National Pension Fund (South Korea), II-2647
National Raisin Company, I-1100
National Recoveries Inc., I-1650
National Social Security Fund, II-2647
National Storage Affiliates, II-3006
National Tobacco Co., II-3365, 3369, 3371
National Van Lines Inc., II-3424
National Veterinary Associates Inc., II-3475
National Wealth Fund (Russia), II-2647
Nations Roof, I-922
Nationwide Group, I-1923-1927, 1929-1931, 1934, 1939, 1941
Nationwide Hotel Management Co., I-1829

Nationwide Mutual Insurance Co., I-1914, 1950
Native, II-2656
Natura & Co., I-1081, II-3553
Natural Gas Pipeline of America, II-2492
Natural Grocers by Vitamin Cottage, I-1689, II-2418
The Nature Conservancy, II-3337
Nature's Path Foods Inc., I-662
Natus Medical Inc., I-1070
Navajo Nation, I-747
Navarro Research & Engineering Inc., II-2445
Navient Corp., I-1650, 2105
Navoi Mining and Metallurgy Combinat, I-1641
Navy Exchange Service Command, II-2307
Navy Federal Credit Union, I-1019
NBC, II-2632, 2762
NCR, II-3005, 3170
Nebraska Furniture Mart, I-219
NEC Corp., II-2305, 2421, 2426
The Neiman Marcus Group Inc., I-1056
Nelnet Inc., I-1650
Nelonen Media, II-3318
NELSON Worldwide, I-1962
Nenault Brilliance, I-572
NENT Group (Nordic Entertainment Group), II-3318
Neon, II-2356
NeoPhotonics Corp., II-2526
NES Global Talent, II-3228
Nest, I-591
Nestlé Purina PetCare Co., II-2670-2671, 2674, 2676, 2678, 2681-2683
Nestlé S.A., I-38, 373, 376, 487-488, 717, 755, 812, 1033-1034, 1390, 1394, 1396, 1399, 1489, II-2310, 2679-2680, 2686, 3131
Nestlé USA Inc., I-719, 1097, 1488, 1491, 1493
Nestlé Waters North America Inc., I-539
NetApp Inc., I-781
NetEase Inc., II-2331
Netflix Inc., II-2538-2539, 2541-2543, 2545-2553, 3315
Netgear Inc., II-2427
Netmarble, II-2338
Netto Marken-Discount, I-1688
Nevell Group Inc., I-929

New Balance Athletics Inc., I-1426
New Best Wire Industrial, I-1882
New Flyer Industries Inc., I-301
New Hope Group Co. Ltd., I-1885, II-2215
New Hope Liuhe Co., II-2178, 2185
New Image Global, II-3371
New Jersey Transit Corp., II-2150, 2153, 2155, 2157, 2162
New Life Church, II-2867
New Mexico Bank & Trust, I-435
New Orleans Regional Transit Authority, II-2159
New Prime Inc., II-3427
New World Van Lines Inc., II-3424
New York City Department of Education, I-1422
New York City Department of Transportation, II-2156
New York City Economic Development Corp., II-2156
New York City Retirement System, II-2645
New York Life Group, I-1942
New York State Lottery Gaming Corp., I-1577
New York State Teachers, II-2645
New York States Common, II-2645
New York Stock Exchange, I-1257
New York Times, II-2762
Newag S.A., II-2831
Newco Enterprises, I-1423
NewCold Advanced, II-3502
Newcrest Mining, I-1641
Newell Brands Inc., I-235, 597, II-3594
Newlyweds Foods, I-559
Newman's Own Inc., I-1493, II-3119
Newman's Own Organics Inc., II-2683
Newmark Group Inc., II-2843-2847, 2851
Newmont Corp., I-1641
News Corp., II-2430
News Entertainment Co., II-2430
NewSouth Windows Solutions L.L.C., I-869
Nexamp Inc., I-925
Nexia Resources, II-3601
Nexstar Media Group, II-3319
Next Level Apparel, II-2806
Next Realty, II-2849
NextCare, I-1753
NextEra Energy Inc., I-1234, II-2715

Nexters, II-2338
Nexus Clinical L.L.C., II-3190
NFI Industries, II-3500, 3503
NFI Transportation, II-3431
NFP Corp., I-1909, 1940
NH Industries, I-70
NIBCO Inc., II-2721
Niceone.sa, I-1180
Niche Bakers Corp., I-395
Nichia Corp., I-2069
Nichirei Logistics Group Inc., II-3502
Nicolet National Bank, I-458
Nicor Gas, II-3458
Nielsen, II-2874
Nike Inc., I-216, 1425, 1429, 1431-1432, 1435-1436, II-2909
Nikken Corp., I-1775
Nikkiso Co. Ltd., II-2825
Nikon Corp., I-595
Nilfisk, II-2920
Nine Dragons Paper Holdings Ltd., II-2604
Nintendo Co. Ltd., II-3476, 3479
Nippon Dental, I-956
Nippon Express, II-3055
Nippon Mektron Ltd., II-2790
Nippon Paint Holdings Co., II-2592
Nippon Paper Industries Co. Ltd., II-2604
Nippon Pet Food Co. Ltd., II-2680
Nippon Shokubai Co. Ltd., II-2733
Nippon Steel Corp., II-3238
Nippon Suisan Kaisha Ltd. (Nissui), II-2990
NISA-Today's Holdings Ltd., I-1442
Nishio Rent All Co., I-1775
Nissan Motor Co., I-33, 344, 365
Nissei Build Kogyo Co. Ltd., I-320
Nisshin Pet Food Inc., II-2680
NLC India Ltd., I-748
NMDC Ltd., I-1992
NNA (Nutréa Nutrition Animale), I-1194
Noa Brands, II-2145
Noble Corp., II-2484
Noble Energy Inc., II-2463
Noble Foods, I-1194
Nofrills, II-2165
NOK Corp., I-1592
Nokia Corp., II-2421, 2424-2425, 3306-3307
Nomad Foods Ltd., I-1489
NomNomNow, II-2666

Nongfu Spring, I-540
Noodles & Company, II-2896
Noon.com, I-1180
Norbord, I-1344, II-3581-3582
Norcal Group, I-1943
Nord Drivesystems, I-1594
Nordex SE, II-3446
Nordic Track, II-3209
Nordlaks Produkter, I-1328
Nordstrom Inc., I-1056, 1434, 2000
Norfolk Dredging, I-912
Norfolk Southern, II-2839
Normet Group Oy, II-2325
Nornickel, II-2432-2433, 2595, 2750
Nortek Control, II-2995
North American Arms Inc., I-1719
North American Central School Bus, II-2979
North Carolina Retirement System, II-2645
North Dakota Mill and Elevator, I-1372
The North Face Inc., II-3213
North Point Ministries, II-2867
North Wind Group, II-2445
Northam Platinum Ltd., II-2750
Northeast Illinois Regional Commuter Railroad Corp., II-2153
Northern Pipe Products Inc., II-2719
The Northern Trust Co., I-417
Northfield Savings Bank, I-453
Northland Concrete & Masonry Co. L.L.C., I-919
NorthMarq Capital L.L.C., II-2845
Northrim Bank, I-405
Northrop Grumman Corp., I-1648-1649, 1658, 1664-1665, 2108, II-2829
NorthStar, I-910-911
Northway Bank, I-433
Northwestern Mutual Group, I-1942
Norway Royal Salmon, I-1328
Norway Savings Bank, I-423
Norwegian Cruise Line, I-1024-1025
NOV Inc., II-2493
Nova Sea, I-1328
Novad Management Consulting L.L.C., I-1654
Novametal Group, II-2434
Novanax Inc., II-3459
Novartis International, I-23, 1134-1136, 1138
Novatek Microelectronics Corp., I-1955-1956

Novo Nordisk A/S, I-504, 1130-1131
Novolex, II-2728
NP Auto Group, I-311
NPC International, I-1454
The NPD Group, II-2874
NPR (National Public Radio), II-2762
NRF Distributors, I-1362
The NRP Group, I-1852
NSG Group, I-1627
NSK Ltd., I-471, 473
NTI Group, II-2612
NTT, I-772
Nu Skin Enterprises Inc., I-1081, II-3278
Nuaxis L.L.C., I-1659
Nucor Corp., I-515
Nufarm, I-689
Nuovo Trasporto Viaggiatori, II-2838
Nutanix Inc., II-3168
Nutreco N.V., I-1885
Nutriavícola S.A., I-1197
Nutrichem Company Ltd., I-687
Nutrien Ag-Solutions, I-52
Nutrien Corp., I-692, 2033
NuVasive Corp., II-2243, 2247
Nuvoton Technology Corp., I-1958
nVent Erico International, I-1189
Nvidia Corp., I-1956, II-3017, 3036
NVR Inc., I-1840, 1842, 1846, 1850
NXP Semiconductors, I-1958, 1960-1961, II-3011
NY Brooklyn Bread, I-557
NYK Line, II-3048-3049, 3051, 3053, 3064
Nyrstar N.V., II-3601
The O2-London, I-262
Oakland Nurseries, I-2037
Oakwood Corp. Housing, II-3039
OB Sports, I-1644
Obasanjo Farms Nigeria Ltd., I-1192
Oberto Sausage Co., II-2199
OBO Bettermann GmbH, I-1189
Occidental Petroleum Corp., II-2465, 2485-2488
OCDetailing Inc., I-318
Ocean Alliance, II-3060, 3062-3063
Ocean Park (Hong Kong), I-180
Ocean Spray Cranberries Inc., I-821, 1100
Oceanfirst Bank NA, I-434
OCESA/CIE, I-801
OCT Parks China, I-182
Octapharma AG, I-1877

Oculens Ltd., I-398
Oden Hughes, I-1852
Odgen Newspapers, II-2429
Odisha Mining Corp., I-1992
Odle Management Group L.L.C., I-1656
O.F. Mossberg & Sons, I-1715, 1717
Offerpad, I-1965
Office Depot L.L.C., I-902
Office (shoe retailer), I-1435
OFS Fitel L.L.C., I-584
Ohana Pacific Bank, I-415
Ohio Industries Co., I-1931
Ohio Public Employees, II-2645
Oilmens Equipment Corp., II-3292
Oiltanking, II-3291
Oji Group, II-2612
Oji Holdings Corp., II-2604
OK Cupid, I-253
Okamoto USA, II-2657
O'Key Group, I-1699
Oklahoma Steel & Wire, I-1303
Old Dominion Freight Line, II-3425
Old Dutch Foods Inc., II-3125
Old Home Kitchens, I-385
Old National Bank, I-418, 427
Old Navy, I-213
Old Republic Insurance Group, I-1921, 1929, 1931, 1954
Old Trapper Smoked Products, II-2199
Old Wisconsin Food Products, II-2194
Oldendorff Carriers, II-3048
Ole Mexican Foods Inc., II-3390
Ole South Properties, I-1846
Olive Garden, II-2884, 2891
Olson Baking Co., I-385
Olson's Greenhouse Gardens, I-1674
Olymel L.P., I-1783
Olympic Steel Inc., II-2297
Olympus Corp., II-2241, 2250
Omaha Steaks International Inc., II-2231
Omega World Travel Inc., II-3413
Omnicom Group, I-24
OmniMax International, I-1720
OmniVision, II-3031-3032
Omron Corp., I-323, II-2306
Omron Healthcare, II-2530
On the Run Pty Ltd., I-1438
Onatel S.A., II-3564
OnDeck Capital Inc., I-2104

One Brands L.L.C., I-839
One Store, I-252
O'Neal Industries Inc., II-2297
Onewater, I-507
OneWeb Ltd., II-2964
Oni Press, I-774
Ontex bvba, II-3553
Opal Foods, I-1202
Opendoor, I-1965
Opici Family Distributing, II-3551
Oppliger Feedyard Inc., I-625
Oppo Mobile, I-638-639, 641
Opportunity Bank of Montana, I-430
Optum Specialty Pharmacy, I-1116
Opus Agency, I-1255
OQEMA GmbH, I-699
Oracle Corp., II-3036, 3166, 3170
Orange County Florida Public Schools, I-1422
Orange County Transportation Authority, II-2160
Orange S.A., II-2629, 3564, 3566, 3572
Orano TN, II-2443-2444, 2446, 3456
Orbia, II-3509
Oregon Ice Cream Co., I-1876
O'Reilly Auto Parts, I-310
Organic Valley Family of Farms, I-1397
Organigram, I-601
Orian Rugs, I-1360
Orica Ltd., I-1262
Orient Cement Ltd., I-646
Oriental Bank, I-444
Oriental Weavers, I-1360, 1821
Origin Bank, I-422
Original Gourmet Food Co., I-829
Orion Corp., I-717, 812
Orion Food Systems L.L.C., I-1003
Orkla Care AB, I-978
Orsted Wind Power, I-1234
Ortho Clinical Diagnostics, I-1068
OSG Corp., II-2289
Oshkosh Corp., I-1658
OSN, II-2550
Osram AG, I-2069, 2071
OTCPharm, I-1135
Otis Worldwide Corp., I-1209
OTK Kart, II-3396
Otter Tail, II-2719
Otto Baum Co. Inc., I-919
Outback Steakhouse, II-2884, 2891
Outdoor Venture Corp., II-3325
Outer Aisle Gourmet L.L.C., I-558

Outfront, I-39
Outlook.com, II-3161
Ovation Travel Group, II-3413
Overstock.com, I-1560, 1801, 1805
Ovostar Union, I-1194
Owens Corning, I-281, 566, 1624, 1905-1906, II-2931
Owl Companies, I-1656
Oxford University, II-3459
Oyo Rooms, I-1828
P H Van Den Brink, II-2181
PABCO Gypsum, II-3493
PABCO Roofing Products, I-1725
Pace Farm, I-1196
Pace-Suburban Bus Division, II-2155, 2160
Pacific Gas & Electric, II-3423, 3458
Pacific Golf Management, I-1644
Pacific Sales Kitchen & Bath Centers L.L.C., I-219
Pacific Western Bank, I-437
Pacific Woodtech Corp., I-1241
Pacific World Corp., I-973
Pactiv Evergreen, II-2561-2564
PAE Holding Corp., I-1657
PAE Inc., I-1657
PagSeguro, II-2275
Pakerin, II-2605
Paladin/PalAmerican Security, II-3000
Palermo Villa Inc., I-1493
Palfingermarine, I-509
Palmetto Automatic Sprinkler Co. Inc., I-917
Palomar Specialty Insurance Co., I-1932
Pamela's Products Inc., I-1010
Pamesa, I-659
Pampered Chef, I-1834
Pan American Silver Corp., II-3084
Pan-O-Gold Baking Co., I-549, 555
Panarama Inc., I-396
Panariagroup, I-658
Panasonic Automotive Systems Co. of America, I-305-306
Panasonic Corp., I-307, 464-465, 595, 642, 1764, 1865, II-2306
Panda Choc Finnfoods, I-831
Panda Express, II-2888, 2896
P&J Arcomet, I-1014
P&O Australia, I-1024
Pandora A/S, I-2000, II-2409
Panduit, II-3575
Panel Rey, I-1727, II-3493

Panera Bread, II-2882, 2888-2889
Panjapol Paper Industry, II-2606
Panolam Surface Systems, I-997
PANTHERx Rare, I-1116
Papa Pita Bakery, I-379, 556
Paper Excellence, II-2816
PAR Pharmaceuticals, I-1129
Paramount Baking Co. Inc., I-556
Paramount Pictures, II-2356
Paramount Recording Studios, II-3194
Paramount Theatre, II-3334
Parexel International, II-2876
Paric Corp., I-915
Paris Baguette, I-768
The Park National Bank, I-439
Park Square Homes, I-1847
Parkdale Advanced Materials Inc., I-1653
Parker-Hannifin Corp., II-2936
Parkland Fuel Corp., I-1439, 1593
Parque De La Costa, I-178
Parque Mundo Aventura, I-178
Parque Xcaret, I-178
Parques Reunidos, I-182
Parrot, II-3455
Parsons Corp., I-1057, 1661
Parsons Music, II-2415
PartnerRe Ltd., I-1951
Partners Group, I-945
Party Planners West, I-1255
Passumpsic Savings Bank, I-453
Patagonia Inc., II-3213
Patek Philippe, II-3507
Patores Inc., I-1400
Patti's Good Life Inc., I-393-394
Paul French Bakery & Café, I-766
Paxton Media Group, II-2429
PayPal, I-1184
PBF Energy Co. L.L.C., II-2467
PC Connection Inc., I-902
P.C. Richard & Son, I-219
PCHome Online, I-1181
PCL Construction Enterprises, I-862-863, 865-866, 870, 907
PCL Construction Services Inc., I-915
PDC Brands, I-1450-1452, 1733
PDV America Inc., II-2467
PDVSA (Petróleos de Venezuela S.A.), II-2466, 2484
Peabody Energy Corp., I-747
Peacock, II-2538
Peak Campus, I-1855

Peapod, II-2517
Pearson, II-2811
Pearson Candy Co., I-850
Peck Madigan Jones, I-2109
Peco Foods, II-2176
Peet's Coffee & Tea, I-758, 763, 769, II-2883
Pei Wei Asian Kitchen, II-2896
Peleton Inc., II-3209
Pelita Cengkareng Paper Co., II-2605
Pengcheng Helmets, I-185
Penguin Random House, I-529, 532-533
Penhall Co., I-910-911
Peninsula Corridor Joint Powers Board, II-2153
Pennsylvania Lottery, I-1577
PennyMac Financial, II-2346
Pennzoil 10-Minute Oil Change, I-317
Penske Automotive Group Inc., I-296
Penske Logistics, II-3431, 3500
Penske Truck, II-3428
Pentagon Federal Credit Union, I-1019
Pentair PLC, II-3509
Penumbra Inc., II-2265-2266
PeopleFun, II-2336
People's United Bank NA, I-410, 425, 433, 453
Pepperidge Farm, I-387, 1006, 1010
Peppertree Capital, II-3573
PepsiCo, I-34, 392, 539, 829, 1394, 1396, 1399, II-3127-3131, 3150
Perdue Farms, II-2180, 2185, 2224
Perdue Foods, II-2176
Perfect World, II-2331
PerfecTint, I-318
Perfetti Van Melle S.p.A., I-812, 817, 842
Performance Contracting Group Inc., I-929
Perkins Eastman, I-261, 1962
Perkins Restaurant & Bakery, II-2887
Perkins+Will, I-261, 1962
Permasteelisa North America, I-918
Permobil, II-2251
Pernod Ricard, I-2086
Perry Homes, I-1845, 1849
Persimmon Homes, I-1838
Perspecta Inc., I-1654, 1663, 1665
Perstorp AB, I-1588

Pet Supermarket, II-2687
Pet Supplies Plus, II-2687
Pet Valu, II-2687
PetCo, II-2687
Petersen-Dean Inc., I-926
Peterson Spring Co., II-3226
Petitti Garden Centers, I-2037
PetLand, II-2687
Petline, II-2680
Petmatrix L.L.C., II-2671
Petra Diamonds, I-1072
Petrochem Middle East, I-703-704
PetroChina, I-706, II-2468, 2738, 3291
Petroncini Impianti S.p.A., I-762
Petróoleo Brasileiro S.A., II-2466
PetSense, II-2687
PetSmart Co., II-2687
Pfizer Inc., I-23, 32, 1119, 1121, 1135, 1138-1141, 1652, II-3459-3460
PFNonwovens, II-2442
PGIM Funds (Prudential), I-1982
PGT Holdings, II-3422
Pharo Cattle Company, I-623
Phibro Animal Health, I-1127
Philip Morris Intl., II-3361
Philips N.V., I-2071, II-2241
Phillips 66 Company, II-2467
Phillips (auction house), I-269
Phoenix Air Group Inc., I-1657
Phoenix Conduit, II-3575
Phoenix Publishing and Media, II-2811
PHW Group, II-2179
PI Industries Ltd., I-688, 711
Piano Distributors, II-2411
Pick 'n Save Metro Market, I-1695
Pico Group, I-1255
Piedmont Candy Co. Inc., I-842
Pierre & Vacancies, II-3039
Pilatus Aircraft Ltd., I-61, 63
Pilgrim's Pride Corp., II-2176, 2180
PillPack, II-2277
Pilot Corp., II-3234, 3594
Pilot Travel Centers, I-1454
Pinduoduo Inc., I-1179, II-2908
Pine Hall Brick, I-560
Pinnacle Bank, I-431, 448
Pinnacle Bank - Wyoming, I-459
Pinnacle Foods, I-1488, II-2599
Pinnacle Property Management, I-1854
Pinnacle Seed Products, I-692

Pinterest, I-1968
Pioneer Natural Resources Co., II-2485-2488
Piper Aircraft Inc., I-61, 63, 71
Pipestone Systems, I-1782
Pipestone Veterinary Services, II-2215
Pirate Brands, II-3118
Pirelli & C. S.p.A., II-3356
Pirelli Tire North America, II-3355
Pitts Enterprises, II-3407
Pittsburgh Tank & Tower Group Inc., I-927
Pizza Hut, I-1453, II-2889
PKF Littlejohn, I-6
Pladis, I-717, 812
Plains Pipeline, II-2491
Planet Fitness, I-1722
Planters Bank & Trust Co., I-428
Plarium, II-2338
Plastic Omnium Auto Inergy Division, II-2727
Plastic Omnium Co., I-304
Plastipak Packaging Inc., II-2727
Plastopil Hazorea, II-2573
Plateau Excavation Inc., I-916
Platinum Auto Wraps, I-318
Play Communications S.A., II-3572
Playboy Enterprises, I-2061
PlayCore, II-2752
Playgendary, II-2335
Playrix Holding, II-2336
Playtech PLC, I-1578
Playtex Products Inc., II-2945
Playtika Ltd., II-2336
Plaza De Sesamo, I-178
Plenty of Fish, I-253-254
Plug Power Inc., I-1865
Plukon Food Group, II-2179
PM-International, I-1081
PNC Bank NA, I-404, 411, 417-418, 421, 424, 426, 429, 434, 437, 439, 443, 454, 456, 458, II-2350
PNC Financial Services Group Inc., I-2105
Pochteca Materias Primas S.A. de C.V., I-700
PODS Enterprises L.L.C., II-3249
The Pokemon Company Intl., I-2061
PokerStars, I-1579
Polaris Inc., I-103
Polaris Shipping Co., II-3048
Polkomtel Sp. z.o.o., II-3572
Pollo Cibao, II-2183

Pollos Eccus, II-2183
Poly Auction, I-269
Polyair Inter Pack, II-2557
Polyconcept North America, II-2806
Polymetal International PLC, II-3084
PolyOne Corp., II-2725
Polyrus Gold International, I-1641
Pomerleau Inc., I-862
Pomp's Tire & Auto Service Inc., II-3345, 3347
Ponsse Oyj, I-854
Pooch Cake, II-2678
POP MART, II-3394
Popcore, II-2335
Popeye's Louisiana Kitchen, II-2885
Port Authority of Allegheny County, II-2152
Port Authority Trans-Hudson Corp., II-2156
Port Imperial Ferry Corporation, II-2156
Portillo's, II-2895
POSCO, II-3238
Post Holdings Inc., I-392, 662
Postmates, I-1402-1403, 1408-1410
Potbelly Sandwich Shop, II-2895
PotlatchDeltic Corp., I-2129, II-3337
Potomac and Rappahannock Transportation Commission, II-2160
Pottery Barn, I-1560
Poultry Growers Assets Trust, II-2208
Power Construction Corp. of China, I-909
Power Home Remodeling, I-869
PowerAdd, I-466
Powerchip Semiconductor Manufacturing Corp., I-1448
POWERHOME Solar, I-926
Powerhouse Gyms International, I-1722
Powerjet, I-77
PowerLeader Science and Technology Group, II-3035
Powertech Technology Inc., II-3014
Poynter Sheet Metal, I-923
PPG Industries Inc., II-2586, 2591-2592
PRA Health, II-2876
Prairie Farms Dairy Inc., I-399, 1033, 1645
Prairie Star Farms, I-1202
Pratt & Whitney Canada, I-78-79

Pratt & Whitney Corp., I-72-74, 76-78
Precision Castparts Corp., I-515, II-2298
Precision Erection Co. Inc., II-2278
Precision Walls Inc., I-929
Pregis Holding Corp., II-2557
The Preiss Company, I-1855-1856
Premier Bank Inc., I-457
Premier Pools & Spas of Dallas & San Antonio, I-928
Premier Pools & Spas of Houston, I-928
Premier Pools & Spas of Sacramento & Central Valley, I-928
Premier Tech, I-2034
Presidential Pools, Spas and Patios, I-928
Prestage Farms, I-1782
Prestone Products Corp., I-690
Pret A Manger, I-770, II-2882
Price Rite, I-1694
Priceline, II-3418
Pricer S.A., I-1203
PricewaterhouseCoopers, I-5-7, 878, II-3414
Pride Mobility Products Corp., II-2251
Priefert Manufacturing, I-1303
Primal Pet Foods, II-2677
Primary Residential Mortgage Inc., II-2347
Prime, II-3429
Prime Group Holdings L.L.C., II-3006
Prime Therapeutics, II-2701
Primerica Group, I-1081, 1942
Primoris Services Corp., I-916
Primrose School Franchising, I-714
Princess Cruises, I-1024-1025
Principal Bank, I-419
Principal Financial Group Inc., I-1942
Printpack Inc., II-2558, 2570, 2728
Prioskolye, I-1194, II-2208
Prisma Medios de Pago, II-2275
ProAmpac L.L.C., II-2558, 2570, 2728
PROAN (Proteína Animal), I-1195, 1200
Proassurance Corp. Group, I-1943
PROBAT, I-762
Procter & Gamble Co., I-26, 32, 34, 38, 41, 53-55, 737, 1059-1062,

1449-1451, 1732-1733, II-2530-2531, 2651-2653, 2656, 2944-2948, 2953, 3140, 3388, 3553-3555
Prodo, II-2208
Productos Toledano, II-2183
Professional Printers, II-2797
ProFlowers, I-1369-1370
Progressive Insurance Group, I-37, 1783, 1914, 1923-1926, 1929, 1938, 1950
Progressive Transportation Services Administration, II-2159
Promotion in Motion Co., I-821, 825
Pronovias, I-209
Prosegur Compagñia de Seguridad S.A., I-616
Prosegur USA, II-3000
Prosek Partners, II-2809
Prosper Funding L.L.C., I-2104
Prosperity Bank, I-440, 449
Proterra, I-301
Providence Health & Services, I-1749
Providence St. Joseph Health, I-1747
Provident Bank, I-434
Prudential Financial Inc., I-1788, 1915
Prudential of America Group, I-1942
PRX, II-2762
PS Logistics, II-3422
PSA Group, I-340, 365
PSA International, II-3064
PSG Dover, II-2825
PT Astra Tol Nusantara, II-3377
PT Citra Marga Nusaphala Persada, II-3377
PT Hutama Karya, II-3377
PT Nusantara Infrastruktur, II-3377
PT Pertamina (Persero), II-2495
PT Timah, II-3341
PT Waskita Karya, II-3377
Public Service Company of Colorado, II-3458
Public Service Electric & Gas Co., II-3458
Public Storage Inc., II-3006
Publicis Groupe, I-24
Publix Super Markets Inc., I-1115, 1683, 1690-1691, 1700, 1702
Pulike Biological Engineering, II-3464
PulteGroup, I-1839, 1842-1850
Puma Energy International S.A., I-1438

Purcell Tire & Rubber Co., II-3346-3347
Pure Barre, I-1722
Pure Fishing Inc., II-3207
Pure Organic, I-825, 840
PureGym, I-1722-1723
Purina Mills L.L.C., I-1884
Purina Pet Care India Pvt Ltd., II-2665
Purple, I-1543, 1801
Purple Liner L.L.C., II-3403
PVH Corp., I-189, 192, 198, 2061, 2131-2132
PwC's PwC Digital Services, I-24
Pyramid Hotel Group, I-1829
Pyramid Poultry Co., II-2177
Pysham Refinery (Russia), I-953
PZL-Mielec, I-71
Qatar Airways Group, I-84, II-3054
QBE Insurance Group, I-1917, 1921, 1937, 1945, 1947
Qdoba Mexican Eats, II-2888, 2894
Qiangli Jucai Opto-Electronic, I-2052
Qingdao Yebio Biological Engineering, II-3464
Qorvo, II-3024
QST International, I-1882
Quad, II-2793-2796
Quad City Bank and Trust Co., I-419
Quadpay, I-256
Quadra Chemicals Ltd., I-701
Quaker Oats Co., I-539, 662, 815, 827, 846, II-2599
Qualcomm, I-1956, 1961, II-2628, 3017-3018, 3022
Quali Desserts Inc., I-399
Quality Distribution Inc., II-3421
Quality Drive Away Inc., II-3426
Quangzhou Baiyunshan Pharmaceutical Group Co. Ltd., I-1133
Quanta Services, I-913
Quantum Foods, I-1192, II-2177
Quantum Rehab, II-2251
Quectel Wireless Solutions, II-2422
Quen Zhou Banglida Technology Industry, II-2733
Quest, II-2993
Quest Aircraft Co., I-71
Quest Nutrition L.L.C., I-839
Quibi, II-2537
Quick Quack Car Wash, I-615
Quicken Loans Inc., II-2346-2347, 2349-2351

Quidsi, II-2277
QuikTrip Corp., I-935, 1437
Química Anastacio, I-700
Quimidroga S.A., I-703
Quimtia S.A., I-700
Quinlan & Fabish Music Co., II-2411
Qunar, II-2521
Qurate Retail Group, I-1805, 2000
QVC Inc., I-2000
Racioppi's Taralles Inc., I-1003
Radian Group, I-1944
Radici, II-2732
Radio City Music Hall, II-3334
Radio Shack, I-885
Rainbow, I-2061
Raising Cane's Chicken Fingers, II-2885, 2888
RAK Ceramics PJSC, I-659, II-2958
Rakha Al-Khaleej International, I-703
Rakuten Inc., I-215
Ralcorp Frozen Bakery Products, I-559
Rallis India Ltd., I-688, 711
Ralph C. Wilson Jr. Foundation, I-666
Ralph Lauren, I-189, 192, 2131
The Ramco Cements Ltd., I-646
Ramsey Popcorn Co. Inc., II-3119
Ranbaxy Laboratories, II-3276
Ranchers & Farmers Mutual Insurance Co., I-1928
R+L Carriers, II-3425
Randolph-Brooks Federal Credit Union, I-1019
Randstad Holding, II-3228, 3230
R&T Plumbing, II-2756
Range Resources Corp., II-2462-2465, 2485-2486
Raritan (Legrand), II-2428
Ravago Chemicals, I-703
Ray Young Food Distributors, I-559
Raychem HTS, I-586
Raydium, I-1955
The Raymond Group, I-929
Raymond James Bank NA, I-412
Raymour & Flanigan, I-1565, 1802
Rayonier Inc., II-3337
Raytheon Technologies Corp., I-1646, 1649, 1658, 1661, 1664-1665, 1667-1668, II-2327, 2829
Razer, I-786
RCA, II-2408

RCB Bank, I-440
RCL Foods Ltd., II-2177
RDH Tire Co., II-3346
Re-Bath L.L.C., I-869
RE/MAX Ability Plus, II-2848
RE/MAX at the Beach, II-2849
RE/MAX Centerstone, II-2848
RE/MAX Essential, II-2849
Real Foods, I-846
Real Pet Food Co. Australia, II-2679
realme, I-633, 639, 641
Realogy Brokerage Group, II-2850
Realtek Semiconductor Corp., I-1956
Reckitt Benckiser Group PLC, I-53-54, 373, 376, 1059, II-2657-2658, 2945
Recology, II-3504
Recreational Equipment Inc., II-3213-3215
Red Bull North America Inc., I-1238
Red Lobster, II-2884, 2891
Red River Bank, I-422
Red Robin Gourmet Burgers and Brews, II-2884
Red Roof Inn, I-1832
Red Wing Shoes, I-1426
Redbox Automated Retail L.L.C., II-2870
Reddit, I-1968
Reddy Ice Holdings Inc., I-1867
Rede, II-2275
Redecan, I-601
Redfin, I-1965, II-2850
RedMed, II-2252
Redner's Warehouse Markets, I-1697, 1705
Redox, I-702
Reed & Mackay, II-3415
Reed Exhibitions, I-942
Refinitiv, I-1323
REG Geismar, I-497
Regal Cinemas, II-2379
Regent Homes, I-1846
Regions Bank, I-404, 407, 412-413, 422, 428-429, 448, II-2348
Regis Corp., I-1730
Reign Beverage Co. L.L.C., I-1238
Reinsurance Group of America Inc., I-1951
Related Companies, I-1853
Reliance Industries Ltd., I-706
Reliance Jio Infocomm Ltd., II-3568
Reliance Retail, I-1678, 1692

Reliance Steel & Aluminum Co., II-2297
Reliant Capital Solutions L.L.C., I-1650
RELX, I-1256, 1646, II-2811
Rema 1000, I-1688
Rembrandt Enterprises, I-1195
Remington Arms Co., I-1715, 1717
Remington Hotels, I-1829
Renasant Bank, I-428, II-2348
Renault Group, I-331, 347, 365-366
Renault Nissan Mitsubishi, I-339-341
Renesas Electronics Corp., I-1958, II-3011, 3029
Renfe Operadora, II-2838
Renfro Corp., I-186
Rengo Group, II-2612
Rent-A-Center Inc., II-2870
Rent-A-Wreck of America, I-311
Rentokil Initial, II-2661-2662
Republic Bank & Trust Co., I-421
Republic National Distributing Co./Young's Market Co., II-3551
Republic Services Inc., II-3504
Republic Tobacco, II-3367, 3371
Residential Design Services, I-1366
ResiPro, I-869
ResMed, II-2235
Resolute Forest Products, I-2128
Resource Group of Companies, II-2179
Resource Management Service, II-3336
Respironics, II-2235, 2252
Restonic Ltd., I-1796
Rethink Robotics, II-2926
REV Recreation Group, II-2859
Revlon Canada Inc., I-977
Revolut, I-403
Rewe Group, I-1441
Reynolds American Inc., I-1165, 1167, II-3363, 3365, 3367, 3369
Reynolds Consumer Products, I-169, II-2614-2615
Reynolds Group, II-2561
RFS Holding, I-1182
RH, I-1565, 1805
Rheem Manufacturing, I-238
Ricchetti Group, I-658
Rich Products Corp., I-385, 395
Richard Mille, II-3507
Richemont S.A., I-2134, II-3507
Richmond American Home, I-1848

Rimowa, I-2121
Rimports USA L.L.C., I-53, 55
Ring, II-2277
Ringpu Bio-technology, II-3464
Rio Tinto, I-159, 166, 1072, 1992
Ripple Brand Collective L.L.C., I-721
Ripple Foods Inc., II-2318
Rite Aid Corp., I-1105, 1108-1109, 1111-1112, 1115, 1744, II-2907
Riverbend Sandler Pools, I-928
Riverview L.L.P., I-1290
RJM International Inc., II-2731
RJ's Licorice Ltd., I-831
RK Mechanical Inc., I-923
R.L. Carriers, II-3428
RMS Cranes, I-1014
ROAR, I-1579
Roaring Fork Transportation Authority, II-2151
ROBE Lighting S.R.O., I-2072
Robert Bosch, I-304-306
Robert Douglas, II-2844
Robert Half International, II-3230
Robert W. Baird & Co., I-1982
Robertet Group, I-695
Robertson Brothers Corp., I-1844
Robinson Helicopter Co., I-60
Roca Group, II-2958
Roche Holding AG, I-504
Roche Inc., I-1068-1069, 1134, 1138
Rocket Farms Inc., I-1674
Rockfon L.L.C., I-626
Rockland Coaches Inc., II-2154
Rockland Trust Co., I-425
Rockstar Inc., I-1238
Rockview Farms, I-1290
Rockwell Automation, I-322-324
Rockwool International, I-1906
Rocky Mountain Bank, I-430
Rocky Mountain Pies, I-394, 398
Rodeway Inn, I-1832
Rodex Fasteners, I-1882
Rogers Wireless Inc., II-3565
Rohde & Schwarz GmbH, II-2829
Roland Corp., II-2415
Rolex S.A., II-3507
Roll20, II-3397
Rollic Games, II-2335
Rollins Inc., II-2661-2662
Rolls-Royce Corp., I-72-73, 75-76, 78-79
Rommel Construction Group, I-917
Rontec PLC, I-1442

Rooms To Go, I-1565, 1802
Rosa Clara, I-209
Rosa Foods Inc., II-3278
Rose Acre Farms, I-1195, 1200, 1202
Roseburg Forest Products Co., I-1241, 1344, II-3588
Rosendin Electric, I-913
Rosneft Oil Co., I-696, II-2466
Ross Stores Inc., I-213, 1803
Rostelecom, II-2629
Rotam Agrochemical Co. Ltd., I-710
Rotary Corp., II-2457
Rottne Industri AB, I-854
Rouseco Inc., II-3367, 3371
Rover Pipeline, II-2492
Rovio Entertainment, II-2336
Royal Barenburg Group, II-3003
Royal Canin India Pvt Ltd., II-2665
Royal Canin Japan Inc., II-2680
Royal Caribbean, I-1024-1025
Royal Dutch Shell, I-690, 696, 1439-1443, 2119, II-2466, 2732
Royal Philips, II-2254
RPM International Inc., I-12, II-2591
R.R. Donnelley, II-2794-2795
RSA Insurance Group, I-1918
RSA Security L.L.C., II-3167
RSB Tobacco, II-3367
RSG Forest Products Inc., I-1306, 2129
RSG Group, I-1722
RSM U.K., I-6
RSM U.S. L.L.P., I-5
RTL Group, II-3315
Ruan Corp., II-3421
Ruan Transportation, II-3431
Rubbermaid, I-1588
Rubio's Coastal Grill, II-2894
Ruder Finn Inc., II-2809
Rudi's Bakery, I-392
Rudolph Foods Co., II-3121
Ruffwear, II-2685
Rug Doctor Inc., I-1059
Ruiz Foods, I-1491
Runsveo AB, I-978
Rush Enterprises Inc., I-296
Rush Street Interactive, I-1573, 1579
Russel Metals Inc., II-2297
Russell Stover Candies Inc., I-727, 852
Russian Aircraft Corp., I-68
Russian Helicopters, I-60, 62
Ruth's Chris Steak House, II-2890

RWE Renewables, I-1234
RWS Group, II-3411
RYAM (Rayonier) Lumber, I-2128
Ryder Supply Chain Solutions, II-3431, 3500, 3503
Ryerson Inc., II-2297
S. Abraham & Sons Inc., I-933
Saab AB, I-68
Saatva, I-1543, 1801
Sabert, II-2563
Sabesp, II-3509
Sabor Sensual, I-395
Sabre, I-1635
Saco Foods Inc., I-719
Saddle Creek Logistics Services, II-3500
Saddleback Church (CA), II-2867
Safelite, I-315
Safeway Inc., I-1681, 1686, 1689, 1698, 1703, 1706, II-2165, 2902
Safilo Group, I-2133
Safran S.A., I-72, 501
Sagely Naturals, I-603
Sager, I-1204
Saia Motor Freight Line, II-3425
SAIC-GM-Wuling, I-331, 349
SAIC Maxus Corp., I-572
SAIC Motor Corp., I-331, 349
Sainbury's, I-1679
Saint-Gobain, I-1627, 1727, 1905-1906, II-3493
Saipem S.p.A., II-2493
Sakata Inx Group, I-1903
Sakku Group, I-1193
Saks Inc., I-1056
Salem Media Group Inc., II-2828
Salesforce.com Inc., II-3166
Sallaum Lines, II-3049
Sallie Mae, I-2105
Sallie Mae Bank, I-452
Sally Beauty Supply, I-990, 1971
SalMar ASA, I-1328
Saltchuk Resources Inc., I-1661
The Salvation Army, I-665
Sam Ash Music Corp., II-2411
Sampo-Rosenlew, I-854
Sam's Cafe, II-2893
Sam's Club, I-902, 1683, 1685, 1689, 1691, 1695, 1698, 1702, 1802, 1834, II-2524, 3495
Samsonite S.A., I-2121, 2123, 2133
Samsung Corp., I-284, 287-291, 307, 462, 464, 609, 633, 639-641, 785, 792, 795-796, 799-800, 880, 900, 1088, 1184, 1448, 1955, 1958, 1960, 2052, 2069, II-2341, 2628, 2789-2790, 3013, 3016-3020, 3031-3032, 3071, 3105, 3161, 3519-3520

Samuel, Son & Co Ltd., II-2297
Samvardhana Motherson Group, I-304
San Diego Association of Governments, II-2160
San Diego Metropolitan Transit System, II-2157
San Diego Tortilla, II-3391
San Fernando, II-2182
San Francisco Bay Area Rapid Transit District, II-2158
San Francisco Bay Area Water Emergency Transportation authority, II-2156
San Francisco Municipal Railway, II-2150, 2152, 2157, 2159, 2161-2162
San Miguel Corp., I-102
San Miguel Pure Foods, II-2178
San Qun, II-2144
San Shing Fastech, I-1882
Sanderson Farms Inc., II-2176, 2180, 2185
SanDisk, I-783
Sandoz, I-1129
S&S Activewear, II-2806
S&S Structures Inc., II 2278
Sandvik AB, II-2289, 2324-2325
Sandvik Materials Technology, II-2434
Sandvik Mining and Rock Technology, I-855
Sandy Spring Bank, I-424
Sangetsu Co. Ltd., II-3494
SanMar, II-2806
Sanofi-Aventis, I-1135-1136
Sanofi Pasteur Inc., II-3462
Sanofi S.A., I-1131, 1138, 1652
Sanoma Media Finland, II-3318
Sanquan Food Co. Ltd., I-1468
Sanrio Company Ltd., I-2061
Sansi, I-2052
Santander Bank NA, I-425, 433-434, 443, 445
Santo Co., I-1134
Sanwa Holdings, I-1586
Sany Heavy Industry Co., I-855, 857-858, II-3445, 3447
SAP SE, II-3166

Saputo Cheese USA Inc., I-674
Saputo Inc., I-1033-1034, 1394
Sargento Foods Inc., I-674
Sarku Japan, II-2896
Sarris Candies Inc., I-823
Satellite Science & Technology Co., II-2733
SATS ASA, I-1723
Saudi Arabian Oil Co., I-696, II-2466, 2495
Saudi Aramco, II-2467
Saudi Basic Industries Corp., I-706, II-2725
Savage Arms Inc., I-1715, 1717
Savannah River Nuclear Solutions L.L.C., I-1651
Save-A-Lot Food Stores, I-1687, 1697, 1705
Savills PLC, II-2843, 2846
SayGames, II-2335
SBA Communications, II-3573
Sbarro, II-2896
Sberbank, II-2274
S.C. Johnson & Son Inc., I-53-54, 597, 737, 1059
Scandinavian Tobacco Group, II-3367, 3371
Scania AB, II-2324
Scapa Group PLC, I-9
SCCY Firearms, I-1716, 1718
SCF Group, II-3053
SCG Ceramics, I-659
SCG Packaging, II-2605-2606
Schaeffler AG, I-471
Schaeffler Group, I-304, 473
Schar USA Inc., I-1010
Schattdecor, I-2026
Schedulers Logistics, II-3499
The Schindler Group, I-1208-1209
Schlumberger Ltd., II-2493
Schluter-Systems, II-2759
Schmitt Music Co., II-2411
Schneider Electric, I-322-324, 731, 2113, II-3290
Schneider National, II-3421, 3428-3429, 3431
Scholastic Corp., II-2811
The School District of Palm Beach County, FL, I-1422
Schoolsfirst Federal Credit Union, I-1019
Schreiber Foods Inc., I-1033
Schuff Steel Co., I-927
Schuh, I-1435

Schuler Group, II-2137
Schullsburg Creamery Inc., I-380
Schuman Cheese, II-3113
Schunk GmbH, II-2342
The Schwan Food Co., I-1489, 1493
Schwan's Mama Rosa's L.L.C., I-1400
Schwenk Donau GbmH & Co. KG, I-1660
Schwenk Zement KG, I-647
Science Applications International Corp., I-1648, 1655, 1657, 1661, 1663
Scientific Games, I-1582
The Scion Group, I-1855-1856
Scopely Inc., II-2338-2339
SCOR SE, I-1951
Scott-Mason Equipment, I-1013
Scotts Miracle-Gro, I-2033-2034, II-3003
SDF, I-1284
SDI Media Group Inc., II-3411
SDIC Jilin Alcohol, I-499
SDL, II-3411
SDP Global, II-2733
Seaboard Foods L.P., I-1782, II-2215
Seaco srl, I-905
SeaCube Container Leasing, I-905
Seadrill Ltd., II-2484
Seagate Technology, I-788
Sealaska Corp., I-1659
Sealed Air Corp., II-2557, 2570, 2573, 2728
Sealy Corp., I-1796
Sears, I-219, 222
Sears Hometown Store, I-219
Seasons Hospice & Palliative Care, I-1749
Seaway Crude Pipeline, II-2491
Seaworld Orlando, I-179
Seaworld Parks and Entertainment, I-182
Second Baptist Church, II-2867
Second Cup Coffee Co., I-764
SecurAmerica, II-3000
Securitas AB, I-1653, II-3001
Securitas Electronic Security, II-3002
Securitas North America, II-3000
Security Bank of Kansas City, I-420
Securus, II-2799
Sedima Group, I-1192
Seiko Epson Corp., I-741
Sekisui Chemical Co., I-1838

Select Demo Services L.L.C., I-910
Select Medical, I-1752
Selective Insurance Group, I-1938, 1949
Selene Finance L.P., I-1654
Sembcorp Marine Ltd., II-3071
Semen Indonesia, I-649
Semiconductor Manufacturing International Corp., I-1448, II-3015
Semmell Concerts Ent. GmbH, I-801
SenderraRx, I-1116
Sendik's Food Market, I-1695
Seneca Foods Corp., II-3111
Seneca Tank, II-3292
Senior Lifestyle, I-1861-1862
Sennheiser Electronic, I-884, II-2415
Senpiliç Gida Sanayi, II-2184
SenseFly, II-3455
Sensient Technologies Corp., I-695
Sentinel Safety & Security Group L.L.C., I-917
Seoul Semiconductor Co. Ltd., I-2069
Sephora, I-990, 1971
Serrato Corp., I-1656
Serta Inc., I-1796
Servatii Inc., I-397
Service Corp. Intl., I-1040
Service Tire Truck Centers Inc., II-3345
ServiceMaster Corp., II-2662
Servisfirst Bank, I-404
SESB (Sabah Electricity), II-3167
Seven & I Holdings Co. Ltd., I-1437-1439, 1443, II-2908
Seven West Media, II-2430
Seventh Generation Inc., I-1059
Severnaya, II-2208
Seville Farms, I-1674
SEW Eurodrive, I-1594
Sexton Group, I-1790
Sexy Hair Concepts, I-1732
Sezzle, I-256
SF Express, II-3067
Sfera, II-2208
SFR Numericable, II-3566
SG360, a Segerdahl Co., II-2794
Shaanqi Automobile Group, I-308
Shaffer Trucking, II-3427
Shagang Group, II-3238
Shahid & Shahid VIP, II-2550
Shandong Fangyuan Nonferrous Metals Group, I-953
Shandong Fu'en Biochemical, I-499

Shandong Gold Group, I-1641
Shandong Lingong Construction Machinery Co., I-857
Shandong Luhua Group Co., I-1294
Shandong Qiaochang Modern Agriculture Co., I-710
Shandong Weifang Rainbow Chemical Co. Ltd., I-687
Shandong Xinhai Mining Technology, II-2433
Shandong Xiwang Food Co., I-1294
Shanghai Construction Group, I-864
Shanghai Disneyland, I-180-181
Shanghai Electric Wind Power Group, II-3290, 3445, 3447
Shanghai Hode Information Technology Co., II-2331
Shanghai Huahong Grace Semiconductor Manufacturing Co., I-1448
Shanghai Institute, II-3463
Shanghai Liangyou Group, I-1294
Shanghai Lilith Technology Co., II-2331
Shanghai M&G Stationery, II-3234
Shanghai Pharmaceutical Group Co. Ltd., I-1133
Shanghai Shen Lian Biomedical Corp., II-3464
Shanghai Youzu Information Technology Corp., II-2331
Shantui Construction Machinery Co. Ltd., I-853
Shanxi Fen Wine Factory Co., II-3547
ShaoXing Royal Tea, II-3304
Sharda Cropchem Ltd., I-688
Sharp Bus Lines Ltd., II-2979
The Shaw Group, I-1351, 1355, 1357-1358
Shawcor Ltd., II-2591
Shawmut Design and Construction, I-870-871
Shaw's Supermarket, I-1694
Shea Homes, I-1848
Sheh Fung Screws, I-1882
Shelf Drilling Ltd., II-2484
Shell Canada Ltd., I-1593
Shell Oil Co., I-935
Shemberg Marketing Corp., II-2993
Shendan Healthy Food, I-1193
Shenghong Group, II-2733
Shennan Circuit Co. Ltd., II-2790
Shenyang Aircraft Corp., I-68

Shenzhen Ganten Food & Beverage, I-540
Shenzhen Neptunus Biological Engineering Co. Ltd., I-1133
Shenzhen Noposion Agrochermicals Co., I-710
Sheraton, I-1833
Sheridan Nurseries, I-2037
Sherritt International, II-2432-2433
The Sherwin-Williams Co., I-1366, 1789, II-2586, 2591-2592
Sherwood Bedding, I-1796
The Shilla Duty Free, II-3419
Shimano Inc., II-3207
Shinsegae Co. Ltd., II-2908
Shinsegae Duty Free, II-3419
Shipt, II-2517
Shire PLC, I-1877
Shiseido Co., I-971, 986, II-2651
Shoe Carnival, I-1433
Shop-Rite, I-1687, 1697
Shopee Mall, I-1181
Shopify, I-1173
Shopko Optical, II-2524
Shoppers Food & Pharmacy, I-1686, 1703, 1706
ShopRite Supermarkets, I-1703-1705, II-2907
Shougang Group, II-3238
Showmax, II-2539
Shree Cement Ltd., I-646
Shunxin Agriculture, II-3547
Shure Inc., I-884, II-2415
Shutterfly, II-2703
SHW Group, I-299
Shwarz Group, II-2910
SIAE Microelettronica, II-2421
Sibanye-Stillwater, II-2595, 2750
Sichuan Leshan Fuhua Tongda Agro-Chemical Technology Co., I-687
SICPA Holding S.A., I-1903
Siegwerk, I-1903
Siemens, I-322-324, 642, 731, 779, 2113, II-2831, 2995, 3290, 3410, 3423, 3443, 3448
Siemens Gamesa Renewable Energy, II-3444-3447
Siemens Healthineers, I-1068, II-2241, 2254
Siemens Mobility, II-2834
Siemer Milling Co., I-1372
Sientra Inc., II-2258
Sierra, I-213
Sierra Nevada Corp., I-1649

Sierra Pacific Industries, I-2129, II-3337
Sierra Wireless, II-2422
Siete Family Foods, II-3391
SIG Combibloc Group, II-2574
SIG Sauer Inc., I-1715-1716, 1718
Sigma Plastics Group, II-2728
Sigma Supplies (Isinya Feeds Ltd.), I-1192
Signature Bank, I-436
Signet Jewelers Ltd., I-2000, 2002
Sika, I-12, 803
Sikorsky Aircraft Corp., I-60, 62, 70
Silgan Holdings Inc., I-610, II-2729
Silgan Plastics L.L.C., II-2727
Silhouette, II-2617
Silicon Laboratories Inc., I-1958
Silicon Ranch, I-925
Silicon Valley Bank, I-408
Silicon Works Co., I-1955
Siliconware Precision Industries, II-3014
Silverlining Inc., I-869
Simmons Bank, I-407, 429, 440
Simmons Bedding Co., I-1796
Simmons Pet Food Inc., II-2674, 2681-2682
Simon & Schuster Inc., I-529, 532-533
Simplehuman, I-1588
Simplot Foods, I-1478
Simplot Grower Solutions, I-52
Simply Delicious Inc., I-815
The Simply Good Foods Co., I-721, 815, 827, 839, II-3278
Simply Layered, I-398
Simply Orange Juice Co., I-2012
Sinaberg-Hansen, I-1328
Sinar Mas Group, II-2605
Sinclair Broadcast Corp., II-3319
Singareni Collieries Co. Ltd., I-748
Singer Equipment Co., I-1419
Singtel, II-3568
Siniat, I-1728
Sino-Agri Leading BioSciences Co. Ltd., I-710
Sinochem Group Co. Ltd., II-2495
Sinochem Plastics Co. Ltd., I-702, 704
Sinopec, I-706, 1443, II-2468, 2738, 3291
Sinopharm, II-3459
Sinotrans Ltd., II-3059
Sinotruk Group, I-308

Sinovac Biotech, II-3459
Sinyavskaya Poultry Farm, I-1194
Sir Speedy Printing, II-2797
Sirva Inc., II-3424
Sisecam, I-1634
Sitronix Technology Corp., I-1955
Sitz Angus, I-623
Six Flags Inc., I-182
Six Flags Mexico, I-178
Sixt SE, I-311-312
SK Hynix Inc., II-3013, 3017, 3019-3020
SK Invictus Holdings L.P., I-1645
Skanska, I-863, 867, 870-871, 907, 909
SKC Communications, II-3289
Skechers USA, I-1425, 1429
SKF Inc., I-471, 473
Skidmore, Owings & Merrill, I-261
SkinnyPop Popcorn L.L.C., I-844, 846, II-3119
Skoda Holding, II-3448
SKW, II-2993
Sky, II-2629
Sky Now TV, II-2549
Skydio Inc., II-3455
Skyline Champion, I-1851
Skyline Equipment, II-2862
SkySea, I-1024
SkyWest, I-86-90, 96
Skyworks Solutions Inc., II-3024
Sleep Number, I-1565, 1796, 1802
Slim Fast Foods Co., I-847
SlingTV, II-2537, 2631
S.M. Wilson & Co., I-915
Small Planet Foods Inc., I-662, 815, 827
Smartfoods Inc., I-844
Smartply, II-3581
SmartStop Self Storage, II-3006
Smashmallow L.L.C., I-833
SMBC Aviation Capital, I-80
SMBC Rail, I-2042-2044
SMC Corp. of America, II-2342, 2760
SME Steel, I-927
Smith & Wesson Corp., I-1715-1719, II-2243
Smith Douglas Homes, I-1839
Smith+Nephew Corp., II-2236, 2240, 2248
Smithfield Armory Inc., I-1715
Smithfield Foods Inc., I-1394, 1782, II-2215

Smithfield Packaged Meats, II-2223
Smiths Medical Inc., II-3474
Smokey Mountain Chew Inc., II-3365, 3369
Smoothie King, II-2883
Smurfit Kappa Group, II-2604
Snap-On Inc., II-3388
SNC-Lavalin Inc., II-2445
SNCF, II-2838
Snetor S.A., I-700, 703
Snider Fleet Solutions, II-3345
Snohomish County PTBA Corp., II-2154
Snowman Logistics, II-3499
Snyder's-Lance Inc., I-823, 850, 1003, 1008, II-3115, 3119, 3121, 3123, 3125, 3134, 3137
Sobeys Inc., I-1593, II-2165
SODAM, I-1073
Sodexo, I-1420-1421
Sodikart, II-3396
Södra Skogsägarma, II-2816
Soitec S.A., II-2715
Solar Turbines, II-3443, 3448
Soller L.L.C., II-3119
Solotech Inc., II-3289
Solstice Studios, II-2356
SoluM, I-1203
Solutionz Inc., II-3289
Solvay S.A., I-469, 612
Somerset Hardwood Flooring Inc., I-1358
Something Sweet Inc., I-398
Sompo Holdings Inc., I-1910, 1912, 1921, 1932, 1937, 1947
Sonae Arauco Deutschland GmbH, II-3581
Sonic Automotive Inc., I-296
Sonic Drive-In, II-2889, 2892
Sonoco Products Co., II-2558, 2561, 2563, 2565, 2575
Sonos Inc., I-894
Sony Corp., I-286, 595, 880, 882, II-2338, 2356, 3031-3032, 3105, 3479, 3519
Sony Music, II-2399-2402
Sotheby's, I-269
Sottera Inc., I-1165, 1167
Souq.com, II-2277
South State Bank NA, I-413, 446
Southco Distributing Co., I-933
Southeastern Container Inc., II-2727
Southeastern Freight Lines, II-3425

Southeastern Pennsylvania Transportation Authority, II-2150, 2153, 2159, 2161-2162
Southerland Inc., I-1796
Southern California Gas Company, II-3458
Southern California Regional Rail Authority, II-2153
Southern Copper Corp., I-958, II-3084
Southern First Bank, I-446
Southern Glazer's Wine and Spirits, II-3551
Southern States Cooperative, I-52
Southern Tire Mart L.L.C., II-3345
Southland Holdings L.L.C., I-1659
Southland Industries Inc., I-920
Southwest Airlines, I-84, 86, 89, 91, 93-95
Southwest Gas Corp., II-3458
Southwestern Energy Co., II-2462-2465
Sovereign Food Investments, II-2177
Sowles Co., I-927
SP Plus Corp., II-2620
Space Exploration Technologies Corp., I-1648
SpaceX, II-2964
Span Construction & Engineering Inc., II-2278
Spangler Candy Co., I-829
Spar Group, I-1684
Spark Thinking, I-1255
Sparrow Health System, I-1750
Specialized Packaging Group, II-2557
Specialty Pharmacy Solutions, I-1116
Spectrum Brands Inc., I-235, 2033, II-2671, 2681
Spectrum Group International Inc., I-1660
Spectrum Health System, I-1750
Speedling Inc., I-1674
Speedway Motorsports Inc., II-2826
Speedy Equipment Rentals, I-1774
Spencer's Retail, I-1678
Spire Missouri Inc., II-3458
Spirit Airlines, I-86-88, 90-94
Spirit Miller Trucking L.L.C., II-3426
Sports Clips Inc., I-1730
SportsDirect.com, I-1435
Spotify, II-2409

Spring Air, I-1796
Spring Education Group, I-714
Springer Nature, II-2811
Springfield Armory Inc., I-1716-1718
Sprint Corp., II-3561
Sprouts Farmers Market, I-1681, 1689, 1698, II-2418
SQM Ltd., II-2774
Squarespace, I-36
SRG Global Inc., II-2729
Sri Trang Gloves Thailand PLC, II-2273
SRS Distribution, I-565
SRT Marine Systems, II-3412
SSA Marine Inc., II-3064
SSAB AB, II-3243
The SSE Hydro, I-262
SSP Group PLC, I-1424
Stacy's Pita Chips Co., I-1006
Stada Arzneimittel, I-1134-1135
Stadler Rail, II-2831
Stafford Crane Group, I-1014
Stafford-Smith Inc., I-1419
Stage Stores Inc., I-1056
Stagecoach, II-2164
Standard & Poor's, I-1017-1018, 1323
Standard Solar Inc., I-925
Stanley Black & Decker, II-3295, 3381-3382, 3384-3385, 3388-3389
Stanley Electric Co., I-2069, 2077
Stanley Martin Homes, I-1850
Stantec Inc., I-261, 1057, 1962, II-3513-3514
Staples Inc., I-902
Star Bulk Carriers Corp., II-3048
Star Cruises, I-1024
Star India, I-1678
Star International Group, I-1946
Star Market, I-1694
Star Snacks Co. L.L.C., II-3134
Starbucks Corp., I-393, 487, 758, 763-766, 768-770, 1423, II-2341, 2878-2879, 2883, 2889
Starion Bank, I-438
Starling Bank, I-403
StarPower Semiconductor, II-3029
Starr Group, I-1921
Stars Group, I-1578
Starwood Capital Group, I-1853
StarzPlay, II-2550
State Compensation Insurance Fund, I-1954

State Employees' Credit Union, I-1019
State Farm Group, I-40, 1914, 1923-1926, 1930, 1932, 1934, 1939, 1942, 1950
State Russian Museum, II-2387
State Street Bank and Trust Co., I-425
State Street Global, I-1981
Staton Corporate and Casual, II-2806
Stauffers of Kissel Hill, I-2037
Ste. Michelle Wine Estates, II-3549
Steak 'N Shake, II-2892
Steel Technologies L.L.C., II-2297
Steel Worx Solutions L.L.C., II-2278
Steelcase Inc., II-3578
Stein's Garden & Home, I-2037
Steinway Hall, II-2411
Steinway Musical Instruments, II-2415
Stellantis N.V., I-345, 1663
Stellar Value Chain, II-3499
Stephens Pipe & Steel, I-1304
Stericycle Inc., I-1090, II-3504
Steris Corp., II-2249
Sterling Sound Inc., II-3194
Sterlite Refinery, I-953
Stevens Transport Inc., II-3427
Stewart Information Services Corp., I-944
The Sticky Toffee Pudding Co., I-399
Stifel Bank and Trust, I-429
STMicroelectronics, I-741, 1958, 1960
STN Group, I-659
STO Building Group, I-871
STO Express, II-3067
Stock Yards Bank & Trust Co., I-421
Stockman Bank of Montana, I-430
Stockmeier Holding GmbH, I-699
Stonemor Partners L.P., I-1040
StonePeak Ceramics, I-1356
Stonex Group Inc., I-1660
Stop & Shop Supermarket Co., I-1694, 1704, II-2907
Stora Enso, II-2604, 2815-2816
StorageMart, II-3006
Storck USA L.P., I-829
Stormshield, II-3167
Storopack, II-2557
Stoughton Trailers, II-3407
Strabag SE, I-909
Strauss Group, I-487, 1078

Stremicks Heritager Foods L.L.C., II-2318
Stretch Island Fruit Sales L.L.C., I-825
Structural Group, I-908
Stryker Corp., II-2240, 2243, 2247-2248, 2254, 2266
Student Transportation Inc., II-2979
Studio Movie Grill, II-2379
Stuffed Puffs L.L.C., I-833
Sturm, Ruger & Co. Inc., I-1715-1719
Stutz Packing Co., I-1645
STX Entertainment, II-2356
STX Offshore & Shipbuilding, II-3071
Subaru Corp., I-344
Sublime Desserts, I-1485
Subsea 7, II-2493
Suburban Propane Partners L.P., II-2808
Suburban Transit Corp., II-2154
Subway, I-1453, II-2879, 2889, 2895
The Suddath Companies, II-3424
Suez North America, II-3514
Suez Water, II-3509
Suffolk Construction, I-866, 868
Sugon, II-3035-3036
Suguna Foods, II-2178
Sulzer Ltd., II-2824
Sumitomo Chemical Corp., I-689, II-3012
Sumitomo Corp., I-1515, 1594, II-2526
Sumitomo Electric Industries, I-306, 585
Sumitomo Heavy Industries, II-3071
Sumitomo Metal Mining Co., II-2432-2433
Sumitomo Rubber Industries Ltd., II-3355-3356
Sumitomo Seika Chemicals, II-2733
Summit Community Bank Inc., I-457
Summit Contracting Group Inc., I-868, 1852
Summit Security Services, II-3000
Sun Art Retail Group, I-1684, II-2903, 2906
Sun Burn L.L.C., II-3095
Sun Gro, I-2034
Sun Holdings Inc., I-1454
Sun Maid Growers, I-821
Sun Pharmaceuticals Co., I-1130

The Sun Products Corp., I-1059-1062
Sun Scaffold & Supply, I-1776
Sun Solar L.L.C., I-924
The Sun Valley Group, I-1674
Sun Valley Masonry Inc., I-919
Sunbelt Rentals, I-1771-1774, 1776
Suncor Energy Inc., I-1439, 1593
Suncore Photovoltaic Technology Co., II-2715
Sundt Construction Inc., II-3513
Sunflower Bank NA, I-435
Sunhaven Farms, I-1783
Suning Appliance Group, I-220
Suning.com Co. Ltd., I-1170, 1172, 1179, 1684, II-2903, 2906, 2908
Sunkist Growers Inc., I-1291
Sunmoon Inc., I-1957
Sunoco Logistics, II-3202
Sunoco L.P., I-935
Sunoco Pipeline, II-2491
Sunpro Solar Inc., I-926
Sunrise Medical Inc., II-2251
Sunrise Senior Living Inc., I-1861
Sunsea Telecommunications, II-2422
Sunshine Biscuits L.L.C., I-1012
Sunshine Mills Inc., II-2674, 2676, 2683
Sunshine Minting Inc., I-1660
Sunstar Group, II-2528, 2530
Sunsweet Growers, I-1100
Suntec Concrete, I-908
Sunterra Farms, I-1783
Suntory Holding Ltd., I-102
Suntuity Solar L.L.C., I-926
Sunward Aircraft, I-71
Sunwoda Electric Vehicle Battery Co., I-467
Sunwood Holding Group, II-3234
Suominen Corp., II-2441
Suominen Nonwovens, II-2442
Super 8, I-1832-1833
Superbrugsen, I-1688
Supercell Oy, II-2331, 2339
Superior Bulk Logistics, II-3421
Superior Metal Services, II-2278
Superior Plus Propane, II-2808
Supermax Healthcare Inc., II-2273
Supersonic, II-2335
SuperTarget, I-1689, 1698
SuperValu, I-1693
Sure Steel Inc., I-927
Sutphin Cattle Company, I-623
Sutton Leasing Inc., I-298

Suzano Papel e Celuloso, II-2814-2815
Suzhou FMC Corp. Care Co. Ltd., I-710
Suzlon Energy Ltd., II-3444
Svenhard's Swedish Bakery, I-393
The Swatch Group Ltd., I-2132, 2134, II-3507
Sweda Co., II-2806
Swedish Match, I-2065, II-3359, 3363, 3365, 3369, 3372
Sweet Loren's L.L.C., I-1097
Swinerton Renewable Energy, I-863, 866, 907, 924
Swisher International, II-3359, 3365, 3369
Swiss Colony Retail Brands L.L.C., I-399
Swiss Krono, I-1359, II-3581
Swiss Re Group, I-1932, 1948
Swiss Re Ltd., I-1951
Swissport International, I-99
SX Brands, II-3367
Sylvan Learning Inc., II-3450
Symantec Corp., II-3171
Symbol Mattress, I-1796
Symrise AG, I-695
Synaptics, I-1955
Synchrony Bank, I-452
Synchrony Financial, II-2640
Syncora Guaranty Inc., I-1936
Synear Food Co. Ltd., I-1468
Synergy Solar, I-925
Syngenta Corp., I-689, II-3004
Syngenta India, I-711
Synovus Bank, I-404, 413, 446
Synta Technology Corp., II-3313
Syntex S.A., I-1134
System C, II-3190
System One, II-3228
Systematic A/S, II-3190
T. Hasegawa, I-695
T. Marzetti Co., I-819
T-Mobile Polska S.A., II-3572
T-Mobile U.S., I-26, 32, 34, 40-41, 628, II-3561-3562
T-Rex Solutions L.L.C., I-1646
TA Instruments, I-1077
Table Talk Pies Inc., I-394
Taco Bell, II-2878, 2889, 2894
Taco Cabana, II-2894
Taco John's, II-2894
Tactile Games, II-2336
Tactile Missiles Corp., II-2327

Tagros Chemicals, I-688
Taiwan Cement Corp., I-651
Taiwan High Speed Rail Corp., II-2838
Taiwan Plastics, II-2733
Taiwan Semiconductor Manufacturing Co., I-1448, II-2628, 3015
Taiyo Yuden Co. Ltd., I-609
TAJIMA Corp., II-3295
Takasago International Corp., I-695
Takeda Pharmaceutical Co. Ltd., I-1120-1121, 1140
Tall Timbers Trust, II-3337
Tampa Bay, II-3219
Tamura Corp., I-321
Tander, I-1699
T&K Toka Co. Ltd., I-1903
Tantan, I-254
Tapestry Inc., I-189, 2046
Target, I-216, 221, 902, 1178, 1432, 1454, 1560, 1596, 1598-1615, 1683, 1686, 1694-1695, 1697, 1744, 1803-1804, 1834, 2000, II-2524, 2902, 2904-2905, 2907, 2909, 3402
Target Cafe, II-2893
Tarkett S.A., I-1351, 1357
TAS Commercial Concrete Construction L.L.C., I-908
Task Force For Global Health, I-665
Taski (Diversey), II-2920
Tastee Caramel Apple Co. Inc., I-819
Tata Motors Ltd., I-366
Tata Steel Group, II-3238
Tate & Lyle PLC, I-1395
Tate Modern, II-2387
Tate's Bake Shop Inc., I-387
Tattoo Goo, II-2264
Taurus International Manufacturing Inc., I-1716, 1718
Taylor Corp., II-2795
Taylor Morrison, I-1839, 1842, 1845, 1847-1848
TBC Corp., I-317, II-3343
TBWA Worldwide, I-25
TC Transcontinental, II-2558, 2570
TCF National Bank, I-426-427
Tchibo, I-767
TCL Electronics, I-880
TCT, II-2836
TD Bank NA, I-410-412, 423, 425, 433-434, 436, 443, 445-446, 453
TDIndustries, I-920
TDK Corp., I-608-609

TEA, I-292
TechnipFMC, I-909, II-2493
Techno Pneu Inc., II-3347
Technology Insurance Co. Inc., I-1954
Techtronic Industries Inc., II-2784, 3381-3382, 3384-3385, 3389
Teclast Electronics Co., II-3021
Tecnam Aircraft, I-71
Tecno Mobil, I-641
Tecon Biology, II-3464
Tecta America Corp., I-922
Teekay Shipping, II-3051
TEG Dainty/TEG Live/TEG MJR, I-801
Tegel Foods Ltd., II-2181
TEGNA Inc., II-3319
Tekni-Plex, II-2561
Tele Norte Leste Participacoes S.A., II-3563
Telecel Faso, II-3564
Telecom Italia, II-3563
Teleflora, I-1369-1370
Telefônica Brasil, II-3563
Telefónica del Peru, II-3571
Telefónica España, II-2629
Telefónica S.A., II-3569
Telehouse, I-772
Telekom Healthcare Solutions, II-3190
Telephone and Data Systems, II-3561
Telia Company, II-3318
TELUS Mobility Inc., II-3565
Temporary Tattoos, II-3297
Tempur-Pedic, I-1796
Tempur Sealy International, I-1802
Tenaris S.A., II-2720
Tencent Cloud, II-3165, 3169
Tencent Holdings Ltd., II-2409
Tencent Mobile Games, II-2331
Tencent Video, II-2540
Tenet Healthcare, I-1747, 1753
The Tennant Co., II-2920, 2928
Tenneco, I-309
Tennessee Farmers Group, I-1934
Tennessee Gas Pipeline, II-2492
Tennessee Titans, II-3219
Tenpay, I-1186
Tenpower, I-462
Teo Seng Capital Bhd., I-1193
Terminal Investment Ltd., II-3064
Terminix International, II-2661
Terminix Service, II-2661

Territorial Savings Bank, I-415
Terumo Corp., II-2266
Tesco PLC, I-1442, 1679, 1693
Tesla Inc., I-331, 347
Tetra Pak, II-2574
Tetra Tech Inc., I-1057, 1252-1253, 1647, II-3514
Teva Pharmaceuticals Ltd., I-504, 1129, 1132
Texas Capital Bank NA, I-449
Texas Eastern Transmission, II-2492
Texas Farm Bureau Mutual Group, I-1934
Texas Instruments Inc., I-589, 741, 1958, II-2789, 3011, 3017, 3104
Texas Lottery Commission, I-1577
Texas Mutual Insurance Co., I-1954
Texas Roadhouse, II-2884, 2891
Texas Teachers, II-2645
Textainer Group Holdings, I-905
Textron Inc., I-57, 61, 65, 71
TFP & TWI Group, I-1922
Thai Beverage PCL, I-102
Thai Union Group, II-2681
Thaisarco Smelting and Refining, II-3341
Thales Group, I-1338-1339, 1668, 1878, II-2422
Thales SEC Transport System, II-2836
Thanasi Foods L.L.C., II-2194, 3137
That's How We Roll L.L.C., II-3113
Theme Parque Nacional del Café, I-178
Therapedic Intl., I-1796
Thermas Dos Laranjais, II-3510
Therme Erding, II-3510
Thermo Fisher Scientific Inc., I-1068, II-2420
Thielmann AG, I-2016
Think Thin L.L.C., I-839
Third Federal Savings and Loan Association of Cleveland, I-439
Thomas Industrial Coatings Inc., I-921
Thomas Sign, II-3325
Thompson Gas L.L.C., II-2808
Thompson Hospitality, I-1420
Thomson Reuters, II-2811, 3172
Thor Industries Inc., II-2859-2861, 3404-3406
Three Squirrels, II-3135
Thrust Aircraft, I-71
ThyssenKrupp AG, I-304, 1208-1209

ThyssenKrupp Materials NA Inc., II-2297
TIAA FSB, I-412
TianJin Lishen Battery Joint-Stock Co. Ltd., I-467
Tianjin Zhonghuan Semiconductor Co. Ltd., II-2715
Tianma Micro-Electronics Co., I-1088
Tianshui Huatian Technology Co. Ltd., II-3014
TianYi Cloud by China Telecom, II-3169
Ticklebelly Desserts, I-399
Tidal Wave Auto Spa, I-615
TietoEVRY Oyj, II-3190
Tiffany & Co., I-2000
Tigercat, I-854
Tigo Energy Inc., II-3021
Tillamook County Creamery, I-674, 1875
Tillman Infrastructure L.L.C., II-3573
Tilray, I-601
Tim Hortons, I-763-764, II-2882, 2886
TIM Vision, II-2546, 2549
Timber Mart, I-1790
The Timken Co., I-471
Tinder, I-253-254
Tingyi Holding Corp., I-540
The Tint Pros, I-318
Titan Co., I-2123
Titan Comics, I-774
Titan Pro, I-52
Titan Solar Power, I-926
T.J. Maxx, I-213, 1435, 1803-1804
The TJX Companies Inc., I-213
TLC, II-2632
TM International, II-3297
Tmall, I-220, 1170, 1172
TMC/Annett Holdings, II-3422
TNT Construction Equipment, I-1776
TNT Crane & Rigging, I-1013
Toagosei Co. Ltd., I-14
Todd Campbell Construction, I-1841
Toei Animation, I-2061
Tokai Carbon Co., I-1994
Tokai Corp., I-2065
Tokio Marine Holdings Inc. Group, I-1911-1912, 1916, 1921, 1928, 1930, 1933, 1935, 1946-1947, 1952
Tokyo Disneyland, I-181

Tokyo Disneyland (Japan), I-180
Tokyo Disneysea, I-181
Tokyo Disneysea (Japan), I-180
Tokyo Electron, II-3007
Tolko Industries Ltd., I-2128, II-3582
Toll Brothers, I-1841, 1844
Tommy's Express Car Wash, I-615
Tomra, II-2911
Tom's of Maine, II-2531
Tonal, II-3189
Tong Ming Enterprise Co. Ltd., I-1882
Tongfu Microelectronics Co. Ltd., II-3014
Tongling Nonferrous Metals Co., I-960
TooFab, I-1971
Tootsie Roll Industries, I-721, 723, 829, 837
Top Glove Corp. Bhd., II-2273
Toppan Printing, I-2026
The Topps Co. Inc., I-837
Toray, I-612, II-2442
The Toro Co., I-2036
Torqeedo, I-1242
Torrent Pharmaceuticals Ltd., I-1130
Toshiba Corp., I-1958, II-3005, 3170, 3290
Total Produce/Dole Food, I-1515
Total Produce PLC, I-1395
Total Quality Logistics, II-3057, 3065
Total S.A., I-696, 1441, II-2715
Toto Ltd., II-2958
Toufayan Bakery Inc., I-379, 556, 1003
Tower Research Capital Europe, I-1979
Town & Country Living, I-1821
Town Bank NA, I-458
Town of Mountain Village, II-2152
Towne Bank, I-454
Townsquare Media Inc., II-2828
Toyo Ink SC Holdings Co. Ltd., I-1903
Toyo/Niihama (Besshi), I-953
Toyo Tanso USA Inc., I-1994
Toyo Tire Corp., II-2936, 3355-3356
Toyofuji Shipping Co. Ltd., II-3049
Toyota Motor Corp., I-33, 339, 341, 344-345, 365-366, 2063
Toyota Tsusho America, II-2297
TP-Link Technologies Co., II-2427

TPV Technology Ltd., I-785
TracFone Wireless, II-3561
Tractor Supply Co., I-1789
Tradebe Environmental Services, I-1742
Trader Joe's, I-1682, 1689, 1694, 1704-1706
Trailwest Bank, I-430
Trane Technologies, I-779
TransAlta, I-1225
Transbank S.A., II-2275
Transcend Information Inc., II-3021
Transcontinental Gas Pipe Line, II-2492
Transcontinental Inc., I-528, II-2795-2796
Transfar Chemicals Group, I-697
TransForce Inc., II-3428
Transfort, II-2151
Transmashholding, II-2833
Transnational Foods Inc., II-3111
Transocean Ltd., II-2484, 2493
TransPerfect Translations, II-3411
Transportation Insights, II-3065
Transwestern, II-2843, 2846
Trautwein, II-2911
Travel and Transport, II-3413
The Travel Corp., II-3416
Travel Leaders Group U.K., II-3415
Travelers Cos. Inc., I-1910-1912, 1914, 1922-1930, 1932, 1934-1935, 1937, 1939, 1941, 1946, 1949-1950, 1952
Travelers Property Casualty Company of America, I-1954
Travelport, I-1635
Tread Wright Inc., II-3347
Treasury Wine Estates Americas Co., II-3549
Tree Top Inc., I-490
Trek Bicycle Co., I-494, 496
Trelleborg Group, II-3348
Tremcar, II-3292
Trend Offset Printing Services, II-2793, 2796
Trendyol, I-1183
TrenItalia, II-2838
Tresidio Homes, I-1841
Trex Company Inc., I-1043-1044, 2125
TRG Group, I-2121
Tri-County Metropolitan Transportation District of Oregon, II-2157
Tri-West Ltd., I-1362

Triad National Security L.L.C., I-1651
Triangle Brick Co., I-560
Tribe Hummus, I-1078
Tribune Media Company, II-2429
Tricio Group, I-1290
Tricolor, II-2629
Tricon Energy Inc., I-699-704
Trident Home Furnishings, I-1821
Trigg Labs, II-2658
Trimac, II-3421
TriMark USA Inc., I-1419
Trimble Inc., I-1667-1668
Trinchero Family Estates, II-3549
Trinity Health, I-1747-1748, 1750
Trinity Industries, I-2042-2044
Trinity Services Group, I-1421
Trinity Solar Inc., I-926
TripAdvisor, I-37, II-3417
Trip.com, II-2521, 3417
Triple T Timberlands J.V., II-3337
Tripod Technology Corp., II-2790
Tripp Lite, II-2783
Triton International, I-905
Triumph Foods L.L.C., II-2215
Triunfo Foods, I-825
TriWest Healthcare Alliance Corp., I-1662
Troon, I-1644
Tropical Smoothie Cafe, II-2883
Tropicana Dole Beverages, I-2012
TruckMovers, II-3426
Truco Enterprises, II-3139
True Homes, I-1842
Truist Bank, I-404, 412-413, 421, 424, 437, 443, 446, 448, 454, 456-457
The Trumpf Group, I-2028
Trung Nguyen Coffee, I-771
Trustbridge Inc., I-1749
Trustmark National Bank, I-404, 428
The Truth Bar L.L.C., I-847
TSC Apparel, II-2806
TSI Inc., I-1879
Tsingshan Group, II-2433
Tsingtao Brewery Co. Ltd., I-102, 481
Tsingtao Brewery Group, I-483
Tsuneishi Shipbuilding, II-3071
TTI Inc., I-1204
TTM Technologies, II-2790
Tuft & Needle, I-1543, 1801
TUI Cruises, I-1025
Tulsa Fruit Company, I-1645

Tumi Inc., I-2133
Tuniu Corp., II-2521
Tupperware, I-1081
Turkey Creek Pork Skins Inc., II-3121
Turkey Hill Dairy, I-1875
Turkish Airlines, II-3054
Turner Construction Co., I-863, 865, 867, 871, 907
Turosi, I-1196, II-2181
TV2 Play, II-2541
TWEE Group, II-2442
Twin Peaks, II-2897
Twitch Interactive, II-2277
Twitter, I-28, 1968, 1970
TWS Marketing Group Inc., I-2012
Tyco International, II-2996
Tycoons Group, I-1882
Typhoon Lagoon at Disney World, II-3510
Tyrolia, II-3208
Tyson Foods Inc., I-1394, 1489, 1885, II-2176, 2180, 2185, 2224
Tyson Pet Products Inc., II-2671
U-blox, II-2422
U-Haul International Inc., II-3006
U-Save Auto Rental News, I-311
Uber Australia, I-1415
Uber Eats, I-1402-1409, 1411-1412
Uber Technologies Inc., I-2082, II-2918
Ubiquiti Inc., I-782
UDS, I-1985
UBS Bank USA, I-452
UC Rusal, I-166
UCI Cinemas, II-2381
UFP Industries, I-1306
U.K. National Lottery, I-1577
Ukrop's Homestyle Foods L.L.C., I-394, 398
Ulta Beauty Inc., I-990
UltraTech Cement Ltd., I-646
Ultratech Cement Ltd., I-651
UMB Bank NA, I-420, 429
Umpqua Bank, I-441, 455
Unbun Foods, I-558
Unfi Supervalu, I-1680
Unicharm Corp., II-2680-2681, 2953
UniFirst Corp., II-3328-3329
UniGroup Inc., II-3424
Unilever PLC, I-487, 490, 978, 1033, 1395-1396, 1449-1450, 1732-1733, 1873, 1875, 2108, II-2651, 2653, 2656, 3140, 3554

Unilumin Group Co., I-2052
Unimicron Tehnology Corp., II-2790
Union Bank and Trust Co., I-431
Union Bank (Vermont), I-453
Union Leasing Inc., I-298
Union Pacific, II-2839
Union Tank Car, I-2043-2044
UnionPay, II-2634-2635
Unique Pretzel Bakery, II-3125
Unisoc, II-3018
Unisys Corp., I-1646
United Aircraft Corp., I-67
United Airlines, I-84, 86-87, 89, 92-93
United Artists, II-2356
United Bakery & Co., I-1003
United Bank, I-446, 454, 456-457
United Bank of Iowa, I-419
United Community Bank, I-413, 446
United Jewish Foundation, I-666
United Launch Alliance L.L.C., I-1649
United Microelectronics Corp., I-1448, II-3015
United Paper PCL, II-2606
United Parcel Service, II-3054, 3068-3069, 3423, 3425, 3428
United Pet Group, II-2681
United Petroleum Pty Ltd., I-1438
United Real Estate, II-2850
United Rentals Inc., I-1771-1772, 1775
United Road Service, II-3426
United Services Automobile Association, I-1914, 1938
United Shipbuilding Corp., II-3071
U.S. Air Force, I-1649
U.S. AutoLogistics, II-3426
United States Bakery, I-379, 388, 549-551, 555, 1003
U.S. Bancorp., II-2640
U.S. Bank NA, I-406, 409, 416-417, 419-421, 427, 429-432, 435, 438-439, 441, 447-448, 455, 458-459
U.S. Bioservices, I-1116
U.S. Cellular Co., II-3561, 3573
United States Cold Storage, II-3501-3502
U.S. Crane & Rigging, I-1014
U.S. Department of Agriculture, I-1645
U.S. Department of Commerce, I-1646

U.S. Department of Education, I-1650
U.S. Department of Energy, I-1651
U.S. Department of Health and Human Services, I-1652
U.S. Department of Homeland Security, I-1653
U.S. Department of Housing and Urban Development, I-1654
U.S. Department of Justice, I-1655
U.S. Department of Labor, I-1656
U.S. Department of State, I-1657
U.S. Department of the Army, I-1658
U.S. Department of the Interior, I-1659
U.S. Department of the Treasury, I-1660
U.S. Department of Transportation, I-1661
U.S. Ecology, I-1742, II-3504
U.S. Farathane L.L.C., II-2729
U.S. Government, I-36, 41, 1655, 1665
U.S. Navy, I-1664
U.S. Physical Therapy, I-1752
U.S. Postal Service, II-2773, 3068-3069
U.S. Renal Care Inc., I-1745
U.S. Veterans Administration, I-1751
U.S. Xpress Enterprises, II-3429
United Supermarkets, I-1696
United Talent Agency, I-50
United Technologies Corp., I-1208, II-2420, 2995
United Way, I-665
United Wholesale Mortgage Corp., II-2346-2347, 2349, 2351
UnitedHealth Group Inc., I-1114-1115, 1662, 1788, 1915, 1919, II-2701
UnitedImaging, II-2241
UniTTEC Co. Ltd., II-2836
Univar Solutions Inc., I-699-701, 704
Univeral Studios Japan, I-181
Universal, II-2356
Universal Brand Development, I-2061
Universal Music, II-2399-2402
Universal Parks and Resorts, I-182
Universal Robot, II-2926
Universal Studios Florida at Universal, I-179
Universal Studios Hollywood, I-179

Universal Studios Japan, I-180
Universal Truckload Services, II-3422
Universal Windows Direct, I-869
University of California Health, I-1747
University of Michigan Credit Inc., I-1020
Univision Communications Inc., II-2632, 2828, 3319
Uno Foods Inc., I-1400
UPL Ltd., I-688-689, 711
UPM, II-2604, 2814-2815
UPS Supply Chain Solutions, II-3055, 3065
Upstream Rehabilitation, I-1752
Uralkali, II-2774
Uranium One, II-3456
Urban One Inc., II-2828
Urban Stems, I-1369
US LBM Holdings Inc., I-565, 1789
USAA Federal Savings Bank, I-449
USAA Group, I-1922-1926, 1939, 1950
USG, I-1725
USG Boral, II-3493
USG Mexico, I-1727
USI Insurance Services L.L.C., I-1909, 1940
UT-Batelle L.L.C., I-1651
Utah Transit Authority, II-2160
UTC Corp., I-1667-1668, II-2829
Utility Trailer Manufacturing, II-3407
Utz Brands Inc., II-3127-3130
Utz Quality Foods, I-823, II-3113, 3118, 3123, 3125
V3Gate Inc., I-1662
Vail Resorts Inc., II-3087
Vaillant Group, I-1768
Valaris, II-2484, 2493
Vale S.A., I-1992, II-2432-2433
Valeo Corp., I-304, 306, 2070
Valero Corp., II-2466-2467
Valley National Bank, I-434
Valley Steel Stamp Inc., I-1719
Vallourec S.A., II-2720
Valmont Industries Inc., II-2715
The Valory Music Co., II-2408
Valvoline Instant Oil Change, I-317
Van Scoyoc Associates, I-2109
Vanguard Group, I-1684, 1980-1982
Vanguard International Semiconductor Corp., I-1448

Vanguard National, II-3407
Vans Inc., I-1433
Varo, I-402
Vatican Museums, II-2387
Vault Comics, I-774
VCA Inc., II-3475
VCC, I-870
Vector Security, II-3002
Ventas, I-1862
Ventev, I-466
Venustech Inc., II-3167
Veolia Energy North America Holdings, II-3237
Veolia Environnement S.A., II-3509
Vera Wang, I-209
Verizon Communications Inc., I-26, 32, 36-37, 628, II-3561-3562
Verizon FiOS, II-2631
Verizon Media, I-28, 42
Vermont Bread Co., I-549
VersaCold Logistics Services, II-3501-3502
Versova Holdings, I-1195, 1200, 1202
Vertical Bridge, II-3573
Vesper Holdings, I-1856
Vestas Wind Systems, II-3444-3447
Veterans Canteen Service, II-2307
Veterans Evaluation Services Inc., I-1662
VF Corp., I-189, 191, 194, 2121
VI-Grade, I-1101
VIA Technologies Inc., II-3009
ViacomCBS, I-36, 40, 2061, II-3319
Viaplay Inc., II-2541, 2549
Vibe Credit Inc., I-1020
Vicat S.A., I-645
Vicolo Operations Inc., I-1400
Vicorp Restaurants Inc., I-398
Victoria's Secret, I-210
Victorinox, I-2121
Videojet Technologies Inc., I-2028
Viettel Perú S.A.C., II-3571
View Homes, I-1849
View Smart Windows, I-1620
Vigo Importing Co., I-1003
Viken Mol AS, II-3052
Viking Direct, I-36
VIKING Life-Saving Equipment, I-509
Village Farms, I-601
Vilmorin, II-3004
Vinci, I-864, 909
Vinyltech, II-2719

VIP Industries Ltd., I-2123
VIP.com, I-1170, 1172, 1179, II-2906
VIPJr, I-1966
VIPKid, I-1966
Virbac Corp., I-1127
Virgin Active, I-1722
Virginia Poultry Growers Cooperative Inc., II-2224
Virtu Financial, I-1979
Visa, II-2634-2635, 2638
Visual Graphic Systems Inc., II-3077
Visual Photonics Epitaxy Co., II-3012
Vital Pharma Inc., I-1238
Vitalant Inc., I-505
Vitamin Shoppe, II-2418
Vitas Healthcare, I-1749
Vivint Smart Home, II-3002
Vivo Communication Technology Co., I-633, 638-639, 641
Viz Media, I-774
VLI Pty. Ltd., II-2325
VMware, II-3168
Vodafone Group, II-2629, 3315, 3567-3568
Voestalpine, I-732, II-2835
VOK DAMS Worldwide, I-1255
Volcano Bay, II-3510
Volkswagen Group, I-33, 331-332, 339-341, 344, 347, 365
Volma Corp., II-3493
Volume Transportation Inc., II-3424
Volvo Cars, I-331-332, 365
Volvo Construction, I-855, II-2324
Voodoo, II-2335
Voortman Cookies Inc., I-387
Vopak Horizon Fujairah Ltd., II-2494
Vopak N.V., II-3291
Vortech Superchargers, II-3262
Vorwerk & Co. KG, I-1081
Vossloh AG, II-2835
Votorantim Cinmentos, I-651
VP Auto, I-292
VP Equipment Rental Pty Ltd., I-1774
VTTI BV, II-2494
W20 Group, II-2809
Wabash National Corp., II-3407
Wabtec, II-2833
Wacker Chemie AG, I-12
Wadi Group, I-1180, 1192
Waffle House, II-2887

Waggin Train, II-2671
Wagner Forest Management, II-3336
Wal-Mart Auto Care Centers, I-317
Wal-Mart Group, I-1684
Walden Security, II-3000
Walgreens, I-1102-1110, 1112, 1114-1116, 1744, II-2902, 2904, 2907
Walk-On's Sports Bistreaux, II-2897
Walker & Dunlop Inc., II-2847
Wall Street English, I-1245
Wallenius Wilhelmsen Ocean, II-3049
Walmart Inc., I-26, 42, 216, 219, 221, 902, 1059, 1102, 1104, 1106-1107, 1110, 1114-1115, 1168, 1178, 1366, 1431-1432, 1434, 1533, 1560, 1596-1615, 1618, 1680, 1682, 1685-1687, 1694-1697, 1744, 1789, 1803-1805, 1834, 2000, II-2517, 2524, 2902-2905, 2907-2910, 3343, 3402, 3495
Walmart Neighborhood Market, I-1689, 1691, 1702
Walmart Specialty Pharmacy, I-1116
Walmart Supercenter, I-1681, 1683, 1689-1691, 1698, 1700, 1702
The Walsh Group, I-863, 868, II-3514
Walsworth, I-528, II-2793, 2796
Walt Disney Co., I-26, 34, 40-41, 182, 2061, II-2356, 3318-3319
Walters & Wolf, I-918
W&P Cementi, I-645
W&W Glass, I-918
Wanli Runda, I-499
Want Want Holdings Ltd., II-2314
Wanty S.A., I-911
Warner Bros., II-2339, 2356
Warner Media, I-2061, II-2762
Warner Music, II-2399-2402, 2408
Waserstrom Co., I-1419
Wash Depot Holdings Inc., I-615
Washington Federal Bank NA, I-435, 441, 455
Washington Iron Works, I-927
Washington Metropolitan Area Transit Authority, II-2150, 2155, 2162
Washington State Board, II-2645
Washington State Ferries, II-2156
Washington Trust Bank, I-455
The Washington Trust Co., of Westerly, I-445
Waste Connections, II-3504

Waste Management Inc., II-3423, 3504
Waste Management Recycle America L.L.C., II-2731
Watson & Son, I-1825
Wawa Inc., I-935, 1437, II-2907
Wayfair Inc., I-1178, 1366, 1560, 1801, 1803-1805, II-2905
Waymouth Farms Inc., II-3137
Wayne Farms L.L.C., II-2176, 2180
W.E. O'Neill Construction, I-870
WE Transport Inc., II-2979
The Weather Company, II-3522
Weatherbeeta, II-2685
Weaver Brothers, I-1202
Weaver Popcorn Co., II-3119
Webcor, I-866, 868, 871
Webster Bank NA, I-410, 445
Webuild S.p.A., I-1251, II-3513
WeChat, I-1184
Weeks Marine Inc., I-912, 1253
Wegmans Food Markets Inc., I-1686, 1703, 1705-1706, II-2902
Weihai Ploumeter Co. Ltd., II-2302
Weis Markets Inc., I-1686, 1697, 1703, 1705, II-2902
Wellpath, I-1746
WellPet L.L.C., II-2681
Wells Enterprises Inc., I-1873, 1875
Wells Fargo & Co., I-1984, 2105, II-2640
Wells Fargo Bank NA, I-404-406, 408-410, 412-413, 416, 419, 424, 427, 430-432, 434-435, 437-438, 441, 443, 446-447, 449, 452, 454-456, 458-459, II-2348
Wells Fargo Home Mortgage Inc., II-2346-2347, 2349, 2351
Wells Fargo Rail, I-2042-2043
Welltower, I-1862
Welocalize, II-3411
Welspun, I-1821
WEM, I-1253
Wemakeprice, II-2519
Wendy's, II-2878, 2889, 2892
Wen's Food Group, I-1885, II-2178, 2185
Wens Foodstuffs Group Co. Ltd., II-2215
Wenzhou Aihao Pen, II-3234
Werner Enterprises, II-3429
Werner Ladder, I-2025
Werner Logistics, II-3431
Wesbanco Bank Inc., I-424, 457

West Bank, I-419
West Elm, I-1560
West Fraser Timber Co., I-2127-2129, II-3588
West Shore Home, I-869
West Virginia University, II-2158
Westat, II-2874
Western Alliance Bank, I-406, 432
Western Bagel Baking Corp., I-379-380
Western Digital Corp., I-788, II-3013
Western Logistics, II-3499
Western Partitions Inc., I-929
Western Specialty Contractors, I-919
Westfalen AG, I-1441
Westinghouse, II-2446
Westlake Building Products, I-566
Westlake Chemical Corp., I-2125, II-2730
Westlake Vinyl PPG, II-3050, 3058
Westmor, II-3292
WestRock, I-545-546, II-2562, 2564-2565, 2604, 2607-2609
Westwood One, II-2762
Wetmaster Co., I-237
Wexford Health, I-1746
Weyerhaeuser, I-1241, 1344, 2127-2129, II-3337, 3582, 3588
WH Group, I-1782
What I Tongreu Industrial Manufacturing Co., I-247
Whataburger, II-2892
Wheaton Worldwide Moving, II-3424
Wheels Inc., I-298
Whipple Superchargers, II-3262
White Castle, II-2892
White Castle Foods Products L.L.C., I-1491
The Whiting-Turner Contracting Co., I-865, 868, 870-871, 907
Whitman's Chocolates, I-727, 852
Whole Foods Market Inc., I-1682, 1685-1686, 1689-1690, 1694, 1700, 1704-1706, II-2277, 2418, 2907
WHSmith, II-3419
Wieland Copper Products, I-954
Wienerschnitzel, II-2896
Wilbur-Ellis Co., I-52, 692
Wildcraft India, I-2123
William Davidson Foundation, I-666
William Hill, I-1578
William Morrison Supermarkets PLC, I-1442

William Wrigley Jr. Co., I-817, 829, 842, 1711-1712
The Williams Group, I-927
Williams-Sonoma Inc., I-1565, 1804-1805
Willis Towers Watson PLC, I-1909
WillScot Corp., I-1775
Wilmington Savings Fund Society FSB, I-411
Wilmington Trust NA, I-411
Wilson Bank and Trust, I-448
Wilson Fuel Co. Ltd., I-1593
Wilsonart, I-997, 2026
Wilsons Auctions, I-295
Winbond Electronics Corp., I-1959
Windey Co. Ltd., II-3445
Window Live Mail, II-3161
Window Nation, I-869
Window World Inc., I-869
Windows USA L.L.C., I-869
The Wine Group Inc., II-3549
Wine Warehouse, II-3551
Winebow Group, II-3551
Wingstop, II-2885, 2888
Winn-Dixie, I-1700
WinnCompanies, I-1854
Winnebago Motorized, II-2860-2861
Winpak Ltd., II-2573, 2728
Winsor Products Co., I-557
Wintec System Co., II-3005
Wisconsin Investment Board, II-2645
Wise Foods Inc., II-3113, 3123
Withum, I-7
WiZink Center, I-262
Wolters Kluwer, II-2811, 3172
Wolverine Tube Inc., I-954
Wonderful Pistachios & Almonds, II-3134
Wondery, II-2762
WooCommerce Checkout, I-1173
Wood (design firm), I-1057, 1253, 1742
Wood-Mizer L.L.C., II-2975
Wood Partners, I-1852
Woodbury Nursery and Azaleas, I-1674
Woodman's Markets, I-1695
WoodSpring Suites, I-1832
Woodstream Corp., II-2660
Woof Gang Bakery, II-2687
Woolworths Ltd., I-1438
Worksman Cycles, I-494
World Energy Paramount, I-497
World English, I-1245

World Medicine, I-1134
World Travel Holdings, II-3413
World Travel Inc., II-3413
World Xinxin Semiconductor Manufacturing Co., II-3015
World's Finest Chocolate Inc., I-727
Worldwide Express, II-3057
Worldwide Flight Services, I-99
Worldwide Sport Nutrition, I-839
Worldwise Inc., II-2670
Worley Ltd., I-1252
Worthington Industries, II-2297
Worzalla Inc., I-528
W.P. Carey Inc., II-3006
WPP, I-24, 1646
W.R. Berkley Corp. Group, I-1949
Wright National Flood Insurance Co., I-1938
WRNN-TV Associates, II-3319
WSL Group, I-1684
WSP, I-1057, 1251, 1253
W.T. Byler Co. Inc., I-916
Wu-Mart Group, I-1684
Wuhu Fanta Wild Water Park, II-3510
Wuliangye Yibin Co. Ltd., II-3547
Wuling Automobile, I-347
Wunderman Thompson, I-25
Wus Group, II-2790
Wuyang Parking, I-320
Wyndham Hotels & Resorts, I-1828
X5 Retail Group, I-1699
XCaliber International Ltd., II-3367
Xcel Energy Inc., I-1234
XCMG Group, I-855, 857-858, 1016
The Xella Group, I-319
Xero, II-3172
Xiamen Golden Dragon Bus Co., I-572
Xiamen King Long United Automotive, I-572
Xi'an Aircraft Industrial Corp., I-69
Xiaomi Corp., I-287-291, 633, 638-641, 895, II-3016, 3519-3520
Xilinx Inc., I-1956
Xinfa Group, I-159, 166
XL Beggars, II-2399-2402
XLerate Group Auctions, I-294
Xochitl Inc., II-3139
XPO Logistics, II-3057, 3065, 3425, 3428, 3430, 3500, 3503
XTX Markets, I-1979
Xylem Inc., II-2823-2824, 3509
Yageo Corp., I-609

Yahoo!, I-215, 1181, II-3161
Yamaha Corp., II-2415, 2426, 2659
Yanghe Distillery, II-3547
The Yankee Candle Co. Inc., I-55, 597
Yaskawa Electric Corp., I-323, 642
Yasso Inc., I-1873
The Yates Companies, I-866
Yazaki, I-305-306
The Yellowstone Bank, I-430
Yelp Inc., I-42
Yew Bio-Pharm Group Inc., I-1291
YH Yonghui Superstores, II-2906
Yihai Kerry Arawana Holdings Co., I-1294
Yihaodian, I-1179
Yili Group, I-1034, II-2314, 3599
Ylei, II-3318
YMCA of the USA, I-665, II-2856
Yogi-Dog, II-2678
Yohe Helmets, I-185
Yokogawa Electric Corp., I-322, 324
Yokohama Rubber Co. Ltd., II-3356
Yokohama Tire Corp., II-2936, 3355
Yonghui Group, I-1684, II-2518, 2903
York Wallcoverings, II-3494
Yoshino Gypsum, II-3493
Yotta Games, II-2339
Young Electric Sign Co., II-3077
Young Living, I-1081, 1971
Young Poong Group, II-2790
YouTube, I-1968
YRC Worldwide Inc., II-3425, 3428
YTL Group, I-649
YTO Express, II-3067
Yuan Longping High-Tech Agriculture, II-3004
Yum! Brands, I-34
Yummy Earth L.L.C., I-831
Yunda Express, II-3067
Yuneec International, II-3455
Yunnan Baiyao Group Co. Ltd., I-1133
Yunnan Chengfeng Nonferrous Metals, II-3341
Yunnan Copper, I-953
Yunnan Tin Group Co., II-3341
Yuri-Farm Ukraine, I-1136
Zachary Confections Inc., I-821
Zalando, I-1182
Zambeef Products PLC, I-1192
Zappe Endeavors Inc., II-3123
Zappos.com, II-2277

Zaxby's, II-2885, 2888
ZD Tech, II-2790
Zee5, II-2544
Zeiders Enterprises Inc., I-1659
Zekelman Industries, II-2720
Zeno Group, II-2809
ZEON Corp., I-469
Zep Inc., I-739
ZF Friedrichshafen, I-304-306, 309
Zhejiang Dahua Technology Co., I-592
Zhejiang Jixiang Motorcycle Fittings, I-185
Zhejiang Ningbo Major Draft Beer Equipment Co. Ltd., I-2016
Zhejiang Uniview Technologies Co., I-592-593
Zhejiang Windey Co. Ltd., II-3447
Zhejiang Wynca Chemical Industry Group Co. Ltd., I-687
Zhengbang Group Co. Ltd., II-2215
Zhengzhou Yutong Bus Co., I-572
Zhongce Rubber Group Co. Ltd., II-3356
Zhongtong Holding Co., I-572
Zhurabek Lab, I-1136
The Ziegenfelder Co., I-1873
ZIEHL Abegg, I-1276
Zig-Zag, I-730
Zignia Live, I-801
Zillow, I-1965
Zimmer Biomet, II-2240, 2243
Zimmer Spine, II-2247
Zions Bancorporation NA, I-406, 416, 432, 452
Zips Car Wash, I-615
Zoe's Kitchen, II-2896
Zoetis Inc., I-1127, II-3461
Zoomlion Heavy Industry, I-855
Zozo, I-215
ZPMC, I-1015
ZTE Corp., II-3306-3307
ZTO Express, II-3067
Zurich Insurance Group, I-1911-1912, 1922, 1927-1929, 1932-1933, 1935, 1937, 1941, 1945, 1947-1949, 1952-1954
Zydeco Pipeline, II-2491
Zydus Pharmaceuticals, I-1129-1130
Zynga Inc., II-2336, 2338

BRANDS INDEX

This index shows 2,615 brands—including names of periodicals, television programs, popular movies, and other "brand-equivalent" names. Each brand name is followed by one or more numerals; these are entry numbers; they are arranged sequentially, with the first mention of the brand shown first. Roman numerals indicate volume number.

100sklepow, II-3160
17xueba, I-257
17zuoye Student, I-257
1800Mattress.com, I-1801
1917, I-1162-1163, II-2359, 2363-2364
1997, II-2361-2362
2 Towns, I-1739
24Liveblog, II-3174
2N, I-889
30 Days Max, II-2361
360 Safe Browser, II-3156
361 Degrees, I-1430
3M Scotch, II-3294
4 Aces, II-3366
44 Cats, I-2061
5 Hour Energy, I-1240
5-Toubun no Hanayome, II-2142
505 Southwestern, I-1469
7 Days Inn, I-1833
A&D, I-372
AARP Bulletin, II-2138
Abbey Road, II-2397
ABC World News Tonight With David Muir, II-3317
Aberdeen, II-3518
Abreva, I-1148
Abreva On The Go, I-1148
Absen, I-1087
Absolut, I-2097
Accolade, II-2239, 2246
Ace, I-1739, II-2272
Acme, II-2986
Adidas, I-202, 207, 1425, 1427-1428, 1430
Adobe Stock, II-3188
Adoring, II-2360
Adú, II-2362
Advance, II-2920
Advil, I-1143
Advil PM, I-1143
Advisa, II-2239

Aeonmed, II-2256
Affy Tapple, I-818
Afrin, I-1156
Afrin No Drip, I-1156
After Hours, II-2390, 2394
AGCO, I-1286
Aha, I-542
Aidells, II-2220
Aimtell, II-3182
Airborne, II-3489
Airborne Original, II-3489
Airheads, I-834
Airheads Xtremes, I-834
Airmate, I-234
Airtable, II-3181
Al Fresco, II-2207
Aladdin, II-2365
Alcatel, II-3106
Alessi, I-1002
Aleve, I-1143
Alfa, II-2920
Align, II-3282
All Betty Crocker Products, I-824
All Danone U.S., I-672, 1869, II-2317, 2321
All Dean Foods, I-1871, II-2311, 2317
All Dreyer's Grand Ice Cream, I-1871
All Fairlife, II-2311
All Frito-Lay Products, II-3126
All Heartland Farms, II-2317
All Hershey's Products, I-722
All In With Chris Hayes, II-3317
All Lamagna Cheese, I-676
All M. Maggio Co., I-676
All Mars Products, I-720, 722, 836
All Mooala Brands, II-2321
Allegra, I-1147
Almay, I-980
Almond Joy, I-722
Alpro, II-2319

Altoids, I-816
Always, II-2955
Always Discreet, II-2950
Always Discreet Boutique, II-2950
Always Infinity, II-2955
Always Maxi, II-2955
Always Radiant, II-2955
Always Ultra Thin, II-2955
Amazfit, II-3521
Amazon, I-1975, II-3160, 3251
Amazon Alexa, I-897
Amazon FireTV, II-3250
American Beauty, II-3196
American Eagle, I-201-202
American Express, II-2633, 2638
American Plating, II-2416
American Standard, II-2753, 2755
Among Us, II-2340
Amy's, I-1477, 1487, 1490, II-3196-3197
Anbesol, I-1148
Andersen, II-3536
Anderson Cooper 360, II-3317
Andre, II-3545
Android, II-3155-3156, 3176-3178, 3191, 3252
Angies Boom Chicka Pop, I-843
Angry Orchard, I-1739
Ankai, I-571
Anker, I-466
Anne's, I-1094
Annie's Homegrown, I-1009, 1092
Annie's Homegrown Organic, I-1095
Annie's Organic Bunny Fruit, I-824
Anta, I-207, 1430
Anthem, I-886
AOL, I-259
Apple, I-284, 287-291, 629-630, 635, 637, 883, 1975, II-3250, 3515, 3521
Apple HomePod, I-897
Apple Mail, II-3161

Applegate Naturals, II-2209
Aquafina, I-541
Aquaphor, I-982, 1150
Aquaphor Baby, I-372
AriZona, I-2005, 2007, II-3303
Arm & Hammer Simply, I-1156
Armani, I-975
Armour Lunch Makers, II-2230
Armour Lunch Makers Cracker Crunchers, II-2230
Asana, II-3181
Aspercreme, I-1142
Assurity, II-2239, 2246
AT&T, I-888
Athens, I-1094
Athleta, I-193
Atkins, I-826, 838, II-3277
Atkinsons Chick-O-Stick, I-849
Atlanta Cheesecake Co., I-389, 1461
Audemars Pigeuet, II-3505
Audi, I-338, 343
Audi e-tron, I-327, 329-330, 335-336
Audi e-tron Sportback, I-329
AudioQuest, I-587
August, II-2998
Aussie Instant Freeze, I-1731
Austin, I-1007
Austin Eastciders, I-1739
Aveeno, II-3088
Aveeno Active, II-3093
Aveeno Active Naturals Clear Complexion, II-3090
Aveeno Active Naturals Positively Radiant, II-3092
Aveeno Baby, I-371-372
Aveeno Baby Calming Comfort, I-371
Avocado, I-1801
Awara, I-1801
Axe Detailer, II-2654
Aylmer, II-2969
Azure, II-2239, 2246
Azure DevOps Server, II-3181
Baby Bottle Pop, I-836
Baby Dove, I-371
Babyganics, I-709
Bacardi, I-2085
Back Buddie, II-2654
Backwoods, II-3358
Bad Boys for Life, I-1162-1163, II-2359, 2361-2364
Bagel Bites, I-1457
Bagel Dots, I-378
Bagels Forever, I-378

Bai, I-2005-2006
Bai Bubbles, I-2007
Bai Cocofusion, I-2005
Baidu, II-3185-3186
Baileys, I-2091
Baked Cheetos, II-3112
Baken-ets, II-3120
Bakers, I-718
Balabala, I-207
Ball Park, II-2222
The Ballad of Songbirds and Snakes, I-522, 524
Ballatore, II-3545
Balmex Complete Protection, I-372
The Balvenie, I-2093
Bamboo Lane, I-845
Bamboo Lane Rollers, I-845
Banana Boat, II-3096
Banana Boat Ultra, II-3096
B&W, I-890, 893
Banquet, I-1477, 1486-1487, II-2200
Banquet Brown 'N Serve, II-2209
Bantam Bagels, I-378
Baojun E-Series, I-333, 336
Bar-S, II-2186, 2206, 2220, 2222
Barber Foods, II-2196
Barcel Takis Fuego, II-3138
Bare, II-3110
Barefoot, II-3548
Barefoot Bubbly, II-3545
Barton Vodka, I-2096
Basil Hayden's, I-2095
Bath & Body Works, II-3088
Batiste, I-1734
Bausch + Lomb Preservision, II-3489
Bayer, I-1143
BDI, I-1556
Becbas, I-245
Beechcraft, I-63
BelGioioso, I-671, 673, 676-677
Bellisio Foods Atkins, I-1477
Bellisio Foods Boston Market, I-1477
belVita, I-386
Ben & Jerry's, I-1869, 1874
The Ben Shapiro Show, II-2762
Benadryl, I-1147
Benefiber, I-1153
Bengay, I-1142
Bertolli, I-1486
Best Western, I-1833
Better Homes and Gardens, I-1973, 2061, II-2138

Betty Crocker Fruit By The Foot, I-824
Betty Crocker Fruit Gushers, I-824
Betty Crocker Fruit Roll Ups, I-824
Betty Crocker Scooby Doo, I-824
Beyond Meat Beyond Burger, II-2229
Beyond Meat Beyond Sausage, II-2229
BFGoodrich, II-3351-3352
BG, II-2416
Biazzo, I-676
BIC BU3, II-3595
BIC Cristal, II-3595
BIC Gel-ocity, II-3595
Big League Chew, I-1710
Big Sexy Hair Spray & Play, I-1731
Big Time Soft Scrub, II-2270
Big's, II-3136
Biktarvy, I-1117
Bing, II-3184, 3186
Biofreeze, I-1142
Bioré, II-3091
Bioron Arnicare, I-1142
Biotene, II-2529
Birds Eye, I-1458-1460, 1462-1463, 1470, 1472, 1479, 1481
Birds Eye C&W, I-1458, 1462, 1472
Birds Eye McKenzie's, I-1462
Birds Eye Southland, I-1481
Birds Eye Steamfresh, I-1458, 1460, 1462, 1470, 1472
Birds Eye Steamfresh Chef's Favorites, I-1479
Birds Eye Steamfresh Veggie Made, I-1479
Birds Eye Voila, I-1486
Birds of Prey, I-1162, II-2359, 2364
Birkenstock, I-1427
Birrittella's, I-1096
Bissell, I-239
Bjorg, II-2319
Black & Decker Baldwin, II-2998
Black & Decker Kwikset, II-2998
Black & Mild, II-3358
Black Velvet, I-2089
The Blacklist, II-3320
Blake's, I-1477
Blistex, I-982
Blu, I-1164, 1166
Blue Bell, I-1871-1872, 1874
Blue Bloods, II-3323
Blue Bonnet, I-581

Blue Bunny, I-1872, 1874
Blue Diamond, II-3133
Blue Diamond Almond Breeze, II-2320
Blue Emu, I-1142
Blue Life Protection Formula, II-2675
Blue Moon, I-478, 484
Blue Ribbon Classics, I-1872
Blue Star, I-223, 242
Bluesound, I-893
Blumen, II-3144
BMW, I-338, 353, 364, II-2370-2372, 2374
BMW i3, I-327, 329
BMW Z4, I-328
Boardwalk Baskin-Robbins, I-1871
Boar's Head, I-671, 675, II-2207
Boat, I-285
Bob Evans, II-2218
Bob Evans Farm Fresh Goodness, II-2218
Bob's Sweet Stripes, I-841
Bodycology, II-3142
BodyKey by Nutrilite, II-3277
Boeing 787, I-75
Bois, II-2416
Boku no Hero Academia, II-2142
Bold Rock, I-1739
Bols Cordials, I-2090
Bolthouse, II-2972
Bonade, II-2416
The Book Thief, I-524
Boomerang's, I-1477
Borden, I-673, 675, II-2311, 2315-2316
Bosch, I-240, 244, 250
Bose, I-893
Boss Baby: Back in Business, II-3321
Boston Baked Beans, I-849
Boudreaux's Butt Paste, I-372
Bounty, I-27
Bowflex, II-3209
Box, II-3162
The Boy, the Mole, the Fox and the Horse, I-522
Brach's Star Brites, I-841
Brain Out, II-2340
Brandy Melville, I-201
Breakstone's, I-680, II-3198
Breakstone's Cottage Doubles, I-680
Breath Savers, I-816
Breathe Right, I-1157

Breathe Right Extra, I-1157
Breitling, II-3505
Breyers, I-1874
Bridgestone, II-3351-3352
Bridgford, I-1094
Bridgford Sweet Baby Ray's, II-2198
Brim's, II-3120
Brookstone, I-2061
Brother, I-787
BSN, II-3283
Bubba Burger, II-2195
Bubble Yum, I-1710
Bubly, I-542
Buchanan, I-2092
Bud, I-478
Bud Light Lime-A-Rita, I-1336
Bud Specialty, I-478
Bud's Best, I-1011
Bud's Light Seltzer, I-1336
Bueno, I-1469
Bugler, II-3366, 3370
Buitoni, II-2626
Bulleit Bourbon, I-2095
Bulletproof, I-848
Burgess, II-2306
Burnett's Vodka, I-2096
Burt's Bees, I-982-983, II-3091
Burt's Bees Baby Bee, I-371-372
Burt's Bees Lip Shimmer, I-984
Busch, I-478, 480
Butler Good Cook, II-2270
Butler Mr. Clean, II-2270
Butler Mr. Clean Ultra Flex, II-2270
Butterball, II-2207
Butterball Everyday, II-2197
Butterfinger, I-722
BYD, I-571
BYD Han EV, I-333
BYD Qin Pro EV, I-333
Cabot, I-576, 671, 673
Cacique, II-2309, 3198
Cal Maine Sunups, I-1201
Calidad, II-3138
Califia Farms, I-759, II-2320-2321
California Pizza Kitchen, I-1474, 1492
Call of Cthulhu, II-3397
The Call of the Wild, II-2359, 2361
Calypso, I-2006
CAMC, II-3438
Camel, II-3360
Camel Snus, II-3368
Campbell's, II-3196-3197
Campbell's Chunky, II-3197

Campbell's Chunky Healthy Request, II-3197
Campbell's Disney Frozen, II-3196
Campbell's Disney Pixar Incredibles 2, II-3196
Campbell's Disney Princess, II-3196
Campbell's Healthy Request, II-3196
Campbell's Light, II-3196
Campfire Giant Roasters, I-832
Campho Phenique, I-1148
Campoverde, I-1465
Canadian Club, I-2088
Canadian LTD, I-2089
Canadian Mist, I-2089
Canine Carry Outs, II-2672
Canon, I-787
Cape Cod, II-3122
Cardini's, I-1021
CareerBuilder, I-1974
Carefree Acti-Fresh, II-2955
CareFusion, II-2256
Caring Hands Elegant Fare, II-2270
Carmex, I-982, 1148
Carnival, I-1023-1024
Carolan's Irish Cream, I-2091
Carslan, I-975, 985
Cartier Watches, II-3505
Case IH, I-1286
Casillero Del Diablo, II-3548
Casio, II-2417
Castrol, I-2114-2116
Cat Kid Comic Club, I-523
Cattleman's Cut, II-2198
Caught in Time, II-2360
CBS Evening News With Norah O'Donnell, II-3317
CBS This Morning, II-3316
Cedar's, II-2147
Celebrity, I-1023
Celestron, II-3313
Cellucor, II-3283
Centrum, II-3489
Centrum Multigummies, II-3489
Centrum Silver, II-3489
CeraVe, II-3088, 3091-3093
Cessna Aircraft, I-63
Cetaphil, II-3088, 3091-3093, 3143, 3146
Chain of Gold, I-524
Challenge, I-576
Champion, I-202
Chanel, I-985
Changes, Justin Bieber, II-2394
Changyu, II-3548

Chaparros, I-1469
Chapstick, I-982
Chapstick Total Hydration, I-982
ChargeBee, II-3183
Charmin, I-27
Charms Blow Pop, I-828
Chatham Village, I-1021
Chatroll, II-3174
Checkr, II-3180
Cheerios, I-661
The Cheesecake Factory, I-389, 1461
Cheetos, I-843, II-3112, 3126
Cheez-It, I-1004-1005
Cheez-It Snap'd, II-3112
Chery eQ, I-333
Chester's, II-3112, 3126
Chevrolet, I-343, 346, 353, 364
Chevrolet Camaro, I-328
Chevrolet Equinox, I-337
Chevrolet Express, II-3467
Chevrolet Silverado, I-337
Chevy Bolt, I-329
Chex Mix Muddy Buddles, I-822
Cheyenne, II-3358
Chicago Fire, II-3323
Chicago Med, II-3323
Chicago PD, II-3323
Chicken of the Sea, II-2986
Chifles, II-3116
Children's Dimetapp, I-1146
Children's Mucinex, I-1146
Chilombo, II-2394
China Resources Beverage, I-538
Chips Ahoy!, I-386
Chivas Regal, I-2092
Chobani, II-2321
Christian Dior, I-985
Chromatica, II-2392
Chrome, II-3155-3157, 3176, 3179
Chromecast, II-3250, 3252
Chronicle: The 20 Greatest Hits, II-2396
Chufi, II-2319
Chuwoobang, II-2973
Cineak, I-1556
Cinema-Tech, I-1556
Cinnamon Toast Crunch, I-661
Ciroc, I-2097
Citrucel, I-1153
Claim Jumper, I-390
Clairol Nice 'n Easy, I-1736
Clairol Root Touch Up, I-1736
Clan MacGregor, I-2094
Claritin, I-1147

Claritin D, I-1147
Clarke, II-2920
Clausthaler, I-480
Clean & Clear, II-3091
Clearasil, II-3090
Clearblue, I-1071
Cleverbridge, II-3183
Clif, II-3283
Clif Bar, I-838
Clif Whole Lotta, I-848
Clinere, I-1149
Clio Plum Beauty, II-2654
Clorox, I-27
Clover Sonoma, I-576, II-2317
Cluny, I-2094
CNN, I-259
CNN Tonight With Don Lemon, II-3317
Coastal Source, I-2075
Coco Lace, I-845
Coco Lite, I-845
Colace, I-1154
Coleen's, I-1002
Cole's, I-548, 553
Colombina Crakenas, I-1011
Colorbeam, I-2075
Combos, II-3124
Comcast NBCUniversal, I-1975
Comen, II-2256
Concord, I-1079
Concord Foods, I-818
Conecuh, II-2220
Confetteria Raffaello, I-849
Continental, II-3352
Control4, I-889, 893, II-2997
Converse, I-1427-1428, 1430
Cooked Perfect, II-2195, 2201
Cook's, II-3545
Cool Whip, II-3535
Cool Whip Mix Ins, II-3535
Cooper, II-3351-3352
Coors, I-478
Copenhagen, II-3364, 3368
Coppertone Sport, II-3096
Corona, I-479, 485
Corven, II-2369
Cosmopolitan, II-2138
Costa, I-1024
Costco Connection, II-2138
Country Archer, II-2198
Country Living, I-1973
Country Time, I-2006
Courtyard by Marriott, I-1833
COVERGIRL Cheekers, I-974

COVERGIRL Classic Color, I-974
COVERGIRL Instant Cheekbones, I-974
COVERGIRL Lash Blast, I-987
COVERGIRL Outlast, I-984
COVERGIRL Perfect Blend, I-980
COVERGIRL Perfect Point Plus, I-980
COVERGIRL TruBlend Undercover, I-976
CoveritLive, II-3174
Covidien, II-2256
Cra Z Art, I-273
Crayola, I-273, II-3142
Crayola Bathtub, I-273
Crayola Disney Princess, I-273
Crayola My First, I-273
Crayola Nickelodeon Paw Patrol, I-273
Crayola Silly Scents, I-273
Crayola Twistables, I-273
Crayola Ultra Clean Color Max, I-273
Cream-O-Land, II-2316
Creative Snacks Naturally Delicious, I-820, 848
Crepini, I-1190
Crest Pro Health, II-2529
Crest Pro Health Advanced, II-2529
Crest Scope Outlast, II-2529
Crestron, I-892, II-2997
Criminal Minds, II 3320
Criss Cross, II-3366
Cristalino Cava, II-3546
Crocs, I-1427
Crown Royal, I-2088
Crown Royal Reserve, I-2088
The Crown, II-3321
CRRC Electric, I-571
Crystal, I-1023
Crystal Farms, I-672-673, 675-677
Culturelle, II-3282
Cummins, I-1243
Cuomo Prime Time, II-3317
Cupcake Sparkling, II-3546
Curad, II-2270
Cutter Backyard, I-709
Cutter Skinsations, I-709
Cytosport, II-3283
D'Addario Woodwinds, II-2416
Daher Socata, I-63
Daikin, I-223, 242
The Daily, II-2762
Daily's, I-2085

Dairy Pure, II-3534
Daisy Brand, I-680, II-3198
Daiya, I-675, 1461
D&D 3.5, II-3397
D&D 5E, II-3397
Dandies, I-832
Danielle Creations, II-2654
Danone, II-2315-2316, 2320, 2322, 3600
Darigold, I-576, II-2311, 2317, 3534
Darrell Lea, I-830
Dasani, I-541
David, II-3136
Dayun, II-3438
De La Rosa, I-832, 849
Dean Foods, I-680, II-2315-2316, 3198
Debrox, I-1149
Deep Eddy, I-2096
The Deep End (Diary of a Wimpy Kid #15), I-523
Degree Men, II-2655
DeKuyper, I-2090
Del Monte Fruit Naturals, II-2785
Del Monte Sun Fresh, II-2785
DeLallo, II-2147, 2649
Delimex, I-1457, 1469
Dell, I-883
Delta, II-2753, 2755
DeMet's Turtles, I-726
Demon Slayer: Mugen Train, II-2364
Denon, I-886, 893
Dentyne Ice, I-1713
Depend, II-2950
Depend Fit Flex, II-2950
Depend Night Defense, II-2950
Depend Silhouette, II-2950
Desitin, I-372
Detroit Diesel, I-1243
Dewar's, I-2092
Di Saronno, I-2091
Dial, II-3145
Dial Complete, II-3145
Diamonds, II-2396
Differin, II-3090
DiGiorno, I-1474, 1492
DiGiorno Pizzeria!, I-1474, 1492
Dior, I-975
Discover, II-2633, 2638
Disqus, II-3158
Dixie Paper Products, I-761
Dockside Classics, II-2986
Docobu 3, II-2361
Dodge Challenger, I-328

Dodge/Ram, II-3432
Dodoni, II-3600
Dog Man, I-522
Dole, I-1465, 2006
Dole Crafted Smoothie Blends, I-1464
Dole Fruit & Veggie Blends, I-1465
Dolittle, II-2359, 2361-2364
Domaine Chandon, II-3545
Dominex, I-1459
Dongfeng, II-3438
Dongfeng Xianglv, I-571
Dongpeng, I-1236
Don't Smile at Me, II-2397
Doritos, II-3126, 3138
Dos Equis XX, I-479, 485
Dots Homestyle Pretzels, II-3124
Doubletree by Hilton, I-1833
Dove, II-2655, 3142-3143, 3146
Dove Advanced Care, II-2655
Dove Deep Moisture, II-3143
Dove Go Fresh Cool Moisture, II-3146
Dove Men+Care, II-2654-2655, 3143, 3146
Dove Promises, I-720
Dove Purely Pampering, II-3146
Downton Abbey–the Movie, I-1163
Downy, I-27
DPVR, I-1743
Dr. Bronner's Magic Soaps, II-3145
Dr. Martens, I-1427
Dr. Seuss' The Grinch, II-2365
Dr. Smith's, I-372
Dr. Teals, II-3142
Dr. Teals Relax & Relief, II-3142
Dr. Teals Restore and Replenish, II-3142
DraftKings, I-258
Dräger, II-2256
Dragonball Z, I-2061
Dream Cloud, I-1801
Dream Cruises, I-1024
Dreyer's, I-1872, 1874
Dropbox, II-3162
DRYFT, II-3362
DS 7 Crossback PHEV, I-334
DSW, I-1427
Dubble Bubble, I-1710
Dubuque Royal Buffet, II-2186
Duck, II-3294
Duck EZ Start, II-3294
DuckDuckGo, II-3184
Ducktrap River, II-2986

Duda, II-3193
Duke's, II-2193
Dulcolax, I-1153-1154
Dunkin', I-757, 760
Duracell, I-465, 468
Duracell Optimum, I-468
Duracell Quantum, I-468
Duracell Ultra, I-468
Duraflame, I-1324
Duraflame Crackleflame, I-1324
Duraflame Gold, I-1324
DuraMax, I-2114-2116
Dutch Farms, I-673, 1201
Dutch Masters, II-3358
Dux, I-1011
Dynasty, I-1190
Dyson, I-234, 239
E-Z Pass, II-3376
Eagle Creek, I-2121
Early Times, I-2095
Earthbound Farm Organic, I-1465
Earwax MD, I-1149
Eastpak, I-2121
Eating Well, I-2061
Echo Falls, II-2986, 3548
Eckrich, II-2220, 2222
Ecosia, II-3184
Edge, II-3155, 3157
Edge Legacy, II-3155, 3157
Edifier, II-3515
Edison, I-245
Edora, II-2239, 2246
Edwards, I-389-390, 1461
Egg Beaters, I-1191
Eggland's Best, I-1201
Egnyte, II-3162
The Eight Hundred, II-2360, 2364
El Monterey, I-1457, 1469, 1490
El Último Tour Del Mundo, II-2393
Electrolux, I-244
e.l.f., I-983
Eliquis, I-1117
Elmer's, I-13
Elmer's Classic Glitter Glue, I-13
Elmer's Glue All, I-13
Elysian, I-484
Emblem, II-2238
Emerald, II-3133
Emergen C, II-3488
Emergence, II-3324
Emmanuel, II-2393
Energizer, I-465, 468
Energizer Max, I-468
Energy, II-2392

English Laundry, I-2061
Enjoy Life, I-718
Ensure, II-3284
Enviro Log, I-1324
EOS, I-982
Epson, I-787
Esie Gel Couture, I-989
eSkill, II-3180
Essie, I-989
Essie Expressie, I-989
Estée Lauder, I-975
Ester-C, II-3488
Esther Price, I-726
Eternal Take, II-2390, 2395
Eucerin, II-3088
Eustachi, I-1149
Evan Williams, I-2095
Evenflo Classic, I-374
Evera, II-2238
Ex-Lax, I-1154
Excedrin, I-1143
Excedrin Migraine, I-1143
Exclusiv, I-2097
Eylea, I-1117
Fabletics, I-193
Facebook, I-1967, 1969, 1975, II-3158, 3485
FAGE, II-3600
Fairlife, II-2315-2316
Fairy Tales, I-1155
Falken, II-3351-3352
FanDuel, I-258
Farm Rich, I-1457
Farma Koukaki, II-3600
Farmer John, II-2206, 2218
Farmland, II-2206-2207, 2309
Father There is Only One 2, II-2362
FAW Jiefang, II-3438
FBI, II-3323
Feit Electric, I-2078
Ferrara Kellogg's, I-824
Ferrero Collection, I-726
Ferrero Nutella & Go, I-1007
Ferrero Rocher, I-726
Fetch-22 (Dog Man #8), I-523
Fibocom Wireless, II-2422
Fila, I-207, 1430
Fine Line, II-2390, 2397
Fire OS, II-3252
Fireball, I-2091
Firefox, II-3155-3157, 3252
Firestone, I-484, II-3351-3352
First Response, I-1071
Fitbit, II-3521

Flav-R-Pac, I-1462, 1470
Fleet, I-1153-1154
Fleet Pedia Lax, I-1153
Flex Tape, II-3294
Flickr, II-3188
Flipz, I-822
Flonase, I-1156
Flonase Sensimist, I-1156
Florida's Natural, I-2011
Foco, I-2007
Folgers, I-757, 760
Folklore, II-2390
Follow Your Heart, I-675
Foot Locker, I-1427-1428
Ford, I-338, 346, 353, 363-364, 1243, II-3432-3434
Ford E-series, II-3467
Ford Explorer, I-337
Ford F-Series, I-337
Ford Mustang, I-328
Ford Transit, II-3467
Ford Transit Connect, II-3467
Forever 21, I-201
Fortify, II-2238
Fortress, I-1556
Fortune Brands, II-2626
Fossil, II-3521
Foster Farms, I-1457, 1490, II-2200-2201
Fotile, I-236
Fotolia, II-3188
Foton, II-3438
Foton AUV, I-571
Founders, I-484
Fox and NFL Thursday Night Football, II-3323
Fox Bet, I-258
Fox News, I-259
Freightliner, II-3432-3435
Freixenet, II-3546
French's, II-2969
Freschetta, I-1474, 1492
Fresh Gourmet, I-1021
Frieda's, I-1190
Friendship, II-3198
Friesland/Campina, II-3600
Frigo, I-673, 676
Frigo Cheese Heads, I-672
Frito-Lay brands, II-3136
Fritos, II-3114
Fritos Flavor Twists, II-3114
Fritos Scoops, II-3114
Froot Loops, I-661
Frosted Flakes, I-661

Frosted Mini-Wheats, I-661
Frozen II, I-1162-1163, II-2365
Fuji Quicksnap Flash, I-596
Fuji Quicksnap Waterproof, I-596
Fuji Super HQ, II-2711
Fuji Superia Xtra, II-2711
Fuji Xerox, I-787
Fujifilm, II-2711
Fujifilm Instax Mini Film, II-2711
Fujifilm Quicksnap Flash 800, I-596
Fun Pops, I-1870
Funyuns, II-3126
Furlani, I-548
Fusebill, II-3183
Future Automation, I-1741
Futuro, II-2272
Futuro Sport, II-2272
GAC Aion S, I-333
Gain, I-27
Galanz, I-236
Galaxy A11, I-630
Galaxy A21s, I-630
Galaxy A51, I-630
Galaxy AO1, I-630
Galbani, I-672, 676
Gallo, II-3548
Gambler, II-3366, 3370
Game, II-3358
Gamesa Saladitas, I-1011
Ganten, I-538
Gaomei Nobles, II-2920
Gardein, II-2229
Gardenscapes, II-2340
Garena Free Fire, II-2340
Garmin, II-3521
Garnier Fructis Sleek & Shine, I-1734
Garnier Nutrisse, I-1736
Garnier Skinactive, II-3091
Garnier Whole Blends, I-1734
Gatorade, II-3222
Gatorade Frost, II-3222
Gatorade Perform, II-3223
Gatorade Performance, II-3222
Gatorade Zero, II-3222
GE Reveal, I-2078
General, II-3351-3352
General Electric, I-246, 2078
General Mills Bugles, II-3114
General Mills Chex Mix, II-3126
General Mills Mott's Medleys, I-824
General Motors, I-1243, II-3432-3433
Gentleman Jack, I-2095

The Gentlemen, II-2363
Germ X, II-3144
Ghirardelli, I-718
Giant, I-496
Gilera, II-2369
Giorgio Armani, I-985
Giovanni Rana, II-2626
Giovanni Rana Organic, II-2626
The Giver, I-524
Glacéau smartwater, I-541
Glenfiddich, I-2093
The Glenlivet, I-2093
Glenmorangie, I-2093
Gmail, II-3161
GMC Savana, II-3467
GMC Sierra, I-337
GNC, II-3283
GoCentral, II-3193
Godiva Goldmark, I-726
Godrej, I-250
Gold Bond, II-3088
Gold Bond Ultimate, II-3093
Gold Leaf, II-2196
Gold Peak, II-3303, 3305
Golden Crisp Fryer Saver, I-1459
Golden Dragon, I-571
Golden Flake, II-3120
Golden Harvest, II-3366, 3370
Golden Hour, II-2392
Good & Plenty, I-830
Good Cook, I-2017
Good Girls, II-3324
Good Housekeeping, I-1973, II-2138
Good Karma, II-2321
Good Morning America, II-3316
Good Sense, II-3136
Good Stuff, II-3366
Goodnites, II-2951
Goodyear, II-3351-3352
Google, I-1975, II-3161, 3184-3186, 3251
Google Cast, II-3252
Google Drive, II-3162
Google Home, I-897
Gorilla, II-3294
Gorilla Glue, I-13
Gorilla Tape, II-3294
Goya, I-1094, 1465, 2007, II-3116
GPX, II-2375
Grand Marnier, I-2091
Grandma's, II-2785
The Great British Baking Show, II-3321
great kid, m.A.A.d city, II-2397

Great Value, I-27
Great Wall, II-3548
Great Wall Ora R1/Black Cat, I-333
Greatest Hits, II-2396-2397
Gree, I-234, 243
Green Giant, I-1463, 1466, 1481
Green Giant Little Green Sprouts Organics, I-1481
Green Giant Nibblers, I-1463
Green Giant Riced Veggies, I-1470
Green Giant Simply Steam, I-1479
Green Giant Steamers, I-1460, 1470, 1472, 1479
Green Giant Valley Fresh Steamers, I-1479
Greenies, II-2672
GreenTree Inn, I-1833
Grey Goose, I-2097
Grey's Anatomy, II-3320
Grime and Punishment (Dog Man #9), I-523
Grizzly, II-3364, 3368
GRK, II-2417
Grown in Idaho, I-1475
Guardians of the Galaxy: Awesome Mix, Vol. 1, II-2397
Guittard, I-718
GVC, I-258
GVM, I-1286
GW ORA R1/Black Cat, I-336
Gwaltney, II-2222
Gymshark, I-193
Haake Beck, I-480
Habitrol, I-1145
HackerRank, II-3180
Hagie, I-1286
Haier, I-236, 243-245, 248-250
Haikyuu, II-2142
Haiten, II-2973
Hako, II-2920
Halo Top, I-1874
Hamilton, II-2256
Hamilton, II-2365
Hamkook, II-3352
Hampton by Hilton, I-1833
Handi Foil, I-170
Handi Foil Bake America, I-170
Handi Foil Bake America Cook-n-Carry, I-170
Handi Foil Bake America iChef, I-170
Handi Foil Cook-n-Carry, I-170
Handi Foil Eco Foil, I-170

Handi Foil Funcolors, I-170
Handi Foil Ultimates, I-170
Handi Works, II-2270
H&M, I-201-202
HangTing Hotel, I-1833
Hankook, II-3351
Hannity, II-3317
Hanover, I-1480
Hanover the Gold Line, I-1460
Hanover The Silver Line, I-1458
Hans Kissle, II-2785
Haosou, II-3185
Happy Apples, I-818
The Happy Egg, I-1201, 1467
Hardy's, II-3548
Haribo Gold Bears, I-834
Harley-Davidson, II-2371
Hask, I-1734
The Hate You Give, I-524
Hatfield, II-2186, 2218
Havoline, I-2114-2116
Hawaiian Punch, I-2005
Hawaiian Tropic, II-3096
Hawaii's Own, I-1464
Health Mart Pharmacy Clearlax, I-1153
Healthy Choice Café Steamers, I-1487
Healthy Hide Good 'n' Fun, II-2672
Hearst, I-1975
Hebrew National, II-2222
Hefty, I-761
Hefty EZ Foil, I-170
Heineken, I-479-480, 485
Heinz, II-2969-2970
Hello Kitty, I-2061
HEOS, I-893
Herbal Essences Bio Renew, I-1734
Herbalife Nutrition, II-3277
Herpecin L, I-1148
Herr's, II-3124
Hershey's, I-718, 720, 722, 822, 851
Hershey's Kisses, I-720
Hershey's Kitchens, I-718
Hershey's Nuggets, I-720
Hershey's Special Dark, I-851
Hewlett-Packard, I-787, 883
HGTV, I-1973
Hi-Tiger, I-1236
Hidrau Model, II-2417
Higer, I-571
Hikvision, I-594
Hiland, I-680, II-2311, 2315-2316, 3534

Hillandale Farms, I-1201
Hillshire Farm, II-2202, 2220
Hillshire Farm Li'l Smokies, II-2220
Hillshire Snacking, II-2230
Hilton Hotels & Resorts, I-1833
Hino, I-1243, II-3432-3434
Hiram Walker Cordials, I-2090
HireRight, II-3180
Hisense, II-3106, 3251
Hitachi, I-223
HLA, I-207
Holiday Inn, I-1833
Holiday Inn Express, I-1833
Holland America, I-1023
Hollister, I-201-202
Hollywood's Bleeding, II-2390, 2395
Holm, I-2075
Holovision, I-889
HomeAdvisor, I-1973
Homeinns, I-1833
Homescapes, II-2340
Honda, I-346, 353, 364, II-2369-2375
Honda Civic, I-337, 353
Honda CR-V, I-337
The Honest Co., II-3556
Honest Diapers, II-2951
Honey Bunches of Oats, I-661
Honey Nut Cheerios, I-661
Hongyan, II-3438
Honor of Kings, II-2340
Hood, I-680, II-2309, 2315, 2317, 2321, 3198
Hood Lactaid, II-2315-2316
Hoover, I-239
Horizon Organic, II-3534
Hormel, II-2206-2207
Hormel Always Tender, II-2203
Hormel Black Label, II-2186
Hormel Gatherings, II-2230
Hormel Party Tray, II-2230
Hot Pink, II-2394
Hot Pockets, I-1490
Hot Stuff, I-1002
Houzz, I-1973
HP Hood, II-2322
Hpnotiq, I-2091
HTC, I-1743
Huadi, I-245
Huang Shang Huang, II-2175
Huawei, I-284, 629, 634-635, 637, II-3518, 3521
Hubba Bubba Bubble Tape, I-1710
Hubba Bubba Max, I-1710

Huberts, I-2006
Huddle, II-3162
Huel, II-3277
Huggies, II-2951
Huggies Natural Care, II-3556
Huggies Pull-Ups, II-2951
Huggies Refreshing Clean, II-3556
Huggies Simply Clean Disney Mickey Mouse & Friends, II-3556
Humira, I-1117
The Hunger Game, I-524
Hungry-Man, I-1487
Hunker, I-1973
Hunter Assassin, II-2340
Huzhu Wendang, I-257
Hyland's, I-1149
Hylands 4 Kids, I-1146
Hyundai, I-326, 346, 353
Hyundai Kona EV, I-327, 330, 334-336
Hyundai Veloster, I-328
I Can't Believe It's Not Butter, I-581
I Can't Believe It's Not Butter Light, I-581
Iams ProActive Health, II-2673, 2675
Ibis, I-1833
IC Realtime, I-594
Ice Breakers, I-816
Ice Breakers Duo, I-816
Ice Breakers Ice Cubes, I-1713
Icy Hot, I-1142
Idea Village Copper Fit, II-2272
If Animals Kissed Goodnight, I-523
If I Know Me, Morgan Wallen, II-2391
IFB, I-250
Ikea, I-1973
Imbruvica, I-1117
Immaculate Baking Co., I-1095
Imoo, II-3518, 3521
Imperial, I-581
Indeed, I-1974
Infor Talent Science, II-3180
Ingraham Angle, II-3317
Insignia, II-3106
InSinkErator, I-245
Instagram, I-1967, 1969
Integra, I-886
IntenseDebate, II-3158
International, I-1243, II-3432-3435
International Delight, I-759
Internet Explorer, II-3155-3157

Into the Pit (Five Nights at Freddy's: Fazbear Frights #1), I-524
Inver House, I-2094
The Invisible Man, II-2359
iOS, II-3176-3178, 3191
iPad, I-259, 892, II-3161
IPC, II-2920
iPhone, II-3161
iPhone 11, I-630
iPhone 12, I-630
iPhone 12 mini, I-630
iPhone 12 Pro Max, I-630
iPhone SE, I-630
Isopure, II-3283
iStock, II-3188
Isuzu, I-1243, II-3432-3433
Ivory, II-3146
IWC, II-3505
iZooto, II-3182
J. Roget, II-3545
Jabra, II-3515
JAC, II-3438
Jack Daniel's, I-2095
Jack Daniel's Tennessee Fire, I-2090
Jack Daniel's Tennessee Honey, I-2090
Jack Link's, II-2193, 2198
Jack Link's Wild, II-2193
Jackpot, II-3358
Jack's, I-1474, 1492
Jagermeister, I-2091
Jamba, I-1464
James Loudspeaker, I-890
JamStands, II-2417
J&J Snack Foods Auntie Annie's, I-1480
Jansen, II-2417
Jansport, I-2121
Jarden Ball, I-2017
JBL, II-3515
Jeep, I-346, 353
Jeep Grand Cherokee, I-337
Jeld-Wen, II-3536
Jell-O, II-2812
Jell-O Temptations, II-2812
Jennie-O, II-2197
Jennie-O All Natural, II-2197
Jergens, II-3088, 3093
Jergens Ultra Healing, II-3093
Jet, II-3518
JiaJia, II-2973
Jiang Ziya: Legend of Deification, II-2360
Jif, II-3224

Jiffy Foil, I-170
Jim Beam Family, I-2095
Jimmy Dean, I-1467, II-2206-2207, 2209, 2218
Jimmy Dean Delights, I-1467
Jimmy's, I-818
Jira, II-3181
Jiu Jiu Ya, II-2175
JLAB, II-3515
Jo San, II-2147
Job, II-3370
Jobs.net, I-1974
JodyJazz, II-2416
John Deere, I-1286
John Morrell, II-2206
John Morrell Nathan's Famous, II-2222
John Soules Foods, II-2200
Johnnie Walker Black, I-2092
Johnnie Walker Red, I-2092
Johnson's, I-371
Johnson's Baby, I-371
Johnson's Bedtime, I-371
Johnson's CottonTouch, I-371
Johnsonville, II-2218, 2220
Johnsonville Beddar with Cheddar, II-2220
Joker, I-1162-1163
Jolly Rancher, I-828
Jones Dairy Farm, II-2209
Jones Golden Brown, II-2209
Jordan, I-1425
José Olé, I-1457, 1469, 1490
Journey's Greatest Hits, II-2396
Joyva, I-848
JR Watkins, II-3145
Jue Wei, II-2175
Jujitsu Kaisen, II-2142
Jumanji: The Next Level, I-1162-1163, II-2359, 2362-2363
Jumex, I-2007
Jupyter, II-3162
Just, I-64, 1191
Just Bare, II-2196
Justin's, II-3224
Juul, I-1164, 1166
Kahlua, I-2091
Kaleidoscope, I-887
Kanban, II-3181
K&M, II-2417
KANS, I-975
Kärcher, II-2920
Kars Sweet N Salty Mix, II-3117
Kashi, I-826

Kawasaki, II-2370-2371, 2375
Keebler, I-1007
Keebler Club, I-1004-1005
Keebler Scooby Doo, I-1009
Keebler Zesta, I-1011
Keepos, II-2649
Keller, II-2369
Keller's, I-576
Kellogg's Eggo, I-1482
Kellogg's Eggo Nutri Grain, I-1482
Kellogg's Eggo Thick & Fluffy, I-1482
Kellogg's Nutri Grain, I-814
Kellogg's Nutri Grain Bars, I-814
Kellogg's Rice Krispies Treats, I-814
Kellogg's Special K, II-3277
Kellogg's Special K Pastry Crisps, I-814
Kemps, I-680, 1869, 1871, II-3198
Kemps Select, II-3534
Kendall, I-2116
Kenworth, II-3433-3435
Kerr, I-2017
Kerrygold, I-576
Ketel One Vodka, I-2097
Kettle, II-3122
Keurig, I-239
Keurig Green Mountain, I-760
Keystone, I-478
Keytruda, I-1117
Khonka, II-3518
Kia, I-338, 346, 353, 364
Kia Niro EV, I-330, 334-335
Kibbles 'n Bits, II-2675
Kimetsu no Yaiba, II-2142
Kind, I-838
Kind Breakfast, I-814
Kind Breakfast Protein, I-814
Kind Healthy Grains, I-826
Kind Minis, I-814
King Long, I-571
King Oscar, II-2982
Kingdom, II-2142
Kingsford, I-663
Kingsford BBQ Bag, I-663
Kingsford Match Light, I-663
Kinky, I-2090
Kirbiker, II-3132
Kirkland Signature, I-27, II-2951
Kit Kat, I-720, 722
Kitfox, I-64
KLN Wiley Wallaby, I-830
Klondike, I-1872
Knives Out, I-1163, II-2359

Knob Creek, I-2095
Knudsen, I-680, II-3198, 3534
Kodak Fun Saver, I-596
Kodak Gold, II-2711
Kodak Max Sport, I-596
Kodak Power Flash, I-596
Kodak Ultra, II-2711
Kodak Ultra Max, II-2711
Kodiak, I-63, II-3364, 3368
Kodiak Cake Power Waffles, I-1482
Kodiak Cakes, I-1009
Kodiak Cakes Bear Bites, I-1009
Kohler, II-2753, 2755
Korbel, II-3545
Kotex Natural Balance Security, II-2956
Kozy Shack, II-2812
Kozy Shack Simply Well, II-2812
Kraft, I-671-673, 677
Kraft Deli Deluxe, I-675
Kraft Heinz Hershey's, II-2812
Kraft Heinz TGI Friday's, I-1457, II-2196
Kraft Jet-Puffed, I-832
Kraft Jet-Puffed Funmallows, I-832
Kraft Jet-Puffed Smoremallows, I-832
Kraft Singles, I-675
Kraft Velveeta, I-675
Krazy Glue, I-13
Kri Kri, II-3600
Kroger, II-2951
KT Tape, II-2272
KT Tape Pro, II-2272
KTM, II-2371
Kuaidui Zuoye, I-257
Kumho, II-3352
Kwikset, II-2997
Kymco, II-2372, 2374
Kyocera, I-787
L.A. Colors, I-983
L.A. Colors Color Craze, I-989
La Croix, I-542
La Grande Dame, II-3546
La Marca Prosecco, II-3546
La Pasta, II-2626
Lagunitas, I-484
Lamb Weston Alexia, I-1471, 1475
Lamb Weston Nathan's Famous, I-1471
Lamb Weston Red Robin, I-1471
Lance, I-1007
Lance Captain's Wafers, I-1007
Lance Fresh, I-849

Lance ToastChee, I-1007
Lance Toasty, I-1007
Lancôme, I-975, 985
Land O'Frost Premium, II-2202
Land O'Lakes, I-576, 581, 675, 1201
Lansinoh, I-374
Larabar, I-814
Largo, II-3366
Las Campanas, I-1469
Las Que No Iban A Salir, II-2393
Last Word-Lawrence O'Donnell, II-3317
Late July Organic, I-1011, II-3138
Latitude 45, II-2986
Laura's Lean Beef, II-2203
Lay's, II-3122, 3132
Lay's Kettle Cooked, II-3122
Lay's Poppables, II-3126
Lay's Stax, II-3122
Lean Cuisine Comfort, I-1487
Lean Cuisine Favorites, I-1487
Lean Cuisine Marketplace, I-1487
Leap, II-2360
Leap (vaping), I-1164
Leblanc, II-2416
Leekumkee, II-2973
Legend: the Best of..., II-2397
Legend of Deification, II-2364
Legends Never Die, II-2390, 2395
L'Eggs Sheer Energy, I-208
L'Eggs Silken Mist, I-208
Legrand AV, I-1741
Leinenkugle Specialty, I-484
Lejiaolexue, I-257
Lender's, I-378
Lenovo, I-787
Level Sleep, I-1801
Leyard, I-1087
LG, I-223, 240, 242, 244, 246, 249-250, 887, 899, II-3106, 3251
Li Ning, I-207, 1430
Li Xiang One EREV, I-333
Liantronics, I-1087
Liberty AV Solutions, I-587
Lice Shield, I-1155
Licefreee!, I-1155
Life Savers, I-828, 841
Life Savers Gummies, I-834
Lil'Dutch Maid, I-1011
Lily's, I-718, 851
Lindt, I-726
Lindt Lindor, I-720, 726
Linux, II-3176-3178
Lipton, II-3303

Lipton Brisk, I-2006, II-3303
Lipton Pure Leaf, II-3303
Liquid I.V., II-3223
Listerine, II-2529
Listerine Pocketpaks, I-816
Listerine Total Care, II-2529
Listerine Ultraclean, II-2529
Litehouse, I-818, 1079, II-2972
Little Debbie, I-386
Little Debbie Nutty Bar, I-386
Little Women, II-2359, 2363
Live Writer Support, II-3174
Liveblog, II-3174
Livefyre, II-3158, 3174
Lloyd, I-223, 242
Loctite, I-13
Loctite Quicktite, I-13
Logic, I-1164
Longhorn, II-3364, 3368
Longines, II-3505
Longmire, II-3321
L'Oréal, I-975
L'Oréal Advanced, I-1731
L'Oréal Colorista, I-1736
L'Oréal Colour Riche, I-984
L'Oréal Ever Pure, I-1734
L'Oréal Excellence, I-1736
L'Oréal Excellence Creme, I-1736
L'Oréal Feria, I-1736
L'Oréal Infallible, I-980, 983
L'Oréal Infallible Full Wear, I-976
L'Oréal Infallible Pro-Last, I-980
L'Oréal Infallible The Super Slim, I-980
L'Oréal Paris, I-985
L'Oréal Root Cover Up, I-1736
L'Oréal Superior Preference, I-1736
L'Oréal Telescopic, I-987
L'Oréal True Match, I-974, 976
L'Oréal Voluminous, I-987
L'Oréal Voluminous Lash, I-987
Louis Kemp Crab Delights, II-2986
Love You Forever, II-2360
Lucifer, II-3321
Lucky Charms, I-661
Ludo King, II-2340
Lululemon, I-193, 201
Luna, I-594
Lunchables, II-2230
Lunchables Uploaded, II-2230
Lundberg, I-845
Lutron, I-2075
Luvs, II-2951

Luyben, II-2416
MAC, I-985
The Macallan, I-2093
Mack, I-1243, II-3433, 3435
MacNaughton, I-2088
MacOS, II-3179
Mac's, II-3120
Magnum, I-1872
Maker's Mark, I-2095
Mama Lucia, II-2201
Mambi, II-3120
The Mandalorian, II-3321
M&M's, I-720
Mangento, II-3160
Manifest, II-3324
Maquet, II-2256
Marantz, I-891
Maratz, I-886
Mariani, I-820, II-2321
Marie Callender's, I-390, 1473, 1477, 1486-1487
Marie's, II-2972
Marifano, II-2649
Marlboro, II-3360
Marriott Hotels, I-1833
Marshmello Fortnite Extended Set, II-2392
Martini & Rossi Asti, II-3546
Marvin, II-3536
Mary B's, I-548, 1094
Marzetti, I-818, 1021, 1079, II-2972
Master Kong, I-538
Mastercard, II-2633-2635, 2638
Mata Piojos, I-1155
Matador by Jack Link's, II-2193
Maui Moisture, I-1734
Maxwell House, I-757
Maybelline, I-975, 985
Maybelline Color Sensational, I-984
Maybelline Cover Stick, I-976
Maybelline EyeStudio Lasting Drama, I-980
Maybelline FaceStudio Master Conceal, I-974, 976
Maybelline Fit Me, I-974, 976
Maybelline Great Lash, I-987
Maybelline Instant Age Rewind, I-976
Maybelline Instant Age Rewind Eraser, I-976
Maybelline Lash, I-987
Maybelline Lifter, I-983

Maybelline SuperStay 24, I-984
Maybelline SuperStay Ink, I-984
Maybelline SuperStay Matte Ink, I-984
Maybelline Tattoo Studio, I-980
Maybelline Unstoppable, I-980
Maytag, I-246
Mazda MX-5 Miata, I-328
McCain, I-1471
McCormick Vodka, I-2096
McIntosh, I-887, 891
Meade, II-3313
Media, I-245
Melissa's, I-1190
Member's Mark, I-27
Mentos, I-841
Mentos Pure Fresh, I-1713
Meow Mix, II-2673
Meow Mix Original Choice, II-2673
Meow Mix Tender Centers, II-2673
Mercedes-Benz, I-338, 353, 364
Mercedes-Benz EQC 400, I-327
Mercedes-Benz GLC300e/de, I-334
Mercedes-Benz Sprinter, II-3467
Metamucil, I-1153-1154
Metgra Home Theater/Ethereal, I-587
Method, II-3145
Mevgal, II-3600
Meyenberg, II-2321
MG ZS EV, I-327
MGA, II-3399
MGM, I-258
MI, II-3518
Michael Angelo's, I-1486
Michelin, II-3352
Michelina's, I-1487
Michelle, II-3545
Michelob, I-478
Microsoft, I-1975, II-3251
Microsoft Frontpage, II-3193
Microsoft OneDrive, II-3162
Microsoft Outlook, II-3161
Microsoft Project, II-3181
Microsoft Windows SharePoint Services, II-3162
Microsoft Xbox, II-3252
Microsoft Xbox 360, II-3481
Microsoft Xbox One, II-3476, 3478, 3481
Microsoft Xbox S, II-3476, 3478
Mid-America Farms Top the Tater, II-3198
Midea, I-234, 236, 243-244, 248

Midnight Sun, I-522, 524
Midway, I-1162
Mighty Sesame Co., I-848
Mike's Hard, I-1336
Mike's Harder, I-1336
Milani, I-974
Milani Keep It Full, I-983
Milano, I-386
Milgard, II-3536
Milk-Bone, II-2672
Milky Way, I-722
Miller, I-1286
Miller High Life, I-478
Miller Lite, I-478
Million Little Things, II-3324
Milos, II-3305
Mimi, II-3518
Mindray, II-2256
Mingua Beef Jerky, II-2198
Mini Babybel, I-671
Minute Maid, I-2005-2007
Minute Maid Premium, I-2010-2011
MinuteMan, II-2920
Mionetto, II-3546
Miralax, I-1153
Miralax Mix in Pax, I-1153
Mission, II-3120, 3138
Mixer, II-3485
Moana, II-2365
Mobil, I-2114-2116
Modelo, I-479, 485
Moën, II-2753, 2755
Monster Energy, I-1239
Monster Energy Zero Ultra, I-1239
MonsterCommerce, II-3160
MoonClerk, II-3183
Morningstar Farms, II-2229
Morningstar Farms Grillers, II-2229
Mother in Law's Kimchi, II-2147
Motomel, II-2369
Motrin IB, I-1143
Mountain Dew Amp Game Fuel, I-2007
Mountain Dew Kickstart, I-2007
Moyer's, I-818
Mr. Boston Cordials, I-2090
Mr. Bubble, II-3142
Mr. Clean, I-738
Mr. Sketch, I-273
Mrs. Cubbison's, I-1021
Mrs. Gerry's, II-2785
Mrs. Meyer's Clean Day, II-3145
Mrs. Smith's, I-390
MSC, I-1024

MSNBC, I-259
Mucinex, I-1147
Mucinex DM, I-1147
Mucinex Fast Max, I-1146-1147
Mucinex Fast Max & Nightshift, I-1146
Mueller, II-2272
Mueller Sport Care, II-2272
Mumm Napa, II-3545
Munch, I-849
Munchkin, I-374
Munchkin Miracle 360 Degree, I-374
Muscle Milk, II-3283-3284
My People, My Homeland, II-2360, 2364
My Turn, II-2390, 2395
Mynavi, I-1974
Nabisco, I-1009
Nabisco Honey Maid, I-1004, 1009
Nabisco Honey Maid Fresh Stacks, I-1009
Nabisco Premium, I-1004, 1011
Nabisco Ritz, I-1004-1005, 1007
Nabisco Ritz Bits, I-1007
Nabisco Ritz Fresh Stacks, I-1004
Nabisco Triscuit, I-1004-1005
Nabisco Wheat Thins, I-1004-1005
Nami Box, I-257
Nasacort, I-1156
Nasoya, I-1190, II-2147
Natrol, I-1158
Natural, I-478
Natural American Spirit, II-3360, 3366
Nature Made, I-1158, II-3282, 3488-3489
Nature Valley, I-814, 826, II-3283
Nature Valley Fruit & Nut, I-826
Nature Valley Protein, I-838
Nature Valley Sweet & Salty Nut, I-826
Nature's Bounty, I-1158, II-3282, 3488
Nature's Bounty Optimal Solutions, II-3488
Nature's Truth, II-3282, 3488
Nature's Way Alive, II-3489
Navage, I-1156
NBC Nightly News With Lester Holt, II-3317
NBC Sunday Night Football, II-3323
NCIS, II-3320, 3323
Nectar, I-1801
NeilMed ClearCanal, I-1149

NeilMed Sinus Rinse, I-1156
Nellie's, I-1201, 1467
Neo G, II-2272
Neosporin, I-1150
Neosporin Plus, I-1150
Nerds, I-836
Nestlé, I-1093
Nestlé Pure Life, I-541
Nestlé Tollhouse, I-718, 1093
Nestlé Tollhouse Ultimates, I-1093
Neutrogena, II-3090-3091
Neutrogena Acne Stress Control, II-3090
Neutrogena Beach, II-3096
Neutrogena Clear Pore, II-3090
Neutrogena Hydro, II-3091
Neutrogena Hydro Boost, II-3092
Neutrogena Moisture, II-3092
Neutrogena Rapid Clear, II-3090
Neutrogena Ultra Sheer, II-3096
New Amsterdam, II-3324
New Amsterdam vodka, I-2096
New Balance, I-1428, 1430
New Belgium, I-484
New Girl, II-3320
New Honor, I-634
New York, I-548
New York Bakery, I-553, 1021
The New York Times, I-259
Newport, II-3360
News Break, I-259
Nextdoor, I-259
Nexxus Comb Thru, I-1731
Nice N Clean, II-3144
Nicoderm CQ, I-1145
Nicorette, I-1144
Nike, I-201-202, 207, 1425, 1427-1428, 1430
Nilfisk, II-2920
Nilla, I-386
Nintendo, II-3251
Nintendo 3DS, II-3476, 3478
Nintendo N64, II-3481
Nintendo NES, II-3481
Nintendo Super NES, II-3481
Nintendo Switch, II-3476-3478, 3481
Nintendo Wii, II-3481
NIO ES6, I-333
Nips, I-828
Nissan, I-338, 343, 346, 353, 364
Nissan Leaf, I-327, 329-330, 336
Nissan NV Van, II-3467
Nissan NV200, II-3467

Nissan Rogue, I-337
Nivea, II-3088, 3093, 3143
Nix, I-1155
Nix Ultra, I-1155
NJOY, I-1164, 1166
No Brand, I-820
No Brand Interstate Meat, II-2203
No Man's Land, II-2198
No Nonsense, I-208
No Nonsense Great Shapes, I-208
Nongfu Spring, I-538
Nordic Track, II-3209
Norwegian, I-1023-1024
NPR News Now, II-2762
Nuby Easy Grip, I-374
Nuby Non-Drip, I-374
Nudges Jerky Cuts, II-2672
Nuk Active Cup, I-374
Nuk Trendline, I-374
Nuun, II-3223
NYX Butter Gloss, I-983
O Sole Mio, II-2626
Oatly, II-2319, 2321-2322
o.b., II-2956
Oberto, II-2198
OCB, II-3370
Ocean Spray Craisins, I-820
Oceania, I-1023
Oculus, I-1743
Odom's Tennessee Pride, II-2218
O'Douls, I-480
Off, I-709
Off Active, I-709
Off Botanicals, I-709
Off Deep Woods, I-709
Off Deep Woods for Sportsmen, I-709
The Office, II-3320
OGX, I-1734
Oh, the Places You'll Go!, I-523
Oh Snap! Pickling Co., II-2147
Ohm, II-3366
Oishi, II-3132
Olay, II-3143, 3146
Olay Active Hydrating, II-3092
Olay Complete, II-3092
Olay Regenerist Retinol24, II-3092
Olay Ultra Moisture, II-3143
Old Smuggler, I-2094
Old Spice, II-2655, 3143
Old Spice High Endurance, II-2655
Old Spice Red Zone, II-2655
Old Trapper, II-2193, 2198
Old Wisconsin, II-2193

Ole Smoky, I-2090
Ole South, II-2209
Olly, I-1158, II-3282
Olympos, II-3600
Omega, II-3505
Omni Safe, II-2270
On-Cor, I-1486
On-Stage, II-2417
On The Border, II-3138
On the Go, I-208
ON!, II-3362
One, I-838
The One and Only Ivan, I-523
One of Us is Lying, I-524
One Piece, II-2142
Oneplus, I-635
Onesignal, II-3182
Onward, II-2359, 2365
Opdivo, I-1117
Opera, II-3155, 3157
Opi, I-989
OPPO, I-629, 634-636
Optimo, II-3358
Optimum Nutrition, II-3283
Orajel, I-1148
Oralabs Sanell, II-3144
Orbit, I-1713
Orchard Valley Harvest, II-3117
Ore-Ida, I-1471, 1475
Ore-Ida Golden Crinkles, I-1475
Ore-Ida Onion Ringers, I-1471
Ore-Ida Tater Tots, I-1475
Oreo, I-386
Oreo Double Stuf, I-386
Organic Valley, II-2315-2317, 3534
Origin Acoustics, I-890
Orion, II-3132
OS X, II-3176-3178
Oscar Mayer, II-2202, 2206-2207, 2222
Oscar Mayer Deli Fresh, II-2202
Oscar Mayer Selects, II-2222
Our Little Rebellion Popcorners, II-3114
The Outsiders, I-524
Over It, Summer Walker, II-2394
Owens, II-2218
Ozark, II-3321
P3, II-2230
Paccar, I-1243
Pacific Foods, II-3196
Pacsun, I-201-202
Pall Mall, II-3360
Palmer's Cocoa Butter, II-3093

Pamela's, I-1009
Pampers, II-2951, 3556
Pampers Aqua Pure, II-3556
Pampers Easy Ups, II-2951
Pampers Sensitive, II-3556
Panasonic, I-236, 465, 889, 899
P&O Australia, I-1024
Panoxyl, II-3090
Pantene Pro V Daily Moisture Renewal, I-1734
Pantum, I-787
Paper Mate Flair, II-3595
Paper Mate Inkjoy, II-3595
Paper Mate Profile, II-3595
Parasite, II-2362-2363
Parent's Choice, II-2951
Parkay, I-581
Patek Philippe, II-3505
Pathfinder, II-3397
Pathfinder Second Edition, II-3397
Patti's Gold Life, II-2812
Pay Day, I-849
Pearsons Salted Nut Roll, I-849
PediaSure, II-3284
Pedigree, II-2675
Pedigree DentaStix, II-2672
Peerless-AV, I-1741
Pella, II-3536
Peloton, II-3209
Pennzoil, I-2114-2116
Penrose Big Mama, II-2193
People, II-2138
Pepperidge Farm, I-548, 553, 1473
Pepperidge Farm Flavor Blasted Goldfish, I-1004-1005
Pepperidge Farm Goldfish, I-1004-1005
Pepperidge Farm Stone Baked, I-548
Pepperidge Goldfish Grahams, I-1009
Perdue, II-2196, 2200
Perdue Harvestland, II-2196
Perdue Perfect Portions, II-2196
Perdue Short Cuts, II-2200-2201
Perdue Simply Smart Organics, II-2200
Perfect Diary, I-985
Perrier, I-542
Pete & Gerry's, I-1201, 1467
Peter Pan, II-3224
Peterbilt, II-3433-3435
PetMatrix DreamBone, II-2672
Peugeot, II-2370
Peugeot 208 EV, I-334

Peugeot 3008 PHEV, I-334
Peugeot e-208, I-330
P.F. Chang's Home Menu, I-1486
Pharmanex, II-3277
Philadelphia, I-677
Philips, I-2078, II-3251
Philips Avent, I-374
Philips Duramax, I-2078
Philips Ecovantage, I-2078
Phillips, II-2256
Philly Gourmet, II-2195
Physicians Formula Powder Palette, I-974
Piaggio, II-2370-2372, 2374-2375
Pico, I-1743
Pictsweet, I-1458-1460, 1462-1463, 1470, 1472, 1481
Pictsweet All Natural, I-1472
Pictsweet Deluxe Steamables, I-1458
Pictsweet Steamables, I-1458, 1460, 1481
Pilatus Aircraft, I-63
Pilgrim's, II-2196
Pillsbury, I-1092-1093, 1095-1096
Pillsbury Big Dix Hershey's Mini Kisses, I-1093
Pillsbury Cinnabon, I-1095
Pillsbury Grands, I-548, 1092, 1094-1095
Pillsbury Grands Cinnabon, I-1095
Pillsbury Grands Flaky Surpreme, I-1095
Pillsbury Pet Ritz, I-1473
Pillsbury Place & Bake, I-1093
Pillsbury Ready to Bake, I-1093
Pillsbury Toaster Strudel, I-1467
Pilot G2, II-3595
Pine Mountain, I-1324
Pine Mountain American Home, I-1324
Pine Mountain First Alert Creosote Buster, I-1324
Pine Mountain Java Log, I-1324
Pine Mountain Ultraflame, I-1324
Pinnacle Vodka, I-2097
Pinterest, I-1967, 1969
Pioneer, I-234, 286
Piper Aircraft, I-63
Pirate's Booty, II-3126
Planters, II-3133
Planters Nutrition, II-3117
Platinum 7X, I-2096
Playboy, I-2061
PlayStation 4, II-3476-3478, 3482

PlayStation 5, II-3476, 3478
Playtex, II-2270
Playtex Sport, II-2956
Please Excuse Me for Being Antisocial, II-2390
Poise, II-2950
Pokémon Go, II-2337
Polar, I-542
Polaroid, I-596
Polestar 2, I-327, 335
Polly-O, I-672, 676
Pom Pom, II-3358
Ponds, II-3092
Pop Ice, I-1870
Popsicle, I-1872
Porsche 718, I-328
Porsche Taycan, I-329
Portland Pie, I-1096
PowerAdd, I-466
Powerade ION4, II-3222
PowerBoss, II-2920
Powrachute, I-64
Prairie Farms, I-680, 1871, II-2311, 2315-2317, 3534
Premier, II-3370
Premier Protein, II-3277, 3284
Premio, II-2220
Prestige Brands, I-1071
Pretzel Crisps Drizzlers, I-822
Prevagen, II-3282
Primatene Mist, I-1156
Primo, II-2969
Princess, I-1023-1024
Pringles, II-3122
Pro-Ject, I-891
ProChem, II-2920
Profile, II-2417
Proform, II-3209
Progresso, II-3197
Progresso Light, II-3197
Progresso Rich & Hearty, II-3197
Progresso Traditional, II-3197
Progresso Vegetable Classics, II-3197
Proline, II-2417
Promised Land, II-2311
A Promised Land, I-522
Promotion in Motion Welch's, I-824
Propel, II-3223
Provamel, II-2319
Prunelax Ciruelax, I-1154
PUBG Mobile, II-2340
Pup-Peroni, II-2672
Pure Protection, II-2951

Pure Protein, I-838, II-3283
Purell, II-3144
Purell Advanced, II-3144
Purina Beggin' Strips, II-2672
Purina Beneful, II-2675
Purina Cat Chow Complete, II-2673
Purina Cat Chow Naturals, II-2673
Purina Dog Chow, II-2675
Purina Friskies Seafood Sensations, II-2673
Purina Kit & Kaboodle, II-2673
Purina One SmartBlend, II-2675
Purina One SmartBlend True Instinct, II-2675
Purnell Old Folks, II-2209
Push Pop, I-836
PushCare, II-3182
PushEngage, II-3182
Pyrex, I-2017
QCY, I-284, II-3515
QQ Browser, II-3156
Quad City, I-64
Quaker, I-845
Quaker Chewy, I-826
Quaker Chewy Dipps, I-826
Quaker Popped, I-845
Quantum Lip Clear Lysine Plus, I-1148
Quectel, II-2422
Queen Anne, I-726
Quest, I-838, II-3283
Quest Bar, I-838
Quik-Lok, II-2417
Qunol, II-3282
Rachael Ray Nutrish, II-2673, 2675
Rachel Maddow, II-3317
Racioppi's, I-1002
Rader Farms, I-1465
Raid, I-709
Ralph Lauren, I-202
Ram, I-346
Ram Pickup, I-337
Ram ProMaster, II-3467
Ram ProMaster City, II-3467
Rans (S-21 Outbound), I-64
Rave 4X Mega, I-1731
Raw, II-3370
Raw Sugar, II-3145
Raymundo's, II-2812
Ray's New York Bagels, I-378
Reader's Digest, II-2138
Realme, I-285, 635-636, II-3515
ReCharge, II-3183
Recurly, II-3183

Red Baron, I-1474, 1492
Red Bird, I-841
Red Bull, I-1236, 1239
Red Bull Sugar Free, I-1239
Red Diamond, II-3305
Red Man, II-3364, 3368
Red Seal, II-3364, 3368
Red Vines, I-830
Reddi-Whip, II-2309
Reddit, I-259, 1967, 1969
Redd's, I-1336
Redmi, I-284
Redmi Note 9 Pro, I-630
Red's, I-1469
Redwood Hill Farm & Creamery, II-2321
Reese's, I-718, 720, 722, 822, 851
Regent, I-1023
Releev, I-1148
Renault, I-326
Renault Captur PHEV, I-334
Renault Zoe, I-330, 334, 336
Reser's, II-2785
Reser's Fine Foods, II-2785
The Resident, II-3324
Resonate, II-2238
REVEL, II-3362
Revlimid, I-1117
Revlon, I-974, II-2654
Revlon ColorSilk Beautiful Color, I-1736
Revlon ColorStay, I-980
Revlon ColorStay Overtime, I-984
Revlon Insta Blush, I-974
Revlon Kiss, I-982
Revlon PhotoReady, I-976
Revlon PhotoReady Candid, I-976
Revlon Super Lustrous, I-983-984
Revlon Ultra HD, I-984
Rhinomed Mute, I-1157
Rhodes, I-554
Rhodes Bake-N-Serv, I-1094
Rich & Rare, I-2089
Richard Mille, II-3505
Rico, II-2416
Ricoh, I-787
Rid, I-1155
Rikunabi 2019, I-1974
Rimmel Stay Glossy, I-983
Ring, II-3102
Ring Relief, I-1149
Ripple, II-2321-2322
Rips, I-830
Road Prince, II-2373

Robam, I-236
Robert Mondavi, II-3548
Roblox, II-2340
Roku, II-3250-3252
Roland, II-2417
Rold Gold, II-3124
Rolex, II-3505
Roost, II-3182
Rothbury Farms, I-1021
Rovner, II-2416
Rowley Jefferson's Awesome Friendly Adventure, I-523
Royal Caribbean, I-1023-1024
Rubbermaid Easy Find Lids, I-2017
Rubbermaid Take Alongs, I-2017
Ruffino Prosecco, II-3546
Ruffles, II-3122
Rugby, I-1144-1145
RumChata, I-2091
Rumours, II-2396-2397
Rumple Minze, I-2091
Russell Stover, I-726, 851
RXBar, I-838, II-3283
Sabrett, II-2222
Sack O'Corn, I-1463
The Sacrifice, II-2360
Safari, II-3155-3157
Safeguard, II-3141
Sage, II-2654
St. Ives, II-3090
Salamander, I-1556
Sally Hansen Color, I-989
Sally Hansen Hard As Nails, I-989
Sally Hansen Insta Dri, I-989
Sally Hansen Miracle, I-989
Salonpas, I-1142
Sambazon, I-1464
Samsung, I-240, 242, 244, 246, 250, 284-285, 287-289, 291, 629-630, 635-637, 787, 883, 887, 899, 1087, II-3106, 3155, 3157, 3161, 3251, 3515, 3521
Samuel Adams, I-484
San Pellegrino, I-542, 2007
SanDisk, I-783
Sanford Sharpie, II-3595
Santa Cruz Organic, I-2006
Santitas, II-3138
Sanus, I-1556
Sara Lee, I-389-390, 1461
Sargento, I-672-673
Sargento Balanced Breaks, II-2230
Sarris Candies, I-822
Savant, I-889, 892, II-2997

Schiff Mega Red, II-3282
Schitt's Creek, II-3320
Schlage, II-2998
Schreiber, I-672
Schwarzkopf got2b, I-1731
Scoob!, I-1162
Scoresby, I-2094
Scotch, I-13, II-3294
Scotch Brite, I-738
Scotch Magic, II-3294
Scotch Sure Start, II-3294
Scott, I-27
ScribbleLive Engage, II-3174
Seabourn, I-1023
Seagram's, I-2088, 2096
Seagram's Escapes, I-1336
Seal the Seasons, I-1465
Sealy, I-1796
Seapoint Farms, I-1458
Seattle International Baking, I-1002
Sebastian Shaper, I-1731
Second Nature, II-3117
Secret, II-2655
Secret Clinical Strength, II-2655
The Secret Life of Pets 2, II-2365
Secret PH Balanced, II-2655
Sega Genesis, II-3481
SelectLeaders, I-1974
Selmer Paris, II-2416
Seneca, II-3110
Senokot, I-1154
Senokot S, I-1154
Senor Rico, II-2812
Sensible Portions Veggie Straw, II-3126
Seoul, II-2147
Seventh Generation, II-3556
SFGate, I-1973
Shacman, II-3438
Shady Brook Farms, II-2197
Shakeology, II-3277
Shameless, II-3320
Shamrock Farms, II-2317
Shape, I-2061, II-2138
SharkNinja, I-239
Sharp, II-3106, 3251
Shea Moisture, I-371, II-3146
Shedd's Country Crock, I-581
Sheep Without A Shepherd, II-2360
Shein, I-201
Shenma, II-3185
Sheraton, I-1833
Shiner, I-484
Shingeki no Kyojin, II-2142

Shiseido, I-975
Shockwave, II-2360
Shoot for the Stars Aim for the Moon, II-2390, 2395
Shopify, II-3160
Shutterstock, II-3188
Siemens, I-236
Sierra Nevada, I-484
Sierra Wireless, II-2422
Siesta, I-663
Signature Pick 5, I-1459, 1463
Silk Almond Light, II-2320
Silk Oat Yeah, II-2309, 2321-2322
SilkRoad RedCarpet, II-3180
The Silver Eyes (Five Nights at Freddy's #1), I-524
Similasan, I-1149
Simple Pleasures, II-2654
Simply Cheetos, II-3112
Simply Concord, I-818
Simply Lemonade, I-2010
Simply Limeade, I-2010
Simply Orange, I-2011
Sinotruk Group, II-3438
Sister Schubert's, I-548, 554
Skechers, I-207, 1425, 1430
SkillSurvey, II-3180
Skinnypop, I-843, 845
Skippy, II-3224
Skittles, I-834
Skoal, II-3364, 3368
Skoda, I-338
Skol Vodka, I-2096
Sky Watcher, II-3313
SkySea, I-1024
Skyworth, II-3251
Skyy, I-2096
Slim Fast, I-848, II-3277
Slim Jim, II-2193
Smart, I-326
Smart Balance, I-581
Smart Mouth, II-2529
Smartfood, I-843
Smartsheet, II-3181
Smash Mallow, I-832
Smiletime, I-596
Smirnoff, I-1336, 2096
Smithfield, II-2203, 2206-2207, 2209
Smucker's, II-3224
Smuckers Uncrustables, I-1490
Snack Factory Pretzel Crisps, I-822, 1004-1005
SnapAV, I-587, 890, 1741
Snapcups, I-761

Snappers', I-822
Snapple, I-2005-2006
Snickers, I-722, 1872
Snyder's of Hanover, II-3124
Snyder's of Hanover 100 Cal Pack, II-3124
Snyder's of Hanover Pretzel Dips, I-822
So Delicious Cocowhip, II-3535
Soapbox, II-3144
Sobieski, I-2097
Softsoap, II-3143, 3145
Sogou, II-3185
Sogou Explorer, II-3156
Soleil, II-3209
Sonex, I-64
Sonic the Hedgehog, I-1162-1163, II-2359, 2361-2364
Sonos, I-890, 893
Sontrol4, I-892
Sony, I-285-286, 290, 883, 886-887, 891, 899, 1743, II-3106, 3251, 3515
Sony PlayStation, II-3252, 3481
Sony PlayStation 2, II-3481
Sony PlayStation 3, II-3481
Sony PlayStation 4, II-3481
S.O.S., I-738
Sour Patch Kid, I-834
Sour Punch, I-830
Southern Comfort, I-2090
Southern Living, I-2061, II-2138
Southern Recipe, II-3120
SOUTHSIDE, II-2391
Soylent, II-3277
Spangler Dum Dum Pops, I-828
Spangler Dum Dums, I-828
Sparkling Ice, I-542
Special K, I-661
Specialty Bakers, I-1473
Spenser Confidential, II-2365
Spindrift, I-542
SpongeBob SquarePants, I-2061
Sports Illustrated, I-2061, II-2138
Spot.IM, II-3158
The Spruce, I-1973
Spy x Family, II-2142
Squarespace, II-3160, 3193
Stacker 2, I-1240
Stacker 2 Extra, I-1240
Stacy's, I-1004-1005
Stagg, II-2417
Stamped: Racism, Antiracism, and You, I-524

Star Cruises, I-1024
Star Trek, I-2061
Star Wars, II-3397
Star Wars Episode IX: The Rise of Skywalker, I-1162-1163, II-2359, 2361-2363
Starbucks, I-757, 759-760
Starbucks Iced Espresso Classics, I-759
Starburst, I-834
Starfinder, II-3397
State Fair, I-1490
Stayfree, II-2955
Steak-umm, II-2195
Stelara, I-1117
Stella Artois, I-479, 485
Stella Doro, I-1002
Sterilite, I-2017
Sterling, II-3180
Steve Madden, I-1427
Stilwell, I-1459
Stock Werther's Original, I-828
Stocksy, II-3188
Stok, I-759
Stokers, II-3364, 3368
Stolichnaya, I-2097
Storify, II-3174
Stouffer's, I-1477, 1486-1487
Stuffed Puffs, I-832
Stumptown, II-3324
Suave, I-1731
Sub-Zero, I-240
Subaru, I-346, 364
Subaru BRZ, I-328
Subway Surfers, II-2340
Sugardale, II-2206-2207
Sun Bum, II-3096
Sun Maid, I-820
Sun Maid Mini Snacks, I-820
Sunbelt Bakery, I-826
Sunchips, II-3126
Sundown, II-3488
Suning Jiu, I-245
Sunmark, I-1144-1145, II-3144
Sunsea Teleommunications, II-2422
Sunshine Krispy, I-1011
Super 8 by Wyndham, I-1833
Super Pretzel, I-1480
Super Pretzel Soft Pretzel Bites, I-1480
Super Pretzel Softstix, I-1480
Supernatural, II-3320
SureCall, I-888
Sutter Home, II-3548

Suzies, I-845
Suzuki, II-2375
Svedka, I-2097
Swaggerty's Farm, II-2218
Swan, I-1150
Swanson, I-1477
SweatyBetty, I-193
Swedish Fish, I-834
Sweet Loren's, I-1093
Swisher Sweets, II-3358
Sylvania, I-2078
Sylvania Double Life, I-2078
Sylvania Super Saver, I-2078
SYM, II-2370, 2374
TAG Heuer, II-3505
Tai Pei, I-1457
Talenti, I-1871, 1874
Tampax, II-2956
Tampax Pearl, II-2956
Tampax Pocket Pearl, II-2956
Tampax Radiant, II-2956
Tampico, I-2005
Taski, II-2920
Tastee, I-818
Tattooed Chef, I-1462, 1481
TCL, II-3106, 3251
TecServ, II-2920
Ten Days Without Mom, II-2361
Ten High, I-2095
Tena, II-2950
Tena Serenity, II-2950
Tenet, II-2361-2364
Tennant, II-2920
Terminator: Dark Fate, I-1162-1163
Terranova Bakery, I-1096
Tesla, I-326, 343, 364
Tesla Model 3, I-327, 329-330, 333-336
Tesla Model S, I-329
Tesla Model X, I-329
Tesla Model Y, I-329, 336
Texas Tamale, I-1469
Thales Group, II-2422
Thayers, II-3091
The Deep End, Jeff Kinney, I-522
The Fame, Lady Gaga, II-2392
Therabreath, II-2529
Theraflu ExpressMax, I-1146
Theraworx Relief, I-1142
Thermador, I-240
Think Thin, I-838
Thinkstock, II-3188
ThinkThin, II-3283
This is Us, II-3323

This One's for You, II-2391
Thorens, I-891
Three Bridges, II-2626
Three Olives, I-2097
Thriller, II-2397
Tiber Balm, I-1142
Tic Tac, I-816
Tide, I-27
Tiger King, II-3321
Tiles Hop, II-2340
Tillamook, I-576, 671, 673, 677, 1874
Tillamook Country Smoker, II-2193, 2198
Timberwolf, II-3364
Tina's, I-1469, 1490
Tito's Handmade Vodka, I-2096
Tizen, II-3252
Tizhio Nengliang, I-1236
Today, II-3316
Tolls by Mail, II-3376
Tombstone, I-1474, 1492
Tom's of Maine, II-3145
Tony's, I-1474, 1492
Too Much and Never Enough, I-522
Tootsie Pops, I-828
Tootsie Roll Child's Play, I-836
Tootsie Roll Pops, I-828
Top, II-3366, 3370
Topo Chico, I-542
Tostitos, II-3138
Tostitos Scoops, II-3138
Totino's Party Pizza, I-1474, 1492
Totino's Pizza Rolls, I-1457
Toto, II-2753, 2755
Toufayan, I-1002
Toy Story 4, II-2365
Toyo, II-3351
Toyota, I-338, 346, 353, 364
Toyota 86, I-328
Toyota Camry, I-337
Toyota Corolla, I-337
Toyota Highlander, I-337
Toyota RAV4, I-337
Toyota Supra, I-328
Toyota Tacoma, I-337
Trans Ocean, II-2986
Traveller, II-2391
Trek, I-496
Trello, II-3181
TRESemmé Moisture Rich, I-1734
TRESemmé Tres Two, I-1731
TRESTwo, I-1731
Tributaries/Clarus, I-587

Trident, I-1713
Trident White, I-1713
Triple Paste, I-372
Trolli Sour Brite Crawlers, I-834
Trolls: World Tour, I-1162
Tropicana Pure Premium, I-2011
True North, I-849
Truly, I-1336
Truth Bar, I-848
Truwhip, II-3535
Tucker Carlson Tonight, II-3317
Tumblr, I-1967, 1969
Turkey Creek, II-3120
Turkey Hill, I-1874, 2010, II-3305
tvOS, II-3252
Tweaker, I-1240
Twin Dragon, I-1190
Twisted, I-1336
Twitch, II-3485
Twitter, I-259, 1967, 1969
Twix, I-722
Twizzlers, I-830
Twizzlers Cherry Kick, I-830
Twizzlers Nibs, I-830
Twizzlers Pull 'n Peel, I-830
Tylenol, I-1143
Tylenol PM, I-1143
Tyson, II-2196, 2200
Tyson Any'tizers, II-2200
Tyson Grilled & Ready, II-2200
U-blox, II-2422
U by Kotex Clean Wear, II-2955
U by Kotex Click, II-2956
U by Kotex Security, II-2955-2956
UC Browser, II-3156-3157
Ultrathon, I-709
The Umbrella Academy, II-3321
Under Armour, I-202, 1428
Unilumin, I-1087
UnionPay, II-2635
Uniqlo, I-207
Unique Splits, II-3124
United Auto, II-2373
United Bakery, I-1002
Unsplash, II-3188
Untamed, I-522
Up & Up, II-2951
Up First, II-2762
Urban Outfitters, I-201
URC, I-892
Utz, II-3112, 3122, 3124
Utz Specials, II-3124
V8 Splash, I-2005
V8 V Fusion Plus Energy, I-2007

Valenti, I-245
Valued Naturals, I-820
Valvoline, I-2114-2116
Vamousse, I-1155
Vampire Diaries, II-3320
Vandoren, II-2416
Vans, I-64, 202, 1427-1428, 1482
Vaseline, II-3088
Vaseline Lip Therapy, I-982
Vaseline Total Moisture, II-3093
Vashon, I-64
Vatti, I-236
Vauxhall, I-338
VELO, II-3362
Ventev, I-466
Verdi Spumante, II-3546
Verizon, I-888, II-3518
Verizon Media, I-1975
The Very Hungry Caterpillar, I-523
Veuve Clicquot, II-3546
ViacomCBS Digital, I-1975
Viafoura, II-3158
Vicks Dayquil, I-1146-1147
Vicks Nyquil, I-1146
Vicks Vapobath, II-3142
Village Naturals Therapy, II-3142
Viper, II-2920
Visa, II-2633-2635, 2638
Visia, II-2238
Visualint, I-594
Vita, II-2986
Vitafusion, II-3488-3489
Vitafusion Fiber Well, I-1154
Vitafusion Power C, II-3488
Vital Farms, I-1201, 1467
Vital Proteins, I-848
Vivartia, II-3600
Vivo, I-629, 634, 636
Vizio, II-3106, 3251
Volkswagen, I-326, 338
Volkswagen e-Golf, I-327, 330
Volkswagen ID.3, I-327, 330, 334-336
Volkswagen ID.4, I-335
Voltas, I-223, 242
Volvo, I-1243
Volvo Truck, II-3435
Volvo XC40 EV, I-335
Volvo XC40 PHEV, I-335
VPX Bang, I-1239-1240
Vtech, II-3518
Vuse, I-1164, 1166
Vuukle, II-3158
Walking Dead, II-3324

The Walt Disney Company, I-1975
Wang Dawei, I-245
Want Want Holdings, II-3132
Wantedly Admin, I-1974
War Horse, I-1236
Warhammer, II-3397
WarnerMedia, I-1975
WasteMaid, I-245
Water Wipes, II-3556
Wavy Lay's, II-3122
Wax + Rx, I-1149
We Were Liars, I-524
WebOS, II-3252
Weebly, II-3193
Weeks & Leo, I-1155
Weinmann, II-2256
Welch's, I-2005
Welch's Fruit 'n Yogurt, I-820
Wella Bar, I-848
Western Star, II-3435
Wet Ones, II-3144
Wewalka, I-1095-1096
What You See is What You Get, II-2390-2391
When We Fall Asleep, Where Do We Go?, II-2397
Where the Crawdads Sing, I-522
Whirlpool, I-236, 242, 244, 246, 248-250
Whisps, II-3112
White Castle, I-1490
White Claw Hard Seltzer, I-1336
White Fragility, I-522
White Owl, II-3358
WhiteWave Land O'Lakes, II-3534
Whitman's Sampler, I-726
Wholly Veggie, I-1459
Wild Turkey, I-2095
Wild Turkey American Honey, I-2090
Wildbrine, II-2147
Will & Grace, II-3324
William Bolthouse Farms, II-2321
Williams, II-2209
Wilson Electronics, I-888
Window Live Mail, II-3161
Windows, II-3176-3179
Windsor, II-2920
Windsor Supreme, I-2089
Wing Hing, I-1190
Winky, II-2812
Winter Gardens, II-2147
Winx Club, I-2061
Wirepath, I-594

Wise Cheez Doodles, II-3112
Wix, II-3193
WixStores, II-3160
Wolf, I-240
Womans Day, II-2138
Wonderful, II-3133
WonderPush, II-3182
The Wonkey Donkey, I-523
WooCommerce, II-3160
Woodford Reserve SBL, I-2095
World of Darkness, II-3397
Wright, II-2206
Wrigley's 5 Cobalt, I-1713
Wrigley's 5 Rain, I-1713
Wrigley's Big Red, I-1710
Wrigley's Doublemint, I-1710
Wrigley's Eclipse, I-1713
Wrigley's Extra, I-1713
Wrigley's Juicy Fruit, I-1710
Wrigley's Spearmint, I-1710
Wrigley's Winterfresh, I-1710
Wuling HongGuang Mini EV, I-333, 336
Wycliff Sparkling, II-3545
Wyman's, I-1465
Wyman's of Maine, I-1465
X 100PRE, II-2393
Xarelto, I-1117
Xbox One, II-3477
XCMG, II-3438
Xiaomi, I-285, 287-291, 629-630, 634-637, 899, II-3251, 3515
XS, I-1236
Xtep, I-207, 1430
Yahoo!, II-3161, 3184, 3186
Yakusoku no Neverland, II-2142
Yale, II-2997-2998
Yamaha, I-886, II-2369-2372, 2374-2375, 2416-2417
Yandex, II-3186
Yardley London, II-3146
Yasso, I-1872
Yellow Trail, II-3548
Yellowstone, II-3324
YHLQMDLG, II-2393
Yoder's, II-2785
Yokohama, II-3351-3352
You, II-3321
Young Sheldon, II-3323
YouTube, I-1967, 1969
YouTube Gaming, II-3485
YSL, I-975
Yuansouti, I-257
Yummallo, I-832

Yutong, I-571
Yves Saint Laurent, I-985
Zachary, I-820
Zanella, II-2369
Zatarain's, I-1486
zBoost, I-888
Zebra F301, II-3595
Zenair, I-64
Zenith, I-64
Zhongtong, I-571
Zhou Hei Ya, II-2175
Zi Yan, II-2175
Zig-Zag, II-3370
Ziploc, I-2017
Ziploc Twist 'n Loc, I-2017
ZipRecruiter, I-1974
Zonin, II-3546
Zootopia, II-2365
Zuora, II-3183
Zuoyebang, I-257
Zurros, I-1002
ZYN, II-3362, 3368
Zyrtec, I-1147

APPENDIX I - INDUSTRIAL CLASSIFICATIONS
SIC COVERAGE

This appendix lists the Standard Industrial Classification Codes (SICs) included in *Market Share Reporter*. Volume and page numbers are shown following each SIC category. NEC stands for not elsewhere classified.

Agricultural Production - Crops

0110 Cash grains, p. I-443
0111 Wheat, pp. II-942-943
0112 Rice, pp. II-776-777
0115 Corn, pp. I-256-257
0116 Soybeans, pp. II-665-667
0119 Cash grains, nec, p. II-655
0131 Cotton, pp. I-263-264
0132 Tobacco, p. II-899
0134 Irish potatoes, pp. II-738-739
0161 Vegetables and melons, pp. I-400, 403, 407-410, II-801
0171 Berry crops, pp. I-400, 403
0172 Grapes, p. I-401
0173 Tree nuts, pp. II-651-653
0174 Citrus fruits, pp. I-401-402, 405-406
0175 Deciduous tree fruits, pp. I-399-403
0179 Fruits and tree nuts, nec, pp. I-400-401, 403, 409
0181 Ornamental nursery products, pp. I-366-367, 444
0182 Food crops grown under cover, pp. II-636, 798
0191 General farms, primarily crop, pp. I-343-344

Agricultural Production - Livestock

0211 Beef cattle feedlots, p. I-167
0212 Beef cattle, except feedlots, pp. I-165-166
0213 Hogs, pp. I-473-474
0214 Sheep and goats, pp. II-811, 959
0241 Dairy farms, pp. I-343-344
0251 Broiler, fryer, and roaster chickens, pp. II-577, 579-581, 587
0252 Chicken eggs, pp. I-318-320
0253 Turkeys and turkey eggs, pp. II-591-592
0271 Fur-bearing animals and rabbits, p. II-704
0273 Animal aquaculture, pp. I-354-355
0279 Animal specialties, nec, pp. I-484, II-716-718, 821

Agricultural Services

0724 Cotton ginning, p. I-263
0742 Veterinary services, specialties, p. II-925
0751 Livestock services, exc. veterinary, p. I-166

Forestry

0811 Timber tracts, pp. II-889-890

Fishing, Hunting, & Trapping

0912 Finfish, pp. I-355-356, 493
0971 Hunting, trapping, game propagation, p. I-494

Metal Mining

1011 Iron ores, pp. I-528-530
1021 Copper ores, pp. I-252-254
1031 Lead and zinc ores, pp. I-543-544, II-962-963
1041 Gold ores, pp. I-434-436
1044 Silver ores, pp. II-822-823
1061 Ferroalloy ores, except vanadium, pp. I-194, 199, II-623, 648-649, 916
1094 Uranium-radium-vanadium ores, pp. II-920-921
1099 Metal ores, nec, pp. I-48, 52, II-604, 690-691, 731, 890-891, 895

Coal Mining

1220 Bituminous coal and lignite mining, pp. I-197-199

Oil & Gas Extraction

1311 Crude petroleum and natural gas, pp. II-656-657, 659-660
1321 Natural gas liquids, pp. II-658-660, 662-663
1381 Drilling oil and gas wells, p. II-661
1389 Oil and gas field services, nec, pp. II-663-664

Nonmetallic Minerals, Except Fuels

1420 Crushed and broken stone, p. I-15
1422 Crushed and broken limestone, p. I-273
1423 Crushed and broken granite, pp. I-272, 443, II-571
1442 Construction sand and gravel, pp. I-229, II-784, 865
1446 Industrial sand, p. II-784
1455 Kaolin and ball clay, p. I-536
1459 Clay and related minerals, nec, p. I-195

1474 Potash, soda, and borate minerals, pp. I-142, II-737-738, 839
1475 Phosphate rock, p. II-719
1479 Chemical and fertilizer mining, nec, pp. I-73, 77, 367, II-784, 869
1499 Miscellaneous nonmetallic minerals, pp. I-286-287, 418, 423, 429, 443-444, 458, II-612, 704, 751, 756-757

General Building Contractors

1500 General building contractors, pp. I-230, 240
1521 Single-family housing construction, pp. I-232-233, 487-490, 492-493
1522 Residential construction, nec, pp. I-231, 491
1540 Nonresidential building construction, p. I-233
1541 Industrial buildings and warehouses, p. I-230
1542 Nonresidential construction, nec, pp. I-230-232, 243

Heavy Construction, Ex. Building

1600 Heavy construction, ex. building, pp. I-232, 241, 505
1611 Highway and street construction, p. I-229
1629 Heavy construction, nec, p. I-242

Special Trade Contractors

1711 Plumbing, heating, air-conditioning, p. I-246
1721 Painting and paper hanging, p. I-244
1731 Electrical work, pp. I-240, 242, 244
1741 Masonry and other stonework, p. I-243
1742 Plastering, drywall, and insulation, p. I-246
1761 Roofing, siding, and sheet metal work, p. I-244
1771 Concrete work, p. I-241
1791 Structural steel erection, p. I-245
1793 Glass and glazing work, p. I-243
1794 Excavation work, p. I-243
1795 Wrecking and demolition work, p. I-241
1796 Installing building equipment, nec, p. I-243
1799 Special trade contractors, nec, pp. I-245, 333-334

Food & Kindred Products

2000 Food and kindred products, pp. I-369-373
2011 Meat packing plants, pp. II-579, 586, 588-589
2013 Sausages and other prepared meats, pp. II-576-578, 581, 583-591
2015 Poultry slaughtering and processing, pp. I-318, II-577, 581-585, 592
2020 Dairy products, p. I-275
2021 Creamery butter, pp. I-153-155
2022 Cheese, natural and processed, pp. I-178-182
2023 Dry, condensed, evaporated products, p. II-943
2024 Ice cream and frozen desserts, pp. I-495-498
2026 Fluid milk, pp. II-613-617, 852, 961
2032 Canned specialties, pp. I-102-103, 161-162, II-851-852
2033 Canned fruits and vegetables, pp. I-533-535
2034 Dehydrated fruits, vegetables, soups, pp. I-294, 404, 406-407
2035 Pickles, sauces, and salad dressings, pp. I-288, II-791-793, 860
2037 Frozen fruits and vegetables, pp. I-388-397
2038 Frozen specialties, nec, pp. I-388-389, 391, 393-398
2041 Flour and other grain mill products, pp. I-365-366
2043 Cereal breakfast foods, pp. I-176-177
2044 Rice milling, p. II-776
2045 Prepared flour mixes and doughs, pp. I-292-293, II-692
2046 Wet corn milling, pp. II-941-942
2047 Dog and cat food, pp. II-709-714, 717
2048 Prepared feeds, nec, p. I-500
2050 Bakery products, p. I-104
2051 Bread, cake, and related products, pp. I-103-108, 146-149, 271
2052 Cookies and crackers, pp. I-105, 266-269
2053 Frozen bakery products, except bread, pp. I-106, 292, 389, 393, 396
2061 Raw cane sugar, p. II-869
2062 Cane sugar refining, p. II-868
2063 Beet sugar, pp. II-867-868
2064 Candy & other confectionery products, pp. I-215-227
2066 Chocolate and cocoa products, pp. I-190-194, 200
2067 Chewing gum, pp. I-215, 453-454
2068 Salted and roasted nuts and seeds, pp. II-830, 832, 835-836
2070 Fats and oils, pp. II-664-665, 668
2075 Soybean oil mills, pp. I-346-347, II-666-667
2076 Vegetable oil mills, nec, pp. I-345-346, II-668-669
2077 Animal and marine fats and oils, pp. I-345-346
2079 Edible fats and oils, nec, p. I-345
2080 Beverages, pp. I-29, 130-131
2082 Malt beverages, pp. I-127-130, 357, 462
2084 Wines, brandy, and brandy spirits, pp. II-946-948
2085 Distilled and blended liquors, pp. I-555-558, II-947
2086 Bottled and canned soft drinks, pp. I-143-144, 329-330, II-839-840, 859
2087 Flavoring extracts and syrups, nec, pp. I-357, 399, 556
2091 Canned and cured fish and seafoods, pp. II-795-797
2092 Fresh or frozen prepared fish, pp. II-796-797
2095 Roasted coffee, pp. I-200-202
2096 Potato chips and similar snacks, pp. II-828-836

2097 Manufactured ice, p. I-495
2098 Macaroni and spaghetti, pp. II-698-699
2099 Food preparations, nec, pp. I-130, 288, 317, 368-371, 373, 484, II-572, 592-593, 705, 741, 749, 853-854, 859, 880-882, 903, 924

Tobacco Products

2100 Tobacco products, p. II-899
2111 Cigarettes, p. II-896
2121 Cigars, p. II-895
2131 Chewing and smoking tobacco, pp. II-896-899

Textile Mill Products

2200 Textile mill products, pp. II-888-889
2211 Broadwoven fabric mills, cotton, p. I-339
2252 Hosiery, nec, p. I-53
2269 Finishing plants, nec, pp. I-186, 338
2273 Carpets and rugs, pp. I-358, 361-362
2281 Yarn spinning mills, p. II-960
2295 Coated fabrics, not rubberized, p. I-338
2297 Nonwoven fabrics, pp. II-649-650, 948, 950
2298 Cordage and twine, p. II-782

Apparel & Other Textile Products

2300 Apparel and other textile products, pp. I-52-55, 57-58
2320 Men's and boys' furnishings, pp. I-55-57
2322 Men's & boys' underwear + nightwear, p. I-56
2323 Men's and boys' neckwear, p. I-56
2326 Men's and boys' work clothing, p. I-55
2330 Women's and misses' outerwear, pp. I-57, 59-60
2335 Women's, junior's, & misses' dresses, p. I-59
2341 Women's and children's underwear, pp. I-55, 59
2391 Curtains and draperies, p. I-476
2392 Housefurnishings, nec, pp. I-477-478
2394 Canvas and related products, p. II-887
2399 Fabricated textile products, nec, p. II-714

Lumber & Wood Products

2421 Sawmills and planing mills, general, pp. I-565, II-958
2426 Hardwood dimension & flooring mills, pp. I-359, 361-362, 566, II-955
2434 Wood kitchen cabinets, p. I-156
2435 Hardwood veneer and plywood, pp. II-955-958
2436 Softwood veneer and plywood, pp. I-566-567, II-957
2448 Wood pallets and skids, p. II-691
2449 Wood containers, nec, pp. I-537, II-958
2451 Mobile homes, pp. I-490, 492
2452 Prefabricated wood buildings, p. I-488

2491 Wood preserving, p. II-955
2493 Reconstituted wood products, pp. II-956-957
2499 Wood products, nec, pp. I-255-256, 330, 348, 353, 542, II-959

Furniture & Fixtures

2500 Furniture and fixtures, pp. I-410-411, 414, II-955
2512 Upholstered household furniture, p. I-413
2514 Metal household furniture, pp. I-412-414
2515 Mattresses and bedsprings, pp. I-411, 413, 476
2520 Office furniture, p. I-414
2531 Public building & related furniture, pp. I-411-412

Paper & Allied Products

2611 Pulp mills, pp. II-749-750
2621 Paper mills, pp. I-194, II-693, 695-696, 898
2631 Paperboard mills, pp. II-693-694
2652 Setup paperboard boxes, pp. I-145-146
2653 Corrugated and solid fiber boxes, p. I-145
2671 Paper coated & laminated, packaging, p. II-696
2672 Paper coated and laminated, nec, p. II-879
2673 Bags: plastics, laminated, & coated, pp. I-167, 373, II-681, 684, 696
2675 Die-cut paper and board, p. II-695
2676 Sanitary paper products, pp. II-785-789, 949-950
2677 Envelopes, p. II-684
2678 Stationery products, p. II-862
2679 Converted paper products, nec, p. II-931

Printing & Publishing

2700 Printing and publishing, p. II-748
2711 Newspapers, p. II-647
2721 Periodicals, pp. I-205, II-569-570
2731 Book publishing, pp. I-139-142, II-748
2732 Book printing, p. I-141
2741 Miscellaneous publishing, pp. I-289-290, 522-525, 559, II-620-622
2750 Commercial printing, p. II-744
2752 Commercial printing, lithographic, pp. I-537-538, II-743
2754 Commercial printing, gravure, p. II-744
2759 Commercial printing, nec, pp. II-719, 743
2771 Greeting cards, pp. I-444-445

Chemicals & Allied Products

2800 Chemicals and allied products, p. I-188
2813 Industrial gases, pp. I-501-502
2816 Inorganic pigments, p. I-185
2819 Industrial inorganic chemicals, nec, pp. I-45, 190, 528, 559

2821 Plastics materials and resins, pp. I-134, II-725, 727-730
2822 Synthetic rubber, p. II-782
2823 Cellulosic manmade fibers, pp. I-351-353
2833 Medicinals and botanicals, pp. I-160-161, II-870-877, 921, 929
2834 Pharmaceutical preparations, pp. I-297-308, II-714
2835 Diagnostic substances, pp. I-284-286
2836 Biological products exc. diagnostic, pp. I-134-135, 425, 498, II-875-876, 921-922
2841 Soap and other detergents, pp. I-282-284, II-837-838
2842 Polishes and sanitation goods, pp. I-196-197
2844 Toilet preparations, pp. I-101, 257-262, 307, 337, 386-387, 460-461, II-672-673, 706-707, 823-825
2851 Paints and allied products, pp. II-688-690
2861 Gum and wood chemicals, p. I-177
2865 Cyclic crudes and intermediates, p. I-183
2869 Industrial organic chemicals, nec, pp. I-133, 183, 185-186
2873 Nitrogenous fertilizers, pp. I-182, 349-351
2874 Phosphatic fertilizers, pp. I-349-350
2875 Fertilizers, mixing only, pp. I-350-351
2879 Agricultural chemicals, nec, pp. I-183-186, 189
2891 Adhesives and sealants, pp. I-3-5
2892 Explosives, p. I-336
2893 Printing ink, pp. I-506-507
2895 Carbon black, p. I-188
2899 Chemical preparations, nec, pp. I-16-17, 184-185, II-727

Petroleum & Coal Products

2911 Petroleum refining, pp. I-133, II-657
2951 Asphalt paving mixtures and blocks, pp. I-77-78
2952 Asphalt felts and coatings, pp. I-78-79
2992 Lubricating oils and greases, pp. I-124, 563-564

Rubber & Misc. Plastics Products

3011 Tires and inner tubes, pp. II-893-894
3021 Rubber and plastics footwear, pp. I-380-381
3053 Gaskets, packing and sealing devices, p. I-424
3069 Fabricated rubber products, nec, pp. II-623, 707
3081 Unsupported plastics film & sheet, p. II-726
3083 Laminated plastics plate & sheet, p. I-539
3084 Plastics pipe, pp. II-724, 726
3085 Plastics bottles, p. II-728
3087 Custom compound purchased resins, p. II-654
3088 Plastics plumbing fixtures, p. II-733
3089 Plastics products, nec, pp. I-278, 348, 362, 537, 565, II-681, 683, 685, 725-727, 877

Leather & Leather Products

3111 Leather tanning and finishing, pp. I-545-546
3140 Footwear, except rubber, pp. I-380-381
3161 Luggage, p. I-565
3171 Women's handbags and purses, pp. I-54, 461, 568

Stone, Clay, & Glass Products

3211 Flat glass, pp. I-430-433
3221 Glass containers, pp. I-430, 432
3229 Pressed and blown glass, nec, pp. I-431, 433
3231 Products of purchased glass, pp. I-84, 431, 434
3241 Cement, hydraulic, pp. I-172-174
3253 Ceramic wall and floor tile, pp. I-175-176, 358, 361
3255 Clay refractories, p. I-149
3261 Vitreous plumbing fixtures, pp. II-733, 789
3262 Vitreous china table & kitchenware, p. I-202
3269 Pottery products, nec, pp. II-739-740
3271 Concrete block and brick, p. I-214
3272 Concrete products, nec, pp. I-88, II-650-651, 723
3273 Ready-mixed concrete, p. I-213
3274 Lime, p. I-554
3275 Gypsum products, pp. I-167, 457-458, II-931
3281 Cut stone and stone products, pp. I-76, 265, 274
3291 Abrasive products, pp. I-1, 196
3292 Asbestos products, p. I-507
3295 Minerals, ground or treated, pp. I-347, 453, 530
3296 Mineral wool, pp. I-507-508, II-617

Primary Metal Industries

3312 Blast furnaces and steel mills, pp. II-861, 863-865
3313 Electrometallurgical products, p. II-571
3315 Steel wire and related products, p. II-950
3317 Steel pipe and tubes, pp. I-528, II-725
3321 Gray and ductile iron foundries, pp. I-386, II-571
3331 Primary copper, p. I-255
3334 Primary aluminum, pp. I-46-48
3339 Primary nonferrous metals, nec, pp. I-157, II-821, 961
3341 Secondary nonferrous metals, pp. I-255, II-570, 648
3351 Copper rolling and drawing, pp. I-46, 252-253, II-954
3353 Aluminum sheet, plate, and foil, pp. I-46, 48
3356 Nonferrous rolling and drawing, nec, pp. II-648, 962
3357 Nonferrous wiredrawing & insulating, pp. I-156-157
3360 Nonferrous foundries (castings), p. I-165
3365 Aluminum foundries, pp. I-385-386
3369 Nonferrous foundries, nec, pp. II-611, 785

3398 Metal heat treating, p. II-609
3399 Primary metal products, nec, p. I-103

Fabricated Metal Products

3411 Metal cans, pp. II-605-606
3412 Metal barrels, drums, and pails, p. II-607
3421 Cutlery, pp. I-251, II-706, 902
3423 Hand and edge tools, nec, p. II-903
3425 Saw blades and handsaws, p. II-793
3429 Hardware, nec, pp. I-462, 562, II-900
3431 Metal sanitary ware, p. II-733
3432 Plumbing fixture fittings and trim, pp. II-732, 734
3433 Heating equipment, except electric, pp. I-468-469, II-723
3441 Fabricated structural metal, p. I-339
3442 Metal doors, sash, and trim, pp. I-423, II-944-945
3443 Fabricated plate work (boiler shops), pp. I-137, II-609
3444 Sheet metalwork, pp. I-195, 456, II-608, 811
3446 Architectural metal work, pp. II-673-674
3448 Prefabricated metal buildings, p. II-605
3452 Bolts, nuts, rivets, and washers, pp. I-137, 462, 499
3462 Iron and steel forgings, p. II-610
3465 Automotive stampings, p. II-611
3466 Crowns and closures, pp. I-163, II-607-608
3469 Metal stampings, nec, pp. I-250-251
3471 Plating and polishing, p. I-321
3479 Metal coating and allied services, p. II-606
3482 Small arms ammunition, pp. I-50, 454
3483 Ammunition, exc. for small arms, nec, p. I-50
3484 Small arms, p. I-455
3489 Ordnance and accessories, nec, p. II-826
3491 Industrial valves, p. II-923
3492 Fluid power valves & hose fittings, p. II-734
3495 Wire springs, p. II-860
3496 Misc. fabricated wire products, p. I-348
3497 Metal foil and leaf, p. I-253
3499 Fabricated metal products, nec, pp. I-539, II-609-610

Industrial Machinery & Equipment

3511 Turbines and turbine generator sets, pp. II-916-918
3519 Internal combustion engines, nec, pp. I-330-331
3523 Farm machinery and equipment, pp. I-341-343
3524 Lawn and garden equipment, p. I-542
3531 Construction machinery, pp. I-227-229
3532 Mining machinery, pp. II-617-618
3534 Elevators and moving stairways, pp. I-88, 321-322, 484
3535 Conveyors and conveying equipment, p. I-250
3536 Hoists, cranes, and monorails, pp. I-269-270, 322, 474, 550
3537 Industrial trucks and tractors, p. I-550
3541 Machine tools, metal cutting types, p. II-569
3544 Special dies, tools, jigs & fixtures, pp. I-503-504, II-853
3545 Machine tool accessories, p. II-608
3546 Power-driven handtools, pp. II-900-902
3548 Welding apparatus, pp. II-939-940
3552 Textile machinery, p. II-887
3553 Woodworking machinery, p. II-794
3554 Paper industries machinery, p. II-696
3556 Food products machinery, p. I-203
3559 Special industry machinery, nec, pp. I-540, II-697, 730-731, 802
3562 Ball and roller bearings, pp. I-126-127
3563 Air and gas compressors, pp. I-207, II-870
3564 Blowers and fans, pp. I-340, II-935
3565 Packaging machinery, p. II-687
3568 Power transmission equipment, nec, pp. I-425, II-751-752
3569 General industrial machinery, nec, pp. I-308, II-778-780
3571 Electronic computers, pp. I-210-212, II-810, 828, 937-938
3572 Computer storage devices, p. I-208
3577 Computer peripheral equipment, nec, pp. I-134, 209, II-889
3578 Calculating and accounting equipment, pp. I-158, II-655-656, 737, 801, 930
3581 Automatic vending machines, p. II-775
3585 Refrigeration and heating equipment, pp. I-63, 67-68, 468-469, II-718
3589 Service industry machinery, nec, p. II-740
3593 Fluid power cylinders & actuators, pp. I-367, II-734
3596 Scales and balances, exc. laboratory, p. II-794

Electronic & Other Electric Equipment

3612 Transformers, except electronic, pp. I-562, II-740, 878, 908
3613 Switchgear and switchboard apparatus, pp. I-195, 336, 417, II-877
3621 Motors and generators, pp. I-44, 429
3624 Carbon and graphite products, p. I-163
3625 Relays and industrial controls, p. II-763
3629 Electrical industrial apparatus, nec, p. I-494
3630 Household appliances, pp. I-64-65, 67-68
3631 Household cooking equipment, pp. I-63, 66, 69
3632 Household refrigerators and freezers, pp. I-64, 69
3633 Household laundry equipment, pp. I-64, 69
3634 Electric housewares and fans, pp. I-65-67, II-778
3639 Household appliances, nec, pp. I-65-66, 68

3641 Electric lamps, pp. I-550-553
3643 Current-carrying wiring devices, pp. I-317, II-720, 760, 877
3644 Noncurrent-carrying wiring devices, p. II-939
3645 Residential lighting fixtures, pp. I-552-553
3647 Vehicular lighting equipment, pp. I-551, 553
3648 Lighting equipment, nec, pp. I-552-553
3651 Household audio and video equipment, pp. I-235-239, II-828
3652 Prerecorded records and tapes, pp. II-636-640
3661 Telephone and telegraph apparatus, pp. I-168-171, II-883
3663 Radio & TV communications equipment, pp. I-442, II-753, 790-791, 866-867, 954
3669 Communications equipment, nec, pp. I-79, 237, 339, 462, II-645-646, 791, 799, 826-827, 882
3672 Printed circuit boards, pp. I-208, II-741-742
3674 Semiconductors and related devices, pp. I-520-521, 540, II-802-809
3675 Electronic capacitors, p. I-162
3679 Electronic components, nec, pp. I-79-81, 168, 290-291, 498, II-612-613, 672, 692
3691 Storage batteries, pp. I-124-125
3692 Primary batteries, dry and wet, p. I-125
3695 Magnetic and optical recording media, p. II-760
3699 Electrical equipment & supplies, nec, pp. I-294, II-908

Transportation Equipment

3711 Motor vehicles and car bodies, pp. I-89-100
3713 Truck and bus bodies, pp. I-151-153, II-914-916, 923-924
3714 Motor vehicle parts and accessories, pp. I-83-85
3715 Truck trailers, p. II-907
3716 Motor homes, pp. II-761-762
3721 Aircraft, pp. I-17-21, II-920
3724 Aircraft engines and engine parts, pp. I-21-23
3728 Aircraft parts and equipment, nec, pp. I-24, II-920
3731 Ship building and repairing, p. II-819
3732 Boat building and repairing, pp. I-136-137
3743 Railroad equipment, pp. II-754-755
3751 Motorcycles, bicycles, and parts, pp. I-131-132, II-629-631
3761 Guided missiles and space vehicles, pp. I-278, II-618
3792 Travel trailers and campers, pp. II-762, 906-907
3795 Tanks and tank components, p. I-73
3799 Transportation equipment, nec, pp. I-29, II-708

Instruments & Related Products

3812 Search and navigation equipment, pp. I-357-358, 442, II-644, 798, 809, 828
3821 Laboratory apparatus and furniture, p. I-539
3823 Process control instruments, pp. I-88-89, 171, 288
3824 Fluid meters and counting devices, p. I-498
3825 Instruments to measure electricity, pp. II-612, 887
3826 Analytical instruments, pp. I-538-539
3827 Optical instruments and lenses, pp. II-722, 884
3829 Measuring & controlling devices, nec, pp. II-602, 879
3841 Surgical and medical instruments, pp. II-594, 598-599, 602
3842 Surgical appliances and supplies, pp. II-594-598, 600-603, 925
3845 Electromedical equipment, pp. II-595, 597
3851 Ophthalmic goods, pp. I-239-240, 547, II-671, 870
3861 Photographic equipment and supplies, pp. I-158-159, II-720-721
3873 Watches, clocks, watchcases & parts, pp. I-197, II-934

Miscellaneous Manufacturing Industries

3911 Jewelry, precious metal, pp. I-435, 531-532, 568, II-703, 822
3914 Silverware and plated ware, pp. I-531, II-823
3931 Musical instruments, pp. II-642-643
3942 Dolls and stuffed toys, p. II-905
3944 Games, toys, and children's vehicles, pp. I-472, II-904-906, 926-928
3949 Sporting and athletic goods, nec, pp. II-854-856
3951 Pens and mechanical pencils, p. II-959
3952 Lead pencils and art goods, pp. I-75, II-959
3991 Brooms and brushes, pp. I-149-150, 262, II-673
3993 Signs and advertising specialities, pp. I-546, II-820-821
3995 Burial caskets, p. I-165
3996 Hard surface floor coverings, nec, pp. I-359-360, II-820
3999 Manufacturing industries, nec, pp. I-102, 159, 310, 423, 550, II-571, 706, 708, 732

Railroad Transportation

4011 Railroads, line-haul operating, p. II-756

Local & Interurban Passenger Transit

4111 Local and suburban transit, pp. II-572, 576
4119 Local passenger transportation, nec, pp. I-49, 555, II-573-575, 777, 819
4141 Local bus charter service, pp. II-572-573, 576
4151 School buses, p. II-795

Trucking & Warehousing

4210 Trucking & courier services, ex. air, pp. II-812, 911-912
4212 Local trucking, without storage, p. II-913
4213 Trucking, except local, pp. II-878, 911-913, 931
4215 Courier services, except by air, pp. I-374-377, II-576, 670, 817-818
4221 Farm product warehousing and storage, p. II-932
4222 Refrigerated warehousing and storage, pp. II-932-933
4225 General warehousing and storage, pp. II-801, 866, 933
4226 Special warehousing and storage, nec, p. II-853

U.S. Postal Service

4311 U.S. Postal Service, p. II-737

Water Transportation

4412 Deep sea foreign trans. of freight, pp. II-813-814, 816-817
4432 Freight trans. on the great lakes, p. II-812
4449 Water transportation of freight, nec, pp. II-813, 815
4481 Deep sea passenger trans., ex. ferry, pp. I-272, II-936
4482 Ferries, pp. II-574, 935
4489 Water passenger transportation, nec, p. II-819
4491 Marine cargo handling, pp. II-736-737, 813, 815, 817

Transportation By Air

4512 Air transportation, scheduled, pp. I-24-28, II-634
4513 Air courier services, pp. II-812, 814
4581 Airports, flying fields, & services, pp. I-28-29

Pipelines, Except Natural Gas

4612 Crude petroleum pipelines, p. II-663

Transportation Services

4720 Passenger transportation arrangement, pp. II-903, 909
4724 Travel agencies, pp. I-434, 486, II-671, 910
4725 Tour operators, p. II-909
4731 Freight transportation arrangement, pp. II-814-817
4741 Rental of railroad cars, p. I-544
4785 Inspection & fixed facilities, pp. II-899-900
4789 Transportation services, nec, p. II-814

Communication

4812 Radiotelephone communications, pp. II-950-954
4813 Telephone communications, exc. radio, pp. II-745, 883
4822 Telegraph & other communications, pp. I-101, 311-316, 524, II-604, 641, 910
4832 Radio broadcasting stations, pp. I-79, II-641, 734-736, 753
4833 Television broadcasting stations, pp. II-884-885
4841 Cable and other pay TV services, pp. I-312, II-675-680, 700-701
4899 Communication services, nec, p. II-954

Electric, Gas, & Sanitary Services

4911 Electric services, pp. I-323-329, II-921
4922 Natural gas transmission, p. II-663
4941 Water supply, p. II-935
4952 Sewerage systems, pp. II-811, 936
4953 Refuse systems, pp. I-462, II-651, 934
4959 Sanitary services, nec, pp. I-246, II-764
4961 Steam and air-conditioning supply, p. II-862

Wholesale Trade - Durable Goods

5023 Homefurnishings, pp. I-362-363, 483
5030 Lumber and construction materials, p. I-150
5043 Photographic equipment and supplies, p. II-721
5047 Medical and hospital equipment, p. II-600
5051 Metals service centers and offices, p. II-610
5063 Electrical apparatus and equipment, p. I-320
5078 Refrigeration equipment and supplies, p. II-763
5083 Farm and garden machinery, p. I-341
5084 Industrial machinery and equipment, p. I-503
5092 Toys and hobby goods and supplies, p. II-904

Wholesale Trade - Nondurable Goods

5113 Industrial & personal service paper, p. II-697
5139 Footwear, p. I-383
5141 Groceries, general line, pp. I-378, 452
5142 Packaged frozen foods, p. I-388
5145 Confectionery, p. I-214
5146 Fish and seafoods, p. I-353
5147 Meats and meat products, p. II-593
5148 Fresh fruits and vegetables, p. I-399
5159 Farm-product raw materials, nec, p. I-247
5162 Plastics materials & basic shapes, p. II-731
5169 Chemicals & allied products, nec, pp. I-182, 186-187
5171 Petroleum bulk stations & terminals, p. II-878
5182 Wine and distilled beverages, p. II-948
5191 Farm supplies, p. I-16

5193 Flowers & florists' supplies, p. I-364
5198 Paints, varnishes, and supplies, p. II-687

Building Materials & Garden Supplies

5211 Lumber and other building materials, p. I-475
5231 Paint, glass, and wallpaper stores, p. II-690
5251 Hardware stores, p. II-732
5261 Retail nurseries and garden stores, p. I-543

General Merchandise Stores

5300 General merchandise stores, pp. I-425-429, II-772-775
5311 Department stores, p. I-281
5331 Variety stores, pp. I-247-248, 292, II-931

Food Stores

5411 Grocery stores, pp. I-445-452, II-670-671
5421 Meat and fish markets, pp. II-593, 797
5431 Fruit and vegetable markets, pp. I-399, 408
5441 Candy, nut, and confectionery stores, p. I-214
5461 Retail bakeries, p. I-104
5499 Miscellaneous food stores, pp. I-160, 467, II-928

Automotive Dealers & Service Stations

5511 New and used car dealers, p. I-82
5521 Used car dealers, pp. I-81-82
5531 Auto and home supply stores, pp. I-85, II-891-892
5541 Gasoline service stations, pp. I-383-385, 424
5551 Boat dealers, p. I-136

Apparel & Accessory Stores

5621 Women's clothing stores, pp. I-60-61
5651 Family clothing stores, p. I-60
5661 Shoe stores, pp. I-381-382

Furniture & Homefurnishings Stores

5712 Furniture stores, pp. I-415-417
5713 Floor covering stores, pp. I-363, 487
5714 Drapery and upholstery stores, p. I-483
5719 Misc. homefurnishings stores, pp. I-416, 477-482, 487
5722 Household appliance stores, pp. I-61-62
5731 Radio, TV, & electronic stores, pp. I-168, 239
5734 Computer and software stores, pp. I-70-71, 210
5736 Musical instrument stores, p. II-641

Eating & Drinking Places

5812 Eating places, pp. I-203-205, 377-380, II-620, 766-772
5813 Drinking places, p. II-649

Miscellaneous Retail

5912 Drug stores and proprietary stores, pp. I-294-297, II-719
5921 Liquor stores, p. I-29
5932 Used merchandise stores, p. II-798
5941 Sporting goods and bicycle shops, p. II-857
5942 Book stores, pp. I-138, II-823
5944 Jewelry stores, pp. I-532-533
5945 Hobby, toy, and game shops, pp. I-472, II-906, 927
5962 Merchandising machine operators, pp. II-924-925
5963 Direct selling establishments, pp. I-288-289, II-619
5984 Liquefied petroleum gas dealers, p. II-747
5989 Fuel dealers, nec, pp. I-30-44
5992 Florists, p. I-364
5993 Tobacco stores and stands, p. II-899
5995 Optical goods stores, p. II-672
5999 Miscellaneous retail stores, nec, pp. I-73-75, 263, II-613, 644, 715-716, 910

Depository Institutions

6011 Federal reserve banks, pp. II-623-624
6020 Commercial banks, p. I-109
6021 National commercial banks, pp. I-110-123
6061 Federal credit unions, p. I-271
6062 State credit unions, p. I-271
6099 Functions related to deposit banking, pp. I-273, II-764

Nondepository Institutions

6111 Federal & fed.-sponsored credit, p. I-561
6141 Personal credit institutions, pp. II-604, 701-703
6153 Short-term business credit, p. I-316
6159 Misc. business credit institutions, pp. I-559-561
6162 Mortgage bankers and correspondents, pp. I-560, II-624-626

Security & Commodity Brokers

6211 Security brokers and dealers, pp. I-526-527
6221 Commodity contracts brokers, dealers, p. I-206
6231 Security and commodity exchanges, p. I-335
6282 Investment advice, pp. I-353, 528

Insurance Carriers

6300 Insurance carriers, pp. I-509-510
6311 Life insurance, p. I-510
6324 Hospital and medical service plans, p. I-511
6331 Fire, marine, and casualty insurance, pp. I-511-520

6351 Surety insurance, pp. I-508-509, 515, 517-519
6371 Pension, health, and welfare funds, pp. II-704-705

Insurance Agents, Brokers, & Service

6411 Insurance agents, brokers, & service, pp. I-508, 510, 519

Real Estate

6531 Real estate agents and managers, pp. I-492, II-757-760

Holding & Other Investment Offices

6719 Holding companies, nec, p. I-475
6722 Management investment, open-end, p. I-527
6794 Patent owners and lessors, pp. I-387-388, II-699
6798 Real estate investment trusts, pp. I-491-492

Hotels & Other Lodging Places

7011 Hotels and motels, pp. I-127, 484-486, II-811
7021 Rooming and boarding houses, p. II-781
7032 Sporting and recreational camps, p. II-761
7041 Membership-basis organization hotels, p. I-476

Personal Services

7213 Linen supply, p. II-888
7215 Coin-operated laundries and cleaning, p. I-541
7216 Drycleaning plants, except rug, p. I-308
7218 Industrial launderers, pp. I-502-503
7231 Beauty shops, pp. I-127, 460
7241 Barber shops, p. I-123
7261 Funeral service and crematories, p. I-277
7291 Tax return preparation services, p. II-880
7299 Miscellaneous personal services, nec, pp. I-287, 385, 461, II-879-880

Business Services

7311 Advertising agencies, pp. I-7-8
7312 Outdoor advertising services, pp. I-7, 9, 12
7313 Radio, TV, publisher representatives, pp. I-5-13, II-735
7322 Adjustment & collection services, p. I-277
7323 Credit reporting services, p. I-270
7335 Commercial photography, p. II-722
7338 Secretarial & court reporting, p. I-265
7342 Disinfecting & pest control services, p. II-708
7349 Building maintenance services, nec, p. I-531
7350 Misc. equipment rental & leasing, p. I-545
7353 Heavy construction equipment rental, pp. I-240, 470-471

7359 Equipment rental & leasing, nec, pp. I-23, 469, II-691, 764
7363 Help supply services, pp. II-860-861
7372 Prepackaged software, pp. I-70-72, 76, 320, II-622, 841-851, 926-928
7373 Computer integrated systems design, pp. I-205, 276
7374 Data processing and preparation, p. I-276
7375 Information retrieval services, pp. I-504-505
7376 Computer facilities management, p. I-208
7378 Computer maintenance & repair, p. I-207
7379 Computer related services, nec, p. II-877
7381 Detective & armored car services, pp. I-164, 525-526
7382 Security systems services, p. II-800
7384 Photofinishing laboratories, p. II-720
7389 Business services, nec, pp. I-13-15, 248-249, 291, 293, 334, 499, 522, II-685-686, 746-747, 765, 827, 851, 908, 928

Auto Repair, Services, & Parking

7514 Passenger car rental, p. I-86
7515 Passenger car leasing, pp. I-82, 96
7521 Automobile parking, pp. I-88, II-697
7532 Top & body repair & paint shops, pp. I-86-87
7533 Auto exhaust system repair shops, p. I-86
7534 Tire retreading and repair shops, p. II-892
7536 Automotive glass replacement shops, p. I-87
7537 Automotive transmission repair shops, p. I-87
7538 General automotive repair shops, p. I-87
7542 Carwashes, pp. I-163-164
7549 Automotive services, nec, p. II-629

Miscellaneous Repair Services

7629 Electrical repair shops, nec, p. I-61
7641 Reupholstery and furniture repair, p. I-415
7699 Repair services, nec, p. I-562

Motion Pictures

7812 Motion picture & video production, pp. I-309, 332-333, II-626-629, 885-887
7819 Services allied to motion pictures, p. II-883
7822 Motion picture and tape distribution, p. II-626
7832 Motion picture theaters, ex drive-in, pp. II-632-634
7833 Drive-in motion picture theaters, p. II-632
7841 Video tape rental, p. I-308

Amusement & Recreation Services

7911 Dance studios, schools, and halls, p. I-276
7922 Theatrical producers and services, pp. I-72, 212, 332, II-889

SIC 7929

7929 Entertainers & entertainment groups, p. I-213
7933 Bowling centers, p. I-145
7941 Sports clubs, managers, & promoters, pp. I-15, II-857-859
7948 Racing, including track operation, p. II-753
7991 Physical fitness facilities, pp. I-456-457, II-853
7992 Public golf courses, p. I-436
7993 Coin-operated amusement devices, p. I-422
7996 Amusement parks, pp. I-50-51, II-935
7997 Membership sports & recreation clubs, p. II-745
7999 Amusement and recreation, nec, pp. I-317, 334, 340, 418-423, II-761

Health Services

8011 Offices & clinics of medical doctors, pp. I-463, 467
8021 Offices and clinics of dentists, p. I-466
8031 Offices of osteopathic physicians, p. I-466
8041 Offices and clinics of chiropractors, p. I-466
8049 Offices of health practitioners, nec, pp. I-465-466
8051 Skilled nursing care facilities, p. II-766
8059 Nursing and personal care, nec, p. I-493
8060 Hospitals, pp. I-463-464
8062 General medical & surgical hospitals, p. I-465
8063 Psychiatric hospitals, p. I-467
8069 Specialty hospitals exc. psychiatric, p. I-465
8071 Medical laboratories, p. I-284
8072 Dental laboratories, p. I-281
8082 Home health care services, p. I-464
8092 Kidney dialysis centers, p. I-463
8093 Specialty outpatient clinics, nec, p. I-340
8099 Health and allied services, nec, pp. I-135, 464, II-600

Legal Services

8111 Legal services, pp. I-250, 547

Educational Services

8211 Elementary and secondary schools, pp. I-317, 331, II-795
8222 Junior colleges, p. II-795
8231 Libraries, pp. I-547-548
8244 Business and secretarial schools, p. I-153
8299 Schools & educational services, nec, pp. II-669, 907-908, 918

Social Services

8322 Individual and family services, pp. I-206, 322
8351 Child day care services, p. I-190
8399 Social services, nec, pp. I-177-178

Market Share Reporter, 32nd Edition

Museums, Botanical, Zoological Gardens

8412 Museums and art galleries, pp. I-471-472, II-635
8422 Botanical and zoological gardens, pp. II-698, 963

Membership Organizations

8611 Business associations, p. I-153
8631 Labor organizations, p. II-919
8641 Civic and social associations, pp. I-271, 483
8651 Political organizations, pp. I-561-562
8661 Religious organizations, p. II-763
8699 Membership organizations, nec, p. I-333

Engineering & Management Services

8711 Engineering services, p. I-282
8712 Architectural services, p. I-72
8713 Surveying services, p. II-920
8721 Accounting, auditing, & bookkeeping, p. I-2
8732 Commercial nonphysical research, pp. II-765-766
8733 Noncommercial research organizations, p. II-766
8742 Management consulting services, pp. I-234, 335
8743 Public relations services, p. II-748
8748 Business consulting, nec, pp. I-234, 335

Services, nec

8999 Services, nec, p. II-939

Justice, Public Order, & Safety

9221 Police protection, p. II-736
9222 Legal counsel and prosecution, p. I-439
9223 Correctional institutions, p. II-745

Finance, Taxation, & Monetary Policy

9311 Finance, taxation, & monetary policy, p. I-440

Administration of Human Resources

9411 Admin. of educational programs, p. I-438
9441 Admin. of social & manpower programs, pp. I-439-441
9451 Administration of veterans' affairs, p. I-441

Environmental Quality & Housing

9512 Land, mineral, wildlife conservation, p. I-440
9531 Housing programs, p. I-439

Administration of Economic Programs

9611 Admin. of general economic programs, pp. I-437-439, 441-442
9631 Regulation, admin. of utilities, p. I-438

9641 Regulation of agricultural marketing, p. I-436
9661 Space research and technology, pp. I-437, II-791, 852

National Security & Intl. Affairs

9711 National security, pp. I-278-280, 440

APPENDIX I - INDUSTRIAL CLASSIFICATIONS
NAICS COVERAGE

This appendix lists the North American Industrial Classification System codes (NAICS) included in *Market Share Reporter*. Volume and page numbers are shown following each NAICS category.

Crop Production

111110 Soybeans, pp. II-665-667
111140 Wheat, pp. I-443, II-942-943
111150 Corn, pp. I-256-257, 443
111160 Rice, pp. I-443, II-776-777
111199 All other grain farming, p. II-655
111211 Potatoes, pp. I-407, 409, II-738-739
111219 Other vegetables & melons, pp. I-400, 403, 407-410, II-738, 801
111310 Orange groves, pp. I-401, 405
111320 Citrus (exc orange) groves, pp. I-401-402, 405-406
111331 Apple orchards, pp. I-399-400, 402-403
111332 Grape vineyards, p. I-401
111333 Strawberries, p. I-400
111334 Berries (exc strawberries), pp. I-400, 403
111335 Tree nuts, pp. II-651-653
111336 Fruit & tree nut combination, pp. I-403, 409
111339 Other noncitrus fruits, pp. I-400-402
111411 Mushroom production, p. II-636
111419 Other food crops grown under cover, p. II-798
111421 Nursery & tree production, p. I-444
111422 Floriculture production, pp. I-366-367, 444
111910 Tobacco, p. II-899
111920 Cotton, pp. I-263-264
111998 Other crop farming, pp. I-343-344

Animal Production

112111 Beef cattle ranching & farming, pp. I-165-166, 344
112112 Cattle feedlots, p. I-167
112120 Dairy cattle & milk production, p. I-343
112210 Hogs & pigs, pp. I-473-474
112310 Chicken eggs, pp. I-318-320
112320 Broilers & other chicken production, pp. II-577, 579-581, 587
112330 Turkey production, pp. II-591-592
112410 Sheep farming, pp. II-811, 959
112420 Goat farming, p. II-811
112511 Finfish farming & fish hatcheries, p. I-354
112519 Other aquaculture, pp. I-355, II-716

112910 Apiculture, p. I-484
112930 Fur-bearing animal production, p. II-704
112990 All other animal production, pp. II-716-718, 821

Forestry and Logging

113110 Timber tract operations, pp. II-889-890

Fishing, Hunting & Trapping

114111 Finfish fishing, pp. I-355-356, 493
114210 Hunting & trapping, p. I-494

Agriculture & Forestry Support Activities

115111 Cotton ginning, p. I-263
115210 Animal production support activities, p. I-166

Oil & Gas Extraction

211120 Crude petroleum extraction, pp. II-659-660
211130 Natural gas extraction, pp. II-656-660, 662-663

Mining (except Oil & Gas)

212111 Bituminous coal & lignite mining, pp. I-197-199
212112 Bituminous coal underground mining, pp. I-197-199
212210 Iron ore, pp. I-528-530
212221 Gold ore, pp. I-434-436
212222 Silver ore, pp. II-822-823
212230 Copper, nickel, lead & zinc mining, pp. I-252-254, 435, 543-544, II-648-649, 962-963
212291 Uranium-radium-vanadium ore, pp. II-920-921
212299 All other metal ore mining, pp. I-48, 52, 194, 199, II-604, 623, 690-691, 731, 890-891, 895, 916
212312 Crushed & broken limestone, pp. I-15, 273
212313 Crushed & broken granite, pp. I-15, 272, 443, II-571
212319 Other crushed & broken stone, pp. I-15, 429

212321 Construction sand & gravel, pp. I-229, II-784, 865
212322 Industrial sand, p. II-784
212324 Kaolin & ball clay, p. I-536
212325 Clay/ceramic/refractory minerals, pp. I-195, 347
212391 Potash/soda/borite mineral mining, pp. I-142, II-737-738, 839
212392 Phosphate rock, p. II-719
212393 Other chemical/fertilizer minerals, pp. I-73, 77, 367, II-784, 869
212399 Other nonmetallic minerals, pp. I-286-287, 418, 423, 443-444, 458, II-612, 704, 751, 756-757

Mining Support Activities

213111 Drilling oil & gas wells, p. II-661
213112 Oil & gas operation support, pp. II-663-664

Utilities

221111 Hydroelectric power generation, pp. I-323-324, 326-329
221112 Fossil fuel electric pwr generation, pp. I-323-324, 326-328, II-921
221113 Nuclear electric power generation, pp. I-323-324, 326-328, II-921
221114 Solar electric power generation, pp. I-327, II-921
221115 Wind electric power generation, pp. I-324-328
221116 Geothermal electric power generation, pp. I-324, 327
221310 Water supply & irrigation systems, p. II-935
221320 Sewage treatment facilities, pp. II-811, 936
221330 Steam & air-conditioning supply, p. II-862

Building Construction

236115 New single-family housing (exc operative), pp. I-230, 233, 240, 487-490, 492-493
236116 New multifamily housing (exc operative), pp. I-230-231, 240, 491
236118 Residential remodelers, pp. I-232-233
236210 Industrial building construction, pp. I-230, 233, 240-241
236220 Commercial & institutional building construction, pp. I-230-233, 243

Heavy & Civil Engineering Construction

237110 Water & sewer line & related structures, pp. I-232, 241, 505
237120 Oil & gas pipeline & related structures, pp. I-241, 505
237130 Power & communication line & related structures, p. I-232
237310 Highway, street, & bridge construction, pp. I-229, 232, 505

Specialty Trade Contractors

238110 Poured concrete foundation & structure contractors, p. I-241
238120 Structural steel & precast concrete contractors, p. I-245
238140 Masonry contractors, p. I-243
238150 Glass & glazing contractors, p. I-243
238160 Roofing contractors, p. I-244
238210 Electrical & other wiring installation contractors, pp. I-240, 242, 244
238220 Plumbing, heating, & air-conditioning contractors, pp. I-243, 246
238310 Drywall & insulation contractors, p. I-246
238320 Painting & wall covering contractors, p. I-244
238390 Other building finishing contractors, p. I-244
238910 Site preparation contractors, pp. I-241-243
238990 All other specialty trade contractors, pp. I-245, 333-334

Food Manufacturing

311111 Dog & cat food manufacturing, pp. II-709-714, 717
311119 Other animal food manufacturing, p. I-500
311211 Flour milling, pp. I-365-366
311212 Rice milling, p. II-776
311221 Wet corn milling, pp. II-941-942
311224 Soybean & other oilseed processing, pp. I-345-347, 370, II-664-669
311225 Fats & oils refining & blending, pp. I-345-346, II-664-665, 668-669
311230 Breakfast cereal manufacturing, pp. I-176-177
311313 Beet sugar manufacturing, pp. II-867-868
311314 Cane sugar manufacturing, pp. II-868-869
311340 Nonchocolate confectionery mfg, pp. I-215-227, 370, 453-454
311351 Chocolate/confectionery mfg, pp. I-190-194, 200
311352 Confectionery mfg, from chocolate, pp. I-190-194, 200
311411 Frozen fruit/juice/vegetable mfg, pp. I-388-397
311412 Frozen specialty food mfg, pp. I-369, 371, 373, 388-389, 391, 393-398
311421 Fruit & vegetable canning, pp. I-371-372, 533-535
311422 Specialty canning, pp. I-102-103, 161-162, 373, II-851-852

311423 Dried & dehydrated food mfg, pp. I-294, 404, 406-407
311511 Fluid milk manufacturing, pp. I-275, 369-370, 372, II-613-617, 852, 961
311512 Creamery butter manufacturing, pp. I-153-155, 275, 371
311513 Cheese manufacturing, pp. I-178-182, 275
311514 Dry/condensed/evaporated dairy mfg, pp. II-613, 943
311520 Ice cream & frozen dessert mfg, pp. I-495-498
311611 Animal (exc poultry) slaughtering, pp. I-372, II-579, 586, 588-589
311612 Meat processed from carcasses, pp. I-369-370, 372, II-576-578, 581, 583-591
311613 Rendering/meat byproduct processing, pp. I-345-346
311615 Poultry processing, pp. I-318, II-577, 581-585, 592
311710 Seafood preparation & packaging, pp. I-345-346, II-795-797
311811 Retail bakeries, p. I-104
311812 Commercial bakeries, pp. I-103-108, 146-149, 271, 369
311813 Frozen cakes/other pastries mfg, pp. I-104, 106, 292, 389, 393, 396
311821 Cookie & cracker manufacturing, pp. I-105, 266-269
311824 Dry pasta, flour mixes & dough manufacturing, pp. I-292-293, II-692, 698-699
311830 Tortilla manufacturing, p. II-903
311911 Roasted nuts & peanut butter mfg, pp. II-830, 832, 835-836, 859
311919 Other snack food manufacturing, pp. I-369, II-828-836
311920 Coffee & tea manufacturing, pp. I-130-131, 200-202, II-880-882
311930 Flavoring syrup & concentrate mfg, pp. I-357, 399, 556
311941 Mayonnaise/dressing/other sauce, pp. I-288, II-791-793, 860
311942 Spice & extract manufacturing, pp. I-188, II-853-854
311991 Perishable prepared food mfg, pp. I-288, 317, 373, 484, II-572, 592-593, 705, 741, 749, 924
311999 Other food manufacturing, pp. I-368-371, II-593, 924

Beverage & Tobacco Product Manufacturing

312111 Soft drink manufacturing, pp. I-130-131, 329-330, 373, II-839-840, 859
312112 Bottled water manufacturing, pp. I-130, 143-144
312113 Ice manufacturing, p. I-495
312120 Breweries, pp. I-29, 127-130, 357, 462
312130 Wineries, pp. I-29, II-946-948
312140 Distilleries, pp. I-29, 555-558
312230 Tobacco manufacturing, pp. II-895-899

Textile Mills

313110 Fiber, yarn, & thread mills, pp. II-888, 960
313210 Broadwoven fabric mills, pp. I-339, II-888-889
313220 Narrow fabric mills & schiffli machine embroidery, p. II-888
313230 Nonwoven fabric mills, pp. II-649-650, 888-889, 948, 950
313240 Knit fabric mills, p. II-889
313310 Textile & fabric finishing mills, pp. I-186, 338
313320 Fabric coating mills, p. I-338

Textile Product Mills

314110 Carpet & rug mills, pp. I-358, 361-362
314120 Curtain & linen mills, p. I-476
314910 Textile bag & canvas mills, p. II-887
314994 Rope/cordage/twine/tire cord/tire fabric mills, p. II-782
314999 Other textile product mills, pp. I-477-478, II-714

Apparel Manufacturing

315110 Hosiery & sock mills, p. I-53
315220 Men's & boys' cut & sew apparel mfg, pp. I-52-58
315240 Women's/girls'/infants' cut & sew apparel mfg, pp. I-52-55, 57-60
315990 Apparel accessories & other apparel mfg, p. I-56

Leather & Allied Product Manufacturing

316110 Leather & hide tanning & finishing, pp. I-545-546
316210 Footwear manufacturing, pp. I-380-381
316992 Women's handbag & purse mfg, pp. I-54, 461, 568
316998 All other leather good mfg, p. I-565

Wood Product Manufacturing

321113 Sawmills, pp. I-565-566, II-955, 958
321114 Wood preservation, p. II-955
321211 Hardwood veneer & plywood mfg, pp. II-955-958
321212 Softwood veneer & plywood mfg, pp. I-566-567, II-957

321219 Reconstituted wood product mfg, pp. II-956-957
321912 Cut stock/resawing lumber/planing, p. II-955
321918 Other millwork (including flooring), pp. I-359, 361-362
321920 Wood container & pallet mfg, pp. I-537, II-691, 958
321991 Manufactured (mobile) home mfg, pp. I-490, 492
321992 Prefabricated wood building mfg, p. I-488
321999 Other wood product manufacturing, pp. I-255-256, 330, 348, 353, 542, II-959

Paper Manufacturing

322110 Pulp mills, pp. II-749-750
322121 Paper (except newsprint) mills, pp. II-693, 695-696, 898
322122 Newsprint mills, p. I-194
322130 Paperboard mills, pp. II-693-694
322211 Corrugated & solid fiber box mfg, p. I-145
322219 Other paperboard container manufacturing, pp. I-145-146
322220 Paper bag & coated & treated paper mfg, pp. I-167, 373, II-696, 879
322230 Stationery product manufacturing, pp. II-684, 862
322291 Sanitary paper product mfg, pp. II-785-789, 949-950
322299 Other converted paper product mfg, pp. II-695, 931

Printing & Related Support Activities

323111 Commercial printing (exc screen & books), pp. I-537-538, II-719, 743-744
323113 Commercial screen printing, p. II-743
323117 Books printing, p. I-141

Petroleum & Coal Products Manufacturing

324110 Petroleum refineries, pp. I-133, II-657
324121 Asphalt paving mixture & block mfg, pp. I-77-78
324122 Asphalt shingle & coating materials, pp. I-78-79
324191 Petroleum lubricating oil & grease, pp. I-124, 563-564

Chemical Manufacturing

325110 Petrochemical manufacturing, pp. I-133, 186, 188
325120 Industrial gas manufacturing, pp. I-188, 501-502
325180 Other basic inorganic chemical mfg, pp. I-185, 188, 528
325194 Cyclic crude/intermediate/gum/wood chemical mfg, pp. I-177, 183
325211 Plastics material & resin mfg, pp. I-134, II-725, 727-730
325212 Synthetic rubber manufacturing, p. II-782
325220 Artificial & synthetic fibers & filaments mfg, pp. I-351-353
325311 Nitrogenous fertilizer mfg, pp. I-182, 349-351
325312 Phosphatic fertilizer manufacturing, pp. I-349-350
325314 Fertilizer (mixing only) mfg, pp. I-350-351
325320 Pesticide, other ag chemicals, pp. I-183-186, 189
325411 Medicinal and botanical mfg, pp. I-160-161, II-870-877, 921, 929
325412 Pharmaceutical preparation mfg, pp. I-297-308, II-714
325413 In-vitro diagnostic substance mfg, pp. I-284-286
325414 Biological product manufacturing, pp. I-134-135, 425, 498, II-875-876, 921-922
325510 Paint & coating mfg, pp. II-688-690
325520 Adhesive manufacturing, pp. I-3-5
325611 Soap & other detergent mfg, pp. I-282-284, II-837-838
325612 Polish & other sanitation good mfg, pp. I-196-197
325620 Toilet preparation manufacturing, pp. I-101, 257-262, 307, 337, 386-387, 460-461, II-672-673, 706-707, 823-825
325910 Printing ink manufacturing, pp. I-506-507
325920 Explosives manufacturing, p. I-336
325991 Custom compounding of resin, p. II-654
325992 Photographic film/paper/plate mfg, p. II-721
325998 All other chemical product mfg, pp. I-13-17, 183-185, 188, 190, 559, II-727

Plastics & Rubber Products Manufacturing

326111 Plastics bag manufacturing, pp. I-373, II-681, 684
326113 Unlaminated plastics film/sheet (exc packaging), p. II-726
326121 Unlaminated plastics profile shape, p. II-726
326122 Plastics pipe & pipe fitting mfg, pp. II-724, 726
326130 Laminated plastics plate/sheet mfg, p. I-539
326160 Plastics bottle manufacturing, p. II-728
326191 Plastics plumbing fixture mfg, p. II-733
326199 Other plastics product mfg, pp. I-278, 348, 359-360, 362, 537, 565, II-681, 683, 685, 706, 725-727, 820, 877

326211 Tire manufacturing (exc retreading), pp. II-893-894
326212 Tire retreading, p. II-892
326299 All other rubber product mfg, pp. II-623, 707

Nonmetallic Mineral Product Manufacturing

327110 Pottery, ceramics, & plumbing fixture mfg, pp. I-202, II-733, 739-740, 789
327120 Clay building material & refractories mfg, pp. I-149, 175-176, 358, 361
327211 Flat glass manufacturing, pp. I-430-433
327212 Other pressed & blown glass, pp. I-431, 433
327213 Glass container manufacturing, pp. I-430, 432
327215 Glass product mfg, purchased glass, pp. I-84, 431, 434
327310 Cement manufacturing, pp. I-172-174
327320 Ready-mix concrete manufacturing, p. I-213
327331 Concrete block and brick mfg, p. I-214
327332 Concrete pipe manufacturing, p. II-723
327390 Other concrete product mfg, pp. I-88, II-650-651
327410 Lime manufacturing, p. I-554
327420 Gypsum product manufacturing, pp. I-167, 457-458, II-931
327910 Abrasive product manufacturing, pp. I-1, 196
327991 Cut stone & stone product mfg, pp. I-76, 265, 274
327992 Ground or treated mineral mfg, pp. I-453, 530
327993 Mineral wool manufacturing, pp. I-507-508, II-617
327999 Other nonmetallic mineral products, p. I-507

Primary Metal Manufacturing

331110 Iron & steel mills & ferroalloy mfg, pp. II-571, 861, 863-865
331210 Iron & steel pipe & tube mfg, pp. I-528, II-725
331222 Steel wire drawing, p. II-950
331313 Alumina refining & primary aluminum production, pp. I-45-48
331315 Aluminum sheet, plate, and foil mfg, pp. I-46, 48
331410 Nonferrous (exc aluminum) smelting & refining, pp. I-157, 255, II-821, 961
331420 Copper rolling/drawing/extruding/alloying, pp. I-46, 252-253, 255, II-954
331491 Nonferrous roll/draw/extrude, pp. II-648, 962
331492 Secondary smelt/refine/alloy, pp. I-103, II-570, 648
331511 Iron foundries, pp. I-386, II-571
331523 Nonferrous die-casting foundries, p. I-165
331524 Aluminum foundries (exc die-casting), pp. I-385-386
331529 Other nonferrous foundries (exc die-casting), pp. II-611, 785

Fabricated Metal Product Manufacturing

332111 Iron and steel forging, p. II-610
332117 Powder metallurgy part mfg, pp. II-609-610
332119 Crown, closure, & other metal stamping mfg, pp. I-163, II-607-608
332215 Metal kitchen cookware, cutlery & flatware mfg, pp. I-250-251, II-706
332216 Saw blade & handtool manufacturing, pp. II-793, 902-903
332311 Prefabricated metal bldg/components, pp. I-137, II-605
332312 Fabricated structural metal mfg, p. I-339
332321 Metal window & door mfg, pp. I-423, II-944-945
332322 Sheet metal work manufacturing, pp. I-195, 456, II-811
332323 Ornamental/architectural metal work, pp. II-673-674
332410 Power boiler & heat exchanger mfg, p. I-137
332420 Metal tank (heavy gauge) mfg, p. II-609
332431 Metal can manufacturing, pp. II-605-606
332439 Other metal container manufacturing, pp. II-607-608
332510 Hardware manufacturing, pp. I-462, 562, II-900
332613 Spring manufacturing, p. II-860
332618 Other fabricated wire product mfg, p. I-348
332722 Bolt/nut/screw/rivet/washer mfg, pp. I-137, 462, 499
332811 Metal heat treating, p. II-609
332812 Metal coating/engraving services, p. II-606
332813 Plating/polishing/anodizing, p. I-321
332911 Industrial valve manufacturing, p. II-923
332912 Fluid power valve & hose fittings, p. II-734
332913 Plumbing fixture fitting/trim mfg, pp. II-732, 734
332991 Ball and roller bearing mfg, pp. I-126-127
332992 Small arms ammunition manufacturing, pp. I-50, 454
332993 Ammunition (exc small arms) mfg, p. I-50
332994 Small arms, ordnance, & accessories mfg, pp. I-455, II-826
332999 Other fabricated metal product mfg, pp. I-253, 539, II-733

Machinery Manufacturing

333111 Farm machinery & equipment mfg, pp. I-341-343
333112 Lawn & garden equipment mfg, p. I-542

Appendix I - Industrial Classifications

333120 Construction machinery mfg, pp. I-227-229
333131 Mining machinery & equipment mfg, pp. II-617-618
333241 Food product machinery mfg, p. I-203
333242 Semiconductor machinery mfg, p. II-802
333243 Sawmill, woodwoking, & paper machinery mfg, pp. II-696, 794
333249 Other industrial machinery mfg, pp. II-731, 778, 887
333314 Optical instrument & lens mfg, pp. II-722, 884
333316 Photograph/photocopy equip mfg, pp. I-158-159, II-720
333318 Other commercial/service machinery, pp. I-158, 540, II-655-656, 697, 730, 737, 740, 775, 801, 908, 930
333413 Ind/commercial fan & blower & air purification mfg, pp. I-340, II-935
333414 Heating equip manufacturing, pp. I-468-469, II-723
333415 AC/heating equip & commercial refrig, pp. I-63, 67-68, 468-469, II-718
333511 Industrial mold manufacturing, pp. I-503-504
333514 Special die/tool/jig/fixture mfg, p. II-853
333515 Cutting/machine tool accessory mfg, p. II-608
333517 Machine tool manufacturing, p. II-569
333611 Turbine & turbine generator mfg, pp. II-916-918
333613 Mechanical pwr transmission equip, pp. I-425, II-751-752
333618 Other engine equipment mfg, pp. I-330-331
333912 Air and gas compressor mfg, pp. I-207, II-870
333921 Elevator & moving stairway mfg, pp. I-88, 321-322, 484
333922 Conveyor & conveying equipment mfg, p. I-250
333923 Overhead crane/hoist/monorail, pp. I-269-270, 322, 474, 550
333924 Industrial truck/tractor/stacker, p. I-550
333991 Power-driven handtool manufacturing, pp. II-900-902
333992 Welding & soldering equipment mfg, pp. II-939-940
333993 Packaging machinery manufacturing, p. II-687
333994 Industrial process furnace/oven mfg, p. I-539
333995 Fluid power cylinder & actuator mfg, pp. I-367, II-734
333997 Scale & balance manufacturing, p. II-794
333999 Other general purpose machinery mfg, pp. I-308, II-778-780

Computer & Electronic Product Manufacturing

334111 Electronic computer manufacturing, pp. I-210-212, II-810, 828, 937-938
334112 Computer storage device mfg, p. I-208
334118 Computer terminal & other computer peripheral mfg, pp. I-134, 209, II-889
334210 Telephone apparatus manufacturing, pp. I-168-171, II-883
334220 Radio/TV/wireless equipment mfg, pp. I-442, II-753, 790-791, 866-867, 954
334290 Other communications equip. mfg, pp. I-79, 237, 339, 462, II-645-646, 791, 799, 826-827, 882
334310 Audio and video equipment mfg, pp. I-79-81, 168, 235-239, 498, II-612, 828
334412 Bare printed circuit board mfg, pp. I-208, II-741-742
334413 Semiconductor & related device mfg, pp. I-520-521, 540, II-802-809
334416 Capacitor/resistor/coil/transformer/other mfg, p. I-162
334419 Other electronic component mfg, pp. I-290-291, II-613, 672, 692
334511 Search/detection/navigation system, pp. I-357-358, 442, II-644, 798, 809, 828
334513 Industrial measure/display/control, pp. I-88-89, 171, 288
334514 Totalizing fuel meter/count device, pp. I-498, II-612
334515 Electricity measuring/testing mfg, p. II-887
334516 Analytical laboratory instrument, pp. I-538-539
334517 Irradiation apparatus manufacturing, pp. II-595, 597
334519 Other measuring, controlling device, pp. I-197, II-879, 934
334613 Magnetic/optical recording media, p. II-760
334614 Software/CD/tape/record reproducing, pp. I-70-72, 76, 320, II-622, 636-640, 841-851, 926-928

Electrical Equip, Appliance & Component Mfg

335110 Electric lamp bulb & part mfg, pp. I-550-553
335121 Res electric light fixture mfg, pp. I-552-553
335129 Other lighting equipment mfg, pp. I-552-553
335210 Small electrical appliance manufacturing, pp. I-65-68
335220 Major household appliance mfg, pp. I-63-69, II-778
335311 Pwr/distribution/spclty transformer, pp. I-562, II-740, 878, 908
335312 Motor & generator mfg, pp. I-44, 429
335313 Switchgear & switchboard apparatus, pp. I-195, 336, 417, II-877
335314 Relay & industrial control mfg, p. II-763
335911 Storage battery manufacturing, pp. I-124-125
335912 Primary battery manufacturing, p. I-125
335921 Fiber optic cable manufacturing, pp. I-156-157

335931 Current-carrying wiring device mfg, pp. I-317, II-720, 760, 877
335932 Noncurrent-carrying wiring device, p. II-939
335991 Carbon and graphite product mfg, p. I-163
335999 Other electrical equip & component, pp. I-294, 494

Transportation Equipment Manufacturing

336111 Automobile manufacturing, pp. I-89-100
336112 Light truck/utility vehicle mfg, pp. I-89-92, 94-100
336211 Motor vehicle body manufacturing, pp. I-84, 151-153, II-914-916, 923-924
336212 Truck trailer manufacturing, p. II-907
336213 Motor home manufacturing, pp. II-761-762
336214 Travel trailer & camper mfg, pp. II-762, 906-907
336310 Gasoline engine & engine parts mfg, pp. I-83-85
336320 Motor vehicle electric/electronic equip mfg, pp. I-84, 551, 553
336330 Motor vehicle steering/suspension, p. I-85
336350 Motor vehicle transmission mfg, p. I-83
336370 Motor vehicle metal stamping, p. II-611
336390 Other motor vehicle parts mfg, pp. I-83, 85
336411 Aircraft manufacturing, pp. I-17-21, II-920
336412 Aircraft engine & engine parts mfg, pp. I-21-23
336413 Other aircraft parts & equip mfg, p. I-24
336414 Guided missile & space vehicle mfg, pp. I-278, II-618
336510 Railroad rolling stock mfg, pp. II-754-755
336611 Ship building and repairing, p. II-819
336612 Boat building, pp. I-136-137
336991 Motorcycle/bicycle/parts mfg, pp. I-131-132, II-629-631
336992 Military armored vehicle/component, p. I-73
336999 Other transporation equipment mfg, pp. I-29, II-708

Furniture & Related Product Manufacturing

337110 Wood kitchen cabinet & countertop, p. I-156
337121 Upholstered household furniture mfg, pp. I-411, 413-414, 476, II-955
337122 Nonupholstered wood furniture, pp. I-411, 414
337124 Metal household furniture mfg, pp. I-411-414
337125 Household furniture, pp. I-410-411, 414
337127 Institutional furniture mfg, pp. I-410-412
337211 Wood office furniture manufacturing, pp. I-410, 414
337212 Custom architectural wood/millwork, p. II-955
337214 Office furniture (exc wood) mfg, pp. I-414, II-955
337910 Mattress manufacturing, pp. I-411, 413, 476

Miscellaneous Manufacturing

339112 Surgical & medical instrument mfg, pp. II-594, 598-599, 602
339113 Surgical appliance & supplies mfg, pp. II-594-603, 925
339115 Ophthalmic goods manufacturing, pp. I-239-240, 547, II-671, 870
339116 Dental laboratories, p. I-281
339910 Jewelry & silverware manufacturing, pp. I-435, 531-532, 568, II-703, 822-823
339920 Sporting & athletic goods mfg, pp. II-854-856
339930 Doll, toy, & game manufacturing, pp. I-472, II-904-906, 926-928
339940 Office supplies (exc paper) manufacturing, pp. I-75, II-959
339950 Sign manufacturing, pp. I-546, II-820-821
339991 Gasket/packing/sealing device mfg, p. I-424
339992 Musical instrument manufacturing, pp. II-642-643
339994 Broom, brush, and mop mfg, pp. I-149-150, 262, II-673
339995 Burial casket manufacturing, p. I-165
339999 All other miscellaneous mfg, pp. I-102, 159, 310, 423, 550, II-571, 708, 732

Merchant Wholesalers, Durable Goods

423220 Home furnishing merchant wholesalers, pp. I-363, 483
423310 Lumber/plywood/millwork/wood panel, p. I-150
423320 Brick, stone & related construction material, p. I-150
423330 Roofing, siding, and insulation material, p. I-150
423410 Photographic equipment & supplies, p. II-721
423450 Medical/dental/hospital equipment & supplies, p. II-600
423510 Metal service centers & other metal wholesalers, p. II-610
423610 Electrical equipment & wiring supplies & related, p. I-320
423740 Refrigeration equipment & supplies, p. II-763
423820 Farm & garden machinery & equipment, p. I-341
423830 Industrial machinery & equipment, p. I-503
423920 Toy & hobby goods & supplies, p. II-904
423990 Other misc durable goods merchant wholesalers, p. II-626

Merchant Wholesalers, Nondurable Goods

424130 Industrial & personal service paper, p. II-697
424340 Footwear merchant wholesalers, p. I-383
424410 General line grocery merchant wholesalers, pp. I-378, 452
424420 Packaged frozen food merchant wholesalers, p. I-388
424450 Confectionery merchant wholesalers, p. I-214
424460 Fish & seafood merchant wholesalers, p. I-353
424470 Meat & meat product merchant wholesalers, p. II-593
424480 Fresh fruit & vegetable merchant wholesalers, p. I-399
424610 Plastics materials & basic forms & shapes, p. II-731
424690 Other chemical & allied products, pp. I-182, 186-187
424710 Petroleum bulk stations and terminals, p. II-878
424820 Wine & distilled alcoholic beverages, p. II-948
424930 Flowers, nursery stock, & florists' supplies, p. I-364
424950 Paint, varnish, & supplies, p. II-687

Wholesale Electronic Markets, Agents, & Brokers

425120 Wholesale trade agents and brokers, p. I-247

Motor Vehicle & Parts Dealers

441110 New car dealers, p. I-82
441120 Used car dealers, pp. I-81-82
441222 Boat dealers, p. I-136
441310 Automotive parts/accessories stores, p. I-85
441320 Tire dealers, pp. II-891-892

Furniture & Home Furnishings Stores

442110 Furniture stores, pp. I-415-417
442210 Floor covering stores, pp. I-362-363, 487
442291 Window treatment stores, p. I-483
442299 All other home furnishings stores, pp. I-480-482, 487, 416, 477-479

Electronics & Appliance Stores

443141 Household appliance stores, pp. I-61-62
443142 Electronics stores, pp. I-70-71, 168, 210, 239

Bldg Material & Garden Equip & Supp Dealers

444110 Home centers, p. I-475
444120 Paint and wallpaper stores, p. II-690
444130 Hardware stores, p. II-732
444190 Other building material dealers, p. I-475
444220 Nursery and garden centers, pp. I-16, 543

Food & Beverage Stores

445110 Supermarkets & other grocery stores, pp. I-445-452, II-670-671
445210 Meat markets, p. II-593
445220 Fish and seafood markets, p. II-797
445230 Fruit and vegetable markets, pp. I-399, 408
445292 Confectionery and nut stores, p. I-214
445299 All other specialty food stores, p. I-160
445310 Beer, wine, and liquor stores, p. I-29

Health & Personal Care Stores

446110 Pharmacies and drug stores, pp. I-294-297, II-719
446120 Cosmetics & perfume stores, p. I-263
446130 Optical goods stores, p. II-672
446191 Food (health) supplement stores, pp. I-467, II-928
446199 Other health & personal care stores, p. II-644

Gasoline Stations

447110 Gas stations w/convenience stores, pp. I-383-385, 424
447190 Other gasoline stations, p. I-424

Clothing & Clothing Accessories Stores

448120 Women's clothing stores, pp. I-60-61
448140 Family clothing stores, p. I-60
448210 Shoe stores, pp. I-381-382
448310 Jewelry stores, pp. I-532-533

Sporting Goods, Hobby, Book, & Music Stores

451110 Sporting goods stores, p. II-857
451120 Hobby, toy, and game stores, pp. I-472, II-906, 927
451140 Musical instrument/supplies stores, p. II-641
451211 Book stores, pp. I-138, II-823

General Merchandise Stores

452210 Department stores, pp. I-281, II-772-775
452311 Warehouse clubs and superstores, pp. I-425-429, II-772-775
452319 All other gen merchandise stores, pp. I-247-248, 292, 425-429, II-772-775, 931

Miscellaneous Store Retailers

453110 Florists, p. I-364
453310 Used merchandise stores, p. II-798
453910 Pet and pet supplies stores, pp. II-715-716
453920 Art dealers, pp. I-73-75
453991 Tobacco stores, p. II-899
453998 Other stores (exc tobacco stores), pp. II-613, 910

Nonstore Retailers

454210 Vending machine operators, pp. II-924-925
454310 Fuel dealers, pp. I-30-44, II-747, 878
454390 Other direct selling establishments, pp. I-288-289

Air Transportation

481111 Scheduled passenger air transport, pp. I-24-28, II-634
481112 Scheduled freight air transport, p. II-634

Rail Transportation

482111 Line-haul railroads, p. II-756

Water Transportation

483111 Deep sea freight transportation, pp. II-813-814, 816-817
483112 Deep sea passenger transportation, p. I-272
483113 Coastal/great lakes freight transport, p. II-812
483114 Coastal/great lakes passenger transport, pp. I-272, II-574, 935-936
483211 Inland water freight transportation, pp. II-813, 815
483212 Inland water passenger transport, p. II-574

Truck Transportation

484110 General freight trucking, local, p. II-812
484121 Gen freight truck/long-distance, pp. II-812, 911-913
484122 Freight/long-distance/<truckload, pp. II-911-913
484230 Special freight trucking, long, pp. II-878, 912, 931

Transit & Ground Passenger Transportation

485112 Commuter rail systems, pp. II-572, 576
485320 Limousine service, pp. I-555, II-575
485410 School & employee bus transport, pp. II-575, 795
485510 Charter bus industry, pp. II-572-573, 576
485999 Other transit/ground passenger transport, pp. II-573-575, 777

Pipeline Transportation

486110 Pipeline transport of crude oil, p. II-663
486210 Pipeline transport of natural gas, p. II-663

Scenic & Sightseeing Transportation

487110 Scenic/sightseeing transport, land, p. II-819
487210 Scenic/sightseeing transport, water, p. II-819

Transportation Support Activities

488111 Air traffic control, p. I-28
488119 Other airport operations, p. I-29
488310 Port and harbor operations, pp. II-736-737, 813, 815, 817
488410 Motor vehicle towing, p. II-629
488490 Road transport support activities, pp. II-899-900
488510 Freight transportation arrangement, pp. II-814-816
488999 Other transport support activities, p. II-814

Postal Service

491110 Postal service, p. II-737

Couriers & Messengers

492110 Couriers & express delivery services, pp. II-576, 812, 814, 817-818
492210 Local messengers/local delivery, pp. I-374-377, II-576

Warehousing & Storage

493110 General warehousing and storage, pp. II-866, 933
493120 Refrigerated warehousing storage, pp. II-932-933
493130 Farm product warehousing storage, p. II-932
493190 Other warehousing and storage, p. II-853

Publishing Industries (exc Internet)

511110 Newspaper publishers, pp. II-647, 748
511120 Periodical publishers, pp. I-205, II-569-570, 748

511130 Book publishers, pp. I-139-142, II-748
511140 Directory & mailing list publishers, pp. I-289-290
511191 Greeting card publishers, pp. I-444-445
511210 Software publishers, pp. I-70-72, 76, 320, II-622, 841-851, 926-928

Motion Picture & Sound Recording Industries

512110 Motion picture & video production, pp. I-309, 332-333, II-626-629, 885-887
512120 Motion picture & video distribution, p. II-626
512131 Motion picture theaters, pp. II-632-634
512132 Drive-in motion picture theaters, p. II-632
512191 Teleproduction/other postproduction, p. II-883
512230 Music publishers, p. II-748
512240 Sound recording studios, p. II-851
512250 Record production & distribution, pp. II-636-640

Broadcasting (except Internet)

515111 Radio networks, pp. I-79, II-641, 734-736
515112 Radio stations, pp. I-79, II-641, 734-736, 753
515120 Television broadcasting, pp. II-884-885
515210 Cable & other subscription programming, pp. II-675-680, 700-701

Telecommunications

517311 Wired telecommunications carriers, pp. I-101, 311-316, 504-505, 524, II-604, 641, 670, 745, 883, 910
517312 Wireless telecommunications (exc satellite), pp. II-950-954
517919 All other telecommunications, pp. I-504-505

Data Processing, Hosting, and Related Services

518210 Data processing, hosting, and related services, pp. I-276, II-877

Other Information Services

519120 Libraries and archives, pp. I-547-548
519130 Internet publishing/broadcasting & web portals, pp. I-205, 522-525, 559, II-570, 620-622, 647, 748

Monetary Authorities-Central Bank

521110 Monetary authorities-central bank, pp. II-623-624

Credit Intermediation Activities

522110 Commercial banking, pp. I-109-123
522130 Credit unions, p. I-271
522210 Credit card issuing, pp. I-109, II-604, 701-703
522220 Sales financing, pp. I-559-561
522292 Real estate credit, pp. I-560, II-624-626
522298 Nondepository credit intermediation, p. I-561
522320 Financial transaction processing, pp. I-316, II-764
522390 Credit intermediation activity, p. I-273

Security, Commodity Contracts & Like Activity

523110 Investment banking & securities, pp. I-526-527
523130 Commodity contracts dealing, p. I-206
523140 Commodity contracts brokerage, p. I-206
523210 Securities and commodity exchanges, p. I-335
523920 Portfolio management, p. I-528
523930 Investment advice, pp. I-353, 528

Insurance Carriers & Related Activities

524113 Direct life insurance carriers, pp. I-509-510
524114 Direct health/medical ins carriers, pp. I-509-511
524126 Direct property/casualty insurance, pp. I-508-519
524128 Other direct insurance carriers, pp. I-515-516, 518, 520
524210 Insurance agencies and brokerages, pp. I-508, 510, 519
524298 All other insurance related activities, p. I-510

Funds, Trusts & Other Financial Vehicles

525110 Pension funds, pp. II-704-705
525910 Open-end investment funds, p. I-527

Real Estate

531110 Lessors residential bldgs/dwellings, pp. I-491-492
531130 Miniwarehouse/self-storage lessors, pp. II-801, 866
531210 Real estate agents/brokers offices, pp. II-757-759
531311 Residential property managers, p. I-492
531320 Offices of real estate appraisers, pp. II-759-760

Rental & Leasing Services

532111 Passenger car rental, p. I-86
532112 Passenger car leasing, pp. I-82, 96
532210 Consumer electronics rental, p. II-764

532281 Formal wear and costume rental, p. I-385
532282 Video tape and disc rental, p. I-308
532284 Recreational goods rental, p. II-761
532310 General rental centers, p. II-764
532411 Commercial transport equip leasing, pp. I-23, 544
532412 Heavy machinery rental & leasing, pp. I-240, 470-471
532420 Office equipment rental & leasing, p. I-545
532490 Other com/industrial equip rental, pp. I-469, 545, II-691

Intangible Asset Lessors (exc Copyrighted Works)

533110 Intangible asset lessors (exc copyrighted works), pp. I-387-388, II-699

Professional, Scientific & Technical Services

541110 Offices of lawyers, pp. I-250, 547
541211 Offices of CPAs, p. I-2
541213 Tax preparation services, p. II-880
541310 Architectural services, p. I-72
541330 Engineering services, p. I-282
541340 Drafting services, p. I-293
541360 Surveying & mapping services (geophysical), p. II-920
541410 Interior design services, p. I-522
541420 Industrial design services, p. I-499
541512 Computer systems design services, pp. I-205, 276, II-877
541513 Computer facilities management, p. I-208
541519 Other computer related services, p. II-877
541611 Admin & general management services, p. I-234
541613 Marketing consulting services, p. I-234
541614 Process/logistics services, p. II-817
541690 Scientific & tech consult services, pp. I-234, 335, II-939
541714 Biotechnology R&D (exc nanotechnology), p. II-766
541720 Social science & humanities R&D, p. II-765
541810 Advertising agencies, pp. I-7-8
541820 Public relations agencies, p. II-748
541840 Media representatives, pp. I-5-13, II-735
541850 Display advertising, pp. I-7, 9, 11-12
541910 Marketing research & polling, pp. II-765-766
541922 Commercial photography, p. II-722
541930 Translation/interpretation services, p. II-908
541940 Veterinary services, p. II-925

Management Companies & Enterprises

551112 Offices of other holding companies, p. I-475

Administrative & Support Services

561312 Executive search services, p. I-335
561320 Temporary help services, pp. II-860-861
561431 Private mail centers, pp. II-746-747, 827
561439 Other business service centers, pp. I-291, II-827
561440 Collection agencies, p. I-277
561450 Credit bureaus, p. I-270
561491 Repossession services, p. II-765
561492 Court reporting/stenotype services, p. I-265
561510 Travel agencies, pp. I-434, 486, II-671, 903, 909-910
561520 Tour operators, pp. II-903, 909
561611 Investigation services, pp. I-525-526
561613 Armored car services, p. I-164
561621 Security services (exc locksmiths), p. II-800
561622 Locksmiths, p. I-562
561710 Exterminating/pest control services, p. II-708
561720 Janitorial services, p. I-531
561790 Other building & dwelling services, p. I-246
561910 Packaging and labeling services, pp. II-685-686
561920 Convention/trade show organizers, pp. I-248-249, 334, II-928

Waste Management & Remediation Services

562211 Hazardous waste treatment/disposal, pp. I-462, II-651
562212 Solid waste landfill, p. II-934
562910 Remediation services, p. II-764

Educational Services

611110 Elementary and secondary schools, pp. I-317, 331, II-795
611210 Junior colleges, p. II-795
611410 Business and secretarial schools, p. I-153
611430 Professional & management training, pp. II-907-908
611519 Other technical and trade schools, p. II-669
611610 Fine arts schools, p. I-276
611691 Exam preparation and tutoring, p. II-918
611710 Educational support services, p. II-918

Ambulatory Health Care Services

621111 Physician offices (exc mental health), pp. I-463, 467
621112 Physician/mental health specialist, p. I-466
621210 Offices of dentists, p. I-466
621310 Offices of chiropractors, p. I-466
621330 Mental health practitioners, pp. I-465-466
621340 Therapists and audiologists, p. I-466
621410 Family planning centers, p. I-340

621492 Kidney dialysis centers, p. I-463
621512 Diagnostic imaging centers, p. I-284
621610 Home health care services, p. I-464
621910 Ambulance services, p. I-49
621991 Blood and organ banks, pp. I-135, II-600
621999 Ambulatory health care services, p. I-464

Hospitals

622110 General medical/surgical hospitals, pp. I-463-465
622210 Psychiatric/substance abuse hospitals, pp. I-464, 467
622310 Specialty hospitals, pp. I-464-465

Nursing & Residential Care Facilities

623110 Nursing care facilities, p. I-493
623210 Res mental retardation facilities, p. II-766
623311 Continuing care retirement community, p. I-493

Social Assistance

624210 Community food services, p. I-206
624230 Emergency and other relief services, p. I-322
624410 Child day care services, p. I-190

Perform Arts, Spectator Sports & Related

711110 Theater companies & dinner theaters, p. II-889
711130 Musical groups and artists, p. I-213
711211 Sports teams and clubs, pp. II-857-859
711212 Racetracks, p. II-753
711219 Other spectator sports, p. I-317
711310 Arts/sports promoters w/facilities, pp. I-72, 212, 332, 418, 420, II-889
711320 Arts/sports promoters wo/facilities, pp. I-212, II-889
711410 Agents & managers for public figures, p. I-15

Museums, Historical Sites & Like Institutions

712110 Museums, p. II-635
712120 Historical sites, pp. I-471-472
712130 Zoos and botanical gardens, p. II-963
712190 Nature parks/similar institutions, p. II-698

Amusement, Gambling, & Recreation Industries

713110 Amusement and theme parks, pp. I-50-51, II-935
713210 Casinos (except casino hotels), pp. I-418-419, 421-422
713290 Other gambling industries, pp. I-340, 419-423

713910 Golf courses and country clubs, pp. I-436, II-745
713940 Fitness/recreational sports centers, pp. I-456-457, II-853
713950 Bowling centers, p. I-145
713990 Amusement/recreation industries, pp. I-334, 422

Accomodation

721110 Hotels (exc casino) & motels, pp. I-476, 484-486, II-811
721191 Bed-and-breakfast inns, p. I-127
721214 Recreational & vacation camps, p. II-761
721310 Rooming and boarding houses, pp. I-476, II-781

Food Services & Drinking Places

722310 Food service contractors, pp. I-378-380, II-770
722320 Caterers, p. I-377
722330 Mobile food services, p. II-619
722410 Drinking places (alcoholic beverages), p. II-649
722513 Limited-service restaurants, pp. I-203, II-620, 766-772
722515 Snack & nonalcoholic beverage bars, pp. I-203-205, II-769

Repair & Maintenance

811111 General automotive repair, p. I-87
811112 Automotive exhaust system repair, p. I-86
811113 Automotive transmission repair, p. I-87
811121 Auto body/interior repair/maintain, pp. I-86-87
811122 Auto glass replacement shops, p. I-87
811192 Car washes, pp. I-163-164
811212 Office machine repair & maintain, p. I-207
811412 Appliance repair & maintenance, p. I-61
811420 Reupholstery and furniture repair, p. I-415

Personal & Laundry Services

812111 Barber shops, p. I-123
812112 Beauty salons, pp. I-127, 460
812113 Nail salons, p. I-460
812191 Diet and weight reducing centers, p. I-287
812210 Funeral homes & services, p. I-277
812220 Cemeteries and crematories, p. I-277
812310 Coin-operated laundries, p. I-541
812320 Dry cleaning & laundry services, p. I-308
812331 Linen supply, p. II-888
812332 Industrial launderers, pp. I-502-503
812922 One-hour photofinishing, p. II-720

812930 Parking lots and garages, pp. I-88, II-697
812990 All other personal services, pp. I-461, II-879-880

Religious/Grantmaking/Prof/Like Organizations

813110 Religious organizations, p. II-763
813311 Human rights organizations, pp. I-177-178
813312 Environ/conserve/wildlife org, p. I-333
813319 Other social advocacy organizations, pp. I-177-178, 271
813910 Business associations, p. I-153
813930 Labor unions/similar organizations, p. II-919
813940 Political organizations, pp. I-561-562
813990 Other similar organizations, p. I-483

General Government Support

921130 Public finance activities, p. I-440

Justice, Public Order & Safety Activities

922120 Police protection, p. II-736
922130 Legal counsel and prosecution, p. I-439
922140 Correctional institutions, p. II-745

Administration of Human Resource Programs

923110 Admin of education programs, p. I-438
923130 Human resource program admin, pp. I-439-441
923140 Administration of veterans' affairs, p. I-441

Administration of Environmental Quality Programs

924120 Admin of conservation programs, p. I-440

Administration of Housing & Community Development

925110 Administration of housing programs, p. I-439

Administration of Economic Programs

926110 General economic program admin, pp. I-437-439, 441-442
926130 Utility regulation & administration, p. I-438
926140 Agricultural marketing regulations, p. I-436

Space Research & Technology

927110 Space research & technology, pp. I-437, II-791, 852

National Security & International Affairs

928110 National security, pp. I-278-280, 440

APPENDIX I - INDUSTRIAL CLASSIFICATIONS
ISIC COVERAGE

This appendix lists the International Standard Industrial Classification Codes (ISICs). Entries in the body of the book are arranged according to topic. Products may be located using either the SIC Coverage listing beginning on page 1141 or the Products, Services, Names, and Issues Index beginning on page 1045.

0110	Growing of crops; market gardening; horticulture
0111	Growing of cereals and other crops nec
0112	Growing of vegetables, horticultural specialties and nursery products
0113	Growing of fruits, nuts, beverage and spice crops
0120	Farming of animals
0121	Farming of cattle, sheep, goats, horses, asses, mules and hinnies; dairy farming
0122	Other animal farming; production of animal products nec
0130	Growing of crops combined with farming of animals (mixed farming)
0140	Agricultural and animal husbandry service activities, except veterinary activities
0150	Hunting, trapping and game propagation including related service activities
0200	Forestry, logging, and related service activities
0500	Fishing, operation of fish hatcheries and fish farms; service activities incidental to fishing
1010	Mining and agglomeration of hard coal
1020	Mining and agglomeration of lignite
1030	Extraction and agglomeration of peat
1110	Extraction of crude petroleum and natural gas
1120	Service activities incidental to oil and gas extraction excluding surveying
1200	Mining of uranium and thorium ores
1310	Mining of iron ores
1320	Mining of non-ferrous metal ores, except uranium and thorium ores
1410	Quarrying of stone, sand and clay
1420	Mining and quarrying, nec
1421	Mining of chemical and fertilizer minerals
1422	Extraction of salt
1429	Other mining and quarrying nec
1510	Production, processing, and preservation of meat, fish, fruit, vegetables, oils and fats
1511	Production, processing and preserving of meat and meat products
1512	Processing and preserving of fish and fish products
1513	Processing and preserving of fruits and vegetables
1514	Manufacture of vegetable and animal oils and fats
1520	Manufacture of dairy products
1530	Manufacture of grain mill products, starches and starch products, and prepared animal feeds
1531	Manufacture of grain mill products
1532	Manufacture of starches and starch products
1533	Manufacture of prepared animal feeds
1540	Manufacture of other food products
1541	Manufacture of bakery products
1542	Manufacture of sugar
1543	Manufacture of cocoa, chocolate, and sugar confectionery
1544	Manufacture of macaroni, noodles, couscous and similar farinaceous products
1549	Manufacture of other food products nec
1550	Manufacture of beverages
1551	Distilling, rectifying and blending of spirits; ethyl alcohol production from fermented materials
1552	Manufacture of wines
1553	Manufacture of malt liquors and malt
1554	Manufacture of soft drinks; production of mineral waters
1600	Manufacture of tobacco products
1710	Spinning, weaving and finishing of textiles
1711	Preparation and spinning of textile fibers; weaving of textiles
1712	Finishing of textiles
1720	Manufacture of other textiles
1721	Manufacture of made-up textile articles, except apparel
1722	Manufacture of carpets and rugs
1723	Manufacture of cordage, rope, twine and netting
1729	Manufacture of other textiles nec
1730	Manufacture of knitted and crocheted fabrics and articles
1810	Manufacture of wearing apparel, except fur apparel

1820	Dressing and dyeing of fur; manufacture of articles of fur
1910	Tanning and dressing of leather; manufacture of luggage, handbags, saddlery and harness
1911	Tanning and dressing of leather
1912	Manufacture of luggage, handbags and the like, saddlery and harness
1920	Manufacture of footwear
2010	Sawmilling and planning of wood
2020	Manufacture of products of wood, cork, straw and plaiting materials
2021	Manufacture of veneer sheets; manufacture of plywood, laminboard, particle board and other panels and boards
2022	Manufacture of builders' carpentry and joinery
2023	Manufacture of wood containers
2029	Manufacture of other products of wood; manufacture of articles of cork, straw and plaiting materials
2101	Manufacture of pulp, paper, and paperboard
2102	Manufacture of corrugated paper and paperboard and of containers of paper and paperboard
2109	Manufacture of other articles of paper and paperboard
2210	Publishing
2211	Publishing of books, brochures, musical books, and other publications
2212	Publishing of newspapers, journals, and periodicals
2213	Publishing of recorded media
2219	Other publishing
2220	Printing and service activities related to printing
2221	Printing
2222	Service activities related to printing
2230	Reproduction of recorded media
2310	Manufacture of coke oven products
2320	Manufacturer of refined petroleum products
2330	Processing of nuclear fuel
2410	Manufacture of basic chemicals
2411	Manufacture of basic chemicals, except fertilizers and nitrogen compounds
2412	Manufacture of fertilizers and nitrogen compounds
2413	Manufacture of plastics in primary forms and of synthetic rubber
2420	Manufacture of other chemical products
2421	Manufacture of pesticides and other agro-chemical products
2422	Manufacture of paints, varnishes, and similar coatings, printing ink and mastics
2423	Manufacture of pharmaceuticals, medicinal chemicals, and botanical products
2424	Manufacture of soap and detergents, cleaning and polishing preparations, perfumes and toilet preparations
2429	Manufacture of other chemical products nec
2430	Manufacture of man-made fibers
2510	Manufacture of rubber products
2511	Manufacture of rubber tires and tubes; retreading and rebuilding of rubber tires
2519	Manufacture of other rubber products
2520	Manufacture of plastic products
2610	Manufacture of glass and glass products
2690	Manufacture of non-metallic minerals products nec
2691	Manufacture of non-structural non-refractory ceramic ware
2692	Manufacture of refractory ceramic products
2693	Manufacture of structural non-refractory clay and ceramic products
2694	Manufacture of cement, lime and plaster
2695	Manufacture of articles of concrete, cement and plaster
2696	Cutting, shaping, and finishing of stone
2699	Manufacture of other non-metallic mineral products nec
2710	Manufacture of basic iron and steel
2720	Manufacture of basic precious and non-ferrous metals
2730	Casting of metals
2731	Casting of iron and steel
2732	Casting of non-ferrous metals
2810	Manufacture of structural metal products, tanks, reservoirs and steam generators
2811	Manufacture of structural metal products
2812	Manufacture of tanks, reservoirs and containers of metals
2813	Manufacture of steam generators, except central heating hot water boilers
2890	Manufacture of other fabricated metal products; metal working service activities
2891	Forging, pressing, stamping and roll-forming of metal; powder metallurgy
2892	Treatment and coating of metals; general mechanical engineering on a fee or contract basis
2893	Manufacture of cutlery, hand tools, and general hardware
2899	Manufacture of other fabricated metal products nec
2910	Manufacture of general purpose machinery
2911	Manufacture of engines and turbines, except aircraft, vehicle and cycle engines

2912	Manufacture of pumps, compressors, taps, and valves	3320	Manufacture of optical instruments and photographic equipment
2913	Manufacture of bearings, gears, gearing and driving elements	3330	Manufacture of watches and clocks
		3410	Manufacture of motor vehicles
2914	Manufacture of ovens, furnaces and furnace burners	3420	Manufacture of bodies (coachwork) for motor vehicles; manufacture of trailers and semi-trailers
2915	Manufacture of lifting and handling equipment	3430	Manufacture of parts and accessories for motor vehicles and their engines
2919	Manufacture of other general purpose machinery		
2920	Manufacture of special purpose machinery	3510	Building and repairing of ships and boats
2921	Manufacture of agricultural and forestry machinery	3511	Building and repairing of ships
		3512	Building and repairing of pleasure and sporting boats
2922	Manufacture of machine-tools		
2923	Manufacture of machinery for metallurgy	3520	Manufacture of railway and tramway locomotives and rolling stock
2924	Manufacture of machinery for mining, quarrying and construction		
		3530	Manufacture of aircraft and spacecraft
2925	Manufacture of machinery for food, beverage, and tobacco processing	3590	Manufacture of transport equipment nec
		3591	Manufacture of motorcycles
2926	Manufacture of machinery for textile, apparel and leather production	3592	Manufacture of bicycles and invalid carriages
		3599	Manufacture of other transport equipment nec
2927	Manufacture of weapons and ammunition	3610	Manufacture of furniture
2929	Manufacture of other special purpose machinery	3690	Manufacturing nec
2930	Manufacture of domestic appliances nec	3691	Manufacture of jewelry and related articles
3000	Manufacture of office, accounting, and computing machinery	3692	Manufacture of musical instruments
		3693	Manufacture of sports goods
3110	Manufacture of electric motors, generators and transformers	3694	Manufacture of games and toys
		3699	Other manufacturing nec
3120	Manufacture of electricity distribution and control apparatus	3710	Recycling of metal waste and scrap
		3720	Recycling of non-metal waste and scrap
3130	Manufacture of insulated wire and cable	4010	Production, collection, and distribution of electricity
3140	Manufacture of accumulators, primary cells, and primary batteries		
		4020	Manufacture of gas; distribution of gaseous fuels through mains
3150	Manufacture of electric lamps and lighting equipment		
		4030	Steam and hot water supply
3190	Manufacture of other electrical equipment nec	4100	Collection, purification, and distribution of water
3210	Manufacture of electronic valves and tubes and other electronic components	4510	Site preparation
		4520	Building of complete constructions or parts thereof; civil engineering
3220	Manufacture of television and radio transmitters and apparatus for line telephony and line telegraphy		
		4530	Building installation
		4540	Building completion
3230	Manufacture of television and radio receivers, sound or video recording or reproducing apparatus, and associated goods	4550	Renting of construction or demolition equipment with operator
		5010	Sale of motor vehicles
3310	Manufacture of medical appliances and instruments and appliances for measuring, checking, testing, navigating, and other purposes, except optical instruments	5020	Maintenance and repair of motor vehicles
		5030	Sale of motor vehicle parts and accessories
		5040	Sale, maintenance and repair of motorcycles and related parts and accessories
		5050	Retail sale of automotive fuel
3311	Manufacture of medical and surgical equipment and orthopedic appliances	5110	Wholesale on a fee or contract basis
		5120	Wholesale of agricultural raw materials, live animals, food, beverages and tobacco
3312	Manufacture of instruments and appliances for measuring, checking, testing, navigating, and other purposes, except industrial process control equipment		
		5121	Wholesale of agricultural raw materials and live animals
		5122	Wholesale of food, beverages, and tobacco
3313	Manufacture of industrial process control equipment	5130	Wholesale of household goods

5131	Wholesale of textiles, clothing, and footwear
5139	Wholesale of other household goods
5140	Wholesale of non-agricultural intermediate products, waste and scrap
5141	Wholesale of solid, liquid and gaseous fuels and related products
5142	Wholesale of metals and metal ores
5143	Wholesale of construction materials, hardware, plumbing and heating equipment and supplies
5149	Wholesale of other intermediate products, waste and scrap
5150	Wholesale of machinery, equipment, and supplies
5190	Other wholesale
5210	Non-specialized retail trade in stores
5211	Retail sale in non-specialized stores with food, beverages, or tobacco predominating
5219	Other retail sale in non-specialized stores
5220	Retail sale of food, beverages, and tobacco in specialized stores
5230	Other retail trade of new goods in specialized stores
5231	Retail sale of pharmaceutical and medical goods, cosmetic and toilet articles
5232	Retail sale of textiles, clothing, footwear, and leather goods
5233	Retail sale of household appliances, articles, and equipment
5234	Retail sale of hardware, paints and glass
5239	Other retail sale in specialized stores
5240	Retail sale of second-hand goods in stores
5250	Retail trade not in stores
5251	Retail sale via mail-order houses
5252	Retail sale via stalls and markets
5259	Other non-store retail sale
5260	Repair of personal and household goods
5510	Hotels; camping sites and other provision of short-stay accommodation
5520	Restaurants, bars and canteens
6010	Transport via railways
6020	Other land transport
6021	Other scheduled passenger land transport
6022	Other non-scheduled passenger land transport
6023	Freight transport by road
6030	Transport via pipelines
6110	Sea and coastal water transport
6120	Inland water transport
6210	Scheduled air transport
6220	Non-scheduled air transport
6300	Supporting and auxiliary transport activities; activities of travel agencies
6301	Cargo handling
6302	Storage and warehousing
6303	Other supporting transport activities
6304	Activities of travel agencies and tour operators; tourist assistance activities nec
6309	Activities of other transport agencies
6410	Post and courier activities
6411	National post activities
6412	Courier activities other than national post activities
6420	Telecommunications
6510	Monetary intermediation
6511	Central banking
6519	Other monetary intermediation
6559	Other financial intermediation nec
6590	Other financial leasing
6591	Financial leasing
6592	Other credit granting
6600	Insurance and pension funding, except compulsory social security
6601	Life insurance
6602	Pension funding
6603	Non-life insurance
6710	Activities auxiliary to financial intermediation, except insurance and pension funding
6711	Administration of financial markets
6712	Security dealing activities
6719	Activities auxiliary to financial intermediation nec
6720	Activities auxiliary to insurance and pension funding
7010	Real estate activities with own or leased property
7020	Real estate activities on a fee or contract basis
7110	Renting of transport equipment
7111	Renting of land transport equipment
7112	Renting of water transport equipment
7113	Renting of air transport equipment
7120	Renting of other machinery and equipment
7121	Renting of agricultural machinery and equipment
7122	Renting of construction and civil engineering machinery and equipment
7123	Renting of office machinery and equipment (including computers)
7129	Renting of other machinery and equipment nec
7130	Renting of personal and household goods nec
7210	Hardware consultancy
7220	Software consultancy and supply
7230	Data processing
7240	Database activities
7250	Maintenance and repair of office, accounting and computing machinery
7290	Other computer related activities
7310	Research and experimental development on natural sciences and engineering (NSE)

7320	Research and experimental development on social sciences and humanities (SSH)	8510	Human health activities
7410	Legal, accounting, bookkeeping, and auditing activities; tax consultancy; market research and public opinion polling; business and management consultancy	8511	Hospital activities
		8512	Medical and dental practice activities
		8519	Other human health activities
		8520	Veterinary activities
		8530	Social work activities
7411	Legal activities	8531	Social work with accommodation
7412	Accounting, book-keeping and auditing activities; tax consultancy	8532	Social work without accommodation
		9000	Sewage and refuse disposal, sanitation, and similar activities
7413	Market research and public opinion polling	9110	Activities of business, employers and professional organizations
7414	Business and management consultancy activities		
7420	Architectural, engineering and other technical activities	9111	Activities of business and employers' organizations
7421	Architectural and engineering activities and related technical consultancy	9112	Activities of professional organizations
		9120	Activities of trade unions
7422	Technical testing and analysis	9190	Activities of other membership organizations
7430	Advertising	9191	Activities of religious organizations
7490	Business activities nec	9192	Activities of political organizations
7491	Labor recruitment and provision of personnel	9199	Activities of other membership organizations nec
7492	Investigation and security activities	9210	Motion picture, radio, television and other entertainment activities
7493	Building-cleaning activities		
7494	Photographic activities	9211	Motion picture and video production and distribution
7495	Packaging activities		
7499	Other business activities nec	9212	Motion picture projection
7510	Administration of the State and the economic and social policy of the community	9213	Radio and television activities
		9214	Dramatic arts, music, and other arts activities
7511	General (overall) public service activities	9219	Other entertainment activities nec
7512	Regulation of the activities of agencies that provide health care, education, cultural service, and other social services, excluding social security	9220	News agencies activities
		9230	Library, archives, museums and other cultural activities
		9231	Library and archives activities
		9232	Museums activities and preservation of historical sites and buildings
7513	Regulation of and contribution to more efficient operation of business		
		9233	Botanical and zoological gardens and nature reserves activities
7514	Ancillary service activities for the Government as a whole		
		9240	Sporting and other recreational activities
7520	Provision of services to the community as a whole	9241	Sporting activities
		9249	Other recreational activities
7521	Foreign affairs	9300	Other service activities
7522	Defense activities	9301	Washing and (dry-) cleaning of textile and fur products
7523	Public order and safety activities		
7530	Compulsory social security activities	9302	Hairdressing and other beauty treatment
8010	Primary education		
8020	Secondary education	9303	Funeral and related activities
8021	General secondary education	9309	Other service activities nec
8022	Technical and vocational secondary education	9500	Private households with employed persons
8030	Higher education		
8090	Adult and other education	9900	Extra-territorial organizations and bodies

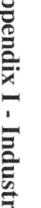

APPENDIX I - INDUSTRIAL CLASSIFICATIONS
HARMONIZED CODE COVERAGE

This appendix lists the Harmonized Code Classifications (HCs). Entries in the body of the book are arranged according to topic. Products may be located using either the SIC Coverage listing beginning on page 1141 or the Products, Services, Names, and Issues Index beginning on page 1045.

01 Live animals
02 Meat and edible meat offal
03 Fish and crustaceans, mollusks and other aquatic invertebrates
04 Dairy produce; birds' eggs; natural honey, edible products of animal origin, not elsewhere specified or included
05 Products of animal origin, not elsewhere specified or included
06 Live trees and other plants; bulbs, roots, and the like; cut flowers and ornamental foliage
07 Edible vegetables and certain roots and tubers
08 Edible fruits and nuts; peel of citrus fruits or melons
09 Coffee, tea, mate, and spices
10 Cereals
11 Products of the milling industry; malt; starches; insulin; wheat gluten
12 Oil seeds and oleaginous fruits; miscellaneous grains, seeds, and fruits; industrial or medicinal plants; straw and fodder
13 Lac; gums, resins and other vegetable saps and extract
14 Vegetable plaiting materials; vegetable products not elsewhere specified or included
15 Animal or vegetable fats and oils and their cleavage products; prepared edible fats; animal or vegetable waxes
16 Preparation of meat, of fish, or of crustaceans, mollusks, or other aquatic invertebrates
17 Sugars and sugar confectionery
18 Cocoa and cocoa preparations
19 Preparations of cereals, flour, starch or milk; bakers' wares
20 Preparations of vegetables, fruits, nuts, or other parts of plants
21 Miscellaneous edible preparations
22 Beverages, spirits, and vinegar
23 Residues and waste from the food industries; prepared animal feed
24 Tobacco and manufactured tobacco substitutes
25 Salt; sulfur; earths and stone; plastering materials, lime and cement
26 Ores, slag, and ash
27 Mineral fuels, mineral oils and products of their distillation; bituminous substances; mineral waxes
28 Inorganic chemicals; organic or inorganic compounds of precious metals, of rare-earth metals, of radioactive elements, or of isotopes
29 Organic chemicals
30 Pharmaceutical products
31 Fertilizers
32 Tanning or dyeing extracts; tannins and their derivatives; dyes, pigments, and other coloring matter; paints and varnishes; putty and other mastics; inks
33 Essential oils and resinoids; perfumery, cosmetic or toilet preparations
34 Soaps; organic surface-active agents; washing preparations; lubricating preparations; artificial waxes; prepared waxes; polishing or scouring preparations; candles and similar articles; modeling pastes; "dental waxes," and dental preparations with a basis of plaster
35 Albuminoidal substances; modified starches; glues; enzymes
36 Explosives; pyrotechnic products; matches; pyrotechnic alloys; certain combustible preparations
37 Photographic or cinematographic goods
38 Miscellaneous chemical products
39 Plastics and articles thereof
40 Rubber and articles thereof
41 Raw hides and skins (other than furskins) and leather
42 Articles of leather; saddlery and harness; travel goods, handbags and similar containers; articles of animal gut (other than silkworm gut)
43 Furskins and artificial fur; manufactures thereof
44 Wood and articles of wood; wood charcoal

45 Cork and articles of cork
46 Manufacturers of stray, of esparto or of other plaiting materials; basketware and wickerwork
47 Pulp of wood or of other fibrous cellulosic material; waste and scrap of paper or paperboard
48 Paper and paperboard; articles of paper pulp, of paper, or of paperboard
49 Printed books, newspapers, pictures, and other products of the printing industry; manuscripts, typescripts, and plans
50 Silk
51 Wool; fine or coarse animal hair; horsehair yarn and woven fabric
52 Cotton
53 Other vegetable textile fibers; paper yarn and woven fabrics of paper yarn
54 Man-made filaments
55 Man-made staple fibers
56 Wadding, felt and nonwovens; special yarns; twine, cordage, ropes and cables and articles thereof
57 Carpets and other textile floor coverings
58 Special woven fabrics; tufted textile fabrics; lace; tapestries; trimmings; embroidery
59 Impregnated, coated, covered or laminated textile fabrics; textile articles of a kind suitable for industrial use
60 Knitted or crocheted fabrics
61 Articles of apparel and clothing accessories, knitted or crocheted
62 Articles of apparel and clothing accessories, not knitted or crocheted
63 Other made-up textile articles; needle craft sets; worn clothing and worn textile articles; rags
64 Footwear, gaiters and the like; parts of such articles
65 Headgear and parts thereof
66 Umbrellas, sun umbrellas, walking sticks, seatsticks, whips, riding crops and parts thereof
67 Prepared feathers and down and articles made of feathers or of down; artificial flowers; articles of human hair
68 Articles of stone, plaster, cement, asbestos, mica or similar materials
69 Ceramic products
70 Glass and glassware
71 Natural or cultured pearls, precious or semiprecious stones, precious metals; metals clad with precious metal, and articles thereof; imitation jewelry; coin
72 Iron and steel
73 Articles of iron or steel
74 Copper and articles thereof
75 Nickel and articles thereof
76 Aluminum and articles thereof
77 Reserved for possible future use
78 Lead and articles thereof
79 Zinc and articles thereof
80 Tin and articles thereof
81 Other base metals; cermets; articles thereof
82 Tools, implements, cutlery, spoons and forks, of base metal; parts thereof of base metal
83 Miscellaneous articles of base metal
84 Nuclear reactors, boilers, machinery and mechanical appliances; parts thereof
85 Electrical machinery and equipment and parts thereof; sound recorders and reproducers, television image and sound recorders and reproducers, and parts and accessories of such articles
86 Railway or tramway locomotives, rolling stock and parts thereof; railway or tramway track fixtures and fittings and parts thereof; mechanical (including electromechanical) traffic signalling equipment of all kinds
87 Vehicles, other than railway or tramway rolling stock, and parts and accessories thereof
88 Aircraft, spacecraft, and parts thereof
89 Ships, boats, and floating structures
90 Optical, photographic, cinematographic, measuring, checking, precision, medical or surgical instruments and apparatus; parts and accessories thereof
91 Clocks and watches and parts thereof
92 Musical instruments; parts and accessories of such articles
93 Arms and ammunition; parts and accessories thereof
94 Furniture; bedding, mattresses, mattress supports, cushions and similar stuffed furnishings; lamps and lighting fittings, not elsewhere specified or included; illuminated signs; illuminated nameplates and the like; prefabricated buildings
95 Toys, games, and sports equipment; parts and accessories thereof
96 Miscellaneous manufactured articles
97 Works of art, collectors' pieces and antiques

APPENDIX II

Annotated Source List

The following listing provides the names, publishers, addresses, telephone and fax numbers (if available), and frequency of publication for the primary sources used in *Market Share Reporter.*

20/20 Magazine, Jobson Publishing L.L.C., 100 Avenue of the Americas, New York, NY 10013-1678, *Telephone*: (212) 274-7000, *Fax*: (212) 431-0500, *Published*: 14x/yr., *Price*: free digital copies available.

2020 ASHA 50 - A Supplement to Seniors Housing Business, France Media Inc., Fourteen Piedmont Center, 3535 Piedmont Rd. NE, Suite 950, Atlanta, GA 30305, *Telephone*: (404) 832-8262, *Fax*: (404) 832-8260, *Published*: annually, *Price*: free to qualified subscribers.

2020 Sosland Publishing's Corporate Profiles State of the Industry Report, Sosland Publishing, 4801 Main Street, Suite 650, Kansas City, MO 64112, *Telephone*: (816) 756-1000, *Fax*: (816) 756-0494, *Published*: annually, *Price*: $45.

5thWave, World Coffee Portal Ltd., Serendipity House, 106 Arlington Road, London NW17HP, United Kingdom, *Telephone*: +44 (0) 20 7691 8800, *Published*: quarterly, *Price*: free digital copies.

Access, Lift & Handlers, KHL Group Southfields, Southview Road, Wadhurst, East Sussex TN5 6TP, United Kingdom, *Telephone*: +44 (0) 1892 784088, *Fax*: +44 (0) 1892 784086, *Published*: 10x/year, *Price*: free to qualified subscribers.

Adhesives & Sealants Industry, BNP Media L.L.C., W. Big Beaver Road, Suite 700, Troy, MI 48084, *Telephone*: (248) 362-3700, *Fax*: (248) 362-0317, *Published*: monthly, *Price*: $232 annually.

Advertising Age, Crain Communications, N. Michigan Ave., Chicago, IL 60601, *Telephone*: (877) 320-1721, *Fax*: (212) 210-0465, *Published*: bimonthly, three times in May, June and October, *Price*: $109 annually.

Aggregates Business Europe, Route One Publishing Ltd., Waterbridge Court, 50 Spital Street, Dartford, Kent, DA1 2DT, United Kingdom, *Telephone*: +44 (0) 1322 612055, *Fax*: +44 (0) 1322 7880633, *Published*: 6x/yr., *Price*: free to qualified subscribers.

Agropages, Stanley Alliance, Room 1301, 13th Floor, CRE Building, 303 Hennessy Road, Wanchai, Hong Kong, *Telephone*: +86-571-8724 5206, *Fax*: +86-571-8724 5207, *Published*: annually, *Price*: free to subscribers.

Air Cargo News, Air Cargo Media, 7th Floor Chancery House, St. Nicholas Way, Sutton, Surrey, SM1 1JB, United Kingdom, *Telephone*: +44 (0) 208 772 8370, *Fax*: +44 (0) 208 652 5218, *Published*: monthly, *Price*: $200 annually.

Airline Business, Reed Business Information, Quadrant House, Sutton, Surrey, SM2 5AS, United Kingdom, *Telephone*: +44 20 8652 4996, *Fax*: +44 20 8652 3814, *Published*: monthly, *Price*: $158 annually.

American Ceramic Society Bulletin, American Ceramic Society, 735 Ceramic Place, Suite 100, Westerville, OH 43086-6136, *Telephone*: (866) 721-3322, *Fax*: (614) 794-5822, *Published*: monthly, *Price*: $75 annually for North American subscribers, $131 annually for international subscribers.

American School & University, Informa USA Inc., 9800 Metcalf Ave., Overland Park, KS 66212, *Telephone*: (215) 752-2787, *Fax*: (913) 514-9520, *Published*: monthly, except combined issues January-February; May-June and November-December, *Price*: $69 annually.

American Vegetable Grower, Meister Media, 37733 Euclid Avenue, Willoughby, OH 44094-5992, *Telephone*: (800) 572-7740, *Fax*: (440) 942-0662, *Published*: monthly, *Price*: $15.95.

Architectural Record, BNP Media, Two Penn Plaza, 9th Floor, New York, NY 10121-2298, *Telephone*: (212) 904-2594, *Fax*: (212) 904-4256, *Published*: monthly, *Price*: $49 annually.

The Art Newspaper, 594 Broadway, Suite 406, New York, NY 10001, *Telephone*: (212) 343-0727, *Fax*: (212) 965-5367, *Published*: monthly, *Price*: $99 annually.

Asia Food & Beverages Report, Consumer Goods Intelligence Pte. Ltd., #10-06 International Plaza, 10 Anson Road, Singapore 079903, *Telephone*: 65 63488973, *Fax*: 65 62275402, *Published*: 6x/yr., *Price*: $300 annually.

Asian Ceramics, Bowhead Media Ltd., 57 Oaks Avenue, Worcester Park, Surrey KT4 8XE, United Kingdom, *Telephone*: +44 (0) 208-123-0839, *Fax*: +44 (0) 207-183 7196, *Published*: monthly, *Price*: $330 annually.

Atlanta Journal-Constitution, 72 Marietta St., NW, Atlanta, GA 30303, *Telephone*: (404) 526 - 5151, *Published*: daily, *Price*: $104.27 annually.

The Atlantic, Atlantic Media Company, 600 New Hampshire Ave., NW, Washington, D.C. 20037, *Telephone*: (202) 266-6000, *Fax*: (202) 266-6001, *Published*: monthly, *Price*: $24.50 annually.

Auto Rental News, Bobit Business Media, 3250 Challenger Street, Torrance, CA 90503, *Telephone*: (888) 274-4580, *Fax*: (847) 647-8064, *Published*: monthly, *Price*: free to qualified subscribers.

Autocar, Haymarket Media Group, Richmond Bridge House, 69 London Road, Twickenham TW 1 3 SP, United Kingdom, *Telephone*: +44 (0) 20 8267 5630, *Published*: weekly, *Price*: 73.98 British pounds sterling (6 months, print and digital).

Automatic Merchandiser, Endeavor Business Media, 1233 Janesville Ave., Fort Atkinson, WI 53538, *Telephone*: (800) 547-7377, *Published*: 7x/yr., *Price*: $37 annually.

Automotive Fleet, Bobit Business Media, 3520 Challenger St., Torrance, CA 90503, *Telephone*: (310) 533-2400, *Fax*: (310) 533-2500, *Published*: monthly, *Price*: free to qualified subscribers.

Automotive News, Crain Communications Inc., 1155 Gratiot Ave., Detroit, MI 48207-2997, *Telephone*: (313) 446-6031, *Fax*: (313) 446-8030, *Published*: weekly, *Price*: $149 annually.

Aviation Week & Space Technology, Informa, 2121 K Street NW, Suite 210, Washington D.C. 20037, *Telephone*: (202) 517-1100, *Published*: biweekly, *Price*: free digital copies.

Baking & Snack, Sosland Publishing Co., 4800 Main St., Suite 100, Kansas City, MO 64112, *Telephone*: (816) 756-1000, *Fax*: (816) 756-0494, *Published*: monthly, *Price*: free to qualified subscribers.

Baltimore Business Journal, American City Business Journals Inc., 111 Market Place, Suite 720, Baltimore, MD 21202, *Telephone*: (410) 576-1161, *Fax*: (410) 752-3112, *Published*: weekly, *Price*: $150 annually, print and digital.

Barron's, Dow Jones & Company Inc., 1211 Ave. of the Americas, New York, NY 10036, *Telephone*: (800)-DOW-JONES, *Fax*: (212) 416-2524, *Published*: weekly, *Price*: $99 annually.

Beauty Packaging, Rodman Media Corp., 25 Philips Pkwy., Suite 200, Montvale, NJ 07645, *Telephone*: (201) 825-2552, *Fax*: (201) 391-1008, *Published*: 8x/yr., *Price*: free digital copies.

Bedding Yearbook - A Supplement to Furniture Today, Gannett Media, 7025 Albert Pick Road, Suite 200, Greensboro NC 27409, *Telephone*: (336) 605-0121, *Fax*: (336) 605-1143, *Published*: annually, *Price*: included with subscription.

Beef, Informa Business Media, 9800 Metcalf Ave., Overland Park, KS 66212, *Telephone*: (800) 441-1410, *Published*: monthly, *Price*: $41 annually.

Best's Review, A.M. Best Co. Inc., 1 Ambest Rd., Oldwick, NJ 08858, *Telephone*: (800) 424-2378, *Fax*: (908) 439-3363, *Published*: monthly, *Price*: $20 annually.

Beverage Dynamics, Beverage Information Group, 40 Richards Ave., 3rd Floor, Suite 312, Nowalk, CT 06851, *Telephone*: (203) 855-8499, *Fax*: (203) 855-9446, *Published*: bimonthly, *Price*: free to qualified subscribers.

Beverage Industry, BNP Media Inc., 2401 W. Big Beaver Rd., Suite 700, Troy, MI 48084-3333, *Telephone*: (800) 952-6643, *Fax*: (847) 763-9538, *Published*: monthly, *Price*: free to qualified subscribers.

BevNet Magazine, BevNET.com Inc., 44 Pleasant St., Suite 110, Watertown, MA 02472, *Telephone*: (617) 231-8800, *Fax*: (617) 812-7740, *Published*: 6x/yr., *Price*: free to qualified subscribers.

Bicycle Retailer & Industry News, 25431 Cabot Road, Suite 204, Laguna Hills, CA 92653, *Telephone*: (949) 206-1677, *Fax*: (949) 206-1675, *Published*: 18x/year, *Price*: $68 annually.

Bike & E-Bike Market Update, No. 193, Tze-Chiang Road, Chang Hua City 50095, Taiwan, *Telephone*: 886-4-7350500, *Fax*: 866-4-7360794, *Published*: quarterly, *Price*: free digital copies.

Biodiesel Magazine, BBI International, 308 2nd Avenue North, Suite 304, Grand Forks, ND 58203, *Telephone*: (701) 746-8385, *Fax*: (701) 746-5367, *Published*: monthly, *Price*: $49.95 annually.

Birmingham Business Journal, 2140 11th Avenue South, Suite 205, Birmingham, AL 35205, *Telephone*: (205) 443-5600, *Fax*: (205) 322-0040, *Published*: weekly, *Price*: $150 annually, print and digital.

The Boston Globe, 1 Exchange Place, Suite 201, Boston, MA 02109-2132, *Telephone*: (617) 929-2000, *Published*: daily, *Price*: $27.72 monthly.

Builder, Hanley-Wood L.L.C., One Thomas Circle, N.W., Suite 600, Washington, D.C. 20005, *Telephone*: (202) 452-0800, *Fax*: (202) 785-1974, *Published*: monthly, *Price*: free to qualified subscribers.

Building Design + Construction, Horizon L.L.C., 3030 W. Salt Creek Lane, Suite 201, Arlington Heights, IL 60005-5025, *Telephone*: (847) 391-1000, *Fax*: (847) 390-0408, *Published*: monthly, *Price*: $146 annually.

Business Insurance, 77 Frankling St., Suite 809, Boston, MA 02110-1510, *Telephone*: (212) 210-0100, *Published*: weekly, *Price*: $97 annually.

Business Standard, Business Standard Ltd., H/3&4 Paragon Centre, Opp Century Mills, P B Marg, Worli, Mumbai – 400013, India, *Telephone*: 91-22-24978456-69, *Fax*: 91-22-24978540, *Published*: monthly, *Price*: Rs 1,499 annually.

Canadian Grocer, Stagnito Partners Canada Inc., 20 Eglinton Avenue West, Suite 1800, Toronto, Ontario, M4R 1K8, Canada, *Telephone*: (800) 268-9119, *Fax*: (416) 764-1523, *Published*: 10x/yr., *Price*: $85 annually.

Candy Industry, Stagnito Communications, 155 Pfingsten Road, Suite 205, Deerfield, IL 60015, *Telephone*: (847) 205-5660 Ext. 4039, *Fax*: (847) 205-5680, *Published*: monthly, *Price*: free to qualified subscribers.

Car Dealer, Blackball Media Ltd., Units 1-2 Warrior Court, 9-11 Mumby Road, Gosport, PO12 1BS, *Telephone*: (020) 8125 3880, *Published*: monthly, *Price*: 60 British pounds sterling annually.

Car Wash Magazine, International Car Wash Association, 350 N. Orleans St., Suite 9000N, Chicago, IL 606054, *Telephone*: (888) 422-8422, *Published*: quarterly, *Price*: free to qualified subscribers.

Casting Source, American Foundry Society, 1695 N. Penny Lane, Schaumburg, IL 60173-4555, *Telephone*: (847) 824-0181, *Fax*: (847) 924-7848, *Published*: bi-monthly, *Price*: $185 annually.

Casual Living, Bridgetown Media, 7025 Albert Pick Road, Suite 200, Greensboro, NC 27409, *Telephone*: (336) 605-0121, *Fax*: (336) 605-1143, *Published*: monthly, *Price*: $69.99 annually.

CE Pro, EH Publishing Inc., 111 Speen Street, Suite 200, P.O. Box 989, Framingham, MA 01701-2000, *Telephone*: (508) 663-1500, *Fax*: (508) 663-1599, *Published*: monthly, *Price*: free digital copies.

Ceramic World Review, Tile Edizioni S.R.L., Via Fossa Buracchione 84, 41126 Baggiovara (MO) - Italy, *Telephone*: +39 059 512 103, *Fax*: +39 059 512 157, *Published*: 5x/yr., *Price*: €70 annually.

Chain Drug Review, Racher Press, 220 5th Ave, New York, NY 10001, *Telephone*: (212) 213-6000, *Fax*: (212) 725-3961, *Published*: 21x/yr., *Price*: free to qualified subscribers.

Charlotte Business Journal, American City Business Journals Inc., 550 S. Caldwell St., Suite 910, Charlotte, NC 28202, *Telephone*: (704) 973-1100, *Fax*: (704) 973-1102, *Published*: weekly, *Price*: $92 annually.

Cheers, EPG Media & Specialty Information, 10405 6th Ave. N, Suite 210, Minneapolis, MN 55441, *Telephone*: (763) 383-4400, *Fax*: (763) 383-4499, *Published*: 6x/yr., *Price*: $35 annually.

Cheese Reporter - Dairy Production Extra, Cheese Reporter Publishing Co., 2810 Crossroads Drive, Suite 3000, Madison, WI 53718, *Telephone*: (608) 246-8430, *Fax*: (608) 246-8431, *Published*: weekly, *Price*: $140 annually.

Chemical & Engineering News, American Chemical Society, 1155 16th Street, N.W., Washington, D.C 20036, *Telephone*: (202) 872-4600, *Fax*: (202) 872-8127, *Published*: weekly, except last week in December, *Price*: $55.70 annually (membership required in American Chemical Society).

Chicago Sun-Times, Chicago Sun-Times, 350 N. Orleans St., 10th Floor, Chicago, IL 60654, *Telephone*: (312) 321-3000, *Fax*: (312) 222-3935, *Published*: daily, *Price*: $4.99 monthly, digital only.

China Chemical Reporter, China National Chemical Centre, 2F, B Unit, No. 33 Anding Road, Chaoyang District, Beijing, 100029, China, *Telephone*: (086) 010-64444031, 64421206, *Fax*: (086) 010-64421206, *Published*: weekly, *Price*: $1,100 annually.

China Fastener World, Fastener World Inc., No. 469, Yu Ping Road, Tainan 70843, Taiwan, *Telephone*: +866-6295 4000, *Fax*: +866-6295 3939, *Published*: quarterly, *Price*: free digital copies.

Cincinnati Business Courier, American City Business Journals Inc., 120 E. 4th Street, Suite 230, Cincinnati, OH 45202, *Telephone*: (513) 621-6665, *Fax*: (513) 621-2462, *Published*: weekly, *Price*: $150 annually, digital and print.

Club Business International, International Health, Racquet Sportsclub Association, 70 Fargo Street, Boston, MA 02210, *Telephone*: (800) 228-4772, *Fax*: (617) 951-0056, *Published*: monthly, *Price*: $74.95 annually.

Coal Age, Mining Media, 11655 Indianapolis Parkway, Suite 306, Jacksonville, FL 32224, *Telephone*: (303) 751-5370, *Fax*: (303) 368-0070, *Published*: monthly, except January and July, *Price*: $75 annually.

Coatings World, Rodman Media Group, 70 Hilltop Road, Ramsey, NJ 07446, *Telephone*: (201) 825-2552, *Fax*: (201) 825-0553, *Published*: monthly, *Price*: free to qualified subscribers.

The College Store Magazine, National Association of College Stores, 500 E. Lorain St., Oberlin, OH 44074, *Telephone*: (800) 622-7498, *Fax*: (440) 775-4769, *Published*: bimonthly, *Price*: digital copies available.

Columbus Business First, American City Business Journals Inc., 303 West Nationwide Blvd., Columbus, OH 43215, *Telephone*: (614) 461-4040, *Fax*: (614) 365-2780, *Published*: weekly, *Price*: $86 annually.

Commercial Baking, Avant Food Media, 1625 Oak Street, Suite 201, Kansas City, MO 64108, *Telephone*: (816) 585-5030, *Published*: quarterly, along with two annual issues, *Price*: free to qualified subscribers.

Composites Manufacturing, American Composites Manufacturers Association, 2000 N. 15th Street, Ste. 250, Arlington, VA 22201, *Telephone*: (703) 525-0511, *Fax*: (703) 525-0743, *Published*: bimonthly, *Price*: free to qualified subscribers.

Contact Lens Spectrum, PentaVision L.L.C., 321 Norristown Road, Suite 150, Ambler, PA 19002, *Telephone*: (800) 869-6882, *Fax*: (866) 658-6156, *Published*: monthly, *Price*: $79 annually.

Control, Putman Media Inc., 1501 E. Woodfield Road, Suite 400N, Schaumburg, IL 60173, *Telephone*: (630) 467-1300, *Fax*: (630) 467-1120, *Published*: monthly, *Price*: $96 annually.

Convenience Store Decisions, WTWH Media, 1111 Superior Ave., 26th Floor, Cleveland, OH 44114, *Telephone*: (888) 543-2447, *Fax*: (216) 453-0617, *Published*: monthly, *Price*: $80 annually.

Convenience Store News, EnsembleIQ, 8550 W. Bryn Mawr Ave., Suite 200, Chicago, IL 60631, *Telephone*: (773) 992-4450, *Fax*: (773) 992-4455, *Published*: 12x/yr., *Price*: $125 annually.

Converting Quarterly, Peterson Publications Inc., 2150 SW Westport Drive, Suite 101, Topeka, KS 66614, *Telephone*: (785) 271-5801, *Published*: quarterly, *Price*: free to qualified subscribers.

Counselor, Advertising Specialty Institute, Bucks County Technology Park, 4800 Street Road, Trevose PA 19053, *Telephone*: (800) 546-1350, *Fax*: (954) 360-0034, *Published*: monthly, *Price*: $9.95 annually.

Countertops & Architectural Surfaces, International Surface Fabricators Association, P.O. Box 627, Ingomar, PA 15127, *Telephone*: (888) 599-IFSA, *Published*: quarterly, *Price*: free to qualified subscribers.

Country Aircheck, 914 18th Avenue, South, Nashville TN 37212, *Telephone*: (615) 320-1450, *Published*: weekly, *Price*: free digital copies.

Crain's Detroit Business, Crain Communications Inc., 1155 Gratiot Ave., Detroit, MI 48207-3187, *Telephone*: (888) 909-9111, *Fax*: (313) 446-0392, *Published*: weekly, except semiweekly the fourth week in May, *Price*: $40.60 annually.

CRN, CMP Media, One Jericho Plaza, Jericho, NY 11753, *Telephone*: (717) 430-2229, *Published*: weekly, *Price*: $199 annually.

CropLife, CropLife Media Group, 37733 Euclid Ave., Willoughby, OH 44094, *Telephone*: (440) 942-2000, *Published*: monthly, *Price*: free to qualified subscribers.

Crossties, Railway Ties Association, 115 Commerce Dr., Suite C, Fayetteville, GA 30214, *Telephone*: (770) 460-5553, *Published*: monthly, *Price*: free digital copies.

Cruise Industry News, 441 Lexington Avenue, Suite 809, New York, NY 10017, *Telephone*: (212) 986-1025, *Fax*: (212) 986-1033, *Published*: quarterly, *Price*: $75 annually.

CSI Magazine, Perspective Publishing, 3 London Wall Buildings, London EC2M 5PD, United Kingdom, *Telephone*: +44 (0) 20 7562 2438, *Published*: monthly, *Price*: €88 Europe; U.K. €68; €98 rest of world.

CSP, Winsight L.L.C., 300 South Riverside Plaza, Suite 1600, Chicago, IL 60606, *Telephone*: (312) 876-0004, *Fax*: (312) 876-1158, *Published*: monthly, *Price*: free to qualified subscribers.

Culinology, Research Chefs Association, 330 N. Wabash Ave., Suite 2000, Chicago, IL 60611, *Telephone*: (313) 321-6861, *Published*: monthly, *Price*: free to qualified subscribers.

Dairy Foods, BNP Media L.L.C., 2401 W. Big Beaver Rd., Suite 700, Troy, MI 48084-3333, *Telephone*: (248) 362-3700, *Fax*: (248) 362-0317, *Published*: monthly, *Price*: free to qualified subscribers.

DBusiness, Hour Media, 117 W. Third St., Royal Oak, MI 48067, *Telephone*: (248) 691-1800, *Fax*: (248) 691-4531, *Published*: monthly, *Price*: $9.95 annually.

Dealerscope, CT Lab Global Media L.L.C., 1500 Spring Garden St., Suite 1200, Philadelphia, PA 19130-4094, *Telephone*: (215) 238-5300, *Published*: 9x/yr., *Price*: $85 annually.

Defense News, Sightline Media Group, 883 Commercial Dr., Springfield, VA 22159-0500, *Telephone*: (800) 368-5718, *Published*: monthly, *Price*: $139 annually.

Demolition & Recycling International, KHL Group, Southfields, Southview Road, Wadhurst East Sussex TN5 6TP, United Kingdom, *Telephone*: +44 (0) 1892 784 088, *Fax*: +44 (0) 1892 784 086, *Published*: monthly, *Price*: free to qualified subscribers.

Direct Selling News, 5800 Democracy Drive, Suite 100, Planto, TX 72024, *Telephone*: (800) 279-5249, *Fax*: (940) 497-9988, *Published*: monthly, *Price*: $50 annually.

Directions - A Supplement to National Cattlemen, National Cattlemen's Beef Association, 9110 E. Nichols Ave., Suite 300, Cenntennial, CO 80112, *Telephone*: (303) 694-0305, *Published*: annually, *Price*: free digital copies.

Door & Window, National Glass Association, 1945 Old Gallows Road, Suie 750, Vienna, VA 22182, *Telephone*: (703) 442-4890, *Fax*: (703) 442-0630, *Published*: 6x/yr., *Price*: $49.95 annually.

DrugStore Management, Millennium Media L.L.C., 3 Chaser Court, Holmdel NJ 07733, *Telephone*: (732) 888-0066, *Published*: annually, *Price*: $50 annually.

The Economist, The Economist Group, 750 3rd Avenue, 5th Floor, New York, NY 10017, *Telephone*: (212) 541-0500, *Fax*: (212) 541-9378, *Published*: weekly, *Price*: $158.25 annually.

Editor & Publisher, 19606 Eagle Crest Drive, Lutz, FL 33549, *Telephone*: (406) 455-0000, *Fax*: (800) 654-5370, *Published*: monthly, *Price*: $99 annually.

Electrical Construction & Maintenance, Informa USA, 9800 Metcalf Avenue, Overland Park, KS 66212, *Telephone*: (913) 967-1782, *Published*: monthly, *Price*: free to qualified subscribers.

The Electrical Distributor, National Association of Electrical Distributors Inc., 1181 Corporate Lake Drive, St. Louis, MO 63132, *Telephone*: (314) 991-9000, *Published*: monthly, *Price*: $40 annually.

Engineering and Mining Journal, Mining Media International Inc., 11655 Central Parkway, Suite 306, Jacksonville, FL 32224, *Telephone*: (904) 721-2925, *Fax*: (904) 721-2930, *Published*: monthly, *Price*: $90 annually.

ENR, BNP Media L.L.C., 2401 W. Big Beaver Rd., Suite 700, Troy, MI 48084-3333, *Telephone*: (248) 362-3700, *Fax*: (248) 362-0317, *Published*: weekly, *Price*: $111 annually, print and digital.

EQ International, 95-C, Sampat Farms, Bicholi Mardana Distt-Indore 452016, Madhya Pradesh, India, *Telephone*: + 91 96441 22268, *Fax*: + 91 96441 33319, *Published*: monthly, *Price*: free to qualified subscribers.

Eurofish, Eurofish International Organization, H.C. Andersens Blvd. 44-46, DK-1553, Copenhagen V, Denmark, *Telephone*: +45 333 777 55, *Published*: 6 issues, *Price*: €100 annually.

Eurofresh Distribution, SARL Publications Agricoles, 51 - rue Camus, BP 20131, France, *Telephone*: +34 962 950 087, *Published*: 6x/yr., *Price*: €59 annually.

Exchange, Exchange Press, 7700 A Street, Lincoln, NE 68510, *Telephone*: (425) 883-9394, *Fax*: (402) 467-6118, *Published*: 6x/yr., *Price*: $38 for one year.

F&L Magazine, F&L Asia Ltd., 22/F, 3 Lockhart Road, Wanchai, Hong Kong, *Telephone*: +852 3183 4143, *Fax*: +852 3753 5122, *Published*: quarterly, *Price*: $105 annually.

Farm Equipment, 16655 W Wisconsin Ave, Brookfield, WI 53005, *Telephone*: (800) 645-8455, *Fax*: (262) 786-5564, *Published*: monthly, *Price*: free to qualified subscribers.

Fast Company, Mansueto Ventures L.L.C., 7 World Trade Center, New York, NY 10007-2195, *Telephone*: (800) 542-6029, *Fax*: (212) 389-5245, *Published*: 7x/yr., *Price*: $19.95 annually.

FDM+C, CCI Media L.L.C., 2240 Country Club Parkway SE, Cedar Rapids, IA, 52403, *Telephone*: (319) 423-8001, *Fax*: (319) 512-7158, *Published*: monthly, with extra issues in April and October, *Price*: $96 annually.

Federal Computer Week, 4300 Canoga Avenue, Suite 1100, Woodland Hills, CA 91307, *Telephone*: (818) 814-5200, *Fax*: (818) 936-0496, *Published*: 7x/yr., *Price*: $25 annually.

Feed Strategy, WATT AgNet, 401 E. State Street, 3rd Floor, Rockford, IL 61104, *Telephone*: (815) 966-5774, *Fax*: (815) 968-0941, *Published*: monthly, *Price*: free digital copies.

Financial Express, B/B1 Express Building, Sector 10, Noida 201301, Uttar Predesh, India, *Telephone*: 079 268 73941, *Fax*: 079 268 73950, *Published*: daily, *Price*: free newsletter.

Financial Post, 1450 Don Mills Rd., Don Mills, Ontario, M3B 2X7, Canada, *Telephone*: (800) 668-7678, *Published*: daily, *Price*: $312 annually.

Financial Times, FT Publications Inc., 14 East 60th Street, New York, NY 21002, *Telephone*: (212) 752-4500, *Fax*: (212) 319-0704, *Published*: daily, except for Sundays and holidays, *Price*: $425 annually.

Fleet Owner, Informa Business Media, 9800 Metcalf Ave., Overland Park, KS 66212, *Telephone*: (866) 505-7173, *Fax*: (913) 967-1898, *Published*: monthly, *Price*: $75 annually.

Flight International, DVW Media, Heidenkampsweg 73-79, 20097 Hamburg, Germany, *Telephone*: +49 40 237 1401, *Published*: monthly, *Price*: $585 annually, print and digital.

Floor Covering News, Roel Productions Inc., 33 Walt Whitman Road, Suite 302, Huntington Station, NY 11746, *Telephone*: (516) 932-7860, *Fax*: (516) 932-7639, *Published*: biweekly, *Price*: $25 annually.

Floor Covering Weekly, Hearst Communications, 300 W. 57th Street, 15th Floor, New York, NY 10019, *Telephone*: (212) 649-7981, *Fax*: (646) 280-1990, *Published*: bimonthly, *Price*: $25 annually.

Floor Focus, Flooring News Corp., 310 Dodds Ave., Suite 301, Chattanooga, TN 37404, *Telephone*: (423) 752-0401, *Fax*: (423) 752-0400, *Published*: monthly, except August, *Price*: $79 annually.

Food Business News, Sosland Publishing Co., 4800 Main St., Suite 100, Kansas City, MO 64112, *Telephone*: 816-756-1000, *Fax*: 816-756-0494, *Published*: monthly, *Price*: free to qualified subscribers.

Food Processing, Putman Media, 555 West Pierce Rd., Suite 301, Itasca, IL 60143, *Telephone*: (630) 467-1300, *Fax*: (630) 467-1179, *Published*: monthly, *Price*: $79.95 annually.

Food Trade News, Best-Met Publishing Co. Inc., 5537 Twin Knolls Road, Suite 438, Columbia, MD 21045, *Telephone*: (410) 730-5013, *Fax*: (410) 740-4680, *Published*: monthly, *Price*: $69 annually.

Food World, Best-Met Publishing Co. Inc., 5537 Twin Knolls Road, Suite 438, Columbia, MD 21045, *Telephone*: (410) 730-5013, *Fax*: (410) 740-4680, *Published*: monthly, *Price*: $48 annually.

Franchise Times, Franchise Times Corporation, 2808 Anthony Lane S., Minneapolis, MN 55418, *Telephone*: (800) 528-3296, *Fax*: (612) 767-3230, *Published*: monthly, *Price*: $35 annually.

Frozen & Refrigerated Buyer, CT Media Partners, P.O. Box 1564, Norwich, VT 05055, *Telephone*: (603) 252-0507, *Published*: 11x/yr., *Price*: free to qualified subscribers.

FSR, Food News Media, 101 Europa, Suite 150, Chapel Hill, NC 27517, *Telephone*: (919) 945-0718, *Published*: monthly, *Price*: free to qualified subscribers.

Furniture Today, Reed Business Information, P.O. Box 2754, High Point, NC 27261-2754, *Telephone*: (336) 605-0121, *Fax*: (336) 605-1143, *Published*: weekly, *Price*: $159.97 annually.

Future Power Technology, Net Resources International, John Carpenter House, John Carpenter Street, London, EC4Y OAN, United Kingdom, *Telephone*: +44 (0) 207 936 6400, *Published*: monthly, *Price*: free digital copies available.

Games & Parks Industry, Facto Edizioni s.r.l., Via Ugo Foscolo, 11-35131, Padova, Italy, *Telephone*: (+39) 049 876 2922, *Published*: 11x/yr., *Price*: €100 for European countries; €130 for extra-European countries.

Gifts & Decorative Accessories, Reed Business Information, 360 Park Ave., New York, NY 10010, *Telephone*: (646) 746-6400, *Fax*: (646) 746-7431, *Published*: monthly, *Price*: free to qualified subscribers.

Glass International, Quartz Business Media Ltd., Quartz House, 20 Clarendon Road, Redhill, Surrey RH1 1QX, United Kingdom, *Telephone*: +44 (0) 1737 855136, *Fax*: +44 (0) 1737 855034, *Published*: monthly, *Price*: 224 British pounds sterling, one year.

Glass Magazine, National Glass Association, 1945 Old Gallows Rd., Suite 750, Vienna, VA 22182-3931, *Telephone*: (703) 442-4890, *Fax*: (703) 442-0630, *Published*: monthly, *Price*: free to qualified subscribers.

Global Cargo Insight, 80-83 Long Lane, London EC1A 9ET, United Kingdom, *Telephone*: + (0) 20 395 0227, *Fax*: + (0) 20 395 0228, *Published*: bimonthly, *Price*: $600 annually, print and digital.

Global Cement Magazine, Pro Global Media Ltd., Ground Floor, Sollis House, 20 Hook Road, Epsom, Surrey, KT19 8TR, United Kingdom, *Telephone*: +44 (0) 1372 743837, *Fax*: +44 (0) 1372 743838, *Published*: monthly, combined issues July-August, *Price*: €15 annually.

Global Gaming Business, Casino Connection Intl., 901 American Pacific Drive, Suite 1180, Henderson, NV 89014, *Telephone*: (702) 248-1565, *Fax*: (702) 248-1567, *Published*: monthly, *Price*: $99 annually.

Global Gypsum Magazine, Pro Global Media Ltd., Ground Floor, Sollis House, 20 Hook Road, Epsom Surrey, United Kingdom, KT19 8TR, *Telephone*: +44 (0) 1372 743837, *Fax*: +44 (0) 1372 743838, *Published*: 6x/yr., *Price*: €250 annually.

Global Trade Magazine, Global Site Location Industries L.L.C., P.O. Box 3183, Van Nuys, CA 91499-0410, *Telephone*: (469) 778-2606, *Published*: 6x/yr., *Price*: $39 annually.

Golf Inc., Cypress Magazines Inc., 7670 Opportunity Road, Suite 105, San Diego CA 92111, *Telephone*: (858) 300-3201, *Published*: quarterly, *Price*: $24 annually.

Greater Wilmington Business Journal, American City Business Journals Inc., 219 Station Road, Suite 202, Wilmington NC 28405, *Telephone*: (910) 343-8600, *Fax*: (910) 343-8660, *Published*: monthly, *Price*: $150 annually, print and digital.

The Griffin Report Northeast Market Review, The Shelby Report, 517 Green Street NW, Gainesville, GA 30501, *Telephone*: (770) 534-8380, *Published*: monthly, *Price*: $56.97 annually, print and digital.

The Grocer, William Reed Publishing Ltd., Broadfield Park, Crawley, RH11 9RT, United Kingdom, *Telephone*: +44 (0) 1293 613400, *Fax*: 44 (0) 1293 610340, *Published*: monthly, *Price*: 266 British pounds sterling, digital and print.

The Guardian, 3-7 Ray Street, London EC1R 3DR, United Kingdom, *Telephone*: 020 7278 2332, *Published*: daily, *Price*: 9.99 British pounds sterling per month.

Guide to Tobacco - A Supplement to Convenience Store News, EnsembleIQ, 8550 W. Bryn Mawr Ave., Suite 200, Chicago, IL 60631, *Telephone*: (773) 992-4450, *Fax*: (773) 992-4455, *Published*: annual, *Price*: free digital copies.

GWI, American Water Intelligence, 2121 E. 6th St., Suite 202, Austin, TX 78702, *Telephone*: (512) 961-5693, *Published*: monthly, *Price*: $1,795 annually, print and digital.

Hardware + Building Supply Dealer, EnsembleIQ, 8550 W. Bryn Mahr Ave., Suite 200, Chicago, IL 60631, *Telephone*: (773) 992-4450, *Fax*: (773) 992-4455, *Published*: monthly, double issues Jul./Aug. and Nov./Dec., *Price*: $191 annually.

The Hardware Connection, Hardware Connection Inc., 919100 Overseas Highway, Tavernier, FL 33070, *Telephone*: (804) 690-0666, *Published*: 8x/yr., *Price*: free to qualified subscribers.

Hardware Retailing, North American Retail Hardware Association, 136 N. Delaware St., Ste. 200, Indianapolis, IN 46204, *Telephone*: (317) 275-9400, *Published*: monthly, *Price*: $50 annually.

Hardwood Floors, National Wood Flooring Association, 111 Chesterfield, Chesterfield, MO 63005, *Telephone*: (800) 422-4556, *Published*: monthly, *Price*: free to qualified subscribers.

Healthcare Sales & Marketing, CL Media Inc., 1420 Walnut Street, Ste. 1100, Philadelphia, PA 19102, *Telephone*: (215) 383-2020, *Published*: 6x/yr., *Price*: free digital copies.

The Hearing Review, Medqor, 7900 College Blvd., Ste. 105, Overland Park, KS 66210, *Telephone*: (913) 955-2749, *Fax*: (913) 894-6932, *Published*: monthly, *Price*: free to qualified subscribers.

Heavy Duty Trucking, Bobit Business Media, 3520 Challenger Street, Torrance, CA 90503, *Telephone*: (310) 533-2451, *Fax*: (949) 261-2904, *Published*: monthly, *Price*: free to qualified subscribers.

HFN, Fairchild Publications, 7 W. 34th Street, New York, NY 10001, *Telephone*: (212) 630-4000, *Published*: weekly, *Price*: $109 annually.

The Hollywood Reporter, 5055 Wilshire Blvd, 6th Floor, Los Angeles, CA 90036, *Telephone*: (313) 525-2000, *Published*: 41 issues a year, *Price*: $199 annually.

Home Accents Today, Bridgetower Media L.L.C., 7025 Albert Pick Road, Suite 200, Greensboro N.C. 27409, *Telephone*: (336) 605-0121, *Fax*: (336) 605-1143, *Published*: monthly, *Price*: $105.97 annually.

Home Furnishings Business, FurnitureCore, 1389 Peachtree St. NE, Suite 310, Atlanta, GA 30079, *Telephone*: (404) 961-3734, *Fax*: (404) 961-3739, *Published*: monthly, *Price*: free digital copies.

Home Textiles Today, BridgeTower Media L.L.C., 7025 Albert Pack Road, Greensboro, NC 27409, *Telephone*: (336) 605-0121, *Fax*: (336) 605-1143, *Published*: monthly, *Price*: $134.97 annually.

HomeWorld Business, ICD Publications, 45 Research Way, Ste. 106, East Setauket, NY 11733, *Telephone*: (631) 246-9300, *Fax*: (631) 246-9496, *Published*: weekly, *Price*: free to qualified subscribers.

Hotel & Motel Management, Advanstar Communications, Inc., 7500 Old Oak Blvd., Cleveland, OH 44130, *Telephone*: (440) 891-2674, *Fax*: (440) 891-3120, *Published*: 21 issues, *Price*: $53.55 annually.

Hotels, Marketing and Technology Group, 1415 N. Dayton St., Chicago, IL 60642, *Telephone*: (312) 274-2200, *Published*: monthly, *Price*: $170 annually.

Household and Personal Products Industry, 25 Philips Parkway, Montvale, NJ 07645, *Telephone*: (201) 825-2552, *Fax*: (201) 825-0553, *Published*: monthly, *Price*: free to qualified subscribers.

IBD Weekly, Investor's Business Daily Inc., 12655 Beatrice Street, Los Angeles, CA 90066-7300, *Telephone*: (310) 448-6000, *Fax*: (310) 577-7301, *Published*: weekly, *Price*: $279 annually.

ICIS Chemical Business, Reed Business Information, Quadrant House, The Quadrant, Sutton, Surrey, SM2 5AS, United Kingdom, *Telephone*: (888) 525-3255, *Fax*: 44 20 8652 3924, *Published*: daily, *Price*: free to qualified subscribers.

IEEE Vehicular Technology Magazine, IEEE Vehicular Technology Society, 3 Park Avenue, 17th Floor, New York, NY 10016, *Telephone*: (212) 419-7900, *Published*: quarterly, *Price*: $402.50 annually.

Indianapolis Business Journal, IBJ Corp., One Monument Circle, Suite 300, Indianapolis, IN 46204, *Telephone*: (317) 634-6200, *Fax*: (317) 263-5060, *Published*: weekly, *Price*: $105 annually.

Industrial Supply, Direct Business Media L.L.C., 401 S. Fort St. W., West Atkinson, WI 53538, *Telephone*: (920) 397-7551, *Fax*: (920) 397-7558, *Published*: bimonthly, *Price*: free to qualified subscribers.

Ink World, Rodman Media, 70 Hilltop Road, Ramsey NJ 07446, *Telephone*: (201) 825-2552, *Fax*: (201) 825-0553, *Published*: monthly, *Price*: free to qualified subscribers.

Innovation & Tech Today, Innovative Properties Worldwide Inc., 1750 Wewatta Street, Suite 1821, Denver, CO 80202, *Telephone*: (720) 476-4920, *Published*: quarterly, *Price*: $19.95, print and digital.

Inside Unmanned Systems, Autonomous Media, 157 Broad Street, Suite 307, Red Bank, NJ 07701, *Telephone*: (732) 741-1964, *Published*: 6x/yr., *Price*: free to qualified subscribers.

Insurance Journal, Wills Publishing, 3570 Camino del Rio North, Ste. 200, San Diego, CA 92108, *Telephone*: (619) 584-1100, *Fax*: (619) 584-1200, *Published*: monthly, *Price*: free to qualified subscribers.

Interior Design, Sandow, 3651 NW 8th Avenue, Boca Raton, FL 33431, *Telephone*: (917) 934-2910, *Published*: 14x/yr., *Price*: $29.95 annually.

Internal Correspondence, ICV2, 448 W. Washington Ave., Madison, WI 53703, *Telephone*: (608) 284-9400, *Fax*: (608) 284-9404, *Published*: monthly, *Price*: $10 annually.

International Boat Industry, Boating Communications Ltd., 9 Pound Lane, Godalming, Surrey, GU7 1BX, United Kingdom, *Telephone*: +44 (0) 208 955 7029, *Published*: 6x/yr., *Price*: $100 annually.

International Construction, KHL Group Ltd., Southfields, Southview Road, Wadhurst, East Sussex, TN5 6TP, United Kingdom, *Telephone*: +44 (0) 1892 784088, *Fax*: +44 (0) 1892 784086, *Published*: monthly, *Price*: free digital copies.

International Fiber Journal, INDA Media, 1100 Crescent Green, Suite 115, Cary, NC 27518, *Telephone*: (919) 459-3700, *Published*: bimonthly, *Price*: $125 annually.

International Rental News, KHL Group Americas L.L.C., 3726 E. Ember Glow Way, Phoenix, AZ 85050, *Telephone*: (480) 659-0578, *Fax*: (480) 659-0678, *Published*: monthly, *Price*: free digital copies.

Intrafish, Intrafish Media USA, 701 Dexter Ave North Ste 410, Seattle, WA 98109, *Telephone*: (206) 282-3474, *Fax*: (206) 282-3470, *Published*: monthly, *Price*: $535 annually.

Investment & Pensions Europe, International Publishers Ltd., 1 Kentish Buildings, 125 Borough High Street, London SE1 1NP, United Kingdom, *Telephone*: + 44 (0) 20 3465 9300, *Published*: 6x/yr., *Price*: free to qualified subscribers.

Investor's Business Daily, 19 West 44th Street, Ste. 804, New York, NY 10036, *Telephone*: (212) 626-7676, *Fax*: (212) 626-7532, *Published*: daily, except weekends and holidays, *Price*: $299 annually.

Journal of Commerce, Commonwealth Business Media, 400 Windsor Corporate Center, 50 Millstone Road, Ste. 200, East Windsor, NJ 08520-1415, *Telephone*: (800) 221-5488, *Fax*: (650) 326-6056, *Published*: weekly, *Price*: $200.65 annually.

Kansas City Business Journal, American City Business Journals Inc., 1100 Main St., Suite 210, Kansas City, MO 64105-5123, *Telephone*: (816) 421-5900, *Fax*: (816) 472-4010, *Published*: weekly, *Price*: $100 annually.

Korea Herald, Huam-ro 4-gil 10 Herald Square, Yongsan-gu, Seoul, South Korea, *Telephone*: +82 2 727-0221, *Fax*: +82 2 727-0240, *Published*: daily, *Price*: 20,000 won per month (in South Korea).

Labels & Labeling, Tarsus Exhibitions & Publishing Ltd., 04U Centre, 649, Office M-03, Phase-5, Udyog Vihar, Gurgaon, Haryana 122001, India, *Telephone*: +86 21 6448-4882, *Fax*: +86 21 6448-4880, *Published*: bimonthly, *Price*: free to qualified subscribers.

The Land Report, Wright's Media, P.O. Box 941187, Plano, TX 75074, *Telephone*: (888) 300-3507, *Published*: 4x/yr., *Price*: $60 annually.

Landscape Architect and Specifier News, Landscape Communications, 14771 Plaza Drive, Suite K, Tustin CA 92780, *Telephone*: (714) 979-5276, *Fax*: (714) 434-3882, *Published*: monthly, *Price*: $65 annually.

Laser Focus World, Endeavor Business Media L.L.C., 61 Split Brook Road, Suite 501, Nashua, NH 03060, *Telephone*: (603) 891-0123, *Published*: monthly, *Price*: free to qualified subscribers.

License Global, UBM Advanstar Inc., 2 Penn Plaza, 15th Floor, New York City, NY 10121, *Telephone*: (212) 600-3000, *Fax*: (212) 600-3050, *Published*: monthly, *Price*: free to qualified subscribers.

Licensing Letter, EPM Communications Inc., 160 Mercer Street, 3rd Floor, New York, N.Y. 10012-3212, *Telephone*: (212) 941-0099, *Fax*: (212) 941-1622, *Published*: monthly, *Price*: $527 annually.

Logging & Sawmilling Journal, P.O. Box 86670, North Vancouver, BC, V7L 4L2, Canada, *Telephone*: (604) 990-9970, *Fax*: (604) 990-9971, *Published*: monthly, *Price*: $58 annually.

Logistics Management, Peerless Media, 281 Route 79, Morganville, NJ 07751, *Telephone*: (508) 663-1553, *Fax*: (877) 330-6449, *Published*: monthly, *Price*: $110 annually.

LP Gas, North Coast Media, 1360 E. 9th St., Suite 1070, Cleveland, OH 44114, *Telephone*: (216) 706-3700, *Fax*: (216) 706-3710, *Published*: monthly, *Price*: $41.95 annually.

Lubes 'n Greases, LNG Publishing Company Inc., 6105 Arlington Blvd., Suite G, Falls Church, VA 22044, *Telephone*: (703) 536-0800, *Fax*: (703) 536-0803, *Published*: monthly, *Price*: free to qualified subscribers.

Manufacturing & Supply Chain, Premier Publishing Ltd., 51 Parkwest Enterprise Centre, Nangor Road, Dublin 12, *Telephone*: + 353 1 612 0880, *Fax*: + 353 1 612 0881, *Published*: 10x/yr., *Price*: €145 annually.

The Manufacturing Confectioner, Manufacturing Confectioner Publishing, 175 Rock Rd., Glen Rock, NJ 07452, *Telephone*: (201) 652-2655, *Fax*: (201) 652-3419, *Published*: monthly, *Price*: $25 annually.

Marijuana Business Magazine, Marijuana Business Daily, 3900 S. Wadsworth Blvd., Suite 100, Denver, CO 80235, *Telephone*: (720) 213-5992, *Published*: 10x/yr., *Price*: free to qualified subscribers.

Marketing News, American Marketing Association, 130 E. Randolph Street, 22nd Floor, Chicago, IL 60601, *Telephone*: (312) 993-9517, *Fax*: (312) 993-7540, *Published*: monthly, except June/July and November/December, *Price*: included in membership in the American Marketing Association.

McKnight's Senior Living, Haymarket Media Inc., 900 Skokie Blvd, Suite 114, Northbrook IL 60062, *Telephone*: (847) 599-2884, *Published*: monthly, *Price*: free to qualified subscribers.

Media Play News, JCH Media, 3988 Monroe Street, Carlsbad, CA 92008, *Telephone*: (760) 573-8225, *Published*: monthly, *Price*: free to qualified subscribers.

Medical Design & Outsourcing, WTWH Media L.L.C., 1111 Superior Ave., 26th Floor, Cleveland, OH 44114, *Telephone*: (888) 543-2447, *Published*: 7x/yr., *Price*: $195 annually.

Medical Marketing & Media, CPS Communications, 7200 West Camino Real, Ste. 215, Boca Raton, FL 33433, *Telephone*: (561) 368-9301, *Fax*: (561) 368-7870, *Published*: monthly, *Price*: $96 annually.

Metal Center News, Sackett Business Media, 1100 Jorie Blvd., Suite 207, Oak Brook, IL 60523, *Telephone*: (630) 571-1067, *Fax*: (630) 572-0689, *Published*: monthly, *Price*: $109 annually.

MHInsider, MH Village Inc., 2600 Five Mile Road NE, Grand Rapids, MI 49525, *Telephone*: (800) 397-2158, *Published*: quarterly, *Price*: free digital copies.

Milling & Baking News, Sosland Publishing Co., 4800 Main St., Suite 100, Kansas City, MO 64112, *Telephone*: (816) 756-1000, *Fax*: (816) 756-0494, *Published*: monthly, *Price*: free digital copies.

Milsat Magazine, Satnews Publishers, 800 Siesta Way, Sonoma, CA 95476, *Telephone*: (707) 939-9306, *Fax*: (707) 939-9235, *Published*: 11x/yr., *Price*: free to qualified subscribers.

Milwaukee Business Journal, American City Business Journals Inc., 825 N Jefferson St., Milwaukee, WI 53202, *Telephone*: (414) 278-7788, *Fax*: (414) 278-7028, *Published*: weekly, *Price*: $140 annually.

Mine, John Carpenter House, John Carpenter Street, London EC4Y OAN, United Kingdom, *Telephone*: +44 207 936 6400, *Published*: monthly, *Price*: free digital copies.

MMR, Racher Press, 220 5th Ave., New York, NY 1001, *Telephone*: (212) 213-6000, *Fax*: (212) 213-6101, *Published*: biweekly, *Price*: $185 annually.

Modern Casting, American Foundrymen's Society, 505 State St., Des Plaines, IL 60016-8399, *Telephone*: (847) 824-0181, *Fax*: (847) 824-7848, *Published*: monthly, *Price*: $60.65 annually.

Modern Machine Shop, Gardner Publications, Inc., 6915 Valley Avenue, Cincinnati, OH 45244, *Telephone*: (513) 527-8800, *Fax*: (513) 527-8801, *Published*: monthly, *Price*: free to qualified subscribers.

Modern Materials Handling, Reed Business Information, 275 Washington St., Newton, MA 02458, *Telephone*: (617) 964-3030, *Fax*: (617) 558-4327, *Published*: monthly, *Price*: free to qualified subscribers.

Modern Tire Dealer, Missions Media L.L.C., 3515 Massillon Road, Suite 350, Uniontown, OH 44685, *Telephone*: (330) 899-2000, *Fax*: (330) 867-0019, *Published*: monthly, *Price*: $65 annually.

The Moodie Davitt Report, Moodie International Limited, Great West House, Great West Road, Brentford, Middlesex TW8 9DF, United Kingdom, *Telephone*: +44 (0) 20 8231 7201, *Fax*: +44 (0) 20 8231 7220, *Published*: monthly, *Price*: free digital copies.

Multi-Unit Franchisee, P.O. Box 20547, San Jose, CA 95160, *Telephone*: (800) 289-4232 ext. 202, *Fax*: (408) 402-5738, *Published*: monthly, *Price*: $49 annually.

Multichannel News, Reed Business Information, 275 Washington St., Newton, MA 02458, *Telephone*: (617) 964-3030, *Fax*: (617) 558-4327, *Published*: monthly, *Price*: $169.99 annually.

Music & Sound Retailer, Retailer Publishing Inc., 25 Willowdale Ave., Port Washington, NY 11050-3779, *Telephone*: (516) 767-2500, *Fax*: (516) 767-9335, *Published*: monthly, *Price*: $18 annually.

Music Trades, 80 West St., Englewood, NJ 07631, *Telephone*: (201) 871-1965, *Fax*: (201) 871-0455, *Published*: monthly, *Price*: $26.6 annually.

Music Week, CMP Information, Tower House, Sovereign Park, Market Harborough, Leicestershire, LE16 9EF, United Kingdom, *Telephone*: +44 (0) 20 7921 5000, *Published*: weekly, *Price*: 215 British pounds sterling, print and digital.

Musical Merchandise Review, Timeless Communications Corp., 6000 S. Eastern Ave., Suite 14-J, Las Vegas, NV 89119, *Telephone*: (702) 479-1879, *Fax*: (702) 554-5340, *Published*: monthly, *Price*: free digital copies.

National Fisherman, Diversified Business Communications, 121 Free Street, Portland ME 04101, *Telephone*: (207) 842-5608, *Fax*: (207) 842-5600, *Published*: monthly, *Price*: $17.95 annually.

National Hog Farmer, Informa PLC, 9800 Metcalf Ave., Overland Park, KS 66212, *Telephone*: (800) 722-5334, *Fax*: (952) 851-4601, *Published*: monthly, *Price*: $51, one year; $100, two years.

National Jeweler, VNU Business Publications USA, Inc., 770 Broadway, Fifth Floor, New York, NY 10003-9595, *Telephone*: (646) 654-4924, *Published*: biweekly, *Price*: $79 annually.

National Liquor News, Food and Beverage Media Pty Ltd., 41 Bridge Road, GLEBE NSW, Australia, 2037, *Telephone*: 02 9660 2113, *Fax*: 02 9660 4119, *Published*: 11x/yr., *Price*: $70 annually.

National Oil & Lube News, Missions Media L.L.C., 4418 74th St., Suite 66, Lubbock, TX 79424, *Telephone*: (800) 796-2577, *Fax*: (806) 762-4023, *Published*: monthly, *Price*: $70 annually.

The National Provisioner, BNP Media L.L.C., 2401 W. Big Beaver Rd., Suite 700, Troy, MI 48084-3333, *Telephone*: (248) 362-3700, *Fax*: (248) 362-0317, *Published*: monthly, *Price*: free to qualified subscribers.

National Underwriter, The National Underwriter Co., 505 Gest St., Cincinnati, OH 45203, *Telephone*: (800) 543-0874, *Fax*: (800) 874-1916, *Published*: weekly, except last week in December, *Price*: $98 annually.

Nation's Restaurant News, Informa USA Inc., 605 3rd Avenue, New York, NY 10036, *Telephone*: (212) 756-5129, *Fax*: (212) 756-5215, *Published*: weekly, *Price*: $149 annually.

Natural Foods Merchandiser, New Hope Natural Media a division of Informa Media Inc., 9800 Metcalf Ave., Overland Park, KS 66212-22162, *Telephone*: (303) 939-8440, *Fax*: (303) 440-8884, *Published*: bimonthly, *Price*: $85 annually.

Nilson Report, 110 Eugenia Place, Suite 100, Carpinteria CA, 93103, *Telephone*: (805) 684-8800, *Published*: 22x/yr., *Price*: $2,195 annually.

Non-Foods Management, Millennium Media, 3 Chaser Court, Holmdel, NJ 07733, *Telephone*: (732) 888-0066, *Fax*: (732) 888-0066, *Published*: annual, *Price*: free digital copies.

The NonProfit Times, NPT Publishing Group, 201 Littleton Road - 2nd Floor, Morris Plains, NJ 07950, *Telephone*: (973) 401-0202, *Fax*: (973)-401-0404, *Published*: biweekly, *Price*: free to qualified subscribers.

Nonwovens Industry, Rodman Publishing, 17 S. Franklin Turnpike, P.O. Box 555, Ramsey, NJ 07446, *Telephone*: (201) 825-2552, *Fax*: (201) 825-0553, *Published*: monthly, *Price*: $48, or free to qualified subscribers.

Northeast Dairy, Northeast Dairy Foods Association, 427 S. Main St., North Syracuse, NY 13212, *Telephone*: (315) 452-MILK, *Published*: quarterly, *Price*: free digital copies.

Nursery Retailer, Brantwood Publications, 2410 Northside Dr., Clearwater, FL 33761, *Telephone*: (727) 786-9771, *Fax*: (727) 786-9772, *Published*: 6x/yr., *Price*: free to qualified subscribers.

Nutfruit Magazine, International Nut & Dried Fruit Council, Carrer de la Fruita Seca, 4 Poligon Tecnoparc, 43204 Reus, Spain, *Telephone*: +34 977-331-416, *Fax*: +34 977-331-028, *Published*: 3x/yr., *Price*: €170 annually.

Nutritional Outlook, MJH Life Sciences, 2 Clarke Drive, Suite 100, Cranbury, NJ 08512, *Telephone*: (609) 716-7777, *Published*: monthly, *Price*: free to qualified subscribers.

Octane, EnsembleIQ, 20 Eglinton Ave. West, Suite 1800, Toronto, Ontario M4R 1K8, Canada, *Telephone*: (416) 256-9908, *Fax*: (888) 889-9522, *Published*: 6x/yr., *Price*: $65 annually.

O'Dwyer's, J.R. O'Dwyer Co. Inc., 271 Madison Ave., New York, NY 10016, *Telephone*: (212) 679-2471, *Fax*: (212) 683-2750, *Published*: monthly, *Price*: free digital copies.

Offshore Technology Focus, Net Resources International, John Carpenter House, John Carpenter Street, London, EC4Y OAN, United Kingdom, *Telephone*: +44 (0) 207 936 6400, *Published*: monthly, *Price*: free to qualified subscribers.

OGV Energy, 11490 Westheimer Road, Suite 925, Houston, TX 77077, *Telephone*: (713) 425-6355, *Published*: monthly, *Price*: free to qualified subscribers.

Oil & Gas Journal, Endeavour Business Media, 1455 West Loop South, Suite 400, Houston, TX 77027, *Telephone*: (713) 621-9720, *Fax*: (713) 963-6285, *Published*: monthly, *Price*: $109 annually.

Oils & Fats International, dmg world media, 1100 Larkspur Landing CircleSuite 255, Larkspur CA 94939, *Telephone*: (415) 464-8500, *Published*: monthly, *Price*: free digital copies.

On-Site Magazine, Rogers Media, One Mount Pleasant Road, 7th Floor, Toronto, Ontario, Canada M4Y 2Y5, *Telephone*: (416) 764-1510, *Fax*: (416) 764-1733, *Published*: monthly, *Price*: free to qualified subscribers.

Orlando Business Journal, American City Business Journals Inc., 255 South Orange Avenue, Suite 700, Orlando, FL 32801, *Telephone*: (407) 649-8470, *Fax*: (407) 420-1625, *Published*: weekly, *Price*: $150 annually, print and digital.

Outreach Magazine, 2230 Oak Ridge Way, Vista, CA 92081-2314, *Telephone*: (760) 940-0600, *Published*: monthly, *Price*: $29.95 annually.

Packaging Strategies, BNP Media L.L.C., 2401 W. Big Beaver Rd., Suite 700, Troy, MI 48084-3333, *Telephone*: (248) 362-3700, *Fax*: (248) 362-0317, *Published*: monthly, *Price*: free to qualified subscribers.

The Packer, Farm Journal Media, 8725 Rosehill Road, Suite 200, Lenexa, KS 66215, *Telephone*: (800) 331-9310, *Published*: weekly, but biweekly in March, June and October, *Price*: $149 annually.

Paint & Coatings Industry, BNP Media L.L.C., 2401 W. Big Beaver Rd., Suite 700, Troy, MI 48084-3333, *Telephone*: (248) 362-3700, *Fax*: (248) 362-0317, *Published*: monthly, *Price*: $184 annually.

Panels & Furniture Asia, Palo Publishing Ltd., Block 16 Kallang Palace, 07-01 Singapore 339156, *Telephone*: (65) 6397 7877, *Fax*: (65) 6396 7177, *Published*: monthly, *Price*: $90 annually.

Paper360°, Tappi, 15 Technology Parkway South, Suite 115, Peachtree Corners, GA 30092, *Telephone*: (800) 332-8686, *Fax*: (770)446-6947, *Published*: bimonthly, *Price*: free digital copies.

Pensions & Investments, Crain Communications Inc., 685 Third Avenue, Tenth Floor, New York, NY 10017-4036, *Telephone*: (212) 210-0100, *Fax*: (212) 210-0117, *Published*: 26x/yr., *Price*: $350 annually.

Perfumer & Flavorist, Allured Business Media, 336 Gundersen Drive, Suite A, Carol Stream, IL 60188, *Telephone*: (630) 653-2155, *Fax*: (630) 653-2192, *Published*: monthly, *Price*: free to qualified subscribers.

Pest Control Technology, 5811 Canal Road, Valley View, OH 44125, *Telephone*: (800) 456-0707, *Fax*: (330) 659-0823, *Published*: monthly, *Price*: $35 annually.

Pet Food & Animal Feed Technology, EDITRICE EDF trend SRL, Corso del Popolo, 31100, Treviso, Italy, *Telephone*: +39 0422 549305, *Fax*: +39 0422 591736, *Published*: monthly, *Price*: free with subscription.

Pet Food Processing Resource Guide, Sosland Publishing, 4801 Main St., Suite 650, Kansas City, MO 64112, *Telephone*: (816) 756-1000, *Fax*: (816) 756-0494, *Published*: annual, *Price*: included with subscription, $24 annually U.S. and Canada.

Petfood Industry, Watt Publishing Company, 122 South Wesley Avenue, Mt. Morris, IL 61054-1497, *Telephone*: (815) 734-4171, *Fax*: (815) 734-5631, *Published*: monthly, *Price*: $84 annually.

PETS International, PETS International & Global Pets Community, P.O. Box 1719, 3800 BS Amersfoot, Netherlands, *Telephone*: +31-33-4225833, *Published*: monthly, *Price*: free digital copies.

Pharmaceutical Executive, MultiMedia Healthcare L.L.C., 2 Clarke Dr., Suite 100, Cranbury, NJ 08512, *Telephone*: (609) 716-7777, *Published*: monthly, *Price*: free to qualified subscribers.

Phoenix Business Journal, American City Business Journals Inc., 101 N. First Ave, Suite 2300, Phoenix, AZ 85003, *Telephone*: 602-230-8400, *Fax*: 602-230-0955, *Published*: weekly, *Price*: $93 annually.

Pittsburgh Business Journal, American City Business Journals Inc., 45 S. 23rd Street, Pittsburgh, PA 15203, *Telephone*: (412) 481-6397, *Fax*: (412) 481-9956, *Published*: monthly, *Price*: $150 annually, print and digital.

PMG Producemarketguide.com, Farm Journal, 1600 Market Street, Suite 1530, Philadelphia, PA 19103, *Telephone*: (714) 383-9982, *Published*: 6x/yr., *Price*: $45 annually.

PMQ Pizza Magazine, PMQ Inc., 605 Edison St., Oxford, MS 38655, *Telephone*: (662) 234-5481, *Fax*: (662) 234-0665, *Published*: 10x/yr., *Price*: $25 annually.

Pollstar, 4697 W. Jacquelyn Ave., Fresno, CA 93722-6413, *Telephone*: (800) 344-7383, *Published*: monthly, *Price*: $349 annually.

Poultry International, WATT Global Media, 401 E. State Street, 3rd Floor, Rockford, IL 61104, *Telephone*: (815) 966-5400, *Published*: monthly, *Price*: free to qualified subscribers.

Poultry Trends, WATT Global Media, 401 E. State Street, 3rd Floor, Rockford, IL 61104, *Telephone*: (815) 966-5574, *Published*: annually, *Price*: $99.

PowerSports Business, EPG Media/Specialty Information Media, 10405 6th Avenue North, Suite 210, Minneapolis MN 55441, *Telephone*: (763) 383-4492, *Fax*: (763) 383-4499, *Published*: 15x/yr., *Price*: $56 annually.

PPF Magazine, Key Media & Research, P.O. Box 569, Garrisonville, VA 22463, *Telephone*: (540) 720-5584, *Fax*: (540) 720-5687, *Published*: quarterly, *Price*: free to qualified subscribers.

Printed Circuit Design & Fab/Circuits Assembly, UPM Media Group Inc., P.O. Box 470, Canton, GA 30169, *Telephone*: (617) 327-4702, *Published*: monthly, *Price*: $80 annually U.S. and Canada; $145 elsewhere.

Printing Impressions, North American Publishing Company, Spring Garden Street, 12th Floor, Philadelphia, PA 19108, *Telephone*: (800) 627-2689, *Fax*: (215) 238-5457, *Published*: weekly, *Price*: $95 annually.

Produce Blueprints Supplement, Blue Book Services Inc., 845 E. Geneva Road, Carol Stream, IL 60188, *Telephone*: (630) 668-3500, *Fax*: (630) 668-0303, *Published*: monthly, *Price*: free digital copies.

Produce News, 800 Kinderkamack Road, Suite 100, Oradell, NJ 07649, *Telephone*: (800) 753-9110, *Fax*: (201) 986-7996, *Published*: semi-monthly, *Price*: $85 annually.

Professional Carwashing & Detailing, Babcox Media Inc., 3550 Parkway, Akron, OH 44333, *Telephone*: (330) 670-1234, *Published*: monthly, *Price*: $74 annually.

Professional Pasta, Avenue Media SRL, Viale Aldini Antonio, 222/4, 40136 Bologna, Italy, *Telephone*: +39 051 656 4311, *Published*: 6x/yr., *Price*: Inside Europe €45; outside Europe, €60.

ProFood World, PMMI Media Group, 401 N. Michigan Ave., Suite 300, Chicago, IL 60611, *Telephone*: (312) 222-1010, *Fax*: (312) 222-1310, *Published*: monthly, *Price*: $55 annually.

Progressive Dairy, 238 West Nez Pence, Jerome, ID 83338, *Telephone*: (208) 324-7513, *Fax*: (208) 324-1133, *Published*: 20x/yr., *Price*: free to qualified subscribers.

Progressive Grocer, EnsembleIQ, 8550 W. Bryn Mawr Ave., Suite 200, Chicago, IL 60601, *Telephone*: (773) 992-4450, *Fax*: (773) 992-4455, *Published*: 18x/yr., *Price*: $129 annually.

ProSales Magazine, One Thomas Circle, N.W., Suite 600, Washington, D.C. 20005, *Telephone*: (202) 736-3308, *Fax*: (202) 736-3406, *Published*: monthy, *Price*: free to qualified subscribers.

Publishers Weekly, Reed Business Information, 360 Park Avenue South, New York, NY 10010, *Telephone*: (646) 746-6758, *Fax*: (646) 746-6631, *Published*: weekly, *Price*: $240 annually.

Qualified Remodeler, SOLA Group Inc., 1880 Oak Ave., Suite 350, Evanston, IL 60201, *Telephone*: (847) 440-3000, *Published*: monthly, *Price*: free to qualified subscribers.

Radio World, Future US Inc., 11 West 42nd Street, 15th Floor, New York, NY 10036, *Telephone*: (212) 378-0448, *Published*: 26x/yr., *Price*: free digital copies.

Radiology Business Journal, TriMed Business Group, 29 E. Madison Street, Suite 440, Chicago, IL 60602, *Telephone*: (401) 383-5660, *Published*: bimonthly, *Price*: free digital copies.

Railway Age, Simmons-Boardman Publishing, 345 Hudson St., New York, NY 10014, *Telephone*: (212) 620-7200, *Fax*: (212) 633-1165, *Published*: monthly, *Price*: $100 annually.

Railway Pro, Summit House, 4-5 Mitchell Street, Edinburgh, EH6 7BD, United Kingdom, *Telephone*: +44 131 618 9828, *Published*: monthly, *Price*: free digital copies.

R&D Magazine, Advantage Business Media, 100 Enterprise Drive, Suite 600, Box 912, Rockaway, NJ 07866-0912, *Telephone*: (973) 920-7000, *Published*: monthly, *Price*: free to qualified subscribers.

Recreation Management, CAB Communications, Inc., 50 North Brockway Street, Suite 4-11, Palatine, IL 60067, *Telephone*: (847) 963-8740, *Fax*: (847) 963-8745, *Published*: monthly, *Price*: free to qualified subscribers.

Redbook - A Supplement to Bake Magazine, Sosland Publishing, 4801 Main Street, Suite 650, Kansas City, MO 64112, *Telephone*: (816) 756-1000, *Fax*: (816) 756-0494, *Published*: yearly, *Price*: free digital copies.

Refrigerated & Frozen Foods, BNP Media L.L.C., 2401 Big Beaver Rd., Suite 700, Troy, MI 48084-3333, *Telephone*: (248) 362-3700, *Fax*: (248) 362-0317, *Published*: 7x/yr., *Price*: free to qualified subscribers.

Refrigerated Transporter, Endeavor Business Media L.L.C., 331 54th Ave. N., Nashville, TN 37209, *Telephone*: (713) 523-8124, *Fax*: (713) 523-8384, *Published*: monthly, *Price*: free to qualified subscribers.

Render, North American Renders Association, 500 Montgomery Street, Suite 310, Alexandria, VA 33210, *Telephone*: (703) 683-0155, *Fax*: (571) 970-2279, *Published*: bimonthly, *Price*: free to qualified subscribers.

Research in Transportation Business & Management, Elsevier, 230 Park Ave., Suite 300, New York, NY 10169, *Telephone*: (212) 989-5800, *Published*: monthly, *Price*: $2,360 annually.

Restaurant Business, Winsight L.L.C., 300 S. Riverside Plaza, Suite 1600, Chicago, IL 60606, *Telephone*: (312) 876-0004, *Fax*: (312) 876-1158, *Published*: 18x/yr., *Price*: free digital copies.

Retail News, Tara Publishing, 14 Upper Fitzwilliam Street, Dublin Ireland, *Telephone*: +353 (0) 1 678 5165, *Fax*: +353 (0) 1 647 7127, *Published*: monthly, *Price*: €104 annually.

Rubber & Plastics News, Crain Communications Inc., 1725 Merriman Road, Akron, OH 44313-5251, *Telephone*: (330) 836-9180, *Fax*: (330) 836-2831, *Published*: weekly, *Price*: $99 annually.

Rubber World, P.O. Box 5451, 1867 W. Market St., Akron, OH 44313-6901, *Telephone*: (330) 864-2122, *Fax*: (330) 864-5298, *Published*: monthly, *Price*: $34 annually.

RugNews.com, Tisch Communications, P.O. Box 18207, Sarasota, FL 34276, *Telephone*: (941) 929-9430, *Published*: weekly, *Price*: free digital newsletter.

Sacramento Business Journal, American City Business Journals Inc., 555 Capitol Street, Suite 200, Sacramento, CA 95818, *Telephone*: (916) 447-7661, *Fax*: (916) 444-7879, *Published*: weekly, *Price*: $150 annually, print and digital.

SatMagazine, 800 Siesta Way, Sonoma, CA 95476, *Telephone*: (707) 939-9306, *Fax*: (707) 939-9235, *Published*: monthly, *Price*: free to qualified subscribers.

SBC Magazine, Structural Building Components Association, 6300 Enterprise Lane, Madison, WI 57319, *Telephone*: (608)310-6706, *Fax*: (608) 274-3329, *Published*: 9x/yr., *Price*: free to qualified subscribers.

School Bus Fleet, Bobit Business Media, 3520 Challenger Street, Torrence, CA 90503, *Telephone*: (310) 376-8788, *Fax*: (310) 376-9043, *Published*: monthly, *Price*: free digital copies.

School Transportation News, STN Media, 700 Torrance Blvd., Suite C, Redondo Beach, California 90277, *Telephone*: (310) 792-2226, *Fax*: (310) 792-2231, *Published*: monthly, *Price*: free to qualified subscribers.

Screen Daily, MBI Ltd, 1st Floor Unit, F2/G, Zetland House, 5-25 Scrutton Street, London EC2A 4HJ, U.K., *Telephone*: +44 (0) 330 222 9414, *Published*: weekly, *Price*: $376 annually.

SDM, BNP Media L.L.C., 2401 W. Big Beaver Rd., Suite 200, Troy, MI 48084, *Telephone*: (248) 362-3700, *Fax*: (248) 362-3717, *Published*: monthly, *Price*: $232 annually.

Security, BNP Media L.L.C., 2401 W. Big Beaver Rd., Suite 700, Troy, MI 48084, *Telephone*: (248) 362-3700, *Fax*: (248) 362-0317, *Published*: monthly, *Price*: free digital copies.

Semiconductor Today, Juno Publishing and Media Solutions Ltd., Suite 133, 20 Winchcombe Street, Cheltenham, GL52 2LY, United Kingdom, *Telephone*: +44 (0) 1869 811577, *Fax*: +44 (0) 1242 291482, *Published*: 10X/yr, *Price*: free to qualified subscribers.

Shooting Industry, Publishers' Development Corp., 13741 Danielson St., Suite A, Poway, CA 92064, *Telephone*: (858) 842-4444, *Published*: monthly, *Price*: $25 annually in U.S; $45 annually internationally.

Signs of the Times, ST Publications, 407 Gilbert Avenue, Cincinnati, OH 45202, *Telephone*: (513) 421-2050, *Fax*: (513) 421-5144, *Published*: 13x/yr., *Price*: $39 annually in U.S.; $59 per year in Canada; $62 per year elsewhere.

Snack Food & Wholesale Bakery, BNP Media L.L.C., 2401 W. Big Beaver Rd., Suite 700, Troy, MI 48084-3333, *Telephone*: (248) 362-3700, *Fax*: (248) 362-0317, *Published*: monthly, *Price*: $152 annually in U.S., $187 annually in Canada,$212 annually internationally.

Snow Magazine, 4020 Kinross Lakes Parkway, Ste. 201, Richfield, OH 44286, *Telephone*: (800) 456-0707, *Fax*: (330) 659-0823, *Published*: monthly, *Price*: free to qualified subscribers.

Sosland Publishing's Corporate Profiles - Milling & Baking News Supplement, Sosland Publishing, 4801 Main Street, Suite 650, Kansas City, MO 64112, *Telephone*: (816) 756-1000, *Fax*: (816) 756-0494, *Published*: annually, *Price*: free to qualified subscribers.

Soundings, Soundings Publications L.L.C., 10 Bokum Road, Essex, CT 06426, *Telephone*: (800) 444-7686, *Fax*: (860) 767-0642, *Published*: monthly, *Price*: $25 annually.

South China Morning Post, 16/F Somerset House, Taikoo Place, 979 King's Road, Quarry Bay, Hong Kong, *Telephone*: (852) 2565-2222, *Fax*: (852) 2811-1048, *Published*: daily, *Price*: $901 annually.

Special Events, 17383 Sunset Boulevard, Suite A220, Pacific Palisades, CA 90272, *Telephone*: (310) 230-7160, *Fax*: (310) 230-7168, *Published*: monthly, *Price*: $48.24 annually.

Spotlight, Mendenhall Associates Inc., 1500 Cedar Bend Drive, Ann Arbor, MI 48105, *Telephone*: (619) 436-0336, *Published*: quarterly, *Price*: free digital copies.

Spray Technology & Marketing, Industry Publications Inc., 140 Littleton Road, Suite 320, Parsippany, NJ 07054, *Telephone*: (973) 331-9545, *Fax*: (973) 331-9547, *Published*: monthly, *Price*: free to qualified subscribers.

Staffing Success, American Staffing Association, 277 S. Washington St., Suite 200, Alexandria, VA 22314, *Telephone*: (703) 253-2020, *Fax*: (703) 253-2053, *Published*: 7x/yr, *Price*: $90 annually.

State of the Industry - A Supplement to Snac World, Snac International., 1600 Wilson Blvd., Suite 650, Arlington, VA 22209, *Telephone*: (703) 836-4500, *Fax*: (800) 628-1334, *Published*: annually, *Price*: free with subscription.

Stone World, BNP Media L.L.C., 210 Route 4 East, Suite 203, Paramus, NJ 07652, *Telephone*: (201) 291-9001, *Fax*: (201) 291-9002, *Published*: monthly, *Price*: free to qualified subscrbers.

Store Brands, Stagnito Business, 570 Lake Cook Rd, Suite 310, Deerfield, IL 60015, *Telephone*: (224) 632-8200, *Fax*: (224) 632-8266, *Published*: monthly, *Price*: free to qualified subscrbers.

Supermarket News, Fairchild Publications, 7 W. 34th St., New York, NY 10001, *Telephone*: (800) 204-4515, *Fax*: (212) 630-4760, *Published*: weekly, *Price*: $195 annually.

Systems Contractor News, Future Publishing Ltd., Quay House, The Ambury, Bath BA1 1UA, United Kingdom, *Telephone*: +44 (0) 1225 442244, *Published*: monthly, *Price*: free to qualified subscrbers.

Tea & Coffee Trade Journal, Bell Publishing, The Maltings, 57 Bath Street, Gravesend, Kent DA 411 ODF, United Kingdom, *Telephone*: +44 (0) 1474 532 202, *Fax*: +44 (0) 1474 532 203, *Published*: monthly, *Price*: $49 annually.

Tecoya Trend, Tecoya Trend Publications, D-66 Oshiwara Industrial Centre, Andheri Malad Link Road, Mumbai, 400 104. Mumbai, *Telephone*: +91 91670 76293, *Fax*: +91 22287 93022, *Published*: daily, *Price*: free digital copies.

Tennis Industry, Tennis Industry and USRSA, P.O. Box 3392, Duluth, GA 30096, *Telephone*: (646) 783-1450, *Published*: 10x/yr., *Price*: $25 annually.

Tile International, Tile Edizioni SRL, Via Fossa Buracchione 84, 41126 Baggiovara (Modena), Italy, *Telephone*: +39 059 512 103, *Fax*: +39 059 512 157, *Published*: quarterly, *Price*: €70 annually.

The Times, The Times, 1 Pennington Street, London E98 1XY, United Kingdom, *Telephone*: 00 44 (0)20 7782 5000, *Fax*: 00 44 (0)20 7782 5046, *Published*: daily, *Price*: 5 British pounds sterling monthly (digital).

Tire Review, Babcox Publications, 3550 Embassy Parkway, Akron, OH 44313, *Telephone*: (330) 670-1234, *Published*: monthly, *Price*: free to qualified subscribers.

TissueMag, Edipap, Via Pordenone 13, 20132 Milano, Italy, *Telephone*: +39 02 2171-1614, *Fax*: +39 05 632-3050, *Published*: monthly, *Price*: free digital copies.

Titanium Today, International Titanium Association, P.O. Box 1300, Eastlake, CO 80614, *Telephone*: (303) 404-2221, *Fax*: (303) 404-9111, *Published*: monthly, *Price*: free digital copies.

Today's Motor Vehicles, GIE Media Inc., 5811 Canal Road, Suite 6, Valley View, OH 44125, *Telephone*: (216) 393-3000, *Published*: monthly, except double issue in Jan/Feb., *Price*: free to qualified subscribers.

Today's Trucking, Newcom Business Media Inc., 451 Attwell, Dr., Toronto, ON, M9W 5C4, Canada, *Telephone*: (416) 614-2200, *Fax*: (416) 614-8861, *Published*: monthly, *Price*: $50 annually.

Trailer Body Builders, Penton Media Inc., 249 W. 17th Street, New York, NY 10011, *Telephone*: (212) 204-4200, *Fax*: (212) 206-3622, *Published*: monthly, *Price*: free to qualified subcribers.

Training, Lakewood Media Group, L.L.C., 5353 Knox Ave. S., Minneapolis, MN 55419, *Telephone*: (847) 559-7596, *Fax*: (847) 291-4816, *Published*: bimonthly, *Price*: $79 annually.

Travel Retail Business, TRBusiness Ltd., 16 The Warren, Worcester Park, Surrey, KT4 7DL, United Kingdom, *Telephone*: +44 (0) 2076 102782, *Fax*: +44 (0) 2083 309449, *Published*: monthly, *Price*: free digital copies.

Trends in Biotechnology, Cell Press, 50 Hampshire St., 5th Floor, Cambridge, MA 02139, *Telephone*: (617) 397-2800, *Published*: monthly, *Price*: $377 annually.

Triad Business Journal, American City Business Journals Inc., 100 South Elm Street, Suite 400, Greensboro, NC 27401, *Telephone*: (336) 271-6539, *Fax*: (336) 574-3607, *Published*: weekly, *Price*: $97 annually.

Turbomachinery International, Multimedia Healthcare L.L.C., 2 Clarke Drive, Suite 100, Cranbury, NJ 08512, *Telephone*: (323) 317-5255, *Published*: 7x/yr., *Price*: free to qualified subscribers.

TV Veupar Journal, ADI Media, C-35, Sector 62, Noida - 201 307 Uttar Pradesh, India, *Telephone*: 91-120-4021200, *Fax*: 91-120-4021280, *Published*: monthly, *Price*: Rs 1,200 crore.

Twice, Future PLC, 11 West 42nd Street, 15th Floor, New York, NY 10010, *Telephone*: (646) 746-6980, *Fax*: (646) 746-7066, *Published*: weekly, *Price*: $143 annually.

USA Today, Gannett Co., 7950 Jones Branch Drive, McLean, VA 22108-0605, *Telephone*: (800) 872-0001, *Published*: Mon.-Fri., *Price*: $146 annually.

Valve World Americas, KCI Publishing Corp., 36 King Street East, Suite 701, Toronto, ON, Canada, *Telephone*: (416) 361-7030, *Fax*: (416) 361-6191, *Published*: 10x/yr., *Price*: $160 annually.

Variety, Reed Business Information, 5700 Wilshire Blvd., Suite 120, Los Angeles, CA 90036, *Telephone*: (323) 857-6600, *Published*: daily, *Price*: $150 annually.

Vision Monday, Jobson Publishing L.L.C., 100 Avenue of the Americas, New York, NY 10013-1678, *Telephone*: (212) 274-7000, *Fax*: (212) 274-0392, *Published*: monthly, *Price*: free to qualified subscribers.

The Voice, Outside Inc., 5720 Flatiron Parkway, Boulder, CO 80301, *Telephone*: (800) 380-9824, *Published*: quarterly, *Price*: free digital copies.

Wall Street Journal, Dow Jones & Co. Inc., 1211 Ave. of the Americas, New York, NY 10281, *Telephone*: (212) 416-2000, *Fax*: (212) 416-2891, *Published*: Mon.-Sat., *Price*: $257.40 annually.

Walls & Ceilings, BNP Media L.L.C., 2401 W. Big Beaver Road, Suite 700, Troy, MI 48084, *Telephone*: (248) 362-3700, *Fax*: (248) 362-5103, *Published*: monthly, *Price*: free to qualified subscribers.

WATTPoultry USA, WATT Global Media, 401 East State Street, 3rd Floor, Rockford, IL 61104, *Telephone*: (815) 966-5574, *Published*: monthly, *Price*: free digital copies; $15 single print copies.

WhatTheyThink, Watt Media Inc., 2038 Ford Parkway, Suite 238, Saint Paul, MN 55116, *Telephone*: (518) 584-8784, *Published*: 10x/yr., *Price*: $95 annually; $125 Canada.

Wine Business Monthly, Wine Communications Group, Inc., 35 Maple St., Sonoma, CA 95476, *Telephone*: (800) 895-9463, *Fax*: (707) 940-3930, *Published*: monthly, *Price*: $39 annually.

Winsight Grocery Business, Winsight L.L.C., 300 S. Riverside Plaza, Suite 1600, Chicago, IL 60606, *Telephone*: (312) 876-0004, *Fax*: (312) 654-2323, *Published*: monthly, *Price*: $60 those in food industry; $120 for others.

Winston-Salem Journal, 2051 E. 5th Street, Winston-Salem, NC, *Telephone*: (336) 727-7308, *Published*: daily, *Price*: $23.83 per month, print and digital.

World Furniture - International Markets Review, C.so Monforte 15, 20122 Milano, Italy, *Telephone*: +39 02 796630, *Fax*: +39 02 780703, *Published*: quarterly, *Price*: $129.45 annually.

World Grain, Sosland Publishing Co., 4801 Main Street, Suite 650, Kansas, MO 64112, *Telephone*: (816) 756-1000, *Fax*: (816) 756-0494, *Published*: monthly, *Price*: free digital copies.